Using the dictionary

In this dictionary you will find

Headwords

The words you want to look up are printed in bold and arranged in a single alphabetical sequence. In addition, there may be sub-heads in bold at the end of main entries for derived forms and phrases.

Synonyms

Synonyms are listed alphabetically, except that distinct senses of a headword are numbered and treated separately.

Under some headwords, in addition to the lists of synonyms given there, a cross-reference printed in SMALL CAPITALS takes you to another entry to provide an extended range of synonyms. These cross-references are marked by the arrowhead symbol ▷.

Related words

Lists of words which are not synonyms but which have a common relationship to the headword (eg, kinds of vehicle listed under *vehicle*) are printed in italic, flagged by the symbol □.

Antonyms

Cross-reference printed in SMALL CAPITALS introduce you to lists of opposites. These cross-references are preceded by the abbreviation *Opp*.

Part-of-speech labels

Part-of-speech labels are given throughout. (See list of abbreviations.) Under each headword, uses as *adjective*, *adverb*, *noun*, and *verb* are separated by the symbol ●.

Illustrative phrases

Meanings of less obvious senses are indicated by illustrative phrases printed in *italic*.

Usage warnings

Usage markers in *italic* precede words which are normally informal, derogatory, etc. (See list of abbreviations.)

Abbreviations used in this dictionary

Parts of speech

adj	adjective
adv	adverb
int	interjection
n	noun
prep	preposition
vb	verb

Other abbreviations

derog	normally used in a derogatory, negative, or uncomplimentary sense
fem	feminine
inf	normally used informally
joc	normally jocular or joking
old use	old-fashioned or obsolete
opp	opposites (antonyms)
plur	plural
poet	poetic
sl	slang
Amer	word or phrase usually regarded as American usage
Fr	word or phrase common in English contexts, but still identifiably French
Ger	ditto German
Gr	ditto Greek
It	ditto Italian
Lat	ditto Latin
Scot	word or phrase usually regarded as Scottish usage
▷	This symbol shows that you will find relevant information if you go to the word indicated.

A

abandon *v* **1** evacuate, leave, quit, vacate, withdraw from. **2** break with, desert, *inf* dump, forsake, jilt, leave behind, *inf* leave in the lurch, maroon, renounce, strand, *inf* throw over, *inf* wash your hands of. **3** *abandon a claim.* abdicate, cancel, cede, *sl* chuck in, discontinue, disown, *inf* ditch, drop, forfeit, forgo, give up, relinquish, resign, surrender, waive, yield.

abbey *n* cathedral, church, convent, friary, monastery, nunnery, priory.

abbreviate *v* abridge, compress, condense, cut, digest, edit, précis, reduce, shorten, summarize, truncate. *Opp* LENGTHEN.

abdicate *v* renounce the throne, *inf* step down. ▷ ABANDON, RESIGN.

abduct *v* carry off, kidnap, *inf* make away with, seize.

abhor *v* detest, execrate, loathe, shudder at. ▷ HATE.

abhorrent *adj* abominable, detestable, execrable, loathsome, nauseating, obnoxious, repellent, revolting. ▷ HATEFUL. *Opp* ATTRACTIVE.

abide *v* **1** accept, bear, endure, put up with, stand, *inf* stomach, suffer, tolerate. **2** ▷ STAY. **abide by** ▷ OBEY.

ability *n* aptitude, bent, brains, capability, capacity, cleverness, competence, expertise, flair, genius, gift, intelligence, knack, *inf* knowhow, knowledge, means, power, proficiency, prowess, resources, scope, skill, strength, talent, training, wit.

ablaze *adj* afire, aflame, aglow, alight, blazing, burning, flaming, lit up, on fire, raging.

able *adj* **1** accomplished, adept, capable, clever, competent, effective, efficient, experienced, expert, *inf* handy, intelligent, masterly, practised, proficient, skilful, skilled, talented. *Opp* INCOMPETENT. **2** allowed, at liberty, authorized, available, eligible, fit, free, permitted, willing. *Opp* UNABLE.

abnormal *adj* aberrant, anomalous, atypical, *inf* bent, bizarre, curious, deformed, deviant, distorted, eccentric, exceptional, extraordinary, freak, funny, idiosyncratic, irregular, *inf* kinky, malformed, odd, peculiar, perverted, queer, singular, strange, uncharacteristic, unnatural, unorthodox, unrepresentative, untypical, unusual, wayward, weird. *Opp* NORMAL.

abolish *v* abrogate, annul, delete, destroy, dispense with, do away with, eliminate, end, eradicate, finish, *inf* get rid of, liquidate, nullify, overturn, put an end to, quash, remove, suppress, terminate, withdraw. *Opp* CREATE.

abominable *adj* abhorrent, appalling, atrocious, awful, base, beastly, brutal, cruel, despicable, detestable, disgusting, dreadful, execrable, foul, hateful, heinous, horrible, inhuman, inhumane, loathsome, nasty, obnoxious, odious, repellent, repugnant, repulsive, revolting, terrible, vile. ▷ UNPLEASANT. *Opp* PLEASANT.

abort *v* **1** be born prematurely, die, miscarry. **2** *abort take-off.* call off, end, halt, nullify, stop, terminate.

abortion *n* **1** miscarriage, premature birth, termination of pregnancy. **2** ▷ MONSTER.

abortive *adj* fruitless, futile, ineffective, pointless, stillborn, unfruitful, unsuccessful, vain. *Opp* SUCCESSFUL.

abound *v* be plentiful, flourish, prevail, swarm, teem, thrive.

abrasive *adj* biting, caustic, galling, grating, harsh, hurtful, irritating, rough, sharp. ▷ UNKIND. *Opp* KIND.

abridge *v* abbreviate, compress, condense, cut, edit, précis, reduce, shorten, summarize, truncate. *Opp* EXPAND.

abridged *adj* abbreviated, bowdlerized, censored, compact, concise, cut, edited, *inf* potted, shortened.

abrupt *adj* **1** hasty, headlong, hurried, precipitate, quick, rapid, sudden, unexpected, unforeseen. **2** *an abrupt drop.* precipitous, sharp, sheer, steep. **3** *an abrupt manner.* blunt, brisk, brusque, curt, discourteous, rude, snappy, terse, uncivil, ungracious. *Opp* GENTLE, GRADUAL.

absent *adj* **1** away, *sl* bunking off, gone, missing, off, out, playing truant, *inf* skiving. *Opp* PRESENT. **2** ▷ ABSENT-MINDED.

absent-minded *adj* absent, absorbed, abstracted, careless, distracted, dreamy, forgetful, inattentive, oblivious, preoccupied, scatterbrained, unaware, unthinking, vague, withdrawn, wool-gathering. *Opp* ALERT.

absolute *adj* **1** categorical, certain, complete, conclusive, decided, definite, downright, genuine, implicit, inalienable, indubitable, *inf* out-and-out, perfect, positive, pure, sheer, sure, thorough, total, unadulterated, unambiguous, unconditional, unequivocal, unmitigated, unqualified, unreserved, unrestricted, utter. **2** *absolute ruler.* autocratic, despotic, dictatorial, omnipotent, totalitarian, tyrannical. **3** *absolute opposites. inf* dead, diametrical, exact.

absorb *v* **1** assimilate, consume, digest, drink in, hold, imbibe, incorporate, ingest, mop up, soak up, suck up, take in. *Opp* EMIT. **2** *absorb a blow.* cushion, deaden, lessen, soften. **3** *absorb a person.* captivate, engage, engross, enthral, fascinate, occupy, preoccupy. ▷ INTEREST. **absorbed** ▷ INTERESTED.

absorbent *adj* absorptive, permeable, pervious, porous, spongy. *Opp* IMPERVIOUS.

absorbing *adj* engrossing, fascinating, gripping, spellbinding. ▷ INTERESTING.

abstain *v* **abstain from** avoid, cease, deny yourself, desist from, eschew, forgo, give up, go without, refrain from, refuse, resist, shun, withhold from.

abstemious *adj* ascetic, frugal, moderate, restrained, self-denying, sparing, temperate. *Opp* SELF-INDULGENT.

abstract *adj* **1** academic, hypothetical, indefinite, intangible, intellectual, metaphysical, notional, philosophical, theoretical, unreal. *Opp* CONCRETE. **2** *abstract art.* non-pictorial, non-representational, symbolic. • *n* outline, précis, résumé, summary, synopsis.

abstruse *adj* complex, cryptic, deep, devious, difficult, enigmatic, esoteric, hard, incomprehensible, mysterious, obscure, perplexing, problematical, profound, unfathomable. *Opp* OBVIOUS.

absurd *adj* crazy, daft, eccentric, farcical, foolish, grotesque, illogical, incongruous, irrational, laughable, ludicrous, nonsensical, outlandish, paradoxical, preposterous, ridiculous, senseless, silly, stupid, surreal, unreasonable, zany. ▷ FUNNY, MAD. *Opp* RATIONAL.

abundant *adj* ample, bountiful, copious, excessive, flourishing, generous, lavish, liberal, luxuriant, overflowing, plentiful, profuse, rampant, rank, rich, well-supplied. *Opp* SCARCE.

abuse *n* **1** assault, ill-treatment, maltreatment, misappropriation, misuse, perversion. **2** *verbal abuse.* curse, execration, imprecation, insult, invective, obscenity, slander, vilification, vituperation. • *v* **1** damage, exploit, harm, hurt, ill-treat, injure, maltreat, misuse, molest, rape, spoil, treat roughly. **2** *abuse verbally*. affront, berate, be rude to, *inf* call names, castigate, curse, defame, denigrate, insult, inveigh against, libel, malign, revile, slander, *inf* smear, sneer at, swear at, vilify, vituperate, wrong.

abusive *adj* acrimonious, angry, censorious, critical, cruel, defamatory, denigrating, derogatory, disparaging, hurtful, impolite, injurious, insulting, libellous, offensive, opprobrious, pejorative, rude, scathing, scornful, scurrilous, slanderous, vituperative. *Opp* POLITE.

abysmal *adj* **1** bottomless, boundless, deep, immeasurable, incalculable, infinite, profound, vast. **2** ▷ BAD.

abyss *n inf* bottomless pit, chasm, crater, fissure, gap, gulf, hole, pit, rift, void.

academic *adj* **1** educational, pedagogical, scholastic. **2** bookish, brainy, clever, erudite, highbrow, intelligent, learned, scholarly, studious. **3** *academic study*. abstract, conjectural, hypothetical, impractical, intellectual, speculative, theoretical. • *n inf* egghead, highbrow, intellectual, scholar, thinker.

accelerate *v* **1** *inf* get a move on, go faster, hasten, pick up speed, quicken, speed up. **2** bring on, expedite, spur on, step up, stimulate.

accent *n* **1** brogue, cadence, dialect, enunciation, intonation, pronunciation, speech pattern, tone. **2** accentuation, beat, emphasis, pulse, rhythm, stress.

accept *v* **1** get, *inf* jump at, receive, take, welcome. **2** acknowledge, admit, bear, put up with, reconcile yourself to, resign yourself to, submit to, suffer, tolerate, undertake. **3** *accept an argument*. abide by, accede to, acquiesce in, agree to, believe in, be reconciled to, consent to, defer to, grant, recognize, *inf* stomach, *inf* swallow, take in. *Opp* REJECT.

acceptable *adj* **1** agreeable, gratifying, pleasant, pleasing, worthwhile. **2** adequate, admissible, moderate, passable, satisfactory, suitable, tolerable. *Opp* UNACCEPTABLE.

acceptance *n* acquiescence, agreement, approval, consent. *Opp* REFUSAL.

accepted *adj* acknowledged, agreed, axiomatic, common, indisputable, recognized, standard, undisputed, unquestioned. *Opp* CONTROVERSIAL.

accessible *adj* approachable, at hand, attainable, available, close, convenient, *inf* handy, within reach. *Opp* INACCESSIBLE.

accessory *n* **1** addition, appendage, attachment, component, extra. **2** ▷ ACCOMPLICE.

accident *n* **1** blunder, chance, coincidence, fate, fluke, fortune, luck, misadventure, mischance, mishap, mistake, *inf* pot luck, serendipity. **2** catastrophe, collision, crash, disaster, *inf* pile-up, wreck.

accidental *adj* arbitrary, casual, chance, coincidental, *inf* fluky, fortuitous, fortunate, haphazard, inadvertent, lucky, random, unexpected, unforeseen, unintended, unintentional, unlucky, unplanned, unpremeditated. *Opp* INTENTIONAL.

acclaim *v* applaud, celebrate, cheer, clap, commend, extol, hail, honour, praise, salute, welcome.

accommodate *v* **1** assist, equip, fit, furnish, help, provide, serve, supply. **2** *accommodate guests*. billet, board, cater for, harbour, house, lodge, provide for, *inf* put up, quarter, shelter, take in. **3** *accommodate yourself to new surroundings*. accustom, adapt, reconcile. **accommodating** ▷ CONSIDERATE.

accommodation *n* board, home, housing, lodgings, pied-à-terre, premises, shelter. □ *apartment*, inf *bedsit*, *boarding house*, inf *digs*, *flat*, *guest house*, *hall of residence*, *hostel*, *hotel*, *inn*, *motel*, *pension*, *rooms*, *self-catering*, *timeshare*, *youth hostel*. ▷ HOUSE.

accompany *v* **1** attend, chaperon, conduct, escort, follow, go with, guard, guide, look after, partner, *inf* tag along with. **2** be associated with, be linked with, belong with, complement, occur with, supplement.

accompanying *adj* associated, attached, attendant, complementary, related.

accomplice *n* abettor, accessory, associate, collaborator, colleague, confederate, conspirator, helper, partner.

accomplish *v* achieve, attain, *inf* bring off, carry out, carry through, complete, consummate, discharge, do successfully, effect, finish, fulfil, realize, succeed in.

accomplished *adj* adept, expert, gifted, polished, proficient, skilful, talented.

accomplishment *n* ability, attainment, expertise, gift, skill, talent.

accord *n* agreement, concord, harmony, rapport, understanding.

account *n* **1** bill, calculation, check, computation, invoice, receipt, reckoning, *inf* score, statement. **2** commentary, description, diary, explanation, history, log, memoir, narrative, record, report, statement, story, tale, *inf* write-up. **3** *of no account.* advantage, benefit, concern, consequence, importance, interest, significance, use, value, worth. **account for** ▷ EXPLAIN.

accumulate *v* accrue, aggregate, amass, assemble, bring together, build up, collect, come together, gather, grow, heap up, hoard, increase, multiply, pile up, stockpile, store up. *Opp* DISPERSE.

accumulation *n inf* build-up, collection, conglomeration, gathering, heap, hoard, mass, stockpile, store.

accurate *adj* authentic, careful, correct, exact, factual, faultless, meticulous, minute, nice, perfect, precise, reliable, scrupulous, sound, *inf* spot-on, true, truthful, unerring, veracious. *Opp* INACCURATE.

accusation *n* allegation, charge, citation, complaint, impeachment, indictment, summons.

accuse *v* attack, blame, bring charges against, censure, charge, condemn, denounce, impeach, impugn, indict, *inf* point the finger at, prosecute, summons, tax. *Opp* DEFEND.

accustomed *adj* common, customary, established, expected, familiar, habitual, normal, ordinary, prevailing, routine, traditional, usual. **get accustomed** ▷ ADAPT.

ache *n* anguish, discomfort, hurt, pain, pang, smart, soreness, throbbing, twinge. • *v* **1** be painful, be sore, hurt, smart, sting, throb. **2** ▷ DESIRE.

achieve *v* **1** accomplish, attain, bring off, carry out, complete, conclude, do successfully, effect, engineer, execute, finish, fulfil, manage, succeed in. **2** *achieve fame.* acquire, earn, gain, get, obtain, reach, win.

acid *adj* sharp, sour, stinging, tangy, tart, vinegary. *Opp* SWEET.

acknowledge *v* **1** accede, accept, acquiesce, admit, allow, concede, confess, confirm, endorse, grant, own up to, profess. *Opp* DENY. **2** *acknowledge a greeting.* answer, react to, reply to, respond to, return. **3** *acknowledge a friend.* greet, hail, recognize, *inf* say hello to. *Opp* IGNORE.

acme *n* apex, crown, height, highest point, peak, pinnacle, summit, top, zenith. *Opp* NADIR.

acquaint *v* announce, apprise, brief, enlighten, inform, make aware, make familiar, notify, reveal, tell.

acquaintance *n* **1** awareness, familiarity, knowledge, understanding. **2** ▷ FRIEND.

acquire *v* buy, come by, earn, get, obtain, procure, purchase.

acquisition *n* accession, addition, *inf* buy, gain, possession, purchase.

acquit *v* absolve, clear, declare innocent, discharge, excuse, exonerate, find innocent, free, *inf* let off, release, reprieve, set free, vindicate. *Opp* CONDEMN. **acquit yourself** ▷ BEHAVE.

acrid *adj* bitter, caustic, pungent, sharp, unpleasant.

acrimonious *adj* abusive, acerbic, angry, bad-tempered, bitter, caustic, hostile, hot-tempered, ill-natured, ill-tempered, irascible, quarrelsome, rancorous, sarcastic, sharp, spiteful, tart, testy, venomous, virulent, waspish. *Opp* PEACEABLE.

act *n* **1** deed, exploit, feat, operation, undertaking. ▷ ACTION. **2** *act of parliament.* bill [= *draft act*], decree, edict, law, regulation, statute. **3** *a stage act.* performance, routine, sketch, turn. • *v* **1** behave, carry on, conduct yourself, deport yourself. **2** function, operate, serve, take effect, work. **3** *Act now!* do something, get involved, take steps. ▷ BEGIN. **4** *act a role.* appear (as), *derog* camp it up, characterize, dramatize, enact, *derog* ham it up, impersonate, mime, mimic, *derog* overact, perform, personify, play, portray, pose as, represent. ▷ PRETEND.

acting *adj* deputy, interim, stand-by, stopgap, substitute, temporary, vice-.

action *n* **1** act, deed, enterprise, exploit, feat, measure, performance, proceeding, step, undertaking, work. **2** activity, drama, energy, enterprise, excitement, exertion, liveliness, movement, vigour, vitality. **3** *action of a play.* events, happenings, story. **4** *action of a watch.* mechanism, operation, working, works. **5** *military action.* ▷ BATTLE.

activate *v* actuate, energize, excite, fire, galvanize, initiate, mobilize, rouse, set in motion, set off, start, stimulate, trigger.

active *adj* **1** animated, brisk, bustling, busy, dynamic, energetic, enthusiastic, functioning, hyperactive, live, lively, militant, nimble, *inf* on the go, restless, sprightly, strenuous, vigorous, vivacious, working. **2** *active support.* committed, dedicated, devoted, diligent, hard-working, industrious, involved, occupied, sedulous, staunch, zealous. *Opp* INACTIVE.

activity *n* **1** action, animation, bustle, commotion, energy, hurly-burly, hustle, industry, life, movement, stir. **2** hobby, interest, job, occupation, pastime, pursuit, task, venture. ▷ WORK.

actor, actress *ns* artist, artiste, lead, leading lady, performer, player, star, supporting actor. ▷ ENTERTAINER. **actors** cast, company, troupe.

actual *adj* authentic, bona fide, confirmed, corporeal, definite, existing, factual, genuine, indisputable, in existence, legitimate, living, material, real, tangible, true, verifiable. *Opp* IMAGINARY.

acute *adj* **1** narrow, pointed, sharp. **2** *acute pain.* excruciating, exquisite, extreme, intense, keen, piercing, racking, severe, sharp, shooting, violent. **3** *an acute mind.* alert, analytical, astute, *inf* cute, discerning, incisive, intelligent, keen, penetrating, perceptive, sharp, subtle. ▷ CLEVER. **4** *an acute problem.* crucial, immediate, important, overwhelming, pressing, serious, urgent. **5** *an acute illness.* critical, sudden. *Opp* CHRONIC, STUPID.

adapt *v* **1** acclimatize, accustom, adjust, attune, become conditioned, become hardened, fit, get accustomed (to), get used (to), habituate, reconcile, suit, tailor, turn. **2** *adapt to a new use.* alter, amend, change, convert, modify, process, rearrange, rebuild, reconstruct, refashion, remake, reorganize, transform. ▷ EDIT.

add *v* annex, append, attach, combine, integrate, join, *inf* tack on, unite. *Opp* DEDUCT. **add to** ▷ INCREASE. **add up (to)** ▷ TOTAL.

addict *n* **1** alcoholic, *sl* junkie, *inf* user. **2** ▷ ENTHUSIAST.

addiction *n* compulsion, craving, dependence, fixation, habit, obsession.

addition *n* **1** adding up, calculation, computation, reckoning, totalling, *inf* totting up. **2** accession, accessory, accretion, addendum, additive, adjunct, admixture, annexe, appendage, appendix, appurtenance, attachment, continuation, development, expansion, extension, extra, increase, increment, postscript, supplement.

additional *adj* added, extra, further, increased, more, new, other, spare, supplementary.

address *n* **1** directions, location, whereabouts. **2** *deliver an address*. discourse, harangue, homily, lecture, sermon, speech, talk. • *v* **1** accost, approach, *inf* buttonhole, greet, hail, salute, speak to, talk to. **2** *address an audience*. give a speech to, harangue, lecture. **address yourself to** ▷ TACKLE.

adept *adj* clever, competent, gifted, practised, proficient. ▷ SKILFUL. *Opp* UNSKILFUL.

adequate *adj* acceptable, all right, average, competent, fair, fitting, middling, *inf* OK, passable, presentable, satisfactory, *inf* so-so, sufficient, tolerable. *Opp* INADEQUATE.

adhere *v* bind, bond, cement, cling, glue, gum, paste. ▷ STICK.

adherent *n* aficionado, devotee, fan, follower, *inf* hanger-on, supporter.

adhesive *adj* glued, gluey, gummed. ▷ STICKY.

adjoining *adj* abutting, adjacent, bordering, contiguous, juxtaposed, neighbouring, next, touching. *Opp* DISTANT.

adjourn *v* break off, defer, discontinue, interrupt, postpone, put off, suspend.

adjournment *n* break, interruption, pause, postponement, recess, stay, suspension.

adjust *v* **1** adapt, alter, amend, balance, change, convert, correct, modify, put right, rectify, regulate, remake, remodel, reorganize, reshape, set, tailor, temper, tune. **2** acclimatize, accommodate, accustom, fit, habituate, reconcile yourself.

administer *v* **1** administrate, conduct affairs, control, direct, govern, lead, manage, organize, oversee, preside over, regulate, rule, run, supervise. **2** *administer justice*. carry out, execute, implement, prosecute. **3** *administer medicine*. dispense, distribute, give, hand out, measure out, mete out, provide, supply.

administrator *n* bureaucrat, civil servant, controller, director, executive, manager, *derog* mandarin, organizer. ▷ CHIEF.

admirable *adj* awe-inspiring, commendable, creditable, deserving, estimable, excellent, exemplary, great, honourable, laudable, marvellous, meritorious, pleasing, praiseworthy, wonderful, worthy. *Opp* CONTEMPTIBLE.

admiration *n* appreciation, awe, commendation, esteem, hero-worship, high regard, honour, praise, respect. *Opp* CONTEMPT.

admire *v* applaud, appreciate, approve of, be delighted by, commend, esteem, have a high opinion of, hero-worship, honour, idolize, laud, look up to, marvel at, praise, respect, revere, think highly of, value, venerate, wonder at. ▷ LOVE. **admiring** ▷ COMPLIMENTARY, RESPECTFUL.

admission *n* **1** access, admittance, entrance, entry. **2** acceptance, acknowledgement, affirmation, concession, confession, declaration, disclosure, revelation. *Opp* DENIAL.

admit *v* **1** accept, allow in, let in, provide a place (in), receive, take in. **2** *admit guilt*. accept, acknowledge, allow, concede, confess, declare, disclose, own up, recognize, reveal, say reluctantly. *Opp* DENY.

adolescence *n* boyhood, girlhood, growing up, puberty, *inf* your teens, youth.

adolescent *adj* boyish, girlish, immature, juvenile, pubescent, teenage, youthful. • *n* boy, girl, juvenile, minor, *inf* teenager, youngster, youth.

adopt *v* **1** appropriate, approve, back, choose, embrace, endorse, follow, *inf* go for, patronize, support, take on, take up. **2** befriend, foster, stand by, take in.

adore *v* adulate, dote on, glorify, honour, love, revere, venerate, worship. ▷ ADMIRE. *Opp* HATE.

adorn *v* beautify, decorate, embellish, garnish, ornament, trim.

adrift *adj* **1** afloat, anchorless, drifting, floating. **2** aimless, astray, directionless, lost, purposeless.

adult *adj* full-grown, full-size, grown-up, marriageable, mature, of age. *Opp* IMMATURE.

adulterate *v* alloy, contaminate, corrupt, debase, dilute, *inf* doctor, pollute, taint, weaken.

advance *n* development, evolution, forward movement, growth, headway, improvement, progress. • *v* **1** approach, bear down, come near, forge ahead, gain ground, go forward, make headway, make progress, move forward, press on, progress, *inf* push on. *Opp* RETREAT. **2** *science advances.* develop, evolve, improve, prosper, thrive. **3** *advance your career.* accelerate, assist, benefit, boost, further, help the progress of, promote. *Opp* HINDER. **4** *advance a theory.* adduce, give, present, propose, submit, suggest. **5** *advance money.* lend, offer, pay, provide, supply. *Opp* WITHHOLD.

advanced *adj* **1** latest, modern, sophisticated, up-to-date. **2** *advanced ideas.* avant-garde, contemporary, experimental, forward-looking, futuristic, imaginative, innovative, new, novel, original, pioneering, progressive, revolutionary, trend-setting, *inf* way-out. **3** *advanced maths.* complex, difficult, hard, higher. **4** *advanced for her age.* grown-up, mature, precocious, sophisticated, well-developed. *Opp* BACKWARD, BASIC.

advantage *n* **1** aid, asset, assistance, benefit, boon, gain, help, profit, usefulness. **2** *have an advantage.* dominance, edge, *inf* head start, superiority. **take advantage of** ▷ EXPLOIT.

advantageous *adj* beneficial, favourable, helpful, positive, profitable, salutary, useful, valuable, worthwhile. ▷ GOOD. *Opp* USELESS.

adventure *n* **1** chance, escapade, exploit, feat, gamble, occurrence, risk, undertaking, venture. **2** danger, excitement, hazard.

adventurous *adj* **1** audacious, bold, brave, courageous, daredevil, daring, *derog* foolhardy, intrepid, *derog* reckless, venturesome. **2** *an adventurous trip.* challenging, dangerous, difficult, exciting, hazardous, risky. *Opp* UNADVENTUROUS.

adversary *n* antagonist, attacker, enemy, foe, opponent.

adverse *adj* **1** attacking, censorious, critical, derogatory, hostile, hurtful, inimical, negative, uncomplimentary, unfavourable, unkind, unsympathetic. **2** *adverse conditions.* deleterious, detrimental, disadvantageous, harmful, inappropriate, opposing, prejudicial, uncongenial, unpropitious. *Opp* FAVOURABLE.

advertise *v* announce, broadcast, display, flaunt, make known, market, merchandise, *inf* plug, proclaim, promote, publicize, *inf* push, show off, tout.

advertisement *n inf* advert, bill, *inf* blurb, circular, commercial, handout, leaflet, notice, placard, *inf* plug, poster, promotion, publicity, sign, *inf* small ad.

advice *n* **1** admonition, counsel, guidance, help, opinion, recommendation, tip, view, warning. **2** ▷ NEWS.

advisable *adj* expedient, judicious, politic, prudent, recommended, sensible. ▷ WISE.

advise *v* **1** admonish, caution, counsel, enjoin, exhort, guide, instruct, recommend, suggest, urge, warn. **2** ▷ INFORM.

adviser *n* confidant(e), consultant, counsellor, guide, mentor.

advocate *n* **1** apologist, backer, champion, proponent, supporter. **2** ▷ LAWYER. ● *v* argue for, back, champion, favour, recommend, speak for, uphold.

aesthetic *adj* artistic, beautiful, cultivated, sensitive, tasteful. *Opp* UGLY.

affair *n* **1** activity, business, concern, interest, issue, matter, project, subject, topic, undertaking. **2** circumstance, episode, event, happening, incident, occurrence, thing. **3** *love affair.* amour, attachment, intrigue, involvement, liaison, relationship, romance.

affect *v* **1** act on, agitate, alter, attack, change, concern, disturb, have an effect on, have an impact on, impinge on, impress, influence, move, perturb, relate to, stir, touch, trouble, upset. **2** *affect an accent.* adopt, assume, feign, *inf* put on. ▷ PRETEND.

affectation *n* artificiality, insincerity, mannerism, posturing. ▷ PRETENCE.

affected *adj* **1** artificial, contrived, insincere, *inf* put on, studied, unnatural. ▷ PRETENTIOUS. **2** *affected by disease.* afflicted, damaged, infected, injured, poisoned, stricken, troubled.

affection *n* attachment, fondness, friendliness, friendship, liking, partiality, *inf* soft spot, tenderness, warmth. ▷ LOVE.

affectionate *adj* caring, doting, fond, kind, tender. ▷ LOVING. *Opp* ALOOF.

affinity *n* closeness, compatibility, kinship, like-mindedness, likeness, rapport, relationship, similarity, sympathy.

affirm *v* assert, aver, avow, declare, maintain, state, swear, testify.

affirmation *n* assertion, avowal, declaration, oath, promise, statement, testimony.

affirmative *adj* agreeing, assenting, concurring, confirming, positive. *Opp* NEGATIVE.

afflict *v* affect, annoy, beset, bother, burden, cause suffering to, distress, harass, harm, hurt, oppress, pain, plague, torment, torture, trouble, try, worry, wound.

affluent *adj* **1** *inf* flush, *sl* loaded, moneyed, prosperous, rich, wealthy, *inf* well-heeled, well-off, well-to-do. **2** *affluent life-style.* expensive, gracious, lavish, opulent, self-indulgent, sumptuous. *Opp* POOR.

afford *v* **1** be rich enough, have the means, manage to give, sacrifice, *inf* stand. **2** ▷ PROVIDE.

afloat *adj* aboard, adrift, floating, on board ship, under sail.

afraid *adj* **1** aghast, agitated, alarmed, anxious, apprehensive, cowardly, cowed, daunted, diffident, faint-hearted, fearful, frightened, hesitant, horrified, intimidated, jittery, nervous, panicky, panic-stricken, reluctant, scared, terrified, timid, timorous, trembling, unheroic, *inf* windy. *Opp* FEARLESS. **2** [*inf*] *I'm afraid I'm late.* apologetic, regretful, sorry. **be afraid** ▷ FEAR.

afterthought *n* addendum, addition, extra, postscript.

age *n* **1** advancing years, decrepitude, dotage, old age, senility. **2** *a bygone age.* days, epoch, era, time. **3** [*inf*] *ages ago.* lifetime, long time. ● *v* degenerate, grow older, look older, mature, mellow, ripen. **aged** ▷ OLD.

agenda *n* list, plan, programme, schedule, timetable.

agent *n* broker, delegate, envoy, executor, *old use* functionary, go-between, intermediary, mediator, middleman, negotiator, proxy, representative, surrogate, trustee.

aggravate *v* **1** add to, augment, compound, exacerbate, exaggerate, increase, inflame, intensify, make worse, worsen. *Opp* ALLEVIATE. **2** [Some think this use wrong.] ▷ ANNOY.

aggressive *adj* antagonistic, assertive, bellicose, belligerent, bullying, *sl* butch, destructive, hostile, *sl* macho, militant, offensive, pugnacious, pushful, *inf* pushy, quarrelsome, violent, warlike. *Opp* DEFENSIVE, PEACEABLE.

aggressor *n* assailant, attacker, instigator, invader.

agile *adj* acrobatic, adroit, deft, fleet, graceful, lissom, lithe, mobile, nimble, quick-moving, sprightly, spry, supple. *Opp* CLUMSY.

agitate *v* **1** beat, churn, froth up, ruffle, shake, stimulate, stir, toss, work up. **2** alarm, arouse, confuse, discomfit, disconcert, excite, fluster, incite, perturb, stir up, trouble, unsettle, upset, worry. *Opp* CALM. **agitated** ▷ EXCITED, NERVOUS.

agitator *n* firebrand, rabblerouser, revolutionary, troublemaker.

agonize *v* hurt, labour, suffer, worry, wrestle.

agony *n* anguish, distress, suffering, torment, torture. ▷ PAIN.

agree *v* **1** accede, acquiesce, admit, allow, assent, be willing, concede, consent, grant, make a contract, pledge yourself, promise, undertake. **2** accord, be unanimous, be united, concur, correspond, fit, get on, harmonize, match, *inf* see eye to eye. *Opp* DISAGREE. **agree on** ▷ CHOOSE. **agree with** ▷ ENDORSE.

agreeable *adj* acceptable, delightful, enjoyable, nice. ▷ PLEASANT. *Opp* DISAGREEABLE.

agreement *n* **1** accord, compatibility, concord, conformity, consensus, consent, consistency, correspondence, harmony, similarity, sympathy, unanimity, unity. **2** alliance, armistice, arrangement, bargain, compact, contract, convention, covenant, deal, *Fr* entente, pact, settlement, treaty, truce, understanding. *Opp* DISAGREEMENT.

agricultural *adj* **1** agrarian, bucolic, pastoral, rural. **2** *agricultural land.* cultivated, farmed, productive, tilled.

agriculture *n* agronomy, crofting, cultivation, farming, husbandry, tilling.

aground *adj* beached, grounded, helpless, marooned, shipwrecked, stranded.

aid *n* assistance, avail, backing, benefit, cooperation, donation, funding, grant, guidance, help, loan, patronage, relief, sponsorship, subsidy, succour, support. • *v* abet, assist, back, benefit, collaborate with, cooperate with, encourage, facilitate, help, *inf* lend a hand, promote, prop up, *inf* rally round, relieve, subsidize, succour, support.

ailing *adj* feeble, infirm, poorly, sick, unwell, weak. ▷ ILL.

ailment *n* affliction, disorder, infirmity, sickness. ▷ ILLNESS.

aim *n* ambition, cause, design, destination, direction, dream, focus, goal, hope, intent, intention, mark, object, objective, plan, purpose, wish. • *v* **1** address, beam, direct, fire at, line up, point, sight, take aim, train, turn, zero in on. **2** *aim to win.* aspire, design, endeavour, essay, intend, plan, propose, resolve, strive, try, want, wish.

aimless *adj* chance, directionless, purposeless, rambling, random, undisciplined, unfocused. *Opp* PURPOSEFUL.

air *n* **1** airspace, atmosphere, ether, heavens, sky. **2** *fresh air.* breath, breeze, draught, wind, *poet* zephyr. **3** *air of authority.* ambience, appearance, aspect, aura, bearing, character, demeanour, feeling, impression, look, manner, mood, style. • *v* **1** aerate, dry off, freshen, ventilate. **2** *air opinions.* articulate, display, exhibit, express, give vent to, make known, make public, vent, voice.

aircraft *n old use* flying-machine. □ *aeroplane, airliner, airship, balloon, biplane, bomber, dirigible, fighter, glider, gunship, hang-glider, helicopter, jet, jumbo, jump-jet, monoplane, plane, seaplane.*

airman *n* aviator, flier, pilot.

airport *n* aerodrome, airfield, air strip, heliport, landing-strip, runway.

airy *adj* breezy, draughty, fresh, open, ventilated. *Opp* STUFFY.

aisle *n* corridor, passage, passageway.

akin *adj* allied, related, similar.

alarm *n* **1** alert, signal, warning. □ *alarm-clock, bell, fire-alarm, siren, whistle.* **2** anxiety, consternation, dismay, fright, nervousness, panic, uneasiness. ▷ FEAR. ● *v* agitate, dismay, distress, panic, *inf* put the wind up, shock, startle, unnerve, worry. ▷ FRIGHTEN. *Opp* REASSURE.

alcohol *n sl* bevvy, *inf* booze, drink, intoxicant, liquor, spirits, wine.

alcoholic *adj* brewed, distilled, fermented, intoxicating, *inf* strong. ● *n* addict, dipsomaniac, drunkard, inebriate. *Opp* TEETOTALLER.

alert *adj* active, alive (to), attentive, awake, careful, eagle-eyed, heedful, lively, observant, on the lookout, on the watch, on your guard, on your toes, perceptive, ready, sensitive, sharp-eyed, vigilant, watchful, wide-awake. *Opp* ABSENT-MINDED, INATTENTIVE. ● *v* advise, alarm, forewarn, make aware, notify, signal, tip off, warn.

alibi *n* excuse, explanation.

alien *adj* extra-terrestrial, foreign, outlandish, strange, unfamiliar. ● *n* foreigner, newcomer, outsider, stranger.

alight *adj* ablaze, aflame, blazing, burning, fiery, ignited, illuminated, lit up, live, on fire. ● *v* come down, come to rest, disembark, dismount, get down, get off, land, touch down.

align *v* **1** arrange in line, line up, straighten up. **2** *align with the opposition.* affiliate, ally, associate, join, side, sympathize.

alike *adj* analogous, cognate, comparable, equivalent, identical, indistinguishable, like, matching, parallel, resembling, similar, twin, uniform. *Opp* DISSIMILAR.

alive *adj* **1** animate, breathing, existing, extant, flourishing, in existence, live, living, *old use* quick. **2** *alive to new ideas.* ▷ ALERT. *Opp* DEAD.

allay *v* calm, check, diminish, ease, mollify, pacify, quell, quench, quieten, reduce, slake (*thirst*), subdue. ▷ ALLEVIATE. *Opp* STIMULATE.

allegation *n* accusation, assertion, charge, claim, declaration, statement, testimony.

allege *v* assert, asseverate, attest, aver, avow, claim, declare, depose, maintain, make a charge, plead, state.

allegiance *n* devotion, duty, faithfulness, fidelity, loyalty.

allergic *adj* antipathetic, averse, hostile, incompatible (with), opposed.

alleviate *v* abate, allay, ameliorate, assuage, check, diminish, ease, lessen, lighten, mitigate, moderate, quell, quench, reduce, relieve, slake (*thirst*), soften, subdue, temper. *Opp* AGGRAVATE.

alliance *n* affiliation, agreement, bloc, cartel, coalition, compact, concordat, confederation, connection, consortium, covenant, entente, federation, guild, marriage, pact, partnership, relationship, treaty, union.

allot *v* allocate, allow, assign, deal out, *inf* dish out, dispense, distribute, *inf* dole out, give out, grant, provide, ration, share out.

allow *v* **1** approve, authorize, consent to, enable, grant permission for, let, license, permit, sanction, *inf* stand, tolerate. *Opp* FORBID. **2** acknowledge, admit, concede, grant, own. **3** ▷ ALLOT. *Opp* DENY.

allowance *n* **1** allocation, measure, portion, quota, ration, share. **2** alimony, annuity, grant, payment, pension, pocket money. **3** *allowance on the full price.* deduction, discount, rebate, reduction. **make allowances for** ▷ TOLERATE.

alloy *n* admixture, aggregate, amalgam, blend, compound, fusion, mixture.

allude *v* **allude to** make an allusion to, mention, refer to, speak of, touch on.

allure *v* attract, beguile, cajole, charm, decoy, draw, entice, fascinate, lead on, lure, magnetize, seduce, tempt.

allusion *n* mention, reference, suggestion.

ally *n* abettor, accessory, accomplice, associate, backer, collaborator, colleague, companion, comrade, confederate, friend, helper, helpmate, *inf* mate, partner, supporter. *Opp* ENEMY. • *v* affiliate, amalgamate, associate, band together, collaborate, combine, confederate, cooperate, form an alliance, fraternize, join, join forces, league, *inf* link up, marry, merge, side, *inf* team up, unite.

almighty *adj* **1** all-powerful, omnipotent, supreme. **2** ▷ BIG.

almost *adv* about, all but, approximately, around, as good as, just about, nearly, not quite, practically, virtually.

alone *adj* apart, by yourself, deserted, desolate, forlorn, friendless, isolated, lonely, lonesome, on your own, separate, single, solitary, solo, unaccompanied, unassisted.

aloof *adj* chilly, cold, cool, detached, disinterested, dispassionate, distant, formal, frigid, haughty, impassive, inaccessible, indifferent, remote, reserved, reticent, self-contained, self-possessed, *inf* standoffish, supercilious, unapproachable, unconcerned, undemonstrative, unemotional, unforthcoming, unfriendly, uninvolved, unresponsive, unsociable, unsympathetic. *Opp* FRIENDLY, SOCIABLE.

aloud *adv* audibly, clearly, distinctly, out loud.

also *adv* additionally, besides, furthermore, in addition, moreover, *joc* to boot, too.

alter *v* adapt, adjust, amend, change, convert, edit, emend, enlarge, modify, reconstruct, reduce, reform, remake, remodel, reorganize, reshape, revise, transform, vary.

alteration *n* adaptation, adjustment, amendment, change, conversion, difference, modification, reorganization, revision, transformation.

alternate *v* come alternately, follow each other, interchange, oscillate, replace each other, rotate, *inf* seesaw, substitute for each other, take turns.

alternative *n* **1** choice, option, selection. **2** back-up, replacement, substitute.

altitude *n* elevation, height.

altogether *adv* absolutely, completely, entirely, fully, perfectly, quite, thoroughly, totally, utterly, wholly.

always *adv* consistently, constantly, continually, continuously, endlessly, eternally, everlastingly, evermore, forever, invariably, perpetually, persistently, regularly, repeatedly, unceasingly, unfailingly, unremittingly.

amalgamate *v* affiliate, ally, associate, band together, blend, coalesce, combine, come together, compound, confederate, form an alliance, fuse, integrate, join, join forces, league, *inf* link up, marry, merge, mix, put together, synthesize, *inf* team up, unite. *Opp* SPLIT.

amateur *adj* inexperienced, lay, unpaid, unqualified. ▷ AMATEURISH. • *n* dabbler, dilettante, enthusiast, layman, non-professional. *Opp* PROFESSIONAL.

amateurish *adj* clumsy, crude, *inf* do-it-yourself, incompetent, inept, inexpert, *inf* roughand-ready, second-rate, shoddy, unpolished, unprofessional, unskilful, unskilled, untrained. *Opp* SKILLED.

amaze *v* astonish, astound, awe, bewilder, confound, confuse, daze, disconcert, dumbfound, *inf* flabbergast, perplex, *inf* rock, shock, stagger, startle, stun, stupefy, surprise. **amazed** ▷ SURPRISED.

amazing *adj* astonishing, astounding, awe-inspiring, breathtaking, exceptional, exciting, extraordinary, *inf* fantastic, incredible, miraculous, notable, phenomenal, prodigious, remarkable, *inf* sensational, shocking, special, staggering, startling, stunning, stupendous, unusual, *inf* wonderful. *Opp* ORDINARY.

ambassador *n* agent, attaché, *Fr* chargé d'affaires, consul, diplomat, emissary, envoy, legate, nuncio, plenipotentiary, representative.

ambiguous *adj* ambivalent, confusing, enigmatic, equivocal, indefinite, indeterminate, puzzling, uncertain, unclear, vague, woolly. ▷ UNCERTAIN. *Opp* DEFINITE.

ambition *n* **1** commitment, drive, energy, enterprise, enthusiasm, *inf* go, initiative, *inf* push, pushfulness, self-assertion, thrust, zeal. **2** aim, aspiration, desire, dream, goal, hope, ideal, intention, object, objective, target, wish.

ambitious *adj* **1** assertive, committed, eager, energetic, enterprising, enthusiastic, go-ahead, *inf* go-getting, hard-working, industrious, keen, *inf* pushy, zealous. **2** *ambitious ideas. inf* big, far-reaching, grand, grandiose, large-scale, unrealistic. *Opp* APATHETIC.

ambivalent *adj* ambiguous, back-handed (*compliment*), confusing, doubtful, equivocal, inconclusive, inconsistent, indefinite, self-contradictory, *inf* two-faced, unclear, uncommitted, unresolved, unsettled. ▷ UNCERTAIN.

ambush *n* ambuscade, attack, snare, surprise attack, trap. • *v* attack, ensnare, entrap, intercept, lie in wait for, pounce on, surprise, swoop on, trap, waylay.

amenable *adj* accommodating, acquiescent, adaptable, agreeable, biddable, complaisant, compliant, cooperative, deferential, docile, open-minded, persuadable, responsive, submissive, tractable, willing. *Opp* OBSTINATE.

amend *v* adapt, adjust, alter, ameliorate, change, convert, correct, edit, emend, improve, make better, mend, modify, put right, rectify, reform, remedy, reorganize, reshape, revise, transform, vary.

amiable *adj* affable, agreeable, amicable, friendly, genial, good-natured, kind-hearted, kindly, likeable, well-disposed. *Opp* UNFRIENDLY.

ammunition *n* buckshot, bullet, cartridge, grenade, missile, projectile, round, shell, shrapnel.

amoral *adj* lax, loose, unethical, unprincipled, without standards. ▷ IMMORAL. *Opp* MORAL.

amorous *adj* affectionate, ardent, carnal, doting, enamoured, erotic, fond, impassioned, loving, lustful, passionate, *sl* randy, sexual, *inf* sexy. *Opp* COLD.

amount *n* aggregate, bulk, entirety, extent, lot, mass, measure, quantity, quantum, reckoning, size, sum, supply, total, value, volume, whole. • *v* **amount to** add up to, aggregate, be equivalent to, come to, equal, make, mean, total.

ample *adj* abundant, bountiful, broad, capacious, commodious, considerable, copious, extensive, fruitful, generous, great, large, lavish, liberal, munificent, plentiful, profuse, roomy, spacious, substantial, unstinting, voluminous. ▷ BIG, PLENTY. *Opp* INSUFFICIENT.

amplify *v* **1** add to, augment, broaden, develop, dilate upon, elaborate, enlarge, expand, expatiate on, extend, fill out, lengthen, make fuller, make longer, supplement. **2** *amplify sound.* boost, heighten, increase, intensify, magnify, make louder, raise the volume. *Opp* DECREASE.

amputate *v* chop off, cut off, dock, lop off, poll, pollard, remove, sever, truncate. ▷ CUT.

amuse *v* absorb, beguile, cheer (up), delight, divert, engross, enliven, entertain, gladden, interest, involve, make laugh, occupy, please, raise a smile, *inf* tickle. *Opp* BORE. **amusing** ▷ ENJOYABLE, FUNNY.

amusement *n* **1** delight, enjoyment, fun, hilarity, laughter, mirth. ▷ MERRIMENT. **2** distraction, diversion, entertainment, game, hobby, interest, joke, leisure activity, pastime, play, pleasure, recreation, sport.

anaemic *adj* bloodless, colourless, feeble, frail, pale, pallid, pasty, sallow, sickly, unhealthy, wan, weak.

analogy *n* comparison, likeness, metaphor, parallel, resemblance, similarity, simile.

analyse *v* anatomize, assay, break down, criticize, dissect, evaluate, examine, interpret, investigate, scrutinize, separate out, take apart, test.

analysis *n* breakdown, critique, dissection, enquiry, evaluation, examination, interpretation, investigation, *inf* post-mortem, scrutiny, study, test. *Opp* SYNTHESIS.

analytical *adj* analytic, critical, *inf* in-depth, inquiring, investigative, logical, methodical, penetrating, questioning, rational, searching, systematic. *Opp* SUPERFICIAL.

anarchy *n* bedlam, chaos, confusion, disorder, disorganization, insurrection, lawlessness, misgovernment, misrule, mutiny, pandemonium, riot. *Opp* ORDER.

ancestor *n* antecedent, forebear, forefather, forerunner, precursor, predecessor, progenitor.

ancestry *n* blood, derivation, descent, extraction, family, genealogy, heredity, line, lineage, origin, parentage, pedigree, roots, stock, strain.

anchor *v* berth, make fast, moor, secure, tie up. ▷ FASTEN.

anchorage *n* harbour, haven, marina, moorings, port, refuge, sanctuary, shelter.

ancient *adj* **1** aged, antediluvian, antiquated, antique, archaic, elderly, fossilized, obsolete, old, old-fashioned, outmoded, out-of-date, passé, superannuated, time-worn, venerable. **2** *ancient times.* bygone, earlier, early, former, *poet* immemorial, *inf* olden, past, prehistoric, primeval, primitive, primordial, remote, *old use* of yore. *Opp* MODERN.

angel *n* archangel, cherub, divine messenger, seraph.

angelic *adj* **1** beatific, blessed, celestial, cherubic, divine, ethereal, heavenly, holy, seraphic, spiritual. **2** *angelic behaviour.* exemplary, innocent, pious, pure, saintly, unworldly, virtuous. ▷ GOOD. *Opp* DEVILISH.

anger *n* angry feelings, annoyance, antagonism, bitterness, choler, displeasure, exasperation, fury, hostility, indignation, ire, irritability, outrage, passion, pique, rage, rancour, resentment, spleen, tantrum, temper, vexation, wrath. • *v inf* aggravate, antagonize, *sl* bug, displease, *inf* drive mad, enrage, exasperate, incense, incite, inflame, infuriate, irritate, madden, make angry, *inf* make someone's blood boil, *inf* needle, outrage, pique, provoke, *inf* rile, vex. ▷ ANNOY. *Opp* PACIFY.

angle *n* **1** bend, corner, crook, nook, point. **2** *a new angle.* approach, outlook, perspective, point of view, position, slant, standpoint, viewpoint. • *v* bend, bevel, chamfer, slant, turn, twist.

angry *adj inf* aerated, apoplectic, bad-tempered, bitter, *inf* bristling, *inf* choked, choleric, cross, disgruntled, enraged, exasperated, excited, fiery, fuming, furious, heated, hostile, *inf* hot under the collar, ill-tempered, incensed, indignant, infuriated, *inf* in high dudgeon, irascible, irate, livid, mad, outraged, provoked, raging, *inf* ratty, raving, resentful, riled, seething, smouldering, *inf* sore, splenetic, *sl* steamed up, stormy, tempestuous, vexed, *inf* ugly, *inf* up in arms, wild, wrathful. ▷ ANNOYED. *Opp* CALM. **be angry, become angry** *inf* be in a paddy, *inf* blow up, boil, bridle, bristle, flare up, *inf* fly off the handle, fulminate, fume, *inf* get steamed up, lose your temper, rage, rant, rave, *inf* see red, seethe, snap, storm. **make angry** ▷ ANGER.

anguish *n* agony, anxiety, distress, grief, heartache, misery, pain, sorrow, suffering, torment, torture, tribulation, woe.

angular *adj* bent, crooked, indented, jagged, sharp-cornered, zigzag. *Opp* STRAIGHT.

animal *adj* beastly, bestial, brutish, carnal, fleshly, inhuman, instinctive, physical, savage, sensual, subhuman, wild. • *n* beast, being, brute, creature, *pl* fauna, organism, *pl* wildlife. □ *amphibian, arachnid, biped, carnivore, herbivore, insect, invertebrate, mammal, marsupial, mollusc, monster, omnivore, pet, quadruped, reptile, rodent, scavenger, vertebrate.* ▷ BIRD, FISH, INSECT. □ *aardvark, antelope, ape, armadillo, baboon, badger, bear, beaver, bison, buffalo, camel, caribou, cat, chamois, cheetah, chimpanzee, chinchilla, chipmunk, coypu, deer, dog, dolphin, donkey, dormouse, dromedary, elephant, elk, ermine, ferret, fox, frog, gazelle, gerbil, gibbon, giraffe, gnu, goat, gorilla, grizzly bear, guinea-pig, hamster, hare, hedgehog, hippopotamus, horse, hyena, ibex, impala, jackal, jaguar, jerboa, kangaroo, koala, lemming, lemur, leopard, lion, llama, lynx, marmoset, marmot, marten, mink, mongoose, monkey, moose, mouse, musquash, ocelot, octopus, opossum, orang-utan, otter, panda, panther, pig, platypus, polar bear, pole-cat, porcupine, porpoise, rabbit, rat, reindeer, rhinoceros, roe, salamander, scorpion, seal, sea-lion, sheep, shrew, skunk, snake, spider, squirrel, stoat, tapir, tiger, toad, vole, wallaby, walrus, weasel, whale, wildebeest, wolf, wolverine, wombat, yak, zebra.*

animate *adj* alive, breathing, conscious, feeling, live, living, sentient. ▷ ANIMATED. *Opp* INANIMATE. • *v* activate, arouse, brighten up, *inf* buck up, cheer up, encourage, energize, enliven, excite, exhilarate, fire, galvanize, incite, inspire, invigorate, kindle, liven up, make lively, move, *inf* pep up, *inf* perk up, quicken, rejuvenate, revitalize, revive, rouse, spark, spur, stimulate, stir, urge, vitalize.

animated *adj* active, alive, bright, brisk, bubbling, busy, cheerful, eager, ebullient, energetic, enthusiastic, excited, exuberant, gay, impassioned, lively, passionate, quick, spirited, sprightly, vibrant, vigorous, vivacious, zestful. *Opp* LETHARGIC.

animation *n* activity, briskness, eagerness, ebullience, energy, enthusiasm, excitement, exhilaration, gaiety, high spirits, life, liveliness, *inf* pep, sparkle, spirit, sprightliness, verve, vigour, vitality, vivacity, zest. *Opp* LETHARGY.

animosity *n* acerbity, acrimony, animus, antagonism, antipathy, asperity, aversion, bad blood, bitterness, dislike, enmity, grudge, hate, hatred, hostility, ill will, loathing, malevolence, malice, malignancy, malignity, odium, rancour, resentment, sarcasm, sharpness, sourness, spite, unfriendliness, venom, vindictiveness, virulence. *Opp* FRIENDLINESS.

annex *v* acquire, appropriate, conquer, occupy, purloin, seize, take over, usurp.

annihilate *v* abolish, destroy, eliminate, eradicate, erase, exterminate, extinguish, extirpate, *inf* finish off, *inf* kill off, *inf* liquidate, nullify, obliterate, raze, slaughter, wipe out.

annotation *n* comment, commentary, elucidation, explanation, footnote, gloss, interpretation, note.

announce *v* **1** advertise, broadcast, declare, disclose, divulge, give notice of, intimate, make public, notify, proclaim, promulgate, propound, publicize, publish, put out, report, reveal, state. **2** *announce a speaker.* introduce, lead into, preface, present.

announcement *n* advertisement, bulletin, communiqué, declaration, disclosure, intimation, notification, proclamation, promulgation, publication, report, revelation, statement.

announcer *n* anchorman, anchorwoman, broadcaster, commentator, compère, disc jockey, DJ, *poet* harbinger, herald, master of ceremonies, *inf* MC, messenger, newscaster, newsreader, reporter, town crier.

annoy *v inf* aggravate, antagonize, *inf* badger, be an annoyance to, bother, *sl* bug, chagrin, displease, distress, drive mad, exasperate, fret, gall, *inf* get at, *inf* get on your nerves, grate, harass, harry, infuriate, irk, irritate, jar, madden, make cross, molest, *inf* needle, *inf* nettle, offend, peeve, pester, pique, *inf* plague, provoke, put out, rankle, rile, *inf* rub up the wrong way, ruffle, *inf* spite, tease, trouble, try (someone's patience), upset, vex, worry. ▷ ANGER. *Opp* PLEASE.

annoyance *n* **1** chagrin, crossness, displeasure, exasperation, irritation, pique, vexation. ▷ ANGER. **2** *Noise is an annoyance. inf* aggravation, bother, harassment, irritant, nuisance, offence, *inf* pain in the neck, pest, provocation, worry.

annoyed *adj* chagrined, cross, displeased, exasperated, *inf* huffy, irritated, jaundiced, *inf* miffed, *inf* needled, *inf* nettled, offended, *inf* peeved, piqued, *inf* put out, *inf* riled, *inf* shirty, *inf* sore, upset, vexed. ▷ ANGRY. *Opp* PLEASED. **be annoyed** *inf* go off in a huff, take offence, *inf* take umbrage.

annoying *adj inf* aggravating, bothersome, displeasing, exasperating, galling, grating, inconvenient, infuriating, irksome, irritating, jarring, maddening, offensive, provocative, provoking, tiresome, troublesome, trying, upsetting, vexatious, vexing, wearisome, worrying.

anoint *v* **1** embrocate, grease, lubricate, oil, rub, smear. **2** bless, consecrate, dedicate, hallow, sanctify.

anonymous *adj* **1** incognito, nameless, unacknowledged, unidentified, unknown, unnamed, unspecified, unsung. **2** *anonymous letters.* unattributed, unsigned. **3** *anonymous style.* characterless, impersonal, nondescript, unidentifiable, unrecognizable, unremarkable.

answer *n* **1** acknowledgement, *inf* comeback, reaction, rejoinder, reply, response, retort, riposte. **2** explanation, outcome, solution. **3** *answer to a charge.* countercharge, defence, plea, rebuttal, refutation, vindication. • *v* **1** acknowledge, give an answer, react, rejoin, reply, respond, retort, return. **2** explain, resolve, solve. **3** *answer a charge.* counter, defend yourself against, disprove, rebut, refute. **4** *answer a need.* correspond to, echo, fit, match up to, meet, satisfy, serve, suffice, suit. **answer back** ▷ ARGUE.

antagonism *n* antipathy, dissension, enmity, friction, opposition, rancour, rivalry, strife. ▷ HOSTILITY.

antagonize *v* alienate, anger, annoy, embitter, estrange, irritate, make an enemy of, offend, provoke, *inf* put off, upset.

anthem *n* canticle, chant, chorale, hymn, introit, paean, psalm.

anthology *n* collection, compendium, compilation, digest, miscellany, selection, treasury.

anticipate *v* **1** forestall, obviate, preclude, pre-empt, prevent. **2** [Many think this use incorrect.] ▷ FORESEE.

anticlimax *n* bathos, *inf* comedown, *inf* damp squib, disappointment, *inf* let-down.

antics *plur n* buffoonery, capers, clowning, escapades, foolery, fooling, *inf* larking-about, pranks, *inf* skylarking, tomfoolery, tricks.

antidote *n* antitoxin, corrective, countermeasure, cure, drug, neutralizing agent, remedy.

antiquarian *n* antiquary, antiques expert, collector, dealer.

antiquated *adj* aged, anachronistic, ancient, antediluvian, archaic, dated, medieval, obsolete, old, old-fashioned, *inf* out, out-dated, outmoded, out-of-date, passé, *inf* past it, *inf* prehistoric, *inf* primeval, primitive, quaint, superannuated, unfashionable. ▷ ANTIQUE. *Opp* NEW.

antique *adj* antiquarian, collectible, historic, old-fashioned, traditional, veteran, vintage. ▷ ANTIQUATED. • *n* collectible, collector's item, curio, curiosity, *Fr* objet d'art, rarity.

antiquity *n* classical times, days gone by, former times, *inf* olden days, the past.

antiseptic *adj* aseptic, clean, disinfectant, disinfected, germ free, germicidal, hygienic, medicated, sanitized, sterile, sterilized, sterilizing, unpolluted.

antisocial *adj* alienated, anarchic, disagreeable, disorderly, disruptive, misanthropic, nasty, obnoxious, offensive, rebellious, rude, troublesome, uncooperative, undisciplined, unruly, unsociable. ▷ UNFRIENDLY. *Opp* SOCIABLE.

anxiety *n* **1** angst, apprehension, concern, disquiet, distress, doubt, dread, fear, foreboding, fretfulness, misgiving, nervousness, qualm, scruple, strain, stress, tension, uncertainty, unease, worry. **2** *anxiety to succeed.* desire, eagerness, enthusiasm, impatience, keenness, longing, solicitude, willingness.

anxious *adj* **1** afraid, agitated, alarmed, apprehensive, concerned, distracted, distraught, distressed, disturbed, edgy, fearful, *inf* fraught, fretful, *inf* jittery, nervous, *inf* nervy, *inf* on edge, overwrought, perturbed, restless, tense, troubled, uneasy, upset, watchful, worried. **2** *anxious to succeed.* avid, careful, desirous, *inf* desperate, *inf* dying, eager, impatient, intent, *inf* itching, keen, longing, solicitous, willing, yearning. **be anxious** ▷ WORRY.

apathetic *adj* casual, cool, dispassionate, dull, emotionless, half-hearted, impassive, inactive, indifferent, indolent, languid, lethargic, listless, passive, phlegmatic, slow, sluggish, tepid, torpid, unambitious, uncommitted, unconcerned, unenterprising, unenthusiastic, unfeeling, uninterested, uninvolved, unmotivated, unresponsive. *Opp* ENTHUSIASTIC.

apathy *n* coolness, inactivity, indifference, lassitude, lethargy, listlessness, passivity, torpor. *Opp* ENTHUSIASM.

apex *n* **1** crest, crown, head, peak, pinnacle, point, summit, tip, top, vertex. **2** *apex of your career.* acme, apogee, climax, consummation, crowning moment, culmination, height, high point, zenith. *Opp* NADIR.

aphrodisiac *adj* arousing, erotic, *inf* sexy, stimulating.

apologetic *adj* ashamed, blushing, conscience-stricken, contrite, penitent, red-faced, regretful, remorseful, repentant, rueful, sorry. *Opp* UNREPENTANT.

apologize *v* ask pardon, be apologetic, express regret, make an apology, repent, say sorry.

apology *n* acknowledgement, confession, defence, excuse, explanation, justification, plea.

apostle *n* crusader, disciple, evangelist, follower, messenger, missionary, preacher, propagandist, proselytizer, teacher.

appal *v* alarm, disgust, dismay, distress, harrow, horrify, nauseate, outrage, revolt, shock, sicken, terrify, unnerve. ▷ FRIGHTEN. **appalling** ▷ ATROCIOUS, BAD, FRIGHTENING.

apparatus *n* appliance, *inf* contraption, device, equipment, gadget, *inf* gear, implement, instrument, machine, machinery, mechanism, *inf* set-up, system, *inf* tackle, tool, utensil.

apparent *adj* blatant, clear, conspicuous, detectable, discernible, evident, manifest, noticeable, observable, obvious, ostensible, overt, patent, perceptible, recognizable, self-explanatory, unconcealed, unmistakable, visible. *Opp* HIDDEN.

apparition *n* chimera, ghost, hallucination, illusion, manifestation, phantasm, phantom, presence, shade, spectre, spirit, *inf* spook, vision, wraith.

appeal *n* **1** application, call, *Fr* cri de coeur, cry, entreaty, petition, plea, prayer, request, solicitation, supplication. **2** allure, attractiveness, charisma, charm, *inf* pull, seductiveness. • *v* ask earnestly, beg, beseech, call, canvass, cry out, entreat, implore, invoke, petition, plead, pray, request, solicit, supplicate. **appeal to** ▷ ATTRACT.

appear *v* **1** arise, arrive, attend, begin, be published, be revealed, be seen, *inf* bob up, come, come into view, come out, *inf* crop up, enter, develop, emerge, *inf* heave into sight, loom, materialize, occur, originate, show, *inf* show up, spring up, surface, turn up. **2** *I appear to be wrong.* look, seem, turn out. **3** *appear in a play.* ▷ PERFORM.

appearance *n* **1** arrival, advent, emergence, presence, rise. **2** *a smart appearance.* air, aspect, bearing, demeanour, exterior, impression, likeness, look, mien, semblance.

appease *v* assuage, calm, conciliate, humour, mollify, pacify, placate, propitiate, quiet, reconcile, satisfy, soothe, *inf* sweeten, tranquillize, win over. *Opp* ANGER.

appendix *n* addendum, addition, annexe, codicil, epilogue, postscript, rider, supplement.

appetite *n* craving, demand, desire, eagerness, fondness, greed, hankering, hunger, keenness, longing, lust, passion, predilection, proclivity, relish, *inf* stomach, taste, thirst, urge, willingness, wish, yearning, *inf* yen, zeal, zest.

appetizing *adj* delicious, *inf* moreish, mouthwatering, tasty, tempting.

applaud *v* acclaim, approve, *inf* bring the house down, cheer, clap, commend, compliment, congratulate, eulogize, extol, *inf* give someone a hand, give someone an ovation, hail, laud, praise, salute. *Opp* CRITICIZE.

applause *n* acclaim, acclamation, approval, cheering, clapping, éclat, ovation, plaudits. ▷ PRAISE.

appliance *n* apparatus, contraption, device, gadget, implement, instrument, machine, mechanism, tool, utensil.

applicant *n* aspirant, candidate, competitor, entrant, interviewee, participant, postulant.

apply *v* **1** administer, affix, bring into contact, lay on, put on, rub on, spread, stick. ▷ FASTEN. **2** *rules apply to all.* appertain, be relevant, have a bearing (on), pertain, refer, relate. **3** *apply common sense.* bring into use, employ, exercise, implement, practise, use, utilize, wield. **apply for** ▷ REQUEST. **apply yourself** ▷ CONCENTRATE.

appoint *v* **1** arrange, authorize, decide on, determine, establish, fix, ordain, prescribe, settle. **2** *appoint you to do a job.* assign, choose, co-opt, delegate, depute, designate, detail, elect, make an appointment, name, nominate, *inf* plump for, select, settle on, vote for.

appointment *n* **1** arrangement, assignation, consultation, date, engagement, fixture, interview, meeting, rendezvous, session, *old use* tryst. **2** choice, choosing, commissioning, election, naming, nomination, selection. **3** job, office, place, position, post, situation.

appreciate *v* **1** admire, applaud, approve of, be grateful for, be sensitive to, cherish, commend, enjoy, esteem, favour, find worthwhile, like, praise, prize, rate highly, regard highly, respect, sympathize with, treasure, value, welcome. **2** *appreciate the facts.* acknowledge, apprehend, comprehend, know, realize, recognize, see, understand. **3** *value appreciates.* build up, escalate, gain, go up, grow, improve, increase, inflate, mount, rise, soar, strengthen. *Opp* DEPRECIATE, DESPISE, DISREGARD.

apprehensive *adj* afraid, concerned, disturbed, edgy, fearful, *inf* jittery, nervous, *inf* nervy, *inf* on edge, troubled, uneasy, worried. ▷ ANXIOUS. *Opp* FEARLESS.

apprentice *n* beginner, learner, novice, probationer, pupil, starter, tiro, trainee.

approach *n* **1** advance, advent, arrival, coming, movement, nearing. **2** access, doorway, entrance, entry, passage, road, way in. **3** *your approach to work.* attitude, course, manner, means, method, mode, *Lat* modus operandi, procedure, style, system, technique, way. **4** *an approach for help.* appeal, application, invitation, offer, overture, proposal, proposition. • *v* **1** advance, bear down, catch up, come near, draw near, gain (on), loom, move towards, near, progress. *Opp* RETREAT. **2** *approach a task*. ▷ BEGIN. **3** *approach someone for help*. ▷ CONTACT.

approachable *adj* accessible, affable, informal, kind, open, relaxed, sympathetic, *inf* unstuffy, well-disposed. ▷ FRIENDLY. *Opp* ALOOF.

appropriate *adj* applicable, apposite, apropos, apt, becoming, befitting, compatible, correct, decorous, deserved, due, felicitous, fit, fitting, germane, happy, just, *old use* meet, opportune, pertinent, proper, relevant, right, seasonable, seemly, suitable, tactful, tasteful, timely, well-judged, well-suited, well-timed. *Opp* INAPPROPRIATE. • *v* annex, arrogate, commandeer, confiscate, expropriate, gain control of, *inf* hijack, requisition, seize, take, take over, usurp. ▷ STEAL.

approval *n* **1** acclaim, acclamation, admiration, applause, appreciation, approbation, commendation, esteem, favour, liking, plaudits, praise, regard, respect, support. *Opp* DISAPPROVAL. **2** acceptance, acquiescence, agreement, assent, authorization, *inf* blessing, confirmation, consent, endorsement, *inf* go-ahead, *inf* green light, licence, mandate, *inf* OK, permission, ratification, sanction, seal, stamp, support, *inf* thumbs up, validation. *Opp* REFUSAL.

approve *v* accede to, accept, affirm, agree to, allow, assent to, authorize, *inf* back, *inf* bless, confirm, consent to, countenance, endorse, *inf* give your blessing to, *inf* go along with, pass, permit, ratify, *inf* rubber-stamp, sanction, sign, subscribe to, support, tolerate, uphold, validate. *Opp* REFUSE, VETO. **approve of** ▷ ADMIRE.

approximate *adj* close, estimated, imprecise, inexact, loose, near, rough. *Opp* EXACT. • *v* **approximate to** approach, be close to, be similar to, border on, come near to, equal roughly, look like, resemble, simulate, verge on.

approximately *adv* about, approaching, around, *Lat* circa, close to, just about, loosely, more or less, nearly, *inf* nigh on, *inf* pushing, roughly, round about.

aptitude *n* ability, bent, capability, facility, fitness, flair, gift, suitability, talent. ▷ SKILL.

arbitrary *adj* **1** capricious, casual, chance, erratic, fanciful, illogical, indiscriminate, irrational, random, subjective, unplanned, unpredictable, unreasonable, whimsical, wilful. *Opp* METHODICAL. **2** *arbitrary rule*. absolute, autocratic, despotic, dictatorial, high-handed, imperious, summary, tyrannical, tyrannous, uncompromising.

arbitrate *v* adjudicate, decide the outcome, intercede, judge, make peace, mediate, negotiate, pass judgement, referee, settle, umpire.

arbitration *n* adjudication, *inf* good offices, intercession, judgement, mediation, negotiation, settlement.

arbitrator *n* adjudicator, arbiter, go-between, intermediary, judge, mediator, middleman, negotiator, ombudsman, peacemaker, referee, *inf* trouble-shooter, umpire.

arch *n* arc, archway, bridge, vault. • *v* arc, bend, bow. ▷ CURVE.

archetype *n* classic, example, ideal, model, original, paradigm, pattern, precursor, prototype, standard.

archives *plur n* annals, chronicles, documents, history, libraries, memorials, museums, papers, records, registers.

ardent *adj* eager, enthusiastic, fervent, hot, impassioned, intense, keen, passionate, warm, zealous. *Opp* APATHETIC.

arduous *adj* backbreaking, demanding, exhausting, gruelling, heavy, herculean, laborious, onerous, punishing, rigorous, severe, strenuous, taxing, tiring, tough, uphill. ▷ DIFFICULT. *Opp* EASY.

area *n* **1** acreage, breadth, expanse, extent, patch, sheet, size, space, square-footage, stretch, surface, tract, width. **2** district, environment, environs, locality, neighbourhood, part, precinct, province, quarter, region, sector, terrain, territory, vicinity, zone. **3** *an area of study*. field, sphere, subject.

argue *v* **1** answer back, *inf* bandy words, bargain, bicker, debate, deliberate, demur, differ, disagree, discuss, dispute, dissent, expostulate, fall out, feud, fight, haggle, have an argument, *inf* have words, object, protest, quarrel, remonstrate, *inf* row, spar, squabble, take exception, wrangle. **2** *argue a case*. assert, claim, contend, demonstrate, hold, maintain, make a case, plead, prove, reason, show, suggest.

argument *n* **1** altercation, bickering, clash, conflict, controversy, difference (of opinion), disagreement, dispute, expostulation, feud, fight, protest, quarrel, remonstration, row, *inf* set-to, squabble, *inf* tiff, wrangle. **2** consultation, debate, defence, deliberation, dialectic, discussion, exposition, polemic. **3** *argument of a lecture*. abstract, case, contention, gist, hypothesis, idea, outline, plot, reasoning, summary, synopsis, theme, thesis, view.

arid *adj* **1** barren, desert, dry, fruitless, infertile, lifeless, parched, sterile, torrid, unproductive, waste, waterless. *Opp* FRUITFUL. **2** *arid work*. boring, dreary, dull, pointless, tedious, uninspired, uninteresting, vapid.

arise *v* come up, crop up, get up, rise. ▷ APPEAR.

aristocrat *n* grandee, lady, lord, noble, nobleman, noblewoman, patrician. ▷ PEER.

aristocratic *adj inf* blueblooded, courtly, élite, gentle, highborn, lordly, noble, patrician, princely, royal, thoroughbred, titled, upper class.

arm *n* appendage, bough, branch, extension, limb, offshoot, projection. • *v* equip, fortify, furnish, provide, supply. **arms** ▷ WEAPON(S).

armed services *pl n* force, forces, troops. □ *air force, army, militia, navy.* □ *cavalry, infantry.* □ *battalion, brigade, cohort, company, corps, foreign legion, garrison, legion, patrol, platoon, rearguard, regiment, reinforcements, squad, squadron, task-force, vanguard.* ▷ FIGHTER, RANK, SOLDIER.

armistice *n* agreement, cease-fire, peace, treaty, truce.

armoury *n* ammunition-dump, arsenal, depot, magazine, ordnance depot, stockpile.

aroma *n* bouquet, fragrance, odour, perfume, redolence, savour, scent, smell, whiff.

arouse *v* awaken, call forth, encourage, foment, foster, kindle, provoke, quicken, stimulate, stir up, *inf* whip up. ▷ CAUSE. *Opp* ALLAY.

arrange *v* **1** adjust, align, array, categorize, classify, collate, display, dispose, distribute, grade, group, lay out, line up, marshal, order, organize, *inf* pigeon-hole, position, put in order, range, rank, set out, sift, sort (out), space out, systematize, tabulate, tidy up. **2** *arrange a party*. bring about, contrive, coordinate, devise, manage, organize, plan, prepare, see to, settle, set up. **3** *arrange music*. adapt, harmonize, orchestrate, score, set.

arrangement *n* **1** adjustment, alignment, design, disposition, distribution, grouping, layout, marshalling, organization, planning, positioning, setting out, spacing, tabulation. ▷ ARRAY. **2** agreement, bargain, compact, contract, deal, pact, scheme, settlement, terms, understanding. **3** *musical arrangement*. adaptation, harmonization, orchestration, setting, version.

array *n* arrangement, assemblage, collection, demonstration, display, exhibition, formation, *inf* line-up, muster, panoply, parade, presentation, show, spectacle. • *v* **1** adorn, apparel, attire, clothe, deck, decorate, dress, equip, fit out, garb, rig out, robe, wrap. **2** ▷ ARRANGE.

arrest *n* apprehension, capture, detention, seizure. ● *v* **1** bar, block, check, delay, end, halt, hinder, impede, inhibit, interrupt, obstruct, prevent, restrain, retard, slow, stem, stop. **2** *arrest a suspect.* apprehend, *inf* book, capture, catch, *inf* collar, detain, have up, hold, *inf* nab, *inf* nick, *inf* pinch, *inf* run in, seize, take into custody, take prisoner.

arrival *n* **1** advent, appearance, approach, coming, entrance, home-coming, landing, return, touchdown. **2** *new arrivals.* caller, newcomer, visitor.

arrive *v* **1** appear, come, disembark, drive up, drop in, enter, get in, land, make an entrance, *inf* roll in, *inf* roll up, show up, touch down, turn up. **2** ▷ SUCCEED. **arrive at** ▷ REACH.

arrogant *adj* boastful, brash, brazen, bumptious, cavalier, *inf* cocky, conceited, condescending, disdainful, egotistical, haughty, *inf* high and mighty, high-handed, imperious, impudent, insolent, lofty, lordly, overbearing, patronizing, pompous, presumptuous, proud, scornful, self-admiring, self-important, smug, snobbish, *inf* snooty, *inf* stuck-up, supercilious, superior, vain. *Opp* MODEST.

arsonist *n* fire-raiser, incendiary, pyromaniac.

art *n* **1** aptitude, artistry, cleverness, craft, craftsmanship, dexterity, expertise, facility, knack, proficiency, skilfulness, skill, talent, technique, touch, trick. **2** artwork, craft, fine art. □ *architecture, batik, carpentry, cloisonné, collage, crochet, drawing, embroidery, enamelling, engraving, etching, fashion design, graphics, handicraft, illustration, jewellery, knitting, linocut, lithography, marquetry, metalwork, modelling, monoprint, needlework, origami, painting, patchwork, photography, pottery, printmaking, sculpture, sewing, sketching, spinning, weaving, woodcut, woodwork.*

artful *adj* astute, canny, clever, crafty, cunning, deceitful, designing, devious, *inf* fly, *inf* foxy, ingenious, knowing, scheming, shrewd, skilful, sly, smart, sophisticated, subtle, tricky, wily. *Opp* NAÏVE.

article *n* **1** item, object, thing. **2** *magazine article.* ▷ WRITING.

articulate *adj* clear, coherent, comprehensible, distinct, eloquent, expressive, fluent, *derog* glib, intelligible, lucid, understandable, vocal. *Opp* INARTICULATE. ● *v* ▷ SPEAK.

articulated *adj* bending, flexible, hinged, jointed.

artificial *adj* **1** fabricated, made-up, man-made, manufactured, synthetic, unnatural. **2** *artificial style.* affected, assumed, bogus, concocted, contrived, counterfeit, factitious, fake, false, feigned, forced, imitation, insincere, laboured, mock, *inf* phoney, pretended, pseudo, *inf* put on, sham, simulated, spurious, unreal. *Opp* NATURAL.

artist *n* craftsman, craftswoman. □ *architect, carpenter, cartoonist, commercial artist, designer, draughtsman, draughtswoman, engraver, goldsmith, graphic designer, illustrator, mason, painter, photographer, potter, printer, sculptor, silversmith, smith, weaver.* ▷ ENTERTAINER, MUSICIAN, PERFORMER.

artistic *adj* aesthetic, attractive, beautiful, creative, cultured, decorative, *inf* designer, imaginative, ornamental, tasteful. *Opp* UGLY.

ascend *v* climb, come up, defy gravity, fly, go up, levitate, lift off, make an ascent, mount, move up, rise, scale, slope up, soar, take off. *Opp* DESCEND.

ascent *n* ascension, climb, gradient, hill, incline, ramp, rise, slope. *Opp* DESCENT.

ascertain *v* confirm, determine, discover, establish, find out, identify, learn, make certain, make sure, settle, verify.

ascetic *adj* abstemious, austere, celibate, chaste, frugal, harsh, hermit-like, plain, puritanical, restrained, rigorous, selfcontrolled, self-denying, selfdisciplined, severe, spartan, strict, temperate. *Opp* SELF-INDULGENT.

ash *n* burnt remains, cinders, clinker, embers.

ashamed *adj* **1** abashed, apologetic, chagrined, chastened, conscience-stricken, contrite, discomfited, distressed, guilty, humbled, humiliated, mortified, penitent, red-faced, remorseful, repentant, rueful, shamefaced, sorry, upset. **2** *ashamed of your nakedness.* bashful, blushing, demure, diffident, embarrassed, modest, prudish, self-conscious, sheepish, shy. *Opp* SHAMELESS.

ask *v* appeal, apply, badger, beg, beseech, catechize, crave, demand, enquire, entreat, implore, importune, inquire, interrogate, invite, petition, plead, pose a question, pray, press, query, question, quiz, request, require, seek, solicit, sue, supplicate. **ask for** ▷ ATTRACT.

asleep *adj* comatose, *inf* dead to the world, dormant, dozing, *inf* fast off, hibernating, inactive, inattentive, *inf* in the land of nod, *sl* kipping, napping, *inf* off, *inf* out like a light, resting, sedated, sleeping, slumbering, snoozing, *inf* sound off, unconscious, under sedation. ▷ NUMB. *Opp* AWAKE.

aspect *n* **1** angle, attribute, characteristic, circumstance, detail, element, facet, feature, quality, side, standpoint, viewpoint. **2** air, appearance, attitude, bearing, countenance, demeanour, expression, face, look, manner, mien, visage. **3** *a southern aspect.* direction, orientation, outlook, position, prospect, situation, view.

asperity *n* abrasiveness, acerbity, acidity, acrimony, astringency, bitterness, churlishness, crossness, harshness, hostility, irascibility, irritability, peevishness, rancour, roughness, severity, sharpness, sourness, venom, virulence. *Opp* MILDNESS.

aspiration *n* aim, ambition, craving, desire, dream, goal, hope, longing, objective, purpose, wish, yearning.

aspire *v* **aspire to** aim for, crave, desire, dream of, hope for, long for, pursue, seek, set your sights on, strive after, want, wish for, yearn for. **aspiring** ▷ POTENTIAL.

assail *v* assault, bombard, pelt, set on. ▷ ATTACK.

assault *n* battery, *inf* GBH, mugging, rape. ▷ ATTACK. • *v* abuse, assail, *inf* beat up, *inf* do over, fall on, fight, fly at, jump on, lash out at, *inf* lay into, mob, molest, mug, *inf* pitch into, pounce on, rape, rush at, set about, set on, strike at, violate, *inf* wade into. ▷ ATTACK.

assemble *v* **1** come together, congregate, convene, converge, crowd, flock, gather, group, herd, join up, meet, rally round, swarm, throng round. **2** accumulate, amass, bring together, collect, gather, get together, marshal, mobilize, muster, pile up, rally, round up. **3** build, construct, erect, fabricate, fit together, make, manufacture, piece together, produce, put together. *Opp* DISMANTLE, DISPERSE.

assembly *n* assemblage, conclave, conference, congregation, congress, convention, convocation, council, gathering, meeting, parliament, rally, synod. ▷ CROWD.

assent *n* acceptance, accord, acquiescence, agreement, approbation, approval, compliance, consent, *inf* go-ahead, permission, sanction, willingness. *Opp* REFUSAL. • *v* accede, accept, acquiesce, agree, approve, be willing, comply, concede, concur, consent, express agreement, give assent, say 'yes', submit, yield. *Opp* REFUSE.

assert *v* affirm, allege, argue, asseverate, attest, claim, contend, declare, emphasize, insist, maintain, proclaim, profess, protest, state, stress, swear, testify. **assert yourself** ▷ INSIST.

assertive *adj* aggressive, assured, authoritative, bold, *inf* bossy, certain, confident, decided, decisive, definite, dogmatic, domineering, emphatic, firm, forceful, insistent, peremptory, *derog* opinionated, positive, *derog* pushy, self-assured, strong, strong-willed, *derog* stubborn, uncompromising. *Opp* SUBMISSIVE.

assess *v* appraise, assay (*metal*), calculate, compute, consider, determine, estimate, evaluate, fix, gauge, judge, price, reckon, review, *inf* size up, value, weigh up, work out.

asset *n* advantage, aid, benefit, blessing, boon, *inf* godsend, good, help, profit, resource, strength, support. **assets** capital, effects, estate, funds, goods, holdings, means, money, possessions, property, resources, savings, securities, valuables, wealth, *inf* worldly goods.

assign *v* **1** allocate, allot, apportion, consign, dispense, distribute, give, hand over, share out. **2** *assign to a job*. appoint, authorize, delegate, designate, nominate, ordain, prescribe, put down, select, specify, stipulate. **3** *assign my success to luck*. accredit, ascribe, attribute, credit.

assignment *n* chore, duty, errand, job, mission, obligation, post, project, responsibility, task. ▷ WORK.

assist *v* abet, advance, aid, back, benefit, boost, collaborate, co-operate, facilitate, further, help, *inf* lend a hand, promote, *inf* rally round, reinforce, relieve, second, serve, succour, support, sustain, work with. *Opp* HINDER.

assistance *n* aid, backing, benefit, collaboration, contribution, co-operation, encouragement, help, patronage, reinforcement, relief, sponsorship, subsidy, succour, support. *Opp* HINDRANCE.

assistant *n* abettor, accessory, accomplice, acolyte, aide, ally, associate, auxiliary, backer, collaborator, colleague, companion, comrade, confederate, deputy, helper, helpmate, *inf* henchman, mainstay, *derog* minion, partner, *inf* right-hand man, *inf* right-hand woman, second, second-in-command, stand-by, subordinate, supporter.

associate *n* ▷ ASSISTANT, FRIEND. ● *v* **1** ally yourself, be friends, combine, consort, fraternize, *inf* gang up, *inf* go around (with), *sl* hang out (with), *inf* hob nob (with), join up, keep company, link up, make friends, mingle, mix, side, socialize. *Opp* DISSOCIATE. **2** *associate snow with winter*. bracket together, connect, put together, relate, *inf* tie up.

association *n* affiliation, alliance, amalgamation, body, brotherhood, cartel, clique, club, coalition, combination, company, confederation, consortium, cooperative, corporation, federation, fellowship, group, league, marriage, merger, organization, partnership, party, society, syndicate, trust, union. ▷ FRIENDSHIP.

assorted *adj* different, differing, *old use* divers, diverse, heterogeneous, manifold, miscellaneous, mixed, motley, multifarious, sundry, varied, various.

assortment *n* agglomeration, array, choice, collection, diversity, farrago, jumble, medley, mélange, miscellany, *inf* mishmash, *inf* mixed bag, mixture, pot-pourri, range, selection, variety.

assume *v* **1** believe, deduce, expect, guess, *inf* have a hunch, have no doubt, imagine, infer, presume, presuppose, suppose, surmise, suspect, take for granted, think, understand. **2** *assume duties*. accept, embrace, take on, undertake. **3** *assume an air of*. acquire, adopt, affect, don, dress up in, fake, feign, pretend, put on, simulate, try on, wear.

assumption *n* belief, conjecture, expectation, guess, hypothesis, premise, premiss, supposition, surmise, theory.

assurance *n* commitment, guarantee, oath, pledge, promise, vow, undertaking, word (of honour).

assure *v* convince, give a promise, guarantee, make sure, persuade, pledge, promise, reassure, swear, vow. **assured** ▷ CONFIDENT.

astonish *v* amaze, astound, baffle, bewilder, confound, daze, *inf* dazzle, dumbfound, electrify, *inf* flabbergast, leave speechless, nonplus, shock, stagger, startle, stun, stupefy, surprise, take aback, take by surprise, *inf* take your breath away, *sl* wow. **astonishing** ▷ AMAZING.

astound *v* ▷ ASTONISH.

astray *adv* adrift, amiss, awry, lost, off course, *inf* off the rails, wide of the mark, wrong.

astute *adj* acute, adroit, artful, canny, clever, crafty, cunning, discerning, *inf* fly, *inf* foxy, guileful, ingenious, intelligent, knowing, observant, perceptive, perspicacious, sagacious, sharp, shrewd, sly, subtle, wily. *Opp* STUPID.

asylum *n* cover, haven, refuge, retreat, safety, sanctuary, shelter.

asymmetrical *adj* awry, crooked, distorted, irregular, lop-sided, unbalanced, uneven, *inf* wonky. *Opp* SYMMETRICAL.

atheist *n* heathen, pagan, sceptic, unbeliever.

athletic *adj* acrobatic, active, energetic, fit, muscular, powerful, robust, sinewy, *inf* sporty, *inf* strapping, strong, sturdy, vigorous, well-built, wiry. *Opp* WEAK.

athletics *n* field events, track events. □ *cross-country, decathlon, discus, high jump, hurdles, javelin, long jump, marathon, pentathlon, pole-vault, relay, running, shot, sprint, triple jump.*

atmosphere *n* **1** aerospace, air, ether, heavens, ionosphere, sky, stratosphere, troposphere. **2** ambience, aura, character, climate, environment, feeling, mood, spirit, tone, *inf* vibes, vibrations.

atom *n inf* bit, crumb, grain, iota, jot, molecule, morsel, particle, scrap, speck, spot, trace.

atone *v* answer, be punished, compensate, do penance, expiate, make amends, make reparation, make up (for), pay the penalty, pay the price, recompense, redeem yourself, redress.

atrocious *adj* abominable, appalling, barbaric, bloodthirsty, brutal, brutish, callous, cruel, diabolical, dreadful, evil, execrable, fiendish, frightful, grim, gruesome, hateful, heartless, heinous, hideous, horrendous, horrible, horrific, horrifying, inhuman, merciless, monstrous, nauseating, revolting, sadistic, savage, shocking, sickening, terrible, vicious, vile, villainous, wicked.

atrocity *n* crime, cruelty, enormity, offence, outrage. ▷ EVIL.

attach *v* **1** add, affix, anchor, append, bind, combine, connect, couple, fix, join, link, secure, stick, tie, unite, weld. ▷ FASTEN. *Opp* DETACH. **2** ascribe, assign, associate, attribute, impute, place, relate to. **attached** ▷ LOVING.

attack *n* **1** aggression, ambush, assault, battery, blitz, bombardment, broadside, cannonade, charge, counter-attack, foray, incursion, invasion, offensive, onset, onslaught, pre-emptive strike, raid, rush, sortie, strike. **2** *verbal attack.* abuse, censure, criticism, diatribe, impugnment, invective, outburst, tirade. **3** *attack of coughing.* bout, convulsion, fit, outbreak, paroxysm, seizure, spasm, stroke, *inf* turn. ● *v* **1** ambush, assail, assault, *inf* beat up, *inf* blast, bombard, charge, counterattack, descend on, *inf* do over, engage, fall on, fight, fly at, invade, jump on, lash out at, *inf* lay into, mob, mug, *inf* pitch into, pounce on, raid, rush, set about, set on, storm, strike at, *inf* wade into. **2** *attack verbally.* abuse, censure, criticize, denounce, impugn, inveigh against, libel, malign, round on, slander, snipe at, traduce, vilify. *Opp* DEFEND. **3** *attack a task.* ▷ BEGIN.

attacker *n* aggressor, assailant, critic, detractor, enemy, intruder, invader, mugger, opponent, persecutor, raider, slanderer. ▷ FIGHTER.

attain *v* accomplish, achieve, acquire, arrive at, complete, earn, fulfil, gain, get, grasp, *inf* make, obtain, *inf* pull off, procure, reach, realize, secure, touch, win.

attempt *n* assault, bid, effort, endeavour, *inf* go, start, try, undertaking. • *v* aim, aspire, do your best, endeavour, essay, exert yourself, *inf* have a crack, *inf* have a go, make a bid, make an assault, make an effort, put yourself out, seek, *inf* spare no effort, strive, *inf* sweat blood, tackle, try, undertake, venture.

attend *v* **1** appear, be present, go (to), frequent, present yourself, *inf* put in an appearance, visit. **2** accompany, chaperon, conduct, escort, follow, guard, usher. **3** *attend carefully.* concentrate, follow, hear, heed, listen, mark, mind, note, notice, observe, pay attention, think, watch. **attend to** assist, care for, help, look after, mind, minister to, nurse, see to, take care of, tend, wait on.

attendant *n* assistant, escort, helper, usher. ▷ SERVANT.

attention *n* **1** alertness, awareness, care, concentration, concern, diligence, heed, notice, recognition, thought, vigilance. **2** *kind attention.* attentiveness, civility, consideration, courtesy, gallantry, good manners, kindness, politeness, regard, respect, thoughtfulness.

attentive *adj* **1** alert, awake, concentrating, heedful, intent, observant, watchful. *Opp* INATTENTIVE. **2** ▷ POLITE. *Opp* RUDE.

attire *n* accoutrements, apparel, array, clothes, clothing, costume, dress, finery, garb, garments, *inf* gear, *old use* habit, outfit, raiment, wear, *old use* weeds. • *v* ▷ DRESS.

attitude *n* **1** air, approach, aspect, bearing, behaviour, carriage, demeanour, disposition, frame of mind, manner, mien, mood, posture, stance. **2** *political attitudes.* approach, belief, feeling, opinion, orientation, outlook, position, standpoint, thought, view, viewpoint.

attract *v* **1** allure, appeal to, beguile, bewitch, bring in, captivate, charm, decoy, enchant, entice, fascinate, *sl* get someone going, interest, inveigle, lure, magnetize, seduce, tempt, *sl* turn someone on. **2** *a magnet attracts iron.* drag, draw, pull, tug at. **3** *attract attention.* ask for, cause, court, encourage, generate, incite, induce, invite, provoke, seek out, *inf* stir up. *Opp* REPEL.

attractive *adj* adorable, alluring, appealing, appetizing, becoming, bewitching, captivating, *inf* catchy (*tune*), charming, *inf* cute, delightful, desirable, disarming, enchanting, endearing, engaging, enticing, enviable, fascinating, fetching, flattering, glamorous, good-looking, gorgeous, handsome, hypnotic, interesting, inviting, irresistible, lovable, lovely, magnetic, personable, pleasing, prepossessing, pretty, quaint, seductive, sought-after, stunning, *inf* taking, tasteful, tempting, winning, winsome. ▷ BEAUTIFUL. *Opp* REPULSIVE.

attribute *n* characteristic, feature, property, quality, trait. • *v* accredit, ascribe, assign, blame, charge, credit, impute, put down, refer, trace back.

audacious *adj* adventurous, courageous, daring, fearless, *derog* foolhardy, intrepid, *derog* rash, *derog* reckless, venturesome. ▷ BOLD. *Opp* TIMID.

audacity *n* boldness, *inf* cheek, effrontery, forwardness, impertinence, impudence, presumptuousness, rashness, *inf* sauce, temerity. ▷ COURAGE.

audible *adj* clear, detectable, distinct, high, loud, noisy, recognizable. *Opp* INAUDIBLE.

audience *n* assembly, congregation, crowd, gathering, house, listeners, meeting, onlookers, *TV* ratings, spectators, *inf* turn-out, viewers.

auditorium *n* assembly room, concert-hall, hall, theatre.

augment *v* add to, amplify, boost, eke out, enlarge, expand, extend, fill out, grow, increase, intensify, magnify, make larger, multiply, raise, reinforce, strengthen, supplement, swell. *Opp* DECREASE.

augur *v* bode, forebode, foreshadow, forewarn, give an omen, herald, portend, predict, promise, prophesy, signal.

augury *n* forecast, forewarning, omen, portent, prophecy, sign, warning.

auspicious *adj* favourable, *inf* hopeful, lucky, positive, promising, propitious. *Opp* OMINOUS.

austere *adj* **1** abstemious, ascetic, chaste, cold, economical, exacting, forbidding, formal, frugal, grave, hard, harsh, hermit-like, parsimonious, puritanical, restrained, rigorous, self-denying, selfdisciplined, serious, severe, sober, spartan, stern, *inf* strait-laced, strict, thrifty, unpampered. **2** *austere dress.* modest, plain, simple, unadorned, unfussy. *Opp* LUXURIOUS, ORNATE.

authentic *adj* accurate, actual, bona fide, certain, dependable, factual, genuine, honest, legitimate, original, real, reliable, true, trustworthy, truthful, undisputed, valid, veracious. ▷ AUTHORITATIVE. *Opp* FALSE.

authenticate *v* certify, confirm, corroborate, endorse, substantiate, validate, verify.

author *n* **1** composer, dramatist, novelist, playwright, poet, scriptwriter. ▷ WRITER. **2** architect, begetter, creator, designer, father, founder, initiator, inventor, maker, mover, organizer, originator, parent, planner, prime mover, producer.

authoritarian *adj* autocratic, *inf* bossy, despotic, dictatorial, dogmatic, domineering, strict, tyrannical.

authoritative *adj* approved, certified, definitive, dependable, official, recognized, sanctioned, scholarly. ▷ AUTHENTIC.

authority *n* **1** approval, authorization, consent, licence, mandate, permission, permit, sanction, warrant. **2** charge, command, control, domination, force, influence, jurisdiction, might, power, prerogative, right, sovereignty, supremacy, sway, weight. **3** *authority on wine. inf* boffin, *inf* buff, connoisseur, expert, scholar, specialist. **the authorities** administration, government, management, officialdom, *inf* powers that be.

authorize *v* accede to, agree to, allow, approve, *inf* back, commission, consent to, empower, endorse, entitle, legalize, license, make official, mandate, *inf* OK, pass, permit, ratify, *inf* rubber-stamp, sanction, sign the order, sign the warrant, validate. **authorized** ▷ OFFICIAL.

automatic *adj* **1** conditioned, habitual, impulsive, instinctive, involuntary, natural, reflex, spontaneous, unconscious, unintentional, unthinking. **2** automated, computerized, electronic, mechanical, programmable, programmed, robotic, self-regulating, unmanned.

autonomous *adj* free, independent, self-determining, selfgoverning, sovereign.

auxiliary *adj* additional, ancillary, assisting, *inf* back-up, emergency, extra, helping, reserve, secondary, spare, subordinate, subsidiary, substitute, supplementary, supporting, supportive.

available *adj* accessible, at hand, convenient, disposable, free, handy, obtainable, procurable, ready, to hand, uncommitted, unengaged, unused, usable. *Opp* INACCESSIBLE.

avaricious *adj* acquisitive, covetous, grasping, greedy, mercenary, miserly.

avenge *v* exact punishment, *inf* get your own back, repay, requite, take revenge.

average *adj* common, commonplace, everyday, mediocre, medium, middling, moderate, normal, regular, *inf* run of the mill, typical, unexceptional, usual. ▷ ORDINARY. *Opp* EXCEPTIONAL. ● *n* mean, mid-point, norm, standard. • *v* equalize, even out, normalize, standardize.

averse *adj* antipathetic, disinclined, hostile, opposed, reluctant, resistant, unwilling.

aversion *n* antagonism, antipathy, dislike, distaste, hostility, reluctance, repugnance, unwillingness. ▷ HATRED.

avert *v* change the course of, deflect, draw off, fend off, parry, prevent, stave off, turn aside, turn away, ward off.

avoid *v* abstain from, be absent from, *inf* beg the question, *inf* bypass, circumvent, dodge, *inf* duck, elude, escape, eschew, evade, fend off, find a way round, get out of the way of, *inf* get round, *inf* give a wide berth to, help (*can't help it*), ignore, keep away from, keep clear of, refrain from, run away from, shirk, shun, side-step, skirt round, *inf* skive off, steer clear of. *Opp* SEEK.

await *v* be ready for, expect, hope for, lie in wait for, look out for, wait for.

awake *adj* **1** aware, conscious, insomniac, open-eyed, restless, sleepless, *inf* tossing and turning, wakeful, wide awake. **2** ▷ ALERT. *Opp* ASLEEP.

awaken *v* alert, animate, arouse, awake, call, excite, kindle, revive, rouse, stimulate, stir up, wake, waken.

award *n* badge, cap, cup, decoration, endowment, grant, medal, prize, reward, scholarship, trophy. • *v* accord, allot, assign, bestow, confer, decorate with, endow, give, grant, hand over, present.

aware *adj* acquainted, alive (to), appreciative, attentive, cognizant, conscious, conversant, familiar, heedful, informed, knowledgeable, mindful, observant, responsive, sensible, sensitive, versed. *Opp* IGNORANT, INSENSITIVE.

awe *n* admiration, amazement, apprehension, dread, fear, respect, reverence, terror, veneration, wonder.

awe-inspiring *adj* awesome, *old use* awful, breathtaking, dramatic, grand, imposing, impressive, magnificent, marvellous, overwhelming, solemn, *inf* stunning, stupendous, sublime, wondrous. ▷ FRIGHTENING, WONDERFUL. *Opp* INSIGNIFICANT.

awful *adj* **1** ▷ AWE-INSPIRING. **2** *awful weather.* ▷ BAD.

awkward *adj* **1** blundering, bungling, clumsy, gauche, gawky, *inf* ham-fisted, inelegant, inept, inexpert, maladroit, uncoordinated, ungainly, ungraceful, unskilful, wooden. **2** *an awkward load.* bulky, cumbersome, inconvenient, unmanageable, unwieldy. **3** *an awkward problem.* annoying, difficult, perplexing, thorny, *inf* ticklish, troublesome, trying, vexatious, vexing. **4** *an awkward silence.* embarrassing, touchy, tricky, uncomfortable, uneasy. **5** *awkward children. inf* bloodyminded, *sl* bolshie, defiant, disobedient, disobliging, exasperating, intractable, misbehaving, naughty, obstinate, perverse, *inf* prickly, rebellious, refractory, rude, stubborn, touchy, uncooperative, undisciplined, unruly, wayward. *Opp* COOPERATIVE, EASY, NEAT.

awning *n* canopy, flysheet, screen, shade, shelter, tarpaulin.

axe *n* battleaxe, chopper, cleaver, hatchet, tomahawk. • *v* cancel, cut, discharge, discontinue, dismiss, eliminate, get rid of, *inf* give the chop to, make redundant, rationalize, remove, sack, terminate, withdraw.

axle *n* rod, shaft, spindle.

B

baby *n* babe, child, infant, newborn, toddler.

babyish *adj* childish, immature, infantile, juvenile, puerile, simple. *Opp* MATURE.

back *adj* dorsal, end, hind, hinder, hindmost, last, rear, rearmost. ● *n* **1** end, hindquarters, posterior, rear, stern, tail, tail-end. **2** reverse, verso. *Opp* FRONT. ● *v* **1** back away, back off, back-pedal, backtrack, *inf* beat a retreat, give way, go backwards, move back, recede, recoil, retire, retreat, reverse. *Opp* ADVANCE. **2** ▷ SUPPORT. **back down** ▷ RETREAT. **back out** ▷ WITHDRAW.

backer *n* advocate, *inf* angel, benefactor, patron, promoter, sponsor, supporter.

background *n* **1** circumstances, context, history, *inf* lead-up, setting, surroundings. **2** breeding, culture, education, experience, grounding, milieu, tradition, training, upbringing.

backing *n* **1** aid, approval, assistance, encouragement, endorsement, funding, grant, help, investment, loan, patronage, sponsorship, subsidy, support. **2** *musical backing.* accompaniment, orchestration, scoring.

backward *adj* **1** regressive, retreating, retrograde, retrogressive, reverse. **2** afraid, bashful, coy, diffident, hesitant, inhibited, modest, reluctant, reserved, reticent, self-effacing, shy, timid, unassertive, unforthcoming. **3** *a backward pupil.* disadvantaged, handicapped, immature, late-starting, retarded, slow, subnormal, underdeveloped, undeveloped. *Opp* FORWARD.

bad *adj* [*Bad* describes anything we don't like. Possible synonyms are almost limitless.] **1** *bad men, deeds.* abhorrent, base, beastly, blameworthy, corrupt, criminal, cruel, dangerous, delinquent, deplorable, depraved, detestable, evil, guilty, immoral, infamous, malevolent, malicious, malignant, mean, mischievous, nasty, naughty, offensive, regrettable, reprehensible, rotten, shameful, sinful, unworthy, vicious, vile, villainous, wicked, wrong. **2** *a bad accident.* appalling, awful, calamitous, dire, disastrous, distressing, dreadful, frightful, ghastly, grave, hair-raising, hideous, horrible, painful, serious, severe, shocking, terrible, unfortunate, unpleasant, violent. **3** *bad driving, work.* abominable, abysmal, appalling, atrocious, awful, cheap, *inf* chronic, defective, deficient, diabolical, disgraceful, dreadful, egregious, execrable, faulty, feeble, *inf* grotty, hopeless, imperfect, inadequate, incompetent, incorrect, ineffective, inefficient, inferior, *inf* lousy, pitiful, poor, *inf* ropy, shoddy, *inf* sorry, substandard, unsound, unsatisfactory, useless, weak, worthless. **4** *bad conditions.* adverse, deleterious, detrimental, discouraging, *inf* frightful, harmful, harsh, hostile, inappropriate, inauspicious, prejudicial, uncongenial, unfortunate, unhelpful, unpropitious. **5** *bad smell.* decayed, decomposing, diseased, foul, loathsome, mildewed, mouldy, nauseating, noxious, objectionable, obnoxious, odious, offensive, polluted, putrid, rancid, repellent, repulsive, revolting, rotten, sickening, smelly, sour, spoiled, tainted, vile. **6** *I feel bad.* ▷ ILL. *Opp* GOOD.

badge *n* chevron, crest, device, emblem, insignia, logo, mark, medal, sign, symbol, token.

bad-tempered *adj* acrimonious, angry, bilious, cantankerous, churlish, crabbed, cross, *inf* crotchety, disgruntled, disobliging, dyspeptic, fretful, gruff, grumbling, grumpy, hostile, hot-tempered, ill-humoured, ill-tempered, irascible, irritable, malevolent, malign, moody, morose, peevish, petulant, quarrelsome, querulous, rude, scowling, short-tempered, shrewish, snappy, *inf* stroppy, sulky, sullen, testy, truculent, unfriendly, unsympathetic. *Opp* GOOD-TEMPERED.

baffle *v inf* bamboozle, bemuse, bewilder, confound, confuse, defeat, *inf* floor, *inf* flummox, foil, frustrate, mystify, perplex, puzzle, *inf* stump, thwart. **baffling** ▷ INEXPLICABLE.

bag *n* basket, carrier, carrier-bag, case, handbag, haversack, holdall, reticule, rucksack, sack, satchel, shopping-bag, shoulder-bag. ▷ BAGGAGE. • *v* capture, catch, ensnare, snare.

baggage *n* accoutrements, bags, belongings, *inf* gear, impedimenta, paraphernalia. ▷ LUGGAGE.

bait *n* allurement, attraction, bribe, carrot, decoy, enticement, inducement, lure, temptation. • *v* annoy, goad, harass, hound, jeer at, *inf* needle, persecute, pester, provoke, tease, torment.

balance *n* **1** scales, weighing-machine. **2** equilibrium, equipoise, poise, stability, steadiness. **3** correspondence, equality, equivalence, evenness, parity, symmetry. **4** *spend a bit & save the balance.* difference, excess, remainder, residue, rest, surplus. • *v* **1** cancel out, compensate for, counteract, counterbalance, counterpoise, equalize, even up, level, make steady, match, neutralize, offset, parallel, stabilize, steady. **2** keep balanced, keep in equilibrium, poise, steady, support. **balanced** ▷ EVEN, IMPARTIAL, STABLE.

bald *adj* **1** baldheaded, bare, hairless, smooth, thin on top. **2** *bald truth.* direct, forthright, plain, simple, stark, straightforward, unadorned, uncompromising.

bale *n* bunch, bundle, pack, package, truss. • *v* **bale out** eject, escape, jump out, parachute down.

ball *n* **1** drop, globe, globule, orb, shot, sphere, spheroid. **2** dance, disco, party, social.

balloon *n* airship, dirigible, hot-air balloon. • *v* ▷ BILLOW.

ballot *n* election, plebiscite, poll, referendum, vote.

ban *n* boycott, embargo, interdiction, moratorium, prohibition, proscription, taboo, veto. • *v* banish, bar, debar, disallow, exclude, forbid, interdict, make illegal, ostracize, outlaw, prevent, prohibit, proscribe, put a ban on, restrict, stop, suppress, veto. *Opp* PERMIT.

banal *adj* boring, clichéd, cliché-ridden, commonplace, *inf* corny, dull, hackneyed, humdrum, obvious, *inf* old hat, ordinary, over-used, pedestrian, platitudinous, predictable, stereotyped, trite, unimaginative, uninteresting, unoriginal, vapid. *Opp* INTERESTING.

band *n* **1** belt, border, fillet, hoop, line, loop, ribbon, ring, strip, stripe, swathe. **2** association, body, clique, club, company, crew, flock, gang, herd, horde, party, society, troop. ▷ GROUP. **3** [*music*] ensemble, group, orchestra.

bandage *n* dressing, gauze, lint, plaster.

bandit *n* brigand, buccaneer, desperado, footpad, gangster, gunman, highwayman, hijacker, marauder, outlaw, pirate, robber, thief.

bandy *adj* bandy-legged, bowed, bow-legged. • *v bandy words.* exchange, interchange, pass, swap, throw, toss. ▷ ARGUE.

bang *n* **1** blow, *inf* box, bump, collision, cuff, knock, punch, slam, smack, stroke, thump, wallop, whack. ▷ HIT. **2** blast, boom, clap, crash, explosion, pop, report, thud, thump. ▷ SOUND.

banish *v* **1** deport, drive out, eject, evict, excommunicate, exile, expatriate, expel, ostracize, oust, outlaw, rusticate, send away, ship away, transport. **2** ban, bar, *inf* black, debar, eliminate, exclude, forbid, get rid of, make illegal, prohibit, proscribe, put an embargo on, remove, restrict, stop, suppress, veto.

bank *n* **1** camber, declivity, dike, earthwork, embankment, gradient, incline, mound, ramp, rampart, ridge, rise, slope, tilt. **2** *river bank.* brink, edge, margin, shore, side. **3** *bank of controls.* array, collection, display, file, group, line, panel, rank, row, series. ● *v* **1** cant, heel, incline, lean, list, pitch, slant, slope, tilt, tip. **2** *bank money.* deposit, save.

bankrupt *adj inf* broke, failed, *sl* gone bust, gone into liquida-tion, insolvent, ruined, spent up, wound up. ▷ POOR. *Opp* SOLVENT.

banner *n* banderole, colours, ensign, flag, pennant, pennon, standard, streamer.

banquet *n inf* binge, *sl* blow-out, dinner, feast, repast, *inf* spread. ▷ MEAL.

banter *n* badinage, chaffing, joking, persiflage, pleasantry, raillery, repartee, ribbing, ridicule, teasing, wordplay.

bar *n* **1** beam, girder, pole, rail, railing, rod, shaft, stake, stick, strut. **2** barricade, barrier, check, deterrent, hindrance, impediment, obstacle, obstruction. **3** band, belt, line, streak, strip, stripe. **4** *bar of soap.* block, cake, chunk, hunk, ingot, lump, nugget, piece, slab, wedge. **5** *drink in a bar.* café, canteen, counter, inn, lounge, pub, public house, saloon, taproom, tavern, wine bar. ● *v* **1** ban, banish, debar, exclude, forbid to enter, keep out, ostracize, outlaw, prevent from entering, prohibit, proscribe. **2** *bar the way.* arrest, block, check, deter, halt, hinder, impede, obstruct, prevent, stop, thwart.

barbarian *adj* ▷ BARBARIC. ● *n* boor, churl, heathen, hun, ignoramus, lout, pagan, philistine, savage, vandal, *sl* yob.

barbaric *adj* barbarous, brutal, brutish, crude, inhuman, primitive, rough, savage, uncivil, uncivilized, uncultivated, wild. ▷ CRUEL. *Opp* CIVILIZED.

bare *adj* **1** bald, denuded, exposed, naked, nude, stark-naked, stripped, unclad, unclothed, uncovered, undressed. **2** *bare moor.* barren, bleak, desolate, featureless, open, treeless, unwooded, windswept. **3** *bare trees.* defoliated, leafless, shorn. **4** *a bare room.* austere, empty, plain, simple, unadorned, undecorated, unfurnished, vacant. **5** *a bare wall.* blank, clean, unmarked. **6** *bare facts.* direct, explicit, hard, honest, literal, open, plain, straightforward, unconcealed, undisguised, unembellished. **7** *the bare minimum.* basic, essential, just adequate, just sufficient, minimal, minimum. ● *v* betray, bring to light, disclose, expose, lay bare, make known, publish, reveal, show, uncover, undress, unmask, unveil.

bargain *n* **1** agreement, arrangement, compact, contract, covenant, deal, negotiation, pact, pledge, promise, settlement, transaction, treaty, understanding. **2** *bargain in the sales. inf* give-away, good buy, good deal, loss-leader, reduced item, *inf* snip, special offer. ● *v* argue, barter, discuss terms, do a deal, haggle, negotiate. **bargain for** ▷ EXPECT.

bark *v* **1** growl, yap. **2** *bark your shin.* abrade, chafe, graze, rub, score, scrape, scratch.

barmaid,

barman *ns* attendant, server, steward, stewardess, waiter, waitress.

barracks *plur n* accommodation, billet, camp, garrison, lodging, quarters.

barrage *n* **1** ▷ BARRIER. **2** *barrage of gunfire.* assault, attack, battery, bombardment, cannonade, fusillade, gunfire, onslaught, salvo, storm, volley.

barrel *n* butt, cask, churn, cistern, drum, hogshead, keg, tank, tub, tun, water-butt.

barren *adj* **1** arid, bare, desert, desolate, dried-up, dry, empty, infertile, lifeless, non-productive, treeless, uncultivated, unproductive, unprofitable, untilled, useless, waste. **2** childless, fruitless, infertile, sterile, sterilized, unfruitful. *Opp* FERTILE.

barricade *n* ▷ BARRIER. ● *v* bar, block off, defend, obstruct.

barrier *n* **1** bar, barrage, barricade, blockade, boom, bulwark, dam, earthwork, embankment, fence, fortification, frontier, hurdle, obstacle, obstruction, palisade, railing, rampart, stockade, wall. **2** *barrier to progress.* check, drawback, handicap, hindrance, impediment, limitation, restriction, stumbling-block.

barter *v* bargain, deal, exchange, negotiate, swap, trade, traffic.

base *adj* contemptible, cowardly, degrading, depraved, despicable, detestable, dishonourable, evil, ignoble, immoral, inferior, low, mean, scandalous, selfish, shabby, shameful, sordid, undignified, unworthy, vulgar, vile. ▷ WICKED. ● *n* **1** basis, bed, bedrock, bottom, core, essentials, foot, footing, foundation, fundamentals, groundwork, infrastructure, pedestal, plinth, rest, root, stand, substructure, support, underpinning. **2** camp, centre, depot, headquarters, post, starting-point, station. ● *v* build, construct, establish, found, ground, locate, position, post, secure, set up, station.

basement *n* cellar, crypt, vault.

bashful *adj* abashed, backward, blushing, coy, demure, diffident, embarrassed, faint-hearted, inhibited, meek, modest, nervous, reserved, reticent, retiring, self-conscious, self-effacing, shamefaced, sheepish, shy, timid, timorous, uneasy, unforthcoming. *Opp* ASSERTIVE.

basic *adj* central, chief, crucial, elementary, essential, foremost, fundamental, important, intrinsic, key, main, necessary, primary, principal, radical, underlying, vital. *Opp* UNIMPORTANT.

basin *n* bath, bowl, container, dish, pool, sink, stoup.

basis *n* base, core, footing, foundation, ground, infrastructure, premise, principle, starting-point, support, underpinning.

bask *v* enjoy, feel pleasure, glory, lie, lounge, luxuriate, relax, sunbathe, wallow.

basket *n* bag, hamper, pannier, punnet, skip, trug.

bastard *n* illegitimate child, *old use* love-child, natural child.

bat *n* club, racket, racquet.

bath *n* douche, jacuzzi, pool, sauna, shower, *inf* soak, *inf* tub, wash.

bathe *v* **1** clean, cleanse, immerse, moisten, rinse, soak, steep, swill, wash. **2** *bathe in the sea.* go swimming, paddle, plunge, splash about, swim, *inf* take a dip.

bathos *n* anticlimax, *inf* come-down, disappointment, *inf* let-down. *Opp* CLIMAX.

baton *n* cane, club, cudgel, rod, staff, stick, truncheon.

batter *v* beat, bludgeon, cudgel, keep hitting, pound. ▷ HIT.

battery *n* **1** artillery-unit, emplacement. **2** *electric battery.* accumulator, cell. **3** *assault and battery.* assault, attack, *inf* beating-up, blows, mugging, onslaught, thrashing, violence.

battle *n* action, air-raid, Armageddon, attack, blitz, brush, campaign, clash, combat, conflict, confrontation, contest, crusade, *inf* dogfight, encounter, engagement, fight, fray, hostilities, offensive, pitched battle, pre-emptive strike, quarrel, *inf* shoot-out, siege, skirmish, strife, struggle, war, warfare. ● *v* ▷ FIGHT.

battlefield *n* arena, battleground, theatre of war.

bawdy *adj* broad, earthy, erotic, lusty, *inf* naughty, racy, *inf* raunchy, ribald, *inf* sexy, *inf* spicy. [*derog syn-*

onyms] *inf* blue, coarse, dirty, immoral, improper, indecent, indecorous, indelicate, lascivious, lecherous, lewd, licentious, obscene, pornographic, prurient, risqué, rude, salacious, smutty, suggestive, titillating, vulgar. *Opp* PROPER.

bawl *v* cry, roar, shout, thunder, wail, yell, yelp.

bay *n* **1** bight, cove, creek, estuary, fjord, gulf, harbour, indentation, inlet, ria, sound. **2** alcove, booth, compartment, niche, nook, opening, recess.

bazaar *n* auction, boot-sale, bring-and-buy, fair, fête, jumble sale, market, sale.

be *v* **1** be alive, breathe, endure, exist, live. **2** *be here all day*. continue, dwell, inhabit, keep going, last, occupy a position, persist, remain, stay, survive. **3** *the next event will be tomorrow*. arise, befall, come about, happen, occur, take place. **4** *want to be a writer*. become, develop into.

beach *n* bank, coast, coastline, foreshore, littoral, sand, sands, seashore, seaside, shore, *poet* strand.

beacon *n* bonfire, fire, flare, light, lighthouse, pharos, signal.

bead *n* blob, drip, drop, droplet, globule, jewel, pearl.

beaker *n* cup, glass, goblet, jar, mug, tankard, tumbler.

beam *n* **1** bar, board, boom, brace, girder, joist, plank, post, rafter, spar, stanchion, stud, support, timber. **2** *beam of light*. gleam, pencil, ray, shaft, stream. ● *v* **1** aim, broadcast, direct, emit, radiate, send out, shine, transmit. **2** *beam happily*. grin, laugh, look radiant, radiate happiness, smile.

bear *v* **1** carry, hold, prop up, shoulder, support, sustain, take. **2** *bear an inscription*. display, exhibit, have, possess, show. **3** *bear gifts*. bring, carry, convey, deliver, fetch, move, take, transfer, transport. **4** *bear pain*. abide, accept, brook, cope with, endure, live with, permit, *inf* put up with, reconcile yourself to, *inf* stand, *inf* stomach, suffer, sustain, tolerate, undergo. **5** *bear children, fruit*. breed, *old use* bring forth, develop, engender, generate, give birth to, produce, spawn, yield. **bear out** ▷ CONFIRM. **bear up** ▷ SURVIVE. **bear witness** ▷ TESTIFY.

bearable *adj* acceptable, endurable, supportable, survivable, sustainable, tolerable.

bearing *n* **1** air, appearance, aspect, attitude, behaviour, carriage, demeanour, deportment, look, manner, mien, poise, posture, presence, stance, style. **2** *evidence had no bearing*. applicability, application, connection, import, pertinence, reference, relation, relationship, relevance, significance. **bearings** aim, course, direction, line, location, orientation, path, position, road, sense of direction, tack, track, way, whereabouts.

beast *n* brute, creature, monster, savage. ▷ ANIMAL.

beastly *adj* abominable, barbaric, bestial, brutal, cruel, savage. ▷ VILE.

beat *n* **1** accent, pulse, rhythm, stress, tempo, throb. **2** *policeman's beat*. course, itinerary, journey, path, rounds, route, way. ● *v* **1** batter, bludgeon, buffet, cane, clout, cudgel, flail, flog, hammer, knock about, lash, *inf* lay into, manhandle, pound, punch, scourge, strike, *inf* tan, thrash, thump, trounce, *inf* wallop, whack, whip. ▷ HIT. **2** *beat eggs*. agitate, blend, froth up, knead, mix, pound, stir, whip, whisk. **3** *heart was beating*. flutter, palpitate, pound, pulsate, race, throb, thump. **4** *beat an opponent*. best, conquer, crush, defeat, excel, get the better of, *inf* lick, master, outclass, outdistance, outdo, outpace, outrun, outwit, overcome, overpower, overthrow, overwhelm, rout, subdue, surpass, *inf* thrash, trounce, vanquish, win against, worst. **beat up** ▷ ATTACK.

beautiful *adj* admirable, aesthetic, alluring, appealing, artistic, attractive, becoming, bewitching, brilliant, captivating, charming, *old use* comely, dainty, decorative, delightful, elegant, enjoyable, exquisite, *old use* fair, fascinating, fetching, fine, good-looking, glamorous, glorious, gorgeous, graceful, handsome, irresistible, lovely, magnificent, neat, picturesque, pleasing, pretty, pulchritudinous, quaint, radiant, ravishing, scenic, seductive, sensuous, sexy, spectacular, splendid, stunning, superb, tasteful, tempting. *Opp* UGLY.

beautify *v* adorn, bedeck, deck, decorate, embellish, garnish, make beautiful, ornament, prettify, *derog* tart up, *inf* titivate. *Opp* DISFIGURE.

beauty *n* allure, appeal, attractiveness, charm, elegance, fascination, glamour, glory, grace, handsomeness, loveliness, magnificence, picturesqueness, prettiness, pulchritude, radiance, splendour.

becalmed *adj* helpless, idle, motionless, still, unmoving.

beckon *v* gesture, motion, signal, summon, wave.

become *v* **1** be transformed into, change into, develop into, grow into, mature into, metamorphose into, turn into. **2** *Red becomes you.* be appropriate to, be becoming to, befit, enhance, fit, flatter, harmonize with, set off, suit. **becoming** ▷ ATTRACTIVE, SUITABLE.

bed *n* **1** resting-place. □ *air-bed, berth, bunk, cot, couch, couchette, cradle, crib, divan, four-poster, hammock, pallet, palliasse, truckle bed, waterbed.* **2** *bed of concrete.* base, foundation, groundwork, layer, substratum. **3** *river bed.* bottom, channel, course, watercourse. **4** *flower bed.* border, garden, patch, plot.

bedclothes *plur n* bedding, bed linen. □ *bedspread, blanket, bolster, continental quilt, counterpane, coverlet, duvet, eiderdown, electric-blanket, mattress, pillow, pillowcase, pillowslip, quilt, sheet, sleeping-bag.*

bedraggled *adj* dirty, dishevelled, drenched, messy, muddy, scruffy, sodden, soiled, stained, unkempt, untidy, wet, wringing. *Opp* SMART.

beer *n* ale, bitter, lager, mild, porter, stout.

befall *v* be the outcome, *old use* betide, chance, come about, *inf* crop up, eventuate, happen, occur, take place, *inf* transpire.

before *adv* already, earlier, in advance, previously, sooner.

befriend *v inf* chat up, *inf* gang up with, get to know, make friends with, make the acquaintance of, *inf* pal up with.

beg *v* **1** *inf* cadge, scrounge, solicit, sponge. **2** *beg a favour.* ask, beseech, cajole, crave, entreat, implore, importune, petition, plead, pray, request, supplicate, wheedle.

beget *v* breed, bring about, cause, create, engender, father, generate, give rise to, procreate, produce, propagate, result in, sire, spawn.

beggar *n* cadger, destitute person, down-and-out, homeless person, mendicant, pauper, ragamuffin, scrounger, sponger, tramp, vagrant. ▷ POOR.

begin *v* **1** activate, approach, attack, be first, broach, commence, conceive, create, embark on, enter into, found, *inf* get cracking, *inf* get going, inaugurate, initiate, inspire, instigate, introduce, kindle, launch, lay the foundations, lead off, move into, move off, open, originate, pioneer, precipitate, provoke, set about, set in motion, set off, set out, set up, *inf* spark off, start, *inf* take steps, take the initiative, take up, touch off, trigger off, undertake. **2** *Spring begins gradually.* appear, arise, break out, come into existence, crop up, emerge, get going, happen, materialize, originate, spring up. *Opp* END.

beginner *n* **1** creator, founder, initiator, inspiration, instigator, originator, pioneer. **2** *only a beginner.* apprentice, fresher, greenhorn, inexperienced person, initiate, learner, novice, recruit, starter, tiro, trainee.

beginning *n* **1** birth, commencement, conception, creation, dawn, embryo, emergence, establishment, foundation, genesis, germ, inauguration, inception, initiation, instigation, introduction, launch, onset, opening, origin, outset, point of departure, rise, source, start, starting-point, threshold. **2** *beginning of a book*. preface, prelude, prologue. *Opp* END.

begrudge *v* be bitter about, covet, envy, grudge, mind, object to, resent.

behave *v* **1** acquit yourself, act, *inf* carry on, comport yourself, conduct yourself, function, operate, perform, react, respond, run, work. **2** *told to behave*. act properly, be good, be on best behaviour.

behaviour *n* actions, attitude, bearing, comportment, conduct, courtesy, dealings, demeanour, deportment, manners, performance, reaction, response, ways.

behead *v* decapitate, guillotine.

behold *v* descry, discern, espy, look at, note, notice, see, set eyes on, view.

being *n* **1** actuality, essence, existence, life, living, reality, solidity, substance. **2** animal, creature, individual, person, spirit, soul.

belated *adj* behindhand, delayed, last-minute, late, overdue, posthumous, tardy, unpunctual.

belch *v* **1** *inf* burp, emit wind. **2** *belch smoke*. discharge, emit, erupt, fume, gush, send out, smoke, spew out, vomit.

belief *n* **1** acceptance, assent, assurance, certainty, confidence, credence, reliance, security, sureness, trust. **2** *religious belief*. attitude, conviction, creed, doctrine, dogma, ethos, faith, feeling, ideology, morality, notion, opinion, persuasion, principles, religion, standards, tenets, theories, views. *Opp* SCEPTICISM.

believe *v* **1** accept, be certain of, count on, credit, depend on, endorse, have faith in, reckon on, rely on, subscribe to, *inf* swallow, swear by, trust. *Opp* DISBELIEVE. **2** assume, consider, *inf* dare say, feel, gather, guess, hold, imagine, judge, know, maintain, postulate, presume, speculate, suppose, take it for granted, think. **make believe** ▷ IMAGINE.

believer *n* adherent, devotee, disciple, fanatic, follower, proselyte, supporter, upholder, zealot. *Opp* ATHEIST.

belittle *v* be unimpressed by, criticize, decry, denigrate, deprecate, depreciate, detract from, disparage, minimize, *inf* play down, slight, speak slightingly of, underrate, undervalue. *Opp* EXAGGERATE, FLATTER, PRAISE.

bell *n* alarm, carillon, chime, knell, peal, signal. ▷ RING.

belligerent *adj* aggressive, antagonistic, argumentative, bellicose, bullying, combative, contentious, defiant, disputatious, fierce, hawkish, hostile, jingoistic, martial, militant, militaristic, provocative, pugnacious, quarrelsome, violent, warlike, warmongering, warring. ▷ UNFRIENDLY. *Opp* PEACEABLE.

belong *v* **1** be owned (by), go (with), pertain (to), relate (to). **2** be at home, feel welcome, have a place. **3** *belong to a club*. be affiliated with, be a member of, be connected with, *inf* be in with.

belongings *plur n* chattels, effects, *inf* gear, goods, impedimenta, possessions, property, things.

belt *n* **1** band, circle, loop. **2** *belt round the waist*. cincture, cummerbund, girdle, girth, sash, strap, waistband, *old use* zone. **3** *green belt*. area, district, line, stretch, strip, swathe, tract, zone.

bemuse *v* befuddle, bewilder, confuse, mix up, muddle, perplex, puzzle, stupefy.

bench *n* **1** form, pew, seat, settle. **2** counter, table, work-bench, worktable. **3** *magistrate's bench*. court, courtroom, judge, magistrate, tribunal.

bend *n* angle, arc, bow, corner, crank, crook, curvature, curve, flexure, loop, turn, turning, twist, zigzag. • *v* **1** arch, be flexible, bow, buckle, coil, contort, crook, curl, curve, deflect, distort, divert, flex, fold, *inf* give, loop, mould, refract, shape, turn, twist, warp, wind, yield. **2** bow, crouch, curtsy, duck, genuflect, kneel, lean, stoop.

benefactor *n inf* angel, backer, *derog* do-gooder, donor, *inf* fairy godmother, patron, philanthropist, promoter, sponsor, supporter, well-wisher.

beneficial *adj* advantageous, benign, constructive, favourable, fruitful, good, health-giving, healthy, helpful, improving, nourishing, nutritious, positive, productive, profitable, rewarding, salubrious, salutary, supportive, useful, valuable, wholesome. *Opp* HARMFUL.

beneficiary *n* heir, heiress, inheritor, legatee, recipient, successor (*to title*).

benefit *n* **1** advantage, asset, blessing, boon, convenience, gain, good thing, help, privilege, prize, profit, service, use. *Opp* DISADVANTAGE. **2** *unemployment benefit*. aid, allowance, assistance, *inf* dole, *inf* hand-out, grant, payment, social security, welfare. • *v* advance, advantage, aid, assist, better, boost, do good to, enhance, further, help, improve, profit, promote, serve.

benevolent *adj* altruistic, beneficent, benign, caring, charitable, compassionate, considerate, friendly, generous, helpful, humane, humanitarian, kind-hearted, kindly, liberal, magnanimous, merciful, philanthropic, supportive, sympathetic, unselfish, warm-hearted. ▷ KIND. *Opp* UNKIND.

benign *adj* gentle, harmless, kind. ▷ BENEFICIAL, BENEVOLENT.

bent *adj* **1** angled, arched, bowed, buckled, coiled, contorted, crooked, curved, distorted, folded, hunched, looped, twisted, warped. **2** [*inf*] *a bent dealer*. corrupt, criminal, dishonest, illegal, immoral, untrustworthy, wicked. *Opp* HONEST, STRAIGHT. • *n* ▷ APTITUDE, BIAS.

bequeath *v* endow, hand down, leave, make over, pass on, settle, will.

bequest *n* endowment, gift, inheritance, legacy, settlement.

bereavement *n* death, loss.

bereft *adj* deprived, destitute, devoid, lacking, robbed, wanting.

berserk *adj inf* beside yourself, crazed, crazy, demented, deranged, frantic, frenetic, frenzied, furious, infuriated, insane, mad, maniacal, rabid, violent, wild. *Opp* CALM. **go berserk** ▷ RAGE, RAMPAGE.

berth *n* **1** bed, bunk, hammock. **2** *berth for ships*. anchorage, dock, harbour, haven, landing-stage, moorings, pier, port, quay, slipway, wharf. • *v* anchor, dock, drop anchor, land, moor, tie up. **give a wide berth to** ▷ AVOID.

beseech *v* ask, beg, entreat, implore, importune, plead, supplicate.

besiege *v* beleaguer, beset, blockade, cut off, encircle, encompass, hem in, isolate, pester, plague, siege, surround.

best *adj* choicest, excellent, finest, first-class, foremost, incomparable, leading, matchless, optimum, outstanding, pre-eminent, superlative, supreme, top, unequalled, unrivalled, unsurpassed.

bestial *adj* animal, beast-like, beastly, brutal, brutish, inhuman, subhuman. ▷ SAVAGE.

bestow *v* award, confer, donate, give, grant, present.

bet *n inf* flutter, gamble, *inf* punt, speculation, stake, wager. • *v* bid, chance, do the pools, enter a lottery, gamble, *inf* have a flutter, hazard, lay bets, *inf* punt, risk, speculate, stake, venture, wager.

betray *v* **1** be a Judas to, be a traitor to, be false to, cheat, conspire against, deceive, denounce, desert, double-cross, give away, *inf* grass on, incriminate, inform against, inform on, jilt, let down, *inf* rat on, report, *inf* sell down the river, sell out, *inf* shop, *inf* tell tales about, *inf* turn Queen's evidence on. **2** *betray secrets.* disclose, divulge, expose, give away, indicate, let out, let slip, manifest, reveal, show, tell.

better *adj* **1** preferable, recommended, superior. **2** convalescent, cured, fitter, healed, healthier, improved, *inf* on the mend, progressing, recovered, recovering, restored. • *v* ▷ IMPROVE, SURPASS.

beware *v* avoid, be alert, be careful, be cautious, be on your guard, guard (against), heed, keep clear (of), look out, mind, shun, steer away (from), take care, take heed, take precautions, watch out, *inf* watch your step.

bewilder *v* baffle, *inf* bam boozle, bemuse, confound, confuse, daze, disconcert, disorientate, distract, floor, *inf* flummox, mislead, muddle, mystify, perplex, puzzle, stump.

bewitch *v* captivate, cast a spell on, charm, enchant, enrapture, fascinate, spellbind.

bias *n* **1** aptitude, bent, inclination, leaning, liking, partiality, penchant, predilection, predisposition, preference, proclivity, proneness, propensity, tendency. **2** [*derog*] bigotry, chauvinism, favouritism, imbalance, injustice, nepotism, one-sidedness, partiality, partisanship, prejudice, racism, sexism, unfairness. • *v* ▷ INFLUENCE.

biased *adj* bigoted, blinkered, chauvinistic, distorted, emotive, influenced, interested, jaundiced, loaded, one-sided, partial, partisan, prejudiced, racist, sexist, slanted, tendentious, unfair, unjust, warped. *Opp* UNBIASED.

bicycle *n inf* bike, cycle, penny-farthing, *inf* push-bike, racer, tandem, *inf* two-wheeler.

bid *n* **1** offer, price, proposal, proposition, tender. **2** *a bid to win.* attempt, *inf* crack, effort, endeavour, *inf* go, try, venture. • *v* **1** make an offer, offer, proffer, propose, tender. **2** ▷ COMMAND.

big *adj* **1** above average, *inf* almighty, ample, astronomical, bold, broad, Brobdingnagian, bulky, burly, capacious, colossal, commodious, considerable, elephantine, enormous, extensive, fat, formidable, gargantuan, generous, giant, gigantic, grand, great, gross, heavy, hefty, high, huge, *inf* hulking, husky, immeasurable, immense, impressive, *inf* jumbo, *inf* king-sized, large, largish, lofty, long, mammoth, massive, mighty, monstrous, monumental, mountainous, overgrown, oversized, prodigious, roomy, sizeable, spacious, stupendous, substantial, swingeing (*increase*), tall, *inf* terrific, thick, *inf* thumping, tidy (*sum*), titanic, towering, *inf* tremendous, vast, voluminous, weighty, *inf* whacking, *inf* whopping, wide. **2** *a big decision.* grave, important, influential, leading, main, major, momentous, notable, powerful, prime, principal, prominent, serious, significant. **3** *a big number.* ▷ INFINITE. **4** *a big name.* ▷ FAMOUS. **5** *a big noise.* ▷ LOUD. *Opp* SMALL.

bigot *n* chauvinist, fanatic, prejudiced person, racist, sexist, zealot.

bigoted *adj* intolerant, one-sided, partial, prejudiced. ▷ BIASED.

bill *n* **1** account, invoice, receipt, statement, tally. **2** advertisement, broadsheet, bulletin, circular, handbill, handout, leaflet, notice, placard, poster, sheet. **3** *a Parliamentary bill.* draft law, proposed law. **4** *a bird's bill.* beak, mandible.

billow *v* balloon, belly, bulge, fill out, heave, puff out, rise, roll, surge, swell, undulate.

bind *v* **1** attach, clamp, combine, connect, fuse, hitch, hold together, join, lash, link, rope, secure, strap, tie, truss, unify, unite, weld. ▷ FASTEN. **2** *bind a wound.* bandage, cover, dress, encase, swathe, wrap. **3** *bound to obey.* compel, constrain, force, necessitate, oblige, require. **binding** ▷ COMPULSORY, FORMAL.

biography *n* autobiography, life, life-story, memoirs, recollections. ▷ WRITING.

bird *n inf* birdie, chick, cock, *joc* feathered friend, fledgling, fowl, hen, nestling. □ *gamebird*, plur *poultry*, *seabird*, *wader*, *waterfowl*, *wildfowl*. □ *albatross*, *auk*, *bittern*, *blackbird*, *budgerigar*, *bullfinch*, *bunting*, *bustard*, *buzzard*, *canary*, *cassowary*, *chaffinch*, *chiff-chaff*, *chough*, *cockatoo*, *coot*, *cormorant*, *corncrake*, *crane*, *crow*, *cuckoo*, *curlew*, *dabchick*, *dipper*, *dove*, *duck*, *dunnock*, *eagle*, *egret*, *emu*, *falcon*, *finch*, *flamingo*, *flycatcher*, *fulmar*, *goldcrest*, *goldfinch*, *goose*, *grebe*, *greenfinch*, *grouse*, *gull*, *hawk*, *heron*, *hoopoe*, *hornbill*, *humming bird*, *ibis*, *jackdaw*, *jay*, *kingfisher*, *kestrel*, *kite*, *kiwi*, *kookaburra*, *lapwing*, *lark*, *linnet*, *macaw*, *magpie*, *martin*, *mina bird*, *moorhen*, *nightingale*, *nightjar*, *nuthatch*, *oriole*, *osprey*, *ostrich*, *ousel*, *owl*, *parakeet*, *parrot*, *partridge*, *peacock*, *peewit*, *pelican*, *penguin*, *peregrine*, *petrel*, *pheasant*, *pigeon*, *pipit*, *plover*, *ptarmigan*, *puffin*, *quail*, *raven*, *redbreast*, *redstart*, *robin*, *rook*, *sandpiper*, *seagull*, *shearwater*, *shelduck*, *shrike*, *skua*, *skylark*, *snipe*, *sparrow*, *sparrowhawk*, *spoonbill*, *starling*, *stonechat*, *stork*, *swallow*, *swan*, *swift*, *teal*, *tern*, *thrush*, *tit*, *toucan*, *turkey*, *turtle-dove*, *vulture*, *wagtail*, *warbler*, *waxwing*, *wheatear*, *woodcock*, *woodpecker*, *wren*, *yellowhammer*.

birth *n* **1** childbirth, confinement, delivery, labour, nativity, parturition. **2** ancestry, background, blood, breeding, derivation, descent, extraction, family, genealogy, line, lineage, parentage, pedigree, race, stock, strain. **3** ▷ BEGINNING. **give birth** bear, calve, farrow, foal. ▷ BEGIN.

bisect *v* cross, cut in half, divide, halve, intersect.

bit *n* **1** atom, bite, block, chip, chunk, crumb, division, dollop, fraction, fragment, gobbet, grain, helping, hunk, iota, lump, modicum, morsel, mouthful, part, particle, piece, portion, sample, scrap, section, segment, share, slab, slice, snippet, soupçon, speck, spot, taste, titbit, trace. **2** *Wait a bit.* flash, instant, *inf* jiffy, minute, moment, second, *inf* tick, time, while.

bite *n* **1** nip, pinch, sting. **2** *a bite to eat.* morsel, mouthful, nibble, snack, taste. ▷ BIT. ● *v* **1** champ, chew, crunch, cut into, gnaw, masticate, munch, nibble, nip, rend, snap, tear at, wound. **2** *An insect bit me.* pierce, sting. **3** *The screw won't bite.* grip, hold.

bitter *adj* **1** acid, acrid, harsh, sharp, sour, unpleasant. **2** *a bitter experience.* calamitous, dire, distasteful, distressing, galling, hateful, heartbreaking, painful, poignant, sorrowful, unhappy, unwelcome, upsetting. **3** *bitter remarks.* acrimonious, acerbic, angry, cruel, cynical, embittered, envious, hostile, jaundiced, jealous, malicious, rancorous, resentful, savage, sharp, spiteful, stinging, vicious, violent, waspish. **4** *a bitter wind.* biting, cold, fierce, freezing, perishing, piercing, raw. *Opp* KIND, MILD, PLEASANT.

bizarre *adj* curious, eccentric, fantastic, freakish, grotesque, odd, outlandish, outré, surreal, weird. ▷ STRANGE. *Opp* ORDINARY.

black *adj* blackish, coal-black, dark, dusky, ebony, funereal, gloomy, inky, jet, jet-black, moonless, murky, pitch-black, pitch-dark, raven, sable, sooty, starless, unlit. ● *v* **1** blacken, polish. **2** ▷ BLACKLIST.

blackleg *n sl* scab, strikebreaker, traitor.

blacklist *v* ban, bar, blackball, boycott, debar, disallow, exclude, ostracize, preclude, proscribe, put an embargo on, refuse to handle, repudiate, snub, veto.

blade *n* dagger, edge, knife, razor, scalpel, vane. ▷ SWORD.

blame *n* accountability, accusation, castigation, censure, charge, complaint, condemnation, criticism, culpability, fault, guilt, imputation, incrimination, liability, onus, *inf* rap, recrimination, reprimand, reproach, reproof, responsibility, *inf* stick, stricture. ● *v* accuse, admonish, censure, charge, chide, condemn, criticize, denounce, *inf* get at, hold responsible, incriminate, rebuke, reprehend, reprimand, reproach, reprove, round on, scold, tax, upbraid. *Opp* EXCUSE.

blameless *adj* faultless, guiltless, innocent, irreproachable, moral, unimpeachable, upright. *Opp* GUILTY.

bland *adj* affable, amiable, banal, boring, calm, characterless, dull, flat, gentle, insipid, mild, nondescript, smooth, soft, soothing, suave, tasteless, trite, unappetizing, unexciting, uninspiring, uninteresting, vapid, watery, weak, *inf* wishy-washy. *Opp* INTERESTING.

blank *adj* **1** bare, clean, clear, empty, plain, spotless, unadorned, unmarked, unused, void. **2** *a blank look.* apathetic, baffled, baffling, dead, *inf* deadpan, emotionless, expressionless, featureless, glazed, immobile, impassive, inane, inscrutable, lifeless, poker-faced, uncomprehending, unresponsive, vacant, vacuous. • *n* **1** emptiness, nothingness, vacuity, vacuum, void. **2** *blanks on a form.* box, break, gap, line, space.

blaspheme *v* curse, execrate, imprecate, profane, swear.

blasphemous *adj* disrespectful, godless, impious, irreligious, irreverent, profane, sacrilegious, sinful, ungodly, wicked. *Opp* REVERENT.

blast *n* **1** gale, gust, wind. **2** blare, din, noise, racket, roar, sound. **3** ▷ EXPLOSION. • *v* ▷ ATTACK, EXPLODE. **blast off** ▷ LAUNCH.

blatant *adj* apparent, barefaced, bold, brazen, conspicuous, evident, flagrant, glaring, obtrusive, obvious, open, overt, shameless, stark, unconcealed, undisguised, unmistakable, visible. *Opp* HIDDEN.

blaze *n* conflagration, fire, flame, flare-up, holocaust, inferno, outburst. • *v* burn, erupt, flame, flare.

bleach *v* blanch, discolour, etiolate, fade, lighten, pale, peroxide (*hair*), whiten.

bleak *adj* bare, barren, blasted, cheerless, chilly, cold, comfortless, depressing, desolate, dismal, dreary, exposed, grim, hopeless, joyless, sombre, uncomfortable, unpromising, windswept, wintry. *Opp* COMFORTABLE, WARM.

bleary *adj* blurred, *inf* blurry, cloudy, dim, filmy, fogged, foggy, fuzzy, hazy, indistinct, misty, murky, obscured, smeary, unclear, watery. *Opp* CLEAR.

blemish *n* blot, blotch, chip, crack, defect, deformity, disfigurement, eyesore, fault, flaw, imperfection, mark, mess, smudge, speck, stain, ugliness. □ *birthmark, blackhead, blister, callus, corn, freckle, mole, naevus, pimple, pustule, scar, spot, verruca, wart, whitlow,* sl *zit.* • *v* deface, disfigure, flaw, mar, mark, scar, spoil, stain, tarnish.

blend *n* alloy, amalgam, amalgamation, combination, composite, compound, concoction, fusion, mélange, mix, mixture, synthesis, union. • *v* **1** amalgamate, coalesce, combine, commingle, compound, fuse, harmonize, integrate, intermingle, intermix, meld, merge, mingle, synthesize, unite. **2** *blend in a bowl.* beat, mix, stir together, whip, whisk.

bless *v* **1** anoint, consecrate, dedicate, grace, hallow, make sacred, ordain, sanctify. **2** *bless God's name.* adore, exalt, extol, glorify, magnify, praise. *Opp* CURSE.

blessed *adj* **1** adored, divine, hallowed, holy, revered, sacred, sanctified. **2** ▷ HAPPY.

blessing *n* **1** benediction, consecration, grace, prayer. **2** approbation, approval, backing, concurrence, consent, leave, permission, sanction, support. **3** *Warmth is a blessing.* advantage, asset, benefit, boon, comfort, convenience, *inf* godsend, help. *Opp* CURSE, MISFORTUNE.

blight *n* affliction, ailment, *old use* bane, cancer, canker, curse, decay, disease, evil, illness, infestation, misfortune, *old use* pestilence, plague, pollution, rot, scourge, sickness, trouble. • *v* ▷ SPOIL.

blind *adj* **1** blinded, eyeless, sightless, unseeing. □ *astigmatic, colour-blind, long-sighted, myopic, near-sighted, short-sighted, suffering from cataract, suffering from glaucoma, visually handicapped.* **2** *blind devotion.* blinkered, heedless, ignorant, inattentive, indifferent, indiscriminate, insensible, insensitive, irrational, mindless, oblivious, prejudiced, unaware, unobservant, unreasoning. ● *n* awning, cover, curtain, screen, shade, shutters. ● *v* **1** dazzle, make blind. **2** ▷ DECEIVE.

blink *v* coruscate, flash, flicker, flutter, gleam, glimmer, shimmer, sparkle, twinkle, wink.

bliss *n* blessedness, delight, ecstasy, euphoria, felicity, gladness, glee, happiness, heaven, joy, paradise, rapture. ▷ PLEASURE. *Opp* MISERY.

bloated *adj* dilated, distended, enlarged, inflated, puffy, swollen.

block *n* **1** bar, brick, cake, chock, chunk, hunk, ingot, lump, mass, piece, slab. **2** ▷ BLOCKAGE. ● *v* **1** bar, barricade, *inf* bung up, choke, clog, close, congest, constrict, dam, fill, impede, jam, obstruct, plug, stop up. **2** *block a plan.* deter, halt, hamper, hinder, hold back, prevent, prohibit, resist, *inf* scotch, *inf* stonewall, stop, thwart.

blockage *n* barrier, block, bottleneck, congestion, constriction, hindrance, impediment, jam, obstacle, obstruction, resistance, stoppage.

blond,

blonde *adjs* bleached, fair, flaxen, golden, light, platinum, silvery, yellow.

bloodshed *n* bloodletting, butchery, carnage, killing, massacre, murder, slaughter, slaying, violence.

bloodthirsty *adj* barbaric, brutal, feral, ferocious, fierce, homicidal, inhuman, murderous, pitiless, ruthless, sadistic, sanguinary, savage, vicious, violent, warlike. ▷ CRUEL. *Opp* HUMANE.

bloody *adj* **1** bleeding, bloodstained, raw. **2** *a bloody battle.* cruel, gory, sanguinary. ▷ BLOODTHIRSTY.

bloom *n* **1** blossom, bud, floret, flower. **2** *bloom of youth.* beauty, blush, flush, glow, prime. ● *v* be healthy, blossom, *poet* blow, bud, burgeon, *inf* come out, develop, flourish, flower, grow, open, prosper, sprout, thrive. *Opp* FADE.

blot *n* **1** blob, blotch, mark, smear, smirch, smudge, *inf* splodge, spot, stain. **2** *blot on the landscape.* blemish, defect, eyesore, fault, flaw, ugliness. ● *v* bespatter, blemish, blotch, blur, disfigure, mar, mark, smudge, spoil, spot, stain. **blot out** ▷ OBLITERATE. **blot your copybook** ▷ MISBEHAVE.

blotchy *adj* blemished, brindled, discoloured, inflamed, marked, patchy, smudged, spotty, streaked, uneven.

blow *n* **1** bang, bash, *inf* belt, *inf* biff, box (*ears*), buffet, bump, clip, clout, clump, concussion, hit, jolt, knock, punch, rap, slap, *inf* slosh, smack, *inf* sock, stroke, swat, swipe, thump, thwack, wallop, welt, whack, whop. **2** *a sad blow.* affliction, *inf* bombshell, calamity, disappointment, disaster, misfortune, shock, surprise, upset. ● *v* blast, breathe, exhale, fan, puff, waft, whine, whirl, whistle. **blow up** **1** dilate, enlarge, expand, fill, inflate, pump up. **2** exaggerate, magnify, make worse, overstate. **3** blast, bomb, burst, detonate, dynamite, erupt, explode, go off, set off, shatter. **4** [*inf*] erupt, get angry, lose your temper, rage.

blue *adj* **1** aquamarine, azure, cerulean, cobalt, indigo, navy, sapphire, sky-blue, turquoise, ultramarine. **2** ▷ BAWDY. **3** ▷ SAD. ● *v* ▷ SQUANDER.

blueprint *n* basis, design, draft, model, outline, pattern, pilot, plan, project, proposal, prototype, scheme.

bluff *v* cozen, deceive, delude, dupe, fool, hoodwink, mislead.

blunder *n* *inf* boob, *inf* botch, *inf* clanger, *sl* cock-up, error, fault, *Fr* faux pas, gaffe, howler, indiscretion, miscalculation, misjudgement, mistake, slip, slip-up, solecism. • *v* be clumsy, *inf* botch up, bumble, bungle, *inf* drop a clanger, err, flounder, *inf* foul up, *sl* goof, go wrong, *inf* make a hash of something, make a mistake, mess up, miscalculate, misjudge, *inf* put your foot in it, slip up, stumble.

blunt *adj* **1** dull, rounded, thick, unpointed, unsharpened, worn. *Opp* SHARP. **2** *blunt criticism.* abrupt, bluff, brusque, candid, curt, direct, downright, forthright, frank, honest, insensitive, outspoken, plain-spoken, rude, straightforward, tactless, unceremonious, undiplomatic. *Opp* TACTFUL. • *v* abate, allay, anaesthetize, dampen, deaden, desensitize, dull, lessen, numb, soften, take the edge off, weaken. *Opp* SHARPEN.

blur *v* bedim, befog, blear, cloud, conceal, confuse, darken, dim, fog, mask, muddle, obscure, smear, unfocus.

blurred *adj* bleary, blurry, clouded, cloudy, confused, dim, faint, foggy, fuzzy, hazy, ill-defined, indefinite, indistinct, misty, nebulous, out of focus, smoky, unclear, unfocused, vague. *Opp* CLEAR.

blurt *v* **blurt out** be indiscreet, *inf* blab, burst out with, come out with, cry out, disclose, divulge, exclaim, *inf* give the game away, let out, let slip, reveal, *inf* spill the beans, tell, utter.

blush *v* be ashamed, colour, flush, glow, go red, redden.

blustering *adj* angry, boasting, boisterous, bragging, bullying, crowing, defiant, domineering, hectoring, noisy, ranting, selfassertive, showing-off, storming, swaggering, threatening, vaunting, violent. *Opp* MODEST.

blustery *adj* gusty, squally, unsettled, windy.

board *n* **1** blockboard, chipboard, clapboard, panel, plank, plywood, scantling, sheet, slab, slat, timber, weatherboard. **2** *board of directors.* cabinet, committee, council, directorate, jury, panel. • *v* **1** accommodate, billet, feed, house, lodge, put up, quarter, stay. **2** *board a bus.* catch, embark (on), enter, get on, go on board.

boast *v sl* be all mouth, *inf* blow your own trumpet, bluster, brag, crow, exaggerate, gloat, praise yourself, *sl* shoot a line, show off, *inf* sing your own praises, swagger, *inf* swank, *inf* talk big, vaunt.

boaster *n inf* big-head, *inf* big mouth, braggadocio, braggart, *inf* loudmouth, *inf* poser, show-off, swaggerer, swank.

boastful *adj inf* big-headed, bragging, *inf* cocky, conceited, egotistical, ostentatious, proud, puffed up, swaggering, swanky, swollen-headed, vain, vainglorious. *Opp* MODEST.

boat *n* craft, ship. ▷ VESSEL.

boatman *n* bargee, coxswain, ferryman, gondolier, lighterman, oarsman, rower, waterman, yachtsman. ▷ SAILOR.

bob *v* be agitated, bounce, dance, hop, jerk, jig about, jolt, jump, leap, move about, nod, oscillate, shake, toss about, twitch. **bob up** ▷ APPEAR.

body *n* **1** anatomy, being, build, figure, form, frame, individual, physique, shape, substance, torso, trunk. **2** cadaver, carcass, corpse, mortal remains, mummy, relics, remains, *sl* stiff. **3** association, band, committee, company, corporation, society. ▷ GROUP. **4** *body of material.* accumulation, agglomeration, collection, corpus, mass.

bodyguard *n* defender, guard, minder, protector.

bog *n* fen, marsh, marshland, mire, morass, mudflats, peat bog, quagmire, quicksands, salt-marsh, *old use* slough, swamp, wetlands. **get bogged down** be hindered, get into difficulties, get stuck, grind to a halt, sink.

bogus *adj* counterfeit, fake, false, fictitious, fraudulent, imitation, *inf* phoney, sham, spurious. *Opp* GENUINE.

Bohemian *adj inf* arty, *old use* beatnik, bizarre, eccentric, hippie, informal, nonconformist, off-beat, unconventional, unorthodox, *inf* way-out, weird.

boil *n* abscess, blister, carbuncle, chilblain, eruption, gathering, gumboil, inflammation, pimple, pock, pustule, sore, spot, tumour, ulcer, *sl* zit. • *v* **1** cook, heat, simmer, stew. **2** bubble, effervesce, foam, seethe, steam. **3** ▷ RAGE.

boisterous *adj* animated, disorderly, exuberant, irrepressible, lively, loud, noisy, obstreperous, riotous, rollicking, rough, rowdy, stormy, tempestuous, tumultuous, undisciplined, unrestrained, unruly, uproarious, wild. *Opp* CALM.

bold *adj* **1** adventurous, audacious, brave, confident, courageous, daredevil, daring, dauntless, enterprising, fearless, *derog* foolhardy, forceful, gallant, hardy, heroic, intrepid, *inf* plucky, *derog* rash, *derog* reckless, resolute, self-confident, unafraid, valiant, valorous, venturesome. **2** [*derog*] *a bold request.* brash, brazen, *inf* cheeky, forward, fresh, impertinent, impudent, insolent, pert, presumptuous, rude, saucy, shameless, unashamed. **3** *bold colours, writing.* big, bright, clear, conspicuous, eye-catching, large, obvious, prominent, pronounced, showy, striking, strong, vivid. *Opp* FAINT, TIMID.

bolster *n* cushion, pillow. • *v* ▷ SUPPORT.

bolt *n* **1** arrow, dart, missile, projectile. **2** peg, pin, rivet, rod, screw. **3** *bolt on a door.* bar, catch, fastening, latch, lock. • *v* **1** bar, close, fasten, latch, lock, secure. **2** *The animals bolted.* abscond, dart away, dash away, escape, flee, fly, run off, rush off. **3** *bolt food.* ▷ EAT. **bolt from the blue** ▷ SURPRISE.

bomb *n* bombshell, explosive. ▷ WEAPON. • *v* ▷ BOMBARD.

bombard *v* **1** assail, assault, attack, batter, blast, blitz, bomb, fire at, pelt, pound, shell, shoot at, strafe. **2** badger, beset, harass, importune, pester, plague.

bombardment *n* attack, barrage, blast, blitz, broadside, burst, cannonade, discharge, fusillade, hail, salvo, volley.

bombastic *adj* extravagant, grandiloquent, grandiose, high-flown, inflated, magniloquent, pompous, turgid.

bond *n* **1** chain, cord, fastening, fetters, handcuffs, manacles, restraints, rope, shackles. **2** *bond of friendship.* affiliation, affinity, attachment, connection, link, relationship, tie, unity. **3** *a legal bond.* agreement, compact, contract, covenant, guarantee, legal document, pledge, promise, word. • *v* ▷ STICK.

bondage *n* enslavement, serfdom, servitude, slavery, subjection, thraldom, vassalage.

bonus *n* **1** bounty, commission, dividend, gift, gratuity, hand-out, honorarium, largesse, payment, *inf* perk, reward, supplement, tip. **2** addition, advantage, benefit, extra, *inf* plus.

bony *adj* angular, emaciated, gangling, gawky, lanky, lean, scraggy, scrawny, skinny, thin, ungainly. *Opp* GRACEFUL, PLUMP.

book *n* booklet, copy, edition, hardback, paperback, publication, tome, volume, work. □ *album, annual, anthology, atlas, bestiary,* old use *chap-book, compendium, concordance, diary, dictionary, digest, directory, encyclopaedia, fiction, gazetteer, guidebook, handbook, hymnal, hymn-book, jotter, ledger, lexicon, libretto, manual, manuscript, missal, notebook, omnibus, picture-book, prayer-book, primer, psalter, reading book, reference book,* music *score, scrap-book, scroll, sketch-book, textbook, thesaurus, vade mecum.* ▷ WRITING. • *v* **1** *book for speeding.* arrest, take your name, write down details. **2** *book in advance.* arrange, buy, engage, order, organize, reserve, sign up.

booklet *n* brochure, leaflet, pamphlet, paperback.

boom *n* **1** bang, blast, crash, explosion, reverberation, roar, rumble. ▷ SOUND. **2** *boom in trade.* bonanza, boost, expansion, growth, improvement, increase, spurt, upsurge, upturn. ▷ PROSPERITY. **3** *boom across a river.* ▷ BARRIER. ● *v* **1** ▷ SOUND. **2** ▷ PROSPER.

boorish *adj* barbarian, ignorant, ill-bred, ill-mannered, loutish, oafish, philistine, uncultured, vulgar. *Opp* CULTURED.

boost *n* aid, encouragement, fillip, impetus, help, lift, push, stimulus. ● *v* advance, aid, assist, augment, bolster, build up, buoy up, encourage, enhance, enlarge, expand, foster, further, give an impetus to, heighten, help, improve, increase, inspire, lift, promote, push up, raise, support, sustain. *Opp* DEPRESS.

booth *n* box, carrel, compartment, cubicle, hut, kiosk, stall, stand.

booty *n* contraband, gains, haul, loot, pickings, pillage, plunder, spoils, *inf* swag, takings, trophies, winnings.

border *n* **1** brim, brink, edge, edging, frame, frieze, frill, fringe, hem, margin, perimeter, periphery, rim, surround, verge. **2** borderline, boundary, frontier, limit. **3** *flower border.* bed, herbaceous border. ● *v* abut on, adjoin, be adjacent to, be alongside, join, share a border with, touch.

bore *v* **1** burrow, drill, mine, penetrate, sink, tunnel. ▷ PIERCE. **2** *bore listeners.* alienate, depress, jade, *inf* leave cold, tire, *inf* turn off, weary. *Opp* INTEREST.

boring *adj* arid, commonplace, dead, dreary, dry, dull, flat, humdrum, long-winded, monotonous, prolix, repetitious, repetitive, soporific, stale, tedious, tiresome, trite, uneventful, unexciting, uninspiring, uninteresting, vapid, wearisome, wordy. *Opp* INTERESTING.

born *adj* congenital, genuine, instinctive, natural, untaught.

borrow *v* adopt, appropriate, be lent, *inf* cadge, copy, crib, make use of, obtain, pirate, plagiarize, *inf* scrounge, *inf* sponge, take, use, usurp. *Opp* LEND.

boss *n* employer, head. ▷ CHIEF.

bossy *adj* aggressive, assertive, authoritarian, autocratic, bullying, despotic, dictatorial, domineering, exacting, hectoring, high-handed, imperious, lordly, magisterial, masterful, officious, oppressive, overbearing, peremptory, *inf* pushy, self-assertive, tyrannical. *Opp* SERVILE.

bother *n* **1** ado, difficulty, disorder, disturbance, fuss, *inf* hassle, problem, *inf* to-do. **2** annoyance, inconvenience, irritation, nuisance, pest, trouble, worry. ● *v* **1** annoy, bewilder, concern, confuse, disconcert, dismay, disturb, exasperate, harass, *inf* hassle, inconvenience, irk, irritate, molest, nag, perturb, pester, plague, trouble, upset, vex, worry. **2** be concerned, be worried, care, mind, take trouble. ▷ TROUBLE.

bottle *n* flask. □ *carafe, carboy, decanter, flagon, jar, jeroboam, magnum, phial, pitcher, vial, wine-bottle.* **bottle up** ▷ SUPPRESS.

bottom *adj* deepest, least, lowest, minimum. ● *n* **1** base, bed, depth, floor, foot, foundation, lowest point, nadir, pedestal, substructure, underneath, underside. *Opp* TOP. **2** basis, essence, grounds, heart, origin, root, source. **3** *your bottom. vulg* arse, backside, behind, *inf* bum, buttocks, *joc* posterior, rear, rump, seat, *inf* sit-upon.

bottomless *adj* deep, immeasurable, unfathomable, unplumbable.

bounce *v* bob, bound, bump, jump, leap, move about, rebound, recoil, ricochet, spring.

bound *adj* **1** certain, committed, compelled, constrained, destined, doomed, duty-bound, fated, forced, obligated, obliged, pledged, required, sure. **2** *bound with rope.* ▷ BIND. ● *v* bob, bounce, caper, frisk, frolic, gambol, hop, hurdle, jump, leap, pounce, romp, skip, spring, vault. **bound for** aimed at, directed towards, going to, heading for, making for, off to, travelling towards.

boundary *n* border, borderline, bounds, brink, circumference, confines, demarcation, edge, end, extremity, fringe, frontier, interface, limit, margin, perimeter, threshold, verge.

boundless *adj* endless, everlasting, immeasurable, incalculable, inexhaustible, infinite, limitless, unbounded, unconfined, unflagging, unlimited, unrestricted, untold. ▷ VAST. *Opp* FINITE.

bounty *n* alms, altruism, beneficence, benevolence, charity, generosity, giving, goodness, kindness, largesse, liberality, munificence, philanthropy, unselfishness.

bouquet *n* **1** arrangement, bunch, buttonhole, corsage, garland, nosegay, posy, spray, wreath. **2** *bouquet of wine*. ▷ SMELL.

bout *n* **1** attack, fit, period, run, spell, stint, stretch, time, turn. **2** battle, combat, competition, contest, encounter, engagement, fight, match, round, *inf* set-to, struggle.

bow *v* **1** bend, bob, curtsy, genuflect, incline, kowtow, nod, prostrate yourself, salaam, stoop. **2** ▷ SUBMIT.

bowels *plur n* **1** entrails, guts, *inf* innards, insides, intestines, viscera, vitals. **2** core, depths, heart, inside.

bower *n* alcove, arbour, bay, gazebo, grotto, hideaway, pavilion, pergola, recess, retreat, sanctuary, shelter, summer-house.

bowl *n* basin, bath, casserole, container, dish, pan, pie-dish, tureen. • *v* fling, hurl, lob, pitch, throw, toss.

box *n* carton, case, chest, container, crate. □ *bin, caddy, canister, cartridge, casket, coffer, coffin, pack, package, punnet, tea-chest, tin, trunk*. • *v inf* engage in fisticuffs, fight, punch, scrap, spar. ▷ HIT.

boxer *n* prize-fighter, sparring partner. □ *bantamweight, cruiserweight, featherweight, flyweight, heavyweight, lightweight, middleweight, welterweight*.

boy *n derog* brat, *inf* kid, lad, schoolboy, son, *derog* stripling, *derog* urchin, youngster, youth.

boycott *n* ban, blacklist, embargo, prohibition. • *v* avoid, black, blackball, blacklist, exclude, *inf* give the cold-shoulder to, ignore, make unwelcome, ostracize, outlaw, prohibit, spurn, stay away from.

bracing *adj* crisp, exhilarating, health-giving, invigorating, refreshing, restorative, stimulating, tonic.

brag *v* crow, gloat, show off. ▷ BOAST.

brain *n* cerebrum, *inf* grey matter, intellect, intelligence, mind, *inf* nous, reason, sense, understanding, wisdom, wit.

brainwash *v* condition, indoctrinate, re-educate.

branch *n* **1** arm, bough, limb, prong, shoot, sprig, stem, twig. **2** department, division, office, offshoot, part, ramification, section, subdivision, wing. • *v* diverge, divide, fork, ramify, split, subdivide. **branch out** ▷ DIVERSIFY.

brand *n* kind, label, line, make, sort, trademark, type, variety. • *v* **1** burn, identify, label, mark, scar, stamp, tag. **2** censure, characterize, denounce, discredit, stigmatize, vilify.

brash *adj* brazen, bumptious, insolent, rash, reckless, rude, self-assertive. ▷ ARROGANT.

bravado *n* arrogance, bluster, braggadocio, machismo, swagger.

brave *adj* adventurous, audacious, bold, chivalrous, cool, courageous, daring, dauntless, determined, fearless, gallant, game, *sl* gutsy, heroic, indomitable, intrepid, lion-hearted, *derog* macho, noble, *inf* plucky, resolute, spirited, stalwart, stoical, stout-hearted, tough, unafraid, uncomplaining, undaunted, unshrinking, valiant, valorous, venturesome. *Opp* COWARDLY.

bravery *n* audacity, boldness, *sl* bottle, courage, daring, dauntlessness, determination, fearlessness, fibre, firmness, fortitude, gallantry, *inf* grit, *inf* guts, heroism, intrepidity, mettle, *inf* nerve, *inf* pluck, prowess, resolution, spirit, *sl* spunk, stoicism, tenacity, valour, will-power. *Opp* COWARDICE.

brawl *n* affray, altercation, *inf* bust-up, clash, *inf* dust-up, fracas, fray, *inf* free-for-all, mêlée, *inf* punch-up, quarrel, row, scrap, scuffle, *inf* set-to, tussle. • *v* ▷ FIGHT.

brazen *adj* barefaced, blatant, cheeky, defiant, flagrant, impertinent, impudent, insolent, rude, shameless, unabashed, unashamed. *Opp* SHAMEFACED.

breach *n* **1** aperture, break, chasm, crack, fissure, gap, hole, opening, rent, space, split. **2** alienation, difference, disagreement, divorce, drifting apart, estrangement, quarrel, rift, rupture, schism, separation, split. **3** *breach of law.* contravention, failure, infringement, offence, transgression, violation.

bread *n* □ *brioche, cob, croissant, French bread, loaf, roll, stick of bread, toast.* ▷ FOOD.

break *n* **1** breach, breakage, burst, chink, cleft, crack, crevice, cut, fissure, fracture, gap, gash, hole, leak, opening, rent, rift, rupture, slit, split, tear. **2** *break from work. inf* breather, breathing-space, hiatus, interlude, intermission, interval, *inf* let-up, lull, pause, respite, rest, tea-break. **3** *break in service.* disruption, halt, interruption, lapse, suspension. • *v* **1** breach, burst, *inf* bust, chip, crack, crumple, crush, damage, demolish, fracture, fragment, knock down, ruin, shatter, shiver, smash, *inf* smash to smithereens, snap, splinter, split, squash, wreck. ▷ DESTROY. **2** *break the law.* contravene, defy, disobey, disregard, fail to observe, flout, go back on, infringe, transgress, violate. **3** *break a record.* beat, better, do more than, exceed, excel, go beyond, outdo, outstrip, pass, surpass. **break down** ▷ ANALYSE, DEMOLISH. **break in** ▷ INTERRUPT, INTRUDE. **break off** ▷ FINISH. **break out** ▷ ESCAPE. **break through** ▷ PENETRATE. **break up** ▷ DISINTEGRATE.

breakdown *n* **1** collapse, destruction, disintegration, downfall, failure, fault, hitch, malfunction, ruin, stoppage. **2** analysis, classification, detailing, dissection, itemization, *inf* rundown.

breakthrough *n* advance, development, discovery, find, improvement, innovation, invention, leap forward, progress, revolution, success.

breakwater *n* groyne, jetty, mole, pier, sea-defence.

breath *n* breeze, gust, murmur, pant, puff, sigh, stir, waft, whiff, whisper.

breathe *vb* **1** exhale, inhale, pant, puff, respire, suspire. **2** hint, let out, tell, whisper.

breathless *adj* exhausted, gasping, out of breath, panting, *inf* puffed, *inf* puffing and blowing, tired out, wheezy, winded.

breed *n* ancestry, clan, family, kind, line, lineage, nation, pedigree, progeny, race, sort, species, stock, strain, type, variety. • *vb* **1** bear young ones, beget young ones, increase, multiply, procreate, produce young, propagate (*plants*), raise young ones, reproduce. **2** *breed contempt.* arouse, cause, create, cultivate, develop, engender, foster, generate, induce, nourish, nurture, occasion.

breeze *n* air-current, breath, draught, waft, wind, *poet* zephyr.

breezy *adj* airy, *inf* blowy, draughty, fresh, gusty, windy.

brevity *n* briefness, compactness, compression, conciseness, concision, curtness, economy, incisiveness, pithiness, shortness, succinctness, terseness.

brew *n* blend, compound, concoction, drink, hash, infusion, liquor, mixture, potion, preparation, punch, stew. • *vb* **1** boil, cook, ferment, infuse, make, simmer, steep, stew. **2** *brew mischief.* concoct, contrive, *inf* cook up, develop, devise, foment, hatch, plan, plot, prepare, scheme, stir up.

bribe *n sl* backhander, bribery, *inf* carrot, enticement, *sl* graft, gratuity, incentive, inducement, *inf* payola, protection money, *inf* sweetener, tip. • *vb* buy off, corrupt, entice, *inf* grease your palm, influence, offer a bribe, pervert, reward, suborn, tempt, tip.

brick *n* block, breeze-block, cube, set, sett, stone.

bridge *n* arch, connection, crossing, link, span, way over. □ *aqueduct, Bailey bridge, drawbridge, flyover, footbridge, overpass, pontoon bridge, suspension bridge, swing bridge, viaduct.* • *vb* connect, cross, fill, join, link, pass over, span, straddle, tie together, traverse, unite.

bridle *vb* check, control, curb, restrain.

brief *adj* **1** cursory, ephemeral, evanescent, fast, fleeting, hasty, limited, little, momentary, passing, quick, sharp, short, short-lived, temporary, transient, transitory. **2** *brief comment.* abbreviated, abridged, compact, compendious, compressed, concise, condensed, crisp, curt, curtailed, incisive, laconic, pithy, shortened, succinct, terse, thumbnail, to the point. *Opp* LONG. • *n* **1** advice, briefing, data, description, directions, information, instructions, orders, outline, plan. **2** *a barrister's brief.* argument, case, defence, dossier, summary. • *vb* advise, coach, direct, enlighten, *inf* fill someone in, give someone the facts, guide, inform, instruct, prepare, prime, *inf* put someone in the picture.

briefs *n* camiknickers, knickers, panties, pants, shorts, trunks, underpants.

brigand *n* bandit, buccaneer, desperado, footpad, gangster, highwayman, marauder, outlaw, pirate, robber, ruffian, thief.

bright *adj* **1** ablaze, aglow, alight, beaming, blazing, burnished, colourful, dazzling, flashing, *derog* flashy, fresh, *derog* gaudy, glaring, gleaming, glistening, glittering, glossy, glowing, incandescent, lambent, light, luminous, lustrous, pellucid, polished, radiant, refulgent, resplendent, scintillating, shimmering, shining, shiny, showy, sparkling, twinkling, vivid. **2** *bright sky.* clear, cloudless, fair, sunny. **3** *bright prospects.* auspicious, favourable, good, hopeful, optimistic, rosy. **4** *a bright smile.* ▷ CHEERFUL. **5** *bright ideas.* ▷ CLEVER. *Opp* DULL.

brighten *vb* **1** cheer (up), enliven, gladden, illuminate, light up, liven up, *inf* perk up, revitalize, smarten up. **2** *The sky brightened.* become sunny, clear up, lighten.

brilliant *adj* **1** coruscating, dazzling, glaring, glittering, glorious, intense, resplendent, scintillating, shining, showy, sparkling, splendid, vivid. ▷ BRIGHT. *Opp* DULL. **2** [*inf*] *a brilliant game.* ▷ EXCELLENT.

brim *n* brink, circumference, edge, limit, lip, margin, peri-meter, periphery, rim, top, verge.

bring *vb* **1** bear, carry, convey, deliver, fetch, take, transfer, transport. **2** *bring a friend.* accompany, conduct, escort, guide, lead, usher. **3** *The play brought great applause.* attract, cause, create, draw, earn, engender, generate, get, give rise to, induce, lead to, occasion, produce, prompt, provoke, result in. **bring about** ▷ CREATE. **bring in** ▷ EARN, INTRODUCE. **bring off** ▷ ACHIEVE. **bring on** ▷ ACCELERATE, CAUSE. **bring out** ▷ EMPHASIZE, PRODUCE. **bring up** ▷ EDUCATE, RAISE.

brink *n* bank, border, boundary, brim, circumference, edge, fringe, limit, lip, margin, perimeter, periphery, rim, skirt, threshold, verge.

brisk *adj* **1** active, alert, animated, bright, businesslike, bustling, busy, crisp, decisive, energetic, fast, keen, lively, nimble, quick, rapid, *inf* snappy, *inf* spanking (*pace*), speedy, spirited, sprightly, spry, vigorous. *Opp* LEISURELY. **2** *a brisk wind.* bracing, enlivening, fresh, invigorating, refreshing, stimulating.

bristle *n* barb, hair, prickle, quill, spine, stubble, thorn, whisker, wire. • *vb* become angry, become defensive, become indignant, bridle, flare up.

brittle *adj* breakable, crackly, crisp, crumbling, delicate, easily broken, fragile, frail, frangible, weak. *Opp* FLEXIBLE, RESILIENT.

broad *adj* **1** ample, capacious, expansive, extensive, great, large, open, roomy, spacious, sweeping, vast, wide. **2** *broad daylight.* clear, full, open, plain, undisguised. **3** *broad outline.* general, imprecise, indefinite, inexact, non-specific, sweeping, undetailed, vague. **4** *broad tastes.* all-embracing, catholic, comprehensive, eclectic, encyclopaedic, universal, wide-ranging. **5** *broad humour.* bawdy, *sl* blue, coarse, earthy, improper, impure, indecent, indelicate, racy, ribald, suggestive, vulgar. ▷ BROAD-MINDED. *Opp* FINITE, NARROW.

broadcast *n* programme, relay, show, telecast, transmission. • *vb* **1** advertise, announce, circulate, disseminate, make known, make public, proclaim, promulgate, publish, relay, report, send out, spread about, televise, transmit. **2** *broadcast seed.* scatter, sow at random.

broadcaster *n* anchor-man, announcer, commentator, compère, disc jockey, DJ, linkman, newsreader, presenter. ▷ ENTERTAINER.

broaden *vb* branch out, build up, develop, diversify, enlarge, expand, extend, increase, open up, spread, widen. *Opp* LIMIT.

broad-minded *adj* all-embracing, balanced, broad, catholic, comprehensive, cosmopolitan, eclectic, enlightened, liberal, open-minded, permissive, tolerant, unbiased, unbigoted, unprejudiced, unshockable. *Opp* NARROW-MINDED.

brochure *n* booklet, broadsheet, catalogue, circular, folder, handbill, leaflet, pamphlet, prospectus, tract.

brooch *n* badge, clasp, clip, fastening.

brood *n* children, clutch (*of eggs*), family, issue, litter, offspring, progeny, young. • *vb* **1** hatch, incubate, sit on. **2** *brood over mistakes.* agonize, dwell (on), *inf* eat your heart out, fret, mope, sulk, worry. ▷ THINK.

brook *n* beck, burn, channel, *poet* rill, rivulet, runnel, stream, watercourse. • *vb* ▷ TOLERATE.

browbeat *vb* badger, bully, coerce, cow, hector, intimidate, tyrannize. ▷ FRIGHTEN.

brown *adj* beige, bronze, buff, chestnut, chocolate, dun, fawn, khaki, ochre, russet, sepia, tan, tawny, terracotta, umber. • *vb* bronze, burn, colour, grill, tan, toast.

browse *vb* **1** crop grass, eat, feed, graze, pasture. **2** *browse in a book.* dip in, flick through, leaf through, look through, peruse, read here and there, scan, skim, thumb through.

bruise *n* black eye, bump, contusion, discoloration, *inf* shiner, welt. • *vb* blacken, crush, damage, discolour, injure, knock, mark. ▷ WOUND.

brush *n* **1** besom, broom. **2** *brush with police.* ▷ CONFLICT. • *vb* **1** comb, groom, scrub, sweep, tidy, whisk. **2** *just brushed the gatepost.* graze, touch. **brush aside** ▷ DISMISS, DISREGARD. **brush-off** ▷ REBUFF. **brush up** ▷ REVISE.

brutal *adj* atrocious, barbaric, barbarous, beastly, bestial, bloodthirsty, bloody, brutish, callous, cold-blooded, cruel, dehumanized, ferocious, hard-hearted, heartless, inhuman, inhumane, merciless, murderous, pitiless, remorseless, ruthless, sadistic, savage, uncivilized, unfeeling, vicious, violent, wild. ▷ UNKIND. *Opp* HUMANE.

brutalize *vb* dehumanize, harden, inure, make brutal.

brute *adj* crude, irrational, mindless, physical, rough, stupid, unfeeling, unthinking. ▷ BRUTISH. • *n* **1** beast, creature, dumb animal. ▷ ANIMAL. **2** [*inf*] *a cruel brute.* barbarian, bully, devil, lout, monster, ruffian, sadist, savage, swine.

brutish *adj* animal, barbaric, barbarous, beastly, bestial, boorish, brutal, coarse, cold-blooded, crude, cruel, *inf* gross, inhuman, insensitive, loutish, mindless, savage, senseless, stupid, subhuman, uncouth, unintelligent, unthinking. *Opp* HUMANE.

bubble *n* air-pocket, blister, hollow, vesicle. • *vb* boil, effervesce, fizz, fizzle, foam, froth, gurgle, seethe, sparkle. **bubbles** effervescence, fizz, foam, froth, head, lather, suds.

bubbly *adj* carbonated, effervescent, fizzy, foaming, seething, sparkling. ▷ LIVELY.

buccaneer *n* adventurer, bandit, brigand, corsair, marauder, pirate, privateer, robber.

bucket *n* can, pail, scuttle, tub.

buckle *n* catch, clasp, clip, fastener, fastening, hasp. • *vb* **1** clasp, clip, do up, fasten, hitch up, hook up, secure. **2** bend, bulge, cave in, collapse, contort, crumple, curve, dent, distort, fold, twist, warp.

bud *n* shoot, sprout. • *vb* begin to grow, burgeon, develop, shoot, sprout. **budding** ▷ POTENTIAL, PROMISING.

budge *vb* **1** change position, give way, move, shift, stir, yield. **2** *can't budge him.* alter, change, dislodge, influence, move, persuade, propel, push, remove, shift, sway.

budget *n* accounts, allocation of funds, allowance, estimate, financial planning, funds, means, resources. • *vb* allocate money, allot resources, allow (for), estimate expenditure, plan your spending, provide (for), ration your spending.

buff *n* ▷ ENTHUSIAST. • *vb* burnish, clean, polish, rub, shine, smooth.

buffer *n* bulwark, bumper, cushion, fender, pad, safeguard, screen, shield, shock-absorber.

buffet *n* **1** bar, café, cafeteria, counter, snack-bar. **2** *a stand-up buffet.* ▷ MEAL. • *vb* ▷ HIT.

bug *n* **1** ▷ INSECT, MICROBE. **2** *bug in a computer program.* breakdown, defect, error, failing, fault, flaw, *inf* gremlin, imperfection, malfunction, mistake, *inf* snarl-up, virus. • *vb* **1** intercept, interfere with, listen in to, spy on, tap. **2** [*sl*] *Untidiness bugs me.* ▷ ANNOY.

build *vb* assemble, construct, develop, erect, fabricate, form, found, *inf* knock together, make, put together, put up, raise, rear, set up. **build up** ▷ INTENSIFY.

builder *n* bricklayer, construction worker, labourer.

building *n* construction, edifice, erection, piece of architecture, *inf* pile, premises, structure. □ *arcade, barn, barracks, basilica, boat-house, bungalow, cabin, castle, cathedral, chapel, chateau, church, cinema, college, complex, cottage, dovecote, factory, farmhouse, flats, fort, fortress, garage, gazebo, gymnasium, hall, hangar, hotel, house, inn, library, lighthouse, mansion, mausoleum, mill, monastery, monument, mosque, museum, observatory, outbuilding, outhouse, pagoda, palace, pavilion, pier, power-station, prison, pub, public house, restaurant, school, shed, shop, silo, skyscraper, stable, storehouse, studio, summer-house, synagogue, temple, theatre, tower, villa, warehouse, windmill.*

bulb *n* **1** corm, tuber. □ *amaryllis, bluebell, crocus, daffodil, freesia, hyacinth, lily, narcissus, snowdrop, tulip.* **2** *electric bulb.* lamp, light.

bulbous *adj* bloated, bulging, convex, distended, ovoid, pear-shaped, pot-bellied, rotund, rounded, spherical, swollen, tuberous.

bulge *n* bump, distension, hump, knob, lump, projection, protrusion, protuberance, rise, swelling. • *vb* belly, billow, dilate, distend, enlarge, expand, project, protrude, stick out, swell.

bulk *n* **1** amplitude, bigness, body, dimensions, extent, immensity, largeness, magnitude, mass, size, substance, volume, weight. **2** *the bulk* *of the work. inf* best part, greater part, majority, preponderance.

bulky *adj* awkward, chunky, cumbersome, large, unwieldy. ▷ BIG.

bulletin *n* account, announcement, communication, communiqué, dispatch, message, newsflash, notice, proclamation, report, statement.

bullion *n* bar, ingot, nugget, solid gold, solid silver.

bull's-eye *n* bull, centre, mark, middle, target.

bully *vb* bludgeon, browbeat, coerce, cow, domineer, frighten, harass, hector, intimidate, oppress, persecute, *inf* pick on, *inf* push around, terrorize, threaten, torment, tyrannize.

bulwark *n* defence, earthwork, fortification, parapet, protection, rampart, redoubt, wall. ▷ BARRIER.

bump *n* **1** bang, blow, buffet, collision, crash, knock, smash, thud, thump. **2** bulge, distension, hump, knob, lump, projection, protrusion, protuberance, rise, swelling, tumescence, welt. ● *vb* **1** bang, collide with, crash into, jar, knock, ram, slam, smash into, strike, thump, wallop. ▷ HIT. **2** bounce, jerk, jolt, shake. **bump into** ▷ MEET. **bump off** ▷ KILL.

bumptious *adj* arrogant, *inf* bigheaded, boastful, brash, *inf* cocky, conceited, egotistic, forward, immodest, officious, overbearing, over-confident, pompous, presumptuous, pretentious, *inf* pushy, self-assertive, self-important, smug, *inf* snooty, *inf* stuck-up, swaggering, vain, vainglorious, vaunting. *Opp* MODEST.

bumpy *adj* **1** bouncy, jarring, jerky, jolting. **2** *a bumpy road.* broken, irregular, jagged, knobbly, lumpy, pitted, rocky, rough, rutted, stony, uneven. *Opp* SMOOTH.

bunch *n* **1** batch, bundle, clump, cluster, collection, heap, lot, number, pack, quantity, set, sheaf, tuft. **2** *bunch of flowers.* bouquet, posy, spray. **3** [*inf*] *bunch of friends.* band, crowd, gang, gathering, mob, party, team, troop. ▷ GROUP. ● *vb* assemble, cluster, collect, congregate, crowd, flock, gather, group, herd, huddle, mass, pack. *Opp* DISPERSE.

bundle *n* bag, bale, bunch, carton, collection, pack, package, packet, parcel, sheaf, truss. ● *vb* bale, bind, enclose, fasten, pack, package, roll, tie, truss, wrap. **bundle out** ▷ EJECT.

bung *n* cork, plug, stopper. ● *vb* ▷ THROW.

bungle *vb* blunder, botch, *sl* cock up, *inf* foul up, fluff, *inf* make a hash of, *inf* make a mess of, *inf* mess up, mismanage, *inf* muck up, *inf* muff, ruin, *inf* screw up, spoil.

buoy *n* beacon, float, marker, mooring buoy, signal. ● *vb* **buoy up** ▷ RAISE.

buoyant *adj* **1** floating, light. **2** *a buoyant mood.* ▷ CHEERFUL.

burden *n* **1** cargo, encumbrance, load, weight. **2** *burden of guilt.* affliction, albatross, anxiety, care, cross, duty, handicap, millstone, obligation, onus, problem, responsibility, sorrow, trial, trouble, worry. ● *vb* afflict, bother, encumber, hamper, handicap, impose on, load (with), *inf* lumber (with), oppress, overload (with), *inf* saddle (with), strain, tax, trouble, weigh down, worry.

burdensome *adj* bothersome, difficult, exacting, hard, heavy, onerous, oppressive, taxing, tiring, troublesome, trying, wearisome, wearying, weighty, worrying. *Opp* EASY.

bureau *n* **1** desk, writing-desk. **2** *travel bureau.* agency, counter, department, office, service.

bureaucracy *n* administration, government, officialdom, paperwork, *inf* red tape, regulations.

burglar *n* cat-burglar, housebreaker, intruder, robber. ▷ THIEF.

burglary *n* break-in, forcible entry, house-breaking, larceny, pilfering, robbery, stealing, theft, thieving.

burgle *vb* break in, pilfer, rob. ▷ STEAL.

burial *n* entombment, funeral, interment, obsequies.

burlesque *n* caricature, imitation, mockery, parody, pastiche, satire, *inf* send-up, spoof, *inf* take-off, travesty.

burly *adj* athletic, beefy, brawny, heavy, hefty, hulking, husky, muscular, powerful, stocky, stout, *inf* strapping, strong, sturdy, thickset, tough, well-built. *Opp* THIN.

burn *n* blister, charring. • *vb* **1** be alight, blaze, flame, flare, flash, flicker, glow, smoke, smoulder, spark, sparkle. **2** carbonize, consume, cremate, destroy by fire, ignite, incinerate, kindle, light, reduce to ashes, set fire to, set on fire. **3** *burn your skin.* blister, brand, char, scald, scorch, sear, shrivel, singe, sting, toast. ▷ FIRE, HEAT.

burning *adj* **1** ablaze, afire, aflame, alight, blazing, flaming, glowing, incandescent, lit up, on fire, raging, smouldering. **2** *burning pain.* biting, blistering, boiling, fiery, hot, inflamed, scalding, scorching, searing, smarting, stinging. **3** *burning chemicals.* acid, caustic, corrosive. **4** *a burning smell.* acrid, pungent, reeking, scorching, smoky. **5** *a burning desire.* acute, ardent, consuming, eager, fervent, flaming, frenzied, heated, impassioned, intense, passionate, red-hot, vehement. **6** *a burning issue.* crucial, important, pertinent, pressing, relevant, urgent, vital.

burrow *n* earth, excavation, hole, retreat, set, shelter, tunnel, warren. • *vb* delve, dig, excavate, mine, tunnel.

burst *vb* **1** break, crack, disintegrate, erupt, explode, force open, give way, open suddenly, part suddenly, puncture, rupture, shatter, split, tear. **2** ▷ RUSH.

bury *vb* cover, embed, enclose, engulf, entomb, immerse, implant, insert, inter, lay to rest, plant, put away, secrete, sink, submerge. ▷ HIDE.

bus *n old use* charabanc, coach, double-decker, minibus, *old use* omnibus.

bushy *adj* bristling, bristly, dense, fluffy, fuzzy, hairy, luxuriant, rough, shaggy, spreading, sticking out, tangled, thick, thick-growing, unruly, untidy.

business *n* **1** affair, concern, duty, function, issue, matter, obligation, problem, question, responsibility, subject, task, topic. **2** calling, career, craft, employment, industry, job, line of work, occupation, profession, pursuit, trade, vocation, work. **3** buying and selling, commerce, dealings, industry, marketing, merchandising, selling, trade, trading, transactions. **4** company, concern, corporation, enterprise, establishment, firm, organization, *inf* outfit, partnership, practice, *inf* set-up, venture.

businesslike *adj* careful, efficient, hard-headed, logical, methodical, neat, orderly, practical, professional, prompt, systematic, well-organized. *Opp* DISORGANIZED.

businessman,

businesswoman *ns* dealer, entrepreneur, executive, financier, industrialist, magnate, manager, merchant, trader, tycoon.

bustle *n* activity, agitation, commotion, excitement, flurry, fuss, haste, hurly-burly, hurry, hustle, movement, restlessness, scurry, stir, *inf* to-do, *inf* toing and froing. • *vb* dart, dash, fuss, hasten, hurry, hustle, make haste, move busily, rush, scamper, scramble, scurry, scuttle, *inf* tear, whirl.

busy *adj* **1** active, assiduous, bustling about, committed, dedicated, diligent, employed, energetic, engaged, engrossed, *inf* hard at it, immersed, industrious, involved, keen, occupied, *inf* on the go, pottering, preoccupied, slaving, *inf* tied up, tireless, *inf* up to your eyes, working. *Opp* IDLE. **2** *busy shops.* bustling, frantic, full, hectic, lively.

busybody *n* gossip, meddler, *inf* Nosey Parker, scandalmonger, snooper, spy. **be a busybody** ▷ INTERFERE.

butt *n* **1** haft, handle, shaft, stock. **2** barrel, cask, water-butt. **3** *cigar butt.* end, remains, remnant, stub. **4** *butt of ridicule.* end, mark, object, subject, target, victim. • *vb* buffet, bump, jab, knock, poke, prod, punch, push, ram, shove, strike, thump. ▷ HIT. **butt in** ▷ INTERRUPT.

buttocks *n* vulg arse, backside, behind, bottom, *vulg* bum, *Amer* butt, *Fr* derrière, fundament, haunches, hindquarters, *joc* posterior, rear, rump, seat.

buttress *n* pier, prop, support. • *vb* brace, prop up, reinforce, shore up, strengthen, support.

buxom *adj* ample, bosomy, *vulg* chesty, full-figured, healthy-looking, plump, robust, rounded, voluptuous. *Opp* THIN.

buy *vb* acquire, come by, gain, get, get on hire purchase, *inf* invest in, obtain, pay for, procure, purchase. *Opp* SELL.

buyer *n* client, consumer, customer, purchaser, shopper.

bypass *vb* avoid, circumvent, dodge, evade, find a way round, get out of, go round, ignore, neglect, omit, side-step, skirt.

by-product *n* adjunct, complement, consequence, corollary, repercussion, result, side-effect.

bystander *n* eyewitness, looker-on, observer, onlooker, passer-by, spectator, watcher, witness.

C

cabin *n* **1** bothy, chalet, cottage, hut, lodge, shack, shanty, shed, shelter. **2** *cabin on a ship.* berth, compartment, deck-house, quarters.

cable *n* **1** chain, cord, flex, guy, hawser, lead, line, mooring, rope, wire. **2** *news by cable.* message, telegram, wire.

cacophonous *adj* atonal, discordant, dissonant, harsh, noisy, unmusical. *Opp* HARMONIOUS.

cacophony *n* atonality, caterwauling, din, discord, disharmony, dissonance, harshness, jangle, noise, racket, row, rumpus, tumult. *Opp* HARMONY.

cadence *n* accent, beat, inflection, intonation, lilt, metre, pattern, rhythm, rise and fall, sound, stress, tune.

cadet *n* beginner, learner, recruit, tiro, trainee.

cadge *vb* ask, beg, scrounge, sponge.

café *n* bar, bistro, brasserie, buffet, cafeteria, canteen, coffee bar, coffee house, coffee shop, diner, restaurant, snack-bar, take-away, tea-room, tea-shop.

cage *n* aviary, coop, enclosure, hutch, pen, pound. • *vb* ▷ CONFINE.

cajole *vb inf* butter up, coax, flatter, inveigle, persuade, seduce.

cake *n* **1** bun, gateau. **2** *cake of soap.* bar, block, chunk, cube, loaf, lump, mass, piece, slab. • *vb* **1** coat, clog, cover, encrust, make dirty, make muddy. **2** coagulate, congeal, consolidate, dry, harden, solidify, thicken.

calamitous *adj* awful, cataclysmic, catastrophic, deadly, devastating, dire, disastrous, distressful, dreadful, fatal, ghastly, ruinous, serious, terrible, tragic, unfortunate, unlucky, woeful.

calamity *n* accident, affliction, cataclysm, catastrophe, disaster, misadventure, mischance, misfortune, mishap, tragedy, tribulation.

calculate *vb* add up, ascertain, assess, compute, count, determine, do sums, enumerate, estimate, evaluate, figure out, find out, gauge, judge, reckon, total, value, weigh, work out. **calculated** ▷ DELIBERATE. **calculating** ▷ CRAFTY.

calibre *n* **1** bore, diameter, gauge, measure, size. **2** ability, capability, capacity, character, competence, distinction, excellence, genius, gifts, importance, merit, proficiency, quality, skill, stature, talent, worth.

call *n* **1** bellow, cry, exclamation, roar, scream, shout, yell. **2** bidding, invitation, signal, summons. **3** *social call.* stay, stop, visit. **4** *no call for it.* cause, demand, excuse, justification, need, occasion, request, requirement. • *vb* **1** bellow, clamour, cry out, exclaim, hail, roar, shout, yell. **2** *call on friends.* drop in, socialize, visit. **3** *called her 'Jane'.* baptize, christen, dub, name. **4** *play called 'Lear'.* entitle, title. **5** *call me at 7.* arouse, awaken, get someone up, rouse, wake, waken. **6** *call a meeting.* convene, gather, invite, order, summon. **7** *call by phone.* contact, dial, phone, ring, telephone. **call for** ▷ FETCH, REQUEST. **call off** ▷ CANCEL. **call someone names** ▷ INSULT.

calligraphy *n* copperplate, handwriting, illumination, lettering, penmanship, script.

calling *n* business, career, employment, job, line of work, métier, occupation, profession, pursuit, trade, vocation, work.

callous *adj* apathetic, cold, cold-hearted, cool, dispassionate, hard-bitten, *inf* hard-boiled, hardened, hard-hearted, *inf* hard-nosed, heartless, inhuman, insensitive, merciless, pitiless, ruthless, *inf* thick-skinned, uncaring, unconcerned, unemotional, unfeeling, unsympathetic. ▷ CRUEL. *Opp* SENSITIVE.

callow *adj* adolescent, *inf* born yesterday, *inf* green, immature, inexperienced, innocent, juvenile, naïve, raw, unsophisticated, *inf* wet behind the ears, young. *Opp* MATURE.

calm *adj* **1** airless, even, flat, glassy, *poet* halcyon (*days*), like a millpond, motionless, placid, quiet, slow-moving, smooth, still, unclouded, unwrinkled, windless. **2** collected, *derog* complacent, composed, controlled, cool, dispassionate, equable, impassive, imperturbable, *inf* laid-back, level-headed, moderate, pacific, passionless, patient, peaceful, poised, quiet, relaxed, restful, restrained, sedate, self-possessed, sensible, serene, tranquil, undemonstrative, unemotional, unexcitable, *inf* unflappable, unhurried, unperturbed, unruffled, untroubled. *Opp* EXCITABLE, STORMY. • *n* flat sea, peace, quietness, stillness, tranquillity. ▷ CALMNESS. • *vb* appease, compose, control, cool, lull, mollify, pacify, placate, quieten, sedate, settle down, smooth, sober down, soothe, tranquillize. *Opp* DISTURB.

calmness *n derog* complacency, composure, equability, equanimity, imperturbability, level-headedness, peace of mind, sang-froid, self-possession, serenity, *inf* unflappability. *Opp* ANXIETY, EXCITEMENT.

camouflage *n* blind, cloak, concealment, cover, disguise, façade, front, guise, mask, pretence, protective colouring, screen, veil. • *vb* cloak, conceal, cover up, disguise, hide, mask, obscure, screen, veil.

camp *n* bivouac, camping-ground, campsite, encampment, settlement.

campaign *n* action, battle, crusade, drive, effort, fight, manoeuvre, movement, offensive, operation, push, struggle, war.

campus *n* grounds, setting, site.

canal *n* channel, waterway.

cancel *vb* abandon, abolish, abort, abrogate, annul, call off, countermand, cross out, delete, drop, eliminate, erase, expunge, frank (*stamps*), give up, invalidate, override, overrule, postpone, quash, repeal, repudiate, rescind, revoke, scrap, *inf* scrub, wipe out, write off. **cancel out** ▷ NEUTRALIZE.

cancer *n* canker, carcinoma, growth, malignancy, melanoma, tumour.

candid *adj* blunt, direct, fair, forthright, frank, honest, ingen-uous, just, *inf* no-nonsense, objective, open, outspoken, plain, sincere, straight, straightforward, transparent, true, truthful, unbiased, undisguised, unequivocal, unflattering, unprejudiced. *Opp* INSINCERE.

candidate *n* applicant, aspirant, competitor, contender, contestant, entrant, nominee, *inf* possibility, pretender (*to throne*), runner, suitor.

cane *n* bamboo, rod, stick. • *vb* ▷ THRASH.

canoe *n* dug-out, kayak.

canopy *n* awning, cover, covering, shade, shelter, umbrella.

canvass *n* campaign, census, enquiry, examination, investigation, market research, opinion poll, poll, probe, scrutiny, survey. • *vb* ask for, campaign, *inf* drum up support, electioneer, seek, solicit.

canyon *n* defile, gap, gorge, gulch, pass, ravine, valley.

cap *n* covering, lid, top. ▷ HAT. • *vb* ▷ COVER.

capable *adj* able, accomplished, adept, clever, competent, effective, effectual, efficient, experienced, expert, gifted, *inf* handy, intelligent, masterly, practised, proficient, qualified, skilful, skilled, talented, trained. *Opp* INCAPABLE. **capable of** apt to, disposed to, equal to, liable to.

capacity *n* **1** content, dimensions, magnitude, room, size, volume. **2** ability, acumen, capability, cleverness, competence, intelligence, potential, power, skill, talent, wit. **3** *in an official capacity*. appointment, duty, function, job, office, place, position, post, province, responsibility, role.

cape *n* **1** cloak, coat, cope, mantle, robe, shawl, wrap. **2** head, headland, peninsula, point, promontory.

caper *vb* bound, cavort, dance, frisk, frolic, gambol, hop, jig about, jump, leap, play, prance, romp, skip, spring.

capital *adj* **1** chief, controlling, first, foremost, important, leading, main, paramount, pre-eminent, primary, principal. **2** *capital letters.* big, block, initial, large, upper-case. **3** ▷ EXCELLENT. • *n* **1** chief city, centre of government. **2** assets, cash, finance, funds, investments, money, principal, property, *sl* (the) ready, resources, riches, savings, stock, wealth, *inf* the wherewithal.

capitulate *vb* acquiesce, be defeated, concede, desist, fall, give in, relent, submit, succumb, surrender, *inf* throw in the towel, yield.

capricious *adj* changeable, erratic, fanciful, fickle, fitful, flighty, impulsive, inconstant, mercurial, moody, quirky, uncertain, unpredictable, unreliable, unstable, variable, wayward, whimsical. *Opp* STEADY.

capsize *vb* flip over, invert, keel over, overturn, tip over, turn over, *inf* turn turtle, turn upside down.

capsule *n* lozenge, medicine, pill, tablet.

captain *n* **1** boss, chief, head, leader. **2** commander, master, officer in charge, pilot, skipper.

caption *n* description, explanation, heading, headline, superscription, title.

captivate *vb* attract, beguile, bewitch, charm, delight, enamour, enchant, enrapture, enslave, ensnare, enthral, entrance, fascinate, hypnotize, infatuate, mesmerize, seduce, *inf* steal your heart, *inf* turn your head, win. *Opp* DISGUST.

captive *adj* caged, captured, chained, confined, detained, enslaved, ensnared, fettered, gaoled, imprisoned, incarcerated, jailed, restricted, secure, taken prisoner, *inf* under lock and key. *Opp* FREE. • *n* convict, detainee, hostage, internee, prisoner, slave.

captivity *n* bondage, confinement, custody, detention, duress, imprisonment, incarceration, internment, protective custody, remand, restraint, servitude, slavery. ▷ PRISON. *Opp* FREEDOM.

capture *n* apprehension, arrest, seizure. • *vb* apprehend, arrest, *inf* bag, bind, catch, *inf* collar, corner, ensnare, entrap, *inf* get, *inf* nab, net, *inf* nick, overpower, secure, seize, snare, take prisoner, trap. ▷ CONQUER. *Opp* LIBERATE.

car *n* automobile, *inf* banger, *joc* bus, *joc* jalopy, motor, motor car, *sl* wheels. □ *cab, convertible, coupé, Dormobile, estate, fastback, hatchback, jeep, Land Rover, limousine, Mini, panda car, patrol car, police car, saloon, shooting brake, sports car, taxi, tourer.* ▷ VEHICLE.

carcass *n* **1** body, cadaver, corpse, meat, remains. **2** *carcass of a car.* framework, hulk, remains, shell, skeleton, structure.

card *n* cardboard, pasteboard. □ *bank card, birthday card, business card, calling card, credit card, get-well card, greetings card, identity card, invitation, membership card, notelet, picture postcard, playing-card, postcard, union card, Valentine, visiting card.*

care *n* **1** attention, carefulness, caution, circumspection, concentration, concern, diligence, exactness, forethought, heed, interest, meticulousness, pains, prudence, solicitude, thoroughness, thought, vigilance, watchfulness. **2** anxiety, burden, concern, difficulty, hardship, problem, responsibility, sorrow, stress, tribulation, vexation, woe, worry. ▷ TROUBLE. **3** *left in my care.* charge, control, custody, guardianship, keeping, management, protection, safe-keeping, ward. • *vb* be troubled, bother, concern yourself, mind, worry. **care for** ▷ LOVE, TEND.

career *n* business, calling, craft, employment, job, livelihood, living, métier, occupation, profession, trade, vocation, work. • *vb* ▷ RUSH.

carefree *adj* **1** blasé, casual, cheery, contented, debonair, easy, easy-going, happy-go-lucky, indifferent, insouciant, *inf* laid-back, light-hearted, nonchalant, relaxed, unconcerned, unworried. ▷ HAPPY. **2** *carefree holiday.* leisured, peaceful, quiet, relaxing, restful, trouble-free, untroubled. *Opp* ANXIOUS.

careful *adj* **1** alert, attentive, cautious, chary, circumspect, heedful, mindful, observant, prudent, solicitous, thoughtful, vigilant, wary, watchful. **2** *careful work.* accurate, conscientious, deliberate, diligent, exhaustive, fastidious, *derog* fussy, judicious, methodical, meticulous, neat, orderly, organized, painstaking, particular, precise, punctilious, responsible, rigorous, scrupulous, systematic, thorough, well-organized. *Opp* CARELESS. **be careful** ▷ BEWARE.

careless *adj* **1** absent-minded, heedless, ill-considered, imprudent, inattentive, incautious, inconsiderate, irresponsible, negligent, rash, reckless, thoughtless, uncaring, unguarded, unthinking, unwary. **2** *careless work.* casual, confused, cursory, disorganized, hasty, imprecise, inaccurate, jumbled, messy, perfunctory, scatter-brained, shoddy, slapdash, slipshod, *inf* sloppy, slovenly, thoughtless, untidy. *Opp* CAREFUL.

carelessness *n* haste, inattention, irresponsibility, negligence, recklessness, *inf* sloppiness, slovenliness, thoughtlessness, untidiness. *Opp* CARE.

caress *vb* cuddle, embrace, fondle, hug, kiss, make love to, *sl* neck with, nuzzle, pat, pet, rub against, smooth, stroke, touch.

caretaker *n* custodian, janitor, keeper, porter, superintendent, warden, watchman.

careworn *adj* gaunt, grim, haggard. ▷ WEARY.

cargo *n* consignment, freight, goods, lading (*bill of lading*), load, merchandise, payload, shipment.

caricature *n* burlesque, cartoon, parody, satire, *inf* send-up, spoof, *inf* take-off, travesty. • *vb* burlesque, distort, exaggerate, imitate, lampoon, make fun of, mimic, mock, overact, overdo, parody, ridicule, satirize, *inf* send up, *inf* take off.

caring *n* concern, kindness, nursing, solicitude.

carnage *n* blood-bath, bloodshed, butchery, havoc, holocaust, killing, massacre, pogrom, shambles, slaughter.

carnal *adj* animal, bodily, erotic, fleshly, natural, physical, sensual, sexual. ▷ LUSTFUL. *Opp* SPIRITUAL.

carnival *n* celebration, fair, festival, festivity, fête, fiesta, fun and games, gala, jamboree, merrymaking, pageant, parade, procession, revelry, show, spectacle.

carp *vb* cavil, find fault, *inf* go on, *inf* gripe, grumble, object, pick holes, quibble, *inf* split hairs, whinge. ▷ COMPLAIN.

carpentry *n* joinery, woodwork.

carriage *n* **1** coach. ▷ VEHICLE. **2** bearing, comportment, demeanour, gait, manner, mien, posture, presence, stance.

carrier *n* **1** bearer, conveyor, courier, delivery-man, delivery-woman, dispatch rider, errand-boy, errand-girl, haulier, messenger, porter, postman, runner. **2** *carrier of a disease.* contact, host, transmitter.

carry *vb* **1** bring, *inf* cart, communicate, ferry, fetch, haul, lead, lift, *inf* lug, manhandle, move, relay, remove, ship, shoulder, take, transfer, transmit, transport. ▷ CONVEY. **2** *carry weight.* bear, hold up, maintain, support. **3** *carry a penalty.* demand, entail, involve, lead to, occasion, require, result in. **carry on** ▷ CONTINUE. **carry out** ▷ DO.

cart *n* barrow, dray, truck, wagon, wheelbarrow. • *vb* ▷ CARRY.

carton *n* box, cartridge, case, container, pack, package, packet.

cartoon *n* animation, caricature, comic strip, drawing, sketch.

cartridge *n* **1** canister, capsule, case, cassette, container, cylinder, tube.

2 *cartridge for a gun*. magazine, round, shell.

carve *vb* **1** slice. ▷ CUT. **2** *carve stone*. *inf* chip away at, chisel, engrave, fashion, hew, incise, sculpture, shape.

cascade *n* cataract, deluge, flood, gush, torrent, waterfall. • *vb* ▷ POUR.

case *n* **1** box, cabinet, carton, casket, chest, container, crate, pack, packaging, suitcase, trunk. ▷ LUGGAGE. **2** *case of mistaken identity*. example, illustration, instance, occurrence, specimen, state of affairs. **3** *rules don't apply in his case*. circumstances, condition, context, plight, predicament, situation, state. **4** *a legal case*. action, argument, cause, dispute, inquiry, investigation, lawsuit, suit.

cash *n* banknotes, bills, change, coins, currency, *inf* dough, funds, hard money, legal tender, money, notes, *inf* (the) ready, *inf* the wherewithal. • *vb* exchange for cash, realize, sell. **cash in on** ▷ PROFIT.

cashier *n* accountant, banker, check-out person, clerk, teller, treasurer. • *vb* ▷ DISMISS.

cask *n* barrel, butt, hogshead, tub, tun, vat.

cast *n* **1** ▷ SCULPTURE. **2** *cast of a play*. characters, company, dramatis personae, performers, players, troupe. • *vb* **1** bowl, chuck, drop, fling, hurl, impel, launch, lob, pelt, pitch, project, scatter, shy, sling, throw, toss. **2** *cast a sculpture*. form, found, mould, shape. ▷ SCULPTURE. **cast off** ▷ SHED, UNTIE.

castaway *adj* abandoned, deserted, exiled, marooned, rejected, shipwrecked, stranded.

caste *n* class, degree, estate, grade, level, position, rank, standing, station, status, stratum.

castigate *vb* censure, chasten, chastise, *old use* chide, correct, discipline, lash, punish, rebuke, reprimand, scold, *inf* tell off. ▷ CRITICIZE.

castle *n* château, citadel, fort, fortress, mansion, palace, stately home, stronghold, tower.

castrate *vb* emasculate, geld, neuter, spay, sterilize, unsex.

casual *adj* **1** accidental, chance, erratic, fortuitous, incidental, irregular, promiscuous, random, serendipitous, sporadic, unexpected, unforeseen, unintentional, unplanned, unpremeditated, unstructured, unsystematic. *Opp* DELIBERATE. **2** *casual attitude*. apathetic, blasé, careless, *inf* couldn't-care-less, easygoing, *inf* free-and-easy, lackadaisical, *inf* laid-back, lax, negligent, nonchalant, offhand, relaxed, *inf* slap-happy, *inf* throwaway, unconcerned, unenthusiastic, unimportant, unprofessional. *Opp* ENTHUSIASTIC. **3** *casual clothes*. comfortable, informal. *Opp* FORMAL.

casualty *n* dead person, death, fatality, injured person, injury, loss, victim, wounded person.

cat *n* kitten, *inf* moggy, *inf* pussy, tabby, tom, tomcat.

catacomb *n* crypt, sepulchre, tomb, underground passage, vault.

catalogue *n* brochure, directory, index, inventory, list, record, register, roll, schedule, table. • *vb* classify, codify, file, index, list, make an inventory of, record, register, tabulate.

catapult *vb* fire, fling, hurl, launch. ▷ THROW.

cataract *n* cascade, falls, rapids, torrent, waterfall.

catastrophe *n* blow, calamity, cataclysm, crushing blow, débâcle, devastation, disaster, fiasco, holocaust, mischance, mishap, ruin, ruination, tragedy, upheaval. ▷ MISFORTUNE.

catch *n* **1** bag, booty, capture, haul, net, prey, prize, take. **2** *suspected a catch*. difficulty, disadvantage, drawback, obstacle, problem, snag, trap, trick. **3** *catch on a door*. bolt, clasp, clip, fastener, fastening, hasp, hook, latch, lock. • *vb* **1** clutch, ensnare, entrap, grab, grasp, grip, hang on to, hold, hook, net, seize, snare, snatch, take, tangle, trap. **2** *catch a thief*. apprehend, arrest, capture, *inf* cop, corner, detect, discover, expose, intercept, *inf* nab, *inf* nobble, stop, surprise, take by surprise, unmask. **3** *caught me unawares*. come upon, discover, find, surprise. **4** *catch a bus.* be in time for, get on. **5** *catch a cold.* become infected by, contract, get. **catch on** ▷ SUCCEED, UNDERSTAND. **catch-phrase** ▷ SAYING. **catch-22** ▷ DILEMMA. **catch up** ▷ OVERTAKE.

catching *adj* communicable, contagious, infectious, spreading, transmissible, transmittable.

catchy *adj* attractive, haunting, memorable, popular, singable, tuneful.

categorical *adj* absolute, authoritative, certain, complete, decided, decisive, definite, direct, dogmatic, downright, emphatic, explicit, express, firm, forceful, *inf* out-and-out, positive, strong, total, unambiguous, unconditional, unequivocal, unmitigated, unqualified, unreserved, utter, vigorous. *Opp* TENTATIVE.

category *n* class, classification, division, grade, group, head, heading, kind, order, rank, ranking, section, sector, set, sort, type, variety.

cater *vb* cook, make arrangements, minister, provide, provision, serve, supply.

catholic *adj* all-embracing, all inclusive, broad, broad-minded, comprehensive, cosmopolitan, eclectic, general, liberal, universal, varied, wide, wide-ranging.

cattle *plur n* beef, bullocks, bulls, calves, cows, heifers, livestock, oxen, steers, stock.

catty *adj inf* bitchy, ill-natured, malevolent, malicious, mean, nasty, rancorous, sly, spiteful, venomous, vicious. ▷ UNKIND. *Opp* KIND.

cause *n* **1** basis, beginning, genesis, grounds, motivation, motive, occasion, origin, reason, root, source, spring, stimulus. **2** agent, author, *old use* begetter, creator, initiator, inspiration, inventor, originator, producer. **3** *cause of his lateness.* excuse, explanation, pretext, reason. **4** *a good cause.* aim, belief, concern, end, ideal, object, purpose, undertaking. • *vb* **1** arouse, awaken, begin, bring about, bring on, create, effect, effectuate, engender, foment, generate, give rise to, incite, kindle, lead to, occasion, precipitate, produce, provoke, result in, set off, spark off, stimulate, trigger off, *inf* whip up. **2** compel, force, induce, motivate.

caustic *adj* **1** acid, astringent, burning, corrosive, destructive. **2** *caustic criticism.* acidulous, acrimonious, biting, bitter, critical, cutting, mordant, pungent, sarcastic, scathing, severe, sharp, stinging, trenchant, virulent, waspish. *Opp* MILD.

caution *n* **1** alertness, attentiveness, care, carefulness, circumspection, discretion, forethought, heed, heedfulness, prudence, vigilance, wariness, watchfulness. **2** *let off with a caution.* admonition, caveat, *inf* dressing-down, injunction, reprimand, *inf* talkingto, *inf* ticking-off, warning. • *vb* **1** advise, alert, counsel, forewarn, inform, *inf* tip off, warn. **2** *cautioned by the police.* admonish, censure, give a warning, reprehend, reprimand, *inf* tell off, *inf* tick off.

cautious *adj* **1** alert, attentive, careful, heedful, prudent, scrupulous, vigilant, watchful. **2** *cautious comments. inf* cagey, calculating, chary, circumspect, deliberate, discreet, gingerly, grudging, guarded, hesitant, judicious, non-committal, restrained, suspicious, tactful, tentative, unadventurous, wary, watchful. *Opp* RECKLESS.

cavalcade *n* march-past, parade, procession, spectacle, troop.

cave *n* cavern, cavity, den, grotto, hole, pothole, underground chamber. • *vb* **cave in** ▷ COLLAPSE, SURRENDER.

cavity *n* cave, crater, dent, hole, hollow, pit.

cease *vb* break off, call a halt, conclude, cut off, desist, discontinue, end, finish, halt, *inf* kick (*a habit*), *inf* knock off, *inf* lay off, leave off, *inf* pack in, *inf* pack up, refrain, stop, terminate. *Opp* BEGIN.

ceaseless *adj* chronic, constant, continual, continuous, endless, everlasting, incessant, interminable, never-ending, non-stop, permanent, perpetual, persistent, relentless, unending, unremitting, untiring. *Opp* INTERMITTENT, TEMPORARY.

celebrate *vb* **1** be happy, have a celebration, let yourself go, *inf* live it up, make merry, *inf* paint the town red, rejoice, revel, *old use* wassail. **2** *celebrate an anniversary*. commemorate, hold, honour, keep, observe, remember. **3** *celebrate a wedding*. officiate at, solemnize. **celebrated** ▷ FAMOUS.

celebration *n* banquet, binge, carnival, commemoration, feast, festivity, *inf* jamboree, *joc* jollification, merry-making, observance, *inf* orgy, party, *inf* rave-up, revelry, *church* service, *inf* shindig, solemnization. □ *anniversary, birthday, festival, fête, gala, jubilee, remembrance, reunion, wedding*.

celebrity *n* **1** ▷ FAME. **2** big name, *inf* bigwig, dignitary, famous person, idol, notability, personality, public figure, star, superstar, VIP, worthy.

celestial *adj* **1** astronomical, cosmic, galactic, interplanetary, interstellar, starry, stellar, universal. **2** *celestial beings*. angelic, blissful, divine, ethereal, godlike, heavenly, seraphic, spiritual, sublime, supernatural, transcendental, visionary.

celibacy *n* bachelorhood, chastity, continence, purity, self-restraint, spinsterhood, virginity.

celibate *adj* abstinent, chaste, continent, immaculate, single, unmarried, unwedded, virgin. • *n* bachelor, spinster, virgin.

cell *n* cavity, chamber, compartment, cubicle, den, enclosure, living space, prison, room, space, unit.

cellar *n* basement, crypt, vault, wine-cellar.

cemetery *n* burial-ground, churchyard, graveyard, necropolis.

censor *vb* amend, ban, bowdlerize, *inf* clean up, cut, edit, exclude, expurgate, forbid, prohibit, remove.

censorious *adj* fault-finding, *inf* holier-than-thou, judgemental, moralistic, Pharisaical, selfrighteous. ▷ CRITICAL.

censure *n* accusation, admonition, blame, castigation, condemnation, criticism, denunciation, diatribe, disapproval, *inf* dressing-down, harangue, rebuke, reprimand, reproach, reprobation, reproof, *inf* slating, stricture, *inf* talking-to, *inf* telling-off, tirade, verbal attack, vituperation. • *vb* admonish, berate, blame, *inf* carpet, castigate, caution, chide, condemn, criticize, denounce, lecture, rebuke, reproach, reprove, scold, take to task, *sl* tear (someone) off a strip, *inf* tell off, *inf* tick off, upbraid.

census *n* count, survey, tally.

central *adj* **1** focal, inner, innermost, interior, medial, middle. **2** *central facts*. chief, crucial, essential, fundamental, important, key, main, major, overriding, pivotal, primary, principal, vital. *Opp* PERIPHERAL.

centralize *vb* amalgamate, bring together, concentrate, rationalize, streamline, unify. *Opp* DISPERSE.

centre *n* bull's-eye, core, focal point, focus, heart, hub, inside, interior, kernel, middle, mid-point, nucleus, pivot. *Opp* PERIMETER. • *vb* concentrate, converge, focus.

centrifugal *adj* dispersing, diverging, moving outwards, scattering, spreading. *Opp* CENTRIPETAL.

centripetal *adj* converging. *Opp* CENTRIFUGAL.

cereal *n* corn, grain. □ *barley, corn on the cob, maize, millet, oats, rice, rye, sweet corn, wheat*.

ceremonial *adj* celebratory, dignified, liturgical, majestic, official, ritual, ritualistic, solemn, stately. ▷ FORMAL. *Opp* INFORMAL.

ceremonious *adj* civil, courteous, courtly, dignified, formal, grand, *derog* pompous, proper, punctilious, *derog* starchy. ▷ POLITE. *Opp* CASUAL.

ceremony *n* **1** celebration, commemoration, *inf* do, event, formal occasion, function, occasion, parade, reception, rite, ritual, service, solemnity. **2** ceremonial, decorum, etiquette, formality, grandeur, pageantry, pomp, pomp and circumstance, protocol, ritual, spectacle.

certain *adj* **1** adamant, assured, confident, constant, convinced, decided, determined, firm, invariable, positive, resolved, satisfied, settled, stable, steady, sure, undoubting, unshakable, unwavering. **2** *certain proof.* absolute, authenticated, categorical, certified, clear, clear-cut, conclusive, convincing, definite, dependable, established, genuine, guaranteed, incontestable, incontrovertible, indubitable, infallible, irrefutable, known, official, plain, reliable, settled, sure, true, trustworthy, unarguable, undeniable, undisputed, undoubted, unmistakable, unquestionable, valid, verifiable. **3** *certain disaster.* destined, fated, guaranteed, imminent, inescapable, inevitable, inexorable, predestined, predictable, unavoidable. **4** *certain to pay up.* bound, compelled, obliged, required, sure. **5** *certain people.* individual, particular, some, specific, unnamed, unspecified. *Opp* UNCERTAIN. **be certain** ▷ KNOW. **for certain** ▷ DEFINITELY. **make certain** ▷ ENSURE.

certainty *n* **1** actuality, certain fact, *inf* foregone conclusion, foreseeable outcome, inevitability, necessity, *inf* sure thing. **2** assertiveness, assurance, authority, certitude, confidence, conviction, knowledge, positiveness, proof, sureness, truth, validity. *Opp* DOUBT.

certificate *n* authorization, award, credentials, degree, diploma, document, guarantee, licence, pass, permit, qualification, warrant.

certify *vb* **1** affirm, asseverate, attest, authenticate, aver, avow, bear witness, confirm, declare, endorse, guarantee, notify, sign, swear, testify, verify, vouch, vouchsafe, warrant, witness. **2** *certify as competent.* authorize, charter, commission, franchise, license, recognize, validate.

chain *n* **1** bonds, coupling, fetters, handcuffs, irons, links, manacles, shackles. **2** *chain of events.* column, combination, concatenation, cordon, line, progression, row, sequence, series, set, string, succession, train. • *vb* bind, clap in irons, fetter, handcuff, link, manacle, shackle, tether, tie. ▷ FASTEN.

chair *n* armchair, carver, deckchair, dining-chair, easy chair, recliner, rocking-chair, throne. ▷ SEAT. • *vb* ▷ PRESIDE.

chairperson *n* chair, chairman, chairwoman, convenor, director, leader, moderator, organizer, president, speaker.

challenge *vb* **1** accost, confront, *inf* have a go at, take on, tax. 2 *challenge to duel.* dare, defy, *old use* demand satisfaction, provoke, summon. **3** *challenge a decision.* argue against, call in doubt, contest, dispute, dissent from, impugn, object to, oppose, protest against, query, question, take exception to.

challenging *adj* inspiring, stimulating, testing, thought-provoking, worthwhile. ▷ DIFFICULT. *Opp* EASY.

chamber *n* cavity, cell, compartment, niche, nook, space. ▷ ROOM.

champion *adj* great, leading, record-breaking, supreme, top, unrivalled, victorious, winning, world-beating. • *n* **1** conqueror, hero, medallist, prize-winner, record-breaker, superman, superwoman, titleholder, victor, winner. **2** *champion of the poor.* backer, defender, guardian, patron, protector, supporter, upholder, vindicator. **3** [*old use*] *champion in lists.* challenger, contender, contestant, fighter, knight, warrior. • *vb* ▷ SUPPORT.

championship *n* competition, contest, series, tournament.

chance *adj* accidental, adventitious, casual, coincidental, *inf* fluky, fortuitous, fortunate, haphazard, inadvertent, incidental, lucky, random, unexpected, unforeseen, unfortunate, unlooked-for, unplanned, unpremeditated. *Opp* DELIBERATE. • *n* **1** accident, coincidence, destiny, fate, fluke, fortune, gamble, hazard, luck, misfortune, serendipity. **2** *chance of rain.* danger, liability, likelihood, possibility, probability, prospect, risk. **3** occasion, opportunity, time, turn. • *vb* **1** ▷ RISK. **2** ▷ HAPPEN.

chancy *adj* dangerous, *inf* dicey, *inf* dodgy, hazardous, *inf* iffy, insecure, precarious, risky, speculative, ticklish, tricky, uncertain, unpredictable, unsafe. *Opp* SAFE.

change *n* **1** adaptation, adjustment, alteration, break, conversion, deterioration, development, difference, diversion, improvement, innovation, metamorphosis, modification, modulation, mutation, new look, rearrangement, refinement, reformation, reorganization, revolution, shift, substitution, swing, transfiguration, transformation, transition, translation, transmogrification, transmutation, transposition, *inf* turn-about, U-turn, variation, variety, vicissitude. **2** *small change.* ▷ CASH. ● *vb* **1** acclimatize, accommodate, accustom, adapt, adjust, affect, alter, amend, convert, diversify, influence, modify, process, rearrange, reconstruct, refashion, reform, remodel, reorganize, reshape, restyle, tailor, transfigure, transform, translate, transmogrify, transmute, vary. **2** *opinions change.* alter, be transformed, *inf* chop and change, develop, fluctuate, metamorphose, move on, mutate, shift, vary. **3** *change one thing for another.* alternate, displace, exchange, replace, substitute, switch, swop, transpose. **4** *change money.* barter, convert, trade in. **change into** ▷ BECOME. **change someone's mind** ▷ CONVERT. **change your mind** ▷ RECONSIDER.

changeable *adj* capricious, chequered (*career*), erratic, fickle, fitful, fluctuating, fluid, inconsistent, inconstant, irregular, mercurial, mutable, protean, shifting, temperamental, uncertain, unpredictable, unreliable, unsettled, unstable, unsteady, *inf* up and down, vacillating, variable, varying, volatile, wavering. *Opp* CONSTANT.

channel *n* **1** aqueduct, canal, conduit, course, dike, ditch, duct, groove, gully, gutter, moat, overflow, pipe, sluice, sound, strait, trench, trough, watercourse, waterway. ▷ STREAM. **2** avenue, means, medium, path, route, way. **3** *TV channel. inf* side, station, waveband, wavelength. ● *vb* conduct, convey, direct, guide, lead, pass on, route, send, transmit.

chant *n* hymn, plainsong, psalm. ▷ SONG. ● *vb* intone. ▷ SING.

chaos *n* anarchy, bedlam, confusion, disorder, disorganization, lawlessness, mayhem, muddle, pandemonium, shambles, tumult, turmoil. *Opp* ORDER.

chaotic *adj* anarchic, confused, deranged, disordered, disorderly, disorganized, haphazard, *inf* haywire, *inf* higgledy-piggledy, jumbled, lawless, muddled, rebellious, riotous, *inf* shambolic, *inf* topsy-turvy, tumultuous, uncontrolled, ungovernable, unruly, untidy, *inf* upside-down. *Opp* ORDERLY.

char *vb* blacken, brown, burn, carbonize, scorch, sear, singe.

character *n* **1** distinctiveness, flavour, idiosyncrasy, individuality, integrity, peculiarity, quality, stamp, taste, uniqueness. ▷ CHARACTERISTIC. **2** *a forceful character.* attitude, constitution, disposition, individuality, make-up, manner, nature, personality, reputation, temper, temperament. **3** *a famous character.* figure, human being, individual, person, personality, *inf* type. **4** *She's a character! inf* case, comedian, comic, eccentric, *inf* nut-case, oddity, *derog* weirdo. **5** *character in a play.* part, persona, portrayal, role. **6** *written characters.* cipher, figure, hieroglyphic, ideogram, letter, mark, rune, sign, symbol, type.

characteristic *adj* **1** [*of an individual*] distinctive, distinguishing, essential, idiosyncratic, individual, particular, peculiar, recognizable, singular, special, specific, symptomatic, unique. **2** [*of a kind*] representative, typical. ● *n* attribute, distinguishing feature, feature, hallmark, idiosyncrasy, mark, peculiarity, property, quality, symptom, trait.

characterize *vb* brand, delineate, depict, describe, differentiate, distinguish, draw, identify, individualize, mark, portray, present, recognize, typify.

charade *n* absurdity, deceit, deception, fabrication, farce, make-believe, masquerade, mockery, *inf* play-acting, pose, pretence, *inf* put-up job, sham.

charge *n* **1** cost, expenditure, expense, fare, fee, payment, postage, price, rate, terms, toll, value. **2** *in my charge.* care, command, control, custody, guardianship, jurisdiction, keeping, protection, responsibility, safe-keeping, supervision, trust. **3** *criminal charges.* accusation, allegation, imputa-tion, indictment. **4** *cavalry charge.* action, assault, attack, drive, incursion, invasion, offensive, onslaught, raid, rush, sally, sortie, strike. • *vb* **1** ask for, debit, exact, levy, make you pay, require. **2** accuse, blame, impeach, indict, prosecute, tax. **3** *charge with a duty.* burden, commit, empower, entrust, give, impose on. **4** *charged us to do our best.* ask, command, direct, enjoin, exhort, instruct. **5** *charge an enemy.* assail, assault, attack, *inf* fall on, rush, set on, storm, *inf* wade into.

charitable *adj* bountiful, generous, humanitarian, liberal, munificent, open-handed, philanthropic, unsparing. ▷ KIND. *Opp* MEAN.

charity *n* **1** affection, altruism, benevolence, bounty, caring, compassion, consideration, generosity, goodness, helpfulness, humanity, kindness, love, mercy, philanthropy, self-sacrifice, sympathy, tender-heartedness, unselfishness, warm-heartedness. **2** *old use* alms, alms-giving, bounty, donation, financial support, gift, *inf* handout, largesse, offering, patronage, poor relief. **3** good cause, the needy, the poor.

charm *n* **1** allure, appeal, attractiveness, charisma, fascination, hypnotic power, lovable nature, lure, magic, magnetism, power, pull, seductiveness. ▷ BEAUTY. **2** *magic charm.* curse, enchantment, incantation, magic, mumbo-jumbo, sorcery, spell, witchcraft, wizardry. **3** *charm on a bracelet.* amulet, lucky charm, mascot, ornament, talisman, trinket. • *vb* allure, attract, beguile, bewitch, cajole, captivate, cast a spell on, decoy, delight, disarm, enchant, enrapture, enthral, entrance, fascinate, hold spellbound, hypnotize, intrigue, lure, mesmerize, please, seduce, soothe, win over.
charming ▷ ATTRACTIVE.

chart *n* diagram, graph, map, plan, sketch-map, table.

charter *vb* **1** employ, engage, hire, lease, rent. **2** ▷ CERTIFY.

chase *vb* drive, follow, go after, hound, hunt, pursue, run after, track, trail.

chasm *n* abyss, canyon, cleft, crater, crevasse, drop, fissure, gap, gulf, hole, hollow, opening, pit, ravine, rift, split, void.

chaste *adj* **1** abstinent, celibate, *inf* clean, continent, good, immaculate, inexperienced, innocent, moral, pure, sinless, uncorrupted, undefiled, unmarried, virgin, virginal, virtuous. *Opp* IMMORAL **2** *chaste dress.* austere, becoming, decent, decorous, maidenly, modest, plain, restrained, severe, simple, tasteful, unadorned. *Opp* INDECENT.

chasten *vb* **1** restrain, subdue. ▷ HUMILIATE. **2** ▷ CHASTISE.

chastise *vb* castigate, chasten, correct, discipline, penalize, rebuke, scold. ▷ PUNISH, REPRIMAND.

chastity *n* abstinence, celibacy, continence, innocence, integrity, maidenhood, morality, purity, restraint, sinlessness, virginity, virtue. *Opp* LUST.

chat *n* chatter, *inf* chin-wag, *inf* chit-chat, conversation, gossip, *inf* heart-to-heart. • *vb* chatter, converse, gossip, *inf* natter, prattle. ▷ TALK.
chat up ▷ WOO.

chauvinist *n* bigot, *inf* MCP (= *male chauvinist pig*), patriot, sexist, xenophobe.

cheap *adj* **1** bargain, budget, cut-price, *inf* dirt-cheap, discount, economical, economy, fair, inexpensive, *inf* knock-down, low-priced, reasonable, reduced, *inf* rockbottom, sale, under-priced. **2** *cheap quality.* base, inferior, poor, second-rate, shoddy, *inf* tatty, tawdry, *inf* tinny, *inf* trashy, worthless. **3** *a cheap insult.* contemptible, crude, despicable, facile, glib, ill-bred, ill-mannered, mean, silly, tasteless, unworthy, vulgar. *Opp* EXPENSIVE, WORTHY.

cheapen *vb* belittle, debase, degrade, demean, devalue, discredit, downgrade, lower the tone (of), popularize, prostitute, vulgarize.

cheat *n* **1** charlatan, cheater, *inf* con-man, counterfeiter, deceiver, double-crosser, extortioner, forger, fraud, hoaxer, impersonator, impostor, mountebank, *inf* phoney, *inf* quack, racketeer, rogue, *inf* shark, swindler, trickster, *inf* twister. **2** artifice, bluff, chicanery, *inf* con, confidence trick, deceit, deception, *sl* fiddle, fraud, hoax, imposture, lie, misrepresentation, pretence, *inf* put-up job, *inf* racket, *inf* ripoff, ruse, sham, swindle, *inf* swizz, treachery, trick. ● *vb* **1** bamboozle, beguile, bilk, *inf* con, deceive, defraud, *sl* diddle, *inf* do, double-cross, dupe, *sl* fiddle, *inf* fleece, fool, hoax, hoodwink, outwit, *inf* rip off, rob, *inf* short-change, swindle, take in, trick. **2** *cheat in an exam.* copy, crib, plagiarize.

check *adj* ▷ CHEQUERED. ● *n* **1** break, delay, halt, hesitation, hiatus, interruption, pause, stop, stoppage, suspension. **2** *medical check.* check-up, examination, *inf* going-over, inspection, investigation, *inf* once-over, scrutiny, test. ● *vb* **1** arrest, bar, block, bridle, control, curb, delay, foil, govern, halt, hamper, hinder, hold back, impede, inhibit, keep in check, obstruct, regulate, rein, repress, restrain, retard, slow down, stem, stop, stunt (*growth*), thwart. **2** *check answers. Amer* check out, compare, cross-check, examine, inspect, investigate, monitor, research, scrutinize, test, verify.

cheek *n* audacity, boldness, brazenness, effrontery, impertinence, impudence, insolence, presumptuousness, rudeness, shamelessness, temerity.

cheeky *adj* arrogant, audacious, bold, brazen, cool, discourteous, disrespectful, flippant, forward, impertinent, impolite, impudent, insolent, insulting, irreverent, mocking, pert, presumptuous, rude, *inf* saucy, shameless, *inf* tongue-in-cheek. *Opp* RESPECTFUL.

cheer *n* **1** acclamation, applause, cry of approval, encouragement, hurrah, ovation, shout of approval. **2** ▷ HAPPINESS. ● *vb* **1** acclaim, applaud, clap, encourage, shout, yell. *Opp* JEER. **2** comfort, console, delight, encourage, exhilarate, gladden, make cheerful, please, solace, uplift. *Opp* SADDEN. **cheer someone up** ▷ COMFORT, ENTERTAIN. **cheer up** ▷ BRIGHTEN. **Cheer up!** *inf* buck up, look happy, *inf* perk up, smile, *sl* snap out of it, take heart.

cheerful *adj* animated, bouncy, bright, buoyant, cheery, *inf* chirpy, contented, convivial, delighted, elated, festive, gay, genial, glad, gleeful, good-humoured, hearty, hopeful, jaunty, jocund, jolly, jovial, joyful, joyous, jubilant, laughing, light, light-hearted, lively, merry, optimistic, *inf* perky, pleased, positive, rapturous, sparkling, spirited, sprightly, sunny, warm-hearted. ▷ HAPPY. *Opp* BAD-TEMPERED, CHEERLESS.

cheerless *adj* bleak, comfortless, dark, depressing, desolate, dingy, disconsolate, dismal, drab, dreary, dull, forbidding, forlorn, frowning, funereal, gloomy, grim, joyless, lacklustre, melancholy, miserable, mournful, sober, sombre, sullen, sunless, uncongenial, unhappy, uninviting, unpleasant, unpromising, woeful, wretched. ▷ SAD. *Opp* CHEERFUL.

chemical *n* compound, element, substance.

chemist *n old use* apothecary, *Amer* drug-store, pharmacist, pharmacy.

chequered *adj* **1** check, crisscross, in squares, like a chessboard, patchwork, tartan, tessellated. **2** *chequered career.* ▷ CHANGEABLE.

cherish *vb* be fond of, care for, cosset, foster, hold dear, keep safe, look after, love, nourish, nurse, nurture, prize, protect, treasure, value.

chest *n* **1** box, caddy, case, casket, coffer, crate, strongbox, trunk. **2** breast, rib-cage, thorax.

chew *vb* bite, champ, crunch, gnaw, grind, masticate, munch, nibble. ▷ EAT. **chew over** ▷ CONSIDER.

chick *n* fledgling, nestling.

chicken *n* bantam, broiler, cockerel, fowl, hen, pullet, rooster.

chief *adj* **1** arch, best, first, greatest, head, highest, in charge, leading, major, most experienced, most honoured, most important, oldest, outstanding, premier, principal, senior, supreme, top, unequalled, unrivalled. **2** *chief facts.* basic, cardinal, central, dominant, especial, essential, foremost, fundamental, high-priority, indispensable, key, main, necessary, overriding, paramount, predominant, primary, prime, salient, significant, substantial, uppermost, vital, weighty. *Opp* UNIMPORTANT. • *n* administrator, authority-figure, *inf* bigwig, *inf* boss, captain, chairperson, chieftain, commander, commanding officer, commissioner, controller, director, employer, executive, foreman, forewoman, *inf* gaffer, *Amer inf* godfather, governor, head, king, leader, manager, managing director, master, mistress, *inf* number one, officer, organizer, overseer, owner, president, principal, proprietor, ringleader, ruler, superintendent, supervisor, *inf* supremo.

chiefly *adv* especially, essentially, generally, in particular, mainly, mostly, particularly, predominantly, primarily, principally, usually.

child *n* **1** adolescent, *inf* babe, baby, *Scot* bairn, *inf* bambino, boy, *derog* brat, girl, *derog* guttersnipe, infant, juvenile, *inf* kid, lad, lass, minor, newborn, *inf* nipper, offspring, *inf* stripling, toddler, *inf* tot, *derog* urchin, youngster, youth. **2** daughter, descendant, heir, issue, offspring, progeny, son.

childhood *n* adolescence, babyhood, boyhood, girlhood, infancy, minority, schooldays, *inf* teens, youth.

childish *adj* babyish, credulous, foolish, immature, infantile, juvenile, puerile. ▷ SILLY. *Opp* MATURE.

childlike *adj* artless, frank, *inf* green, guileless, ingenuous, innocent, naïve, natural, simple, trustful, unaffected, unsophisticated. *Opp* ARTFUL.

chill *n* ▷ COLD. • *vb* cool, freeze, keep cold, make cold, refrigerate. *Opp* WARM.

chilly *adj* **1** cold, cool, crisp, fresh, frosty, icy, *inf* nippy, *inf* parky, raw, sharp, wintry. **2** *a chilly greeting.* aloof, cool, dispassionate, frigid, hostile, ill-disposed, remote, reserved, *inf* standoffish, unforthcoming, unfriendly, unresponsive, unsympathetic, unwelcoming. *Opp* WARM.

chime *n* carillon, peal, striking, tintinnabulation, tolling. • *vb* ▷ RING.

chimney *n* flue, funnel, smokestack.

china *n* porcelain. ▷ CROCKERY.

chink *n* **1** cleft, crack, cranny, crevice, cut, fissure, gap, opening, rift, slit, slot, space, split. **2** ▷ SOUND.

chip *n* **1** bit, flake, fleck, fragment, piece, scrap, shard, shaving, shiver, slice, sliver, splinter, wedge. **2** *a chip in a cup.* crack, damage, flaw, gash, nick, notch, scratch, snick. • *vb* break, crack, damage, gash, nick, notch, scratch, splinter. **chip away** ▷ CHISEL. **chip in** ▷ CONTRIBUTE, INTERRUPT.

chisel *vb* carve, *inf* chip away, cut, engrave, fashion, model, sculpture, shape.

chivalrous *adj* bold, brave, chivalric, courageous, courteous, courtly, gallant, generous, gentlemanly, heroic, honourable, knightly, noble, polite, respectable, true, trustworthy, valiant, valorous, worthy. *Opp* COWARDLY, RUDE.

choice *adj* ▷ EXCELLENT. • *n* **1** alternative, dilemma, need to choose, option. **2** *make your choice.* choosing, decision, election, liking, nomination, pick, preference, say, vote. **3** *a choice of food.* array, assortment, diversity, miscellany, mixture, range, selection, variety.

choke *vb* **1** asphyxiate, garrotte, smother, stifle, strangle, suffocate, throttle. **2** *choke in smoke.* cough, gag, gasp, retch. **3** *choked with traffic.* block, *inf* bung up, clog, close, congest, constrict, dam, fill, jam, obstruct, smother, stop up. **choke back** ▷ SUPPRESS.

choose *vb* adopt, agree on, appoint, decide on, determine on, distinguish, draw lots for, elect, establish, fix on, identify, isolate, name, nominate, opt for, pick out, *inf* plump for, prefer, select, settle on, show a preference for, single out, vote for.

choosy *adj* dainty, discerning, discriminating, exacting, fastidious, finical, finicky, fussy, *inf* hard to please, nice, particular, pernickety, *inf* picky, selective. *Opp* INDIFFERENT.

chop *vb* cleave, cut, hack, hew, lop, slash, split. ▷ CUT. **chop and change** ▷ CHANGE.

chopper *n* axe, cleaver.

choppy *adj* roughish, ruffled, turbulent, uneven, wavy. *Opp* SMOOTH.

chore *n* burden, drudgery, duty, errand, job, task, work.

chorus *n* **1** choir, choral society, vocal ensemble. **2** *join in the chorus.* refrain, response.

christen *vb* anoint, baptize, call, dub, name.

chronic *adj* **1** ceaseless, constant, continuing, deep-rooted, habitual, incessant, incurable, ineradicable, ingrained, lasting, lifelong, lingering, long-lasting, long-lived, long-standing, never-ending, non-stop, permanent, persistent, unending. *Opp* ACUTE, TEMPORARY. **2** [*inf*] *chronic driving.* ▷ BAD.

chronicle *n* account, annals, archive, chronology, description, diary, history, journal, narrative, record, register, saga, story.

chronological *adj* consecutive, in order, sequential.

chronology *n* **1** almanac, calendar, diary, journal, log, schedule, timetable. **2** *establish the chronology.* dating, order, sequence, timing.

chubby *adj* buxom, dumpy, plump, podgy, portly, rotund, round, stout, tubby. ▷ FAT. *Opp* THIN.

chunk *n* bar, block, brick, chuck, *inf* dollop, hunk, lump, mass, piece, portion, slab, wad, wedge, *inf* wodge.

church *n* abbey, basilica, cathedral, chapel, convent, monastery, nunnery, parish church, priory.

churchyard *n* burial-ground, cemetery, graveyard.

chute *n* channel, incline, ramp, rapid, slide, slope.

cinema *n* films, *old use* flicks, *Amer* motion pictures, *inf* movies, *inf* pictures.

circle *n* **1** annulus, band, circlet, disc, hoop, ring. □ *belt, circuit, circulation, circumference, circumnavigation, coil, cordon, curl, curve, cycle, ellipse, girdle, globe, gyration, lap, loop, orb, orbit, oval, revolution, rotation, round, sphere, spiral, tour, turn, wheel, whirl, whorl.* **2** *circle of friends.* association, band, body, clique, club, company, fellowship, fraternity, gang, party, set, society. ▷ GROUP. ● *vb* **1** circulate, circumnavigate, circumscribe, coil, compass, corkscrew, curl, curve, go round, gyrate, loop, orbit, pirouette, pivot, reel, revolve, rotate, spin, spiral, swirl, swivel, tour, turn, wheel, whirl, wind. **2** *trees circle the lawn.* encircle, enclose, encompass, girdle, hem in, ring, skirt, surround.

circuit *n* journey round, lap, orbit, revolution, tour.

circuitous *adj* curving, devious, indirect, labyrinthine, mean-dering, oblique, rambling, roundabout, serpentine, tortuous, twisting, winding, zigzag. *Opp* DIRECT.

circular *adj* **1** annular, discoid, ring-like, round. **2** *circular conversation.* circumlocutory, cyclic, periphrastic, repeating, repetitive, roundabout, tautologous. ● *n* advertisement, leaflet, letter, notice, pamphlet.

circulate *vb* **1** go round, move about, move round, orbit. ▷ CIRCLE. **2** *circulate gossip.* advertise, disseminate, distribute, issue, make known, noise abroad, promulgate, publicize, publish, *inf* put about, send round, spread about.

circulation *n* **1** flow, movement, pumping, recycling. **2** broadcasting, diffusion, dissemination, distribution, promulgation, publication, spreading, transmission. **3** *newspaper circulation.* distribution, sales-figures.

circumference *n* border, boundary, circuit, edge, exterior, fringe, limit, margin, outline, outside, perimeter, periphery, rim, verge.

circumstance *n* affair, event, happening, incident, occasion, occurrence. **circumstances 1** background, causes, conditions, considerations, context, contingencies, details, factors, facts, influences, particulars, position, situation, state of affairs, surroundings. **2** finances, income, resources.

circumstantial *adj* conjectural, deduced, inferred, unprovable. *Opp* PROVABLE.

cistern *n* bath, container, reservoir, tank.

citadel *n* acropolis, bastion, castle, fort, fortification, fortress, garrison, stronghold, tower.

cite *vb* adduce, advance, *inf* bring up, enumerate, mention, name, quote, *inf* reel off, refer to, specify.

citizen *n* burgess, commoner, denizen, dweller, freeman, householder, inhabitant, national, native, passport-holder, ratepayer, resident, subject, taxpayer, voter.

city *n* capital, conurbation, metropolis, town, urban district.

civil *adj* **1** affable, civilized, considerate, courteous, obliging, respectful, urbane, well-bred, well-mannered. ▷ POLITE. *Opp* IMPOLITE. **2** *civil administration*. civilian, domestic, internal, national. *Opp* MILITARY. **3** *civil liberties*. communal, public, social, state. **civil rights** freedom, human rights, legal rights, liberty, political rights. **civil servant** administrator, bureaucrat, *derog* mandarin.

civilization *n* achievements, attainments, culture, customs, mores, organization, refinement, sophistication, urbanity, urbanization.

civilize *vb* cultivate, domesticate, educate, enlighten, humanize, improve, make better, organize, refine, socialize, urbanize.

civilized *adj* advanced, cultivated, cultured, democratic, developed, domesticated, educated, enlightened, humane, orderly, polite, refined, sociable, social, sophisticated, urbane, urbanized, well-behaved, well-run. *Opp* UNCIVILIZED.

claim *vb* **1** ask for, collect, command, demand, exact, insist on, request, require, take. **2** affirm, allege, argue, assert, attest, contend, declare, insist, maintain, pretend, profess, state.

clairvoyant *adj* extra-sensory, oracular, prophetic, psychic, telepathic. • *n* fortune-teller, oracle, prophet, seer, sibyl, soothsayer.

clamber *vb* climb, crawl, move awkwardly, scramble.

clammy *adj* close, damp, dank, humid, moist, muggy, slimy, sticky, sweaty, wet.

clamour *n* babel, commotion, din, hubbub, hullabaloo, noise, outcry, racket, row, screeching, shouting, storm, uproar. • *vb* call out, cry out, exclaim, shout, yell.

clan *n* family, house, tribe.

clannish *adj* *derog* cliquish, close, close-knit, insular, isolated, narrow, united.

clap *n* bang, crack, crash, report, smack. ▷ SOUND. • *vb* **1** applaud, *sl* put your hands together, show approval. **2** *clap on the back*. ▷ HIT.

clarify *vb* **1** clear up, define, elucidate, explain, explicate, gloss, illuminate, make clear, simplify, *inf* spell out, throw light on. *Opp* CONFUSE. **2** *clarify wine*. cleanse, clear, filter, purify, refine. *Opp* CLOUD.

clash *vb* **1** bang, clang, clank, crash, resonate, ring. ▷ SOUND. **2** ▷ CONFLICT. **3** *The events clashed*. ▷ COINCIDE.

clasp *n* **1** brooch, buckle, catch, clip, fastener, fastening, hasp, hook, pin. **2** cuddle, embrace, grasp, grip, hold, hug. • *vb* **1** ▷ FASTEN. **2** cling to, clutch, embrace, enfold, grasp, grip, hold, hug, squeeze. **3** *clasp your hands*. hold together, wring.

class *n* **1** category, classification, division, domain, genre, genus, grade, group, kind, league, order, quality, rank, set, sort, species, sphere, type. **2** *social class*. caste, degree, descent, extraction, grouping, lineage, pedigree, standing, station, status. □ *aristocracy, bourgeoisie, commoners, (the) commons, gentry, lower* *class, middle class, nobility, proletariat, ruling class, serfs, upper class, upper-middle class, (the) workers, working class.* **3** *class in school.* band, form, *Amer* grade, group, set, stream, year. ● *vb* ▷ CLASSIFY.

classic *adj* **1** abiding, ageless, deathless, enduring, established, exemplary, flawless, ideal, immortal, lasting, legendary, masterly, memorable, notable, outstanding, perfect, time-honoured, undying, unforgettable, *inf* vintage. ▷ EXCELLENT. *Opp* COMMONPLACE, EPHEMERAL. **2** *a classic case.* archetypal, characteristic, copybook, definitive, model, paradigmatic, regular, standard, typical, usual. *Opp* UNUSUAL. ● *n* masterpiece, masterwork, model.

classical *adj* **1** ancient, Attic, Greek, Hellenic, Latin, Roman. **2** *classical style.* austere, dignified, elegant, pure, restrained, simple, symmetrical, well-proportioned. **3** *classical music.* established, harmonious, highbrow, serious.

classification *n* categorization, codification, ordering, organization, systematization, tabulation, taxonomy. ▷ CLASS.

classify *vb* arrange, bracket together, catalogue, categorize, class, grade, group, order, organize, *inf* pigeon-hole, put into sets, sort, systematize, tabulate. **classified** ▷ SECRET.

clause *n* article, condition, item, paragraph, part, passage, provision, proviso, section, subsection.

claw *n* nail, talon. ● *vb* graze, injure, lacerate, maul, rip, scrape, scratch, slash, tear.

clean *adj* **1** decontaminated, dirt-free, disinfected, hygienic, immaculate, laundered, perfect, polished, sanitary, scrubbed, spotless, sterile, sterilized, tidy, unadulterated, unsoiled, unstained, unsullied, washed, wholesome. **2** *clean water.* clarified, clear, distilled, fresh, pure, purified, unpolluted. **3** *clean paper.* blank, new, plain, uncreased, unmarked, untouched, unused. **4** *a clean edge.* neat, regular, smooth, straight, tidy. **5** *a clean fight.* chivalrous, fair, honest, honourable, sporting, sportsmanlike. **6** *clean fun.* chaste, decent, good, innocent, moral, respectable, upright, virtuous. *Opp* DIRTY. ● *vb* cleanse, clear up, tidy up, wash. □ *bath, bathe, brush, buff, decontaminate, deodorize, disinfect, dry-clean, dust, filter, flush, groom, hoover, launder, mop, polish, purge, purify, rinse, sand-blast, sanitize, scour, scrape, scrub, shampoo, shower, soap, sponge, spring-clean, spruce up, sterilize, swab, sweep, swill, vacuum, wipe, wring out. Opp* CONTAMINATE. **make a clean breast of** ▷ CONFESS.

clean-shaven *adj* beardless, shaved, shaven, shorn, smooth.

clear *adj* **1** clean, colourless, crystalline, glassy, limpid, pellucid, pure, transparent. **2** *clear weather.* cloudless, fair, fine, sunny, starlit, unclouded. *Opp* CLOUDY. **3** *clear colours.* bright, lustrous, shining, sparkling, strong, vivid. **4** *clear conscience.* blameless, easy, guiltless, innocent, quiet, satisfied, sinless, undisturbed, untarnished, untroubled, unworried. **5** *clear handwriting.* bold, clean, definite, distinct, explicit, focused, legible, positive, recognizable, sharp, simple, visible, well-defined. **6** *clear sound.* audible, clarion (*call*), distinct, penetrating, sharp. **7** *clear instructions.* clear-cut, coherent, comprehensible, explicit, intelligible, lucid, perspicuous, precise, specific, straightforward, unambiguous, understandable, unequivocal, well-presented. **8** *clear case of cheating.* apparent, blatant, clear-cut, conspicuous, evident, glaring, indisputable, manifest, noticeable, obvious, palpable, perceptible, plain, pronounced, straightforward, unconcealed, undisguised, unmistakable. *Opp* UNCERTAIN. **9** *clear space.* empty, free, open, passable, uncluttered, uncrowded, unhampered, unhindered, unimpeded, unobstructed. ● *vb* **1** disappear, evaporate, fade, melt away, vanish. **2** become clear, brighten, clarify, lighten, uncloud. **3** clean, make clean, make transparent, polish, wipe. **4** *clear weeds.* disentangle, eliminate, get rid of, remove, strip. **5** *clear a drain.* clean out, free, loosen, open up, unblock, unclog. **6** *clear of blame.* absolve, acquit, exculpate, excuse, exonerate, free, *inf* let off, liberate, release, vindicate. **7** *clear a building.* empty, evacuate. **8** *clear a fence.* bound over, jump, leap over, pass over, spring over, vault. **clear away** ▷ REMOVE. **clear off** ▷ DEPART. **clear up** ▷ CLEAN, EXPLAIN.

clearing *n* gap, glade, opening, space.

cleave *vb* divide, halve, rive, slit, split. ▷ CUT.

clench *vb* **1** clamp up, close tightly, double up, grit (*your teeth*), squeeze tightly. **2** clasp, grasp, grip, hold.

clergyman *n* archbishop, ayatollah, bishop, canon, cardinal, chaplain, churchman, cleric, curate, deacon, *fem* deaconess, dean, divine, ecclesiastic, evangelist, friar, guru, imam, *inf* man of the cloth, minister, missionary, monk, padre, parson, pastor, preacher, prebend, prelate, priest, rabbi, rector, vicar. *Opp* LAYMAN.

clerical *adj* **1** *clerical and administrative work.* office, secretarial, *inf* white-collar. **2** *a clerical collar.* canonical, ecclesiastical, episcopal, ministerial, monastic, pastoral, priestly, rabbinical, sacerdotal, spiritual.

clerk *n* assistant, bookkeeper, computer operator, copyist, filing clerk, office boy, office girl, office worker, *inf* pen-pusher, receptionist, recorder, scribe, secretary, shorthand-typist, stenographer, typist, word-processor operator.

clever *adj* able, academic, accomplished, acute, adept, adroit, apt, artful, artistic, astute, *inf* brainy, bright, brilliant, canny, capable, *derog* crafty, creative, *derog* cunning, *inf* cute, *inf* deep, deft, dextrous, discerning, expert, *derog* foxy, gifted, guileful, *inf* handy, imaginative, ingenious, intellectual, intelligent, inventive, judicious, keen, knowing, knowledgeable, observant, penetrating, perceptive, percipient, perspicacious, precocious, quick, quick-witted, rational, resourceful, sagacious, sensible, sharp, shrewd, skilful, skilled, slick, *derog* sly, smart, subtle, talented, *derog* wily, wise, witty. *Opp* STUPID, UNSKILFUL. **clever person** *inf* egghead, expert, genius, *derog* know-all, mastermind, prodigy, sage, *derog* smart alec, *derog* smart-arse, virtuoso, wizard.

cleverness *n* ability, acuteness, astuteness, brilliance, *derog* cunning, expertise, ingenuity, intellect, intelligence, mastery, quickness, sagacity, sharpness, shrewdness, skill, subtlety, talent, wisdom, wit. *Opp* STUPIDITY.

cliché *n* banality, *inf* chestnut, commonplace, hackneyed phrase, platitude, stereotype, truism, well-worn phrase.

client *n plur* clientele, consumer, customer, patient, patron, shopper, user.

cliff *n* bluff, crag, escarpment, precipice, rock-face, scar, sheer drop.

climate *n* **1** ▷ WEATHER. **2** *climate of opinion.* ambience, atmosphere, aura, disposition, environment, feeling, mood, spirit, temper, trend.

climax *n* **1** acme, apex, apogee, crisis, culmination, head, highlight, high point, peak, summit, zenith. *Opp* BATHOS. **2** *sexual climax.* orgasm.

climb *n* ascent, grade, gradient, hill, incline, pitch, rise, slope. • *vb* **1** ascend, clamber up, defy gravity, go up, levitate, lift off, mount, move up, scale, shin up, soar, swarm up, take off. **2** incline, rise, slope up. **3** *climb a mountain.* conquer, reach the top of. **climb down** ▷ DESCEND.

clinch *vb* agree, close, complete, conclude, confirm, decide, determine, finalize, make certain of, ratify, secure, settle, shake hands on, sign, verify.

cling *vb* adhere, attach, fasten, fix, hold fast, stick. **cling to** ▷ EMBRACE.

clinic *n* health centre, infirmary, medical centre, sick-bay, surgery.

clip *n* **1** ▷ FASTENER. **2** *clip from a film.* bit, cutting, excerpt, extract, fragment, part, passage, portion, quotation, section, snippet, trailer. • *vb* **1** pin, staple. ▷ FASTEN. **2** crop, dock, prune, shear, snip, trim. ▷ CUT.

cloak *n* **1** cape, cope, mantle, poncho, robe, wrap. ▷ COAT. **2** ▷ COVER. • *vb* cover, disguise, mantle, mask, screen, shroud, veil, wrap. ▷ HIDE.

clock *n* time-piece. □ *alarm-clock, chronometer, dial, digital clock, grandfather clock, hourglass, pendulum clock, sundial, watch.*

clog *vb* block, *inf* bung up, choke, close, congest, dam, fill, impede, jam, obstruct, plug, stop up.

close *adj* **1** accessible, adjacent, adjoining, at hand, convenient, handy, near, neighbouring, point-blank. **2** *close friends.* affectionate, attached, dear, devoted, familiar, fond, friendly, intimate, loving, *inf* thick. **3** *close comparison.* alike, analogous, comparable, compatible, corresponding, related, resembling, similar. **4** *a close crowd.* compact, compressed, congested, cramped, crowded, dense, *inf* jam-packed, packed, thick. **5** *close scrutiny.* attentive, careful, concentrated, detailed, minute, painstaking, precise, rigorous, searching, thorough. **6** *close with information.* confidential, private, reserved, reticent, secretive, taciturn. **7** *close with money.* illiberal, mean, *inf* mingy, miserly, niggardly, parsimonious, penurious, stingy, tight, tight-fisted, ungenerous. **8** *close atmosphere.* airless, confined, fuggy, humid, muggy, oppressive, stale, stifling, stuffy, suffocating, sweltering, unventilated, warm. *Opp* DISTANT, OPEN. • *n* **1** cessation, completion, conclusion, culmination, end, finish, stop, termination. **2** cadence, coda, finale. **3** *close of a play.* denouement, last act. • *vb* **1** bolt, fasten, lock, make inaccessible, padlock, put out of bounds, seal, secure, shut. **2** *close a road.* bar, barricade, block, make impassable, obstruct, seal off, stop up. **3** *close proceedings.* complete, conclude, culminate, discontinue, end, finish, stop, terminate, *inf* wind up. **4** *close a gap.* fill, join up, make smaller, reduce, shorten. *Opp* OPEN.

closed *adj* **1** fastened, locked, sealed, shut. **2** completed, concluded, done with, ended, finished, over, resolved, settled, tied up.

clot *n* embolism, lump, mass, thrombosis. • *vb* coagulate, coalesce, congeal, curdle, make lumps, set, solidify, stiffen, thicken.

cloth *n* fabric, material, stuff, textile. □ *astrakhan, bouclé, brocade, broderie anglaise, buckram, calico, cambric, candlewick, canvas, cashmere, cheesecloth, chenille, chiffon, chintz, corduroy, cotton, crepe, cretonne, damask, denim, dimity, drill, drugget, elastic, felt, flannel, flannelette, gabardine, gauze, georgette, gingham, hessian, holland, lace, lamé, lawn, linen, lint, mohair, moiré, moquette, muslin, nankeen, nylon, oilcloth, oilskin, organdie, organza, patchwork, piqué, plaid, plissé, plush, polycotton, polyester, poplin, rayon, sackcloth, sacking, sailcloth, sarsenet, sateen, satin, satinette, seersucker, serge, silk, stockinet, taffeta, tapestry, tartan, terry, ticking, tulle, tussore, tweed, velour, velvet, velveteen, viscose, voile, winceyette, wool, worsted.*

clothe *vb* accoutre, apparel, array, attire, cover, deck, drape, dress, fit out, garb, *inf* kit out, outfit, robe, swathe, wrap up. *Opp* STRIP. **clothe yourself in** ▷ WEAR.

clothes *plur n* apparel, attire, *inf* clobber, clothing, costume, dress, ensemble, finery, garb, garments, *inf* gear, *inf* get-up, outfit, *old use* raiment, *inf* rig-out, *sl* togs, trousseau, underclothes, uniform, vestments, wardrobe, wear, weeds. □ *anorak, apron, blazer, blouse, bodice, breeches, caftan, cagoule, cape, cardigan, cassock, chemise, chuddar, cloak, coat, crinoline, culottes, décolletage, doublet, dress, dressing-gown, duffel coat, dungarees, frock, gaiters, gauntlet, glove, gown, greatcoat, gym-slip, habit, housecoat, jacket, jeans, jerkin, jersey, jodhpurs, jumper, kilt, knickers, leg-warmers, leotard, livery, loincloth, lounge suit, mackintosh, mantle, miniskirt, muffler, neck-tie, négligé, nightclothes, nightdress, oilskins, overalls, overcoat, pants, parka, pinafore, poncho, pullover, pyjamas, raincoat,* *robe, rompers, sari, sarong, scarf, shawl, shirt, shorts, singlet, skirt, slacks, smock, sock, sou'wester, spats, stocking, stole, suit, surplice, sweater, sweatshirt, tail-coat, tie, tights, trousers, trunks, t-shirt, tunic, tutu, uniform, waistcoat, wet-suit, wind-cheater, wrap, yashmak.* ▷ HAT, SHOE, UNDERCLOTHES.

cloud *n* billow, haze, mist, rain cloud, storm cloud. ● *vb* blur, conceal, cover, darken, dull, eclipse, enshroud, hide, mantle, mist up, obfuscate, obscure, screen, shroud, veil.

cloudless *adj* bright, clear, starlit, sunny, unclouded. *Opp* CLOUDY.

cloudy *adj* **1** dark, dismal, dull, gloomy, grey, leaden, lowering, overcast, sullen, sunless. *Opp* CLOUDLESS. **2** *cloudy windows.* blurred, blurry, dim, misty, opaque, steamy, unclear. **3** *cloudy liquid.* hazy, milky, muddy, murky. *Opp* CLEAR.

clown *n* buffoon, comedian, comic, fool, funnyman, jester, joker. ▷ IDIOT.

club *n* **1** bat, baton, bludgeon, cosh, cudgel, mace, staff, stick, truncheon. **2** association, brotherhood, circle, company, federation, fellowship, fraternity, group, guild, league, order, organization, party, set, sisterhood, society, sorority, union. ● *vb* ▷ HIT. **club together** ▷ COMBINE.

clue *n* hint, idea, indication, indicator, inkling, key, lead, pointer, sign, suggestion, suspicion, tip, tip-off, trace.

clump *n* bunch, bundle, cluster, collection, mass, shock (*of hair*), thicket, tuft. ▷ GROUP.

clumsy *adj* **1** awkward, blundering, bumbling, bungling, fumbling, gangling, gawky, graceless, *inf* ham-fisted, heavy-handed, hulking, inelegant, lumbering, maladroit, shambling, uncoordinated, ungainly, ungraceful, unskilful. *Opp* SKILFUL. **2** amateurish, badly-made, bulky, cumbersome, heavy, inconvenient, inelegant, large, ponderous, rough, shapeless, unmanageable, unwieldy. *Opp* NEAT. **3** *a clumsy remark.* boorish, gauche, ill-judged, inappropriate, indelicate, indiscreet, inept, insensitive, tactless, uncouth, undiplomatic, unsubtle, unsuitable.

cluster *n* assembly, batch, bunch, clump, collection, crowd, gathering, knot. ▷ GROUP. ● *vb* ▷ GATHER.

clutch *n* clasp, control, evil embrace, grasp, grip, hold, possession, power. ● *vb* catch, clasp, cling to, grab, grasp, grip, hang on to, hold on to, seize, snatch, take hold of.

clutter *n* chaos, confusion, disorder, jumble, junk, litter, lumber, mess, mix-up, muddle, odds and ends, rubbish, tangle, untidiness. ● *vb* be scattered about, fill, lie about, litter, make untidy, *inf* mess up, muddle, strew.

coach *n* **1** bus, carriage, *old use* charabanc. **2** *games coach.* instructor, teacher, trainer, tutor. ● *vb* direct, drill, exercise, guide, instruct, prepare, teach, train, tutor.

coagulate *vb* clot, congeal, curdle, *inf* jell, set, solidify, stiffen, thicken.

coarse *adj* **1** bristly, gritty, hairy, harsh, lumpy, prickly, rough, scratchy, sharp, stony, uneven, unfinished. *Opp* FINE, SOFT. **2** *coarse language.* bawdy, blasphemous, boorish, common, crude, earthy, foul, immodest, impolite, improper, impure, indecent, indelicate, offensive, ribald, rude, smutty, uncouth, unrefined, vulgar. *Opp* REFINED.

coast *n* beach, coastline, littoral, seaboard, seashore, seaside, shore. ● *vb* cruise, drift, free-wheel, glide, sail, skim, slide, slip.

coastal *adj* maritime, nautical, naval, seaside.

coat *n* **1** □ *anorak, blazer, cagoule, cardigan, dinner-jacket, doublet, duffel coat, greatcoat, jacket, jerkin, mackintosh, overcoat, raincoat, tail-coat, tunic, tuxedo, waistcoat, wind-cheater.* **2** *an animal's coat.* fleece, fur, hair, hide, pelt, skin. **3** *coat of paint.* coating, cover, film, finish, glaze, layer, membrane, overlay, patina, sheet, veneer, wash. ▷ COVERING. ● *vb* ▷ COVER. **coat of arms** ▷ CREST.

coax *vb* allure, beguile, cajole, charm, decoy, entice, induce, inveigle, manipulate, persuade, tempt, urge, wheedle.

cobble *vb* **cobble together** botch, knock up, make, mend, patch up, put together.

code *n* **1** etiquette, laws, manners, regulations, rule-book, rules, system. **2** *message in code.* cipher, secret language, signals, sign-system.

coerce *vb* bludgeon, browbeat, bully, compel, constrain, dragoon, force, frighten, intimidate, press-gang, pressurize, terrorize.

coercion *n* browbeating, brute force, bullying, compulsion, conscription, constraint, duress, force, intimidation, physical force, pressure, *inf* strong-arm tactics, threats.

coffer *n* box, cabinet, case, casket, chest, crate, trunk.

cog *n* ratchet, sprocket, tooth.

cogent *adj* compelling, conclusive, convincing, effective, forceful, forcible, indisputable, irresistible, logical, persuasive, potent, powerful, rational, sound, strong, unanswerable, weighty, well-argued. ▷ COHERENT. *Opp* IRRATIONAL.

cohere *vb* bind, cake, cling together, coalesce, combine, consolidate, fuse, hang together, hold together, join, stick together, unite.

coherent *adj* articulate, cohering, cohesive, connected, consistent, integrated, logical, lucid, orderly, organized, rational, reasonable, reasoned, sound, structured, systematic, unified, united, well-ordered, well-structured. ▷ COGENT. *Opp* INCOHERENT.

coil *n* circle, convolution, corkscrew, curl, helix, kink, loop, ring, roll, screw, spiral, twirl, twist, vortex, whirl, whorl. • *vb* bend, curl, entwine, loop, roll, snake, spiral, turn, twine, twirl, twist, wind, writhe.

coin *n* **1** bit, piece. **2** [*plur*] cash, change, coppers, loose change, silver, small change. ▷ MONEY. • *vb* **1** forge, make, mint, mould, stamp. **2** *coin a name.* conceive, concoct, create, devise, dream up, fabricate, hatch, introduce, invent, make up, originate, produce, think up.

coincide *vb* accord, agree, be congruent, be identical, be in unison, be the same, clash, coexist, come together, concur, correspond, fall together, happen together, harmonize, line up, match, square, synchronize, tally.

coincidence *n* **1** accord, agreement, coexistence, concurrence, conformity, congruence, congruity, correspondence, harmony, similarity. **2** *meet by coincidence.* accident, chance, fluke, luck.

cold *adj* **1** arctic, biting, bitter, bleak, chill, chilly, cool, crisp, cutting, draughty, freezing, fresh, frosty, glacial, heatless, ice-cold, icy, inclement, keen, *inf* nippy, numbing, *inf* parky, penetrating, perishing, piercing, polar, raw, shivery, Siberian, snowy, unheated, wintry. **2** *cold hands.* blue with cold, chilled, dead, frostbitten, frozen, numbed, shivering, shivery. **3** *a cold heart.* aloof, apathetic, callous, cold-blooded, cool, cruel, distant, frigid, hard, hard-hearted, heartless, indifferent, inhospitable, inhuman, insensitive, passionless, phlegmatic, reserved, standoffish, stony, uncaring, unconcerned, undemonstrative, unemotional, unenthusiastic, unfeeling, unkind, unresponsive, unsympathetic. ▷ UNFRIENDLY. *Opp* HOT, KIND. • *n* **1** chill, coldness, coolness, freshness, iciness, low temperature, wintriness. *Opp* HEAT. **2** *cold in the head.* catarrh, *inf* flu, influenza, *inf* the sniffles. **feel the cold** freeze, quiver, shake, shiver, shudder, suffer from hypothermia, tremble.

cold-blooded *adj* barbaric, brutal, callous, hard-hearted, inhuman, inhumane, merciless, pitiless, ruthless, savage. ▷ CRUEL. *Opp* HUMANE.

cold-hearted *adj* apathetic, cool, dispassionate, frigid, heartless, impassive, impersonal, indifferent, insensitive, thick-skinned, uncaring, unemotional, unfeeling, unkind, unresponsive, unsympathetic. ▷ UNFRIENDLY. *Opp* FRIENDLY.

collaborate *vb* **1** band together, cooperate, join forces, *inf* pull together, team up, work together. **2** [*derog*] collude, connive, conspire, join the opposition, *inf* rat, turn traitor.

collaboration *n* **1** association, concerted effort, cooperation, partnership, tandem, teamwork. **2** [*derog*] collusion, connivance, conspiracy, treachery.

collaborator *n* **1** accomplice, ally, assistant, associate, co-author, colleague, confederate, fellow-worker, helper, helpmate, partner, *joc* partner-in-crime, teammate. **2** *collaborator with an enemy.* blackleg, *inf* Judas, quisling, *inf* scab, traitor, turncoat.

collapse *n* break-down, break-up, cave-in, destruction, downfall, end, fall, ruin, ruination, subsidence, wreck. • *vb* **1** break down, break up, buckle, cave in, crumble, crumple, deflate, disintegrate, double up, fall apart, fall down, fall in, fold up, give way, *inf* go west, sink, subside, tumble down. **2** *collapse in the heat.* become ill, *inf* bite the dust, black out, *inf* crack up, faint, founder, *inf* go under, *inf* keel over, pass out, *old use* swoon. **3** *sales collapsed.* become less, crash, deteriorate, diminish, drop, fail, slump, worsen.

collapsible *adj* adjustable, folding, retractable, telescopic.

colleague *n* associate, business partner, fellow-worker. ▷ COLLABORATOR.

collect *vb* **1** accumulate, agglomerate, aggregate, amass, assemble, bring together, cluster, come together, concentrate, congregate, convene, converge, crowd, forgather, garner, gather, group, harvest, heap, hoard, lay up, muster, pile up, put by, rally, reserve, save, scrape together, stack up, stockpile, store. *Opp* DISPERSE. **2** *collect money for charity.* be given, raise, secure, take. **3** *collect goods from a shop.* acquire, bring, fetch, get, load up, obtain, pick up.

collected ▷ CALM.

collection *n* **1** accumulation, array, assemblage, assortment, cluster, conglomeration, heap, hoard, mass, pile, set, stack, store. ▷ GROUP. **2** *old use* alms-giving, flag-day, free-will offering, offertory, voluntary contributions, *inf* whip-round.

collective *adj* combined, common, composite, co-operative, corporate, democratic, group, joint, shared, unified, united. *Opp* INDIVIDUAL.

college *n* academy, conservatory, institute, polytechnic, school, university.

collide *vb* **collide with** bump into, cannon into, crash into, knock, meet, run into, slam into, smash into, strike, touch. ▷ HIT.

collision *n* accident, bump, clash, crash, head-on collision, impact, knock, pile-up, scrape, smash, wreck.

colloquial *adj* chatty, conversational, everyday, informal, slangy, vernacular. *Opp* FORMAL.

colonist *n* colonizer, explorer, pioneer, settler. *Opp* NATIVE.

colonize *vb* occupy, people, populate, settle in, subjugate.

colony *n* **1** dependency, dominion, possession, protectorate, province, settlement, territory. **2** ▷ GROUP.

colossal *adj* Brobdingnagian, elephantine, enormous, gargantuan, giant, gigantic, herculean, huge, immense, *inf* jumbo, mammoth, massive, mighty, monstrous, monumental, prodigious, titanic, towering, vast. ▷ BIG. *Opp* SMALL.

colour *n* **1** coloration, colouring, hue, pigment, pigmentation, shade, tincture, tinge, tint, tone. □ *amber, azure, beige, black, blue, bronze, brown, buff, carroty, cherry, chestnut, chocolate, cobalt, cream, crimson, dun, fawn, gilt, gold, golden, green, grey, indigo, ivory, jet-black, khaki, lavender, maroon, mauve, navy blue, ochre, olive, orange, pink, puce, purple, red, rosy, russet, sandy, scarlet, silver, tan, tawny, turquoise, vermilion, violet, white, yellow.* **2** *colour in your cheeks.* bloom, blush, flush, glow, rosiness, ruddiness. • *vb* **1** colour-wash, crayon, dye, paint, pigment, shade, stain, tinge, tint. **2** blush, bronze, brown, burn, flush, redden, tan. *Opp* FADE. **3** *coloured by prejudice.* affect, bias, distort, impinge on, influence, pervert, prejudice, slant, sway. **colours** ▷ FLAG.

colourful *adj* **1** bright, brilliant, chromatic, gaudy, iridescent, multicoloured, psychedelic, showy, vibrant. **2** *colourful personality.* dashing, distinctive, dynamic, eccentric, energetic, exciting, flamboyant, flashy, florid, glamorous, unusual, vigorous. **3** *colourful description.* graphic, interesting, lively, picturesque, rich, stimulating, striking, telling, vivid. *Opp* COLOURLESS.

colouring *n* colourant, dye, pigment, pigmentation, stain, tincture. ▷ COLOUR.

colourless *adj* **1** albino, ashen, blanched, faded, grey, monochrome, neutral, pale, pallid, sickly, wan, *inf* washed out, waxen. ▷ WHITE. **2** bland, boring, characterless, dingy, dismal, dowdy, drab, dreary, dull, insipid, lacklustre, lifeless, ordinary, tame, uninspiring, uninteresting, vacuous, vapid. *Opp* COLOURFUL.

column *n* **1** pilaster, pile, pillar, pole, post, prop, shaft, support, upright. **2** *newspaper column.* article, feature, leader, leading article, piece. **3** *column of soldiers.* cavalcade, file, line, procession, queue, rank, row, string, train.

comb *vb* **1** arrange, groom, neaten, smarten up, spruce up, tidy, untangle. **2** *comb the house.* hunt through, ransack, rummage through, scour, search thoroughly.

combat *n* action, battle, bout, clash, conflict, contest, duel, encounter, engagement, fight, skirmish, struggle, war, warfare. • *vb* battle against, contend against, contest, counter, defy, face up to, grapple with, oppose, resist, stand up to, strive against, struggle against, tackle, withstand. ▷ FIGHT.

combination *n* aggregate, alloy, amalgam, blend, compound, concoction, concurrence, conjunction, fusion, marriage, mix, mixture, synthesis, unification. **2** alliance, amalgamation, association, coalition, confederacy, confederation, consortium, conspiracy, federation, grouping, link-up, merger, partnership, syndicate, union.

combine *vb* **1** add together, amalgamate, bind, blend, bring together, compound, fuse, incorporate, integrate, intertwine, interweave, join, link, *inf* lump together, marry, merge, mingle, mix, pool, put together, synthesize, unify, unite. *Opp* DIVIDE. **2** *combine as a team.* ally, associate, band together, club together, coalesce, connect, cooperate, form an alliance, gang together, gang up, join forces, team up. *Opp* DISPERSE.

combustible *adj* flammable, inflammable. *Opp* INCOMBUSTIBLE.

come *vb* **1** advance, appear, approach, arrive, draw near, enter, get to, move (towards), near, reach, visit. **2** *take what comes.* happen, materialize, occur, put in an appearance, show up. **come about** ▷ HAPPEN. **come across** ▷ FIND. **come apart** ▷ DISINTEGRATE. **come clean** ▷ CONFESS. **come out with** ▷ SAY. **come round** ▷ RECOVER. **come up** ▷ ARISE. **come upon** ▷ FIND.

comedian *n* buffoon, clown, comic, fool, humorist, jester, joker, wag. ▷ ENTERTAINER.

comedy *n* buffoonery, clowning, facetiousness, farce, hilarity, humour, jesting, joking, satire, slapstick, wit.

comfort *n* **1** aid, cheer, consolation, encouragement, help, moral support, reassurance, relief, solace, succour, sympathy. **2** *living in comfort.* abundance, affluence, contentment, cosiness, ease, luxury, opulence, plenty, relaxation, well-being. *Opp* DISCOMFORT, POVERTY. • *vb* assuage, calm, cheer up, console, ease, encourage, gladden, hearten, help, reassure, relieve, solace, soothe, succour, sympathize with.

comfortable *adj* **1** *inf* comfy, convenient, cosy, easy, padded, reassuring, relaxing, roomy, snug, soft, upholstered, warm. **2** *comfortable clothes.* informal, loose-fitting, well-fitting, well-made. **3** *a comfortable life.* affluent, agreeable, contented, happy, homely, luxurious, pleasant, prosperous, relaxed, restful, serene, tranquil, untroubled, well-off. *Opp* UNCOMFORTABLE.

comic *adj* absurd, amusing, comical, diverting, droll, facetious, farcical, funny, hilarious, humorous, hysterical, jocular, joking, laughable, ludicrous, *inf* priceless, *inf* rich, ridiculous, sarcastic, sardonic, satirical, side-splitting, silly, uproarious, waggish, witty. *Opp* SERIOUS. ● *n* **1** ▷ COMEDIAN. **2** ▷ MAGAZINE.

command *n* **1** behest, bidding, commandment, decree, directive, edict, injunction, instruction, mandate, order, requirement, ultimatum, writ. **2** authority, charge, control, direction, government, jurisdiction, management, oversight, power, rule, sovereignty, supervision, sway. **3** *command of a language.* grasp, knowledge, mastery. ● *vb* **1** adjure, *old use* bid, charge, compel, decree, demand, direct, enjoin, instruct, ordain, order, prescribe, request, require. **2** *command a ship.* administer, be in charge of, control, direct, govern, have authority over, head, lead, manage, reign over, rule, supervise.

commandeer *vb* appropriate, confiscate, hijack, impound, requisition, seize, sequester, take over.

commander *n* captain, commandant, commanding-officer, general, head, leader, officer-in-charge. ▷ CHIEF.

commemorate *vb* be a memorial to, be a reminder of, celebrate, honour, immortalize, keep alive the memory of, memorialize, pay your respects to, pay homage to, pay tribute to, remember, salute, solemnize.

commence *vb* embark on, enter on, inaugurate, initiate, launch, open, set off, set out, set up, start. ▷ BEGIN. *Opp* FINISH.

commend *vb* acclaim, applaud, approve of, compliment, congratulate, eulogize, extol, praise, recommend. *Opp* CRITICIZE.

commendable *adj* admirable, creditable, deserving, laudable, meritorious, praiseworthy, worthwhile. ▷ GOOD. *Opp* DEPLORABLE.

comment *n* animadversion, annotation, clarification, commentary, criticism, elucidation, explanation, footnote, gloss, interjection, interpolation, mention, note, observation, opinion, reaction, reference, remark, statement. ● *vb* animadvert, criticize, elucidate, explain, interject, interpolate, interpose, mention, note, observe, opine, remark, say, state.

commentary *n* **1** account, broadcast, description, report. **2** *commentary on a poem.* analysis, criticism, critique, discourse, elucidation, explanation, interpretation, notes, review.

commentator *n* announcer, broadcaster, journalist, reporter.

commerce *n* business, buying and selling, dealings, financial transactions, marketing, merchandising, trade, trading, traffic, trafficking.

commercial *adj* business, economic, financial, mercantile, monetary, money-making, pecuniary, profitable, profit-making, trading. ● *n inf* advert, advertisement, *inf* break, *inf* plug.

commiserate *vb* be sorry (for), be sympathetic, comfort, condole, console, feel (for), grieve, mourn, show sympathy (for), sympathize. *Opp* CONGRATULATE.

commission *n* **1** appointment, promotion, warrant. **2** *commission to do a job.* booking, order, request. **3** *commission on a sale.* allowance, *inf* cut, fee, percentage, *inf* rake-off, reward. **4** ▷ COMMITTEE.

commit *vb* **1** be guilty of, carry out, do, enact, execute, perform, perpetrate. **2** *commit to safe-keeping.* consign, deliver, deposit, entrust, give, hand over, put away, transfer. **commit yourself** ▷ PROMISE.

commitment *n* **1** assurance, duty, guarantee, liability, pledge, promise, undertaking, vow, word. **2** *commitment to a cause.* adherence, dedication, determination, devotion, involvement, loyalty, zeal. **3** *social* *commitments*. appointment, arrangement, engagement.

committed *adj* active, ardent, *inf* card-carrying, dedicated, devoted, earnest, enthusiastic, fervent, firm, keen, passionate, resolute, single-minded, staunch, unwavering, wholehearted, zealous. *Opp* APATHETIC.

committee *n* body, council, panel. □ *assembly, board, cabinet, caucus, commission, convention, junta, jury, parliament, quango, synod, think-tank, working party*. ▷ GROUP, MEETING.

common *adj* **1** average, *inf* common or garden, conventional, customary, daily, everyday, familiar, frequent, habitual, normal, ordinary, plain, popular, prevalent, regular, routine, *inf* run-of-the-mill, standard, stock, traditional, typical, undistinguished, unexceptional, unsurprising, usual, well-known, widespread, workaday. ▷ COMMONPLACE. **2** *common knowledge*. accepted, collective, communal, general, joint, mutual, open, popular, public, shared, universal. **3** *the common people*. lower class, lowly, plebeian, proletarian. **4** [*inf*] *Don't be common!* boorish, churlish, coarse, crude, disreputable, ill-bred, inferior, loutish, low, rude, uncouth, unrefined, vulgar, *inf* yobbish. *Opp* ARISTOCRATIC, DISTINCTIVE, UNUSUAL. ● *n* heath, park, parkland.

commonplace *adj* banal, boring, forgettable, hackneyed, humdrum, mediocre, obvious, ordinary, pedestrian, plain, platitudinous, predictable, prosaic, routine, standard, trite, unexciting, unremarkable. ▷ COMMON. *Opp* MEMORABLE. ● *n* ▷ PLATITUDE.

commotion *n inf* ado, agitation, *inf* bedlam, bother, brawl, *inf* brouhaha, *inf* bust-up, chaos, clamour, confusion, contretemps, din, disorder, disturbance, excitement, ferment, flurry, fracas, fray, furore, fuss, hubbub, hullabaloo, incident, *inf* kerfuffle, noise, *inf* palaver, pandemonium, *inf* punch-up, quarrel, racket, riot, row, rumpus, sensation, *inf* shemozzle, *inf* stir, *inf* to-do, tumult, turbulence, turmoil, unrest, upheaval, uproar, upset.

communal *adj* collective, common, general, joint, mutual, open, public, shared. *Opp* PRIVATE.

communicate *vb* **1** commune, confer, converse, correspond, discuss, get in touch, interrelate, make contact, speak, talk, write (to). **2** *communicate information*. advise, announce, broadcast, convey, declare, disclose, disseminate, divulge, express, get across, impart, indicate, inform, intimate, make known, mention, network, notify, pass on, proclaim, promulgate, publish, put across, put over, relay, report, reveal, say, show, speak, spread, state, transfer, transmit, write. **3** *communicate a disease*. give, infect someone with, pass on, spread, transfer, transmit. **4** *The passage communicates with the kitchen*. be connected, lead (to).

communication *n* **1** communicating, communion, contact, interaction, *old use* intercourse. □ *announcement, bulletin, cable, card, communiqué, conversation, correspondence, dialogue, directive, dispatch, document, fax, gossip,* inf *grapevine, information, intelligence, intimation, letter,* inf *memo, memorandum, message, news, note, notice, proclamation, report, rumour, signal, statement, talk, telegram, transmission, wire, word of mouth, writing*. □ *CB, computer, intercom, radar, telegraph, telephone, teleprinter, walkie-talkie*. **2** *mass communication*. mass media, the media. □ *advertising, broadcasting, cable television, magazines, newspapers, the press, radio, satellite, telecommunication, television*.

communicative *adj* articulate, *inf* chatty, frank, informative, open, outgoing, responsive, sociable. ▷ TALKATIVE. *Opp* SECRETIVE.

community *n* colony, commonwealth, commune, country, kibbutz, nation, society, state. ▷ GROUP.

commute *vb* **1** adjust, alter, curtail, decrease, lessen, lighten, mitigate, reduce, shorten. **2** ▷ TRAVEL.

compact *adj* **1** close-packed, compacted, compressed, consolidated, dense, firm, heavy, packed, solid, tight-packed. *Opp* LOOSE. **2** handy, neat, portable, small. **3** abbreviated, abridged, brief, compendious, compressed, concentrated, condensed, short, small, succinct, terse. ▷ CONCISE. *Opp* LARGE. ● *n* ▷ AGREEMENT.

companion *n* accomplice, assistant, associate, chaperone, colleague, comrade, confederate, confidant(e), consort, *inf* crony, escort, fellow, follower, *inf* henchman, mate, partner, stalwart. ▷ FRIEND, HELPER.

company *n* **1** companionship, fellowship, friendship, society. **2** [*inf*] *company for tea.* callers, guests, visitors. **3** *mixed company.* assemblage, association, band, body, circle, club, community, coterie, crew, crowd, ensemble, entourage, gang, gathering, society, throng, troop, troupe (*of actors*). **4** *trading company.* business, cartel, concern, conglomerate, consortium, corporation, establishment, firm, house, line, organization, partnership, *inf* set-up, syndicate, union. ▷ GROUP.

comparable *adj* analogous, cognate, commensurate, compatible, corresponding, equal, equivalent, matching, parallel, proportionate, related, similar, twin. *Opp* DISSIMILAR.

compare *vb* check, contrast, correlate, draw parallels (between), equate, juxtapose, liken, make comparisons, make connections (between), measure (against), relate (to), set side by side, weigh (against). **compare with** ▷ EQUAL.

comparison *n* analogy, comparability, contrast, correlation, difference, distinction, juxtaposition, likeness, parallel, relationship, resemblance, similarity.

compartment *n* alcove, area, bay, berth, booth, cell, chamber, *inf* cubbyhole, cubicle, division, hole, kiosk, locker, niche, nook, partition, pigeonhole, section, slot, space, subdivision.

compatible *adj* **1** harmonious, like-minded, similar, well-matched. ▷ FRIENDLY. **2** *compatible claims.* accordant, congruent, consistent, consonant, matching, reconcilable. *Opp* INCOMPATIBLE.

compel *vb* bind, bully, coerce, constrain, dragoon, drive, exact, force, impel, make, necessitate, oblige, order, press, press-gang, pressurize, require, *inf* shanghai, urge.

compendium *n* abridgement, abstract, anthology, collection, condensation, digest, handbook, summary.

compensate *vb* **1** atone, *inf* cough up, expiate, indemnify, make amends, make good, make reparation, make restitution, make up for, pay back, pay compensation, recompense, redress, reimburse, remunerate, repay, requite. **2** counterbalance, counterpoise, even up, neutralize, offset.

compensation *n* amends, damages, indemnity, recompense, refund, reimbursement, reparation, repayment, restitution.

compère *n* anchor-man, announcer, disc jockey, host, hostess, linkman, Master of Ceremonies, MC, presenter.

compete *vb* **1** be a contestant, enter, participate, perform, take part, take up the challenge. **2** be in competition, conflict, contend, emulate, oppose, rival, strive, struggle, undercut, vie. ▷ FIGHT. *Opp* COOPERATE. **compete with** ▷ RIVAL.

competent *adj* able, acceptable, accomplished, adept, adequate, capable, clever, effective, effectual, efficient, experienced, expert, fit, *inf* handy, practical, proficient, qualified, satisfactory, skilful, skilled, trained, workmanlike, worthwhile. *Opp* INCOMPETENT.

competition *n* **1** competitiveness, conflict, contention, emulation, rivalry, struggle. **2** challenge, championship, contest, event, game, heat, match, quiz, race, rally, series, tournament, trial.

competitive *adj* **1** aggressive, antagonistic, combative, contentious, cut-throat, hard-fought, keen, lively, sporting, well-fought. **2** *competitive prices.* average, comparable with others, fair, moderate, reasonable, similar to others.

competitor *n* adversary, antagonist, candidate, challenger, contender, contestant, entrant, finalist, opponent, participant, rival.

compile *vb* accumulate, amass, arrange, assemble, collate, collect, compose, edit, gather, marshal, organize, put together.

complain *vb inf* beef, *inf* bellyache, *sl* bind, carp, cavil, find fault, fuss, *inf* gripe, groan, *inf* grouch, grouse, grumble, lament, moan, object, protest, wail, whine, *inf* whinge. *Opp* PRAISE. **complain about** ▷ CRITICIZE.

complaint *n* **1** accusation, *inf* beef, charge, condemnation, criticism, grievance, *inf* gripe, grouse, grumble, moan, objection, protest, stricture, whine, whinge. **2** *a medical complaint.* affliction, ailment, disease, disorder, infection, malady, malaise, sickness, upset. ▷ ILLNESS.

complaisant *adj* accommodating, acquiescent, amenable, biddable, compliant, cooperative, deferential, docile, obedient, obliging, pliant, polite, submissive, tractable, willing. *Opp* OBSTINATE.

complement *n* **1** completion, *inf* finishing touch, perfection. **2** *a full complement.* aggregate, capacity, quota, sum, total. • *vb* add to, complete, make whole, perfect, round off, top up.

complementary *adj* interdependent, matching, reciprocal, toning, twin.

complete *adj* **1** comprehensive, entire, exhaustive, full, intact, total, unabbreviated, unabridged, uncut, unedited, unexpurgated, whole. **2** accomplished, achieved, completed, concluded, done, ended, finished, over. ▷ PERFECT. **3** *a complete disaster.* absolute, arrant, downright, extreme, *inf* out-and-out, outright, pure, rank, sheer, thorough, thoroughgoing, total, unmitigated, unmixed, unqualified, utter, *inf* wholesale. *Opp* INCOMPLETE. • *vb* **1** accomplish, achieve, carry out, clinch, close, conclude, crown, do, end, finalize, finish, fulfil, perfect, perform, round off, terminate, *inf* top off, *inf* wind up. **2** *complete forms.* answer, fill in.

complex *adj* complicated, composite, compound, convoluted, elaborate, *inf* fiddly, heterogeneous, intricate, involved, *inf* knotty (*problem*), labyrinthine, manifold, mixed, multifarious, multiple, multiplex, ornate, perplexing, problematical, sophisticated, tortuous, *inf* tricky. *Opp* SIMPLE.

complexion *n* appearance, colour, colouring, look, pigmentation, skin, texture.

complicate *vb* compound, confound, confuse, elaborate, entangle, make complicated, mix up, muddle, *inf* screw up, *inf* snarl up, tangle, twist. *Opp* SIMPLIFY. **complicated** ▷ COMPLEX.

complication *n* complexity, confusion, convolution, difficulty, dilemma, intricacy, *inf* mix-up, obstacle, problem, ramification, setback, snag, tangle.

compliment *n* accolade, admiration, appreciation, approval, commendation, congratulations, encomium, eulogy, felicitations, flattery, honour, panegyric, plaudits, praise, testimonial, tribute. • *vb* applaud, commend, congratulate, *inf* crack up, eulogize, extol, felicitate, flatter, give credit, laud, pay homage to, praise, salute, speak highly of. *Opp* INSULT.

complimentary *adj* admiring, appreciative, approving, commendatory, congratulatory, encomiastic, eulogistic, favourable, flattering, *derog* fulsome, generous, laudatory, panegyrical, rapturous, supportive. *Opp* ABUSIVE, CONTEMPTUOUS, CRITICAL.

comply *vb* abide (by), accede, accord, acquiesce, adhere (to), agree, assent, be in accordance, coincide, concur, consent, correspond (to), defer, fall in (with), fit in, follow, fulfil, harmonize, keep (to), match, meet, obey, observe, perform, respect, satisfy, square (with), submit, suit, yield. ▷ CONFORM. *Opp* DEFY.

component *n* bit, constituent, element, essential part, ingredient, item, part, piece, *inf* spare, spare part, unit.

compose *vb* **1** build, compile, constitute, construct, fashion, form, frame, make, put together. **2** *compose music.* arrange, create, devise, imagine, make up, produce, write. **3** *compose yourself.* calm, control, pacify, quieten, soothe, tranquillize. **be composed of** ▷ COMPRISE. **composed** ▷ CALM.

composition *n* **1** assembly, constitution, creation, establishment, formation, formulation, *inf* make-up, setting up. **2** balance, configuration, layout, organization, structure. **3** *a literary composition.* article, essay, story. ▷ WRITING. **4** *a musical composition.* opus, piece, work. ▷ MUSIC.

compound *adj* complex, complicated, composite, intricate, involved, multiple. *Opp* SIMPLE. • *n* **1** alloy, amalgam, blend, combination, composite, composition, fusion, mixture, synthesis. **2** *compound for cattle. Amer* corral, enclosure, pen, run. • *vb* ▷ COMBINE, COMPLICATE.

comprehend *vb* appreciate, apprehend, conceive, discern, fathom, follow, grasp, know, perceive, realize, see, take in, *inf* twig, understand.

comprehensible *adj* clear, easy, intelligible, lucid, meaningful, plain, self-explanatory, simple, straightforward, understandable. *Opp* INCOMPREHENSIBLE.

comprehensive *adj* allembracing, broad, catholic, compendious, complete, detailed, encyclopaedic, exhaustive, extensive, far-reaching, full, inclusive, indiscriminate, sweeping, thorough, total, universal, wholesale, wide-ranging. *Opp* SELECTIVE.

compress *vb* abbreviate, abridge, compact, concentrate, condense, constrict, contract, cram, crush, flatten, *inf* jam, précis, press, shorten, squash, squeeze, stuff, summarize, telescope, truncate. *Opp* EXPAND. **compressed** ▷ COMPACT, CONCISE.

comprise *vb* be composed of, comprehend, consist of, contain, cover, embody, embrace, include, incorporate, involve.

compromise *n* bargain, concession, *inf* give-and-take, *inf* halfway house, middle course, middle way, settlement. • *vb* **1** concede a point, go to arbitration, make concessions, meet halfway, negotiate a settlement, reach a formula, settle, *inf* split the difference, strike a balance. **2** *compromise your reputation.* damage, discredit, disgrace, dishonour, imperil, jeopardize, prejudice, risk, undermine, weaken. **compromising** ▷ SHAMEFUL.

compulsion *n* **1** coercion, duress, force, necessity, restraint, restriction. **2** *compulsion to smoke.* addiction, drive, habit, impulse, pressure, urge.

compulsive *adj* **1** besetting, compelling, driving, instinctive, involuntary, irresistible, overpowering, overwhelming, powerful, uncontrollable, urgent. **2** *compulsive drinker.* addicted, habitual, incorrigible, incurable, obsessive, persistent.

compulsory *adj* binding, contractual, *Fr* de rigueur, enforceable, essential, imperative, imposed, incumbent, indispensable, inescapable, mandatory, necessary, obligatory, official, prescribed, required, requisite, set, statutory, stipulated, unavoidable. *Opp* OPTIONAL.

compunction *n* contrition, hesitation, pang of conscience, qualm, regret, remorse, scruple, self-reproach.

compute *vb* add up, ascertain, assess, calculate, count, determine, estimate, evaluate, measure, reckon, total, work out.

computer *n* mainframe, micro, microcomputer, mini-computer, PC, personal computer, robot, word-processor.

comrade *n* associate, colleague, companion. ▷ FRIEND.

conceal *vb* blot out, bury, camouflage, cloak, cover up, disguise, envelop, gloss over, hide, hush up, keep dark, keep quiet, keep secret, mask, obscure, screen, secrete, suppress, veil. *Opp* REVEAL. **concealed** ▷ HIDDEN.

concede *vb* accept, acknowledge, admit, agree, allow, confess, grant, make a concession, own, profess, recognize. **concede defeat** capitulate, *inf* cave in, cede, give in, resign, submit, surrender, yield.

conceit *n* arrogance, boastfulness, egotism, self-admiration, self-esteem, self-love, vanity. ▷ PRIDE.

conceited *adj* arrogant, *inf* bigheaded, boastful, bumptious, *inf* cocksure, *inf* cocky, egocentric, egotistic(al), grand, haughty, *inf* high and mighty, immodest, narcissistic, overweening, pleased with yourself, proud, self-centred, self-important, self-satisfied, smug, snobbish, *inf* snooty, *inf* stuck-up, supercilious, *inf* swollen-headed, *inf* toffee-nosed, vain, vainglorious. *Opp* MODEST.

conceive *vb* **1** become pregnant. **2** *conceive a plan.* conjure up, contrive, create, design, devise, *inf* dream up, envisage, evolve, form, formulate, frame, germinate, hatch, imagine, initiate, invent, make up, originate, plan, plot, produce, realize, suggest, think up, visualize, work out. ▷ THINK.

concentrate *n* distillation, essence, extract. • *vb* **1** apply yourself, attend, be absorbed, be attentive, engross yourself, think, work hard. **2** accumulate, centralize, centre, cluster, collect, congregate, converge, crowd, focus, gather, mass. *Opp* DISPERSE. **3** *concentrate a liquid.* condense, reduce, thicken. *Opp* DILUTE. **concentrated 1** ▷ INTENSIVE. **2** condensed, evaporated, reduced, strong, thick, undiluted.

conception *n* **1** begetting, conceiving, fathering, fertilization, genesis, impregnation, initiation, origin. ▷ BEGINNING. **2** ▷ IDEA.

concern *n* **1** attention, care, charge, consideration, heed, interest, regard. **2** *no concern of yours.* affair, business, involvement, matter, problem, responsibility, task. **3** *matter for concern.* anxiety, burden, disquiet, distress, fear, malaise, solicitude, worry. **4** *business concern.* business, company, corporation, enterprise, establishment, firm, organization. • *vb* affect, be important to, be relevant to, interest, involve, matter to, pertain to, refer to, relate to.

concerned *adj* **1** *concerned parents.* bothered, caring, distressed, disturbed, fearful, perturbed, solicitous, touched, troubled, uneasy, unhappy, upset, worried. ▷ ANXIOUS. **2** *the people concerned.* connected, implicated, interested, involved, referred to, relevant. ▷ RESPONSIBLE.

concerning *prep* about, apropos of, germane to, involving, re, regarding, relating to, relevant to, with reference to, with regard to.

concert *n* performance, programme, show. ▷ ENTERTAINMENT, MUSIC.

concerted *adj* collaborative, collective, combined, cooperative, joint, mutual, shared, united.

concession *n* adjustment, allowance, reduction.

concise *adj* brief, compact, compendious, compressed, concentrated, condensed, epigrammatic, laconic, pithy, short, small, succinct, terse. ▷ ABRIDGED. *Opp* DIFFUSE.

conclude *vb* **1** cease, close, complete, culminate, end, finish, round off, stop, terminate. **2** assume, decide, deduce, gather, infer, judge, reckon, suppose, surmise. ▷ THINK.

conclusion *n* **1** close, completion, culmination, end, epilogue, finale, finish, peroration, rounding-off, termination. **2** answer, belief, decision, deduction, inference, interpretation, judgement, opinion, outcome, resolution, result, solution, upshot, verdict.

conclusive *adj* certain, convincing, decisive, definite, persuasive, unambiguous, unanswerable, unequivocal, unquestionable. *Opp* INCONCLUSIVE.

concoct *vb* contrive, cook up, counterfeit, devise, fabricate, feign, formulate, hatch, invent, make up, plan, prepare, put together, think up.

concord *n* agreement, euphony, harmony, peace.

concrete *adj* actual, definite, existing, factual, firm, material, objective, palpable, physical, real, solid, substantial, tactile, tangible, touchable, visible. *Opp* ABSTRACT.

concur *vb* accede, accord, agree, assent. ▷ COMPLY.

concurrent *adj* coexisting, coinciding, concomitant, contemporaneous, contemporary, overlapping, parallel, simultaneous, synchronous.

condemn *vb* **1** blame, castigate, censure, criticize, damn, decry, denounce, deplore, deprecate, disapprove of, disparage, execrate, rebuke, reprehend, reprove, revile, *inf* slam, *inf* slate, upbraid. *Opp* COMMEND. **2** convict, find guilty, judge, pass judgement, prove guilty, punish, sentence. *Opp* ACQUIT.

condensation *n* haze, mist, precipitation, *inf* steam, water-drops.

condense *vb* **1** abbreviate, abridge, compress, contract, curtail, précis, reduce, shorten, summarize, synopsize. *Opp* EXPAND. **2** *condense a liquid.* concentrate, distil, reduce, solidify, thicken. *Opp* DILUTE.

condescend *vb* deign, demean yourself, humble yourself, lower yourself, stoop. **condescending** ▷ HAUGHTY.

condition *n* **1** case, circumstance, *inf* fettle, fitness, form, health, *inf* nick, order, shape, situation, state, *inf* trim, working order. **2** limitation, obligation, prerequisite, proviso, qualification, requirement, requisite, restriction, stipulation, terms. **3** *medical condition.* ▷ ILLNESS. • *vb* acclimatize, accustom, brainwash, educate, mould, prepare, re-educate, *inf* soften up, teach, train.

conditional *adj* dependent, limited, provisional, qualified, restricted, safeguarded, *inf* with strings attached. *Opp* UNCONDITIONAL.

condone *vb* allow, connive at, disregard, endorse, excuse, forgive, ignore, let someone off, overlook, pardon, tolerate.

conducive *adj* advantageous, beneficial, encouraging, favourable, helpful, supportive. **be conducive to** ▷ ENCOURAGE.

conduct *n* **1** actions, attitude, bearing, behaviour, comportment, demeanour, deportment, manners, ways. **2** *conduct of affairs.* administration, control, direction, discharge, government, guidance, handling, leading, management, operation, organization, regulation, running, supervision. • *vb* **1** administer, be in charge of, chair, command, control, direct, escort, govern, handle, head, look after, manage, organize, oversee, preside over, regulate, rule, run, steer, superintend, supervise, usher. **2** *conduct me home.* accompany, escort, guide, lead, pilot, take, usher. **3** *conduct electricity.* carry, channel, convey, transmit. **conduct yourself** ▷ BEHAVE.

confer *vb* **1** accord, award, bestow, give, grant, honour with, impart, invest, present. **2** compare notes, consult, converse, debate, deliberate, discourse, discuss, exchange ideas, *inf* put your heads together, seek advice. ▷ TALK.

conference *n* colloquium, congress, consultation, convention, council, deliberation, discussion, forum, seminar, symposium. ▷ MEETING.

confess *vb* acknowledge, admit, be truthful, *inf* come clean, concede, disclose, divulge, *inf* make a clean breast (of), own up, unbosom yourself, unburden yourself.

confession *n* acknowledgement, admission, declaration, disclosure, expression, profession, revelation.

confide *vb* consult, open your heart, speak confidentially, *inf* spill the beans, *inf* tell all, tell secrets, unbosom yourself, trust.

confidence *n* **1** belief, certainty, credence, faith, hope, optimism, positiveness, reliance, trust. **2** aplomb, assurance, boldness, composure, conviction, firmness, nerve, panache, self-assurance, self-confidence, self-possession, self-reliance, spirit, verve.

Opp DOUBT, HESITATION. **have confidence in** ▷ TRUST.

confident *adj* **1** certain, convinced, hopeful, optimistic, positive, sanguine, sure, trusting. **2** *a confident person.* assertive, assured, bold, *derog* cocksure, composed, cool, definite, fearless, secure, self-assured, self-confident, self-possessed, self-reliant, unafraid. *Opp* DOUBTFUL.

confidential *adj* **1** classified, *inf* hush-hush, intimate, *inf* off the record, personal, private, restricted, secret, suppressed, top secret. **2** *confidential secretary.* personal, private, trusted.

confine *vb* bind, box in, cage, circumscribe, constrain, *inf* coop up, cordon off, cramp, curb, detain, enclose, gaol, hedge in, hem in, *inf* hold down, immure, incarcerate, isolate, keep in, limit, localize, restrain, restrict, rope off, shut in, shut up, surround, wall up. ▷ IMPRISON. *Opp* FREE.

confirm *vb* **1** authenticate, back up, bear out, corroborate, demonstrate, endorse, establish, fortify, give credence to, justify, lend force to, prove, reinforce, settle, show, strengthen, substantiate, support, underline, vindicate, witness to. **2** *confirm a deal.* authorize, *inf* clinch, formalize, guarantee, make legal, make official, ratify, sanction, validate, verify.

confiscate *vb* appropriate, commandeer, expropriate, impound, remove, seize, sequester, sequestrate, take away, take possession of.

conflict *n* **1** antagonism, antipathy, contention, contradiction, difference, disagreement, discord, dissension, friction, hostility, incompatibility, inconsistency, opposition, strife. **2** altercation, battle, *inf* brush, clash, combat, confrontation, contest, dispute, encounter, engagement, feud, fight, quarrel, row, *inf* set-to, skirmish, struggle, war, warfare, wrangle. • *vb inf* be at odds, be at variance, be incompatible, clash, compete, contend, contradict, contrast, *inf* cross swords, differ, disagree, oppose each other. ▷ FIGHT, QUARREL.

conform *vb* acquiesce, agree, be good, behave conventionally, blend in, *inf* do what you are told, fit in, *inf* keep in step, obey, *inf* see eye to eye, *inf* toe the line. ▷ COMPLY.

conformist *n* conventional person, traditionalist, yes-man. *Opp* REBEL.

conformity *n* complaisance, compliance, conventionality, obedience, orthodoxy, submission, uniformity.

confront *vb* accost, argue with, attack, brave, challenge, defy, encounter, face up to, meet, oppose, resist, stand up to, take on, withstand. *Opp* AVOID.

confuse *vb* **1** disarrange, disorder, distort, entangle, garble, jumble, *inf* mess up, mingle, mix up, muddle, tangle, *inf* throw into disarray, upset. **2** *rules confuse me.* agitate, baffle, befuddle, bemuse, bewilder, confound, disconcert, disorientate, distract, *inf* flummox, fluster, mislead, mystify, perplex, puzzle, *inf* rattle, *inf* throw. **3** *confuse twins.* fail to distinguish. **confusing** ▷ PUZZLING.

confused *adj* **1** chaotic, disordered, disorderly, disorganized, *inf* higgledy-piggledy, jumbled, messy, mixed up, muddled, *inf* screwed-up, *sl* shambolic, *inf* topsy-turvy, twisted. **2** *confused ideas.* aimless, contradictory, disconnected, disjointed, garbled, incoherent, inconsistent, irrational, misleading, obscure, rambling, unclear, unsound, unstructured, woolly. **3** *confused mind.* addled, addle-headed, baffled, bewildered, dazed, disorientated, distracted, flustered, fuddled, *inf* in a tizzy, inebriated, muddle-headed, *inf* muzzy, mystified, non-plussed, perplexed, puzzled. ▷ MAD. *Opp* ORDERLY.

confusion *n* **1** *inf* ado, anarchy, bedlam, bother, chaos, clutter, commotion, confusion, din, disorder, disorganization, disturbance, fuss, hubbub, hullabaloo, jumble, maelstrom, *inf* mayhem, mêlée, mess, *inf* mix-up, muddle, pandemonium, racket, riot, rumpus, shambles, tumult, turbulence, turmoil, upheaval, uproar, welter, whirl. **2** *mental confusion*. bemusement, bewilderment, disorientation, distraction, mystification, perplexity, puzzlement. *Opp* ORDER.

congeal *vb* clot, coagulate, coalesce, condense, curdle, freeze, harden, *inf* jell, set, solidify, stiffen, thicken.

congenial *adj* acceptable, agreeable, amicable, companionable, compatible, genial, kindly, suitable, sympathetic, understanding, well-suited. ▷ FRIENDLY. *Opp* UNCONGENIAL.

congenital *adj* hereditary, inborn, inbred, inherent, inherited, innate, natural.

congested *adj* blocked, choked, clogged, crammed, crowded, full, jammed, obstructed, overcrowded, stuffed. *Opp* CLEAR.

congratulate *vb* applaud, compliment, felicitate, praise.

congregate *vb* assemble, cluster, collect, come together, convene, converge, crowd, forgather, gather, get together, mass, meet, muster, rally, rendezvous, swarm, throng. ▷ GROUP.

conjure *vb* bewitch, charm, compel, enchant, invoke, raise, rouse, summon. **conjure up** ▷ PRODUCE.

conjuring *n* illusions, legerdemain, magic, sleight of hand, tricks, wizardry.

connect *vb* **1** attach, combine, couple, engage, fix, interlock, join, link, put on, switch on, tie, turn on, unite. ▷ FASTEN. **2** associate, bracket together, compare, make a connection between, put together, relate, tie up. *Opp* SEPARATE.

connection *n* affinity, association, bond, coherence, contact, correlation, correspondence, interrelationship, link, relationship, relevance, tie, *inf* tie-up, unity. *Opp* SEPARATION.

conquer *vb* **1** annex, beat, best, capture, checkmate, crush, defeat, get the better of, humble, *inf* lick, master, occupy, outdo, overcome, overpower, overrun, overthrow, overwhelm, possess, prevail over, quell, rout, seize, silence, subdue, subject, subjugate, succeed against, surmount, take, *inf* thrash, triumph over, vanquish, worst. ▷ WIN. **2** *conquer a mountain*. climb, reach the top of.

conquest *n* annexation, appropriation, capture, defeat, domination, invasion, occupation, overthrow, subjection, subjugation, *inf* takeover. ▷ VICTORY.

conscience *n* compunction, ethics, honour, fairness, misgivings, morality, morals, principles, qualms, reservations, scruples, standards.

conscientious *adj* accurate, attentive, careful, diligent, dutiful, exact, hard-working, high-minded, honest, meticulous, painstaking, particular, punctilious, responsible, rigorous, scrupulous, serious, thorough. *Opp* CARELESS.

conscious *adj* **1** alert, awake, aware, compos mentis, sensible. **2** *a conscious act*. calculated, deliberate, intended, intentional, knowing, planned, premeditated, self-conscious, studied, voluntary, waking, wilful. *Opp* UNCONSCIOUS.

consecrate *vb* bless, dedicate, devote, hallow, make sacred, sanctify. *Opp* DESECRATE.

consecutive *adj* continuous, following, one after the other, running (*3 days running*), sequential, succeeding, successive.

consent *n* acquiescence, agreement, approval, assent, concurrence, imprimatur, permission, seal of approval. • *vb* accede, acquiesce, agree, approve, comply, concede, concur, conform, submit, undertake, yield. *Opp* REFUSE. **consent to** ▷ ALLOW.

consequence *n* **1** aftermath, byproduct, corollary, effect, end, *inf* follow-up, issue, outcome, repercussion, result, sequel, side-effect, upshot. **2** *of no consequence*. account, concern, importance, moment, note, significance, value, weight.

consequent *adj* consequential, ensuing, following, resultant, resulting, subsequent.

conservation *n* careful management, economy, good husbandry, maintenance, preservation, protection, safeguarding, saving, upkeep. *Opp* DESTRUCTION.

conservationist *n* ecologist, environmentalist, *inf* green, preservationist.

conservative *adj* **1** conventional, die-hard, hidebound, moderate, narrow-minded, old-fashioned, reactionary, sober, traditional, unadventurous. **2** *conservative estimate.* cautious, moderate, reasonable, understated, unexaggerated. **3** *conservative politics.* right-of-centre, right-wing, Tory. *Opp* PROGRESSIVE. • *n* conformist, die-hard, reactionary, right-winger, Tory, traditionalist.

conserve *vb* be economical with, hold in reserve, keep, look after, maintain, preserve, protect, safeguard, save, store up, use sparingly. *Opp* DESTROY, WASTE.

consider *vb* **1** *inf* chew over, cogitate, contemplate, deliberate, discuss, examine, meditate, mull over, muse, ponder, puzzle over, reflect, ruminate, study, *inf* turn over, weigh up. ▷ THINK. **2** believe, deem, judge, reckon.

considerable *adj* appreciable, big, biggish, comfortable, fairly important, fairly large, noteworthy, noticeable, perceptible, reasonable, respectable, significant, sizeable, substantial, *inf* tidy (amount), tolerable, worthwhile. *Opp* NEGLIGIBLE.

considerate *adj* accommodating, altruistic, attentive, caring, charitable, cooperative, friendly, generous, gracious, helpful, kind, kind-hearted, kindly, neighbourly, obliging, polite, sensitive, solicitous, sympathetic, tactful, thoughtful, unselfish. *Opp* SELFISH.

consign *vb* commit, convey, deliver, devote, entrust, give, hand over, pass on, relegate, send, ship, transfer.

consignment *n* batch, cargo, delivery, load, lorry-load, shipment, vanload.

consist *vb* **consist of** add up to, amount to, be composed of, be made of, comprise, contain, embody, include, incorporate, involve.

consistent *adj* **1** constant, dependable, faithful, predictable, regular, reliable, stable, steadfast, steady, unchanging, undeviating, unfailing, uniform, unvarying. **2** *The stories are consistent.* accordant, compatible, congruous, conso-nant, in accordance, in agreement, in harmony, of a piece. *Opp* INCONSISTENT.

console *vb* calm, cheer, comfort, ease, encourage, hearten, relieve, solace, soothe, succour, sympathize with.

consolidate *vb* make secure, make strong, reinforce, stabilize, strengthen. *Opp* WEAKEN.

consort *vb* **consort with** accompany, associate with, befriend, be friends with, be seen with, fraternize with, *inf* gang up with, keep company with, mix with.

conspicuous *adj* apparent, blatant, clear, discernible, distinguished, dominant, eminent, evident, flagrant, glaring, impressive, manifest, marked, notable, noticeable, obtrusive, obvious, ostentatious, outstanding, patent, perceptible, plain, prominent, pronounced, self-evident, shining (*example*), showy, striking, unconcealed, unmistakable, visible. *Opp* INCONSPICUOUS.

conspiracy *n* cabal, collusion, connivance, *inf* frame-up, insider dealing, intrigue, machinations, plot, *inf* racket, scheme, stratagem, treason.

conspirator *n* plotter, schemer, traitor, *inf* wheeler-dealer.

conspire *vb* be in league, collude, combine, connive, cooperate, hatch a plot, have designs, intrigue, plot, scheme.

constant *adj* **1** ceaseless, chronic, consistent, continual, continuous, endless, eternal, everlasting, fixed, immutable, incessant, invariable, neverending, non-stop, permanent, perpetual, persistent, predictable, regular, relentless, repeated, stable, steady, sustained, unbroken, unchanging, unending, unflagging, uniform, uninterrupted, unremitting, unvarying. **2** *a constant friend.* dedicated, dependable, determined, devoted, faithful, firm, indefatigable, loyal, reliable, resolute, staunch, steadfast, tireless, true, trustworthy, trusty, unswerving, unwavering. *Opp* CHANGEABLE.

constitute *vb* appoint, bring together, compose, comprise, create, establish, form, found, inaugurate, make (up), set up.

construct *vb* assemble, build, create, engineer, erect, fabricate, fashion, fit together, form, *inf* knock together, make, manufacture, pitch (*tent*), produce, put together, put up, set up. *Opp* DEMOLISH.

construction *n* **1** assembly, building, creation, erecting, erection, manufacture, production, putting-up, setting-up. **2** building, edifice, erection, structure.

constructive *adj* advantageous, beneficial, cooperative, creative, helpful, positive, practical, productive, useful, valuable, worthwhile. *Opp* DESTRUCTIVE.

consult *vb* confer, debate, discuss, exchange views, *inf* put your heads together, refer (to), seek advice, speak (to), *inf* talk things over. ▷ QUESTION.

consume *vb* **1** devour, digest, drink, eat, *inf* gobble up, *inf* guzzle, *inf* put away, swallow. **2** *consume energy.* absorb, deplete, drain, eat into, employ, exhaust, expend, swallow up, use up, utilize.

contact *n* connection, join, junction, touch, union. ▷ COMMUNICATION. ● *vb* apply to, approach, call on, communicate with, correspond with, *inf* drop a line to, get hold of, get in touch with, make overtures to, notify, phone, ring, sound out, speak to, talk to, telephone.

contagious *adj* catching, communicable, infectious, spreading, transmittable.

contain *vb* **1** accommodate, enclose, hold. **2** be composed of, comprise, consist of, embody, embrace, include, incorporate, involve. **3** *contain your anger.* check, control, curb, hold back, keep back, limit, repress, restrain, stifle.

container *n* holder, receptacle, repository, vessel. ▷ BAG, BARREL, BOTTLE, BOWL, BOX, CUP, DISH, GLASS, LUGGAGE, POT.

contaminate *vb* adulterate, befoul, corrupt, debase, defile, dirty, foul, infect, poison, pollute, soil, spoil, stain, sully, taint. *Opp* PURIFY.

contemplate *vb* **1** eye, gaze at, look at, observe, regard, stare at, survey, view, watch. ▷ SEE. **2** cogitate, consider, day-dream, deliberate, examine, meditate, mull over, muse, plan, ponder, reflect, ruminate, study, work out. ▷ THINK. **3** envisage, expect, intend, propose.

contemporary *adj* **1** *contemporary with me at school.* coeval, coexistent, coinciding, concurrent, contemporaneous, simultaneous, synchronous. **2** *contemporary music.* current, fashionable, the latest, modern, newest, novel, present-day, topical, *inf* trendy, up-to-date, *inf* with-it.

contempt *n* abhorrence, contumely, derision, detestation, disdain, disgust, dislike, disrespect, loathing, ridicule, scorn. ▷ HATRED. *Opp* ADMIRATION. **feel contempt for** ▷ DESPISE.

contemptible *adj* base, beneath contempt, despicable, detestable, discreditable, disgraceful, dishonourable, disreputable, ignominious, inferior, loathsome, low-down, mean, odious, pitiful, *inf* shabby, shameful, worthless, wretched. ▷ HATEFUL. *Opp* ADMIRABLE.

contemptuous *adj* arrogant, belittling, condescending, derisive, disdainful, dismissive, disrespectful, haughty, *inf* holier-than-thou, imperious, insolent, insulting, jeering, lofty, patronizing, sarcastic, scathing, scornful, sneering, *sl* snide, snobbish, *inf* snooty, *sl* snotty, supercilious, superior, withering. *Opp* RESPECTFUL. **be contemptuous of** ▷ DESPISE.

contend *vb* **1** compete, contest, cope, dispute, grapple, oppose, rival, strive, struggle, vie. ▷ FIGHT, QUARREL. **2** *contend that you're innocent.* affirm, allege, argue, assert, claim, declare, maintain, plead.

content *adj* ▷ CONTENTED. ● *n* **1** constituent, element, ingredient, part. **2** ▷ CONTENTMENT. ● *vb* ▷ SATISFY.

contented *adj* cheerful, comfortable, *derog* complacent, content, fulfilled, gratified, peaceful, pleased, relaxed, satisfied, serene, smiling, smug, uncomplaining, untroubled, well-fed. ▷ HAPPY. *Opp* DISSATISFIED.

contentment *n* comfort, content, contentedness, ease, fulfilment, relaxation, satisfaction, serenity, smugness, tranquillity, well-being. ▷ HAPPINESS. *Opp* DISSATISFACTION.

contest *n* ▷ COMPETITION, FIGHT. ● *vb* **1** compete for, contend for, fight for, *inf* make a bid for, strive for, struggle for, take up the challenge of, vie for. **2** *contest a decision.* argue against, challenge, debate, dispute, doubt, oppose, query, question, refute, resist.

contestant *n* candidate, competitor, contender, entrant, opponent, participant, player, rival.

context *n* background, environment, frame of reference, framework, milieu, position, setting, situation, surroundings.

continual *adj* eternal, everlasting, frequent, limitless, ongoing, perennial, perpetual, recurrent, regular, repeated. ▷ CONTINUOUS. *Opp* OCCASIONAL.

continuation *n* **1** continuance, extension, maintenance, prolongation, protraction, resumption. **2** addition, appendix, postscript, sequel, supplement.

continue *vb* **1** carry on, endure, go on, keep on, last, linger, persevere, persist, proceed, pursue, remain, stay, *inf* stick at, survive, sustain. **2** *continue after lunch. inf* pick up the threads, recommence, restart, resume. **3** *continue a series.* extend, keep going, keep up, lengthen, maintain, prolong.

continuous *adj* ceaseless, constant, continuing, endless, incessant, interminable, lasting, never-ending, nonstop, permanent, persistent, relentless, *inf* round-the-clock, *inf* solid, sustained, unbroken, unceasing, unending, uninterrupted, unremitting. ▷ CHRONIC, CONTINUAL. *Opp* INTERMITTENT.

contour *n* curve, form, outline, relief, shape.

contract *n* agreement, bargain, bond, commitment, compact, concordat, covenant, deal, indenture, lease, pact, settlement, treaty, understanding, undertaking. ● *vb* **1** become denser, become smaller, close up, condense, decrease, diminish, draw together, dwindle, fall away, lessen, narrow, reduce, shrink, shrivel, slim down, thin out, wither. *Opp* EXPAND. **2** agree, arrange, close a deal, covenant, negotiate a deal, promise, sign an agreement, undertake. **3** *contract a disease.* become infected by, catch, develop, get.

contraction *n* **1** diminution, narrowing, shortening, shrinkage, shrivelling. **2** abbreviation, diminutive, shortened form.

contradict *vb* argue with, challenge, confute, controvert, deny, disagree with, dispute, gainsay, impugn, oppose, speak against.

contradictory *adj* antithetical, conflicting, contrary, different, discrepant, incompatible, inconsistent, irreconcilable, opposed, opposite. *Opp* COMPATIBLE.

contraption *n* apparatus, contrivance, device, gadget, invention, machine, mechanism.

contrary *adj* **1** conflicting, contradictory, converse, different, opposed, opposite, other, reverse. **2** *contrary winds.* adverse, hostile, inimical, opposing, unfavourable. **3** *a contrary child.* awkward, cantankerous, defiant, difficult, disobedient, disobliging, disruptive, intractable, obstinate, perverse, rebellious, *inf* stroppy, stubborn, subversive, uncooperative, unhelpful, wayward, wilful. *Opp* HELPFUL.

contrast *n* antithesis, comparison, difference, differentiation, disparity, dissimilarity, distinction, divergence, foil, opposition. *Opp* SIMILARITY. ● *vb* **1** compare, differentiate, discriminate, distinguish, emphasize differences, make a distinction, set one against the other. **2** be set off (by), clash, conflict, deviate (from), differ (from). **contrasting** ▷ DISSIMILAR.

contribute *vb* add, bestow, *inf* chip in, donate, *inf* fork out, furnish, give, present, provide, put up, subscribe, supply. **contribute to** ▷ SUPPORT.

contribution *n* **1** donation, fee, gift, grant, *inf* hand-out, offering, payment, sponsorship, subscription. **2** addition, encouragement, input, support. ▷ HELP.

contributor *n* **1** backer, benefactor, donor, giver, helper, patron, sponsor, subscriber, supporter. **2** ▷ WRITER.

control *n* **1** administration, authority, charge, command, curb, direction, discipline, government, grip, guidance, influence, jurisdiction, leadership, management, mastery, orderliness, organization, oversight, power, regulation, restraint, rule, strictness, supervision, supremacy, sway. **2** button, dial, handle, key, lever, switch. • *vb* **1** administer, *inf* be at the helm, be in charge, *inf* boss, command, conduct, cope with, deal with, direct, dominate, engineer, govern, guide, handle, have control of, lead, look after, manage, manipulate, order about, oversee, regiment, regulate, rule, run, superintend, supervise. **2** *control animals.* check, confine, contain, curb, hold back, keep in check, master, repress, restrain, subdue, suppress.

controversial *adj* **1** arguable, controvertible, debatable, disputable, doubtful, problematical, questionable. *Opp* ACCEPTED. **2** argumentative, contentious, dialectic, litigious, polemical, provocative.

controversy *n* altercation, argument, confrontation, contention, debate, disagreement, dispute, dissension, issue, polemic, quarrel, war of words, wrangle.

convalesce *vb* get better, improve, make progress, mend, recover, recuperate, regain strength.

convalescent *adj* getting better, healing, improving, making progress, *inf* on the mend, recovering, recuperating.

convene *vb* bring together, call, convoke, summon. ▷ GATHER.

convenient *adj* accessible, appropriate, at hand, available, commodious, expedient, handy, helpful, labour-saving, nearby, neat, opportune, serviceable, suitable, timely, usable, useful. *Opp* INCONVENIENT.

convention *n* **1** custom, etiquette, formality, matter of form, practice, rule, tradition. **2** ▷ ASSEMBLY.

conventional *adj* **1** accepted, accustomed, commonplace, correct, customary, decorous, expected, formal, habitual, mainstream, orthodox, prevalent, received, *inf* run-of-the-mill, standard, straight, traditional, unadventurous, unimaginative, unoriginal, unsurprising. ▷ ORDINARY. **2** [*derog*] bourgeois, conservative, hidebound, pedestrian, reactionary, rigid, stereotyped, *inf* stuffy. *Opp* UNCONVENTIONAL.

converge *vb* coincide, combine, come together, join, link up, meet, merge, unite. *Opp* DIVERGE.

conversation *n inf* chat, *inf* chinwag, colloquy, communication, conference, dialogue, discourse, discussion, exchange of views, gossip, *inf* heart-to-heart, intercourse, *inf* natter, palaver, phone-call, *inf* powwow, tête-à-tête. ▷ TALK.

convert *vb* change someone's mind, convince, persuade, re-educate, reform, regenerate, rehabilitate, save, win over. ▷ CHANGE.

convey *vb* **1** bear, bring, carry, conduct, deliver, export, ferry, fetch, forward, import, move, send, shift, ship, shuttle, take, taxi, transfer, transport. **2** *convey a message.* communicate, disclose, impart, imply, indicate, mean, relay, reveal, signify, tell, transmit.

convict *n* condemned person, criminal, culprit, felon, malefactor, prisoner, wrongdoer. • *vb* condemn, declare guilty, prove guilty, sentence. *Opp* ACQUIT.

conviction *n* **1** assurance, certainty, confidence, firmness. **2** *religious con-*

viction. belief, creed, faith, opinion, persuasion, position, principle, tenet, view.

convince *vb* assure, *inf* bring round, convert, persuade, prove to, reassure, satisfy, sway, win over. **convincing** ▷ PERSUASIVE.

convulsion *n* **1** disturbance, eruption, outburst, tremor, turbulence, upheaval. **2** [*medical*] attack, fit, paroxysm, seizure, spasm.

convulsive *adj* jerky, shaking, spasmodic, *inf* twitchy, uncontrolled, uncoordinated, violent, wrenching.

cook *vb* concoct, heat up, make, prepare, warm up. □ *bake, barbecue, boil, braise, brew, broil, casserole, coddle, fry, grill, pickle, poach, roast, sauté, scramble, simmer, steam, stew, toast*. **cook up** ▷ PLOT.

cooking *n* baking, catering, cookery, cuisine.

cool *adj* **1** chilled, chilly, coldish, iced, refreshing, unheated. ▷ COLD. *Opp* HOT. **2** calm, collected, composed, dignified, elegant, *inf* laid-back, level-headed, phlegmatic, quiet, relaxed, self-possessed, sensible, serene, unexcited, unflustered, unruffled, urbane. ▷ BRAVE. **3** [*derog*] aloof, apathetic, cold-blooded, dispassionate, distant, frigid, half-hearted, indifferent, lukewarm, negative, offhand, reserved, *inf* stand-offish, unconcerned, unemotional, unenthusiastic, unfriendly, uninvolved, unresponsive, unsociable, unwelcoming. *Opp* PASSIONATE. **4** [*inf*] *cool customer*. ▷ INSOLENT. ● *vb* **1** chill, freeze, ice, refrigerate. *Opp* HEAT. **2** *cool your enthusiasm*. abate, allay, assuage, calm, dampen, diminish, lessen, moderate, *inf* pour cold water on, quiet, temper. *Opp* INFLAME.

cooperate *vb* act in concert, collaborate, combine, conspire, help each other, *inf* join forces, *inf* pitch in, *inf* play along, *inf* play ball, *inf* pull together, support each other, unite, work as a team, work together. *Opp* COMPETE.

cooperation *n* assistance, collaboration, cooperative effort, coordination, help, joint action, mutual support, teamwork. *Opp* COMPETITION.

cooperative *adj* **1** accommodating, comradely, constructive, hard-working, helpful to each other, keen, obliging, supportive, united, willing, working as a team. **2** *cooperative effort*. collective, combined, communal, concerted, coordinated, corporate, joint, shared.

cope *vb* get by, make do, manage, survive, win through. **cope with** ▷ ENDURE, MANAGE.

copious *adj* abundant, ample, bountiful, extravagant, generous, great, huge, inexhaustible, large, lavish, liberal, luxuriant, overflowing, plentiful, profuse, unsparing, unstinting. *Opp* SCARCE.

copy *n* **1** carbon copy, clone, counterfeit, double, duplicate, facsimile, fake, forgery, imitation, likeness, model, pattern, photocopy, print, replica, representation, reproduction, tracing, transcript, twin, Xerox. **2** *copy of a book*. edition, volume. ● *vb* **1** borrow, counterfeit, crib, duplicate, emulate, follow, forge, imitate, photocopy, plagiarize, print, repeat, reproduce, simulate, transcribe. **2** ape, imitate, impersonate, mimic, parrot.

cord *n* cable, catgut, lace, line, rope, strand, string, twine, wire.

cordon *n* barrier, chain, fence, line, ring, row. **cordon off** ▷ ISOLATE.

core *n* **1** centre, heart, inside, middle, nucleus. **2** *core of a problem*. central issue, crux, essence, gist, heart, kernel, *sl* nitty-gritty, nub.

cork *n* bung, plug, stopper.

corner *n* **1** angle, crook, joint. **2** bend, crossroads, intersection, junction, turn, turning. **3** *a quiet corner*. hideaway, hiding-place, hole, niche, nook, recess, retreat. ● *vb* capture, catch, trap.

corporation *n* **1** company, concern, enterprise, firm, organization. **2** council, local government.

corpse *n* body, cadaver, carcass, mortal remains, remains, skeleton, *sl* stiff.

correct *adj* **1** accurate, authentic, confirmed, exact, factual, faithful, faultless, flawless, genuine, literal, precise, reliable, right, strict, true, truthful, verified. **2** *correct manners*. acceptable, appropriate, fitting, just, normal, proper, regular, standard, suitable, tactful, unexceptionable, well-mannered. *Opp* WRONG. • *vb* **1** adjust, alter, cure, *inf* debug, put right, rectify, redress, remedy, repair. **2** *correct pupils' work*. assess, mark. **3** ▷ REPRIMAND.

correspond *vb* accord, agree, be congruous, be consistent, coincide, concur, conform, correlate, fit, harmonize, match, parallel, square, tally. **corresponding** ▷ EQUIVALENT. **correspond with** communicate with, send letters to, write to.

correspondence *n* letters, memoranda, *inf* memos, messages, notes, writings.

correspondent *n* contributor, journalist, reporter. ▷ WRITER.

corridor *n* hall, hallway, passage, passageway.

corrode *vb* **1** consume, eat into, erode, oxidize, rot, rust, tarnish. **2** crumble, deteriorate, disintegrate, tarnish.

corrugated *adj* creased, *inf* crinkly, fluted, furrowed, lined, puckered, ribbed, ridged, wrinkled.

corrupt *adj inf* bent, bribable, criminal, crooked, debauched, decadent, degenerate, depraved, *inf* dirty, dishonest, dishonourable, dissolute, evil, false, fraudulent, illegal, immoral, iniquitous, low, perverted, profligate, rotten, sinful, unethical, unprincipled, unscrupulous, unsound, untrustworthy, venal, vicious, wicked. *Opp* HONEST. • *vb* **1** bribe, divert, *inf* fix, influence, pervert, suborn, subvert. **2** *corrupt the innocent*. debauch, deprave, lead astray, make corrupt, seduce, tempt.

cosmetics *plur n* make-up, toiletries.

cosmic *adj* boundless, endless, infinite, limitless, universal.

cosmopolitan *adj* international, multicultural, sophisticated, urbane. *Opp* PROVINCIAL.

cost *n* amount, charge, expenditure, expense, fare, figure, outlay, payment, price, rate, tariff, value. • *vb* be valued at, be worth, fetch, go for, realize, sell for, *inf* set you back.

costume *n* apparel, attire, clothing, dress, fancy-dress, garb, garments, *inf* get-up, livery, outfit, period dress, raiment, robes, uniform, vestments. ▷ CLOTHES.

cosy *adj* comfortable, *inf* comfy, easy, homely, intimate, reassuring, relaxing, restful, secure, snug, soft, warm. *Opp* UNCOMFORTABLE.

council *n* committee, conclave, convention, convocation, corporation, gathering, meeting. ▷ ASSEMBLY.

counsel *n* ▷ LAWYER. • *vb* advise, discuss (with), give help, guide, listen to your views.

count *vb* **1** add up, calculate, check, compute, enumerate, estimate, figure out, keep account of, *inf* notch up, number, reckon, score, take stock of, tell, total, *inf* tot up, work out. **2** be important, have significance, matter, signify. **count on** ▷ EXPECT.

countenance *n* air, appearance, aspect, demeanour, expression, face, features, look, visage. • *vb* ▷ APPROVE.

counter *n* **1** bar, sales-point, service-point, table. **2** chip, disc, marker, piece, token. • *vb* answer, *inf* come back at, contradict, defend yourself against, hit back at, parry, react to, rebut, refute, reply to, resist, ward off.

counteract *vb* act against, annul, be an antidote to, cancel out, counterbalance, fight against, foil, invalidate, militate against, negate, neutralize, offset, oppose, resist, thwart, withstand, work against.

counterbalance *vb* balance, compensate for, counteract, counterpoise, counterweight, equalize.

counterfeit *adj* artificial, bogus, copied, ersatz, fake, false, feigned, forged, fraudulent, imitation, make-believe, meretricious, pastiche, *inf* phoney, *inf* pretend, *inf* pseudo, sham, simulated, spurious, synthetic. *Opp* GENUINE. • *vb* copy, fake, falsify, feign, forge, imitate, pretend, *inf* put on, sham, simulate.

countless *adj* endless, immeasurable, incalculable, infinite, innumerable, limitless, many, measureless, myriad, numberless, numerous, unnumbered, untold. *Opp* FINITE.

country *n* **1** canton, commonwealth, domain, empire, kingdom, land, nation, people, power, principality, realm, state, territory. **2** *open country.* countryside, green belt, landscape, scenery.

couple *n* brace, duo, pair, twosome. • *vb* **1** combine, connect, fasten, hitch, join, link, match, pair, unite, yoke. **2** ▷ MATE.

coupon *n* tear-off slip, ticket, token, voucher.

courage *n* audacity, boldness, *sl* bottle, bravery, daring, dauntlessness, determination, fearlessness, fibre, firmness, fortitude, gallantry, *inf* grit, *inf* guts, heroism, indomitability, intrepidity, mettle, *inf* nerve, patience, *inf* pluck, prowess, resolution, spirit, *sl* spunk, stoicism, tenacity, valour, will-power. *Opp* COWARDICE.

courageous *adj* audacious, bold, brave, cool, daring, dauntless, determined, fearless, gallant, game, *sl* gutsy, heroic, indomitable, intrepid, lion-hearted, noble, *inf* plucky, resolute, spirited, stalwart, stoical, stout-hearted, tough, unafraid, uncomplaining, undaunted, unshrinking, valiant, valorous. *Opp* COWARDLY.

course *n* **1** bearings, circuit, direction, line, orbit, path, route, track, way. **2** *course of events.* advance, continuation, development, movement, passage, passing, progress, progression, succession. **3** *course of lectures.* curriculum, programme, schedule, sequence, series, syllabus.

court *n* **1** assizes, bench, court martial, high court, lawcourt, magistrates' court. **2** entourage, followers, palace, retinue. **3** ▷ COURTYARD. • *vb* **1** *inf* ask for, attract, invite, provoke, seek, solicit. **2** date, *inf* go out with, make advances to, make love to, try to win, woo.

courteous *adj* civil, considerate, gentlemanly, ladylike, urbane, well-bred, well-mannered. ▷ POLITE.

courtier *n* attendant, follower, lady, lord, noble, page, steward.

courtyard *n* court, enclosure, forecourt, patio, *inf* quad, quadrangle, yard.

cover *n* **1** ▷ COVERING. **2** binding, case, dust-jacket, envelope, file, folder, portfolio, wrapper. **3** camouflage, cloak, concealment, cover-up, deception, disguise, façade, front, hiding-place, mask, pretence, refuge, sanctuary, shelter, smokescreen. **4** *air cover.* defence, guard, protection, support. • *vb* **1** blot out, bury, camouflage, cap, carpet, cloak, clothe, cloud, coat, conceal, curtain, disguise, drape, dress, encase, enclose, enshroud, envelop, face, hide, hood, mantle, mask, obscure, overlay, overspread, plaster, protect, screen, shade, sheathe, shield, shroud, spread over, surface, tile, veil, veneer, wrap up. **2** *cover expenses.* be enough for, match, meet, pay for, suffice for. **3** *talk covered many subjects.* comprise, contain, deal with, embrace, encompass, include, incorporate, involve, treat.

covering *n* blanket, canopy, cap, carpet, casing, cladding, cloak, coat, coating, cocoon, cover, crust, facing, film, incrustation, layer, lid, mantle, outside, pall, rind, roof, screen, sheath, sheet, shell, shield, shroud, skin, surface, tarpaulin, top, veil, veneer, wrapping. ▷ BEDCLOTHES.

coward *n inf* chicken, craven, deserter, runaway, *inf* wimp.

cowardice *n* cowardliness, desertion, evasion, faint-heartedness, *inf* funk, shirking, spinelessness, timidity. ▷ FEAR. *Opp* COURAGE.

cowardly *adj* abject, afraid, base, chicken-hearted, cowering, craven, dastardly, faint-hearted, fearful, *inf* gutless, *inf* lily-livered, pusillanimous, spineless, submissive, timid, timorous, unchivalrous, ungallant, unheroic, *inf* wimpish, *sl* yellow. ▷ FRIGHTENED. *Opp* COURAGEOUS.

cower *vb* cringe, crouch, flinch, grovel, hide, quail, shiver, shrink, skulk, tremble.

coy *adj* arch, bashful, coquettish, demure, diffident, embarrassed, evasive, hesitant, modest, reserved, reticent, retiring, self-conscious, sheepish, shy, timid, unforthcoming. *Opp* BOLD.

crack *n* **1** breach, break, chink, chip, cleavage, cleft, cranny, craze, crevice, fissure, flaw, fracture, gap, opening, rift, rupture, slit, split. **2** ▷ JOKE. ● *vb* **1** break, chip, fracture, snap, splinter, split. **2** ▷ HIT, SOUND. **crack up** ▷ DISINTEGRATE.

craft *n* **1** handicraft, job, skilled work, technique, trade. ▷ CRAFTSMANSHIP, CUNNING. **2** *a sea-going craft.* ▷ VESSEL. ● *vb* ▷ MAKE.

craftsmanship *n* art, artistry, cleverness, craft, dexterity, expertise, handiwork, knack, *inf* know-how, workmanship. ▷ SKILL.

crafty *adj* artful, astute, calculating, canny, cheating, clever, conniving, cunning, deceitful, designing, devious, *inf* dodgy, *inf* foxy, furtive, guileful, ingenious, knowing, machiavellian, manipulative, scheming, shifty, shrewd, sly, *inf* sneaky, tricky, wily. *Opp* HONEST, NAÏVE.

craggy *adj* jagged, rocky, rough, rugged, steep, uneven.

cram *vb* **1** compress, crowd, crush, fill, force, jam, overcrowd, overfill, pack, press, squeeze, stuff. **2** ▷ STUDY.

cramped *adj* close, crowded, narrow, restricted, tight, uncomfortable. *Opp* ROOMY.

crane *n* davit, derrick, hoist.

crash *n* **1** bang, boom, clash, explosion. ▷ SOUND. **2** accident, bump, collision, derailment, disaster, impact, knock, pile-up, smash, wreck. **3** *crash on the stock market.* collapse, depression, failure, fall. ● *vb* **1** bump, collide, knock, lurch, pitch, smash. ▷ HIT. **2** collapse, crash-dive, dive, fall, plummet, plunge, topple.

crate *n* box, carton, case, packing-case, tea-chest.

crater *n* abyss, cavity, chasm, hole, hollow, opening, pit.

crawl *vb* **1** clamber, creep, edge, inch, slither, squirm, worm, wriggle. **2** [*inf*] be obsequious, cringe, fawn, flatter, grovel, *sl* suck up, toady.

craze *n* diversion, enthusiasm, fad, fashion, infatuation, mania, novelty, obsession, passion, pastime, rage, *inf* thing, trend, vogue.

crazy *adj* **1** berserk, crazed, delirious, demented, deranged, frantic, frenzied, hysterical, insane, lunatic, *inf* potty, *inf* scatty, unbalanced, unhinged, wild. ▷ MAD. **2** *crazy comedy.* daft, eccentric, farcical, idiotic, *inf* knockabout, ludicrous, ridiculous, *sl* wacky, zany. ▷ ABSURD. **3** *crazy ideas.* confused, foolish, ill-considered, illogical, impractical, irrational, senseless, silly, unrealistic, unreasonable, unwise. ▷ STUPID. **4** ▷ ENTHUSIASTIC. *Opp* SENSIBLE.

creamy *adj* milky, oily, rich, smooth, thick, velvety.

crease *n* corrugation, crinkle, fold, furrow, groove, line, pleat, pucker, ridge, ruck, tuck, wrinkle. ● *vb* crimp, crinkle, crumple, crush, fold, furrow, pleat, pucker, ridge, ruck, rumple, wrinkle.

create *vb old use* beget, begin, be the creator of, breed, bring about, bring into existence, build, cause, compose, conceive, concoct, constitute, construct, design, devise, *inf* dream up, engender, engineer, establish, father, forge, form, found, generate, give rise to, hatch, imagine, institute, invent, make up, manufacture, occasion, originate, produce, set up, shape, sire, think up. ▷ MAKE. *Opp* DESTROY.

creation *n* **1** beginning, birth, building, conception, constitution, construction, establishing, formation, foundation, generation, genesis, inception, institution, making, origin, procreation, production, shaping. **2** achievement, brainchild, concept, effort, handiwork, invention, product, work of art. *Opp* DESTRUCTION.

creative *adj* artistic, clever, fecund, fertile, imaginative, ingenious, inspired, inventive, original, positive, productive, resourceful, talented. *Opp* DESTRUCTIVE.

creator *n* architect, artist, author, begetter, builder, composer, craftsman, designer, deviser, discoverer, initiator, inventor, maker, manufacturer, originator, painter, parent, photographer, potter, producer, sculptor, smith, weaver, writer.

creature *n* beast, being, brute, mortal being, organism. ▷ ANIMAL.

credentials *n* authorization, documents, identity card, licence, passport, permit, proof of identity, warrant.

credible *adj* believable, conceivable, convincing, imaginable, likely, persuasive, plausible, possible, reasonable, tenable, thinkable, trustworthy. *Opp* INCREDIBLE.

credit *n* approval, commendation, distinction, esteem, fame, glory, honour, *inf* kudos, merit, praise, prestige, recognition, reputation, status, tribute. ● *vb* **1** accept, believe, *inf* buy, count on, depend on, endorse, have faith in, reckon on, rely on, subscribe to, *inf* swallow, swear by, trust. *Opp* DOUBT. **2** *credit you with sense.* ascribe to, assign to, attach to, attribute to. **3** *credit £10 to my account.* add, enter. *Opp* DEBIT.

creditable *adj* admirable, commendable, estimable, good, honourable, laudable, meritorious, praiseworthy, respectable, well thought of, worthy. *Opp* UNWORTHY.

credulous *adj* easily taken in, *inf* green, gullible, *inf* soft, trusting, unsuspecting. ▷ NAÏVE. *Opp* SCEPTICAL.

creed *n* belief, conviction, doctrine, dogma, faith, principle, teaching, tenet.

creek *n* bay, cove, estuary, harbour, inlet.

creep *vb* crawl, edge, inch, move quietly, move slowly, pussyfoot, slink, slip, slither, sneak, steal, tiptoe, worm, wriggle, writhe.

creepy *adj* disturbing, eerie, frightening, ghostly, hair-raising, macabre, ominous, scary, sinister, spine-chilling, *inf* spooky, supernatural, threatening, uncanny, unearthly, weird.

crest *n* **1** comb, plume, tuft. **2** *crest of a hill.* apex, brow, crown, head, peak, pinnacle, ridge, summit, top. **3** badge, coat of arms, design, device, emblem, heraldic device, insignia, seal, shield, sign, symbol.

crevice *n* break, chink, cleft, crack, cranny, fissure, furrow, groove, rift, slit, split.

crew *n* band, company, gang, party, team. ▷ GROUP.

crime *n* delinquency, dishonesty, *old use* felony, illegality, law-breaking, lawlessness, misconduct, misdeed, misdemeanour, offence, *inf* racket, sin, transgression of the law, violation, wrongdoing. □ *abduction, arson, assassination, blackmail, burglary, extortion, hijacking, hooliganism, kidnapping, manslaughter, misappropriation, mugging, murder, pilfering, piracy, poaching, rape, robbery, shop-lifting, smuggling, stealing, terrorism, theft, treason, vandalism.*

criminal *adj inf* bent, corrupt, *inf* crooked, culpable, dishonest, felonious, illegal, illicit, indictable, lawless, nefarious, *inf* shady, unlawful. ▷ WICKED, WRONG. *Opp* LAWFUL. ● *n inf* baddy, convict, *inf* crook, culprit, delinquent, desperado, felon, gangster, knave, lawbreaker, malefactor, miscreant, offender, outlaw, recidivist, ruffian, scoundrel, *old use* transgressor, villain, wrongdoer. □ *bandit, brigand, buccaneer, defaulter, gunman, highwayman,* sl *hoodlum, hooligan, pickpocket, racketeer, receiver, swindler, thug,* ▷ CRIME.

cringe *vb* blench, cower, crouch, dodge, duck, flinch, grovel, quail, quiver, recoil, shrink back, shy away, tremble, wince.

cripple *vb* **1** disable, dislocate, fracture, hamper, hamstring, incapacitate, lame, maim, mutilate, paralyse, weaken. **2** damage, make useless, put out of action, sabotage, spoil. **crippled** ▷ HANDICAPPED.

crisis *n* calamity, catastrophe, climax, critical moment, danger, difficulty, disaster, emergency, predicament, problem, turning point.

crisp *adj* **1** breakable, brittle, crackly, crispy, crunchy, fragile, friable, hard and dry. **2** ▷ BRACING, BRISK.

criterion *n* measure, principle, standard, touchstone, yardstick.

critic *n* **1** analyst, authority, commentator, judge, pundit, reviewer. **2** attacker, detractor.

critical *adj* **1** captious, carping, censorious, criticizing, deprecatory, depreciatory, derogatory, disapproving, disparaging, faultfinding, hypercritical, judgemental, *inf* nit-picking, *derog* Pharisaical, scathing, slighting, uncomplimentary, unfavourable. *Opp* COMPLIMENTARY. **2** analytical, discerning, discriminating, intelligent, judicious, perceptive, probing, sharp. **3** *critical moment.* basic, crucial, dangerous, decisive, important, key, momentous, pivotal, vital. *Opp* UNIMPORTANT.

criticism *n* **1** censure, condemnation, diatribe, disapproval, disparagement, reprimand, reproach, stricture, tirade, verbal attack. **2** *literary criticism.* analysis, appraisal, appreciation, assessment, commentary, critique, elucidation, evaluation, judgement, valuation.

criticize *vb* **1** belittle, berate, blame, carp, *inf* cast aspersions on, castigate, censure, *old use* chide, condemn, complain about, decry, disapprove of, disparage, fault, find fault with, *inf* flay, *inf* get at, impugn, *inf* knock, *inf* lash, *inf* pan, *inf* pick holes in, *inf* pitch into, *inf* rap, rate, rebuke, reprimand, satirize, scold, *inf* slam, *inf* slate, snipe at. *Opp* PRAISE. **2** analyse, appraise, assess, evaluate, discuss, judge, review.

crockery *n* ceramics, china, crocks, dishes, earthenware, porcelain, pottery, tableware. □ *basin, bowl, coffee-cup, coffee-pot, cup, dinner plate, dish, jug, milk-jug, mug, plate,* Amer *platter, pot, sauceboat, saucer, serving dish, side plate, soup bowl, sugar-bowl, teacup, teapot,* old use *trencher, tureen.*

crook *n* **1** angle, bend, corner, hook. **2** ▷ CRIMINAL.

crooked *adj* **1** angled, askew, awry, bendy, bent, bowed, contorted, curved, curving, deformed, gnarled, lopsided, misshapen, off-centre, tortuous, twisted, twisty, warped, winding, zigzag. ▷ INDIRECT. **2** ▷ CRIMINAL.

crop *n* gathering, harvest, produce, sowing, vintage, yield. ● *vb* bite off, browse, clip, graze, nibble, shear, snip, trim. ▷ CUT. **crop up** ▷ ARISE.

cross *adj* bad-tempered, cantankerous, crotchety, *inf* grumpy, ill-tempered, irascible, irate, irritable, peevish, short-tempered, testy, tetchy, upset, vexed. ▷ ANGRY, ANNOYED. *Opp* GOOD-TEMPERED. ● *n* **1** intersection, X. **2** *a cross to bear.* affliction, burden, difficulty, grief, misfortune, problem, sorrow, trial, tribulation, trouble, worry. **3** *cross of breeds.* amalgam, blend, combination, cross-breed, half-way house, hybrid, mixture, mongrel. ● *vb* **1** criss-cross, intersect, meet, zigzag. **2** *cross a river.* bridge, ford, go across, pass over, span, traverse. **3** *cross someone.* annoy, block, frustrate, hinder, impede, interfere with, oppose, stand in the way of, thwart. **cross out** ▷ CANCEL. **cross swords** ▷ CONFLICT.

crossing *vb* **1** bridge, causeway, flyover, ford, level-crossing, overpass, pedestrian crossing, pelican crossing, stepping-stones, subway, underpass, zebra crossing. **2** *sea crossing.* ▷ JOURNEY.

crossroads *n* interchange, intersection, junction.

crouch *vb* bend, bow, cower, cringe, duck, kneel, squat, stoop.

crowd *n* **1** army, assemblage, assembly, bunch, circle, cluster, collection, company, crush, flock, gathering, horde, host, mass, mob, multitude, pack, press, rabble, swarm, throng. ▷ GROUP. **2** *a football crowd.* audience, gate, spectators. ● *vb* assemble, bundle, cluster, collect, compress, congregate, cram, crush, flock, gather, get together, herd, huddle, jam, jostle, mass, muster, overcrowd, pack, *inf* pile, press, push, squeeze, swarm, throng.

crowded *adj* congested, cramped, full, jammed, *inf* jam-packed, jostling, overcrowded, overflowing, packed, swarming, teeming, thronging. *Opp* EMPTY.

crown *n* **1** circlet, coronet, diadem, tiara. **2** *crown of a hill.* apex, brow, head, peak, ridge, summit, top. • *vb* **1** anoint, appoint, enthrone, install. **2** cap, complete, conclude, consummate, culminate, finish off, perfect, round off, top.

crucial *adj* central, critical, decisive, essential, important, major, momentous, pivotal, serious. *Opp* UNIMPORTANT.

crude *adj* **1** natural, raw, unprocessed, unrefined. **2** *crude work.* amateurish, awkward, bungling, clumsy, inartistic, incompetent, inelegant, inept, makeshift, primitive, rough, rudimentary, unpolished, unskilful, unworkmanlike. *Opp* REFINED. **3** ▷ VULGAR.

cruel *adj* atrocious, barbaric, barbarous, beastly, bestial, bloodthirsty, bloody, brutal, callous, cold-blooded, cold-hearted, diabolical, ferocious, fiendish, fierce, flinty, grim, hard, hard-hearted, harsh, heartless, hellish, implacable, inexorable, inhuman, inhumane, malevolent, merciless, murderous, pitiless, relentless, remorseless, ruthless, sadistic, savage, severe, sharp, spiteful, stern, stony-hearted, tyrannical, unfeeling, unjust, unkind, unmerciful, unrelenting, vengeful, venomous, vicious, violent. *Opp* KIND.

cruelty *n* barbarity, bestiality, bloodthirstiness, brutality, callousness, cold-bloodedness, ferocity, hard-heartedness, heartlessness, inhumanity, malevolence, ruthlessness, sadism, savagery, unkindness, viciousness, violence.

cruise *n* sail, voyage. ▷ TRAVEL.

crumb *n* bit, bite, fragment, grain, morsel, particle, scrap, shred, sliver, speck.

crumble *vb* break into pieces, break up, crush, decay, decompose, deteriorate, disintegrate, fall apart, fragment, grind, perish, pound, powder, pulverize.

crumbly *adj* friable, granular, powdery. *Opp* SOLID.

crumple *vb* crease, crinkle, crush, dent, fold, mangle, pucker, rumple, wrinkle.

crunch *vb* break, champ, chew, crush, grind, masticate, munch, scrunch, smash, squash.

crusade *n* campaign, drive, holy war, jehad, movement, struggle, war.

crush *n* congestion, jam. ▷ CROWD. • *vb* **1** break, bruise, compress, crumple, crunch, grind, mangle, mash, pound, press, pulp, pulverize, shiver, smash, splinter, squash, squeeze. **2** *crush opponents.* humiliate, mortify, overwhelm, quash, rout, thrash, vanquish. ▷ CONQUER.

crust *n* incrustation, outer layer, outside, rind, scab, shell, skin, surface. ▷ COVERING.

crux *n* centre, core, crucial issue, essence, heart, nub.

cry *n* battle-cry, bellow, call, caterwaul, ejaculation, exclamation, hoot, howl, outcry, roar, scream, screech, shout, shriek, whoop, yell, yelp, yowl. • *vb* bawl, blubber, grizzle, howl, keen, shed tears, snivel, sob, wail, weep, whimper, whinge. **cry off** ▷ WITHDRAW. **cry out** ▷ SHOUT.

crypt *n* basement, catacomb, cellar, grave, sepulchre, tomb, undercroft, vault.

cryptic *adj* arcane, cabbalistic, coded, concealed, enigmatic, esoteric, hidden, mysterious, mystical, obscure, occult, perplexing, puzzling, recondite, secret, unclear, unintelligible, veiled. *Opp* INTELLIGIBLE.

cuddle *vb* caress, clasp lovingly, dandle, embrace, fondle, hold closely, huddle against, hug, kiss, make love, nestle against, nurse, pet, snuggle up to.

cudgel *n* baton, bludgeon, cane, club, cosh, stick, truncheon. • *vb* batter, beat, bludgeon, cane, *inf* clobber, cosh, pound, pummel, thrash, thump, *inf* thwack. ▷ HIT.

cue *n* hint, prompt, reminder, sign, signal.

culminate *vb* build up to, climax, conclude, reach a finale, rise to a peak. ▷ END.

culpable *adj* blameworthy, criminal, guilty, knowing, liable, punishable, reprehensible, wrong. ▷ DELIBERATE. *Opp* INNOCENT.

culprit *n* delinquent, malefactor, miscreant, offender, troublemaker, wrongdoer. ▷ CRIMINAL.

cult *n* **1** craze, fan-club, fashion, following, devotees, party, school, trend, vogue. **2** *religious cult.* ▷ DENOMINATION.

cultivate *vb* **1** dig, farm, fertilize, hoe, manure, mulch, plough, prepare, rake, till, turn, work. **2** grow, plant, produce, raise, sow, take cuttings, tend. **3** *cultivate a friendship.* court, develop, encourage, foster, further, improve, promote, pursue, try to achieve.

cultivated *adj* **1** agricultural, farmed, planted, prepared, tilled. **2** ▷ CULTURED.

cultivation *n* agriculture, agronomy, breeding, culture, farming, gardening, growing, horticulture, husbandry, nurturing.

cultural *adj* aesthetic, artistic, civilized, civilizing, educational, elevating, enlightening, highbrow, improving, intellectual.

culture *n* **1** art, background, civilization, customs, education, learning, mores, traditions, way of life. **2** ▷ CULTIVATION.

cultured *adj* artistic, civilized, cultivated, discriminating, educated, elegant, erudite, highbrow, knowledgeable, polished, refined, scholarly, sophisticated, wellbred, well-educated, well-read. *Opp* IGNORANT.

cunning *adj* **1** artful, devious, dodgy, guileful, insidious, knowing, machiavellian, sly, subtle, tricky, wily. ▷ CRAFTY. **2** adroit, astute, ingenious, skilful. ▷ CLEVER. • *n* **1** artfulness, chicanery, craft, craftiness, deceit, deception, deviousness, duplicity, guile, slyness, trickery. **2** cleverness, expertise, ingenuity, skill.

cup *n* **1** beaker, bowl, chalice, glass, goblet, mug, tankard, teacup, tumbler, wine-glass. **2** award, prize, trophy.

cupboard *n* cabinet, chiffonier, closet, dresser, filing-cabinet, food-cupboard, larder, locker, sideboard, wardrobe.

curable *adj* operable, remediable, treatable. *Opp* INCURABLE.

curb *vb* bridle, check, contain, control, deter, hamper, hinder, hold back, impede, inhibit, limit, moderate, repress, restrain, restrict, subdue, suppress. *Opp* ENCOURAGE.

curdle *vb* clot, coagulate, congeal, go lumpy, go sour, thicken.

cure *n* **1** antidote, corrective, medication, nostrum, palliative, panacea, prescription, remedy, restorative, solution, therapy, treatment. ▷ MEDICINE. **2** deliverance, healing, recovery, recuperation, restoration, revival. • *vb* alleviate, correct, counteract, ease, *inf* fix, heal, help, mend, palliate, put right, rectify, relieve, remedy, repair, restore, solve, treat. *Opp* AGGRAVATE.

curiosity *n* inquisitiveness, interest, interference, meddling, nosiness, prying, snooping.

curious *adj* **1** inquiring, inquisitive, interested, probing, puzzled, questioning, searching. **2** interfering, intrusive, meddlesome, *inf* nosy, prying. **3** ▷ STRANGE. **be curious** ▷ PRY.

curl *n* bend, coil, curve, kink, loop, ringlet, scroll, spiral, swirl, turn, twist, wave, whorl. • *vb* **1** bend, coil, corkscrew, curve, entwine, loop, spiral, turn, twine, twist, wind, wreathe, writhe. **2** *curl your hair.* crimp, frizz, perm.

curly *adj* crimped, curled, curling, frizzy, fuzzy, kinky, permed, wavy. *Opp* STRAIGHT.

current *adj* **1** alive, contemporary, continuing, existing, extant, fashionable, living, modern, ongoing, present, present-day, prevailing, prevalent, reigning, remaining, surviving, *inf* trendy, up-to-date. **2** *current passport.* usable, valid. *Opp* OLD. • *n* course, draught, drift, flow, jet, river, stream, tide, trend, undercurrent, undertow.

curriculum *n* course, programme of study, syllabus.

curse *n* blasphemy, exclamation, expletive, imprecation, malediction, oath, obscenity, profanity, swear-word. ▷ EVIL. *Opp* BLESSING. ● *vb* blaspheme, damn, fulminate, swear, utter curses. *Opp* BLESS. **cursed** ▷ HATEFUL.

cursory *adj* brief, careless, casual, desultory, fleeting, hasty, hurried, perfunctory, quick, slapdash, superficial. *Opp* THOROUGH.

curt *adj* abrupt, blunt, brief, brusque, concise, crusty, gruff, laconic, monosyllabic, offhand, rude, sharp, short, snappy, succinct, tart, terse, unceremonious, uncommunicative, ungracious. ▷ RUDE. *Opp* EXPANSIVE.

curtail *vb* abbreviate, abridge, break off, contract, cut short, decrease, diminish, *inf* dock, guillotine, halt, lessen, lop, prune, reduce, restrict, shorten, stop, terminate, trim, truncate. *Opp* EXTEND.

curtain *n* blind, drape, drapery, hanging, screen. ● *vb* drape, mask, screen, shroud, veil. ▷ HIDE.

curtsy *vb* bend the knee, bow, genuflect, salaam.

curve *n* arc, arch, bend, bow, bulge, camber, circle, convolution, corkscrew, crescent, curl, curvature, cycloid, loop, meander, spiral, swirl, trajectory, turn, twist, undulation, whorl. ● *vb* arc, arch, bend, bow, bulge, camber, coil, corkscrew, curl, loop, meander, snake, spiral, swerve, swirl, turn, twist, wind. ▷ CIRCLE.

curved *adj* concave, convex, convoluted, crescent, crooked, curvilinear, curving, curvy, rounded, serpentine, shaped, sinuous, sweeping, swelling, tortuous, turned, undulating, whorled.

cushion *n* bean-bag, bolster, hassock, headrest, pad, pillow. ● *vb* absorb, bolster, deaden, lessen, mitigate, muffle, protect from, reduce the effect of, soften, support.

custodian *n* caretaker, curator, guardian, keeper, overseer, superintendent, warden, warder, *inf* watchdog, watchman.

custody *n* **1** care, charge, guardianship, keeping, observation, possession, preservation, protection, safekeeping. **2** *in police custody.* captivity, confinement, detention, imprisonment, incarceration, remand.

custom *n* **1** convention, etiquette, fashion, form, formality, habit, institution, manner, observance, policy, practice, procedure, routine, tradition, usage, way, wont. **2** *A shop needs custom.* business, buyers, customers, patronage, support, trade.

customary *adj* accepted, accustomed, common, commonplace, conventional, established, everyday, expected, fashionable, general, habitual, normal, ordinary, popular, prevailing, regular, routine, traditional, typical, usual, wonted. *Opp* UNUSUAL.

customer *n* buyer, client, consumer, patron, purchaser, shopper. *Opp* SELLER.

cut *n* **1** gash, graze, groove, incision, laceration, nick, notch, opening, rent, rip, slash, slice, slit, snick, snip, split, stab, tear. ▷ INJURY. **2** *cut in prices.* cut-back, decrease, fall, lowering, reduction, saving. ● *vb* **1** amputate, axe, carve, chip, chisel, chop, cleave, clip, crop, dice, dissect, divide, dock, engrave, fell, gash, gouge, grate, graze, guillotine, hack, halve, hew, incise, knife, lacerate, lance, lop, mince, mow, nick, notch, open, pare, pierce, poll, pollard, prune, reap, rive, saw, scalp, score, sever, share, shave, shear, shred, slash, slice, slit, snick, snip, split, stab, subdivide, trim, whittle, wound. **2** abbreviate, abridge, bowdlerize, censor, condense, curtail, digest, edit, précis, shorten, summarize, truncate. ▷ REDUCE. **cut and dried** ▷ DEFINITE. **cut in** ▷ INTERRUPT. **cut off** ▷ REMOVE, STOP. **cut short** ▷ CURTAIL.

cutlery *n inf* eating irons. □ *bread-knife, butter-knife, carving knife, cheese knife, dessert-spoon, fish knife, fish fork, fork, knife, ladle, salad servers, spoon, steak knife, tablespoon, teaspoon.*

cutter *n* □ *axe, billhook, chisel, chopper, clippers, harvester, guillotine, lawnmower, mower, saw, scalpel, scissors, scythe, secateurs, shears, sickle.* ▷ KNIFE.

cutting *adj* acute, biting, caustic, incisive, keen, mordant, sarcastic, satirical, sharp, trenchant. ▷ HURTFUL.

cycle *n* **1** circle, repetition, revolution, rotation, round, sequence, series. **2** bicycle, *inf* bike, moped, *inf* motor bike, motor cycle, pennyfarthing, scooter, tandem, tricycle. ● *vb* ▷ TRAVEL.

cyclic *adj* circular, recurring, repeating, repetitive, rotating.

cynical *adj* doubting, *inf* hard, incredulous, misanthropic, mocking, negative, pessimistic, questioning, sceptical, sneering. *Opp* OPTIMISTIC.

D

dabble *vb* **1** dip, paddle, splash, wet. **2** *dabble in a hobby.* potter about, tinker, work casually.

dabbler *n* amateur, dilettante, potterer.

dagger *n* bayonet, blade, *old use* dirk, knife, kris, poniard, stiletto.

daily *adj* diurnal, everyday, quotidian, regular.

dainty *adj* **1** charming, delicate, exquisite, fine, graceful, meticulous, neat, nice, pretty, skilful. **2** choosy, discriminating, fastidious, finicky, fussy, genteel, mincing, sensitive, squeamish, well-mannered. **3** *a dainty morsel.* appealing, appetizing, choice, delectable, delicious. *Opp* CLUMSY, GROSS.

dally *vb* dawdle, delay, *inf* dillydally, hang about, idle, linger, loaf, loiter, play about, procrastinate, saunter, *old use* tarry, waste time.

dam *n* bank, barrage, barrier, dike, embankment, wall, weir. ● *vb* block, check, hold back, obstruct, restrict, stanch, stem, stop.

damage *n* destruction, devastation, harm, havoc, hurt, injury, loss, mutilation, sabotage. ● *vb* **1** blemish, break, buckle, burst, *inf* bust, chip, crack, cripple, deface, destroy, disable, disfigure, *inf* do mischief to, flaw, fracture, harm, hurt, immobilize, impair, incapacitate, injure, make inoperative, make useless, mar, mark, mutilate, *inf* play havoc with, ruin, rupture, sabotage, scar, scratch, spoil, strain, vandalize, warp, weaken, wound, wreck. **damaged** ▷ FAULTY. **damages** ▷ COMPENSATION. **damaging** ▷ HARMFUL.

damn *vb* attack, berate, castigate, censure, condemn, criticize, curse, denounce, doom, execrate, sentence, swear at.

damnation *n* doom, everlasting fire, hell, perdition, ruin. *Opp* SALVATION.

damp *adj* clammy, dank, dewy, dripping, drizzly, foggy, humid, misty, moist, muggy, perspiring, rainy, soggy, steamy, sticky, sweaty, unaired, unventilated, wet, wettish. *Opp* DRY. ● *vb* **1** dampen, humidify, moisten, sprinkle. **2** ▷ DISCOURAGE.

dance *n* choreography, dancing. □ *ball, barn-dance, ceilidh, disco, discothèque,* inf *hop,* inf *knees-up, party,* inf *shindy, social, square dance.* □ *ballet, ballroom dancing, break-dancing, country dancing, disco dancing, flamenco dancing, folk dancing, Latin-American dancing, limbo dancing, morris dancing, old-time dancing, tap-dancing.* □ *bolero, cancan, conga, fandango, fling, foxtrot, gavotte, hornpipe, jig, mazurka, minuet, polka, polonaise, quadrille, quickstep, reel, rumba, square dance, tango, waltz.* ● *vb* caper, cavort, frisk, frolic, gambol, hop about, jig, jive, jump, leap, prance, rock, skip, *joc* trip the light fantastic, whirl.

danger *n* **1** crisis, distress, hazard, insecurity, jeopardy, menace, peril, pitfall, trouble, uncertainty. **2** *danger of frost.* chance, liability, possibility, risk, threat.

dangerous *adj* **1** alarming, breakneck, *inf* chancy, critical, destructive, explosive, grave, *sl* hairy, harmful, hazardous, insecure, menacing, *inf* nasty, noxious, perilous, precarious, reckless, risky, threatening, toxic, uncertain, unsafe. **2** *dangerous men.* desperate, ruthless, treacherous, unmanageable, unpredictable, violent, volatile, wild. *Opp* HARMLESS.

dangle *vb* be suspended, depend, droop, flap, hang, sway, swing, trail, wave about.

dank *adj* chilly, clammy, damp, moist, unaired.

dappled *adj* blotchy, brindled, dotted, flecked, freckled, marbled, motley, mottled, particoloured, patchy, pied, speckled, spotted, stippled, streaked, varicoloured, variegated.

dare *vb* **1** gamble, have the courage, risk, take a chance, venture. **2** challenge, defy, provoke, taunt. **daring** ▷ BOLD.

dark *adj* **1** black, blackish, cheerless, clouded, cloudy, coal-black, dim, dingy, dismal, drab, dreary, dull, dusky, funereal, gloomy, glowering, glum, grim, inky, moonless, murky, overcast, pitch-black, pitch-dark, *poet* sable, shadowy, shady, sombre, starless, stygian, sullen, sunless, tenebrous, unilluminated, unlighted, unlit. **2** *dark colours*. dense, heavy, strong. **3** *dark complexion*. black, brown, dark-skinned, dusky, swarthy, tanned. **4** ▷ HIDDEN, MYSTERIOUS. *Opp* LIGHT, PALE.

darken *vb* **1** become overcast, cloud over. **2** blacken, dim, eclipse, obscure, overshadow, shade. *Opp* LIGHTEN.

darling *n inf* apple of your eye, beloved, *inf* blue-eyed boy, dear, dearest, favourite, honey, love, loved one, pet, sweet, sweetheart, true love.

dart *n* arrow, bolt, missile, shaft. • *vb* bound, fling, flit, fly, hurtle, leap, move suddenly, shoot, spring, *inf* whiz, *inf* zip. ▷ DASH.

dash *n* **1** chase, race, run, rush, sprint, spurt. • *vb* **1** bolt, chase, dart, fly, hasten, hurry, move quickly, race, run, rush, speed, sprint, tear, *inf* zoom. **2** ▷ HIT.

dashing *adj* animated, dapper, dynamic, elegant, lively, smart, spirited, stylish, vigorous.

data *plur n* details, evidence, facts, figures, information, statistics.

date *n* **1** day. ▷ TIME. **2** *date with a friend*. appointment, assignation, engagement, fixture, meeting, rendezvous. **out-of-date** ▷ OBSOLETE. **up-to-date** ▷ MODERN.

daunt *vb* alarm, depress, deter, discourage, dishearten, dismay, intimidate, overawe, put off, unnerve. ▷ FRIGHTEN. *Opp* ENCOURAGE.

dawdle *vb* be slow, dally, delay, *inf* dilly-dally, hang about, idle, lag behind, linger, loaf about, loiter, move slowly, straggle, *inf* take it easy, *inf* take your time, trail behind. *Opp* HURRY.

dawn *n* day-break, first light, *inf* peep of day, sunrise. ▷ BEGINNING.

day *n* **1** daylight, daytime, light. **2** age, epoch, era, period, time.

day-dream *n* dream, fantasy, hope, illusion, meditation, pipe-dream, reverie, vision, woolgathering. • *vb* dream, fantasize, imagine, meditate.

daze *vb* benumb, paralyse, shock, stun, stupefy. ▷ AMAZE.

dazzle *vb* blind, confuse, disorientate. **dazzling** ▷ BRILLIANT.

dead *adj* **1** cold, dead and buried, deceased, departed, *inf* done for, inanimate, inert, killed, late, lifeless, perished, rigid, stiff. *Opp* ALIVE. **2** *dead language*. died out, extinct, obsolete. **3** *dead with cold*. deadened, insensitive, numb, paralysed, without feeling. **4** *dead battery, engine*. burnt out, defunct, flat, inoperative, not going, not working, no use, out of order, unresponsive, used up, useless, worn out. **5** *a dead party*. boring, dull, moribund, slow, uninteresting. *Opp* LIVELY. **6** *dead centre*. ▷ EXACT. **dead person** ▷ CORPSE. **dead to the world** ▷ ASLEEP.

deaden *vb* **1** anaesthetize, desensitize, dull, numb, paralyse. **2** blunt, check, cushion, damp, diminish, hush, lessen, mitigate, muffle, mute, quieten, reduce, smother, soften, stifle, suppress, weaken.

deadlock *n* halt, impasse, stalemate, standstill, stop, stoppage, tie.

deadly *adj* dangerous, destructive, fatal, lethal, mortal, noxious, terminal. ▷ HARMFUL. *Opp* HARMLESS.

deafen *vb* make deaf, overwhelm. **deafening** ▷ LOUD.

deal *n* **1** agreement, arrangement, bargain, contract, pact, settlement, transaction, understanding. **2** amount, quantity, volume. ● *vb* **1** allot, apportion, assign, dispense, distribute, divide, *inf* dole out, give out, share out. **2** *deal someone a blow.* administer, apply, deliver, give, inflict, mete out. **3** *deal in stocks and shares.* buy and sell, do business, trade, traffic. **deal with** ▷ MANAGE, TREAT.

dealer *n* agent, broker, distributor, merchant, retailer, shopkeeper, stockist, supplier, trader, tradesman, vendor, wholesaler.

dear *adj* **1** adored, beloved, close, darling, intimate, loved, precious, treasured, valued, venerated. ▷ LOVABLE. *Opp* HATEFUL. **2** costly, exorbitant, expensive, high-priced, over-priced, *inf* pricey. *Opp* CHEAP. ● *n* ▷ DARLING.

death *n* **1** decease, demise, dying, loss, passing. ▷ END. **2** casualty, fatality. **put to death** ▷ EXECUTE.

debase *vb* belittle, commercialize, degrade, demean, depreciate, devalue, diminish, lower the tone of, pollute, reduce the value of, ruin, soil, spoil, sully, vulgarize.

debatable *adj* arguable, contentious, controversial, controvertible, disputable, doubtful, dubious, moot (*point*), open to doubt, open to question, problematical, questionable, uncertain, unsettled, unsure. *Opp* CERTAIN.

debate *n* argument, conference, consultation, controversy, deliberation, dialectic, discussion, disputation, dispute, polemic. ● *vb* argue, *inf* chew over, consider, deliberate, discuss, dispute, *inf* mull over, question, reflect on, weigh up, wrangle.

debit *vb* cancel, remove, subtract, take away. *Opp* CREDIT.

debris *n* bits, detritus, flotsam, fragments, litter, pieces, remains, rubbish, rubble, ruins, waste, wreckage.

debt *n* account, arrears, bill, debit, dues, indebtedness, liability, obligation, score, what you owe. **in debt** bankrupt, defaulting, insolvent. ▷ POOR.

decadent *adj* corrupt, debased, debauched, declining, degenerate, dissolute, immoral, self-indulgent. *Opp* MORAL.

decay *vb* atrophy, break down, corrode, crumble, decompose, degenerate, deteriorate, disintegrate, dissolve, fall apart, fester, go bad, go off, mortify, moulder, oxidize, perish, putrefy, rot, shrivel, spoil, waste away, weaken, wither.

deceit *n* artifice, cheating, chicanery, craftiness, cunning, deceitfulness, dishonesty, dissimulation, double-dealing, duplicity, guile, hypocrisy, insincerity, lying, misrepresentation, pretence, sham, slyness, treachery, trickery, underhandedness, untruthfulness. ▷ DECEPTION. *Opp* HONESTY.

deceitful *adj* cheating, crafty, cunning, deceiving, deceptive, designing, dishonest, double-dealing, duplicitous, false, fraudulent, furtive, hypocritical, insincere, lying, secretive, shifty, sneaky, treacherous, *inf* tricky, *inf* two-faced, underhand, unfaithful, untrustworthy, wily. *Opp* HONEST.

deceive *vb inf* bamboozle, be an impostor, beguile, betray, blind, bluff, cheat, *inf* con, defraud, delude, *inf* diddle, double-cross, dupe, fool, *inf* fox, *inf* have on, hoax, hoodwink, *inf* kid, *inf* lead on, lie, mislead, mystify, *inf* outsmart, outwit, pretend, swindle, *inf* take for a ride, *inf* take in, trick.

decelerate *vb* brake, decrease speed, go slower, lose speed, slow down. *Opp* ACCELERATE.

decent *adj* **1** acceptable, appropriate, becoming, befitting, chaste, courteous, decorous, delicate, fitting, honourable, modest, polite, presentable, proper, pure, respectable, seemly, sensitive, suitable, tasteful. *Opp* INDECENT. **2** [*inf*] *a decent meal.* agreeable, nice, pleasant, satisfactory. ▷ GOOD. *Opp* BAD.

deception *n* bluff, cheat, *inf* con, confidence trick, cover-up, deceit, fake, feint, *inf* fiddle, fraud, hoax, imposture, lie, pretence, ruse, sham, stratagem, subterfuge, swindle, trick, wile. ▷ DECEIT.

deceptive *adj* ambiguous, deceiving, delusive, dishonest, distorted, equivocal, evasive, fallacious, false, fraudulent, illusory, insincere, lying, mendacious, misleading, specious, spurious, treacherous, unreliable, wrong. *Opp* GENUINE.

decide *vb* adjudicate, arbitrate, choose, conclude, determine, elect, fix on, judge, make up your mind, opt for, pick, reach a decision, resolve, select, settle. **decided** ▷ DEFINITE.

decipher *vb* disentangle, *inf* figure out, read, work out. ▷ DECODE.

decision *n* conclusion, decree, finding, judgement, outcome, result, ruling, verdict.

decisive *adj* **1** conclusive, convincing, crucial, final, influential, positive, significant. **2** *decisive action.* certain, confident, decided, definite, determined, firm, forceful, forthright, incisive, resolute, strong-minded, sure, unhesitating. *Opp* TENTATIVE.

declaration *n* affirmation, announcement, assertion, avowal, confirmation, deposition, disclosure, edict, manifesto, notice, proclamation, profession, promulgation, pronouncement, protestation, revelation, statement, testimony.

declare *vb* affirm, announce, assert, attest, avow, broadcast, certify, claim, confirm, contend, disclose, emphasize, insist, maintain, make known, proclaim, profess, pronounce, protest, report, reveal, show, state, swear, testify, *inf* trumpet forth, witness. ▷ SAY.

decline *n* decrease, degeneration, deterioration, diminuendo, downturn, drop, fall, falling off, loss, recession, reduction, slump, worsening. • *vb* **1** decrease, degenerate, deteriorate, die away, diminish, drop away, dwindle, ebb, fail, fall off, flag, lessen, peter out, reduce, shrink, sink, slacken, subside, tail off, taper off, wane, weaken, wilt, worsen. *Opp* IMPROVE. **2** *decline an invitation.* abstain from, forgo, refuse, reject, *inf* turn down, veto. *Opp* ACCEPT.

decode *vb inf* crack, decipher, explain, figure out, interpret, make out, read, solve, understand, unravel, unscramble.

decompose *vb* break down, decay, disintegrate, go off, moulder, putrefy, rot.

decorate *vb* **1** adorn, array, beautify, *old use* bedeck, colour, deck, *inf* do up, embellish, embroider, festoon, garnish, make beautiful, ornament, paint, paper, *derog* prettify, refurbish, renovate, smarten up, spruce up, *derog* tart up, trim, wallpaper. **2** give a medal to, honour, reward.

decoration *n* **1** accessories, adornment, arabesque, elaboration, embellishment, finery, flourishes, ornament, ornamentation, trappings, trimmings. **2** award, badge, colours, medal, order, ribbon, star.

decorative *adj* elaborate, fancy, non-functional, ornamental, ornate. *Opp* FUNCTIONAL.

decorous *adj* appropriate, becoming, befitting, correct, dignified, fitting, genteel, polite, presentable, proper, refined, respectable, sedate, seemly, staid, suitable, well-behaved. ▷ DECENT. *Opp* INDECOROUS.

decorum *n* correctness, decency, dignity, etiquette, good form, good manners, gravity, modesty, politeness, propriety, protocol, respectability, seemliness.

decoy *n* bait, distraction, diversion, enticement, inducement, lure, red herring, stool-pigeon, trap. • *vb* allure, attract, bait, draw, entice, inveigle, lead, lure, seduce, tempt, trick.

decrease *n* abatement, contraction, curtailment, cut, cut-back, decline, de-escalation, diminuendo, diminution, downturn, drop, dwindling, easing-off, ebb, fall, falling off, lessening, lowering, reduction, shrinkage, wane. *Opp* INCREASE. • *vb* **1** abate, curtail, cut, ease off, lower, reduce, slim down, turn down. **2** condense, contract, decline, die away, diminish, dwindle, fall off, lessen, peter out, shrink, slacken, subside, *inf* tail off, taper off, wane. *Opp* INCREASE.

decree *n* act, command, declaration, dictate, dictum, directive, edict, enactment, fiat, injunction, judgement, law, mandate, order, ordinance, proclamation, promulgation, regulation, ruling, statute. • *vb* command, decide, declare, determine, dictate, direct, ordain, order, prescribe, proclaim, promulgate, pronounce, rule.

decrepit *adj* battered, broken down, derelict, dilapidated, feeble, frail, infirm, ramshackle, tumbledown, weak, worn out. ▷ OLD.

dedicate *vb* **1** commit, consecrate, devote, give, hallow, pledge, sanctify, set apart. **2** *dedicate a book.* address, inscribe. **dedicated** ▷ KEEN, LOYAL.

dedication *n* **1** adherence, allegiance, commitment, devotion, enthusiasm, faithfulness, fidelity, loyalty, single-mindedness, zeal. **2** inscription.

deduce *vb* conclude, divine, draw the conclusion, extrapolate, gather, glean, infer, *inf* put two and two together, reason, surmise, *sl* suss out, understand, work out.

deduct *vb inf* knock off, subtract, take away. *Opp* ADD.

deduction *n* **1** allowance, decrease, diminution, discount, reduction, removal, subtraction, withdrawal. **2** conclusion, finding, inference, reasoning, result.

deed *n* **1** accomplishment, achievement, act, action, adventure, effort, endeavour, enterprise, exploit, feat, performance, stunt, undertaking. **2** ▷ DOCUMENT.

deep *adj* **1** abyssal, bottomless, chasmic, fathomless, profound, unfathomable, unplumbed, yawning. **2** *deep feelings.* earnest, extreme, genuine, heartfelt, intense, serious, sincere. **3** *deep in thought.* absorbed, concentrating, engrossed, immersed, lost, preoccupied, rapt, thoughtful. **4** *deep matters.* abstruse, arcane, esoteric, intellectual, learned, obscure, recondite. ▷ DIFFICULT. **5** *deep sleep.* heavy, sound. **6** *deep colour.* dark, rich, strong, vivid. **7** *deep sound.* bass, booming, growling, low, low-pitched, resonant, reverberating, sonorous. *Opp* SHALLOW, SUPERFICIAL, THIN.

deface *vb* blemish, damage, disfigure, harm, impair, injure, mar, mutilate, ruin, spoil, vandalize.

defeat *n* beating, conquest, downfall, *inf* drubbing, failure, humiliation, *inf* licking, overthrow, *inf* put-down, rebuff, repulse, reverse, rout, setback, subjugation, thrashing, trouncing. *Opp* VICTORY. • *vb* baulk, beat, best, be victorious over, check, checkmate, *inf* clobber, confound, conquer, crush, destroy, *inf* flatten, foil, frustrate, get the better of, *sl* hammer, *inf* lay low, *inf* lick, master, outdo, outvote, outwit, overcome, overpower, overthrow, overwhelm, prevail over, put down, quell, repulse, rout, ruin, *inf* smash, stop, subdue, subjugate, suppress, *inf* thrash, thwart, triumph over, trounce, vanquish, whip, win a victory over. *Opp* LOSE. **be defeated** ▷ LOSE. **defeated** ▷ UNSUCCESSFUL.

defect *n* blemish, *computing* bug, deficiency, error, failing, fault, flaw, imperfection, inadequacy, irregularity, lack, mark, mistake, shortcoming, shortfall, spot, stain, want, weakness, weak point. • *vb* change sides, desert, go over.

defective *adj* broken, deficient, faulty, flawed, *inf* gone wrong, imperfect, incomplete, *inf* on the blink, unsatisfactory, wanting, weak. *Opp* PERFECT.

defence *n* **1** cover, deterrence, guard, protection, safeguard, security, shelter, shield. ▷ BARRIER. **2** alibi, apologia, apology, case, excuse, explanation, justification, plea, testimony, vindication.

defenceless *adj* exposed, helpless, impotent, insecure, powerless, unguarded, unprotected, vulnerable, weak.

defend *vb* **1** cover, fight for, fortify, guard, keep safe, preserve, protect, safeguard, screen, secure, shelter, shield, *inf* stick up for, watch over. **2** argue for, champion, justify, plead for, speak up for, stand by, stand up for, support, uphold, vindicate. *Opp* ATTACK.

defendant *n* accused, appellant, offender, prisoner.

defensive *adj* **1** cautious, defending, protective, wary, watchful. **2** apologetic, faint-hearted, self-justifying. *Opp* AGGRESSIVE.

defer *vb* **1** adjourn, delay, hold over, lay aside, postpone, prorogue (*parliament*), put off, *inf* shelve, suspend. **2** ▷ YIELD.

deference *n* acquiescence, compliance, obedience, submission. ▷ RESPECT.

defiant *adj* aggressive, antagonistic, belligerent, bold, brazen, challenging, daring, disobedient, headstrong, insolent, insubordinate, mutinous, obstinate, rebellious, recalcitrant, refractory, self-willed, stubborn, truculent, uncooperative, unruly, unyielding. *Opp* COOPERATIVE.

deficient *adj* defective, inadequate, insufficient, lacking, meagre, scanty, scarce, short, sketchy, unsatisfactory, wanting, weak. *Opp* ADEQUATE, EXCESSIVE.

defile *vb* contaminate, corrupt, degrade, desecrate, dirty, dishonour, foul, infect, make dirty, poison, pollute, soil, stain, sully, taint, tarnish.

define *vb* **1** be the boundary of, bound, circumscribe, delineate, demarcate, describe, determine, fix, limit, mark off, mark out, outline, specify. **2** *define a word.* clarify, explain, formulate, give the meaning of, interpret, spell out.

definite *adj* apparent, assured, categorical, certain, clear, clear-cut, confident, confirmed, cut-and-dried, decided, determined, discernible, distinct, emphatic, exact, explicit, express, fixed, incisive, marked, noticeable, obvious, particular, perceptible, plain, positive, precise, pronounced, settled, specific, sure, unambiguous, unequivocal, unmistakable, well-defined. *Opp* VAGUE.

definitely *adv* beyond doubt, certainly, doubtless, for certain, indubitably, positively, surely, unquestionably, without doubt, without fail.

definition *n* **1** clarification, elucidation, explanation, interpretation. **2** clarity, clearness, focus, precision, sharpness.

definitive *adj* agreed, authoritative, complete, conclusive, correct, decisive, final, last (*word*), official, permanent, reliable, settled, standard, ultimate, unconditional. *Opp* PROVISIONAL.

deflect *vb* avert, deviate, divert, fend off, head off, intercept, parry, prevent, sidetrack, swerve, switch, turn aside, veer, ward off.

deformed *adj* bent, buckled, contorted, crippled, crooked, defaced, disfigured, distorted, gnarled, grotesque, malformed, mangled, misshapen, mutilated, twisted, ugly, warped.

defraud *vb inf* con, *inf* diddle, embezzle, *inf* fleece, rob, swindle. ▷ CHEAT.

deft *adj* adept, adroit, agile, clever, dextrous, expert, handy, neat, *inf* nifty, nimble, proficient, quick, skilful. *Opp* CLUMSY.

defy *vb* **1** challenge, confront, dare, disobey, face up to, flout, *inf* kick against, rebel against, refuse to obey, resist, stand up to, withstand. **2** baffle, beat, defeat, elude, foil, frustrate, repel, repulse, resist, thwart, withstand.

degenerate *adj* ▷ CORRUPT. ● *vb* become worse, decline, deteriorate, *inf* go to the dogs, regress, retrogress, sink, slip, weaken, worsen. *Opp* IMPROVE.

degrade *vb* **1** cashier, demote, depose, downgrade. **2** abase, brutalize, cheapen, corrupt, debase, dehumanize, deprave, desensitize, dishonour, harden, humiliate, mortify. **degrading** ▷ SHAMEFUL.

degree *n* **1** calibre, class, grade, order, position, rank, standard, standing, station, status. **2** extent, intensity, level, measure.

deify *vb* idolize, treat as a god, venerate, worship.

deign *vb* concede, condescend, demean yourself, lower yourself, stoop, vouchsafe.

deity *n* creator, divinity, god, goddess, godhead, idol, immortal, power, spirit, supreme being.

dejected *adj* depressed, disconsolate, dispirited, down, downcast, downhearted, heavy-hearted, in low spirits. ▷ SAD.

delay *n* check, deferment, deferral, filibuster, hiatus, hitch, hold-up, interruption, moratorium, pause, postponement, setback, stay (*of execution*), stoppage, wait. ● *vb* **1** check, defer, detain, halt, hinder, hold over, hold up, impede, keep back, keep waiting, make late, obstruct, postpone, put back, put off, retard, set back, slow down, stay, stop, suspend. **2** be late, be slow, *inf* bide your time, dally, dawdle, *inf* dilly-dally, *inf* drag your feet, *inf* get bogged down, hang about, hang back, hang fire, hesitate, lag, linger, loiter, mark time, pause, *inf* play for time, procrastinate, stall, *old use* tarry, temporize, vacillate, wait. *Opp* HURRY.

delegate *n* agent, ambassador, emissary, envoy, go-between, legate, messenger, nuncio, plenipotentiary, representative, spokesperson. ● *vb* appoint, assign, authorize, charge, commission, depute, designate, empower, entrust, mandate, nominate.

delegation *n* commission, deputation, mission.

delete *vb* blot out, cancel, cross out, cut out, edit out, efface, eliminate, eradicate, erase, expunge, obliterate, remove, rub out, strike out, wipe out.

deliberate *adj* **1** arranged, calculated, cold-blooded, conscious, contrived, culpable, designed, intended, intentional, knowing, malicious, organized, planned, prearranged, preconceived, premeditated, prepared, purposeful, studied, thought out, wilful, worked out. **2** careful, cautious, circumspect, considered, diligent, measured, methodical, orderly, painstaking, regular, slow, thoughtful, unhurried, watchful. *Opp* HASTY, INSTINCTIVE. ● *vb* ▷ THINK.

delicacy *n* **1** accuracy, care, cleverness, daintiness, discrimination, exquisiteness, fineness, finesse, fragility, intricacy, precision, sensitivity, subtlety, tact. **2** *delicacies to eat.* rarity, speciality, treat.

delicate *adj* **1** dainty, diaphanous, easily broken, easily damaged, elegant, exquisite, feathery, fine, flimsy, fragile, frail, gauzy, gentle, intricate, light, sensitive, slender, soft, tender. *Opp* TOUGH. **2** *delicate work.* accurate, careful, clever, deft, precise, skilled. *Opp* CLUMSY. **3** *delicate flavour, colour.* faint, mild, muted, pale, slight, subtle. **4** *delicate health.* feeble, puny, sickly, squeamish, unhealthy, weak. **5** *delicate problem.* awkward, confidential, embarrassing, private, problematical, prudish, *inf* sticky, ticklish, touchy. **6** *delicate handling.* considerate, diplomatic, discreet, judicious, prudent, sensitive, tactful. *Opp* CRUDE.

delicious *adj* appetizing, choice, delectable, enjoyable, luscious, *inf* mouth-watering, *inf* nice, palatable, savoury, *inf* scrumptious, succulent, tasty, tempting, toothsome, *sl* yummy.

delight *n* bliss, delectation, ecstasy, enchantment, enjoyment, felicity, gratification, happiness, joy, paradise, pleasure, rapture, satisfaction. • *vb* amuse, bewitch, captivate, charm, cheer, divert, enchant, enrapture, entertain, enthral, entrance, fascinate, gladden, gratify, please, ravish, thrill, transport. *Opp* DISMAY. **delighted** ▷ HAPPY, PLEASED.

delightful *adj* agreeable, attractive, captivating, charming, congenial, delectable, diverting, enjoyable, *inf* nice, pleasant, pleasing, pleasurable, rewarding, satisfying, spell-binding. ▷ BEAUTIFUL.

delinquent *n* culprit, defaulter, hooligan, lawbreaker, malefactor, miscreant, offender, roughneck, ruffian, *inf* tear-away, vandal, wrongdoer, young offender. ▷ CRIMINAL.

delirious *adj inf* beside yourself, crazy, demented, deranged, distracted, ecstatic, excited, feverish, frantic, frenzied, hysterical, incoherent, irrational, light-headed, rambling, wild. ▷ DRUNK, MAD. *Opp* SANE, SOBER.

deliver *vb* **1** bear, bring, carry, cart, convey, distribute, give out, hand over, make over, present, purvey, supply, surrender, take round, transfer, transport, turn over. **2** *deliver a lecture.* announce, broadcast, express, give, make, read. ▷ SPEAK. **3** *deliver a blow.* administer, aim, deal, direct, fire, inflict, launch, strike, throw. ▷ HIT. **4** ▷ RESCUE.

delivery *n* **1** conveyance, dispatch, distribution, shipment, transmission, transportation. **2** *a delivery of goods.* batch, consignment. **3** *delivery of a speech.* enunciation, execution, implementation, performance, presentation. **4** childbirth, confinement, parturition.

deluge *n* downpour, flood, inundation, rainfall, rainstorm, rush, spate. • *vb* drown, engulf, flood, inundate, overwhelm, submerge, swamp.

delusion *n* dream, fantasy, hallucination, illusion, mirage, misconception, mistake, self-deception.

delve *vb* burrow, dig, explore, investigate, probe, research, search.

demand *n old use* behest, claim, command, desire, expectation, importunity, insistence, need, order, request, requirement, requisition, want. • *vb* call for, claim, cry out for, exact, expect, insist on, necessitate, order, request, require, requisition, want. ▷ ASK. **demanding** ▷ DIFFICULT, IMPORTUNATE. **in demand** ▷ POPULAR.

demean *vb* abase, cheapen, debase, degrade, disgrace, humble, humiliate, lower, make (yourself) cheap, *inf* put (yourself) down, sacrifice (your) pride, undervalue. **demeaning** ▷ SHAMEFUL.

democratic *adj* **1** classless, egalitarian. **2** chosen, elected, elective, popular, representative. *Opp* TOTALITARIAN.

demolish *vb* break down, bulldoze, dismantle, flatten, knock down, level, pull down, raze, tear down, topple, undo, wreck. ▷ DESTROY. *Opp* BUILD.

demon *n* devil, evil spirit, fiend, goblin, imp, spirit.

demonstrable *adj* conclusive, confirmable, evident, incontrovertible, indisputable, irrefutable, palpable, positive, provable, undeniable, unquestionable, verifiable.

demonstrate *vb* **1** confirm, describe, display, embody, establish, evince, exemplify, exhibit, explain, expound, express, illustrate, indicate, manifest, prove, represent, show, substantiate, teach, typify, verify. **2** lobby, march, parade, picket, protest, rally.

demonstration *n* **1** confirmation, description, display, evidence, exhibition, experiment, expression, illustration, indication, manifestation, presentation, proof, representation, show, substantiation, test, trial, verification. **2** *inf* demo, march, parade, picket, protest, rally, sit-in, vigil.

demonstrative *adj* affectionate, effusive, emotional, fulsome, loving, open, uninhibited, unreserved, unrestrained. *Opp* RETICENT.

demote *vb* downgrade, put down, reduce, relegate. *Opp* PROMOTE.

demure *adj* bashful, coy, diffident, modest, prim, quiet, reserved, reticent, retiring, sedate, shy, sober, staid. *Opp* CONCEITED.

den *n* hideaway, hide-out, hiding-place, hole, lair, private place, retreat, sanctuary, secret place, shelter.

denial *n* abnegation, contradiction, disavowal, disclaimer, negation, refusal, refutation, rejection, renunciation, repudiation, veto. *Opp* ADMISSION.

denigrate *vb* belittle, blacken the reputation of, criticize, decry, disparage, impugn, malign, *inf* put down, *inf* run down, sneer at, speak slightingly of, traduce, *inf* turn your nose up, vilify. ▷ DESPISE. *Opp* PRAISE.

denomination *n* **1** category, class, classification, designation, kind, size, sort, species, type, value. **2** church, communion, creed, cult, order, persuasion, schism, school, sect.

denote *vb* be the sign for, designate, express, indicate, mean, represent, signal, signify, stand for, symbolize.

denouement *n* climax, *inf* pay-off, resolution, solution, *inf* sorting out, *inf* tidying up, unravelling. ▷ END.

denounce *vb* accuse, attack verbally, betray, blame, brand, censure, complain about, condemn, criticize, declaim against, decry, fulminate against, *inf* hold forth against, impugn, incriminate, inform against, inveigh against, pillory, report, reveal, stigmatize, *inf* tell off, vilify, vituperate. *Opp* PRAISE.

dense *adj* **1** close, compact, concentrated, heavy, impassable, impenetrable, *inf* jam-packed, lush, massed, packed, solid, thick, tight, viscous. *Opp* THIN. **2** ▷ STUPID.

dent *n* concavity, depression, dimple, dint, dip, hollow, indentation, pit. • *vb* bend, buckle, crumple, knock in.

denude *vb* bare, defoliate, deforest, expose, remove, strip, unclothe, uncover. *Opp* CLOTHE.

deny *vb* **1** contradict, controvert, disagree with, disclaim, disown, dispute, gainsay, negate, oppose, rebuff, refute, reject, repudiate. *Opp* AGREE. **2** begrudge, deprive of, disallow, refuse, withhold. *Opp* GRANT. **deny yourself** ▷ ABSTAIN.

depart *vb* **1** abscond, begin a journey, *inf* check out, *inf* clear off, decamp, disappear, embark, emigrate, escape, exit, go away, *sl* hit the road, leave, make off, *inf* make tracks, *inf* make yourself scarce, migrate, move away, move off, *inf* push off, quit, retire, retreat, run away, run off, *sl* scarper, *sl* scram, set forth, set off, set out, start, take your leave, vanish, withdraw. **2** ▷ DEVIATE. **departed** ▷ DEAD.

department *n* **1** branch, division, office, part, section, sector, subdivision, unit. **2** [*inf*] *not my department.* area, concern, domain, field, function, job, line, province, responsibility, specialism, sphere.

departure *n* disappearance, embarkation, escape, exit, exodus, going, retirement, retreat, withdrawal. *Opp* ARRIVAL.

depend *vb* **depend on** *inf* bank on, be dependent on, count on, hinge on, need, pivot on, put your faith in, *inf* reckon on, rely on, rest on, trust.

dependable *adj* conscientious, consistent, faithful, honest, regular, reliable, safe, sound, steady, true, trustworthy, unfailing. *Opp* UNRELIABLE.

dependence *n* **1** confidence, need, reliance, trust. **2** ▷ ADDICTION.

dependent *adj* **dependent on** **1** conditional on, connected with, controlled by, determined by, liable to, relative to, subject to, vulnerable to. *Opp* INDEPENDENT. **2** *dependent on* *drugs*. addicted to, enslaved by, *inf* hooked on, reliant on.

depict *vb* delineate, describe, draw, illustrate, narrate, outline, paint, picture, portray, represent, reproduce, show, sketch.

deplete *vb* consume, cut, decrease, drain, lessen, reduce, use up. *Opp* INCREASE.

deplorable *adj* awful, blameworthy, discreditable, disgraceful, disreputable, dreadful, execrable, lamentable, regrettable, reprehensible, scandalous, shameful, shocking, unfortunate, unworthy. ▷ BAD. *Opp* COMMENDABLE.

deplore *vb* **1** grieve over, lament, mourn, regret. **2** ▷ CONDEMN.

deploy *vb* arrange, bring into action, distribute, manage, position, use systematically, utilize.

deport *vb* banish, exile, expatriate, expel, remove, send abroad, transport.

depose *vb* demote, dethrone, dismiss, displace, get rid of, oust, remove, *inf* topple.

deposit *n* **1** advance payment, down-payment, initial payment, part-payment, retainer, security, stake. **2** accumulation, alluvium, dregs, layer, lees, precipitate, sediment, silt, sludge. • *vb* **1** drop, *inf* dump, lay down, leave, *inf* park, place, precipitate, put down, set down. **2** *deposit money*. bank, pay in, save.

depot *n* **1** arsenal, base, cache, depository, dump, hoard, store, storehouse. **2** *bus depot*. garage, headquarters, station, terminus.

deprave *vb* brutalize, corrupt, debase, degrade, influence, pervert. **depraved** ▷ CORRUPT.

depreciate *vb* **1** become less, decrease, deflate, drop, fall, go down, lessen, lower, reduce, slump, weaken. *Opp* APPRECIATE. **2** ▷ DISPARAGE.

depress *vb* **1** burden, cast down, discourage, dishearten, dismay, dispirit, enervate, grieve, lower the spirits of, make sad, oppress, sadden, tire, upset, weary. *Opp* CHEER. **2** *depress the market*. bring down, deflate, make less active, push down, undermine, weaken. *Opp* BOOST. **depressed**, **depressing** ▷ SAD.

depression *n* **1** *inf* blues, dejection, desolation, despair, despondency, gloom, glumness, heaviness, hopelessness, low spirits, melancholy, misery, pessimism, sadness, weariness. *Opp* HAPPINESS. **2** cavity, concavity, dent, dimple, dip, excavation, hole, hollow, impression, indentation, pit, recess, rut, sunken area. *Opp* BUMP. **3** *economic depression*. decline, hard times, recession, slump. *Opp* BOOM, HIGH.

deprive *vb* **deprive of** deny, dispossess of, prevent from using, refuse, rob of, starve of, strip of, take away, withdraw, withhold. **deprived** ▷ POOR.

deputize *vb* **deputize for** act as deputy, act as stand-in for, cover for, do the job of, replace, represent, stand in for, substitute for, take over from, understudy.

deputy *n* agent, ambassador, assistant, delegate, emissary, *inf* fill-in, locum, proxy, relief, replacement, representative, reserve, second-in-command, spokesperson, *inf* stand-in, substitute, supply, surrogate, understudy, vice-captain, vice-president.

derelict *adj* abandoned, broken down, decrepit, deserted, desolate, dilapidated, forgotten, forlorn, forsaken, neglected, overgrown, ruined, run-down, tumbledown, uncared-for, untended.

derivation *n* ancestry, descent, etymology, extraction, origin, root. ▷ BEGINNING.

derive *vb* acquire, borrow, collect, crib, draw, extract, gain, gather, get, glean, *inf* lift, obtain, pick up, procure, receive, secure, take. **be derived** ▷ ORIGINATE.

descend *vb* **1** climb down, come down, drop, fall, go down, move down, plummet, plunge, sink, swoop down. **2** decline, dip, incline, slant, slope. **3** alight, disembark, dismount, get down, get off. *Opp* ASCEND. **be descended** ▷ ORIGINATE. **descend on** ▷ ATTACK.

descendant *n* child, heir, scion, successor. *Opp* ANCESTOR. **descendants** family, issue, line, lineage, offspring, posterity, progeny, *old use* seed.

descent *n* **1** declivity, dip, drop, fall, incline, slant, slope, way down. *Opp* ASCENT. **2** *aristocratic descent*. ancestry, background, blood, derivation, extraction, family, genealogy, heredity, lineage, origin, parentage, pedigree, stock, strain.

describe *vb* **1** characterize, define, delineate, depict, detail, explain, express, give an account of, narrate, outline, portray, present, recount, relate, report, represent, sketch, speak of, tell about. **2** *describe a circle*. draw, mark out, trace.

description *n* account, characterization, commentary, definition, delineation, depiction, explanation, narration, outline, portrait, portrayal, report, representation, sketch, story, word-picture.

descriptive *adj* colourful, detailed, explanatory, expressive, graphic, illustrative, pictorial, vivid.

desecrate *vb* abuse, contaminate, corrupt, debase, defile, degrade, dishonour, pervert, pollute, profane, treat blasphemously, treat disrespectfully, treat irreverently, vandalize, violate, vitiate. *Opp* REVERE.

desert *adj* arid, barren, desolate, dry, infertile, isolated, lonely, sterile, uncultivated, unfrequented, uninhabited, waterless, wild. *Opp* FERTILE. • *n* dust bowl, wasteland, wilderness. • *vb* **1** abandon, betray, forsake, give up, jilt, leave, *inf* leave in the lurch, maroon, quit, *inf* rat on, renounce, strand, vacate, *inf* walk out on, *inf* wash your hands of. **2** abscond, decamp, defect, go absent, run away. **deserted** ▷ EMPTY, LONELY.

deserter *n* absconder, absentee, apostate, backslider, betrayer, defector, escapee, fugitive, outlaw, renegade, runaway, traitor, truant, turncoat.

deserve *vb* be good enough for, be worthy of, earn, justify, merit, rate, warrant. **deserving** ▷ WORTHY.

design *n* **1** blueprint, conception, draft, drawing, model, pattern, plan, proposal, prototype, sketch. **2** mark, style, type, version. **3** arrangement, composition, configuration, form, pattern, shape. **4** *wander without design*. aim, end, goal, intention, object, objective, purpose, scheme. • *vb* conceive, construct, contrive, create, delineate, devise, draft, draw, draw up, fashion, form, intend, invent, lay out, make, map out, originate, outline, plan, plot, project, propose, scheme, shape, sketch, think up. **designing** ▷ CRAFTY. **have designs** ▷ PLOT.

designer *n* architect, artist, author, contriver, creator, deviser, inventor, originator.

desire *n* **1** ache, ambition, appetite, craving, fancy, hankering, hunger, *inf* itch, longing, requirement, thirst, urge, want, wish, yearning, *inf* yen. **2** avarice, covetousness, cupidity, greed, miserliness, rapacity. **3** *sexual desire*. ardour, libido, love, lust, passion. • *vb* ache for, ask for, aspire to, covet, crave, dream of, fancy, hanker after, *inf* have a yen for, hope for, hunger for, *inf* itch for, like, long for, lust after, need, pine for, prefer, pursue, *inf* set your heart on, set your sights on, strive after, thirst for, want, wish for, yearn for.

desolate *adj* **1** abandoned, bare, barren, benighted, bleak, cheerless, depressing, deserted, dismal, dreary, empty, forsaken, gloomy, *inf* god-forsaken, inhospitable, isolated, lonely, remote, unfrequented, uninhabited, wild, windswept. **2** bereft, companionless, dejected, depressed, despairing, disconsolate, distressed, forlorn, forsaken, inconsolable, lonely, melancholy, miserable, neglected, solitary, suicidal, wretched. ▷ SAD. *Opp* CHEERFUL.

despair *n* anguish, dejection, depression, desperation, despondency, hopelessness, pessimism, resignation, wretchedness. ▷ MISERY. • *vb* give in, give up, lose heart, lose hope, quit, surrender. *Opp* HOPE.

desperate *adj* **1** *inf* at your wits' end, beyond hope, despairing, inconsolable, wretched. **2** *desperate situation.* acute, bad, critical, dangerous, drastic, grave, hopeless, irretrievable, pressing, serious, severe, urgent. **3** *desperate criminals.* dangerous, foolhardy, impetuous, rash, reckless, violent, wild. **4** ▷ ANXIOUS.

despise *vb* be contemptuous of, condemn, deride, disapprove of, disdain, feel contempt for, hate, have a low opinion of, look down on, *inf* put down, scorn, sneer at, spurn, undervalue. ▷ DENIGRATE. *Opp* ADMIRE.

despondent *adj* dejected, depressed, discouraged, disheartened, down, downcast, *inf* down in the mouth, melancholy, morose, pessimistic, sad, sorrowful. ▷ MISERABLE.

despotic *adj* absolute, arbitrary, authoritarian, autocratic, dictatorial, domineering, oppressive, totalitarian, tyrannical. *Opp* DEMOCRATIC.

destination *n* goal, objective, purpose, stopping-place, target, terminus.

destined *adj* **1** foreordained, ineluctable, inescapable, inevitable, intended, ordained, predestined, predetermined, preordained, unavoidable. **2** *destined to fail.* bound, certain, doomed, fated, meant.

destiny *n* chance, doom, fate, fortune, karma, kismet, lot, luck, providence.

destitute *adj* bankrupt, deprived, down-and-out, homeless, impecunious, impoverished, indigent, insolvent, needy, penniless, poverty-stricken, *inf* skint. ▷ POOR. *Opp* WEALTHY.

destroy *vb* abolish, annihilate, blast, break down, burst, *inf* bust, crush, *inf* decimate, demolish, devastate, devour, dismantle, dispose of, do away with, eliminate, eradicate, erase, exterminate, extinguish, extirpate, finish off, flatten, fragment, get rid of, knock down, lay waste, level, liquidate, make useless, nullify, pull down, pulverize, put out of existence, raze, root out, ruin, sabotage, sack, scuttle, shatter, smash, stamp out, undo, uproot, vaporize, wipe out, wreck, write off. ▷ DEFEAT, END, KILL. *Opp* CONSERVE, CREATE.

destruction *n* annihilation, damage, *inf* decimation, demolition, depredation, devastation, elimination, end, eradication, erasure, extermination, extinction, extirpation, havoc, holocaust, liquidation, overthrow, pulling down, ruin, ruination, shattering, smashing, undoing, uprooting, wiping out, wrecking. ▷ KILLING. *Opp* CONSERVATION, CREATION.

destructive *adj* adverse, antagonistic, baleful, baneful, calamitous, catastrophic, damaging, dangerous, deadly, deleterious, detrimental, devastating, disastrous, fatal, harmful, injurious, internecine, lethal, malignant, negative, pernicious, pestilential, ruinous, violent. *Opp* CONSTRUCTIVE.

detach *vb* cut loose, cut off, disconnect, disengage, disentangle, divide, free, isolate, part, pull off, release, remove, segregate, separate, sever, take off, tear off, uncouple, undo, unfasten, unfix, unhitch. *Opp* ATTACH.
detached ▷ ALOOF, IMPARTIAL, SEPARATE.

detail *n* aspect, circumstance, complexity, complication, component, element, fact, factor, feature, ingredient, intricacy, item, *plur* minutiae, nicety, particular, point, refinement, respect, specific, technicality.

detailed *adj inf* blow-by-blow, complete, complex, comprehensive, descriptive, exact, exhaustive, full, *derog* fussy, giving all details, *derog* hair-splitting, intricate, itemized, minute, particularized, specific. *Opp* GENERAL.

detain *vb* **1** arrest, capture, confine, gaol, hold, imprison, intern. **2** buttonhole, delay, hinder, hold up, impede, keep, keep waiting, restrain, retard, slow, stop, waylay.

detect *vb* ascertain, become aware of, diagnose, discern, discover, expose, feel, *inf* ferret out, find, hear, identify, locate, note, notice, observe, perceive, *inf* put your finger on, recognize, reveal, scent, see, sense, sight, smell, sniff out, spot, spy, taste, track down, uncover, unearth, unmask.

detective *n* investigator, policeman, policewoman, *inf* private eye, sleuth, *inf* snooper.

detention *n* captivity, confinement, custody, imprisonment, incarceration, internment.

deter *vb* check, daunt, discourage, dismay, dissuade, frighten off, hinder, impede, intimidate, obstruct, prevent, put off, repel, send away, stop, *inf* turn off, warn off. *Opp* ENCOURAGE.

deteriorate *vb* crumble, decay, decline, degenerate, depreciate, disintegrate, fall off, get worse, *inf* go downhill, lapse, relapse, slip, weaken, worsen. *Opp* IMPROVE.

determination *n inf* backbone, commitment, courage, dedication, doggedness, drive, firmness, fortitude, *inf* grit, *inf* guts, perseverance, persistence, pertinacity, resoluteness, resolution, resolve, single-mindedness, spirit, steadfastness, *derog* stubbornness, tenacity, willpower.

determine *vb* **1** arbitrate, clinch, conclude, decide, establish, find out, identify, judge, settle. **2** choose, decide on, fix on, resolve, select. **3** *What determined your choice?* affect, condition, dictate, govern, influence, regulate.

determined *adj* adamant, assertive, bent (*on success*), certain, convinced, decided, decisive, definite, dogged, firm, insistent, intent, *derog* obstinate, persistent, pertinacious, purposeful, resolute, resolved, single-minded, steadfast, strong-minded, strong-willed, *derog* stubborn, sure, tenacious, tough, unwavering. *Opp* IRRESOLUTE.

deterrent *n* barrier, caution, check, curb, difficulty, discouragement, disincentive, dissuasion, hindrance, impediment, obstacle, restraint, threat, *inf* turn-off, warning. *Opp* ENCOURAGEMENT.

detest *vb* abhor, abominate, despise, execrate, loathe. ▷ HATE.

detour *n* deviation, diversion, indirect route, roundabout route. **make a detour** ▷ DEVIATE.

detract *vb* **detract from** diminish, lessen, lower, reduce, take away from.

detrimental *adj* damaging, deleterious, disadvantageous, harmful, hurtful, inimical, injurious, prejudicial, unfavourable. *Opp* ADVANTAGEOUS.

devastate *vb* **1** damage severely, demolish, destroy, flatten, lay waste, level, obliterate, overwhelm, ravage, raze, ruin, sack, waste, wreck. **2** ▷ DISMAY.

develop *vb* **1** advance, age, arise, *inf* blow up, come into existence, evolve, flourish, get better, grow, improve, mature, move on, progress, ripen. *Opp* REGRESS. **2** *develop habits.* acquire, contract, cultivate, evolve, foster, get, pick up. **3** *develop ideas.* amplify, augment, elaborate, enlarge on, expatiate on, unfold, work up. **4** *business developed.* branch out, build up, diversify, enlarge, expand, extend, increase, swell.

development *n* **1** advance, betterment, change, enlargement, evolution, expansion, extension, *inf* forward march, furtherance, gain, growth, improvement, increase, progress, promotion, regeneration, reinforcement, spread. **2** happening, incident, occurrence, outcome, result, upshot. **3** *industrial development.* building, conversion, exploitation, use.

deviate *vb* branch off, depart, digress, diverge, drift, err, go astray, go round, make a detour, stray, swerve, turn aside, turn off, vary, veer, wander.

device *n* **1** apparatus, appliance, contraption, contrivance, gadget, implement, instrument, invention, machine, tool, utensil. **2** dodge, expedient, gambit, gimmick, manoeuvre, plan, ploy, ruse, scheme, stratagem, stunt, tactic, trick, wile. **3** *heraldic device.* badge, crest, design, figure, logo, motif, shield, sign, symbol, token.

devil *n* demon, fiend, imp, spirit. **The Devil** the Adversary, Beelzebub, the Evil One, Lucifer, Mephistopheles, *inf* Old Nick, the Prince of Darkness, Satan.

devilish *adj* demoniac(al), demonic, diabolic(al), fiendish, hellish, impish, infernal, inhuman, Mephisophelian, satanic. ▷ EVIL. *Opp* ANGELIC.

devious *adj* **1** circuitous, crooked, deviating, indirect, periphrastic, rambling, round-about, sinuous, tortuous, wandering, winding. **2** [*derog*] calculating, cunning, deceitful, evasive, insincere, misleading, scheming, *inf* slippery, sly, sneaky, treacherous, underhand, wily. ▷ DISHONEST. *Opp* DIRECT.

devise *vb* arrange, conceive, concoct, contrive, *inf* cook up, create, design, engineer, form, formulate, frame, imagine, invent, make up, plan, plot, prepare, project, scheme, think out, think up, work out.

devoted *adj* committed, dedicated, enthusiastic, faithful, loving, staunch, true, unswerving, wholehearted, zealous. ▷ LOYAL. *Opp* DISLOYAL, HALF-HEARTED.

devotee *n inf* addict, aficionado, *inf* buff, enthusiast, fan, follower, *sl* freak, supporter.

devotion *n* allegiance, attachment, commitment, dedication, devotedness, enthusiasm, fanaticism, fervour, loyalty, zeal. ▷ LOVE, PIETY.

devour *vb* consume, demolish, eat up, engulf, swallow up, take in. ▷ DESTROY, EAT.

devout *adj* God-fearing, godly, holy, religious, sincere, spiritual. ▷ PIOUS. *Opp* IRRELIGIOUS.

dexterous *adj* adroit, agile, deft, nimble, quick, sharp, skilful. ▷ CLEVER. *Opp* CLUMSY.

diabolical *adj* evil, fiendish, inhuman, satanic, wicked. ▷ DEVILISH. *Opp* SAINTLY.

diagnose *vb* detect, determine, distinguish, find, identify, isolate, name, pinpoint, recognize.

diagnosis *n* analysis, conclusion, explanation, identification, interpretation, opinion, pronouncement, verdict.

diagram *n* chart, drawing, figure, flow-chart, graph, illustration, outline, picture, plan, representation, sketch, table.

dial *n* clock, digital display, face, instrument, pointer, speedometer.

dialect *n* accent, argot, brogue, cant, creole, idiom, jargon, language, patois, phraseology, pronunciation, register, slang, speech, tongue, vernacular.

dialogue *n inf* chat, *inf* chin-wag, colloquy, communication, conference, conversation, debate, discourse, discussion, duologue, exchange, interchange, *old use* intercourse, meeting, oral communication, talk, *inf* tête-à-tête.

diary *n* annals, appointment book, calendar, chronicle, engagement book, journal, log, record.

dictate *vb* **1** read aloud, speak slowly. **2** command, decree, direct, enforce, give orders, impose, *inf* lay down the law, make the rules, ordain, order, prescribe, state categorically.

dictator *n* autocrat, *inf* Big Brother, despot, tyrant. ▷ RULER.

dictatorial *adj* absolute, arbitrary, authoritarian, autocratic, *inf* bossy, despotic, dogmatic, dominant, domineering, illiberal, imperious, intolerant, omnipotent, oppressive, overbearing, repressive, totalitarian, tyrannical, undemocratic. *Opp* DEMOCRATIC.

dictionary *n* concordance, glossary, lexicon, thesaurus, vocabulary, wordbook.

didactic *adj* instructive, lecturing, pedagogic, pedantic.

die *vb* **1** *inf* bite the dust, *inf* breathe your last, cease to exist, come to the end, decease, depart, expire, fall, *inf* give up the ghost, *sl* kick the bucket, lay down your life, lose your life, pass away, *sl* peg out, perish, *sl* pop off, *sl* snuff it, starve. **2** decline, decrease, die away, disappear, droop, dwindle, ebb, end, fade, fail, fizzle out, go out, languish, lessen, peter out, stop, subside, vanish, wane, weaken, wilt, wither.

diet *n* fare, food, intake, nourishment, nutriment, nutrition, sustenance. • *vb* abstain, *inf* cut down, deny yourself, fast, lose weight, ration yourself, reduce, slim.

differ *vb* **1** be different, be distinct, contrast, deviate, diverge, show differences, vary. **2** argue, be at odds, be at variance, clash, conflict, contradict, disagree, dispute, dissent, fall out, *inf* have a difference, oppose each other, quarrel, take issue with each other. *Opp* AGREE.

difference *n* **1** alteration, change, comparison, contrast, development, deviation, differential, differentiation, discrepancy, disparity, dissimilarity, distinction, diversity, incompatibility, incongruity, inconsistency, modification, nuance, unlikeness, variation, variety. *Opp* SIMILARITY. **2** argument, clash, conflict, controversy, debate, disagreement, disharmony, dispute, dissent, quarrel, strife, tiff, wrangle. *Opp* AGREEMENT.

different *adj* **1** assorted, clashing, conflicting, contradictory, contrasting, deviating, discordant, discrepant, disparate, dissimilar, distinguishable, divergent, diverse, heterogeneous, ill-matched, incompatible, inconsistent, miscellaneous, mixed, multifarious, opposed, opposite, *inf* poles apart, several, sundry, unlike, varied, various. *Opp* SIMILAR. **2** abnormal, altered, anomalous, atypical, bizarre, changed, distinct, distinctive, eccentric, extraordinary, fresh, individual, irregular, new, original, particular, peculiar, personal, revolutionary, separate, singular, special, specific, strange, uncommon, unconventional, unique, unorthodox, unusual. *Opp* CONVENTIONAL.

differentiate *vb* contrast, discriminate, distinguish, tell apart.

difficult *adj* **1** abstruse, advanced, baffling, complex, complicated, deep, *inf* dodgy, enigmatic, hard, intractable, intricate, involved, *inf* knotty, *inf* nasty, obscure, perplexing, problematical, *inf* thorny, ticklish, tricky. **2** arduous, awkward, backbreaking, burdensome, challenging, daunting, demanding, exacting, exhausting, formidable, gruelling, heavy, herculean, *inf* killing, laborious, onerous, punishing, rigorous, severe, strenuous, taxing, tough, uphill. **3** *difficult children.* annoying, disruptive, fussy, headstrong, intractable, obstinate, obstreperous, refractory, stubborn, tiresome, troublesome, trying, uncooperative, unfriendly, unhelpful, unresponsive, unruly. *Opp* COOPERATIVE, EASY.

difficulty *n* adversity, challenge, complication, dilemma, embarrassment, enigma, *inf* fix, *inf* hang-up, hardship, *inf* hiccup, hindrance, hurdle, impediment, *inf* jam, *inf* mess, obstacle, perplexity, *inf* pickle, pitfall, plight, predicament, problem, puzzle, quandary, snag, *inf* spot, straits, *inf* stumbling-block, tribulation, trouble, *inf* vexed question.

diffident *adj* backward, bashful, coy, distrustful, doubtful, fearful, hesitant, hesitating, inhibited, insecure, introvert, meek, modest, nervous, private, reluctant, reserved, retiring, self-effacing, sheepish, shrinking, shy, tentative, timid, timorous, unadventurous, unassuming, underconfident, unsure, withdrawn. *Opp* CONFIDENT.

diffuse *adj* digressive, discursive, long-winded, loose, meandering, rambling, spread out, unstructured, vague, *inf* waffly, wandering. ▷ WORDY. *Opp* CONCISE. ● *vb* ▷ SPREAD.

dig *vb* **1** burrow, delve, excavate, gouge, hollow, mine, quarry, scoop, tunnel. **2** cultivate, fork over, *inf* grub up, till, trench, turn over. **3** jab, nudge, poke, prod, punch, shove, thrust. **dig out** ▷ FIND. **dig up** disinter, exhume.

digest *n* ▷ SUMMARY. ● *vb* **1** absorb, assimilate, dissolve, ingest, process, utilize. ▷ EAT. **2** consider, ponder, study, take in, understand.

digit *n* **1** figure, integer, number, numeral. **2** finger, toe.

dignified *adj* august, becoming, calm, courtly, decorous, distinguished, elegant, exalted, formal, grand, grave, imposing, impressive, lofty, lordly, majestic, noble, proper, refined, regal, sedate, serious, sober, solemn, stately, tasteful, upright. ▷ PROUD. *Opp* UNBECOMING.

dignitary *n inf* high-up, important person, luminary, notable, official, *inf* VIP, worthy.

dignity *n* calmness, courtliness, decorum, elegance, eminence, formality, glory, grandeur, *Lat* gravitas, gravity, greatness, honour, importance, majesty, nobility, propriety, regality, respectability, seriousness, sobriety, solemnity, stateliness. ▷ PRIDE.

digress *vb* depart, deviate, diverge, drift, get off the subject, *inf* go off at a tangent, *inf* lose the thread, ramble, stray, veer, wander.

dilapidated *adj* badly maintained, broken down, crumbling, decayed, decrepit, derelict, falling apart, falling down, in disrepair, in ruins, neglected, ramshackle, rickety, ruined, *inf* run-down, shaky, tottering, tumbledown, uncared-for.

dilemma *n inf* catch-22, deadlock, difficulty, doubt, embarrassment, *inf* fix, impasse, *inf* jam, *inf* mess, *inf* pickle, plight, predicament, problem, quandary, *inf* spot, stalemate.

diligent *adj* assiduous, busy, careful, conscientious, constant, devoted, earnest, energetic, hardworking, indefatigable, industrious, meticulous, painstaking, persevering, persistent, pertinacious, punctilious, scrupulous, sedulous, studious, thorough, tireless. *Opp* LAZY.

dilute *vb* adulterate, reduce the strength of, thin, water down, weaken. *Opp* CONCENTRATE.

dim *adj* **1** bleary, blurred, clouded, cloudy, dark, dingy, dull, faint, fogged, foggy, fuzzy, gloomy, grey, hazy, ill-defined, imperceptible, indistinct, indistinguishable, misty, murky, nebulous, obscure, obscured, pale, shadowy, sombre, unclear, vague, weak. **2** ▷ STUPID. *Opp* BRIGHT. ● *vb* **1** blacken, cloud, darken, dull, make dim, mask, obscure, shade, shroud. **2** become dim, fade, go out, lose brightness, lower. *Opp* BRIGHTEN. **take a dim view** ▷ DISAPPROVE.

dimensions *plur n* capacity, extent, magnitude, measurements, proportions, scale, scope, size. ▷ MEASUREMENT.

diminish *vb* **1** abate, become less, contract, curtail, decline, decrease, depreciate, die down, dwindle, ease off, ebb, fade, lessen, *inf* let up, lower, peter out, recede, reduce, shorten, shrink, shrivel, slow down, subside, wane, *inf* wind down. ▷ CUT. *Opp* INCREASE. **2** belittle, cheapen, demean, deprecate, devalue, disparage, minimize, undervalue. *Opp* EXAGGERATE.

diminutive *adj* microscopic, midget, miniature, minuscule, minute, tiny, undersized. ▷ SMALL.

din *n* blaring, clamour, clangour, clatter, commotion, crash, hubbub, hullabaloo, noise, outcry, pandemonium, racket, roar, row, rumpus, shouting, tumult, uproar. ▷ SOUND.

dingy *adj* colourless, dark, depressing, dim, dirty, discoloured, dismal, drab, dreary, dull, faded, gloomy, grimy, murky, old, seedy, shabby, smoky, soiled, sooty, worn. *Opp* BRIGHT.

dining-room *n* cafeteria, carvery, refectory, restaurant.

dinner *n* banquet, feast. ▷ MEAL.

dip *n* **1** concavity, declivity, dent, depression, fall, hole, hollow, incline, slope. **2** *dip in the sea.* bathe, dive, immersion, plunge, soaking, swim. • *vb* **1** decline, descend, dive, fall, go down, sag, sink, slope down, slump, subside. **2** douse, drop, duck, dunk, immerse, lower, plunge, submerge. **take a dip** ▷ BATHE.

diplomacy *n* adroitness, delicacy, discretion, finesse, negotiation, skill, tact, tactfulness.

diplomat *n* ambassador, consul, government representative, negotiator, official, peacemaker, politician, representative, tactician.

diplomatic *adj* careful, considerate, delicate, discreet, judicious, polite, politic, prudent, sensitive, subtle, tactful, thoughtful, understanding. *Opp* TACTLESS.

direct *adj* **1** non-stop, shortest, straight, unbroken, undeviating, uninterrupted, unswerving. **2** blunt, candid, categorical, clear, decided, explicit, express, forthright, frank, honest, open, outspoken, plain, point-blank, sincere, straightforward, *derog* tactless, to the point, unambiguous, uncomplicated, *derog* undiplomatic, unequivocal, uninhibited, unqualified, unreserved. **3** *direct experience.* empirical, firsthand, *inf* from the horse's mouth, personal. **4** *direct opposites.* absolute, complete, diametrical, exact, head-on, *inf* out-and-out, utter. *Opp* INDIRECT. • *vb* **1** address, escort, guide, indicate the way, point, route, send, show the way, tell the way, usher. **2** aim, focus, level, target, train, turn. **3** administer, be in charge of, command, conduct, control, govern, handle, lead, manage, mastermind, oversee, regulate, rule, run, stage-manage, superintend, supervise, take charge of. **4** *direct someone to do something.* advise, bid, charge, command, counsel, enjoin, instruct, order, require, tell.

direction *n* aim, approach, (compass) bearing, course, orientation, path, point of the compass, road, route, tack, track, way. **directions** guidance, guidelines, instructions, orders, plans.

director *n* administrator, *inf* boss, executive, governor, manager, managing director, organizer, president, principal. ▷ CHIEF.

directory *n* catalogue, index, list, register.

dirt *n* **1** dust, excrement, filth, garbage, grime, impurity, mess, mire, muck, ooze, ordure, pollution, slime, sludge, smut, soot, stain. ▷ OBSCENITY, RUBBISH. **2** clay, earth, loam, mud, soil.

dirty *adj* **1** befouled, begrimed, besmirched, bespattered, black, dingy, dusty, filthy, foul, grimy, grubby, marked, messy, mucky, muddy, nasty, scruffy, shabby, slatternly, smeary, smudged, soiled, sooty, sordid, spotted, squalid, stained, sullied, tarnished, travel-stained, uncared for, unclean, untidy, unwashed. **2** *dirty water.* cloudy, contaminated, impure, muddy, murky, poisoned, polluted, tainted, untreated. **3** *dirty tactics.* dishonest, dishonourable, illegal, *inf* low-down, mean, rough, treacherous, unfair, ungentlemanly, unscrupulous, unsporting, unsportsmanlike. ▷ CORRUPT. **4** *dirty talk.* coarse, crude, improper, indecent, offensive, rude, smutty, vulgar. ▷ OBSCENE. *Opp* CLEAN. • *vb* befoul, foul, make dirty, mark, *inf* mess up, smear, smudge, soil, spatter, spot, stain, streak, tarnish. ▷ DEFILE. *Opp* CLEAN.

disability *n* affliction, complaint, defect, disablement, handicap, impairment, incapacity, infirmity, weakness.

disable *vb* cripple, damage, debilitate, enfeeble, *inf* hamstring, handicap, immobilize, impair, incapacitate, injure, lame, maim, make useless, mutilate, paralyse, put out of action, ruin, weaken. **disabled** ▷ HANDICAPPED.

disadvantage *n* drawback, handicap, hardship, hindrance, impediment, inconvenience, liability, *inf* minus, nuisance, privation, snag, trouble, weakness.

disagree *vb* argue, bicker, clash, conflict, contend, differ, dispute, dissent, diverge, fall out, fight, quarrel, squabble, wrangle. **disagree with** ▷ OPPOSE.

disagreeable *adj* disgusting, distasteful, nasty, objectionable, obnoxious, offensive, *inf* off-putting, repellent, sickening, unsavoury. ▷ UNPLEASANT. *Opp* PLEASANT.

disagreement *n* altercation, argument, clash, conflict, contention, controversy, debate, difference, discrepancy, disharmony, disparity, dispute, dissension, dissent, divergence, incompatibility, inconsistency, misunderstanding, opposition, quarrel, squabble, strife, *inf* tiff, variance, wrangle. *Opp* AGREEMENT.

disappear *vb* **1** become invisible, cease to exist, clear, die out, disperse, dissolve, dwindle, ebb, evanesce, evaporate, fade, melt away, recede, vanish, vaporize, wane. ▷ DIE. **2** depart, escape, flee, fly, go, pass out of sight, run away, walk away, withdraw. *Opp* APPEAR.

disappoint *vb* be worse than expected, chagrin, *inf* dash your hopes, disenchant, disillusion, dismay, displease, dissatisfy, fail to satisfy, *inf* let down, upset, vex. ▷ FRUSTRATE. *Opp* SATISFY. **disappointed** disillusioned, frustrated, *inf* let down, unsatisfied. ▷ SAD.

disapproval *n* anger, censure, condemnation, criticism, disapprobation, disfavour, dislike, displeasure, dissatisfaction, hostility, reprimand, reproach. *Opp* APPROVAL.

disapprove *vb* **disapprove of** be displeased by, belittle, blame, censure, condemn, criticize, denounce, deplore, deprecate, dislike, disparage, frown on, jeer at, look askance at, make unwelcome, object to, regret, reject, *inf* take a dim view of, take exception to. *Opp* APPROVE. **disapproving** ▷ CRITICAL.

disarm *vb* **1** demilitarize, demobilize, disband troops, make powerless, take weapons from. **2** charm, mollify, pacify, placate.

disaster *n* accident, act of God, blow, calamity, cataclysm, catastrophe, crash, débâcle, failure, fiasco, *inf* flop, *inf* mess-up, misadventure, mischance, misfortune, mishap, reverse, tragedy, *inf* wash-out. *Opp* SUCCESS.

disastrous *adj* appalling, awful, calamitous, cataclysmic, catastrophic, crippling, destructive, devastating, dire, dreadful, fatal, ruinous, terrible, tragic. *Opp* SUCCESSFUL.

disbelieve *vb* be sceptical of, discount, discredit, doubt, have no faith in, mistrust, reject, suspect. *Opp* BELIEVE. **disbelieving** ▷ INCREDULOUS.

disc *n* **1** circle, counter, plate, token. **2** album, CD, LP, record, single. **3** [*computing*] CD-ROM, disk, diskette, floppy disk, hard disk.

discard *vb* abandon, cast off, *inf* chuck away, dispense with, dispose of, *inf* ditch, dump, eliminate, get rid of, jettison, junk, reject, scrap, shed, throw away, toss out.

discern *vb* be aware of, be sensitive to, detect, discover, discriminate, distinguish, make out, mark, notice, observe, perceive, recognize, spy. ▷ SEE. **discerning** ▷ PERCEPTIVE.

discernible *adj* detectable, distinguishable, measurable, perceptible. ▷ NOTICEABLE.

discharge *n* **1** release, dismissal. **2** emission, excretion, ooze, pus, secretion, suppuration. • *vb* **1** belch, eject, emit, expel, exude, give off, give out, pour out, produce, release, secrete, send out, spew, spit out. **2** *discharge guns*. detonate, explode, fire, let off, shoot. **3** *discharge employees*. dismiss, fire, make redundant, remove, sack, throw out. **4** *discharge a prisoner*. absolve, acquit, allow to leave, clear, dismiss, excuse, exonerate, free, let off, liberate, pardon, release. **5** *discharge duties*. accomplish, carry out, execute, fulfil, perform.

disciple *n* acolyte, adherent, admirer, apostle, apprentice, devotee, follower, learner, proselyte, pupil, scholar, student, supporter.

disciplinarian *n* authoritarian, autocrat, despot, dictator, *inf* hardliner, *inf* hard taskmaster, martinet, *inf* slave-driver, *inf* stickler, tyrant.

discipline *n* **1** control, drilling, indoctrination, instruction, management, strictness, system, training. **2** good behaviour, obedience, order, orderliness, routine, self-control, self-restraint. • *vb* **1** break in, coach, control, drill, educate, govern, indoctrinate, instruct, keep in check, manage, restrain, school, train. **2** castigate, chasten, chastise, correct, penalize, punish, rebuke, reprimand, reprove, scold. **disciplined** ▷ OBEDIENT.

disclaim *vb* deny, disown, forswear, reject, renounce, repudiate. *Opp* ACKNOWLEDGE.

disclose *vb* divulge, expose, let out, make known. ▷ REVEAL.

discolour *vb* bleach, dirty, fade, mark, spoil the colour of, stain, tarnish, tinge.

discomfort *n* ache, care, difficulty, distress, hardship, inconvenience, irritation, soreness, uncomfortableness, uneasiness. ▷ PAIN. *Opp* COMFORT.

disconcert *vb* agitate, bewilder, confuse, discomfit, distract, disturb, fluster, nonplus, perplex, *inf* put off, puzzle, *inf* rattle, ruffle, throw off balance, trouble, unsettle, upset, worry. *Opp* REASSURE.

disconnect *vb* break off, cut off, detach, disengage, divide, part, sever, switch off, take away, turn off, uncouple, undo, unhitch, unhook, unplug. **disconnected** ▷ INCOHERENT.

discontented *adj* annoyed, disgruntled, displeased, dissatisfied, *inf* fed up, restless, sulky, unhappy, unsettled.

discord *n* **1** argument, conflict, contention, difference of opinion, disagreement, disharmony, dispute, friction, incompatibility, strife. ▷ QUARREL. **2** [*music*] cacophony, clash, jangle. ▷ NOISE. *Opp* HARMONY.

discordant *adj* **1** conflicting, contrary, differing, disagreeing, dissimilar, divergent, incompatible, incongruous, inconsistent, opposed, opposite. ▷ QUARRELSOME. **2** atonal, cacophonous, clashing, dissonant, grating, grinding, harsh, jangling, jarring, shrill, strident, tuneless, unmusical. *Opp* HARMONIOUS.

discount *n* abatement, allowance, concession, cut, deduction, *inf* markdown, rebate, reduction. • *vb* disbelieve, dismiss, disregard, gloss over, ignore, overlook, reject.

discourage *vb* **1** cow, damp, dampen, daunt, demoralize, depress, disenchant, dishearten, dismay, dispirit, frighten, inhibit, intimidate, overawe, *inf* put down, *inf* put off, scare, *inf* throw cold water on, unman, unnerve. **2** *discourage vandalism*. check, deflect, deter, dissuade, hinder, prevent, put an end to, repress, restrain, slow down, stop, suppress. *Opp* ENCOURAGE.

discouragement *n* constraint, *inf* damper, deterrent, disincentive, hindrance, impediment, obstacle, restraint, setback. *Opp* ENCOURAGEMENT.

discourse *n* **1** ▷ CONVERSATION. **2** dissertation, essay, monograph, paper, speech, thesis, treatise. ▷ WRITING. • *vb* ▷ SPEAK.

discover *vb* ascertain, bring to light, come across, detect, *inf* dig up, disclose, *inf* dredge up, explore, expose, *inf* ferret out, find, hit on, identify, learn, light upon, locate, notice, observe, perceive, recognize, reveal, search out, spot, *sl* sus out, track down, turn up, uncover, unearth. ▷ INVENT. *Opp* HIDE.

discoverer *n* creator, explorer, finder, initiator, inventor, originator, pioneer, traveller.

discovery *n* breakthrough, conception, detection, disclosure, exploration, *inf* find, innovation, invention, recognition, revelation.

discredit *vb* attack, calumniate, challenge, defame, disbelieve, disgrace, dishonour, disprove, *inf* explode, prove false, raise doubts about, refuse to believe, ruin the reputation of, show up, slander, slur, smear, vilify.

discreet *adj* careful, cautious, chary, circumspect, considerate, delicate, diplomatic, guarded, judicious, low-key, mild, muted, polite, politic, prudent, restrained, sensitive, soft, subdued, tactful, thoughtful, understated, wary. *Opp* INDISCREET.

discrepancy *n* conflict, difference, disparity, dissimilarity, divergence, incompatibility, incongruity, inconsistency, variance. *Opp* SIMILARITY.

discretion *n* circumspection, diplomacy, good sense, judgement, maturity, prudence, responsibility, sensitivity, tact, wisdom. *Opp* TACTLESSNESS.

discriminate *vb* **1** differentiate, distinguish, draw a distinction, separate, tell apart. **2** be biased, be intolerant, be prejudiced, show discrimination. **discriminating** ▷ PERCEPTIVE.

discrimination *n* **1** discernment, good taste, insight, judgement, perceptiveness, refinement, selectivity, subtlety, taste. **2** [*derog*] bias, bigotry, chauvinism, favouritism, intolerance, male chauvinism, prejudice, racialism, racism, sexism, unfairness. *Opp* IMPARTIALITY.

discuss *vb* argue about, confer about, consider, consult about, debate, deliberate, examine, *inf* put heads together about, talk about, *inf* weigh up the pros and cons of, write about. ▷ TALK.

discussion *n* argument, colloquy, confabulation, conference, consideration, consultation, conversation, debate, deliberation, dialogue, discourse, examination, exchange of views, *inf* powwow, symposium. ▷ TALK.

disdainful *adj* contemptuous, jeering, mocking, scornful, sneering, supercilious, superior. ▷ PROUD.

disease *n* affliction, ailment, blight, *inf* bug, complaint, *inf* condition, contagion, disorder, infection, infirmity, malady, plague, sickness. ▷ ILLNESS.

diseased *adj* ailing, infirm, sick, unwell. ▷ ILL.

disembark *vb* alight, debark, detrain, get off, go ashore, land. *Opp* EMBARK.

disfigure *vb* blemish, damage, deface, deform, distort, impair, injure, make ugly, mar, mutilate, ruin, scar, spoil. *Opp* BEAUTIFY.

disgrace *n* **1** blot, contumely, degradation, discredit, dishonour, disrepute, embarrassment, humiliation, ignominy, obloquy, odium, opprobrium, scandal, shame, slur, stain, stigma. **2** ▷ OUTRAGE.

disgraceful *adj* contemptible, degrading, dishonourable, embarrassing, humiliating, ignominious, shameful, shaming, wicked. ▷ BAD.

disgruntled *adj* annoyed, cross, disaffected, disappointed, discontented, dissatisfied, *inf* fed up, grumpy, moody, sulky, sullen. ▷ BAD-TEMPERED.

disguise *n* camouflage, cloak, costume, cover, fancy dress, front, *inf* get-up, impersonation, make-up, mask, pretence, smoke-screen. ● *vb* blend into the background, camouflage, conceal, cover up, dress up, falsify, gloss over, hide, make inconspicuous, mask, misrepresent, screen, shroud, veil. **disguise yourself as** ▷ IMPERSONATE.

disgust *n* abhorrence, antipathy, aversion, contempt, detestation, dislike, distaste, hatred, loathing, nausea, outrage, repugnance, repulsion, revulsion, sickness. ● *vb* appal, be distasteful to, displease, horrify, nauseate, offend, outrage, put off, repel, revolt, shock, sicken, *inf* turn your stomach. *Opp* PLEASE. **disgusting** ▷ HATEFUL.

dish *n* **1** basin, bowl, casserole, container, plate, *old use* platter, tureen. **2** concoction, food, item on the menu, recipe. **dish out** ▷ DISTRIBUTE. **dish up** ▷ SERVE.

dishearten *vb* depress, deter, discourage, dismay, put off, sadden. *Opp* ENCOURAGE. **disheartened** ▷ SAD.

dishevelled *adj* bedraggled, disarranged, disordered, knotted, matted, messy, ruffled, rumpled, *inf* scruffy, slovenly, tangled, tousled, uncombed, unkempt, untidy. *Opp* NEAT.

dishonest *adj inf* bent, cheating, corrupt, criminal, crooked, deceitful, deceiving, deceptive, devious, dishonourable, disreputable, false, fraudulent, hypocritical, immoral, insincere, lying, mendacious, misleading, perfidious, *inf* shady, *inf* slippery, specious, swindling, thieving, treacherous, *inf* twofaced, *inf* underhand, unethical, unprincipled, unscrupulous, untrustworthy, untruthful. *Opp* HONEST.

dishonour *n inf* black mark, blot, degradation, discredit, disgrace, humiliation, ignominy, indignity, loss of face, obloquy, opprobrium, reproach, scandal, shame, slander, slur, stain, stigma. *Opp* HONOUR. ● *vb* **1** abuse, affront, debase, defile, degrade, disgrace, offend, profane, shame, slight. **2** ▷ RAPE.

dishonourable *adj* base, blameworthy, compromising, despicable, discreditable, disgraceful, disgusting, dishonest, disloyal, disreputable, ignoble, ignominious, improper, infamous, mean, outrageous, perfidious, reprehensible, scandalous, shabby, shameful, shameless, treacherous, unchivalrous, unethical, unprincipled, unscrupulous, untrustworthy, unworthy, wicked. ▷ CORRUPT. *Opp* HONOURABLE.

disillusion *vb* disabuse, disappoint, disenchant, enlighten, reveal the truth to, undeceive.

disinfect *vb* chlorinate, clean, cleanse, decontaminate, fumigate, purge, purify, sanitize, sterilize.

disinfectant *n* antiseptic, decontaminant, fumigant, germicide.

disinherit *vb* cut off, cut out of a will, deprive someone of his/her birthright, deprive someone of his/her inheritance.

disintegrate *vb* break into pieces, break up, come apart, crack up, crumble, decay, decompose, degenerate, deteriorate, fall apart, lose coherence, moulder, rot, shatter, smash, splinter.

disinterested *adj* detached, dispassionate, impartial, impersonal, neutral, objective, unbiased, uninvolved, unprejudiced. *Opp* BIASED.

disjointed *adj* aimless, broken up, confused, desultory, disconnected, dislocated, disordered, disunited, divided, incoherent, jumbled, loose, mixed up, muddled, rambling, separate, split up, unconnected, uncoordinated, wandering. *Opp* COHERENT.

dislike *n* animus, antagonism, antipathy, aversion, contempt, detestation, disapproval, disfavour, disgust, distaste, hatred, hostility, ill will, loathing, repugnance, revulsion. ● *vb* avoid, despise, detest, disapprove of, feel dislike for, scorn, *inf* take against. ▷ HATE. *Opp* LOVE.

dislocate *vb* disengage, disjoint, displace, misplace, *inf* put out, put out of joint.

disloyal *adj* apostate, faithless, false, insincere, perfidious, recreant, renegade, seditious, subversive, treacherous, treasonable, *inf* two-faced, unfaithful, unreliable, untrue, untrustworthy. *Opp* LOYAL.

disloyalty *n* betrayal, doubledealing, duplicity, faithlessness, falseness, inconstancy, infidelity, perfidy, treachery, treason, unfaithfulness. *Opp* LOYALTY.

dismal *adj* bleak, cheerless, depressing, dreary, dull, funereal, gloomy, grey, grim, joyless, miserable, sombre, wretched. ▷ SAD.

dismantle *vb* demolish, knock down, strike, strip down, take apart, take down. *Opp* ASSEMBLE.

dismay *n* agitation, alarm, anxiety, apprehension, consternation, depression, disappointment, discouragement, distress, dread, gloom, horror, pessimism. ▷ FEAR. • *vb* alarm, appal, daunt, depress, devastate, disappoint, discompose, discourage, disgust, dishearten, dispirit, distress, horrify, scare, shock, take aback, unnerve. ▷ FRIGHTEN. *Opp* PLEASE.

dismiss *vb* **1** disband, discard, free, let go, *inf* pack off, release, send away, *inf* send packing. **2** belittle, brush aside, discount, disregard, drop, give up, *inf* pooh-pooh, reject, repudiate, set aside, shelve, shrug off, wave aside. **3** *dismiss a worker. inf* axe, banish, cashier, disband, discharge, *inf* fire, get rid of, give notice to, *inf* give someone his/her cards, give the push to, lay off, make redundant, sack.

disobedient *adj* anarchic, contrary, defiant, delinquent, disorderly, disruptive, fractious, headstrong, insubordinate, intractable, mutinous, obdurate, obstinate, obstreperous, perverse, rebellious, recalcitrant, refractory, riotous, selfwilled, stubborn, uncontrollable, undisciplined, ungovernable, unmanageable, unruly, wayward, wild, wilful. ▷ NAUGHTY. *Opp* OBEDIENT.

disobey *vb* **1** be disobedient, mutiny, protest, rebel, revolt, rise up, strike. **2** break, contravene, defy, disregard, flout, ignore, infringe, oppose, rebel against, resist, transgress, violate. *Opp* OBEY.

disorder *n* **1** anarchy, chaos, clamour, confusion, disarray, disorderliness, disorganization, disturbance, fighting, fracas, fuss, jumble, lawlessness, mess, muddle, rumpus, *inf* shambles, tangle, tumult, untidiness, uproar. ▷ COMMOTION. *Opp* ORDER. **2** ▷ ILLNESS.

disorderly *adj* ▷ DISOBEDIENT, DISORGANIZED.

disorganized *adj* aimless, careless, chaotic, confused, disorderly, haphazard, illogical, jumbled, messy, muddled, rambling, scatter-brained, *inf* slapdash, *inf* slipshod, *inf* sloppy, slovenly, straggling, unmethodical, unplanned, unstructured, unsystematic, untidy. *Opp* SYSTEMATIC.

disown *vb* cast off, disclaim knowledge of, renounce, repudiate.

disparage *vb* belittle, demean, depreciate, discredit, insult, *inf* put down, slight, undervalue. ▷ CRITICIZE. **disparaging** ▷ UNCOMPLIMENTARY.

dispassionate *adj* calm, composed, cool, equable, even-tempered, level-headed, sober. ▷ IMPARTIAL, UNEMOTIONAL. *Opp* EMOTIONAL.

dispatch *n* bulletin, communiqué, document, letter, message, report. • *vb* **1** consign, convey, forward, mail, post, send, ship, transmit. **2** ▷ KILL.

dispense *vb* **1** allocate, allot, apportion, assign, deal out, disburse, distribute, dole out, give out, issue, measure out, mete out, parcel out, provide, ration out, share. **2** *dispense medicine.* make up, prepare, supply. **dispense with** ▷ OMIT, REMOVE.

disperse *vb* **1** break up, decentralize, devolve, disband, dismiss, dispel, dissipate, distribute, divide up, drive away, send away, send in different directions, separate, spread, stray. *Opp* GATHER. **2** disappear, dissolve, melt away, scatter, spread out, vanish.

displace *vb* **1** disarrange, dislocate, dislodge, disturb, misplace, move, put out of place, shift. **2** crowd out, depose, dispossess, evict, expel, oust, replace, succeed, supersede, supplant, take the place of, unseat, usurp.

display *n* **1** array, demonstration, exhibition, manifestation, pageant, parade, presentation, show, spectacle. **2** ceremony, ostentation, pageantry, pomp, showing off. • *vb* advertise, air, betray, demonstrate, disclose, exhibit, expose, flaunt, flourish, give evidence of, parade, present, produce, put on show, reveal, set out, show, show off, unfold, unfurl, unveil, vaunt. *Opp* HIDE.

displease *vb* anger, offend, *inf* put out, upset. ▷ ANNOY.

disposable *adj* **1** at your disposal, available, spendable, usable. **2** biodegradable, expendable, non-returnable, replaceable, *inf* throw-away.

dispose *vb* adjust, arrange, array, distribute, group, order, organize, place, position, put, set out, situate. **disposed** ▷ LIABLE. **dispose of** ▷ DESTROY, DISCARD.

disproportionate *adj* excessive, incommensurate, incongruous, inequitable, inordinate, out of proportion, unbalanced, uneven, unreasonable. *Opp* PROPORTIONAL.

disprove *vb* confute, contradict, controvert, demolish, discredit, *inf* explode, invalidate, negate, rebut, refute, show to be wrong. *Opp* PROVE.

dispute *n* ▷ QUARREL. • *vb* argue against, challenge, contest, contradict, controvert, deny, disagree with, doubt, fault, gainsay, impugn, object to, oppose, *inf* pick holes in, quarrel with, query, question, raise doubts about, take exception to. ▷ DEBATE. *Opp* ACCEPT.

disqualify *vb* bar, debar, declare ineligible, exclude, preclude, prohibit, reject, turn down.

disregard *vb* brush aside, despise, discount, dismiss, disobey, exclude, *inf* fly in the face of, forget, ignore, leave out, *inf* make light of, miss out, neglect, omit, overlook, pass over, pay no attention to, *inf* pooh-pooh, reject, shrug off, skip, slight, snub, turn a blind eye to. *Opp* HEED.

disreputable *adj* dishonest, dishonourable, *inf* dodgy, dubious, infamous, questionable, raffish, *inf* shady, suspect, suspicious, unconventional, unreliable, unsound, untrustworthy. *Opp* REPUTABLE.

disrespectful *adj* bad-mannered, blasphemous, derisive, discourteous, disparaging, impolite, impudent, inconsiderate, insolent, insulting, irreverent, mocking, scornful, uncivil, uncomplimentary, unmannerly. ▷ RUDE. *Opp* RESPECTFUL.

disrupt *vb* agitate, break up, confuse, disconcert, dislocate, disorder, disturb, interfere with, interrupt, intrude on, spoil, throw into disorder, unsettle, upset.

dissatisfaction *n* annoyance, chagrin, disappointment, discontentment, dismay, displeasure, disquiet, exasperation, frustration, irritation, malaise, mortification, regret, unhappiness. *Opp* SATISFACTION.

dissatisfied *adj* disaffected, disappointed, discontented, disgruntled, displeased, fed up, frustrated, unfulfilled, unsatisfied. ▷ UNHAPPY. *Opp* CONTENTED.

dissident *n derog* agitator, apostate, dissenter, independent thinker, nonconformer, protester, rebel, recusant, *inf* refusenik, revolutionary. *Opp* CONFORMIST.

dissimilar *adj* antithetical, clashing, conflicting, contrasting, different, disparate, distinct, distinguishable, divergent, diverse, heterogeneous, incompatible, irreconcilable, opposite, unlike, unrelated, various. *Opp* SIMILAR.

dissipate *vb* **1** break up, diffuse, disappear, disperse, scatter. **2** distribute, fritter away, spread about, squander, throw away, use up, waste. **dissipated** ▷ IMMORAL.

dissociate *vb* back away, cut off, detach, disengage, distance, divorce, isolate, segregate. ▷ SEPARATE. *Opp* ASSOCIATE.

dissolve *vb* **1** become liquid, decompose, deliquesce, dematerialize, diffuse, disappear, disintegrate, disperse, liquefy, melt away, vanish. **2** *dissolve a meeting.* adjourn, break up, cancel, disband, dismiss, divorce, end, sever, split up, suspend, terminate, *inf* wind up.

dissuade *vb* **dissuade from** advise against, argue out of, deter from, discourage from, persuade not to, put off, remonstrate against, warn against. *Opp* PERSUADE.

distance *n* **1** breadth, extent, gap, *inf* haul, interval, journey, length, measurement, mileage, range, reach, separation, space, span, stretch, width. **2** aloofness, coolness, haughtiness, isolation, remoteness, separation, *inf* standoffishness, unfriendliness. • *vb* **distance yourself** be unfriendly, detach yourself, dissociate yourself, keep away, keep your distance, remove yourself, separate yourself, set yourself apart, stay away. *Opp* INVOLVE.

distant *adj* **1** far, far-away, far-flung, *inf* god-forsaken, inaccessible, outlying, out-of-the-way, remote, removed. *Opp* CLOSE. **2** aloof, cool, formal, frigid, haughty, reserved, reticent, stiff, unapproachable, unenthusiastic, unfriendly, withdrawn. *Opp* FRIENDLY.

distasteful *adj* disgusting, displeasing, nasty, nauseating, objectionable, offensive, *inf* off-putting, repugnant, revolting, unpalatable. ▷ UNPLEASANT. *Opp* PLEASANT.

distinct *adj* **1** apparent, clear, clear-cut, definite, evident, noticeable, obvious, palpable, patent, perceptible, plain, precise, recognizable, sharp, unambiguous, unequivocal, unmistakable, visible, well-defined. *Opp* INDISTINCT. **2** contrasting, detached, different, discrete, dissimilar, distinguishable, individual, separate, special, *Lat* sui generis, unconnected, unique.

distinction *n* **1** contrast, difference, differentiation, discrimination, dissimilarity, distinctiveness, dividing line, division, individuality, particularity, peculiarity, separation. *Opp* SIMILARITY. **2** *distinction of being first.* celebrity, credit, eminence, excellence, fame, glory, greatness, honour, importance, merit, prestige, renown, reputation, superiority.

distinctive *adj* characteristic, different, distinguishing, idiosyncratic, individual, inimitable, original, peculiar, personal, singular, special, striking, typical, uncommon, unique. *Opp* COMMON.

distinguish *vb* **1** choose, decide, differentiate, discriminate, judge, make a distinction, separate, tell apart. **2** ascertain, determine, discern, know, make out, perceive, pick out, recognize, see, single out, tell. **distinguished** ▷ FAMOUS.

distort *vb* **1** bend, buckle, contort, deform, misshape, twist, warp, wrench. **2** alter, exaggerate, falsify, garble, misrepresent, pervert, slant, tamper with, twist, violate. **distorted** ▷ GNARLED, FALSE.

distract *vb* bewilder, bother, confound, confuse, deflect, disconcert, distress, divert, harass, mystify, perplex, puzzle, rattle, sidetrack, trouble, worry. **distracted** ▷ DISTRAUGHT, MAD.

distraction *n* **1** disturbance, diversion, interference, interruption, temptation, *inf* upset. **2** agitation, befuddlement, bewilderment, confusion, delirium, frenzy, insanity, madness. **3** ▷ DIVERSION.

distraught *adj* agitated, *inf* beside yourself, distracted, distressed, disturbed, emotional, excited, frantic, hysterical, overcome, overwrought, troubled, upset, worked up. ▷ ANXIOUS. *Opp* CALM.

distress *n* adversity, affliction, angst, anguish, anxiety, danger, desolation, difficulty, discomfort, dismay, fright, grief, heartache, misery, pain, poverty, privation, sadness, sorrow, stress, suffering, torment, tribulation, trouble, unhappiness, woe, worry, wretchedness. ▷ PAIN. • *vb* afflict, alarm, bother, *inf* cut up, dismay, disturb, frighten, grieve, harass, harrow, hurt, make miserable, oppress, pain, perplex, perturb, plague, sadden, scare, shake, shock, terrify, torment, torture, trouble, upset, vex, worry, wound. *Opp* COMFORT.

distribute *vb* allocate, allot, apportion, arrange, assign, circulate, deal out, deliver, *inf* dish out, dispense, disperse, dispose of, disseminate, divide out, *inf* dole out, give out, hand round, issue, mete out, partition, pass round, scatter, share out, spread, strew, take round. *Opp* COLLECT.

district *n* area, community, department, division, locality, neighbourhood, parish, part, partition, precinct, province, quarter, region, sector, territory, vicinity, ward, zone.

distrust *vb* be distrustful of, disbelieve, doubt, have misgivings about, have qualms about, mistrust, question, suspect. *Opp* TRUST.

distrustful *adj* cautious, chary, cynical, disbelieving, distrusting, doubtful, dubious, sceptical, suspicious, uncertain, uneasy, unsure, wary. *Opp* TRUSTFUL.

disturb *vb* **1** agitate, alarm, annoy, bother, discompose, disrupt, distract, distress, excite, fluster, frighten, hassle, interrupt, intrude on, perturb, pester, ruffle, scare, shake, startle, stir up, trouble, unsettle, upset, worry. **2** confuse, disorder, interfere with, jumble up, *inf* mess about with, move, muddle, rearrange, reorganize. **disturbed** ▷ DISTRAUGHT.

disturbance *n* disruption, interference, upheaval, upset. ▷ COMMOTION.

disunited *adj* divided, opposed, polarized, split. *Opp* UNITED.

disunity *n* difference, disagreement, discord, disharmony, disintegration, division, fragmentation, incoherence, opposition, polarization. *Opp* UNITY.

disused *adj* abandoned, archaic, closed, dead, discarded, discontinued, idle, neglected, obsolete, superannuated, unused, withdrawn. ▷ OLD. *Opp* CURRENT.

ditch *n* aqueduct, channel, dike, drain, gully, gutter, moat, trench, watercourse. • *vb* ▷ ABANDON.

dive *vb* crash-dive, descend, dip, drop, duck, fall, go snorkelling, go under, jump, leap, nosedive, pitch, plummet, plunge, sink, submerge, subside, swoop.

diverge *vb* branch, deviate, divide, fork, go off at a tangent, part, radiate, ramify, separate, split, spread, subdivide. ▷ DIFFER. *Opp* CONVERGE.

diverse *adj* assorted, different, dissimilar, distinct, divergent, diversified, heterogeneous, miscellaneous, mixed, multifarious, varied, various.

diversify *vb* branch out, broaden out, develop, divide, enlarge, expand, extend, spread out, vary.

diversion *n* **1** detour, deviation. **2** amusement, distraction, entertainment, fun, game, hobby, interest, pastime, play, recreation, relaxation, sport.

divert *vb* **1** alter, avert, change direction, deflect, deviate, rechannel, redirect, reroute, shunt, sidetrack, switch, turn aside. **2** amuse, beguile, cheer up, delight, distract, engage, entertain, keep happy, occupy, recreate, regale. **diverting** ▷ FUNNY.

divide *vb* **1** branch, detach, diverge, fork, move apart, part, separate, sunder. **2** allocate, allot, apportion, break up, cut up, deal out, dispense, distribute, dole out, give out, halve, measure out, mete out, parcel out, pass round, share out. **3** *divide a party.* cause disagreement in, disunite, polarize, split. **4** *divide into sets.* arrange, categorize, classify, grade, group, sort out, subdivide. *Opp* GATHER, UNITE.

divine *adj* angelic, celestial, godlike, hallowed, heavenly, holy, immortal, mystical, religious, sacred, saintly, seraphic, spiritual, superhuman, supernatural, transcendental. *Opp* MORTAL. • *n* ▷ CLERGYMAN. • *vb* ▷ PROPHESY.

divinity *n* **1** ▷ GOD. **2** religion, religious studies, theology.

division *n* **1** allocation, allotment, apportionment, cutting up, dividing, partition, segmentation, separation, splitting. **2** disagreement, discord, disunity, feud, quarrel, rupture, schism, split. **3** alcove, compartment, part, recess, section, segment. **4** *division between rooms, lands.* border, borderline, boundary line, demarcation, divider, dividing wall, fence, frontier, margin, partition, screen. **5** *division of a business.* branch, department, section, subdivision, unit.

divorce *n* annulment, *inf* breakup, decree nisi, dissolution, separation, *inf* split-up. • *vb* annul marriage, dissolve marriage, part, separate, *inf* split up.

dizziness *n* faintness, giddiness, light-headedness, vertigo.

dizzy *adj* bewildered, confused, dazed, faint, giddy, light-headed, muddled, reeling, shaky, swimming, unsteady, *inf* woozy.

do *vb* **1** accomplish, achieve, bring about, carry out, cause, commit, complete, effect, execute, finish, fulfil, implement, initiate, instigate, organize, perform, produce, undertake. **2** *do the garden.* arrange, attend to, cope with, deal with, handle, look after, manage, work at. **3** *do sums.* answer, give your mind to, puzzle out, solve, think out, work out. **4** *Will this do?* be acceptable, be enough, be satisfactory, be sufficient, be suitable, satisfy, serve, suffice. **5** *Do as you like.* act, behave, conduct yourself, perform. **do away with** ▷ ABOLISH. **do up** ▷ DECORATE, FASTEN.

docile *adj* cooperative, domesticated, obedient, submissive, tractable. ▷ TAME.

dock *n* berth, boatyard, dockyard, dry dock, harbour, haven, jetty, landing-stage, marina, pier, port, quay, slipway, wharf. • *vb* **1** anchor, berth, drop anchor, land, moor, put in, tie up. **2** ▷ CUT.

doctor *n* general practitioner, *inf* GP, *inf* medic, medical officer, medical practitioner, *inf* MO, physician, *derog* quack, surgeon.

doctrine *n* axiom, belief, conviction, *Lat* credo, creed, dogma, maxim, orthodoxy, postulate, precept, principle, teaching, tenet, theory, thesis.

document *n* certificate, charter, chronicle, deed, diploma, form, instrument, legal document, licence, manuscript, *inf* MS, paper, parchment, passport, policy, print-out, record, typescript, visa, warrant, will. • *vb* ▷ RECORD.

documentary *adj* **1** authenticated, chronicled, recorded, substantiated, written. **2** factual, historical, non-fiction, real life.

dodge *n* contrivance, device, knack, manoeuvre, ploy, *sl* racket, ruse, scheme, stratagem, subterfuge, trick, *inf* wheeze. • *vb* **1** avoid, duck, elude, escape, evade, fend off, move out of the way, sidestep, swerve, turn away, veer, weave. **2** *dodge work.* shirk, *inf* skive, *inf* wriggle out of. **3** *dodge a question.* equivocate, fudge, hedge, quibble, *inf* waffle.

dog *n* bitch, *inf* bow-wow, *derog* cur, dingo, hound, mongrel, pedigree, pup, puppy, whelp. • *vb* ▷ FOLLOW.

dogma *n* article of faith, belief, conviction, creed, doctrine, orthodoxy, precept, principle, teaching, tenet, truth.

dogmatic *adj* arbitrary, assertive, authoritarian, authoritative, categorical, certain, dictatorial, doctrinaire, *inf* hard-line, hidebound, imperious, inflexible, intolerant, legalistic, narrow-minded, obdurate, opinionated, pontifical, positive. ▷ STUBBORN. *Opp* AMENABLE.

dole *n* [*inf*] benefit, income support, social security, unemployment benefit. **dole out** ▷ DISTRIBUTE. **on the dole** ▷ UNEMPLOYED.

doll *n inf* dolly, figure, marionette, puppet, rag doll.

domestic *adj* **1** family, household, in the home, private. **2** *domestic air service.* indigenous, inland, internal, national.

domesticated *adj* house-broken, house-trained, tame, tamed, trained. *Opp* WILD.

dominant *adj* **1** biggest, chief, commanding, conspicuous, eyecatching, highest, imposing, largest, main, major, obvious, outstanding, pre-eminent, prevailing, primary, principal, tallest, uppermost, widespread. **2** ascendant, controlling, dominating, domineering, governing, influential, leading, powerful, predominant, presiding, reigning, ruling, supreme.

dominate *vb* **1** be dominant, be in the majority, control, direct, govern, influence, lead, manage, master, monopolize, outnumber, preponderate, prevail, rule, subjugate, take control, tyrannize. **2** dwarf, look out over, overshadow, tower over.

domineering *adj* authoritarian, autocratic, *inf* bossy, despotic, dictatorial, high-handed, oppressive, overbearing, *inf* pushy, strict, tyrannical. *Opp* SUBMISSIVE.

donate *vb* contribute, give, grant, hand over, make a donation, present, subscribe, supply.

donation *n* alms, contribution, freewill offering, gift, offering, present, subscription.

donor *n* backer, benefactor, contributor, giver, philanthropist, provider, sponsor, supplier, supporter.

doom *n* destiny, end, fate, fortune, karma, kismet, lot.

doomed *adj* **1** condemned, destined, fated, intended, ordained, predestined. **2** *a doomed enterprise.* accursed, bedevilled, cursed, damned, hopeless, ill-fated, ill-starred, luckless, star-crossed, unlucky.

door *n* barrier, doorway, entrance, exit, French window, gate, gateway, opening, portal, postern, revolving door, swing door, way out.

dormant *adj* **1** asleep, comatose, hibernating, inactive, inert, passive, quiescent, quiet, resting, sleeping. **2** *dormant talent.* hidden, latent, potential, unrevealed, untapped, unused. *Opp* ACTIVE.

dose *n* amount, dosage, measure, portion, prescribed amount, quantity. • *vb* administer, dispense, prescribe.

dossier *n* file, folder, records, set of documents.

dot *n* decimal point, fleck, full stop, iota, jot, mark, point, speck, spot. • *vb* fleck, mark with dots, punctuate, speckle, spot, stipple.

dote *vb* **dote on** adore, idolize, worship. ▷ LOVE.

double *adj* coupled, doubled, dual, duple, duplicated, paired, twin, twofold, two-ply. • *n* clone, copy, counterpart, *Ger* doppelgänger, duplicate, *inf* look-alike, opposite, *inf* spitting image, twin. • *vb* duplicate, increase, multiply by two, reduplicate, repeat. **double back** ▷ RETURN. **double up** ▷ COLLAPSE.

double-cross *vb* cheat, deceive, let down, trick. ▷ BETRAY.

doubt *n* **1** agnosticism, anxiety, apprehension, confusion, cynicism, diffidence, disbelief, disquiet, distrust, fear, hesitation, incredulity, indecision, misgiving, mistrust, perplexity, qualm, reservation, scepticism, suspicion, worry. **2** *doubt about meaning.* ambiguity, difficulty, dilemma, problem, query, question, uncertainty. *Opp* CERTAINTY. • *vb* be dubious, be sceptical about, disbelieve, distrust, fear, feel uncertain about, have doubts about, have misgivings about, have reservations about, hesitate, lack confidence, mistrust, query, question, suspect. *Opp* TRUST.

doubtful *adj* **1** agnostic, cynical, diffident, disbelieving, distrustful, dubious, hesitant, incredulous, sceptical, suspicious, tentative, uncertain, unclear, unconvinced, undecided, unsure. **2** *a doubtful decision.* ambiguous, debatable, dubious, equivocal, *inf* iffy, inconclusive, problematical, questionable, suspect, vague, worrying. **3** *a doubtful ally.* irresolute, uncommitted, unreliable, untrustworthy, vacillating, wavering. *Opp* CERTAIN, DEPENDABLE.

dowdy *adj* colourless, dingy, drab, dull, *inf* frumpish, old-fashioned, shabby, *inf* sloppy, slovenly, *inf* tatty, unattractive, unstylish. *Opp* SMART.

downfall *n* collapse, defeat, overthrow, ruin, undoing.

downhearted *adj* dejected, depressed, discouraged, *inf* down, downcast, miserable, unhappy. ▷ SAD.

downward *adj* declining, descending, downhill, easy, falling, going down. *Opp* UPWARD.

downy *adj* feathery, fleecy, fluffy, furry, fuzzy, soft, velvety, woolly.

drab *adj* cheerless, colourless, dingy, dismal, dowdy, dreary, dull, flat, gloomy, grey, grimy, lacklustre, shabby, sombre, unattractive, uninteresting. *Opp* BRIGHT.

draft *n* **1** first version, notes, outline, plan, rough version, sketch. **2** *bank draft*. cheque, order, postal order. • *vb* block out, compose, delineate, draw up, outline, plan, prepare, put together, sketch out, work out, write a draft of.

drag *vb* **1** draw, haul, lug, pull, tow, trail, tug. **2** *time drags*. be boring, crawl, creep, go slowly, linger, loiter, lose momentum, move slowly, pass slowly.

drain *n* channel, conduit, culvert, dike, ditch, drainage, drainpipe, duct, gutter, outlet, pipe, sewer, trench, water-course. • *vb* **1** bleed, clear, draw off, dry out, empty, evacuate, extract, pump out, remove, tap, take off. **2** drip, ebb, leak out, ooze, seep, strain, trickle. **3** *drain resources*. consume, deplete, exhaust, sap, spend, use up.

drama *n* **1** acting, dramatics, dramaturgy, histrionics, improvisation, stagecraft, theatre, theatricals, thespian arts. **2** comedy, dramatization, farce, melodrama, musical, opera, operetta, pantomime, performance, play, production, screenplay, script, show, stage version, TV version, tragedy. **3** *real-life drama*. action, crisis, excitement, suspense, turmoil.

dramatic *adj* **1** histrionic, stage, theatrical, thespian. **2** *dramatic gestures*. exaggerated, flamboyant, large, overdone, showy. **3** ▷ EXCITING.

dramatist *n* dramaturge, playwright, scriptwriter.

dramatize *vb* **1** adapt, make into a play. **2** exaggerate, make too much of, overdo, overplay, overstate.

drape *n old use* arras, curtain, drapery, hanging, screen, tapestry, valance. • *vb* cover, decorate, festoon, hang, swathe.

drastic *adj* desperate, dire, draconian, extreme, far-reaching, forceful, harsh, radical, rigorous, severe, strong, vigorous.

draught *n* **1** breeze, current, movement, puff, wind. **2** *draught of ale*. dose, drink, gulp, measure, pull, swallow, *inf* swig.

draw *n* **1** attraction, enticement, lure, *inf* pull. **2** dead-heat, dead-lock, stalemate, tie. **3** competition, lottery, raffle. • *vb* **1** drag, haul, lug, pull, tow, tug. **2** *draw a crowd*. allure, attract, bring in, coax, entice, invite, lure, persuade, pull in, win over. **3** *draw a sword*. extract, remove, take out, unsheathe, withdraw. **4** *draw lots*. choose, pick, select. **5** *draw a conclusion*. arrive at, come to, deduce, formulate, infer, work out. **6** *draw water*. drain, let (*blood*), pour, pump, syphon, tap. **7** *draw 1-1*. be equal, finish equal, tie. **8** *draw pictures*. depict, map out, mark out, outline, paint, pen, pencil, portray, represent, sketch, trace. **draw out** ▷ EXTEND. **draw up** ▷ DRAFT, HALT.

drawback *n* defect, difficulty, disadvantage, hindrance, hurdle, impediment, obstacle, obstruction, problem, snag, stumbling block.

drawing *n* cartoon, design, graphics, illustration, outline, sketch. ▷ PICTURE.

dread *n* anxiety, apprehension, awe, *inf* cold feet, dismay, fear, *inf* the jitters, nervousness, perturbation, qualm, trepidation, uneasiness, worry. ● *vb* be afraid of, shrink from, view with horror. ▷ FEAR.

dreadful *adj* alarming, appalling, awful, dire, distressing, evil, fearful, frightful, ghastly, grisly, gruesome, harrowing, hideous, horrible, horrifying, indescribable, monstrous, shocking, terrible, tragic, unspeakable, upsetting, wicked. ▷ BAD, FRIGHTENING.

dream *n* **1** daydream, delusion, fantasy, hallucination, illusion, mirage, nightmare, reverie, trance, vision. **2** ambition, aspiration, ideal, pipedream, wish. ● *vb* conjure up, daydream, fancy, fantasize, hallucinate, have a vision, imagine, think. **dream up** ▷ INVENT.

dreary *adj* bleak, boring, cheerless, depressing, dismal, dull, gloomy, joyless, sombre, uninteresting. ▷ MISERABLE.

dregs *n* deposit, grounds (*of coffee*), lees, precipitate, remains, residue, sediment.

drench *vb* douse, drown, flood, inundate, saturate, soak, souse, steep, wet thoroughly.

dress *n* **1** apparel, attire, clothing, costume, garb, garments, *inf* gear, *inf* get-up, outfit, *old use* raiment. ▷ CLOTHES. **2** frock, gown, robe, shift. ● *vb* **1** array, attire, clothe, cover, fit out, provide clothes for, put clothes on, robe. **2** *dress a wound.* attend to, bandage, bind up, care for, put a dressing on, tend, treat. *Opp* UNCOVER.

dressing *n* bandage, compress, plaster, poultice.

dribble *vb* **1** drool, slaver, slobber. **2** drip, flow, leak, ooze, run, seep, trickle.

drift *n* **1** accumulation, bank, dune, heap, mound, pile, ridge. **2** *drift of a speech.* ▷ GIST. ● *vb* **1** be carried, coast, float, meander, move casually, move slowly, ramble, roam, rove, stray, waft, walk aimlessly, wander. **2** *snow drifts.* accumulate, gather, make drifts, pile up.

drill *n* **1** discipline, exercises, instruction, practice, *sl* square-bashing, training. ● *vb* **1** coach, discipline, exercise, indoctrinate, instruct, practise, rehearse, school, teach, train. **2** bore, penetrate, perforate, pierce.

drink *n* **1** beverage, *inf* bevvy, *inf* cuppa, *inf* dram, draught, glass, *inf* gulp, *inf* night-cap, *inf* nip, pint, *joc* potation, sip, swallow, swig, *inf* tipple, tot. **2** alcohol, *inf* booze, *joc* grog, *joc* liquid refreshment, liquor. □ *ale, beer, bourbon, brandy, champagne, chartreuse, cider, cocktail, Cognac, crème de menthe, gin, Kirsch, lager, mead, perry,* inf *plonk, port, punch, rum, schnapps, shandy, sherry, vermouth, vodka, whisky, wine.* ● *vb* **1** gulp, guzzle, imbibe, *inf* knock back, lap, partake of, *old use* quaff, sip, suck, swallow, swig, *inf* swill. **2** *inf* booze, carouse, get drunk, *inf* indulge, tipple, tope.

drip *n* bead, dribble, drop, leak, splash, spot, tear, trickle. ● *vb* dribble, drizzle, drop, fall in drips, leak, plop, splash, sprinkle, trickle, weep.

drive *n* **1** excursion, jaunt, journey, outing, ride, run, *inf* spin, trip. **2** aggressiveness, ambition, determination, energy, enterprise, enthusiasm, *inf* get-up-and-go, impetus, industry, initiative, keenness, motivation, persistence, *inf* push, vigour, vim, zeal. **3** campaign, crusade, effort. ● *vb* **1** bang, dig, hammer, hit, impel, knock, plunge, prod, push, ram, sink, stab, strike, thrust. **2** coerce, compel, constrain, force, oblige, press, urge. **3** *drive a car.* control, direct, guide, handle, herd, manage, pilot, propel, send, steer. ▷ TRAVEL. **drive out** ▷ EXPEL.

droop *vb* be limp, bend, dangle, fall, flop, hang, sag, slump, wilt, wither.

drop *n* **1** bead, blob, bubble, dab, drip, droplet, globule, pearl, spot, tear. **2** dash, *inf* nip, small quantity, *inf* tot. **3** *a steep drop.* declivity, descent, dive, escarpment, fall, incline, plunge, precipice, scarp. **4** *a drop in price.* cut, decrease, reduction, slump. *Opp* RISE. ● *vb* **1** collapse, descend, dip, dive, fall, go down, jump down, lower, nosedive, plummet, *inf* plump, plunge, sink, slump, subside, swoop, tumble. **2** *drop from a team.* eliminate, exclude, leave out, omit. **3** *drop a friend.* abandon, desert, discard, *inf* dump, forsake, give up, jilt, leave, reject, scrap, shed. **drop behind** ▷ LAG. **drop in on** ▷ VISIT. **drop off** ▷ SLEEP.

drown *vb* **1** engulf, flood, immerse, submerge, swamp. ▷ KILL. **2** *noise drowned my voice.* be louder than, overpower, overwhelm, silence.

drowsy *adj* dozing, dozy, heavyeyed, listless, *inf* nodding off, sleepy, sluggish, somnolent, soporific, tired, weary. *Opp* LIVELY.

drudgery *n* chore, donkey-work, *inf* grind, labour, slavery, *inf* slog, toil, travail. ▷ WORK.

drug *n* **1** cure, medicament, medication, medicine, *old use* physic, remedy, treatment. **2** *inf* dope, narcotic, opiate. □ *analgesic, antidepressant, barbiturate, hallucinogen, pain-killer, sedative, stimulant, tonic, tranquillizer.* □ *caffeine, cannabis, cocaine, digitalis, hashish, heroin, insulin, laudanum, marijuana, morphia, nicotine, opium, phenobarbitone, quinine.* • *vb* anaesthetize, *inf* dope, dose, give a drug to, *inf* knock out, medicate, poison, sedate, stupefy, tranquillize, treat.

drum *n* **1** ▷ BARREL. **2** □ *bass-drum, bongo-drum, kettledrum, side-drum, snare-drum, tambour, tenor-drum,* plur *timpani, tom-tom.*

drunk *adj* delirious, fuddled, incapable, inebriate, inebriated, intoxicated, maudlin. [*slang*] blotto, bombed, boozed-up, canned, high, legless, merry, paralytic, pickled, pie-eyed, pissed, plastered, sloshed, soused, sozzled, stoned, tanked, tiddly, tight, tipsy. *Opp* SOBER.

drunkard *n* alcoholic, *inf* boozer, *sl* dipso, dipsomaniac, drunk, *inf* sot, tippler, toper, *sl* wino. *Opp* TEETOTALLER.

dry *adj* **1** arid, baked, barren, dead, dehydrated, desiccated, moistureless, parched, scorched, shrivelled, sterile, thirsty, waterless. *Opp* WET. **2** *a dry book.* boring, dreary, dull, flat, prosaic, stale, tedious, tiresome, uninspired, uninteresting. *Opp* LIVELY. **3** *dry humour. inf* dead-pan, droll, expressionless, laconic, lugubrious, unsmiling. • *vb* become dry, dehumidify, dehydrate, desiccate, go hard, make dry, parch, shrivel, wilt, wither.

dual *adj* binary, coupled, double, duplicate, linked, paired, twin.

dubious *adj* **1** ▷ DOUBTFUL. **2** *a dubious character. inf* fishy, *inf* shady, suspect, suspicious, unreliable, untrustworthy.

duck *vb* **1** avoid, bend, bob down, crouch, dip down, dodge, evade, sidestep, stoop, swerve, take evasive action. **2** immerse, plunge, push under, submerge.

due *adj* **1** in arrears, outstanding, owed, owing, payable, unpaid. **2** *due consideration.* adequate, appropriate, decent, deserved, expected, fitting, just, mature, merited, proper, requisite, right, rightful, scheduled, sufficient, suitable, wellearned. • *n* deserts, entitlement, merits, reward, rights. **dues** ▷ DUTY.

dull *adj* **1** dim, dingy, dowdy, drab, dreary, faded, flat, gloomy, lacklustre, lifeless, matt, plain, shabby, sombre, subdued. **2** *a dull sky.* cloudy, dismal, grey, heavy, leaden, murky, overcast, sullen, sunless. **3** *a dull sound.* deadened, indistinct, muffled, muted. **4** *a dull student.* dense, dim, dim-witted, obtuse, slow, *inf* thick, unimaginative, unintelligent, unresponsive. ▷ STUPID. **5** *a dull edge.* blunt, blunted, unsharpened. **6** *dull talk.* boring, commonplace, dry, monotonous, prosaic, stodgy, tame, tedious, unexciting, uninteresting. *Opp* BRIGHT, SHARP.

dumb *adj* inarticulate, *inf* mum, mute, silent, speechless, tongue-tied, unable to speak.

dummy *n* **1** copy, counterfeit, duplicate, imitation, mock-up, model, reproduction, sample, sham, simulation, substitute, toy. **2** doll, figure, manikin, puppet.

dump *n* **1** junkyard, rubbish-heap, tip. **2** *arms dump*. arsenal, cache, depot, hoard, store. ● *vb* deposit, discard, dispose of, *inf* ditch, drop, empty out, get rid of, jettison, offload, *inf* park, place, put down, reject, scrap, throw away, throw down, tip, unload.

dune *n* drift, hillock, hummock, mound, sand-dune.

dungeon *n* old use donjon, gaol, keep, lock-up, oubliette, pit, prison, vault.

duplicate *adj* alternative, copied, corresponding, identical, matching, second, twin. ● *n* carbon copy, clone, copy, double, facsimile, imitation, likeness, *inf* look-alike, match, photocopy, photostat, replica, reproduction, twin, Xerox. ● *vb* copy, do again, double up on, photocopy, print, repeat, reproduce, Xerox.

durable *adj* enduring, hard-wearing, heavy-duty, indestructible, long-lasting, permanent, resilient, stout, strong, substantial, thick, tough. *Opp* IMPERMANENT, WEAK.

dusk *n* evening, gloaming, gloom, sundown, sunset, twilight.

dust *n* dirt, grime, grit, particles, powder.

dusty *adj* **1** chalky, crumbly, dry, fine, friable, gritty, powdery, sandy, sooty. **2** *a dusty room*. dirty, filthy, grimy, grubby, mucky, uncleaned, unswept.

dutiful *adj* attentive, careful, compliant, conscientious, devoted, diligent, faithful, hard-working, loyal, obedient, obliging, punctilious, reliable, responsible, scrupulous, thorough, trustworthy, willing. *Opp* IRRESPONSIBLE.

duty *n* **1** allegiance, faithfulness, loyalty, obedience, obligation, onus, responsibility, service. **2** assignment, business, charge, chore, function, job, office, role, stint, task, work. **3** charge, customs, dues, fee, impost, levy, tariff, tax, toll.

dwarf *adj* ▷ SMALL. ● *n* midget, pigmy. ● *vb* dominate, look bigger than, overshadow, tower over.

dwell *vb* abide, be accommodated, live, lodge, reside, stay. **dwell in** ▷ INHABIT.

dwelling *n* abode, domicile, habitation, home, lodging, quarters, residence. ▷ HOUSE.

dying *adj* declining, expiring, fading, failing, moribund, obsolescent. *Opp* ALIVE.

dynamic *adj* active, committed, driving, eager, energetic, enterprising, enthusiastic, forceful, *inf* go-ahead, *derog* go-getting, high-powered, lively, motivated, powerful, pushful, *derog* pushy, spirited, vigorous, zealous. *Opp* APATHETIC.

E

eager *adj* agog, animated, anxious (*to please*), ardent, avid, bursting, committed, craving, desirous, earnest, enthusiastic, excited, fervent, fervid, hungry, impatient, intent, interested, *inf* itching, keen, *inf* keyed up, longing, motivated, passionate, *inf* raring (*to* go), voracious, yearning, zealous. *Opp* APATHETIC.

eagerness *n* alacrity, anxiety, appetite, ardour, avidity, commitment, desire, earnestness, enthusiasm, excitement, fervour, hunger, impatience, intentness, interest, keenness, longing, motivation, passion, thirst, zeal. *Opp* APATHY.

early *adj* **1** advance, ahead of time, before time, first, forward, premature. *Opp* LATE. **2** ancient, antiquated, initial, original, primeval, primitive. ▷ OLD. *Opp* RECENT.

earn *vb* **1** be paid, *inf* bring in, *inf* clear, draw, fetch in, gain, get, *inf* gross, make, make a profit of, net, obtain, pocket, realize, receive, *inf* take home, work for, yield. **2** attain, be worthy of, deserve, merit, qualify for, warrant, win.

earnest *adj* **1** assiduous, committed, conscientious, dedicated, determined, devoted, diligent, eager, hardworking, industrious, involved, purposeful, resolved, zealous. *Opp* CASUAL. **2** grave, heartfelt, impassioned, serious, sincere, sober, solemn, thoughtful, well-meant.

earnings *plur n* income, salary, stipend, wages. ▷ PAY.

earth *n* clay, dirt, ground, humus, land, loam, soil, topsoil.

earthenware *n* ceramics, china, crockery, *inf* crocks, porcelain, pots, pottery.

earthly *adj* corporeal, human, material, materialistic, mortal, mundane, physical, secular, temporal, terrestrial, worldly. *Opp* SPIRITUAL.

earthquake *n* quake, shock, tremor, upheaval.

earthy *adj* bawdy, coarse, crude, down to earth, frank, lusty, ribald, uninhibited. ▷ OBSCENE.

ease *n* **1** aplomb, calmness, comfort, composure, contentment, enjoyment, happiness, leisure, luxury, peace, quiet, relaxation, repose, rest, serenity, tranquillity. **2** dexterity, easiness, effortlessness, facility, nonchalance, simplicity, skill, speed, straightforwardness. *Opp* DIFFICULTY. • *vb* **1** allay, alleviate, assuage, calm, comfort, decrease, lessen, lighten, mitigate, moderate, pacify, quell, quieten, reduce, relax, relieve, slacken, soothe, tranquillize. **2** edge, guide, inch, manoeuvre, move gradually, slide, slip, steer.

easy *adj* **1** carefree, comfortable, contented, cosy, *inf* cushy, effortless, leisurely, light, painless, peaceful, pleasant, relaxed, relaxing, restful, serene, soft, tranquil, undemanding, unexacting, unhurried, untroubled. **2** clear, elementary, facile, foolproof, *inf* idiot-proof, manageable, plain, simple, straightforward, uncomplicated, understandable, user-friendly. **3** ▷ EASYGOING. *Opp* DIFFICULT.

easygoing *adj* accommodating, affable, amenable, calm, carefree, casual, cheerful, docile, even-tempered, flexible, forbearing, *inf* free and easy, friendly, genial, *inf* happy-go-lucky, indulgent, informal, *inf* laid-back, *derog* lax, lenient, liberal, mellow, natural, nonchalant, open, patient, permissive, placid, relaxed, tolerant, unexcitable, unruffled, *derog* weak. *Opp* STRICT.

eat *vb* consume, devour, digest, feed on, ingest, live on, *old use* partake of, swallow. □ *bite, bolt, champ, chew, crunch, gnaw, gobble, gorge, gormandize, graze, grind, gulp, guzzle,* inf *make a pig of yourself, masticate, munch, nibble, overeat, peck,* inf *scoff,* inf *slurp,* inf *stuff (yourself), taste,* inf *tuck in,* inf *wolf.* □ *banquet, breakfast, dine, feast, lunch, snack,* old use *sup.* **eat away, eat into** ▷ ERODE.

eatable *adj* digestible, edible, fit to eat, good, palatable, safe to eat, wholesome. ▷ TASTY. *Opp* INEDIBLE.

ebb *vb* fall, flow back, go down, recede, retreat, subside. ▷ DECLINE.

eccentric *adj* **1** aberrant, abnormal, anomalous, atypical, bizarre, cranky, curious, freakish, grotesque, idiosyncratic, *sl* kinky, odd, outlandish, out of the ordinary, peculiar, preposterous, quaint, queer, quirky, singular, strange, unconventional, unusual, *sl* wacky, *inf* way-out, *inf* weird, *inf* zany. ▷ ABSURD, MAD. **2** *eccentric circles.* irregular, off-centre. • *n inf* character, *inf* crackpot, crank, *inf* freak, individualist, nonconformist, *inf* oddball, oddity, *inf* weirdie, *inf* weirdo.

echo *vb* **1** resound, reverberate, ring, sound again. **2** ape, copy, duplicate, emulate, imitate, mimic, mirror, reiterate, repeat, reproduce, say again.

eclipse *vb* **1** block out, blot out, cloud, darken, dim, extinguish, obscure, veil. ▷ COVER. **2** excel, outdo, outshine, overshadow, *inf* put in the shade, surpass, top.

economic *adj* budgetary, business, financial, fiscal, monetary, money-making, trading.

economical *adj* **1** careful, cheeseparing, frugal, parsimonious, provident, prudent, sparing, thrifty. ▷ MISERLY. *Opp* WASTEFUL. **2** *an economical meal.* cheap, cost-effective, inexpensive, lowpriced, money-saving, reasonable, *inf* value-for-money. *Opp* EXPENSIVE.

economize *vb* be economical, cut back, retrench, save, *inf* scrimp, skimp, spend less, *inf* tighten your belt. *Opp* SQUANDER.

economy *n* **1** frugality, *derog* meanness, *derog* miserliness, parsimony, providence, prudence, saving, thrift. *Opp* WASTE. **2** *the national economy.* budget, economic affairs, wealth. **3** ▷ BREVITY.

ecstasy *n* bliss, delight, delirium, elation, enthusiasm, euphoria, exaltation, fervour, frenzy, gratification, happiness, joy, rapture, thrill, trance, *old use* transport.

ecstatic *adj* blissful, delighted, delirious, elated, enraptured, enthusiastic, euphoric, exhilarated, exultant, fervent, frenzied, gleeful, joyful, orgasmic, overjoyed, *inf* over the moon, rapturous, transported. ▷ HAPPY.

eddy *n* circular movement, maelstrom, swirl, vortex, whirl, whirlpool, whirlwind. • *vb* move in circles, spin, swirl, turn, whirl.

edge *n* **1** border, boundary, brim, brink, circumference, frame, kerb, limit, lip, margin, outline, perimeter, periphery, rim, side, verge. **2** *edge of town.* outlying parts, outskirts, suburbs. **3** *edge on a knife.* acuteness, keenness, sharpness. **4** *edge of a curtain.* edging, fringe, hem, selvage. • *vb* **1** bind, border, fringe, hem, make an edge for, trim. **2** *edge away.* crawl, creep, inch, move stealthily, sidle, slink, steal, work your way, worm.

edible *adj* digestible, eatable, fit to eat, palatable, safe to eat, wholesome. ▷ TASTY. *Opp* INEDIBLE.

edit *vb* adapt, alter, amend, arrange, assemble, compile, get ready, modify, organize, prepare, put together, select, supervise the production of. □ *abridge, annotate, bowdlerize, censor, clean up, condense, copy-edit, correct, cut, dub, emend, expurgate, format, polish, proof-read, rearrange, rephrase, revise, rewrite, select, shorten, splice* (film).

edition *n* **1** copy, issue, number. **2** impression, printing, print-run, publication, version.

educate *vb* bring up, civilize, coach, counsel, cultivate, discipline, drill, edify, enlighten, guide, improve, inculcate, indoctrinate, inform, instruct, lecture, nurture, rear, school, teach, train, tutor.

educated *adj* cultured, enlightened, erudite, knowledgeable, learned, literate, numerate, sophisticated, trained, well-bred, well-read.

education *n* coaching, curriculum, enlightenment, guidance, indoctrination, instruction, schooling, syllabus, teaching, training, tuition. □ *academy, college, conservatory, polytechnic, sixth-form college, tertiary college, university.* ▷ SCHOOL, TEACHING.

eerie *adj inf* creepy, frightening, ghostly, mysterious, *inf* scary, spectral, *inf* spooky, strange, uncanny, unearthly, unnatural, weird.

effect *n* **1** aftermath, conclusion, consequence, impact, influence, issue, outcome, repercussion, result, sequel, upshot. **2** feeling, illusion, impression, sensation, sense. • *vb* accomplish, achieve, bring about, bring in, carry out, cause, create, effectuate, enforce, execute, implement, initiate, make, produce, put into effect, secure.

effective *adj* **1** able, capable, competent, effectual, efficacious, functional, impressive, potent, powerful, productive, proficient, real, serviceable, strong, successful, useful, worthwhile. ▷ EFFICIENT. **2** *an effective argument.* cogent, compelling, convincing, meaningful, persuasive, striking, telling. *Opp* INEFFECTIVE.

effeminate *adj* camp, effete, girlish, *inf* pansy, *inf* sissy, unmanly, weak, womanish. *Opp* MANLY.

effervesce *vb* bubble, ferment, fizz, foam, froth, sparkle.

effervescent *adj* bubbling, bubbly, carbonated, fizzy, foaming, frothy, gassy, sparkling.

efficient *adj* businesslike, cost-effective, economic, productive, streamlined, thrifty. ▷ EFFECTIVE. *Opp* INEFFICIENT.

effort *n* **1** application, diligence, *inf* elbow grease, endeavour, exertion, industry, labour, pains, strain, stress, striving, struggle, toil, *old use* travail, trouble, work. **2** *a brave effort.* attempt, endeavour, go, try, venture. **3** *a successful effort.* accomplishment, achievement, exploit, feat, job, outcome, product, production, result.

effusive *adj* demonstrative, ebullient, enthusiastic, exuberant, fulsome, gushing, lavish, *inf* over the top, profuse, voluble. *Opp* RETICENT.

egoism *n* egocentricity, egotism, narcissism, pride, self-centredness, self-importance, self-interest, selfishness, self-love, self-regard, vanity.

egotistical *adj* egocentric, self-admiring, self-centred, selfish. ▷ CONCEITED.

eject *vb* **1** banish, *inf* boot out, *inf* bundle out, deport, discharge, dismiss, drive out, evict, exile, expel, get rid of, *inf* kick out, oust, push out, put out, remove, sack, send out, shoot out, *inf* shove out, throw out, turn out. **2** ▷ EMIT.

elaborate *adj* **1** complex, complicated, detailed, exhaustive, intricate, involved, meticulous, minute, painstaking, thorough, well worked out. **2** *elaborate décor.* baroque, busy, Byzantine, decorative, fancy, fantastic, fussy, grotesque, intricate, ornamental, ornamented, ornate, rococo, showy. *Opp* SIMPLE. • *vb* add to, adorn, amplify, complicate, decorate, develop, embellish, enlarge on, enrich, expand, expatiate on, fill out, flesh out, give details of, improve on, ornament. *Opp* SIMPLIFY.

elapse *vb* go by, lapse, pass, slip by.

elastic *adj* bendy, bouncy, ductile, expandable, flexible, plastic, pliable, pliant, resilient, rubbery, *inf* springy, stretchable, *inf* stretchy, yielding. *Opp* RIGID.

elderly *adj* ageing, *inf* getting on, oldish. ▷ OLD.

elect *adj* [*goes after noun*] *president elect.* [*synonyms used after noun*] designate, to be; [*synonyms before noun*] chosen, elected, prospective, selected. • *vb* adopt, appoint, choose, name, nominate, opt for, pick, select, vote for.

election *n* ballot, choice, plebiscite, poll, referendum, selection, vote, voting.

electioneer *vb* campaign, canvass.

electorate *n* constituents, electors, voters.

electric *adj* **1** battery-operated, electrical, mains-operated. **2** *electric atmosphere.* electrifying. ▷ EXCITING.

electricity *n* current, energy, power, power supply.

elegant *adj* artistic, beautiful, chic, courtly, cultivated, dapper, debonair, dignified, exquisite, fashionable, fine, genteel, graceful, gracious, handsome, luxurious, modish, noble, pleasing, *inf* plush, *inf* posh, refined, smart, soigné(e), sophisticated, splendid, stately, stylish, suave, tasteful, urbane, well-bred. *Opp* INELEGANT.

elegy *n* dirge, lament, requiem.

element *n* **1** component, constituent, detail, essential, factor, feature, fragment, hint, ingredient, part, piece, small amount, trace, unit. **2** *in your element.* domain, environment, habitat, medium, sphere, territory. **elements** ▷ RUDIMENTS, WEATHER.

elementary *adj* basic, early, first, fundamental, initial, introductory, primary, principal, rudimentary, simple, straightforward, uncomplicated, understandable. ▷ EASY. *Opp* ADVANCED.

elevate *vb* exalt, hold up, lift, make higher, promote, rear. ▷ RAISE. **elevated** ▷ HIGH, NOBLE.

elicit *vb* bring out, call forth, derive, draw out, evoke, extort, extract, get, obtain, wrest, wring.

eligible *adj* acceptable, allowed, appropriate, authorized, available, competent, equipped, fit, fitting, proper, qualified, suitable, worthy. *Opp* INELIGIBLE.

eliminate *vb* **1** abolish, annihilate, delete, destroy, dispense with, do away with, eject, end, eradicate, exterminate, extinguish, finish off, get rid of, put an end to, remove, stamp out. ▷ KILL. **2** cut out, drop, exclude, knock out, leave out, omit, reject.

élite *n* aristocracy, best, *inf* cream, first-class people, flower, meritocracy, nobility, top people, *inf* upper crust.

eloquent *adj* articulate, expressive, fluent, forceful, *derog* glib, moving, persuasive, plausible, powerful, unfaltering. *Opp* INARTICULATE.

elude *vb* avoid, circumvent, dodge, *inf* duck, escape, evade, foil, get away from, *inf* give (someone) the slip, shake off, slip away from.

elusive *adj* **1** *inf* always on the move, evasive, fugitive, hard to find, slippery. **2** *elusive meaning.* ambiguous, baffling, deceptive, hard to pin down, indefinable, intangible, puzzling, shifting.

emaciated *adj* anorectic, atrophied, bony, cadaverous, gaunt, haggard, shrivelled, skeletal, skinny, starved, underfed, undernourished, wasted away, wizened. ▷ THIN.

emancipate *vb* deliver, discharge, enfranchise, free, give rights to, let go, liberate, loose, manumit, release, set free, unchain. *Opp* ENSLAVE.

embankment *n* bank, causeway, dam, earthwork, mound, rampart.

embark *vb* board, depart, go aboard, leave, set out. *Opp* DISEMBARK. **embark on** ▷ BEGIN.

embarrass *vb* abash, chagrin, confuse, discomfit, discompose, disconcert, discountenance, disgrace, distress, fluster, humiliate, *inf* make you blush, mortify, *inf* put you on the spot, shame, *inf* show up, upset.

embarrassed ▷ ASHAMED. **embarrassing** ▷ AWKWARD, SHAMEFUL.

embellish *vb* adorn, beautify, deck, decorate, embroider, garnish, ornament, *sl* tart up, *inf* titivate. ▷ ELABORATE.

embezzle *vb* appropriate, misapply, misappropriate, peculate, *inf* put your hand in the till, take fraudulently. ▷ STEAL.

embezzlement *n* fraud, misappropriation, misuse of funds, peculation, stealing, theft.

embittered *adj* acid, bitter, disillusioned, envious, rancorous, resentful, sour. ▷ ANGRY.

emblem *n* badge, crest, device, image, insignia, mark, regalia, seal, sign, symbol, token.

embody *vb* **1** exemplify, express, incarnate, manifest, personify, reify, represent, stand for, symbolize. **2** bring together, combine, comprise, embrace, enclose, gather together, include, incorporate, integrate, involve, take in, unite.

embrace *vb* **1** clasp, cling to, cuddle, enfold, fondle, grasp, hold, hug, kiss, snuggle up to. **2** *embrace new ideas.* accept, espouse, receive, take on, welcome. **3** ▷ EMBODY.

embryonic *adj* early, immature, just beginning, rudimentary, underdeveloped, undeveloped, unformed. *Opp* MATURE.

emerge *vb* appear, arise, be revealed, come out, come to light, come to notice, emanate, *old use* issue forth, leak out, *inf* pop up, proceed, surface, transpire, *inf* turn out.

emergency *n* crisis, danger, difficulty, exigency, predicament, serious situation.

emigrate *vb* depart, go abroad, leave, quit, relocate, resettle, set out.

eminent *adj* august, celebrated, conspicuous, distinguished, elevated, esteemed, exalted, familiar, famous, great, high-ranking, honoured, illustrious, important, notable, noted, noteworthy, outstanding, pre-eminent, prominent, renowned, well-known. *Opp* LOWLY.

emit *vb* belch, discharge, disgorge, ejaculate, eject, exhale, expel, exude, give off, give out, issue, radiate, send out, spew out, spout, transmit, vent, vomit.

emotion *n* agitation, excitement, feeling, fervour, passion, sentiment, warmth. ▷ ANGER, LOVE, etc.

emotional *adj* **1** ardent, demonstrative, enthusiastic, excited, fervent, fiery, heated, hot-headed, impassioned, intense, irrational, moved, passionate, romantic, stirred, touched, warm-hearted, *inf* worked up. ▷ ANGRY, LOVING, etc. **2** *emotional language.* affecting, biased, emotive, heartfelt, heart-rending, inflammatory, loaded, moving, pathetic, poignant, prejudiced, provocative, sentimental, stirring, subjective, tear-jerking, tender, touching. *Opp* UNEMOTIONAL.

emphasis *n* accent, attention, force, gravity, importance, intensity, priority, prominence, strength, stress, urgency, weight.

emphasize *vb* accent, accentuate, bring out, dwell on, focus on, foreground, give emphasis to, highlight, impress, insist on, make obvious, *inf* play up, point up, *inf* press home, *inf* rub it in, show clearly, spotlight, stress, underline, underscore.

emphatic *adj* affirmative, assertive, categorical, confident, dogmatic, definite, firm, forceful, insistent, positive, pronounced, resolute, strong, uncompromising, unequivocal. *Opp* TENTATIVE.

empirical *adj* experiential, experimental, observed, practical, pragmatic. *Opp* THEORETICAL.

employ *vb* **1** commission, engage, enlist, have on the payroll, hire, pay, sign up, take on, use the services of. **2** apply, use, utilize.

employed *adj* active, busy, earning, engaged, hired, involved, in work, occupied, practising, working. ▷ BUSY. *Opp* UNEMPLOYED.

employee *n old use* hand, *inf* underling, worker. **employees** staff, workforce.

employer *n* boss, chief, *inf* gaffer, *inf* governor, head, manager, owner, proprietor, taskmaster.

employment *n* business, calling, craft, job, line, livelihood, living, métier, occupation, profession, pursuit, trade, vocation, work.

empty *adj* **1** bare, blank, clean, clear, deserted, desolate, forsaken, hollow, unfilled, unfurnished, uninhabited, unladen, unoccupied, unused, vacant, void. *Opp* FULL. **2** *empty threats.* futile, idle, impotent, ineffective, insincere, meaningless, pointless, purposeless, senseless, silly, unreal, worthless. • *vb* clear, discharge, drain, eject, evacuate, exhaust, pour out, remove, take out, unload, vacate, void. *Opp* FILL.

enable *vb* aid, allow, approve, assist, authorize, charter, empower, entitle, equip, facilitate, franchise, help, license, make it possible, permit, provide the means, qualify, sanction. *Opp* PREVENT.

enchant *vb* allure, beguile, bewitch, captivate, cast a spell on, charm, delight, enrapture, enthral, entrance, fascinate, hypnotize, mesmerize, spellbind. **enchanting** ▷ ATTRACTIVE.

enchantment *n* charm, conjuration, magic, sorcery, spell, witchcraft, wizardry. ▷ DELIGHT.

enclose *vb* bound, box, cage, case, cocoon, conceal, confine, contain, cover, encase, encircle, encompass, enfold, envelop, fence in, hedge in, hem in, immure, insert, limit, package, parcel up, pen, restrict, ring, secure, sheathe, shut in, shut up, surround, wall in, wall up, wrap. ▷ IMPRISON.

enclosure *n* **1** arena, cage, compound, coop, corral, court, courtyard, farmyard, field, fold, paddock, pen, pound, ring, run, sheepfold, stockade, sty, yard. **2** *enclosure in an envelope.* contents, inclusion, insertion.

encounter *n* **1** confrontation, meeting. **2** [*military*] battle, brush, clash, dispute, skirmish, struggle. ▷ FIGHT. • *vb* chance upon, clash with, come upon, confront, contend with, *inf* cross swords with, face, grapple with, happen upon, have an encounter with, meet, *inf* run into.

encourage *vb* **1** abet, advocate, animate, applaud, cheer, *inf* egg on, embolden, give hope to, hearten, incite, inspire, invite, persuade, prompt, rally, reassure, rouse, spur on, support, urge. **2** *encourage sales.* aid, be an incentive to, be conducive to, boost, engender, foster, further, generate, help, increase, induce, promote, stimulate. *Opp* DISCOURAGE.

encouragement *n* applause, approval, boost, cheer, exhortation, incentive, incitement, inspiration, reassurance, *inf* shot in the arm, stimulation, stimulus, support. *Opp* DISCOURAGEMENT.

encouraging *adj* comforting, heartening, hopeful, inspiring, optimistic, positive, promising, reassuring. ▷ FAVOURABLE.

encroach *vb* enter, impinge, infringe, intrude, invade, make inroads, trespass, violate.

end *n* **1** boundary, edge, extreme, extremity, limit, pole, tip. **2** cessation, close, coda, completion, conclusion, culmination, curtain (*of play*), denouement (*of plot*), ending, expiration, expiry, finale, finish, *inf* pay-off, resolution. **3** *journey's end.* destination, home, termination, terminus. **4** *end of a queue.* back, rear, tail. **5** *end of your life.* destiny, destruction, doom, extinction, fate, passing, ruin. ▷ DEATH. **6** *an end in view.* aim, aspiration, consequence, design, effect, intention, objective, outcome, plan, purpose, result, upshot. *Opp* BEGINNING. • *vb* **1** abolish, break off, bring to an end, complete, conclude, cut off, destroy, discontinue, *inf* drop, eliminate, exterminate, finalize, *inf* get rid of, halt, phase out, *inf* put an end to, *inf* round off, ruin, scotch, terminate, *inf* wind up. **2** break up, cease, close, come to an end, culminate, die, disappear, expire, fade away, finish, *inf* pack up, reach a climax, stop. *Opp* BEGIN.

endanger *vb* expose to risk, imperil, jeopardize, put at risk, threaten. *Opp* PROTECT.

endearing *adj* appealing, attractive, captivating, charming, disarming, enchanting, engaging, likable, lovable, sweet, winning, winsome. *Opp* REPULSIVE.

endeavour *vb* aim, aspire, attempt, do your best, exert yourself, strive, try.

endless *adj* **1** boundless, immeasurable, inexhaustible, infinite, limitless, measureless, unbounded, unfailing, unlimited. **2** abiding, ceaseless, constant, continual, continuous, enduring, eternal, everlasting, immortal, incessant, interminable, never-ending, nonstop, perpetual, persistent, unbroken, undying, unending, uninterrupted.

endorse *vb* **1** advocate, agree with, approve, authorize, *inf* back, condone, confirm, *inf* OK, sanction, set your seal of approval to, subscribe to, support. **2** *endorse a cheque.* countersign, sign.

endurance *n* determination, fortitude, patience, perseverance, persistence, pertinacity, resolution, stamina, staying-power, strength, tenacity.

endure *vb* **1** carry on, continue, exist, last, live on, persevere, persist, prevail, remain, stay, survive. **2** bear, cope with, experience, go through, *inf* put up with, stand, *inf* stick, *inf* stomach, submit to, suffer, *sl* sweat it out, tolerate, undergo, weather, withstand. **enduring** ▷ ENDLESS.

enemy *n* adversary, antagonist, assailant, attacker, competitor, foe, opponent, opposition, the other side, rival, *inf* them. *Opp* FRIEND.

energetic *adj* active, animated, brisk, dynamic, enthusiastic, fast, forceful, hard-working, high-powered, indefatigable, lively, powerful, quick-moving, spirited, strenuous, tireless, unflagging, vigorous, zestful. *Opp* LETHARGIC.

energy *n* **1** animation, ardour, *inf* dash, drive, dynamism, élan, enthusiasm, exertion, fire, force, forcefulness, *inf* get-up-and-go, *inf* go, life, liveliness, might, *inf* pep, spirit, stamina, strength, verve, vigour, *inf* vim, vitality, vivacity, zeal, zest. *Opp* LETHARGY. **2** fuel, power.

enforce *vb* administer, apply, carry out, compel, execute, implement, impose, inflict, insist on, prosecute, put into effect, require, stress. *Opp* WAIVE.

engage *vb* **1** contract with, employ, enlist, hire, recruit, sign up, take on. **2** *cogs engage.* bite, fit together, interlock. **3** *engage to do something.* ▷ PROMISE. **4** *engaged me in gossip.* ▷ OCCUPY. **5** *engage in sport.* ▷ PARTICIPATE.

engaged *adj* **1** affianced, betrothed, *old use* plighted, *old use* promised, *old use* spoken for. **2** ▷ BUSY.

engagement *n* **1** betrothal, promise to marry, *old use* troth. **2** *social engagements.* appointment, arrangement, commitment, date, fixture, meeting, obligation, rendezvous. **3** ▷ BATTLE.

engine *n* **1** machine, motor. □ *diesel, electric, internalcombustion, jet, outboard, petrol, steam, turbine, turbo-jet, turbo-prop.* **2** locomotive.

engineer *n* mechanic, technician. ● *vb* ▷ CONSTRUCT, DEVISE.

engrave *vb* carve, chisel, etch, inscribe. ▷ CUT.

enigma *n* conundrum, mystery, *inf* poser, problem, puzzle, riddle.

enjoy *vb* **1** admire, appreciate, bask in, be happy in, delight in, *inf* go in for, indulge in, *inf* lap up, luxuriate in, rejoice in, relish, revel in, savour, take pleasure from, take pleasure in. ▷ LIKE. **2** benefit from, experience, have, take advantage of, use. **enjoy yourself** celebrate, *inf* gad about, *inf* have a fling, have a good time, make merry.

enjoyable *adj* agreeable, amusing, delicious, delightful, diverting, entertaining, gratifying, likeable, *inf* nice, pleasurable, rewarding, satisfying. ▷ PLEASANT. *Opp* UNPLEASANT.

enlarge *vb* amplify, augment, blow up, broaden, build up, develop, dilate, distend, diversify, elongate, expand, extend, fill out, grow, increase, inflate, lengthen, magnify, multiply, spread, stretch, supplement, swell, wax, widen. *Opp* DECREASE. **enlarge on** ▷ ELABORATE.

enlighten *vb* edify, illuminate, inform, make aware. ▷ TEACH.

enlist *vb* **1** conscript, engage, enrol, impress, muster, recruit, sign up. **2** *enlist in the army.* enrol, enter, join up, register, sign on, volunteer. **3** *enlist help.* ▷ OBTAIN.

enliven *vb* animate, arouse, brighten, cheer up, energize, inspire, *inf* pep up, quicken, rouse, stimulate, vitalize, wake up.

enormous *adj* Brobdingnagian, colossal, elephantine, gargantuan, giant, gigantic, gross, huge, hulking, immense, *inf* jumbo, mammoth, massive, mighty, monstrous, mountainous, prodigious, stupendous, titanic, towering, tremendous, vast. ▷ BIG. *Opp* SMALL.

enough *adj* adequate, ample, as much as necessary, sufficient.

enquire *vb* ask, beg, demand, entreat, implore, inquire, query, question, quiz, request. **enquire about** ▷ INVESTIGATE.

enrage *vb* incense, inflame, infuriate, madden, provoke. ▷ ANGER.

enslave *vb* disenfranchise, dominate, make slaves of, subject, subjugate, take away the rights of. *Opp* EMANCIPATE.

ensure *vb* confirm, guarantee, make certain, make sure, secure.

entail *vb* call for, demand, give rise to, involve, lead to, necessitate, require.

enter *vb* **1** arrive, come in, get in, go in, infiltrate, invade, move in, step in. *Opp* DEPART. **2** dig into, penetrate, pierce, puncture, push into. **3** *enter a contest.* engage in, enlist in, enrol in, *inf* go in for, join, participate in, sign up for, take part in, take up, volunteer for. **4** *enter names on a list.* add, inscribe, insert, note down, put down, record, register, set down, sign, write. *Opp* REMOVE. **enter into** ▷ BEGIN.

enterprise *n* **1** adventure, effort, endeavour, operation, programme, project, undertaking, venture. **2** adventurousness, ambition, boldness, courage, daring, determination, drive, energy, *inf* get-up-and-go, initiative, *inf* push. **3** business, company, concern, firm, organization.

enterprising *adj* adventurous, ambitious, bold, courageous, daring, determined, eager, energetic, enthusiastic, *inf* go-ahead, *derog* go-getting, hard-working, imaginative, indefatigable, industrious, intrepid, keen, purposeful, *inf* pushful, *derog* pushy, resourceful, spirited, venturesome, vigorous, zealous. *Opp* UNADVENTUROUS.

entertain *vb* **1** amuse, cheer up, delight, divert, keep amused, make laugh, occupy, please, regale, *inf* tickle. *Opp* BORE. **2** *entertain friends.* accommodate, be host to, be hostess to, cater for, give hospitality to, *inf* put up, receive, treat, welcome. **3** *entertain an idea.* accept, agree to, approve, consent to, consider, contemplate, harbour, support, take seriously. *Opp* IGNORE. **entertaining** ▷ INTERESTING.

entertainer *n* artist, artiste, performer. □ *acrobat, actor, actress, ballerina, broadcaster, busker, clown, comedian, comic, compère, conjurer, dancer, disc jockey, DJ, impersonator, jester, juggler, lion-tamer, magician, matador, mime artist, minstrel, singer, stunt man, toreador, trapeze artist, trouper, ventriloquist.* ▷ MUSICIAN.

entertainment *n* **1** amusement, distraction, diversion, enjoyment, fun, night-life, pastime, play, pleasure, recreation, sport. **2** divertissement, exhibition, extravaganza, performance, presentation, production, show, spectacle. □ *ballet, bullfight, cabaret, casino, ceilidh, cinema, circus, concert, dance, disco, discothèque, fair, firework display, flower show, gymkhana, motor show, nightclub, pageant, pantomime, play, radio, recital, recitation, revue, rodeo, son et lumière, tattoo, television, variety show, waxworks, zoo.* ▷ DANCE, DRAMA, MUSIC, SPORT.

enthusiasm *n* **1** ambition, ardour, avidity, commitment, drive, eagerness, excitement, exuberance, *derog* fanaticism, fervour, gusto, keenness, panache, passion, relish, spirit, verve, zeal, zest. *Opp* APATHY. **2** craze, diversion, *inf* fad, hobby, interest, passion, pastime.

enthusiast *n* addict, adherent, admirer, aficionado, *inf* buff, champion, devotee, fan, fanatic, *sl* fiend, *sl* freak, lover, supporter, zealot.

enthusiastic *adj* ambitious, ardent, avid, committed, *inf* crazy, delighted, devoted, eager, earnest, ebullient, energetic, excited, exuberant, fervent, fervid, hearty, impassioned, interested, involved, irrepressible, keen, lively, *inf* mad (about), *inf* mad keen, motivated, optimistic, passionate, positive, rapturous, raring (*to go*), spirited, unqualified, unstinting, vigorous, wholehearted, zealous. *Opp* APATHETIC. **be enthusiastic** enthuse, get excited, *inf* go into raptures, *inf* go overboard, rave.

entice *vb* allure, attract, cajole, coax, decoy, inveigle, lead on, lure, persuade, seduce, tempt, trap, wheedle.

entire *adj* complete, full, intact, sound, total, unbroken, undivided, uninterrupted, whole.

entitle *vb* **1** call, christen, designate, dub, name, style, term, title. **2** *A licence entitles you to drive.* allow, authorize, empower, enable, justify, license, permit, qualify, warrant.

entitlement *n* claim, ownership, prerogative, right, title.

entity *n* article, being, object, organism, thing, whole.

entrails *plur n* bowels, guts, *inf* innards, inner organs, *inf* insides, intestines, viscera.

entrance *n* **1** access, admission, admittance. **2** appearance, arrival, coming, entry. **3** door, doorway, gate, gateway, ingress, opening, portal, turnstile, way in. **4** ante-room, entrance hall, foyer, lobby, passage, passageway, porch, vestibule. *Opp* EXIT.

entrant *n* applicant, candidate, competitor, contender, contestant, entry, participant, player, rival.

entreat *vb* ask, beg, beseech, implore, importune, petition, sue, supplicate. ▷ REQUEST.

entry *n* **1** insertion, item, jotting, listing, note, record. **2** ▷ ENTRANCE. **3** ▷ ENTRANT.

envelop *vb* cloak, cover, enclose, enfold, enshroud, enwrap, shroud, swathe, veil, wrap. ▷ HIDE.

envelope *n* cover, sheath, wrapper, wrapping.

enviable *adj* attractive, covetable, desirable, favourable, sought-after.

envious *adj* begrudging, bitter, covetous, dissatisfied, *inf* greeneyed, *inf* green with envy, grudging, jaundiced, jealous, resentful.

environment *n* circumstances, conditions, context, ecosystem, environs, habitat, location, milieu, setting, situation, surroundings, territory.

envisage *vb* anticipate, contemplate, dream of, envision, fancy, forecast, foresee, imagine, picture, predict, visualize.

envy *n* bitterness, covetousness, cupidity, desire, discontent, dissatisfaction, ill-will, jealousy, longing, resentment. • *vb* begrudge, grudge, resent.

ephemeral *adj* brief, evanescent, fleeting, fugitive, impermanent, momentary, passing, short-lived, temporary, transient, transitory. *Opp* PERMANENT.

epidemic *adj* general, pandemic, prevalent, spreading, universal, widespread. ● *n* outbreak, pestilence, plague, rash, upsurge.

episode *n* **1** affair, event, happening, incident, matter, occurrence. **2** chapter, instalment, part, passage, scene, section.

epitome *n* **1** archetype, embodiment, essence, exemplar, incarnation, personification, quintessence, representation, type. **2** ▷ SUMMARY.

equal *adj* balanced, coextensive, commensurate, congruent, correspondent, egalitarian, even, fair, identical, indistinguishable, interchangeable, level, like, matched, matching, proportionate, regular, the same, symmetrical, uniform. ▷ EQUIVALENT. *Opp* UNEQUAL. ● *n* clone, compeer, counterpart, equivalent, fellow, peer, twin. ● *vb* **1** balance, correspond to, draw with, tie with. **2** *No one equals Caruso.* be in the same class as, compare with, match, parallel, resemble, rival, vie with.

equality *n* **1** balance, congruence, correspondence, equivalence, identity, similarity, uniformity. *Opp* BIAS. **2** *social equality.* egalitarianism, evenhandedness, fairness, justice, parity. *Opp* INEQUALITY.

equalize *vb* balance, catch up, compensate, even up, level, make equal, match, regularize, *inf* square, standardize.

equate *vb* assume to be equal, compare, juxtapose, liken, match, parallel, set side by side.

equilibrium *n* balance, equanimity, equipoise, evenness, poise, stability, steadiness, symmetry.

equip *vb* accoutre, arm, array, attire, caparison, clothe, dress, fit out, fit up, furnish, *inf* kit out, outfit, provide, stock, supply.

equipment *n* accoutrements, apparatus, appurtenances, *sl* clobber, furnishings, *inf* gear, *inf* hardware, implements, instruments, kit, machinery, materials, outfit, paraphernalia, plant, *inf* rig, *inf* stuff, supplies, tackle, *inf* things, tools, trappings. ▷ CLOTHES.

equivalent *adj* alike, analogous, comparable, corresponding, fair, interchangeable, parallel, proportionate, *Lat* pro rata, similar, synonymous. ▷ EQUAL.

equivocal *adj* ambiguous, circumlocutory, equivocating, evasive, noncommittal, oblique, periphrastic, questionable, roundabout, suspect.

equivocate *vb inf* beat about the bush, be equivocal, dodge the issue, fence, *inf* have it both ways, hedge, prevaricate, quibble, waffle.

era *n* age, date, day, epoch, period, time.

eradicate *vb* eliminate, erase, get rid of, root out, uproot. ▷ DESTROY.

erase *vb* cancel, cross out, delete, efface, eradicate, expunge, obliterate, rub out, wipe away, wipe off. ▷ REMOVE.

erect *adj* perpendicular, rigid, standing, straight, upright, vertical. ● *vb* build, construct, elevate, establish, lift up, make upright, pitch (*a tent*), put up, raise, set up.

erode *vb* abrade, corrode, eat away, eat into, gnaw away, grind down, wash away, wear away.

erotic *adj* amatory, amorous, aphrodisiac, arousing, lubricious, lustful, *sl* randy, *sl* raunchy, seductive, sensual, venereal, voluptuous. ▷ SEXY.

err *vb* be mistaken, be naughty, *sl* boob, *inf* get it wrong, go astray, go wrong, misbehave, miscalculate, sin, *inf* slip up, transgress.

errand *n* assignment, commission, duty, job, journey, mission, task, trip.

erratic *adj* **1** aberrant, capricious, changeable, fickle, fitful, fluctuating, inconsistent, irregular, shifting, spasmodic, sporadic, uneven, unpredictable, unreliable, unstable, unsteady, variable, wayward. *Opp* REGULAR. **2** aimless, directionless, haphazard, meandering, wandering.

error *n inf* bloomer, blunder, *sl* boob, *Lat* corrigendum, *Lat* erratum, fallacy, falsehood, fault, flaw, gaffe, *inf* howler, inaccuracy, inconsistency, inexactitude, lapse, misapprehension, miscalculation, misconception, misprint, mistake, misunderstanding, omission, oversight, sin, *inf* slip-up, solecism, transgression, *old use* trespass, wrongdoing. ▷ WRONG.

erupt *vb* be discharged, be emitted, belch, break out, burst out, explode, gush, issue, pour out, shoot out, spew, spout, spurt, vomit.

eruption *n* burst, discharge, emission, explosion, outbreak, outburst, rash.

escapade *n* adventure, exploit, *inf* lark, mischief, practical joke, prank, scrape, stunt.

escape *n* **1** bolt, breakout, departure, flight, flit, getaway, jail-break, retreat, running away. **2** discharge, emission, leak, leakage, seepage. **3** *escape from reality.* avoidance, distraction, diversion, escapism, evasion, relaxation, relief. • *vb* **1** abscond, *inf* beat it, bolt, break free, break out, *inf* cut and run, decamp, disappear, *sl* do a bunk, elope, flee, fly, get away, *inf* give someone the slip, run away, *sl* scarper, slip away, *inf* slip the net, *inf* take to your heels, *inf* turn tail. **2** discharge, drain, leak, ooze, pour out, run out, seep. **3** *escape the nasty jobs.* avoid, dodge, duck, elude, evade, get away from, shirk, *sl* skive off.

escapism *n* day-dreaming, fantasy, pretence, unreality, wishful thinking.

escort *n* **1** bodyguard, convoy, guard, guide, pilot, protection, protector, safe-conduct. **2** *royal escort.* attendant, entourage, retinue, train. **3** *escort at a dance.* chaperon, companion, *inf* date, partner. • *vb* accompany, attend, chaperon, conduct, guard, *inf* keep an eye on, *inf* keep tabs on, look after, protect, shepherd, stay with, usher, watch.

essence *n* **1** centre, character, core, cornerstone, crux, essential quality, heart, kernel, life, meaning, nature, pith, quiddity, quintessence, soul, spirit, substance. **2** concentrate, decoction, elixir, extract, flavouring, fragrance, perfume, scent, tincture.

essential *adj* basic, characteristic, chief, crucial, elementary, fundamental, important, indispensable, inherent, innate, intrinsic, irreplaceable, key, leading, main, necessary, primary, principal, quintessential, requisite, vital. *Opp* INESSENTIAL.

establish *vb* **1** base, begin, constitute, construct, create, decree, found, form, inaugurate, initiate, institute, introduce, organize, originate, set up, start. **2** *establish yourself in a job.* confirm, ensconce, entrench, install, lodge, secure, settle, station. **3** *establish facts.* accept, agree, authenticate, certify, confirm, corroborate, decide, demonstrate, fix, prove, ratify, recognize, show to be true, substantiate, verify.

established *adj* deep-rooted, deep-seated, indelible, ineradicable, ingrained, long-lasting, long-standing, permanent, proven, reliable, respected, rooted, secure, traditional, well-known, well-tried. *Opp* NEW.

establishment *n* **1** composition, constitution, creation, formation, foundation, inauguration, inception, institution, introduction, setting up. **2** *a well-run establishment.* business, company, concern, enterprise, factory, household, institution, office, organization, shop.

estate *n* **1** area, development, domain, land. **2** assets, belongings, capital, chattels, effects, fortune, goods, inheritance, lands, possessions, property, wealth.

esteem *n* admiration, credit, estimation, favour, honour, regard, respect, reverence, veneration. • *vb* ▷ RESPECT.

estimate *n* appraisal, approximation, assessment, calculation, conjecture, estimation, evaluation, guess, *inf* guesstimate, judgement, opinion, price, quotation, reckoning, specification, valuation. • *vb* appraise, assess, calculate, compute, conjecture, consider, count up, evaluate, gauge, guess, judge, project, reckon, surmise, think out, weigh up, work out.

estimation *n* appraisal, appreciation, assessment, calculation, computation, consideration, estimate, evaluation, judgement, opinion, rating, view.

estuary *n* creek, *Scot* firth, fjord, inlet, *Scot* loch, river mouth.

eternal *adj* ceaseless, deathless, endless, everlasting, heavenly, immeasurable, immortal, infinite, lasting, limitless, measureless, never-ending, permanent, perpetual, timeless, unchanging, undying, unending, unlimited. ▷ CONTINUAL. *Opp* OCCASIONAL, TRANSIENT.

eternity *n* afterlife, eternal life, immortality, infinity, perpetuity.

ethical *adj* decent, fair, good, honest, just, moral, noble, principled, righteous, upright, virtuous. *Opp* IMMORAL.

ethnic *adj* cultural, folk, national, racial, traditional, tribal.

etiquette *n* ceremony, civility, code of behaviour, conventions, courtesy, decency, decorum, form, formalities, manners, politeness, propriety, protocol, rules of behaviour, standards of behaviour.

evacuate *vb* **1** clear, deplete, drain, move out, remove, send away, void. **2** abandon, decamp from, desert, empty, forsake, leave, pull out of, quit, relinquish, vacate, withdraw from.

evade *vb* **1** avoid, *inf* chicken out of, circumvent, dodge, duck, elude, escape from, fend off, flinch from, get away from, shirk, shrink from, shun, sidestep, *inf* skive, steer clear of, turn your back on. **2** *evade a question.* fudge, hedge, parry. ▷ EQUIVOCATE. *Opp* CONFRONT.

evaluate *vb* appraise, assess, calculate the value of, estimate, judge, value, weigh up.

evaporate *vb* dehydrate, desiccate, disappear, disperse, dissipate, dissolve, dry up, evanesce, melt away, vanish, vaporize.

evasive *adj* ambiguous, *inf* cagey, circumlocutory, deceptive, devious, disingenuous, equivocal, equivocating, inconclusive, indecisive, indirect, *inf* jesuitical, misleading, noncommittal, oblique, prevaricating, roundabout, *inf* shifty, sophistical, uninformative. *Opp* DIRECT.

even *adj* **1** flat, flush, horizontal, level, plane, smooth, straight, true. **2** *even pulse.* consistent, constant, equalized, measured, metrical, monotonous, proportional, regular, rhythmical, symmetrical, unbroken, uniform, unvarying. **3** *even scores.* balanced, equal, identical, level, matching, the same. **4** ▷ EVEN-TEMPERED. *Opp* IRREGULAR. **even out** ▷ FLATTEN. **even up** ▷ EQUALIZE. **get even** ▷ RETALIATE.

evening *n* dusk, *poet* eventide, *poet* gloaming, nightfall, sundown, sunset, twilight.

event *n* **1** affair, business, chance, circumstance, contingency, episode, eventuality, experience, happening, incident, occurrence. **2** conclusion, consequence, effect, issue, outcome, result, upshot. **3** activity, ceremony, entertainment, function, occasion. **4** *sporting event.* bout, championship, competition, contest, engagement, fixture, game, match, meeting, tournament.

even-tempered *adj* balanced, calm, composed, cool, equable, even, impassive, imperturbable, pacific, peaceable, peaceful, placid, poised, reliable, self-possessed, serene, stable, steady, tranquil, unemotional, unexcitable, unruffled. *Opp* EXCITABLE.

eventual *adj* concluding, consequent, destined, due, ensuing, expected, final, last, overall, probable, resultant, resulting, ultimate.

everlasting *adj* ceaseless, deathless, endless, eternal, immortal, incorruptible, infinite, lasting, limitless, measureless, never-ending, permanent, perpetual, persistent, timeless, unchanging, undying, unending. *Opp* TRANSIENT.

evermore *adv* always, eternally, for ever, unceasingly.

evict *vb* dislodge, dispossess, eject, expel, *sl* give (someone) the boot, *inf* kick out, oust, put out, remove, throw out, *inf* turf out, turn out.

evidence *n* attestation, certification, confirmation, corroboration, data, demonstration, deposition, documentation, facts, grounds, information, proof, sign, statement, statistics, substantiation, testimony. **give evidence** ▷ TESTIFY.

evident *adj* apparent, certain, clear, discernible, manifest, noticeable, obvious, palpable, patent, perceptible, plain, self-explanatory, unambiguous, undeniable, unmistakable, visible. *Opp* UNCERTAIN.

evil *adj* **1** amoral, atrocious, base, black-hearted, blasphemous, corrupt, criminal, cruel, depraved, devilish, diabolical, dishonest, fiendish, foul, harmful, hateful, heinous, hellish, immoral, impious, infamous, iniquitous, irreligious, machiavellian, malevolent, malicious, malignant, nefarious, pernicious, perverted, reprobate, satanic, sinful, sinister, treacherous, ungodly, unprincipled, unrighteous, vicious, vile, villainous, wicked, wrong. ▷ BAD. *Opp* GOOD. **2** *evil smell.* foul, nasty, pestilential, poisonous, troublesome, unspeakable, vile. ▷ UNPLEASANT. *Opp* PLEASANT. ● *n* **1** amorality, blasphemy, corruption, criminality, cruelty, depravity, dishonesty, fiendishness, heinousness, immorality, impiety, iniquity, *old use* knavery, malevolence, malice, mischief, pain, sin, sinfulness, suffering, treachery, turpitude, ungodliness, unrighteousness, vice, viciousness, villainy, wickedness, wrongdoing. ▷ CRIME. **2** *Poverty is an evil.* affliction, bane, calamity, catastrophe, curse, disaster, enormity, hardship, harm, ill, misfortune, wrong.

evocative *adj* atmospheric, convincing, descriptive, emotive, graphic, imaginative, provoking, realistic, stimulating, suggestive, vivid.

evoke *vb* arouse, awaken, call up, conjure up, elicit, excite, inspire, invoke, kindle, produce, provoke, raise, rouse, stimulate, stir up, suggest, summon up.

evolution *n* advance, development, emergence, formation, growth, improvement, maturation, maturing, progress, unfolding.

evolve *vb* derive, descend, develop, emerge, grow, improve, mature, modify gradually, progress, unfold.

exact *adj* **1** accurate, correct, dead (*centre*), detailed, faithful, faultless, flawless, meticulous, painstaking, precise, punctilious, right, rigorous, scrupulous, specific, *inf* spot-on, strict, true, truthful, veracious. *Opp* IMPRECISE. **2** *exact copy.* identical, indistinguishable, literal, perfect. ● *vb* claim, compel, demand, enforce, extort, extract, get, impose, insist on, obtain, require. **exacting** ▷ DIFFICULT.

exaggerate *vb* **1** amplify, embellish, embroider, enlarge, inflate, *inf* lay it on thick, magnify, make too much of, maximize, overdo, overemphasize, overestimate, overstate, *inf* pile it on, *inf* play up. *Opp* MINIMIZE. **2** ▷ CARICATURE. **exaggerated** ▷ EXCESSIVE.

exalt *vb* boost, elevate, lift, promote, raise, uplift. ▷ PRAISE. **exalted** ▷ HIGH.

examination *n* **1** analysis, appraisal, assessment, audit, catechism, *inf* exam, inspection, investigation, *inf* oral, paper, post-mortem, review, scrutiny, study, survey, test, *inf* viva, *Lat* viva voce. **2** [*medical*] *inf* check-up, scan. **3** *police examination.* cross-examination, enquiry, inquiry, inquisition, interrogation, probe, questioning, trial.

examine *vb* **1** analyse, appraise, audit (*accounts*), check, *inf* check out, explore, inquire into, inspect, investigate, peruse, probe, research, scan, scrutinize, sift, sort out, study, *sl* sus out, test, vet, weigh up. **2** *examine a* *witness.* catechize, cross-examine, cross-question, *inf* grill, interrogate, *inf* pump, question, sound out, try.

example *n* **1** case, illustration, instance, occurrence, sample, specimen. **2** *example to follow.* ideal, lesson, model, paragon, pattern, prototype. **make an example of** ▷ PUNISH.

exasperate *vb inf* aggravate, drive mad, gall, infuriate, irk, irritate, *inf* needle, pique, provoke, rile, vex. ▷ ANNOY.

excavate *vb* burrow, dig, gouge out, hollow out, mine, scoop out, unearth.

exceed *vb* beat, be more than, do more than, go beyond, go over, outnumber, outshine, outstrip, overstep, overtake, pass, transcend. ▷ EXCEL.

exceedingly *adv* amazingly, especially, exceptionally, excessively, extraordinarily, extremely, outstandingly, specially, unusually, very.

excel *vb* beat, be excellent, better, do best, eclipse, outclass, outdo, outshine, shine, stand out, surpass, top. ▷ EXCEED.

excellent *adj inf* ace, admirable, *inf* brilliant, *old use* capital, champion, choice, consummate, *sl* cracking, distinguished, esteemed, estimable, exceptional, exemplary, extraordinary, *inf* fabulous, *inf* fantastic, fine, first-class, first-rate, flawless, gorgeous, great, high-class, ideal, impressive, magnificent, marvellous, model, notable, outstanding, perfect, *inf* phenomenal, remarkable, *inf* smashing, splendid, sterling, *inf* stunning, *inf* super, superb, superlative, supreme, surpassing, *inf* terrific, *inf* tip-top, *old use* top-hole, *inf* top-notch, top-ranking, *inf* tremendous, unequalled, wonderful. *Opp* BAD.

except *vb* exclude, leave out, omit.

exception *n* **1** exclusion, omission, rejection. **2** abnormality, anomaly, departure, deviation, eccentricity, freak, irregularity, oddity, peculiarity, quirk, rarity. **take exception** ▷ OBJECT.

exceptional *adj* **1** aberrant, abnormal, anomalous, atypical, curious, deviant, eccentric, extraordinary, extreme, isolated, memorable, notable, odd, out-of-the-ordinary, peculiar, phenomenal, quirky, rare, remarkable, singular, solitary, special, strange, surprising, uncommon, unconventional, unexpected, unheard-of, unique, unparalleled, unprecedented, unpredictable, untypical, unusual. **2** ▷ EXCELLENT. *Opp* ORDINARY.

excerpt *n* citation, clip, extract, fragment, highlight, part, passage, quotation, section, selection.

excess *n* **1** abundance, glut, overabundance, overflow, *inf* overkill, profit, redundancy, superabundance, superfluity, surfeit, surplus. *Opp* SCARCITY. **2** debauchery, dissipation, extravagance, intemperance, overindulgence, profligacy, wastefulness. *Opp* MODERATION.

excessive *adj* **1** disproportionate, exaggerated, extravagant, extreme, fanatical, immoderate, inordinate, intemperate, needless, overdone, prodigal, profligate, profuse, superfluous, undue, unnecessary, unneeded, wasteful. ▷ HUGE. *Opp* INADEQUATE. **2** *excessive prices.* exorbitant, extortionate, unjustifiable, unrealistic, unreasonable. *Opp* MODERATE.

exchange *n* deal, interchange, reciprocity, replacement, substitution, *inf* swap, switch. • *vb* bargain, barter, change, convert (*currency*), interchange, reciprocate, replace, substitute, *inf* swap, switch, *inf* swop, trade, trade in, traffic. **exchange words** ▷ TALK.

excitable *adj inf* bubbly, chattery, edgy, emotional, explosive, fidgety, fiery, highly-strung, hot-tempered, irrepressible, jumpy, lively, mercurial, nervous, passionate, quick-tempered, restive, temperamental, unstable, volatile. *Opp* CALM.

excite *vb* **1** agitate, amaze, animate, arouse, awaken, discompose, disturb, elate, electrify, enthral, exhilarate, fluster, *inf* get going, incite, inflame, interest, intoxicate, make excited, move, perturb, provoke, rouse, stimulate, stir up, thrill, titillate, *inf* turn on, upset, urge, *inf* wind up, *inf* work up. **2** *excite interest*. activate, cause, elicit, encourage, engender, evoke, fire, generate, kindle, motivate, produce, set off, whet. *Opp* CALM.

excited *adj* agitated, boisterous, delirious, eager, enthusiastic, excitable, exuberant, feverish, frantic, frenzied, heated, *inf* het up, hysterical, impassioned, intoxicated, lively, moved, nervous, overwrought, restless, spirited, vivacious, wild. *Opp* APATHETIC.

excitement *n* action, activity, adventure, agitation, animation, commotion, delirium, drama, eagerness, enthusiasm, furore, fuss, heat, intensity, *inf* kicks, passion, stimulation, suspense, tension, thrill, unrest.

exciting *adj* cliff-hanging, dramatic, electric, electrifying, eventful, fast-moving, galvanizing, gripping, heady, hair-raising, inspiring, intoxicating, *inf* nailbiting, provocative, riveting, rousing, sensational, spectacular, spine-tingling, stimulating, stirring, suspenseful, tense, thrilling. ▷ AMAZING. *Opp* BORING.

exclaim *vb* bawl, bellow, blurt out, call, cry out, *old use* ejaculate, shout, utter, vociferate, yell. ▷ SAY.

exclamation *n* bellow, call, cry, *old use* ejaculation, expletive, interjection, oath, shout, swear-word, utterance, vociferation, yell.

exclude *vb* ban, banish, bar, blacklist, debar, disallow, disown, eject, except, excommunicate, expel, forbid, interdict, keep out, leave out, lock out, omit, ostracize, oust, outlaw, prohibit, proscribe, put an embargo on, refuse, reject, repudiate, rule out, shut out, veto. ▷ REMOVE. *Opp* INCLUDE.

exclusive *adj* **1** limiting, restricted, sole, unique, unshared. **2** *an exclusive club*. clannish, classy, closed, fashionable, *sl* posh, private, restrictive, select, selective, snobbish, *inf* upmarket.

excreta *plur n* droppings, dung, excrement, faeces, manure, sewage, waste matter.

excrete *vb* defecate, evacuate the bowels, go to the lavatory, relieve yourself.

excursion *n* cruise, expedition, jaunt, journey, outing, ramble, tour, trip, voyage. ▷ TRAVEL.

excuse *n* alibi, apology, defence, explanation, extenuation, justification, mitigation, palliation, plea, pretext, rationalization, reason, vindication. • *vb* **1** apologize for, condone, disregard, explain away, forgive, ignore, justify, mitigate, overlook, pardon, pass over, sanction, tolerate, vindicate, warrant. **2** absolve, acquit, clear, discharge, exculpate, exempt, exonerate, free, let off, *inf* let off the hook, liberate, release. *Opp* BLAME.

execute *vb* **1** accomplish, achieve, bring off, carry out, complete, discharge, do, effect, enact, finish, implement, perform, *inf* pull off. **2** kill, put to death. □ *behead, burn, crucify, decapitate, electrocute, garrotte, gas, guillotine, hang, lynch, shoot, stone.*

executive *n* administrator, *inf* boss, director, manager, officer. ▷ CHIEF.

exemplary *adj* admirable, commendable, faultless, flawless, ideal, model, perfect, praiseworthy, unexceptionable.

exemplify *vb* demonstrate, depict, embody, illustrate, personify, represent, show, symbolize, typify.

exempt *vb* except, exclude, excuse, free, let off, *inf* let off the hook, liberate, release, spare.

exercise *n* **1** action, activity, aerobics, callisthenics, effort, exertion, games, gymnastics, PE, sport, *inf* warm-up, *inf* work-out. **2** *military exercises*. discipline, drill, manoeuvres, operation, practice, training. • *vb* **1** apply, bring to bear, display, effect, employ, execute, exert, expend, implement, put to use, show, use, utilize, wield. **2** *exercise your body*. discipline, drill, exert, jog, keep fit, practise, train, *inf* work out. **3** ▷ WORRY.

exertion *n* action, effort, endeavour, strain, striving, struggle. ▷ WORK.

exhaust *n* discharge, effluent, emission, fumes, gases, smoke. ● *vb* **1** consume, deplete, dissipate, drain, dry up, empty, expend, finish off, *inf* run through, sap, spend, use up, void. **2** debilitate, enervate, *inf* fag, fatigue, prostrate, tax, tire, wear out, weary. **exhausted** ▷ BREATHLESS, WEARY.

exhausting *adj* arduous, backbreaking, crippling, debilitating, demanding, difficult, enervating, fatiguing, gruelling, hard, laborious, punishing, severe, strenuous, taxing, tiring, wearying.

exhaustion *n* debility, fatigue, lassitude, tiredness, weakness, weariness.

exhaustive *adj inf* all-out, careful, comprehensive, full-scale, intensive, meticulous, thorough. *Opp* INCOMPLETE.

exhibit *vb* **1** arrange, display, offer, present, put up, set up, show. **2** *exhibit knowledge*. air, betray, brandish, demonstrate, disclose, evidence, express, *derog* flaunt, indicate, manifest, *derog* parade, reveal, *derog* show off. *Opp* HIDE.

exhibition *n* demonstration, display, *inf* expo, exposition, presentation, show.

exhilarating *adj* bracing, cheering, enlivening, exciting, invigorating, refreshing, rejuvenating, stimulating, tonic, uplifting. ▷ HAPPY.

exhort *vb* advise, encourage, harangue, *inf* give a pep talk to, lecture, sermonize, urge.

exile *n* **1** banishment, deportation, expatriation, expulsion, transportation. **2** deportee, displaced person, émigré, expatriate, outcast, refugee, wanderer. ● *vb* ban, banish, bar, deport, drive out, eject, evict, expatriate, expel, oust, send away, transport.

exist *vb* **1** be, be found, be in existence, be real, happen, occur. **2** abide, continue, endure, hold out, keep going, last, live, remain alive, subsist, survive. **existing** ▷ ACTUAL, CURRENT, LIVING.

existence *n* actuality, being, continuance, life, living, persistence, reality, survival.

exit *n* **1** barrier, door, doorway, egress, gate, gateway, opening, portal, way out. **2** *a hurried exit*. departure, escape, evacuation, exodus, flight, leave-taking, retreat, withdrawal. ● *vb* ▷ DEPART.

exorbitant *adj* disproportionate, excessive, extortionate, extravagant, high, inordinate, outrageous, profiteering, prohibitive, *inf* sky-high, *inf* steep, *inf* stiff, *inf* swingeing, top, unjustifiable, unrealistic, unreasonable, unwarranted. ▷ EXPENSIVE. *Opp* REASONABLE.

exotic *adj* **1** alien, faraway, foreign, remote, romantic, unfamiliar, wonderful. **2** bizarre, colourful, different, exciting, extraordinary, foreign-looking, novel, odd, outlandish, peculiar, rare, singular, strange, striking, unfamiliar, unusual, weird. *Opp* ORDINARY.

expand *vb* **1** amplify, augment, broaden, build up, develop, diversify, elaborate, enlarge, extend, fill out, heighten, increase, make bigger, make longer, prolong. **2** become bigger, dilate, distend, grow, increase, lengthen, open out, stretch, swell, thicken, widen. *Opp* CONTRACT.

expanse *n* area, breadth, extent, range, sheet, space, spread, stretch, sweep, surface, tract.

expansive *adj* **1** affable, amiable, communicative, effusive, extrovert, friendly, genial, open, outgoing, sociable, well-disposed. ▷ TALKATIVE. *Opp* TACITURN. **2** ▷ BROAD. *Opp* NARROW.

expect *vb* **1** anticipate, await, bank on, bargain for, be prepared for, contemplate, count on, envisage, forecast, foresee, have faith in, hope for, imagine, look forward to, plan for, predict, prophesy, reckon on, wait for. **2** *expect obedience.* consider necessary, demand, insist on, look for, rely on, require, want. **3** *I expect he'll come.* assume, believe, conjecture, guess, imagine, judge, presume, presuppose, suppose, surmise, think. **expected** ▷ PREDICTABLE.

expectant *adj* **1** eager, hopeful, *inf* keyed up, *inf* on tenterhooks, optimistic, ready. **2** *inf* expecting, pregnant.

expedient *adj* advantageous, advisable, appropriate, apropos, beneficial, convenient, desirable, helpful, judicious, opportune, politic, practical, pragmatic, profitable, propitious, prudent, right, sensible, suitable, to your advantage, useful, worthwhile. • *n* contrivance, device, *inf* dodge, manoeuvre, means, measure, method, *inf* ploy, recourse, resort, ruse, scheme, stratagem, tactics.

expedition *n* crusade, excursion, exploration, journey, mission, pilgrimage, quest, raid, safari, tour, trek, trip, undertaking, voyage.

expel *vb* **1** ban, banish, cast out, *inf* chuck out, dismiss, drive out, eject, evict, exile, exorcise, *inf* fire, *inf* kick out, oust, remove, *inf* sack, send away, throw out, turn out, *inf* turf out. **2** *expel fumes.* belch, discharge, emit, exhale, give out, push out, send out, spew out.

expend *vb* consume, disburse, *sl* dish out, employ, pay out, spend, use.

expendable *adj* disposable, inessential, insignificant, replaceable, *inf* throw-away, unimportant.

expense *n* charge, cost, disbursement, expenditure, fee, outgoings, outlay, overheads, payment, price, rate, spending.

expensive *adj* costly, dear, generous, high-priced, over-priced, precious, *inf* pricey, *inf* steep, *inf* up-market, valuable. ▷ EXORBITANT. *Opp* CHEAP.

experience *n* **1** familiarity, involvement, observation, participation, practice, taking part. **2** background, expertise, *inf* know-how, knowledge, *Fr* savoir faire, skill, understanding, wisdom. **3** *a nasty experience.* adventure, circumstance, episode, event, happening, incident, occurrence, ordeal, trial. • *vb* encounter, endure, face, go through, have a taste of, know, meet, practise, sample, suffer, test out, try, undergo. **experienced** ▷ EXPERT.

experiment *n* demonstration, investigation, *inf* practical, proof, research, test, trial, try-out. • *vb* do experiments, examine, investigate, make tests, probe, research, test, try out.

experimental *adj* **1** exploratory, on trial, pilot, provisional, tentative, trial. **2** *experimental evidence.* empirical, experiential, proved, tested.

expert *adj* able, *inf* ace, *inf* brilliant, capable, competent, *inf* crack, experienced, knowing, knowledgeable, master, masterly, practised, professional, proficient, qualified, skilful, skilled, sophisticated, specialized, trained, wellversed, worldly-wise. ▷ CLEVER. *Opp* UNSKILFUL. • *n inf* ace, authority, connoisseur, *inf* dab hand, genius, *derog* know-all, master, *inf* old hand, professional, pundit, specialist, veteran, virtuoso, *derog* wiseacre, *inf* wizard. *Opp* AMATEUR.

expertise *n* adroitness, dexterity, expertness, judgement, *inf* know-how, knowledge, *Fr* savoir faire, skill.

expire *vb* become invalid, cease, come to an end, discontinue, finish, *inf* run out, terminate. ▷ DIE.

explain *vb* **1** clarify, clear up, decipher, decode, define, demonstrate, describe, disentangle, elucidate, expound, *inf* get across, *inf* get over, gloss, illustrate, interpret, make clear, make plain, provide an explanation, resolve, shed light on, simplify, solve, *inf* sort out, spell out, teach, translate, unravel. **2** *explain a mistake.* account for, excuse, give reasons for, justify, legitimatize, legitimize, make excuses for, rationalize, vindicate.

explanation *n* **1** account, analysis, clarification, definition, demonstration, description, elucidation, exegesis, explication, exposition, gloss, illustration, interpretation, key, meaning, rubric, significance, solution, translation. **2** cause, excuse, justification, motivation, motive, rationalization, reason, vindication.

explanatory *adj* descriptive, expository, helpful, illuminating, illustrative, interpretive, revelatory.

explicit *adj* categorical, clear, definite, detailed, direct, exact, express, frank, graphic, manifest, open, outspoken, patent, plain, positive, precise, put into words, said, specific, *inf* spelt out, spoken, stated, straightforward, unambiguous, unconcealed, unequivocal, unhidden, unreserved, well-defined. *Opp* IMPLICIT.

explode *vb* **1** backfire, blast, blow up, burst, detonate, erupt, go off, make an explosion, set off, shatter. **2** *explode a theory.* debunk, destroy, discredit, disprove, put an end to, rebut, refute, reject.

exploit *n* achievement, adventure, attainment, deed, enterprise, feat. • *vb* **1** build on, capitalize on, *inf* cash in on, develop, make capital out of, make use of, profit by, profit from, trade on, use, utilize, work on. **2** *exploit people. inf* bleed, enslave, ill-treat, impose on, keep down, manipulate, *inf* milk, misuse, oppress, *inf* rip off, *inf* squeeze dry, take advantage of, treat unfairly, withhold rights from.

explore *vb* **1** break new ground, probe, prospect, reconnoitre, scout, search, survey, tour, travel through. **2** *explore a problem.* analyse, examine, inspect, investigate, look into, probe, research, scrutinize, study.

explosion *n* **1** bang, blast, boom, burst, clap, crack, detonation, discharge, eruption, firing, report. **2** *explosion of anger.* fit, outbreak, outburst, *inf* paddy, paroxysm, spasm.

explosive *adj* dangerous, highly-charged, liable to explode, sensitive, unstable, volatile. *Opp* STABLE. • *n* cordite, dynamite, gelignite, gunpowder, TNT.

exponent *n* **1** executant, interpreter, performer, player. **2** advocate, champion, defender, expounder, presenter, propagandist, proponent, supporter, upholder.

expose *vb* bare, betray, dig up, disclose, display, exhibit, lay bare, reveal, show (up), uncover, unearth, unmask. ▷ REVEAL. *Opp* HIDE.

express *vb* air, articulate, disclose, give vent to, make known, phrase, put into words, release, vent, ventilate, voice, word. ▷ COMMUNICATE.

expression *n* **1** cliché, formula, phrase, phraseology, remark, statement, term, turn of phrase, usage, utterance, wording. ▷ SAYING. **2** articulation, confession, declaration, disclosure, revelation, statement. **3** *expression in your voice.* accent, depth, emotion, expressiveness, feeling, intensity, intonation, nuance, pathos, sensibility, sensitivity, sympathy, tone, understanding. **4** *expression on your face.* air, appearance, aspect, countenance, face, look, mien. □ *beam, frown, glare, glower, grimace, grin, laugh, leer, long face, lour, lower, poker-face, pout, scowl, smile, smirk, sneer, wince, yawn.*

expressionless *adj* **1** blank, *inf* dead-pan, emotionless, empty, glassy, impassive, inscrutable, poker-faced, straight-faced, uncommunicative, wooden. **2** boring, dull, flat, monotonous, uninspiring, unmodulated, unvarying. *Opp* EXPRESSIVE.

expressive *adj* **1** indicative, meaningful, mobile, revealing, sensitive, significant, striking, suggestive, telling. **2** articulate, eloquent, lively, modulated, varied. *Opp* EXPRESSIONLESS.

exquisite *adj* delicate, elegant, fine, intricate, refined, skilful, well-crafted. ▷ BEAUTIFUL. *Opp* CRUDE.

extend *vb* **1** add to, broaden, build up, develop, draw out, enlarge, expand, increase, keep going, lengthen, make longer, open up, pad out, perpetuate, prolong, protract, *inf* spin out, spread, stretch, widen. **2** *extend a deadline*. defer, delay, postpone, put back, put off. **3** *extend your hand*. give, hold out, offer, outstretch, present, proffer, put out, raise, reach out, stick out, stretch out. **4** *The garden extends to the fence*. continue, range, reach.

extensive *adj* broad, comprehensive, expansive, far-ranging, far-reaching, sweeping, vast, wide, wide-spread. ▷ LARGE.

extent *n* amount, area, bounds, breadth, compass, degree, dimensions, distance, expanse, length, limit, magnitude, measure, measurement, proportions, quantity, range, reach, scale, scope, size, space, spread, sweep, width.

exterior *adj* external, outer, outside, outward, superficial. ● *n* coating, covering, façade, front, outside, shell, skin, surface. *Opp* INTERIOR.

exterminate *vb* annihilate, destroy, eliminate, eradicate, extirpate, get rid of, obliterate, put an end to, root out, terminate. ▷ KILL.

external *adj* exterior, outer, outside, outward, superficial. *Opp* INTERNAL.

extinct *adj* burnt out, dead, defunct, died out, exterminated, extinguished, gone, inactive, vanished. ▷ OLD. *Opp* LIVING.

extinguish *vb* blow out, damp down, douse, put out, quench, slake, smother, snuff out, switch off. ▷ DESTROY. *Opp* KINDLE.

extort *vb* blackmail, bully, coerce, exact, extract, force, obtain by force.

extra *adj* accessory, added, additional, ancillary, auxiliary, excess, further, left-over, more, other, reserve, spare, superfluous, supernumerary, supplementary, surplus, temporary, unneeded, unused, unwanted.

extract *n* **1** concentrate, concentration, decoction, distillation, essence, quintessence. **2** abstract, citation, *inf* clip, clipping, cutting, excerpt, passage, quotation, selection. ● *vb* **1** draw out, extricate, pull out, remove, take out, withdraw. **2** *extract a confession*. extort, force out, *inf* winkle out, *inf* worm out, wrench, wrest, wring. **3** *extract what you need*. choose, cull, derive, distil, gather, glean, quote, select. ▷ OBTAIN.

extraordinary *adj* abnormal, amazing, astonishing, astounding, awe-inspiring, bizarre, breathtaking, curious, exceptional, extreme, fantastic, *inf* funny, incredible, marvellous, miraculous, mysterious, mystical, notable, noteworthy, odd, outstanding, peculiar, *inf* phenomenal, prodigious, queer, rare, remarkable, *inf* sensational, signal, singular, special, staggering, strange, striking, stunning, stupendous, surprising, *inf* unbelievable, uncommon, unheard-of, unimaginable, unique, unprecedented, unusual, *inf* weird, wonderful. *Opp* ORDINARY.

extravagance *n* excess, immoderation, improvidence, lavish-ness, overindulgence, overspending, prodigality, profligacy, self-indulgence, wastefulness. *Opp* ECONOMY.

extravagant *adj* exaggerated, excessive, flamboyant, grandiose, immoderate, improvident, lavish, outrageous, overblown, overdone, pretentious, prodigal, profligate, profuse, reckless, self-indulgent, *inf* showy, spendthrift, uneconomical, unreasonable, unthrifty, wasteful. ▷ EXPENSIVE. *Opp* ECONOMICAL.

extreme *adj* **1** acute, drastic, excessive, greatest, intensest, maximum, severest, *inf* terrific, utmost. ▷ EXTRAORDINARY. **2** distant, endmost, farthest, furthest, furthermost, last, outermost, remotest, ultimate, uttermost. **3** *extreme opinions*. absolute, avant-garde, exaggerated, extravagant, extremist, fanatical, *inf* hard-line, immoderate, intemperate, intransigent, left-wing, militant, obsessive, outrageous, radical, right-wing, uncompromising, *inf* way-out, zealous. ● *n* bottom, bounds, edge, end, extremity, left wing, limit, maximum, minimum, opposite, pole, right wing, top, ultimate.

extroverted *adj* active, confident, exhibitionist, outgoing, positive. ▷ SOCIABLE. *Opp* INTROVERTED.

exuberant *adj* **1** animated, boisterous, *inf* bubbly, buoyant, eager, ebullient, effervescent, energetic, enthusiastic, excited, exhilarated, exultant, high-spirited, irrepressible, lively, spirited, sprightly, vivacious. ▷ CHEERFUL. **2** *exuberant decoration.* baroque, exaggerated, highly-decorated, ornate, overdone, rich, rococo. **3** *exuberant growth.* abundant, copious, lush, luxuriant, overflowing, profuse, rank, teeming. *Opp* AUSTERE.

exultant *adj* delighted, ecstatic, elated, joyful, jubilant, *inf* on top of the world, overjoyed, rejoicing. ▷ EXUBERANT.

eye *n* **1** eyeball, *inf* peeper. **2** discernment, perception, sight, vision. ● *vb* contemplate, examine, inspect, look at, observe, regard, scrutinize, study, watch. ▷ SEE.

eye-witness *n* bystander, looker-on, observer, onlooker, passer-by, spectator, watcher, witness.

F

fabric *n* **1** material, stuff, textile. ▷ CLOTH. **2** *fabric of a building*. constitution, construction, framework, make-up, structure, substance.

fabulous *adj* **1** fabled, fairy-tale, fanciful, fictitious, imaginary, legendary, mythical, story-book. **2** ▷ EXCELLENT.

face *n* **1** appearance, countenance, features, lineaments, look, *sl* mug, *old use* physiognomy, visage. ▷ EXPRESSION. **2** *face of building*. aspect, covering, exterior, façade, facet, front, outside, side, surface. • *vb* **1** be opposite, front, look towards, overlook. **2** *face danger*. appear before, brave, come to terms with, confront, cope with, defy, encounter, experience, face up to, meet, oppose, square up to, stand up to, tackle. **3** *face a wall with plaster*. clad, coat, cover, dress, finish, overlay, sheathe, veneer.

facetious *adj* cheeky, flippant, impudent, irreverent. ▷ FUNNY.

facile *adj* **1** cheap, easy, effortless, hasty, obvious, quick, simple, superficial, unconsidered. **2** *facile talker*. fluent, glib, insincere, plausible, ready, shallow, slick, *inf* smooth.

facility *n* **1** adroitness, alacrity, ease, expertise, fluency, *derog* glibness, skill, smoothness. **2** *a useful facility*. amenity, convenience, help, provision, resource, service.

fact *n* actuality, certainty, *Fr* fait accompli, reality, truth. *Opp* FICTION. **the facts** circumstances, data, details, evidence, information, *sl* the lowdown, particulars, statistics.

factor *n* aspect, cause, circumstance, component, consideration, constituent, contingency, detail, determinant, element, fact, influence, ingredient, item, parameter, part, particular.

factory *n* assembly line, forge, foundry, manufacturing plant, mill, plant, refinery, shop-floor, works, workshop.

factual *adj* **1** accurate, *Lat* bona fide, circumstantial, correct, demonstrable, empirical, faithful, genuine, matter-of-fact, objective, plain, prosaic, provable, realistic, straightforward, true, unadorned, unbiased, undistorted, unemotional, unimaginative, unvarnished, valid, verifiable, well-documented. *Opp* FALSE. **2** *a factual film*. biographical, documentary, historical, real-life. *Opp* FICTIONAL.

faculty *n* ability, aptitude, capability, capacity, flair, genius, gift, knack, power, talent.

fade *vb* **1** blanch, bleach, darken, dim, discolour, dull, etiolate, grow pale, whiten. *Opp* BRIGHTEN. **2** become less, decline, decrease, diminish, disappear, dwindle, evanesce, fail, melt away, vanish, wane, weaken. **3** *flowers fade*. droop, flag, perish, shrivel, wilt, wither.

fail *vb* **1** abort, be a failure, be unsuccessful, break down, close down, come to an end, *inf* come to grief, come to nothing, *sl* conk out, *inf* crash, cut out, fall through, *inf* fizzle out, *inf* flop, *inf* fold, fold up, founder, give up, go bankrupt, *inf* go bust, go out of business, meet with disaster, miscarry, misfire, *inf* miss out, peter out, stop working. **2** *fail in health*. decay, decline, deteriorate, diminish, disappear, dwindle, ebb, fade, get worse, give out, melt away, vanish, wane, weaken. **3** *fail to do something*. forget, neglect, omit. **4** *fail someone*. abandon, disappoint, *inf* let down. *Opp* IMPROVE, SUCCEED.

failing *n* blemish, defect, fault, flaw, foible, imperfection, shortcoming, weakness, weak spot.

failure *n* **1** abandonment, defeat, disappointment, disaster, downfall, fiasco, *inf* flop, loss, miscarriage, *inf* wash-out, wreck. **2** breakdown, collapse, crash, stoppage. **3** *failure to do your duty.* dereliction, neglect, omission, remissness. *Opp* SUCCESS.

faint *adj* **1** blurred, blurry, dim, faded, feeble, hazy, ill-defined, indistinct, misty, muzzy, pale, pastel (*colours*), shadowy, unclear, vague. **2** *faint smell.* delicate, slight. **3** *faint sounds.* distant, hushed, low, muffled, muted, soft, stifled, subdued, thin, weak. **4** *faint in the head.* dizzy, exhausted, feeble, giddy, light-headed, unsteady, vertiginous, weak, *inf* woozy. *Opp* CLEAR, STRONG. • *vb* become unconscious, black out, collapse, *inf* flake out, *inf* keel over, pass out, swoon.

fair *adj* **1** blond, blonde, flaxen, golden, light, yellow. **2** *fair weather.* bright, clear, clement, cloudless, dry, favourable, fine, pleasant, sunny. *Opp* DARK. **3** *a fair decision.* disinterested, evenhanded, fair-minded, honest, honourable, impartial, just, lawful, legitimate, nonpartisan, open-minded, proper, right, unbiased, unprejudiced, upright. *Opp* UNJUST. **4** *a fair standard.* acceptable, adequate, average, indifferent, mediocre, middling, moderate, ordinary, passable, reasonable, respectable, satisfactory, *inf* so-so, tolerable. *Opp* UNACCEPTABLE. **5** ▷ BEAUTIFUL. • *n* **1** amusement-park, fair-ground, fun-fair. **2** bazaar, carnival, exhibition, festival, fête, gala, market, sale, show.

fairly *adv* moderately, pretty, quite, rather, reasonably, somewhat, tolerably, up to a point.

faith *n* **1** assurance, belief, certitude, confidence, credence, reliance, sureness, trust. *Opp* DOUBT. **2** conviction, creed, devotion, doctrine, dogma, persuasion, religion.

faithful *adj* **1** constant, dependable, devoted, dutiful, honest, loyal, reliable, staunch, steadfast, trusted, trusty, trustworthy, unswerving. **2** *a faithful account.* accurate, close, consistent, exact, factual, literal, precise. ▷ TRUE. *Opp* FALSE.

fake *adj* artificial, bogus, concocted, counterfeit, ersatz, factitious, false, fictitious, forged, fraudulent, imitation, invented, made-up, mock, *sl* phoney, pretended, sham, simulated, spurious, synthetic, trumped-up, unfounded, unreal. *Opp* GENUINE. • *n* **1** copy, counterfeit, duplicate, forgery, hoax, imitation, replica, reproduction, sham, simulation. **2** charlatan, cheat, fraud, hoaxer, humbug, impostor, mountebank, *sl* phoney, quack. • *vb* affect, copy, counterfeit, dissemble, falsify, feign, forge, fudge, imitate, make believe, mock up, pretend, put on, reproduce, sham, simulate.

fall *n* **1** collapse, crash, decline, decrease, depreciation, descent, dip, dive, downswing, downturn, drop, lowering, nosedive, plunge, reduction, slant, slump, tumble. **2** *fall of a fortress.* capitulation, capture, defeat, overthrow, seizure, submission, surrender. • *vb* **1** collapse, *inf* come a cropper, crash down, dive, drop down, founder, go down, keel over, overbalance, pitch, plummet, plunge, sink, slump, spiral, stumble, topple, trip over, tumble. **2** become less, become lower, decline, decrease, diminish, dwindle, ebb, lessen, subside. **3** descend, drop, fall away, slope down. **4** *curtains fell in folds.* be suspended, cascade, dangle, dip down, hang. **5** *silence fell.* come, come about, happen, occur, settle. **6** ▷ DIE. **7** ▷ SURRENDER. **fall apart** ▷ DISINTEGRATE. **fall back** ▷ RETREAT. **fall behind** ▷ LAG. **fall down, fall in** ▷ COLLAPSE. **fall off** ▷ DECLINE. **fall out** ▷ QUARREL. **fall through** ▷ FAIL.

fallacy *n* delusion, error, flaw, miscalculation, misconception, mistake, solecism.

fallible *adj* erring, frail, human, imperfect, liable to make mistakes, uncertain, unpredictable, unreliable, weak. *Opp* INFALLIBLE.

fallow *adj* dormant, resting, uncultivated, unplanted, unsown, unused.

false *adj* **1** deceptive, distorted, erroneous, fabricated, fallacious, faulty, fictitious, flawed, imprecise, inaccurate, incorrect, inexact, invalid, misleading, mistaken, spurious, unfactual, unsound, untrue, wrong. ▷ FAKE. **2** *false friends.* deceitful, dishonest, disloyal, double-dealing, double-faced, faithless, lying, treacherous, unfaithful, unreliable, untrustworthy. *Opp* TRUE. **false name** ▷ PSEUDONYM.

falsehood *n* fabrication, *inf* fib, fiction, lie, prevarication, *inf* story, untruth, *sl* whopper.

falsify *vb* alter, *inf* cook (*the books*), counterfeit, distort, exaggerate, fake, forge, *inf* fudge, imitate, misrepresent, mock up, oversimplify, pervert, simulate, slant, tamper with, tell lies about, twist.

falter *vb* **1** become weaker, flag, flinch, hesitate, hold back, lose confidence, pause, quail, stagger, stumble, totter, vacillate, waver. *Opp* PERSIST. **2** stammer, stutter. **faltering** ▷ HESITANT.

fame *n* acclaim, celebrity, distinction, eminence, glory, honour, illustriousness, importance, *inf* kudos, name, *derog* notoriety, pre-eminence, prestige, prominence, public esteem, renown, reputation, repute, *inf* stardom.

familiar *adj* **1** accustomed, common, conventional, current, customary, everyday, frequent, habitual, mundane, normal, ordinary, predictable, regular, routine, stock, traditional, usual, well-known. *Opp* STRANGE. **2** *familiar language. inf* chatty, close, confidential, *derog* forward, *inf* free-andeasy, *derog* impudent, informal, intimate, near, *derog* presumptuous, relaxed, sociable, unceremonious. ▷ FRIENDLY. *Opp* FORMAL. **familiar with** acquainted with, *inf* at home with, aware of, conscious of, expert in, informed about, knowledgeable about, trained in, versed in.

family *n* **1** brood, children, *inf* flesh and blood, generation, issue, kindred, *old use* kith and kin, litter, *inf* nearest and dearest, offspring, progeny, relations, relatives, *inf* tribe. **2** ancestry, blood, clan, dynasty, extraction, forebears, genealogy, house, line, lineage, pedigree, race, strain, tribe. □ *ancestor, descendant.* □ *aunt, brother, child, cousin, daughter, father, fiancé(e), forefather, foster-child, foster-parent, godchild, godparent, grandchild, grandparent, guardian, husband,* Amer *junior, kinsman, kinswoman, mother, nephew, next-of-kin, niece, parent, sibling, sister, son, step-child, step-parent, uncle, ward, widow, widower, wife.*

famine *n* dearth, hunger, lack, malnutrition, scarcity, shortage, starvation, want. *Opp* PLENTY.

famished *adj* craving, famishing, hungry, *inf* peckish, ravenous, starved, starving.

famous *adj* acclaimed, big, celebrated, distinguished, eminent, exalted, famed, glorious, great, historic, honoured, illustrious, important, legendary, lionized, notable, noted, *derog* notorious, outstanding, popular, prominent, proverbial, renowned, revered, time-honoured, venerable, well-known, world-famous. *Opp* UNKNOWN.

fan *n* **1** blower, extractor, propeller, ventilator. **2** *a soccer fan.* addict, admirer, aficionado, *inf* buff, devotee, enthusiast, fanatic, *inf* fiend, follower, *inf* freak, lover, supporter. ▷ FANATIC.

fanatic *n* activist, adherent, bigot, extremist, fiend, freak, maniac, militant, zealot.

fanatical *adj* bigoted, excessive, extreme, fervent, fervid, immoderate, irrational, maniacal, militant, obsessive, overenthusiastic, passionate, rabid, single-minded, zealous. *Opp* MODERATE.

fanciful *adj* capricious, chimerical, fancy, fantastic, illusory, imaginary, imagined, make-believe, unrealistic, whimsical.

fancy *adj* decorative, elaborate, embellished, embroidered, intricate, ornamented, ornate. ▷ FANCIFUL. • *n* ▷ IMAGINATION, WHIM. • *vb* **1** conjure up, dream of, envisage, imagine, picture, visualize. ▷ THINK. **2** be attracted to, crave, *inf* have a yen for, like, long for, prefer, want, wish for. ▷ DESIRE.

fantastic *adj* **1** absurd, amazing, elaborate, exaggerated, extraordinary, extravagant, fabulous, fanciful, far-fetched, grotesque, imaginative, implausible, incredible, odd, quaint, remarkable, rococo, strange, surreal, unbelievable, unlikely, unrealistic, weird. **2** ▷ EXCELLENT. *Opp* ORDINARY.

fantasy *n* chimera, day-dream, delusion, dream, fancy, hallucination, illusion, imagination, invention, make-believe, mirage, pipe-dream, reverie, vision. *Opp* REALITY.

far *adj* distant, far-away, far-off, outlying, remote. *Opp* NEAR.

farcical *adj* absurd, foolish, ludicrous, preposterous, ridiculous, silly. ▷ FUNNY.

fare *n* **1** charge, cost, fee, payment, price, ticket. **2** *festive fare*. ▷ FOOD.

farewell *adj* goodbye, last, leaving, parting, valedictory. • *n* departure, leave-taking, *inf* send-off, valediction. ▷ GOODBYE.

farm *n* farmhouse, farmstead, *old use* grange. □ *arable farm, croft, dairy farm, fish farm, fruit farm, livestock farm, organic farm, plantation, poultry farm, ranch, smallholding.*

farming *n* agriculture, agronomy, crofting, cultivation, foodproduction, husbandry.

fascinate *vb* allure, attract, beguile, bewitch, captivate, charm, delight, enchant, engross, enthral, entice, entrance, hypnotize, interest, mesmerize, rivet, spellbind. **fascinating** ▷ ATTRACTIVE.

fashion *n* **1** convention, manner, method, mode, way. **2** craze, cut, *inf* fad, line, look, pattern, rage, style, taste, trend, vogue.

fashionable *adj Fr* [à] la mode, chic, contemporary, current, elegant, *inf* in, in vogue, the latest, modern, modish, popular, smart, *inf* snazzy, sophisticated, stylish, tasteful, *inf* trendy, up-to-date, *inf* with it. *Opp* UNFASHIONABLE.

fast *adv* at full tilt, briskly, in no time, post-haste, quickly, rapidly, swiftly. • *adj* **1** breakneck, brisk, expeditious, express, hasty, headlong, high-speed, hurried, lively, *inf* nippy, precipitate, quick, rapid, smart, *inf* spanking, speedy, supersonic, swift, unhesitating. *Opp* SLOW. **2** *fast on the rocks*. attached, bound, fastened, firm, fixed, immobile, immovable, secure, tight. **3** *fast colours*. indelible, lasting, permanent, stable. **4** *fast living*. ▷ IMMORAL. • *vb* abstain, deny yourself, diet, go hungry, go without food, starve. *Opp* INDULGE.

fasten *vb* affix, anchor, attach, batten, bind, bolt, buckle, button, chain, clamp, clasp, cling, close, connect, couple, do up, fix, grip, hitch, hook, knot, join, lace, lash, latch on, link, lock, make fast, moor, nail, padlock, paste, peg, pin, rivet, rope, screw down, seal, secure, solder, staple, strap, tack, tape, tether, tie, unite, weld. ▷ STICK. *Opp* UNDO.

fastener *n* bond, connection, connector, coupling, fastening, link, linkage. □ *anchor, bolt, buckle, button, catch, chain, clamp, clasp, clip, dowel, dowel-pin, drawing-pin, glue, gum, hasp, hook, knot, lace, latch, lock, mooring, nail, padlock, painter, paste, peg, pin, rivet, rope, safety-pin, screw, seal, Sellotape, solder, staple, strap, string, tack, tape, tether, tie, toggle, Velcro, wedge, zip.*

fastidious *adj* choosy, dainty, delicate, discriminating, finical, finicky, fussy, hard to please, nice, particular, *inf* pernickety, *inf* picky, selective, squeamish.

fat *adj* **1** bloated, *inf* broad in the beam, bulky, chubby, corpulent, dumpy, flabby, fleshy, gross, heavy, massive, obese, overweight, paunchy, plump, podgy, portly, pot-bellied, pudgy, rotund, round, solid, squat, stocky, stout, thick, tubby, weighty, well-fed. ▷ BIG. **2** *fat meat.* fatty, greasy, oily. *Opp* LEAN. ● *n* □ *adipose tissue, blubber, butter, dripping, grease, lard, margarine, oil, suet.*

fatal *adj* **1** deadly, final, incurable, lethal, malignant, mortal, terminal. **2** ▷ DISASTROUS.

fatality *n* casualty, death, loss.

fate *n* **1** chance, destiny, doom, fortune, karma, kismet, lot, luck, nemesis, *inf* powers above, predestination, providence, the stars. **2** death, demise, destruction, disaster, downfall, end, ruin.

fated *adj* certain, cursed, damned, decreed, destined, doomed, foreordained, inescapable, inevitable, intended, predestined, predetermined, preordained, sure.

father *n* begetter, *inf* dad, *inf* daddy, *inf* pa, *inf* papa, parent, *old use* pater, *inf* pop, sire.

fatigue *n* debility, exhaustion, feebleness, languor, lassitude, lethargy, tiredness, weakness, weariness. ● *vb* debilitate, drain, enervate, exhaust, tire, weaken, weary. **fatigued** ▷ WEARY.

fault *n* **1** blemish, defect, deficiency, demerit, failing, failure, fallacy, flaw, foible, frailty, imperfection, inaccuracy, malfunction, snag, weakness. **2** blunder, *inf* boob, error, failing, *Fr* faux pas, gaffe, *inf* howler, indiscretion, lapse, miscalculation, misconduct, misdeed, mistake, negligence, offence, omission, oversight, peccadillo, shortcoming, sin, slip, transgression, *old use* trespass, vice, wrongdoing. **3** *It was my fault.* accountability, blame, culpability, guilt, liability, responsibility. ● *vb* ▷ CRITICIZE.

faultless *adj* accurate, correct, exemplary, flawless, ideal, in mint condition, irreproachable, sinless, unimpeachable. ▷ PERFECT. *Opp* FAULTY.

faulty *adj* broken, damaged, defective, deficient, flawed, illogical, imperfect, inaccurate, incomplete, incorrect, inoperative, invalid, not working, out of order, shop-soiled, unusable, useless. *Opp* FAULTLESS.

favour *n* **1** acceptance, approbation, approval, bias, favouritism, friendliness, goodwill, grace, liking, partiality, preference, support. **2** *Do me a favour.* benefit, courtesy, gift, good deed, good turn, indulgence, kindness, service. ● *vb* **1** approve of, be in sympathy with, champion, choose, commend, esteem, *inf* fancy, *inf* go for, like, opt for, prefer, show favour to, think well of, value. *Opp* DISLIKE. **2** abet, advance, back, be advantageous to, befriend, forward, promote, support. ▷ HELP. *Opp* HINDER.

favourable *adj* **1** advantageous, appropriate, auspicious, beneficial, benign, convenient, following (*wind*), friendly, generous, helpful, kind, opportune, positive, promising, propitious, reassuring, suitable, supportive, sympathetic, understanding, well-disposed. **2** *a favourable review.* approving, commendatory, complimentary, congratulatory, encouraging, enthusiastic, laudatory. **3** *a favourable reputation.* agreeable, desirable, enviable, good, pleasing, satisfactory. *Opp* UNFAVOURABLE.

favourite *adj* beloved, best, choice, chosen, dearest, esteemed, ideal, liked, loved, popular, preferred, selected, well-liked. ● *n* **1** choice, pick, preference. **2** *inf* apple of your eye, darling, idol, pet.

fear *n* alarm, anxiety, apprehension, apprehensiveness, awe, concern, consternation, cowardice, cravenness, diffidence, dismay, doubt, dread, faint-heartedness, foreboding, fright, *inf* funk, horror, misgiving, nervousness, panic, phobia, qualm, suspicion, terror, timidity, trepidation, uneasiness, worry. ▷ PHOBIA. *Opp* COURAGE. ● *vb* be afraid of, dread, quail at, shrink from, suspect, tremble at, worry about.

fearful *adj* **1** alarmed, apprehensive, frightened, nervous, panic-stricken, scared, terrified, timid. ▷ AFRAID. *Opp* FEARLESS. **2** ▷ FEARSOME.

fearless *adj* bold, brave, dauntless, intrepid, resolute, stoical, unafraid, unconcerned, undaunted, valiant, valorous. ▷ COURAGEOUS. *Opp* FEARFUL.

fearsome *adj* appalling, aweinspiring, awesome, daunting, dreadful, fearful, frightful, intimidating, terrible, terrifying. ▷ FRIGHTENING.

feasible *adj* **1** achievable, attainable, easy, possible, practicable, practical, realizable, viable, workable. *Opp* IMPRACTICAL. **2** *a feasible scenario.* credible, likely, plausible, reasonable. *Opp* IMPLAUSIBLE.

feast *n* banquet, *sl* blow-out, dinner, *inf* spread. ▷ MEAL. ● *vb* dine, gorge, gormandize, *inf* wine and dine. ▷ EAT.

feat *n* accomplishment, achievement, act, action, attainment, deed, exploit, performance.

feather *n* plume, quill. **feathers** down, plumage.

feathery *adj* downy, fluffy, light, wispy.

feature *n* **1** aspect, attribute, characteristic, circumstance, detail, facet, hall mark, idiosyncrasy, mark, peculiarity, point, property, quality, trait. **2** *newspaper feature.* article, column, item, piece, report, story. ● *vb* **1** emphasize, focus on, give prominence to, highlight, *inf* play up, present, promote, show up, *inf* spotlight, *inf* star, stress. **2** *feature in a film.* act, appear, figure, participate, perform, play a role, star, take a part. **features** ▷ FACE.

fee *n* bill, charge, cost, dues, emolument, fare, payment, price, remuneration, subscription, sum, tariff, terms, toll, wage.

feeble *adj* **1** ailing, debilitated, decrepit, delicate, enfeebled, exhausted, faint, fragile, frail, helpless, ill, impotent, inadequate, ineffective, infirm, languid, listless, poorly, powerless, puny, sickly, slight, useless, weak. *Opp* STRONG. **2** effete, feckless, hesitant, incompetent, indecisive, ineffectual, irresolute, *inf* namby-pamby, spineless, vacillating, weedy, wimpish, *inf* wishy-washy. **3** *feeble excuses.* flimsy, insubstantial, lame, paltry, poor, tame, thin, unconvincing.

feed *vb* **1** cater for, give food to, nourish, nurture, provender, provide for, provision, strengthen, suckle, support, sustain, *inf* wine and dine. **2** dine, eat, fare, graze, pasture. **feed on** ▷ EAT.

feel *vb* **1** caress, finger, fondle, handle, hold, manipulate, maul, *inf* paw, pet, stroke, touch. **2** *feel your way.* explore, fumble, grope. **3** *feel the cold.* be aware of, be conscious of, detect, discern, experience, know, notice, perceive, sense, suffer, undergo. **4** *It feels cold.* appear, give a feeling of, seem. **5** *feel something's true.* believe, consider, deem, guess, *inf* have a feeling, *inf* have a hunch, intuit, judge, think.

feeling *n* **1** sensation, sense of touch, sensitivity. **2** ardour, emotion, fervour, passion, sentiment, warmth. **3** *religious feelings.* attitude, belief, consciousness, guess, hunch, idea, impression, instinct, intuition, notion, opinion, perception, thought, view. **4** *a feeling for music.* fondness, responsiveness, sensibility, sympathy, understanding. **5** [*inf*] *a party feeling.* atmosphere, aura, mood, tone, *inf* vibrations.

fell *vb* bring down, chop down, cut down, flatten, *inf* floor, knock down, mow down, prostrate. ▷ KILL.

female *adj* ▷ FEMININE. *Opp* MALE. ● *n* □ *aunt*, old use *damsel*, *daughter*, old use *débutante*, *fiancé*, *girl*, *girlfriend*, *grandmother*, *lady*, inf *lass*, *lesbian*, old use *maid*, old use *maiden*, old use *mistress*, *mother*, *niece*, *sister*, *spinster*, old use or sexist *wench*, *wife*, *woman*. □ *bitch*, *cow*, *doe*, *ewe*, *hen*, *lioness*, *mare*, *nanny-goat*, *sow*, *tigress*, *vixen*.

feminine *adj derog of men* effeminate, female, *derog* girlish, ladylike, womanly. *Opp* MASCULINE.

fen *n* bog, lowland, marsh, morass, quagmire, slough, swamp.

fence *n* barricade, barrier, fencing, hedge, hurdle, obstacle, paling, palisade, railing, rampart, stockade, wall, wire. • *vb* **1** bound, circumscribe, confine, coop up, encircle, enclose, hedge in, immure, pen, restrict, surround, wall in. **2** ▷ FIGHT.

fend *vb* **fend for yourself** care for yourself, do for yourself, *inf* get along, *inf* get by, look after yourself, *inf* scrape along, support yourself, survive. **fend off** ▷ REPEL.

ferment *n* ▷ COMMOTION. • *vb* **1** boil, bubble, effervesce, *inf* fizz, foam, froth, rise, seethe, work. **2** agitate, excite, foment, incite, instigate, provoke, rouse, stir up.

ferocious *adj* bestial, bloodthirsty, brutal, cruel, feral, fiendish, fierce, harsh, inhuman, merciless, murderous, pitiless, sadistic, savage, vicious, wild. *Opp* GENTLE.

ferry *n* ▷ VESSEL. • *vb* carry, export, fetch, import, shift, ship, shuttle, take across, taxi, transport. ▷ CONVEY.

fertile *adj* abundant, fecund, fertilized, flourishing, fruitful, lush, luxuriant, productive, prolific, rich, teeming, well-manured. *Opp* STERILE.

fertilize *vb* **1** impregnate, inseminate, pollinate. **2** cultivate, dress, enrich, feed, make fertile, manure, mulch, nourish, top-dress.

fertilizer *n* compost, dressing, dung, manure, mulch, nutrient.

fervent *adj* animated, ardent, avid, burning, committed, devout, eager, earnest, emotional, enthusiastic, excited, fanatical, fervid, fiery, frenzied, heated, impassioned, intense, keen, passionate, rapturous, spirited, vehement, vigorous, warm, wholehearted, zealous. *Opp* COOL.

fervour *n* ardour, eagerness, energy, enthusiasm, excitement, fervency, fire, heat, intensity, keenness, passion, sparkle, spirit, vehemence, vigour, warmth, zeal.

fester *vb* become infected, become inflamed, become poisoned, decay, discharge, gather, go bad, go septic, mortify, ooze, putrefy, rot, run, suppurate, ulcerate.

festival *n* anniversary, carnival, celebration, commemoration, fair, feast, fête, fiesta, gala, holiday, jamboree, jubilee. ▷ FESTIVITY.

festive *adj* celebratory, cheerful, cheery, convivial, gay, gleeful, jolly, jovial, joyful, joyous, light-hearted, merry, uproarious. ▷ HAPPY.

festivity *n* celebration, conviviality, entertainment, feasting, festive occasion, *inf* jollification, jollity, jubilation, merrymaking, merriment, mirth, rejoicing, revelry, revels. ▷ PARTY.

fetch *vb* **1** bear, bring, call for, carry, collect, convey, get, import, obtain, pick up, retrieve, transfer, transport. **2** *fetch a good price.* be bought for, bring in, earn, go for, make, produce, raise, realize, sell for. **fetching** ▷ ATTRACTIVE.

feud *n* animosity, antagonism, *inf* bad blood, conflict, dispute, enmity, grudge, hostility, rivalry, strife, vendetta. ▷ QUARREL.

fever *n* delirium, feverishness, high temperature.

feverish *adj* **1** burning, febrile, fevered, flushed, hot, inflamed, trembling. *Opp* COOL. **2** *feverish activity.* agitated, excited, frantic, frenetic, frenzied, hectic, hurried, impatient, passionate, restless.

few *adj inf* few and far between, hardly any, inadequate, infrequent, rare, scarce, sparse, sporadic, *inf* thin on the ground, uncommon. *Opp* MANY.

fibre *n* **1** filament, hair, strand, thread. **2** *moral fibre.* backbone, character, determination, spirit, tenacity, toughness. ▷ COURAGE.

fickle *adj* capricious, changeable, changing, disloyal, erratic, faithless, flighty, inconsistent, inconstant, mercurial, mutable, treacherous, undependable, unfaithful, unpredictable, unreliable, unstable, unsteady, *inf* up and down, vacillating, variable, volatile. *Opp* CONSTANT.

fiction *n* concoction, deception, fabrication, fantasy, figment of the imagination, flight of fancy, invention, lies, story-telling, *inf* tall story. ▷ WRITING. *Opp* FACT.

fictional *adj* fabulous, fanciful, imaginary, invented, legendary, made-up, make-believe, mythical, story-book. *Opp* FACTUAL.

fictitious *adj* apocryphal, assumed, fabricated, deceitful, fraudulent, imagined, invented, made-up, spurious, unreal, untrue. ▷ FALSE. *Opp* GENUINE.

fiddle *vb* interfere, meddle, play about, tamper. ▷ FIDGET. **fiddling** ▷ TRIVIAL.

fidget *vb* be restless, *inf* fiddle about, fret, frisk about, fuss, jerk about, *inf* jiggle, *inf* mess about, move restlessly, *inf* play about, shuffle, squirm, twitch, worry, wriggle about.

fidgety *adj* agitated, frisky, impatient, jittery, jumpy, nervous, on edge, restive, restless, *inf* twitchy, uneasy. *Opp* CALM.

field *n* **1** arable land, clearing, enclosure, grassland, *poet* glebe, green, *old use* mead, meadow, paddock, pasture. **2** *a games field.* arena, ground, pitch, playing-field, recreation ground, stadium. **3** *field of activity.* area, *inf* department, domain, province, sphere, subject, territory.

fiend *n* **1** demon, devil, evil spirit, goblin, hobgoblin, imp, Satan, spirit. **2** ▷ FANATIC.

fierce *adj* **1** angry, barbaric, barbarous, bloodthirsty, bloody, brutal, cold-blooded, cruel, dangerous, fearsome, ferocious, fiendish, fiery, homicidal, inhuman, merciless, murderous, pitiless, ruthless, sadistic, savage, untamed, vicious, violent, wild. **2** *fierce opposition.* active, aggressive, competitive, eager, furious, heated, intense, keen, passionate, relentless, strong, unrelenting. *Opp* GENTLE.

fiery *adj* **1** ablaze, afire, aflame, aglow, blazing, burning, fierce, flaming, glowing, heated, hot, incandescent, raging, red, red-hot. **2** *a fiery temper.* angry, ardent, choleric, excitable, fervent, furious, hotheaded, intense, irascible, irritable, livid, mad, passionate, touchy, violent. *Opp* COOL.

fight *n* action, affray, attack, battle, bout, brawl, *inf* brush, *inf* bust-up, clash, combat, competition, conflict, confrontation, contest, counterattack, dispute, dogfight, duel, *inf* dustup, encounter, engagement, feud, *old use* fisticuffs, fracas, fray, *inf* free-for-all, hostilities, joust, match, mêlée, *inf* punch-up, raid, riot, rivalry, row, scramble, scrap, scrimmage, scuffle, *inf* set-to, skirmish, squabble, strife, struggle, tussle, war, wrangle. ▷ QUARREL. ● *vb* **1** attack, battle, box, brawl, *inf* brush, clash, compete, conflict, contend, do battle, duel, engage, exchange blows, fence, feud, grapple, have a fight, joust, quarrel, row, scrap, scuffle, skirmish, spar, squabble, stand up (to), strive, struggle, *old use* tilt, tussle, wage war, wrestle. **2** *fight a decision.* campaign against, contest, defy, oppose, protest against, resist, take a stand against.

fighter *n* aggressor, antagonist, attacker, belligerent, campaigner, combatant, contender, contestant, defender. □ *archer, boxer,* inf *brawler, champion, duellist, freedom fighter, gladiator, guerrilla, gunman, knight, marine, marksman, mercenary, partisan, prize-fighter, pugilist, sniper, swordsman, terrorist, warrior, wrestler.* ▷ SOLDIER.

figure *n* **1** amount, cipher, digit, integer, number, numeral, sum, symbol, value. **2** diagram, drawing, graph, illustration, outline, picture, plate, representation. **3** *plump figure.* body, build, form, outline, physique, shape, silhouette. **4** *bronze figure.* ▷ SCULPTURE. **5** *well-known figure.* ▷ PERSON. ● *vb*

▷ FEATURE. **figure out** ▷ CALCULATE, UNDERSTAND. **figures** ▷ STATISTICS.

file *n* **1** binder, box-file, case, cover, documentation, document-case, dossier, folder, portfolio, ring-binder. **2** *single file.* column, line, procession, queue, rank, row, stream, string, train. • *vb* **1** arrange, categorize, classify, enter, pigeon-hole, organize, put away, record, register, store, systematize. **2** *file through a door.* march, parade, proceed in a line, stream, troop.

fill *vb* **1** be full of, block, *inf* bung up, caulk, clog, close up, cram, crowd, flood, inflate, jam, load, obstruct, pack, plug, refill, replenish, seal, stock up, stop up, *inf* stuff, *inf* top up. *Opp* EMPTY. **2** *fill a need.* answer, fulfil, furnish, meet, provide, satisfy, supply. **3** *fill a post.* execute, hold, occupy, take over, take up. **fill out** ▷ SWELL.

filling *n* contents, *inf* innards, insides, padding, stuffing, wadding.

film *n* **1** coat, coating, cover, covering, haze, layer, membrane, mist, overlay, screen, sheet, skin, slick, tissue, veil. **2** cartoon, *old use* flick, motion picture, movie, picture, video, videotape.

filter *n* colander, gauze, membrane, mesh, riddle, screen, sieve, strainer. • *vb* clarify, filtrate, percolate, purify, refine, screen, sieve, sift, strain.

filth *n* decay, dirt, effluent, garbage, grime, *inf* gunge, impurity, muck, mud, ordure, pollution, putrescence, refuse, rubbish, scum, sewage, slime, sludge, trash. ▷ EXCRETA.

filthy *adj* **1** begrimed, caked, defiled, dirty, disgusting, dusty, foul, grimy, grubby, impure, messy, mucky, muddy, nasty, polluted, scummy, slimy, smelly, soiled, sooty, sordid, squalid, stinking, tainted, uncleaned, unkempt, unwashed, vile. **2** ▷ OBSCENE. *Opp* CLEAN.

final *adj* clinching, closing, concluding, conclusive, decisive, dying, end, eventual, finishing, last, settled, terminal, terminating, ultimate. *Opp* INITIAL.

finalize *vb* clinch, complete, conclude, settle, *inf* sew up, *inf* wrap up.

finance *n* accounting, banking, business, commerce, economics, investment, stocks and shares. • *vb* back, fund, guarantee, invest in, pay for, provide money for, subsidize, support, underwrite. **finances** assets, bank account, budget, capital, cash, funds, holdings, income, money, resources, wealth, *inf* the wherewithal.

financial *adj* economic, fiscal, monetary, pecuniary.

find *vb* **1** acquire, arrive at, become aware of, *inf* bump into, chance upon, come across, come upon, detect, diagnose, dig out, dig up, discover, encounter, espy, expose, *inf* ferret out, happen on, hit on, identify, learn, light on, locate, meet, note, notice, observe, *inf* put your finger on, reach, recognize, reveal, spot, stumble on, uncover, unearth. **2** *find lost property.* get back, recover, rediscover, regain, repossess, retrieve, trace, track down. **3** *found me a job.* give, pass on, procure, provide, supply. *Opp* LOSE.

finding *n* conclusion, decision, decree, judgement, pronouncement, verdict.

fine *adj* **1** admirable, beautiful, choice, classic, commendable, excellent, first-class, handsome, noble, select, superior, worthy. ▷ GOOD. **2** *fine workmanship.* consummate, craftsmanlike, meticulous, skilful, skilled. **3** *fine sand.* minute, powdery, soft. **4** *fine fabric.* dainty, delicate, exquisite, flimsy, fragile, silky. **5** *a fine point.* acute, keen, narrow, sharp, slender, slim, thin. **6** *a fine distinction.* fine-drawn, discriminating, hair-splitting, nice, precise, subtle. **7** *fine weather.* bright, clear, cloudless, dry, fair, nice, pleasant, sunny. • *n* charge, forfeit, penalty.

finish *n* **1** cessation, close, completion, conclusion, culmination, end, ending, finale, resolution, result, termination. **2** *finish on furniture.* appearance, completeness, gloss, lustre, patina, perfection, polish, shine, smoothness, surface, texture. • *vb* **1** accomplish, achieve, break off, bring to an end, cease, clinch, complete, conclude, discontinue, end, finalize, fulfil, halt, pack up, perfect, phase out, reach the end, round off, say goodbye, sign off, stop, take your leave, terminate, *inf* wind up, *inf* wrap up. **2** consume, drink up, eat up, empty, exhaust, expend, get through, *inf* polish off, *inf* say goodbye to, use up. **finish off** ▷ KILL.

finite *adj* bounded, calculable, controlled, countable, definable, defined, determinate, fixed, known, limited, measurable, numbered, rationed, restricted. *Opp* INFINITE.

fire *n* **1** blaze, burning, combustion, conflagration, flames, holocaust, inferno, pyre. **2** fireplace, grate, hearth. □ *boiler, bonfire, brazier, convector, electric fire, forge, furnace, gas fire, immersion-heater, incinerator, kiln, oven, radiator, stove.* **3** *fire in your veins.* ▷ PASSION. • *vb* **1** bake, burn, heat, ignite, kindle, light, put a light to, set alight, set fire to, spark off. **2** animate, awaken, enkindle, enliven, excite, incite, inflame, inspire, motivate, rouse, stimulate, stir. **3** *fire a gun or missile.* catapult, detonate, discharge, explode, launch, let off, propel, set off, shoot, trigger off. **4** *fire a worker.* dismiss, make redundant, sack, throw out. **fire at** ▷ BOMBARD. **hang fire** ▷ DELAY.

fireproof *adj* flameproof, incombustible, non-flammable. *Opp* INFLAMMABLE.

fire-raiser *n* arsonist, pyromaniac.

firm *adj* **1** compact, compressed, congealed, dense, hard, inelastic, inflexible, rigid, set, solid, stable, stiff, unyielding. **2** *firm on the rocks.* anchored, embedded, fast, fastened, fixed, immovable, secure, steady, tight. **3** *firm convictions.* adamant, decided, determined, dogged, obstinate, persistent, resolute, unshakeable, unwavering. **4** *a firm price.* agreed, settled, unchangeable. **5** *firm friends.* constant, dependable, devoted, faithful, loyal, reliable. • *n* business, company, concern, corporation, establishment, organization, partnership.

first *adj* **1** cardinal, chief, dominant, foremost, head, highest, key, leading, main, outstanding, paramount, predominant, primary, prime, principal, top, uppermost. **2** *first steps.* basic, elementary, fundamental, initial, introductory, preliminary, rudimentary. **3** *first inhabitants.* aboriginal, archetypal, earliest, eldest, embryonic, oldest, original, primeval. **first-class, first-rate** ▷ EXCELLENT.

fish *n* □ *brill, brisling, carp, catfish, chub, cod, coelacanth, conger, cuttlefish, dab, dace, eel, flounder, goldfish, grayling, gudgeon, haddock, hake, halibut, herring, jellyfish, lamprey, ling, mackerel, minnow, mullet, perch, pike, pilchard, piranha, plaice, roach, salmon, sardine, sawfish, shark, skate, sole, sprat, squid, starfish, stickleback, sturgeon, swordfish,* inf *tiddler, trout, tuna, turbot, whitebait, whiting.* • *vb* angle, go fishing, trawl.

fisher *n* angler, fisherman, trawlerman.

fit *adj* **1** adapted, adequate, applicable, apposite, appropriate, apropos, apt, becoming, befitting, correct, decent, equipped, fitting, good enough, proper, right, satisfactory, seemly, sound, suitable, suited, timely. **2** able, capable, competent, in good form, on form, prepared, ready, strong, well enough. ▷ HEALTHY. *Opp* UNFIT. • *n* attack, bout, convulsion, eruption, explosion, outbreak, outburst, paroxysm, seizure, spasm, spell. • *vb* **1** accord with, become, be fitting for, conform with, correspond to, correspond with, go with, harmonize with, suit. **2** *fit things into place.* arrange, assemble, build, construct, dovetail, install, interlock, join, match, position, put in place, put together. **fit out, fit up** ▷ EQUIP.

fix *n inf* catch-22, corner, difficulty, dilemma, *inf* hole, *inf* jam, mess, *inf* pickle, plight, predicament, problem, quandary. • *vb* **1** attach, bind, connect, embed, implant, install, join, link, make firm, plant, position, secure, stabilize, stick. ▷ FASTEN. **2** *fix a price.* agree, appoint, arrange, arrive at, conclude, confirm, decide, define, establish, finalize, name, ordain, set, settle, sort out, specify. **3** *fix a broken window.* correct, make good, mend, put right, rectify, remedy, repair.

fixture *n* date, engagement, event, game, match, meeting.

fizz *vb* bubble, effervesce, fizzle, foam, froth, hiss, sizzle, sparkle, sputter.

fizzy *adj* bubbly, effervescent, foaming, sparkling.

flag *n* banner, bunting, colours, ensign, jack, pennant, pennon, standard, streamer. • *vb* **1** ▷ SIGNAL. **2** *enthusiasm flagged.* ▷ DECLINE.

flake *n* bit, chip, leaf, scale, scurf, shaving, slice, sliver, splinter, wafer.

flame *n* blaze, light, tongue. ▷ FIRE. • *vb* ▷ FLARE.

flap *vb* beat, flutter, oscillate, slap, sway, swing, thrash about, thresh about, wag, waggle, wave about.

flare *vb* **1** blaze, brighten, burst out, erupt, flame, shine. ▷ BURN. **2** ▷ WIDEN.

flash *vb* coruscate, dazzle, flicker, glare, glint, glitter, light up, reflect, scintillate, shine, spark, sparkle, twinkle. ▷ BURN.

flat *adj* **1** calm, even, horizontal, level, smooth, unbroken, unruffled. **2** outstretched, prone, prostrate, recumbent, spread-eagled, spread out, supine. **3** *a flat voice.* bland, boring, dead, dry, dull, featureless, insipid, lacklustre, lifeless, monotonous, spiritless, stale, tedious, tired, unexciting, uninteresting, unmodulated, unvarying. **4** *a flat tyre.* blown out, burst, deflated, punctured. • *n* apartment, bedsitter, flatlet, maisonette, penthouse, rooms, suite.

flatten *vb* **1** compress, even out, iron out, level out, press, roll, smooth, straighten. **2** crush, demolish, devastate, level, raze, run over, squash, trample. ▷ DESTROY. **3** *flatten an opponent.* fell, floor, knock down, prostrate. ▷ DEFEAT.

flatter *vb* be flattering to, *inf* butter up, compliment, court, curry favour with, fawn on, humour, *inf* play up to, praise, *sl* suck up to, *inf* toady to. *Opp* INSULT. **flattering** ▷ COMPLIMENTARY, OBSEQUIOUS.

flatterer *n inf* crawler, *inf* creep, groveller, lackey, sycophant, time-server, *inf* toady, *inf* yes-man.

flattery *n* adulation, blandishments, *inf* blarney, *inf* boot-licking, cajolery, fawning, *inf* flannel, insincerity, obsequiousness, servility, *inf* soft soap, sycophancy, unctuousness.

flavour *n* **1** savour, taste. ▷ FLAVOURING. **2** air, ambience, atmosphere, aura, character, characteristic, feel, feeling, property, quality, spirit, stamp, style. • *vb* add flavour to, add taste to, season, spice.

flavouring *n* additive, essence, extract, seasoning.

flaw *n* break, defect, error, fallacy, fault, imperfection, inaccuracy, loophole, mistake, shortcoming, slip, split, weakness. ▷ BLEMISH. **flawed** ▷ IMPERFECT.

flawless *adj* accurate, clean, faultless, immaculate, mint, pristine, sound, spotless, undamaged, unmarked. ▷ PERFECT. *Opp* IMPERFECT.

flee *vb* abscond, *inf* beat a retreat, *sl* beat it, bolt, clear off, cut and run, decamp, disappear, escape, fly, get away, hurry off, *inf* make a run for it, make off, retreat, run away, *sl* scarper, take flight, *inf* take to your heels, vanish, withdraw.

fleet *n* armada, convoy, flotilla, navy, squadron, task force.

fleeting *adj* brief, ephemeral, evanescent, fugitive, impermanent, momentary, mutable, passing, short, short-lived, temporary, transient, transitory. *Opp* PERMANENT.

flesh *n* carrion, fat, meat, muscle, tissue.

flex *n* cable, cord, extension, lead, wire. • *vb* ▷ BEND.

flexible *adj* **1** bendable, *inf* bendy, elastic, flexile, floppy, giving, limp, lithe, plastic, pliable, pliant, rubbery, soft, springy, stretchy, supple, whippy, willowy, yielding. **2** adjustable, alterable, fluid, mutable, open, provisional, variable. **3** *a flexible person*. accommodating, adaptable, amenable, compliant, conformable, co-operative, docile, easygoing, malleable, open-minded, responsive, tractable, willing. *Opp* RIGID.

flicker *vb* blink, flap, flutter, glimmer, gutter, quiver, shake, shimmer, sparkle, tremble, twinkle, vibrate, waver.

flight *n* **1** journey, trajectory. **2** ▷ ESCAPE.

flimsy *adj* **1** breakable, brittle, delicate, fine, fragile, frail, insubstantial, light, loose, slight, thin, weak. **2** *a flimsy building*. decrepit, dilapidated, gimcrack, jerry-built, makeshift, rickety, shaky, tottering, wobbly. **3** *a flimsy argument*. feeble, implausible, inadequate, superficial, trivial, unbelievable, unconvincing, unsatisfactory. *Opp* STRONG.

flinch *vb* blench, cower, cringe, dodge, draw back, duck, falter, jerk away, jump, quail, quake, recoil, shrink back, shy away, start, swerve, wince. **flinch from** ▷ EVADE.

fling *vb* bowl, *inf* bung, cast, *inf* chuck, heave, hurl, launch, lob, pelt, pitch, propel, send, *inf* shy, *inf* sling, throw, toss.

flippant *adj* cheeky, facetious, facile, *inf* flip, frivolous, light-hearted, shallow, superficial, thoughtless, unserious. *Opp* SERIOUS.

flirt *n female* coquette, *male* philanderer, *inf* tease. • *vb sl* chat someone up, lead someone on, make love, philander, toy with someone's affections.

flirtatious *adj* amorous, coquettish, flirty, *derog* philandering, playful, *derog* promiscuous, teasing.

float *vb* **1** be poised, be suspended, bob, drift, glide, hang, hover, sail, swim, waft. **2** *float a ship*. launch. *Opp* SINK.

flock *n* assembly, congregation, crowd, drove, gathering, herd, horde, multitude, swarm. ▷ GROUP. • *vb* ▷ GATHER.

flog *vb* beat, birch, cane, chastise, flagellate, flay, lash, scourge, thrash, whip. ▷ HIT.

flood *n* **1** cataract, deluge, downpour, flash-flood, inundation, overflow, rush, spate, stream, tidal wave, tide, torrent. **2** abundance, excess, glut, plethora, quantity, superfluity, surfeit, surge. • *vb* cover, deluge, drown, engulf, fill up, immerse, inundate, overflow, overwhelm, saturate, sink, submerge, swamp.

floor *n* **1** floorboards, flooring. **2** deck, level, storey, tier.

flop *vb* **1** collapse, dangle, droop, drop, fall, flag, flap about, hang down, sag, slump, topple, tumble, wilt. **2** ▷ FAIL.

floppy *adj* dangling, droopy, flabby, hanging, loose, limp, pliable, soft. ▷ FLEXIBLE. *Opp* RIGID.

flounder *vb* **1** blunder, flail, fumble, grope, move clumsily, plunge about, stagger, struggle, stumble, tumble, wallow. **2** falter, get confused, make mistakes, talk aimlessly.

flourish *n* ▷ GESTURE. • *vb* **1** be fruitful, be successful, bloom, blossom, boom, burgeon, develop, do well, flower, grow, increase, *inf* perk up, progress, prosper, strengthen, succeed, thrive. **2** *flourish an umbrella*. brandish, flaunt, gesture with, shake, swing, twirl, wag, wave, wield.

flow *n* cascade, course, current, drift, ebb, effusion, flood, gush, outpouring, spate, spurt, stream, tide, trickle. • *vb* bleed, cascade, course, dribble, drift, drip, ebb, flood, flush, glide, gush, issue, leak, move in a stream, ooze, overflow, pour, purl, ripple, roll, run, seep, spill, spring, spurt, squirt, stream, swirl, trickle, well, well up.

flower *n* **1** bloom, blossom, bud, floret, petal. □ *begonia, bluebell, buttercup, campanula, campion, candytuft, carnation, catkin, celandine, chrysanthemum, coltsfoot, columbine, cornflower, cowslip, crocus, crowfoot, cyclamen, daffodil, dahlia, daisy, dandelion, forget-me-not, foxglove, freesia, geranium, gladiolus, gypsophila, harebell, hollyhock, hyacinth, iris, jonquil, kingcup, lilac, lily, lupin, marguerite, marigold, montbretia, nasturtium, orchid, pansy, pelargonium, peony, periwinkle, petunia, phlox, pink, polyanthus, poppy, primrose, rhododendron, rose, saxifrage, scabious, scarlet pimpernel, snowdrop, speedwell, sunflower, tulip, violet, wallflower, water-lily.* • *vb* bloom, blossom, *poet* blow, bud, burgeon, come out, have flowers, open out, unfold. ▷ FLOURISH. **bunch of flowers** arrangement, bouquet, corsage, garland, posy, spray, wreath.

fluctuate *vb* alternate, be unsteady, change, go up and down, oscillate, seesaw, shift, swing, vacillate, vary, waver.

fluent *adj* articulate, effortless, eloquent, expressive, *derog* facile, felicitous, flowing, *derog* glib, natural, polished, ready, smooth, voluble, unhesitating. *Opp* HESITANT.

fluff *n* down, dust, feathers, floss, fuzz, thistledown.

fluffy *adj* downy, feathery, fibrous, fleecy, furry, fuzzy, hairy, light, silky, soft, velvety, wispy, woolly.

fluid *adj* **1** aqueous, flowing, gaseous, liquefied, liquid, melted, molten, running, *inf* runny, sloppy, watery. *Opp* SOLID. **2** *a fluid situation.* adjustable, alterable, changing, flexible, mutable, open, variable, undefined. • *n* gas, liquid, liquor, plasma, vapour.

fluke *n* accident, chance, serendipity, stroke of good luck, twist of fate.

flush *vb* **1** blush, colour, glow, go red, redden. **2** *flush a lavatory.* clean out, cleanse, flood, *inf* pull the plug, rinse out, wash out. **3** *flush from a hiding-place.* chase out, drive out, expel, send up.

fluster *vb* agitate, bewilder, bother, distract, flurry, perplex, put off, put out, *inf* rattle, *inf* throw, upset. ▷ CONFUSE.

flutter *vb* bat (*eyelid*), flap, flicker, flit, fluctuate, move agitatedly, oscillate, palpitate, quiver, shake, tremble, twitch, vacillate, vibrate, wave.

fly *vb* **1** ascend, flit, glide, hover, rise, sail, soar, swoop, take flight, take wing. **2** *fly a plane.* aviate, pilot, take off in. **3** *fly a flag.* display, flap, flutter, hang up, hoist, raise, show, wave. **4** *fly from danger.* flee, hurry, move quickly, run. ▷ ESCAPE. **fly at** ▷ ATTACK. **fly in the face of** ▷ DISREGARD.

flying *n* aeronautics, air-travel, aviation, flight, *inf* jetting.

foam *n* **1** bubbles, effervescence, froth, head (*on beer*), lather, scum, spume, suds. **2** sponge. • *vb* boil, bubble, effervesce, fizz, froth, lather, make foam.

focus *n* **1** clarity, correct adjustment, sharpness. **2** centre, core, focal point, heart, hub, pivot, target. • *vb* aim, centre, concentrate, direct attention, fix attention, home in, spotlight.

fog *n* bad visibility, cloud, haze, miasma, mist, smog, vapour.

foggy *adj* blurred, blurry, clouded, cloudy, dim, hazy, indistinct, misty, murky, obscure. *Opp* CLEAR.

foil *vb* baffle, block, check, circumvent, frustrate, halt, hamper, hinder, obstruct, outwit, prevent, stop, thwart. ▷ DEFEAT.

foist *vb inf* fob off, get rid of, impose, offload, palm off.

fold *n* **1** bend, corrugation, crease, crinkle, furrow, gather, hollow, knife-edge, line, pleat, pucker, wrinkle. **2** *fold for sheep.* ▷ ENCLOSURE. • *vb* **1** bend, crease, crimp, crinkle, double over, jack-knife, overlap, pleat, ply, pucker, tuck in, turn over. **2** close, collapse, let down, put down, shut. **3** *fold in your arms.* clasp, clip, embrace, enclose, enfold, entwine, envelop, hold, hug, wrap. **4** *business folded.* ▷ FAIL.

folk *n* clan, nation, people, the population, the public, race, society, tribe.

follow *vb* **1** accompany, chase, come after, dog, escort, go after, hound, hunt, keep pace with, pursue, replace, shadow, stalk, succeed, supersede, supplant, *inf* tag along with, tail, take the place of, track, trail. **2** *follow a path.* keep to, trace. **3** *follow rules.* abide by, adhere to, attend to, comply with, conform to, heed, honour, obey, observe, pay attention to, stick to, submit to, take notice of. **4** *follow my example.* adopt, be guided by, conform to, copy, imitate, mimic, mirror. **5** *follow an argument.* appreciate, comprehend, grasp, keep up with, take in, understand. **6** *follow football.* admire, be a fan of, keep abreast of, know about, take an interest in, support. **7** *It doesn't follow.* be inevitable, be logical, come about, ensue, happen, have the consequence, mean, result. **following** ▷ SUBSEQUENT.

folly *n* foolishness, insanity, lunacy, madness. ▷ STUPIDITY.

foment *vb* arouse, incite, instigate, kindle, provoke, rouse, stir up. ▷ STIMULATE.

fond *adj* **1** adoring, affectionate, caring, loving, tender, warm. **2** *a fond hope.* ▷ FOOLISH. **be fond of** ▷ LOVE.

fondle *vb* caress, cuddle, handle, pat, pet, snuggle, squeeze, touch.

food *n* aliment, *old use* bread, *old use* comestibles, cooking, cuisine, delicacies, diet, *inf* eatables, *inf* eats, fare, feed, fodder, foodstuff, forage, *inf* grub, *inf* junk food, *old use* meat, *sl* nosh, nourishment, nutriments, provender, provisions, rations, recipe, refreshments, sustenance, swill, *old use* tuck, *old use* viands, *old use* victuals. ▷ MEAL.

fool *n* **1** [*most synonyms inf*] ass, blockhead, booby, buffoon, dim-wit, dope, dunce, dunderhead, dupe, fat-head, half-wit, ignoramus, mug, muggins, mutt, ninny, nit, nitwit, simpleton, sucker, twerp, wally. ▷ IDIOT. **2** clown, comedian, comic, coxcomb, entertainer, jester. • *vb inf* bamboozle, bluff, cheat, *inf* con, cozen, deceive, defraud, delude, dupe, fleece, gull, *inf* have on, hoax, hoodwink, *inf* kid, mislead, *inf* string along, swindle, take in, tease, trick. **fool about** ▷ MISBEHAVE.

foolish *adj* absurd, asinine, brainless, childish, crazy, daft, *inf* dopey, *inf* dotty, fatuous, feather-brained, feeble-minded, *old use* fond, frivolous, *inf* half-baked, hare-brained, idiotic, illogical, immature, inane, infantile, irrational, *inf* jokey, laughable, light-hearted, ludicrous, mad, meaningless, mindless, misguided, naïve, nonsensical, playful, pointless, preposterous, ridiculous, scatter-brained, *inf* scatty, senseless, shallow, silly, simple, simple-minded, simplistic, *inf* soppy, stupid, thoughtless, unintelligent, unreasonable, unsound, unwise, witless. *Opp* WISE.

foot *n* **1** claw, hoof, paw, trotter. **2** ▷ BASE.

footprint *n* footmark, spoor, track.

forbid *vb* ban, bar, debar, deny, deter, disallow, exclude, interdict, make illegal, outlaw, preclude, prevent, prohibit, proscribe, refuse, rule out, say no to, stop, veto. *Opp* ALLOW.

forbidden *adj* **1** against the law, taboo, unlawful, wrong. **2** *a forbidden area.* closed, out of bounds, restricted, secret.

forbidding *adj* gloomy, grim, menacing, ominous, stern, threatening, uninviting, unwelcoming. ▷ UNFRIENDLY. *Opp* FRIENDLY.

force *n* **1** aggression, *inf* armtwisting, coercion, compulsion, constraint, drive, duress, effort, might, power, pressure, strength, vehemence, vigour, violence. **2** effect, energy, impact, intensity, momentum, shock. **3** *a military force.* army, body, group, troops. **4** *force of an argument.* cogency, effectiveness, persuasiveness, rightness, thrust, validity, weight. • *vb* **1** *inf* bulldoze, coerce, compel, constrain, drive, impel, impose on, make, oblige, order, press-gang, pressurize. **2** *force a door.* break open, burst open, prise open, smash, use force on, wrench. **3** *force something on someone.* impose, inflict.

foreboding *n* anxiety, apprehension, dread, fear, feeling, foreshadowing, forewarning, intimation, intuition, misgiving, omen, portent, premonition, presentiment, suspicion, warning, worry.

forecast *n* augury, expectation, outlook, prediction, prognosis, prognostication, projection, prophecy. • *vb* ▷ FORESEE.

forefront *n* avant-garde, front, lead, vanguard.

foreign *adj* **1** distant, exotic, faraway, outlandish, remote, strange, unfamiliar, unknown. **2** alien, external, immigrant, imported, incoming, international, outside, overseas, visiting. **3** *foreign ideas.* extraneous, odd, uncharacteristic, unnatural, untypical, unusual, unwanted. *Opp* NATIVE.

foreigner *n* alien, immigrant, newcomer, outsider, overseas visitor, stranger. *Opp* NATIVE.

foremost *adj* first, leading, main, primary, supreme. ▷ CHIEF.

forerunner *n* advance messenger, harbinger, herald, precursor, predecessor. ▷ ANCESTOR.

foresee *vb* anticipate, envisage, expect, forecast, picture. ▷ FORETELL.

foresight *n* anticipation, caution, far-sightedness, forethought, looking ahead, perspicacity, planning, preparation, prudence, readiness, vision.

forest *n* coppice, copse, jungle, plantation, trees, woodland, woods.

foretaste *n* advance warning, augury, example, foreknowledge, forewarning, indication, omen, premonition, preview, sample, specimen, *inf* tip-off, trailer, *inf* try-out.

foretell *vb* augur, *old use* bode, forebode, foreshadow, forewarn, give a foretaste of, herald, portend, predict, presage, prognosticate, prophesy, signify. ▷ FORESEE.

forethought *n* anticipation, caution, far-sightedness, foresight, looking ahead, perspicacity, planning, preparation, prudence, readiness, vision.

forewarning *n* advance warning, augury, omen, premonition, *inf* tip-off. ▷ FORETASTE.

forfeit *n* confiscation, damages, fee, fine, penalty, sequestration. • *vb* abandon, give up, let go, lose, pay up, relinquish, renounce, surrender.

forge *n* furnace, smithy, workshop. • *vb* **1** beat into shape, cast, construct, hammer out, manufacture, mould, shape, work. **2** coin, copy, counterfeit, fake, falsify, imitate, make illegally, reproduce. **forge ahead** ▷ ADVANCE.

forgery *n* copy, counterfeit, *inf* dud, fake, fraud, imitation, *inf* phoney, replica, reproduction.

forget *vb* **1** be forgetful, dismiss from your mind, disregard, fail to remember, ignore, leave out, lose track (of), miss out, neglect, omit, overlook, skip, suffer from amnesia, unlearn. **2** be without, leave behind, lose. *Opp* REMEMBER.

forgetful *adj* absent-minded, amnesiac, careless, distracted, inattentive, neglectful, negligent, oblivious, preoccupied, unconscious, unmindful, unreliable, vague, *inf* woolly-minded.

forgivable *adj* allowable, excusable, justifiable, negligible, pardonable, petty, understandable, venial. *Opp* UNFORGIVABLE.

forgive *vb* **1** absolve, acquit, clear, exculpate, excuse, exonerate, indulge, *inf* let off, pardon, spare. **2** *forgive a crime.* condone, ignore, make allowances for, overlook, pass over.

forgiveness *n* absolution, amnesty, clemency, compassion, exculpation, exoneration, grace, indulgence, leniency, mercy, pardon, reprieve, tolerance. *Opp* RETRIBUTION.

forgiving *adj* clement, compassionate, forbearing, generous, magnanimous, merciful, tolerant, understanding. ▷ KIND. *Opp* VENGEFUL.

forgo *vb* abandon, abstain from, do without, forswear, give up, go without, omit, pass up, relinquish, renounce, sacrifice, turn down, waive.

forked *adj* branched, cleft, divergent, divided, fork-like, pronged, split, V-shaped.

forlorn *adj* abandoned, alone, bereft, deserted, forsaken, friendless, lonely, outcast, solitary, unloved. ▷ SAD.

form *n* **1** appearance, arrangement, cast, character, configuration, design, format, framework, genre, guise, kind, manifestation, manner, model, mould, nature, pattern, plan, semblance, sort, species, structure, style, system, type, variety. **2** *human form.* anatomy, body, build, figure, frame, outline, physique, shape, silhouette. **3** *your form in school.* class, grade, group, level, set, stream, tutor-group. **4** *good form.* behaviour, convention, custom, etiquette, fashion, manners, practice. **5** *an application form.* document, paper. **6** *in good form.* condition, *inf* fettle, fitness, health, performance, spirits. **7** ▷ SEAT. • *vb* **1** bring into existence, cast, constitute, construct, create, design, establish, forge, found, give form to, make, model, mould, organize, produce, shape. **2** appear, arise, come into existence, develop, grow, materialize, take shape. **3** *form a team.* act as, compose, comprise, make up, serve as. **4** *form a habit.* acquire, cultivate, develop, get.

formal *adj* **1** aloof, ceremonial, ceremonious, conventional, cool, correct, customary, dignified, *inf* dressed-up, orthodox, *inf* posh, *derog* pretentious, proper, punctilious, ritualistic, solemn, sophisticated, stately, *inf* starchy, stiff, stiffnecked, unbending, unfriendly. **2** *formal language.* academic, impersonal, official, precise, reserved, specialist, stilted, technical, unemotional. **3** *a formal agreement.* binding, contractual, enforceable, legal, *inf* signed and sealed. **4** *a formal design.* calculated, geometrical, orderly, organized, regular, rigid, symmetrical. *Opp* INFORMAL.

format *n* appearance, design, layout, plan, shape, size, style.

former *adj* bygone, departed, ex-, last, late, old, one-time, past, previous, prior, recent. **the former** earlier, first, first-mentioned. *Opp* LATTER.

formidable *adj* awe-inspiring, awesome, challenging, daunting, difficult, dreadful, fearful, frightening, intimidating, large-scale, *inf* mind-boggling, onerous, overwhelming, prodigious, taxing. *Opp* EASY.

formula *n* **1** form of words, ritual, rubric, spell, wording. **2** *formula for success.* blueprint, method, prescription, procedure, recipe, rule, technique, way.

formulate *vb* **1** articulate, codify, define, express clearly, set out in detail, specify, systematize. **2** concoct, create, devise, evolve, form, invent, map out, originate, plan, work out.

forsake *vb* abandon, break off from, desert, forgo, forswear, give up, jettison, jilt, leave, quit, renounce, repudiate, surrender, throw over, *inf* turn your back on, vacate.

fort *n* camp, castle, citadel, fortification, fortress, garrison, stronghold, tower.

forthright *adj* blunt, candid, decisive, direct, outspoken, plain-speaking, straightforward, unequivocal, unhesitating, uninhibited. ▷ FRANK. *Opp* EVASIVE.

fortify *vb* **1** buttress, defend, garrison, protect, reinforce, secure against attack, shore up. **2** bolster, boost, brace, buoy up, cheer, embolden, encourage, hearten, invigorate, lift the morale of, reassure, stiffen the resolve of, strengthen, support, sustain. *Opp* WEAKEN.

fortitude *n* backbone, bravery, courage, determination, endurance, firmness, heroism, patience, resolution, stoicism, tenacity, valour, will-power. ▷ COURAGE. *Opp* COWARDICE.

fortunate *adj* auspicious, blessed, favourable, lucky, opportune, propitious, prosperous, providential, timely. ▷ HAPPY.

fortune *n* **1** accident, chance, destiny, fate, fortuity, karma, kismet, luck, providence. **2** affluence, assets, estate, holdings, inheritance, means, *inf* millions, money, opulence, *inf* pile, possessions, property, prosperity, riches, treasure, wealth.

fortune-teller *n* clairvoyant, crystal-gazer, futurologist, oracle, palmist, prophet, seer, soothsayer, star-gazer, sybil.

forward *adj* **1** advancing, front, frontal, head-first, leading, onward, progressive. **2** *forward planning.* advance, early, forward-looking, future, well-advanced. **3** *a forward child.* advanced, assertive, bold, brazen, cheeky, confident, familiar, *inf* fresh, impertinent, impudent, insolent, over-confident, precocious, presumptuous, pushful, *inf* pushy, shameless, uninhibited. *Opp* BACKWARD. ● *vb* **1** dispatch, expedite, freight, post on, re-address, send, send on, ship, transmit, transport. **2** *forward your career.* accelerate, advance, encourage, facilitate, foster, further, hasten, help along, *inf* lend a helping hand to, promote, speed up, support. ▷ HELP. *Opp* HINDER.

foster *vb* **1** advance, cultivate, encourage, further, nurture, promote, stimulate. ▷ HELP. **2** *foster a child.* adopt, bring up, care for, look after, maintain, nourish, nurse, raise, rear, take care of.

foul *adj* **1** bad, contaminated, disagreeable, disgusting, fetid, filthy, hateful, impure, infected, loathsome, nasty, nauseating, nauseous, noisome, obnoxious, offensive, polluted, putrid, repellent, repugnant, repulsive, revolting, rotten, sickening, smelly, squalid, stinking, vile. ▷ DIRTY, SMELLING. **2** *foul crimes.* abhorrent, abominable, atrocious, beastly, cruel, evil, ignominious, monstrous, scandalous, shameful, vicious, villainous, violent, wicked. **3** *foul language.* abusive, bawdy, blasphemous, coarse, common, crude, impolite, improper, indecent, insulting, licentious, offensive, rude, uncouth, vulgar. ▷ OBSCENE. **4** *foul weather.* foggy, rainy, rough, stormy, violent, windy. ▷ UNPLEASANT. **5** *foul play.* against the rules, dishonest, forbidden, illegal, invalid, prohibited, unfair, unsportsmanlike. *Opp* CLEAN, FAIR. ● *n* infringement, violation. ● *vb* ▷ DIRTY. **foul up** ▷ MUDDLE.

found *vb* **1** begin, bring about, create, endow, establish, fund, *inf* get going, inaugurate, initiate, institute, organize, originate, provide money for, raise, set up, start. **2** base, build, construct, erect, ground, rest, set.

foundation *n* **1** beginning, endowment, establishment, founding, inauguration, initiation, institution, organizing, setting up, starting. **2** base, basement, basis, bottom, cornerstone, foot, footing, substructure, underpinning. **3** *foundations of science.* basic principle, element, essential, fundamental, origin, *plur* rudiments.

founder *vb* abort, be wrecked, *inf* come to grief, fail, fall through, go down, miscarry, sink.

fountain *n* font, fount, fountain-head, jet, source, spout, spray, spring, well, well-spring.

foyer *n* ante-room, entrance, entrance hall, hall, lobby, reception.

fraction *n* division, part, portion, section, subdivision.

fracture *n* break, breakage, chip, cleavage, cleft, crack, fissure, gap, opening, rent, rift, rupture, split. ● *vb* breach, break, cause a fracture in, chip, cleave, crack, rupture, separate, split, suffer a fracture in.

fragile *adj* ▷ FRAIL.

fragment *n* atom, bit, chip, crumb, *plur* debris, morsel, part, particle, piece, portion, remnant, scrap, shard, shiver, shred, sliver, *plur* smithereens, snippet, speck. • *vb* ▷ BREAK.

fragmentary *adj inf* bitty, broken, disconnected, disintegrated, disjointed, fragmented, imperfect, in bits, incoherent, incomplete, in fragments, partial, scattered, scrappy, sketchy, uncoordinated. *Opp* COMPLETE.

fragrance *n* aroma, bouquet, nose (*of wine*), odour, perfume, redolence, scent, smell.

fragrant *adj* aromatic, odorous, perfumed, redolent, scented, sweet-smelling.

frail *adj* breakable, brittle, dainty, delicate, easily damaged, feeble, flimsy, fragile, insubstantial, light, *derog* puny, rickety, slight, thin, unsound, unsteady, vulnerable, weak, *derog* weedy. ▷ ILL. *Opp* STRONG.

frame *n* **1** bodywork, chassis, construction, scaffolding, structure. ▷ FRAMEWORK. **2** *photo frame.* border, case, casing, edge, edging, mount, mounting. • *vb* **1** box in, enclose, mount, set off, surround. **2** ▷ COMPOSE. **frame of mind** ▷ ATTITUDE.

framework *n* bare bones, frame, outline, plan, shell, skeleton, support, trellis.

frank *adj* blunt, candid, direct, downright, explicit, forthright, genuine, *inf* heart-to-heart, honest, ingenuous, *inf* no-nonsense, open, outright, outspoken, plain, plain-spoken, revealing, serious, sincere, straightforward, straight from the heart, to the point, trustworthy, truthful, unconcealed, undisguised, unreserved. *Opp* INSINCERE.

frantic *adj* agitated, anxious, berserk, *inf* beside yourself, crazy, delirious, demented, deranged, desperate, distraught, excitable, feverish, *inf* fraught, frenetic, frenzied, furious, hectic, hurried, hysterical, mad, overwrought, panicky, rabid, uncontrollable, violent, wild, worked up. *Opp* CALM.

fraud *n* **1** cheating, chicanery, *inf* con-trick, counterfeit, deceit, deception, dishonesty, double-dealing, duplicity, fake, forgery, hoax, imposture, pretence, *inf* put-up job, ruse, sham, *inf* sharp practice, swindle, trick, trickery. **2** charlatan, cheat, *inf* con-man, hoaxer, humbug, impostor, mountebank, *sl* phoney, *inf* quack, rogue, scoundrel, swindler.

fraudulent *adj inf* bent, bogus, cheating, corrupt, counterfeit, criminal, *inf* crooked, deceitful, devious, *inf* dirty, dishonest, double-dealing, duplicitous, fake, false, forged, illegal, lying, *sl* phoney, sham, specious, swindling, underhand, unscrupulous. *Opp* HONEST.

fray *n* brawl, commotion, conflict, disturbance, fracas, mêlée, quarrel, rumpus. ▷ FIGHT.

frayed *adj* chafed, rough-edged, tattered, threadbare, unravelled, worn. ▷ RAGGED.

freak *adj* aberrant, abnormal, anomalous, atypical, bizarre, exceptional, extraordinary, freakish, odd, peculiar, queer, rare, unaccountable, unforeseeable, unpredictable, unusual, weird. *Opp* NORMAL. • *n* **1** aberration, abnormality, abortion, anomaly, curiosity, deformity, irregularity, monster, monstrosity, mutant, oddity, *inf* one-off, quirk, rarity, sport, variant. **2** ▷ FANATIC.

free *adj* **1** able, allowed, at leisure, at liberty, idle, independent, loose, not working, uncommitted, unconfined, unconstrained, unencumbered, unfixed, unrestrained, untrammelled. **2** *free from slavery.* emancipated, freeborn, let go, liberated, released, unchained, unfettered, unshackled. **3** *a free country.* autonomous, democratic, independent, self-governing, sovereign. **4** *free access.* accessible, clear, open, permitted, unhindered, unimpeded, unrestricted. **5** *free gifts.* complimentary, gratis, *sl* on the house, unasked-for, unsolicited, without charge. **6** *free space.* available, empty, uninhabited, unoccupied, vacant. **7** *free with money.* bounteous, casual, charitable, generous, lavish, liberal, munificent, ready, unstinting, willing. • *vb* **1** absolve, acquit, clear, deliver, discharge, disenthral, emancipate, enfranchise, exculpate, exonerate, let go, let off, let out, liberate, loose, make free, manumit, pardon, parole, ransom, release, reprieve, rescue, save, set free, spare, turn loose, unchain, unfetter, unleash, unlock, unloose. *Opp* CONFINE. **2** *free tangled ropes.* clear, disengage, disentangle, extricate, loose, unbind, undo, unknot, untie. *Opp* TANGLE. **free and easy** ▷ INFORMAL.

freedom *n* **1** autonomy, independence, liberty, self-determination, self-government, sovereignty. *Opp* CAPTIVITY. **2** deliverance, emancipation, exemption, immunity, liberation, release. **3** *freedom to choose.* ability, *Fr* carte blanche, discretion, free hand, latitude, leeway, leisure, licence, opportunity, permission, power, privilege, right, scope.

freeze *vb* **1** become ice, become solid, congeal, harden, ice over, ice up, solidify, stiffen. **2** chill, cool, make cold, numb. **3** *freeze food.* chill, deep-freeze, dry-freeze, ice, refrigerate. **4** *freeze the frame.* fix, hold, immobilize, keep still, paralyse, peg, petrify, stand still, stick, stop. **freezing** ▷ COLD.

freight *n* cargo, consignment, goods, haul, load, merchandise, payload, shipment.

frenzy *n* agitation, delirium, derangement, excitement, fever, fit, fury, hysteria, insanity, lunacy, madness, mania, outburst, paroxysm, passion, turmoil.

frequent *adj* common, constant, continual, countless, customary, everyday, familiar, habitual, incessant, innumerable, many, normal, numerous, ordinary, persistent, recurrent, recurring, regular, reiterative, repeated, usual. *Opp* INFREQUENT. • *vb* ▷ HAUNT.

fresh *adj* **1** additional, alternative, different, extra, just arrived, new, recent, supplementary, unfamiliar, up-to-date. **2** alert, energetic, healthy, invigorated, lively, *inf* perky, rested, revived, sprightly, spry, tingling, vigorous, vital. **3** *a fresh recruit.* callow, *inf* green, inexperienced, naïve, raw, unsophisticated, untried, *inf* wet behind the ears. **4** *fresh water.* clear, drinkable, potable, pure, refreshing, sweet, uncontaminated. **5** *fresh air.* airy, circulating, cool, unpolluted, ventilated. **6** *a fresh wind.* bracing, breezy, invigorating, moderate, sharp, stiff, strongish. **7** *fresh food.* healthy, natural, newly gathered, unprocessed, untreated, wholesome. **8** *fresh sheets.* clean, crisp, laundered, untouched, unused, washed-and-ironed. **9** *fresh colours.* bright, clean, glowing, just painted, renewed, restored, sparkling, unfaded, vivid. *Opp* OLD, STALE.

fret *vb* **1** agonize, be anxious, brood, lose sleep, worry. **2** ▷ ANNOY.

fretful *adj* anxious, distressed, disturbed, edgy, irritable, irritated, jittery, peevish, petulant, restless, testy, touchy, worried. ▷ BAD-TEMPERED. *Opp* CALM.

friction *n* **1** abrading, abrasion, attrition, chafing, fretting, grating, resistance, rubbing, scraping. **2** ▷ CONFLICT.

friend *n* acquaintance, associate, *inf* buddy, *inf* chum, companion, comrade, confidant(e), *inf* crony, intimate, *inf* mate, *inf* pal, partner, pen-friend, playfellow, playmate, supporter, well-wisher. ▷ ALLY, LOVER. *Opp* ENEMY. **be friends** ▷ ASSOCIATE. **make friends with** ▷ BEFRIEND.

friendless *adj* abandoned, alienated, alone, deserted, estranged, forlorn, forsaken, isolated, lonely, ostracized, shunned, shut out, solitary, unattached, unloved.

friendliness *n* benevolence, camaraderie, conviviality, devotion, esteem, familiarity, goodwill, helpfulness, hospitality, kindness, neighbourliness, regard, sociability, warmth. *Opp* HOSTILITY.

friendly *adj* accessible, affable, affectionate, agreeable, amiable, amicable, approachable, attached, benevolent, benign, *inf* chummy, civil, close, clubbable, companionable, compatible, comradely, conciliatory, congenial, convivial, cordial, demonstrative, expansive, favourable, genial, good-natured, gracious, helpful, hospitable, intimate, kind, kind-hearted, kindly, likeable, *inf* matey, neighbourly, outgoing, *inf* pally, sympathetic, tender, *inf* thick, warm, welcoming, well-disposed. ▷ FAMILIAR, LOVING, SOCIABLE. *Opp* UNFRIENDLY.

friendship *n* affection, alliance, amity, association, attachment, closeness, comradeship, fellowship, fondness, harmony, intimacy, rapport, relationship. ▷ FRIENDLINESS, LOVE. *Opp* HOSTILITY.

fright *n* **1** jolt, scare, shock, surprise. **2** alarm, apprehension, consternation, dismay, dread, fear, horror, panic, terror, trepidation.

frighten *vb* agitate, alarm, appal, browbeat, bully, cow, *inf* curdle your blood, daunt, dismay, distress, harrow, horrify, intimidate, make afraid, *inf* make your blood run cold, make your hair stand on end, menace, panic, persecute, *inf* petrify, *inf* put the wind up, scare, *inf* scare stiff, shake, shock, startle, terrify, terrorize, threaten, traumatize, tyrannize, unnerve, upset. ▷ DISCOURAGE. *Opp* REASSURE.

frightened *adj* afraid, aghast, alarmed, anxious, appalled, apprehensive, *inf* chicken, cowardly, craven, daunted, fearful, harrowed, horrified, horror-struck, panicky, panic-stricken, petrified, scared, shocked, terrified, terrorstricken, trembling, unnerved, upset, *inf* windy.

frightening *adj* alarming, appalling, blood-curdling, *inf* creepy, daunting, dire, dreadful, eerie, fearful, fearsome, formidable, ghostly, grim, hair-raising, horrifying, intimidating, petrifying, scary, sinister, spine-chilling, *inf* spooky, terrifying, traumatic, uncanny, unnerving, upsetting, weird, worrying. ▷ FRIGHTFUL.

frightful *adj* **1** awful, ghastly, grisly, gruesome, harrowing, hideous, horrible, horrid, horrific, macabre, shocking, terrible. ▷ FRIGHTENING. **2** ▷ BAD.

fringe *n* **1** borders, boundary, edge, limits, marches, margin, outskirts, perimeter, periphery. **2** border, edging, flounce, frill, gathering, ruffle, trimming, valance.

frisky *adj* active, animated, coltish, frolicsome, high-spirited, jaunty, lively, perky, playful, skittish, spirited, sprightly.

frivolity *n* childishness, facetiousness, flippancy, levity, light-heartedness, nonsense, playing about, silliness, triviality. ▷ FUN.

frivolous *adj* casual, childish, facetious, flighty, *inf* flip, flippant, foolish, inconsequential, insignificant, irresponsible, jocular, joking, minor, nugatory, paltry, petty, pointless, puerile, ridiculous, shallow, silly, stupid, superficial, trifling, trivial, trumpery, unimportant, unserious, vacuous, worthless. *Opp* SERIOUS.

frock *n* dress, gown, robe.

frolic *vb* caper, cavort, curvet, dance, frisk about, gambol, have fun, hop about, *inf* horse about, jump about, lark around, leap about, *inf* make whoopee, play about, prance, revel, rollick, romp, skip, skylark, sport.

front *adj* facing, first, foremost, leading, most advanced. • *n* **1** anterior, bow (*of ship*), façade, face, facing, forefront, foreground, frontage, head, nose, obverse, van, vanguard. **2** battle area, danger zone, front line. **3** *a brave front.* appearance, aspect, bearing, blind, *inf* cover-up, demeanour, disguise, expression, look, mask, pretence, show. *Opp* BACK.

frontal *adj* direct, facing, head-on, oncoming, straight.

frontier *n* border, borderline, boundary, bounds, limit, marches, pale.

froth *n* bubbles, effervescence, foam, head (*on beer*), lather, scum, spume, suds.

frown *vb inf* give a dirty look, glare, glower, grimace, knit your brows, look sullen, lour, lower, scowl. **frown on** ▷ DISAPPROVE.

fruit *n* □ *apple, apricot, avocado, banana, berry, bilberry, blackberry, cherry, coconut, crabapple, cranberry, currant, damson, date, fig, gooseberry, grape, grapefruit, greengage, guava, hip, kiwi fruit, lemon, lichee, lime, litchi, loganberry, lychee, mango, medlar, melon, mulberry, nectarine, olive, orange, papaw, pawpaw, peach, pear, pineapple, plum, pomegranate, prune, quince, raisin, raspberry, satsuma, sloe, strawberry, sultana, tangerine, tomato, ugli.*

fruitful *adj* **1** abundant, bounteous, bountiful, copious, fecund, fertile, flourishing, lush, luxurious, plenteous, productive, profuse, prolific, rich. **2** advantageous, beneficial, effective, gainful, profitable, rewarding, successful, useful, well-spent, worthwhile. *Opp* FRUITLESS.

fruitless *adj* **1** barren, sterile, unfruitful, unproductive. **2** abortive, bootless, disappointing, futile, ineffective, ineffectual, pointless, profitless, unavailing, unprofitable, unrewarding, unsuccessful, useless, vain. *Opp* FRUITFUL.

frustrate *vb* baffle, balk, baulk, block, check, disappoint, discourage, foil, halt, hamstring, hinder, impede, inhibit, nullify, prevent, *inf* scotch, stop, stymie, thwart. ▷ DEFEAT. *Opp* ENCOURAGE.

frustrated *adj* disappointed, embittered, loveless, lovesick, resentful, thwarted, unfulfilled, unsatisfied.

fuel *n* □ *anthracite, butane, charcoal, coal, coke, derv, diesel, electricity, gas, gasoline, kindling, logs, methylated spirit, nuclear fuel, oil, paraffin, peat, petrol, propane, tinder, wood.* ● *vb* encourage, feed, inflame, keep going, nourish, put fuel on, stoke up, supply with fuel.

fugitive *adj* ▷ TRANSIENT. ● *n* deserter, escapee, escaper, refugee, renegade, runaway.

fulfil *vb* **1** accomplish, achieve, bring about, bring off, carry off, carry out, complete, consummate, discharge, do, effect, effectuate, execute, implement, make come true, perform, realize. **2** *fulfil a need.* answer, comply with, conform to, meet, obey, respond to, satisfy.

full *adj* **1** brimming, bursting, *inf* chock-a-block, *inf* chock-full, congested, crammed, crowded, filled, jammed, *inf* jam-packed, loaded, overflowing, packed, replete, solid, stuffed, topped-up, well-filled, well-stocked, well-supplied. **2** *a full stomach.* gorged, sated, satiated, satisfied, well-fed. **3** *the full story.* complete, comprehensive, detailed, entire, exhaustive, plenary, thorough, total, unabridged, uncensored, uncut, unedited, unexpurgated, whole. **4** *full speed.* extreme, greatest, highest, maximum, top, utmost. **5** *a full figure.* ample, broad, buxom, fat, large, plump, rounded, voluptuous, well-built. **6** *a full skirt.* baggy, generous, voluminous, wide. *Opp* EMPTY, INCOMPLETE, SMALL.

full-grown *adj* adult, grown-up, mature, ready, ripe.

fumble *vb* grope at, feel, handle awkwardly, mishandle, stumble, touch clumsily.

fume *vb* emit fumes, smoke, smoulder. **fuming** ▷ ANGRY.

fumes *plur n* exhaust, fog, gases, pollution, smog, smoke, vapour.

fun *n* amusement, clowning, diversion, enjoyment, entertainment, festivity, *inf* fooling around, frolic, *inf* fun-and-games, gaiety, games, *inf* high jinks, high spirits, horseplay, jocularity, jokes, joking, *joc* jollification, jollity, laughter, merriment, merrymaking, mirth, pastimes, play, playfulness, pleasure, pranks, recreation, romp, *inf* skylarking, sport, teasing, tomfoolery. ▷ FRIVOLITY. **make fun of** ▷ MOCK.

function *n* **1** aim, purpose, *Fr* raison d'être, use. ▷ JOB. **2** *an official function.* affair, ceremony, *inf* do, event, occasion, party, reception. • *vb* act, behave, go, operate, perform, run, work.

functional *adj* functioning, practical, serviceable, useful, utilitarian, working. *Opp* DECORATIVE.

fund *n* cache, hoard, *inf* kitty, mine, pool, reserve, reservoir, stock, store, supply, treasurehouse. **funds** capital, endowments, investments, reserves, resources, riches, savings, wealth. ▷ MONEY.

fundamental *adj* axiomatic, basic, cardinal, central, crucial, elementary, essential, important, key, main, necessary, primary, prime, principal, quintessential, rudimentary, underlying. *Opp* INESSENTIAL.

funeral *n* burial, cremation, entombment, exequies, interment, obsequies, Requiem Mass, wake.

funereal *adj* dark, depressing, dismal, gloomy, grave, mournful, sepulchral, solemn, sombre. ▷ SAD. *Opp* CHEERFUL.

funnel *n* chimney, smoke-stack. • *vb* channel, direct, filter, pour.

funny *adj* **1** absurd, amusing, comic, comical, crazy, *inf* daft, diverting, droll, eccentric, entertaining, facetious, farcical, foolish, grotesque, hilarious, humorous, *inf* hysterical, ironic, jocose, jocular, *inf* killing, laughable, ludicrous, mad, merry, nonsensical, preposterous, *inf* priceless, *inf* rich, ridiculous, risible, sarcastic, sardonic, satirical, *inf* side-splitting, silly, slapstick, uproarious, waggish, witty, zany. *Opp* SERIOUS. **2** ▷ PECULIAR.

fur *n* bristles, coat, down, fleece, hair, hide, pelt, skin, wool.

furious *adj* **1** boiling, enraged, fuming, incensed, infuriated, irate, livid, mad, raging, savage, wrathful. ▷ ANGRY. **2** *furious activity.* agitated, fierce, frantic, frenzied, intense, tempestuous, tumultuous, turbulent, violent, wild. *Opp* CALM.

furnish *vb* **1** decorate, equip, fit out, fit up, *inf* kit out. **2** *furnish information.* afford, give, grant, provide, supply.

furniture *n* antiques, chattels, effects, equipment, fitments, fittings, fixtures, furnishings, household goods, *inf* movables, possessions. □ *armchair, bed, bench, bookcase, bunk, bureau, cabinet, chair, chesterfield, chest of drawers, chiffonier, commode, cot, couch, cradle, cupboard, cushion, desk, divan, drawer, dresser, dressing-table, easel, fender, filing-cabinet, fireplace, mantelpiece, ottoman, overmantel, pelmet, pew, pouffe, rocking-chair, seat, settee, sideboard, sofa, stool, suite, table, trestle-table, wardrobe, workbench.*

furrow *n* channel, corrugation, crease, cut, ditch, drill, fissure, fluting, gash, groove, hollow, line, rut, score, scratch, track, trench, wrinkle.

furrowed *adj* **1** creased, crinkled, corrugated, fluted, grooved, ploughed, ribbed, ridged, rutted, scored. **2** *furrowed brow.* frowning, lined, worried, wrinkled. *Opp* SMOOTH.

furry *adj* bristly, downy, feathery, fleecy, fuzzy, hairy, woolly.

further *adj* accessory, additional, another, auxiliary, extra, fresh, more, new, other, spare, supplementary.

furthermore *adv* additionally, also, besides, moreover, too.

furtive *adj* clandestine, concealed, conspiratorial, covert, deceitful, disguised, hidden, mysterious, private, secret, secretive, shifty, sly, *inf* sneaky, stealthy, surreptitious, underhand, untrustworthy. ▷ CRAFTY. *Opp* BLATANT.

fury *n* ferocity, fierceness, force, intensity, madness, power, rage, savagery, tempestuousness, turbulence, vehemence, violence, wrath. ▷ ANGER.

fuse *vb* amalgamate, blend, coalesce, combine, commingle, compound, consolidate, join, meld, melt, merge, mix, solder, unite, weld.

fusillade *n* barrage, burst, firing, outburst, salvo, volley.

fuss *n* ▷ COMMOTION. • *vb* agitate, bother, complain, *inf* create, fidget, *inf* flap, *inf* get worked up, grumble, make a commotion, worry.

fussy *adj* **1** carping, choosy, difficult, discriminating, *inf* faddy, fastidious, *inf* finicky, hard to please, niggling, *inf* nit-picking, particular, *inf* pernickety, scrupulous, squeamish. **2** *fussy decorations*. Byzantine, complicated, detailed, elaborate, fancy, ornate, overdone, rococo.

futile *adj* abortive, absurd, barren, bootless, empty, foolish, forlorn, fruitless, hollow, impotent, ineffective, ineffectual, pointless, profitless, silly, sterile, unavailing, unproductive, unprofitable, unsuccessful, useless, vain, wasted, worthless. *Opp* FRUITFUL.

future *adj* approaching, awaited, coming, destined, expected, forthcoming, impending, intended, planned, prospective, subsequent, unborn. • *n* expectations, outlook, prospects, time to come, tomorrow. *Opp* PAST.

fuzz *n* down, floss, fluff, hair.

fuzzy *adj* **1** downy, feathery, fleecy, fluffy, frizzy, furry, linty, woolly. **2** bleary, blurred, cloudy, dim, faint, hazy, ill-defined, indistinct, misty, obscure, out of focus, shadowy, unclear, unfocused, vague. *Opp* CLEAR.

G

gadget *n* apparatus, appliance, contraption, contrivance, device, implement, instrument, invention, machine, tool, utensil.

gag *n* ▷ JOKE. • *vb* check, curb, keep quiet, muffle, muzzle, prevent from speaking, quiet, silence, stifle, still, suppress.

gaiety *n* brightness, cheerfulness, colourfulness, delight, exhilaration, felicity, glee, happiness, high spirits, hilarity, jollity, joyfulness, joyousness, light-heartedness, liveliness, merriment, merrymaking, mirth.

gain *n* achievement, acquisition, advantage, asset, attainment, benefit, dividend, earnings, income, increase, proceeds, profit, return, revenue, winnings, yield. *Opp* LOSS. • *vb* **1** acquire, bring in, capture, collect, earn, garner, gather in, get, harvest, make, net, obtain, pick up, procure, profit, realize, reap, receive, win. *Opp* LOSE. **2** *gain your objective.* achieve, arrive at, attain, get to, reach, secure. *Opp* MISS. **gain on** approach, catch up with, close the gap, close with, go faster than, leave behind, overhaul, overtake.

gainful *adj* advantageous, beneficial, fruitful, lucrative, paid, productive, profitable, remunerative, rewarding, useful, worthwhile.

gala *n* carnival, celebration, fair, festival, festivity, fête, *inf* jamboree, party.

gale *n* blast, cyclone, hurricane, outburst, storm, tempest, tornado, typhoon, wind.

gallant *adj* attentive, chivalrous, courageous, courteous, courtly, dashing, fearless, gentlemanly, gracious, heroic, honourable, intrepid, magnanimous, noble, polite, valiant, well-bred. ▷ BRAVE. *Opp* VILLAINOUS.

gallows *plur n* gibbet, scaffold.

gamble *vb* back, bet, chance, draw lots, game, *inf* have a flutter, hazard, lay bets, risk money, speculate, stake money, *inf* take a chance, take risks, *inf* try your luck, venture, wager.

game *adj* ▷ BRAVE, WILLING. • *n* **1** amusement, diversion, entertainment, frolic, fun, jest, joke, *inf* lark, *inf* messing about, pastime, play, playing, recreation, romp, sport. **2** competition, contest, match, round, tournament. ▷ SPORT. **3** animals, game-birds, prey, quarry. **give the game away** ▷ REVEAL.

gang *n* band, crew, crowd, mob, pack, ring, team. ▷ GROUP. **gang together**, **gang up** ▷ COMBINE.

gangster *n* bandit, brigand, criminal, *inf* crook, desperado, gunman, hoodlum, hooligan, mafioso, mugger, racketeer, robber, ruffian, thug, tough.

gaol *n* borstal, cell, custody, dungeon, guardhouse, jail, *Amer* penitentiary, prison. • *vb* confine, detain, imprison, incarcerate, intern, *inf* send down, send to prison, *inf* shut away, shut up.

gaoler *n* guard, jailer, prison officer, *sl* screw, warder.

gap *n* **1** aperture, breach, break, cavity, chink, cleft, crack, cranny, crevice, gulf, hole, opening, rent, rift, rip, space, void. **2** breathing-space, discontinuity, hiatus, interlude, intermission, interruption, interval, lacuna, lapse, lull, pause, recess, respite, rest, suspension, wait. **3** *gap between political parties.* difference, disagreement, discrepancy, disparity, distance, divergence, division, incompatibility, inconsistency.

gape *vb* **1** open, part, split, yawn. **2** *inf* gawp, gaze, *inf* goggle, stare.

garbage *n* debris, detritus, junk, litter, muck, refuse, scrap, trash, waste. ▷ RUBBISH.

garble *vb* corrupt, distort, falsify, misconstrue, misquote, misrepresent, mutilate, pervert, slant, twist, warp. ▷ CONFUSE.

garden *n* allotment, patch, plot, yard. □ *arbour, bed, border, herbaceous border, lawn, orchard, patio, pergola, rock garden, rose garden, shrubbery, terrace, vegetable garden, walled garden, water garden, window-box.* **gardens** grounds, park.

gardening *n* cultivation, horticulture.

garish *adj* bright, Brummagem, cheap, crude, flamboyant, flashy, gaudy, harsh, loud, lurid, meretricious, ostentatious, raffish, showy, startling, tasteless, tawdry, vivid, vulgar. *Opp* DRAB, TASTEFUL.

garment *n* apparel, attire, clothing, costume, dress, garb, habit, outfit. ▷ CLOTHES.

garrison *n* **1** contingent, detachment, force, unit. **2** barracks, camp, citadel, fort, fortification, fortress, station, stronghold.

gas *n* exhalation, exhaust, fumes, miasma, vapour.

gash *vb* chop, cleave, cut, incise, lacerate, score, slash, slit, split, wound.

gasp *vb* blow, breathe with difficulty, choke, fight for breath, gulp, *inf* huff and puff, pant, puff, snort, wheeze. **gasping** ▷ BREATHLESS, THIRSTY.

gate *n* access, barrier, door, entrance, entry, exit, gateway, kissing-gate, opening, passage, *poet* portal, portcullis, turnstile, way in, way out, wicket, wicket-gate.

gather *vb* **1** accumulate, amass, assemble, bring together, build up, cluster, collect, come together, concentrate, congregate, convene, crowd, flock, forgather, get together, group, grow, heap up, herd, hoard, huddle together, marshal, mass, meet, mobilize, muster, pick up, pile up, rally, round up, stockpile, store up, swarm, throng. *Opp* DISPERSE. **2** *gather flowers.* cull, garner, glean, harvest, pick, pluck, reap. **3** *I gather he's ill.* assume, be led to believe, conclude, deduce, guess, infer, learn, surmise, understand.

gathering *n* assembly, conclave, congress, convention, convocation, function, *inf* get-together, meeting, party, rally, social. ▷ GROUP.

gaudy *adj* bright, Brummagem, cheap, crude, flamboyant, flashy, garish, harsh, loud, lurid, meretricious, ostentatious, raffish, showy, startling, tasteless, tawdry, vivid, vulgar. *Opp* DRAB, TASTEFUL.

gauge *n* **1** bench-mark, criterion, guide-line, measurement, norm, standard, test, yardstick. **2** capacity, dimensions, extent, measure, size, span, thickness, width. • *vb* ▷ ESTIMATE, MEASURE.

gaunt *adj* **1** bony, cadaverous, emaciated, haggard, hollow-eyed, lanky, lean, pinched, raw-boned, scraggy, scrawny, skeletal, starving, underweight, wasted away. ▷ THIN. *Opp* PLUMP. **2** *a gaunt ruin.* bare, bleak, desolate, dreary, forbidding, grim, stark, stern, unfriendly. *Opp* ATTRACTIVE.

gawky *adj* awkward, blundering, clumsy, gangling, gauche, inept, lumbering, maladroit, uncoordinated, ungainly, ungraceful, unskilful. *Opp* GRACEFUL.

gay *adj* **1** animated, bright, carefree, cheerful, colourful, festive, fun-loving, jolly, jovial, joyful, light-hearted, lively, merry, sparkling, sunny, vivacious. ▷ HAPPY. **2** ▷ HOMOSEXUAL.

gaze *vb* contemplate, gape, look, regard, stare, view, wonder (at).

gear *n* accessories, accoutrements, apparatus, appliances, baggage, belongings, equipment, *inf* get-up, harness, implements, instruments, kit, luggage, materials, paraphernalia, rig, stuff, tackle, things, tools, trappings. ▷ CLOTHES.

gem *n* gemstone, jewel, precious stone, *sl* sparkler.

general *adj* **1** accepted, accustomed, collective, common, communal, conventional, customary, everyday, familiar, habitual, normal, ordinary, popular, prevailing, prevalent, public, regular, *inf* run-of-the-mill, shared, typical, usual. **2** *general discussion.* across-the-board, all-embracing, blanket, broad-based, catholic, comprehensive, diversified, encyclopaedic, extensive, far-ranging, far-reaching, global, heterogeneous, hybrid, inclusive, sweeping, universal, wholesale, wide-ranging, widespread, worldwide. **3** *a general idea.* approximate, broad, ill-defined, imprecise, indefinite, inexact, in outline, loose, simplified, superficial, unclear, undefined, unspecific, vague. *Opp* SPECIFIC.

generally *adv* as a rule, broadly, chiefly, commonly, in the main, mainly, mostly, normally, on the whole, predominantly, principally, usually.

generate *vb* beget, breed, bring about, cause, create, engender, father, give rise to, make, originate, procreate, produce, propagate, sire, spawn, *inf* whip up.

generosity *n* bounty, largesse, liberality, munificence, philanthropy.

generous *adj* **1** benevolent, big-hearted, bounteous, bountiful, charitable, disinterested, forgiving, *inf* free, impartial, kind, liberal, magnanimous, munificent, noble, open, open-handed, philanthropic, public-spirited, unmercenary, unprejudiced, unselfish, unsparing, unstinting. **2** *generous gifts.* handsome, princely, undeserved, unearned, valuable. ▷ EXPENSIVE. **3** *generous portions.* abundant, ample, copious, lavish, plentiful, sizeable, substantial. ▷ BIG. *Opp* MEAN, SELFISH.

genial *adj* affable, agreeable, amiable, cheerful, convivial, cordial, easygoing, good-natured, happy, jolly, jovial, kindly, pleasant, relaxed, sociable, sunny, warm, warm-hearted. ▷ FRIENDLY. *Opp* UNFRIENDLY.

genitals *plur n* genitalia, *inf* private parts, pudenda, sex organs.

genius *n* **1** ability, aptitude, bent, brains, brilliance, capability, flair, gift, intellect, intelligence, knack, talent, wit. **2** academic, *inf* egghead, expert, intellectual, *derog* know-all, mastermind, thinker, virtuoso.

genteel *adj derog* affected, chivalrous, courtly, gentlemanly, ladylike, mannered, overpolite, patrician, *inf* posh, refined, stylish, *inf* upper-crust. ▷ POLITE.

gentle *adj* **1** amiable, biddable, compassionate, docile, easygoing, good-tempered, harmless, humane, kind, kindly, lenient, loving, meek, merciful, mild, moderate, obedient, pacific, passive, peace-loving, pleasant, quiet, soft-hearted, sweet-tempered, sympathetic, tame, tender. **2** *gentle music.* low, muted, peaceful, reassuring, relaxing, soft, soothing. **3** *gentle wind.* balmy, delicate, faint, light, soft, warm. **4** *a gentle hint.* indirect, polite, subtle, tactful. **5** *a gentle hill.* easy, gradual, imperceptible, moderate, slight, steady. *Opp* HARSH, SEVERE.

genuine *adj* **1** actual, authentic, authenticated, *Lat* bona fide, legitimate, original, proper, *sl* pukka, real, sterling, veritable. **2** *genuine feelings.* candid, devout, earnest, frank, heartfelt, honest, sincere, true, unaffected, unfeigned. *Opp* FALSE.

germ *n* **1** basis, beginning, embryo, genesis, cause, nucleus, origin, root, seed, source, start. **2** bacterium, *inf* bug, microbe, micro-organism, virus.

germinate *vb* begin to grow, bud, develop, grow, root, shoot, spring up, sprout, start growing, take root.

gesture *n* action, flourish, gesticulation, indication, motion, movement, sign, signal. • *vb* gesticulate, indicate, motion, sign, signal. □ *beckon, bow, nod, point, salute, shake your head, shrug, smile, wave, wink.*

get *vb* **1** acquire, be given, bring, buy, come by, come in possession of, earn, fetch, gain, get hold of, inherit, *inf* land, *inf* lay hands on, obtain, pick up, procure, purchase, receive, retrieve, secure, take, win. **2** *get her by phone.* contact, get in touch with, reach, speak to. **3** *get a cold.* catch, come down with, contract, develop, fall ill with, suffer from. **4** *get a criminal.* apprehend, arrest, capture, catch, *inf* collar, *inf* nab, *sl* pinch, seize. **5** *get him to help.* cajole, cause, induce, influence, persuade, prevail on, *inf* twist someone's arm, wheedle. **6** *get tea.* cook, make ready, prepare. **7** *get what he means.* absorb, appreciate, apprehend, comprehend, fathom, follow, glean, grasp, know, take in, understand, work out. **8** *get what he says.* catch, distinguish, hear, make out. **9** *get somewhere.* arrive, come, go, journey, reach, travel. **10** *get cold.* become, grow, turn. **get across** ▷ COMMUNICATE. **get ahead** ▷ PROSPER. **get at** ▷ CRITICIZE. **get away** ▷ ESCAPE. **get down** ▷ DESCEND. **get in** ▷ ENTER. **get off** ▷ DESCEND. **get on** ▷ PROSPER. **get out** ▷ LEAVE. **get together** ▷ GATHER.

getaway *n* escape, flight, retreat.

ghastly *adj* appalling, awful, deathlike, dreadful, frightening, frightful, grim, grisly, gruesome, hideous, horrible, macabre, nasty, shocking, terrible, upsetting. ▷ UNPLEASANT.

ghost *n* apparition, banshee, *inf* bogey, *Ger* doppelgänger, ghoul, hallucination, illusion, phantasm, phantom, poltergeist, shade, shadow, spectre, spirit, *inf* spook, vision, visitant, wraith. **give up the ghost** ▷ DIE.

ghostly *adj* creepy, disembodied, eerie, frightening, illusory, phantasmal, scary, sinister, spectral, *inf* spooky, supernatural, uncanny, unearthly, weird, wraith-like.

giant *adj* ▷ GIGANTIC. • *n* colossus, Goliath, leviathan, monster, ogre, superhuman, titan, *inf* whopper.

giddiness *n* dizziness, faintness, unsteadiness, vertigo.

giddy *adj* dizzy, faint, light-headed, reeling, silly, spinning, unbalanced, unsteady, vertiginous.

gift *n* **1** benefaction, bonus, bounty, charity, contribution, donation, favour, *inf* give-away, grant, gratuity, *inf* hand-out, honorarium, largesse, offering, present, tip. **2** ability, aptitude, bent, capability, capacity, facility, flair, genius, knack, power, strength, talent.

gifted *adj* able, capable, expert, skilful, skilled, talented. ▷ CLEVER.

gigantic *adj* Brobdingnagian, colossal, elephantine, enormous, gargantuan, giant, herculean, huge, immense, *inf* jumbo, *inf* king-size, mammoth, massive, mighty, monstrous, prodigious, titanic, towering, vast. ▷ BIG. *Opp* SMALL.

giggle *vb* snicker, snigger, titter. ▷ LAUGH.

gimcrack *adj* cheap, *inf* cheap and nasty, flimsy, rubbishy, shoddy, tawdry, trashy, trumpery, useless, worthless.

gimmick *n* device, ploy, ruse, stratagem, stunt, subterfuge, trick.

girder *n* bar, beam, joist, rafter.

girdle *n* band, belt, corset, waistband. • *vb* ▷ SURROUND.

girl *n sl* bird, *old use* damsel, daughter, débutante, fiancée, girlfriend, hoyden, lass, *old use* maid, *old use* maiden, *inf* miss, schoolgirl, tomboy, virgin, *old use or sexist* wench. ▷ WOMAN.

girth *n* circumference, measurement round, perimeter.

gist *n* core, direction, drift, essence, general sense, main idea, meaning, nub, pith, point, quintessence, significance.

give *vb* **1** accord, allocate, allot, allow, apportion, assign, award, bestow, confer, contribute, deal out, *inf* dish out, distribute, *inf* dole out, donate, endow, entrust, *inf* fork out, furnish, give away, give out, grant, hand over, lend, let (someone) have, offer, pass over, pay, present, provide, ration out, render, share out, supply. **2** *give information*. deliver, display, express, impart, issue, notify, publish, put across, put into words, reveal, set out, show, tell, transmit. **3** *give a shout*. emit, let out, utter, voice. **4** *give medicine*. administer, dispense, dose with, impose, inflict, mete out, prescribe. **5** *give a party*. arrange, organize, provide, put on, run, set up. **6** *give trouble*. cause, create, engender, occasion. **7** *give under pressure*. be flexible, bend, buckle, collapse, distort, fail, fall apart, give way, warp, yield. *Opp* RECEIVE, TAKE. **give away** ▷ BETRAY. **give in** ▷ SURRENDER. **give off**, **give out** ▷ EMIT. **give up** ▷ ABANDON, SURRENDER.

glad *adj* **1** content, delighted, gratified, joyful, overjoyed, pleased. ▷ HAPPY. *Opp* GLOOMY. **2** *glad to help*. disposed, eager, inclined, keen, ready, willing. *Opp* RELUCTANT.

glamorize *vb* idealize, romanticize.

glamorous *adj* alluring, appealing, colourful, dazzling, enviable, exciting, exotic, fascinating, glittering, prestigious, romantic, smart, spectacular, wealthy. ▷ BEAUTIFUL.

glamour *n* allure, appeal, attraction, brilliance, charm, excitement, fascination, glitter, high-life, lustre, magic, romance. ▷ BEAUTY.

glance *vb* glimpse, have a quick look, peek, peep, scan, skim, *sl* take a dekko. ▷ LOOK.

glare *vb* **1** frown, *inf* give a nasty look, glower, *inf* look daggers, lour, lower, scowl, stare angrily. **2** blaze, dazzle, flare, reflect, shine. ▷ LIGHT. **glaring** ▷ BRIGHT.

glass *n* **1** crystal, glassware. **2** glazing, pane, plate-glass, window. **3** looking-glass, mirror, reflector. **4** beaker, drinking-glass, goblet, tumbler, wine-glass. **5** optical instrument. □ *binoculars, field-glasses, goggles, magnifying glass, microscope, opera-glasses, telescope, spyglass*. **glasses** *inf* specs, spectacles. □ *bifocals, contact-lenses, eyeglass, lorgnette, monocle, pince-nez, reading glasses, sun-glasses, trifocals*.

glasshouse *n* conservatory, greenhouse, hothouse, orangery, vinery.

glassy *adj* **1** glazed, gleaming, glossy, icy, polished, shining, shiny, smooth, vitreous. **2** *glassy stare*. ▷ EXPRESSIONLESS.

glaze *vb* burnish, enamel, gloss, lacquer, polish, shellac, shine, varnish.

gleam *vb* flash, glimmer, glint, glisten, glow, reflect, shine. ▷ LIGHT. **gleaming** ▷ BRIGHT.

gleeful *adj* cheerful, delighted, ecstatic, exuberant, exultant, gay, jovial, joyful, jubilant, overjoyed, pleased, rapturous, triumphant. ▷ HAPPY. *Opp* SAD.

glib *adj* articulate, facile, fast-talking, fluent, insincere, plausible, quick, ready, shallow, slick, smooth, smooth-tongued, suave, superficial, unctuous. ▷ TALKATIVE. *Opp* INARTICULATE, SINCERE.

glide *vb* coast, drift, float, fly, freewheel, glissade, hang, hover, move smoothly, sail, skate, ski, skid, skim, slide, slip, soar, stream.

glimpse *n* glance, look, peep, sight, *inf* squint, view. • *vb* discern, distinguish, espy, get a glimpse of, make out, notice, observe, see briefly, sight, spot, spy.

glisten *vb* flash, gleam, glimmer, glint, glitter, reflect, shine. ▷ LIGHT.

glitter *vb* coruscate, flash, scintillate, spark, sparkle, twinkle. ▷ LIGHT. **glittering** ▷ BRIGHT.

gloat *vb* boast, brag, *inf* crow, exult, glory, rejoice, *inf* rub it in, show off, triumph.

global *adj* broad, far-reaching, international, pandemic, total, universal, wide-ranging, worldwide. *Opp* LOCAL.

globe *n* **1** ball, globule, orb, sphere. **2** earth, planet, world.

gloom *n* blackness, cloudiness, darkness, dimness, dullness, dusk, murk, murkiness, obscurity, semi-darkness, shade, shadow, twilight. ▷ DEPRESSION.

gloomy *adj* **1** cheerless, cloudy, dark, depressing, dim, dingy, dismal, dreary, dull, glum, grim, heavy, joyless, murky, obscure, overcast, shadowy, shady, sombre. **2** *a gloomy mood.* depressed, downhearted, lugubrious, mournful, pessimistic, saturnine. ▷ SAD. *Opp* CHEERFUL.

glorious *adj* **1** celebrated, distinguished, eminent, famed, famous, heroic, illustrious, noble, noted, renowned, triumphant. **2** *glorious weather.* beautiful, bright, brilliant, dazzling, delightful, excellent, fine, gorgeous, grand, impressive, lovely, magnificent, majestic, marvellous, outstanding, pleasurable, resplendent, spectacular, splendid, *inf* super, superb, wonderful. *Opp* ORDINARY.

glory *n* **1** credit, distinction, eminence, fame, honour, *inf* kudos, praise, prestige, renown, repute, reputation, success, triumph. **2** *glory to God.* adoration, exaltation, glorification, gratitude, homage, praise, thanksgiving, veneration, worship **3** *glory of sunrise.* brightness, brilliance, grandeur, magnificence, majesty, radiance, splendour, wonder. ▷ BEAUTY.

gloss *n* **1** brightness, brilliance, burnish, finish, glaze, gleam, lustre, polish, sheen, shine, varnish. **2** annotation, comment, definition, elucidation, exegesis, explanation, footnote, marginal note, note, paraphrase. • *vb* annotate, comment on, define, elucidate, explain, interpret, paraphrase. **gloss over** ▷ CONCEAL.

glossary *n* dictionary, phrasebook, vocabulary, word-list.

glossy *adj* bright, burnished, glassy, glazed, gleaming, glistening, lustrous, polished, reflective, shiny, silky, sleek, smooth, waxed. *Opp* DULL.

glove *n* gauntlet, mitt, mitten.

glow *n* **1** burning, fieriness, heat, incandescence, luminosity, lustre, phosphorescence, radiation, red-heat, redness. **2** ardour, blush, enthusiasm, fervour, flush, passion, rosiness, warmth. • *vb* blush, flush, gleam, incandesce, light up, phosphoresce, radiate heat, redden, smoulder, warm up. ▷ LIGHT.

glower *vb* frown, glare, lour, lower, scowl, stare angrily.

glowing *adj* **1** aglow, bright, hot, incandescent, lambent, luminous, phosphorescent, radiant, red, red-hot, white-hot. **2** *glowing praise.* complimentary, enthusiastic, fervent, passionate, warm.

glue *n* adhesive, cement, fixative, gum, paste, sealant, size, wallpaper-paste. • *vb* affix, bond, cement, fasten, fix, gum, paste, seal, stick.

glum *adj* cheerless, displeased, gloomy, grim, heavy, joyless, lugubrious, moody, mournful, *inf* out of sorts, saturnine, sullen. ▷ SAD. *Opp* CHEERFUL.

glut *n* abundance, excess, over-abundance, overflow, overprovision, plenty, superfluity, surfeit, surplus. *Opp* SCARCITY.

glutton *n joc* good trencherman, gormandizer, gourmand, *inf* greedy-guts, guzzler, *inf* pig.

gluttonous *adj* gormandizing, greedy, *inf* hoggish, *inf* piggish, insatiable, ravenous, voracious.

gnarled *adj* bent, bumpy, contorted, crooked, distorted, knobbly, knotted, knotty, lumpy, rough, rugged, twisted, warped.

gnaw *vb* bite, chew, erode, wear away. ▷ EAT.

go *n* attempt, chance, *inf* crack, opportunity, *inf* shot, *inf* stab, try, turn. • *vb* **1** advance, begin, be off, commence, decamp, depart, disappear, embark, escape, get away, get going, get moving, get out, get under way, leave, make off, move, *inf* nip along, pass along, pass on, proceed, retire, retreat, run, set off, set out, *inf* shove off, start, take off, take your leave, vanish, *old use* wend your way, withdraw. ▷ RUN, TRAVEL, WALK. **2** die, fade, fail, give way. **3** extend, lead, reach, stretch. **4** *car won't go.* act, function, operate, perform, run, work. **5** *bomb went bang.* give off, make, produce, sound. **6** *Time goes slowly.*

elapse, lapse, pass. **7** *go sour.* become, grow, turn. **8** *Milk goes in the fridge.* belong, feel at home, have a proper place, live. **go away** ▷ DEPART. **go down** ▷ DESCEND, SINK. **go in for** ▷ LIKE. **go into** ▷ INVESTIGATE. **go off** ▷ EXPLODE. **go on** ▷ CONTINUE. **go through** ▷ SUFFER. **go to** ▷ VISIT. **go together** ▷ MATCH. **go with** ▷ ACCOMPANY. **go without** ▷ ABSTAIN.

goad *vb* badger, *inf* chivvy, egg on, *inf* hassle, needle, prick, prod, prompt, spur, urge. ▷ STIMULATE.

go-ahead *adj* ambitious, enterprising, forward-looking, progressive, resourceful. • *n* approval, *inf* green light, permission, sanction, *inf* say-so, *inf* thumbs-up.

goal *n* aim, ambition, aspiration, design, end, ideal, intention, object, objective, purpose, target.

gobble *vb* bolt, devour, gulp, guzzle. ▷ EAT.

go-between *n* agent, broker, envoy, intermediary, liaison, mediator, messenger, middleman, negotiator. **act as go-between** ▷ MEDIATE.

god,

goddess *ns* deity, divinity, godhead, spirit. **God** the Almighty, the Creator, the supreme being. **the gods** the immortals, the pantheon, the powers above.

godsend *n inf* bit of good luck, blessing, boon, gift, miracle, *inf* stroke of good fortune, windfall.

golden *adj* **1** aureate, gilded, gilt. **2** *golden hair.* blond, blonde, flaxen, yellow.

good *adj* **1** acceptable, admirable, agreeable, appropriate, approved of, commendable, delightful, enjoyable, esteemed, *inf* fabulous, fair, *inf* fantastic, fine, gratifying, happy, *inf* incredible, lovely, marvellous, nice, perfect, *inf* phenomenal, pleasant, pleasing, praiseworthy, proper, remarkable, right, satisfactory, *inf* sensational, sound, splendid, suitable, *inf* super, superb, useful, valid, valuable, wonderful, worthy. ▷ EXCELLENT. **2** *a good person.* angelic, benevolent, caring, charitable, chaste, considerate, decent, dependable, dutiful, ethical, friendly, helpful, holy, honest, honourable, humane, incorruptible, innocent, just, law-abiding, loyal, merciful, moral, noble, obedient, personable, pure, reliable, religious, righteous, saintly, sound, *inf* straight, thoughtful, true, trustworthy, upright, virtuous, well-behaved, well-mannered, worthy. ▷ KIND. **3** *a good worker.* able, accomplished, capable, conscientious, efficient, gifted, proficient, skilful, skilled, talented. ▷ CLEVER. **4** *good work.* careful, competent, correct, creditable, efficient, meritorious, neat, orderly, presentable, professional, thorough, well-done. **5** *good food.* beneficial, delicious, eatable, healthy, nourishing, nutritious, tasty, well-cooked, wholesome. **6** *a good book.* classic, exciting, great, interesting, readable, well-written. *Opp* BAD. **good-humoured** ▷ GOOD-TEMPERED. **good-looking** ▷ HANDSOME. **good-natured** ▷ GOOD-TEMPERED. **good person** *inf* angel, *inf* jewel, philanthropist, *inf* saint, Samaritan, worthy. **goods 1** belongings, chattels, effects, possessions, property. **2** commodities, freight, load, merchandise, produce, stock, wares.

goodbye *n* farewell, departure, leave-taking, parting words, send-off, valediction. □ *adieu, adios, arrivederci, auf Wiedersehen, au revoir, bon voyage, cheerio, ciao, so long.*

good-tempered *adj* accommodating, amenable, amiable, benevolent, benign, cheerful, cheery, considerate, cooperative, cordial, friendly, genial, good-humoured, good-natured, helpful, in a good mood, obliging, patient, pleasant, relaxed, smiling, sympathetic, thoughtful, willing. ▷ KIND. *Opp* BAD-TEMPERED.

gorge *vb* be greedy, fill up, gormandize, guzzle, indulge yourself, *inf* make a pig of yourself, overeat, *inf* stuff yourself. ▷ EAT.

gorgeous *adj* colourful, dazzling, glorious, magnificent, resplendent, showy, splendid, sumptuous. ▷ BEAUTIFUL.

gory *adj* blood-stained, bloody, grisly, gruesome, sanguinary, savage.

gospel *n* creed, doctrine, good news, good tidings, message, religion, revelation, teaching, testament.

gossip *n* **1** casual talk, chatter, *inf* the grapevine, hearsay, prattle, rumour, scandal, small talk, *inf* tattle, *inf* tittle-tattle. **2** *inf* blab, busybody, chatterbox, *inf* Nosey Parker, rumourmonger, scandalmonger, telltale. • *vb inf* blab, chat, chatter, *inf* natter, prattle, spread scandal, *inf* tattle, tell tales, *inf* tittle-tattle. ▷ TALK.

gouge *vb* chisel, dig, gash, hollow, incise, scoop. ▷ CUT.

gourmet *n Fr* bon viveur, connoisseur, epicure, gastronome, *derog* gourmand.

govern *vb* **1** administer, be in charge of, command, conduct affairs, control, direct, guide, head, lead, look after, manage, oversee, preside over, reign, rule, run, steer, superintend, supervise. **2** *govern your anger.* bridle, check, control, curb, discipline, keep in check, keep under control, master, regulate, restrain, tame.

government *n* administration, authority, bureaucracy, conduct of state affairs, constitution, control, direction, domination, management, oversight, regime, regulation, rule, sovereignty, supervision, surveillance, sway. □ *commonwealth, democracy, dictatorship, empire, federation, kingdom, monarchy, oligarchy, republic.*

gown *n* dress, frock. ▷ CLOTHES.

grab *vb* appropriate, arrogate, *inf* bag, capture, catch, clutch, *inf* collar, commandeer, expropriate, get hold of, grasp, hold, *inf* nab, pluck, seize, snap up, snatch, usurp.

grace *n* **1** attractiveness, beauty, charm, ease, elegance, fluidity, gracefulness, loveliness, poise, refinement, softness, tastefulness. **2** *God's grace.* beneficence, benevolence, compassion, favour, forgiveness, goodness, graciousness, kindness, love, mercy. **3** *grace before meals.* blessing, prayer, thanksgiving.

graceful *adj* **1** agile, balletic, deft, dignified, easy, elegant, flowing, fluid, natural, nimble, pliant, slender, slim, smooth, supple, willowy. ▷ BEAUTIFUL. **2** *graceful compliments.* courteous, courtly, delicate, kind, polite, refined, suave, tactful, urbane. *Opp* GRACELESS.

graceless *adj* **1** awkward, clumsy, gangling, gawky, inelegant, maladroit, uncoordinated, ungainly. ▷ CLUMSY. *Opp* GRACEFUL. **2** *graceless manners.* boorish, gauche, inept, tactless, uncouth. ▷ RUDE.

gracious *adj* **1** affable, agreeable, civilized, cordial, courteous, dignified, elegant, friendly, good-natured, pleasant, polite, with grace. ▷ KIND. **2** clement, compassionate, forgiving, generous, indulgent, lenient, magnanimous, pitying, sympathetic. ▷ MERCIFUL. **3** *gracious living.* affluent, expensive, lavish, luxurious, opulent, selfindulgent, sumptuous.

grade *n* category, class, condition, degree, echelon, estate, level, mark, notch, point, position, quality, rank, rung, situation, standard, standing, status, step. • *vb* **1** arrange, categorize, classify, differentiate, group, organize, range, size, sort. **2** *grade students' work.* assess, evaluate, mark, rank, rate.

gradient *n* ascent, bank, declivity, hill, incline, rise, slope.

gradual *adj* continuous, easy, even, gentle, leisurely, moderate, regular, slow, steady, unhurried, unspectacular. *Opp* SUDDEN.

graduate *vb* **1** become a graduate, be successful, get a degree, pass, qualify. **2** *graduate a measuring-rod.* calibrate, divide into graded sections, gradate, mark off, mark with a scale.

graft *vb* implant, insert, join, splice.

grain *n* **1** atom, bit, crumb, fleck, fragment, granule, iota, jot, mite, molecule, morsel, mote, particle, scrap, seed, speck, trace. **2** ▷ CEREAL.

grand *adj* **1** aristocratic, august, dignified, eminent, glorious, great, important, imposing, impressive, lordly, magnificent, majestic, noble, opulent, palatial, regal, royal, splendid, stately, sumptuous, superb. ▷ BIG. **2** [*derog*] haughty, *inf* high-and-mighty, lofty, patronizing, pompous, posh, *inf* upper crust. ▷ GRANDIOSE. *Opp* MODEST.

grandiloquent *adj* bombastic, elaborate, florid, flowery, fustian, high-flown, inflated, melodramatic, ornate, poetic, pompous, rhetorical, turgid. ▷ GRANDIOSE. *Opp* SIMPLE.

grandiose *adj* affected, ambitious, exaggerated, extravagant, flamboyant, *inf* flashy, grand, highfalutin, ostentatious, overdone, *inf* over the top, pretentious, showy. ▷ GRANDILOQUENT. *Opp* MODEST.

grant *n* allocation, allowance, annuity, award, benefaction, bursary, concession, contribution, donation, endowment, expenses, gift, honorarium, investment, loan, pension, scholarship, sponsorship, subsidy, subvention. • *vb* **1** allocate, allot, allow, assign, award, bestow, confer, donate, give, pay, provide, supply. **2** *grant that I'm right.* accede, accept, acknowledge, admit, agree, concede, consent, vouchsafe.

graph *n* chart, column-graph, diagram, grid, pie chart, table.

graphic *adj* clear, descriptive, detailed, lifelike, lucid, photographic, plain, realistic, representational, vivid, well-drawn.

grapple *vb* clutch (at), grab, seize, tackle, wrestle. ▷ GRASP, FIGHT. **grapple with** *grapple with a problem.* attend to, come to grips with, contend with, cope with, deal with, engage with, get involved with, handle, *inf* have a go at, manage, try to solve.

grasp *vb* **1** catch, clasp, clutch, get hold of, *inf* get your hands on, grab, grapple with, grip, hang on to, hold, *inf* nab, seize, snatch, take hold of. **2** *grasp an idea.* appreciate, apprehend, comprehend, *inf* cotton on to, follow, *inf* get the drift of, get the hang of, get the point of, learn, master, realize, take in, understand. **grasping** ▷ GREEDY.

grass *n* downland, field, grassland, green, lawn, meadow, pasture, playing-field, prairie, savannah, steppe, *poet* sward, turf, veld. • *vb* ▷ INFORM.

grate *n* fireplace, hearth. • *vb* cut, grind, rasp, shred, triturate. **grate on** ▷ ANNOY. **grating** ▷ ANNOYING, HARSH.

grateful *adj* appreciative, beholden, gratified, indebted, obliged, thankful. *Opp* UNGRATEFUL.

gratify *vb* delight, fulfil, indulge, pander to, please, satisfy.

gratis *adj* complimentary, free, free of charge, gratuitous, without charge.

gratitude *n* appreciation, gratefulness, thankfulness, thanks.

gratuitous *adj* **1** ▷ GRATIS. **2** *gratuitous insults.* baseless, groundless, inappropriate, needless, unasked-for, uncalled-for, undeserved, unjustifiable, unmerited, unnecessary, unprovoked, unsolicited, unwarranted. *Opp* JUSTIFIABLE.

gratuity *n* bonus, *inf* perk, *Fr* pourboire, present, recompense, reward, tip.

grave *adj* **1** acute, critical, crucial, dangerous, important, *inf* life and death, major, momentous, perilous, pressing, serious, severe, significant, terminal (*illness*), threatening, urgent, vital, weighty, worrying. **2** *a grave offence.* criminal, indictable, punishable. **3** *a grave look.* dignified, earnest, grim, long-faced, pensive, sedate, serious, severe, sober, solemn, sombre, subdued, thoughtful, unsmiling. ▷ SAD. *Opp* CHEERFUL, TRIVIAL. • *n* barrow, burial-place, crypt, *inf* last resting-place, mausoleum, sepulchre, tomb, tumulus, vault. ▷ GRAVESTONE.

gravel *n* grit, pebbles, shingle, stones.

gravestone *n* headstone, memorial, monument, tombstone.

graveyard *n* burial-ground, cemetery, churchyard, necropolis.

gravity *n* **1** acuteness, danger, importance, magnitude, momentousness, seriousness, severity, significance, weightiness. **2** *behave with gravity.* ceremony, dignity, earnestness, *Lat* gravitas, pomp, reserve, sedateness, sobriety, solemnity. **3** *force of gravity.* attraction, gravitation, heaviness, ponderousness, pull, weight.

graze *n* abrasion, laceration, raw spot, scrape, scratch. ▷ WOUND.

grease *n* fat, lubrication, oil.

greasy *adj* **1** buttery, fatty, oily, slippery, slithery, smeary, waxy. **2** *greasy manner.* fawning, flattering, fulsome, grovelling, ingratiating, slick, *inf* smarmy, sycophantic, toadying, unctuous.

great *adj* **1** colossal, enormous, extensive, giant, gigantic, grand, huge, immense, large, massive, prodigious, *inf* tremendous, vast. ▷ BIG. **2** *great pain.* acute, considerable, excessive, extreme, intense, marked, pronounced. ▷ SEVERE. **3** *great events.* grand, imposing, large-scale, momentous, serious, significant, spectacular, weighty. ▷ IMPORTANT. **4** *great music.* brilliant, classic, *inf* fabulous, famous, *inf* fantastic, fine, first-rate, outstanding, wonderful. ▷ EXCELLENT. **5** *a great athlete.* able, celebrated, distinguished, eminent, gifted, notable, noted, prominent, renowned, talented, well-known. ▷ FAMOUS. **6** *a great friend.* chief, close, dedicated, devoted, faithful, fast, loyal, main, true, valued. **7** *a great reader.* active, ardent, assiduous, eager, enthusiastic, frequent, habitual, keen, passionate, zealous. **8** ▷ GOOD. *Opp* SMALL, UNIMPORTANT.

greed *n* **1** appetite, craving, gluttony, gormandizing, hunger, insatiability, intemperance, overeating, ravenousness, selfindulgence, voraciousness, voracity. **2** *greed for wealth.* acquisitiveness, avarice, covetousness, cupidity, desire, rapacity, self-interest. ▷ SELFISHNESS.

greedy *adj* **1** famished, gluttonous, gormandizing, *inf* hoggish, hungry, insatiable, intemperate, omnivorous, *inf* piggish, ravenous, self-indulgent, starving, voracious. *Opp* ABSTEMIOUS. **2** *greedy for wealth.* acquisitive, avaricious, avid, covetous, desirous, eager, grasping, materialistic, mean, mercenary, miserly, *inf* moneygrubbing, rapacious, selfish. *Opp* UNSELFISH. **be greedy** ▷ GORGE. **greedy person** ▷ GLUTTON.

green *adj* **1** grassy, greenish, leafy, verdant. □ *emerald, grass-green, jade, khaki, lime, olive, pea-green, turquoise.* **2** ▷ IMMATURE.

greenery *n* foliage, leaves, plants, vegetation.

greet *vb* accost, acknowledge, address, give a greeting to, hail, receive, salute, *inf* say hello to, usher in, welcome.

greeting *n* salutation, reception, welcome. **greetings** compliments, congratulations, felicitations, good wishes, regards.

grey *adj* ashen, blackish, colourless, greying, grizzled, grizzly, hoary, leaden, livid, pearly, silver, silvery, slate-grey, smoky, sooty, whitish. ▷ GLOOMY.

grid *n* framework, grating, grille, lattice, network.

grief *n* affliction, anguish, dejection, depression, desolation, despondency, distress, heartache, heartbreak, melancholy, misery, mourning, pain, regret, remorse, sadness, sorrow, suffering, tragedy, unhappiness, woe, wretchedness. ▷ PAIN. *Opp* HAPPINESS. **come to grief** ▷ FAIL.

grievance *n* **1** calamity, damage, hardship, harm, indignity, injury, injustice. **2** allegation, *inf* bone to pick, charge, complaint, *inf* gripe, objection.

grieve *vb* **1** afflict, cause grief, depress, dismay, distress, hurt, pain, sadden, upset, wound. *Opp* PLEASE.

2 be in mourning, feel grief, *inf* eat your heart out, fret, lament, mope, mourn, suffer, wail, weep. *Opp* REJOICE.

grim *adj* alarming, appalling, awful, cruel, dire, dour, dreadful, fearsome, fierce, forbidding, formidable, frightening, frightful, frowning, ghastly, grisly, gruesome, harsh, hideous, horrible, *inf* horrid, inexorable, inflexible, joyless, louring, menacing, merciless, ominous, pitiless, relentless, ruthless, savage, severe, sinister, stark, stern, sullen, surly, terrible, threatening, unattractive, uncompromising, unfriendly, unpleasant, unrelenting, unsmiling, unyielding. ▷ GLOOMY. *Opp* CHEERFUL.

grime *n* dirt, dust, filth, grit, muck, scum, soot.

grind *vb* **1** abrade, comminute, crumble, crush, erode, granulate, grate, mill, pound, powder, pulverize, rasp, triturate. **2** file, polish, sand, sandpaper, scrape, sharpen, smooth, wear away, whet. **3** *grind your teeth*. gnash, grate, grit, rub together. **grind away** ▷ WORK. **grind down** ▷ OPPRESS.

grip *n* clasp, clutch, grasp, handclasp, hold, purchase, stranglehold. ▷ CONTROL. ● *vb* **1** clasp, clutch, get a grip of, grab, grasp, hold, seize, take hold of. **2** *grip the imagination*. absorb, compel, engage, engross, enthral, entrance, fascinate, hypnotize, mesmerize, rivet, spellbind. **come to grips with** ▷ TACKLE.

grisly *adj* appalling, awful, bloody, disgusting, dreadful, fearful, frightful, ghastly, ghoulish, gory, grim, gruesome, hair-raising, hideous, horrible, *inf* horrid, horrifying, macabre, nauseating, repellent, repulsive, revolting, sickening, terrible.

gristly *adj* leathery, rubbery, tough, uneatable.

gritty *adj* abrasive, dusty, grainy, granular, gravelly, harsh, rasping, rough, sandy.

groan *vb* **1** cry out, lament, moan, sigh, wail, whimper, whine. **2** ▷ COMPLAIN.

groom *n* **1** ostler, stable-lad, stableman. **2** bridegroom, husband. ● *vb* **1** brush, clean, make neat, neaten, preen, smarten up, spruce up, tidy, *inf* titivate. **2** *groom someone for a job*. coach, drill, educate, get ready, prepare, prime, train up, tutor.

groove *n* channel, cut, fluting, furrow, gouge, gutter, hollow, indentation, rut, score, scratch, slot, striation, track.

grope *vb* cast about, feel about, fish, flounder, fumble, search blindly.

gross *adj* **1** bloated, massive, obese, overweight, repellent, repulsive, revolting. ▷ FAT. **2** churlish, coarse, crude, rude, unrefined, unsophisticated, vulgar. **3** *gross injustice*. blatant, flagrant, glaring, manifest, monstrous, obvious, outrageous, shameful. **4** *gross income*. before tax, inclusive, overall, total, whole.

grotesque *adj* absurd, bizarre, curious, deformed, distorted, fantastic, freakish, gnarled, incongruous, ludicrous, macabre, malformed, misshapen, monstrous, outlandish, preposterous, queer, ridiculous, strange, surreal, twisted, ugly, unnatural, weird.

ground *n* **1** clay, dirt, earth, loam, mud, soil. **2** area, land, property, surroundings, terrain. **3** campus, estate, garden, park. **4** *sports ground*. arena, court, field, pitch, playground, playing-field, recreation ground, stadium. **5** *grounds for complaint*. argument, base, basis, case, cause, excuse, evidence, foundation, justification, motive, proof, rationale, reason. ● *vb* **1** base, establish, found, set, settle. **2** coach, educate, instruct, prepare, teach, train, tutor. **3** beach, run ashore, shipwreck, strand, wreck.

groundless *adj* baseless, chimerical, false, gratuitous, hypothetical, illusory, imaginary, irrational, motiveless, needless, speculative, suppositional, uncalled for, unfounded, unjustifiable, unjustified, unproven, unreasonable, unsound, unsubstantiated, unsupported, unwarranted.

group *n* **1** [*people*] alliance, assemblage, assembly, association, band, bevy, body, brotherhood, *inf* bunch, cadre, cartel, caste, caucus, circle, clan, class, *derog* clique, club, cohort, colony, committee, community, company, conclave, congregation, consortium, contingent, corps, coterie, coven, crew, crowd, delegation, faction, family, federation, force, fraternity, gang, gathering, guild, horde, host, knot, league, meeting, *derog* mob, multitude, number, organization, party, phalanx, picket, platoon, posse, *derog* rabble, ring, sect, *derog* shower, sisterhood, society, squad, squadron, swarm, syndicate, team, throng, troop, troupe, union, unit. **2** [*things, animals*] accumulation, agglomeration, assemblage, assortment, batch, battery (*guns*), brood (*chicks*), bunch, bundle, category, class, clump, cluster, clutch (*eggs*), collection, combination, conglomeration, constellation, convoy, covey (*birds*), fleet, flock, gaggle (*geese*), galaxy, grouping, heap, herd, hoard, host, litter, mass, pack, pile, pride (*lions*), school, set, shoal (*fish*), species. **3** ▷ MUSICIAN. ● *vb* **1** arrange, assemble, assort, bracket together, bring together, categorize, classify, collect, deploy, gather, herd, marshal, order, organize, put together, set out, sort. **2** associate, band, cluster, come together, congregate, crowd, flock, gather, get together, herd, make groups, swarm, team up, throng.

grovel *vb* abase yourself, be humble, cower, *inf* crawl, *inf* creep, cringe, demean yourself, fawn, flatter, ingratiate yourself, *inf* kowtow, *inf* lick someone's boots, prostrate yourself, snivel, *inf* suck up, *inf* toady. **grovelling** ▷ OBSEQUIOUS.

grow *vb* **1** augment, become bigger, broaden, build up, burgeon, come to life, develop, emerge, enlarge, evolve, expand, extend, fill out, flourish, flower, germinate, improve, increase, lengthen, live, make progress, mature, multiply, mushroom, progress, proliferate, prosper, put on growth, ripen, rise, shoot up, spread, spring up, sprout, survive, swell, thicken, thrive. **2** *grow roses.* cultivate, farm, help along, nurture, produce, propagate, raise. **3** *grow older.* become, get, turn.

grown-up *adj* adult, fully-grown, mature, well-developed.

growth *n* **1** accretion, advance, augmentation, broadening, burgeoning, development, enlargement, evolution, expansion, extension, flowering, getting bigger, growing, improvement, increase, maturation, maturing, progress, proliferation, prosperity, spread, success. **2** crop, harvest, plants, produce, vegetation, yield. **3** cancer, cyst, excrescence, lump, swelling, tumour.

grub *n* **1** caterpillar, larva, maggot. **2** ▷ FOOD. ● *vb* ▷ DIG.

grudge *n* ▷ RESENTMENT. ● *vb* begrudge, covet, envy, resent.

grudging *adj* cautious, envious, guarded, half-hearted, hesitant, jealous, reluctant, resentful, secret, unenthusiastic, ungracious, unkind, unwilling. *Opp* ENTHUSIASTIC.

gruelling *adj* arduous, backbreaking, crippling, demanding, exhausting, fatiguing, laborious, punishing, severe, stiff, strenuous, taxing, tiring, tough, uphill, wearying. ▷ DIFFICULT. *Opp* EASY.

gruesome *adj* appalling, awful, bloody, disgusting, dreadful, fearful, fearsome, frightful, ghastly, ghoulish, gory, grim, grisly, hair-raising, hideous, horrible, *inf* horrid, horrific, horrifying, macabre, repellent, repugnant, revolting, shocking, sickening, terrible.

gruff *adj* **1** guttural, harsh, hoarse, husky, rasping, rough, throaty. **2** ▷ BAD-TEMPERED.

grumble *vb inf* beef, fuss, *inf* gripe, *inf* grouch, grouse, make a fuss, *inf* moan, object, protest, *inf* whinge. ▷ COMPLAIN.

guarantee *n* assurance, bond, oath, obligation, pledge, promise, surety, undertaking, warranty, word of honour. • *vb* **1** assure, certify, give a guarantee, pledge, promise, swear, undertake, vouch, vow. **2** ensure, make sure of, reserve, secure, stake a claim to.

guard *n* bodyguard, *inf* bouncer, custodian, escort, guardian, *sl* heavy, lookout, *sl* minder, patrol, picket, *sl* screw, security-guard, sentinel, sentry, warder, watchman. • *vb* be on guard over, care for, defend, keep safe, keep watch on, look after, mind, oversee, patrol, police, preserve, prevent from escaping, protect, safeguard, secure, shelter, shield, stand guard over, supervise, tend, watch, watch over. **on your guard** ▷ ALERT.

guardian *n* **1** adoptive parent, foster-parent. **2** champion, custodian, defender, keeper, preserver, protector, trustee, warden. ▷ GUARD.

guess *n* assumption, conjecture, estimate, feeling, *sl* guesstimate, guesswork, hunch, hypothesis, intuition, opinion, prediction, *inf* shot in the dark, speculation, supposition, surmise, suspicion, theory. • *vb* assume, conclude, conjecture, divine, estimate, expect, fancy, feel, have a hunch, have a theory, *inf* hazard a guess, hypothesize, imagine, intuit, judge, make a guess, postulate, predict, *inf* reckon, speculate, suppose, surmise, suspect, think likely, work out.

guest *n* **1** caller, company, visitor. **2** *hotel guests.* boarder, customer, lodger, patron, resident, tenant.

guidance *n* advice, briefing, counselling, direction, guidelines, guiding, help, instruction, leadership, management, *inf* spoon-feeding, *inf* taking by the hand, teaching, tips.

guide *n* **1** courier, escort, leader, navigator, pilot. **2** adviser, counsellor, director, guru, mentor. **3** atlas, directory, gazetteer, guidebook, handbook, *Lat* vade mecum. • *vb* **1** conduct, direct, escort, lead, manoeuvre, navigate, pilot, shepherd, show the way, steer, supervise, usher. **2** advise, brief, control, counsel, educate, give guidance to, govern, help along, influence, instruct, regulate, *inf* take by the hand, teach, train, tutor. *Opp* MISLEAD.

guilt *n* **1** blame, blameworthiness, criminality, culpability, fault, guiltiness, liability, responsibility, sinfulness, wickedness, wrongdoing. **2** *a look of guilt.* bad conscience, contriteness, contrition, dishonour, guilty feelings, penitence, regret, remorse, self-accusation, self-reproach, shame, sorrow. *Opp* INNOCENCE.

guiltless *adj* above suspicion, blameless, clear, faultless, free, honourable, immaculate, innocent, in the right, irreproachable, pure, sinless, untarnished, untroubled, virtuous. *Opp* GUILTY.

guilty *adj* **1** at fault, blameable, blameworthy, culpable, in the wrong, liable, reprehensible, responsible. **2** *a guilty look.* apologetic, ashamed, conscience-stricken, contrite, penitent, *inf* red-faced, regretful, remorseful, repentant, rueful, shamefaced, sheepish, sorry. *Opp* GUILTLESS, SHAMELESS.

gullible *adj* credulous, easily taken in, *inf* green, impressionable, inexperienced, innocent, naïve, suggestible, trusting, unsophisticated, unsuspecting, unwary. *Opp* WARY.

gulp *n* mouthful, swallow, *inf* swig. • *vb* **1** bolt down, gobble, swallow, *inf* wolf. ▷ EAT. **2** *inf* knock back, quaff, *inf* swig. ▷ DRINK. **3** *gulp back tears.* check, choke back, stifle, suppress.

gumption *n* cleverness, *inf* common sense, enterprise, initiative, judgement, *inf* nous, resourcefulness, sense, wisdom.

gun *n plur* artillery, firearm. □ *airgun, automatic, blunderbuss, cannon, machine-gun, mortar, musket, pistol, revolver, rifle, shot-gun,* plur *small arms, sub-*

machine-gun, tommy-gun. **gun down** ▷ SHOOT.

gunfire *n* cannonade, cross-fire, firing, gunshots, salvo.

gunman *n* assassin, bandit, criminal, desperado, fighter, gangster, killer, murderer, sniper, terrorist.

gurgle *vb* babble, bubble, burble, ripple, purl, splash.

gush *n* burst, cascade, eruption, flood, flow, jet, outpouring, overflow, rush, spout, spurt, squirt, stream, tide, torrent. • *vb* **1** come in a gush, cascade, flood, flow freely, overflow, pour, run, rush, spout, spurt, squirt, stream, well up. **2** be enthusiastic, be sentimental, bubble over, fuss, *inf* go on, prattle on, talk on. **gushing** ▷ EFFUSIVE, SENTIMENTAL.

gusto *n* appetite, delight, enjoyment, enthusiasm, excitement, liveliness, pleasure, relish, satisfaction, spirit, verve, vigour, zest.

gut *vb* **1** clean, disembowel, draw, eviscerate, remove the guts of. **2** *gut a building*. clear, despoil, empty, loot, pillage, plunder, ransack, ravage, remove the contents of, sack, strip.

guts *plur n* **1** alimentary canal, belly, bowels, entrails, *inf* innards, insides, intestines, stomach, viscera. **2** ▷ COURAGE.

gutter *n* channel, conduit, ditch, drain, duct, guttering, sewer, sluice, trench, trough.

gypsy *n* nomad, Romany, traveller, wanderer.

gyrate *vb* circle, pirouette, revolve, rotate, spin, spiral, swivel, turn, twirl, wheel, whirl.

H

habit *n* **1** convention, custom, pattern, policy, practice, routine, rule, usage, *old use* wont. **2** attitude, bent, disposition, inclination, manner, mannerism, penchant, predisposition, proclivity, propensity, quirk, tendency, way. **3** *bad habit.* addiction, compulsion, craving, dependence, fixation, obsession, vice.

habitable *adj* in good repair, inhabitable, liveable, usable. *Opp* UNINHABITABLE.

habitual *adj* **1** accustomed, common, conventional, customary, established, expected, familiar, fixed, frequent, natural, normal, ordinary, predictable, regular, ritual, routine, set, settled, standard, traditional, typical, usual, *old use* wonted. **2** addictive, besetting, chronic, established, ineradicable, ingrained, obsessive, persistent, recurrent. **3** *habitual smokers.* addicted, conditioned, confirmed, dependent, hardened, *inf* hooked, inveterate, persistent.

hack *vb* carve, chop, gash, hew, mangle, mutilate, slash. ▷ CUT.

hackneyed *adj* banal, clichéd, cliché-ridden, commonplace, conventional, *inf* corny, familiar, feeble, obvious, overused, pedestrian, platitudinous, predictable, stale, stereotyped, stock, threadbare, tired, trite, uninspired, unoriginal. *Opp* NEW.

haggard *adj inf* all skin and bone, careworn, drawn, emaciated, exhausted, gaunt, hollow-cheeked, hollow-eyed, pinched, run-down, scraggy, scrawny, shrunken, thin, tired out, ugly, unhealthy, wasted, weary, withered, worn out, *inf* worried to death. *Opp* HEALTHY.

haggle *vb* argue, bargain, barter, discuss terms, negotiate, quibble, wrangle. ▷ QUARREL.

hail *vb* **1** accost, address, call to, greet, signal to. **2** ▷ ACCLAIM.

hair *n* **1** beard, bristles, curls, fleece, fur, hank, locks, mane, *inf* mop, moustache, shock, tresses, whiskers. **2** coiffure, cut, haircut, *inf* hair-do, hairstyle, style. □ *bob, braid, bun, crew-cut, dreadlocks, fringe, Mohican,* inf *perm, permanent wave, pigtail, plait, pony-tail, quiff, ringlets, short back and sides, sideboards, sideburns, tonsure, top-knot.* **3** *false hair.* hair-piece, toupee, wig.

hairdresser *n* barber, coiffeur, coiffeuse, hair-stylist.

hairless *adj* bald, bare, cleanshaven, naked, shaved, shaven, smooth. *Opp* HAIRY.

hairy *adj* bearded, bristly, downy, feathery, fleecy, furry, fuzzy, hirsute, long-haired, shaggy, stubbly, woolly. *Opp* HAIRLESS.

half-hearted *adj* apathetic, cool, easily distracted, feeble, indifferent, ineffective, lackadaisical, listless, lukewarm, nonchalant, passive, perfunctory, phlegmatic, uncaring, uncommitted, unconcerned, unenthusiastic, unreliable, wavering, weak, *inf* wishywashy. *Opp* ENTHUSIASTIC.

hall *n* **1** auditorium, concert-hall, lecture room, theatre. **2** corridor, entrance-hall, foyer, hallway, lobby, passage, passageway, vestibule.

hallowed *adj* blessed, consecrated, dedicated, holy, honoured, revered, reverenced, sacred, sacrosanct, worshipped.

hallucinate *vb* day-dream, dream, fantasize, *inf* have a trip, have hallucinations, *inf* see things, see visions.

hallucination *n* apparition, chimera, day-dream, delusion, dream, fantasy, figment of the imagination, illusion, mirage, vision. ▷ GHOST.

halt *n* break, cessation, close, end, interruption, pause, standstill, stop, stoppage, termination. ● *vb* **1** arrest, block, break off, cease, check, curb, end, impede, obstruct, stop, terminate. **2** come to a halt, come to rest, desist, discontinue, draw up, pull up, quit, stop, wait. *Opp* START. **halting** ▷ HESITANT, IRREGULAR.

halve *vb* bisect, cut by half, cut in half, decrease, divide into halves, lessen, reduce by half, share equally, split in two.

hammer *n* mallet, sledge-hammer. ● *vb inf* bash, batter, beat, drive, knock, pound, smash, strike. ▷ DEFEAT, HIT.

hamper *vb* baulk, block, curb, curtail, delay, encumber, entangle, fetter, foil, frustrate, handicap, hinder, hold back, hold up, impede, inhibit, interfere with, obstruct, prevent, restrain, restrict, retard, shackle, slow down, thwart, trammel. *Opp* HELP.

hand *n* **1** fist, *sl* mitt, palm, *inf* paw. **2** *hand on a dial.* index, indicator, pointer. **3** [*old use*] *factory hands.* ▷ WORKER. ● *vb* convey, deliver, give, offer, pass, present, submit. **at hand** ▷ HANDY. **give a hand** ▷ HELP. **hand down** ▷ BEQUEATH. **hand over** ▷ SURRENDER. **hand round** ▷ DISTRIBUTE. **lend a hand** ▷ HELP. **to hand** ▷ HANDY.

handicap *n* **1** barrier, burden, disadvantage, difficulty, drawback, encumbrance, hindrance, impediment, inconvenience, limitation, *inf* minus, nuisance, obstacle, problem, restraint, restriction, shortcoming, stumbling-block. *Opp* ADVANTAGE. **2** defect, disability, impairment. ● *vb* be a handicap to, burden, check, curb, disable, disadvantage, encumber, hamper, hinder, hold back, impede, limit, restrain, restrict, retard, trammel. *Opp* HELP.

handicapped *adj* [*Some synonyms may cause offence*] autistic, bedridden, blind, crippled, deaf, disabled, disadvantaged, dumb, dyslexic, incapacitated, invalid, lame, limbless, maimed, mute, paralysed, paraplegic, retarded, slow, spastic, unsighted. ▷ ILL.

handiwork *n* achievement, creation, doing, invention, production, responsibility, work.

handle *n* grip, haft, handgrip, helve, hilt, knob, stock (*of rifle*). ● *vb* **1** caress, feel, finger, fondle, grasp, hold, *inf* maul, pat, *inf* paw, stroke, touch, treat. **2** *handle situations, people.* conduct, contend with, control, cope with, deal with, direct, guide, look after, manage, manipulate, tackle, treat. ▷ ORGANIZE. **3** *car handles well.* manoeuvre, operate, respond, steer, work. **4** *handle goods.* deal in, do trade in, market, sell, stock, touch, traffic in.

handsome *adj* **1** admirable, attractive, beautiful, comely, elegant, fair, fine-looking, good-looking, personable, tasteful. *Opp* UGLY. **2** *handsome gift.* big, bountiful, generous, goodly, gracious, large, liberal, magnanimous, munificent, sizeable, unselfish, valuable. *Opp* MEAN.

handy *adj* **1** convenient, easy to use, helpful, manageable, practical, serviceable, useful, well-designed, worth having. **2** *handy with tools.* adept, capable, clever, competent, practical, proficient, skilful. **3** *keep tools handy.* accessible, at hand, available, close at hand, easy to reach, get-at-able, nearby, reachable, ready, to hand. *Opp* AWKWARD, INACCESSIBLE.

hang *vb* **1** be suspended, dangle, depend, droop, flap, flop, sway, swing, trail down. **2** *hang washing.* attach, drape, fasten, fix, peg up, pin up, stick up, suspend. **3** *hang in the air.* drift, float, hover. **hang about** ▷ DAWDLE. **hang back** ▷ HESITATE. **hanging** ▷ PENDENT. **hangings** ▷ DRAPE. **hang on** ▷ WAIT. **hang on to** ▷ KEEP.

hank *n* coil, length, loop, piece, skein.

hanker *vb* ache, covet, crave, desire, fancy, *inf* have a yen, hunger, itch, long, pine, thirst, want, wish, yearn.

haphazard *adj* accidental, adventitious, arbitrary, casual, chance, chaotic, confusing, disorderly, disorganized, fortuitous, *inf* higgledy-piggledy, *inf* hit-or-miss, illogical, irrational, random, serendipitous, unforeseen, unplanned, unstructured, unsystematic. *Opp* ORDERLY.

happen *vb* arise, befall, *old use* betide, chance, come about, crop up, emerge, follow, materialize, occur, result, take place, *inf* transpire, *inf* turn out. **happen on** ▷ FIND.

happening *n* accident, affair, chance, circumstance, episode, event, incident, occasion, occurrence, phenomenon.

happiness *n* bliss, cheer, cheerfulness, contentment, delight, ecstasy, elation, enjoyment, euphoria, exhilaration, exuberance, felicity, gaiety, gladness, glee, *inf* heaven, high spirits, joy, joyfulness, joyousness, jubilation, light-heartedness, merriment, pleasure, pride, rapture, well-being. *Opp* SADNESS.

happy *adj* **1** beatific, blessed, blissful, *poet* blithe, buoyant, cheerful, cheery, contented, delighted, ecstatic, elated, enraptured, euphoric, exhilarated, exuberant, exultant, felicitous, festive, gay, glad, gleeful, good-humoured, gratified, grinning, halcyon (*days*), *inf* heavenly, high-spirited, idyllic, jocose, jocular, jocund, joking, jolly, jovial, joyful, joyous, jubilant, laughing, light-hearted, lively, merry, *inf* on top of the world, overjoyed, *inf* over the moon, pleased, proud, radiant, rapturous, rejoicing, relaxed, satisfied, smiling, *inf* starry-eyed, sunny, thrilled, triumphant. *Opp* SAD. **2** *a happy accident*. advantageous, appropriate, apt, auspicious, beneficial, convenient, favourable, felicitous, fortuitous, fortunate, lucky, opportune, propitious, timely, welcome, well-timed.

harangue *n* diatribe, exhortation, lecture, *inf* pep talk, tirade. ▷ SPEECH. • *vb* chivvy, encourage, exhort, lecture, pontificate, preach, sermonize. ▷ SPEAK, TALK.

harass *vb* annoy, attack, badger, bait, bother, chivvy, disturb, harry, *inf* hassle, hound, irritate, molest, nag, persecute, pester, *inf* pick on, *inf* plague, torment, trouble, vex, worry.

harassed *adj inf* at the end of your tether, careworn, distraught, distressed, exhausted, frayed, pressured, strained, stressed, tired, weary, worn out.

harbour *n* anchorage, dock, haven, jetty, landing-stage, marina, mooring, pier, port, quay, safe haven, shelter, wharf. • *vb* **1** conceal, give asylum to, give refuge to, give sanctuary to, hide, protect, shelter, shield. **2** *harbour a grudge*. cherish, cling on to, hold on to, keep in mind, maintain, nurse, nurture, retain.

hard *adj* **1** adamantine, compact, compressed, dense, firm, flinty, frozen, hardened, impenetrable, impervious, inflexible, rigid, rocky, solid, solidified, steely, stiff, stony, unbreakable, unyielding. **2** *hard labour*. arduous, back-breaking, exhausting, fatiguing, formidable, gruelling, harsh, heavy, laborious, onerous, rigorous, severe, stiff, strenuous, taxing, tiring, tough, uphill, wearying. **3** *a hard problem*. baffling, complex, complicated, confusing, difficult, enigmatic, insoluble, intricate, involved, knotty, perplexing, puzzling, tangled, *inf* thorny. **4** *a hard heart*. callous, cold, cruel, *inf* hard-boiled, hard-hearted, harsh, heartless, hostile, inflexible, intolerant, merciless, obdurate, pitiless, ruthless, severe, stern, strict, unbending, unfeeling, unfriendly, unkind. **5** *a hard blow*. forceful, heavy, powerful, strong, violent. **6** *hard times*. austere, bad, calamitous, disagreeable, distressing, grim, intolerable, painful, unhappy, unpleasant. **7** *a hard worker*. assiduous, conscientious, devoted, indefatigable, industrious, keen, persistent, unflagging, untiring, zealous. *Opp* EASY, SOFT. **hard-headed** ▷ BUSINESSLIKE. **hard-hearted** ▷ CRUEL. **hard up** ▷ POOR. **hard-wearing** ▷ DURABLE.

harden *vb* bake, cake, clot, coagulate, congeal, freeze, gel, jell, ossify, petrify, reinforce, set, solidify, stiffen, strengthen, toughen. *Opp* SOFTEN.

hardly *adv* barely, faintly, only just, rarely, scarcely, seldom, with difficulty.

hardship *n* adversity, affliction, austerity, bad luck, deprivation, destitution, difficulty, distress, misery, misfortune, need, privation, suffering, *inf* trials and tribulations, trouble, unhappiness, want.

hardware *n* equipment, implements, instruments, ironmongery, machinery, tools.

hardy *adj* **1** durable, fit, healthy, hearty, resilient, robust, rugged, strong, sturdy, tough, vigorous. *Opp* TENDER. **2** ▷ BOLD.

harm *n* abuse, damage, detriment, disadvantage, disservice, havoc, hurt, inconvenience, injury, loss, mischief, misfortune, pain, unhappiness, *inf* upset, wrong. ▷ EVIL. • *vb* abuse, be harmful to, damage, hurt, ill-treat, impair, injure, maltreat, misuse, ruin, spoil, wound. *Opp* BENEFIT.

harmful *adj* addictive, bad, baleful, damaging, dangerous, deadly, deleterious, destructive, detrimental, disadvantageous, evil, fatal, hurtful, injurious, lethal, malign, negative, noxious, pernicious, poisonous, prejudicial, ruinous, unfavourable, unhealthy, unpleasant, unwholesome. *Opp* BENEFICIAL, HARMLESS.

harmless *adj* acceptable, benign, gentle, innocent, innocuous, inoffensive, mild, non-addictive, non-toxic, safe, tame, unobjectionable. *Opp* HARMFUL.

harmonious *adj* **1** concordant, consonant, *inf* easy on the ear, euphonious, harmonizing, melodious, musical, sweet-sounding, tonal, tuneful. *Opp* DISCORDANT. **2** *a harmonious meeting.* agreeable, amicable, compatible, congenial, congruous, cooperative, friendly, integrated, like-minded, sympathetic.

harmonize *vb* agree, balance, be in harmony, blend, cooperate, coordinate, correspond, go together, match, suit each other, tally, tone in.

harmony *n* **1** assonance, concord, consonance, euphony, tunefulness. **2** accord, agreement, amity, balance, compatibility, conformity, congruence, cooperation, friendliness, goodwill, like-mindedness, peace, rapport, sympathy, togetherness, understanding. *Opp* DISCORD.

harness *n* equipment, *inf* gear, straps, tackle. • *vb* control, domesticate, exploit, keep under control, make use of, mobilize, tame, use, utilize.

harsh *adj* **1** abrasive, bristly, coarse, hairy, rough, scratchy. **2** *harsh sounds.* cacophonous, croaking, croaky, disagreeable, discordant, dissonant, grating, gravelly, grinding, gruff, guttural, hoarse, husky, irritating, jarring, rasping, raucous, rough, screeching, shrill, squawking, stertorous, strident, unpleasant. **3** *harsh colours, light.* bright, brilliant, dazzling, gaudy, glaring, lurid. **4** *harsh smell.* acrid, bitter, sour, unpleasant. **5** *harsh conditions.* arduous, austere, comfortless, difficult, hard, severe, stressful, tough. **6** *harsh criticism, treatment.* abusive, acerbic, bitter, blunt, brutal, cruel, Draconian, frank, hard-hearted, hurtful, impolite, merciless, outspoken, pitiless, severe, sharp, stern, strict, uncivil, unforgiving, unkind, unrelenting, unsympathetic, untempered. *Opp* GENTLE.

harvest *n* crop, gathering-in, produce, reaping, return, yield. • *vb* bring in, collect, garner, gather, glean, mow, pick, reap, take in.

hash *n* **1** goulash, stew. **2** *inf* botch, confusion, farrago, *inf* hotchpotch, jumble, mess, *inf* mishmash, mixture. **make a hash of** ▷ BUNGLE.

hassle *n* altercation, argument, bother, confusion, difficulty, disagreement, disturbance, fighting, fuss, harassment, inconvenience, making difficulties, nuisance, persecution, problem, struggle, trouble, upset. ● *vb* ▷ HARASS, QUARREL.

haste *n* dispatch, hurry, impetuosity, precipitateness, quickness, rashness, recklessness, rush, urgency. ▷ SPEED.

hasty *adj* **1** abrupt, fast, foolhardy, headlong, hot-headed, hurried, ill-considered, immediate, impetuous, impulsive, incautious, instantaneous, *inf* pell-mell, precipitate, quick, rapid, rash, reckless, speedy, sudden, summary (*justice*), swift. **2** *hasty work*. brief, careless, cursory, hurried, illconsidered, perfunctory, rushed, short, slapdash, superficial, thoughtless, unthinking. *Opp* CAREFUL, SLOW.

hat *n* head-dress. □ *Balaclava, bearskin, beret, biretta, boater, bonnet, bowler, busby, cap, coronet, crash-helmet, crown, deerstalker, diadem, fez, fillet, headband, helmet, hood, mitre, skullcap, sombrero, sou'wester, stetson, sun-hat, tiara, top hat, toque, trilby, turban, wig, wimple, yarmulke.*

hatch *vb* **1** brood, incubate. **2** conceive, concoct, contrive, *inf* cook up, design, devise, *inf* dream up, formulate, invent, plan, plot, scheme, think up.

hate *n* **1** ▷ HATRED. **2** *a pet hate*. abomination, aversion, *Fr* bête noire, dislike, loathing. ● *vb* abhor, abominate, be averse to, be hostile to, be revolted by, *inf* can't bear, *inf* can't stand, deplore, despise, detest, dislike, execrate, fear, find intolerable, loathe, object to, recoil from, resent, scorn, shudder at. *Opp* LIKE, LOVE.

hateful *adj* abhorred, abhorrent, abominable, accursed, awful, contemptible, cursed, *inf* damnable, despicable, detestable, disgusting, distasteful, execrable, foul, hated, heinous, horrible, *inf* horrid, loathsome, nasty, nauseating, obnoxious, odious, offensive, repellent, repugnant, repulsive, revolting, vile. ▷ EVIL. *Opp* LOVABLE.

hatred *n* abhorrence, animosity, antagonism, antipathy, aversion, contempt, detestation, dislike, enmity, execration, hate, hostility, ill-will, intolerance, loathing, misanthropy, odium, repugnance, revulsion. *Opp* LOVE.

haughty *adj* arrogant, boastful, bumptious, cavalier, *inf* cocky, conceited, condescending, disdainful, egotistical, *inf* highand-mighty, *inf* hoity-toity, imperious, lofty, lordly, offhand, patronizing, pompous, presumptuous, pretentious, proud, self-admiring, self-important, smug, snobbish, *inf* snooty, *inf* stuck-up, supercilious, superior, *inf* uppish, vain. *Opp* MODEST.

haul *vb* carry, cart, convey, drag, draw, heave, *inf* lug, move, pull, tow, trail, transport, tug.

haunt *vb* **1** frequent, *inf* hang around, keep returning to, loiter about, patronize, spend time at, visit regularly. **2** *haunt the mind*. beset, linger in, obsess, plague, prey on, torment.

have *vb* **1** be in possession of, keep, maintain, own, possess, use, utilize. **2** *house has six rooms*. comprise, consist of, contain, embody, hold, include, incorporate, involve. **3** *have fun, illness*. be subject to, endure, enjoy, experience, feel, go through, know, live through, put up with, suffer, tolerate, undergo. **4** *have presents*. accept, acquire, be given, gain, get, obtain, procure, receive. **5** *thieves had the lot*. *inf* get away with, remove, retain, secure, steal, take. **6** *have a snack*. consume, eat, drink, partake of, swallow. **7** *have a party*. arrange, hold, organize, prepare, set up. **8** *have guests*. be host to, cater for, entertain, put up. **have on** ▷ HOAX. **have to** be compelled to, be forced to, have an obligation to, must, need to, ought to, should. **have up** ▷ ARREST.

haven *n* asylum, refuge, retreat, safety, sanctuary, shelter. ▷ HARBOUR.

havoc *n* carnage, chaos, confusion, damage, desolation, destruction, devastation, disorder, disruption, *inf* mayhem, *inf* rack and ruin, ruin, *inf* shambles, upset, waste, wreckage.

hazard *n* chance, danger, jeopardy, peril, risk, threat. • *vb* dare, gamble, jeopardize, risk, stake, take a chance with, venture.

hazardous *adj* chancy, dangerous, *inf* dicey, fraught with danger, parlous, perilous, precarious, risky, *inf* ticklish, *inf* tricky, uncertain, unpredictable, unsafe. *Opp* SAFE.

haze *n* cloud, film, fog, mist, steam, vapour.

hazy *adj* **1** blurred, blurry, clouded, cloudy, dim, faint, foggy, fuzzy, indefinite, milky, misty, obscure, unclear. **2** ▷ VAGUE. *Opp* CLEAR.

head *adj* ▷ CHIEF. • *n* **1** brain, cranium, skull. **2** *head for figures.* ability, brains, capacity, imagination, intelligence, intellect, mind, understanding. **3** *head of a mountain.* apex, crown, highest point, peak, summit, top, vertex. **4** boss, director, employer, leader, manager, ruler. ▷ CHIEF. **5** *head of a school.* headmaster, headmistress, head teacher, principal. **6** *head of a river.* ▷ SOURCE. • *vb* **1** be in charge of, command, control, direct, govern, guide, lead, manage, rule, run, superintend, supervise. **2** *head for home.* aim, go, make, *inf* make a beeline, point, set out, start, steer, turn. **head off** ▷ DEFLECT. **lose your head** ▷ PANIC. **off your head** ▷ MAD.

heading *n* caption, headline, rubric, title.

headquarters *n* administration, base, depot, head office, *inf* HQ, main office, *inf* nerve-centre.

heal *vb* **1** become healthy, get better, improve, knit, mend, recover, recuperate, unite. **2** cure, make better, minister to, nurse, rejuvenate, remedy, renew, restore, revitalize, tend, treat. **3** *heal differences.* patch up, put right, reconcile, repair, settle.

health *n* **1** condition, constitution, fettle, form, shape, trim. **2** *the picture of health.* fitness, robustness, soundness, strength, vigour, well-being.

healthy *adj* **1** active, blooming, fine, fit, flourishing, good, *inf* hale-and-hearty, hearty, *inf* in fine fettle, in good shape, lively, perky, robust, sound, strong, sturdy, vigorous, well. **2** bracing, health-giving, hygienic, invigorating, salubrious, sanitary, wholesome. *Opp* ILL, UNHEALTHY.

heap *n* accumulation, assemblage, bank, collection, hill, hoard, mass, mound, mountain, pile, stack. • *vb* accumulate, amass, bank up, collect, gather, hoard, mass, pile, stack, stockpile, store. **heaps** ▷ PLENTY.

hear *vb* **1** attend to, catch, *old use* hearken to, heed, listen to, overhear, pay attention to, pick up. **2** *hear evidence.* examine, investigate, judge, try. **3** *hear news.* be told, discover, find out, gather, get, *inf* get wind of, learn, receive.

hearing *n* case, inquest, inquiry, trial.

heart *n* **1** *sl* ticker. **2** centre, core, crux, essence, focus, hub, inside, kernel, marrow, middle, *sl* nitty-gritty, nub, nucleus, pith. **3** affection, compassion, concern, courage, feeling, goodness, humanity, kindness, love, pity, sensitivity, sympathy, tenderness, understanding, warmth.

heartbreaking *adj* bitter, distressing, grievous, heart-rending, pitiful, tragic.

heartbroken *adj* broken-hearted, dejected, desolate, despairing, dispirited, grieved, inconsolable, miserable, *inf* shattered. ▷ SAD.

hearten *vb* boost, cheer up, encourage, strengthen, uplift.

heartless *adj* callous, cold, icy, inhuman, pitiless, ruthless, steely, stony, unconcerned, unemotional, unkind, unsympathetic. ▷ CRUEL.

hearty *adj* **1** enthusiastic, exuberant, friendly, genuine, healthy, heartfelt, lively, positive, robust, sincere, spirited, strong, vigorous, warm. *Opp* HALF-HEARTED. **2** *a hearty dinner.* ▷ BIG.

heat *n* **1** calorific value, fever, fieriness, glow, hotness, incandescence, warmth. **2** closeness, heat-wave, high temperature, hot weather, humidity, sultriness, torridity, warmth. **3** *heat of the moment.* anger, ardour, eagerness, enthusiasm, excitement, fervour, feverishness, fury, impetuosity, violence. ▷ PASSION. *Opp* COLD. ● *vb* bake, blister, boil, burn, cook, *inf* frizzle, fry, grill, inflame, make hot, melt, reheat, roast, scald, scorch, simmer, sizzle, smoulder, steam, stew, swelter, toast, warm. *Opp* COOL. **heated** ▷ FERVENT, HOT.

heath *n* common land, moor, moorland, open country, waste land, wilderness.

heathen *adj* atheistic, barbaric, godless, idolatrous, infidel, irreligious, pagan, philistine, savage, unenlightened. ● *n* atheist, barbarian, heretic, idolater, infidel, pagan, philistine, savage, sceptic, unbeliever.

heave *vb* **1** drag, draw, haul, hoist, lift, lug, move, pull, raise, tow, tug. **2** ▷ THROW. **heave into sight** ▷ APPEAR. **heave up** ▷ VOMIT.

heaven *n* **1** after-life, Elysium, eternal rest, the hereafter, the next world, nirvana, paradise. **2** bliss, contentment, delight, ecstasy, felicity, happiness, joy, perfection, pleasure, rapture, Utopia. *Opp* HELL.

heavenly *adj* angelic, beatific, beautiful, blissful, celestial, delightful, divine, exquisite, glorious, lovely, other-worldly, *inf* out of this world, saintly, spiritual, sublime, unearthly, wonderful.

heavy *adj* **1** bulky, burdensome, compact, concentrated, dense, hefty, immovable, large, leaden, massive, ponderous, unwieldy, weighty. ▷ BIG, FAT. **2** *heavy work.* arduous, demanding, difficult, hard, exhausting, laborious, onerous, strenuous, tough. **3** *heavy rain.* penetrating, pervasive, severe, torrential. **4** *a heavy crop.* abundant, copious, laden, loaded, profuse, thick. **5** *a heavy heart.* burdened, depressed, gloomy, miserable, sorrowful. ▷ SAD. **6** [*inf*] *a heavy lecture.* deep, dull, intellectual, intense, serious, tedious, wearisome. *Opp* LIGHT. **heavy-handed** ▷ CLUMSY. **heavy-hearted** ▷ SAD.

hectic *adj* animated, boisterous, brisk, bustling, busy, chaotic, excited, feverish, frantic, frenetic, frenzied, hurried, hyperactive, lively, mad, overactive, restless, riotous, rumbustious, *inf* rushed off your feet, turbulent, wild. *Opp* LEISURELY.

hedge *n* barrier, fence, hedgerow, screen. ● *vb inf* beat about the bush, be evasive, equivocate, *inf* hum and haw, quibble, stall, temporize, waffle. **hedge in** ▷ ENCLOSE.

hedonistic *adj* epicurean, extravagant, intemperate, luxurious, pleasure-loving, self-indulgent, sensual, sybaritic, voluptuous. *Opp* PURITANICAL.

heed *vb* attend to, bear in mind, concern yourself about, consider, follow, keep to, listen to, mark, mind, note, notice, obey, observe, pay attention to, regard, take notice of. *Opp* DISREGARD.

heedful *adj* attentive, careful, concerned, considerate, mindful, observant, sympathetic, taking notice, vigilant, watchful. *Opp* HEEDLESS.

heedless *adj* blind, careless, deaf, inattentive, inconsiderate, neglectful, oblivious, reckless, regardless, thoughtless, uncaring, unconcerned, unmindful, unobservant, unsympathetic. *Opp* HEEDFUL.

heel *vb* careen, incline, lean, list, tilt, tip.

hefty *adj* beefy, brawny, bulky, burly, heavy, heavyweight, hulking, husky, large, massive, mighty, muscular, powerful, robust, rugged, solid, substantial, *inf* strapping, strong, tough. ▷ BIG. *Opp* SLIGHT.

height *n* **1** altitude, elevation, level, tallness, vertical measurement. **2** crag, fell, hill, mound, mountain, peak, prominence, ridge, summit, top. **3** *height of your career.* acme, apogee, climax, crest, culmination, extreme, high point, maximum, peak, pinnacle, zenith.

heighten *vb* add to, amplify, augment, boost, build up, elevate, enhance, improve, increase, intensify, lift up, magnify, make higher, maximize, raise, reinforce, sharpen, strengthen, supplement. *Opp* LOWER, REDUCE.

hell *n* **1** eternal punishment, Hades, infernal regions, lower regions, nether world, *sl* the other place, underworld. **2** ▷ MISERY. *Opp* HEAVEN.

help *n* advice, aid, assistance, avail, backing, benefit, boost, collaboration, contribution, cooperation, encouragement, friendship, guidance, moral support, patronage, relief, remedy, succour, support. *Opp* HINDRANCE. • *vb* **1** abet, advise, aid, aid and abet, assist, back, befriend, be helpful, boost, collaborate, contribute, co-operate, encourage, facilitate, forward, further the interests of, *inf* give a hand, *inf* lend a hand, profit, promote, prop up, *inf* rally round, serve, side with, *derog* spoon-feed, stand by, subsidize, succour, support, take pity on. *Opp* HINDER. **2** *linctus helps a cough.* alleviate, benefit, cure, ease, improve, lessen, make easier, relieve, remedy. **3** *can't help it.* ▷ AVOID, PREVENT.

helper *n* abettor, accessory, accomplice, ally, assistant, associate, collaborator, colleague, confederate, deputy, helpmate, *inf* henchman, partner, *inf* right-hand man, second, supporter, *inf* willing hands.

helpful *adj* **1** accommodating, benevolent, caring, considerate, constructive, cooperative, favourable, friendly, helping, kind, neighbourly, obliging, practical, supportive, sympathetic, thoughtful, willing. **2** *a helpful comment.* advantageous, beneficial, informative, instructive, profitable, useful, valuable, worthwhile. **3** *a helpful tool.* convenient, easy to use, handy, manageable, practical, serviceable, useful, well designed, worth having. *Opp* UNHELPFUL, USELESS.

helping *adj* ▷ HELPFUL. • *n* amount, *inf* dollop, plateful, portion, ration, serving, share.

helpless *adj* abandoned, crippled, defenceless, dependent, deserted, destitute, disabled, exposed, feeble, handicapped, impotent, incapable, in difficulties, infirm, lame, marooned, powerless, stranded, unprotected, vulnerable. *Opp* INDEPENDENT.

herald *n* **1** announcer, courier, messenger, town crier. **2** *herald of spring.* forerunner, harbinger, omen, precursor, sign. • *vb* advertise, announce, indicate, make known, proclaim, promise, publicize. ▷ FORETELL.

herd *n* bunch, flock, mob, pack, swarm, throng. ▷ GROUP. • *vb* assemble, collect, congregate, drive, gather, group together, round up, shepherd.

hereditary *adj* **1** ancestral, bequeathed, family, handed down, inherited, passed down, passed on, willed. **2** congenital, constitutional, genetic, inborn, inbred, inherent, inheritable, innate, native, natural, transmissible, transmittable.

heresy *n* blasphemy, dissent, idolatry, nonconformity, rebellion, *inf* stepping out of line, unorthodox ideas.

heretic *n* apostate, blasphemer, dissenter, free-thinker, iconoclast, nonconformist, rebel, renegade, unorthodox thinker. *Opp* BELIEVER.

heretical *adj* apostate, atheistic, blasphemous, dissenting, freethinking, heathen, iconoclastic, idolatrous, impious, irreligious, nonconformist, pagan, rebellious, unorthodox. *Opp* ORTHODOX.

heritage *n* birthright, culture, history, inheritance, legacy, past, tradition.

hermit *n* anchoress, anchorite, eremite, monk, recluse, solitary.

hero, heroine *ns* champion, conqueror, daredevil, exemplar, ideal, idol, luminary, protagonist, star, superman, *inf* superstar, superwoman, victor, winner.

heroic *adj* adventurous, audacious, bold, brave, chivalrous, courageous, daring, dauntless, doughty, epic, fearless, gallant, herculean, intrepid, lion-hearted, noble, selfless, staunch, steadfast, stout-hearted, superhuman, unafraid, valiant, valorous. *Opp* COWARDLY.

hesitant *adj* cautious, diffident, dithering, faltering, halfhearted, halting, hesitating, indecisive, irresolute, nervous, *inf* shillyshallying, shy, stammering, stumbling, stuttering, tentative, timid, uncertain, uncommitted, undecided, underconfident, unsure, vacillating, wary, wavering. *Opp* DECISIVE, FLUENT.

hesitate *vb* **1** be hesitant, be indecisive, *inf* be in two minds, delay, demur, *inf* dilly-dally, dither, equivocate, falter, halt, hang back, haver, *inf* hum and haw, pause, put it off, *inf* shilly-shally, shrink back, teeter, temporize, think twice, vacillate, wait, waver. **2** stammer, stumble, stutter.

hesitation *n* caution, delay, diffidence, dithering, doubt, indecision, irresolution, nervousness, reluctance, *inf* shilly-shallying, uncertainty, vacillation, wavering.

hidden *adj* **1** camouflaged, concealed, covered, disguised, enclosed, invisible, obscured, out of sight, private, shrouded, *inf* under wraps, undetectable, unnoticeable, unseen, veiled. *Opp* VISIBLE. **2** *hidden meaning*. abstruse, arcane, coded, covert, cryptic, dark, esoteric, implicit, mysterious, mystical, obscure, occult, recondite, secret, unclear. *Opp* OBVIOUS.

hide *n* fur, leather, pelt, skin. • *vb* **1** blot out, bury, camouflage, cloak, conceal, cover, curtain, disguise, eclipse, enclose, mantle, mask, obscure, put away, put out of sight, screen, secrete, shelter, shroud, veil, wrap up. **2** *go into hiding*. *inf* go to ground, *inf* hole up, keep hidden, *inf* lie low, lurk, shut yourself away, take cover. **3** *hide facts*. censor, *inf* hush up, repress, silence, suppress, withhold.

hideous *adj* appalling, beastly, disgusting, dreadful, frightful, ghastly, grim, grisly, grotesque, gruesome, macabre, nauseous, odious, repellent, repulsive, revolting, shocking, sickening, terrible. ▷ UGLY. *Opp* BEAUTIFUL.

hiding-place *n* den, haven, hide, hideaway, *inf* hide-out, *inf* hideyhole, lair, refuge, retreat, sanctuary.

hierarchy *n* grading, ladder, *inf* pecking-order, ranking, scale, sequence, series, social order, system.

high *adj* **1** elevated, extending upwards, high-rise, lofty, raised, soaring, tall, towering. **2** aristocratic, chief, distinguished, eminent, exalted, important, leading, powerful, prominent, royal, top, upper. **3** *high prices*. dear, excessive, exorbitant, expensive, extravagant, outrageous, *inf* steep, unreasonable. **4** *high winds*. exceptional, extreme, great, intense, *inf* stiff, stormy, strong. **5** *a high reputation*. favourable, good, noble, respected, virtuous. **6** *high sounds*. acute, high-pitched, penetrating, piercing, sharp, shrill, soprano, squeaky, treble. *Opp* LOW. **high-and-mighty** ▷ ARROGANT. **high-class** ▷ EXCELLENT. **high-handed** ▷ ARROGANT. **high-minded** ▷ MORAL. **high-powered** ▷ POWERFUL. **high-speed** ▷ FAST. **high-spirited** ▷ LIVELY.

highbrow *adj* **1** academic, bookish, brainy, cultured, intellectual, *derog* pretentious, sophisticated. **2** *highbrow books*. classical, cultural, deep, difficult, educational, improving, serious. *Opp* LOWBROW.

highlight *n* best moment, climax, high spot, peak, top point.

hilarious *adj* boisterous, cheerful, cheering, entertaining, jolly, jovial, lively, merry, mirthful, rollicking, side-splitting, uproarious. ▷ FUNNY.

hill *n* **1** elevation, eminence, foothill, height, hillock, hillside, hummock, knoll, mound, mount, mountain, peak, prominence, ridge, summit. □ *brae, down, fell, pike, stack, tor, wold.* **2** acclivity, ascent, declivity, drop, gradient, incline, ramp, rise, slope.

hinder *vb* arrest, bar, be a hindrance to, check, curb, delay, deter, endanger, frustrate, get in the way of, hamper, handicap, hit, hold back, hold up, impede, keep back, limit, obstruct, oppose, prevent, restrain, restrict, retard, sabotage, slow down, slow up, stand in the way of, stop, thwart. *Opp* HELP.

hindrance *n* bar, barrier, burden, check, curb, deterrent, difficulty, disadvantage, *inf* drag, drawback, encumbrance, handicap, hitch, impediment, inconvenience, limitation, obstacle, obstruction, restraint, restriction, snag, stumbling-block. *Opp* HELP.

hinge *n* articulation, joint, pivot. ● *vb* depend, hang, rest, revolve, turn.

hint *n* **1** allusion, clue, idea, implication, indication, inkling, innuendo, insinuation, pointer, shadow, sign, suggestion, tip, *inf* tip-off. **2** *a hint of herbs.* dash, taste, tinge, touch, trace, undertone, whiff. ● *vb* allude, give a hint, imply, indicate, insinuate, intimate, mention, suggest, tip off.

hire *vb* book, charter, employ, engage, lease, pay for the use of, rent, sign on, take on. **hire out** lease out, let, rent out, take payment for.

hiss *vb* buzz, fizz, purr, rustle, sizzle, whir, whizz.

historic *adj* celebrated, eminent, epoch-making, famed, famous, important, momentous, notable, outstanding, remarkable, renowned, significant, well-known. *Opp* INSIGNIFICANT.

historical *adj* actual, authentic, documented, factual, real, real-life, recorded, true, verifiable. *Opp* FICTITIOUS.

history *n* **1** antiquity, bygone days, heritage, historical events, the old days, the past. **2** annals, biography, chronicles, diaries, narratives, records.

histrionic *adj* actorish, dramatic, theatrical.

hit *n* **1** blow, bull's eye, collision, impact, shot, stroke. **2** success, triumph, *inf* winner. ● *vb* **1** bang, bash, baste, batter, beat, belt, biff, birch, box, bludgeon, buffet, bump, butt, cane, cannon into, clap, clip, clobber, clock, clonk, clout, club, collide with, cosh, crack, crash into, cudgel, cuff, dash, deliver a blow, drive, elbow, flagellate, flail, flick, flip, flog, hammer, head, head-butt, impact, jab, jar, jog, kick, knee, knock, lam, lambaste, lash, nudge, pat, poke, pound, prod, pummel, punch, punt, putt, ram, rap, run into, scourge, slam, slap, slog, slosh, slug, smack, smash, smite, sock, spank, stab, strike, stub, swat, swipe, tan, tap, thrash, thump, thwack, wallop, whack, wham, whip. **2** *The slump hit sales.* affect, attack, bring disaster to, check, damage, do harm to, harm, have an effect on, hinder, hurt, make suffer, ruin. **hit back** ▷ RETALIATE. **hit on** ▷ DISCOVER.

hoard *n* accumulation, cache, collection, fund, heap, pile, reserve, stockpile, store, supply, treasure-trove. ● *vb* accumulate, amass, assemble, collect, gather, keep, lay in, lay up, mass, pile up, put away, put by, save, stockpile, store, treasure. *Opp* SQUANDER, USE.

hoarse *adj* croaking, grating, gravelly, growling, gruff, harsh, husky, rasping, raucous, rough, throaty.

hoax *n* cheat, *inf* con, confidence trick, deception, fake, fraud, humbug, imposture, joke, *inf* leg-pull, practical joke, spoof, swindle, trick. ● *vb* bluff, cheat, *inf* con, cozen, deceive, defraud, delude, dupe, fool, gull, *inf* have on, hoodwink, lead on, mislead, *inf* pull someone's leg, swindle, *inf* take for a ride, take in, trick. ▷ TEASE.

hoaxer *n* *inf* con-man, impostor, joker, practical joker, trickster. ▷ CHEAT.

hobble *vb* dodder, falter, limp, shuffle, stagger, stumble, totter. ▷ WALK.

hobby *n* amateur interest, avocation, diversion, interest, pastime, pursuit, recreation, relaxation, sideline.

hoist *n* block-and-tackle, crane, davit, jack, lift, pulley, tackle, winch, windlass. ● *vb* elevate, heave, lift, pull up, raise, winch up.

hold *n* **1** clasp, clutch, foothold, grasp, grip, purchase, toehold. **2** *a hold over someone.* ascendancy, authority, control, dominance, influence, leverage, mastery, power, sway. ● *vb* **1** bear, carry, catch, clasp, clench, cling to, clutch, cradle, embrace, enfold, grasp, grip, hang on to, have, hug, keep, possess, retain, seize, support, take. **2** *hold a suspect.* arrest, confine, coop up, detain, imprison, keep in custody, restrain. **3** *hold an opinion.* believe in, stick to, subscribe to, swear to. **4** *hold a pose.* continue, keep up, maintain, occupy, preserve, retain, sustain. **5** *hold a party.* celebrate, conduct, convene, have, organize. **6** *jug holds a litre.* contain, enclose, have a capacity of, include. **7** *My offer holds.* be unaltered, carry on, continue, endure, hold out, keep on, last, persist, remain unchanged, stay. **hold back** ▷ RESTRAIN. **hold forth** ▷ SPEAK, TALK. **hold out** ▷ OFFER, PERSIST. **hold over, hold up** ▷ DELAY. **hold-up** ▷ ROBBERY.

hole *n* **1** abyss, burrow, cave, cavern, cavity, chamber, chasm, crater, dent, depression, excavation, fault, fissure, hollow, indentation, niche, pit, pocket, pot-hole, recess, shaft, tunnel. **2** aperture, breach, break, chink, crack, cut, eyelet, fissure, gap, gash, leak, opening, orifice, perforation, puncture, rip, slit, slot, split, tear, vent.

holiday *n* bank holiday, break, day off, furlough, half-term, leave, recess, respite, rest, sabbatical, time off, vacation.

holiness *n* devotion, divinity, faith, godliness, piety, *derog* religiosity, sacredness, saintliness, *derog* sanctimoniousness, sanctity, venerability.

hollow *adj* **1** empty, unfilled, vacant, void. **2** cavernous, concave, deep, depressed, dimpled, indented, recessed, sunken. **3** *a hollow laugh, victory.* cynical, false, futile, insincere, insubstantial, meaningless, pointless, valueless, worthless. ● *n* bowl, cave, cavern, cavity, concavity, crater, dent, depression, dimple, dint, dip, dish, excavation, furrow, hole, indentation, pit, trough. ▷ VALLEY. **hollow out** ▷ EXCAVATE.

holocaust *n* **1** conflagration, firestorm, inferno. **2** annihilation, bloodbath, destruction, devastation, extermination, genocide, massacre, pogrom.

holy *adj* **1** blessed, consecrated, dedicated, devoted, divine, hallowed, heavenly, revered, sacred, sacrosanct, venerable. **2** *holy pilgrims.* devout, faithful, God-fearing, godly, immaculate, *derog* pietistic, pious, prayerful, pure, religious, reverent, reverential, righteous, saintly, *derog* sanctimonious, sinless, unsullied. *Opp* IRRELIGIOUS.

home *n* **1** abode, accommodation, base, domicile, dwelling, dwelling-place, habitation, household, lodging, quarters, residence. ▷ HOUSE. **2** birthplace, native land. **3** *derog* institution. □ old use *almshouse, convalescent home, hospice, nursing-home,* old use *poorhouse, rest home, retirement home, retreat, shelter.*

homeless *adj* abandoned, destitute, dispossessed, down-and-out, evicted, exiled, forsaken, itinerant, nomadic, outcast, rootless, unhoused, vagrant, wandering. ● *plur n* beggars, refugees, tramps, vagabonds, vagrants.

homely *adj* comfortable, congenial, cosy, easygoing, friendly, informal, intimate, modest, natural, relaxed, simple, unaffected, unassuming, unpretentious, unsophisticated. ▷ FAMILIAR. *Opp* FORMAL, SOPHISTICATED.

homogeneous *adj* akin, alike, comparable, compatible, consistent, identical, indistinguishable, matching, similar, uniform, unvarying. *Opp* DIFFERENT.

homosexual *adj inf* camp, gay, lesbian, *derog* queer.

honest *adj* above-board, blunt, candid, conscientious, direct, equitable, fair, forthright, frank, genuine, good, honourable, impartial, incorruptible, just, law-abiding, legal, legitimate, moral, *inf* on the level, open, outspoken, plain, principled, pure, reliable, respectable, scrupulous, sincere, square (*deal*), straight, straightforward, trustworthy, trusty, truthful, unbiased, unequivocal, unprejudiced, upright, veracious, virtuous. *Opp* DISHONEST.

honesty *n* **1** fairness, goodness, honour, integrity, morality, probity, rectitude, reliability, scrupulousness, sense of justice, trustworthiness, truthfulness, uprightness, veracity, virtue. *Opp* DECEIT. **2** bluntness, candour, directness, frankness, outspokenness, plainness, sincerity, straightforwardness.

honorary *adj* nominal, titular, unofficial, unpaid.

honour *n* **1** acclaim, accolade, compliment, credit, esteem, fame, good name, *inf* kudos, regard, renown, reputation, repute, respect, reverence, veneration. **2** distinction, duty, importance, pleasure, privilege. **3** *a sense of honour.* decency, dignity, honesty, integrity, loyalty, morality, nobility, principle, rectitude, righteousness, sincerity, uprightness, virtue. • *vb* acclaim, admire, applaud, celebrate, commemorate, commend, dignify, esteem, give credit to, glorify, pay homage to, pay respects to, pay tribute to, praise, remember, respect, revere, reverence, show respect to, sing the praises of, value, venerate, worship.

honourable *adj* admirable, chivalrous, creditable, decent, estimable, ethical, fair, good, high-minded, irreproachable, just, law-abiding, loyal, moral, noble, principled, proper, reputable, respectable, respected, righteous, sincere, *inf* straight, trustworthy, trusty, upright, venerable, virtuous, worthy. ▷ HONEST. *Opp* DISHONOURABLE.

hoodwink *vb* bluff, cheat, *inf* con, cozen, deceive, defraud, delude, dupe, fool, gull, *inf* have on, hoax, lead on, mislead, *inf* pull the wool over someone's eyes, swindle, *inf* take for a ride, take in, trick.

hook *n* barb, crook, peg. ▷ FASTENER. • *vb* **1** ▷ FASTEN. **2** *hook a fish.* capture, catch, take.

hooligan *n* bully, delinquent, hoodlum, lout, mugger, rough, ruffian, *inf* tearaway, thug, tough, troublemaker, vandal, *inf* yob. ▷ CRIMINAL.

hoop *n* band, circle, girdle, loop, ring.

hop *vb* bound, caper, dance, jump, leap, limp, prance, skip, spring, vault.

hope *n* **1** ambition, aspiration, craving, day-dream, desire, dream, longing, wish, yearning. **2** *hope of better weather.* assumption, conviction, expectation, faith, likelihood, optimism, promise, prospect. • *vb inf* anticipate, aspire, be hopeful, believe, contemplate, count on, desire, expect, foresee, have faith, have hope, look forward (to), trust, wish. *Opp* DESPAIR.

hopeful *adj* **1** assured, confident, expectant, optimistic, positive, sanguine. **2** *hopeful signs.* auspicious, cheering, encouraging, favourable, heartening, promising, propitious, reassuring. *Opp* HOPELESS.

hopefully *adv* **1** confidently, expectantly, optimistically, with hope. **2** [*inf*] *Hopefully I'll be better tomorrow.* all being well, most likely, probably. [Many think this use of *hopefully* is wrong]

hopeless *adj* **1** defeatist, demoralized, despairing, desperate, disconsolate, fatalist, negative, pessimistic, resigned, wretched. **2** *a hopeless situation.* daunting, depressing, impossible, incurable, irremediable, irreparable, irreversible. **3** [*inf*] *He's hopeless!* feeble, inadequate, incompetent, inefficient, poor, useless, weak, worthless. *Opp* HOPEFUL.

horde *n* band, crowd, gang, mob, swarm, throng, tribe. ▷ GROUP.

horizontal *adj* even, flat, level, lying down, prone, prostrate, supine. *Opp* VERTICAL.

horrible *adj* awful, beastly, disagreeable, dreadful, ghastly, hateful, horrid, loathsome, macabre, nasty, objectionable, odious, offensive, revolting, terrible, unkind. ▷ HORRIFIC, UNPLEASANT. *Opp* PLEASANT.

horrific *adj* appalling, atrocious, blood-curdling, disgusting, dreadful, frightening, frightful, grisly, gruesome, hair-raising, harrowing, horrendous, horrifying, nauseating, shocking, sickening, spine-chilling, unacceptable, unnerving, unthinkable.

horrify *vb* alarm, appal, disgust, frighten, harrow, nauseate, outrage, scare, shock, sicken, stun, terrify, unnerve. **horrifying** ▷ HORRIFIC.

horror *n* **1** abhorrence, antipathy, aversion, detestation, disgust, dislike, dismay, distaste, dread, fear, hatred, loathing, panic, repugnance, revulsion, terror. **2** awfulness, frightfulness, ghastliness, gruesomeness, hideousness.

horse *n* bronco, carthorse, *old use* charger, cob, colt, filly, foal, *childish* gee-gee, gelding, hack, hunter, *old use* jade, mare, mount, mule, mustang, *inf* nag, *old use* palfrey, piebald, pony, race-horse, roan, skewbald, stallion, steed, warhorse.

horseman, horsewoman *ns* cavalryman, equestrian, jockey, rider.

hospitable *adj* cordial, courteous, generous, gracious, receptive, sociable, welcoming. ▷ FRIENDLY. *Opp* INHOSPITABLE.

hospital *n* clinic, convalescent home, dispensary, health centre, hospice, infirmary, medical centre, nursing home, sanatorium, sick bay.

hospitality *n* **1** accommodation, catering, entertainment. **2** cordiality, courtesy, friendliness, generosity, sociability, warmth, welcome.

host *n* **1** army, crowd, mob, multitude, swarm, throng, troop. ▷ GROUP. **2** ▷ COMPÈRE.

hostage *n* captive, pawn, prisoner, surety.

hostile *adj* **1** aggressive, antagonistic, antipathetic, attacking, averse, bellicose, belligerent, combative, confrontational, ill-disposed, inhospitable, inimical, malevolent, militant, opposed, oppressive, pugnacious, resentful, rival, unfriendly, unsympathetic, unwelcoming, warlike, warring. ▷ ANGRY. *Opp* FRIENDLY. **2** *hostile conditions.* adverse, contrary, opposing, unfavourable, unhelpful, unpropitious. ▷ BAD. *Opp* FAVOURABLE.

hostility *n* aggression, animosity, animus, antagonism, bad feeling, belligerence, confrontation, dissension, enmity, estrangement, friction, incompatibility, malevolence, malice, opposition, pugnacity, rancour, resentment, strife, unfriendliness. ▷ HATRED. *Opp* FRIENDSHIP. **hostilities** ▷ WAR.

hot *adj* **1** baking, blistering, boiling, burning, close, fiery, flaming, humid, oppressive, *inf* piping, red-hot, roasting, scalding, scorching, searing, sizzling, steamy, stifling, sultry, summery, sweltering, thermal, torrid, tropical, warm, white-hot. **2** *hot temper.* ardent, eager, emotional, excited, fervent, fervid, feverish, fierce, heated, hotheaded, impatient, impetuous, inflamed, intense, passionate, violent. **3** *hot taste.* acrid, biting, gingery, peppery, piquant, pungent, spicy, strong. *Opp* COLD, COOL. **hot-tempered** ▷ BAD-TEMPERED. **hot under the collar** ▷ ANGRY.

hotel *n* guest house, hostel, *joc* hostelry, inn, lodge, motel, pension. ▷ ACCOMMODATION.

hound *n* ▷ DOG. • *vb* annoy, badger, chase, harass, harry, hunt, nag, persecute, pester, pursue.

house *n old use* abode, domicile, dwelling, dwelling-place, habitation, home, homestead, house-hold, place, residence. □ *apartment*, inf *back-to-back*, *bungalow*, *chalet*, *cottage*, *council house*, *croft*, *detached house*, *farmhouse*, *flat*, *grange*, *hovel*, *homestead*, *hut*, *igloo*, *lodge*, *maisonette*, *manor*, *manse*, *mansion*, *penthouse*, inf *prefab*, *public house*, *rectory*, inf *semi*, *semi-detached house*, *shack*, *shanty*, *terraced house*, *thatched house*, inf *two-up two-down*, *vicarage*, *villa*. ● *vb* accommodate, billet, board, domicile, harbour, keep, lodge, place, *inf* put up, quarter, shelter, take in.

household *n* establishment, family, home, ménage, *inf* set-up.

hovel *n* cottage, *inf* dump, hole, hut, shack, shanty, shed.

hover *vb* **1** be suspended, drift, float, flutter, fly, hang, poise. **2** be indecisive, dally, dither, *inf* hang about, hang around, hesitate, linger, loiter, pause, vacillate, wait about, waver.

howl *vb* bay, bellow, cry, roar, shout, ululate, wail, yowl.

hub *n* axis, centre, core, focal point, focus, heart, middle, nucleus, pivot.

huddle *n* ▷ GROUP. ● *vb* **1** cluster, converge, crowd, flock, gather, group, heap, herd, jam, jumble, pile, press, squeeze, swarm, throng. **2** cuddle, curl up, hug, nestle, snuggle.

hue *n* cast, complexion, dye, nuance, shade, tincture, tinge, tint, tone. ▷ COLOUR. **hue and cry** ▷ OUTCRY.

hug *vb* clasp, cling to, crush, cuddle, embrace, enfold, fold in your arms, hold close, huddle together, nestle together, nurse, snuggle against, squeeze.

huge *adj* **1** Brobdingnagian, colossal, elephantine, enormous, gargantuan, giant, gigantic, *inf* hulking, immense, imposing, impressive, *inf* jumbo, majestic, mammoth, massive, mighty, *inf* monster, monstrous, monumental, mountainous, prodigious, stupendous, titanic, towering, *inf* tremendous, vast, weighty, *inf* whopping. ▷ BIG. **2** *huge number*. ▷ INFINITE. *Opp* SMALL.

hulk *n* **1** body, carcass, frame, hull, shell, wreck. **2** *a clumsy hulk*. lout, lump, oaf.

hulking *adj* awkward, bulky, cumbersome, heavy, ungainly, unwieldy. ▷ BIG, CLUMSY.

hull *n* body, framework, structure.

hum *vb* buzz, drone, murmur, purr, sing, thrum, vibrate, whirr. **hum and haw** ▷ HESITATE.

human *adj* **1** anthropoid, hominid, hominoid, mortal. **2** *human feeling*. kind, rational, reasonable, sensible, sensitive, sympathetic, thoughtful. ▷ HUMANE. *Opp* INHUMAN. **human beings** folk, humanity, mankind, men and women, mortals, people.

humane *adj* altruistic, benevolent, charitable, civilized, compassionate, feeling, forgiving, good, human, humanitarian, kind-hearted, loving, magnanimous, merciful, philanthropic, pitying, refined, sympathetic, tender, understanding, unselfish, warm-hearted. ▷ KIND. *Opp* INHUMANE.

humble *adj* **1** deferential, docile, meek, modest, *derog* obsequious, polite, reserved, respectful, self-effacing, *derog* servile, submissive, subservient, *derog* sycophantic, unassertive, unassuming, unostentatious, unpresuming, unpretentious. *Opp* PROUD. **2** *humble birth*. base, commonplace, ignoble, inferior, insignificant, low, lowly, mean, obscure, ordinary, plebeian, poor, simple, undistinguished, unimportant, unprepossessing, unremarkable. ● *vb* ▷ HUMILIATE.

humid *adj* clammy, damp, dank, moist, muggy, steamy, sticky, sultry, sweaty.

humiliate *vb* abase, abash, break, break someone's spirit, bring someone down, chagrin, chasten, crush, deflate, degrade, demean, discredit, disgrace, embarrass, humble, make someone ashamed, *inf* make someone eat humble pie, *inf* make someone feel small, mortify, *inf* put someone down, *inf* put someone in his/her place, shame, *inf* show someone up, *inf* take someone down a peg. **humiliating** ▷ SHAMEFUL.

humiliation *n* abasement, chagrin, degradation, discredit, disgrace, dishonour, embarrassment, ignominy, indignity, loss of face, mortification, obloquy, shame.

humility *n* deference, humbleness, lowliness, meekness, modesty, self-abasement, self-effacement, *derog* servility, shyness, unpretentiousness. *Opp* PRIDE.

humorous *adj* absurd, amusing, comic, comical, diverting, droll, entertaining, facetious, farcical, funny, hilarious, *inf* hysterical, ironic, jocose, jocular, *inf* killing, laughable, merry, *inf* priceless, risible, sarcastic, sardonic, satirical, *inf* side-splitting, slapstick, uproarious, waggish, whimsical, witty, zany. *Opp* SERIOUS.

humour *n* **1** absurdity, badinage, banter, comedy, drollness, facetiousness, fun, incongruity, irony, jesting, jocularity, jokes, joking, merriment, quips, raillery, repartee, satire, *inf* sense of fun, waggishness, wit, witticism, wittiness. **2** *in a good humour.* disposition, frame of mind, mood, spirits, state of mind, temper.

hump *n* **1** bulge, bump, curve, growth, hunch, knob, lump, node, projection, protrusion, protuberance, swelling, tumescence. **2** *hump in the ground.* barrow, hillock, hummock, mound, rise, tumulus. ● *vb* **1** arch, bend, crook, curl, curve, hunch, raise. **2** *hump a load.* drag, heave, hoist, lift, lug, raise, shoulder.

hunch *n* **1** ▷ HUMP. **2** feeling, guess, idea, impression, inkling, intuition, premonition, presentiment, suspicion. ● *vb* arch, bend, crook, curl, curve, huddle, hump, raise, shrug.

hunger *n* **1** appetite, craving, greed, ravenousness, voracity. **2** deprivation, famine, lack of food, malnutrition, starvation, want. ● *vb* ▷ DESIRE.

hungry *adj* aching, avid, covetous, craving, eager, emaciated, famished, famishing, greedy, longing, *inf* peckish, ravenous, starved, starving, underfed, undernourished, voracious.

hunt *n* chase, pursuit, quest, search. ▷ HUNTING. ● *vb* **1** chase, course, dog, ferret, hound, poach, pursue, stalk, track, trail. **2** *hunt for lost property. inf* check out, enquire after, ferret out, look for, rummage, search for, seek, trace, track down.

hunter *n* huntsman, huntswoman, predator, stalker, trapper.

hunting *n* blood-sports, coursing, poaching, stalking, trapping.

hurdle *n* **1** barricade, barrier, fence, hedge, jump, obstacle, wall. **2** bar, check, complication, difficulty, handicap, hindrance, impediment, obstruction, problem, restraint, snag, stumbling block.

hurl *vb* cast, catapult, chuck, dash, fire, fling, heave, launch, *inf* let fly, pelt, pitch, project, propel, send, shy, sling, throw, toss.

hurricane *n* cyclone, storm, tempest, tornado, typhoon, whirlwind.

hurry *n* ▷ HASTE. ● *vb* **1** *inf* belt, *inf* buck up, chase, dash, dispatch, *inf* fly, *inf* get a move on, hasten, hurtle, hustle, make haste, move quickly, rush, *inf* shift, speed, *inf* step on it, work faster. **2** *hurry a process.* accelerate, expedite, press on with, quicken, speed up. *Opp* DELAY. **hurried** ▷ HASTY.

hurt *vb* **1** ache, be painful, burn, pinch, smart, sting, suffer pain, throb, tingle. **2** *hurt physically.* abuse, afflict, agonize, bruise, cause pain to, cripple, cut, disable, injure, maim, misuse, mutilate, torture, wound. **3** *hurt mentally.* affect, aggrieve, be hurtful to, *inf* cut to the quick, depress, distress, grieve, humiliate, insult, offend, pain, sadden, torment, upset. **4** *hurt things.* damage, harm, impair, mar, ruin, sabotage, spoil.

hurtful *adj* biting, cruel, cutting, damaging, derogatory, detrimental, distressing, hard to bear, harmful, injurious, malicious, nasty, painful, sarcastic, scathing, spiteful, uncharitable, unkind, upsetting, vicious, wounding. *Opp* KIND.

hurtle *vb* charge, chase, dash, fly, plunge, race, rush, shoot, speed, tear.

hush *int* be quiet! be silent! *inf* hold your tongue! *sl* pipe down! *inf* shut up! • *vb* ▷ SILENCE. **hush up** ▷ SUPPRESS.

hustle *vb* **1** bustle, hasten, hurry, jostle, rush, scamper, scurry. **2** *hustled me away.* coerce, compel, force, push, shove, thrust.

hut *n* cabin, den, hovel, lean-to, shack, shanty, shed, shelter.

hybrid *n* amalgam, combination, composite, compound, cross, cross-breed, half-breed, mixture, mongrel.

hygiene *n* cleanliness, health, sanitariness, sanitation, wholesomeness.

hygienic *adj* aseptic, clean, disinfected, germ-free, healthy, pure, salubrious, sanitary, sterile, sterilized, unpolluted, wholesome. *Opp* UNHEALTHY.

hypnotic *adj* fascinating, irresistible, magnetic, mesmeric, mesmerizing, sleep-inducing, soothing, soporific, spellbinding.

hypnotize *vb* bewitch, captivate, cast a spell over, dominate, enchant, entrance, fascinate, gain power over, magnetize, mesmerize, *inf* put to sleep, spellbind, *inf* stupefy.

hypocrisy *n* cant, deceit, deception, double-dealing, double standards, double-talk, double-think, duplicity, falsity, *inf* humbug, inconsistency, insincerity.

hypocritical *adj* deceptive, double-dealing, double-faced, duplicitous, false, inconsistent, insincere, Pharisaical, *inf* phoney, self-deceiving, self-righteous, *inf* two-faced.

hypothesis *n* conjecture, guess, postulate, premise, proposition, speculation, supposition, theory, thesis.

hypothetical *adj* academic, alleged, assumed, conjectural, groundless, imaginary, presumed, putative, speculative, supposed, suppositional, theoretical, unreal.

hysteria *n* frenzy, hysterics, madness, mania, panic.

hysterical *adj* berserk, beside yourself, crazed, delirious, demented, distraught, frantic, frenzied, irrational, mad, overemotional, rabid, raving, uncontrollable, wild.

I

ice *n* black ice, floe, frost, glacier, iceberg, icicle, rime.

icy *adj* **1** arctic, chilling, freezing, frosty, frozen, glacial, polar, Siberian. ▷ COLD. **2** *icy roads.* glassy, slippery, *inf* slippy, slithery.

idea *n* **1** abstraction, attitude, belief, concept, conception, conjecture, construct, conviction, doctrine, hypothesis, notion, opinion, philosophy, principle, sentiment, teaching, tenet, theory, thought, view. **2** *a bright idea.* brainwave, design, fancy, guess, inspiration, plan, proposal, scheme, suggestion. **3** *idea of a poem.* intention, meaning, point. **4** *idea of what to expect.* clue, guidelines, impression, inkling, intimation, model, pattern, perception, suspicion, vision.

ideal *adj* **1** best, classic, complete, excellent, faultless, model, optimum, perfect, supreme, unsurpassable. **2** *an ideal world.* chimerical, dream, hypothetical, illusory, imaginary, unattainable, unreal, Utopian, visionary. • *n* **1** acme, criterion, epitome, exemplar, model, paragon, pattern, standard. **2** ▷ PRINCIPLE.

idealistic *adj* high-minded, impractical, over-optimistic, quixotic, romantic, starry-eyed, unrealistic. *Opp* REALISTIC.

idealize *vb* apotheosize, deify, exalt, glamorize, glorify, *inf* put on a pedestal, romanticize. ▷ IDOLIZE.

identical *adj* alike, comparable, congruent, corresponding, duplicate, equal, equivalent, indistinguishable, interchangeable, like, matching, the same, similar, twin. *Opp* DIFFERENT.

identifiable *adj* detectable, discernible, distinctive, distinguishable, familiar, known, named, noticeable, perceptible, recognizable, unmistakable. *Opp* UNIDENTIFIABLE.

identify *vb* **1** distinguish, label, mark, name, pick out, pinpoint, *inf* put a name to, recognize, single out, specify, spot. **2** *identify an illness.* detect, diagnose, discover. **identify with** empathize with, feel for, *inf* put yourself in the shoes of, relate to, sympathize with.

identity *n* **1** *inf* ID, name. **2** character, distinctiveness, individuality, nature, particularity, personality, selfhood, singularity, uniqueness.

ideology *n* assumptions, beliefs, creed, convictions, ideas, philosophy, principles, tenets, theories, underlying attitudes.

idiom *n* argot, cant, choice of words, dialect, expression, jargon, language, manner of speaking, parlance, phrase, phraseology, phrasing, turn of phrase, usage.

idiomatic *adj* colloquial, natural, vernacular, well-phrased.

idiosyncrasy *n* characteristic, eccentricity, feature, habit, individuality, mannerism, oddity, peculiarity, quirk, trait.

idiosyncratic *adj* characteristic, distinctive, eccentric, individual, odd, peculiar, personal, quirky, singular, unique. *Opp* COMMON.

idiot *n* [*most synonyms inf*] ass, blockhead, bonehead, booby, chump, clot, cretin, dim-wit, dolt, dope, duffer, dumb-bell, dummy, dunce, dunderhead, fat-head, fool, half-wit, ignoramus, imbecile, moron, nincompoop, ninny, nitwit, simpleton, twerp, twit.

idiotic *adj* absurd, asinine, crazy, foolish, half-witted, imbecile, insane, irrational, mad, moronic, nonsensical, ridiculous, senseless. ▷ STUPID. *Opp* SENSIBLE.

idle *adj* **1** dormant, inactive, inoperative, in retirement, not working, redundant, retired, unemployed, unoccupied, unproductive, unused. **2** apathetic, good-for-nothing, indolent, lackadaisical, lazy, shiftless, slothful, slow, sluggish, torpid, uncommitted, work-shy. **3** *idle speculation.* casual, frivolous, futile, pointless, worthless. *Opp* BUSY. ● *vb* be lazy, dawdle, do nothing, *inf* hang about, *inf* kill time, laze, loaf, loll, lounge about, *inf* mess about, potter, slack, stagnate, take it easy, vegetate. *Opp* WORK.

idler *n inf* good-for-nothing, *inf* layabout, *inf* lazybones, loafer, malingerer, shirker, *inf* skiver, slacker, sluggard, wastrel.

idol *n* **1** deity, effigy, fetish, god, graven image, icon, statue. **2** *pop idol.* celebrity, *inf* darling, favourite, hero, *inf* pin-up, star, *inf* superstar.

idolize *vb* adore, adulate, hero-worship, lionize, look up to, revere, reverence, venerate, worship. ▷ IDEALIZE.

idyllic *adj* Arcadian, bucolic, charming, delightful, happy, idealized, lovely, pastoral, peaceful, perfect, picturesque, rustic, unspoiled.

ignite *vb* burn, catch fire, fire, kindle, light, set alight, set on fire, spark off, touch off.

ignoble *adj* base, churlish, cowardly, despicable, disgraceful, dishonourable, infamous, low, mean, selfish, shabby, uncharitable, unchivalrous, unworthy. *Opp* NOBLE.

ignorance *n* inexperience, innocence, unawareness, unconsciousness, unfamiliarity. ▷ STUPIDITY. *Opp* KNOWLEDGE.

ignorant *adj* **1** ill-informed, innocent, lacking knowledge, oblivious, unacquainted, unaware, unconscious, unfamiliar (with), uninformed, unwitting. **2** benighted, *inf* clueless, illiterate, uncouth, uncultivated, uneducated, unenlightened, unlettered, unscholarly, unsophisticated. ▷ IMPOLITE, STUPID. *Opp* CLEVER, KNOWLEDGEABLE.

ignore *vb* disobey, disregard, leave out, miss out, neglect, omit, overlook, pass over, reject, *inf* shut your eyes to, skip, slight, snub, take no notice of, *inf* turn a blind eye to.

ill *adj* **1** ailing, bad, bedridden, bilious, *inf* dicky, diseased, feeble, frail, *inf* funny, *inf* groggy, indisposed, infected, infirm, invalid, nauseated, nauseous, *inf* off-colour, *inf* out of sorts, pasty, poorly, queasy, queer, *inf* seedy, sick, sickly, suffering, *inf* under the weather, unhealthy, unwell, valetudinarian, weak. *Opp* HEALTHY. **2** *ill effects.* bad, damaging, detrimental, evil, harmful, injurious, unfavourable, unfortunate, unlucky. *Opp* GOOD. ● *plur n* the infirm, invalids, patients, the sick, sufferers, victims. **be ill** ail, languish, sicken. **ill-advised** ▷ MISGUIDED. **ill-bred** ▷ RUDE. **ill-fated** ▷ UNLUCKY. **ill-humoured** ▷ BAD-TEMPERED. **ill-mannered** ▷ RUDE. **ill-natured** ▷ UNKIND. **ill-omened** ▷ UNLUCKY. **ill-tempered** ▷ BAD-TEMPERED. **ill-treat** ▷ MISTREAT.

illegal *adj* actionable, against the law, banned, black-market, criminal, felonious, forbidden, illicit, invalid, irregular, outlawed, prohibited, proscribed, unauthorized, unconstitutional, unlawful, unlicensed, wrong, wrongful. ▷ ILLEGITIMATE. *Opp* LEGAL.

illegible *adj* indecipherable, indistinct, obscure, unclear, unreadable. *Opp* LEGIBLE.

illegitimate *adj* **1** against the rules, improper, inadmissible, incorrect, invalid, irregular, spurious, unauthorized, unjustifiable, unreasonable, unwarranted. ▷ ILLEGAL. **2** bastard, born out of wedlock, natural. *Opp* LEGITIMATE.

illiterate *adj* unable to read, uneducated, unlettered. ▷ IGNORANT. *Opp* LITERATE.

illness *n* abnormality, affliction, ailment, allergy, attack, blight, *inf* bug, complaint, condition, contagion, disability, disease, disorder, epidemic, fever, fit, health problem, indisposition, infection, infirmity, malady, malaise, pestilence, plague, sickness, *inf* trouble, *inf* turn, *inf* upset, weakness. ▷ WOUND.

illogical *adj* absurd, fallacious, inconsequential, inconsistent, invalid, irrational, senseless, unreasonable, unsound. ▷ SILLY. *Opp* LOGICAL.

illuminate *vb* **1** brighten, decorate with lights, light up, make brighter, reveal. **2** clarify, clear up, elucidate, enlighten, explain, explicate, throw light on.

illusion *n* **1** apparition, conjuring trick, day-dream, deception, delusion, dream, fancy, fantasy, figment of the imagination, hallucination, mirage. **2** *under an illusion.* error, false impression, misapprehension, misconception, mistake.

illusory *adj* chimerical, deceptive, deluding, delusive, fallacious, false, illusive, imagined, misleading, mistaken, sham, unreal, untrue. ▷ IMAGINARY. *Opp* REAL.

illustrate *vb* **1** demonstrate, elucidate, exemplify, explain, instance, show. **2** adorn, decorate, embellish, illuminate, ornament. **3** depict, draw pictures of, picture, portray.

illustration *n* **1** case in point, demonstration, example, exemplar, instance, sample, specimen. **2** decoration, depiction, diagram, drawing, figure, photograph, picture, sketch. ▷ IMAGE.

image *n* **1** imitation, likeness, projection, reflection, representation. ▷ PICTURE. **2** carving, effigy, figure, icon, idol, statue. **3** *the image of her mother.* counterpart, double, likeness, spitting-image, twin.

imaginary *adj* fabulous, fanciful, fictional, fictitious, hypothetical, imagined, insubstantial, invented, legendary, made-up, mythical, mythological, non-existent, supposed, unreal, visionary. ▷ ILLUSORY. *Opp* REAL.

imagination *n* artistry, creativity, fancy, ingenuity, insight, inspiration, inventiveness, *inf* mind's eye, originality, resourcefulness, sensitivity, thought, vision.

imaginative *adj* artistic, attractive, beautiful, clever, creative, fanciful, ingenious, innovative, inspired, inspiring, inventive, original, poetic, resourceful, sensitive, thoughtful, unusual, visionary, vivid. *Opp* UNIMAGINATIVE.

imagine *vb* **1** conceive, conjure up, *inf* cook up, create, dream up, envisage, fancy, fantasize, invent, make believe, make up, picture, pretend, see, think of, think up, visualize. **2** assume, believe, conjecture, guess, infer, judge, presume, suppose, surmise, suspect, think.

imitate *vb* **1** ape, burlesque, caricature, counterfeit, duplicate, echo, guy, mimic, parody, parrot, portray, reproduce, satirize, send up, simulate, *inf* take off, travesty. ▷ IMPERSONATE. **2** copy, emulate, follow, match, model yourself on.

imitation *adj* artificial, copied, counterfeit, dummy, ersatz, man-made, mock, model, *inf* phoney, reproduction, sham, simulated, synthetic. *Opp* REAL. • *n* **1** copying, duplication, emulation, mimicry, repetition. **2** *inf* clone, copy, counterfeit, dummy, duplicate, fake, forgery, impersonation, impression, likeness, *inf* mock-up, model, parody, reflection, replica, reproduction, sham, simulation, *inf* take-off, toy, travesty.

immature *adj* adolescent, babyish, backward, callow, childish, *inf* green, inexperienced, infantile, juvenile, new, puerile, undeveloped, unripe, young, youthful. *Opp* MATURE.

immediate *adj* **1** instant, instantaneous, prompt, quick, speedy, sudden, swift, unhesitating, unthinking. **2** *immediate need.* current, present, pressing, top-priority, urgent. **3** *immediate neighbours.* adjacent, close, closest, direct, near, nearest, neighbouring, next.

immediately *adv* at once, directly, forthwith, instantly, now, promptly, *inf* right away, straight away, unhesitatingly.

immense *adj* Brobdingnagian, colossal, elephantine, enormous, gargantuan, giant, gigantic, great, huge, *inf* hulking, immeasurable, imposing, impressive, incalculable, *inf* jumbo, large, mammoth, massive, mighty, *inf* monster, monstrous, monumental, mountainous, prodigious, stupendous, titanic, towering, *inf* tremendous, vast, *inf* whopping. ▷ BIG. *Opp* SMALL.

immerse *vb* bathe, dip, drench, drown, duck, dunk, inundate, lower, plunge, sink, submerge. **immersed** ▷ BUSY, INTERESTED.

immersion *n* baptism, dipping, ducking, plunge, submersion.

immigrant *n* alien, arrival, incomer, newcomer, outsider, settler.

imminent *adj* about to happen, approaching, close, coming, foreseeable, forthcoming, impending, looming, menacing, near, threatening.

immobile *adj* **1** ▷ IMMOVABLE. **2** frozen, inexpressive, inflexible, rigid. *Opp* MOBILE.

immobilize *vb* cripple, damage, disable, make immobile, paralyse, put out of action, sabotage, stop.

immoral *adj* abandoned, base, conscienceless, corrupt, debauched, degenerate, depraved, dishonest, dissipated, dissolute, evil, *inf* fast, impure, indecent, irresponsible, licentious, loose, low, profligate, promiscuous, *inf* rotten, sinful, unchaste, unethical, unprincipled, unscrupulous, vicious, villainous, wanton, wrong. ▷ WICKED. *Opp* MORAL. **immoral person** blackguard, cheat, degenerate, liar, libertine, profligate, rake, reprobate, scoundrel, sinner, villain, wrongdoer.

immortal *adj* **1** ageless, ceaseless, deathless, endless, eternal, everlasting, incorruptible, indestructible, never-ending, perpetual, sempiternal, timeless, unchanging, undying, unending, unfading. **2** *immortal beings.* divine, godlike, legendary, mythical. *Opp* MORTAL.

immortalize *vb* apotheosize, beatify, canonize, commemorate, deify, enshrine, keep alive, make immortal, make permanent, memorialize, perpetuate.

immovable *adj* **1** anchored, fast, firm, fixed, immobile, immobilized, motionless, paralysed, riveted, rooted, secure, set, settled, solid, static, stationary, still, stuck, unmoving. **2** ▷ IMMUTABLE.

immune *adj* exempt, free, immunized, inoculated, invulnerable, protected, resistant, safe, unaffected, vaccinated. *Opp* VULNERABLE.

immunize *vb* inoculate, vaccinate.

immutable *adj* constant, dependable, enduring, eternal, fixed, invariable, lasting, obdurate, permanent, perpetual, reliable, settled, stable, steadfast, unalterable, unchangeable, unswerving, unvarying. ▷ RESOLUTE. *Opp* CHANGEABLE.

impact *n* **1** bang, blow, bump, collision, concussion, contact, crash, knock, smash. **2** bearing, consequence, effect, force, impression, influence, repercussions, reverberations, shock, thrust. • *vb* ▷ HIT.

impair *vb* cripple, damage, harm, injure, mar, ruin, spoil, weaken.

impale *vb* pierce, run through, skewer, spear, spike, spit, stab, stick, transfix.

impartial *adj* balanced, detached, disinterested, dispassionate, equitable, even-handed, fair, fair-minded, just, neutral, non-partisan, objective, open-minded, unbiased, uninvolved, unprejudiced. *Opp* BIASED.

impartiality *n* balance, detachment, disinterest, fairness, justice, neutrality, objectivity, open-mindedness. *Opp* BIAS.

impassable *adj* blocked, closed, obstructed, unusable.

impatient *adj* **1** anxious, eager, keen, impetuous, precipitate, *inf* raring. **2** agitated, chafing, edgy, fidgety, fretful, irritable, nervous, restive, restless, uneasy. **3** *an impatient manner.* abrupt, brusque, curt, hasty, intolerant, irascible, irritable, quick-tempered, short-tempered, snappish, snappy, testy. *Opp* APATHETIC, PATIENT.

impede *vb* arrest, bar, be an impediment to, check, curb, delay, deter, frustrate, get in the way of, hamper, handicap, hinder, *inf* hit, hold back, hold up, keep back, limit, obstruct, oppose, prevent, restrain, restrict, retard, sabotage, slow down, slow up, stand in the way of, stop, thwart. *Opp* HELP.

impediment *n* **1** bar, barrier, burden, check, curb, deterrent, difficulty, disadvantage, *inf* drag, drawback, encumbrance, hindrance, inconvenience, limitation, obstacle, obstruction, restraint, restriction, snag, stumbling-block. **2** ▷ HANDICAP.

impending *adj* about to happen, approaching, close, coming, foreseeable, forthcoming, imminent, looming, menacing, near, *inf* on the horizon, threatening.

impenetrable *adj* **1** dense, hard, resilient, solid, strong. ▷ IMPERVIOUS. **2** impregnable, invincible, inviolable, invulnerable, safe, secure, unassailable, unconquerable. *Opp* VULNERABLE. **3** *impenetrable language.* inaccessible, incomprehensible, inscrutable, unfathomable, *inf* unget-at-able. *Opp* ACCESSIBLE.

imperceptible *adj* faint, gradual, inappreciable, inaudible, indistinguishable, infinitesimal, insignificant, invisible, microscopic, minute, negligible, slight, small, subtle, tiny, unclear, undetectable, unnoticeable, vague. ▷ SMALL. *Opp* PERCEPTIBLE.

imperceptive *adj* impercipient, inattentive, slow, uncritical, undiscriminating, unobservant, unresponsive. ▷ STUPID. *Opp* PERCEPTIVE.

imperfect *adj* blemished, broken, chipped, cracked, damaged, defective, deficient, faulty, flawed, incomplete, incorrect, marred, partial, patchy, shop-soiled, spoilt, unfinished, wanting. *Opp* PERFECT.

imperfection *n* blemish, damage, defect, deficiency, error, failing, fault, flaw, foible, frailty, inadequacy, infirmity, peccadillo, shortcoming, weakness. *Opp* PERFECTION.

impermanent *adj* changing, destructible, ephemeral, evanescent, fleeting, momentary, passing, shifting, short-lived, temporary, transient, transitory, unstable. ▷ CHANGEABLE. *Opp* PERMANENT.

impersonal *adj* aloof, businesslike, cold, cool, correct, detached, disinterested, dispassionate, distant, formal, hard, inhuman, mechanical, objective, official, remote, stiff, unapproachable, unemotional, unfriendly, unprejudiced, unsympathetic, without emotion, wooden. *Opp* FRIENDLY.

impersonate *vb* disguise yourself as, do impressions of, dress up as, masquerade as, mimic, pass yourself off as, portray, pose as, pretend to be, *inf* take off. ▷ IMITATE.

impertinent *adj* bold, brazen, cheeky, *inf* cocky, *inf* cool, discourteous, disrespectful, forward, fresh, impolite, impudent, insolent, insubordinate, insulting, irreverent, pert, saucy. ▷ RUDE. *Opp* RESPECTFUL.

impervious *adj* **1** hermetic, impenetrable, impermeable, non-porous, solid, waterproof, water-repellent, watertight. *Opp* POROUS. **2** ▷ RESISTANT.

impetuous *adj* abrupt, careless, eager, hasty, headlong, hot-headed, impulsive, incautious, offhand, precipitate, quick, rash, reckless, speedy, spontaneous, *inf* spur-of-the-moment, *inf* tearing, thoughtless, unplanned, unpremeditated, unthinking, violent. *Opp* CAUTIOUS.

impetus *n* boost, drive, encouragement, energy, fillip, force, impulse, incentive, inspiration, momentum, motivation, power, push, spur, stimulation, stimulus, thrust.

impiety *n* blasphemy, godlessness, irreverence, profanity, sacrilege, sinfulness, ungodliness, unrighteousness, wickedness. *Opp* PIETY.

impious *adj* blasphemous, godless, irreligious, irreverent, profane, sacrilegious, sinful, unholy. ▷ WICKED. *Opp* PIOUS.

implausible *adj* doubtful, dubious, far-fetched, feeble, improbable, questionable, suspect, unconvincing, unlikely, unreasonable, weak. *Opp* PLAUSIBLE.

implement *n* apparatus, appliance, contrivance, device, gadget, instrument, mechanism, tool, utensil. • *vb* accomplish, achieve, bring about, carry out, effect, enforce, execute, fulfil, perform, put into effect, put into practice, realize, try out.

implicate *vb* associate, concern, connect, embroil, enmesh, ensnare, entangle, entrap, include, incriminate, inculpate, involve, show involvement in.

implication *n* **1** hidden meaning, hint, innuendo, insinua-tion, overtone, purport, significance. **2** *implication in crime.* association, connection, embroilment, entanglement, inclusion, involvement.

implicit *adj* **1** hinted at, implied, indirect, inherent, insinuated, tacit, understood, undeclared, unexpressed, unsaid, unspoken, unstated, unvoiced. *Opp* EXPLICIT. **2** *implicit faith.* ▷ ABSOLUTE.

imply *vb* **1** hint, indicate, insinuate, intimate, mean, point to, suggest. **2** ▷ SIGNIFY.

impolite *adj* discourteous, disrespectful, ill-bred, ill-mannered, uncivil, vulgar. ▷ RUDE. *Opp* POLITE.

import *vb* bring in, buy in, introduce, ship in. ▷ CONVEY.

important *adj* **1** basic, big, cardinal, central, chief, consequential, critical, epoch-making, essential, foremost, fundamental, grave, historic, key, main, major, momentous, newsworthy, noteworthy, once in a lifetime, outstanding, pressing, primary, principal, rare, salient, serious, signal, significant, strategic, substantial, urgent, valuable, vital, weighty. **2** celebrated, distinguished, eminent, famous, great, high-ranking, influential, known, leading, notable, noted, powerful, pre-eminent, prominent, renowned, top-level, well-known. *Opp* UNIMPORTANT. **be important** ▷ MATTER.

importunate *adj* demanding, impatient, insistent, persistent, pressing, relentless, urgent, unremitting.

importune *vb* badger, harass, hound, pester, plague, plead with, press, solicit, urge. ▷ ASK.

impose *vb* charge with, decree, dictate, enforce, exact, fix, foist, force, inflict, insist on, introduce, lay, levy, prescribe, set. **impose on** ▷ BURDEN, EXPLOIT. **imposing** ▷ IMPRESSIVE.

impossible *adj* hopeless, impracticable, impractical, inconceivable, insoluble, insuperable, insurmountable, *inf* not on, out of the question, unachievable, unattainable, unimaginable, unobtainable, unthinkable, unviable, unworkable. *Opp* POSSIBLE.

impotent *adj* debilitated, decrepit, emasculated, enervated, helpless, inadequate, incapable, incompetent, ineffective, ineffectual, inept, infirm, powerless, unable. ▷ WEAK. *Opp* POTENT.

impracticable *adj* not feasible, unachievable, unworkable, useless. ▷ IMPOSSIBLE. *Opp* PRACTICABLE.

impractical *adj* academic, idealistic, quixotic, romantic, theoretical, unrealistic, visionary. *Opp* PRACTICAL.

imprecise *adj* ambiguous, approximate, careless, estimated, fuzzy, guessed, hazy, ill-defined, inaccurate, inexact, inexplicit, loose, *inf* sloppy, undefined, unscientific, vague, *inf* waffly, *inf* woolly. *Opp* PRECISE.

impregnable *adj* impenetrable, invincible, inviolable, invulnerable, safe, secure, strong, unassailable, unconquerable. *Opp* VULNERABLE.

impress *vb* **1** affect, be memorable to, excite, influence, inspire, leave its mark on, move, persuade, *inf* stick in the mind of, stir, touch. **2** *impress* *a mark*. emboss, engrave, imprint, mark, print, stamp.

impression *n* **1** effect, impact, influence, mark. **2** belief, consciousness, fancy, feeling, hunch, idea, memory, notion, opinion, recollection, sense, suspicion, view. **3** dent, hollow, imprint, indentation, mark, print, stamp. **4** imitation, impersonation, mimicry, parody, *inf* take-off. **5** *impression of a book*. edition, printing, reprint.

impressionable *adj* easily influenced, gullible, inexperienced, naïve, persuadable, receptive, responsive, suggestible, susceptible.

impressive *adj* affecting, august, awe-inspiring, awesome, commanding, distinguished, evocative, exciting, formidable, grand, *derog* grandiose, great, imposing, magnificent, majestic, memorable, moving, powerful, redoubtable, remarkable, splendid, stately, stirring, striking, touching. ▷ BIG. *Opp* INSIGNIFICANT.

imprison *vb* cage, commit to prison, confine, detain, gaol, immure, incarcerate, intern, jail, keep in custody, keep under house arrest, *inf* keep under lock and key, lock away, lock up, *inf* put away, remand, *inf* send down, shut in, shut up. *Opp* FREE.

imprisonment *n* confinement, custody, detention, duress, gaol, house arrest, incarceration, internment, jail, remand, restraint.

improbable *adj* absurd, doubtful, dubious, far-fetched, *inf* hard to believe, implausible, incredible, preposterous, questionable, unbelievable, unconvincing, unexpected, unlikely. *Opp* PROBABLE.

impromptu *adj inf* ad-lib, extempore, extemporized, improvised, impulsive, made-up, offhand, *inf* off the cuff, *inf* off the top of your head, *inf* on the spur of the moment, spontaneous, unplanned, unpremeditated, unprepared, unrehearsed, unscripted. ▷ IMPULSIVE. *Opp* REHEARSED.

improper *adj* **1** ill-judged, ill-timed, inappropriate, incorrect, infelicitous, inopportune, irregular, mistaken, out of place, uncalled-for, unfit, unseemly, unsuitable, unwarranted. ▷ WRONG. **2** ▷ INDECENT. *Opp* PROPER.

impropriety *n* inappropriateness, incorrectness, indecency, indelicacy, infelicity, insensitivity, irregularity, rudeness, unseemliness. ▷ OBSCENITY. *Opp* PROPRIETY.

improve *vb* **1** advance, develop, get better, grow, increase, *inf* look up, move on, progress, *inf* take a turn for the better. **2** *improve after illness*. convalesce, *inf* pick up, rally, recover, recuperate, revive, strengthen, *inf* turn the corner. **3** *improve your ways*. ameliorate, amend, better, correct, enhance, enrich, make better, mend, polish (up), rectify, refine, reform, revise. **4** *improve a home*. decorate, extend, modernize, rebuild, recondition, refurbish, renovate, repair, touch up, update, upgrade. *Opp* WORSEN.

improvement *n* **1** advance, amelioration, betterment, correction, development, enhancement, gain, increase, progress, rally, recovery, reformation, upswing, upturn. **2** *home improvements*. alteration, extension, *inf* face-lift, modernization, modification, renovation.

improvise *vb* **1** *inf* ad-lib, concoct, contrive, devise, invent, make do, make up, *inf* throw together. **2** extemporize, perform impromptu, play by ear, vamp.

impudent *adj* audacious, bold, *inf* cheeky, disrespectful, forward, *inf* fresh, impertinent, insolent, pert, presumptuous, saucy. ▷ RUDE. *Opp* RESPECTFUL.

impulse *n* **1** drive, force, impetus, motive, pressure, push, stimulus, thrust. **2** caprice, desire, instinct, urge, whim.

impulsive *adj* automatic, emotional, hare-brained, hasty, headlong, hot-headed, impetuous, instinctive, intuitive, involuntary, madcap, precipitate, rash, reckless, *inf* snap, spontaneous, *inf* spur-of-the-moment, sudden, thoughtless, unconscious, unplanned, unpremeditated, unthinking, wild. ▷ IMPROMPTU. *Opp* DELIBERATE.

impure *adj* **1** adulterated, contaminated, defiled, foul, infected, polluted, tainted, unclean, unwholesome. ▷ DIRTY. **2** ▷ INDECENT.

impurity *n* contamination, defilement, infection, pollution, taint. ▷ DIRT.

inaccessible *adj* cut off, deserted, desolate, godforsaken, impassable, impenetrable, inconvenient, isolated, lonely, *inf* off the beaten track, outlying, out of reach, out-of-the-way, private, remote, solitary, unavailable, unfrequented, *inf* unget-at-able, unobtainable, unreachable, unusable. *Opp* ACCESSIBLE.

inaccurate *adj* erroneous, fallacious, false, faulty, flawed, imperfect, imprecise, incorrect, inexact, misleading, mistaken, unfaithful, unreliable, unsound, untrue, vague, wrong. *Opp* ACCURATE.

inactive *adj* asleep, dormant, hibernating, idle, immobile, inanimate, indolent, inert, languid, lazy, lethargic, out of action, passive, quiescent, quiet, sedentary, sleepy, slothful, slow, sluggish, somnolent, torpid, unemployed, unoccupied, vegetating. *Opp* ACTIVE.

inadequate *adj* deficient, disappointing, faulty, imperfect, incompetent, incomplete, ineffective, insufficient, limited, meagre, mean, niggardly, *inf* pathetic, scanty, scarce, *inf* skimpy, sparse, unacceptable, unsatisfactory, unsuitable. *Opp* ADEQUATE.

inadvisable *adj* foolish, illadvised, imprudent, misguided, unwise. ▷ SILLY. *Opp* WISE.

inanimate *adj* cold, dead, dormant, immobile, inactive, insentient, lifeless, motionless, spiritless, unconscious. *Opp* ANIMATE.

inappropriate *adj* ill-judged, ill-suited, ill-timed, improper, inapplicable, inapposite, incompatible, incongruous, incorrect, inept, inopportune, irrelevant, out of place, tactless, tasteless, unbecoming, unbefitting, unfit, unseasonable, unseemly, unsuitable, unsuited, untimely, wrong. *Opp* APPROPRIATE.

inarticulate *adj* dumb, faltering, halting, hesitant, mumbling, mute, shy, silent, speechless, stammering, stuttering, tongue-tied, voiceless. ▷ INCOHERENT. *Opp* ARTICULATE.

inattentive *adj* absent-minded, abstracted, careless, day-dreaming, distracted, dreaming, drifting, heedless, *inf* in a world of your own, lacking concentration, negligent, preoccupied, rambling, remiss, slack, unobservant, vague, wandering, wool-gathering. *Opp* ATTENTIVE.

inaudible *adj* imperceptible, mumbled, quiet, silenced, silent, stifled, undetectable, undistinguishable, unheard. ▷ FAINT. *Opp* AUDIBLE.

incapable *adj* **1** clumsy, helpless, impotent, inadequate, incompetent, ineffective, ineffectual, inept, powerless, stupid, unable, unfit, unqualified, useless, weak. *Opp* CAPABLE. **2** ▷ DRUNK.

incentive *n* bait, *inf* carrot, encouragement, enticement, impetus, incitement, inducement, lure, motivation, reward, stimulus, *inf* sweetener.

incessant *adj* ceaseless, chronic, constant, continual, continuous, endless, eternal, everlasting, interminable, never-ending, non-stop, perennial, permanent, perpetual, persistent, relentless, unbroken, unceasing, unending, unremitting. *Opp* INTERMITTENT, TEMPORARY.

incident *n* **1** affair, circumstance, episode, event, fact, happening, occasion, occurrence, proceeding. **2** *a nasty incident.* accident, confrontation, disturbance, fight, scene, upset. ▷ COMMOTION.

incidental *adj* accidental, adventitious, attendant, casual, chance, fortuitous, inessential, minor, odd, random, secondary, serendipitous, subordinate, subsidiary, unplanned. *Opp* ESSENTIAL.

incipient *adj* beginning, developing, early, embryonic, growing, new, rudimentary, starting.

incisive *adj* acute, clear, concise, cutting, decisive, direct, penetrating, percipient, precise, sharp, telling, trenchant. *Opp* VAGUE.

incite *vb* awaken, encourage, excite, fire, foment, inflame, inspire, prompt, provoke, rouse, spur on, stimulate, stir, urge, whip up, work up.

inclination *n* affection, bent, bias, disposition, fondness, habit, instinct, leaning, liking, partiality, penchant, predilection, predisposition, preference, proclivity, propensity, readiness, tendency, trend, willingness. ▷ DESIRE.

incline *n* acclivity, ascent, declivity, descent, drop, grade, gradient, hill, pitch, ramp, rise, slope. • *vb* angle, ascend, bank, bend, bow, descend, drop, gravitate, lean, rise, slant, slope, tend, tilt, tip, veer. **inclined (to)** ▷ LIABLE.

include *vb* **1** add in, blend in, combine, comprehend, comprise, consist of, contain, embody, embrace, encompass, incorporate, involve, make room for, mix, subsume, take in. **2** *The price includes tea.* allow for, cover, take into account. *Opp* EXCLUDE.

incoherent *adj* confused, disconnected, disjointed, disordered, disorganized, garbled, illogical, incomprehensible, inconsistent, irrational, jumbled, mixed up, muddled, rambling, scrambled, unclear, unconnected, unstructured, unsystematic. ▷ INARTICULATE. *Opp* COHERENT.

incombustible *adj* fireproof, fire-resistant, flameproof, nonflammable. *Opp* COMBUSTIBLE.

income *n* earnings, gain, interest, pay, pension, proceeds, profits, receipts, return, revenue, salary, takings, wages. *Opp* EXPENSE.

incoming *adj* **1** approaching, arriving, entering, coming, landing, new, next, returning. **2** *incoming tide.* flowing, rising. *Opp* OUTGOING.

incompatible *adj* antipathetic, at variance, clashing, conflicting, contradictory, contrasting, different, discordant, discrepant, incongruous, inconsistent, irreconcilable, mismatched, opposed, unsuited. *Opp* COMPATIBLE.

incompetent *adj* **1** bungling, clumsy, feckless, gauche, helpless, *inf* hopeless, incapable, ineffective, ineffectual, inefficient, inexperienced, maladroit, unfit, unqualified, unskilled, untrained. **2** bungled, inadequate, inexpert, unacceptable, unsatisfactory, unskilful, useless. *Opp* COMPETENT.

incomplete *adj* abbreviated, abridged, *inf* bitty, deficient, edited, expurgated, faulty, fragmentary, imperfect, insufficient, partial, selective, shortened, sketchy, unfinished, unpolished, wanting. *Opp* COMPLETE.

incomprehensible *adj* abstruse, arcane, baffling, beyond comprehension, cryptic, deep, enigmatic, esoteric, illegible, impenetrable, indecipherable, meaningless, mysterious, mystifying, obscure, opaque, *inf* over my head, perplexing, puzzling, recondite, strange, too difficult, unclear, unfathomable, unintelligible. *Opp* COMPREHENSIBLE.

inconceivable *adj* implausible, impossible to understand, incredible, *inf* mind-boggling, staggering, unbelievable, undreamed-of, unimaginable, unthinkable. *Opp* CREDIBLE.

inconclusive *adj* ambiguous, equivocal, indecisive, indefinite, interrogative, open, open-ended, questionable, uncertain, unconvincing, unresolved, *inf* up in the air. *Opp* CONCLUSIVE.

incongruous *adj* clashing, conflicting, contrasting, discordant, ill-matched, ill-suited, inappropriate, incompatible, inconsistent, irreconcilable, odd, out of keeping, out of place, surprising, uncoordinated, unsuited. ▷ ABSURD. *Opp* COMPATIBLE.

inconsiderate *adj* careless, cruel, heedless, insensitive, intolerant, negligent, rude, self-centred, selfish, tactless, thoughtless, uncaring, unconcerned, unfriendly, ungracious, unhelpful, unkind, unsympathetic, unthinking. *Opp* CONSIDERATE.

inconsistent *adj* capricious, changeable, erratic, fickle, inconstant, patchy, unpredictable, unreliable, unstable, *inf* up-and-down, variable. ▷ INCOMPATIBLE. *Opp* CONSISTENT.

inconspicuous *adj* camouflaged, concealed, discreet, hidden, insignificant, in the background, invisible, modest, ordinary, out of sight, plain, restrained, retiring, self-effacing, small, unassuming, unobtrusive, unostentatious. *Opp* CONSPICUOUS.

inconvenience *n* annoyance, bother, discomfort, disruption, drawback, encumbrance, hindrance, impediment, irritation, nuisance, trouble. • *vb* annoy, bother, discommode, disturb, incommode, irk, irritate, *inf* put out, trouble.

inconvenient *adj* annoying, awkward, bothersome, cumbersome, difficult, embarrassing, ill-timed, inopportune, irksome, irritating, tiresome, troublesome, unsuitable, untimely, untoward, unwieldy. *Opp* CONVENIENT.

incorporate *vb* admit, combine, comprehend, comprise, consist of, contain, embody, embrace, encompass, include, involve, mix in, subsume, take in, take into account, unite. *Opp* EXCLUDE.

incorrect *adj* erroneous, fallacious, false, faulty, imprecise, improper, inaccurate, inexact, mendacious, misinformed, misleading, mistaken, specious, untrue. *Opp* CORRECT.

incorrigible *adj* confirmed, *inf* dyed-in-the-wool, habitual, hardened, *inf* hopeless, impenitent, incurable, inveterate, irredeemable, obdurate, shameless, unalterable, unreformable, unrepentant. ▷ WICKED.

incorruptible *adj* **1** honest, honourable, just, moral, sound, *inf* straight, true, trustworthy, unbribable, upright. *Opp* CORRUPT. **2** ▷ EVERLASTING.

increase *n* addition, amplification, augmentation, boost, build-up, crescendo, development, enlargement, escalation, expansion, extension, gain, growth, increment, inflation, intensification, proliferation, rise, spread, upsurge, upturn. • *vb* **1** add to, advance, amplify, augment, boost, broaden, build up, develop, enlarge, expand, extend, improve, lengthen, magnify, make bigger, maximize, multiply, prolong, put up, raise, *inf* step up, strengthen, stretch, swell, widen. **2** escalate, gain, get bigger, grow, intensify, proliferate, *inf* snowball, spread, wax. *Opp* DECREASE.

incredible *adj* beyond belief, far-fetched, implausible, impossible, improbable, inconceivable, miraculous, surprising, unbelievable, unconvincing, unimaginable, unlikely, untenable, unthinkable. ▷ EXTRAORDINARY. *Opp* CREDIBLE.

incredulous *adj* disbelieving, distrustful, doubtful, dubious, mistrustful, questioning, sceptical, suspicious, unbelieving, uncertain, unconvinced. *Opp* CREDULOUS.

incriminate *vb* accuse, blame, charge, embroil, implicate, inculpate, indict, involve, *inf* point the finger at. *Opp* EXCUSE.

incur *vb* earn, expose yourself to, get, lay yourself open to, provoke, run up, suffer.

incurable *adj* **1** fatal, hopeless, inoperable, irremediable, irreparable, terminal, untreatable. *Opp* CURABLE. **2** ▷ INCORRIGIBLE.

indebted *adj old use* beholden, bound, grateful, obliged, thankful, under an obligation.

indecent *adj inf* blue, coarse, crude, dirty, immodest, impolite, improper, impure, indelicate, insensitive, naughty, obscene, offensive, risqué, rude, *inf* sexy, *inf* smutty, suggestive, titillating, unprintable, unrepeatable, unsuitable, vulgar. ▷ INDECOROUS. *Opp* DECENT.

indecisive *adj* doubtful, equivocal, evasive, *inf* in two minds, irresolute, undecided. ▷ HESITANT, INDEFINITE. *Opp* DECISIVE. **be indecisive** ▷ HESITATE.

indecorous *adj* churlish, ill-bred, inappropriate, *inf* in bad taste, tasteless, unbecoming, uncouth, undignified, unseemly, vulgar. ▷ INDECENT. *Opp* DECOROUS.

indefensible *adj* incredible, insupportable, unjustifiable, unpardonable, unreasonable, unsound, untenable, vulnerable, weak. ▷ WRONG.

indefinite *adj* ambiguous, blurred, confused, dim, general, ill-defined, imprecise, indeterminate, inexact, inexplicit, *inf* leaving it open, neutral, obscure, uncertain, unclear, unsettled, unspecific, unspecified, unsure, vague. ▷ INDECISIVE. *Opp* DEFINITE.

indelible *adj* fast, fixed, indestructible, ineffaceable, ineradicable, ingrained, lasting, unfading, unforgettable. ▷ PERMANENT.

indentation *n* cut, dent, depression, dimple, dip, furrow, groove, hollow, indent, mark, nick, notch, pit, recess, score, serration, toothmark, zigzag.

independence *n* **1** autonomy, freedom, individualism, liberty, nonconformity, self-confidence, self-reliance, self-sufficiency. **2** autarchy, home rule, self-determination, self-government, self-rule, sovereignty.

independent *adj* **1** carefree, *inf* footloose, free, freethinking, individualistic, nonconformist, non-partisan, open-minded, private, self-confident, selfreliant, separate, spontaneous, unbeholden, unbiased, uncommitted, unconventional, unprejudiced, untrammelled, without ties. **2** autonomous, liberated, neutral, non-aligned, self-determining, self-governing, sovereign.

indescribable *adj* beyond words, indefinable, inexpressible, stunning, unspeakable, unutterable.

indestructible *adj* durable, enduring, eternal, everlasting, immortal, imperishable, ineradicable, lasting, permanent, shatter-proof, solid, strong, tough, toughened, unbreakable.

index *n* **1** catalogue, directory, guide, key, register, table (*of contents*). **2** ▷ INDICATOR.

indicate *vb* announce, betoken, communicate, convey, denote, describe, designate, display, evidence, express, give an indication (*of*), give notice of, imply, intimate, make known, manifest, mean, notify, point out, register, reveal, say, show, signal, signify, specify, spell, stand for, suggest, symbolize, warn.

indication *n* augury, clue, evidence, forewarning, hint, inkling, intimation, omen, portent, sign, signal, suggestion, symptom, token, warning.

indicator *n* clock, dial, display, gauge, index, instrument, marker, meter, needle, pointer, screen, sign, signal.

indifferent *adj* **1** aloof, apathetic, blasé, bored, casual, cold, cool, detached, disinterested, dispassionate, distant, half-hearted, impassive, incurious, insouciant, neutral, nonchalant, not bothered, uncaring, unconcerned, unemotional, unenthusiastic, unexcited, unimpressed, uninterested, uninvolved, unmoved. ▷ IMPARTIAL. *Opp* ENTHUSIASTIC. **2** commonplace, fair, mediocre, middling, moderate, *inf* nothing to write home about, *inf* poorish, undistinguished, unexciting. ▷ ORDINARY. *Opp* EXCELLENT.

indigestion *n* dyspepsia, flatulence, heartburn.

indignant *adj* *inf* aerated, annoyed, cross, disgruntled, exasperated, furious, heated, infuriated, *inf* in high dudgeon, irate, irked, irritated, livid, mad, *inf* miffed, *inf* peeved, piqued, provoked, *inf* put out, riled, sore, upset, vexed. ▷ ANGRY.

indirect *adj* **1** *inf* all round the houses, ambagious, bendy, circuitous, devious, erratic, long, meandering, oblique, rambling, roundabout, roving, tortuous, twisting, winding, zigzag. **2** *an indirect insult.* ambiguous, backhanded, circumlocutory, disguised, equivocal, euphemistic, evasive, implicit, implied, oblique. *Opp* DIRECT.

indiscreet *adj* careless, foolish, ill-advised, ill-considered, ill-judged, impolite, impolitic, incautious, injudicious, insensitive, tactless, undiplomatic, unguarded, unthinking, unwise. *Opp* DISCREET.

indiscriminate *adj* aimless, careless, casual, confused, desultory, general, haphazard, *inf* hit or miss, imperceptive, miscellaneous, mixed, promiscuous, random, uncritical, undifferentiated, undiscerning, undiscriminating, uninformed, unplanned, unselective, unsystematic, wholesale. *Opp* SELECTIVE.

indispensable *adj* basic, central, compulsory, crucial, essential, imperative, important, key, mandatory, necessary, needed, obligatory, required, requisite, vital. *Opp* UNNECESSARY.

indisputable *adj* absolute, accepted, acknowledged, axiomatic, beyond doubt, certain, clear, definite, evident, incontestable, incontrovertible, indubitable, irrefutable, positive, proved, proven, self-evident, sure, unanswerable, unarguable, undeniable, undisputed, undoubted, unimpeachable, unquestionable. *Opp* DEBATABLE.

indistinct *adj* **1** bleary, blurred, confused, dim, dull, faint, fuzzy, hazy, ill-defined, indefinite, misty, obscure, shadowy, unclear, vague. **2** deadened, muffled, mumbled, muted, slurred, unintelligible, woolly. *Opp* DISTINCT.

indistinguishable *adj* alike, identical, interchangeable, the same, twin, undifferentiated. *Opp* DIFFERENT.

individual *adj* characteristic, different, distinct, distinctive, exclusive, idiosyncratic, individualistic, particular, peculiar, personal, private, separate, singular, special, specific, unique. *Opp* COLLECTIVE, GENERAL. ● *n* ▷ PERSON.

indoctrinate *vb* brainwash, implant, instruct, re-educate, train. ▷ TEACH.

induce *vb* **1** coax, encourage, incite, influence, inspire, motivate, persuade, press, prevail on, stimulate, sway, *inf* talk into, tempt, urge. *Opp* DISCOURAGE. **2** *induce a fever.* bring on, cause, effect, engender, generate, give rise to, lead to, occasion, produce, provoke.

inducement *n* attraction, bait, bribe, encouragement, enticement, incentive, spur, stimulus, *inf* sweetener.

indulge *vb* be indulgent to, cosset, favour, give in to, gratify, humour, mollycoddle, pamper, pander to, spoil, *inf* spoonfeed, treat. *Opp* DEPRIVE. **indulge in** ▷ ENJOY. **indulge yourself** be self-indulgent, drink too much, eat too much, give in to temptation, overdo it, overeat, spoil yourself, succumb, yield.

indulgent *adj* compliant, easygoing, fond, forbearing, forgiving, genial, kind, lenient, liberal, overgenerous, patient, permissive, tolerant. *Opp* STRICT.

industrious *adj* assiduous, busy, conscientious, diligent, dynamic, earnest, energetic, enterprising, hard-working, involved, keen, laborious, persistent, pertinacious, productive, sedulous, tireless, unflagging, untiring, zealous. *Opp* LAZY.

industry *n* **1** business, commerce, manufacturing, production, trade. **2** activity, application, commitment, determination, diligence, dynamism, effort, energy, enterprise, industriousness, keenness, labour, perseverance, persistence, sedulousness, tirelessness, toil, zeal. ▷ WORK. *Opp* LAZINESS.

inedible *adj* bad for you, harmful, indigestible, nauseating, *inf* off, poisonous, rotten, tough, uneatable, unpalatable, unwholesome. *Opp* EDIBLE.

ineffective *adj* **1** fruitless, futile, *inf* hopeless, inept, unconvincing, unproductive, unsuccessful, useless, vain, worthless. **2** disorganized, feckless, feeble, idle, impotent, inadequate, incapable, incompetent, ineffectual, inefficient, powerless, shiftless, unenterprising, weak. *Opp* EFFECTIVE.

inefficient *adj* **1** extravagant, prodigal, uneconomic, wasteful. **2** ▷ INEFFECTIVE. *Opp* EFFICIENT.

inelegant *adj* awkward, clumsy, crude, gauche, graceless, inartistic, rough, uncouth, ungainly, unpolished, unskilful, unsophisticated, unstylish. ▷ UGLY. *Opp* ELEGANT.

ineligible *adj* disqualified, inappropriate, *inf* out of the running, *inf* ruled out, unacceptable, unauthorized, unfit, unqualified, unsuitable, unworthy. *Opp* ELIGIBLE.

inept *adj* **1** awkward, bumbling, bungling, clumsy, gauche, incompetent, inexpert, maladroit, unskilful, unskilled. **2** ▷ INAPPROPRIATE.

inequality *n* contrast, difference, discrepancy, disparity, dissimilarity, imbalance, incongruity, prejudice. *Opp* EQUALITY.

inert *adj* apathetic, dormant, idle, immobile, inactive, inanimate, lifeless, passive, quiescent, quiet, slow, sluggish, static, stationary, still, supine, torpid. *Opp* LIVELY.

inertia *n* apathy, deadness, idleness, immobility, inactivity, indolence, lassitude, laziness, lethargy, listlessness, numbness, passivity, sluggishness, torpor. *Opp* LIVELINESS.

inessential *adj* dispensable, expendable, minor, needless, non-essential, optional, ornamental, secondary, spare, superfluous, unimportant, unnecessary. *Opp* ESSENTIAL.

inevitable *adj* assured, *inf* bound to happen, certain, destined, fated, ineluctable, inescapable, inexorable, ordained, predictable, sure, unavoidable. ▷ RELENTLESS.

inexcusable *adj* ▷ UNFORGIVABLE.

inexpensive *adj* ▷ CHEAP.

inexperienced *adj inf* born yesterday, callow, *inf* green, immature, inexpert, innocent, naïve, new, probationary, raw, unaccustomed, unfledged, uninitiated, unskilled, unsophisticated, untried, *inf* wet behind the ears, young. *Opp* EXPERT.

inexplicable *adj* baffling, bewildering, confusing, enigmatic, incomprehensible, inscrutable, insoluble, mysterious, mystifying, perplexing, puzzling, strange, unaccountable, unexplainable, unfathomable, unsolvable. *Opp* STRAIGHTFORWARD.

infallible *adj* certain, dependable, faultless, foolproof, impeccable, perfect, reliable, sound, sure, trustworthy, unbeatable, unerring, unfailing. *Opp* FALLIBLE.

infamous *adj* disgraceful, disreputable, ill-famed, notorious, outrageous, well-known. ▷ WICKED.

infant *n* baby, *inf* toddler, *inf* tot. ▷ CHILD.

infantile *adj* [*derog*] adolescent, babyish, childish, immature, juvenile, puerile. ▷ SILLY. *Opp* MATURE.

infatuated *adj* besotted, charmed, enchanted, *inf* head over heels, in love, obsessed, *inf* smitten.

infatuation *n inf* crush, obsession, passion. ▷ LOVE.

infect *vb* **1** blight, contaminate, defile, poison, pollute, spoil, taint. **2** affect, influence, inspire, touch. **infected** ▷ SEPTIC.

infection *n* blight, contagion, contamination, epidemic, pestilence, pollution, virus. ▷ ILLNESS.

infectious *adj* catching, communicable, contagious, spreading, transmissible, transmittable.

infer *vb* assume, conclude, deduce, derive, draw a conclusion, extrapolate, gather, guess, reach the conclusion, surmise, understand, work out.

inferior *adj* **1** humble, junior, lesser, lower, lowly, mean, menial, secondary, second-class, servile, subordinate, subsidiary, unimportant. **2** cheap, indifferent, mediocre, poor, shoddy, tawdry, *inf* tinny. *Opp* SUPERIOR. ● *n* ▷ SUBORDINATE.

infertile *adj* barren, sterile, unfruitful, unproductive.

infest *vb* infiltrate, overrun, pervade, plague. **infested** alive, crawling, swarming, teeming, verminous.

infidelity *n* **1** adultery, unfaithfulness. **2** ▷ DISLOYALTY.

infiltrate *vb* enter secretly, insinuate, intrude, penetrate, spy on.

infinite *adj* astronomical, big, boundless, countless, endless, eternal, everlasting, immeasurable, immense, incalculable, indeterminate, inestimable, inexhaustible, innumerable, interminable, limitless, multitudinous, never-ending, numberless, perpetual, uncountable, undefined, unending, unfathomable, unlimited, unnumbered, untold. ▷ HUGE. *Opp* FINITE.

infinity *n* endlessness, eternity, infinite distance, infinite quantity, infinitude, perpetuity, space.

infirm *adj* bedridden, crippled, elderly, feeble, frail, lame, old, poorly, senile, sickly, unwell. ▷ ILL, WEAK. *Opp* HEALTHY.

inflame *vb* arouse, encourage, excite, fire, foment, goad, ignite, incense, incite, kindle, madden, provoke, rouse, stimulate, stir up, work up. ▷ ANGER. *Opp* COOL. **inflamed** ▷ PASSIONATE, SEPTIC.

inflammable *adj* burnable, combustible, flammable, volatile. *Opp* INCOMBUSTIBLE.

inflammation *n* abscess, boil, infection, irritation, redness, sore, soreness, swelling.

inflate *vb* **1** blow up, dilate, distend, enlarge, puff up, pump up, swell. **2** ▷ EXAGGERATE.

inflexible *adj* **1** adamantine, firm, hard, hardened, immovable, rigid, solid, stiff, unbending, unyielding. **2** adamant, entrenched, fixed, immutable, inexorable, intractable, intransigent, obdurate, obstinate, *inf* pig-headed, refractory, resolute, rigorous, strict, stubborn, unalterable, unchangeable, uncompromising, unhelpful. *Opp* FLEXIBLE.

inflict *vb* administer, apply, deal out, enforce, force, impose, mete out, perpetrate, wreak.

influence *n* ascendancy, authority, control, direction, dominance, effect, guidance, hold, impact, leverage, power, pressure, pull, sway, weight. ● *vb* **1** affect, bias, change, control, direct, dominate, exert influence on, guide, impinge on, impress, manipulate, modify, motivate, move, persuade, prejudice, prompt, put pressure on, stir, sway. **2** *influence a judge.* bribe, corrupt, lead astray, suborn, tempt.

influential *adj* authoritative, compelling, controlling, convincing, dominant, effective, far-reaching, forceful, guiding, important, inspiring, leading, moving, persuasive, potent, powerful, prestigious, significant, strong, telling, weighty. *Opp* UNIMPORTANT.

influx *n* flood, flow, inflow, inundation, invasion, rush, stream.

inform *vb* **1** advise, apprise, brief, communicate to, enlighten, *inf* fill in, give information to, instruct, leak, notify, *inf* put in the picture, teach, tell, *inf* tip off. **2** *inf* blab, give information, *sl* grass, *sl* peach, *sl* rat, *inf* sneak, *inf* split on, *inf* tell, *inf* tell tales. **inform against** ▷ BETRAY. **informed** ▷ KNOWLEDGEABLE.

informal *adj* **1** approachable, casual, comfortable, cosy, easy, easygoing, everyday, familiar, free and easy, friendly, homely, natural, ordinary, relaxed, simple, unceremonious, unofficial, unpretentious, unsophisticated. **2** *informal language.* chatty, colloquial, personal, slangy, vernacular. **3** *an informal design.* asymmetrical, flexible, fluid, intuitive, irregular, spontaneous. *Opp* FORMAL.

information *n* **1** announcement, briefing, bulletin, communication, enlightenment, instruction, message, news, report, statement, *old use* tidings, *inf* tip-off, word. **2** data, database, dossier, evidence, facts, intelligence, knowledge, statistics.

informative *adj* communicative, edifying, educational, enlightening, factual, giving information, helpful, illuminating, instructive, meaningful, revealing, useful. *Opp* MEANINGLESS.

informer *n sl* grass, informant, spy, *sl* stool-pigeon, *inf* tell-tale, traitor.

infrequent *adj* exceptional, intermittent, irregular, occasional, *inf* once in a blue moon, rare, spasmodic, uncommon, unusual. *Opp* FREQUENT.

infringe *vb* breach, break, contravene, defy, disobey, disregard, flout, ignore, overstep, sin against, transgress, violate.

ingenious *adj* adroit, artful, astute, brilliant, clever, complex, crafty, creative, cunning, deft, imaginative, inspired, intelligent, intricate, inventive, neat, original, resourceful, shrewd, skilful, *inf* smart, subtle, talented. *Opp* UNIMAGINATIVE.

ingenuous *adj* artless, childlike, frank, guileless, honest, innocent, naïve, open, plain, simple, sincere, trusting, unaffected, uncomplicated, unsophisticated. *Opp* SOPHISTICATED.

ingredient *n* component, constituent, element, factor, *plur* makings, part.

inhabit *vb old use* abide in, colonize, dwell in, live in, make your home in, occupy, people, populate, possess, reside in, settle in, set up home in.

inhabitable *adj* habitable, in good repair, liveable, usable. *Opp* UNINHABITABLE.

inhabitant *n* citizen, *old use* denizen, dweller, inmate, native, occupant, occupier, *plur* population, resident, settler, tenant, *plur* townsfolk, *plur* townspeople.

inherent *adj* built-in, congenital, essential, fundamental, hereditary, immanent, inborn, inbred, indwelling, ingrained, intrinsic, native, natural.

inherit *vb* be the inheritor of, be left, *inf* come into, receive as an inheritance, succeed to. **inherited** ▷ HEREDITARY.

inheritance *n* bequest, birthright, estate, fortune, heritage, legacy, patrimony.

inhibit *vb* bridle, check, control, curb, discourage, frustrate, hinder, hold back, prevent, quell, repress, restrain. **inhibited** ▷ REPRESSED, SHY.

inhibition *n* **1** bar, barrier, check, constraint, curb, impediment, interference, restraint, stricture. **2** blockage, diffidence, *inf* hang-up, repression, reserve, self-consciousness, shyness.

inhospitable *adj* antisocial, reclusive, reserved, solitary, standoffish, unkind, unsociable, unwelcoming. ▷ UNFRIENDLY. **2** bleak, cold, comfortless, desolate, grim, hostile, lonely. *Opp* HOSPITABLE.

inhuman *adj* animal, barbaric, barbarous, bestial, bloodthirsty, brutish, diabolical, fiendish, merciless, pitiless, ruthless, savage, unnatural, vicious. ▷ INHUMANE. *Opp* HUMAN.

inhumane *adj* cold-hearted, cruel, hard, hard-hearted, heartless, inconsiderate, insensitive, uncaring, uncharitable, uncivilized, unfeeling, unkind, unsympathetic. ▷ INHUMAN. *Opp* HUMANE.

initial *adj* beginning, commencing, earliest, first, inaugural, incipient, introductory, opening, original, primary, starting. *Opp* FINAL.

initiate *vb* activate, actuate, begin, commence, enter upon, get going, get under way, inaugurate, instigate, institute, introduce, launch, originate, set going, set in motion, set up, start, take the initiative, trigger.

initiative *n* ambition, drive, dynamism, enterprise, *inf* get-up-and-go, inventiveness, lead, leadership, originality, resourcefulness. **take the initiative** ▷ INITIATE.

injection *n inf* fix, inoculation, *inf* jab, vaccination.

injure *vb* break, crush, cut, damage, deface, disfigure, harm, hurt, ill-treat, impair, mar, ruin, spoil, vandalize. ▷ WOUND.

injurious *adj* **1** damaging, deleterious, destructive, detrimental, harmful, insalubrious, painful, ruinous. **2** ▷ ABUSIVE.

injury *n* damage, harm, hurt, mischief. ▷ WOUND.

injustice *n* bias, bigotry, discrimination, dishonesty, favouritism, illegality, inequality, inequity, one-sidedness, oppression, partiality, partisanship, prejudice, unfairness, unlawfulness, wrong, wrongness. *Opp* JUSTICE.

inn *n old use* hostelry, hotel, *inf* local, pub, tavern.

inner *adj* central, concealed, hidden, innermost, inside, interior, internal, intimate, inward, mental, middle, private, secret. *Opp* OUTER.

innocence *n* **1** goodness, honesty, incorruptibility, purity, righteousness, sinlessness, virtue. **2** [*derog*] gullibility, inexperience, naïvety, simple-mindedness.

innocent *adj* **1** above suspicion, angelic, blameless, chaste, childlike, faultless, free from blame, guiltless, harmless, honest, immaculate, incorrupt, inoffensive, pure, righteous, sinless, spotless, untainted, virginal, virtuous. *Opp* CORRUPT, GUILTY. **2** artless, childlike, credulous, *inf* green, guileless, gullible, inexperienced, ingenuous, naïve, simple, simple-minded, trusting, unsophisticated.

innovation *n* change, departure, invention, new feature, novelty, reform, revolution.

innovator *n* discoverer, experimenter, inventor, pioneer, reformer, revolutionary.

innumerable *adj* countless, many, numberless, uncountable, untold. ▷ INFINITE.

inquest *n* hearing. ▷ INQUIRY.

inquire *vb* ask, explore, investigate, seek information, *inf* probe, search, survey. ▷ ENQUIRE.

inquiry *n* cross-examination, examination, inquest, inquisition, interrogation, investigation, poll, *inf* post-mortem, *inf* probe, referendum, review, study, survey.

inquisitive *adj* curious, impertinent, indiscreet, inquiring, interfering, intrusive, investigative, meddlesome, meddling, *inf* nosy, probing, prying, questioning, sceptical, searching, *inf* snooping, spying. **be inquisitive** ▷ PRY.

insane *adj inf* crazy, deranged, lunatic, *inf* mental, psychotic, unbalanced, unhinged. ▷ MAD. *Opp* SANE.

inscription *n* dedication, engraving, epigraph, superscription, writing.

insect *n inf* bug, *inf* creepy-crawly. □ *ant, aphid, bee, beetle, blackfly, butterfly, cicada, cockchafer, cockroach, crane-fly, cricket, daddy-long-legs, damselfly, dragonfly, earwig, firefly, fly, glow-worm, gnat, grasshopper, hornet, ladybird, locust, mantis, mayfly, midge, mosquito, moth, sawfly, termite, tsetse (fly), wasp, weevil.*

insecure *adj* **1** dangerous, flimsy, loose, precarious, rickety, rocky, shaky, unsafe, unsound, unstable, unsteady, unsupported, weak, wobbly. **2** *an insecure feeling.* anxious, apprehensive, defenceless, exposed, open, uncertain, underconfident, unprotected, vulnerable, worried. *Opp* SECURE.

insensible *adj* anaesthetized, benumbed, *inf* dead to the world, inert, insensate, insentient, knocked out, numb, *inf* out, senseless, unaware, unconscious. *Opp* CONSCIOUS.

insensitive *adj* **1** anaesthetized, dead, numb, unresponsive. **2** boorish, callous, crass, cruel, imperceptive, obtuse, tactless, *inf* thick-skinned, thoughtless, uncaring, unfeeling, unsympathetic. *Opp* SENSITIVE.

inseparable *adj* always together, attached, indissoluble, indivisible, integral.

insert *vb* drive in, embed, implant, intercalate, interject, interleave, interpolate, interpose, introduce, place in, *inf* pop in, push in, put in, stick in, tuck in.

inside *adj* central, indoor, inner, innermost, interior, internal. • *n* bowels, centre, contents, core, heart, indoors, interior, lining, middle. *Opp* OUTSIDE. **insides** ▷ ENTRAILS.

insidious *adj* creeping, deceptive, furtive, pervasive, secretive, stealthy, subtle, surreptitious, treacherous, underhand. ▷ CRAFTY.

insignificant *adj* forgettable, inconsiderable, irrelevant, insubstantial, lightweight, meaningless, minor, negligible, paltry, small, trifling, trivial, undistinguished, unimportant, unimpressive, valueless, worthless. *Opp* SIGNIFICANT.

insincere *adj* artful, crafty, deceitful, deceptive, devious, dishonest, disingenuous, dissembling, false, feigned, flattering, *inf* foxy, hollow, hypocritical, lying, *inf* mealy-mouthed, mendacious, perfidious, *inf* phoney, pretended, *inf* put on, *inf* smarmy, sycophantic, treacherous, *inf* two-faced, untrue, untruthful, wily. *Opp* SINCERE.

insist *vb* **1** assert, asseverate, aver, avow, declare, emphasize, hold, maintain, state, stress, swear, take an oath, vow. **2** assert yourself, be assertive, command, persist, *inf* put your foot down, stand firm, *inf* stick to your guns. **insist on** ▷ DEMAND.

insistent *adj* assertive, demanding, dogged, emphatic, firm, forceful, importunate, inexorable, obstinate, peremptory, persistent, relentless, repeated, resolute, stubborn, unrelenting, unremitting, urgent.

insolence *n* arrogance, boldness, *inf* cheek, defiance, disrespect, effrontery, impertinence, impudence, incivility, insubordination, *inf* lip, presumptuousness, rudeness, *inf* sauce.

insolent *adj* arrogant, audacious, bold, brazen, *inf* cheeky, contemptuous, defiant, disdainful, disrespectful, forward, *inf* fresh, impertinent, impolite, impudent, insubordinate, insulting, offensive, pert, presumptuous, saucy, shameless, sneering, uncivil. ▷ RUDE. *Opp* POLITE.

insoluble *adj* baffling, enigmatic, incomprehensible, inexplicable, mystifying, puzzling, strange, unaccountable, unanswerable, unfathomable, unsolvable. *Opp* SOLUBLE.

insolvent *adj* bankrupt, *inf* bust, failed, ruined. ▷ POOR.

inspect *vb* check, examine, *sl* give it the once over, investigate, peruse, pore over, scan, scrutinize, study, survey, vet.

inspection *n* check, check-up, examination, *inf* going-over, investigation, review, scrutiny, survey.

inspector *n* controller, examiner, investigator, official, scrutineer, superintendent, supervisor, tester.

inspiration *n* **1** creativity, genius, imagination, muse. **2** enthusiasm, impulse, incitement, influence, motivation, prompting, spur, stimulation, stimulus. **3** *a sudden inspiration.* brainwave, idea, insight, revelation, thought.

inspire *vb* activate, animate, arouse, awaken, *inf* egg on, encourage, energize, enthuse, fire, galvanize, influence, inspirit, instigate, kindle, motivate, prompt, provoke, quicken, reassure, set off, spark off, spur, stimulate, stir, support.

instability *n* capriciousness, change, changeableness, fickleness, fluctuation, flux, impermanence, inconstancy, insecurity, mutability, precariousness, shakiness, transience, uncertainty, unpredictability, unreliability, unsteadiness, *inf* ups-and-downs, vacillation, variability, variations, weakness. *Opp* STABILITY.

install *vb* ensconce, establish, fit, fix, instate, introduce, place, plant, position, put in, settle, set up, situate, station. *Opp* REMOVE.

instalment *n* **1** payment, rent, rental. **2** chapter, episode, part.

instance *n* case, example, exemplar, illustration, occurrence, precedent, sample.

instant *adj* direct, fast, immediate, instantaneous, on-the-spot, prompt, quick, rapid, speedy, split-second, swift, unhesitating, urgent. • *n* flash, *inf* jiffy, moment, point of time, second, split second, *inf* tick, *inf* trice, *inf* twinkling.

instigate *vb* activate, begin, be the instigator of, bring about, cause, encourage, foment, generate, incite, initiate, inspire, kindle, prompt, provoke, set up, start, stimulate, stir up, urge, *inf* whip up.

instigator *n* agitator, fomenter, inciter, initiator, inspirer, leader, mischief-maker, provoker, ringleader, troublemaker.

instil *vb inf* din into, imbue, implant, inculcate, indoctrinate, infuse, ingrain, inject, insinuate, introduce.

instinct *n* bent, faculty, feel, feeling, guesswork, hunch, impulse, inclination, instinctive urge, intuition, presentiment, propensity, sixth-sense, the subconscious, tendency, urge.

instinctive *adj* automatic, congenital, constitutional, *inf* gut, impulsive, inborn, inbred, inherent, innate, instinctual, intuitive, involuntary, irrational, mechanical, native, natural, reflex, spontaneous, subconscious, unconscious, unreasoning, unthinking, visceral. *Opp* DELIBERATE.

institute *n* ▷ INSTITUTION. • *vb* begin, create, establish, fix up, found, inaugurate, initiate, introduce, launch, open, organize, originate, pioneer, set up, start.

institution *n* **1** creation, establishing, formation, founding, inauguration, inception, initiation, introduction, launching, opening, setting-up. **2** academy, asylum, college, establishment, foundation, home, hospital, institute, organization, school, *inf* set-up. **3** convention, custom, habit, practice, ritual, routine, rule, tradition.

instruct *vb* **1** coach, drill, educate, indoctrinate, inform, lecture, prepare, school, teach, train, tutor. **2** authorize, brief, charge, command, direct, enjoin, give the order, order, require, tell.

instruction *n* **1** briefing, coaching, demonstration, drill, education, guidance, indoctrination, lecture, lesson, schooling, teaching, training, tuition, tutorial, tutoring. **2** authorization, brief, charge, command, direction, directive, order, requisition.

instructive *adj* didactic, edifying, educational, enlightening, helpful, illuminating, improving, informational, informative, instructional, revealing.

instructor *n* adviser, coach, trainer, tutor. ▷ TEACHER.

instrument *n* apparatus, appliance, contraption, device, equipment, gadget, implement, machine, mechanism, tool, utensil. **musical instrument** □ *accordion, bagpipes, banjo, bassoon, bugle, castanets, celesta, cello, clarinet, clavichord, clavier, concertina, cor anglais, cornet, cymbals, double-bass, drum, dulcimer, euphonium, fiddle, fife, flugelhorn, flute, fortepiano, French horn, glockenspiel, gong, guitar, harmonica, harmonium, harp, harpsichord, horn, hurdy-gurdy, kettledrum, keyboard, lute, lyre, mouth-organ, oboe, organ, piano, piccolo, pipes, recorder, saxophone, sitar, spinet, synthesizer, tambourine, timpani, triangle, trombone, trumpet, tuba, tubular bells, ukulele, viol, viola, violin, virginals, xylophone, zither.*

instrumental *adj* active, advantageous, beneficial, contributory, helpful, influential, supportive, useful, valuable.

insubordinate *adj* defiant, disobedient, insurgent, mutinous, rebellious, riotous, seditious, undisciplined, unruly. ▷ IMPERTINENT. *Opp* OBEDIENT.

insufficient *adj* deficient, disappointing, inadequate, incomplete, little, meagre, mean, niggardly, *inf* pathetic, poor, scanty, scarce, short, skimpy, sparse, unsatisfactory. *Opp* EXCESSIVE, SUFFICIENT.

insular *adj* closed, cut-off, isolated, limited, narrow, narrow-minded, parochial, provincial, remote, separated. *Opp* BROADMINDED, COSMOPOLITAN.

insulate *vb* **1** cocoon, cover, cushion, enclose, isolate, lag, protect, shield, surround, wrap up. **2** cut off, detach, isolate, keep apart, quarantine, segregate, separate.

insult *n* abuse, affront, aspersion, *inf* cheek, contumely, defamation, impudence, indignity, insulting behaviour, libel, *inf* put-down, rudeness, slander, slight, slur, snub. • *vb* abuse, affront, be rude to, *inf* call names, *inf* cock a snook at, defame, dishonour, disparage, libel, mock, offend, outrage, patronize, revile, slander, slang, slight, sneer at, snub, *inf* thumb your nose at, vilify. *Opp* COMPLIMENT. **insulting** ▷ RUDE.

insuperable *adj* insurmountable, overwhelming, unconquerable. ▷ IMPOSSIBLE.

insurance *n* assurance, cover, indemnification, indemnity, policy, protection, security.

insure *vb* cover yourself, indemnify, protect, take out insurance.

intact *adj* complete, entire, integral, solid, sound, unbroken, undamaged, whole. ▷ PERFECT.

intangible *adj* abstract, airy, disembodied, elusive, ethereal, evanescent, fleeting, impalpable, imperceptible, imponderable, incorporeal, indefinite, insubstantial, invisible, shadowy, unreal, vague. *Opp* TANGIBLE.

integral *adj* **1** basic, constituent, essential, fundamental, indispensable, intrinsic, irreplaceable, necessary, requisite. *Opp* INESSENTIAL. **2** *an integral unit.* attached, complete, full, indivisible, whole. *Opp* SEPARATE.

integrate *vb* amalgamate, assemble, blend, bring together, coalesce, combine, consolidate, desegregate, fuse, harmonize, join, knit, merge, mix, put together, unify, unite, weld. *Opp* SEPARATE.

integrity *n* **1** decency, fidelity, goodness, honesty, honour, incorruptibility, loyalty, morality, principle, probity, rectitude, reliability, righteousness, sincerity, trustworthiness, uprightness, veracity, virtue. **2** ▷ UNITY.

intellect *n inf* brains, cleverness, genius, mind, rationality, reason, sense, understanding, wisdom, *old use* wit. ▷ INTELLIGENCE.

intellectual *adj* **1** academic, *inf* bookish, cerebral, cultured, educated, scholarly, studious, thinking, thoughtful. ▷ INTELLIGENT. **2** cultural, deep, difficult, educational, highbrow, improving, thought-provoking. • *n* academic, *inf* egghead, genius, highbrow, intellectual person, *inf* mastermind, *inf* one of the intelligentsia, savant, thinker.

intelligence *n* **1** ability, acumen, alertness, astuteness, brainpower, *inf* brains, brightness, brilliance, capacity, cleverness, discernment, genius, *inf* grey matter, insight, intellect, judgement, keenness, mind, *inf* nous, perceptiveness, perspicaciousness, perspicacity, quickness, reason, sagacity, sense, sharpness, shrewdness, understanding, wisdom, wit, wits. **2** data, facts, information, knowledge, *inf* low-down, news, notification, report, *inf* tip-off, warning. **3** espionage, secret service, spying.

intelligent *adj* able, acute, alert, astute, brainy, bright, brilliant, *inf* canny, clever, discerning, educated, intellectual, knowing, penetrating, perceptive, percipient, perspicacious, profound, quick, ratiocinative, rational, reasonable, sagacious, sensible, sharp, shrewd, *inf* smart, thinking, thoughtful, trenchant, wise, *inf* with it, witty. *Opp* STUPID.

intelligible *adj* clear, comprehensible, decipherable, fathomable, legible, logical, lucid, meaningful, plain, straightforward, unambiguous, understandable. *Opp* INCOMPREHENSIBLE.

intend *vb* aim, aspire, contemplate, design, determine, have in mind, mean, plan, plot, propose, purpose, resolve, scheme.

intense *adj* **1** ardent, burning, consuming, deep, eager, earnest, emotional, fanatical, fervent, fervid, impassioned, passionate, powerful, profound, serious, strong, towering, vehement, violent, zealous. *Opp* COOL, HALF-HEARTED. **2** *intense pain.* acute, agonizing, excruciating, extreme, fierce, great, harsh, keen, severe, sharp. *Opp* SLIGHT.

intensify *vb* add to, aggravate, augment, become greater, boost, build up, deepen, emphasize, escalate, fire, focus, fuel, heighten, *inf* hot up, increase, magnify, make greater, quicken, raise, redouble, reinforce, sharpen, *inf* step up, strengthen, whet. *Opp* REDUCE.

intensive *adj inf* all-out, comprehensive, concentrated, detailed, exhaustive, high-powered, thorough, unremitting.

intent *adj* absorbed, attentive, bent, committed, concentrated, concentrating, determined, eager, engrossed, enthusiastic, firm, focused, keen, occupied, preoccupied, resolute, set, steadfast, watchful, zealous. *Opp* CASUAL. • *n* ▷ INTENTION.

intention *n* aim, ambition, design, end, goal, intent, object, objective, plan, point, purpose, target.

intentional *adj* calculated, conscious, contrived, deliberate, designed, intended, knowing, planned, pre-arranged, preconceived, premeditated, prepared, studied, wilful. *Opp* ACCIDENTAL.

intercept *vb* ambush, arrest, block, catch, check, cut off, deflect, head off, impede, interrupt, obstruct, stop, thwart, trap.

intercourse *n* **1** communication, conversation, dealings, interaction, traffic. **2** *sexual intercourse.* carnal knowledge, coition, coitus, congress, copulation, intimacy, love-making, mating, rape, sex, union.

interest *n* **1** attention, attentiveness, care, commitment, concern, curiosity, involvement, notice, regard, scrutiny. **2** *of no interest.* consequence, importance, moment, note, significance, value. **3** *leisure interests.* activity, diversion, hobby, pastime, preoccupation, pursuit, relaxation. • *vb* absorb, appeal to, arouse the curiosity of, attract, capture the imagination of, captivate, concern, divert, enchant, engage, engross, entertain, enthral, fascinate, intrigue, involve, occupy, preoccupy, stimulate, *inf* turn on. ▷ EXCITE. *Opp* BORE.

interested *adj* **1** absorbed, attentive, curious, engrossed, enthusiastic, immersed, intent, involved, keen, occupied, preoccupied, rapt, responsive, riveted. *Opp* UNINTERESTED. **2** concerned, involved, partial. ▷ BIASED. *Opp* DISINTERESTED.

interesting *adj* absorbing, appealing, attractive, challenging, compelling, curious, engaging, engrossing, entertaining, enthralling, fascinating, gripping, imaginative, important, intriguing, inviting, original, piquant, *often ironic* riveting, spellbinding, unpredictable, unusual, varied. *Opp* BORING.

interfere *vb* be a busybody, butt in, interrupt, intervene, intrude, meddle, obtrude, *inf* poke your nose in, pry, snoop, *inf* stick your oar in, tamper. **interfere with** ▷ OBSTRUCT. **interfering** ▷ NOSY.

interim *adj* half-time, halfway, provisional, stopgap, temporary.

interior *adj* ▷ INTERNAL. • *n* centre, core, depths, heart, inside, middle, nucleus.

interlude *n* entr'acte, intermezzo, intermission. ▷ INTERVAL.

intermediary *n* agent, ambassador, arbiter, arbitrator, broker, go-between, mediator, middleman, negotiator, referee, spokesperson, umpire.

intermediate *adj* average, *inf* betwixt and between, halfway, intermediary, intervening, mean, medial, median, middle, midway, *inf* neither one thing nor the other, neutral, *inf* sitting on the fence, transitional.

intermittent *adj* broken, discontinuous, erratic, fitful, irregular, occasional, *inf* on and off, periodic, random, recurrent, spasmodic, sporadic. *Opp* CONTINUOUS.

internal *adj* **1** inner, inside, interior. *Opp* EXTERNAL. **2** confidential, hidden, intimate, inward, personal, private, secret, undisclosed.

international *adj* cosmopolitan, global, intercontinental, universal, worldwide.

interpret *vb* clarify, clear up, construe, decipher, decode, define, elucidate, explain, explicate, expound, gloss, make clear, make sense of, paraphrase, render, rephrase, reword, simplify, sort out, translate, understand, unravel, work out.

interpretation *n* clarification, definition, elucidation, explanation, gloss, paraphrase, reading, rendering, translation, understanding, version.

interrogation *n* cross-examination, debriefing, examination, grilling, inquisition, questioning, *inf* third degree.

interrogative *adj* asking, inquiring, inquisitive, interrogatory, investigatory, questioning.

interrupt *vb* **1** *inf* barge in, break in, butt in, *inf* chime in, *inf* chip in, cut in, disrupt, disturb, heckle, hold up, interfere, intervene, intrude, punctuate, obstruct, spoil. **2** break off, call a halt to, cut off, cut short, discontinue, halt, stop, suspend, terminate.

interruption *n* break, check, disruption, division, gap, halt, hiatus, interference, intrusion, stop, suspension. ▷ INTERVAL.

intersect *vb* bisect each other, converge, criss-cross, cross, divide, meet, pass across each other.

interval *n* **1** adjournment, break, *inf* breather, breathing-space, delay, distance, gap, hiatus, interruption, lapse, lull, opening, pause, recess, respite, rest, space, void, wait. **2** entr'acte, interlude, intermezzo, intermission.

intervene *vb* **1** come between, elapse, happen, occur, pass. **2** arbitrate, butt in, intercede, interfere, interpose, interrupt, intrude, mediate, *inf* step in.

interview *n* appraisal, audience, duologue, formal discussion, meeting, questioning, selection procedure, vetting. • *vb* appraise, ask questions, evaluate, examine, interrogate, question, sound out, vet.

interweave *vb* criss-cross, entwine, interlace, intertwine, knit, tangle, weave together.

intestines *plur n* bowels, entrails, innards, insides, offal.

intimate *adj* **1** affectionate, close, familiar, informal, loving, sexual. ▷ FRIENDLY. **2** *intimate details*. confidential, detailed, exhaustive, personal, private, secret. • *n* ▷ FRIEND. • *vb* ▷ INDICATE.

intimidate *vb* alarm, browbeat, bully, coerce, cow, daunt, dismay, frighten, hector, make afraid, menace, overawe, persecute, petrify, scare, terrify, terrorize, threaten, tyrannize.

intolerable *adj* excruciating, impossible, insufferable, insupportable, unacceptable, unbearable, unendurable. *Opp* TOLERABLE.

intolerant *adj* biased, bigoted, chauvinistic, classist, discriminatory, dogmatic, illiberal, narrow-minded, one-sided, opinionated, prejudiced, racist, sexist, uncharitable, unsympathetic, xenophobic. *Opp* TOLERANT.

intonation *n* accent, delivery, inflection, modulation, pronunciation, sound, speech pattern, tone.

intoxicate *vb* addle, inebriate, make drunk, stupefy. **intoxicated** ▷ DRUNK, EXCITED. **intoxicating** ▷ ALCOHOLIC, EXCITING.

intricate *adj* complex, complicated, convoluted, delicate, detailed, elaborate, entangled, fancy, *inf* fiddly, involved, *inf* knotty, labyrinthine, ornate, sophisticated, tangled, tortuous. *Opp* SIMPLE.

intrigue *n* ▷ PLOT. ● *vb* **1** appeal to, arouse the curiosity of, attract, beguile, captivate, capture the interest of, engage, engross, excite the curiosity of, fascinate, interest, stimulate, *inf* turn on. *Opp* BORE.

intrinsic *adj* basic, essential, fundamental, immanent, inborn, inbred, in-built, inherent, native, natural, proper, real.

introduce *vb* **1** acquaint, make known, present. **2** announce, give an introduction to, lead into, preface. **3** add, advance, bring in, bring out, broach, create, establish, inaugurate, initiate, inject, insert, interpose, launch, make available, offer, phase in, pioneer, put forward, set up, start, suggest, usher in. ▷ BEGIN.

introduction *n* foreword, *inf* intro, *inf* lead-in, opening, overture, preamble, preface, prelude, prologue. ▷ BEGINNING.

introductory *adj* basic, early, first, fundamental, inaugural, initial, opening, prefatory, preliminary, preparatory, starting. *Opp* FINAL.

introverted *adj* contemplative, introspective, inward-looking, meditative, pensive, quiet, reserved, retiring, self-contained, shy, thoughtful, unsociable, withdrawn. *Opp* EXTROVERTED.

intrude *vb* break in, butt in, eavesdrop, encroach, gatecrash, interfere, interpose, interrupt, intervene, join uninvited, obtrude, *inf* snoop.

intruder *n* **1** eavesdropper, gatecrasher, infiltrator, interloper, *inf* uninvited guest. **2** burglar, housebreaker, invader, prowler, raider, robber, *inf* snooper, thief, trespasser.

intuition *n* insight, perceptiveness, percipience. ▷ INSTINCT.

invade *vb* descend on, encroach on, enter, impinge on, infest, infringe, march into, occupy, overrun, penetrate, raid, subdue, violate. ▷ ATTACK.

invalid *adj* **1** null and void, out-of-date, unacceptable, unusable, void, worthless. **2** fallacious, false, illogical, incorrect, irrational, spurious, unconvincing, unfounded, unreasonable, unscientific, unsound, untenable, untrue, wrong. *Opp* VALID. **3** ▷ ILL. ● *n* cripple, incurable, patient, sufferer, valetudinarian.

invaluable *adj* incalculable, inestimable, irreplaceable, precious, priceless, useful. ▷ VALUABLE. *Opp* WORTHLESS.

invariable *adj* certain, changeless, constant, eternal, even, immutable, inflexible, permanent, predictable, regular, reliable, rigid, solid, stable, steady, unalterable, unchangeable, unchanging, unfailing, uniform, unvarying, unwavering. *Opp* VARIABLE.

invasion *n* **1** encroachment, incursion, infiltration, inroad, intrusion, onslaught, raid, violation. ▷ ATTACK. **2** colony, flood, horde, infestation, spate, stream, swarm, throng.

invasive *adj* burgeoning, increasing, mushrooming, profuse, proliferating, relentless, unstoppable.

invent *vb* coin, conceive, concoct, construct, contrive, *inf* cook up, create, design, devise, discover, *inf* dream up, fabricate, formulate, *inf* hit upon, imagine, improvise, make up, originate, plan, put together, think up, trump up.

invention *n* **1** brainchild, coinage, contrivance, creation, design, discovery. **2** contraption, device, gadget. **3** deceit, fabrication, falsehood, fantasy, fiction, figment, lie. **4** ▷ INVENTIVENESS.

inventive *adj* clever, creative, enterprising, fertile, imaginative, ingenious, innovative, inspired, original, resourceful. *Opp* BANAL.

inventiveness *n* creativity, genius, imagination, ingenuity, inspiration, invention, originality, resourcefulness.

inventor *n* architect, author, *inf* boffin, creator, designer, discoverer, maker, originator.

inverse *adj* opposite, reversed, transposed.

invert *vb* capsize, overturn, reverse, transpose, turn upside down, upset.

invest *vb* **1** buy stocks and shares, play the market, speculate. **2** lay out, put to work, *inf* sink, use profitably, venture. **invest in** ▷ BUY.

investigate *vb* analyse, consider, enquire about, examine, explore, follow up, gather evidence about, *inf* go into, inquire into, look into, probe, research, scrutinize, sift (*evidence*), study, *inf* suss out, weigh up.

investigation *n* enquiry, examination, inquiry, inquisition, inspection, *inf* post-mortem, *inf* probe, quest, research, review, scrutiny, search, study, survey.

invidious *adj* discriminatory, objectionable, offensive, undesirable, unfair, unjust, unwarranted.

invigorating *adj* bracing, enlivening, exhilarating, fresh, healthful, health-giving, healthy, refreshing, rejuvenating, revitalizing, salubrious, stimulating, tonic, vitalizing. *Opp* EXHAUSTING.

invincible *adj* impregnable, indestructible, indomitable, insuperable, invulnerable, strong, unassailable, unbeatable, unconquerable, unstoppable.

invisible *adj* camouflaged, concealed, covered, disguised, hidden, imperceptible, inconspicuous, obscured, out of sight, secret, undetectable, unnoticeable, unnoticed, unseen. *Opp* VISIBLE.

invite *vb* **1** ask, encourage, request, summon, urge. **2** attract, entice, solicit, tempt. **inviting** ▷ ATTRACTIVE.

invoice *n* account, bill, list, statement.

invoke *vb* appeal to, call for, cry out for, entreat, implore, pray for, solicit, supplicate.

involuntary *adj* automatic, conditioned, impulsive, instinctive, mechanical, reflex, spontaneous, unconscious, uncontrollable, unintentional, unthinking, unwitting. *Opp* DELIBERATE.

involve *vb* **1** comprise, contain, embrace, entail, hold, include, incorporate, take in. **2** affect, concern, interest, touch. **3** *involve in crime*. embroil, implicate, include, incriminate, inculpate, *inf* mix up. **involved** ▷ BUSY, COMPLEX.

involvement *n* **1** activity, interest, participation. **2** association, complicity, entanglement, partnership.

ironic *adj* derisive, double-edged, ironical, mocking, sarcastic, satirical, wry.

irony *n* double meaning, mockery, paradox, sarcasm, satire.

irrational *adj* absurd, arbitrary, biased, crazy, emotional, emotive, illogical, insane, mad, nonsensical, prejudiced, senseless, subjective, surreal, unconvincing, unintelligent, unreasonable, unreasoning, unsound, unthinking, wild. ▷ SILLY. *Opp* RATIONAL.

irregular *adj* **1** erratic, fitful, fluctuating, halting, haphazard, intermittent, occasional, random, spasmodic, sporadic, unequal, unpredictable, unpunctual, variable, varying, wavering. **2** abnormal, anomalous, eccentric, exceptional, extraordinary, illegal, improper, odd, peculiar, quirky, unconventional, unofficial, unplanned, unscheduled, unusual. **3** *irregular surface*. broken, bumpy, jagged, lumpy, patchy, pitted, ragged, rough, uneven, up and down. *Opp* REGULAR.

irrelevant *adj inf* beside the point, extraneous, immaterial, impertinent, inapplicable, inapposite, inappropriate, inessential, malapropos, *inf* neither here nor there, pointless, unconnected, unnecessary, unrelated. *Opp* RELEVANT.

irreligious *adj* agnostic, atheistic, godless, heathen, humanist, impious, irreverent, pagan, sinful, uncommitted, unconverted, ungodly, unrighteous, wicked. *Opp* RELIGIOUS.

irreparable *adj* hopeless, incurable, irrecoverable, irremediable, irretrievable, irreversible, lasting, permanent, unalterable.

irreplaceable *adj* inimitable, priceless, unique. ▷ RARE.

irrepressible *adj* boisterous, bouncy, *inf* bubbling, buoyant, ebullient, resilient, uncontrollable, ungovernable, uninhibited, unmanageable, unrestrainable, unstoppable, vigorous. ▷ LIVELY. *Opp* LETHARGIC.

irresistible *adj* compelling, inescapable, inexorable, irrepressible, not to be denied, overpowering, overriding, overwhelming, persuasive, powerful, relentless, seductive, strong, unavoidable, uncontrollable. *Opp* WEAK.

irresolute *adj* doubtful, fickle, flexible, *inf* hedging your bets, indecisive, open to compromise, tentative, uncertain, undecided, vacillating, wavering, weak, weak-willed. ▷ HESITANT. *Opp* RESOLUTE.

irresponsible *adj* antisocial, careless, conscienceless, devilmay-care, feckless, immature, immoral, inconsiderate, negligent, rash, reckless, selfish, shiftless, thoughtless, unethical, unreliable, unthinking, untrustworthy, wild. *Opp* RESPONSIBLE.

irreverent *adj* blasphemous, disrespectful, impious, irreligious, profane, sacrilegious, ungodly, unholy. ▷ RUDE. *Opp* REVERENT.

irrevocable *adj* binding, final, fixed, hard and fast, immutable, irreparable, irretrievable, irreversible, permanent, settled, unalterable, unchangeable.

irrigate *vb* flood, inundate, supply water to, water.

irritable *adj* bad-tempered, cantankerous, choleric, crabby, cross, crotchety, crusty, curmudgeonly, dyspeptic, easily annoyed, edgy, fractious, grumpy, ill-humoured, ill-tempered, impatient, irascible, oversensitive, peevish, pettish, petulant, *inf* prickly, querulous, *inf* ratty, short-tempered, snappy, testy, tetchy, touchy, waspish. ▷ ANGRY. *Opp* EVEN-TEMPERED.

irritate *vb* **1** cause irritation, itch, rub, tickle, tingle. **2** ▷ ANNOY.

island *n plur* archipelago, atoll, coral reef, isle, islet.

isolate *vb* cloister, cordon off, cut off, detach, exclude, insulate, keep apart, place apart, quarantine, seclude, segregate, separate, sequester, set apart, shut off, shut out, single out. **isolated** ▷ SOLITARY.

issue *n* **1** affair, argument, controversy, dispute, matter, point, problem, question, subject, topic. **2** conclusion, consequence, effect, end, impact, outcome, *inf* payoff, repercussions, result, upshot. **3** *issue of a magazine.* copy, edition, instalment, number, printing, publication, version. • *vb* **1** appear, come out, emerge, erupt, flow out, gush, leak, rise, spring. **2** announce, bring out, broadcast, circulate, declare, disseminate, distribute, give out, make public, print, produce, promulgate, publicize, publish, put out, release, send out, supply.

itch *n* **1** irritation, prickling, tickle, tingling. **2** ache, craving, desire, hankering, hunger, impatience, impulse, longing, need, restlessness, thirst, urge, wish, yearning, *inf* yen. • *vb* **1** be irritated, prickle, tickle, tingle. **2** ▷ DESIRE.

item *n* **1** article, bit, component, contribution, entry, ingredient, lot, matter, object, particular, thing. **2** *item in a newspaper.* account, article, feature, notice, piece, report.

J

jab *vb* dig, elbow, nudge, poke, prod, stab, thrust. ▷ HIT.

jacket *n* casing, cover, covering, envelope, folder, sheath, skin, wrapper, wrapping. ▷ COAT.

jaded *adj* **1** ▷ WEARY. **2** bored, *inf* fed up, gorged, listless, sated, satiated, *inf* sick and tired, surfeited. *Opp* LIVELY.

jagged *adj* angular, barbed, broken, chipped, denticulate, indented, irregular, notched, ragged, rough, serrated, sharp, snagged, spiky, toothed, uneven, zigzag. *Opp* SMOOTH.

jail, jailer *ns* ▷ GAOL, GAOLER.

jam *n* **1** blockage, bottleneck, congestion, crush, obstruction, press, squeeze, stoppage, throng. ▷ CROWD. **2** difficulty, dilemma, embarrassment, *inf* fix, *inf* hole, *inf* hot water, *inf* pickle, plight, predicament, quandary, tight corner, trouble. **3** conserve, jelly, marmalade, preserve. ● *vb* **1** block, *inf* bung up, clog, congest, cram, crowd, crush, fill, force, pack, obstruct, overcrowd, ram, squash, squeeze, stop up, stuff. **2** prop, stick, wedge.

jar *n* amphora, carafe, container, crock, ewer, glass, jug, mug, pitcher, pot, receptacle, urn, vessel. ▷ BOTTLE. *vb* **1** jerk, jog, jolt, *inf* rattle, shake, shock, upset. **2** *That noise jars on me.* grate, grind, *inf* jangle. ▷ ANNOY. **jarring** ▷ HARSH.

jargon *n* argot, cant, creole, dialect, idiom, language, patois, slang, vernacular.

jaunt *n* excursion, expedition, outing, tour, trip. ▷ JOURNEY.

jaunty *adj* alert, breezy, bright, brisk, buoyant, carefree, *inf* cheeky, debonair, frisky, lively, perky, spirited, sprightly. ▷ HAPPY.

jazzy *adj* **1** animated, rhythmic, spirited, swinging, syncopated, vivacious. ▷ LIVELY. *Opp* SEDATE. **2** *jazzy colours.* bold, clashing, contrasting, flashy, gaudy, loud.

jealous *adj* **1** bitter, covetous, envious, *inf* green-eyed, *inf* green with envy, grudging, jaundiced, resentful. **2** *jealous of your reputation.* careful, possessive, protective, vigilant, watchful.

jeer *vb* barrack, boo, chaff, deride, disapprove, gibe, heckle, hiss, *inf* knock, laugh, make fun (of), mock, scoff, sneer, taunt, *inf* twit. ▷ RIDICULE. *Opp* CHEER.

jeopardize *vb* endanger, gamble, imperil, menace, put at risk, risk, threaten, venture.

jerk *vb* jar, jiggle, jog, jolt, lurch, move jerkily, move suddenly, pluck, pull, *inf* rattle, shake, tug, tweak, twist, twitch, wrench, *inf* yank.

jerky *adj* bouncy, bumpy, convulsive, erratic, fitful, jolting, jumpy, rough, shaky, spasmodic, *inf* stopping and starting, twitchy, uncontrolled, uneven. *Opp* STEADY.

jest *n*, *vb* ▷ JOKE.

jester *n* buffoon, clown, comedian, comic, fool, joker.

jet *adj* ▷ BLACK. ● *n* **1** flow, fountain, gush, rush, spout, spray, spurt, squirt, stream. **2** nozzle, sprinkler.

jetty *n* breakwater, groyne, landing-stage, mole, pier, quay, wharf.

jewel *n* brilliant, gem, gemstone, ornament, precious stone, *inf* rock, *inf* sparkler. ▷ JEWELLERY. □ *amber, cairngorm, carnelian, coral, diamond, emerald, garnet, ivory, jade, jasper, jet, lapis lazuli, moonstone, onyx, opal, pearl,* *rhinestone, ruby, sapphire, topaz, turquoise.*

jeweller *n* goldsmith, silversmith.

jewellery *n* gems, jewels, ornaments, treasure, *inf* sparklers. □ *bangle, beads, bracelet, brooch, chain, charm, clasp, cuff-links, earring, locket, necklace, pendant, pin, ring, signet ring, tie-pin, watch, watch-chain.*

jilt *vb* abandon, break with, desert, *inf* ditch, drop, *inf* dump, forsake, *inf* give someone the brush-off, leave behind, *inf* leave in the lurch, renounce, repudiate, *inf* throw over, *inf* wash your hands of.

jingle *n* **1** doggerel, rhyme, song, tune, verse. **2** chinking, clinking, jangling, ringing, tinkling, tintinnabulation. • *vb* chime, chink, clink, jangle, ring, tinkle. ▷ SOUND.

job *n* **1** activity, assignment, charge, chore, duty, errand, function, housework, mission, operation, project, pursuit, responsibility, role, stint, task, undertaking, work. **2** appointment, business, calling, career, craft, employment, livelihood, living, métier, occupation, position, post, profession, sinecure, trade, vocation.

jobless *adj* out of work, redundant, unemployed, unwaged.

jocular *adj* cheerful, gay, glad, gleeful, happy, jocund, jokey, joking, jolly, jovial, joyous, jubilant, merry, overjoyed, rejoicing. *Opp* SAD, SERIOUS.

jog *vb* **1** bounce, jar, jerk, joggle, jolt, knock, nudge, shake. ▷ HIT. **2** *jog the memory.* activate, arouse, prompt, refresh, remind, set off, stimulate, stir. **3** *jog round the park.* exercise, lope, run, trot.

join *n* connection, joint, knot, link, mend, seam. • *vb* **1** add, amalgamate, attach, combine, connect, couple, dock, dovetail, fit, fix, juxtapose, knit, link, marry, merge, put together, splice, tack on, unite, yoke. ▷ FASTEN. *Opp* SEPARATE. **2** abut, adjoin, border on, come together, converge, meet, touch, verge on. **3** *join a crowd.* accompany, associate with, follow, go with, *inf* latch on to, tag along with, team up with. **4** *join a club.* affiliate with, become a member of, enlist in, enrol in, participate in, register for, sign up for, subscribe to, volunteer for. *Opp* LEAVE.

joint *adj* collaborative, collective, combined, common, communal, concerted, cooperative, corporate, general, mutual, shared, united. *Opp* SEPARATE. • *n* articulation, connection, hinge, junction, union.

joist *n* beam, girder, rafter.

joke *n inf* crack, funny story, *inf* gag, *old use* jape, jest, laugh, *inf* one-liner, pleasantry, pun, quip, wisecrack, witticism. • *vb* banter, be facetious, clown, fool about, have a laugh, jest, make jokes, quip, tease.

jolly *adj* cheerful, delighted, gay, glad, gleeful, grinning, high-spirited, jocose, jocular, jocund, joking, jovial, joyful, joyous, jubilant, laughing, merry, playful, rejoicing, rosy-faced, smiling, sportive. ▷ HAPPY. *Opp* SAD.

jolt *vb* **1** bounce, bump, jar, jerk, jog, shake, twitch. ▷ HIT. **2** *jolted me into action.* astonish, disturb, nonplus, shake up, shock, startle, stun, surprise.

jostle *vb* crowd in on, hustle, press, push, shove.

jot *vb* **jot down** note, scribble, take down. ▷ WRITE.

journal *n* **1** gazette, magazine, monthly, newsletter, newspaper, paper, periodical, publication, review, weekly. **2** account, annals, chronicle, diary, dossier, history, log, memoir, record, scrapbook.

journalist *n* broadcaster, columnist, contributor, correspondent, *derog* hack, *inf* newshound, newspaperman, newspaperwoman, pressman, reporter, writer.

journey *n* excursion, expedition, itinerary, jaunt, mission, odyssey, outing, peregrination, progress, route, tour, transition, travelling, trip, wandering. □ *cruise, drive, flight, hike, joyride, pilgrimage, ramble, ride, run, safari, sail, sea crossing, sea passage, trek, voyage, walk.* • *vb* ▷ TRAVEL.

joy *n* bliss, cheer, cheerfulness, delight, ecstasy, elation, euphoria, exaltation, exhilaration, exultation, felicity, gaiety, gladness, glee, gratification, happiness, high spirits, hilarity, jocularity, joviality, joyfulness, joyousness, jubilation, light-heartedness, merriment, mirth, pleasure, rapture, rejoicing, triumph. *Opp* SORROW.

joyful *adj* buoyant, cheerful, delighted, ecstatic, elated, euphoric, exhilarated, exultant, gay, glad, gleeful, jocund, jolly, jovial, joyous, jubilant, light-hearted, merry, overjoyed, pleased, rapturous, rejoicing, triumphant. ▷ HAPPY. *Opp* SAD.

jubilee *n* anniversary, celebration, commemoration, festival.

judge *n* **1** *sl* beak, justice, magistrate. **2** adjudicator, arbiter, arbitrator, moderator, referee, umpire. **3** *judge of wine.* authority, connoisseur, critic, expert, reviewer. ● *vb* **1** condemn, convict, examine, pass judgement on, pronounce judgement on, punish, sentence, try. **2** adjudicate, mediate, moderate, referee, umpire. **3** believe, conclude, consider, decide, decree, deem, determine, estimate, gauge, guess, reckon, rule, suppose. **4** *judge others.* appraise, assess, criticize, evaluate, give your opinion of, rate, rebuke, scold, sit in judgement on, size up, weigh.

judgement *n* **1** arbitration, award, conclusion, conviction, decision, decree, *old use* doom, finding, outcome, penalty, punishment, result, ruling, verdict. **2** *use your judgement.* acumen, common sense, discernment, discretion, discrimination, expertise, good sense, reason, wisdom. ▷ INTELLIGENCE. **3** *in my judgement.* assessment, belief, estimation, evaluation, idea, impression, mind, notion, opinion, point of view, valuation.

judicial *adj* **1** forensic, legal, official. **2** ▷ JUDICIOUS.

judicious *adj* appropriate, astute, careful, circumspect, considered, diplomatic, discerning, discreet, discriminating, enlightened, expedient, judicial, politic, prudent, sage, sensible, shrewd, sober, thoughtful, well-advised, well-judged. ▷ WISE.

jug *n* bottle, carafe, container, decanter, ewer, flagon, flask, jar, pitcher, vessel.

juggle *vb* alter, *inf* cook, *inf* doctor, falsify, *inf* fix, manipulate, misrepresent, move about, rearrange, rig, tamper.

juice *n* drink, extract, fluid, liquid, sap.

juicy *adj* lush, moist, soft, *inf* squelchy, succulent, wet. *Opp* DRY.

jumble *n* chaos, clutter, confusion, disarray, disorder, farrago, hotchpotch, mess, muddle, tangle. ● *vb* confuse, disarrange, disorganize, *inf* mess up, mingle, mix up, muddle, shuffle, tangle. *Opp* ARRANGE.

jump *n* **1** bounce, bound, hop, leap, pounce, skip, spring, vault. **2** ditch, fence, gap, gate, hurdle, obstacle. **3** *a jump in prices.* ▷ RISE. ● *vb* **1** bounce, bound, caper, dance, frisk, frolic, gambol, hop, leap, pounce, prance, skip, spring. **2** *jump a fence.* clear, hurdle, vault. **3** *jump in surprise.* flinch, recoil, start, wince. **jump on** ▷ ATTACK. **make someone jump** ▷ STARTLE.

junction *n* confluence, connection, corner, crossroads, interchange, intersection, joining, juncture, *inf* link-up, meeting, points, T-junction, union.

jungle *n* forest, rain-forest, tangle, undergrowth, woods.

junior *adj* inferior, lesser, lower, minor, secondary, subordinate, subsidiary, younger. *Opp* SENIOR.

junk *n* clutter, debris, flotsam and jetsam, garbage, litter, lumber, oddments, odds and ends, refuse, rubbish, rummage, scrap, trash, waste. ● *vb* ▷ DISCARD.

just *adj* apt, deserved, equitable, ethical, even-handed, fair, fair-minded, honest, impartial, justified, lawful, legal, legitimate, merited, neutral, proper, reasonable, rightful, right-minded, unbiased, unprejudiced, upright. ▷ MORAL. *Opp* UNJUST.

justice *n* **1** equity, even-handedness, fair-mindedness, fair play, impartiality, integrity, legality, neutrality, objectivity, right. ▷ MORALITY. **2** the law, legal proceedings, the police, punishment, retribution, vengeance.

justifiable *adj* acceptable, allowable, defensible, excusable, forgivable, justified, lawful, legitimate, pardonable, permissible, reasonable, understandable, warranted. *Opp* UNJUSTIFIABLE.

justify *vb* condone, defend, exculpate, excuse, exonerate, explain, explain away, forgive, legitimate, legitimize, pardon, rationalize, substantiate, support, sustain, uphold, validate, vindicate, warrant.

jut *vb* beetle, extend, overhang, poke out, project, protrude, stick out. *Opp* RECEDE.

juvenile *adj* **1** babyish, childish, immature, infantile, puerile, unsophisticated. **2** adolescent, *inf* teenage, underage, young, youthful. *Opp* MATURE.

K

keen *adj* **1** active, ambitious, anxious, ardent, assiduous, avid, bright, clever, committed, dedicated, devoted, diligent, eager, enthusiastic, fervent, fervid, industrious, intelligent, intense, intent, interested, motivated, passionate, quick, zealous. **2** *a keen knife*. knife-edged, piercing, razorsharp, sharp, sharpened. **3** *a keen wit*. acerbic, acid, acute, biting, clever, cutting, discerning, incisive, lively, mordant, observant, pungent, rapier-like, sarcastic, satirical, scathing, shrewd, sophisticated, stinging. **4** *keen eyesight*. acute, clear, fine, perceptive, sensitive. **5** *a keen wind*. bitter, cold, extreme, icy, intense, penetrating, severe. **6** *keen prices*. competitive, low, rock-bottom. *Opp* APATHETIC, DULL.

keep *vb* **1** accumulate, amass, conserve, guard, hang on to, hoard, hold, maintain, preserve, protect, put aside, put away, retain, safeguard, save, store, stow away, withhold. **2** *keep going*. carry on, continue, do again and again, do for a long time, keep on, persevere in, persist in. **3** *keep left*. remain, stay. **4** *keep a family*. be responsible for, care for, cherish, feed, finance, foster, guard, have charge of, look after, maintain, manage, mind, own, pay for, protect, provide for, subsidize, support, take charge of, tend, watch over. **5** *keep a birthday*. celebrate, commemorate, mark, observe, solemnize. **6** *food keeps in the fridge*. be preserved, be usable, last, survive, stay fresh, stay good. **7** *won't keep you*. block, check, confine, curb, delay, detain, deter, get in the way of, hamper, hinder, hold up, impede, imprison, obstruct, prevent, restrain, retard. **keep still** ▷ STAY. **keep to** ▷ FOLLOW, OBEY. **keep up** ▷ PROLONG, SUSTAIN.

keeper *n* caretaker, curator, custodian, gaoler, guard, guardian, *inf* minder, warden, warder.

kernel *n* centre, core, essence, heart, middle, nub, pith.

key *n* **1** answer, clarification, clue, explanation, indicator, pointer, secret, solution. **2** *key to a map*. glossary, guide, index, legend.

keyboard *n* □ *accordion, celesta, clavichord, clavier, fortepiano, harmonium, harpsichord, organ, piano,* old use *pianoforte, spinet, synthesizer, virginals.*

kick *vb* boot, heel, punt. ▷ HIT.

kidnap *vb* abduct, capture, carry off, run away with, seize, snatch.

kill *vb* annihilate, assassinate, be the killer of, *sl* bump off, butcher, cull, decimate, destroy, *inf* dispatch, *inf* do away with, *sl* do in, execute, exterminate, *inf* finish off, *inf* knock off, liquidate, martyr, massacre, murder, put down, put to death, put to sleep, slaughter, slay, *inf* snuff out, take life, *Amer sl* waste. □ *behead, brain, choke, crucify, decapitate, disembowel, drown, electrocute, eviscerate, garrotte, gas, guillotine, hang, knife, lynch, poison, pole-axe, shoot, smother, stab, starve, stifle, stone, strangle, suffocate, throttle.*

killer *n* assassin, butcher, cutthroat, destroyer, executioner, exterminator, gunman, *sl* hit man, murderer, slayer.

killing *n* annihilation, assassination, bloodbath, bloodshed, butchery, carnage, decimation, destruction, elimination, eradication, euthanasia, execution, extermination, extinction, fratricide, genocide, homicide, infanticide, liquidation, manslaughter, martyrdom, massacre, matricide, murder, parricide, patricide, pogrom, regicide, slaughter, sororicide, suicide, unlawful killing, uxoricide.

kin *n* clan, family, *inf* folks, kindred, kith and kin, relations, relatives.

kind *adj* accommodating, affable, affectionate, agreeable, altruistic, amenable, amiable, amicable, approachable, attentive, avuncular, beneficent, benevolent, benign, bountiful, brotherly, caring, charitable, comforting, compassionate, congenial, considerate, cordial, courteous, encouraging, fatherly, favourable, friendly, generous, genial, gentle, good-natured, good-tempered, gracious, helpful, hospitable, humane, humanitarian, indulgent, kind-hearted, kindly, lenient, loving, merciful, mild, motherly, neighbourly, nice, obliging, patient, philanthropic, pleasant, polite, public-spirited, sensitive, sisterly, soft-hearted, sweet, sympathetic, tactful, tender, tender-hearted, thoughtful, tolerant, understanding, unselfish, warm, warm-hearted, well-intentioned, well-meaning, well-meant. *Opp* UNKIND. • *n* brand, breed, category, class, description, family, form, genre, genus, make, manner, nature, persuasion, race, set, sort, species, style, type, variety.

kindle *vb* **1** burn, fire, ignite, light, set alight, set fire to, spark off. **2** ▷ AROUSE.

king *n* **1** crowned head, His Majesty, monarch, ruler, sovereign. **2** ▷ CHIEF.

kingdom *n* country, empire, land, monarchy, realm.

kink *n* **1** bend, coil, crimp, crinkle, curl, knot, loop, tangle, twist, wave. **2** ▷ QUIRK.

kiosk *n* booth, stall. □ *bookstall, news-stand, telephone-box.*

kiss *vb* caress, embrace, *sl* neck, osculate, *old use* spoon. ▷ TOUCH.

kit *n* accoutrements, apparatus, appurtenances, baggage, effects, equipment, gear, *joc* impedimenta, implements, luggage, outfit, paraphernalia, rig, supplies, tackle, tools, tools of the trade, utensils.

kitchen *n* cookhouse, galley, kitchenette, scullery.

knack *n* ability, adroitness, aptitude, art, bent, dexterity, expertise, facility, flair, genius, gift, habit, intuition, *inf* know-how, skill, talent, trick, *inf* way.

knapsack *n* backpack, haversack, rucksack.

knead *vb* manipulate, massage, pound, press, pummel, squeeze, work.

kneel *vb* bend, bow, crouch, fall to your knees, genuflect, stoop.

knickers *plur n old use* bloomers, boxer-shorts, briefs, drawers, panties, pants, shorts, trunks, underpants.

knife *n* blade. □ *butter-knife, carving-knife, clasp-knife, cleaver, dagger, flick-knife, machete, penknife, pocket-knife, scalpel, sheath knife.* • *vb* cut, pierce, slash, stab. ▷ KILL, WOUND.

knit *vb* **1** crochet, weave. **2** bind, combine, connect, fasten, heal, interlace, interweave, join, knot, link, marry, mend, tie, unite. **knit your brow** ▷ FROWN.

knob *n* boss, bulge, bump, handle, lump, projection, protrusion, protuberance, stud, swelling.

knock *vb* **1** bang, *inf* bash, buffet, bump, pound, rap, smack, *old use* smite, strike, tap, thump. ▷ HIT. **2** ▷ CRITICIZE. **knock down** ▷ DEMOLISH. **knock off** ▷ CEASE. **knock out** ▷ STUN.

knot *n* **1** bond, bow, ligature, tangle, tie. **2** ▷ GROUP. • *vb* bind, do up, entangle, entwine, join, knit, lash, link, tether, tie, unite. ▷ FASTEN. *Opp* UNTIE.

know *vb* **1** be certain, have confidence, have no doubt. **2** *know facts.* be cognizant of, be familiar with, be knowledgeable about, comprehend, discern, have experience of, have in mind, realize, remember, understand. **3** *know a person.* be acquainted with, be a friend of, be friends with.

4 differentiate, distinguish, identify, make out, perceive, recognize, see.

know-all *n* expert, pundit, *inf* show-off, wiseacre.

knowing *adj* astute, clever, conspiratorial, cunning, discerning, experienced, expressive, meaningful, perceptive, shrewd. ▷ CUNNING, KNOWLEDGEABLE. *Opp* INNOCENT.

knowledge *n* **1** data, facts, information, intelligence, *sl* low-down. **2** acquaintance, awareness, background, cognition, competence, consciousness, education, erudition, experience, expertise, familiarity, grasp, insight, *inf* know-how, learning, lore, memory, science, scholarship, skill, sophistication, technique, training. *Opp* IGNORANCE.

knowledgeable *adj Fr* au fait, aware, cognizant, conversant, educated, enlightened, erudite, experienced, expert, familiar (with), *sl* genned up, informed, *inf* in the know, learned, scholarly, versed (in), well-informed. *Opp* IGNORANT.

L

label *n* brand, docket, hallmark, identification, imprint, logo, marker, sticker, tag, ticket, trademark. • *vb* brand, call, categorize, class, classify, define, describe, docket, identify, mark, name, pigeon-hole, stamp, tag.

laborious *adj* **1** arduous, back-breaking, difficult, exhausting, fatiguing, gruelling, hard, heavy, herculean, onerous, stiff, strenuous, taxing, tiresome, tough, uphill, wearisome, wearying. *Opp* EASY. **2** *a laborious style.* artificial, contrived, forced, heavy, laboured, overdone, overworked, pedestrian, ponderous, strained, unnatural. *Opp* FLUENT.

labour *n* **1** *inf* donkey-work, drudgery, effort, exertion, industry, navvying, *inf* pains, slavery, strain, *inf* sweat, toil, work. **2** employees, *old use* hands, wage-earners, workers, workforce. **3** childbirth, contractions, delivery, labour pains, parturition, *old use* travail. • *vb* drudge, exert yourself, navvy, *inf* slave, strain, strive, struggle, *inf* sweat, toil, travail. ▷ WORK. **laboured** ▷ LABORIOUS.

labourer *n* blue-collar worker, employee, *old use* hand, manual worker, *inf* navvy, wage-earner, worker.

labour-saving *adj* convenient, handy, helpful, time-saving.

labyrinth *n* complex, jungle, maze, network, tangle.

lace *n* **1** filigree, mesh, net, netting, openwork, tatting, web. **2** bootlace, cord, shoelace, string, thong. • *vb* ▷ FASTEN.

lacerate *vb* claw, cut, gash, graze, mangle, rip, scrape, scratch, slash, tear. ▷ WOUND.

lack *n* absence, dearth, deficiency, deprivation, famine, insufficiency, need, paucity, privation, scarcity, shortage, want. *Opp* PLENTY. • *vb* be lacking in, be short of, be without, miss, need, require, want.

lacking *adj* defective, deficient, inadequate, insufficient, short, unsatisfactory, weak. ▷ STUPID.

laden *adj* burdened, *inf* chock-full, fraught, full, hampered, loaded, oppressed, piled high, weighed down.

lady *n* **1** wife, woman. ▷ FEMALE. **2** aristocrat, peeress. ▷ TITLE.

ladylike *adj* aristocratic, courtly, cultured, dainty, decorous, elegant, genteel, modest, noble, polished, posh, prim and proper, *derog* prissy, refined, respectable, well-born, well-bred. ▷ POLITE.

lag *vb* **1** be slow, *inf* bring up the rear, come last, dally, dawdle, delay, drop behind, fall behind, go too slow, hang about, hang back, idle, linger, loiter, saunter, straggle, trail. **2** *lag pipes.* insulate, wrap up.

lair *n* den, hide-out, hiding-place, refuge, resting-place, retreat, shelter.

lake *n* boating-lake, lagoon, lido, *Scot* loch, mere, pool, pond, reservoir, sea, tarn, water.

lame *adj* **1** crippled, disabled, halting, handicapped, hobbled, hobbling, incapacitated, limping, maimed, spavined. **2** *a lame leg.* dragging, game, *inf* gammy, injured, stiff. **3** *a lame excuse.* feeble, flimsy, inadequate, poor, tame, thin, unconvincing, weak. • *vb* cripple, disable, hobble, incapacitate, maim. **be lame** ▷ LIMP.

lament *n* dirge, elegy, lamentation, moaning, monody, mourning, requiem, threnody. ● *vb* bemoan, bewail, complain, cry, deplore, express your sorrow, grieve, keen, mourn, regret, shed tears, sorrow, wail, weep.

lamentable *adj* deplorable, regrettable, unfortunate, unhappy. ▷ SAD.

lamentation *n* complaints, crying, grief, grieving, lamenting, moaning, mourning, regrets, sobbing, tears, wailing, weeping.

lamp *n* bulb, fluorescent lamp, headlamp, lantern, standard lamp, street light, torch. ▷ LIGHT.

land *n* **1** coast, ground, landfall, shore, *joc* terra firma. **2** *lie of the land.* geography, landscape, terrain, topography. **3** country, fatherland, homeland, motherland, nation, region, state, territory. **4** earth, farmland, soil. **5** *land you own.* estate, grounds, property. ● *vb* **1** alight, arrive, berth, come ashore, come to rest, disembark, dismount, dock, end a journey, get down, go ashore, light, reach landfall, settle, touch down. **2** *land yourself a job.* ▷ GET.

landing *n* **1** docking, re-entry, return, splashdown, touchdown. **2** alighting, arrival, deplaning, disembarkation. **3** ▷ LANDING-STAGE.

landing-stage *n* berth, dock, harbour, jetty, landing, pier, quay, wharf.

landlady,

landlord *ns* **1** host, hostess, hotelier, *old use* innkeeper, licensee, publican, restaurateur. **2** landowner, lessor, letter, manager, manageress, owner, proprietor.

landmark *n* **1** feature, guidepost, high point, identification, visible feature. **2** milestone, new era, turning-point, watershed.

landscape *n* aspect, countryside, outlook, panorama, prospect, rural scene, scene, scenery, view, vista.

language *n* **1** parlance, speech, tongue. □ *argot, cant, colloquialism, dialect, formal language, idiolect, idiom, informal language, jargon, journalese, lingua franca,* inf *lingo, patois, register, slang, vernacular.* **2** linguistics. □ *etymology, lexicography, orthography, philology, phonetics, psycholinguistics, semantics, semiotics, sociolinguistics.* **3** *computer language.* code, system of signs.

languid *adj* apathetic, *inf* droopy, feeble, inactive, inert, lackadaisical, lazy, lethargic, slow, sluggish, torpid, unenthusiastic, weak. *Opp* ENERGETIC.

languish *vb* decline, flag, lose momentum, mope, pine, slow down, stagnate, suffer, sulk, waste away, weaken, wither. *Opp* FLOURISH.

lank *adj* **1** drooping, lifeless, limp, long, straight, thin. **2** ▷ LANKY.

lanky *adj* angular, awkward, bony, gangling, gaunt, lank, lean, long, scraggy, scrawny, skinny, tall, thin, ungraceful, weedy. *Opp* GRACEFUL, STURDY.

lap *n* **1** knees, thighs. **2** circle, circuit, course, orbit, revolution. ● *vb* ▷ DRINK.

lapse *n* **1** backsliding, blunder, decline, error, failing, fault, flaw, mistake, omission, relapse, shortcoming, slip, *inf* slip-up, temporary failure, weakness. **2** *lapse of time.* break, gap, hiatus, *inf* hold-up, intermission, interruption, interval, lacuna, lull, pause. ● *vb* **1** decline, deteriorate, diminish, drop, fall, sink, slide, slip, slump, subside. **2** *My membership lapsed.* become invalid, expire, finish, run out, stop, terminate.

large *adj* above average, abundant, ample, big, bold, broad, bulky, burly, capacious, colossal, commodious, considerable, copious, elephantine, enormous, extensive, fat, formidable, gargantuan, generous, giant, gigantic, grand, great, heavy, hefty, high, huge, *inf* hulking, immense, immeasurable, impressive, incalculable, infinite, *inf* jumbo, *inf* king-sized, largish, lofty, long, mammoth, massive, mighty, monstrous, monumental, mountainous, outsize, overgrown, oversized, prodigious, *inf* roomy, sizeable, spacious, substantial, swingeing (*increase*), tall, thick, *inf* thumping, *inf* tidy (*sum*), titanic, towering, *inf* tremendous, vast, voluminous, weighty, *inf* whacking, *inf* whopping, wide. *Opp* SMALL.

larva *n* caterpillar, grub, maggot.

lash *n* ▷ WHIP. ● *vb* **1** beat, birch, cane, flail, flog, scourge, strike, thrash, whip. ▷ HIT. **2** ▷ CRITICIZE.

last *adj* closing, concluding, final, furthest, hindmost, latest, most recent, rearmost, terminal, terminating, ultimate. *Opp* FIRST. ● *vb* carry on, continue, endure, hold, hold out, keep on, linger, live, persist, remain, stay, survive, *inf* wear well. *Opp* DIE, FINISH. **lasting** ▷ PERMANENT.

late *adj* **1** behindhand, belated, delayed, dilatory, overdue, slow, tardy, unpunctual. **2** *a late edition.* current, last, new, recent, up-to-date. **3** *the late king.* dead, deceased, departed, ex-, former, past, previous.

latent *adj* dormant, hidden, invisible, potential, undeveloped, undiscovered.

latitude *n inf* elbow-room, freedom, leeway, liberty, room, scope, space.

latter *adj* closing, concluding, last, last-mentioned, later, recent, second. *Opp* FORMER.

lattice *n* criss-cross, framework, grid, mesh, trellis.

laugh *vb* beam, be amused, burst into laughter, chortle, chuckle, *sl* fall about, giggle, grin, guffaw, roar with laughter, simper, smile, smirk, sneer, snicker, snigger, *inf* split your sides, titter. **laugh at** ▷ RIDICULE.

laughable *adj* absurd, derisory, ludicrous, preposterous, ridiculous. ▷ FUNNY.

laughing-stock *n* butt, figure of fun, victim.

laughter *n* chuckling, giggling, guffawing, hilarity, *inf* hysterics, laughing, laughs, merriment, mirth, snickering, sniggering, tittering. ▷ RIDICULE.

launch *vb* **1** begin, embark on, establish, float, found, inaugurate, initiate, open, organize, set in motion, set off, set up, start. **2** blast off, catapult, dispatch, fire, propel, send off, set off, shoot.

lavatory *n* bathroom, cloakroom, convenience, *inf* Gents, *inf* Ladies, latrine, *inf* loo, *inf* men's room, *childish* potty, *old use* privy, public convenience, toilet, urinal, water-closet, WC, *inf* women's room.

lavish *adj* **1** abundant, bountiful, copious, exuberant, free, generous, liberal, luxuriant, luxurious, munificent, opulent, plentiful, profuse, sumptuous, unselfish, unsparing, unstinting. **2** excessive, extravagant, improvident, prodigal, self-indulgent, wasteful. *Opp* ECONOMICAL.

law *n* **1** act, bill [= *draft law*], bylaw, commandment, decree, directive, edict, injunction, mandate, measure, order, ordinance, pronouncement, regulation, rule, statute. **2** *laws of science.* axiom, formula, postulate, principle, proposition, theory. **3** *laws of decency.* code, convention, practice. **4** *court of law.* justice, litigation.

law-abiding *adj* compliant, decent, disciplined, good, honest, obedient, orderly, peaceable, peaceful, respectable, well-behaved. *Opp* LAWLESS.

lawful *adj* allowable, allowed, authorized, constitutional, documented, just, justifiable, legal, legitimate, permissible, permitted, prescribed, proper, recognized, regular, right, rightful, valid. *Opp* ILLEGAL.

lawless *adj* anarchic, anarchical, badly-behaved, chaotic, disobedient, disorderly, illdisciplined, insubordinate, mutinous, rebellious, riotous, rowdy, seditious, turbulent, uncontrolled, undisciplined, ungoverned, unregulated, unrestrained, unruly, wild. ▷ WICKED. *Opp* LAW-ABIDING.

lawlessness *n* anarchy, chaos, disobedience, disorder, mob-rule, rebellion, rioting. *Opp* ORDER.

lawyer *n* advocate, barrister, counsel, legal representative, member of the bar, solicitor.

lax *adj* careless, casual, easygoing, flexible, indulgent, lenient, loose, neglectful, negligent, permissive, relaxed, remiss, slack, slipshod, unreliable, vague. *Opp* STRICT.

laxative *n* aperient, enema, purgative.

lay *vb* **1** apply, arrange, deposit, leave, place, position, put down, rest, set down, set out, spread. **2** *lay foundations.* build, construct, establish. **3** *lay the blame on someone.* ascribe, assign, attribute, burden, charge, impose, plant, *inf* saddle. **4** *lay plans.* concoct, create, design, organize, plan, set up. **lay bare** ▷ REVEAL. **lay bets** ▷ GAMBLE. **lay by** ▷ STORE. **lay down the law** ▷ DICTATE. **lay in** ▷ STORE. **lay into** ▷ ATTACK. **lay low** ▷ DEFEAT. **lay off something** ▷ CEASE. **lay someone off** ▷ DISMISS. **lay to rest** ▷ BURY. **lay up** ▷ STORE. **lay waste** ▷ DESTROY.

layer *n* **1** coat, coating, covering, film, sheet, skin, surface, thickness. **2** *layer of rock.* seam, stratum, substratum. **in layers** laminated, layered, sandwiched, stratified.

layman *n* **1** amateur, nonspecialist, untrained person. *Opp* PROFESSIONAL. **2** [*church*] layperson, member of the congregation, parishioner, unordained person. *Opp* CLERGYMAN.

laze *vb* be lazy, do nothing, idle, lie about, loaf, lounge, relax, sit about, unwind.

laziness *n* dilatoriness, idleness, inactivity, indolence, lethargy, loafing, lounging about, shiftlessness, slackness, sloth, slowness, sluggishness, torpor. *Opp* INDUSTRY.

lazy *adj* **1** dilatory, easily pleased, easygoing, idle, inactive, indolent, languid, lethargic, listless, shiftless, *inf* skiving, slack, slothful, slow, sluggish, torpid, unenterprising, work-shy. **2** peaceful, quiet, relaxing. *Opp* ENERGETIC, INDUSTRIOUS. **be lazy** ▷ LAZE. **lazy person** ▷ SLACKER.

lead *n* **1** direction, example, guidance, leadership, model, pattern, precedent. **2** *lead on a crime.* clue, hint, line, tip, tip-off. **3** *lead in a race.* first place, front, spearhead, van, vanguard. **4** *lead in a play.* chief part, hero, heroine, principal, protagonist, starring role, title role. **5** cable, flex, wire. **6** *dog's lead.* chain, leash, strap. • *vb* **1** conduct, draw, escort, guide, influence, pilot, prompt, show the way, steer, usher. **2** be in charge of, captain, command, direct, govern, head, manage, preside over, rule, *inf* skipper, superintend, supervise. **3** be first, be in front, be in the lead, go first, head the field. **4** *lead the field.* beat, defeat, excel, outdo, outstrip, precede, surpass, vanquish. *Opp* FOLLOW. **lead astray** ▷ MISLEAD. **leading** ▷ CHIEF, INFLUENTIAL. **lead off** ▷ BEGIN.

leader *n* **1** ayatollah, boss, captain, chieftain, commander, conductor, courier, demagogue, director, figurehead, godfather, guide, head, patriarch, premier, prime minister, principal, ringleader, superior, *inf* supremo. ▷ CHIEF, RULER. **2** *leader in a newspaper.* editorial, leading article.

leaf *n* **1** blade, foliage, frond, greenery. **2** folio, page, sheet.

leaflet *n* advertisement, bill, booklet, brochure, circular, flyer, folder, handbill, handout, notice, pamphlet.

league *n* alliance, association, coalition, confederation, *derog* conspiracy, federation, fraternity, guild, society, union. ▷ GROUP. **be in league with** ▷ CONSPIRE.

leak *n* **1** discharge, drip, emission, escape, exudation, leakage, oozing, seepage, trickle. **2** aperture, break, chink, crack, crevice, cut, fissure, flaw, hole, opening, perforation, puncture, rent, split, tear. **3** *security leak.* disclosure, revelation. • *vb* **1** discharge, drip, escape, exude, ooze, percolate, seep, spill, trickle. **2** *leak secrets.* disclose, divulge, give away, let out, let slip, *inf* let the cat out of the bag about, make known, pass on, reveal, *inf* spill the beans about.

leaky *adj* cracked, dripping, holed, perforated, punctured.

lean *adj* angular, bony, emaciated, gangling, gaunt, hungry-looking, lanky, long, rangy, scraggy, scrawny, skinny, slender, slim, spare, thin, weedy, wiry. *Opp* FAT. • *vb* **1** bank, careen, heel over, incline, keel over, list, slant, slope, tilt, tip. **2** loll, prop yourself up, recline, rest, support yourself.

leaning *n* bent, bias, favouritism, inclination, instinct, liking, partiality, penchant, predilection, preference, propensity, readiness, taste, tendency, trend.

leap *vb* **1** bound, clear (*a fence*), hop over, hurdle, jump, leapfrog, skip over, spring, vault. **2** caper, cavort, dance, frisk, frolic, gambol, hop, prance, romp. **3** *leap on someone*. ambush, attack, pounce.

learn *vb* acquire, ascertain, assimilate, become aware of, become proficient in, be taught, *inf* catch on, commit to memory, discover, find out, gain, gain understanding of, gather, grasp, master, memorize, *inf* mug up, pick up, remember, study, *inf* swot up. **learned** ▷ ACADEMIC, EDUCATED.

learner *n* apprentice, beginner, cadet, initiate, L-driver, novice, pupil, scholar, starter, student, trainee, tiro.

learning *n* culture, education, erudition, information, knowledge, lore, scholarship, wisdom.

lease *n* agreement, contract. • *vb* charter, hire out, let, rent out, sublet.

least *adj* fewest, lowest, minimum, negligible, poorest, slightest, smallest, tiniest.

leather *n* chamois, hide, skin, suede.

leave *n* **1** authorization, consent, dispensation, liberty, licence, permission, sanction. **2** *leave from work*. absence, free time, furlough, holiday, recess, sabbatical, time off, vacation. • *vb* **1** *inf* be off, *inf* check out, decamp, depart, disappear, *sl* do a bunk, escape, exeunt [*they go out*], exit [*he/she goes out*], get away, get out, go away, go out, *sl* hop it, *inf* pull out, *sl* push off, retire, retreat, run away, say goodbye, set off, *inf* take off, take your leave, withdraw. **2** abandon, desert, evacuate, forsake, vacate. **3** *leave your job*. *inf* chuck in, *inf* drop out of, give up, quit, relinquish, renounce, resign from, retire from, *inf* walk out of, *inf* wash your hands of. **4** *leave it there*. allow to stay, *inf* let alone, let be. **5** *left it here*. deposit, place, position, put down, set down. **6** *left it somewhere*. forget, lose, mislay. **7** *leave it to you*. assign, cede, consign, entrust, refer, relinquish. **8** *leave in a will*. bequeath, hand down, will. **leave off** ▷ STOP. **leave out** ▷ OMIT.

lecture *n* **1** address, discourse, disquisition, instruction, lesson, paper, speech, talk, treatise. **2** *lecture on bad manners*. diatribe, harangue, sermon. ▷ REPRIMAND. • *vb* **1** be a lecturer, teach. **2** discourse, give a lecture, harangue, *inf* hold forth, pontificate, preach, sermonize, speak, talk formally. **3** ▷ REPRIMAND.

lecturer *n* don, fellow, instructor, professor, speaker, teacher, tutor.

ledge *n* mantel, overhang, projection, ridge, shelf, sill, step, windowsill.

left *adj, n* **1** left-hand, port [= *left facing bow of ship*], sinistral. **2** *left wing in politics*. communist, Labour, leftist, liberal, Marxist, progressive, radical, *derog* red, revolutionary, socialist. *Opp* RIGHT.

leg *n* **1** limb, member, *inf* peg, *inf* pin, shank. □ *ankle, calf, foot, hock, knee, shin, thigh*. **2** brace, column, pillar, prop, support, upright. **3** *leg of a journey*. lap, length, part, section, stage, stretch. **pull someone's leg** ▷ HOAX.

legacy *n* bequest, endowment, estate, inheritance.

legal *adj* **1** above-board, acceptable, admissible, allowable, allowed, authorized, constitutional, just, lawful, legalized, legitimate, licensed, licit, permitted, permissible, proper, regular, right, rightful, valid. *Opp* ILLEGAL. **2** *legal proceedings.* forensic, judicial, judiciary.

legalize *vb* allow, authorize, legitimate, legitimize, license, make legal, normalize, permit, regularize, validate. *Opp* BAN.

legend *n* epic, folk-tale, myth, saga, tradition. ▷ STORY.

legendary *adj* **1** apocryphal, epic, fabled, fabulous, fictional, fictitious, imaginary, invented, made-up, mythical, non-existent, story-book, traditional. **2** *a legendary name.* ▷ FAMOUS.

legible *adj* clear, decipherable, distinct, intelligible, neat, plain, readable, understandable. *Opp* ILLEGIBLE.

legitimate *adj* **1** authentic, genuine, proper, real, regular, true. ▷ LEGAL. **2** *a legitimate deception.* ethical, just, justifiable, moral, proper, reasonable, right. *Opp* ILLEGITIMATE. ● *vb* ▷ LEGALIZE.

leisure *n* breathing-space, ease, holiday, liberty, opportunity, quiet, recreation, relaxation, relief, repose, respite, rest, spare time, time off.

leisurely *adj* easy, gentle, lingering, peaceful, relaxed, relaxing, restful, unhurried. ▷ SLOW. *Opp* BRISK.

lend *vb* advance, loan. *Opp* BORROW.

length *n* **1** distance, extent, footage, measure, measurement, mileage, reach, size, span, stretch. **2** duration, period, stretch, term.

lengthen *vb* continue, drag out, draw out, elongate, enlarge, expand, extend, get longer, increase, make longer, *inf* pad out, prolong, protract, pull out, stretch. *Opp* SHORTEN.

lenient *adj* charitable, easygoing, forbearing, forgiving, gentle, humane, indulgent, merciful, mild, permissive, soft, soft-hearted, sparing, tolerant. ▷ KIND. *Opp* STRICT.

less *adj* fewer, reduced, shorter, smaller. *Opp* MORE.

lessen *vb* **1** assuage, cut, deaden, decrease, ease, lighten, lower, make less, minimize, mitigate, reduce, relieve, tone down. **2** abate, become less, decline, decrease, die away, diminish, dwindle, ease off, let up, moderate, slacken, subside, tail off, weaken. *Opp* INCREASE.

lesson *n* **1** class, drill, instruction, laboratory, lecture, practical, seminar, session, task, teaching, tutorial, workshop. **2** *a moral lesson.* admonition, example, moral, warning.

let *vb* **1** agree to, allow to, authorize to, consent to, enable to, give permission to, license to, permit to, sanction to. **2** *let a house.* charter, contract out, hire, lease, rent. **let alone**, **let be** ▷ LEAVE. **let go, let loose** ▷ LIBERATE. **let off** ▷ FIRE. **let out** ▷ LIBERATE. **let someone off** ▷ ACQUIT. **let up** ▷ LESSEN.

letdown *n* anti-climax, disappointment, disillusionment, *inf* wash-out.

lethal *adj* deadly, fatal, mortal, poisonous.

lethargic *adj* apathetic, comatose, dull, heavy, inactive, indifferent, indolent, languid, lazy, listless, phlegmatic, sleepy, slow, slothful, sluggish, torpid. ▷ WEARY. *Opp* ENERGETIC.

lethargy *n* apathy, idleness, inactivity, indolence, inertia, laziness, listlessness, slothfulness, slowness, sluggishness, torpor, weariness. *Opp* ENERGY.

letter *n* **1** character, consonant, sign, symbol, vowel. **2** *old use* billet-doux, card, communication, dispatch, epistle, message, missive, note, postcard. **letters** correspondence, junk mail, mail, post.

level *adj* **1** even, flat, flush, horizontal, plane, regular, smooth, straight, true, uniform. **2** horizontal. **3** *level scores.* balanced, even, equal, matching, *inf* neck-and-neck, the same. *Opp* UNEVEN. ● *n* **1** altitude, depth, elevation, height, value. **2** degree, echelon, grade, plane, position, rank, *inf* rung on the ladder, stage, standard, standing, status. **3** *level in a building.* floor, storey. ● *vb* **1** even out, flatten, rake, smooth.

2 bulldoze, demolish, destroy, devastate, knock down, lay low, raze, tear down, wreck. **level-headed** ▷ SENSIBLE.

lever *vb* force, prise, wrench.

liable *adj* **1** accountable, answerable, blameworthy, responsible. **2** *liable to fall over.* apt, disposed, inclined, in the habit of, likely, minded, predisposed, prone, ready, susceptible, tempted, vulnerable, willing.

liaison *n* **1** communication, contact, cooperation, liaising, linkage, links, mediation, relationship, tie. **2** ▷ AFFAIR.

liar *n* deceiver, false witness, *inf* fibber, perjurer, *inf* story-teller.

libel *n* calumny, defamation, denigration, insult, lie, misrepresentation, obloquy, scandal, slander, slur, smear, vilification. ● *vb* blacken the name of, calumniate, defame, denigrate, disparage, malign, misrepresent, slander, slur, smear, write lies about, traduce, vilify.

libellous *adj* calumnious, cruel, damaging, defamatory, disparaging, false, hurtful, insulting, lying, malicious, mendacious, scurrilous, slanderous, untrue, vicious.

liberal *adj* **1** abundant, ample, bounteous, bountiful, copious, free, generous, lavish, munificent, open-handed, plentiful, unstinting. **2** *liberal attitudes.* big-hearted, broad-minded, charitable, easygoing, enlightened, fair-minded, humanitarian, indulgent, impartial, latitudinarian, lenient, magnanimous, open-minded, permissive, philanthropic, tolerant, unbiased, unbigoted, unopinionated, unprejudiced, unselfish. *Opp* NARROW-MINDED. **3** *liberal politics.* progressive, radical, reformist. *Opp* CONSERVATIVE.

liberalize *vb* broaden, ease, enlarge, make more liberal, moderate, open up, relax, soften, widen.

liberate *vb* deliver, discharge, disenthral, emancipate, enfranchise, free, let go, let loose, let out, loose, manumit, ransom, release, rescue, save, set free, untie. *Opp* CAPTURE, SUBJUGATE.

liberty *n* autonomy, emancipation, independence, liberation, release, self-determination, self-rule. ▷ FREEDOM. **at liberty** ▷ FREE.

licence *n* **1** certificate, credentials, document, papers, permit, warrant. **2** ▷ FREEDOM.

license *vb* **1** allow, approve, authorize, certify, commission, empower, entitle, give a licence to, permit, sanction, validate. **2** buy a licence for, make legal.

lid *n* cap, cover, covering, top.

lie *n* deceit, dishonesty, disinformation, fabrication, falsehood, falsification, *inf* fib, fiction, invention, misrepresentation, prevarication, untruth, *inf* whopper. *Opp* TRUTH. ● *vb* **1** *inf* be economical with the truth, bluff, commit perjury, deceive, falsify the facts, *inf* fib, perjure yourself, prevaricate, tell lies. **2** be horizontal, be prone, be prostrate, be recumbent, be supine, lean back, lounge, recline, repose, rest, sprawl, stretch out. **3** *The house lies in a valley.* be, be found, be located, be situated, exist. **lie low** ▷ HIDE.

life *n* **1** being, existence, living. **2** activity, animation, dash, élan, energy, enthusiasm, exuberance, *inf* go, liveliness, soul, sparkle, spirit, sprightliness, verve, vigour, vitality, vivacity, zest. **3** autobiography, biography, memoir, story.

lifeless *adj* **1** comatose, dead, deceased, inanimate, inert, insensate, insensible, killed, motionless, unconscious. **2** *lifeless desert.* arid, bare, barren, desolate, empty, sterile, uninhabited, waste. **3** *a lifeless performance.* apathetic, boring, dull, flat, heavy, lacklustre, lethargic, slow, torpid, unexciting, wooden. *Opp* LIVELY, LIVING.

lifelike *adj* authentic, convincing, faithful, graphic, natural, photographic, realistic, true-to-life, vivid. *Opp* UNREALISTIC.

lift *n* elevator, hoist. ● *vb* **1** buoy up, carry, elevate, heave up, hoist, jack up, pick up, pull up, raise, rear. **2** ascend, fly, lift off, rise, soar. **3** boost, cheer, enhance, improve, promote. **4** ▷ STEAL.

light *adj* **1** lightweight, portable, underweight, weightless. *Opp* HEAVY. **2** bright, illuminated, lit-up, well-lit. *Opp* DARK. **3** *light work.* ▷ EASY. **4** *a light wind.* ▷ GENTLE. **5** *a light touch.* ▷ DELICATE. **6** *light colours.* ▷ PALE. **7** *a light heart.* ▷ CHEERFUL. **8** *light traffic.* ▷ SPARSE. ● *n* **1** beam, blaze, brightness, brilliance, effulgence, flare, flash, fluorescence, glare, gleam, glint, glitter, glow, halo, illumination, incandescence, luminosity, lustre, phosphorescence, radiance, ray, reflection, scintillation, shine, sparkle, twinkle. □ *candlelight, daylight, firelight, gaslight, moonlight, starlight, sunlight, torchlight, twilight.* □ *arc light, beacon, bulb, candelabra, candle, chandelier, electric light, flare, floodlight, fluorescent lamp, headlamp, headlight, lamp, lantern, laser, lighthouse, lightship, neon light, pilot light, searchlight, spotlight, standard lamp, street light, strobe, stroboscope, taper, torch, traffic lights.* ● *vb* **1** fire, ignite, kindle, put a match to, set alight, set fire to, switch on. *Opp* EXTINGUISH. **2** ▷ LIGHTEN. **bring to light** ▷ DISCOVER. **give light, reflect light** be bright, be luminous, be phosphorescent, blaze, blink, burn, coruscate, dazzle, flash, flicker, glare, gleam, glimmer, glint, glisten, glitter, glow, radiate, reflect, scintillate, shimmer, shine, spark, sparkle, twinkle. **light-headed** ▷ DIZZY. **light-hearted** ▷ CHEERFUL. **light up** ▷ LIGHTEN. **shed light on** ▷ EXPLAIN.

lighten *vb* **1** cast light on, floodlight, illuminate, irradiate, light up, shed light on, shine on. **2** *The sky lightened.* become lighter, brighten, cheer up, clear. **3** ▷ LESSEN.

lighthouse *n* beacon, light, lightship, warning-light.

like *adj* akin to, analogous to, close to, cognate with, comparable to, congruent with, corresponding to, equal to, equivalent to, identical to, parallel to, similar to. ● *n* liking, partiality, predilection, preference. ● *vb* admire, approve of, appreciate, be attracted to, be fond of, be interested in, be keen on, be partial to, be pleased by, delight in, enjoy, find pleasant, *sl* go for, *inf* go in for, have a high regard for, *inf* have a weakness for, prefer, relish, revel in, take pleasure in, *inf* take to, welcome. ▷ LOVE. *Opp* HATE.

likeable *adj* admirable, attractive, charming, congenial, endearing, interesting, lovable, nice, personable, pleasant, pleasing. ▷ FRIENDLY. *Opp* HATEFUL.

likelihood *n* chance, hope, possibility, probability, prospect.

likely *adj* **1** anticipated, expected, feasible, foreseeable, plausible, possible, predictable, probable, reasonable, unsurprising. **2** *a likely candidate.* able, acceptable, appropriate, convincing, credible, favourite, fitting, hopeful, promising, qualified, suitable, *inf* tipped to win. **3** *likely to come.* apt, disposed, inclined, liable, prone, ready, tempted, willing. *Opp* UNLIKELY.

liken *vb* compare, equate, juxtapose, match.

likeness *n* **1** affinity, analogy, compatibility, congruity, correspondence, resemblance, similarity. *Opp* DIFFERENCE. **2** copy, depiction, drawing, duplicate, facsimile, image, model, picture, portrait, replica, representation, reproduction, study.

liking *n* affection, affinity, appetite, eye, fondness, inclination, partiality, penchant, predilection, predisposition, preference, propensity, *inf* soft spot, taste, weakness. ▷ LOVE. *Opp* HATRED.

limb *n* appendage, member, offshoot, projection. □ *arm, bough, branch, flipper, foreleg, forelimb, leg, wing.*

limber *vb* **limber up** exercise, get ready, loosen up, prepare, warm up.

limbo *n* **in limbo** abandoned, forgotten, in abeyance, left out, neglected, neither one thing nor the other, *inf* on hold, *inf* on the back burner, unattached.

limit *n* **1** border, boundary, bounds, brink, confines, demarcation line, edge, end, extent, extreme point, frontier, perimeter. **2** ceiling, check, curb, cut-off point, deadline, inhibition, limitation, maximum, restraint, restriction, stop, threshold. • *vb* bridle, check, circumscribe, confine, control, curb, define, fix, hold in check, put a limit on, ration, restrain, restrict. **limited** ▷ FINITE, INADEQUATE.

limitation *n* **1** ▷ LIMIT. **2** defect, deficiency, fault, inadequacy, shortcoming, weakness.

limitless *adj* boundless, countless, endless, everlasting, immeasurable, incalculable, inexhaustible, infinite, innumerable, never-ending, numberless, perpetual, renewable, unbounded, unconfined, unending, unimaginable, unlimited, unrestricted. ▷ VAST. *Opp* FINITE.

limp *adj inf* bendy, drooping, flabby, flaccid, flexible, *inf* floppy, lax, loose, pliable, sagging, slack, soft, weak, wilting, yielding. ▷ WEARY. *Opp* RIGID. • *vb* be lame, falter, hobble, hop, stagger, totter.

line *n* **1** band, borderline, boundary, contour, contour line, dash, mark, streak, striation, strip, stripe, stroke, trail. **2** corrugation, crease, *inf* crow's feet, fold, furrow, groove, score, wrinkle. **3** cable, cord, flex, hawser, lead, rope, string, thread, wire. **4** chain, column, cordon, crocodile, file, procession, queue, rank, row, series. **5** *railway line.* branch, main line, route, service, track. • *vb* **1** mark with lines, rule, score, streak, striate, underline. **2** *line the street.* border, edge, fringe. **3** *line a garment.* cover the inside, insert a lining, pad, reinforce. **line up** ▷ ALIGN, QUEUE.

linger *vb* continue, dally, dawdle, delay, dither, endure, hang about, hover, idle, lag, last, loiter, pause, persist, procrastinate, remain, *inf* shilly-shally, stay, stay behind, *inf* stick around, survive, temporize, wait about. *Opp* HURRY.

lining *n* inner coat, inner layer, interfacing, liner, padding.

link *n* **1** bond, connection, connector, coupling, join, joint, linkage, tie, yoke. ▷ FASTENER. **2** affiliation, alliance, association, communication, interdependence, liaison, partnership, relationship, *inf* tie-up, twinning, union. • *vb* **1** amalgamate, associate, attach, compare, concatenate, connect, couple, interlink, join, juxtapose, make a link, merge, network, relate, see a link, twin, unite, yoke. ▷ FASTEN.

lip *n* brim, brink, edge, rim.

liquefy *vb* become liquid, dissolve, liquidize, melt, run, thaw. *Opp* SOLIDIFY.

liquid *adj* aqueous, flowing, fluid, liquefied, melted, molten, running, *inf* runny, sloppy, *inf* sloshy, thin, watery, wet. *Opp* SOLID. • *n* fluid, juice, liquor, solution, stock.

liquidate *vb* annihilate, destroy, *inf* do away with, *inf* get rid of, remove, silence, wipe out. ▷ KILL.

liquor *n* **1** alcohol, *sl* booze, *sl* hard stuff, intoxicants, *sl* shorts, spirits, strong drink. **2** ▷ LIQUID.

list *n* catalogue, column, directory, file, index, inventory, listing, register, roll, roster, rota, schedule, shopping-list, table. • *vb* **1** catalogue, enumerate, file, index, itemize, make a list of, note, record, register, tabulate, write down. **2** bank, careen, heel, incline, keel over, lean, slant, slope, tilt, tip.

listen *vb* attend, concentrate, eavesdrop, *old use* hark, hear, heed, *inf* keep your ears open, lend an ear, overhear, pay attention, take notice.

listless *adj* apathetic, enervated, feeble, heavy, languid, lazy, lethargic, lifeless, phlegmatic, sluggish, tired, torpid, unenthusiastic, uninterested, weak. ▷ WEARY. *Opp* LIVELY.

literal *adj* close, exact, faithful, matter of fact, plain, prosaic, strict, unimaginative, verbatim, word for word.

literary *adj* **1** cultured, educated, erudite, imaginative, learned, refined, scholarly, well-read, widely-read. **2** *literary style.* ornate, *derog* pedantic, poetic, polished, rhetorical, *derog* self-conscious, sophisticated, stylish.

literate *adj* **1** educated, wellread. **2** accurate, correct, readable, well-written.

literature *n* books, brochures, circulars, creative writing, handbills, handouts, leaflets, pamphlets, papers, writings. □ *autobiography, biography, comedy, crime fiction, criticism, drama, epic, essay, fantasy, fiction, folk-tale, journalism, myth and legend, novels, parody, poetry, propaganda, prose, romance, satire, science fiction, tragedy.* ▷ WRITING.

lithe *adj* agile, flexible, limber, lissom, loose-jointed, pliable, pliant, supple. *Opp* STIFF.

litter *n* bits and pieces, clutter, debris, fragments, garbage, jumble, junk, mess, odds and ends, refuse, rubbish, trash, waste. • *vb* clutter, fill with litter, make untidy, *inf* mess up, scatter, strew.

little *adj* **1** *inf* baby, bantam, compact, concise, diminutive, *inf* dinky, dwarf, exiguous, fine, fractional, infinitesimal, lean, lilliputian, microscopic, midget, *inf* mini, miniature, minuscule, minute, narrow, petite (*woman*), *inf* pint-sized, *inf* pocket-sized, *inf* poky, portable, pygmy, short, slender, slight, small, *inf* teeny, thin, tiny, toy, undergrown, undersized, *inf* wee, *inf* weeny. *Opp* BIG. **2** *little food.* inadequate, insufficient, meagre, mean, *inf* measly, miserly, modest, niggardly, parsimonious, *inf* piddling, scanty, skimpy, stingy, ungenerous, unsatisfactory. **3** *of little importance.* inconsequential, insignificant, minor, negligible, nugatory, slim (*chance*), slight, trifling, trivial, unimportant.

live *adj* **1** ▷ LIVING. **2** *a live fire.* ▷ ALIGHT. **3** *a live issue.* contemporary, current, important, pressing, relevant, topical, vital. *Opp* DEAD. • *vb* **1** breathe, continue, endure, exist, flourish, function, last, persist, remain, stay alive, survive. *Opp* DIE. **2** be accommodated, dwell, lodge, reside, room, stay. **3** *live on £20 a week.* fare, *inf* get along, keep going, make a living, pay the bills, subsist. **live in** ▷ INHABIT. **live on** ▷ EAT.

liveliness *n* activity, animation, boisterousness, bustle, dynamism, energy, enthusiasm, exuberance, *inf* go, gusto, high spirits, spirit, sprightliness, verve, vigour, vitality, vivacity, zeal. *Opp* APATHY.

lively *adj* active, agile, alert, animated, boisterous, bubbly, bustling, busy, cheerful, colourful, dashing, eager, energetic, enthusiastic, exciting, expressive, exuberant, frisky, gay, high-spirited, irrepressible, jaunty, jazzy, jolly, merry, nimble, *inf* perky, playful, quick, spirited, sprightly, stimulating, strong, vigorous, vital, vivacious, vivid, *inf* zippy. ▷ HAPPY. *Opp* APATHETIC.

livestock *n* cattle, farm animals.

living *adj* active, actual, alive, animate, breathing, existing, extant, flourishing, functioning, live, *old use* quick, sentient, surviving, vigorous, vital. ▷ LIVELY. *Opp* DEAD, EXTINCT. • *n* income, livelihood, occupation, subsistence, way of life.

load *n* **1** burden, cargo, consignment, freight, lading, lorry-load, shipment, van-load. **2** *load of responsibility. inf* albatross, anxiety, care, *inf* cross, encumbrance, *inf* millstone, onus, trouble, weight, worry. • *vb* **1** burden, encumber, fill, heap, overwhelm, pack, pile, ply, saddle, stack, stow, weigh down. **2** *load a gun.* charge, prime. **loaded** ▷ BIASED, LADEN, WEALTHY.

loafer *n* idler, *inf* good-fornothing, layabout, *inf* lazybones, lounger, shirker, *sl* skiver, vagrant, wastrel.

loan *n* advance, credit, mortgage. • *vb* advance, allow, credit, lend.

loathe *vb* abhor, abominate, be averse to, be revolted by, despise, detest, dislike, execrate, find intolerable, hate, object to, recoil from, resent, scorn, shudder at. *Opp* LOVE.

lobby *n* **1** ante-room, corridor, entrance hall, entry, foyer, hall, hallway, porch, reception, vestibule. **2** *environmental lobby*. campaign, campaigners, pressure-group, supporters. ● *vb* persuade, petition, pressurize, try to influence, urge.

local *adj* **1** adjacent, adjoining, nearby, neighbouring, serving the locality. **2** *local politics*. community, limited, narrow, neighbourhood, parochial, particular, provincial, regional. *Opp* GENERAL, NATIONAL. ● *n* **1** inhabitant, resident, townsman, townswoman. **2** ▷ PUB.

locality *n* area, catchment area, community, district, location, neighbourhood, parish, region, residential area, town, vicinity, zone.

localize *vb* concentrate, confine, contain, enclose, keep within bounds, limit, narrow down, pin down, restrict. *Opp* SPREAD.

locate *vb* **1** come across, detect, discover, find, identify, *inf* lay your hands on, *inf* run to earth, search out, track down, unearth. **2** build, establish, find a place for, found, place, position, put, set up, site, situate, station.

location *n* **1** locale, locality, place, point, position, setting, site, situation, spot, venue, whereabouts. **2** *film locations*. background, scene, setting.

lock *n* bar, bolt, catch, clasp, fastening, hasp, latch, padlock. ● *vb* bolt, close, fasten, padlock, seal, secure, shut. **lock away** ▷ IMPRISON. **lock out** ▷ EXCLUDE. **lock up** ▷ IMPRISON.

lodge *n* ▷ HOUSE. ● *vb* **1** accommodate, billet, board, house, *inf* put up. **2** abide, dwell, live, *inf* put up, reside, stay, stop. **3** *lodge a complaint*. enter, file, make formally, put on record, record, register, submit.

lodger *n* boarder, guest, inmate, paying guest, resident, tenant.

lodgings *n* accommodation, apartment, billet, boarding-house, *inf* digs, lodging-house, *sl* pad, quarters, rooms, shelter, *sl* squat, temporary home.

lofty *adj* **1** elevated, high, imposing, majestic, noble, soaring, tall, towering. **2** ▷ ARROGANT.

log *n* **1** timber, wood. **2** account, diary, journal, record.

logic *n* clarity, deduction, intelligence, logical thinking, ratiocination, rationality, reasonableness, reasoning, sense, validity.

logical *adj* clear, cogent, coherent, consistent, deductive, intelligent, methodical, rational, reasonable, sensible, sound, *inf* step-by-step, structured, systematic, valid, well-reasoned, well-thought-out, wise. *Opp* ILLOGICAL.

loiter *vb* be slow, dally, dawdle, hang back, linger, *inf* loaf about, *inf* mess about, skulk, *inf* stand about, straggle.

lone *adj* isolated, separate, single, solitary, solo, unaccompanied. ▷ LONELY.

lonely *adj* **1** abandoned, alone, forlorn, forsaken, friendless, lonesome, loveless, neglected, outcast, reclusive, retiring, solitary, unsociable, withdrawn. ▷ SAD. **2** *inf* cut off, deserted, desolate, distant, far-away, isolated, *inf* off the beaten track, out of the way, remote, secluded, unfrequented, uninhabited.

long *adj* big, drawn out, elongated, endless, extended, extensive, great, interminable, large, lasting, lengthy, longish, prolonged, protracted, slow, stretched, sustained, time-consuming, unending. ● *vb* crave, hanker, have a longing (for), hunger, *inf* itch, pine, thirst, wish, yearn. **long for** ▷ DESIRE. **long-lasting, long-lived** ▷ PERMANENT. **long-standing** ▷ OLD. **long-suffering** ▷ PATIENT. **long-winded** ▷ TEDIOUS.

longing *n* appetite, craving, desire, hankering, hunger, *inf* itch, need, thirst, urge, wish, yearning, *inf* yen.

look *n* **1** gaze, glance, glimpse, observation, peek, peep, sight, *inf* squint, view. **2** air, appearance, aspect, attractiveness, bearing, beauty, complexion, countenance, demeanour, expression, face, looks, manner, mien. • *vb* **1** behold, *inf* cast your eye, consider, contemplate, examine, eye, gape, *inf* gawp, gaze, glance, glimpse, goggle, have a look, inspect, observe, ogle, pay attention (to), peek, peep, peer, read, regard, scan, scrutinize, see, skim through, squint, stare, study, survey, *sl* take a dekko, take note (of), view, watch. **2** *The house looks south.* face, overlook. **3** *look pleased.* appear, seem. **look after** ▷ TEND. **look down on** ▷ DESPISE. **look for** ▷ SEEK. **look into** ▷ INVESTIGATE. **look out** ▷ BEWARE. **look up to** ▷ ADMIRE.

look-out *n* guard, sentinel, sentry, watchman.

loom *vb* appear, arise, dominate, emerge, hover, impend, materialize, menace, rise, stand out, stick up, take shape, threaten, tower.

loop *n* bend, bow, circle, coil, curl, eye, hoop, kink, noose, ring, turn, twist, whorl. • *vb* bend, coil, curl, entwine, make a loop, turn, twist, wind.

loophole *n* escape, *inf* get-out, *inf* let-out, outlet, way out.

loose *adj* **1** detachable, detached, disconnected, independent, insecure, loosened, movable, moving, scattered, shaky, unattached, unconnected, unfastened, unsteady, wobbly. **2** *loose animals.* at large, at liberty, escaped, free, free-range, released, roaming, uncaged, unconfined, unfettered, unrestricted, untied. **3** *loose hair.* dangling, hanging, spread out, straggling, trailing. **4** *loose clothing.* baggy, *inf* floppy, loose-fitting, slack, unbuttoned. **5** *loose thinking.* broad, careless, casual, diffuse, general, ill-defined, illogical, imprecise, inexact, informal, lax, rambling, rough, *inf* sloppy, unscientific, unstructured, vague. *Opp* PRECISE, SECURE, TIGHT. **6** ▷ IMMORAL. • *vb* ▷ FREE, LOOSEN.

loosen *vb* **1** ease off, free, let go, loose, make loose, relax, release, separate, slacken, unfasten, unloose, untie. ▷ UNDO. **2** become loose, come adrift, open up. *Opp* TIGHTEN.

loot *n* booty, contraband, haul, *inf* ill-gotten gains, plunder, prize, spoils, *inf* swag, takings. • *vb* despoil, pillage, plunder, raid, ransack, ravage, rifle, rob, sack, steal from.

lopsided *adj* askew, asymmetrical, awry, *inf* cockeyed, crooked, one-sided, tilting, unbalanced, unequal, uneven.

lord *n* aristocrat, noble, peer. □ *baron, count, duke, earl,* old use *thane, viscount.* ▷ RULER.

lose *vb* **1** be deprived of, cease to have, drop, find yourself without, forfeit, forget, leave (somewhere), mislay, misplace, miss, part with, stray from. *Opp* FIND. **2** admit defeat, be defeated, capitulate, *inf* come to grief, fail, get beaten, get thrashed, succumb, suffer defeat. *Opp* WIN. **3** *lose your chance.* fritter, let slip, squander, waste. **4** *lose pursuers.* escape from, evade, get rid of, give the slip, leave behind, outrun, shake off, throw off. **losing** ▷ UNSUCCESSFUL.

loser *n* the defeated, runner-up, the vanquished. *Opp* WINNER.

loss *n* bereavement, damage, defeat, deficit, depletion, deprivation, destruction, diminution, disappearance, erosion, failure, forfeiture, impairment, privation, reduction, sacrifice. *Opp* GAIN. **losses** casualties, deaths, death toll, fatalities.

lost *adj* **1** abandoned, departed, destroyed, disappeared, extinct, forgotten, gone, irrecoverable, irretrievable, left behind, mislaid, misplaced, missing, strayed, untraceable, vanished. **2** absorbed, daydreaming, dreamy, distracted, engrossed, preoccupied, rapt. **3** corrupt, damned, fallen. ▷ WICKED.

lot *n a lot in a sale.* ▷ ITEM. **a lot of, lots of** ▷ PLENTY. **draw lots** ▷ GAMBLE. **the lot** all (of), everything, the whole thing, *inf* the works.

lotion *n* balm, cream, embrocation, liniment, ointment, pomade, salve, unguent.

lottery *n* **1** raffle, sweepstake. **2** gamble, speculation, venture.

loud *adj* **1** audible, blaring, booming, clamorous, clarion (*call*), deafening, ear-splitting, echoing, fortissimo, high, noisy, penetrating, piercing, raucous, resounding, reverberant, reverberating, roaring, rowdy, shrieking, shrill, sonorous, stentorian, strident, thundering, thunderous, vociferous. **2** *loud colours*. ▷ GAUDY. *Opp* QUIET.

lounge *n* drawing-room, front room, living-room, parlour, salon, sitting-room. • *vb* be idle, be lazy, dawdle, hang about, idle, *inf* kill time, laze, loaf, lie around, loiter, *inf* loll about, *inf* mess about, *inf* mooch about, relax, *inf* skive, slouch, slump, sprawl, stand about, take it easy, vegetate, waste time.

lout *n* boor, churl, rude person, oaf, *inf* yob.

lovable *adj* adorable, appealing, attractive, charming, cuddly, *inf* cute, *inf* darling, dear, enchanting, endearing, engaging, fetching, likeable, lovely, pleasing, taking, winning, winsome. *Opp* HATEFUL.

love *n* **1** admiration, adoration, adulation, affection, ardour, attachment, attraction, desire, devotion, fancy, fervour, fondness, infatuation, liking, passion, regard, tenderness, warmth. ▷ FRIENDSHIP. **2** beloved, darling, dear, dearest, loved one. ▷ LOVER. • *vb* **1** admire, adore, be charmed by, be fond of, be infatuated by, be in love with, care for, cherish, desire, dote on, fancy, *inf* have a crush on, have a passion for, idolize, lose your heart to, lust after, treasure, value, want, worship. ▷ LIKE. *Opp* HATE. **in love** besotted, devoted, enamoured, fond, *inf* head over heels, infatuated. **love affair** affair, amour, courtship, intrigue, liaison, relationship, romance. **make love** be intimate, *inf* canoodle, caress, copulate, court, cuddle, embrace, flirt, fornicate, have intercourse, have sex, kiss, mate, *sl* neck, *inf* pet, philander, *old use* spoon, woo. ▷ SEX.

loved *adj* beloved, cherished, darling, dear, dearest, esteemed, favourite, precious, treasured, valued, wanted.

loveless *adj* cold, frigid, heartless, passionless, undemonstrative, unfeeling, unloving, unresponsive. *Opp* LOVING. ▷ UNLOVED.

lovely *adj* appealing, attractive, charming, delightful, enjoyable, fine, good, nice, pleasant, pretty, sweet. ▷ BEAUTIFUL. *Opp* NASTY.

lover *n* admirer, boyfriend, companion, concubine, fiancé(e), *old use* follower, friend, gigolo, girlfriend, *inf* intended, mate, mistress, *old use* paramour, suitor, sweetheart, *sl* toy boy, valentine.

lovesick *adj* frustrated, languishing, lovelorn, pining.

loving *adj* admiring, adoring, affectionate, amorous, ardent, attached, brotherly, caring, close, concerned, dear, demonstrative, devoted, doting, fatherly, fond, friendly, inseparable, kind, maternal, motherly, passionate, paternal, protective, sisterly, tender, warm. ▷ FRIENDLY, SEXY. *Opp* LOVELESS.

low *adj* **1** flat, low-lying, sunken. **2** *low trees*. little, short, squat, stumpy, stunted. **3** *low status*. abject, base, degraded, humble, inferior, junior, lesser, lower, lowly, menial, miserable, modest, servile. **4** *low behaviour*. churlish, coarse, common, cowardly, crude, *old use* dastardly, disreputable, ignoble, mean, nasty, vulgar, wicked. ▷ IMMORAL. **5** *low sounds*. gentle, indistinct, muffled, murmurous, muted, pianissimo, quiet, soft, subdued, whispered. **6** *low notes*. bass, deep, reverberant. *Opp* HIGH. **in low spirits** ▷ SAD. **low point** ▷ NADIR.

lowbrow *adj* accessible, easy, ordinary, pop, popular, *derog* rubbishy, simple, straightforward, *derog* trashy, *derog* uncultured, undemanding, unpretentious, unsophisticated. *Opp* HIGHBROW.

lower *vb* **1** dip, drop, haul down, let down, take down. **2** *lower prices.* bring down, cut, decrease, discount, lessen, mark down, reduce, *inf* slash. **3** *lower the volume.* abate, diminish, quieten, tone down, turn down. **4** *lower yourself.* abase, belittle, debase, degrade, demean, discredit, disgrace, humble, humiliate, stoop. *Opp* RAISE.

lowly *adj* base, humble, insignificant, little-known, low, low-born, meek, modest, obscure, unimportant. ▷ ORDINARY. *Opp* EMINENT.

loyal *adj* committed, constant, dedicated, dependable, devoted, dutiful, faithful, honest, patriotic, reliable, sincere, stable, staunch, steadfast, steady, true, trustworthy, trusty, unswerving, unwavering. *Opp* DISLOYAL.

loyalty *n* allegiance, constancy, dedication, dependability, devotion, duty, faithfulness, fealty, fidelity, honesty, patriotism, reliability, staunchness, steadfastness, trustworthiness. *Opp* DISLOYALTY.

lubricate *vb* grease, oil.

luck *n* **1** accident, chance, coincidence, destiny, fate, *inf* fluke, fortune, serendipity. **2** *wished her luck.* *inf* break, good fortune, happiness, prosperity, success.

lucky *adj* **1** accidental, appropriate, chance, *inf* fluky, fortuitous, opportune, providential, timely, unintentional, unplanned, welcome. **2** blessed, favoured, fortunate, successful. ▷ HAPPY. **3** *lucky number.* advantageous, auspicious. *Opp* UNLUCKY.

luggage *n* baggage, belongings, *inf* gear, impedimenta, paraphernalia, *inf* things. □ *bag, basket, box, brief-case, case, chest, hamper, handbag, hand luggage, haversack, holdall, knapsack, pannier,* old use *portmanteau, purse, rucksack, satchel, suitcase, trunk, wallet.*

lukewarm *adj* **1** room temperature, tepid, warm. **2** apathetic, cool, half-hearted, indifferent, unenthusiastic.

lull *n* break, calm, delay, gap, halt, hiatus, interlude, interruption, interval, lapse, *inf* let-up, pause, respite, rest, silence. ● *vb* calm, hush, pacify, quell, quieten, soothe, subdue, tranquillize.

lumber *n* **1** beams, boards, planks, timber, wood. **2** bits and pieces, clutter, jumble, junk, litter, odds and ends, rubbish, trash, *inf* white elephants. ● *vb* **1** blunder, move clumsily, shamble, trudge. **2** ▷ BURDEN.

luminous *adj* bright, glowing, luminescent, lustrous, phosphorescent, radiant, refulgent, shining. ▷ LIGHT.

lump *n* **1** ball, bar, bit, block, cake, chunk, clod, clot, cube, *inf* dollop, gob, gobbet, hunk, ingot, mass, nugget, piece, slab, wad, wedge, *inf* wodge. **2** boil, bulge, bump, carbuncle, cyst, excrescence, growth, hump, knob, node, nodule, protrusion, protuberance, spot, swelling, tumescence, tumour. ● *vb* **lump together** ▷ COMBINE.

lunacy *n* delirium, dementia, derangement, frenzy, hysteria, illogicality, insanity, madness, mania, psychosis, unreason. ▷ STUPIDITY.

lunatic *adj* ▷ MAD. ● *n* *inf* crackpot, *inf* crank, *inf* loony, madman, madwoman, maniac, *inf* mental case, *inf* nutcase, *inf* nutter, psychopath, psychotic.

lunge *vb* **1** jab, stab, strike, thrust. **2** charge, dash, dive, lurch, plunge, pounce, rush, spring, throw yourself.

lurch *vb* heave, lean, list, lunge, pitch, plunge, reel, roll, stagger, stumble, sway, totter, wallow. **leave in the lurch** ▷ ABANDON.

lure *vb* allure, attract, bait, charm, coax, decoy, draw, entice, induce, inveigle, invite, lead on, persuade, seduce, tempt.

lurid *adj* **1** bright, gaudy, glaring, glowing, striking, vivid. **2** ▷ SENSATIONAL.

lurk *vb* crouch, hide, lie in wait, lie low, prowl, skulk, steal.

luscious *adj* appetizing, delectable, delicious, juicy, mouth-watering, rich, succulent, sweet, tasty.

lust *n* **1** carnality, concupiscence, desire, lasciviousness, lechery, libido, licentiousness, passion, sensuality, sexuality. **2** appetite, craving, greed, hunger, itch, longing.

lustful *adj* carnal, concupiscent, erotic, lascivious, lecherous, lewd, libidinous, licentious, on heat, passionate, *sl* randy, salacious, sensual, *sl* turned on. ▷ SEXY.

lustrous *adj* burnished, glazed, gleaming, glossy, metallic, polished, reflective, sheeny, shiny.

luxuriant *adj* **1** abundant, ample, copious, dense, exuberant, fertile, flourishing, green, lush, opulent, plenteous, plentiful, profuse, prolific, rank, rich, teeming, thick, thriving, verdant. **2** ▷ ORNATE. *Opp* SPARSE.

luxurious *adj* comfortable, costly, expensive, extravagant, grand, hedonistic, lavish, lush, magnificent, opulent, pampered, *inf* plush, *inf* posh, rich, *inf* ritzy, self-indulgent, splendid, sumptuous, sybaritic, voluptuous. *Opp* SPARTAN.

luxury *n* affluence, comfort, ease, enjoyment, extravagance, grandeur, hedonism, high living, indulgence, magnificence, opulence, pleasure, relaxation, self-indulgence, splendour, sumptuousness, voluptuousness.

lying *adj* crooked, deceitful, deceptive, dishonest, double-dealing, duplicitous, false, hypocritical, inaccurate, insincere, mendacious, misleading, perfidious, unreliable, untrustworthy, untruthful. *Opp* TRUTHFUL. • *n* deceit, deception, dishonesty, duplicity, falsehood, *inf* fibbing, hypocrisy, mendacity, perfidy, perjury, prevarication.

lyrical *adj* emotional, expressive, impassioned, inspired, melodious, musical, poetic, rapturous, rhapsodic, song-like, sweet, tuneful. *Opp* PROSAIC.

M

macabre *adj* eerie, fearsome, frightful, ghoulish, grim, grisly, grotesque, gruesome, morbid, *inf* sick, unhealthy, weird.

machine *n* appliance, contraption, contrivance, device, engine, gadget, implement, instrument, mechanism, motor, robot, tool. ▷ MACHINERY.

machinery *n* **1** apparatus, equipment, gear, machines, plant. **2** constitution, method, organization, procedure, structure, system.

mackintosh *n* anorak, cape, mac, sou'wester, waterproof. ▷ COAT.

mad *adj* **1** *inf* batty, berserk, *inf* bonkers, *inf* certified, *inf* crackers, crazed, crazy, *inf* daft, delirious, demented, deranged, disordered, distracted, *inf* dotty, eccentric, fanatical, frantic, frenzied, hysterical, insane, irrational, *inf* loony, lunatic, maniacal, manic, *inf* mental, moonstruck, *Lat* non compos mentis, *inf* nutty, *inf* off your head, *inf* off your rocker, *inf* out of your mind, possessed, *inf* potty, psychotic, *inf* queer in the head, *inf* round the bend, *inf* round the twist, *inf* screwy, *inf* touched, unbalanced, unhinged, unstable, *inf* up the pole, wild. *Opp* SANE. **2** *a mad comedy.* ▷ ABSURD. **3** ▷ ANGRY. **4** ▷ ENTHUSIASTIC.

madden *vb* anger, craze, derange, *inf* drive crazy, enrage, exasperate, excite, incense, inflame, infuriate, irritate, make you mad, *inf* make your blood boil, *inf* make you see red, provoke, *inf* send you round the bend, unhinge, vex.

madman,
madwoman *ns inf* crackpot, *inf* crank, eccentric, *inf* loony, lunatic, maniac, *inf* mental case, *inf* nutcase, *inf* nutter, psychopath, psychotic.

madness *n* delirium, dementia, derangement, eccentricity, folly, frenzy, hysteria, illogicality, insanity, lunacy, mania, mental illness, psychosis, unreason. ▷ STUPIDITY.

magazine *n* **1** comic, journal, monthly, newspaper, pamphlet, paper, periodical, publication, quarterly, weekly. **2** *magazine of weapons.* ammunition dump, armoury, arsenal, storehouse.

magic *adj* **1** conjuring, miraculous, mystic, necromantic, supernatural. **2** bewitching, charming, enchanting, entrancing, magical, spellbinding. • *n* **1** black magic, charm, enchantment, hocus-pocus, incantation, *inf* mumbo-jumbo, necromancy, occultism, sorcery, spell, voodoo, witchcraft, witchery, wizardry. **2** conjuring, illusion, legerdemain, sleight of hand, trickery, tricks.

magician *n* conjuror, enchanter, enchantress, illusionist, magus, necromancer, sorcerer, *old use* warlock, witch, witch-doctor, wizard.

magnetic *adj* alluring, attractive, bewitching, captivating, charismatic, charming, compelling, engaging, enthralling, entrancing, fascinating, hypnotic, inviting, irresistible, seductive, spellbinding. *Opp* REPULSIVE.

magnetism *n* allure, appeal, attractiveness, charisma, charm, drawing power, fascination, irresistibility, lure, power, pull, seductiveness.

magnificent *adj* awe-inspiring, beautiful, distinguished, excellent, fine, glorious, gorgeous, grand, grandiose, great, imposing, impressive, majestic, marvellous, noble, opulent, *inf* posh, regal, resplendent, rich, spectacular, splendid, stately, sumptuous, superb, wonderful. *Opp* ORDINARY.

magnify *vb* **1** amplify, augment, *inf* blow up, enlarge, expand, increase, intensify, make larger. *Opp* SHRINK. **2** *magnify difficulties. inf* blow up out of proportion, dramatize, exaggerate, heighten, inflate, make too much of, maximize, overdo, overestimate, overstate. *Opp* MINIMIZE.

magnitude *n* bigness, enormousness, extent, greatness, immensity, importance, size.

mail *n* correspondence, letters, parcels, post. • *vb* dispatch, forward, post, send.

maim *vb* cripple, disable, hamstring, handicap, incapacitate, lame, mutilate. ▷ WOUND.

main *adj* basic, biggest, cardinal, central, chief, critical, crucial, dominant, dominating, essential, first, foremost, fundamental, greatest, largest, leading, major, most important, outstanding, paramount, predominant, pre-eminent, prevailing, primary, prime, principal, special, strongest, supreme, top, vital. *Opp* MINOR.

mainly *adv* above all, as a rule, chiefly, especially, essentially, first and foremost, generally, in the main, largely, mostly, normally, on the whole, predominantly, primarily, principally, usually.

maintain *vb* **1** carry on, continue, hold to, keep going, keep up, perpetuate, persevere in, persist in, preserve, retain, stick to, sustain. **2** *maintain a car.* care for, keep in good condition, look after, service, take care of. **3** *maintain a family.* feed, keep, pay for, provide for, stand by, support. **4** *maintain your innocence.* affirm, allege, argue, assert, aver, claim, contend, declare, defend, insist, proclaim, profess, state, uphold.

maintenance *n* **1** care, conservation, looking after, preservation, repairs, servicing, upkeep. **2** alimony, allowance, contribution, subsistence, support.

majestic *adj* august, awe-inspiring, awesome, dignified, distinguished, elevated, exalted, glorious, grand, grandiose, imperial, imposing, impressive, kingly, lofty, lordly, magisterial, magnificent, monumental, noble, pompous, princely, queenly, regal, royal, splendid, stately, striking, sublime.

majesty *n* awesomeness, dignity, glory, grandeur, kingliness, loftiness, magnificence, nobility, pomp, royalty, splendour, stateliness, sublimity.

major *adj* bigger, chief, considerable, extensive, greater, important, key, larger, leading, outstanding, principal, serious, significant. ▷ MAIN. *Opp* MINOR.

majority *n* **1** *inf* best part, *inf* better part, bulk, greater number, mass, preponderance. **2** adulthood, coming of age, manhood, maturity, womanhood. **be in the majority** ▷ DOMINATE.

make *n* brand, kind, model, sort, type, variety. • *vb* **1** assemble, beget, bring about, build, compose, constitute, construct, contrive, craft, create, devise, do, engender, erect, execute, fabricate, fashion, forge, form, frame, generate, invent, make up, manufacture, mass-produce, originate, produce, put together, think up. **2** *make dinner.* concoct, cook, *inf* fix, prepare. **3** *make clothes.* knit, *inf* run up, sew, weave. **4** *make an effigy.* carve, cast, model, mould, sculpt, shape. **5** *make a speech.* deliver, pronounce, utter. ▷ SPEAK. **6** *made her chairperson.* appoint, elect, nominate, ordain. **7** *make P into B.* alter, change, convert, modify, transform, turn. **8** *make a fortune.* earn, gain, get, obtain, receive. **9** *make a good employee.* become, change into, grow into, turn into. **10** *make your objective.* accomplish, achieve, arrive at, attain, catch, get to, reach, win. **11** *2 + 2 makes 4.* add up to, amount to, come to, total. **12** *make rules.* agree, arrange, codify, decide on, draw up, establish, fix, write. **13** *make her happy.* cause to become, render.

14 *make trouble.* bring about, carry out, cause, give rise to, provoke, result in. **15** *make them obey.* coerce, compel, constrain, force, induce, oblige, order, pressurize, prevail on, require. **make amends** ▷ COMPENSATE. **make believe** ▷ IMAGINE. **make fun of** ▷ RIDICULE. **make good** ▷ PROSPER. **make love** ▷ LOVE. **make off** ▷ DEPART. **make off with** ▷ STEAL. **make out** ▷ UNDERSTAND. **make up** ▷ INVENT. **make up for** ▷ COMPENSATE. **make up your mind** ▷ DECIDE.

make-believe *adj* fanciful, feigned, imaginary, made-up, mock, *inf* pretend, pretended, sham, simulated, unreal. • *n* dream, fantasy, play-acting, pretence, self-deception, unreality.

maker *n* architect, author, builder, creator, director, manufacturer, originator, producer.

makeshift *adj* emergency, improvised, provisional, stopgap, temporary.

maladjusted *adj* disturbed, muddled, neurotic, unbalanced.

male *adj* manly, masculine, virile. • *n* □ *bachelor,* inf *bloke, boy, boyfriend,* inf *bridegroom, brother, chap,* inf *codger, father, fellow, gentleman, groom,* inf *guy, husband, lad, lover, man, son,* inf *squire, uncle, widower.* □ *buck, bull, cock, dog, ram, stallion, tom(cat). Opp* FEMALE.

malefactor *n* delinquent, lawbreaker, offender, villain, wrongdoer. ▷ CRIMINAL.

malice *n* animosity, *inf* bitchiness, bitterness, *inf* cattiness, enmity, hatred, hostility, ill-will, malevolence, maliciousness, malignity, nastiness, rancour, spite, spitefulness, vengefulness, venom, viciousness, vindictiveness.

malicious *adj inf* bitchy, bitter, *inf* catty, evil, evil-minded, hateful, ill-natured, malevolent, malignant, mischievous, nasty, rancorous, revengeful, sly, spiteful, vengeful, venomous, vicious, villainous, vindictive, wicked. *Opp* KIND.

malignant *adj* dangerous, deadly, destructive, fatal, harmful, injurious, life-threatening, poisonous, *inf* terminal, uncontrollable, virulent. ▷ MALICIOUS.

malleable *adj* ductile, plastic, pliable, soft, tractable, workable. *Opp* BRITTLE.

malnutrition *n* famine, hunger, starvation, undernourishment.

man *n* **1** [*either sex*] ▷ MANKIND. **2** ▷ MALE. • *vb* cover, crew, provide staff for, staff.

manage *vb* **1** administer, be in charge of, be manager of, command, conduct, control, direct, dominate, govern, head, lead, look after, mastermind, operate, organize, oversee, preside over, regulate, rule, run, superintend, supervise, take care of, take control of, take over. **2** *manage your jobs.* accomplish, achieve, bring about, carry out, contend with, cope with, deal with, do, finish, get through, handle, manipulate, muddle through, perform, sort out, succeed in, undertake. **3** *Can you manage?* cope, fend for yourself, *inf* make it, scrape by, shift for yourself, succeed, survive. **4** *can manage £10.* afford, spare.

manageable *adj* **1** acceptable, convenient, easy to manage, handy, neat, reasonable. *Opp* AWKWARD. **2** amenable, compliant, controllable, disciplined, docile, governable, submissive, tame, tractable. ▷ OBEDIENT. *Opp* DISOBEDIENT.

manager,
manageress *ns* administrator, *inf* boss, chief, controller, director, executive, foreman, forewoman, governor, head, organizer, overseer, proprietor, ruler, superintendent, supervisor. ▷ CHIEF.

mandatory *adj* compulsory, essential, necessary, needed, obligatory, required, requisite.

mangle *vb* butcher, cripple, crush, cut, damage, deform, disfigure, hack, injure, lacerate, maim, maul, mutilate, ruin, spoil, squash, tear, wound.

mangy *adj* dirty, filthy, motheaten, nasty, scabby, scruffy, shabby, slovenly, squalid, *inf* tatty, unkempt, wretched.

manhandle *vb* **1** carry, haul, heave, hump, lift, manoeuvre, move, pull, push. **2** abuse, batter, *inf* beat up, ill-treat, knock about, maltreat, mistreat, misuse, *inf* rough up, treat roughly.

mania *n* craving, craze, enthusiasm, fad, fetish, frenzy, infatuation, obsession, passion, preoccupation, rage. ▷ MADNESS.

maniac *n* lunatic, psychopath, psychotic. ▷ MADMAN.

manifest *adj* apparent, blatant, clear, conspicuous, discernible, evident, explicit, glaring, noticeable, obvious, patent, plain, recognizable, undisguised, visible. • *vb* ▷ SHOW.

manifesto *n* declaration, policy statement.

manipulate *vb* **1** feel, massage, rub, stimulate. **2** *manipulate people*. control, direct, engineer, exploit, guide, handle, influence, manage, manoeuvre, orchestrate, steer.

mankind *n Lat* homo sapiens, human beings, humanity, humankind, the human race, man, men and women, mortals, people.

manly *adj* chivalrous, gallant, heroic, *inf* macho, male, mannish, masculine, strong, swashbuckling, vigorous, virile. ▷ BRAVE. *Opp* EFFEMINATE.

man-made *adj* artificial, imitation, manufactured, massproduced, processed, simulated, synthetic, unnatural. *Opp* NATURAL.

manner *n* **1** approach, fashion, means, method, mode, procedure, process, style, technique, way. **2** air, aspect, attitude, bearing, behaviour, character, conduct, demeanour, deportment, disposition, look, mien. **3** *all manner of things*. genre, kind, sort, type, variety.

manners *plur n* behaviour, breeding, civility, conduct, courtesy, decorum, etiquette, gentility, politeness, protocol, refinement, social graces.

mannerism *n* characteristic, habit, idiosyncrasy, peculiarity, quirk, trait.

manoeuvre *n* device, dodge, gambit, intrigue, move, operation, plan, plot, ploy, ruse, scheme, stratagem, strategy, tactics, trick. • *vb* contrive, engineer, guide, jockey, manipulate, move, navigate, negotiate, pilot, steer.

manoeuvres *plur n* army exercise, operation, training.

mansion *n* castle, château, manor, manor-house, palace, stately home, villa. ▷ HOUSE.

mantle *n* cape, cloak, covering, hood, shawl, shroud, wrap. • *vb* ▷ COVER.

manufacture *vb* assemble, build, construct, create, fabricate, make, mass-produce, prefabricate, process, put together, *inf* turn out. **manufactured** ▷ MAN-MADE.

manufacturer *n* factory-owner, industrialist, maker, producer.

manure *n* compost, dung, fertilizer, *inf* muck.

manuscript *n* document, papers, script. ▷ BOOK.

many *adj* abundant, assorted, copious, countless, diverse, frequent, innumerable, multifarious, myriad, numberless, numerous, profuse, *inf* umpteen, uncountable, untold, varied, various. *Opp* FEW.

map *n* chart, diagram, plan.

mar *vb* blight, blot, damage, deface, disfigure, harm, hurt, impair, ruin, spoil, stain, taint, tarnish, wreck.

marauder *n* bandit, buccaneer, invader, pirate, plunderer, raider.

march *n* cortège, demonstration, march-past, parade, procession, progress. • *vb* file, pace, parade, step, stride, troop. ▷ WALK.

margin *n* **1** border, boundary, brink, edge, frieze, perimeter, periphery, rim, side, verge. **2** allowance, latitude, leeway, room, scope, space.

marginal *adj* borderline, doubtful, insignificant, minimal, negligible, peripheral, slight, small, unimportant.

marital *adj* conjugal, matrimonial, nuptial.

mark *n* **1** blemish, blot, blotch, dent, dot, fingermark, *plur* graffiti, impression, line, marking, pockmark, print, scar, scratch, scribble, smear, smudge, smut, *inf* splotch, spot, stain, *plur* stigmata, streak, trace, vestige. **2** *mark of breeding.* characteristic, feature, indication, indicator, marker, token. **3** *identifying mark.* badge, brand, device, emblem, fingerprint, hallmark, label, seal, sign, stamp, standard, symbol, trademark. • *vb* **1** blemish, blot, brand, bruise, cut, damage, deface, dent, dirty, disfigure, draw on, make a mark on, mar, scar, scratch, scrawl over, scribble on, smudge, spot, stain, stamp, streak, tattoo, write on. **2** *mark pupils' work.* appraise, assess, correct, evaluate, grade, tick. **3** *mark my words.* attend to, heed, listen to, mind, note, notice, observe, pay attention to, take note of, take seriously, *inf* take to heart, watch.

market *n* auction, bazaar, exchange, fair, marketplace, sale. ▷ SHOP. • *vb* advertise, deal in, make available, merchandise, peddle, promote, put on the market, retail, sell, *inf* tout, trade, trade in, try to sell, vend.

marksman *n* crack shot, gunman, sharpshooter, sniper.

maroon *vb* abandon, cast away, desert, forsake, isolate, leave, put ashore, strand.

marriage *n* **1** matrimony, partnership, union, wedlock. **2** nuptials, union, wedding. □ *bigamy, monogamy, polygamy.*

marriageable *adj* adult, mature, nubile.

marry *vb* espouse, *inf* get hitched, *inf* get spliced, join in matrimony, *inf* tie the knot, unite, wed.

marsh *n* bog, fen, marshland, morass, mud, mudflats, quagmire, quicksands, saltings, saltmarsh, *old use* slough, swamp, wetland.

marshal *vb* arrange, assemble, collect, deploy, draw up, gather, group, line up, muster, organize, set out.

martial *adj* aggressive, bellicose, belligerent, militant, military, pugnacious, soldierly, warlike. *Opp* PEACEABLE.

marvel *n* miracle, phenomenon, wonder. • *vb* **marvel at** admire, applaud, be amazed by, be astonished by, be surprised by, gape at, praise, wonder at.

marvellous *adj* admirable, amazing, astonishing, astounding, breathtaking, excellent, exceptional, extraordinary, *inf* fabulous, *inf* fantastic, glorious, impressive, incredible, magnificent, miraculous, out of the ordinary, *inf* out of this world, phenomenal, praiseworthy, prodigious, remarkable, *inf* sensational, spectacular, splendid, staggering, stunning, stupendous, *inf* super, superb, surprising, *inf* terrific, unbelievable, wonderful, wondrous. *Opp* ORDINARY.

masculine *adj* boyish, *inf* butch, gentlemanly, heroic, *inf* macho, male, manly, mannish, muscular, powerful, strong, vigorous, virile. *Opp* FEMININE.

mash *vb* beat, crush, grind, mangle, pound, pulp, pulverize, smash, squash.

mask *n* camouflage, cloak, cover, cover-up, disguise, façade, front, guise, screen, shield, veil, visor. • *vb* blot out, camouflage, cloak, conceal, cover, disguise, hide, obscure, screen, shield, shroud, veil.

masonry *n* bricks, brickwork, stone, stonework.

mass *adj* comprehensive, general, large-scale, popular, universal, wholesale, widespread. • *n* **1** accumulation, agglomeration, aggregation, body, bulk, *inf* chunk, collection, concretion, conglomeration, *inf* dollop, heap, hoard, *inf* hunk, *inf* load, lot, lump, mound, mountain, pile, profusion, quantity, stack, volume. **2** ▷ GROUP. ● *vb* accumulate, aggregate, amass, assemble, collect, congregate, convene, flock together, gather, marshal, meet, mobilize, muster, pile up, rally.

massacre *vb* annihilate, slaughter. ▷ KILL.

massage *vb* knead, manipulate, rub.

mast *n* aerial, flagpole, maypole, pylon, transmitter.

master *n* **1** *inf* boss, employer, governor, keeper, lord, overseer, owner, person in charge, proprietor, ruler, taskmaster. ▷ CHIEF. **2** captain, skipper. **3** *master of an art. inf* ace, authority, expert, genius, maestro, mastermind, virtuoso. **4** ▷ TEACHER. ● *vb* **1** become expert in, *inf* get off by heart, *inf* get the hang of, grasp, know, learn, understand. **2** break in, bridle, check, conquer, control, curb, defeat, dominate, *inf* get the better of, govern, manage, overcome, overpower, quell, regulate, repress, rule, subdue, subjugate, suppress, tame, triumph over, vanquish.

masterly *adj* accomplished, adroit, consummate, dexterous, excellent, expert, masterful, matchless, practised, proficient, skilful, skilled, unsurpassable.

mastermind *n* architect, brains, conceiver, contriver, creator, engineer, expert, genius, intellectual, inventor, manager, originator, planner, prime mover. ● *vb* carry through, conceive, contrive, devise, direct, engineer, execute, manage, organize, originate, plan, plot. ▷ MANAGE.

masterpiece *n* best work, *Fr* chef-d'oeuvre, classic, *inf* hit, *Lat* magnum opus, masterwork, *Fr* pièce de résistance.

match *n* **1** bout, competition, contest, duel, game, test match, tie, tournament, tourney. **2** *met my match.* complement, counterpart, double, equal, equivalent, twin. **3** *a good match.* combination, fit, pair, similarity. **4** *a love match.* alliance, friendship, marriage, partnership, relationship, union. ● *vb* **1** agree, accord, be compatible, be equivalent, be the same, be similar, blend, coincide, combine, compare, coordinate, correspond, fit, *inf* go together, harmonize, suit, tally, tie in, tone in. *Opp* CONTRAST. **2** ally, combine, fit, join, link up, marry, mate, pair off, pair up, put together, team up. *Opp* SPLIT. **matching** ▷ SIMILAR.

mate *n* **1** *inf* better half, companion, consort, helpmeet, husband, partner, spouse, wife. ▷ FRIEND. **2** assistant, associate, collaborator, colleague, helper. ● *vb* become partners, copulate, couple, have intercourse, *inf* have sex, join, marry, *inf* pair up, unite, wed.

material *adj* concrete, corporeal, palpable, physical, solid, substantial, tangible. ● *n* **1** fabric, stuff, textile. ▷ CLOTH. **2** components, constituents, content, data, facts, ideas, information, matter, notes, resources, statistics, stuff, subject matter, substance, supplies, things.

materialize *vb* appear, become visible, emerge, occur, take shape, *inf* turn up.

mathematics *plur n* mathematical science, *inf* maths, number work. □ *addition, algebra, arithmetic, calculus, division, geometry, multiplication, operational research, statistics, subtraction, trigonometry.*

matted *adj* knotted, tangled, uncombed, unkempt. ▷ DISHEVELLED.

matter *n* **1** body, material, stuff, substance. **2** discharge, pus, suppuration. **3** *a matter of life and death.* affair, business, concern, episode, event, fact, incident, issue, occurrence, question, situation, subject, thing, topic. **4** *What's the matter?* difficulty, problem, trouble, upset, worry. ● *vb* be important, be of consequence, be significant, count, make a difference, mean something, signify. **matter-of-fact** ▷ PROSAIC.

mature *adj* **1** adult, advanced, experienced, full-grown, grown-up, nubile, of age, perfect, sophisticated, well-developed. **2** mellow, ready, ripe, seasoned. *Opp* IMMATURE. • *vb* age, come to fruition, develop, grow up, mellow, reach maturity, ripen.

maturity *n* adulthood, completion, majority, mellowness, perfection, readiness, ripeness.

maul *vb* claw, injure, *inf* knock about, lacerate, mangle, manhandle, mutilate, paw, savage, treat roughly, wound.

maximize *vb* **1** add to, augment, build up, increase, make the most of. **2** inflate, magnify, overdo, overstate. ▷ EXAGGERATE. *Opp* MINIMIZE.

maximum *adj* biggest, extreme, full, fullest, greatest, highest, largest, maximal, most, peak, supreme, top, topmost, utmost, uttermost. • *n* apex, ceiling, climax, extreme, highest point, peak, pinnacle, top, upper limit, zenith. *Opp* MINIMUM.

maybe *adv* conceivably, perhaps, possibly.

maze *n* complex, confusion, convolution, labyrinth, network, tangle, web.

meadow *n* field, *old use* mead, paddock, pasture.

meagre *adj* deficient, inadequate, insufficient, lean, mean, paltry, poor, puny, scanty, skimpy, slight, sparse, thin, unsatisfying. ▷ SMALL. *Opp* GENEROUS.

meal *n inf* blow-out, *old use* collation, repast, *inf* spread. □ *banquet, barbecue, breakfast, buffet, dinner,* inf *elevenses, feast, high tea, lunch, luncheon, picnic, snack, supper, take-away, tea, tea-break,* old use *tiffin.*

mean *adj* **1** beggarly, *inf* cheese-paring, close, close-fisted, illiberal, *inf* mingy, miserly, niggardly, parsimonious, *inf* penny-pinching, selfish, sparing, stingy, *inf* tight, tight-fisted, ungenerous. **2** *a mean disposition.* callous, churlish, contemptible, cruel, despicable, hard-hearted, ignoble, ill-tempered, malicious, nasty, shabby, shameful, small-minded, *inf* sneaky, spiteful, uncharitable, unkind, vicious. **3** *a mean dwelling.* base, common, humble, inferior, insignificant, low, lowly, miserable, poor, shabby, squalid, wretched. *Opp* GENEROUS, VALUABLE. • *vb* **1** augur, betoken, communicate, connote, convey, denote, *inf* drive at, express, foretell, *inf* get over, herald, hint at, imply, indicate, intimate, portend, presage, refer to, represent, say, show, signal, signify, specify, spell out, stand for, suggest, symbolize. **2** *I mean to succeed.* aim, desire, have in mind, hope, intend, plan, propose, purpose, want, wish. **3** *The job means long hours.* entail, involve, necessitate.

meander *vb* ramble, rove, snake, twist and turn, wander, wind, zigzag.
meandering ▷ TWISTY.

meaning *n* connotation, content, definition, denotation, drift, explanation, force, gist, idea, implication, import, importance, interpretation, message, point, purport, purpose, relevance, sense, significance, signification, substance, thrust, value.

meaningful *adj* deep, eloquent, expressive, meaning, pointed, positive, pregnant, relevant, serious, significant, suggestive, telling, tell-tale, weighty, worthwhile. *Opp* MEANINGLESS.

meaningless *adj* **1** absurd, coded, incomprehensible, incoherent, inconsequential, irrelevant, nonsensical, pointless, senseless. **2** *meaningless compliments.* empty, flattering, hollow, insincere, shallow, silly, sycophantic, vacuous, worthless. *Opp* MEANINGFUL.

means *n* **1** ability, capacity, channel, course, fashion, machinery, manner, medium, method, mode, process, way. **2** *private means.* ▷ WEALTH.

measurable *adj* appreciable, considerable, perceptible, quantifiable, reasonable, significant. *Opp* NEGLIGIBLE.

measure *n* **1** allocation, allowance, amount, amplitude, extent, magnitude, portion, quantity, quota, range, ration, scope, size, unit. ▷ MEASURE-

MENT. **2** criterion, *inf* litmus test, standard, test, touchstone, yardstick. **3** *measures to curb crime.* act, action, bill, control, course of action, expedient, law, means, procedure, step. • *vb* assess, calculate, calibrate, compute, count, determine, estimate, gauge, judge, mark out, meter, plumb (*depth*), quantify, rank, rate, reckon, survey, take measurements of, weigh. **measure out** ▷ DISPENSE.

measurement *n* amount, calculation, dimensions, extent, figure, mensuration, size. ▷ MEASURE. □ *area, breadth, bulk, capacity, depth, distance, height, length, mass, speed, time, volume, weight, width.* □ *acreage, footage, mileage, tonnage.*

meat *n* flesh. ▷ FOOD. □ *bacon, beef, chicken, game, gammon, ham, lamb, mutton, pork, poultry, turkey, veal, venison.* □ *brawn, breast, burger, brisket, chine, chops, chuck, cutlet, fillet, flank, hamburger, leg, loin, mince, offal, paté, potted meat, rib, rissole, rump, sausage, scrag, shoulder, silverside, sirloin, spare-rib, steak, topside, tripe.*

mechanic *n* engineer, technician.

mechanical *adj* **1** automated, automatic, machine-driven, technological. **2** cold, habitual, impersonal, inhuman, instinctive, lifeless, matter-of-fact, perfunctory, reflex, routine, soulless, unconscious, unemotional, unfeeling, unimaginative, uninspired, unthinking. *Opp* HUMAN.

mechanize *vb* automate, bring up to date, computerize, equip with machines, modernize.

medal *n* award, decoration, honour, medallion, prize, reward, trophy.

medallist *n* champion, victor, winner.

meddle *vb inf* be a busybody, butt in, interfere, *inf* poke your nose in, pry, snoop, tamper.

mediate *vb* act as go-between, act as mediator, arbitrate, intercede, liaise, negotiate.

mediator *n* arbiter, arbitrator, broker, conciliator, go-between, intercessor, intermediary, judge, liaison officer, middleman, moderator, negotiator, peacemaker, referee, umpire.

medicinal *adj* curative, healing, medical, remedial, restorative, therapeutic.

medicine *n* **1** healing, surgery, therapeutics, therapy, treatment. **2** cure, dose, drug, medicament, medication, nostrum, panacea, *old use* physic, prescription, remedy, treatment. □ *anaesthetic, antibiotic, antidote, antiseptic, aspirin, capsule, gargle, herbal remedy, iodine, inhaler, linctus, lotion, lozenge, narcotic, ointment, pain-killer, pastille, penicillin, pill, sedative, suppository, tablet, tonic, tranquillizer.*

mediocre *adj* amateurish, average, *inf* common-or-garden, commonplace, everyday, fair, indifferent, inferior, medium, middling, moderate, ordinary, passable, pedestrian, poorish, *inf* run-of-the-mill, second-rate, *inf* so-so, undistinguished, unexceptional, unexciting, uninspired, unremarkable, weakish. *Opp* OUTSTANDING.

meditate *vb* be lost in thought, brood, cerebrate, chew over, cogitate, consider, contemplate, deliberate, mull things over, muse, ponder, pray, reflect, ruminate, think, turn over.

meditation *n* cerebration, contemplation, deliberation, musing, prayer, reflection, rumination, thought, yoga.

meditative *adj* brooding, contemplative, pensive, prayerful, rapt, reflective, ruminative, thoughtful.

medium *adj* average, intermediate, mean, medial, median, mid, middle, middling, mid-sized, midway, moderate, normal, ordinary, standard, usual. • *n* **1** average, centre, compromise, mean, middle, midpoint, norm. **2** agency, approach, channel, form, means, method, mode, vehicle, way. **3** clairvoyant, seer, spiritualist. **the media, mass media** ▷ COMMUNICATION.

meek *adj* acquiescent, compliant, deferential, docile, forbearing, gentle, humble, long-suffering, lowly, mild, modest, non-militant, obedient, patient, peaceable, quiet, resigned, retiring, self-effacing, shy, soft, spineless, submissive, tame, timid, tractable, unambitious, unassuming, unprotesting, weak, *inf* wimpish. *Opp* AGGRESSIVE.

meet *vb* **1** *inf* bump into, chance upon, collide with, come across, confront, contact, encounter, face, happen on, have a meeting with, run across, run into, see. **2** be introduced to, make the acquaintance of. **3** come and fetch, greet, *inf* pick up, rendezvous with, welcome. **4** assemble, collect, come together, congregate, convene, forgather, gather, have a meeting, muster, rally, rendezvous. **5** *The ends don't meet.* abut, adjoin, come together, connect, converge, cross, intersect, join, link up, merge, touch, unite. **6** *meet a request.* acquiesce in, agree to, answer, comply with, deal with, fulfil, *inf* measure up to, observe, pay, satisfy, settle, take care of. **7** *meet difficulties.* encounter, endure, experience, go through, suffer, undergo.

meeting *n* **1** assembly, gathering, *inf* get-together, *inf* powwow. □ *audience, board, briefing, cabinet, caucus, committee, conclave, conference, congregation, congress, convention, council, discussion group, forum, prayer meeting, rally, seminar, service, synod.* **2** appointment, assignation, date, engagement, *inf* get-together, rendezvous, *old use* tryst. **3** *chance meeting.* confrontation, contact, encounter. **4** *meeting of lines, roads.* confluence (*of rivers*), convergence, crossing, crossroads, intersection, joining, junction, T-junction, union.

melancholy *adj* cheerless, dejected, depressed, depressing, despondent, disconsolate, dismal, dispirited, dispiriting, *inf* down, down-hearted, forlorn, gloomy, glum, joyless, lifeless, low, lugubrious, melancholic, miserable, moody, morose, mournful, sombre, sorrowful, unhappy, woebegone, woeful. ▷ SAD. *Opp* CHEERFUL. ● *n* ▷ SADNESS.

mellow *adj* **1** mature, rich, ripe, smooth, sweet. **2** *mellow mood.* agreeable, amiable, comforting, cordial, genial, gentle, happy, kindly, peaceful, pleasant, reassuring, soft, subdued, warm. *Opp* HARSH. ● *vb* age, develop, improve with age, mature, ripen, soften, sweeten.

melodious *adj* dulcet, *inf* easy on the ear, euphonious, harmonious, lyrical, mellifluous, melodic, sweet, tuneful.

melodramatic *adj* emotional, exaggerated, *inf* hammy, histrionic, overdone, overdrawn, *inf* over the top, sensationalized, sentimental, theatrical.

melody *n* air, song, strain, subject, theme, tune.

melt *vb* deliquesce, dissolve, liquefy, soften, thaw, unfreeze. **melt away** ▷ DISAPPEAR.

member *n* associate, colleague, fellow, life-member, paid-up member.

memorable *adj* catchy (*tune*), distinguished, extraordinary, haunting, historic, impressive, indelible, ineradicable, never-to-beforgotten, notable, outstanding, remarkable, striking, unforgettable.

memorial *n* cairn, cenotaph, gravestone, headstone, monument, plaque, reminder, statue, tablet, tomb.

memorize *vb* commit to memory, *inf* get off by heart, learn, learn by rote, learn parrot-fashion, remember, retain.

memory *n* **1** ability to remember, recall, retention. **2** impression, recollection, reminder, reminiscence, souvenir. **3** *memory of the dead.* fame, honour, name, remembrance, reputation, respect.

menace *n* danger, peril, threat, warning. ● *vb* alarm, bully, cow, intimidate, terrify, terrorize, threaten. ▷ FRIGHTEN.

mend *vb* **1** fix, patch up, put right, rectify, remedy, renew, renovate, repair, restore. □ *beat out, darn, patch, replace parts, sew up, solder, stitch up, touch up, weld.* **2** *mend your ways.* ameliorate, amend, correct, cure, improve, make better, reform, revise. **3** *mend after illness.* convalesce, get better, heal, improve, recover, recuperate.

menial *adj* base, boring, common, degrading, demeaning, humble, inferior, insignificant, low, lowly, servile, slavish, subservient, unskilled, unworthy. • *n inf* dogsbody, lackey, minion, slave, underling. ▷ SERVANT.

mental *adj* **1** abstract, cerebral, cognitive, conceptual, intellectual, rational, theoretical. **2** *mental illness.* emotional, psychological, subjective, temperamental. ▷ MAD.

mentality *n* attitude, bent, character, disposition, frame of mind, inclination, *inf* make-up, outlook, personality, predisposition, propensity, psychology, set, temperament, way of thinking.

mention *vb* acknowledge, allude to, animadvert on, bring up, broach, cite, comment on, disclose, draw attention to, enumerate, hint at, *inf* let drop, let out, make known, make mention, name, note, observe, pay tribute to, point out, quote, recognize, refer to, remark, report, reveal, say, speak about, touch on, write about.

mercenary *adj* acquisitive, avaricious, covetous, grasping, greedy, *inf* money-mad, venal. • *n* ▷ FIGHTER.

merchandise *n* commodities, goods, items for sale, produce, products, stock. • *vb* ▷ ADVERTISE.

merchant *n* broker, dealer, distributor, retailer, salesman, seller, shopkeeper, stockist, supplier, trader, tradesman, tradeswoman, vendor, wholesaler.

merciful *adj* beneficent, benevolent, charitable, clement, compassionate, forbearing, forgiving, generous, gracious, humane, humanitarian, indulgent, kind, kind-hearted, kindly, lenient, liberal, magnanimous, mild, pitying, *inf* soft, soft-hearted, sympathetic, tender-hearted, tolerant. *Opp* MERCILESS.

merciless *adj* barbaric, barbarous, brutal, callous, cold, cruel, cut-throat, hard, hard-hearted, harsh, heartless, indifferent, inexorable, inflexible, inhuman, inhumane, intolerant, malevolent, pitiless, relentless, remorseless, rigorous, ruthless, savage, severe, stern, stony-hearted, strict, tyrannical, unbending, unfeeling, unforgiving, unkind, unmerciful, unrelenting, unremitting, vicious. *Opp* MERCIFUL.

mercy *n* beneficence, benignity, charity, clemency, compassion, feeling, forbearance, forgiveness, generosity, grace, humaneness, humanity, indulgence, kind-heartedness, kindness, leniency, love, pity, quarter, sympathy, understanding.

merge *vb* **1** amalgamate, blend, coalesce, combine, come together, confederate, consolidate, fuse, integrate, join together, link up, mingle, mix, pool, put together, unite. **2** *motorways merge.* converge, join, meet. *Opp* SEPARATE.

merit *n* credit, distinction, excellence, good, goodness, importance, quality, strength, talent, value, virtue, worth, worthiness. • *vb* be entitled to, be worthy of, deserve, earn, have a right to, incur, justify, rate, warrant.

meritorious *adj* admirable, commendable, estimable, exemplary, honourable, laudable, praiseworthy, worthy.

merriment *n* amusement, cheerfulness, conviviality, exuberance, gaiety, glee, good cheer, high spirits, hilarity, jocularity, joking, jollity, joviality, *inf* larking about, laughter, levity, light-heartedness, liveliness, mirth, vivacity. ▷ MERRYMAKING.

merry *adj* bright, *inf* bubbly, carefree, cheerful, cheery, *inf* chirpy, convivial, festive, fun-loving, gay, glad, hilarious, jocular, jolly, jovial, joyful, joyous, light-hearted, lively, mirthful, rollicking, spirited, vivacious. ▷ HAPPY. *Opp* SERIOUS.

merrymaking *n* carousing, celebration, conviviality, festivity, frolic, fun, *inf* fun and games, *inf* jollification, *inf* junketing, merriment, revelry, roistering, sociability, *old use* wassailing. ▷ PARTY.

mesh *n* grid, lace, lacework, lattice, lattice-work, net, netting, network, reticulation, screen, sieve, tangle, tracery, trellis, web, webbing.

mess *n* **1** chaos, clutter, confusion, dirt, disarray, disorder, hotchpotch, jumble, litter, *inf* mishmash, muddle, *inf* shambles, tangle, untidiness. ▷ CONFUSION, DIRT. **2** *made a mess of it.* *inf* botch, failure, *inf* hash, *inf* mix-up. **3** *got into a mess.* difficulty, dilemma, *inf* fix, *inf* jam, *inf* pickle, plight, predicament, problem, trouble. • *vb* **mess about** amuse yourself, loaf, loiter, lounge about, *inf* monkey about, *inf* muck about, *inf* play about. **make a mess of** ▷ BUNGLE, MUDDLE. **mess up** ▷ MUDDLE. **mess up a job** ▷ BUNGLE.

message *n* announcement, bulletin, cable, communication, communiqué, dispatch, information, intelligence, letter, memo, memorandum, missive, news, note, notice, report, statement, *old use* tidings.

messenger *n* bearer, carrier, courier, dispatch-rider, emissary, envoy, errand-boy, errand-girl, go-between, harbinger, herald, intermediary, legate, Mercury, messenger-boy, messenger-girl, nuncio, postman, runner.

messy *adj* blowzy, careless, chaotic, cluttered, dirty, dishevelled, disorderly, filthy, grubby, mucky, muddled, *inf* shambolic, slapdash, sloppy, slovenly, unkempt, untidy. *Opp* NEAT.

metallic *adj* **1** gleaming, lustrous, shiny. **2** clanking, clinking, ringing.

metaphorical *adj* allegorical, figurative, non-literal, symbolic. *Opp* LITERAL.

method *n* **1** approach, fashion, *inf* knack, manner, means, methodology, mode, *Lat* modus operandi, plan, procedure, process, programme, recipe, scheme, style, technique, trick, way. **2** arrangement, design, discipline, neatness, order, orderliness, organization, pattern, routine, structure, system.

methodical *adj* businesslike, careful, deliberate, disciplined, logical, meticulous, neat, ordered, orderly, organized, painstaking, precise, rational, regular, routine, structured, systematic, tidy. *Opp* DISORGANIZED.

meticulous *adj* accurate, exact, exacting, fastidious, *inf* finicky, painstaking, particular, perfectionist, precise, punctilious, scrupulous, thorough. *Opp* CARELESS.

microbe *n* bacillus, bacterium, *inf* bug, germ, micro-organism, virus.

middle *adj* central, centre, halfway, inner, inside, intermediate, intervening, mean, medial, median, mid, middle-of-the-road, midway, neutral. • *n* bull's eye, centre, core, crown (*of road*), focus, half-way point, heart, hub, inside, middle position, midpoint, midst, nucleus.

middling *adj* average, fair, *inf* fair to middling, indifferent, mediocre, moderate, modest, *inf* nothing to write home about, ordinary, passable, run-of-the-mill, *inf* so-so, unremarkable. *Opp* OUTSTANDING.

might *n* capability, capacity, energy, force, muscle, potency, power, strength, superiority, vigour.

mighty *adj* brawny, dominant, doughty, energetic, enormous, forceful, great, hefty, muscular, potent, powerful, robust, *inf* strapping, strong, sturdy, vigorous, weighty. ▷ BIG. *Opp* WEAK.

migrate *vb* emigrate, go, immigrate, move, relocate, resettle, settle, travel.

mild *adj* **1** affable, amiable, conciliatory, docile, easygoing, equable, forbearing, forgiving, gentle, good-tempered, harmless, indulgent, inoffensive, kind, kindly, lenient, meek, merciful, modest, non-violent, pacific, peaceable, placid, quiet, *inf* soft, soft-hearted, submissive, sympathetic, tractable, unassuming, understanding, yielding. **2** *mild weather.* balmy, calm, clement, fair, peaceful, pleasant, serene, temperate, warm. **3** *a mild illness.* insignificant, minor, modest, slight, trivial, unimportant. **4** *mild flavour.* bland, delicate, faint, mellow, soothing, subtle. *Opp* SEVERE, STRONG.

mildness *n* affability, amiability, clemency, docility, forbearance, gentleness, kindness, leniency, moderation, placidity, softness, sympathy, tenderness. *Opp* ASPERITY.

militant *adj* active, aggressive, assertive, attacking, combative, fierce, hostile, positive, pugnacious. *Opp* PASSIVE. • *n* activist, extremist, *inf* hawk, partisan.

militaristic *adj* bellicose, belligerent, combative, fond of fighting, hawkish, hostile, pugnacious, warlike. *Opp* PEACEABLE.

military *adj* armed, belligerent, combatant, enlisted, fighting, martial, uniformed, warlike. *Opp* CIVIL.

militate *vb* **militate against** cancel out, counter, counteract, countervail, discourage, hinder, oppose, prevent, resist.

milk *vb* bleed, drain, exploit, extract, tap, wring.

milky *adj* chalky, cloudy, misty, opaque, whitish. *Opp* CLEAR.

mill *n* **1** factory, foundry, plant, shop, works, workshop. **2** crusher, grinder, quern, watermill, windmill. • *vb* crush, granulate, grate, grind, pound, powder, pulverize. **mill about** move aimlessly, seethe, swarm, throng, wander.

mimic *n* caricaturist, imitator, impersonator, impressionist. • *vb* ape, caricature, copy, do impressions of, echo, imitate, impersonate, lampoon, look like, *inf* make fun of, mirror, mock, parody, parrot, pretend to be, reproduce, ridicule, satirize, simulate, sound like, *inf* take off.

mind *n* **1** astuteness, brain, brainpower, brains, cleverness, *inf* grey matter, head, insight, intellect, intelligence, judgement, memory, mental power, perception, psyche, rationality, reason, reasoning, remembrance, sagacity, sapience, sense, shrewdness, thinking, understanding, wisdom, wit, wits. **2** attitude, belief, bias, disposition, humour, inclination, intention, opinion, outlook, persuasion, plan, point of view, position, view, viewpoint, way of thinking, wishes. • *vb* **1** attend to, care for, guard, keep an eye on, look after, take care of, take charge of, watch. **2** *mind the warning.* be careful about, beware of, heed, listen to, look out for, mark, note, obey, pay attention to, remember, take notice of, watch out for. **3** *won't mind if he's late.* be annoyed, be bothered, be offended, be resentful, bother, care, complain, disapprove, grumble, object, take offence, worry. **be in two minds** ▷ HESITATE. **make up your mind** ▷ DECIDE. **out of your mind** ▷ MAD.

mindful *adj* alert, attentive, aware, conscious, heedful, *inf* on the lookout, vigilant, watchful. ▷ CAREFUL. *Opp* CARELESS.

mindless *adj* brainless, fatuous, idiotic, obtuse, senseless, thick, thoughtless, unintelligent, unthinking, witless. ▷ STUPID. *Opp* INTELLIGENT.

mine *n* **1** coalfield, colliery, excavation, opencast mine, pit, quarry, shaft, tunnel, working. **2** *mine of information.* fund, repository, source, store, storehouse, supply, treasury, vein, wealth. • *vb* dig, excavate, extract, quarry, remove, scoop out, unearth.

mineral *n* metal, ore, rock.

mingle *vb* amalgamate, associate, blend, circulate, combine, commingle, fraternize, get together, *inf* hobnob, intermingle, intermix, join, merge, mix, move about, *inf* rub shoulders, socialize, unite.

miniature *adj* baby, diminutive, dwarf, pocket, pygmy, reduced, scaled-down, small-scale, tiny, toy. ▷ SMALL.

minimal *adj* least, minimum, negligible, nominal, slightest, smallest, token.

minimize *vb* **1** cut down, decrease, diminish, lessen, pare, prune, reduce. **2** *minimize problems*. belittle, decry, depreciate, devalue, gloss over, make light of, play down, underestimate, undervalue. *Opp* MAXIMIZE.

minimum *adj* bottom, least, littlest, lowest, minimal, minutest, nominal, *inf* rock-bottom, slightest, smallest. • *n* least, lowest, minimum amount, minimum quantity, nadir. *Opp* MAXIMUM.

minister *n* ▷ CLERGYMAN, OFFICIAL. • *vb* **minister to** aid, assist, attend to, care for, help, look after, nurse, see to, support, wait on.

minor *adj* inconsequential, inferior, insignificant, lesser, little, negligible, petty, secondary, smaller, subordinate, subsidiary, trivial, unimportant. ▷ SMALL. *Opp* MAJOR. • *n* ▷ ADOLESCENT, CHILD.

minstrel *n* balladeer, bard, entertainer, jongleur, musician, singer, troubadour.

mint *adj* brand-new, first-class, fresh, immaculate, new, perfect, unblemished, unmarked, unused. • *n* fortune, heap, *inf* packet, pile, stack, unlimited supply, vast amount. • *vb* cast, coin, forge, make, manufacture, produce, stamp out, strike.

minute *adj* diminutive, dwarf, infinitesimal, insignificant, lilliputian, microscopic, *inf* mini, miniature, minuscule, *inf* pint-sized, pocket, pygmy, tiny. ▷ SMALL.

minutes *plur n* log, notes, proceedings, record, résumé, summary, transactions.

miracle *n* marvel, miraculous event, mystery, wonder.

miraculous *adj* abnormal, extraordinary, incredible, inexplicable, magic, magical, mysterious, paranormal, phenomenal, preternatural, remarkable, supernatural, unaccountable, unbelievable, unexplainable. ▷ MARVELLOUS.

mirage *n* delusion, hallucination, illusion, vision.

mire *n* bog, fen, marsh, morass, mud, ooze, quagmire, quicksand, slime, *old use* slough, swamp. ▷ DIRT.

mirror *n* glass, looking-glass, reflector, speculum. • *vb* echo, reflect, repeat, send back.

misadventure *n* accident, calamity, catastrophe, disaster, ill fortune, mischance, misfortune, mishap.

misanthropic *adj* anti-social, cynical, mean, nasty, surly, unfriendly, unpleasant, unsociable. *Opp* PHILANTHROPIC.

misappropriate *vb* defalcate, embezzle, expropriate, peculate. ▷ STEAL.

misbehave *vb* be a nuisance, be bad, behave badly, be mischievous, *inf* blot your copybook, *inf* carry on, commit an offence, default, disobey, do wrong, err, fool about, make mischief, *inf* mess about, *inf* muck about, offend, *inf* play about, play up, *inf* raise Cain, sin, transgress.

misbehaviour *n* badness, delinquency, disobedience, disorderliness, horseplay, indiscipline, insubordination, mischief, mischief-making, misconduct, misdemeanour, naughtiness, rowdyism, rudeness, sin, vandalism, wrongdoing.

miscalculate *vb* *inf* boob, err, *inf* get it wrong, go wrong, make a mistake, miscount, misjudge, misread, overestimate, overrate, overvalue, *inf* slip up, underestimate, underrate.

miscarriage *n* *miscarriage of justice*. breakdown, collapse, defeat, error, failure, perversion.

miscarry *vb* **1** abort, *inf* lose a baby, suffer a miscarriage. **2** break down, *inf* come to grief, come to nothing, fail, fall through, founder, go wrong, misfire. *Opp* SUCCEED.

miscellaneous *adj* assorted, different, *old use* divers, diverse, heterogeneous, manifold, mixed, motley, multifarious, sundry, varied, various.

miscellany *n* assortment, diversity, gallimaufry, hotchpotch, jumble, medley, mélange, *inf* mixed bag, mixture, pot-pourri, *inf* ragbag, variety.

mischief *n* **1** devilment, devilry, escapade, impishness, misbehaviour, misconduct, *inf* monkey business, naughtiness, playfulness, prank, rascality, roguishness, scrape, *inf* shenanigans, trouble. **2** damage, difficulty, evil, harm, hurt, injury, misfortune, trouble.

mischievous *adj* annoying, badly behaved, boisterous, disobedient, elvish, fractious, frolicsome, full of mischief, impish, lively, naughty, playful, *inf* puckish, rascally, roguish, sportive, uncontrollable, *inf* up to no good. ▷ WICKED. *Opp* WELL-BEHAVED.

miser *n* hoarder, miserly person, niggard, *inf* Scrooge, *inf* skinflint. *Opp* SPENDTHRIFT.

miserable *adj* **1** broken-hearted, crestfallen, *inf* cut up, dejected, depressed, desolate, despairing, despondent, disappointed, disconsolate, dismayed, dispirited, distressed, doleful, *inf* down, downcast, downhearted, forlorn, friendless, gloomy, glum, grief-stricken, heartbroken, hopeless, in low spirits, *inf* in the doldrums, *inf* in the dumps, joyless, lachrymose, languishing, lonely, low, melancholy, moping, mournful, sad, sorrowful, suicidal, tearful, uneasy, unfortunate, unhappy, unlucky, woebegone, woeful, wretched. **2** churlish, cross, disagreeable, discontented, *inf* grumpy, ill-natured, mean, miserly, morose, pessimistic, sour, sulky, sullen, surly, taciturn, unfriendly, unhelpful, unsociable. **3** *miserable living conditions.* abject, awful, bad, deplorable, destitute, disgraceful, distressing, heart-breaking, hopeless, impoverished, inadequate, inhuman, lamentable, pathetic, pitiable, pitiful, poor, shameful, sordid, soul-destroying, squalid, vile, uncivilized, uncomfortable, vile, worthless, wretched. **4** *miserable weather.* cheerless, damp, depressing, dismal, dreary, grey, inclement, sunless, unpleasant, wet. *Opp* HAPPY, PLEASANT.

miserly *adj* avaricious, *inf* cheese-paring, *inf* close, *inf* close-fisted, covetous, economical, grasping, greedy, mean, mercenary, mingy, niggardly, parsimonious, penny-pinching, penurious, sparing, stingy, *inf* tight, *inf* tight-fisted. *Opp* GENEROUS.

misery *n* **1** angst, anguish, anxiety, bitterness, dejection, depression, despair, desperation, despondency, discomfort, distress, dolour, gloom, grief, heartache, heartbreak, *inf* hell, hopelessness, melancholy, sadness, sorrow, suffering, unhappiness, woe, wretchedness. *Opp* HAPPINESS. **2** adversity, affliction, deprivation, destitution, hardship, indigence, misfortune, need, oppression, penury, poverty, privation, squalor, suffering, *inf* trials and tribulations, tribulation, trouble, want, wretchedness.

misfire *vb* abort, fail, fall through, *inf* flop, founder, go wrong, miscarry. *Opp* SUCCEED.

misfortune *n* accident, adversity, affliction, bad luck, blow, calamity, catastrophe, contretemps, curse, disappointment, disaster, evil, hard luck, hardship, ill-luck, misadventure, mischance, mishap, reverse, setback, tragedy, trouble, vicissitude.

misguided *adj* erroneous, foolish, ill-advised, ill-judged, inappropriate, incorrect, inexact, misinformed, misjudged, misled, mistaken, unfounded, unjust, unsound, unwise. ▷ WRONG.

misjudge *vb* get wrong, guess wrongly, *inf* jump to the wrong conclusion, make a mistake, misinterpret, overestimate, overvalue, underestimate, undervalue. ▷ MISCALCULATE.

mislay *vb* lose, mislocate, misplace, put in the wrong place.

mislead *vb* bluff, confuse, delude, fool, give misleading information to, give a wrong impression to, lead astray, *inf* lead up the garden path, lie to, misdirect, misguide, misinform, outwit, *inf* take for a ride, take in, *inf* throw off the scent, trick. ▷ DECEIVE. **misleading** ▷ DECEPTIVE, PUZZLING.

miss *vb* **1** absent yourself from, avoid, be absent from, be too late for, dodge, escape, evade, fail to keep, forget, forgo, let go, lose, play truant from, *inf* skip, *inf* skive off. **2** *miss a target.* be wide of, fail to hit, fall short of. **3** *miss absent friends.* feel nostalgia for, grieve for, lament, long for, need, pine for, want, yearn for. **miss out** ▷ OMIT.

misshapen *adj* awry, bent, contorted, corkscrew, crippled, crooked, crumpled, deformed, disfigured, distorted, gnarled, grotesque, knotted, malformed, monstrous, screwed up, tangled, twisted, twisty, ugly, warped. *Opp* PERFECT.

missile *n* projectile. □ *arrow, ballistic missile, bomb, boomerang, brickbat, bullet, dart, grenade, guided missile, rocket, shell, shot, torpedo.* ▷ WEAPON.

missing *adj* absent, disappeared, lost, mislaid, *inf* skiving, straying, truant, unaccounted-for. *Opp* PRESENT.

mission *n* **1** delegation, deputation, expedition, exploration, journey, sortie, task-force, voyage. **2** *mission in life.* aim, assignment, calling, commitment, duty, function, goal, job, life's work, métier, objective, occupation, profession, purpose, quest, undertaking, vocation. **3** *evangelical mission.* campaign, crusade, holy war.

missionary *n* campaigner, crusader, evangelist, minister, preacher, proselytizer.

mist *n* **1** cloud, drizzle, fog, haze, smog, vapour. **2** condensation, film, steam.

mistake *n inf* bloomer, blunder, *inf* boob, *inf* botch, *inf* clanger, erratum, error, false step, fault, *Fr* faux pas, gaffe, *inf* howler, inaccuracy, indiscretion, lapse, misapprehension, miscalculation, misconception, misjudgement, misprint, misspelling, misunderstanding, omission, oversight, slip, slip-up, solecism, wrong move. • *vb* confuse, *inf* get the wrong end of the stick, get wrong, misconstrue, misinterpret, misjudge, misread, misunderstand, mix up, *inf* take the wrong way.

mistaken *adj* erroneous, distorted, false, faulty, ill-judged, inaccurate, inappropriate, incorrect, inexact, misguided, misinformed, unfounded, unjust, unsound. ▷ WRONG. *Opp* CORRECT.

mistimed *adj* badly timed, early, inconvenient, inopportune, late, unseasonable, untimely. *Opp* OPPORTUNE.

mistreat *vb* abuse, batter, damage, harm, hurt, ill-treat, ill-use, injure, *inf* knock about, maltreat, manhandle, misuse, molest, treat roughly.

mistress *n* [*mostly old use*] **1** chief, head, keeper, owner, person in charge, proprietor. **2** ▷ TEACHER. **3** ▷ LOVER.

mistrust *n* apprehension, *inf* chariness, distrust, doubt, misgiving, reservation, scepticism, suspicion, uncertainty, unsureness, wariness. • *vb* be sceptical about, be suspicious of, be wary of, disbelieve, distrust, doubt, fear, have doubts about, have misgivings about, have reservations about, question, suspect. *Opp* TRUST.

misty *adj* bleary, blurred, blurry, clouded, cloudy, dim, faint, foggy, fuzzy, hazy, indistinct, murky, obscure, opaque, shadowy, smoky, steamy, unclear, vague. *Opp* CLEAR.

misunderstand *vb inf* get the wrong end of the stick, get wrong, misapprehend, miscalculate, misconceive, misconstrue, mishear, misinterpret, misjudge, misread, miss the point of, mistake, mistranslate. *Opp* UNDERSTAND.

misunderstanding *n* **1** error, failure of understanding, false impression, misapprehension, miscalculation, misconception, misconstruction, misinterpretation, misjudgement, misreading, mistake, *inf* mix up, wrong idea. **2** argument, *inf* contretemps, controversy, difference of opinion, disagreement, discord, dispute. ▷ QUARREL.

misuse *n* abuse, careless use, corruption, ill-treatment, ill-use, maltreatment, misapplication, misappropriation, mishandling, mistreatment, perversion. • *vb* **1** damage, harm, mishandle, treat carelessly. **2** *misuse an animal.* abuse, batter, damage, harm, hurt, ill-treat, ill-use, injure, *inf* knock about, maltreat, manhandle, mistreat, molest, treat roughly. **3** *misuse funds.* fritter away, misappropriate, squander, use wrongly, waste.

mitigate *vb* abate, allay, alleviate, decrease, ease, extenuate, lessen, lighten, make milder, moderate, palliate, qualify, reduce, relieve, soften, *inf* take the edge off, temper, tone down. *Opp* AGGRAVATE.

mix *n* amalgam, assortment, blend, combination, compound, range, variety. • *vb* **1** alloy, amalgamate, blend, coalesce, combine, commingle, compound, confuse, diffuse, emulsify, fuse, homogenize, integrate, intermingle, join, jumble up, make a mixture, meld, merge, mingle, mix up, muddle, put together, shuffle, stir together, unite. *Opp* SEPARATE. **2** *mix with people.* ▷ SOCIALIZE.

mixed *adj* **1** assorted, different, diverse, heterogeneous, miscellaneous, varied, various. **2** *mixed with other things.* adulterated, alloyed, diluted, impure. **3** *mixed ingredients.* amalgamated, combined, composite, hybrid, integrated, joint, mongrel, united. **4** *mixed feelings.* ambiguous, ambivalent, confused, equivocal, muddled, uncertain.

mixture *n* **1** alloy, amalgam, amalgamation, association, assortment, blend, collection, combination, composite, compound, concoction, conglomeration, emulsion, farrago, fusion, gallimaufry, *inf* hotchpotch, intermingling, jumble, medley, mélange, merger, mess, mingling, miscellany, *inf* mishmash, mix, *inf* motley collection, pastiche, potpourri, selection, suspension, synthesis, variety. **2** cross-breed, half-caste, hybrid, mongrel.

moan *n* complaint, grievance, lament, lamentation. • *vb* **1** complain, grieve, *inf* grouse, grumble, lament. **2** cry, groan, keen, sigh, ululate, wail, weep, whimper, whine. ▷ SOUND.

mob *n inf* bunch, crowd, gang, herd, horde, host, multitude, pack, press, rabble, riot, *inf* shower, swarm, throng. ▷ GROUP. • *vb* besiege, crowd round, hem in, jostle, surround, swarm round, throng round.

mobile *adj* **1** itinerant, motorized, movable, portable, transportable, travelling, unfixed. **2** able to move, active, agile, independent, moving, nimble, *inf* on the go, *inf* up and about. **3** *mobile features.* animated, changeable, changing, expressive, flexible, fluid, plastic, shifting. *Opp* IMMOVABLE.

mobilize *vb* activate, assemble, call up, conscript, enlist, enrol, gather, get together, levy, marshal, muster, organize, rally, stir up, summon.

mock *adj* artificial, counterfeit, ersatz, fake, false, imitation, make-believe, man-made, *inf* pretend, sham, simulated, substitute. • *vb* decry, deride, disparage, flout, gibe at, insult, jeer at, lampoon, laugh at, make fun of, make sport of, parody, poke fun at, ridicule, satirize, scoff at, scorn, *inf* send up, sneer at, tantalize, taunt, tease, travesty. ▷ MIMIC.

mockery *n* derision, insults, jeering, laughter, ridicule, scorn. □ *burlesque,* *caricature*, *lampoon*, *parody*, *sarcasm*, *satire*, inf *send-up*, inf *spoof*, inf *take-off*, *travesty*.

mocking *adj* contemptuous, derisive, disparaging, disrespectful, insulting, irreverent, jeering, rude, sarcastic, satirical, scornful, taunting, teasing, uncomplimentary, unkind. *Opp* RESPECTFUL.

mode *n* **1** approach, configuration, manner, medium, method, *Lat* modus operandi, procedure, set-up, system, technique, way. **2** ▷ FASHION.

model *adj* **1** imitation, miniature, scaled-down, toy. **2** *model pupil.* exemplary, ideal, perfect, unequalled. ● *n* **1** archetype, copy, dummy, effigy, facsimile, image, imitation, likeness, miniature, *inf* mock-up, paradigm, prototype, replica, representation, scale model, toy. **2** *model of excellence.* byword, epitome, example, exemplar, ideal, nonpareil, paragon, pattern, standard, yardstick. **3** *artist's model.* poser, sitter, subject. **4** *latest model.* brand, design, kind, mark, type, version. **5** *fashion model.* mannequin. ● *vb* carve, fashion, form, make, mould, sculpt, shape. **model yourself on** ▷ IMITATE.

moderate *adj* **1** average, balanced, calm, cautious, commonsensical, cool, deliberate, fair, judicious, medium, middle, *inf* middle-of-the-road, middling, modest, normal, ordinary, rational, reasonable, respectable, sensible, sober, steady, temperate, unexceptional, usual. *Opp* EXTREME. **2** *moderate winds.* gentle, light, mild. ● *vb* **1** abate, become less extreme, decline, decrease, die down, ease off, subside. **2** blunt, calm, check, curb, dull, ease, keep down, lessen, make less extreme, mitigate, modify, modulate, mollify, reduce, regulate, restrain, slacken, subdue, temper, tone down.

moderately *adv* comparatively, fairly, passably, *inf* pretty, quite, rather, reasonably, somewhat, to some extent.

moderation *n* balance, caution, common sense, fairness, reasonableness, restraint, reticence, sobriety, temperance.

modern *adj* advanced, avant-garde, contemporary, current, fashionable, forward-looking, fresh, futuristic, in vogue, latest, modish, new, newfangled, novel, present, present-day, progressive, recent, stylish, *inf* trendy, up-to-date, up-to-the-minute, *inf* with it. *Opp* OLD.

modernize *vb* bring up-to-date, *inf* do up, improve, make modern, rebuild, redesign, redo, refurbish, regenerate, rejuvenate, renovate, revamp, update.

modest *adj* **1** diffident, humble, inconspicuous, lowly, meek, plain, quiet, reserved, restrained, reticent, retiring, self-effacing, simple, unassuming, unobtrusive, unostentatious, unpretentious. *Opp* CONCEITED. **2** bashful, chaste, coy, decent, demure, discreet, proper, seemly, self-conscious, shamefaced, shy, simple. **3** *a modest income.* limited, medium, middling, moderate, normal, ordinary, reasonable, unexceptional. *Opp* EXCESSIVE.

modesty *n* **1** humbleness, humility, lowliness, meekness, reserve, restraint, reticence, self-effacement, simplicity. *Opp* OSTENTATION. **2** *modesty about undressing.* bashfulness, coyness, decency, demureness, discretion, propriety, seemliness, self-consciousness, shame, shyness.

modify *vb* adapt, adjust, alter, amend, change, convert, improve, reconstruct, redesign, remake, remodel, reorganize, revise, reword, rework, transform, vary. ▷ MODERATE.

modulate *vb* adjust, balance, change key, change the tone, lower the tone, moderate, regulate, soften, tone down.

moist *adj* affected by moisture, clammy, damp, dank, dewy, humid, misty, *inf* muggy, rainy, *inf* runny, steamy, watery, wettish. ▷ WET. *Opp* DRY.

moisten *vb* damp, dampen, humidify, make moist, moisturize, soak, spray, wet. *Opp* DRY.

moisture *n* condensation, damp, dampness, dankness, dew, humidity, liquid, precipitation, spray, steam, vapour, water, wet, wetness.

molest *vb* abuse, accost, annoy, assault, attack, badger, bother, disturb, harass, harry, hassle, hector, ill-treat, interfere with, irk, irritate, manhandle, mistreat, *inf* needle, persecute, pester, plague, set on, tease, torment, vex, worry.

molten *adj* fluid, liquefied, liquid, melted, soft.

moment *n* **1** flash, instant, *inf* jiffy, minute, second, split second, *inf* tick, *inf* trice, *inf* twinkling of an eye, *inf* two shakes. **2** *a historic moment.* hour, juncture, occasion, opportunity, point in time, stage, time.

momentary *adj* brief, ephemeral, evanescent, fleeting, fugitive, hasty, passing, quick, short, short-lived, temporary, transient, transitory. *Opp* PERMANENT.

momentous *adj* consequential, critical, crucial, decisive, epoch-making, fateful, grave, historic, important, portentous, serious, significant, weighty. *Opp* UNIMPORTANT.

monarch *n* crowned head, emperor, empress, king, potentate, queen, ruler, tsar.

monarchy *n* domain, empire, kingdom, realm.

money *n* affluence, arrears, assets, bank-notes, *inf* bread, capital, cash, change, cheque, coin, copper, credit card, credit transfer, currency, damages, debt, dividend, *inf* dough, dowry, earnings, endowment, estate, expenditure, finance, fortune, fund, grant, income, interest, investment, legal tender, loan, *inf* lolly, *old use* lucre, mortgage, *inf* nest-egg, notes, outgoings, patrimony, pay, penny, pension, pocket-money, proceeds, profit, *inf* the ready, remittance, resources, revenue, riches, salary, savings, silver, sterling, takings, tax, traveller's cheque, wage, wealth, *inf* the wherewithal, winnings.

mongrel *n* cross-breed, cur, half-breed, hybrid, mixed breed.

monitor *n* **1** detector, guardian, prefect, supervisor, watchdog. **2** *TV monitor.* screen, set, television, TV, VDU, visual display unit. • *vb* audit, check, examine, *inf* keep an eye on, oversee, record, supervise, trace, track, watch.

monk *n* brother, friar, hermit.

monkey *n* ape, primate, simian. □ *baboon, chimpanzee, gibbon, gorilla, marmoset, orang-utan.*

monopolize *vb* control, *inf* corner the market in, dominate, have a monopoly of, *inf* hog, keep for yourself, own, shut others out of, take over. *Opp* SHARE.

monotonous *adj* boring, colourless, dreary, dull, featureless, flat, level, repetitious, repetitive, soporific, tedious, tiresome, tiring, toneless, unchanging, uneventful, unexciting, uniform, uninteresting, unvarying, wearisome. *Opp* INTERESTING.

monster *n* abortion, beast, bogeyman, brute, demon, devil, fiend, freak, giant, horror, monstrosity, monstrous creature, mutant, ogre, troll.

monstrous *adj* **1** colossal, elephantine, enormous, gargantuan, giant, gigantic, great, huge, hulking, immense, *inf* jumbo, mammoth, mighty, prodigious, titanic, towering, tremendous, vast. ▷ BIG. **2** *a monstrous crime.* abhorrent, atrocious, awful, beastly, brutal, cruel, devilish, disgusting, dreadful, evil, ghoulish, grisly, gross, gruesome, heinous, hideous, *inf* horrendous, horrible, horrific, horrifying, inhuman, nightmarish, obscene, outrageous, repulsive, shocking, terrible, ugly, villainous, wicked. ▷ EVIL.

monument *n* cairn, cenotaph, cross, gravestone, headstone, mausoleum, memorial, obelisk, pillar, prehistoric remains, relic, reminder, shrine, tomb, tombstone.

monumental *adj* **1** aweinspiring, awesome, classic, enduring, epoch-making, grand, historic, impressive, large-scale, lasting, major, memorable, unforgettable. ▷ BIG. **2** *a monumental plaque*. commemorative, memorial.

mood *n* **1** attitude, disposition, frame of mind, humour, inclination, nature, spirit, state of mind, temper, vein. **2** atmosphere, feeling, tone. ▷ ANGRY, HAPPY, SAD, etc. **in the mood** ▷ READY.

moody *adj* abrupt, bad-tempered, cantankerous, capricious, changeable, crabby, cross, crotchety, depressed, depressive, disgruntled, erratic, fickle, gloomy, grumpy, *inf* huffy, ill-humoured, inconstant, irritable, melancholy, mercurial, miserable, morose, peevish, petulant, *inf* short, short-tempered, snappy, sulky, sullen, temperamental, testy, *inf* touchy, unpredictable, unreliable, unstable, volatile. ▷ SAD.

moor *n* fell, heath, moorland, wasteland. • *vb* anchor, berth, dock, make fast, secure, tie up. ▷ FASTEN.

mope *vb* be sad, brood, despair, grieve, languish, *inf* moon, pine, sulk.

moral *adj* **1** blameless, chaste, decent, ethical, good, highminded, honest, honourable, incorruptible, innocent, irreproachable, just, law-abiding, noble, principled, proper, pure, respectable, responsible, right, righteous, sinless, trustworthy, truthful, upright, upstanding, virtuous. **2** *a moral tale*. allegorical, cautionary, didactic, moralistic, moralizing. *Opp* IMMORAL. • *n* lesson, maxim, meaning, message, point, precept, principle, teaching. **morals** ▷ MORALITY. **moral tale** allegory, cautionary tale, fable, parable.

morale *n* attitude, cheerfulness, confidence, *Fr* esprit de corps, *inf* heart, mood, self-confidence, self-esteem, spirit, state of mind.

morality *n* behaviour, conduct, decency, ethics, ethos, fairness, goodness, honesty, ideals, integrity, justice, morals, principles, propriety, rectitude, righteousness, rightness, scruples, standards, uprightness, virtue.

moralize *vb* lecture, philosophize, pontificate, preach, sermonize.

morbid *adj* black (*humour*), brooding, dejected, depressed, ghoulish, gloomy, grim, grotesque, gruesome, lugubrious, macabre, melancholy, monstrous, morose, pathological, pessimistic, *inf* sick, sombre, unhappy, unhealthy, unpleasant, unwholesome. *Opp* CHEERFUL.

more *adj* added, additional, extra, further, increased, longer, new, other, renewed, supplementary. *Opp* LESS.

moreover *adv* also, as well, besides, further, furthermore, in addition, *old use* to boot, too.

morose *adj* bad-tempered, churlish, depressed, gloomy, glum, grim, humourless, ill-natured, melancholy, moody, mournful, pessimistic, saturnine, sour, sulky, sullen, surly, taciturn, unhappy, unsociable. ▷ SAD. *Opp* CHEERFUL.

morsel *n* bite, crumb, fragment, gobbet, mouthful, nibble, piece, sample, scrap, small amount, soupçon, spoonful, taste, titbit. ▷ BIT.

mortal *adj* **1** ephemeral, human, passing, temporal, transient. *Opp* IMMORTAL. **2** *mortal sickness*. deadly, fatal, lethal, terminal. **3** *mortal enemies*. deadly, implacable, irreconcilable, remorseless, sworn, unrelenting. • *n* creature, human being, man, person, soul, woman.

mortality *n* **1** corruptibility, humanity, impermanence, transience. **2** *infant mortality*. death-rate, dying, fatalities, loss of life.

mortify *vb* abash, chagrin, chasten, *inf* crush, deflate, embarrass, humble, humiliate, *inf* put down, shame.

mostly *adv* chiefly, commonly, generally, largely, mainly, normally, predominantly, primarily, principally, typically, usually.

moth-eaten *adj* antiquated, decrepit, holey, mangy, ragged, shabby, *inf* tatty. ▷ OLD.

mother *n old use* dam, *inf* ma, *inf* mamma, *old use* mater, *inf* mum, *inf* mummy, parent. • *vb* care for, cherish, coddle, comfort, cuddle, fuss over, indulge, look after, love, nourish, nurse, nurture, pamper, protect, spoil, take care of.

motherly *adj* caring, kind, maternal, protective. ▷ LOVING.

motif *n* decoration, design, device, figure, idea, leitmotif, ornament, pattern, symbol, theme.

motion *n* action, activity, agitation, change, commotion, development, evolution, move, movement, progress, rise and fall, shift, stir, stirring, to and fro, travel, travelling, trend. • *vb* ▷ GESTURE.

motionless *adj* at rest, calm, frozen, immobile, inanimate, inert, lifeless, paralysed, peaceful, resting, stagnant, static, stationary, still, stockstill, unmoving. *Opp* MOVING.

motivate *vb* activate, actuate, arouse, cause, drive, egg on, encourage, excite, galvanize, goad, incite, induce, influence, inspire, instigate, move, occasion, persuade, prompt, provoke, push, rouse, spur, stimulate, stir, urge.

motive *n* aim, ambition, cause, drive, encouragement, end, enticement, grounds, impulse, incentive, incitement, inducement, inspiration, instigation, intention, lure, motivation, object, provocation, purpose, push, rationale, reason, spur, stimulation, stimulus, thinking.

motor *n* ▷ ENGINE, VEHICLE. • *vb* drive, go by car. ▷ TRAVEL.

mottled *adj* blotchy, brindled, dappled, flecked, freckled, marbled, patchy, spattered, speckled, spotted, spotty, streaked, streaky, variegated.

motto *n* adage, aphorism, catchphrase, maxim, precept, proverb, rule, saw, saying, slogan.

mould *n* blight, fungus, growth, mildew. • *vb* cast, fashion, forge, form, model, *inf* sculpt, shape, stamp, work.

mouldy *adj* carious, damp, decaying, decomposing, fusty, mildewed, mouldering, musty, putrefying, rotten, stale.

mound *n* bank, dune, elevation, heap, hill, hillock, hummock, hump, knoll, pile, stack, tumulus.

mount *n* ▷ MOUNTAIN. • *vb* **1** ascend, clamber up, climb, fly up, go up, rise, rocket upwards, scale, shoot up, soar. *Opp* DESCEND. **2** *mount a horse.* get astride, get on, jump onto. **3** *savings mount.* accumulate, build up, escalate, expand, get bigger, grow, increase, intensify, multiply, pile up, swell. *Opp* DECREASE. **4** *mount a picture.* display, exhibit, frame, install, prepare, put in place, put on, set up.

mountain *n* alp, arête, *Scot* ben, elevation, eminence, height, hill, mound, mount, peak, prominence, range, ridge, sierra, summit, tor, volcano.

mountainous *adj* alpine, craggy, daunting, formidable, high, hilly, precipitous, rocky, rugged, steep, towering. ▷ BIG.

mourn *vb* bemoan, bewail, fret, go into mourning, grieve, keen, lament, mope, pine, regret, wail, weep. *Opp* REJOICE.

mournful *adj* dismal, distressed, distressing, doleful, funereal, gloomy, grief-stricken, grieving, heartbreaking, heartbroken, lamenting, lugubrious, melancholy, plaintive, plangent, sad, sorrowful, tearful, tragic, unhappy, woeful. *Opp* CHEERFUL.

mouth *n* **1** *inf* chops, *sl* gob, jaws, *sl* kisser, lips, maw, muzzle, palate. **2** *mouth of cave.* aperture, door, doorway, entrance, exit, gate, gateway, inlet, opening, orifice, outlet, vent, way in. **3** *mouth of a river.* delta, estuary, outflow. • *vb* articulate, enunciate, form, pronounce. ▷ SAY.

mouthful *n* bite, gobbet, gulp, morsel, sip, spoonful, swallow, taste.

movable *adj* adjustable, changeable, detachable, floating, mobile, portable, transferable, transportable, unfixed, variable. *Opp* IMMOVABLE.

move *n* **1** act, action, deed, device, dodge, gambit, manoeuvre, measure, movement, ploy, ruse, step, stratagem, *inf* tack, tactic. **2** *a career move.* change, changeover, relocation, shift, transfer. **3** *your move.* chance, go, opportunity, turn. • *vb* **1** *move about.* be agitated, be astir, budge, change places, change position, fidget, flap, roll, shake, shift, stir, swing, toss, tremble, turn, twist, twitch, wag, *inf* waggle, wave, *inf* wiggle. **2** *move along.* cruise, fly, jog, journey, make headway, make progress, march, pass, proceed, travel, walk. **3** *move quickly.* bolt, *inf* bowl along, canter, career, dash, dart, flit, flounce, fly, gallop, hasten, hurry, hurtle, hustle, *inf* nip, race, run, rush, shoot, speed, stampede, streak, sweep along, sweep past, *inf* tear, *inf* zip, *inf* zoom. **4** *move slowly.* amble, crawl, dawdle, drift, stroll. **5** *move gracefully.* dance, flow, glide, skate, skim, slide, slip, sweep. **6** *move awkwardly.* dodder, falter, flounder, lumber, lurch, pitch, shuffle, stagger, stumble, sway, totter, trip, trundle. **7** *move stealthily.* crawl, creep, edge, slink, slither. **8** *move things.* carry, export, import, relocate, shift, ship, transfer, transplant, transport, transpose. **9** *moved him to act.* encourage, impel, influence, inspire, persuade, prompt, stimulate, urge. **10** *move the crowd's feelings.* affect, arouse, enrage, fire, impassion, rouse, stir, touch. **11** *moved to improve the situation.* act, do something, make a move, take action. **move away** ▷ DEPART. **move back** ▷ RETREAT. **move down** ▷ DESCEND. **move in** ▷ ENTER. **move round** ▷ CIRCULATE, ROTATE. **move towards** ▷ APPROACH. **move up** ▷ ASCEND.

movement *n* **1** action, activity, migration, motion, shifting, stirring. ▷ GESTURE, MOVE. **2** *movement towards green issues.* change, development, drift, evolution, progress, shift, swing, tendency, trend. **3** *a political movement.* campaign, crusade, drive, faction, group, organization, party. **4** *military movements.* exercise, operation.

movie *n* film, *inf* flick, motion picture.

moving *adj* **1** active, alive, astir, dynamic, flowing, going, in motion, mobile, movable, on the move, travelling, under way. *Opp* MOTIONLESS. **2** *a moving tale.* affecting, emotional, emotive, exciting, heart-rending, heart-warming, inspirational, inspiring, pathetic, poignant, spine-tingling, stirring, *inf* tear-jerking, thrilling, touching.

mow *vb* clip, cut, scythe, shear, trim.

muck *n* dirt, droppings, dung, excrement, faeces, filth, grime, *inf* gunge, manure, mess, mire, mud, ooze, ordure, rubbish, scum, sewage, slime, sludge.

mucky *adj* dirty, filthy, foul, grimy, grubby, messy, muddy, scummy, slimy, soiled, sordid, squalid. *Opp* CLEAN.

mud *n* clay, dirt, mire, muck, ooze, silt, slime, sludge, slurry, soil.

muddle *n* chaos, clutter, confusion, disorder, *inf* hotchpotch, jumble, mess, *inf* mishmash, *inf* mix up, *inf* shambles, tangle, untidiness. • *vb* **1** bemuse, bewilder, confound, confuse, disorient, disorientate, mislead, perplex, puzzle. *Opp* CLARIFY. **2** disarrange, disorder, disorganize, entangle, *inf* foul up, jumble, make a mess of, *inf* mess up, mix up, scramble, shuffle, tangle. *Opp* TIDY.

muddy *adj* **1** caked, dirty, filthy, messy, mucky, soiled. **2** *muddy water.* cloudy, impure, misty, opaque. **3** *muddy ground.* boggy, marshy, sloppy, sodden, soft, spongy, waterlogged, wet. *Opp* CLEAN, FIRM.

muffle *vb* **1** cloak, conceal, cover, enclose, enfold, envelop, shroud, swathe, wrap up. **2** *muffle noise.* damp, dampen, deaden, disguise, dull, hush, mask, mute, quieten, silence, soften, stifle, still, suppress, tone down.

muffled *adj* damped, deadened, dull, fuzzy, indistinct, muted, silenced, stifled, suppressed, unclear, woolly. *Opp* CLEAR.

mug *n* beaker, cup, *old use* flagon, pot, tankard. • *vb* assault, beat up, jump on, molest, rob, set on, steal from. ▷ ATTACK. **mug up** ▷ LEARN.

mugger *n* attacker, hooligan, robber, ruffian, thief, thug. ▷ CRIMINAL.

mugging *n* attack, robbery, street crime. ▷ CRIME.

muggy *adj* clammy, close, damp, humid, moist, oppressive, steamy, sticky, stuffy, sultry, warm.

multiple *adj* complex, compound, double, many, numerous, plural, quadruple, quintuple, triple.

multiplicity *n* abundance, array, complex, diversity, number, plurality, profusion, variety.

multiply *vb* **1** double, quadruple, quintuple, *inf* times, triple. **2** become numerous, breed, increase, proliferate, propagate, reproduce, spread.

multitude *n* crowd, host, large number, legion, lots, mass, myriad, swarm, throng. ▷ GROUP.

mumble *vb* be inarticulate, murmur, mutter, speak indistinctly, swallow your words.

munch *vb* bite, chew, champ, chomp, crunch, eat, gnaw, masticate.

mundane *adj* banal, common, commonplace, down-to-earth, dull, everyday, familiar, human, material, physical, practical, quotidian, routine, temporal, worldly. ▷ ORDINARY. *Opp* EXTRAORDINARY, SPIRITUAL.

municipal *adj* borough, city, civic, community, district, local, public, town, urban.

murder *n* assassination, fratricide, genocide, homicide, infanticide, killing, manslaughter, matricide, parricide, patricide, regicide, sororicide, unlawful killing, uxoricide. • *vb* ▷ KILL.

murderer *n* assassin, *inf* butcher, cutthroat, gunman, homicide, killer, slayer.

murderous *adj* barbarous, bloodthirsty, bloody, brutal, cruel, dangerous, deadly, fell, ferocious, fierce, homicidal, inhuman, pitiless, ruthless, savage, vicious, violent.

murky *adj* clouded, cloudy, dark, dim, dismal, dreary, dull, foggy, funereal, gloomy, grey, misty, muddy, obscure, overcast, shadowy, sombre. *Opp* CLEAR.

murmur *n* background noise, buzz, drone, grumble, hum, mutter, rumble, susurration, undertone, whisper. • *vb* drone, hum, moan, mumble, mutter, rumble, speak in an undertone, whisper. ▷ GRUMBLE, TALK.

muscular *adj* athletic, *inf* beefy, brawny, broad-shouldered, burly, hefty, *inf* hulking, husky, powerful, powerfully built, robust, sinewy, *inf* strapping, strong, sturdy, tough, well-built, well-developed, wiry. *Opp* WEAK.

muse *vb* cogitate, consider, contemplate, deliberate, meditate, mull over, ponder, reflect, ruminate, study, think.

mushy *adj* pulpy, spongy, squashy. ▷ SOFT.

music *n* harmony. □ *blues, chamber music, choral music, classical music, dance music, disco music, folk, instrumental music, jazz, orchestral music, plain-song, pop, ragtime, reggae, rock, soul, swing.* □ *anthem, ballad, cadenza, calypso, canon, cantata, canticle, carol, chant, concerto, dance, dirge, duet, étude, fanfare, fugue, hymn, improvisation, intermezzo, lullaby, march, musical, nocturne, nonet, octet, opera, operetta, oratorio, overture, prelude, quartet, quintet, rhapsody, rondo, scherzo, sea shanty, septet, sextet, sonata, song, spiritual, symphony, toccata, trio.*

musical *adj* euphonious, harmonious, lyrical, melodious, pleasant, sweet-sounding, tuneful. **musical instrument** ▷ INSTRUMENT.

musician *n* composer, music-maker, performer, player, singer. □ *accompanist, bass, bugler, cellist, clarinettist, conductor, contralto, drummer, fiddler, flautist, guitarist, harpist, instrumentalist, maestro, minstrel, oboist, organist, percussionist, pianist, piper, soloist, soprano, tenor, timpanist, treble, trombonist, trumpeter, violinist, virtuoso, vocalist.* **musicians** □ *band, choir, chorus, consort, duet, duo, ensemble, group, nonet, octet, orchestra, quartet, quintet, septet, sextet, trio.*

muster *vb* assemble, call together, collect, come together, convene, convoke, gather, get together, group, marshal, mobilize, rally, round up, summon.

musty *adj* airless, damp, dank, fusty, mildewed, mildewy, mouldy, smelly, stale, stuffy, unventilated.

mutant *n* abortion, anomaly, deviant, freak, monster, monstrosity, sport, variant.

mutation *n* alteration, deviance, evolution, metamorphosis, modification, transfiguration, transformation, transmutation, variation. ▷ CHANGE.

mute *adj* dumb, quiet, silent, speechless, tacit, taciturn, tight-lipped, tongue-tied, voiceless. • *vb* damp, dampen, deaden, dull, hush, make quieter, mask, muffle, quieten, silence, soften, stifle, still, suppress, tone down.

mutilate *vb* cripple, damage, deface, disable, disfigure, dismember, injure, lame, maim, mangle, mar, spoil, vandalize, wound.

mutinous *adj* contumacious, defiant, disobedient, insubordinate, insurgent, insurrectionary, rebellious, refractory, revolutionary, seditious, subversive, ungovernable, unmanageable, unruly. *Opp* OBEDIENT.

mutiny *n* defiance, disobedience, insubordination, insurgency, insurrection, rebellion, revolt, revolution, sedition, subversion, unruliness, uprising. • *vb* agitate, be mutinous, disobey, rebel, revolt, rise up, strike.

mutter *vb* drone, grumble, mumble, murmur, speak in an undertone, whisper. ▷ GRUMBLE, TALK.

mutual *adj* common, interactive, joint, reciprocal, reciprocated, requited, shared.

muzzle *n* jaws, mouth, nose, snout. • *vb* censor, gag, restrain, silence, stifle, suppress.

mysterious *adj* arcane, baffling, bewildering, bizarre, confusing, cryptic, curious, dark, enigmatic, incomprehensible, inexplicable, inscrutable, insoluble, magical, miraculous, mystical, mystifying, obscure, perplexing, puzzling, recondite, secret, strange, uncanny, unexplained, unfathomable, unknown, weird. *Opp* STRAIGHTFORWARD.

mystery *n* conundrum, enigma, miracle, problem, puzzle, question, riddle, secret.

mystical *adj* abnormal, arcane, cabalistic, ineffable, metaphysical, mysterious, occult, other-worldly, preternatural, religious, spiritual, supernatural. *Opp* MUNDANE.

mystify *vb* baffle, *inf* bamboozle, *inf* beat, bewilder, confound, confuse, *inf* flummox, fool, hoax, perplex, puzzle, *inf* stump.

myth *n* **1** allegory, fable, legend, mythology, symbolism. **2** fabrication, falsehood, fiction, invention, make-believe, pretence, untruth.

mythical *adj* **1** allegorical, fabled, fabulous, legendary, mythic, mythological, poetic, symbolic. **2** false, fanciful, fictional, imaginary, invented, make-believe, non-existent, pretended, unreal. *Opp* REAL.

N

nadir *n* bottom, depths, low point, zero. *Opp* ZENITH.

nag *n* ▷ HORSE. ● *vb* annoy, badger, chivvy, find fault with, goad, *inf* go on at, harass, hector, *inf* henpeck, keep complaining, pester, *inf* plague, scold, worry.

nail *n* pin, spike, stud, tack. ● *vb* ▷ FASTEN.

naïve *adj* artless, *inf* born yesterday, candid, childlike, credulous, *inf* green, guileless, gullible, inexperienced, ingenuous, innocent, open, simple, simple-minded, stupid, trustful, trusting, unsophisticated, unsuspecting, unwary. *Opp* ARTFUL.

naked *adj* bare, denuded, disrobed, exposed, in the nude, nude, stark-naked, stripped, unclothed, unconcealed, uncovered, undraped, undressed.

name *n* **1** alias, appellation, Christian name, first name, forename, given name, *inf* handle, identity, nickname, nom de plume, pen name, personal name, pseudonym, sobriquet, surname, title. **2** denomination, designation, epithet, term. ● *vb* **1** baptize, call, christen, dub, style. **2** *name a book.* entitle, label. **3** *named him man of the match.* appoint, choose, commission, delegate, designate, elect, nominate, select, single out, specify. **named** ▷ SPECIFIC.

nameless *adj* **1** anonymous, incognito, unheard-of, unidentified, unnamed, unsung. **2** *nameless horrors.* dreadful, horrible, indescribable, inexpressible, shocking, unmentionable, unspeakable, unutterable.

nap *n* catnap, doze, *inf* forty winks, rest, *inf* shut-eye, siesta, sleep, snooze.

narrate *vb* chronicle, describe, detail, recount, rehearse, relate, repeat, report, retail, tell, unfold.

narration *n* commentary, reading, recital, recitation, relation, storytelling, telling, voiceover.

narrative *n* account, chronicle, description, history, report, story, tale, *inf* yarn.

narrator *n* author, chronicler, raconteur, reporter, storyteller.

narrow *adj* attenuated, close, confined, constricted, constricting, cramped, enclosed, fine, limited, restricted, slender, slim, thin, tight. *Opp* WIDE.

narrow-minded *adj* biased, bigoted, conservative, conventional, hidebound, illiberal, inflexible, insular, intolerant, narrow, old-fashioned, parochial, petty, prejudiced, prim, prudish, puritanical, reactionary, rigid, small-minded, straitlaced, *inf* stuffy. *Opp* BROAD-MINDED.

nasty *adj* [*Nasty* refers to anything you do not like. The range of synonyms is almost limitless: we give only a selection here.] bad, beastly, dangerous, difficult, dirty, disagreeable, disgusting, distasteful, foul, hateful, horrible, loathsome, *sl* lousy, objectionable, obnoxious, obscene, *inf* off-putting, repulsive, revolting, severe, sickening, unkind, unpleasant. *Opp* NICE.

nation *n* civilization, community, country, domain, land, people, population, power, race, realm, society, state, superpower.

national *adj* **1** ethnic, popular, racial. **2** *a national emergency.* countrywide, general, nationwide, state, widespread. • *n* citizen, inhabitant, native, resident, subject.

nationalism *n* chauvinism, jingoism, loyalty, patriotism, xenophobia.

native *adj* **1** aboriginal, indigenous, local, original. **2** *native wit.* congenital, hereditary, inborn, inbred, inherent, inherited, innate, mother (*wit*), natural. • *n* aborigine, life-long resident.

natural *adj* **1** common, everyday, habitual, normal, ordinary, predictable, regular, routine, standard, typical, usual. **2** *natural feelings.* healthy, hereditary, human, inborn, inherited, innate, instinctive, intuitive, kind, maternal, native, paternal, proper, right. **3** *a natural smile.* artless, authentic, candid, genuine, guileless, sincere, spontaneous, unaffected, unpretentious, unselfconscious, unstudied. **4** *natural resources.* crude (*oil*), raw, unadulterated, unprocessed, unrefined. **5** *a natural leader.* born, congenital, untaught. *Opp* UNNATURAL.

nature *n* **1** countryside, creation, ecology, environment, natural history, scenery, wildlife. **2** attributes, character, complexion, constitution, disposition, essence, humour, make-up, manner, personality, properties, quality, temperament, traits. **3** category, description, kind, sort, species, type, variety.

naughty *adj* **1** bad, badly-behaved, bad-mannered, boisterous, contrary, defiant, delinquent, disobedient, disorderly, disruptive, fractious, headstrong, impish, impolite, incorrigible, insubordinate, intractable, misbehaved, mischievous, obstinate, obstreperous, perverse, playful, puckish, rascally, rebellious, refractory, roguish, rude, self-willed, stubborn, troublesome, uncontrollable, undisciplined, ungovernable, unmanageable, unruly, wayward, wicked, wild, wilful. **2** [*inf*] cheeky, improper, ribald, risqué, shocking, *inf* smutty, vulgar. ▷ OBSCENE. *Opp* POLITE, WELL BEHAVED.

nauseate *vb* disgust, offend, repel, revolt, sicken.

nauseous *adj* disgusting, foul, loathsome, nauseating, offensive, repulsive, revolting, sickening, stomach-turning.

nautical *adj* marine, maritime, naval, seafaring, seagoing, yachting.

navigate *vb* captain, direct, drive, guide, handle, manoeuvre, map-read, pilot, sail, skipper, steer.

navy *n* armada, convoy, fleet, flotilla.

near *adj* **1** abutting, adjacent, adjoining, bordering, close, connected, contiguous, immediate, nearby, neighbouring, next-door. **2** *Christmas is near.* approaching, coming, forthcoming, imminent, impending, looming, *inf* round the corner. **3** *near friends.* close, dear, familiar, intimate, related. *Opp* DISTANT.

nearly *adv* about, all but, almost, approaching, approximately, around, as good as, close to, just about, not quite, practically, roughly, virtually.

neat *adj* **1** adroit, clean, dainty, deft, dexterous, elegant, *inf* natty, orderly, organized, pretty, *inf* shipshape, smart, *inf* spick and span, spruce, straight, systematic, tidy, trim, uncluttered, well-kept. **2** accurate, expert, methodical, meticulous, precise, skilful. **3** *neat alcohol.* pure, *inf* straight, unadulterated, undiluted. *Opp* CLUMSY, UNTIDY.

necessary *adj* compulsory, destined, essential, fated, imperative, important, indispensable, ineluctable, inescapable, inevitable, inexorable, mandatory, needed, needful, obligatory, predestined, required, requisite, unavoidable, vital. *Opp* UNNECESSARY.

necessity *n* **1** compulsion, essential, inevitability, *inf* must, need, obligation, prerequisite, requirement, requisite, *Lat* sine qua non. **2** beggary, destitution, hardship, indigence, need, penury, poverty, privation, shortage, suffering, want.

need *n* call, demand, lack, requirement, want. ▷ NECESSITY. • *vb* be short of, call for, crave, demand, depend on, lack, miss, rely on, require, want.

needless *adj* excessive, gratuitous, pointless, redundant, superfluous, unnecessary.

needy *adj* badly off, destitute, *inf* hard up, impecunious, impoverished, indigent, necessitous, penurious, poverty-stricken, underpaid. ▷ POOR.

negate *vb* annul, cancel out, deny, gainsay, invalidate, nullify, oppose.

negative *adj* adversarial, antagonistic, *inf* anti, contradictory, destructive, disagreeing, dissenting, grudging, nullifying, obstructive, opposing, pessimistic, uncooperative, unenthusiastic, unresponsive, unwilling. • *n* denial, no, refusal, rejection, veto. *Opp* POSITIVE.

neglect *n* carelessness, dereliction of duty, disregard, inadvertence, inattention, indifference, negligence, oversight, slackness. • *vb* abandon, be remiss about, disregard, forget, ignore, leave alone, let slide, lose sight of, miss, omit, overlook, pay no attention to, shirk, skip. **neglected** ▷ DERELICT.

negligent *adj* careless, forgetful, heedless, inattentive, inconsiderate, indifferent, irresponsible, lax, offhand, reckless, remiss, slack, sloppy, slovenly, thoughtless, uncaring, unthinking. *Opp* CAREFUL.

negligible *adj* imperceptible, inconsequential, inconsiderable, insignificant, minor, nugatory, paltry, petty, slight, small, tiny, trifling, trivial, unimportant. *Opp* CONSIDERABLE.

negotiate *vb* arbitrate, bargain, come to terms, confer, deal, discuss terms, haggle, intercede, make arrangements, mediate, parley, transact.

negotiation *n* arbitration, bargaining, conciliation, debate, diplomacy, discussion, mediation, parleying, transaction.

negotiator *n* agent, ambassador, arbitrator, broker, conciliator, diplomat, go-between, intercessor, intermediary, mediator, middleman.

neighbourhood *n* area, community, district, environs, locality, place, purlieus, quarter, region, surroundings, vicinity, zone.

neighbouring *adj* adjacent, adjoining, attached, bordering, close, closest, connecting, contiguous, near, nearby, nearest, next-door, surrounding.

neighbourly *adj* civil, considerate, friendly, helpful, kind, sociable, thoughtful, well-disposed.

nerve *n* coolness, determination, firmness, fortitude, resolution, resolve, will-power. ▷ COURAGE.

nervous *adj* afraid, agitated, anxious, apprehensive, disturbed, edgy, excitable, fearful, fidgety, flustered, fretful, highly-strung, ill-at-ease, *inf* in a tizzy, insecure, *inf* jittery, *inf* jumpy, *inf* nervy, neurotic, on edge, *inf* on tenterhooks, *inf* rattled, restive, restless, ruffled, shaky, shy, strained, tense, timid, *inf* touchy, *inf* twitchy, uneasy, unnerved, unsettled, *inf* uptight, worried. ▷ FRIGHTENED. *Opp* CALM.

nestle *vb* cuddle, curl up, huddle, nuzzle, snuggle.

net *n* lace, lattice-work, mesh, netting, network, web. • *vb* **1** capture, catch, enmesh, ensnare, trammel, trap. **2** *net £200 a week*. accumulate, bring in, clear, earn, get, make, realize, receive, *inf* take home.

network *n* **1** *inf* criss-cross, grid, labyrinth, lattice, maze, mesh, net, netting, tangle, tracery, web. **2** complex, organization, system.

neurosis *n* abnormality, anxiety, depression, mental condition, obsession, phobia.

neurotic *adj* anxious, distraught, disturbed, irrational, maladjusted, nervous, obsessive, overwrought, unbalanced, unstable.

neuter *adj* ambiguous, ambivalent, asexual, indeterminate, uncertain. • *vb* castrate, *inf* doctor, emasculate, geld, spay, sterilize.

neutral *adj* **1** detached, disinterested, dispassionate, fair, impartial, indifferent, non-aligned, non-belligerent, non-partisan, objective, unaffiliated, unaligned, unbiased, uncommitted, uninvolved, unprejudiced. *Opp* BIASED. **2** *neutral colours.* characterless, colourless, drab, dull, indefinite, indeterminate, intermediate, neither one thing nor the other, pale, vague. *Opp* DISTINCTIVE.

neutralize *vb* annul, cancel out, compensate for, counteract, counterbalance, invalidate, make ineffective, make up for, negate, nullify, offset, wipe out.

new *adj* **1** brand-new, clean, different, fresh, mint, strange, unfamiliar, unheard of, untried, unused. **2** *new ideas.* advanced, contemporary, current, different, fashionable, latest, modern, modernistic, newfangled, novel, original, recent, revolutionary, *inf* trendy, up-to-date. **3** *new data.* added, additional, changed, extra, further, just arrived, supplementary, unexpected, unknown. *Opp* OLD.

newcomer *n* alien, arrival, immigrant, new boy, new girl, outsider, settler, stranger.

news *n* account, advice, announcement, bulletin, communication, communiqué, dispatch, headlines, information, intelligence, *inf* the latest, message, newscast, newsflash, newsletter, notice, press-release, proclamation, report, rumour, statement, *old use* tidings, word.

newspaper *n inf* daily, gazette, journal, paper, periodical, *inf* rag, tabloid.

next *adj* **1** adjacent, adjoining, closest, nearest, neighbouring, next-door. **2** *the next moment.* following, soonest, subsequent, succeeding.

nice *adj* **1** accurate, careful, delicate, discriminating, exact, fine, hair-splitting, meticulous, precise, punctilious, scrupulous, subtle. **2** *nice manners.* dainty, elegant, fastidious, fussy, particular, *inf* pernickety, polished, refined, well-mannered. **3** [*inf*: In this sense, nice refers to anything which you like. The range of synonyms is almost limitless: we give only a selection here.] acceptable, agreeable, amiable, attractive, beautiful, delicious, delightful, friendly, good, gratifying, kind, likeable, pleasant, satisfactory, welcome. *Opp* NASTY.

niche *n* alcove, corner, hollow, nook, recess.

nickname *n* alias, sobriquet.

niggardly *adj* mean, miserly, parsimonious, stingy.

nimble *adj* acrobatic, active, adroit, agile, brisk, deft, dextrous, limber, lithe, lively, *inf* nippy, quick-moving, sprightly, spry, swift. *Opp* CLUMSY.

nip *vb* bite, clip, pinch, snag, snap at, squeeze.

nobility *n* **1** dignity, glory, grandeur, greatness, high-mindedness, integrity, magnanimity, morality, nobleness, uprightness, virtue, worthiness. **2** *the nobility.* aristocracy, élite, gentry, nobles, peerage, the ruling classes, *inf* the upper crust.

noble *adj* **1** aristocratic, *inf* blue-blooded, courtly, distinguished, élite, gentle, high-born, high-ranking, patrician, princely, royal, thoroughbred, titled, upper-class. **2** *noble deeds.* brave, chivalrous, courageous, gallant, glorious, heroic. **3** *noble thoughts.* elevated, high-flown, honourable, lofty, magnanimous, moral, upright, virtuous, worthy. **4** *noble music.* dignified, elegant, grand, great, imposing, impressive, magnificent, majestic, splendid, stately. *Opp* BASE, COMMON. ● *n* aristocrat, gentleman, gentlewoman, grandee, lady, lord, nobleman, noblewoman, patrician, peer, peeress.

nod *vb* bend, bob, bow. **nod off** ▷ SLEEP.

noise *n inf* babel, bawling, bedlam, blare, cacophony, *inf* caterwauling, clamour, clangour, clatter, commotion, din, discord, *inf* fracas, hubbub, *inf* hullabaloo, outcry, pandemonium, *inf* racket, row, *inf* rumpus, screaming, screeching, shouting, shrieking, tumult, uproar, yelling. ▷ SOUND. *Opp* SILENCE.

noiseless *adj* inaudible, mute, muted, quiet, silent, soft, soundless, still. *Opp* NOISY.

noisy *adj* blaring, boisterous, booming, cacophonous, chattering, clamorous, deafening, discordant, dissonant, ear-splitting, fortissimo, harsh, loud, raucous, resounding, reverberating, rowdy, screaming, screeching, shrieking, shrill, strident, talkative, thunderous, tumultuous, unmusical, uproarious, vociferous. *Opp* NOISELESS.

nomadic *adj* itinerant, peripatetic, roving, travelling, vagrant, wandering, wayfaring.

nominal *adj* **1** formal, in name only, ostensible, self-styled, *inf* so-called, supposed, theoretical, titular. **2** *a nominal sum*. insignificant, minimal, minor, small, token.

nominate *vb* appoint, choose, designate, elect, name, propose, put forward, *inf* put up, recommend, select, specify.

non-existent *adj* chimerical, fictional, fictitious, hypothetical, imaginary, imagined, legendary, made-up, mythical, unreal. *Opp* REAL.

nonplus *vb* amaze, baffle, confound, disconcert, dumbfound, flummox, perplex, puzzle, render speechless.

nonsense *n* **1** [Most synonyms *inf*] balderdash, bilge, boloney, bosh, bunk, bunkum, claptrap, codswallop, double-Dutch, drivel, eyewash, fiddlesticks, foolishness, gibberish, gobbledegook, mumbo jumbo, piffle, poppycock, rot, rubbish, silliness, stuff and nonsense, stupidity, tommy-rot, trash, tripe, twaddle. **2** *The plan was a nonsense*. absurdity, inanity, mistake, nonsensical idea.

nonsensical *adj* absurd, asinine, crazy, *inf* daft, fatuous, foolish, idiotic, illogical, impractical, inane, incomprehensible, irrational, laughable, ludicrous, mad, meaningless, preposterous, ridiculous, senseless, stupid, unreasonable. ▷ SILLY. *Opp* SENSIBLE.

non-stop *adj* ceaseless, constant, continual, continuous, endless, eternal, incessant, interminable, perpetual, persistent, *inf* round-the-clock, steady, unbroken, unending, uninterrupted, unremitting.

norm *n* criterion, measure, model, pattern, rule, standard, type, yardstick.

normal *adj* **1** accepted, accustomed, average, common, commonplace, conventional, customary, established, everyday, familiar, general, habitual, natural, ordinary, orthodox, predictable, prosaic, quotidian, regular, routine, *inf* run-of-the-mill, standard, typical, universal, unsurprising, usual. **2** *a normal person*. balanced, healthy, rational, reasonable, sane, stable, *inf* straight, well-adjusted. *Opp* ABNORMAL.

normalize *vb* legalize, regularize, regulate, return to normal.

nose *n* **1** nostrils, proboscis, snout. **2** *nose of a boat*. bow, front, prow. ● *vb* enter cautiously, insinuate yourself, intrude, nudge your way, penetrate, probe, push, shove. **nose about** ▷ PRY.

nostalgia *n* longing, memory, pining, regret, reminiscence, sentiment, sentimentality, yearning.

nostalgic *adj* emotional, maudlin, regretful, romantic, sentimental, wistful, yearning.

nosy *adj* curious, eavesdropping, inquisitive, interfering, meddlesome, prying.

notable *adj* celebrated, conspicuous, distinctive, distinguished, eminent, evident, extraordinary, famous, illustrious, important, impressive, memorable, noted, noteworthy, noticeable, obvious, outstanding, pre-eminent, prominent, rare, remarkable, renowned, singular, striking, uncommon, unforgettable, unusual, well-known. *Opp* ORDINARY.

note *n* **1** billet-doux, chit, communication, correspondence, epistle, jotting, letter, *inf* memo, memorandum, message, postcard. **2** annotation, comment, cross-reference, explanation, footnote, gloss, jotting, marginal note. **3** *a note in your voice.* feeling, quality, sound, tone. **4** *a £5 note.* banknote, bill, currency, draft. • *vb* **1** enter, jot down, record, scribble, write down. **2** *note mentally.* detect, discern, discover, feel, find, heed, mark, mind, notice, observe, pay attention to, remark, register, see, spy, take note of. **noted** ▷ FAMOUS.

noteworthy *adj* exceptional, extraordinary, rare, remarkable, uncommon, unique, unusual. *Opp* ORDINARY.

nothing *n cricket* duck, *tennis* love, *old use* naught, *football* nil, nought, zero, *sl* zilch.

notice *n* **1** advertisement, announcement, handbill, handout, intimation, leaflet, message, note, notification, placard, poster, sign, warning. **2** attention, awareness, cognizance, consciousness, heed, note, regard. • *vb* be aware, detect, discern, discover, feel, find, heed, make out, mark, mind, note, observe, pay attention to, perceive, register, remark, see, spy, take note. **give notice** ▷ NOTIFY, WARN.

noticeable *adj* appreciable, audible, clear, clear-cut, considerable, conspicuous, detectable, discernible, distinct, distinguishable, manifest, marked, measurable, notable, observable, obtrusive, obvious, overt, palpable, perceivable, perceptible, plain, prominent, pronounced, salient, significant, striking, unconcealed, unmistakable, visible. *Opp* IMPERCEPTIBLE.

notify *vb* acquaint, advise, alert, announce, apprise, give notice, inform, make known, proclaim, publish, report, tell, warn.

notion *n* apprehension, belief, concept, conception, fancy, hypothesis, idea, impression, *inf* inkling, opinion, sentiment, theory, thought, understanding, view.

notorious *adj* disgraceful, disreputable, flagrant, ill-famed, infamous, outrageous, overt, patent, scandalous, shocking, talked about, undisguised, undisputed, well-known. ▷ FAMOUS, WICKED.

nourish *vb* feed, maintain, nurse, nurture, provide for, strengthen, support, sustain. **nourishing** ▷ NUTRITIOUS.

nourishment *n* diet, food, goodness, nutrient, nutriment, nutrition, sustenance, *old use* victuals.

novel *adj* different, fresh, imaginative, innovative, new, odd, original, rare, singular, startling, strange, surprising, uncommon, unconventional, unfamiliar, untested, unusual. *Opp* FAMILIAR. • *n* best-seller, *inf* blockbuster, fiction, novelette, novella, romance, story. ▷ WRITING.

novelty *n* **1** freshness, newness, oddity, originality, strangeness, surprise, unfamiliarity, uniqueness. **2** bauble, curiosity, gimmick, knick-knack, ornament, souvenir, trifle, trinket.

novice *n* amateur, apprentice, beginner, *inf* greenhorn, inexperienced person, initiate, learner, probationer, tiro, trainee.

now *adv* at once, at present, here and now, immediately, instantly, just now, nowadays, promptly, *inf* right now, straight away, today.

noxious *adj* corrosive, foul, harmful, nasty, noisome, objectionable, poisonous, polluting, sulphureous, sulphurous, unwholesome.

nub *n* centre, core, crux, essence, gist, heart, kernel, nucleus, pith, point.

nucleus *n* centre, core, heart, kernel, middle.

nude *adj* bare, disrobed, exposed, in the nude, naked, stark-naked, stripped, unclothed, uncovered, undressed.

nudge *vb* bump, dig, elbow, hit, jab, jog, jolt, poke, prod, push, shove, touch.

nuisance *n* annoyance, bother, burden, inconvenience, irritant, irritation, *inf* pain, pest, plague, trouble, vexation, worry.

nullify *vb* abolish, annul, cancel, do away with, invalidate, negate, neutralize, quash, repeal, rescind, revoke, stultify.

numb *adj* anaesthetized, *inf* asleep, benumbed, cold, dead, deadened, frozen, immobile, insensible, insensitive, paralysed, senseless, suffering from pins and needles. *Opp* SENSITIVE. • *vb* anaesthetize, benumb, deaden, desensitize, drug, dull, freeze, immobilize, make numb, paralyse, stun, stupefy.

number *n* **1** digit, figure, integer, numeral, unit. **2** aggregate, amount, *inf* bunch, collection, crowd, multitude, quantity, sum, total. ▷ GROUP. **3** *musical number.* item, piece, song. **4** *a number of a magazine.* copy, edition, impression, issue, printing, publication. • *vb* add up to, total, work out at. ▷ COUNT.

numerous *adj* abundant, copious, countless, endless, incalculable, infinite, innumerable, many, multitudinous, myriad, numberless, plentiful, several, uncountable, untold. *Opp* FEW.

nun *n* abbess, mother-superior, novice, prioress, sister.

nurse *n* **1** district-nurse, *old use* matron, sister. **2** nanny, nursemaid. • *vb* **1** care for, look after, minister to, nurture, tend, treat. **2** breast-feed, feed, suckle, wet-nurse. **3** cherish, coddle, cradle, cuddle, dandle, hold, hug, mother, pamper.

nursery *n* **1** crèche, kindergarten, nursery school. **2** garden centre, market garden.

nurture *vb* bring up, cultivate, educate, feed, look after, nourish, nurse, rear, tend, train.

nut *n* kernel. □ *almond, brazil, cashew, chestnut, cob-nut, coconut, filbert, hazel, peanut, pecan, pistachio, walnut.*

nutrient *n* fertilizer, goodness, nourishment.

nutriment *n* food, goodness, nourishment, nutrition, sustenance.

nutritious *adj* alimentary, beneficial, good for you, health-giving, healthy, nourishing, sustaining, wholesome.

O

oasis *n* **1** spring, watering-hole, well. **2** asylum, haven, refuge, resort, retreat, safe harbour, sanctuary.

oath *n* **1** assurance, avowal, guarantee, pledge, promise, undertaking, vow, word of honour. **2** blasphemy, curse, exclamation, expletive, *inf* four-letter word, imprecation, malediction, obscenity, profanity, swearword.

obedient *adj* acquiescent, amenable, biddable, compliant, conformable, deferential, disciplined, docile, duteous, dutiful, law-abiding, manageable, submissive, subservient, tamed, tractable, well-behaved, well-trained. *Opp* DISOBEDIENT.

obese *adj* corpulent, gross, overweight. ▷ FAT.

obey *vb* abide by, accept, acquiesce in, act in accordance with, adhere to, agree to, be obedient to, be ruled by, bow to, carry out, comply with, conform to, defer to, do what you are told, execute, follow, fulfil, give in to, heed, honour, implement, keep to, mind, observe, perform, *inf* stick to, submit to, take orders from. *Opp* DISOBEY.

object *n* **1** article, body, entity, item, thing. **2** aim, end, goal, intent, intention, objective, point, purpose, reason. **3** *object of ridicule.* butt, destination, target. • *vb* argue, be opposed, carp, cavil, complain, demur, disapprove, dispute, dissent, expostulate, *sl* grouse, grumble, make an objection, *inf* mind, *inf* moan, oppose, protest, quibble, raise objections, raise questions, remonstrate, take a stand, take exception. *Opp* ACCEPT, AGREE.

objection *n* argument, cavil, challenge, complaint, demur, demurral, disapproval, exception, opposition, outcry, protest, query, question, quibble, refusal, remonstration.

objectionable *adj* abhorrent, detestable, disagreeable, disgusting, dislikeable, displeasing, distasteful, foul, hateful, insufferable, intolerable, loathsome, nasty, nauseating, noisome, obnoxious, odious, offensive, *inf* off-putting, repellent, repugnant, repulsive, revolting, sickening, unacceptable, undesirable, unwanted. ▷ UNPLEASANT. *Opp* ACCEPTABLE.

objective *adj* **1** detached, disinterested, dispassionate, factual, impartial, impersonal, neutral, open-minded, outward-looking, rational, scientific, unbiased, uncoloured, unemotional, unprejudiced. **2** *objective evidence.* empirical, existing, observable, real. *Opp* SUBJECTIVE. • *n* aim, ambition, aspiration, design, destination, end, goal, hope, intent, intention, object, point, purpose, target.

obligation *n* commitment, compulsion, constraint, contract, duty, liability, need, requirement, responsibility. ▷ PROMISE. *Opp* OPTION.

obligatory *adj* binding, compulsory, essential, mandatory, necessary, required, requisite, unavoidable. *Opp* OPTIONAL.

oblige *vb* **1** coerce, compel, constrain, force, make, require. **2** *Please oblige me.* accommodate, gratify, indulge, please. **obliged** ▷ BOUND, GRATEFUL. **obliging** ▷ HELPFUL, POLITE.

oblique *adj* **1** angled, askew, aslant, canted, declining, diagonal, inclined, leaning, listing, raked, rising, skewed, slanted, slanting, slantwise, sloping, tilted. **2** *an oblique insult.* backhanded, circuitous, circumlocutory, devious, implicit, implied, indirect, roundabout. ▷ EVASIVE. *Opp* DIRECT.

obliterate *vb* blot out, cancel, cover over, delete, destroy, efface, eliminate, eradicate, erase, expunge, extirpate, leave no trace of, rub out, wipe out.

oblivion *n* **1** anonymity, darkness, disregard, extinction, limbo, neglect, obscurity. **2** amnesia, coma, forgetfulness, ignorance, insensibility, obliviousness, unawareness, unconsciousness.

oblivious *adj* forgetful, heedless, ignorant, insensible, insensitive, unacquainted, unaware, unconscious, unfeeling, uninformed, unmindful, unresponsive. *Opp* AWARE.

obscene *adj* abominable, bawdy, *inf* blue, coarse, corrupting, crude, debauched, degenerate, depraved, dirty, disgusting, distasteful, filthy, foul, foul-mouthed, gross, immodest, immoral, improper, impure, indecent, indecorous, indelicate, *inf* kinky, lecherous, lewd, loathsome, nasty, *inf* off-colour, offensive, outrageous, perverted, pornographic, prurient, repulsive, ribald, risqué, rude, salacious, scatological, scurrilous, shameful, shameless, shocking, *inf* sick, smutty, suggestive, unchaste, vile, vulgar. ▷ OBJECTIONABLE, SEXY. *Opp* DECENT.

obscenity *n* abomination, blasphemy, coarseness, dirtiness, evil, filth, foulness, grossness, immorality, impropriety, indecency, lewdness, licentiousness, offensiveness, outrage, perversion, pornography, profanity, scurrility, vileness. ▷ SWEARWORD.

obscure *adj* **1** blurred, clouded, concealed, covered, dark, dim, faint, foggy, hazy, hidden, inconspicuous, indefinite, indistinct, masked, misty, murky, nebulous, secret, shadowy, shady, shrouded, unclear, unlit, unrecognizable, vague, veiled. *Opp* CLEAR. **2** *an obscure joke.* arcane, baffling, complex, cryptic, delphic, enigmatic, esoteric, incomprehensible, mystifying, perplexing, puzzling, recherché, recondite, strange. *Opp* OBVIOUS. **3** *an obscure poet.* forgotten, minor, undistinguished, unfamiliar, unheard of, unimportant, unknown, unnoticed. *Opp* FAMOUS. ● *vb* block out, blur, cloak, cloud, conceal, cover, darken, disguise, eclipse, envelop, hide, make obscure, mask, obfuscate, overshadow, screen, shade, shroud, veil. *Opp* CLARIFY.

obsequious *adj* abject, *inf* bootlicking, crawling, cringing, deferential, effusive, fawning, flattering, fulsome, *inf* greasy, grovelling, ingratiating, insincere, mealy-mouthed, menial, *inf* oily, servile, *inf* smarmy, submissive, subservient, sycophantic, unctuous. **be obsequious** ▷ GROVEL.

observant *adj* alert, astute, attentive, aware, careful, eagle-eyed, heedful, mindful, on the lookout, *inf* on the qui vive, perceptive, percipient, quick, sharp-eyed, shrewd, vigilant, watchful, with eyes peeled. *Opp* INATTENTIVE.

observation *n* **1** attention (to), examination, inspection, monitoring, scrutiny, study, surveillance, viewing, watching. **2** comment, note, opinion, reaction, reflection, remark, response, sentiment, statement, thought, utterance.

observe *vb* **1** consider, contemplate, detect, discern, examine, *inf* keep an eye on, look at, monitor, note, notice, perceive, regard, scrutinize, see, spot, spy, stare at, study, view, watch, witness. **2** *observe rules.* abide by, adhere to, comply with, conform to, follow, heed, honour, keep, obey, pay attention to, respect. **3** *observe Easter.* celebrate, commemorate, keep, mark, recognize, remember, solemnize. **4** *observed that it was badly acted.* animadvert (on), comment, declare, explain, make an observation, mention, reflect, remark, say, state.

observer *n* beholder, bystander, commentator, eyewitness, looker-on, onlooker, spectator, viewer, watcher, witness.

obsess *vb* become an obsession with, bedevil, consume, control, dominate, grip, haunt, monopolize, plague, possess, preoccupy, rule, take hold of.

obsession *n* addiction, *inf* bee in your bonnet, conviction, fetish, fixation, *inf* hang-up, *inf* hobby-horse, *Fr* idée fixe, infatuation, mania, passion, phobia, preoccupation, *sl* thing.

obsessive *adj* addictive, compulsive, consuming, controlling, dominating, haunting, passionate.

obsolescent *adj* ageing, aging, declining, dying out, fading, going out of use, losing popularity, moribund, *inf* on the way out, waning.

obsolete *adj* anachronistic, antiquated, antique, archaic, dated, dead, discarded, disused, extinct, old-fashioned, *inf* old hat, out-dated, out-of-date, outmoded, passé, primitive, superannuated, superseded, unfashionable. ▷ OLD. *Opp* CURRENT.

obstacle *n* bar, barricade, barrier, block, blockage, catch, check, difficulty, hindrance, hurdle, impediment, obstruction, problem, restriction, snag, *inf* stumbling-block.

obstinate *adj* adamant, *sl* bloody-minded, defiant, determined, dogged, firm, headstrong, immovable, inflexible, intractable, intransigent, *inf* mulish, obdurate, persistent, pertinacious, perverse, *inf* pig-headed, refractory, resolute, rigid, self-willed, single-minded, *inf* stiff-necked, stubborn, tenacious, uncooperative, unreasonable, unyielding, wilful, wrong-headed. *Opp* AMENABLE.

obstreperous *adj* awkward, boisterous, disorderly, irrepressible, naughty, rough, rowdy, *inf* stroppy, turbulent, uncontrollable, undisciplined, unmanageable, unruly, vociferous, wild. ▷ NOISY. *Opp* WELL-BEHAVED.

obstruct *vb* arrest, bar, block, bring to a standstill, check, curb, delay, deter, frustrate, halt, hamper, hinder, hold up, impede, inhibit, interfere with, interrupt, occlude, prevent, restrict, retard, slow down, stand in the way of, *inf* stonewall, stop, *inf* stymie, thwart. *Opp* HELP.

obtain *vb* **1** acquire, attain, be given, bring, buy, capture, come by, come into possession of, earn, elicit, enlist (*help*), extort, extract, find, gain, get, get hold of, *inf* lay your hands on, *inf* pick up, procure, purchase, receive, secure, seize, take possession of, win. **2** *rules still obtain.* apply, be in force, be in use, be relevant, be valid, exist, prevail, stand.

obtrusive *adj* blatant, conspicuous, forward, importunate, inescapable, interfering, intrusive, meddling, meddlesome, noticeable, out of place, prominent, unwanted, unwelcome. ▷ OBVIOUS. *Opp* INCONSPICUOUS.

obtuse *adj* dense, dull, imperceptive, slow, slow-witted. ▷ STUPID. *Opp* CLEVER.

obviate *vb* avert, forestall, make unnecessary, preclude, prevent, remove, take away.

obvious *adj* apparent, bald, blatant, clear, clear-cut, conspicuous, distinct, evident, eye-catching, flagrant, glaring, gross, inescapable, intrusive, manifest, notable, noticeable, obtrusive, open, overt, palpable, patent, perceptible, plain, prominent, pronounced, recognizable, self-evident, self-explanatory, straightforward, unconcealed, undisguised, undisputed, unmistakable, visible. *Opp* HIDDEN, OBSCURE.

occasion *n* **1** chance, circumstance, moment, occurrence, opportunity, time. **2** *no occasion for rudeness.* call, cause, excuse, grounds, justification, need, reason. **3** *a happy occasion.* affair, celebration, ceremony, event, function, *inf* get-together, happening, incident, occurrence, party.

occasional *adj* casual, desultory, fitful, infrequent, intermittent, irregular, odd, *inf* once in a while, periodic, random, rare, scattered, spasmodic, sporadic, uncommon, unpredictable. *Opp* FREQUENT, REGULAR.

occult *adj* ▷ SUPERNATURAL. • *n* black arts, black magic, cabbalism, diabolism, occultism, sorcery, the supernatural, witchcraft.

occupant *n* denizen, householder, incumbent, inhabitant, lessee, lodger, occupier, owner, resident, tenant.

occupation *n* **1** incumbency, lease, occupancy, possession, residency, tenancy, tenure, use. **2** appropriation, colonization, conquest, invasion, oppression, seizure, subjection, subjugation, suzerainty, *inf* takeover, usurpation. **3** appointment, business, calling, career, employment, job, *inf* line, métier, position, post, profession, situation, trade, vocation, work. **4** *leisure occupation*. activity, diversion, entertainment, hobby, interest, pastime, pursuit, recreation.

occupy *vb* **1** dwell in, inhabit, live in, move into, reside in, take up residence in, tenant. **2** *occupy space*. fill, take up, use, utilize. **3** capture, colonize, conquer, garrison, invade, overrun, possess, subjugate, take over, take possession of. **4** *occupy your time*. absorb, busy, divert, engage, engross, involve, preoccupy. **occupied** ▷ BUSY.

occur *vb* appear, arise, befall, be found, chance, come about, come into being, *old use* come to pass, *inf* crop up, develop, exist, happen, manifest itself, materialize, *inf* show up, take place, *inf* transpire, *inf* turn out, *inf* turn up.

occurrence *n* affair, case, circumstance, development, event, happening, incident, manifestation, matter, occasion, phenomenon, proceeding.

odd *adj* **1** *odd numbers*. uneven. *Opp* EVEN. **2** *an odd sock*. extra, left over, *inf* one-off, remaining, single, spare, superfluous, surplus, unmatched, unused. **3** *odd jobs*. casual, irregular, miscellaneous, occasional, part-time, random, sundry, varied, various. **4** *odd behaviour*. abnormal, anomalous, atypical, bizarre, *inf* cranky, curious, deviant, different, eccentric, exceptional, extraordinary, freak, funny, idiosyncratic, incongruous, inexplicable, *inf* kinky, outlandish, out of the ordinary, peculiar, puzzling, queer, rare, singular, strange, uncharacteristic, uncommon, unconventional, unexpected, unusual, weird. *Opp* NORMAL.

oddments *plur n* bits, bits and pieces, fragments, *inf* junk, leftovers, litter, odds and ends, offcuts, remnants, scraps, shreds, unwanted pieces.

odious *adj* detestable, execrable, loathsome, offensive, repugnant, repulsive. ▷ HATEFUL.

odorous *adj* fragrant, odoriferous, perfumed, scented. ▷ SMELLING.

odour *n* aroma, bouquet, fragrance, nose, redolence, scent, smell, stench, *inf* stink.

odourless *adj* deodorized, unscented. *Opp* ODOROUS.

offence *n* **1** breach, crime, fault, felony, infringement, lapse, malefaction, misdeed, misdemeanour, outrage, peccadillo, sin, transgression, trespass, violation, wrong, wrongdoing. **2** anger, annoyance, disgust, displeasure, hard feelings, indignation, irritation, pique, resentment, *inf* upset. **give offence** ▷ OFFEND.

offend *vb* **1** affront, anger, annoy, cause offence, chagrin, disgust, displease, embarrass, give offence, hurt your feelings, insult, irritate, make angry, *inf* miff, outrage, pain, provoke, *inf* put your back up, revolt, rile, sicken, slight, snub, upset, vex. **2** *offend against the law*. do wrong, transgress, violate. **be offended** be annoyed, *inf* take umbrage.

offender *n* criminal, culprit, delinquent, evil-doer, guilty party, lawbreaker, malefactor, miscreant, outlaw, sinner, transgressor, wrongdoer.

offensive *adj* **1** abusive, annoying, antisocial, coarse, detestable, disagreeable, disgusting, displeasing, disrespectful, embarrassing, foul, impolite, improper, indecent, insulting, loathsome, nasty, nauseating, nauseous, noxious, objectionable, obnoxious, *inf* off-putting, repugnant, revolting, rude, sickening, unpleasant, unsavoury, vile, vulgar. ▷ OBSCENE. *Opp* PLEASANT. **2** *offensive action*. aggressive, antagonistic, attacking, belligerent, hostile, threatening, warlike. *Opp* PEACEABLE. ● *n* ▷ ATTACK.

offer *n* bid, proposal, proposition, suggestion, tender. ● *vb* **1** bid, extend, give the opportunity of, hold out, make an offer of, make available, proffer, put forward, put up, suggest. **2** *offer to help*. come forward, propose, *inf* show willing, volunteer.

offering *n* contribution, donation, gift, oblation, offertory, present, sacrifice.

offhand *adj* **1** abrupt, aloof, careless, cavalier, cool, curt, off-handed, perfunctory, unceremonious, uncooperative, uninterested. ▷ CASUAL. **2** ▷ IMPROMPTU.

office *n* **1** bureau, room, workplace, workroom. **2** appointment, assignment, commission, duty, function, job, occupation, place, position, post, responsibility, role, situation, work.

officer *n* **1** adjutant, aide-de-camp, CO, commandant, commanding officer. **2** *police officer*. constable, PC, policeman, policewoman, WPC. **3** ▷ OFFICIAL.

official *adj* accredited, approved, authentic, authoritative, authorized, bona fide, certified, formal, lawful, legal, legitimate, licensed, organized, proper, recognized, true, trustworthy, valid. ▷ FORMAL. ● *n* administrator, agent, appointee, authorized person, bureaucrat, dignitary, executive, functionary, mandarin, officer, organizer, representative, responsible person. □ *bailiff, captain, chief, clerk of court, commander, commissioner, consul, customs officer, director, elder* (of church), *equerry, governor, manager, marshal, mayor, mayoress, minister, monitor, ombudsman, overseer, prefect, president, principal, proctor, proprietor, registrar, sheriff, steward, superintendent, supervisor, usher.*

officiate *vb* adjudicate, be in charge, be responsible, chair (*a meeting*), conduct, have authority, manage, preside, referee, *inf* run (*a meeting*), umpire.

officious *adj inf* bossy, bumptious, *inf* cocky, dictatorial, forward, impertinent, interfering, meddlesome, meddling, overzealous, *inf* pushy, self-appointed, self-important.

offset *vb* cancel out, compensate for, counteract, counterbalance, make amends for, make good, make up for, redress. ▷ BALANCE.

offshoot *n* branch, by-product, derivative, development, *inf* spin-off, subsidiary product.

offspring *n* [*sing*] baby, child, descendant, heir, successor. [*plur*] brood, family, fry, issue, litter, progeny, *old use* seed, spawn, young.

often *adv* again and again, *inf* all the time, commonly, constantly, continually, frequently, generally, habitually, many times, regularly, repeatedly, time after time, time and again, usually.

oil *vb* grease, lubricate.

oily *adj* **1** buttery, fat, fatty, greasy, oleaginous. **2** *an oily manner*. ▷ OBSEQUIOUS.

ointment *n* balm, cream, embrocation, emollient, liniment, lotion, paste, salve, unguent.

old *adj* **1** ancient, antediluvian, antiquated, antique, crumbling, decayed, decaying, decrepit, dilapidated, early, historic, medieval, obsolete, primitive, quaint, ruined, superannuated, time-worn, venerable, veteran, vintage. ▷ OLD-FASHIONED. **2** *old times*. bygone, classical, forgotten, former, (*time*) immemorial, *old use* olden, past, prehistoric, previous, primeval, primitive, primordial, remote. **3** *old people*. advanced in years, aged, *inf* doddery, elderly, geriatric, *inf* getting on, grey-haired, hoary, *inf* in your dotage, long-lived, oldish, *inf* past it, senile. **4** *old customs*. age-old, enduring, established, lasting, long-standing, time-honoured, traditional, well-established. **5** *old clothes*. moth-eaten, ragged, scruffy, shabby, threadbare, worn, worn-out. **6** *old bread*. dry, stale. **7** *old tickets*. cancelled, expired, invalid, used. **8** *an old hand*. experienced, expert, familiar, mature, practised, skilled, veteran. *Opp* NEW, YOUNG. **old age** *inf* declining years, decrepitude, *inf* dotage, senility. **old person** centenarian, *inf* fogey, *inf* fogy, nonagenarian, octogenarian, pensioner, septuagenarian.

old-fashioned *adj* anachronistic, antiquated, archaic, backward-looking, conventional, dated, fusty, hackneyed, narrow-minded, obsolete, old, *inf* old hat, out of date, out of touch, outdated, outmoded, passé, pedantic, prim, proper, prudish, reactionary, time-honoured, traditional, unfashionable. *Opp* MODERN. **old-fashioned person** *inf* fogey, *inf* fogy, *inf* fuddy-duddy, pedant, reactionary, *inf* square.

omen *n* augury, auspice, foreboding, forewarning, harbinger, indication, portent, premonition, presage, prognostication, sign, token, warning, *inf* writing on the wall.

ominous *adj* baleful, dire, fateful, forbidding, foreboding, grim, ill-omened, ill-starred, inauspicious, lowering, menacing, portentous, prophetic, sinister, threatening, unfavourable, unlucky, unpromising, unpropitious, warning. *Opp* AUSPICIOUS.

omission *n* **1** deletion, elimination, exception, excision, exclusion. **2** failure, gap, neglect, negligence, oversight, shortcoming.

omit *vb* **1** cross out, cut, dispense with, drop, edit out, eliminate, erase, except, exclude, ignore, jump, leave out, miss out, overlook, pass over, reject, skip, strike out. **2** fail, forget, neglect.

omnipotent *adj* all-powerful, almighty, invincible, supreme, unconquerable.

oncoming *adj* advancing, approaching, facing, looming, nearing.

onerous *adj* burdensome, demanding, heavy, laborious, taxing. ▷ DIFFICULT.

one-sided *adj* **1** biased, bigoted, partial, partisan, prejudiced. **2** *one-sided game*. ill-matched, unbalanced, unequal, uneven.

onlooker *n* bystander, eyewitness, looker-on, observer, spectator, watcher, witness.

only *adj* lone, one, single, sole, solitary, unique. • *adv* barely, exclusively, just, merely, simply, solely.

ooze *vb* bleed, discharge, emit, exude, leak, secrete, seep, weep.

opaque *adj* cloudy, dark, dim, dull, filmy, hazy, impenetrable, muddy, murky, obscure, turbid, unclear. *Opp* CLEAR.

open *adj* **1** agape, ajar, gaping, unbolted, unfastened, unlocked, unsealed, unwrapped, wide, wide-open, yawning. **2** accessible, available, exposed, free, public, revealed, unenclosed, unprotected, unrestricted. **3** *open space*. bare, broad, clear, empty, extensive, spacious, treeless, uncrowded, undefended, unfenced, unobstructed, vacant. **4** *open arms*. extended, outstretched, spread out, unfolded. **5** *open nature*. artless, candid, communicative, flexible, frank, generous, guileless, honest, innocent, magnanimous, open-minded, responsive, sincere, straightforward, transparent, uninhibited. **6** *open defiance*. apparent, barefaced, blatant, conspicuous, downright, evident, flagrant, obvious, outspoken, overt, plain, unconcealed, undisguised, visible. **7** *an open question*. arguable, debatable, moot, problematical, unanswered, undecided, unresolved, unsettled. *Opp* CLOSED, HIDDEN. • *vb* **1** unbar, unblock, unbolt, unclose, uncork, undo, unfasten, unfold, unfurl, unlatch, unlock, unroll, unseal, untie, unwrap. **2** become open, gape, yawn. **3** *open proceedings*. activate, begin, commence, establish, *inf* get going, inaugurate, initiate, *inf* kick off, launch, set in motion, set up, start. *Opp* CLOSE.

opening *adj* first, inaugural, initial, introductory. *Opp* FINAL. • *n* **1** aperture, breach, break, chink, cleft, crack, crevice, cut, door, doorway, fissure, gap, gash, gate, gateway, hatch, hole, leak, mouth, orifice, outlet, rent, rift, slit, slot, space, split, tear, vent. **2** beginning, birth, commencement, dawn, inauguration, inception, initiation, launch, outset, start. **3** *a business opening*. *inf* break, chance, opportunity, way in.

operate *vb* **1** act, function, go, perform, run, work. **2** *operate a machine*. control, deal with, drive, handle, manage, use, work. **3** *operate on a patient*. do an operation, perform surgery.

operation *n* **1** control, direction, function, functioning, management, operating, performance, running, working. **2** action, activity, business, campaign, effort, enterprise, exercise, manoeuvre, movement, procedure, proceeding, process, project, transaction, undertaking, venture. **3** [*medical*] biopsy, surgery, transplant.

operational *adj* functioning, going, in operation, in use, in working order, operating, operative, running, *inf* up and running, usable, working.

operative *adj* **1** ▷ OPERATIONAL. **2** *the operative word*. crucial, important, key, principal, relevant, significant. • *n* ▷ WORKER.

opinion *n* assessment, attitude, belief, comment, conclusion, conjecture, conviction, estimate, feeling, guess, idea, impression, judgement, notion, perception, point of view, sentiment, theory, thought, view, viewpoint, way of thinking.

opponent *n* adversary, antagonist, challenger, competitor, contender, contestant, enemy, foe, opposer, opposition, rival. *Opp* ALLY.

opportune *adj* advantageous, appropriate, auspicious, beneficial, convenient, favourable, felicitous, fortunate, good, happy, lucky, propitious, right, suitable, timely, well-timed. *Opp* INCONVENIENT.

opportunity *n inf* break, chance, moment, occasion, opening, possibility, time.

oppose *vb* argue with, attack, be at variance with, be opposed to, challenge, combat, compete against, confront, contend with, contest, contradict, controvert, counter, counterattack, defy, disagree with, disapprove of, dissent from, face, fight, object to, obstruct, *inf* pit your wits against, quarrel with, resist, rival, stand up to, *inf* take a stand against, take issue with, withstand. *Opp* SUPPORT. **opposed** ▷ HOSTILE, OPPOSITE.

opposite *adj* **1** antithetical, conflicting, contradictory, contrasting, converse, different, hostile, incompatible, inconsistent, opposed, opposing, rival. **2** contrary, reverse. **3** *your opposite number*. corresponding, equivalent, facing, matching, similar. • *n* antithesis, contrary, converse, reverse.

opposition *n* antagonism, antipathy, competition, defiance, disapproval, enmity, hostility, objection, resistance, scepticism, unfriendliness. ▷ OPPONENT. *Opp* SUPPORT.

oppress *vb* abuse, afflict, burden, crush, depress, encumber, enslave, exploit, grind down, harass, intimidate, keep under, maltreat, overburden, persecute, pressurize, *inf* ride roughshod over, subdue, subjugate, terrorize, *inf* trample on, tyrannize, weigh down.

oppressed *adj* browbeaten, downtrodden, enslaved, exploited, misused, persecuted, subjugated, tyrannized.

oppression *n* abuse, despotism, enslavement, exploitation, harassment, injustice, maltreatment, persecution, pressure, subjection, subjugation, suppression, tyranny.

oppressive *adj* **1** brutal, cruel, despotic, harsh, repressive, tyrannical, undemocratic, unjust. **2** airless, close, heavy, hot, humid, muggy, stifling, stuffy, suffocating, sultry.

optimism *n* buoyancy, cheerfulness, confidence, hope, idealism, positiveness. *Opp* PESSIMISM.

optimistic *adj* buoyant, cheerful, confident, expectant, hopeful, idealistic, *inf* looking on the bright side, positive, sanguine. *Opp* PESSIMISTIC.

optimum *adj* best, finest, firstclass, first-rate, highest, ideal, maximum, most favourable, perfect, prime, superlative, top.

option *n* alternative, chance, choice, election, possibility, selection.

optional *adj* avoidable, discretionary, dispensable, elective, inessential, possible, unforced, unnecessary, voluntary. *Opp* COMPULSORY.

oral *adj* by mouth, said, spoken, unwritten, uttered, verbal, vocal, voiced.

oratory *n* declamation, eloquence, enunciation, fluency, *inf* gift of the gab, grandiloquence, magniloquence, rhetoric, speaking, speech making.

orbit *n* circuit, course, path, revolution, trajectory. • *vb* circle, encircle, go round, travel round.

orbital *adj* circular, encircling.

orchestrate *vb* **1** arrange, compose. **2** ▷ ORGANIZE.

ordeal *n* affliction, anguish, difficulty, distress, hardship, misery, *inf* nightmare, pain, suffering, test, torture, trial, tribulation, trouble.

order *n* **1** arrangement, array, classification, codification, disposition, lay-out, *inf* line-up, neatness, organization, pattern, progression, sequence, series, succession, system, tidiness. **2** calm, control, discipline, good behaviour, government, harmony, law and order, obedience, orderliness, peace, peacefulness, quiet, rule. **3** *social orders*. caste, category, class, degree, group, hierarchy, kind, level, rank, sort, status. **4** *in good order*. condition, repair, state. **5** *orders to be obeyed*. command, decree, direction, directive, edict, fiat, injunction, instruction, law, mandate, ordinance, regulation, requirement, rule. **6** *an order for goods*. application, booking, commission, demand, mandate, request, requisition, reservation. **7** *religious orders*. association, brotherhood, community, fraternity, group, guild, lodge, sect, sisterhood, society, sodality, sorority. *Opp* DISORDER. • *vb* **1** arrange, categorize, classify, codify, lay out, organize, put in order, sort out, tidy up. **2** *old use* bid, charge, command, compel, decree, demand, direct, enjoin, instruct, ordain, require, tell. **3** apply for, ask for, book, reserve, requisition, send away for.

orderly *adj* **1** careful, methodical, neat, organized, regular, symmetrical, systematic, tidy, well-arranged, well-organized, well-prepared. *Opp* CONFUSED, DISORGANIZED. **2** civilized, controlled, decorous, disciplined, law-abiding, peaceable, polite, restrained, well-behaved, well-mannered. *Opp* UNDISCIPLINED.

ordinary *adj* accustomed, average, common, *inf* common or garden, commonplace, conventional, customary, established, everyday, fair, familiar, habitual, humble, *inf* humdrum, indifferent, mediocre, medium, middling, moderate, modest, mundane, nondescript, normal, orthodox, passable, pedestrian, plain, prosaic, quotidian, reasonable, regular, routine, *inf* run-of-the-mill, satisfactory, simple, *inf* so-so, standard, stock, traditional, typical, undistinguished, unexceptional, unexciting, unimpressive, uninspired, uninteresting, unpretentious, unremarkable, unsurprising, usual, well-known, workaday. *Opp* EXTRAORDINARY.

organic *adj* **1** animate, biological, growing, live, living, natural. **2** *an organic whole*. coherent, coordinated, evolving, integral, integrated, methodical, organized, structured, systematic.

organism *n* animal, being, cell, creature, living thing, plant.

organization *n* **1** arrangement, categorization, classification, codification, composition, coordination, logistics, organizing, planning, regimentation, *inf* running, structuring. **2** *a business organization.* alliance, association, body, business, club, combine, company, concern, confederation, conglomerate, consortium, corporation, federation, firm, group, institute, institution, league, network, *inf* outfit, party, society, syndicate, union.

organize *vb* **1** arrange, catalogue, categorize, classify, codify, compose, coordinate, group, order, *inf* pigeonhole, put in order, rearrange, regiment, *inf* run, sort, sort out, structure, systematize, tabulate, tidy up. *Opp* JUMBLE. **2** build, coordinate, create, deal with, establish, make arrangements for, manage, mobilize, orchestrate, plan, put together, run, *inf* see to, set up, take care of. **organized** ▷ OFFICIAL, SYSTEMATIC.

orgy *n* Bacchanalia, *inf* binge, debauch, *inf* fling, party, *inf* rave-up, revel, revelry, Saturnalia, *inf* spree.

orient *vb* acclimatize, accommodate, accustom, adapt, adjust, condition, familiarize, orientate, position.

oriental *adj* Asiatic, eastern, far-eastern.

origin *n* **1** base, basis, beginning, birth, cause, commencement, cradle, creation, dawn, derivation, foundation, fount, fountainhead, genesis, inauguration, inception, launch, outset, provenance, root, source, start, well-spring. *Opp* END. **2** *humble origins.* ancestry, background, descent, extraction, family, genealogy, heritage, lineage, parentage, pedigree, start in life, stock.

original *adj* **1** aboriginal, archetypal, earliest, first, initial, native, primal, primitive, primordial. **2** *original antiques.* actual, authentic, genuine, real, true, unique. **3** *original ideas.* creative, first-hand, fresh, imaginative, ingenious, innovative, inspired, inventive, new, novel, resourceful, thoughtful, unconventional, unfamiliar, unique, unusual. *Opp* HACKNEYED.

originate *vb* **1** arise, be born, be derived, be descended, begin, come, commence, crop up, derive, emanate, emerge, issue, proceed, spring up, start, stem. **2** beget, be the inventor of, bring about, coin, conceive, create, design, discover, engender, found, give birth to, inaugurate, initiate, inspire, institute, introduce, invent, launch, mastermind, pioneer, produce, think up.

ornament *n* accessory, adornment, bauble, beautification, decoration, embellishment, embroidery, enhancement, filigree, frill, frippery, garnish, gewgaw, ornamentation, tracery, trimming, trinket. ▷ JEWELLERY. • *vb* adorn, beautify, deck, decorate, dress up, elaborate, embellish, emblazon, emboss, embroider, enhance, festoon, garnish, prettify, trim.

ornamental *adj* attractive, decorative, fancy, flashy, pretty, showy.

ornate *adj* arabesque, baroque, *inf* busy, decorated, elaborate, fancy, flamboyant, florid, flowery, fussy, luxuriant, ornamented, overdone, pretentious, rococo. *Opp* PLAIN.

orphan *n* foundling, stray, waif.

orthodox *adj* accepted, accustomed, approved, authorized, common, conformist, conservative, conventional, customary, established, mainstream, normal, official, ordinary, prevailing, recognized, regular, standard, traditional, usual, well-established. *Opp* UNCONVENTIONAL.

ostensible *adj* alleged, apparent, outward, pretended, professed, *inf* put-on, reputed, specious, supposed, visible. *Opp* REAL.

ostentation *n* affectation, display, exhibitionism, flamboyance, *inf* flashiness, flaunting, parade, pretention, pretentiousness, self-advertisement, show, showing-off, *inf* swank. *Opp* MODESTY.

ostentatious *adj* flamboyant, *inf* flashy, pretentious, showy, *inf* swanky, vainglorious. ▷ BOASTFUL. *Opp* MODEST.

ostracize *vb* avoid, banish, *inf* black, blackball, blacklist, boycott, cast out, cold-shoulder, *inf* cut, *inf* cut dead, exclude, excommunicate, expel, isolate, reject, *inf* send to Coventry, shun, shut out, snub. *Opp* BEFRIEND.

oust *vb* banish, drive out, eject, expel, *inf* kick out, remove, replace, *inf* sack, supplant, take over from, unseat.

outbreak *n* epidemic, *inf* flare-up, plague, rash, upsurge.

outburst *n* attack, effusion, eruption, explosion, fit, flood, outbreak, outpouring, paroxysm, rush, spasm, surge, upsurge.

outcast *n* castaway, displaced person, exile, leper, outlaw, outsider, pariah, refugee, reject, untouchable.

outcome *n* conclusion, consequence, effect, end-product, result, sequel, upshot.

outcry *n* cry of disapproval, dissent, hue and cry, objection, opposition, protest, protestation, remonstrance.

outdo *vb* beat, defeat, exceed, excel, *inf* get the better of, outbid, outdistance, outrun, outshine, outstrip, outweigh, overcome, surpass, top, trump.

outdoor *adj* alfresco, open-air, out of doors, outside.

outer *adj* **1** exterior, external, outside, outward, superficial, surface. **2** distant, further, outlying, peripheral, remote. *Opp* INNER.

outfit *n* **1** accoutrements, attire, costume, ensemble, equipment, garb, *inf* gear, *inf* get-up, *inf* rig, suit, trappings, *inf* turn-out. **2** ▷ ORGANIZATION.

outgoing *adj* **1** *outgoing president.* departing, emeritus, ex-, former, last, leaving, past, retiring. **2** *outgoing tide.* ebbing, falling, retreating. **3** ▷ SOCIABLE. *Opp* INCOMING. **outgoings** ▷ EXPENSE.

outing *n* excursion, expedition, jaunt, picnic, ride, tour, trip.

outlast *vb* outlive, survive.

outlaw *n* bandit, brigand, criminal, deserter, desperado, fugitive, highwayman, marauder, outcast, renegade, robber. • *vb* ban, exclude, forbid, prohibit, proscribe. ▷ BANISH.

outlet *n* **1** channel, discharge, duct, egress, escape route, exit, mouth, opening, orifice, safety valve, vent, way out. **2** ▷ SHOP.

outline *n* **1** abstract, *inf* bare bones, diagram, digest, draft, framework, plan, précis, résumé, *inf* rough idea, *inf* rundown, scenario, skeleton, sketch, summary, synopsis, thumbnail sketch. **2** contour, figure, form, profile, shadow, shape, silhouette. • *vb* delineate, draft, give the gist of, give the outline, plan out, précis, rough out, sketch out, summarize.

outlook *n* **1** aspect, panorama, scene, sight, vantage point, view, vista. **2** *your mental outlook.* angle, attitude, frame of mind, opinion, perspective, point of view, position, slant, standpoint, viewpoint. **3** *the weather outlook.* expectations, forecast, *inf* look-out, prediction, prognosis, prospect.

outlying *adj* distant, far-away, far-flung, far-off, outer, outermost, remote. *Opp* CENTRAL.

output *n* achievement, crop, harvest, production, productivity, result, yield.

outrage *n* **1** atrocity, crime, *inf* disgrace, enormity, indignity, outrageous act, scandal, *inf* sensation, violation. **2** anger, bitterness, disgust, fury, horror, indignation, resentment, revulsion, shock, wrath. • *vb* ▷ ANGER.

outrageous *adj* **1** abominable, atrocious, barbaric, beastly, bestial, criminal, cruel, disgraceful, disgusting, execrable, infamous, iniquitous, monstrous, nefarious, notorious, offensive, preposterous, revolting, scandalous, shocking, unspeakable, unthinkable, vile, villainous, wicked. **2** *outrageous prices*. excessive, extortionate, extravagant, immoderate, unreasonable. *Opp* REASONABLE.

outside *adj* **1** exterior, external, facing, outer, outward, superficial, surface, visible. **2** *outside interference*. alien, extraneous, foreign. **3** *outside chance*. ▷ REMOTE. ● *n* appearance, case, casing, exterior, façade, face, front, look, shell, skin, surface.

outsider *n* alien, foreigner, *inf* gatecrasher, guest, immigrant, interloper, intruder, invader, newcomer, non-member, non-resident, outcast, stranger, trespasser, visitor.

outskirts *plur n* borders, edge, environs, fringe, margin, outer areas, periphery, purlieus, suburbs. *Opp* CENTRE.

outspoken *adj* blunt, candid, direct, explicit, forthright, frank, plain-spoken, tactless, unambiguous, undiplomatic, unequivocal, unreserved. ▷ HONEST. *Opp* EVASIVE.

outstanding *adj* **1** above the rest, celebrated, conspicuous, distinguished, dominant, eminent, excellent, exceptional, extraordinary, first-class, first-rate, great, important, impressive, memorable, notable, noteworthy, noticeable, predominant, pre-eminent, prominent, remarkable, singular, special, striking, superior, top rank, unrivalled. ▷ FAMOUS. *Opp* ORDINARY. **2** ▷ OVERDUE.

outward *adj* apparent, evident, exterior, external, manifest, noticeable, observable, obvious, ostensible, outer, outside, superficial, surface, visible.

outwit *vb* deceive, dupe, fool, *inf* get the better of, gull, hoax, hoodwink, make a fool of, outfox, outmanoeuvre, *inf* outsmart, *inf* put one over on, *inf* take in, trick. ▷ CHEAT.

oval *adj* egg-shaped, ellipsoidal, elliptical, oviform, ovoid.

ovation *n* acclaim, acclamation, applause, cheering, plaudits, praise.

overcast *adj* black, clouded, cloudy, dark, dismal, dull, gloomy, grey, leaden, lowering, murky, sombre, starless, stormy, sunless, threatening. *Opp* CLOUDLESS.

overcoat *n* greatcoat, mackintosh, top-coat, trench-coat.

overcome *adj* at a loss, beaten, *inf* bowled over, *inf* done in, exhausted, overwhelmed, prostrate, speechless. ● *vb* ▷ OVERTHROW.

overcrowded *adj* congested, crammed, crawling, filled to capacity, full, jammed, *inf* jampacked, overloaded, packed.

overdue *adj* **1** belated, delayed, late, slow, tardy, unpunctual. *Opp* EARLY. **2** *overdue bills*. due, outstanding, owing, unpaid, unresolved, unsettled.

overeat *vb* be greedy, eat too much, feast, gorge, gormandize, *inf* guzzle, indulge yourself, *inf* make a pig of yourself, overindulge, *inf* stuff yourself.

overflow *vb* brim over, flood, pour over, run over, spill, well up.

overgrown *adj* **1** outsize, oversized. ▷ BIG. **2** *overgrown garden*. overrun, rank, tangled, uncut, unkempt, untidy, untrimmed, unweeded, weedy, wild.

overhang *vb* beetle, bulge, jut, project, protrude, stick out.

overhaul *vb* **1** check over, examine, *inf* fix, inspect, mend, rebuild, recondition, refurbish, renovate, repair, restore, service. **2** ▷ OVERTAKE.

overhead *adj* aerial, elevated, high, overhanging, raised, upper.

overlook *vb* **1** fail to notice, forget, leave out, miss, neglect, omit. **2** condone, disregard, excuse, gloss over, ignore, let pass, make allowances for, pardon, pass over, pay no attention to, *inf* shut your eyes to, *inf* turn a blind eye to, *inf* write off. **3** *overlook a lake*. face, front, have a view of, look at, look down on, look on to.

overpower *vb* ▷ OVERTHROW.

overpowering *adj* compelling, consuming, inescapable, insupportable, irrepressible, irresistible, overriding, overwhelming, powerful, strong, unbearable, uncontrollable, unendurable.

oversee *vb* administer, be in charge of, control, direct, invigilate, *inf* keep an eye on, preside over, superintend, supervise, watch over.

oversight *n* **1** carelessness, dereliction of duty, error, failure, fault, mistake, omission. **2** *oversight of a job.* administration, control, direction, management, supervision, surveillance.

overstate *vb inf* blow up out of proportion, embroider, exaggerate, magnify, make too much of, maximize, overemphasize, overstress.

overt *adj* apparent, blatant, clear, evident, manifest, obvious, open, patent, plain, unconcealed, undisguised, visible. *Opp* SECRET.

overtake *vb* catch up with, gain on, leave behind, outdistance, outpace, outstrip, overhaul, pass.

overthrow *n* conquest, defeat, destruction, mastery, rout, subjugation, suppression, unseating. • *vb* beat, bring down, conquer, crush, deal with, defeat, depose, dethrone, get the better of, *inf* lick, master, oust, overcome, overpower, overturn, overwhelm, rout, *inf* send packing, subdue, *inf* topple, triumph over, unseat, vanquish, win against.

overtone *n* association, connotation, hint, implication, innuendo, reverberation, suggestion, undertone.

overturn *vb* **1** capsize, flip, invert, keel over, knock over, spill, tip over, topple, turn over, *inf* turn turtle, turn upside down, up-end, upset. **2** ▷ OVERTHROW.

overwhelm *vb* **1** engulf, flood, immerse, inundate, submerge, swamp. **2** ▷ OVERTHROW. **overwhelming** ▷ OVERPOWERING.

owe *vb* be in debt, have debts.

owing *adj* due, outstanding, overdue, owed, payable, unpaid, unsettled. **owing to** because of, caused by, on account of, resulting from, thanks to, through.

own *vb* be the owner of, have, hold, possess. **own up** ▷ CONFESS.

owner *n* freeholder, holder, landlady, landlord, possessor, proprietor.

P

pace *n* **1** step, stride. **2** *a fast pace.* gait, *inf* lick, movement, quickness, rate, speed, tempo, velocity. • *vb* ▷ WALK.

pacify *vb* appease, assuage, calm, conciliate, humour, mollify, placate, quell, quieten, soothe, subdue, tame, tranquillize. *Opp* ANGER.

pack *n* **1** bale, box, bundle, package, packet, parcel. **2** backpack, duffel bag, haversack, kitbag, knapsack, rucksack. **3** ▷ GROUP. • *vb* **1** bundle (up), fill, load, package, parcel up, put, put together, store, stow, wrap up. **2** compress, cram, crowd, jam, overcrowd, press, ram, squeeze, stuff, tamp down, wedge. **pack off** ▷ DISMISS. **pack up** ▷ FINISH.

pact *n* agreement, alliance, armistice, arrangement, bargain, compact, concord, concordat, contract, covenant, deal, *Fr* entente, league, peace, settlement, treaty, truce, understanding.

pad *n* **1** cushion, filler, hassock, kneeler, padding, pillow, stuffing, wad. **2** jotter, memo pad, notebook, stationery, writing pad. • *vb* cushion, fill, line, pack, protect, stuff, upholster, wad. **pad out** ▷ EXTEND.

padding *n* **1** filling, protection, upholstery, stuffing, wadding. **2** prolixity, verbiage, verbosity, *inf* waffle, wordiness.

paddle *n* oar, scull. • *vb* **1** propel, row, scull. **2** dabble, splash about, wade.

paddock *n* enclosure, field, meadow, pasture.

pagan *adj* atheistic, godless, heathen, idolatrous, infidel, irreligious, polytheistic, unchristian. • *n* atheist, heathen, infidel, savage, unbeliever.

page *n* **1** folio, leaf, recto, sheet, side, verso. **2** errand-boy, messenger, page-boy.

pageant *n* ceremony, display, extravaganza, parade, procession, show, spectacle, tableau.

pageantry *n* ceremony, display, formality, grandeur, magnificence, pomp, ritual, show, spectacle, splendour.

pain *n* ache, aching, affliction, agony, anguish, cramp, crick, discomfort, distress, headache, hurt, irritation, ordeal, pang, smart, smarting, soreness, spasm, stab, sting, suffering, tenderness, throb, throes, toothache, torment, torture, twinge. • *vb* ▷ HURT.

painful *adj* **1** aching, *inf* achy, agonizing, burning, cruel, excruciating, *old use* grievous, hard to bear, hurting, inflamed, piercing, raw, severe, sharp, smarting, sore, *inf* splitting (*head*), stabbing, stinging, tender, throbbing. **2** distressing, harrowing, hurtful, laborious, *inf* traumatic, trying, unpleasant, upsetting, vexing. **3** *a painful decision.* difficult, hard, troublesome, uncongenial. *Opp* PAINLESS. **be painful** ▷ HURT.

painkiller *n* anaesthetic, analgesic, anodyne, palliative, sedative.

painless *adj* comfortable, easy, effortless, pain-free, simple, trouble-free, undemanding. *Opp* PAINFUL.

paint *n* colour, colouring, dye, pigment, stain, tint. □ *distemper, emulsion, enamel, gloss paint, lacquer, matt paint, oil-colour, oil-paint, oils, pastel, primer, tempera, undercoat, varnish, water-colour, whitewash.* • *vb* **1** apply paint to, coat, colour, cover, daub, decorate, dye, enamel, gild, lacquer, redecorate, stain, tint, touch up, varnish, whitewash. **2** delineate, depict, describe, picture, portray, represent.

painter *n* artist, decorator, illustrator, miniaturist.

painting *n* fresco, landscape, miniature, mural, oil-painting, portrait, still-life, water-colour.

pair *n* brace, couple, duet, duo, mates, partners, partnership, set of two, twins, twosome. • *vb* **pair off**, **pair up** couple, double up, find a partner, get together, join up, *inf* make a twosome, match up, *inf* pal up, team up.

palace *n* castle, château, mansion, official residence, stately home. ▷ HOUSE.

palatable *adj* acceptable, agreeable, appetizing, easy to take, eatable, edible, nice to eat, pleasant, tasty. *Opp* UNPALATABLE.

palatial *adj* aristocratic, grand, large-scale, luxurious, majestic, opulent, *inf* posh, splendid, stately, upmarket.

pale *adj* **1** anaemic, ashen, blanched, bloodless, cadaverous, colourless, corpse-like, *inf* deathly, drained, etiolated, ghastly, ghostly, ill-looking, pallid, pasty, *inf* peaky, sallow, sickly, unhealthy, wan, *inf* washed-out, *inf* whey-faced, white, whitish. **2** *pale colours.* bleached, dim, faded, faint, light, pastel, subtle, weak. *Opp* BRIGHT. • *vb* become pale, blanch, blench, dim, etiolate, fade, lighten, lose colour, whiten.

pall *n* cloth, mantle, shroud, veil. ▷ COVERING. • *vb* become boring, become uninteresting, cloy, irritate, jade, sate, satiate, weary.

palliative *adj* alleviating, calming, reassuring, sedative, soothing. • *n* painkiller, sedative, tranquillizer.

palpable *adj* apparent, corporeal, evident, manifest, obvious, patent, physical, real, solid, substantial, tangible, touchable, visible. *Opp* INTANGIBLE.

palpitate *vb* beat, flutter, pound, pulsate, quiver, shiver, throb, tremble, vibrate.

paltry *adj* contemptible, inconsequential, insignificant, petty, *inf* piddling, pitiable, puny, trifling, unimportant, worthless. ▷ SMALL. *Opp* IMPORTANT.

pamper *vb* coddle, cosset, humour, indulge, mollycoddle, overindulge, pet, spoil, spoonfeed.

pamphlet *n* booklet, brochure, bulletin, catalogue, circular, flyer, folder, handbill, handout, leaflet, notice, tract.

pan *n* container, utensil. □ *billycan, casserole, frying-pan, pot, saucepan, skillet.* • *vb* ▷ CRITICIZE.

panache *n* animation, brio, confidence, dash, élan, energy, enthusiasm, flair, flamboyance, flourish, savoir-faire, self-assurance, spirit, style, swagger, verve, zest.

pandemonium *n* babel, bedlam, chaos, confusion, hubbub, noise, rumpus, turmoil, uproar. ▷ COMMOTION.

pander *n* go-between, *inf* pimp, procurer. • *vb* **pander to** bow to, cater for, fulfil, gratify, humour, indulge, please, provide, satisfy.

pane *n* glass, light, panel, sheet of glass, window.

panel *n* **1** insert, pane, panelling, rectangle, *plur* wainscot. **2** committee, group, jury, team.

panic *n* alarm, consternation, *inf* flap, horror, hysteria, stampede, terror. • *vb* become panic-stricken, *inf* fall apart, *inf* flap, *inf* go to pieces, *inf* lose your head, *inf* lose your nerve, overreact, stampede. ▷ FEAR.

panic-stricken *adj* alarmed, *inf* beside yourself, disorientated, frantic, frenzied, horrified, hysterical, *inf* in a cold sweat, *inf* in a tizzy, jumpy, overexcited, panicky, panic-struck, terror-stricken, undisciplined, unnerved, worked-up. ▷ FRIGHTENED. *Opp* CALM.

panorama *n* landscape, perspective, prospect, scene, view, vista.

panoramic *adj* commanding, extensive, scenic, sweeping, wide.

pant *vb* blow, breathe quickly, gasp, *inf* huff and puff, puff, wheeze. **panting** ▷ BREATHLESS.

pants *n* **1** *old use* bloomers, boxer shorts, briefs, camiknickers, drawers, knickers, panties, pantihose, shorts, *inf* smalls, trunks, underpants, *inf* undies, Y-fronts. **2** ▷ TROUSERS.

paper *n* **1** folio, leaf, sheet. □ *A4 (A1, A2, etc), card, cardboard, cartridge paper, foolscap, manila, notepaper, papyrus, parchment, postcard, quarto, stationery, tissue-paper, toilet paper, tracing-paper, vellum, wallpaper, wrapping-paper, writing-paper.* **2** certificate, credentials, deed, document, form, *inf* ID, identification, licence, record. **3** *the daily paper. inf* daily, journal, newspaper, *inf* rag, tabloid. **4** *an academic paper.* article, discourse, dissertation, essay, monograph, thesis, treatise.

parable *n* allegory, exemplum, fable, moral tale. ▷ WRITING.

parade *n* cavalcade, ceremony, column, cortège, display, file, march-past, motorcade, pageant, procession, review, show, spectacle. ● *vb* **1** assemble, file past, form up, line up, make a procession, march past, present yourself, process. ▷ WALK. **2** ▷ DISPLAY.

paradise *n* Eden, Elysium, heaven, Shangri-La, Utopia.

paradox *n* absurdity, anomaly, contradiction, incongruity, inconsistency, self-contradiction.

paradoxical *adj* absurd, anomalous, conflicting, contradictory, illogical, improbable, incongruous, self-contradictory.

parallel *adj* **1** equidistant. **2** *parallel events.* analogous, cognate, contemporary, corresponding, equivalent, like, matching, similar. ● *n* **1** analogue, counterpart, equal, likeness, match. **2** analogy, comparison, correspondence, equivalence, kinship, resemblance, similarity. ● *vb* be parallel to, be parallel with, compare with, correspond to, duplicate, echo, equate with, keep pace with, match, remind you of, run alongside.

paralyse *vb* anaesthetize, cripple, deactivate, deaden, desensitize, disable, freeze, halt, immobilize, incapacitate, lame, numb, petrify, stop, stun.

paralysed *adj* crippled, dead, desensitized, disabled, handicapped, immobile, immovable, incapacitated, lame, numb, palsied, paralytic, paraplegic, rigid, unusable, useless.

paralysis *n* deadness, immobility, numbness, palsy, paraplegia.

paraphernalia *plur n* accessories, apparatus, baggage, belongings, chattels, *inf* clobber, effects, equipment, gear, impedimenta, materials, *inf* odds and ends, possessions, property, *inf* rig, stuff, tackle, things, trappings.

paraphrase *vb* explain, interpret, put into other words, rephrase, restate, reword, rewrite, translate.

parcel *n* bale, box, bundle, carton, case, pack, package, packet. **parcel out** ▷ DIVIDE. **parcel up** ▷ PACK.

parch *vb* bake, burn, dehydrate, desiccate, dry, scorch, shrivel, wither. **parched** ▷ DRY, THIRSTY.

pardon *n* absolution, amnesty, condonation, discharge, exculpation, exoneration, forgiveness, indulgence, mercy, release, reprieve. ● *vb* absolve, condone, exculpate, excuse, exonerate, forgive, free, grant pardon, let off, overlook, release, remit, reprieve, set free, spare.

pardonable *adj* allowable, condonable, excusable, forgivable, justifiable, minor, negligible, petty, understandable, venial *(sin)*. *Opp* UNFORGIVABLE.

parent *n* begetter, father, guardian, mother, procreator, progenitor.

parentage *n* ancestry, birth, descent, extraction, family, line, lineage, pedigree, stock.

park *n* common, gardens, green, recreation ground. □ *amusement park, arboretum, botanical gardens, car-park, estate, national park, nature reserve, parkland, reserve, theme park.* • *vb* deposit, leave, place, position, put, station, store. **park yourself** ▷ SETTLE.

parliament *n* assembly, conclave, congress, convocation, council, diet, government, legislature, lower house, senate, upper house.

parody *n* burlesque, caricature, distortion, imitation, lampoon, mimicry, satire, *inf* send-up, *inf* spoof, *inf* take-off, travesty. • *vb* ape, burlesque, caricature, guy, imitate, lampoon, mimic, satirize, *inf* send up, *inf* take off, travesty. ▷ RIDICULE.

parry *vb* avert, block, deflect, evade, fend off, push away, repel, repulse, stave off, ward off.

part *n* **1** bit, branch, component, constituent, department, division, element, fraction, fragment, ingredient, parcel, particle, percentage, piece, portion, ramification, scrap, section, sector, segment, shard, share, single item, subdivision, unit. **2** department, faction, party, section, subdivision, unit. **3** *part of a book.* chapter, episode. **4** *part of a town.* area, district, neighbourhood, quarter, region, sector, vicinity. **5** *part of the body.* limb, member, organ. **6** *part in a play.* cameo, character, role. • *vb* **1** cut off, detach, disconnect, divide, pull apart, separate, sever, split, sunder. *Opp* JOIN. **2** break away, depart, go away, leave, part company, quit, say goodbye, separate, split up, take leave, withdraw. *Opp* MEET. **part with** ▷ RELINQUISH. **take part** ▷ PARTICIPATE.

partial *adj* **1** imperfect, incomplete, limited, qualified, unfinished. *Opp* COMPLETE. **2** *partial judge.* biased, one-sided, partisan, prejudiced, unfair. *Opp* IMPARTIAL. **be partial to** ▷ LIKE.

participate *vb* assist, be active, be involved, contribute, cooperate, engage, enter, help, join in, partake, share, take part.

participation *n* activity, assistance, complicity, contribution, cooperation, engagement, involvement, partnership, sharing.

particle *n* **1** bit, crumb, dot, drop, fragment, grain, hint, iota, jot, mite, morsel, *old use* mote, piece, scintilla, scrap, shred, sliver, *inf* smidgen, speck, trace. **2** atom, electron, molecule, neutron.

particular *adj* **1** distinct, idiosyncratic, individual, peculiar, personal, singular, specific, uncommon, unique, unmistakable. **2** *particular with detail.* exact, nice, painstaking, precise, rigorous, scrupulous, thorough. **3** *gave particular pleasure.* especial, exceptional, important, marked, notable, noteworthy, outstanding, significant, special, unusual. **4** *particular about food.* choosy, critical, discriminating, fastidious, finical, finicky, fussy, meticulous, nice, *inf* pernickety, selective. *Opp* GENERAL, EASYGOING. **particulars** circumstances, details, facts, information, *sl* low-down.

parting *n* departure, farewell, going away, leave-taking, leaving, saying goodbye, separation, splitting up, valediction.

partisan *adj* biased, bigoted, blinkered, devoted, factional, fanatical, narrow-minded, one-sided, partial, prejudiced, sectarian, unfair. *Opp* IMPARTIAL. • *n* adherent, devotee, fanatic, follower, freedom fighter, guerrilla, resistance fighter, supporter, underground fighter, zealot.

partition *n* **1** break-up, division, separation, splitting up. **2** barrier, panel, room-divider, screen, wall. • *vb* cut up, divide, parcel out, separate off, share out, split up, subdivide.

partner *n* **1** accessory, accomplice, ally, assistant, associate, *inf* bedfellow, collaborator, colleague, companion, comrade, confederate, helper, *inf* mate, *sl* sidekick. **2** consort, husband, mate, spouse, wife.

partnership *n* **1** affiliation, alliance, association, combination, company, confederation, cooperative, syndicate. **2** collaboration, complicity, cooperation. **3** marriage, relationship, union.

party *n* **1** celebration, *inf* do, festivity, function, gathering, *inf* get-together, *inf* jollification, *inf* knees-up, merrymaking, *inf* rave-up, *inf* shindig, social gathering. □ *ball, banquet, barbecue, ceilidh, dance,* inf *disco, discothèque, feast,* inf *hen-party, house-warming, orgy, picnic, reception, reunion,* inf *stag-party, tea-party, wedding.* **2** *a political party.* alliance, association, bloc, cabal, *inf* camp, caucus, clique, coalition, faction, junta, league, sect, side. ▷ GROUP.

pass *n* **1** canyon, col, cut, defile, gap, gorge, gully, opening, passage, ravine, valley, way through. **2** *identity pass.* authority, authorization, clearance, *inf* ID, licence, passport, permission, permit, safe-conduct, ticket, warrant. • *vb* **1** go beyond, go by, move on, move past, outstrip, overhaul, overtake, proceed, progress, *inf* thread your way. **2** *time passes.* disappear, elapse, fade, go away, lapse, tick by, vanish. **3** *pass drinks.* circulate, deal out, deliver, give, hand over, offer, present, share, submit, supply, transfer. **4** *pass a resolution.* agree, approve, authorize, confirm, decree, enact, establish, ordain, pronounce, ratify, validate. **5** *I pass! inf* give in, opt out, say nothing, waive your rights. **pass away** ▷ DIE. **pass on** ▷ TRANSFER. **pass out** ▷ FAINT. **pass over** ▷ IGNORE.

passable *adj* **1** acceptable, adequate, admissible, allowable, all right, fair, indifferent, mediocre, middling, moderate, not bad, ordinary, satisfactory, *inf* so-so, tolerable. *Opp* UNACCEPTABLE. **2** clear, navigable, open, traversable, unblocked, unobstructed, usable. *Opp* IMPASSABLE.

passage *n* **1** corridor, entrance, hall, hallway, lobby, passageway, vestibule. **2** *passage of time.* advance, flow, lapse, march, movement, moving on, passing, progress, progression, transition. **3** *sea passage.* crossing, cruise, voyage. ▷ JOURNEY. **4** *through passage.* pass, route, thoroughfare, tunnel, way through. ▷ OPENING. **5** *passage from a book.* citation, episode, excerpt, extract, paragraph, part, piece, portion, quotation, scene, section, selection.

passenger *n* commuter, rider, traveller, voyager.

passer-by *n* bystander, onlooker, witness.

passion *n* appetite, ardour, avidity, avidness, commitment, craving, craze, desire, drive, eagerness, emotion, enthusiasm, fanaticism, fervency, fervour, fire, flame, frenzy, greed, heat, hunger, infatuation, intensity, keenness, love, lust, mania, obsession, strong feeling, suffering, thirst, urge, urgency, vehemence, zeal, zest.

passionate *adj* ardent, aroused, avid, burning, committed, eager, emotional, enthusiastic, excited, fanatical, fervent, fiery, frenzied, greedy, heated, hot, hungry, impassioned, infatuated, inflamed, intense, lustful, manic, obsessive, roused, sexy, strong, urgent, vehement, violent, worked up, zealous. *Opp* APATHETIC.

passive *adj* apathetic, complaisant, compliant, deferential, docile, impassive, inert, inactive, long-suffering, malleable, non-violent, patient, phlegmatic, pliable, quiescent, receptive, resigned, sheepish, submissive, supine, tame, tractable, unassertive, unmoved, unresisting, yielding. ▷ CALM. *Opp* ACTIVE.

past *adj* bygone, dead, *inf* dead and buried, earlier, ended, finished, forgotten, former, gone, historical, late, olden (*days*), *inf* over and done with, previous, recent, sometime. • *n* antiquity, days gone by, former times, history, old days, olden days, past times. *Opp* FUTURE.

e *adj* brooding, cogitating, plative, day-dreaming, *inf* far-*nf* in a brown study, lost in , meditative, reflective, rumin-houghtful.

n beggary, destitution, rishment, indigence, lack, poverty, scarcity, want.

e *n* **1** folk, human beings, nity, humans, individuals, and gentlemen, mankind, men omen, mortals, persons. **2** citi-, citizens, community, elect-*inf* grass roots, *Gr* hoi polloi, , *inf* the plebs, populace, popu-, the public, society, subjects. *r own people*. clan, family, kins-kith and kin, nation, race, rela-, relatives, tribe. ● *vb* colonize, nhabit, occupy, overrun, popu-settle.

eive *vb* **1** become aware of, sight of, descry, detect, discern, over, distinguish, espy, glimpse, , identify, make out, note, ce, observe, recognize, see, spot. ppreciate, apprehend, compre-d, deduce, feel, *inf* figure out, ner, grasp, infer, know, realize, se, understand.

ceptible *adj* appreciable, aud-, detectable, discernible, distinct, tinguishable, evident, identifiable, anifest, marked, notable, notice-le, observable, obvious, palpable, rceivable, plain, recognizable, mistakable, visible. *Opp* IMPERCEPTI-E.

rception *n* appreciation, ap-rehension, awareness, cognition, omprehension, consciousness, iscernment, insight, instinct, intu-ion, knowledge, observation, per-pective, realization, recognition, ensation, sense, understanding, view.

erceptive *adj* acute, alert, astute, attentive, aware, clever, discerning, discriminating, observant, penetrat-ing, percipient, perspicacious, quick, responsive, sensitive, sharp, sharp-eyed, shrewd, sympathetic, under-standing. ▷ INTELLIGENT.

perch *n* rest, resting-place, roost. ● balance, rest, roost, settle, sit.

percussion *n* □ *bell, castanets, celest chime bar, cymbal, glockenspiel, gong kettledrum, maracas, rattle, tambourine timpani, triangle, tubular bells, vibra phone, whip, wood block, xylophone* ▷ DRUM.

perdition *n* damnation, doom downfall, hell, hellfire, ruin, ruina-tion.

perfect *adj* **1** absolute, complete, completed, consummate, excellent, exemplary, faultless, finished, flaw-less, ideal, immaculate, incompar-able, matchless, mint, superlative, unbeatable, undamaged, unexcep-tionable, unqualified, whole. **2** blameless, irreproachable, pure, sinless, spotless, unimpeachable. **3** accurate, authentic, correct, exact, faithful, immaculate, impeccable, precise, tailor-made, true. *Opp* IMPER-FECT. ● *vb* bring to fruition, bring to perfection, carry through, complete, consummate, effect, execute, finish, fulfil, make perfect, realize, *inf* see through.

perfection *n* **1** beauty, complete-ness, excellence, faultlessness, flaw-lessness, ideal, precision, purity, wholeness. *Opp* IMPERFECTION. **2** *the per-fection of a plan*. accomplishment, achievement, completion, consum-mation, end, fruition, fulfilment, realization.

perforate *vb* bore through, drill, penetrate, pierce, prick, punch, punc-ture, riddle.

perform *vb* **1** accomplish, achieve, bring about, carry on, carry out, commit, complete, discharge, dis-patch, do, effect, execute, finish, ful-fil, *inf* pull off. **2** behave, function, go, operate, run, work. **3** *perform on stage*. act, appear, dance, feature, fig-ure, take part. **4** *perform a play, song*. enact, mount, play, present, produce, put on, render, represent, serenade, sing, stage.

performance *n* **1** accomplishment, achievement, carrying out, comple-

paste *n* **1** adhesive, fixative, glue, gum. **2** pâté, spread. ● *vb* fix, glue, stick. ▷ FASTEN.

pastiche *n* blend, composite, com-pound, *inf* hotchpotch, mess, miscel-lany, mixture, *inf* motley collection, patchwork, selection.

pastime *n* activity, amusement, avocation, distraction, diversion, en-tertainment, fun, game, hobby, leisure activity, occupation, play, recreation, relaxation, sport.

pastoral *adj* **1** agrarian, agricultural, Arcadian, bucolic, country, farming, idyllic, outdoor, provincial, rural, rus-tic. ▷ PEACEFUL. *Opp* URBAN. **2** *pastoral duties*. clerical, ecclesiastical, minis-terial, parochial, priestly.

pasture *n* field, grassland, grazing, mead, meadow, paddock, pasturage.

pat *vb* caress, dab, slap, stroke, tap. ▷ TOUCH.

patch *n* darn, mend, piece, rein-forcement, repair. ● *vb* cover, darn, fix, mend, reinforce, repair, sew up, stitch up.

patchy *adj inf* bitty, blotchy, chang-ing, dappled, erratic, inconsistent, irregular, speckled, spotty, uneven, unpredictable, variable, varied, vary-ing. *Opp* UNIFORM.

patent *adj* apparent, blatant, clear, conspicuous, evident, flagrant, mani-fest, obvious, open, plain, self-evident, transparent, undisguised, visible.

path *n* **1** alley, bridle-path, bridle-way, esplanade, footpath, footway, pathway, pavement, *Amer* sidewalk, towpath, track, trail, walk, walkway, way. ▷ ROAD. **2** approach, course, direction, flight path, orbit, route, trajectory, way.

pathetic *adj* **1** affecting, distressing, emotional, emotive, heartbreaking, heart-rending, lamentable, moving, piteous, pitiable, pitiful, plaintive, poignant, stirring, touching, tragic. ▷ SAD. **2** ▷ INADEQUATE.

pathos *n* emotion, feeling, pity, poignancy, sadness, tragedy.

patience *n* **1** calmness, composure, endurance, equanimity, forbearance, fortitude, leniency, long-suffering, resignation, restraint, self-control, serenity, stoicism, toleration, *inf* unflappability. **2** *work with patience*. assiduity, determination, diligence, doggedness, endurance, firmness, perseverance, persistence, pertina-city, *inf* stickability, tenacity.

patient *adj* **1** accommodating, acqui-escent, calm, compliant, composed, docile, easygoing, even-tempered, forbearing, forgiving, lenient, long-suffering, mild, philosophical, quiet, resigned, self-possessed, serene, sto-ical, submissive, tolerant, uncom-plaining. **2** *a patient worker*. assiduous, determined, diligent, dogged, persevering, persistent, steady, tenacious, unhurried, untir-ing. *Opp* IMPATIENT. ● *n* case, invalid, outpatient, sufferer.

patriot *n derog* chauvinist, loyalist, nationalist, *derog* xenophobe.

patriotic *adj derog* chauvinistic, *derog* jingoistic, loyal, nationalistic, *derog* xenophobic.

patriotism *n derog* chauvinism, *derog* jingoism, loyalty, nationalism, *derog* xenophobia.

patrol *n* **1** beat, guard, policing, sentry-duty, surveillance, vigilance, watch. **2** guard, lookout, patrolman, sentinel, sentry, watchman. ● *vb* be on patrol, defend, guard, inspect, keep a lookout, make the rounds, police, protect, stand guard, tour, walk the beat, watch over.

patron *n* **1** advocate, *inf* an-gel, backer, benefactor, champion, defender, helper, philanthropist, pro-moter, sponsor, subscriber, sup-porter. **2** *patron of a shop*. client, customer, frequenter, *inf* regular, shopper.

patronage *n* backing, business, cus-tom, help, sponsorship, support, trade.

patronize *vb* **1** back, be a patron of, bring trade to, buy from, deal with, encourage, frequent, give patronage to, shop at, support. **2** *be patronizing towards.* humiliate, *inf* look down on, *inf* look down your nose at, *inf* put down, talk down to. **patronizing** ▷ SUPERIOR.

pattern *n* **1** arrangement, decoration, design, device, figuration, figure, motif, ornamentation, sequence, shape, system, tessellation. **2** archetype, criterion, example, exemplar, guide, ideal, model, norm, original, paragon, precedent, prototype, sample, specimen, standard, yardstick.

pause *n* break, *inf* breather, breathing space, caesura, check, delay, gap, halt, hesitation, hiatus, hold-up, interlude, intermission, interruption, interval, lacuna, lapse, *inf* let-up, lull, moratorium, respite, rest, standstill, stop, stoppage, suspension, wait. • *vb* break off, delay, falter, halt, hang back, have a pause, hesitate, hold, mark time, rest, stop, *inf* take a break, *inf* take a breather, wait.

pave *vb* asphalt, concrete, cover with paving, flag, *old use* macadamize, *inf* make up, surface, tarmac, tile. **pave the way** ▷ PREPARE.

pavement *n* footpath, *Amer* sidewalk. ▷ PATH.

pay *n* cash in hand, compensation, dividend, earnings, emoluments, fee, gain, honorarium, income, money, payment, profit, recompense, reimbursement, remittance, return, salary, settlement, stipend, take-home pay, wages. • *vb* **1** *inf* cough up, *inf* fork out, give, grant, hand over, proffer, recompense, remunerate, requite, spend, *inf* stump up. **2** *pay debts.* bear the cost of, clear, compensate, *inf* foot, honour, indemnify, meet, pay back, pay off, pay up, refund, reimburse, repay, settle. **3** *crime doesn't pay.* avail, benefit, be profitable, pay off, produce results, prove worthwhile, yield a return. **4** *pay for mistakes.* be punished, suffer. ▷ ATONE. **pay back** ▷ RETALIATE.

payment *n* advance, alimony, allowance, charge, commission, compensation, contribution, cost, deposit, disbursement, donation, expenditure, fare, fee, figure, fine, instalment, loan, outgoings, outlay, pocket-money, premium, price, ransom, rate, remittance, reward, royalty, *inf* sub, subscription, subsistence, supplement, surcharge, tip, toll, wage. *Opp* INCOME.

peace *n* **1** accord, agreement, amity, conciliation, concord, friendliness, harmony, order. *Opp* CONFLICT. **2** alliance, armistice, cease-fire, pact, treaty, truce. *Opp* WAR. **3** *peace of mind.* calm, calmness, peace and quiet, peacefulness, placidity, quiet, repose, serenity, silence, stillness, tranquillity. *Opp* ANXIETY.

peaceable *adj* amicable, civil, conciliatory, cooperative, friendly, gentle, harmonious, inoffensive, mild, non-violent, pacific, peace-loving, placid, temperate, understanding. *Opp* QUARRELSOME.

peaceful *adj* balmy, calm, easy, gentle, pacific, placid, pleasant, quiet, relaxing, restful, serene, slow-moving, soothing, still, tranquil, undisturbed, unruffled, untroubled. *Opp* NOISY, STORMY.

peacemaker *n* adjudicator, appeaser, arbitrator, conciliator, diplomat, intercessor, intermediary, mediator, reconciler, referee, umpire.

peak *n* **1** apex, brow, cap, crest, crown, eminence, hill, mountain, pinnacle, point, ridge, summit, tip, top. **2** *peak of your career.* acme, apogee, climax, consummation, crisis, crown, culmination, height, highest point, zenith.

peal *n* carillon, chime, chiming, clangour, knell, reverberation, ringing, tintinnabulation, toll. • *vb* chime, clang, resonate, ring, ring the changes, sound, toll.

peasant *n* [*derog*] boor, bumpkin, churl, oaf, rustic, serf, swain, village idiot, yokel.

pebbles *plur n* cobbles, gravel, stones.

peculiar *adj* **1** aberrant, abnormal, anomalous, atypical, bizarre, curi-

ous, deviant, eccentric, exceptional, freakish, funny, odd, offbeat, outlandish, out of the ordinary, quaint, queer, quirky, strange, surprising, uncommon, unconventional, unusual, weird. **2** *your peculiar style.* characteristic, different, distinctive, identifiable, idiosyncratic, individual, natural, particular, personal, private, singular, special, unique, unmistakable. *Opp* COMMON, ORDINARY.

peculiarity *n* abnormality, characteristic, difference, distinctiveness, eccentricity, foible, idiosyncrasy, individuality, mannerism, oddity, outlandishness, quirk, singularity, speciality, trait, uniqueness.

pedantic *adj* **1** academic, bookish, donnish, dry, formal, humourless, learned, old-fashioned, pompous, scholarly, schoolmasterly, stiff, stilted, *inf* stuffy. **2** *inf* by the book, doctrinaire, exact, fastidious, fussy, inflexible, *inf* nit-picking, precise, punctilious, strict, unimaginative. *Opp* INFORMAL, LAX.

peddle *vb inf* flog, hawk, market, *inf* push, sell, traffic in, vend.

pedestrian *adj* **1** pedestrianized, traffic-free. **2** banal, boring, dreary, dull, commonplace, flat-footed, lifeless, mundane, prosaic, run-of-the-mill, tedious, unimaginative, uninteresting. ▷ ORDINARY. • *n inf* foot-slogger, foot-traveller, stroller, walker.

pedigree *adj* pure-bred, thoroughbred. • *n* ancestry, blood, descent, extraction, family, family history, genealogy, line, lineage, parentage, roots, stock, strain.

pedlar *n old use* chapman, *inf* cheapjack, *old use* colporteur, door-to-door salesman, hawker, *inf* pusher, seller, street-trader, trafficker, vendor.

peel *n* coating, rind, skin. • *vb* denude, flay, hull, pare, skin, strip. ▷ UNDRESS.

peep *vb* **1** glance, have a look, peek, squint. ▷ LOOK. **2** ▷ SHOW.

peer *n* aristocrat, grandee, noble, nobleman, noblewoman, patrician,

titled
ess, du
chione
• *vb* ha
squint
nobilit
peers,
peer-gr

peevish
crabby,
grumpy,
ulant, q
waspish.

peg *n* bo
thole-pin.

pelt *n* coat,
bombard, s

pen *n* **1** coo
fold, hutch,
felt-tip, four

penalize *vb*
a penalty on,

penalty *n* fin
ISHMENT. **pay t**

penance *n* an
trition, penite
paration. **do p**

pendent *adj*
loose, pendulou
ing, swinging, t

pending *adj* abo
coming, *inf* hang
impending, *inf* i
cided, waiting.

penetrate *vb* **1** b
through, drill int
get through, infilt
hole, perforate, pi
ture, stab, stick in.
filter through, impr
through, permeate
into, suffuse.

penitent *adj* apolog
stricken, contrite, reg
ful, repentant, ruefu
sorry. *Opp* UNREPENTANT

pennon *n* banner, f
standard, streamer.

pension *n* annuity, be
pension, superannuatio

pensiv
contem
away, i
though
ative, t

penur
impov
need,

peopl
huma
ladies
and w
zenry
orate
natio
lation
3 *you*
men,
tions
fill, i
late,

perc
catch
disc
hea
not
2 a
her
gat
sen

per
ibl
dis
ma
ab
pe
ur
BL

pe

tion, doing, execution, fulfilment. **2** act, behaviour, conduct, deception, exhibition, exploit, feat, play-acting, pretence. **3** *stage performance.* acting, début, impersonation, interpretation, play, playing, portrayal, presentation, production, rendition, representation. □ *concert, dress rehearsal, first night, last night, matinée, première, preview, rehearsal, show, sketch, turn.*

performer *n* actor, actress, artist, artiste, player, singer, star, *inf* superstar, thespian, trouper. ▷ ENTERTAINER.

perfume *n* **1** aroma, bouquet, fragrance, odour, scent. ▷ SMELL. **2** aftershave, eau de Cologne, scent, toilet water.

perfunctory *adj* apathetic, automatic, brief, cursory, dutiful, fleeting, half-hearted, hurried, inattentive, indifferent, mechanical, offhand, routine, superficial, uncaring, unenthusiastic, uninterested, uninvolved, unthinking. *Opp* ENTHUSIASTIC.

perhaps *adv* conceivably, maybe, *old use* peradventure, *old use* perchance, possibly.

peril *n* danger, hazard, insecurity, jeopardy, risk, susceptibility, threat, vulnerability.

perilous *adj* dangerous, hazardous, insecure, risky, uncertain, unsafe, vulnerable. *Opp* SAFE.

perimeter *n* border, borderline, boundary, bounds, circumference, confines, edge, fringe, frontier, limit, margin, periphery, verge.

period *n* **1** duration, interval, phase, season, session, span, spell, stage, stint, stretch, term, while. **2** aeon, age, epoch, era. ▷ TIME.

periodic *adj* cyclical, intermittent, occasional, recurrent, repeated, spasmodic, sporadic.

peripheral *adj* **1** distant, on the perimeter, outer, outermost, outlying. **2** borderline, incidental, inessential, irrelevant, marginal, minor, nonessential, secondary, tangential, unimportant, unnecessary. *Opp* CENTRAL.

perish *vb* **1** be destroyed, be killed, die, expire, fall, lose your life, meet your death, pass away. **2** crumble away, decay, decompose, disintegrate, go bad, rot.

perishable *adj* biodegradable, destructible, liable to perish, unstable. *Opp* PERMANENT.

perjury *n* bearing false witness, lying, mendacity.

permanent *adj* abiding, ceaseless, changeless, chronic, constant, continual, continuous, durable, endless, enduring, eternal, everlasting, fixed, immutable, incessant, incurable, indestructible, indissoluble, ineradicable, interminable, invariable, irreparable, irreversible, lasting, lifelong, long-lasting, never-ending, nonstop, ongoing, perennial, perpetual, persistent, stable, steady, unalterable, unceasing, unchanging, undying, unending. *Opp* TEMPORARY.

permeate *vb* diffuse, filter through, flow through, impregnate, infiltrate, penetrate, percolate, pervade, saturate, soak through, spread through.

permissible *adj* acceptable, admissible, allowable, allowed, excusable, lawful, legal, legitimate, licit, permitted, proper, right, sanctioned, tolerable, valid, venial (*sin*). *Opp* UNACCEPTABLE.

permission *n* agreement, approbation, approval, acquiescence, assent, authority, authorization, consent, dispensation, franchise, *inf* go-ahead, *inf* green light, leave, licence, *inf* rubber stamp, sanction, seal of approval, stamp of approval, support. ▷ PERMIT.

permissive *adj* acquiescent, consenting, easygoing, indulgent, latitudinarian, lenient, liberal, libertarian, tolerant.

permit *n* authority, authorization, certification, charter, licence, order, pass, passport, ticket, visa, warrant. • *vb* admit, agree to, allow, approve of, authorize, consent to, endorse, enfranchise, give an opportunity for, give permission for, give your blessing to, legalize, license, make possible, sanction, *old use* suffer, support, tolerate.

perpendicular *adj* at right angles, erect, plumb, straight up and down, upright, vertical.

perpetual *adj* abiding, ageless, ceaseless, chronic, constant, continual, continuous, endless, enduring, eternal, everlasting, frequent, immortal, immutable, incessant, incurable, indestructible, ineradicable, interminable, invariable, lasting, long-lasting, never-ending, non-stop, ongoing, perennial, permanent, persistent, protracted, recurrent, recurring, repeated, *old use* sempiternal, timeless, unceasing, unchanging, undying, unending, unfailing, unremitting. *Opp* TEMPORARY.

perpetuate *vb* continue, eternalize, eternize, extend, immortalize, keep going, maintain, make permanent, preserve.

perplex *vb* baffle, *inf* bamboozle, befuddle, bewilder, confound, confuse, disconcert, distract, dumbfound, muddle, mystify, nonplus, puzzle, *inf* stump, *inf* throw, worry.

perquisite *n* benefit, bonus, *inf* consideration, emolument, extra, fringe benefit, gratuity, *inf* perk, tip.

persecute *vb* abuse, afflict, annoy, badger, bother, bully, discriminate against, harass, hector, hound, ill-treat, intimidate, maltreat, martyr, molest, oppress, pester, *inf* put the screws on, suppress, terrorize, torment, torture, trouble, tyrannize, victimize, worry.

persist *vb* be diligent, be steadfast, carry on, continue, endure, go on, *inf* hang on, hold out, *inf* keep at it, keep going, *inf* keep it up, keep on, last, linger, persevere, *inf* plug away, remain, *inf* soldier on, stand firm, stay, *inf* stick at it. *Opp* CEASE.

persistent *adj* **1** ceaseless, chronic, constant, continual, continuous, endless, eternal, everlasting, incessant, interminable, lasting, long-lasting, never-ending, obstinate, permanent, perpetual, persisting, recurrent, recurring, remaining, repeated, unending, unrelenting, unrelieved, unremitting. *Opp* BRIEF, INTERMITTENT. **2** assiduous, determined, dogged, hard-working, indefatigable, patient, persevering, pertinacious, relentless, resolute, steadfast, steady, stubborn, tenacious, tireless, unflagging, untiring, unwavering, zealous. *Opp* LAZY.

person *n* adolescent, adult, baby, being, *inf* body, character, child, *inf* customer, figure, human, human being, individual, infant, mortal, personage, soul, *inf* type, woman. ▷ MAN, PEOPLE, WOMAN.

persona *n* character, exterior, façade, guise, identity, image, part, personality, role, self-image.

personal *adj* **1** distinct, distinctive, exclusive, idiosyncratic, individual, inimitable, particular, peculiar, private, special, unique, your own. *Opp* GENERAL. **2** *a personal appearance.* actual, in person, in the flesh, live, physical. **3** *personal letters.* confidential, friendly, individual, informal, intimate, private, secret. *Opp* PUBLIC. **4** *personal friends.* bosom, close, dear, familiar, intimate, known. **5** *personal remarks.* belittling, critical, derogatory, disparaging, insulting, offensive, pejorative, rude, slighting, unfriendly. **6** *personal knowledge.* direct, empirical, experiential, first-hand.

personality *n* **1** attractiveness, character, charisma, charm, disposition, identity, individuality, magnetism, *inf* make-up, nature, persona, psyche, temperament. **2** *inf* big name, celebrity, idol, luminary, name, public figure, star, superstar.

personification *n* allegorical representation, embodiment, epitome, human likeness, incarnation, living image, manifestation.

personify *vb* allegorize, embody, epitomize, exemplify, give human shape to, incarnate, manifest, personalize, represent, stand for, symbolize, typify.

personnel *n* employees, manpower, people, staff, workers, workforce.

perspective *n* angle, approach, attitude, outlook, point of view, position, prospect, slant, standpoint, view, viewpoint.

persuade *vb* bring round, cajole, coax, convert, convince, entice, exhort, importune, induce, influence, inveigle, press, prevail upon, prompt, talk into, tempt, urge, use persuasion, wheedle (into), win over. *Opp* DISSUADE.

persuasion *n* **1** argument, blandishment, brainwashing, cajolery, coaxing, conditioning, enticement, exhortation, inducement, persuading, propaganda, reasoning. **2** affiliation, belief, conviction, creed, denomination, faith, religion, sect.

persuasive *adj* cogent, compelling, conclusive, convincing, credible, effective, efficacious, eloquent, forceful, influential, logical, plausible, potent, reasonable, sound, strong, telling, unarguable, valid, watertight. *Opp* UNCONVINCING.

pertain *vb* appertain, apply, be relevant, have bearing, have reference, have relevance, refer. **pertain to** affect, concern.

pertinent *adj* apposite, appropriate, apropos, apt, fitting, germane, relevant, suitable. *Opp* IRRELEVANT.

perturb *vb* agitate, alarm, bother, confuse, discomfit, discompose, disconcert, disquiet, distress, disturb, fluster, frighten, make anxious, ruffle, scare, shake, trouble, unnerve, unsettle, upset, vex, worry. *Opp* REASSURE.

peruse *vb* examine, inspect, look over, read, run your eye over, scan, scrutinize, study.

pervade *vb* affect, diffuse, fill, filter through, flow through, impregnate, penetrate, percolate, permeate, saturate, spread through, suffuse.

pervasive *adj* general, inescapable, insidious, omnipresent, penetrating, permeating, pervading, prevalent, rife, ubiquitous, universal, widespread.

perverse *adj* adamant, contradictory, contrary, disobedient, fractious, headstrong, illogical, inappropriate, inflexible, intractable, intransigent, obdurate, obstinate, peevish, *inf* pigheaded, rebellious, refractory, self-willed, stubborn, tiresome, uncooperative, unhelpful, unreasonable, wayward, wilful, wrong-headed. *Opp* REASONABLE.

perversion *n* **1** corruption, distortion, falsification, misrepresentation, misuse, twisting. **2** aberration, abnormality, depravity, deviance, deviation, immorality, impropriety, *inf* kinkiness, perversity, unnaturalness, vice, wickedness.

pervert *n* debauchee, degenerate, deviant, perverted person, profligate. • *vb* **1** bend, deflect, distort, divert, falsify, misrepresent, perjure, subvert, twist, undermine. **2** *pervert a witness.* bribe, corrupt, lead astray.

perverted *adj* abnormal, amoral, bad, corrupt, debauched, degenerate, depraved, deviant, dissolute, eccentric, evil, immoral, improper, *inf* kinky, profligate, sick, twisted, unnatural, unprincipled, warped, wicked, wrong. ▷ OBSCENE. *Opp* NATURAL.

pessimism *n* cynicism, despair, despondency, fatalism, gloom, hopelessness, negativeness, resignation, unhappiness. *Opp* OPTIMISM.

pessimistic *adj* bleak, cynical, defeatist, despairing, despondent, fatalistic, gloomy, hopeless, melancholy, morbid, negative, resigned, unhappy. ▷ SAD. *Opp* OPTIMISTIC.

pest *n* **1** annoyance, bane, bother, curse, irritation, nuisance, *inf* pain in the neck, *inf* thorn in your flesh, trial, vexation. **2** *inf* bug, *inf* creepy-crawly, insect, parasite, *plur* vermin.

pester *vb* annoy, badger, bait, besiege, bother, *inf* get under someone's skin, harass, harry, *inf* hassle, irritate, molest, nag, nettle, plague, provoke, torment, trouble, worry.

pestilence *n* blight, curse, epidemic, pandemic, plague, scourge. ▷ ILLNESS.

pet *n inf* apple of your eye, darling, favourite, idol. • *vb* caress, cuddle, fondle, kiss, nuzzle, pat, stroke. ▷ TOUCH.

petition *n* appeal, application, entreaty, list of signatures, plea, request, solicitation, suit, supplication. • *vb* appeal to, call upon, deliver a petition to, entreat, importune, solicit, sue, supplicate. ▷ ASK.

petty *adj* **1** inconsequential, insignificant, minor, niggling, small, trivial, trifling. ▷ UNIMPORTANT. *Opp* IMPORTANT. **2** *petty complaints.* grudging, mean, nit-picking, small-minded, ungenerous. *Opp* GENEROUS.

phase *n* development, period, season, spell, stage, state, step. ▷ TIME. **phase in** ▷ INTRODUCE. **phase out** ▷ FINISH.

phenomenal *adj* amazing, astonishing, astounding, exceptional, extraordinary, *inf* fantastic, incredible, marvellous, *inf* mind-boggling, miraculous, notable, outstanding, prodigious, rare, remarkable, *inf* sensational, singular, staggering, stunning, unbelievable, unorthodox, unusual, *inf* wonderful. *Opp* ORDINARY.

phenomenon *n* **1** circumstance, event, experience, fact, happening, incident, occasion, occurrence, sight. **2** *an unusual phenomenon.* curiosity, marvel, miracle, phenomenal person, phenomenal thing, prodigy, rarity, sensation, spectacle, wonder.

philanthropic *adj* altruistic, beneficent, benevolent, bountiful, caring, charitable, generous, humane, humanitarian, magnanimous, munificent, public-spirited, ungrudging. ▷ KIND. *Opp* MISANTHROPIC.

philanthropist *n* altruist, benefactor, donor, giver, *inf* Good Samaritan, humanitarian, patron, provider, sponsor.

philistine *adj* boorish, ignorant, lowbrow, materialistic, uncivilized, uncultivated, uncultured, unenlightened, unlettered, vulgar.

philosopher *n* sage, student of philosophy, thinker.

philosophical *adj* **1** abstract, academic, analytical, erudite, esoteric, ideological, impractical, intellectual, learned, logical, metaphysical, rational, reasoned, scholarly, theoretical, thoughtful, wise. **2** calm, collected, composed, detached, equable, imperturbable, judicious, patient, reasonable, resigned, serene, sober, stoical, unemotional, unruffled. *Opp* EMOTIONAL.

philosophize *vb* analyse, moralize, pontificate, preach, rationalize, reason, sermonize, theorize, think things out.

philosophy *n* **1** epistemology, ideology, logic, metaphysics, rationalism, thinking. **2** *philosophy of life.* attitude, convictions, outlook, set of beliefs, tenets, values, viewpoint, wisdom.

phlegmatic *adj* apathetic, cold, cool, frigid, impassive, imperturbable, indifferent, lethargic, passive, placid, slow, sluggish, stoical, stolid, torpid, undemonstrative, unemotional, unenthusiastic, unfeeling, uninvolved, unresponsive. *Opp* EXCITABLE.

phobia *n* anxiety, aversion, dislike, dread, *inf* hang-up, hatred, horror, loathing, neurosis, obsession, repugnance, revulsion. ▷ FEAR. □ *agoraphobia* (open space), *arachnophobia* (spiders), *claustrophobia* (enclosed space), *xenophobia* (foreigners).

phone *vb* call, dial, *inf* give a buzz, ring, telephone.

phoney *adj* affected, artificial, assumed, bogus, cheating, contrived, counterfeit, deceitful, ersatz, factitious, fake, faked, false, fictitious, fraudulent, hypocritical, imitation, insincere, mock, pretended, *inf* pseudo, *inf* put-on, *inf* put-up, sham, spurious, synthetic, trick, unreal. *Opp* REAL.

photocopy *vb* copy, duplicate, photostat, print off, reproduce, *inf* run off.

photograph *n* enlargement, exposure, negative, *inf* photo, picture, plate, positive, print, shot, slide, *inf* snap, snapshot, transparency. • *vb* film, shoot, snap, take a photograph of.

photographic *adj* **1** accurate, exact, faithful, graphic, lifelike, naturalistic, realistic, representational, true to life. **2** *photographic memory*. pictorial, retentive, visual.

phrase *n* clause, expression. ▷ SAYING. • *vb* ▷ SAY.

phraseology *n* diction, expression, idiom, language, parlance, phrasing, style, turn of phrase, wording.

physical *adj* actual, bodily, carnal, concrete, corporal, corporeal, earthly, fleshly, incarnate, material, mortal, palpable, physiological, real, solid, substantial, tangible. *Opp* INTANGIBLE, SPIRITUAL.

physician *n* consultant, doctor, general practitioner, *inf* GP, *inf* medic, medical practitioner, specialist.

physiological *adj* anatomical, bodily, physical. *Opp* PSYCHOLOGICAL.

physique *n* body, build, figure, form, frame, muscles, physical condition, shape.

pick *n* **1** choice, election, option, preference, selection. **2** best, cream, élite, favourite, flower, pride. • *vb* **1** cast *(actor)*, choose, decide on, elect, fix on, make a choice of, name, nominate, opt for, prefer, select, settle on, single out, vote for. **2** *pick flowers*. collect, cull, cut, gather, harvest, pluck, pull off, take. **pick on** ▷ BULLY. **pick up** ▷ GET, IMPROVE.

pictorial *adj* diagrammatic, graphic, illustrated, realistic, representational, vivid.

picture *n* **1** delineation, depiction, image, likeness, outline, portrayal, profile, representation. □ *abstract, cameo, caricature, cartoon, collage, design, doodle, drawing, engraving, etching, fresco,* plur *graffiti,* plur *graphics, icon, identikit, illustration, landscape, montage, mosaic, mural, oil-painting, old master, painting, photofit, photograph, pin-up, plate, portrait, print, reproduction, self-portrait, silhouette, sketch, slide,* inf *snap, snapshot, still life, transfer, transparency, triptych,* Fr *trompe l'oeil, video, vignette*. **2** film, movie, moving picture, video. ▷ FILM. • *vb* **1** caricature, delineate, depict, display, doodle, draw, engrave, etch, evoke, film, illustrate, outline, paint, photograph, portray, print, represent, show, sketch, video. **2** *picture the future*. conceive, describe, dream up, envisage, envision, fancy, imagine, see in your mind's eye, think up, visualize.

picturesque *adj* **1** attractive, charming, colourful, idyllic, lovely, pleasant, pretty, quaint, scenic, *inf* story-book. ▷ BEAUTIFUL. *Opp* UNATTRACTIVE. **2** *picturesque language*. colourful, descriptive, expressive, graphic, imaginative, poetic, vivid. *Opp* PROSAIC.

pie *n* flan, pasty, patty, quiche, tart, tartlet, turnover, vol-au-vent.

piece *n* **1** bar, bit, bite, block, chip, chunk, crumb, division, *inf* dollop, fraction, fragment, grain, helping, hunk, length, lump, morsel, part, particle, portion, quantity, remnant, sample, scrap, section, segment, shard, share, shred, slab, slice, sliver, snippet, speck, stick, tablet, *inf* titbit, wedge. **2** component, constituent, element, spare part, unit. **3** *piece of music, work*. article, composition, example, instance, item, number, passage, specimen, work. ▷ MUSIC, WRITING. **piece together** ▷ ASSEMBLE.

pied *adj* dappled, flecked, mottled, particoloured, patchy, piebald, spotted, variegated.

pier *n* **1** breakwater, jetty, landing-stage, quay, wharf. ▷ DOCK. **2** buttress, column, pile, pillar, post, support, upright.

pierce *vb* bayonet, bore through, cut, drill, enter, go through, impale, jab, lance, make a hole in, penetrate, perforate, poke through, prick, punch, puncture, riddle, skewer, spear, spike, spit, stab, stick into, thrust into, transfix, tunnel through, wound. **piercing** ▷ SHARP.

piety *n* dedication, devotedness, devotion, devoutness, faith, godliness, holiness, piousness, religion, *derog* religiosity, saintliness, sanctity. *Opp* IMPIETY.

pig *n* boar, hog, *inf* piggy, piglet, runt, sow, swine.

pile *n* **1** abundance, accumulation, agglomeration, collection, concentration, conglomeration, deposit, heap, hoard, *inf* load, mass, mound, *inf* mountain, plethora, quantity, stack, stockpile, supply, *inf* tons. **2** column, pier, post, support, upright. ● *vb* accumulate, amass, assemble, bring together, build up, collect, concentrate, deposit, gather, heap, hoard, load, mass, stack up, stockpile, store.

pilfer *vb inf* filch, *inf* pinch, rob, shoplift. ▷ STEAL.

pilgrim *n* crusader, *old use* palmer. ▷ TRAVELLER.

pill *n* bolus, capsule, lozenge, pastille, pellet, pilule, tablet. ▷ MEDICINE.

pillage *n* buccaneering, depredation, despoliation, devastation, looting, marauding, piracy, plunder, plundering, ransacking, rape, rapine, robbery, robbing, sacking, stealing, stripping. ● *vb* despoil, devastate, loot, maraud, plunder, raid, ransack, ravage, raze, rob, sack, steal, strip, vandalize.

pillar *n* baluster, caryatid, column, pier, pilaster, pile, post, prop, shaft, stanchion, support, upright.

pilot *n* **1** airman, *old use* aviator, captain, flier. **2** coxswain, helmsman, navigator, steersman. ● *vb* conduct, convey, direct, drive, fly, guide, lead, navigate, shepherd, steer.

pimple *n* blackhead, boil, eruption, pustule, spot, swelling, *sl* zit. **pimples** acne, rash.

pin *n old use* bodkin, bolt, brooch, clip, dowel, drawing-pin, hatpin, nail, peg, rivet, safety-pin, spike, staple, thole, tiepin. ● *vb* clip, nail, pierce, staple, tack, transfix. ▷ FASTEN.

pinch *vb* **1** crush, grip, hurt, nip, press, squeeze, tweak. **2** ▷ STEAL.

pine *vb* mope, mourn, sicken, waste away. **pine for** ▷ WANT.

pinnacle *n* **1** acme, apex, cap, climax, consummation, crest, crown, crowning point, height, highest point, peak, summit, top, zenith. **2** *pinnacle on a roof*. spire, steeple, turret.

pioneer *n* **1** colonist, discoverer, explorer, frontiersman, frontierswoman, pathfinder, settler, trailblazer. **2** innovator, inventor, originator, pace-maker, trend-setter. ● *vb* begin, *inf* bring out, create, develop, discover, establish, experiment with, found, inaugurate, initiate, institute, introduce, invent, launch, open up, originate, set up, start.

pious *adj* **1** dedicated, devoted, devout, faithful, god-fearing, godly, good, holy, moral, religious, reverent, reverential, saintly, sincere, spiritual, virtuous. *Opp* IMPIOUS. **2** [*derog*] *inf* goody-goody, *inf* holier-than-thou, hypocritical, insincere, mealy-mouthed, Pharisaical, pietistic, sanctimonious, self-righteous, self-satisfied, *inf* smarmy, unctuous. *Opp* SINCERE.

pip *n* **1** pit, seed, stone. **2** mark, spot, star. **3** bleep, blip, sound, stroke.

pipe *n* conduit, channel, duct, hose, hydrant, line, main, pipeline, piping, tube. ● *vb* **1** carry along a pipe, carry along a wire, channel, convey, deliver, supply, transmit. **2** *pipe a tune*. blow, play, sound, *inf* tootle, whistle. **pipe up** ▷ SPEAK. **piping** ▷ HOT, SHRILL.

piquant *adj* **1** appetizing, pungent, salty, sharp, spicy, tangy, tart, tasty. *Opp* BLAND. **2** *a piquant notion*. arresting, exciting, interesting, provocative, stimulating. *Opp* BANAL.

pirate *n* buccaneer, *old use* corsair, marauder, privateer, sea rover. ▷ THIEF. • *vb* ▷ PLAGIARIZE.

pit *n* **1** abyss, chasm, crater, depression, ditch, excavation, hole, hollow, pothole, rut, trench, well. **2** coalmine, colliery, mine, mineshaft, quarry, shaft, working.

pitch *n* **1** bitumen, tar. **2** *pitch of a roof.* angle, gradient, incline, slope, steepness, tilt. **3** *musical pitch.* frequency, tuning. **4** *soccer pitch.* arena, ground, playing-field, stadium. • *vb* **1** erect, put up, raise, set up. **2** *pitch stones.* bowl, *inf* bung, cast, *inf* chuck, fire, fling, heave, hurl, launch, lob, sling, throw, toss. **3** *pitch into the water.* dive, drop, fall headlong, plummet, plunge, *inf* take a nosedive, topple. **pitch about** ▷ TOSS. **pitch in** ▷ COOPERATE. **pitch into** ▷ ATTACK.

piteous *adj* affecting, distressing, heartbreaking, heart-rending, lamentable, miserable, moving, pathetic, pitiable, pitiful, plaintive, poignant, touching, woeful, wretched. ▷ SAD.

pitfall *n* catch, danger, difficulty, hazard, peril, snag, trap.

pitiful *adj* **1** abject, contemptible, deplorable, hopeless, inadequate, incompetent, insignificant, laughable, mean, *inf* miserable, *inf* pathetic, pitiable, ridiculous, sorry, trifling, unimportant, useless, worthless. *Opp* ADMIRABLE. **2** ▷ PITEOUS.

pitiless *adj* bloodthirsty, brutal, callous, cruel, ferocious, hard, heartless, inexorable, inhuman, merciless, relentless, ruthless, sadistic, unfeeling, unrelenting, unrelieved, unremitting, unsympathetic. *Opp* MERCIFUL.

pitted *adj* dented, eaten away, eroded, *inf* holey, marked, pockmarked, rough, scarred, uneven. *Opp* SMOOTH.

pity *n* charity, clemency, commiseration, compassion, condolence, feeling, forbearance, forgiveness, grace, humanity, kindness, leniency, love, mercy, regret, *old use* ruth, softness, sympathy, tenderness, understanding, warmth. *Opp* CRUELTY. • *vb inf* bleed for, commiserate with, *inf* feel for, feel sorry for, show pity for, sympathize with, weep for.

pivot *n* axis, axle, centre, fulcrum, gudgeon, hinge, hub, pin, point of balance, spindle, swivel. • *vb* hinge, revolve, rotate, spin, swivel, turn, twirl, whirl.

placard *n* advert, advertisement, bill, notice, poster, sign.

placate *vb* appease, calm, conciliate, humour, mollify, pacify, soothe.

place *n* **1** area, country, district, locale, locality, location, locus, neighbourhood, part, point, position, quarter, region, scene, setting, site, situation, *inf* spot, town, venue, vicinity, *inf* whereabouts. **2** *a place in society.* condition, degree, estate, function, grade, job, mission, niche, office, position, rank, role, standing, station, status. **3** *a place to live.* ▷ HOUSE. **4** *a place to sit.* ▷ SEAT. • *vb* **1** deposit, dispose, *inf* dump, lay, leave, locate, pinpoint, plant, position, put down, rest, set down, set out, settle, situate, stand, station, *inf* stick. **2** arrange, categorize, class, classify, grade, order, position, put in order, rank, sort. **3** *can't place it.* identify, put a name to, put into context, recognize, remember.

placid *adj* **1** collected, composed, cool, equable, even-tempered, imperturbable, level-headed, mild, phlegmatic, restful, sensible, stable, steady, unexcitable. **2** calm, motionless, peaceful, quiet, tranquil, unruffled, untroubled. *Opp* EXCITABLE, STORMY.

plagiarize *vb* appropriate, borrow, copy, *inf* crib, imitate, infringe copyright, *inf* lift, pirate, purloin, reproduce. ▷ STEAL.

plague *n* **1** affliction, bane, blight, calamity, contagion, epidemic, infection, outbreak, pandemic, pestilence. ▷ ILLNESS. **2** infestation, invasion, nuisance, scourge, swarm, visitation. • *vb* afflict, annoy, be a nuisance to, bother, distress, disturb, harass, harry, hound, irritate, molest, *inf* nag, persecute, pester, torment, torture, trouble, vex, worry.

plain *adj* **1** apparent, audible, certain, clear, comprehensible, definite, distinct, evident, intelligible, legible, lucid, manifest, obvious, patent, simple, transparent, unambiguous, understandable, unmistakable, visible, well-defined. *Opp* OBSCURE. **2** *plain speech*. basic, blunt, candid, direct, downright, explicit, forthright, frank, honest, informative, outspoken, plain-spoken, prosaic, sincere, straightforward, unequivocal, unvarnished. **3** *plain living*. austere, drab, everyday, frugal, homely, modest, ordinary, simple, Spartan, stark, unadorned, unattractive, undecorated, unexciting, unprepossessing, unpretentious, unremarkable, workaday. *Opp* SOPHISTICATED. ● *n* grassland, pampas, pasture, prairie, savannah, steppe, tundra, veld.

plaintive *adj* doleful, melancholy, mournful, plangent, sorrowful, wistful. ▷ SAD.

plan *n* **1** *inf* bird's-eye view, blueprint, chart, design, diagram, drawing, layout, map, representation, sketch-map. **2** *a plan of action*. aim, course of action, design, formula, idea, intention, method, plot, policy, procedure, programme, project, proposal, proposition, *inf* scenario, scheme, strategy, system. ● *vb* **1** arrange, concoct, contrive, design, devise, draw up a plan, formulate, invent, map out, *inf* mastermind, organize, outline, plot, prepare, scheme, think out, work out. **2** *I plan to go away*. aim, conspire, contemplate, envisage, expect, intend, mean, propose, think of.

planned ▷ DELIBERATE.

plane *adj* even, flat, flush, level, smooth, uniform. ● *n* **1** flat surface, level, surface. **2** ▷ AIRCRAFT.

planet *n* globe, orb, satellite, sphere, world. □ *Earth, Jupiter, Mars, Mercury, Neptune, Pluto, Saturn, Uranus, Venus.*

plank *n* beam, board, planking, timber.

planning *n* arrangement, design, drafting, forethought, organization, preparation, setting up, thinking out.

plant *n* greenery, growth, undergrowth, vegetation. □ *annual, bulb, cactus, cereal, climber, fern, flower, fungus, grass, herb, lichen, moss, perennial, shrub, tree, vegetable, vine, water-plant, weed.* ▷ FLOWER, TREE, VEGETABLE. **2** *a manufacturing plant*. factory, foundry, mill, shop, works, workshop. **3** *industrial plant*. apparatus, equipment, machinery, machines. ● *vb* **1** bed out, set out, sow, transplant. **2** locate, place, position, put, situate, station.

plaster *n* **1** mortar, stucco. **2** dressing, sticking-plaster. ● *vb* apply, bedaub, coat, cover, daub, smear, spread.

plastic *adj* ductile, flexible, malleable, pliable, shapable, soft, supple, workable. □ *bakelite, celluloid, polystyrene, polythene, polyurethane, polyvinyl, PVC, vinyl.*

plate *n* **1** *old use* charger, dinner-plate, dish, platter, salver, side-plate, soup-plate, *old use* trencher. **2** lamina, lamination, layer, leaf, pane, panel, sheet, slab, stratum. **3** *plates in a book*. illustration, *inf* photo, photograph, picture, print. **4** *a dental plate*. dentures, false teeth. ● *vb* anodize, coat, cover, electroplate, galvanize (*with zinc*), gild (*with gold*).

platform *n* **1** dais, podium, rostrum, stage, stand. **2** *political platform*. ▷ POLICY.

platitude *n* banality, cliché, commonplace, truism.

plausible *adj* **1** acceptable, believable, conceivable, credible, imaginable, likely, logical, persuasive, possible, probable, rational, reasonable, sensible, tenable, thinkable. *Opp* IMPLAUSIBLE. **2** deceptive, glib, meretricious, misleading, specious, smooth, sophistical.

play *n* **1** amusement, diversion, entertainment, frivolity, fun, *inf* fun and games, *inf* horseplay, joking, make-believe, merrymaking, playing, pretending, recreation, revelry, *inf* skylarking, sport. **2** *play in moving parts.* flexibility, freedom, freedom of movement, *inf* give, latitude, leeway, looseness, movement, tolerance. **3** ▷ DRAMA. ● *vb* **1** amuse yourself, caper, cavort, disport yourself, enjoy yourself, fool about, frisk, frolic, gambol, *inf* have a good time, have fun, *inf* mess about, romp, sport. **2** *play a game.* join in, participate, take part. **3** *play an opponent.* challenge, compete against, oppose, rival, take on, vie with. **4** *play a role.* act, depict, impersonate, perform, portray, pretend to be, represent, take the part of. **5** *play an instrument.* make music on, perform on, strum. **6** *play the radio.* have on, listen to, operate, put on, switch on. play about ▷ MISBEHAVE. **play along, play ball** ▷ COOPERATE. **play down** ▷ MINIMIZE. **play for time** ▷ DELAY. **play it by ear** ▷ IMPROVISE. **play up** ▷ MISBEHAVE. **play up to** ▷ FLATTER.

player *n* **1** athlete, competitor, contestant, participant, sportsman, sportswoman. **2** actor, actress, artiste, entertainer, instrumentalist, musician, performer, soloist, Thespian, trouper. ▷ ENTERTAINER, MUSICIAN.

playful *adj* active, cheerful, coltish, facetious, flirtatious, frisky, frolicsome, fun-loving, good-natured, high-spirited, humorous, impish, jesting, *inf* jokey, joking, kittenish, light-hearted, lively, mischievous, puckish, roguish, skittish, spirited, sportive, sprightly, teasing, *inf* tongue-in-cheek, vivacious, waggish. *Opp* SERIOUS.

plea *n* **1** appeal, entreaty, invocation, petition, prayer, request, solicitation, suit, supplication. **2** argument, excuse, explanation, justification, pretext, reason.

plead *vb* **1** appeal, ask, beg, beseech, cry out, demand, entreat, implore, importune, petition, request, seek, solicit, supplicate. **2** allege, argue, assert, aver, declare, maintain, reason, swear.

pleasant *adj* acceptable, affable, agreeable, amiable, approachable, attractive, balmy, beautiful, charming, cheerful, congenial, decent, delicious, delightful, enjoyable, entertaining, excellent, fine, friendly, genial, gentle, good, gratifying, *inf* heavenly, hospitable, kind, likeable, lovely, mellow, mild, nice, palatable, peaceful, pleasing, pleasurable, pretty, reassuring, relaxed, satisfying, soothing, sympathetic, warm, welcome, welcoming. *Opp* ANNOYING, UNPLEASANT.

please *vb* **1** amuse, cheer up, content, delight, divert, entertain, give pleasure to, gladden, gratify, humour, make happy, satisfy, suit. **2** *Do what you please.* ▷ WANT. **pleasing** ▷ PLEASANT.

pleased *adj inf* chuffed, *derog* complacent, contented, delighted, elated, euphoric, glad, grateful, gratified, *sl* over the moon, satisfied, thankful, thrilled. ▷ HAPPY. *Opp* ANNOYED.

pleasure *n* **1** bliss, comfort, contentment, delight, ecstasy, enjoyment, euphoria, fulfilment, gladness, gratification, happiness, joy, rapture, satisfaction, solace. **2** amusement, diversion, entertainment, fun, luxury, recreation, self-indulgence.

pleat *n* crease, flute, fold, gather, tuck.

plebiscite *n* ballot, poll, referendum, vote.

pledge *n* **1** assurance, covenant, guarantee, oath, pact, promise, undertaking, vow, warranty, word. **2** *a pledge left at a pawnbroker's.* bail, bond, collateral, deposit, pawn, security, surety. ● *vb* agree, commit yourself, contract, give your word, guarantee, promise, swear, undertake, vouch, vouchsafe, vow.

plenary *adj* full, general, open.

plentiful *adj* abounding, abundant, ample, bounteous, bountiful, bristling, bumper (*crop*), copious, generous, inexhaustible, lavish, liberal, overflowing, plenteous, profuse, prolific. *Opp* SCARCE. **be plentiful** ▷ ABOUND.

plenty *n* abundance, adequacy, affluence, cornucopia, excess, fertility, flood, fruitfulness, glut, *inf* heaps, *inf* lashings, *inf* loads, a lot, *inf* lots, *inf* masses, more than enough, much, *inf* oceans, *inf* oodles, *inf* piles, plentitude, plentifulness, plethora, prodigality, profusion, prosperity, quantities, *inf* stacks, sufficiency, superabundance, surfeit, surplus, *inf* tons, wealth. *Opp* SCARCITY.

pliable *adj* **1** bendable, *inf* bendy, ductile, flexible, plastic, pliant, springy, supple. **2** *a pliable character.* adaptable, compliant, docile, easily influenced, easily led, easily persuaded, impressionable, manageable, persuadable, receptive, responsive, susceptible, suggestible, tractable, yielding.

plod *vb* **1** slog, tramp, trudge. ▷ WALK. **2** drudge, grind on, labour, *inf* peg away, persevere, *inf* plug away, toil. ▷ WORK.

plot *n* **1** acreage, allotment, area, estate, garden, lot, parcel, patch, smallholding, tract. **2** *a plot of a novel.* chain of events, narrative, organization, outline, scenario, story, storyline, thread. **3** *a subversive plot.* cabal, conspiracy, intrigue, machination, plan, scheme. • *vb* **1** chart, compute, draw, map out, mark, outline, plan, project. **2** *plot to rob a bank.* collude, conspire, have designs, intrigue, machinate, scheme. **3** *plot a crime.* arrange, *inf* brew, conceive, concoct, *inf* cook up, design, devise, dream up, hatch.

pluck *n* ▷ COURAGE. *vb* **1** collect, gather, harvest, pick, pull off, remove. **2** grab, jerk, pull, seize, snatch, tear away, tweak, yank. **3** *pluck a chicken.* denude, remove feathers from, strip. **4** *pluck a violin.* play pizzicato, strum, twang.

plug *n* **1** bung, cork, stopper. **2** ▷ ADVERTISEMENT. • *vb* **1** block up, *inf* bung up, close, cork, fill, jam, seal, stop up, stuff up. **2** advertise, commend, mention frequently, promote, publicize, puff, recommend. **plug away** ▷ WORK.

plumb *adv* **1** accurately, *inf* dead, exactly, precisely, *inf* slap. **2** perpendicularly, vertically. • *vb* fathom, measure, penetrate, probe, sound.

plumbing *n* heating system, pipes, water-supply.

plume *n* feather, *plur* plumage, quill.

plump *adj* ample, buxom, chubby, dumpy, overweight, podgy, portly, pudgy, *inf* roly-poly, rotund, round, squat, stout, tubby, *inf* well-upholstered. ▷ FAT. *Opp* THIN. **plump for** ▷ CHOOSE.

plunder *n* booty, contraband, loot, pickings, pillage, prize, spoils, swag, takings. • *vb* capture, despoil, devastate, lay waste, loot, maraud, pillage, raid, ransack, ravage, rifle, rob, sack, seize, spoil, steal from, strip, vandalize.

plunge *vb* **1** descend, dip, dive, drop, engulf, fall, fall headlong, hurtle, immerse, jump, leap, lower, nosedive, pitch, plummet, sink, submerge, swoop, tumble. **2** force, push, stick, thrust.

poach *vb* **1** hunt, steal. **2** ▷ COOK.

pocket *n* bag, container, pouch, receptacle. • *vb* ▷ TAKE.

pod *n* case, hull, shell.

poem *n inf* ditty, *inf* jingle, piece of poetry, rhyme, verse. □ *ballad, ballade, doggerel, eclogue, elegy, epic, epithalamium, haiku, idyll, lay, limerick, lyric, nursery-rhyme, pastoral, ode, sonnet, vers libre.* ▷ VERSE.

poet *n* bard, lyricist, minstrel, poetaster, rhymer, rhymester, sonneteer, versifier. ▷ WRITER.

poetic *adj* emotive, *derog* flowery, imaginative, lyrical, metrical, musical, poetical. *Opp* PROSAIC.

poignant *adj* affecting, distressing, heartbreaking, heartfelt, heart-rending, moving, painful, pathetic, piquant, piteous, pitiful, stirring, tender, touching, upsetting. ▷ SAD.

point *n* **1** apex, peak, prong, sharp end, spike, spur, tine, tip. **2** *a point in space.* location, place, position, site, situation, spot. **3** *a point in time.*

instant, juncture, moment, second, stage, time. **4** *decimal point*. dot, full stop, mark, speck, spot. **5** *the point of an argument*. aim, burden, crux, drift, end, essence, gist, goal, heart, import, intention, meaning, motive, nub, object, objective, pith, purpose, quiddity, relevance, significance, subject, substance, theme, thrust, use, usefulness. **6** *points to raise*. aspect, detail, idea, item, matter, particular, question, thought, topic. **7** *good points in her character*. attribute, characteristic, facet, feature, peculiarity, property, quality, trait. • *vb* **1** call attention to, direct attention to, draw attention to, indicate, point out, show, signal. **2** aim, direct, guide, lead, steer. **pointed** ▷ SHARP. **to the point** ▷ RELEVANT.

pointer *n* arrow, hand (*of clock*), indicator.

pointless *adj* aimless, fatuous, fruitless, futile, inane, ineffective, senseless, silly, unproductive, useless, vain, worthless. ▷ STUPID.

poise *n* aplomb, assurance, balance, calmness, composure, coolness, dignity, equanimity, equilibrium, equipoise, imperturbability, presence, sang-froid, self-confidence, self-control, self-possession, serenity, steadiness. • *vb* balance, be poised, hover, keep in balance, support, suspend.

poised *adj* **1** balanced, hovering, in equilibrium, standing, steady, teetering, wavering. **2** *poised to begin*. keyed up, prepared, ready, set, standing by, waiting. **3** *a poised performer*. assured, calm, composed, cool, cool-headed, dignified, self-confident, self-possessed, serene, suave, *inf* unflappable, unruffled, urbane.

poison *n* bane, toxin, venom. • *vb* **1** adulterate, contaminate, infect, pollute, taint. ▷ KILL. **2** *poison the mind*. corrupt, defile, deprave, envenom, pervert, prejudice, subvert, warp. **poisoned** ▷ DIRTY, POISONOUS.

poisonous *adj* deadly, fatal, infectious, lethal, mephitic, miasmic, mortal, noxious, poisoned, septic, toxic, venomous, virulent.

poke *vb* butt, dig, elbow, goad, jab, jog, nudge, prod, stab, stick, thrust. ▷ HIT. **poke about** ▷ SEARCH. **poke fun at** ▷ RIDICULE. **poke out** ▷ PROTRUDE.

poky *adj* confined, cramped, inconvenient, restrictive, uncomfortable. ▷ SMALL. *Opp* SPACIOUS.

polar *adj* antarctic, arctic, freezing, glacial, icy, Siberian. ▷ COLD.

polarize *vb* diverge, divide, move to opposite positions, separate, split.

pole *n* **1** bar, beanpole, column, flagpole, mast, post, rod, shaft, spar, staff, stake, standard, stick, stilt, upright. **2** *opposite poles*. end, extreme, limit. **poles apart** ▷ DIFFERENT.

police *n sl* the Bill, constabulary, *sl* the fuzz, *inf* the law, police force, policemen. • *vb* control, guard, keep in order, keep the peace, monitor, oversee, patrol, protect, provide a police presence, supervise, watch over.

policeman, policewoman *ns inf* bobby, constable, *sl* cop, *sl* copper, detective, *Fr* gendarme, inspector, officer, PC, police constable, *sl* rozzer, woman police constable, WPC.

policy *n* **1** approach, code of conduct, custom, guidelines, *inf* line, method, practice, principles, procedure, protocol, regulations, rules, stance, strategy, tactics. **2** intentions, manifesto, plan of action, platform, programme, proposals.

polish *n* **1** brightness, brilliance, finish, glaze, gleam, gloss, lustre, sheen, shine, smoothness, sparkle. **2** beeswax, French polish, oil, shellac, varnish, wax. **3** *His manners show polish*. *inf* class, elegance, finesse, grace, refinement, sophistication, style, suavity, urbanity. • *vb* brighten, brush up, buff up, burnish, French-polish, gloss, rub down, rub up, shine, smooth, wax. **polish off** ▷ FINISH. **polish up** ▷ IMPROVE.

polished *adj* **1** bright, burnished, glassy, gleaming, glossy, lustrous, shining, shiny. **2** *polished manners.* civilized, *inf* classy, cultivated, cultured, debonair, elegant, expert, faultless, fine, finished, flawless, genteel, gracious, impeccable, perfect, perfected, polite, *inf* posh, refined, soigné(e), sophisticated, suave, urbane. *Opp* ROUGH.

polite *adj* agreeable, attentive, chivalrous, civil, considerate, correct, courteous, courtly, cultivated, deferential, diplomatic, discreet, euphemistic, formal, gallant, genteel, gentlemanly, gracious, ladylike, obliging, polished, proper, respectful, tactful, thoughtful, well-bred, well-mannered, well-spoken. *Opp* RUDE.

political *adj* **1** administrative, civil, diplomatic, governmental, legislative, parliamentary, state. **2** activist, factional, militant, partisan, party-political. □ *anarchist, capitalist, communist, conservative, democrat, fascist, Labour, leftist, left-wing, liberal, Marxist, moderate, monarchist, nationalist, Nazi, parliamentarian, radical, republican, revolutionary, rightist, right-wing, socialist, Tory,* old use *Whig.*

politics *n* diplomacy, government, political affairs, political science, public affairs, statecraft, statesmanship. □ *anarchy, capitalism, communism, democracy, dictatorship, martial law, monarchy, oligarchy, republic.*

poll *n* **1** ballot, election, vote. **2** canvass, census, plebiscite, referendum, survey. ● *vb* ballot, canvass, question, sample, survey.

pollute *vb* adulterate, befoul, blight, contaminate, corrupt, defile, dirty, foul, infect, poison, soil, taint.

pomp *n* brilliance, ceremonial, ceremony, display, formality, glory, grandeur, magnificence, ostentation, pageantry, ritual, show, solemnity, spectacle, splendour.

pompous *adj* affected, arrogant, bombastic, conceited, grandiloquent, grandiose, haughty, *inf* highfalutin, imperious, long-winded, magisterial, ornate, ostentatious, overbearing, pedantic, pontifical, posh, pretentious, self-important, sententious, showy, smug, snobbish, *inf* snooty, *inf* stuck-up, *inf* stuffy, supercilious, turgid, vain, vainglorious. ▷ PROUD. *Opp* MODEST.

ponderous *adj* **1** awkward, bulky, burdensome, cumbersome, heavy, hefty, huge, massive, unwieldy, weighty. *Opp* LIGHT. **2** *a ponderous style.* dreary, dull, elephantine, heavy-handed, humourless, inflated, laboured, lifeless, long-winded, overdone, pedestrian, plodding, prolix, slow, stilted, stodgy, tedious, tiresome, verbose, *inf* windy. *Opp* LIVELY.

pool *n* lagoon, lake, mere, oasis, paddling-pool, pond, puddle, swimming-pool, tarn. ● *vb* ▷ COMBINE.

poor *adj* **1** badly off, bankrupt, beggarly, *inf* broke, deprived, destitute, disadvantaged, *inf* down-and-out, *inf* hard up, homeless, impecunious, impoverished, in debt, indigent, insolvent, necessitous, needy, *inf* on your uppers, penniless, penurious, poverty-stricken, *sl* skint, straitened, underpaid, underprivileged. **2** *poor soil.* barren, exhausted, infertile, sterile, unfruitful, unproductive. **3** *a poor salary.* inadequate, insufficient, low, meagre, mean, scanty, small, sparse, unprofitable, unrewarding. **4** *poor in health. inf* below par, poorly. ▷ ILL. **5** *poor quality.* amateurish, bad, cheap, defective, deficient, disappointing, faulty, imperfect, inferior, low-grade, mediocre, paltry, second-rate, shoddy, substandard, unacceptable, unsatisfactory, useless, worthless. **6** *poor child!* forlorn, hapless, ill-fated, luckless, miserable, pathetic, pitiable, sad, unfortunate, unhappy, unlucky, wretched. *Opp* GOOD, LARGE, LUCKY, RICH. ● *plur n* beggars, the destitute, down-and-outs, the homeless, paupers, tramps, the underprivileged, vagrants, wretches.

populace *n* commonalty, *derog Gk* hoi polloi, masses, people, public, *derog* rabble, *derog* riff-raff.

popular *adj* **1** accepted, acclaimed, *inf* all the rage, approved, celebrated, famous, fashionable, favoured, favourite, *inf* in, in demand, liked, lionized, loved, renowned, sought-after, *inf* trendy, well-known, well-liked, well-received. *Opp* UNPOPULAR. **2** *popular opinion.* average, common, conventional, current, democratic, general, of the people, ordinary, predominant, prevailing, representative, standard, universal.

popularize *vb* **1** make popular, promote, spread. **2** *popularize classics.* make easy, simplify, *derog* tart up.

populate *vb* colonize, dwell in, fill, inhabit, live in, occupy, overrun, people, reside in, settle.

population *n* citizenry, citizens, community, denizens, folk, inhabitants, natives, occupants, people, populace, public, residents.

populous *adj* crowded, full, heavily populated, jammed, overcrowded, overpopulated, packed, swarming, teeming.

porch *n* doorway, entrance, lobby, portico.

pore *vb* **pore over** examine, go over, peruse, read, scrutinize, study.

pornographic *adj* arousing, *inf* blue, erotic, explicit, exploitative, sexual, sexy, titillating. ▷ OBSCENE.

porous *adj* absorbent, cellular, holey, penetrable, permeable, pervious, spongy. *Opp* IMPERVIOUS.

port *n* anchorage, dock, dockyard, harbour, haven, marina, mooring, sea-port.

portable *adj* compact, convenient, easy to carry, handy, light, lightweight, manageable, mobile, movable, pocket, pocket-sized, small, transportable. *Opp* UNWIELDY.

porter *n* **1** caretaker, concierge, doorkeeper, doorman, gatekeeper, janitor, security-guard, watchman. **2** baggage-handler, bearer, carrier.

portion *n* allocation, allowance, bit, chunk, division, fraction, fragment, helping, hunk, measure, part, percentage, piece, quantity, quota, ration, scrap, section, segment, serving, share, slice, sliver, subdivision, wedge. **portion out** ▷ SHARE.

portrait *n* depiction, image, likeness, picture, portrayal, profile, representation, self-portrait. ▷ PICTURE.

portray *vb* **1** delineate, depict, describe, evoke, illustrate, paint, picture, represent, show. **2** ▷ IMPERSONATE.

pose *n* **1** attitude, position, posture, stance. **2** act, affectation, attitudinizing, façade, masquerade, pretence. • *vb* **1** keep still, model, sit, strike a pose. **2** attitudinize, *inf* be a poser, be a poseur, posture, *inf* put on airs, show off. **3** *pose a question.* advance, ask, broach, posit, postulate, present, put forward, submit, suggest. **pose as** ▷ IMPERSONATE.

poser *n* **1** dilemma, enigma, problem, puzzle, question, riddle. **2** ▷ POSEUR.

poseur *n* attitudinizer, exhibitionist, fraud, impostor, masquerader, *inf* phoney, *inf* poser, pretender, *inf* show-off.

posh *adj inf* classy, elegant, fashionable, formal, grand, lavish, luxurious, ostentatious, rich, showy, smart, snobbish, stylish, sumptuous, *inf* swanky, *inf* swish.

position *n* **1** locality, location, locus, place, placement, point, reference, site, situation, spot, whereabouts. **2** *an awkward position.* circumstances, condition, predicament, situation, state. **3** *position of the body.* angle, pose, posture, stance. **4** *intellectual position.* assertion, attitude, contention, hypothesis, opinion, outlook, perspective, principle, proposition, standpoint, thesis, view, viewpoint. **5** *position in a firm.* appointment, degree, employment, function, grade, job, level, niche, occupation, place, post, rank, role, standing, station, status, title. • *vb* arrange, deploy, dispose, fix, locate, place, put, settle, site, situate, stand, station.

positive *adj* **1** affirmative, assured, categorical, certain, clear, conclusive, confident, convinced, decided, definite, emphatic, explicit, firm, incontestable, incontrovertible, irrefutable, real, sure, undeniable, unequivocal. **2** *positive advice.* beneficial, constructive, helpful, optimistic, practical, useful, worthwhile. *Opp* NEGATIVE.

possess *vb* **1** be in possession of, enjoy, have, hold, own. **2** be gifted with, embody, embrace, include. **3** *possess territory.* acquire, control, dominate, govern, invade, occupy, rule, seize, take over. **4** *possess a person.* bewitch, captivate, cast a spell over, charm, enthral, haunt, hypnotize, obsess.

possessions *plur n* assets, belongings, chattels, effects, estate, fortune, goods, property, riches, things, wealth, worldly goods.

possessive *adj* clinging, dominating, domineering, jealous, overbearing, proprietorial, protective, selfish. ▷ GREEDY.

possibility *n* capability, chance, danger, feasibility, likelihood, odds, opportunity, plausibility, potential, potentiality, practicality, probability, risk.

possible *adj* achievable, admissible, attainable, conceivable, credible, *inf* doable, feasible, imaginable, likely, obtainable, *inf* on, plausible, potential, practicable, practical, probable, prospective, realizable, reasonable, tenable, thinkable, viable, workable. *Opp* IMPOSSIBLE.

possibly *adv* God willing, *inf* hopefully, if possible, maybe, *old use* peradventure, *old use* perchance, perhaps.

post *n* **1** baluster, bollard, brace, capstan, column, gate-post, leg, newel, pale, paling, picket, pier, pile, pillar, pole, prop, pylon, shaft, stake, stanchion, standard, starting-post, strut, support, upright, winning-post. **2** *a sentry's post.* location, place, point, position, station. **3** *post in a firm.* appointment, assignment, employment, function, job, occupation, office, place, position, situation, task, work. **4** airmail, cards, delivery, junk mail, letters, mail, packets, parcels, postcards. • *vb* **1** advertise, announce, display, pin up, proclaim, promulgate, publicize, publish, put up, stick up. **2** *post a letter.* dispatch, mail, send, transmit. **3** *post a sentry.* appoint, assign, locate, place, position, set, situate, station.

poster *n* advertisement, announcement, bill, broadsheet, circular, display, flyer, notice, placard, sign.

posterity *n* descendants, future generations, heirs, issue, offspring, progeny, successors.

postpone *vb* adjourn, defer, delay, extend, hold over, keep in abeyance, lay aside, put back, put off, *inf* put on ice, *inf* put on the back burner, *inf* shelve, stay, suspend, temporize.

postscript *n* addendum, addition, afterthought, codicil (*to will*), epilogue, *inf* PS.

postulate *vb* assume, hypothesize, posit, propose, suppose, theorize.

posture *n* **1** appearance, bearing, carriage, deportment, pose, position, stance. **2** ▷ ATTITUDE.

posy *n* bouquet, bunch of flowers, buttonhole, corsage, nosegay, spray.

pot *n* basin, bowl, casserole, cauldron, container, crock, crucible, dish, jar, pan, saucepan, stewpot, teapot, urn, vessel.

potent *adj* **1** effective, forceful, formidable, influential, intoxicating (*drink*), mighty, overpowering, overwhelming, powerful, puissant, strong, vigorous. ▷ STRONG. **2** *a potent argument.* ▷ PERSUASIVE. *Opp* WEAK.

potential *adj* **1** aspiring, budding, embryonic, future, *inf* hopeful, intending, latent, likely, possible, probable, promising, prospective, *inf* would-be. **2** *potential disaster.* imminent, impending, looming, threatening. • *n* aptitude, capability, capacity, possibility, resources.

potion *n* brew, concoction, decoction, dose, draught, drink, drug, elixir, liquid, medicine, mixture, philtre, potation, tonic.

potter *vb* dabble, do odd jobs, fiddle about, loiter, mess about, tinker, work.

pottery *n* ceramics, china, crockery, crocks, earthenware, porcelain, stoneware, terracotta.

pouch *n* bag, pocket, purse, reticule, sack, wallet.

poultry *n* □ *bantam, chicken, duck, fowl, goose, guinea-fowl, hen, pullet, turkey.*

pounce *vb* ambush, attack, drop on, jump on, leap on, seize, snatch, spring at, strike, swoop down on, take by surprise.

pound *n* compound, corral, enclosure, pen. • *vb* batter, beat, crush, grind, hammer, knead, mash, powder, pulp, pulverize, smash. ▷ HIT.

pour *vb* **1** cascade, course, discharge, disgorge, flood, flow, gush, run, spew, spill, spout, spurt, stream. **2** *pour wine.* decant, empty, serve, tip.

poverty *n* **1** beggary, bankruptcy, debt, destitution, hardship, impecuniousness, indigence, insolvency, necessity, need, penury, privation, want. **2** *a poverty of talent.* absence, dearth, insufficiency, lack, paucity, scarcity, shortage. *Opp* WEALTH.

powder *n* dust, particles, talc. • *vb* **1** atomize, comminute, crush, granulate, grind, pound, pulverize, reduce to powder. **2** besprinkle, coat, cover with powder, dredge, dust, sprinkle.

powdered *adj* **1** ▷ POWDERY. **2** dehydrated, dried, freeze-dried.

powdery *adj* chalky, crumbly, crushed, disintegrating, dry, dusty, fine, friable, granular, granulated, ground, loose, powdered, pulverized, sandy. *Opp* SOLID, WET.

power *n* **1** ability, capability, capacity, competence, drive, energy, faculty, force, might, muscle, potential, skill, talent, vigour. **2** *power to arrest.* authority, privilege, right. **3** *power of a tyrant.* ascendancy, *inf* clout, command, control, dominance, domination, dominion, influence, mastery, omnipotence, oppression, potency, rule, sovereignty, supremacy, sway. ▷ STRENGTH. *Opp* WEAKNESS.

powerful *adj* authoritative, cogent, commanding, compelling, consuming, convincing, dominant, dynamic, effective, effectual, energetic, forceful, high-powered, influential, invincible, irresistible, mighty, muscular, omnipotent, overpowering, overwhelming, persuasive, potent, sovereign, vigorous, weighty. ▷ STRONG. *Opp* POWERLESS.

powerless *adj* defenceless, disabled, feeble, helpless, impotent, incapable, incapacitated, ineffective, ineffectual, paralysed, unable, unfit. ▷ WEAK. *Opp* POWERFUL.

practicable *adj* achievable, attainable, *inf* doable, feasible, performable, possible, practical, realistic, sensible, viable, workable. *Opp* IMPRACTICABLE.

practical *adj* **1** applied, empirical, experimental. **2** businesslike, capable, competent, down-to-earth, efficient, expert, hard-headed, matter-of-fact, *inf* no-nonsense, pragmatic, proficient, realistic, sensible, skilled. **3** *a practical tool.* convenient, functional, handy, usable, useful, utilitarian. **4** ▷ PRACTICABLE. *Opp* IMPRACTICAL, THEORETICAL. **practical joke** ▷ TRICK.

practically *adv* almost, close to, just about, nearly, to all intents and purposes, virtually.

practice *n* **1** action, actuality, application, doing, effect, operation, reality, use. **2** *inf* dummy-run, exercise, practising, preparation, rehearsal, *inf* run-through, training, *inf* try-out, *inf* work-out. **3** *common practice.* convention, custom, habit, modus operandi, routine, tradition, way, wont. **4** *a doctor's practice.* business, office, work.

practise *vb* **1** do exercises, drill, exercise, prepare, rehearse, train, warm up, *inf* work out. **2** *practise what* *you preach.* apply, carry out, do, engage in, follow, make a practice of, perform, put into practice.

praise *n* **1** acclaim, acclamation, accolade, admiration, adulation, applause, approbation, approval, commendation, compliment, congratulation, encomium, eulogy, homage, honour, ovation, panegyric, plaudits, testimonial, thanks, tribute. **2** *praise to God.* adoration, devotion, glorification, worship. • *vb* **1** acclaim, admire, applaud, cheer, clap, commend, compliment, congratulate, *inf* crack up, eulogize, extol, give a good review of, marvel at, offer praise to, pay tribute to, *inf* rave about, recommend, *inf* say nice things about, show approval of. *Opp* CRITICIZE. **2** *praise God.* adore, exalt, glorify, honour, laud, magnify, worship. *Opp* CURSE.

praiseworthy *adj* admirable, commendable, creditable, deserving, laudable, meritorious, worthy. ▷ GOOD. *Opp* BAD.

pram *n* baby-carriage, *old use* perambulator, push-chair.

prance *vb* bound, caper, cavort, dance, frisk, frolic, gambol, hop, jig about, jump, leap, play, romp, skip, spring.

prattle *vb* babble, blather, chatter, gabble, maunder, *inf* rattle on, *inf* witter on.

pray *vb* beseech, call upon, invoke, say prayers, supplicate. ▷ ASK.

prayer *n* collect, devotion, entreaty, invocation, litany, meditation, petition, praise, supplication.

prayer-book *n* breviary, missal.

preach *vb* **1** deliver a sermon, evangelize, expound, proselytize, spread the Gospel. **2** expatiate, give moral advice, harangue, *inf* lay down the law, lecture, moralize, pontificate, sermonize.

preacher *n* cleric, crusader, divine, ecclesiastic, evangelist, minister, missionary, moralist, pastor, revivalist. ▷ CLERGYMAN.

prearranged *adj* arranged beforehand, fixed, planned, predetermined, prepared, rehearsed, thought out. *Opp* SPONTANEOUS.

precarious *adj* dangerous, *inf* dicey, *inf* dodgy, dubious, hazardous, insecure, perilous, risky, rocky, shaky, slippery, treacherous, uncertain, unreliable, unsafe, unstable, unsteady, vulnerable, wobbly. *Opp* SAFE.

precaution *n* anticipation, defence, insurance, preventive measure, protection, provision, safeguard, safety measure.

precede *vb* be in front of, come before, go ahead, go before, go in front, herald, introduce, lead, lead into, pave the way for, preface, prefix, start, usher in. *Opp* FOLLOW.

precious *adj* **1** costly, expensive, invaluable, irreplaceable, priceless, valuable. *Opp* WORTHLESS. **2** adored, beloved, darling, dear, loved, prized, treasured, valued, venerated.

precipice *n* bluff, cliff, crag, drop, escarpment, precipitous face, rock.

precipitate *adj* breakneck, hasty, headlong, meteoric, premature. ▷ QUICK. • *vb* accelerate, advance, bring on, cause, encourage, expedite, further, hasten, hurry, incite, induce, instigate, occasion, provoke, spark off, trigger off.

precipitation *n* □ *dew, downpour, drizzle, hail, rain, rainfall, shower, sleet, snow, snowfall.*

precipitous *adj* abrupt, perpendicular, sharp, sheer, steep, vertical.

precise *adj* **1** accurate, clear-cut, correct, defined, definite, distinct, exact, explicit, fixed, measured, right, specific, unambiguous, unequivocal, well-defined. *Opp* IMPRECISE. **2** *precise work.* careful, critical, exacting, fastidious, faultless, finicky, flawless, meticulous, nice, perfect, punctilious, rigorous, scrupulous. *Opp* CARELESS.

preclude *vb* avert, avoid, bar, debar, exclude, forestall, frustrate, impede, make impossible, obviate, pre-empt, prevent, prohibit, rule out, thwart.

precocious *adj* advanced, forward, gifted, mature, quick. ▷ CLEVER. *Opp* BACKWARD.

preconception *n* assumption, bias, expectation, preconceived idea, predisposition, prejudgement, prejudice, presupposition.

predatory *adj* acquisitive, avaricious, covetous, extortionate, greedy, hunting, marauding, pillaging, plundering, preying, rapacious, ravenous, voracious.

predecessor *n* ancestor, antecedent, forebear, forefather, forerunner, precursor.

predetermined *adj* **1** fated, destined, doomed, ordained, predestined. **2** agreed, prearranged, pre-planned, recognized, *inf* set up.

predicament *n* crisis, difficulty, dilemma, embarrassment, emergency, *inf* fix, impasse, *inf* jam, *inf* mess, *inf* pickle, plight, problem, quandary, situation, state.

predict *vb* augur, forebode, forecast, foresee, foreshadow, foretell, foretoken, forewarn, hint, intimate, presage, prognosticate, prophesy, tell fortunes.

predictable *adj* anticipated, certain, expected, foreseeable, foreseen, likely, *inf* on the cards, probable, sure, unsurprising. *Opp* UNPREDICTABLE.

predominant *adj* ascendant, chief, dominating, leading, main, preponderant, prevailing, prevalent, primary, ruling, sovereign.

predominate *vb* be in the majority, control, dominate, *inf* have the upper hand, hold sway, lead, outnumber, outweigh, preponderate, prevail, reign, rule.

pre-eminent *adj* distinguished, eminent, excellent, incomparable, matchless, outstanding, peerless, supreme, unrivalled, unsurpassed.

pre-empt *vb* anticipate, appropriate, arrogate, expropriate, forestall, seize, take over.

preface *n* exordium, foreword, introduction, *inf* lead-in, overture, preamble, prelude, proem, prolegomenon, prologue. • *vb* begin, introduce, lead into, open, precede, prefix, start.

prefer *vb* advocate, *inf* back, be partial to, choose, fancy, favour, *inf* go for, incline towards, like, like better, opt for, pick out, *inf* plump for, *inf* put your money on, recommend, select, single out, think preferable, vote for, want.

preferable *adj* advantageous, better, better-liked, chosen, desirable, favoured, likely, nicer, preferred, recommended, wanted. *Opp* OBJECTIONABLE.

preference *n* **1** choice, fancy, favourite, liking, option, pick, selection, wish. **2** favouritism, inclination, partiality, predilection, prejudice, proclivity.

preferential *adj* advantageous, better, biased, favourable, favoured, privileged, showing favouritism, special, superior.

pregnant *adj* **1** carrying a child, expectant, *inf* expecting, gestating, gravid, parturient, *old use* with child. **2** *pregnant remark*. ▷ MEANINGFUL.

prejudice *n* bias, bigotry, chauvinism, discrimination, dogmatism, fanaticism, favouritism, intolerance, jingoism, leaning, narrow-mindedness, partiality, partisanship, predilection, predisposition, prejudgement, racialism, racism, sexism, unfairness, xenophobia. *Opp* TOLERANCE. • *vb* **1** bias, colour, incline, influence, interfere with, make prejudiced, predispose, sway. **2** *prejudice your chances*. damage, harm, injure, ruin, spoil, undermine.

prejudiced *adj* biased, bigoted, chauvinist, discriminatory, illiberal, intolerant, jaundiced, jingoistic, leading (*question*), loaded, narrow-minded, one-sided, parochial, partial, partisan, racist, sexist, tendentious, unfair, xenophobic. *Opp* IMPARTIAL. **prejudiced person** bigot, chauvinist, fanatic, racist, sexist, zealot.

prejudicial *adj* damaging, deleterious, detrimental, disadvantageous, harmful, inimical, injurious, unfavourable.

preliminary *adj* advance, earliest, early, experimental, exploratory, first, inaugural, initial, introductory, opening, prefatory, preparatory, qualifying, tentative, trial. ● *n* ▷ PRELUDE.

prelude *n* beginning, *inf* curtain-raiser, exordium, introduction, opener, opening, overture, preamble, precursor, preface, preliminary, preparation, proem, prolegomenon, prologue, start, starter, *inf* warm-up. *Opp* CONCLUSION, POSTSCRIPT.

premature *adj* abortive, before time, early, hasty, ill-timed, precipitate, *inf* previous, too early, too soon, undeveloped, untimely. *Opp* LATE.

premeditated *adj* calculated, conscious, considered, contrived, deliberate, intended, intentional, planned, prearranged, preconceived, predetermined, preplanned, studied, wilful. *Opp* SPONTANEOUS.

premiss *n* assertion, assumption, basis, grounds, hypothesis, proposition, supposition, thesis.

premonition *n* anxiety, fear, foreboding, forewarning, *inf* funny feeling, *inf* hunch, indication, intuition, misgiving, omen, portent, presentiment, suspicion, warning, worry.

preoccupied *adj* **1** absorbed, engaged, engrossed, immersed, interested, involved, obsessed, sunk, taken up, wrapped up. **2** absent-minded, abstracted, day-dreaming, distracted, faraway, inattentive, lost in thought, musing, pensive, pondering, rapt, reflecting, thoughtful.

preparation *n* arrangements, briefing, *inf* gearing up, getting ready, groundwork, making provision, measures, organization, plans, practice, preparing, setting up, spadework, training.

prepare *vb* **1** arrange, cook, devise, *inf* do what's necessary, *inf* fix up, get ready, make arrangements, make ready, organize, pave the way, plan, process, set up. ▷ MAKE. **2** *prepare for exams. inf* cram, practise, revise, study, *inf* swot. **3** *prepare pupils for exams.* brief, coach, educate, equip, instruct, rehearse, teach, train, tutor. **prepared** ▷ PRE-ARRANGED, READY. **prepare yourself** be prepared, be ready, brace yourself, discipline yourself, fortify yourself, steel yourself.

preposterous *adj* bizarre, excessive, extreme, grotesque, monstrous, outrageous, surreal, unreasonable, unthinkable. ▷ ABSURD.

prerequisite *adj* compulsory, essential, indispensable, mandatory, necessary, obligatory, prescribed, required, requisite, specified, stipulated. *Opp* OPTIONAL. ● *n* condition, essential, necessity, precondition, proviso, qualification, requirement, requisite, *Lat* sine qua non, stipulation.

prescribe *vb* advise, assign, command, demand, dictate, direct, fix, impose, instruct, lay down, ordain, order, recommend, require, specify, stipulate, suggest.

presence *n* **1** attendance, closeness, companionship, company, nearness, propinquity, proximity, society. **2** air, appearance, aura, bearing, comportment, demeanour, impressiveness, mien, personality, poise, self-assurance, self-possession.

present *adj* **1** adjacent, at hand, close, here, in attendance, nearby. **2** contemporary, current, existing, extant, present-day, up-to-date. ● *n* **1** *inf* here and now, today. **2** alms, bonus, bounty, charity, contribution, donation, endowment, gift, grant, gratuity, handout, offering, tip. ● *vb* **1** award, bestow, confer, dispense, distribute, donate, give, hand over, offer. **2** *present evidence.* adduce, bring forward, demonstrate, display, exhibit, furnish, proffer, put forward, reveal, set out, show, submit. **3** *present a guest.* announce, introduce, make known. **4** *present a play.* act, bring out, perform, put on, stage. **present yourself** ▷ ATTEND, REPORT.

presentable *adj* acceptable, adequate, all right, clean, decent, decorous, fit to be seen, good enough, neat, passable, proper, respectable, satisfactory, suitable, tidy, tolerable, *inf* up to scratch, worthy.

presently *adv old use* anon, before long, by and by, *inf* in a jiffy, shortly, soon.

preserve *n* **1** conserve, jam, jelly, marmalade. **2** *wildlife preserve.* reservation, reserve, sanctuary. • *vb* **1** care for, conserve, defend, guard, keep, lay up, look after, maintain, perpetuate, protect, retain, safeguard, save, secure, stockpile, store, support, sustain, uphold, watch over. *Opp* DESTROY. **2** *preserve food.* bottle, can, chill, cure, dehydrate, dry, freeze, freeze-dry, irradiate, jam, pickle, refrigerate, salt, tin. **3** *preserve a corpse.* embalm, mummify.

preside *vb* be in charge, chair, officiate, take charge, take the chair. **preside over** ▷ GOVERN.

press *n* magazines, the media, newspapers. • *vb* **1** apply pressure to, compress, condense, cram, crowd, crush, depress, force, gather, *inf* jam, push, shove, squash, squeeze, subject to pressure. **2** *press laundry.* flatten, iron, smooth. **3** *press someone to stay.* ask, beg, bully, coerce, constrain, dragoon, entreat, exhort, implore, importune, induce, *inf* lean on, persuade, pressure, pressurize, put pressure on, request, require, urge. **pressing** ▷ URGENT.

pressure *n* **1** burden, compression, force, heaviness, load, might, power, stress, weight. **2** *pressure of modern life.* adversity, affliction, constraints, demands, difficulties, exigencies, *inf* hassle, hurry, oppression, problems, strain, stress, urgency. • *vb* ask, beg, bully, coerce, constrain, dragoon, entreat, exhort, implore, importune, induce, *inf* lean on, persuade, press, pressurize, put pressure on, request, require, urge.

prestige *n* cachet, celebrity, credit, distinction, eminence, esteem, fame, glory, good name, honour, importance, influence, *inf* kudos, regard, renown, reputation, respect, standing, stature, status.

prestigious *adj* acclaimed, august, celebrated, creditable, distinguished, eminent, esteemed, estimable, famed, famous, highly-regarded, high-ranking, honourable, honoured, important, influential, pre-eminent, renowned, reputable, respected, significant, wellknown. *Opp* INSIGNIFICANT.

presume *vb* **1** assume, believe, conjecture, gather, guess, hypothesize, imagine, infer, postulate, suppose, surmise, suspect, *inf* take for granted, *inf* take it, think. **2** *He presumed to correct me.* be presumptuous enough, dare, have the effrontery, make bold, take the liberty, venture.

presumptuous *adj* arrogant, bold, brazen, *inf* cheeky, conceited, forward, impertinent, impudent, insolent, over-confident, *inf* pushy, shameless, unauthorized, unwarranted. ▷ PROUD.

pretence *n* act, acting, affectation, appearance, artifice, camouflage, charade, counterfeiting, deception, disguise, display, dissembling, dissimulation, excuse, façade, falsification, feigning, feint, fiction, front, guise, hoax, *inf* humbug, hypocrisy, insincerity, invention, lying, make-believe, masquerade, pose, posing, posturing, pretext, ruse, sham, show, simulation, subterfuge, trickery, wile. ▷ DECEIT.

pretend *vb* **1** act, affect, allege, behave insincerely, bluff, counterfeit, deceive, disguise, dissemble, dissimulate, fake, feign, fool, hoax, hoodwink, imitate, impersonate, *inf* kid, lie, *inf* make out, mislead, perform, play a part, play-act, pose, posture, profess, purport, put on an act, sham, simulate, take someone in, trick. **2** ▷ IMAGINE. **3** ▷ CLAIM.

pretender *n* aspirant, claimant, rival, suitor.

pretentious *adj* affected, *inf* arty, conceited, exaggerated, extravagant, grandiose, *inf* highfalutin, inflated, ostentatious, overblown, *inf* over the top, pompous, showy, *inf* snobbish, superficial. *Opp* UNPRETENTIOUS.

pretext *n* cloak, cover, disguise, excuse, pretence.

pretty *adj* appealing, attractive, *inf* bonny, charming, *inf* cute, dainty, delicate, *inf* easy on the eye, fetching, good-looking, lovely, nice, pleasing, *derog* pretty-pretty, winsome. ▷ BEAUTIFUL. *Opp* UGLY. ● *adv* fairly, moderately, quite, rather, reasonably, somewhat, tolerably. *Opp* VERY.

prevail *vb* be prevalent, hold sway, predominate, preponderate, succeed, triumph, *inf* win the day. ▷ WIN. **prevailing** ▷ PREVALENT.

prevalent *adj* accepted, ascendant, chief, common, commonest, current, customary, dominant, dominating, effectual, established, extensive, familiar, fashionable, general, governing, influential, main, mainstream, normal, ordinary, orthodox, pervasive, popular, powerful, predominant, prevailing, principal, ruling, ubiquitous, universal, usual, widespread. *Opp* UNUSUAL.

prevaricate *vb inf* beat about the bush, be evasive, cavil, deceive, equivocate, *inf* fib, hedge, lie, mislead, quibble, temporize.

prevent *vb* anticipate, avert, avoid, baffle, bar, block, check, control, curb, deter, fend off, foil, forestall, frustrate, hamper, *inf* head off, *inf* help (*can't help it*), hinder, impede, inhibit, inoculate against, intercept, *inf* nip in the bud, obstruct, obviate, preclude, pre-empt, prohibit, *inf* put a stop to, restrain, save, stave off, stop, take precautions against, thwart, ward off. ▷ FORBID. *Opp* ENCOURAGE.

preventive *adj* anticipatory, counteractive, deterrent, obstructive, precautionary, pre-emptive, preventative.

previous *adj* **1** above-mentioned, aforementioned, aforesaid, antecedent, earlier, erstwhile, foregoing, former, past, preceding, prior. *Opp* SUBSEQUENT. **2** ▷ PREMATURE.

prey *n* kill, quarry, victim. ● *vb* **prey on** eat, feed on, hunt, kill, live off. ▷ EXPLOIT.

price *n* **1** amount, charge, cost, *inf* damage, expenditure, expense, fare, fee, figure, outlay, payment, rate, sum, terms, toll, value, worth. **2** *Give me a price.* estimate, offer, quotation, valuation. ▷ PAYMENT. **pay the price for** ▷ ATONE.

priceless *adj* **1** costly, dear, expensive, incalculable, inestimable, invaluable, irreplaceable, precious, *inf* pricey, rare, valuable. *Opp* WORTHLESS. **2** ▷ FUNNY.

prick *vb* **1** bore into, jab, lance, perforate, pierce, punch, puncture, riddle, stab, sting. **2** ▷ STIMULATE.

prickle *n* **1** barb, bristle, bur, needle, spike, spine, thorn. **2** irritation, itch, pricking, prickling, tingle, tingling. ● *vb* irritate, itch, make your skin crawl, scratch, sting, tingle.

prickly *adj* **1** barbed, bristly, rough, scratchy, sharp, spiky, spiny, stubbly, thorny, unshaven. *Opp* SMOOTH. **2** ▷ IRRITABLE.

pride *n* **1** *Fr* amour propre, gratification, happiness, honour, pleasure, satisfaction, self-respect, self-satisfaction. ▷ DIGNITY. **2** *her pride and joy.* jewel, treasure, treasured possession. **3** *pride before a fall.* arrogance, being proud, *inf* big-headedness, boastfulness, conceit, egotism, haughtiness, hubris, megalomania, narcissism, overconfidence, presumption, self-admiration, self-esteem, self-importance, self-love, smugness, snobbery, snobbishness, vainglory, vanity. *Opp* HUMILITY.

priest *n* confessor, Druid, lama, minister, preacher. ▷ CLERGYMAN.

priggish *adj* conservative, fussy, *inf* goody-goody, haughty, moralistic, prudish, self-righteous, sententious, stiff-necked, *inf* stuffy. ▷ PRIM.

prim *adj* demure, fastidious, formal, inhibited, narrow-minded, precise, *inf* prissy, proper, prudish, *inf* starchy, strait-laced. *Opp* BROADMINDED.

primal *adj* **1** early, earliest, first, original, primeval, primitive, primordial. **2** ▷ PRIMARY.

primarily *adv* basically, chiefly, especially, essentially, firstly, fundamentally, generally, mainly, mostly, particularly, predominantly, preeminently, principally.

primary *adj* basic, cardinal, chief, dominant, first, foremost, fundamental, greatest, important, initial, leading, main, major, outstanding, paramount, predominant, preeminent, primal, prime, principal, supreme, top.

prime *adj* **1** best, first-class, first-rate, foremost, select, superior, top, top-quality. ▷ EXCELLENT. **2** ▷ PRIMARY. ● *vb* get ready, prepare.

primitive *adj* **1** aboriginal, ancient, barbarian, early, first, prehistoric, primeval, savage, uncivilized, uncultivated. **2** *primitive technology*. antediluvian, backward, basic, *inf* behind the times, crude, elementary, obsolete, rough, rudimentary, simple, simplistic, undeveloped. ▷ OLD. **3** *primitive art*. childlike, crude, naïve, unpolished, unrefined, unsophisticated. *Opp* ADVANCED, SOPHISTICATED.

principal *adj* basic, cardinal, chief, dominant, dominating, first, foremost, fundamental, greatest, highest, important, key, leading, main, major, outstanding, paramount, predominant, pre-eminent, prevailing, primary, prime, starring, supreme, top. ● *n* **1** ▷ CHIEF. **2** *the principal in a play*. diva, hero, heroine, lead, leading role, prima ballerina, protagonist, star.

principle *n* **1** assumption, axiom, belief, creed, criterion, doctrine, dogma, ethic, idea, ideal, maxim, notion, precept, proposition, rule, standard, teaching, tenet, truism, truth, values. **2** *a person of principle*. conscience, high-mindedness, honesty, honour, ideals, integrity, morality, probity, scruples, standards, uprightness, virtue. **principles** basics, elements, essentials, fundamentals, laws, philosophy, theory.

print *n* **1** impression, imprint, indentation, mark, stamp. **2** characters, fount, lettering, letters, printing, text, type, typeface. **3** copy, duplicate, engraving, etching, facsimile, linocut, lithograph, monoprint, photograph, reproduction, silk screen, woodcut. ▷ PICTURE. ● *vb* **1** copy, impress, imprint, issue, publish, run off, stamp. **2** ▷ WRITE.

prior *adj* earlier, erstwhile, former, late, old, onetime, previous.

priority *n* first place, greater importance, precedence, preference, prerogative, right-of-way, seniority, superiority, urgency.

prise *vb* force, lever, prize, wrench.

prison *n old use* approved school, *old use* Borstal, cell, *sl* clink, custody, detention centre, dungeon, gaol, guardhouse, house of correction, jail, *inf* lock-up, *Amer* penitentiary, oubliette, reformatory, *sl* stir, youth custody centre. ▷ CAPTIVITY.

prisoner *n* captive, convict, detainee, *inf* gaolbird, hostage, inmate, internee, lifer, *inf* old lag, *inf* trusty.

privacy *n* concealment, isolation, monasticism, quietness, retirement, retreat, seclusion, secrecy, solitude.

private *adj* **1** exclusive, individual, particular, personal, privately owned, reserved. **2** classified, confidential, *inf* hush-hush, *inf* off the record, restricted, secret, top secret, undisclosed. **3** *a private meeting*. clandestine, closed, covert, intimate, surreptitious. **4** *a private hideaway*. concealed, hidden, inaccessible, isolated, little-known, quiet, secluded, sequestered, solitary, unknown, withdrawn. *Opp* PUBLIC.

privilege *n* advantage, benefit, concession, entitlement, exemption, freedom, immunity, licence, prerogative, right.

privileged *adj* **1** advantaged, authorized, élite, entitled, favoured, honoured, immune, licensed, powerful, protected, sanctioned, special, superior. **2** ▷ WEALTHY.

prize *n* accolade, award, jackpot, *inf* purse, reward, trophy, winnings. ● *vb* **1** appreciate, approve of, cherish, esteem, hold dear, like, rate highly, regard, revere, treasure, value. **2** ▷ PRISE.

probable *adj* believable, convincing, credible, expected, feasible, likely, *inf* odds-on, plausible, possible, predictable, presumed, undoubted, unquestioned. *Opp* IMPROBABLE.

probationer *n* apprentice, beginner, inexperienced worker, learner, novice, tiro.

probe *n* enquiry, examination, exploration, inquiry, investigation, research, scrutiny, study. ● *vb* **1** delve, dig, penetrate, plumb, poke, prod. **2** *probe a problem.* examine, explore, go into, inquire into, investigate, look into, research into, scrutinize, study.

problem *n* **1** brain-teaser, conundrum, enigma, mystery, *inf* poser, puzzle, question, riddle. **2** *a worrying problem.* burden, *inf* can of worms, complication, difficulty, dilemma, dispute, *inf* facer, *inf* headache, *inf* hornet's nest, predicament, quandary, set-back, snag, trouble, worry.

problematic *adj* complicated, controversial, debatable, difficult, disputed, doubtful, enigmatic, hard to deal with, *inf* iffy, intractable, moot (*point*), problematical, puzzling, questionable, sensitive, taxing, *inf* tricky, uncertain, unsettling, worrying. *Opp* STRAIGHTFORWARD.

procedure *n* approach, conduct, course of action, *inf* drill, formula, method, methodology, *Lat* modus operandi, plan of action, policy, practice, process, routine, scheme, strategy, system, technique, way.

proceed *vb* **1** advance, carry on, continue, follow, forge ahead, *inf* get going, go ahead, go on, make headway, make progress, move along, move forward, *inf* press on, progress. **2** arise, be derived, begin, develop, emerge, grow, originate, spring up, start. ▷ RESULT.

proceedings *plur n* **1** events, *inf* goings-on, happenings, things. **2** *legal proceedings.* action, lawsuit, procedure, process. **3** *proceedings of a meeting.* annals, business, dealings, *inf* doings, matters, minutes, records, report, transactions.

proceeds *plur n* earnings, gain, gate, income, profit, receipts, returns, revenue, takings. ▷ MONEY.

process *n* **1** function, method, operation, procedure, proceeding, system, technique. **2** *process of ageing.* course, development, evolution, experience, progression. ● *vb* **1** alter, change, convert, deal with, make usable, manage, modify, organize, prepare, refine, transform, treat. **2** ▷ PARADE.

procession *n* cavalcade, chain, column, cortège, file, line, march, march-past, motorcade, pageant, parade, sequence, string, succession, train.

proclaim *vb* **1** announce, advertise, assert, declare, give out, make known, profess, promulgate, pronounce, publish. **2** ▷ DECREE.

procrastinate *vb* be dilatory, be indecisive, dally, defer a decision, delay, *inf* dilly-dally, dither, *inf* drag your feet, equivocate, evade the issue, hesitate, *inf* hum and haw, pause, *inf* play for time, postpone, put things off, *inf* shilly-shally, stall, temporize, vacillate, waver.

procure *vb* acquire, buy, come by, find, get, *inf* get hold of, *inf* lay your hands on, obtain, *inf* pick up, purchase, requisition.

prod *vb* dig, elbow, goad, jab, nudge, poke, push, urge on. ▷ HIT, URGE.

prodigal *adj* excessive, extravagant, immoderate, improvident, irresponsible, lavish, profligate, reckless, self-indulgent, wasteful. *Opp* THRIFTY.

prodigy *n* curiosity, freak, genius, marvel, miracle, phenomenon, rarity, sensation, talent, virtuoso, *inf* whizz kid, wonder, *Ger* Wunderkind.

produce *n* crop, harvest, output, yield. ▷ PRODUCT. • *vb* **1** assemble, bring out, cause, compose, conjure up, construct, create, cultivate, develop, fabricate, form, generate, give rise to, grow, initiate, invent, make, manufacture, originate, provoke, result in, supply, think up, turn out, yield. **2** *produce evidence.* advance, bring out, disclose, display, exhibit, furnish, introduce, offer, present, provide, put forward, reveal, show, supply, throw up. **3** *produce children.* bear, beget, breed, give birth to, raise, rear. **4** *produce a play.* direct, mount, present, put on, stage.

product *n* **1** artefact, by-product, commodity, end-product, goods, merchandise, output, produce, production. **2** consequence, effect, fruit, issue, outcome, result, upshot, yield.

productive *adj* **1** beneficial, busy, constructive, creative, effective, efficient, gainful (*employment*), inventive, profitable, profitmaking, remunerative, rewarding, useful, valuable, worthwhile. **2** *a productive garden.* abundant, bounteous, bountiful, fecund, fertile, fruitful, lush, prolific, vigorous. *Opp* UNPRODUCTIVE.

profess *vb* **1** affirm, announce, assert, asseverate, aver, confess, confirm, declare, maintain, state, vow. **2** *profess to be an expert.* allege, claim, make out, pretend, purport.

profession *n* **1** business, calling, career, craft, employment, job, line of work, métier, occupation, trade, vocation, work. **2** *profession of love.* acknowledgement, affirmation, announcement, assertion, avowal, confession, declaration, statement, testimony.

professional *adj* **1** able, authorized, educated, experienced, expert, knowledgeable, licensed, official, proficient, qualified, skilled, trained. *Opp* AMATEUR. **2** full-time, paid. **3** *professional work.* businesslike, competent, conscientious, efficient, masterly, proper, skilful, thorough, well-done. *Opp* UNPROFESSIONAL. • *n* expert, professional player, professional worker.

proficient *adj* able, accomplished, adept, capable, competent, efficient, expert, gifted, professional, skilled, talented. *Opp* INCOMPETENT.

profile *n* **1** contour, outline, shape, side view, silhouette. **2** *personal profile.* account, biography, *Lat* curriculum vitae, sketch, study.

profit *n* advantage, benefit, excess, gain, interest, proceeds, return, revenue, surplus, yield. • *vb* **1** advance, avail, benefit, further the interests of, pay, serve. ▷ HELP. **2** *profit from a sale.* capitalize (on), *inf* cash in, earn money, gain, *inf* make a killing, make a profit, make money. **profit by, profit from** ▷ EXPLOIT.

profitable *adj* advantageous, beneficial, commercial, enriching, fruitful, gainful, lucrative, money-making, paying, productive, profit-making, remunerative, rewarding, useful, valuable, well-paid, worthwhile. *Opp* UNPROFITABLE.

profiteer *n* black-marketeer, exploiter, extortionist, racketeer. • *vb* exploit, extort, fleece, overcharge.

profligate *adj* **1** abandoned, debauched, degenerate, depraved, dissolute, immoral, libertine, licentious, loose, perverted, promiscuous, sinful, sybaritic, unprincipled, wanton. ▷ WICKED. **2** extravagant, prodigal, reckless, spendthrift, wasteful.

profound *adj* **1** deep, heartfelt, intense, sincere. **2** *a profound discussion.* abstruse, arcane, erudite, esoteric, imponderable, informed, intellectual, knowledgeable, learned, penetrating, philosophical, recondite, sagacious, scholarly, serious, thoughtful, wise. **3** *profound silence.* absolute, complete, extreme, fundamental, perfect, thorough, total, unqualified. *Opp* SUPERFICIAL.

profuse *adj* abundant, ample, bountiful, copious, extravagant, exuberant, generous, lavish, luxuriant, plentiful, productive, prolific, superabundant, thriving, unsparing, unstinting. *Opp* MEAN, SPARSE.

programme *n* **1** agenda, bill of fare, calendar, curriculum, *inf* line-up, listing, menu, plan, routine, schedule, scheme, syllabus, timetable. **2** *a TV programme*. broadcast, performance, presentation, production, show, transmission.

progress *n* **1** advance, breakthrough, development, evolution, forward movement, furtherance, gain, growth, headway, improvement, march (*of time*), maturation, progression, *inf* step forward. **2** journey, route, travels, way. **3** *progress in a career*. advancement, betterment, elevation, promotion, rise, *inf* step up. • *vb* advance, *inf* come on, develop, *inf* forge ahead, go forward, go on, make headway, make progress, move forward, press forward, press on, proceed, prosper. ▷ IMPROVE. *Opp* REGRESS, STAGNATE.

progression *n* **1** ▷ PROGRESS. **2** chain, concatenation, course, flow, order, row, sequence, series, string, succession.

progressive *adj* **1** accelerating, advancing, continuing, continuous, developing, escalating, gradual, growing, increasing, ongoing, steady. **2** *progressive ideas*. advanced, avant-garde, contemporary, dynamic, enterprising, forward-looking, *inf* go-ahead, modernistic, radical, reformist, revisionist, revolutionary, up-to-date. *Opp* CONSERVATIVE.

prohibit *vb* ban, bar, block, censor, check, *inf* cut out, debar, disallow, exclude, foil, forbid, hinder, impede, inhibit, interdict, make illegal, outlaw, place an embargo on, preclude, prevent, proscribe, restrict, rule out, shut out, stop, taboo, veto. *Opp* ALLOW.

prohibitive *adj* discouraging, excessive, exorbitant, impossible, *inf* out of reach, out of the question, unreasonable, unthinkable.

project *n* activity, assignment, contract, design, enterprise, idea, job, piece of research, plan, programme, proposal, scheme, task, undertaking, venture. • *vb* **1** concoct, contrive, design, devise, invent, plan, propose, scheme, think up. **2** beetle, bulge, extend, jut out, overhang, protrude, stand out, stick out. **3** *project into space*. cast, *inf* chuck, fling, hurl, launch, lob, propel, shoot, throw. **4** *project light*. cast, flash, shine, throw out. **5** *project future profits*. estimate, forecast, predict.

proliferate *vb* burgeon, flourish, grow, increase, multiply, mushroom, reproduce, thrive.

prolific *adj* **1** abundant, bounteous, bountiful, copious, fruitful, numerous, plenteous, profuse, rich. **2** *a prolific writer*. creative, fertile, productive. *Opp* UNPRODUCTIVE.

prolong *vb* delay, *inf* drag out, draw out, elongate, extend, increase, keep up, lengthen, make longer, *inf* pad out, protract, *inf* spin out, stretch out. *Opp* SHORTEN.

prominent *adj* **1** conspicuous, discernible, distinguishable, evident, eye-catching, large, notable, noticeable, obtrusive, obvious, pronounced, recognizable, salient, significant, striking. *Opp* INCONSPICUOUS. **2** bulging, jutting out, projecting, protruding, protuberant, sticking out. **3** celebrated, distinguished, eminent, familiar, foremost, illustrious, important, leading, major, much-publicized, noted, outstanding, public, renowned. ▷ FAMOUS. *Opp* UNKNOWN.

promiscuous *adj* casual, haphazard, indiscriminate, irresponsible, non-selective, random, undiscriminating. ▷ IMMORAL. *Opp* MORAL.

promise *n* **1** assurance, commitment, compact, contract, covenant, guarantee, oath, pledge, undertaking, vow, word, word of honour. **2** *actor with promise*. capability, expectation(s), latent ability, potential, promising qualities, talent. • *vb* **1** agree, assure, commit yourself, consent, contract, engage, give a promise, give your word, guarantee, pledge, swear, take an oath, undertake, vow. **2** *The clouds promise rain.* augur, *old use* betoken, forebode, foretell, hint at, indicate, presage, prophesy, show signs of, suggest.

promising *adj* auspicious, budding, encouraging, favourable, hopeful, likely, optimistic, propitious, talented, *inf* up-and-coming.

promontory *n* cape, foreland, headland, peninsula, point, projection, ridge, spit, spur.

promote *vb* **1** advance, elevate, exalt, give promotion, move up, prefer, raise, upgrade. **2** *promote a product.* advertise, back, boost, champion, encourage, endorse, further, help, make known, market, patronize, *inf* plug, popularize, publicize, *inf* push, recommend, sell, speak for, sponsor, support. ▷ HELP.

promoter *n* backer, champion, patron, sponsor, supporter.

promotion *n* **1** advancement, elevation, preferment, rise, upgrading. **2** *promotion of a product.* advertising, backing, encouragement, furtherance, marketing, publicity, recommendation, selling, sponsorship.

prompt *adj* eager, efficient, expeditious, immediate, instantaneous, on time, punctual, timely, unhesitating, willing. ▷ QUICK. *Opp* UNPUNCTUAL. • *n* cue, line, reminder. • *vb* advise, coax, egg on, encourage, exhort, help, incite, influence, inspire, jog the memory, motivate, nudge, persuade, prod, provoke, remind, rouse, spur, stimulate, urge.

prone *adj* **1** face down, flat, horizontal, lying, on your front, prostrate, stretched out. *Opp* SUPINE. **2** *prone to colds.* apt, disposed, given, inclined, liable, likely, predisposed, subject, susceptible, tending, vulnerable. *Opp* IMMUNE.

prong *n* point, spike, spur, tine.

pronounce *vb* **1** articulate, aspirate, enunciate, express, put into words, say, sound, speak, utter, vocalize, voice. **2** *pronounce judgement.* announce, assert, asseverate, declare, decree, judge, make known, proclaim, state. ▷ SPEAK.

pronounced *adj* clear, conspicuous, decided, definite, distinct, evident, inescapable, marked, noticeable, obvious, prominent, recognizable, striking, unambiguous, undisguised, unmistakable, well-defined.

pronunciation *n* accent, articulation, delivery, diction, elocution, enunciation, inflection, intonation, modulation, speech.

proof *n* **1** authentication, certification, confirmation, corroboration, demonstration, evidence, facts, grounds, substantiation, testimony, validation, verification. **2** *the proof of the pudding.* criterion, judgement, measure, test, trial.

prop *n* brace, buttress, crutch, post, stay, strut, support, truss, upright. • *vb* **1** bolster, brace, buttress, hold up, reinforce, shore up, support, sustain. **2** lean, rest, stand.

propaganda *n* advertising, brainwashing, disinformation, indoctrination, persuasion, publicity.

propagate *vb* **1** breed, generate, increase, multiply, produce, proliferate, reproduce. **2** *propagate ideas.* circulate, disseminate, pass on, promote, promulgate, publish, spread, transmit. **3** *propagate plants.* grow from seed, layer, sow, take cuttings.

propel *vb* drive, force, impel, launch, move, *inf* pitchfork, push, send, set in motion, shoot, spur, thrust, urge.

propeller *n* rotor, screw, vane.

proper *adj* **1** becoming, conventional, decent, decorous, delicate, dignified, formal, genteel, gentlemanly, grave, in good taste, ladylike, modest, polite, *derog* prim, *derog* prudish, respectable, sedate, seemly, serious, solemn, tactful, tasteful. **2** acceptable, accepted, advisable, apposite, appropriate, apropos, apt, deserved, fair, fitting, just, lawful, legal, normal, orthodox, rational, sensible, suitable, unexceptionable, usual, valid. **3** *the proper time.* accurate, correct, exact, precise, right. **4** *the proper place.* allocated, distinctive, individual, own, particular, reserved, separate, special, unique. *Opp* IMPROPER.

property *n* **1** assets, belongings, capital, chattels, effects, fortune, *inf* gear, goods, holdings, patrimony, possessions, resources, riches, wealth. **2** acreage, buildings, estate, land, premises. **3** attribute, characteristic, feature, hallmark, idiosyncrasy, oddity, peculiarity, quality, quirk, trait.

prophecy *n* augury, crystal-gazing, divination, forecast, foretelling, fortune-telling, oracle, prediction, prognosis, prognostication, vaticination.

prophesy *vb* augur, bode, divine, forecast, foresee, foreshadow, foretell, portend, predict, presage, prognosticate, promise, vaticinate.

prophet *n* clairvoyant, forecaster, fortune-teller, oracle, seer, sibyl, soothsayer.

prophetic *adj* apocalyptic, farseeing, oracular, predictive, prescient, prognostic, prophesying, sibylline.

propitious *adj* advantageous, auspicious, favourable, fortunate, happy, lucky, opportune, promising, providential, rosy, timely, well-timed.

proportion *n* **1** balance, comparison, correlation, correspondence, distribution, equivalence, ratio, statistical relationship. **2** allocation, fraction, part, percentage, piece, quota, ration, section, share. ▷ NUMBER, QUANTITY. **proportions** dimensions, extent, magnitude, measurements, size, volume.

proportional *adj* analogous, balanced, commensurate, comparable, corresponding, equitable, in proportion, just, proportionate, relative, symmetrical. *Opp* DISPROPORTIONATE.

proposal *n* bid, declaration, draft, motion, offer, plan, project, proposition, recommendation, scheme, statement, suggestion, tender.

propose *vb* **1** advance, ask for, *inf* come up with, present, propound, put forward, recommend, submit, suggest. **2** aim, have in mind, intend, mean, offer, plan, purpose. **3** *propose a candidate.* nominate, put forward, put up, sponsor.

propriety *n* appropriateness, aptness, correctness, courtesy, decency, decorum, delicacy, dignity, etiquette, fairness, fitness, formality, gentility, good form, good manners, gravity, justice, modesty, politeness, *derog* prudishness, refinement, respectability, sedateness, seemliness, sensitivity, suitability, tact, tastefulness. *Opp* IMPROPRIETY.

prosaic *adj* **1** clear, direct, down to earth, factual, matter-of-fact, plain, simple, straightforward, to the point, unadorned, understandable, unemotional, unsentimental, unvarnished. **2** [*derog*] characterless, clichéd, commonplace, dry, dull, flat, hackneyed, lifeless, monotonous, mundane, pedestrian, prosy, routine, stereotyped, trite, unfeeling, unimaginative, uninspired, uninspiring, unpoetic, unromantic. ▷ ORDINARY. *Opp* POETIC.

prosecute *vb* **1** accuse, arraign, bring an action against, bring to trial, charge, indict, institute legal proceedings against, prefer charges against, put on trial, sue, take legal proceedings against, take to court. **2** ▷ PURSUE.

prospect *n* **1** aspect, landscape, outlook, panorama, perspective, scene, seascape, sight, spectacle, view, vista. **2** *prospect of fine weather.* anticipation, chance, expectation, hope, likelihood, opportunity, possibility, probability, promise. • *vb* explore, quest, search, survey.

prospective *adj* anticipated, approaching, awaited, coming, expected, forthcoming, future, imminent, impending, intended, likely, looked-for, negotiable, pending, possible, potential, probable.

prospectus *n* announcement, brochure, catalogue, leaflet, manifesto, pamphlet, programme, scheme, syllabus.

prosper *vb* become prosperous, be successful, *inf* boom, burgeon, develop, do well, fare well, flourish, *inf* get ahead, *inf* get on, *inf* go from strength to strength, grow, *inf* make good, *inf* make your fortune, profit, progress, strengthen, succeed, thrive. *Opp* FAIL.

prosperity *n* affluence, *inf* bonanza, *inf* boom, good fortune, growth, opulence, plenty, profitability, riches, success, wealth.

prosperous *adj* affluent, *inf* blooming, *inf* booming, buoyant, expanding, flourishing, fruitful, healthy, moneyed, moneymaking, productive, profitable, prospering, rich, successful, thriving, vigorous, wealthy, *inf* well-heeled, well-off, well-to-do. *Opp* UNSUCCESSFUL.

prostitute *n old use* bawd, call girl, *old use* camp follower, *old use* courtesan, *old use* harlot, *inf* hooker, streetwalker, *old use* strumpet, *inf* tart, toy boy, trollop, whore. • *vb* cheapen, debase, degrade, demean, devalue, lower, misuse.

prostrate *adj* ▷ OVERCOME, PRONE. • *vb prostrate yourself* abase yourself, bow, kneel, kowtow, lie flat, submit. ▷ GROVEL.

protagonist *n* chief actor, contender, contestant, hero, heroine, lead, leading figure, principal, title role.

protect *vb* care for, cherish, conserve, defend, escort, guard, harbour, insulate, keep, keep safe, look after, mind, preserve, provide cover for, safeguard, screen, secure, shield, stand up for, support, take care of, tend, watch over. *Opp* ENDANGER, NEGLECT.

protection *n* **1** care, conservation, custody, defence, guardianship, patronage, preservation, safekeeping, safety, security, tutelage. **2** barrier, buffer, bulwark, cloak, cover, guard, insulation, screen, shelter, shield.

protective *adj* **1** fireproof, insulating, preservative, protecting, sheltering, shielding, waterproof. **2** *protective parents.* careful, defensive, heedful, jealous, paternalistic, possessive, solicitous, vigilant, watchful.

protector *n* benefactor, bodyguard, champion, defender, guard, guardian, *sl* minder, patron.

protest *n* **1** complaint, cry of disapproval, demur, demurral, dissent, exception, grievance, *inf* gripe, *inf* grouse, grumble, objection, opposition, outcry, protestation, remonstrance. **2** *inf* demo, demonstration, march, rally. • *vb* **1** appeal, argue, challenge a decision, complain, cry out, expostulate, express disapproval, fulminate, *inf* gripe, *inf* grouse, grumble, make a protest, *inf* moan, object, remonstrate, take exception. **2** demonstrate, *inf* hold a demo, march. **3** *protest your innocence.* affirm, assert, asseverate, aver, declare, insist on, profess, swear.

protracted *adj* endless, extended, interminable, long-drawn-out, long-winded, never-ending, prolonged, spun-out. ▷ LONG. *Opp* SHORT.

protrude *vb* balloon, bulge, extend, jut out, overhang, poke out, project, stand out, stick out, stick up, swell.

protruding *adj* bulbous, bulging, distended, gibbous, humped, jutting, overhanging, projecting, prominent, protuberant, swollen, tumescent.

proud *adj* **1** appreciative, delighted, glad, gratified, happy, honoured, pleased, satisfied. **2** *a proud bearing.* brave, dignified, independent, self-respecting. **3** *a proud history.* august, distinguished, glorious, great, honourable, illustrious, noble, reputable, respected, splendid, worthy. **4** [*derog*] arrogant, *inf* big-headed, boastful, bumptious, *inf* cocksure, *inf* cocky, conceited, disdainful, egocentric, egotistical, grand, haughty, *inf* high and mighty, immodest, lordly, narcissistic, self-centred, self-important, self-satisfied, smug, snobbish, *inf* snooty, *inf* stuck-up, supercilious, *inf* swollen-headed, *inf* toffee-nosed, vain, vainglorious. *Opp* MODEST.

provable *adj* demonstrable, verifiable. *Opp* UNPROVABLE.

prove *vb* ascertain, assay, attest, authenticate, *inf* bear out, certify, check, confirm, corroborate, demonstrate, establish, explain, justify, show to be true, substantiate, test, verify. *Opp* DISPROVE.

proven *adj* accepted, proved, reliable, tried and tested, trustworthy, undoubted, unquestionable, valid, verified. *Opp* DOUBTFUL, THEORETICAL.

proverb *n* adage, maxim, *old use* saw. ▷ SAYING.

proverbial *adj* aphoristic, axiomatic, clichéd, conventional, customary, famous, legendary, time-honoured, traditional, well-known.

provide *vb* afford, allot, allow, arrange for, cater, contribute, donate, endow, equip, *inf* fix up with, *inf* fork out, furnish, give, grant, lay on, lend, make provision, offer, present, produce, purvey, spare, stock, supply, yield.

providence *n* destiny, divine intervention, fate, fortune, karma, kismet.

provident *adj* careful, economical, far-sighted, forward-looking, frugal, judicious, prudent, thrifty.

providential *adj* felicitous, fortunate, happy, lucky, opportune, timely.

provincial *adj* **1** local, regional. *Opp* NATIONAL. **2** [*derog*] backward, boorish, bucolic, insular, narrow-minded, parochial, rural, rustic, small-minded, uncultivated, uncultured, unsophisticated. *Opp* COSMOPOLITAN.

provisional *adj* conditional, interim, stopgap, temporary, tentative, transitional. *Opp* DEFINITIVE, PERMANENT.

provisions *plur n* food, foodstuff, groceries, provender, rations, requirements, stocks, stores, subsistence, supplies, *old use* victuals.

proviso *n* condition, exception, limitation, provision, qualification, requirement, restriction, rider, stipulation.

provocation *n inf* aggravation, cause, challenge, grievance, grounds, incentive, incitement, inducement, justification, motivation, motive, reason, stimulus, taunts, teasing.

provocative *adj* **1** alluring, arousing, erotic, pornographic, *inf* raunchy, seductive, sensual, sensuous, *inf* sexy, tantalizing, tempting. **2** *inf* aggravating, annoying, infuriating, irksome, irritating, maddening, provoking, teasing, vexing.

provoke *vb* **1** activate, arouse, awaken, bring about, call forth, cause, elicit, encourage, excite, foment, generate, give rise to, induce, initiate, inspire, instigate, kindle, motivate, promote, prompt, spark off, start, stimulate, stir up, urge on, work up. **2** *inf* aggravate, anger, annoy, enrage, exasperate, gall, *inf* get on your nerves, goad, incense, incite, inflame, infuriate, insult, irk, irritate, madden, offend, outrage, pique, rile, rouse, tease, torment, upset, vex, *inf* wind up, worry. *Opp* PACIFY.

prowess *n* **1** ability, adeptness, adroitness, aptitude, cleverness, competence, dexterity, excellence, expertise, genius, mastery, proficiency, skill, talent. **2** *prowess in battle.* boldness, bravery, courage, daring, doughtiness, gallantry, heroism, mettle, spirit, valour.

prowl *vb* creep, lurk, roam, rove, skulk, slink, sneak, steal. ▷ WALK.

proximity *n* **1** closeness, nearness, propinquity. **2** locality, neighbourhood, vicinity.

prudent *adj* advisable, careful, cautious, circumspect, discreet, economical, far-sighted, frugal, judicious, politic, proper, provident, reasonable, sagacious, sage, sensible, shrewd, thoughtful, thrifty, vigilant, watchful, wise. *Opp* UNWISE.

prudish *adj* decorous, easily shocked, illiberal, intolerant, narrow-minded, old-fashioned, *inf* old-maidish, priggish, prim, *inf* prissy, proper, puritanical, rigid, shockable, strait-laced, strict. *Opp* BROAD-MINDED.

prune *vb* clip, cut back, lop, pare down, trim. ▷ CUT.

pry *vb* be curious, be inquisitive, be nosy, delve, *inf* ferret, inquire, interfere, intrude, investigate, meddle, *inf* nose about, peer, poke about, *inf* poke your nose in, search, *inf* snoop, *inf* stick your nose in. **prying** ▷ INQUISITIVE.

pseudonym *n* alias, assumed name, false name, incognito, nickname, *Fr* nom de plume, pen-name, sobriquet, stage name.

psychic *adj* clairvoyant, extrasensory, magical, mental, metaphysical, mystic, occult, preternatural, psychical, spiritual, supernatural, telepathic. • *n* astrologer, clairvoyant, crystal-gazer, fortune-teller, medium, mind-reader, spiritualist, telepathist.

psychological *adj* cerebral, emotional, mental, subconscious, subjective, subliminal, unconscious. *Opp* PHYSIOLOGICAL.

pub *n old use* alehouse, bar, *sl* boozer, cocktail lounge, *old use* hostelry, inn, *inf* local, public house, saloon, tavern, wine bar.

puberty *n* adolescence, growing-up, juvenescence, pubescence, sexual maturity, *inf* teens.

public *adj* **1** accessible, available, common, familiar, free, known, open, shared, unconcealed, unrestricted, visible, well-known. **2** *public support.* civic, civil, collective, communal, community, democratic, general, majority, national, popular, social, universal. **3** *a public figure.* ▷ PROMINENT. *Opp* PRIVATE. • *n the public.* citizens, the community, the country, the nation, people, the populace, society, voters.

publication *n* **1** appearance, issuing, printing, production. ▷ BOOK, MAGAZINE. **2** advertising, announcement, broadcasting, declaration, disclosure, dissemination, proclamation, promulgation, publicizing, reporting.

publicity *n* **1** attention, *inf* ballyhoo, fame, *inf* hype, limelight, notoriety. **2** advertising, marketing, promotion. ▷ ADVERTISEMENT.

publicize *vb* advertise, *sl* hype, *inf* plug, promote, *old use* puff. ▷ PUBLISH.

publish *vb* **1** bring out, circulate, issue, make available, print, produce, put on sale, release. **2** *publish secrets.* advertise, announce, break the news about, broadcast, communicate, declare, disclose, disseminate, divulge, issue a statement about, *inf* leak, make known, make public, proclaim, promulgate, publicize, *inf* put about, report, reveal, spread.

pucker *vb* compress, contract, crease, crinkle, draw together, purse, screw up, squeeze, tighten, wrinkle.

puerile *adj* babyish, boyish, childish, immature, infantile, juvenile. ▷ SILLY.

puff *n* **1** blast, blow, breath, draught, flurry, gust, whiff, wind. **2** *a puff of smoke.* cloud, wisp. • *vb* **1** blow, breathe heavily, gasp, huff, pant, wheeze. **2** *puff at a cigar. inf* drag, draw, inhale, pull, smoke, suck. **3** *sails puffed by the wind.* balloon, billow, distend, enlarge, inflate, rise, swell.

pugnacious *adj* aggressive, antagonistic, argumentative, bellicose, belligerent, combative, contentious, disputatious, excitable, fractious, hostile, hottempered, litigious, militant, unfriendly, warlike. ▷ QUARRELSOME. *Opp* PEACEABLE.

pull *vb* **1** drag, draw, haul, lug, tow, trail. *Opp* PUSH. **2** jerk, pluck, rip, tug, wrench, *inf* yank. **3** *pull a tooth.* extract, pull out, remove, take out. **pull off** ▷ DETACH. **pull out** ▷ WITHDRAW. **pull round** ▷ RECOVER. **pull someone's leg** ▷ TEASE. **pull through** ▷ RECOVER. **pull together** ▷ COOPERATE. **pull up** ▷ HALT.

pulp *n* mash, mush, paste, pap, purée. • *vb* crush, liquidize, mash, pound, pulverize, purée, smash, squash.

pulsate *vb* beat, drum, oscillate, palpitate, pound, pulse, quiver, reverberate, throb, tick, vibrate.

pulse *n* beat, drumming, oscillation, pounding, pulsation, rhythm, throb, ticking, vibration.

pump *vb* drain, draw off, empty, force, raise, siphon. **pump up** blow up, fill, inflate.

punch *vb* **1** beat, *sl* biff, box, *inf* clout, cuff, jab, poke, prod, pummel, slog, *sl* slug, *sl* sock, strike, thump. ▷ HIT. **2** ▷ PIERCE.

punctual *adj* in good time, *inf* on the dot, on time, prompt. *Opp* UNPUNCTUAL.

punctuate *vb* **1** insert punctuation, point. **2** *punctuated by applause.* break, interrupt, intersperse, *inf* pepper.

punctuation *n* marks, points, stops. □ *accent, apostrophe, asterisk, bracket, caret, cedilla, colon, comma, dash, exclamation mark, full stop, hyphen, question mark, quotation marks, speech marks, semicolon.*

puncture *n* blow-out, burst, burst tyre, *inf* flat, flat tyre, hole, leak, opening, perforation, pin-prick, rupture. ● *vb* deflate, go through, let down, penetrate, perforate, pierce, prick, rupture.

pungent *adj* **1** aromatic, hot, peppery, piquant, seasoned, sharp, spicy, strong, tangy. **2** acid, acrid, astringent, caustic, *inf* chemically, harsh, sour, stinging. **3** *pungent criticism.* biting, bitter, incisive, mordant, sarcastic, scathing, trenchant.

punish *vb* castigate, chasten, chastise, correct, discipline, exact retribution from, impose punishment on, inflict punishment on, *inf* make an example of, pay back, penalize, *inf* rap over the knuckles, scold, *inf* teach someone a lesson.

punishment *n* chastisement, correction, discipline, forfeit, imposition, *inf* just deserts, penalty, punitive measure, retribution, revenge, sentence. □ *banishment, beating, the birch,* old use *Borstal, the cane, capital punishment, cashiering, confiscation of property, corporal punishment, detention, excommunication, execution, exile, fine, flogging, gaol,* inf *hiding, imprisonment, jail, keelhauling, lashing, pillory, prison, probation, scourging, spanking, the stocks, torture, whipping.*

punitive *adj* disciplinary, penal, retaliatory, retributive, revengeful, vindictive.

puny *adj* diminutive, dwarf, feeble, frail, sickly, stunted, underdeveloped, undernourished, undersized. ▷ SMALL. *Opp* LARGE, STRONG.

pupil *n* apprentice, beginner, disciple, follower, learner, novice, protégé(e), scholar, schoolboy, schoolchild, schoolgirl, student, tiro.

puppet *n* doll, dummy, finger-puppet, glove-puppet, hand-puppet, marionette, string-puppet.

purchase *n* **1** acquisition, *inf* buy (*a good buy*), investment. **2** grasp, grip, hold, leverage, support. ● *vb* acquire, buy, get, invest in, obtain, pay for, procure, secure.

pure *adj* **1** authentic, genuine, neat, real, solid, sterling, straight, unadulterated, unalloyed, undiluted. **2** *pure food.* eatable, germ-free, hygienic, natural, pasteurized, uncontaminated, untainted, wholesome. **3** *pure water.* clean, clear, distilled, drinkable, fresh, potable, sterile, unpolluted. **4** *pure in morals.* blameless, chaste, decent, good, impeccable, innocent, irreproachable, maidenly, modest, moral, proper, sinless, stainless, virginal, virtuous. **5** *pure genius.* absolute, complete, downright, *inf* out-and-out, perfect, sheer, thorough, total, true, unmitigated, unqualified, utter. **6** *pure science.* abstract, academic, conjectural, conceptual, hypothetical, speculative, theoretical. *Opp* IMPURE, PRACTICAL.

purgative *n* aperient, cathartic, enema, laxative, purge.

purge *vb* **1** clean out, cleanse, clear, depurate, empty, purify, wash out. **2** *purge your opponents.* eject, eliminate, eradicate, expel, get rid of, liquidate, oust, remove, root out.

purify *vb* clarify, clean, cleanse, decontaminate, depurate, disinfect, distil, filter, fumigate, make pure, purge, refine, sanitize, sterilize.

puritan *n* fanatic, *derog* killjoy, moralist, *derog* prude, zealot.

puritanical *adj* ascetic, austere, moralistic, narrow-minded, pietistic, prim, proper, prudish, rigid, self-denying, self-disciplined, severe, stern, stiff-necked, strait-laced, strict, temperate, unbending, uncompromising. *Opp* HEDONISTIC.

purpose *n* **1** aim, ambition, aspiration, design, end, goal, hope, intent, intention, motivation, motive, object, objective, outcome, plan, point, rationale, result, target, wish. **2** determination, devotion, drive, firmness, persistence, resolution, resolve, steadfastness, tenacity, will, zeal. **3** *purpose of a tool.* advantage, application, benefit, good (*what's the good of it?*), point, practicality, use, usefulness, utility, value. • *vb* ▷ INTEND.

purposeful *adj* calculated, decided, decisive, deliberate, determined, devoted, firm, persistent, positive, resolute, steadfast, *derog* stubborn, tenacious, unwavering, wilful, zealous. ▷ INTENTIONAL. *Opp* HESITANT.

purposeless *adj* aimless, bootless, empty, gratuitous, meaningless, pointless, senseless, unnecessary, useless, vacuous, wanton. *Opp* MEANINGFUL, USEFUL.

purposely *adv* consciously, deliberately, intentionally, knowingly, on purpose, wilfully.

purse *n* bag, handbag, moneybag, pocketbook, pouch, wallet.

pursue *vb* **1** chase, follow, go after, go in pursuit of, harry, hound, hunt, keep up with, run after, shadow, stalk, *inf* tail, trace, track down, trail. **2** aim for, aspire to, be committed to, carry on, conduct, continue, dedicate yourself to, engage in, follow up, *inf* go for, persevere in, persist in, proceed with, prosecute, *inf* stick with, strive for, try for. **3** *pursue truth.* inquire into, investigate, quest after, search for, seek.

pursuit *n* **1** chase, chasing, following, harrying, *inf* hue and cry, hunt, hunting, pursuing, shadowing, stalking, tracking down, trail. **2** *leisure pursuits.* activity, employment, enthusiasm, hobby, interest, obsession, occupation, pastime, pleasure, speciality, specialization.

push *vb* **1** advance, drive, force, hustle, impel, jostle, move, nudge, poke, press, prod, propel, set in motion, shove, thrust. **2** *push a button.* depress, press. **3** *push into a space.* compress, cram, crowd, crush, insert, jam, pack, put, ram, squash, squeeze. **4** *push someone to act.* browbeat, bully, coerce, compel, constrain, dragoon, encourage, force, hurry, importune, incite, induce, influence, *inf* lean on, motivate, nag, persuade, pressurize, prompt, put pressure on, spur, stimulate, urge. **5** *push a new product.* advertise, boost, make known, market, *inf* plug, promote, publicize. *Opp* PULL. **push around** ▷ BULLY. **push off** ▷ DEPART. **push on** ▷ ADVANCE.

put *vb* **1** arrange, assign, commit, consign, deploy, deposit, dispose, fix, hang, lay, leave, locate, park, place, *inf* plonk, position, rest, set down, settle, situate, stand, station. **2** *put a question.* express, formulate, frame, phrase, say, state, utter, voice, word, write. **3** *put a proposal.* advance, bring forward, offer, outline, present, propose, submit, suggest, tender. **4** *put blame on someone.* attach, attribute, cast, fix, impose, inflict, lay, *inf* pin. **put across** ▷ COMMUNICATE. **put back** ▷ RETURN. **put by** ▷ SAVE. **put down** ▷ KILL, SUPPRESS. **put in** ▷ INSERT, INSTALL. **put off** ▷ POSTPONE. **put out** ▷ EJECT, EXTINGUISH. **put over** ▷ COMMUNICATE. **put right** ▷ REPAIR. **put someone up** ▷ ACCOMMODATE. **put up** ▷ RAISE. **put your foot down** ▷ INSIST. **put your foot in it** ▷ BLUNDER.

putative *adj* alleged, assumed, conjectural, presumed, reputed, rumoured, supposed, suppositious.

putrefy *vb* decay, decompose, go bad, go off, moulder, rot, spoil.

putrid *adj* bad, corrupt, decaying, decomposing, fetid, foul, mouldy, putrefying, rotten, rotting, spoilt.

puzzle *n inf* brain-teaser, conundrum, difficulty, dilemma, enigma, mystery, paradox, *inf* poser, problem, quandary, question, riddle. • *vb* baffle, bewilder, confound, confuse, *inf* floor, *inf* flummox, mystify, nonplus, perplex, set thinking, *inf* stump, *inf* stymie, worry. **puzzle out** ▷ SOLVE. **puzzle over** ▷ CONSIDER.

puzzling *adj* ambiguous, baffling, bewildering, confusing, cryptic, enigmatic, impenetrable, inexplicable, insoluble, *inf* mind-boggling, mysterious, mystifying, perplexing, strange, unaccountable, unanswerable, unfathomable, worrying. *Opp* STRAIGHTFORWARD.

pygmy *adj* dwarf, lilliputian, midget, tiny. ▷ SMALL.

Q

quadrangle *n* cloisters, courtyard, enclosure, *inf* quad, yard.

quagmire *n* bog, fen, marsh, mire, morass, mud, quicksand, *old use* slough, swamp.

quail *vb* back away, be apprehensive, blench, cower, cringe, falter, flinch, quake, recoil, show fear, shrink, tremble, wince.

quaint *adj* antiquated, antique, charming, curious, eccentric, fanciful, fantastic, odd, offbeat, old-fashioned, old-world, outlandish, peculiar, picturesque, strange, *inf* twee, unconventional, unexpected, unfamiliar, unusual, whimsical.

quake *vb* convulse, heave, move, quaver, quiver, rock, shake, shiver, shudder, stagger, sway, tremble, vibrate, wobble.

qualification *n* **1** ability, aptitude, capability, capacity, certification, competence, eligibility, experience, fitness, *inf* know-how, knowledge, proficiency, quality, skill, suitability, training. **2** certificate, degree, diploma, doctorate, first degree, Master's degree, matriculation. **3** *agree without qualification.* caveat, condition, exception, limitation, modification, proviso, reservation, restriction.

qualified *adj* **1** able, capable, certificated, competent, equipped, experienced, expert, fit, practised, professional, proficient, skilled, trained, well-informed. *Opp* UNSKILLED. **2** *qualified applicants.* appropriate, eligible, suitable. **3** *qualified praise.* cautious, conditional, equivocal, guarded, half-hearted, limited, modified, provisional, reserved, restricted. *Opp* UNCONDITIONAL.

qualify *vb* **1** authorize, empower, entitle, equip, fit, make eligible, permit, sanction. **2** become eligible, get through, *inf* make the grade, meet requirements, pass. **3** *qualify your praise.* abate, lessen, limit, mitigate, moderate, modulate, restrain, restrict, soften, temper, weaken.

quality *n* **1** calibre, class, condition, excellence, grade, rank, sort, standard, status, value, worth. **2** *personal qualities.* attribute, characteristic, distinction, feature, mark, peculiarity, property, trait.

quandary *n inf* catch-22, *inf* cleft stick, confusion, difficulty, dilemma, perplexity, plight, predicament, uncertainty.

quantity *n* aggregate, amount, bulk, consignment, dosage, dose, expanse, extent, length, load, lot, magnitude, mass, measurement, number, part, portion, proportion, quantum, sum, total, volume, weight. ▷ MEASURE.

quarrel *n* altercation, argument, bickering, clash, conflict, confrontation, contention, controversy, debate, difference, disagreement, discord, disharmony, dispute, dissension, division, feud, *inf* hassle, misunderstanding, row, *inf* ructions, rupture, *inf* scene, schism, *inf* slanging match, split, squabble, strife, *inf* tiff, vendetta, wrangle. • *vb* argue, *inf* be at loggerheads, *inf* be at odds, bicker, clash, conflict, contend, *inf* cross swords, differ, disagree, dispute, dissent, *inf* fall out, feud, haggle, misunderstand one another, *inf* row, squabble, wrangle. ▷ FIGHT. **quarrel with** ▷ DISPUTE.

quarrelsome *adj* aggressive, angry, argumentative, bad-tempered, cantankerous, choleric, contentious, contrary, cross, defiant, disagreeable, dyspeptic, explosive, fractious, impatient, irascible, irritable, peevish, petulant, querulous, quick-tempered, *inf* stroppy, testy, truculent, unfriendly, volatile ▷ PUGNACIOUS. *Opp* PEACEABLE.

quarry *n* **1** game, kill, object, prey, victim. **2** excavation, mine, pit, working. • *vb* dig out, excavate, extract, mine.

quarter *n* area, district, division, locality, neighbourhood, part, region, section, sector, territory, vicinity, zone. • *vb* accommodate, billet, board, house, lodge, *inf* put up, shelter, station. **quarters** abode, accommodation, barracks, billet, domicile, dwelling-place, home, housing, living quarters, lodgings, residence, rooms, shelter.

quash *vb* **1** abolish, annul, cancel, invalidate, overrule, overthrow, reject, rescind, reverse, revoke. **2** ▷ QUELL.

quaver *vb* falter, fluctuate, oscillate, pulsate, quake, quiver, shake, shiver, shudder, tremble, vibrate, waver.

quay *n* berth, dock, harbour, jetty, landing-stage, pier, wharf.

queasy *adj* bilious, *inf* green, *inf* groggy, nauseated, nauseous, *inf* poorly, *inf* queer, sick, unwell. ▷ ILL.

queer *adj* **1** aberrant, abnormal, anomalous, atypical, bizarre, curious, different, eerie, exceptional, extraordinary, *inf* fishy, freakish, *inf* funny, incongruous, inexplicable, irrational, mysterious, odd, offbeat, outlandish, peculiar, puzzling, quaint, remarkable, *inf* rum, singular, strange, unaccountable, uncanny, uncommon, unconventional, unexpected, unnatural, unorthodox, unusual, weird. **2** *inf* cranky, deviant, eccentric, questionable, *inf* shady (*customer*), *inf* shifty, suspect, suspicious. ▷ MAD. *Opp* NORMAL. **3** ▷ ILL. **4** ▷ HOMOSEXUAL.

quell *vb* **1** crush, overcome, put down, quash, repress, subdue, suppress. **2** *quell fears.* allay, alleviate, calm, mitigate, moderate, mollify, pacify, soothe, tranquillize.

quench *vb* **1** allay, appease, cool, sate, satisfy, slake. **2** *quench a fire.* damp down, douse, extinguish, put out, smother, snuff out, stifle, suppress.

quest *n* crusade, expedition, exploration, hunt, mission, pilgrimage, pursuit, search, voyage of discovery. • *vb* **quest after** ▷ SEEK.

question *n* **1** *inf* brain-teaser, conundrum, demand, enquiry, inquiry, *inf* poser, query, request, riddle. **2** *an unresolved question.* argument, controversy, debate, difficulty, dispute, doubt, misgiving, mystery, objection, problem, puzzle, uncertainty. • *vb* **1** ask, catechize, cross-examine, crossquestion, debrief, enquire of, examine, *inf* grill, inquire of, interrogate, interview, probe, *inf* pump, quiz. **2** *question a decision.* argue over, be sceptical about, call into question, cast doubt upon, challenge, dispute, doubt, enquire about, impugn, inquire about, object to, oppose, quarrel with, query.

questionable *adj* arguable, borderline, debatable, disputable, doubtful, dubious, *inf* iffy, moot, problematical, *inf* shady (*customer*), suspect, suspicious, uncertain, unclear, unprovable, unreliable.

questionnaire *n* catechism, opinion poll, question sheet, quiz, survey, test.

queue *n* chain, column, concatenation, *inf* crocodile, file, line, line-up, procession, row, string, succession, tail-back, train. • *vb* fall in, form a queue, line up, wait in a queue.

quibble *n* ▷ OBJECTION. • *vb inf* bandy words, be evasive, carp, cavil, equivocate, *inf* nit-pick, object, pettifog, *inf* split hairs, wrangle.

quick *adj* **1** breakneck, brisk, expeditious, express, fast, *old use* fleet, headlong, high-speed, *inf* nippy, precipitate, rapid, *inf* smart (*pace*), *inf* spanking, speedy, swift. **2** *a quick reaction.* adroit, agile, animated, brisk, deft, dexterous, energetic, lively, nimble, spirited, spry, vigorous. **3** *a quick response.* abrupt, early, hasty, hurried, immediate, instant, instantaneous, perfunctory, precipitate, prompt, punctual, ready, sudden, summary, unhesitating. **4** *a quick mind.* acute, alert, apt, astute, bright, clever, intelligent, perceptive, quick-witted, sharp, shrewd, smart. *Opp* SLOW. **5** *a quick rest.* brief, fleeting, momentary, passing, perfunctory, short, short-lived, temporary, transitory. **6** [*old use*] *the quick and the dead.* ▷ ALIVE. *Opp* SLOW.

quicken *vb* **1** accelerate, expedite, go faster, hasten, hurry, speed up. **2** ▷ AROUSE.

quiet *adj* **1** inaudible, noiseless, silent, soundless. **2** *quiet music.* hushed, low, pianissimo, soft, *It* sotto voce. **3** *a quiet person.* composed, contemplative, contented, gentle, introverted, meditative, meek, mild, modest, peaceable, reserved, retiring, shy, taciturn, thoughtful, uncommunicative, unforthcoming, unsociable, withdrawn. **4** *a quiet life.* cloistered, sheltered, tranquil, unadventurous, unexciting, untroubled. **5** *a quiet place.* isolated, lonely, peaceful, private, secluded, sequestered, undisturbed, unfrequented. **6** *quiet weather.* calm, motionless, placid, restful, serene, still. *Opp* BUSY, NOISY, RESTLESS.

quieten *vb* **1** calm, compose, hush, lull, pacify, sedate, soothe, subdue, tranquillize. **2** deaden, dull, muffle, mute, reduce the volume of, silence, soften, stifle, suppress, tone down.

quirk *n* aberration, caprice, crotchet, eccentricity, idiosyncrasy, kink, oddity, peculiarity, trick, whim.

quit *vb* **1** abandon, decamp from, depart from, desert, exit from, forsake, go away from, leave, walk out (on), withdraw. **2** abdicate, discontinue, drop, give up, leave, *inf* pack it in, relinquish, renounce, repudiate, resign from, retire from, withdraw from. **3** [*inf*] *Quit pushing!* cease, desist from, discontinue, leave off, stop.

quite *adv* [NB: the two senses are almost opposite.] **1** *Yes, I've quite finished.* absolutely, altogether, completely, entirely, perfectly, thoroughly, totally, unreservedly, utterly, wholly. **2** *quite good, but not perfect.* comparatively, fairly, moderately, *inf* pretty, rather, relatively, somewhat, to some extent.

quits *adj* equal, even, level, repaid, revenged, square.

quiver *vb* flicker, fluctuate, flutter, oscillate, palpitate, pulsate, quake, quaver, shake, shiver, shudder, tremble, vibrate, wobble.

quixotic *adj* fanciful, foolhardy, idealistic, impracticable, impractical, romantic, *inf* starry-eyed, unrealistic, unrealizable, unselfish, Utopian, visionary. *Opp* REALISTIC.

quiz *n* competition, exam, examination, questioning, questionnaire, quiz-game, test. • *vb* ▷ QUESTION.

quizzical *adj* amused, comical, curious, intrigued, perplexed, puzzled, queer, questioning.

quota *n* allocation, allowance, apportionment, assignment, *inf* cut, part, portion, proportion, ration, share.

quotation *n* **1** allusion, citation, *inf* clip, cutting, excerpt, extract, passage, piece, reference, selection. **2** estimate, price, tender, valuation.

quote *vb* **1** cite, instance, mention, produce a quotation from, refer to, repeat, reproduce. **2** *quote a price.* estimate, tender.

R

rabble *n* crowd, gang, herd, *Gk* hoi polloi, horde, mob, *inf* riffraff, swarm, throng. ▷ GROUP.

race *n* **1** breed, clan, ethnic group, family, folk, genus, kind, lineage, nation, people, species, stock, tribe, variety. **2** chase, competition, contention, contest, heat, rivalry. □ *cross-country, greyhound race, horse-race, hurdles, marathon, motor-race, regatta, relay, road-race, rowing, scramble, speedway, sprint, steeple-chase, stock-car race, swimming, track event.* ● *vb* **1** *I'll race you!* compete with, contest with, have a race with, try to beat. **2** *race along.* career, dash, *inf* fly, gallop, hasten, hurry, move fast, run, rush, speed, sprint, *inf* tear, *inf* zip, *inf* zoom.

racetrack *n* cinder-track, circuit, dog-track, lap, racecourse.

racial *adj* ethnic, folk, genetic, national, tribal.

racism *n* bias, bigotry, chauvinism, discrimination, intolerance, prejudice, racialism, xenophobia. □ *anti-Semitism, apartheid.*

racist *adj* biased, bigoted, chauvinist, discriminatory, intolerant, prejudiced, racialist, xenophobic. □ *anti-Semitic.*

rack *n* frame, framework, holder, scaffold, scaffolding, shelf, stand, support. ● *vb* ▷ TORTURE.

radiant *adj* **1** beaming, bright, brilliant, effulgent, gleaming, glorious, glowing, incandescent, luminous, phosphorescent, refulgent, shining. **2** *The bride was radiant.* ▷ HAPPY.

radiate *vb* beam, diffuse, emanate, emit, give off, gleam, glow, send out, shed, shine, spread, transmit.

radical *adj* **1** basic, cardinal, deep-seated, elementary, essential, fundamental, primary, principal, profound. **2** complete, comprehensive, drastic, entire, exhaustive, thorough, thoroughgoing. **3** *radical politics.* extreme, extremist, fanatical, far-reaching, revolutionary, *derog* subversive. *Opp* MODERATE, SUPERFICIAL.

radio *n* CB, *sl* ghettoblaster, portable, receiver, set, *inf* transistor, transmitter, walkie-talkie, *old use* wireless. ● *vb* broadcast, send out, transmit.

rafter *n* beam, girder, joist.

rage *n* ▷ ANGER. ● *vb* be angry, boil, fume, go berserk, lose control, rave, *inf* see red, seethe, storm.

ragged *adj* **1** chafed, frayed, in ribbons, old, patched, patchy, ravelled, rent, ripped, rough, rough-edged, shabby, shaggy, tattered, tatty, threadbare, torn, unkempt, unravelled, untidy, worn out. **2** *ragged line.* denticulated, disorganized, erratic, irregular, jagged, serrated, uneven, zigzag.

rags *plur n* bits and pieces, cloths, fragments, old clothes, remnants, ribbons, scraps, shreds, tatters.

raid *n* assault, attack, blitz, foray, incursion, inroad, invasion, onslaught, sally, sortie, strike, surprise attack, swoop. ● *vb* **1** assault, attack, descend on, invade, pounce on, rush, storm, swoop down on. **2** loot, maraud, pillage, plunder, ransack, rifle, rob, sack, steal from, strip.

raider *n* attacker, brigand, invader, looter, marauder, outlaw, pillager, pirate, plunderer, ransacker, robber, rustler, thief.

railway *n* line, permanent way, *Amer* railroad, rails, track. □ *branch line,* *cable railway, funicular, light railway, main line, metro, mineral line, monorail, mountain railway, narrow gauge, rack-and-pinion, rapid transit system, siding, standard gauge, tramway, tube, underground.* ▷ TRAIN.

rain *n* cloudburst, deluge, downpour, drizzle, precipitation, raindrops, rainfall, rainstorm, shower, squall. • *vb inf* bucket down, drizzle, pelt, pour, *inf* rain cats and dogs, spit, teem.

rainy *adj* damp, drizzly, showery, wet.

raise *vb* **1** elevate, heave up, hoist, hold up, jack up, lift, loft, pick up, put up, rear. **2** *raise prices.* augment, boost, increase, inflate, put up, *inf* up. **3** *raise to a higher rank.* exalt, prefer, promote, upgrade. **4** *raise a monument.* build, construct, create, erect, set up. **5** *raise hopes.* activate, arouse, awaken, build up, buoy up, encourage, engender, enlarge, excite, foment, foster, heighten, incite, kindle, motivate, provoke, rouse, stimulate, uplift. **6** *raise animals, children, crops.* breed, bring up, care for, cultivate, educate, farm, grow, look after, nurture, produce, propagate, rear. **7** *raise money.* amass, collect, get, make, receive, solicit. **8** *raise questions.* advance, bring up, broach, express, instigate, introduce, mention, moot, originate, pose, present, put forward, suggest. *Opp* LOWER, REDUCE. **raise from the dead** ▷ RESURRECT. **raise the alarm** ▷ WARN.

rally *n* **1** assembly, *inf* demo, demonstration, gathering, march, mass meeting, protest. **2** ▷ COMPETITION. • *vb* **1** assemble, convene, get together, marshal, muster, organize, round up, summon. **2** come together, reassemble, reform, regroup. **3** *rally after illness.* ▷ RECOVER.

ram *vb* **1** bump, butt, collide with, crash into, slam into, smash into, strike. ▷ HIT. **2** compress, cram, crowd, crush, drive, force, jam, pack, press, push, squash, squeeze, tamp down, wedge.

ramble *n* hike, tramp, trek, walk. • *vb* **1** hike, range, roam, rove, tramp, trek, stroll, wander. ▷ WALK. **2** digress, drift, *inf* lose the thread, maunder, *inf* rabbit on, *inf* rattle on, talk aimlessly, wander, *inf* witter on.

rambling *adj* **1** circuitous, indirect, labyrinthine, meandering, roundabout, tortuous, twisting, wandering, winding, zigzag. *Opp* DIRECT. **2** aimless, circumlocutory, confused, diffuse, digressive, disconnected, discursive, disjointed, illogical, incoherent, jumbled, muddled, periphrastic, unstructured, verbose, wordy. *Opp* COHERENT. **3** *a rambling house.* asymmetrical, extensive, irregular, large, sprawling, straggling, straggly. *Opp* COMPACT.

ramification *n* branch, byproduct, complication, consequence, division, effect, extension, implication, offshoot, result, subdivision, upshot.

ramp *n* acclivity, gradient, incline, rise, slope.

rampage *n* frenzy, riot, tumult, uproar, vandalism, violence. • *vb* behave violently, go berserk, go wild, lose control, race about, run amok, run riot, rush about, storm about. **on the rampage** ▷ WILD.

ramshackle *adj* broken-down, crumbling, decrepit, derelict, dilapidated, flimsy, jerry-built, rickety, ruined, run-down, shaky, tottering, tumbledown, unsafe, unstable, unsteady. *Opp* SOLID.

random *adj* accidental, adventitious, aimless, arbitrary, casual, chance, fortuitous, haphazard, *inf* hit-or-miss, indiscriminate, irregular, serendipitous, stray, unconsidered, unplanned, unpremeditated, unspecific, unsystematic. *Opp* DELIBERATE, SYSTEMATIC.

range *n* **1** area, compass, distance, extent, field, gamut, limit, orbit, radius, reach, scope, span, spectrum, sphere, spread, sweep. **2** *a wide range of goods.* diversity, selection, variety. **3** *range of mountains.* chain, file, line, rank, row, series, string, tier. • *vb*

1 differ, extend, fluctuate, go, reach, run the gamut, spread, stretch, vary. **2** ▷ RANK. **3** ▷ ROAM.

rank *adj* **1** *rank growth.* ▷ ABUNDANT. **2** *rank smell.* ▷ SMELLING. ● *n* **1** column, file, formation, line, order, queue, row, series, tier. **2** birth, blood, caste, class, condition, degree, echelon, estate, grade, level, position, standing, station, status, stratum, title. ● *vb* arrange, array, assort, categorize, class, classify, grade, graduate, line up, order, organize, range, rate, set out in order, sort.

ransack *vb* **1** comb, explore, go through, rake through, rummage through, scour, search, *inf* turn upside down. **2** *ransack a shop.* despoil, loot, pillage, plunder, raid, ravage, rob, sack, strip, wreck.

ransom *n* payment, *inf* payoff, price, redemption. ● *vb* buy the release of, deliver, redeem.

rap *vb* **1** knock, strike, tap. ▷ HIT. **2** ▷ CRITICIZE.

rape *n* **1** assault, sexual attack. **2** ▷ PILLAGE. ● *vb* assault, defile, deflower, dishonour, force yourself on, *inf* have your way with, *old use* ravish, violate.

rapid *adj* alacritous, breakneck, brisk, expeditious, express, fast, *old use* fleet, hasty, headlong, high-speed, hurried, immediate, impetuous, instant, instantaneous, *inf* lightning, *inf* nippy, precipitate, prompt, quick, smooth, speedy, swift, unchecked, uninterrupted. *Opp* SLOW.

rapids *plur n* cataract, current, waterfall, white water.

rapture *n* bliss, delight, ecstasy, elation, euphoria, exaltation, happiness, joy, pleasure, thrill, transport.

rare *adj* abnormal, atypical, curious, exceptional, extraordinary, *inf* few and far between, infrequent, irreplaceable, limited, occasional, odd, out of the ordinary, peculiar, scarce, singular, special, strange, surprising, uncommon, unfamiliar, unusual. *Opp* COMMON.

rascal *n* blackguard, *old use* bounder, devil, good-fornothing, imp, knave, mischiefmaker, miscreant, ne'er-do-well, rapscallion, rogue, *inf* scallywag, scamp, scoundrel, troublemaker, villain, wastrel. ▷ CRIMINAL.

rash *adj* careless, foolhardy, harebrained, hasty, headlong, headstrong, heedless, hotheaded, hurried, ill-advised, ill-considered, impetuous, imprudent, impulsive, incautious, indiscreet, injudicious, madcap, precipitate, reckless, risky, thoughtless, unthinking, wild. *Opp* CAREFUL. ● *n* **1** efflorescence, eruption, spots. **2** *a rash of thefts.* ▷ OUTBREAK.

rasp *vb* **1** abrade, file, grate, rub, scrape. **2** *rasp orders.* croak, screech, speak hoarsely. ▷ SPEAK. **rasping** ▷ HARSH.

rate *n* **1** gait, pace, speed, tempo, velocity. **2** amount, charge, cost, fare, fee, figure, payment, price, scale, tariff, wage. ● *vb* **1** appraise, assess, class, classify, compute, consider, estimate, evaluate, gauge, grade, judge, measure, prize, put a price on, rank, reckon, regard, value, weigh. **2** *rate a prize.* be worthy of, deserve, merit. **3** ▷ REPRIMAND.

rather *adv* **1** fairly, moderately, *inf* pretty, quite, relatively, slightly, somewhat. **2** *would rather have tea than coffee.* more willingly, preferably, sooner.

ratify *vb* approve, authorize, confirm, endorse, sanction, sign, validate, verify.

rating *n* classification, evaluation, grade, grading, mark, order, placing, ranking.

ratio *n* balance, correlation, correspondence, fraction, percentage, proportion, relationship.

ration *n* allocation, allotment, allowance, amount, helping, measure, percentage, portion, quota, share. ● *vb* allocate, allot, apportion, conserve, control, distribute fairly, dole out, give out, limit, parcel out, restrict, share equally. **rations** food, necessaries, necessities, provisions, stores, supplies.

rational *adj* balanced, clear-headed, commonsense, enlightened, intelligent, judicious, logical, lucid, normal, ratiocinative, reasonable, reasoned, reasoning, sane, sensible, sound, thoughtful, wise. *Opp* IRRATIONAL.

rationale *n* argument, case, cause, excuse, explanation, grounds, justification, logical basis, principle, reason, reasoning, theory, vindication.

rationalize *vb* **1** account for, be rational about, elucidate, excuse, explain, justify, make rational, provide a rationale for, ratiocinate, think through, vindicate. **2** ▷ REORGANIZE.

rattle *vb* **1** clatter, vibrate. **2** agitate, jar, *inf* jiggle about, joggle, jolt, shake about. **3** [*inf*] *rattled him by booing*. alarm, discomfit, discompose, disconcert, disturb, fluster, frighten, make nervous, put off, unnerve, upset, worry. **rattle off** ▷ RECITE. **rattle on** ▷ RAMBLE, TALK.

raucous *adj* ear-splitting, harsh, husky, grating, jarring, noisy, rasping, rough, screeching, shrill, squawking, strident.

ravage *vb* damage, despoil, destroy, devastate, lay waste, loot, pillage, plunder, raid, ransack, ruin, sack, spoil, wreak havoc on, wreck.

rave *vb* **1** be angry, fulminate, fume, rage, rant, roar, storm, thunder. **2** be enthusiastic, enthuse, *inf* go into raptures, *inf* gush, rhapsodize.

ravenous *adj* famished, hungry, insatiable, ravening, starved, starving, voracious. ▷ GREEDY.

ravish *vb* **1** bewitch, captivate, capture, charm, delight, enchant, entrance, spellbind, transport. **2** ▷ RAPE. **ravishing** ▷ BEAUTIFUL.

raw *adj* **1** fresh, rare (*steak*), uncooked, underdone, unpre-pared, wet (*fish*). **2** *raw materials*. crude, natural, unprocessed, unrefined, untreated. **3** *raw recruits*. *inf* green, ignorant, immature, inexperienced, innocent, new, unseasoned, untrained, untried. **4** *raw skin*. bloody, chafed, grazed, inflamed, painful, red, rough, scraped, scratched, sensitive, sore, tender, vulnerable. **5** *raw wind*. ▷ COLD.

ray *n* **1** bar, beam, laser, pencil, shaft, streak, stream. **2** *a ray of hope*. flicker, gleam, glimmer, hint, indication, scintilla, sign, trace.

raze *vb* bulldoze, demolish, destroy, flatten, level, tear down.

razor *n* □ *cut-throat razor, disposable razor, electric razor, safety razor*.

reach *n* compass, distance, orbit, range, scope, sphere. ● *vb* **1** achieve, arrive at, attain, come to, get hold of, get to, go as far as, grasp, *inf* make, take, touch. **2** *reach for the salt*. put out your hand, stretch, try to get. **3** *reach me by phone*. communicate with, contact, get in touch with. **reach out** ▷ EXTEND.

react *vb* act, answer, behave, conduct yourself, reciprocate, reply, respond, retaliate, retort, take revenge. **react to** ▷ COUNTER.

reaction *n* answer, backlash, *inf* come-back, counter, countermove, effect, feedback, parry, reciprocation, reflex, rejoinder, reply, reprisal, response, retaliation, retort, revenge, riposte.

reactionary *adj* conservative, die-hard, old-fashioned, rightist, right-wing, *inf* stick-in-the-mud, traditionalist, unprogressive. *Opp* PROGRESSIVE.

read *vb* **1** devour, *inf* dip into, glance at, interpret, look over, peruse, pore over, review, scan, skim, study. **2** *can't read the handwriting*. decipher, decode, interpret, make out, understand.

readable *adj* **1** absorbing, compulsive, easy, engaging, enjoyable, entertaining, gripping, interesting, stimulating, well-written. *Opp* BORING. **2** clear, comprehensible, decipherable, distinct, intelligible, legible, neat, plain, understandable. *Opp* ILLEGIBLE.

readily *adv* cheerfully, eagerly, easily, effortlessly, freely, gladly, happily, promptly, quickly, ungrudgingly, unhesitatingly, voluntarily, willingly.

ready *adj* **1** accessible, *inf* all set, arranged, at hand, available, complete, convenient, done, finalized, finished, fit, obtainable, prepared, primed, ripe, set, set up, waiting. **2** *ready to help*. agreeable, consenting, content, disposed, eager, equipped, *inf* game, glad, inclined, in the mood, keen, *inf* keyed up, liable, likely, minded, of a mind, open, organized, pleased, poised, predisposed, primed, *inf* psyched up, raring (*to go*), trained, willing. **3** *ready wit*. acute, adroit, alert, apt, facile, immediate, prompt, quick, quick-witted, rapid, sharp, smart, speedy. *Opp* SLOW, UNPREPARED.

real *adj* **1** actual, authentic, certain, corporeal, everyday, existing, factual, genuine, material, natural, ordinary, palpable, physical, pure, realistic, tangible, visible. **2** authenticated, *Lat* bona fide, legal, legitimate, official, valid, verifiable. **3** *real friends*. dependable, positive, reliable, sound, true, trustworthy, worthy. **4** *real grief*. earnest, heartfelt, honest, sincere, truthful, unaffected, undoubted, unfeigned, unquestionable. *Opp* FALSE.

realism *n* **1** authenticity, fidelity, naturalism, verisimilitude. **2** *realism in business*. clear-sightedness, common sense, objectivity, practicality, pragmatism.

realistic *adj* **1** businesslike, clear-sighted, commonsense, down-to-earth, feasible, hardheaded, *inf* hard-nosed, levelheaded, logical, matter-of-fact, *inf* no-nonsense, objective, possible, practicable, practical, pragmatic, rational, sensible, tough, unemotional, unsentimental, viable, workable. **2** *realistic pictures*. authentic, convincing, faithful, graphic, lifelike, natural, recognizable, representational, true-to-life, truthful, vivid. **3** *realistic prices*. acceptable, adequate, fair, genuine, justifiable, moderate, reasonable. *Opp* UNREALISTIC.

reality *n* actuality, authenticity, certainty, empirical knowledge, experience, fact, life, *inf* nittygritty, real life, the real world, truth, verity. *Opp* FANTASY.

realize *vb* **1** accept, appreciate, apprehend, be aware of, become conscious of, *inf* catch on to, comprehend, conceive of, *inf* cotton on to, grasp, know, perceive, recognize, see, sense, *inf* twig, understand, *inf* wake up to. **2** *realize an ambition*. accomplish, achieve, bring about, complete, effect, effectuate, fulfil, implement, make a reality of, obtain, perform, put into effect. **3** *realize a price*. *inf* bring in, *inf* clear, earn, fetch, make, net, obtain, produce.

realm *n* country, domain, empire, kingdom, monarchy, principality.

reap *vb* **1** cut, garner, gather in, glean, harvest, mow. **2** *reap a reward*. acquire, bring in, collect, get, obtain, receive, win.

rear *adj* back, end, hind, hinder, hindmost, last, rearmost. *Opp* FRONT. • *n* **1** back, end, stern (*of ship*), tail-end. **2** ▷ BUTTOCKS. • *vb* **1** breed, bring up, care for, cultivate, educate, feed, look after, nurse, nurture, produce, raise, train. **2** *rear your head*. elevate, hold up, lift, raise, uplift. **3** ▷ BUILD.

rearrange *vb* change round, regroup, reorganize, switch round, swop round, transpose. ▷ CHANGE.

rearrangement *n* anagram, reorganization, transposition. ▷ CHANGE.

reason *n* **1** apology, argument, case, cause, defence, excuse, explanation, grounds, incentive, justification, motive, occasion, pretext, rationale, vindication. **2** brains, common sense, *inf* gumption, intelligence, judgement, logic, mind, *inf* nous, perspicacity, rationality, reasonableness, sanity, sense, understanding, wisdom, wit. ▷ REASONING. **3** *reason for living*. aim, goal, intention, motivation, motive, object, objective, point, purpose, spur, stimulus. • *vb* **1** act rationally, calculate, cerebrate, conclude, consider, deduce, estimate, figure out, hypothesize, infer, intellectualize, judge, *inf* put two and two together, ratiocinate, resolve, theorize, think, use your head, work out. **2** *I reasoned with her.* argue, debate, discuss, expostulate, remonstrate.

reasonable *adj* **1** calm, helpful, honest, intelligent, rational, realistic, sane, sensible, sincere, sober, thinking, thoughtful, unemotional, wise. **2** *reasonable argument.* arguable, believable, credible, defensible, justifiable, logical, plausible, practical, reasoned, sound, tenable, viable, well-thought-out. **3** *reasonable prices.* acceptable, appropriate, average, cheap, competitive, conservative, fair, inexpensive, moderate, ordinary, proper, right, suitable, tolerable, unexceptionable. *Opp* IRRATIONAL.

reasoning *n* analysis, argument, case, *derog* casuistry, cerebration, deduction, dialectic, hypothesis, line of thought, logic, proof, rationalization, *derog* sophistry, theorizing, thinking.

reassure *vb* assure, bolster, buoy up, calm, cheer, comfort, encourage, give confidence to, hearten, *inf* set someone's mind at rest, support, uplift. *Opp* ALARM, THREATEN. **reassuring** ▷ SOOTHING, SUPPORTIVE.

rebel *adj* ▷ REBELLIOUS. ● *n* anarchist, apostate, dissenter, freedom fighter, heretic, iconoclast, insurgent, malcontent, maverick, mutineer, nonconformist, recusant, resistance fighter, revolutionary, schismatic. ● *vb* be a rebel, disobey, dissent, fight, *inf* kick over the traces, mutiny, refuse to obey, revolt, rise up, *inf* run riot, *inf* take a stand. *Opp* CONFORM. **rebel against** ▷ DEFY.

rebellion *n* contumacy, defiance, disobedience, insubordination, insurgency, insurrection, mutiny, rebelliousness, resistance, revolt, revolution, rising, schism, sedition, uprising.

rebellious *adj inf* bolshie, breakaway, contumacious, defiant, difficult, disaffected, disloyal, disobedient, incorrigible, insubordinate, insurgent, intractable, malcontent, mutinous, obstinate, quarrelsome, rebel, recalcitrant, refractory, resistant, revolting, revolutionary, seditious, uncontrollable, ungovernable, unmanageable, unruly, wild. *Opp* OBEDIENT.

rebirth *n* reawakening, regeneration, renaissance, renewal, resurgence, resurrection, return, revival.

rebound *vb inf* backfire, *inf* boomerang, bounce, misfire, recoil, ricochet, spring back.

rebuff *n inf* brush-off, check, discouragement, refusal, rejection, slight, snub. ● *vb* cold-shoulder, decline, discourage, refuse, reject, repulse, slight, snub, spurn, turn down.

rebuild *n* reassemble, reconstruct, recreate, redevelop, refashion, regenerate, remake. ▷ RECONDITION.

rebuke *vb* admonish, castigate, censure, chide, reprehend, reproach, reprove, scold, upbraid. ▷ REPRIMAND.

recall *vb* **1** bring back, call in, summon, withdraw. **2** ▷ REMEMBER.

recede *vb* abate, decline, dwindle, ebb, fall back, go back, lessen, regress, retire, retreat, return, shrink back, sink, slacken, subside, wane, withdraw.

receipt *n* **1** account, acknowledgement, bill, proof of purchase, sales slip, ticket. **2** *receipt of goods.* acceptance, delivery, reception. **receipts** gains, gate, income, proceeds, profits, return, takings.

receive *vb* **1** accept, acquire, be given, be paid, be sent, collect, come by, come into, derive, earn, gain, get, gross, inherit, make, net, obtain, take. **2** *receive an injury.* bear, be subjected to, endure, experience, meet with, suffer, sustain, undergo. **3** *receive visitors.* accommodate, admit, entertain, greet, let in, meet, show in, welcome. *Opp* GIVE.

recent *adj* brand-new, contemporary, current, fresh, just out, latest, modern, new, novel, present-day, up-to-date, young. *Opp* OLD.

reception *n* **1** greeting, response, welcome. **2** ▷ PARTY.

receptive *adj* amenable, favourable, flexible, interested, open, open-minded, responsive, susceptible, sympathetic, tractable, welcoming, well-disposed. *Opp* RESISTANT.

recess *n* **1** alcove, apse, bay, cavity, corner, cranny, hollow, indentation, niche, nook. **2** adjournment, break, *inf* breather, breathing-space, interlude, intermission, interval, respite, rest, time off.

recession *n* decline, depression, downturn, slump.

recipe *n* directions, formula, instructions, method, plan, prescription, procedure, technique.

reciprocal *adj* corresponding, exchanged, joint, mutual, requited, returned, shared.

reciprocate *vb* exchange, give the same in return, match, repay, requite, return.

recital *n* **1** concert, performance, programme. **2** *recital of events.* account, description, narration, narrative, recounting, rehearsal, relation, repetition, story, telling. ▷ RECITATION.

recitation *n* declaiming, declamation, delivery, monologue, narration, performance, presentation, reading, *old use* rendition, speaking, telling.

recite *vb* articulate, declaim, deliver, narrate, perform, present, quote, *inf* rattle off, recount, reel off, rehearse, relate, repeat, speak, tell.

reckless *adj* **1** brash, careless, *inf* crazy, daredevil, *inf* devil-maycare, foolhardy, harebrained, *inf* harum-scarum, hasty, heedless, impetuous, imprudent, impulsive, inattentive, incautious, indiscreet, injudicious, irresponsible, *inf* mad, madcap, negligent, rash, thoughtless, unconsidered, unwise, wild. *Opp* CAREFUL. **2** *reckless criminals.* dangerous, desperate, hardened, violent.

reckon *vb* **1** add up, appraise, assess, calculate, compute, count, enumerate, estimate, evaluate, figure out, gauge, number, tally, total, value, work out. **2** ▷ THINK.

reclaim *vb* **1** get back, *inf* put in for, recapture, recover, regain. **2** *reclaim derelict land.* make usable, redeem, regenerate, reinstate, rescue, restore, salvage, save.

recline *vb* lean back, lie, loll, lounge, repose, rest, sprawl, stretch out.

recluse *n* anchoress, anchorite, hermit, loner, monk, nun, solitary.

recognizable *adj* detectable, distinctive, distinguishable, identifiable, known, noticeable, perceptible, undisguised, unmistakable, visible.

recognize *vb* **1** detect, diagnose, discern, distinguish, identify, know, name, notice, perceive, pick out, place (*can't place him*), *inf* put a name to, recall, recollect, remember, see, spot. **2** *recognize your faults.* accept, acknowledge, admit to, appreciate, be aware of, concede, confess, grant, realize, understand. **3** *recognize someone's rights.* approve of, *inf* back, endorse, legitimize, ratify, sanction, support, validate.

recoil *vb* blench, draw back, falter, flinch, jerk back, jump, quail, shrink, shy away, start, wince. ▷ REBOUND.

recollect *vb* hark back to, recall, reminisce about, summon up, think back to. ▷ REMEMBER.

recommend *vb* **1** advise, advocate, counsel, exhort, prescribe, propose, put forward, suggest, urge. **2** applaud, approve of, *inf* back, commend, favour, *inf* plug, praise, *inf* push, *inf* put in a good word for, speak well of, support, vouch for. ▷ ADVERTISE.

recommendation *n* advice, advocacy, approbation, approval, *inf* backing, commendation, counsel, favourable mention, reference, seal of approval, support, testimonial.

reconcile *vb* bring together, *old use* conciliate, harmonize, make friendly again, placate, reunite, settle differences between. **be reconciled to**

accept, adjust to, resign yourself to, submit to.

recondition *vb* make good, overhaul, rebuild, renew, renovate, repair, restore.

reconnaissance *n* examination, exploration, inspection, investigation, observation, *inf* recce, reconnoitring, scouting, spying, survey.

reconnoitre *vb inf* case, *inf* check out, examine, explore, gather intelligence (about), inspect, investigate, patrol, scout, scrutinize, spy, survey, *sl* suss out.

reconsider *vb* be converted, change your mind, come round, reappraise, reassess, re-examine, rethink, review your position, think better of.

reconstruct *vb* act out, mock up, recreate, rerun. ▷ REBUILD.

record *n* **1** account, annals, archives, catalogue, chronicle, diary, documentation, dossier, file, journal, log, memorandum, minutes, narrative, note, register, report, transactions. **2** best performance, best time. **3** ▷ RECORDING. • *vb* **1** chronicle, document, enter, inscribe, list, log, minute, note, put down, register, set down, take down, transcribe, write down. **2** *record on tape.* keep, preserve, tape, tape-record, video.

recording *n* performance, release. □ *album, audio-tape, cassette, CD, compact disc, digital recording, disc, long-playing record, LP, mono recording, record, single, stereo recording, tape, tape-recording, tele-recording, video, video-cassette, video disc, videotape.*

record-player *n* CD player, gramophone, midi system, *old use* phonograph, record deck, turntable.

recount *vb* communicate, describe, detail, impart, narrate, recite, relate, report, tell, unfold.

recover *vb* **1** find, get back, get compensation for, make good, make up for, recapture, reclaim, recoup, regain, repossess, restore, retrieve, salvage, trace, track down, win back. **2** *inf* be on the mend, come round, convalesce, *inf* get back on your feet, get better, heal, improve, mend, *inf* pull round, *inf* pull through, rally, recuperate, regain your strength, revive, survive, *inf* take a turn for the better.

recovery *n* **1** recapture, reclamation, repossession, restoration, retrieval, salvage, salvaging. **2** *recovery from illness.* advance, convalescence, cure, deliverance, healing, improvement, progress, rally, recuperation, revival, upturn.

recreation *n* amusement, distraction, diversion, enjoyment, entertainment, fun, games, hobby, leisure, pastime, play, pleasure, refreshment, relaxation, sport.

recrimination *n* accusation, *inf* come-back, counter-attack, countercharge, reprisal, retaliation, retort.

recruit *n* apprentice, beginner, conscript, *inf* greenhorn, initiate, learner, neophyte, *inf* new boy, new girl, novice, tiro, trainee. *Opp* VETERAN. • *vb* advertise for, conscript, draft in, engage, enlist, enrol, *old use* impress, mobilize, muster, register, sign on, sign up, take on.

rectify *vb* amend, correct, cure, *inf* fix, make good, put right, repair, revise.

recumbent *adj* flat, flat on your back, horizontal, lying down, prone, reclining, stretched out, supine. *Opp* UPRIGHT.

recuperate *vb* convalesce, get better, heal, improve, mend, rally, regain strength, revive. ▷ RECOVER.

recur *vb* be repeated, come back again, happen again, persist, reappear, repeat, return.

recurrent *adj* chronic, cyclical, frequent, intermittent, iterative, periodic, persistent, recurring, regular, repeated, repetitive, returning. ▷ CONTINUAL.

recycle *vb* reclaim, recover, retrieve, reuse, salvage, use again.

red *adj* bloodshot, blushing, embarrassed, fiery, flaming, florid, flushed, glowing, inflamed, rosy, rubicund, ruddy. □ *auburn, blood-red, brick-red, cardinal, carmine, carroty, cerise, cherry, chestnut, crimson, damask, flame-coloured, foxy, magenta, maroon, orange, pink, rose, roseate, ruby, scarlet, titian, vermilion, wine-coloured.* **red herring** ▷ DECOY.

redden *vb* blush, colour, flush, glow.

redeem *vb* buy back, cash in, exchange for cash, reclaim, recover, re-purchase, trade in, win back. ▷ LIBERATE. **redeem yourself** ▷ ATONE.

redolent *adj* **1** aromatic, fragrant, perfumed, scented, smelling. **2** *redolent of the past.* reminiscent, suggestive.

reduce *vb* **1** abate, abbreviate, abridge, clip, compress, curtail, cut, cut back, cut down, decimate, decrease, detract from, devalue, dilute, diminish, *inf* dock (*wages*), *inf* ease up on, halve, impair, lessen, limit, lower, make less, minimize, moderate, narrow, prune, shorten, shrink, simplify, *inf* slash, slim down, tone down, trim, truncate, weaken, whittle. **2** become less, contract, dwindle, shrink. **3** *reduce a liquid.* concentrate, condense, thicken. **4** *reduce to rubble.* break up, destroy, grind, pulp, pulverize, triturate. **5** *reduce to poverty.* degrade, demote, downgrade, humble, impoverish, move down, put down, ruin. *Opp* INCREASE, RAISE.

reduction *n* **1** contraction, curtailment, *inf* cutback, deceleration (*of speed*), decimation, decline, decrease, diminution, drop, impairment, lessening, limitation, loss, moderation, narrowing, remission, shortening, shrinkage, weakening. **2** *reduction in price.* concession, cut, depreciation, devaluation, discount, rebate, refund. *Opp* INCREASE.

redundant *adj* excessive, inessential, non-essential, superfluous, supernumerary, surplus, too many, unnecessary, unneeded, unwanted. *Opp* NECESSARY.

reek *n* stench, stink. ▷ SMELL.

reel *n* bobbin, spool. ● *vb* falter, lurch, pitch, rock, roll, spin, stagger, stumble, sway, totter, waver, whirl, wobble. **reel off** ▷ RECITE.

refer *vb* **refer to 1** allude to, bring up, cite, comment on, draw attention to, make reference to, mention, name, point to, quote, speak of, specify, touch on. **2** *refer one person to another.* direct to, guide to, hand over to, pass on to, recommend to, send to. **3** *refer to the dictionary.* consult, go to, look up, resort to, study, turn to.

referee *n* adjudicator, arbiter, arbitrator, judge, mediator, umpire.

reference *n* **1** allusion, citation, example, illustration, instance, intimation, mention, note, quotation, referral, remark. **2** endorsement, recommendation, testimonial.

refill *vb* fill up, refuel, renew, replenish, top up.

refine *vb* **1** clarify, cleanse, clear, decontaminate, distil, process, purify, treat. **2** *refine manners.* civilize, cultivate, improve, perfect, polish.

refined *adj* **1** aristocratic, civilized, courteous, courtly, cultivated, cultured, delicate, dignified, discerning, discriminating, educated, elegant, fastidious, genteel, gentlemanly, gracious, ladylike, nice, polished, polite, *inf* posh, precise, *derog* pretentious, *derog* prissy, sensitive, sophisticated, stylish, subtle, tasteful, *inf* upper-crust, urbane, well-bred, well brought-up. *Opp* RUDE. **2** *refined oil.* clarified, distilled, processed, purified, treated. *Opp* CRUDE.

refinement *n* **1** breeding, *inf* class, courtesy, cultivation, delicacy, discernment, discrimination, elegance, finesse, gentility, graciousness, polish, *derog* pretentiousness, sensitivity, sophistication, style, subtlety, taste, urbanity. **2** *refinements in design.* alteration, change, enhancement, improvement, modification, perfection.

reflect *vb* **1** echo, mirror, return, send back, shine back, throw back. **2** brood, cerebrate, *inf* chew things over, consider, contemplate, deliberate, meditate, ponder, remind yourself, reminisce, ruminate. ▷ THINK. **3** *Her success reflects her hard work.* bear witness to, correspond to, demonstrate, evidence, exhibit, illustrate, indicate, match, point to, reveal, show.

reflection *n* **1** echo, image, likeness. **2** *reflection of hard work.* demonstration, evidence, indication, manifestation, result. **3** *no reflection on you.* aspersion, censure, criticism, discredit, imputation, reproach, shame, slur. **4** *time for reflection.* cerebration, cogitation, contemplation, deliberation, meditation, pondering, rumination, self-examination, study, thinking, thought.

reflective *adj* **1** glittering, lustrous, reflecting, shiny, silvery. **2** ▷ THOUGHTFUL.

reform *vb* **1** ameliorate, amend, become better, better, change, convert, correct, improve, make better, mend, put right, reconstruct, rectify, remodel, reorganize, save. **2** *reform a system.* purge, reconstitute, regenerate, revolutionize.

refrain *vb* **refrain from** abstain from, avoid, cease, desist from, do without, eschew, forbear, leave off, *inf* quit, renounce, stop.

refresh *vb* **1** cool, energize, enliven, fortify, freshen, invigorate, *inf* perk up, quench the thirst of, reanimate, rejuvenate, renew, restore, resuscitate, revitalize, revive, slake (*thirst*). **2** *refresh the memory.* activate, awaken, jog, prod, prompt, remind, stimulate.

refreshing *adj* **1** bracing, cool, enlivening, exhilarating, inspiriting, invigorating, restorative, reviving, stimulating, thirst-quenching, tingling, tonic. *Opp* EXHAUSTING. **2** *a refreshing change.* different, fresh, interesting, new, novel, original, unexpected, unfamiliar, unforeseen, unpredictable, welcome. *Opp* BORING.

refreshments *plur n* drinks, eatables, *inf* eats, *inf* nibbles, snack. ▷ DRINK, FOOD.

refrigerate *vb* chill, cool, freeze, ice, keep cold.

refuge *n* asylum, *inf* bolt-hole, cover, harbour, haven, *inf* hideaway, hideout, *inf* hidey-hole, hiding-place, protection, retreat, safety, sanctuary, security, shelter, stronghold.

refugee *n* displaced person, émigré, exile, fugitive, outcast, runaway.

refund *n* rebate, repayment. ● *vb* give back, pay back, recoup, reimburse, repay, return.

refusal *n inf* brush-off, denial, disagreement, disapproval, rebuff, rejection, veto. *Opp* ACCEPTANCE.

refuse *n* detritus, dirt, garbage, junk, litter, rubbish, trash, waste. ● *vb* baulk at, decline, deny, disallow, *inf* jib at, *inf* pass up, rebuff, reject, repudiate, say no to, spurn, turn down, veto, withhold. *Opp* ACCEPT, GRANT.

refute *vb* counter, discredit, disprove, negate, prove wrong, rebut.

regain *vb* be reunited with, find, get back, recapture, reclaim, recoup, recover, repossess, retake, retrieve, return to, win back.

regal *adj derog* haughty, imperial, kingly, lordly, majestic, noble, palatial, *derog* pompous, princely, queenly, royal, stately. ▷ SPLENDID.

regard *n* **1** gaze, look, scrutiny, stare. **2** attention, care, concern, consideration, deference, heed, notice, reference, respect, sympathy, thought. **3** admiration, affection, appreciation, approbation, approval, deference, esteem, favour, honour, love, respect, reverence, veneration. ● *vb* **1** behold, contemplate, eye, gaze at, keep an eye on, look at, note, observe, scrutinize, stare at, view, watch. **2** *regarded me as a liability.* account, consider, deem, esteem, judge, look upon, perceive, rate, reckon, respect, think of, value, view, weigh up.

regarding *prep* about, apropos, concerning, connected with, involving, on the subject of, pertaining to, *inf* re, respecting, with reference to, with regard to.

regardless *adj* **regardless of** careless about, despite, heedless of, indifferent to, neglectful of, notwithstanding, unconcerned about, unmindful of.

regime *n* administration, control, discipline, government, leadership, management, order, reign, rule, system.

regiment *vb* arrange, control, discipline, organize, regulate, systematize.

region *n* area, country, department, district, division, expanse, land, locality, neighbourhood, part, place, province, quarter, sector, territory, tract, vicinity, zone.

register *n* archives, catalogue, chronicle, diary, directory, file, index, inventory, journal, ledger, list, record, roll, tally. ● *vb* **1** enlist, enrol, enter your name, join, sign on. **2** *register a complaint.* catalogue, enter, list, log, make official, minute, present, record, set down, submit, write down. **3** *register emotion.* betray, display, divulge, express, indicate, manifest, reflect, reveal, show. **4** *register in a hotel. inf* check in, sign in. **5** *register what someone says.* keep in mind, make a note of, mark, notice, take account of.

regress *vb* backslide, degenerate, deteriorate, fall back, go back, move backwards, retreat, retrogress, revert, slip back. *Opp* PROGRESS.

regret *n* **1** bad conscience, compunction, contrition, guilt, penitence, pricking of conscience, remorse, repentance, self-accusation, self-condemnation, self-reproach, shame. **2** disappointment, grief, sadness, sorrow, sympathy. ● *vb* accuse yourself, bemoan, be regretful, be sad, bewail, deplore, deprecate, feel remorse, grieve (about), lament, mourn, repent (of), reproach yourself, rue, weep (over).

regretful *adj* apologetic, ashamed, conscience-stricken, contrite, disappointed, guilty, penitent, remorseful, repentant, rueful, sorry. ▷ SAD. *Opp* UNREPENTANT.

regrettable *adj* deplorable, disappointing, distressing, lamentable, reprehensible, sad, shameful, undesirable, unfortunate, unhappy, unlucky, unwanted, upsetting, woeful, wrong.

regular *adj* **1** consistent, constant, equal, even, fixed, measured, ordered, predictable, recurring, repeated, rhythmic, steady, symmetrical, systematic, uniform, unvarying. □ *daily, hourly, monthly, weekly, yearly.* **2** *a regular procedure.* accustomed, common, commonplace, conventional, customary, established, everyday, familiar, frequent, habitual, known, normal, official, ordinary, orthodox, prevailing, proper, routine, scheduled, standard, traditional, typical, usual. **3** *a regular supporter.* dependable, faithful, reliable. *Opp* IRREGULAR. ● *n inf* faithful, frequenter, habitué, regular customer, patron.

regulate *vb* **1** administer, conduct, control, direct, govern, manage, monitor, order, organize, oversee, restrict, supervise. **2** *regulate temperature.* adjust, alter, balance, change, get right, moderate, modify, set, vary.

regulation *n* by-law, commandment, decree, dictate, directive, edict, law, order, ordinance, requirement, restriction, rule, ruling, statute.

rehearsal *n* dress rehearsal, *inf* dry run, exercise, practice, preparation, *inf* read-through, *inf* runthrough, *inf* try-out.

rehearse *vb* drill, go over, practise, prepare, *inf* run over, *inf* run through, try out.

rehearsed *adj* calculated, practised, pre-arranged, premeditated, prepared, scripted, studied, thought out. *Opp* IMPROMPTU.

reign *n* administration, ascendancy, command, empire, government, jurisdiction, kingdom, monarchy, power, rule, sovereignty. ● *vb* be king, be on the throne, be queen, command, govern, have power, hold sway, rule, *inf* wear the crown.

reincarnation *n* rebirth, return to life, transmigration.

reinforce *vb* **1** back up, bolster, buttress, fortify, give strength to, hold up, prop up, stay, stiffen, strengthen, support, toughen. **2** *reinforce an army.* add to, assist, augment, help, increase the size of, provide reinforcements for, supplement.

reinforcements *plur n* additional troops, auxiliaries, back-up, help, reserves, support.

reinstate *vb* recall, rehabilitate, restore, take back, welcome back. *Opp* DISMISS.

reject *vb* **1** cast off, discard, discount, dismiss, eliminate, exclude, jettison, *inf* junk, put aside, scrap, send back, throw away, throw out. **2** *reject friends.* disown, *inf* drop, *inf* give someone the cold shoulder, jilt, rebuff, renounce, repel, repudiate, repulse, *inf* send packing, shun, spurn, turn your back on. **3** *reject an invitation.* brush aside, decline, refuse, say no to, turn down, veto. *Opp* ACCEPT, ADOPT.

rejoice *vb* be happy, celebrate, delight, exult, glory, revel, triumph. *Opp* GRIEVE.

relapse *n* degeneration, deterioration, recurrence *(of illness)*, regression, reversion, *inf* set-back, worsening. ● *vb* backslide, degenerate, deteriorate, fall back, have a relapse, lapse, regress, retreat, revert, sink back, slip back, weaken.

relate *vb* **1** communicate, describe, detail, divulge, impart, make known, narrate, present, recite, recount, rehearse, report, reveal, tell. **2** ally, associate, compare, connect, consider together, coordinate, correlate, couple, join, link. **relate to 1** appertain to, apply to, bear upon, be relevant to, concern, *inf* go with, pertain to, refer to. **2** *relate to other people.* be friends with, empathize with, fraternize with, handle, have a relationship with, identify with, socialize with, understand.

related *adj* affiliated, akin, allied, associated, cognate, comparable, connected, consanguineous, interconnected, interdependent, interrelated, joined, joint, linked, mutual, parallel, reciprocal, relative, similar, twin. ▷ RELEVANT. *Opp* UNRELATED.

relation *n* **1** *old use* kinsman, *old use* kinswoman, *plur* kith and kin, member of the family, relative. ▷ FAMILY. **2** *relation of a story.* ▷ NARRATION.

relationship *n* **1** affiliation, affinity, association, attachment, bond, closeness, connection, consanguinity, correlation, correspondence, interconnection, interdependence, kinship, link, parallel, pertinence, rapport, ratio, tie, understanding. ▷ SIMILARITY. *Opp* CONTRAST. **2** affair, *inf* intrigue, *inf* liaison, love affair, romance, sexual relations. ▷ FRIENDSHIP.

relative *adj* ▷ RELATED, RELEVANT. **relative to** commensurate (with), comparative, proportional, proportionate. *Opp* UNRELATED. ● *n* ▷ RELATION.

relax *vb* **1** be easy, be relaxed, calm down, cool down, feel at home, *inf* let go, *inf* put your feet up, rest, *inf* slow down, *inf* take it easy, unbend, unwind. *Opp* TENSION. **2** *relax your vigilance.* abate, curb, decrease, diminish, ease off, lessen, loosen, mitigate, moderate, reduce, release, relieve, slacken, soften, temper, *inf* tone down, unclench, unfasten, weaken. *Opp* INCREASE.

relaxation *n* **1** ease, informality, loosening up, relaxing, repose, rest, unwinding. ▷ RECREATION. *Opp* TENSION. **2** abatement, alleviation, diminution, lessening, *inf* let-up, mitigation, moderation, remission, slackening, weakening. *Opp* INCREASE.

relaxed *adj derog* blasé, calm, carefree, casual, comfortable, contented, cool, cosy, easygoing, *inf* free and easy, friendly, good-humoured, happy, *inf* happy-golucky, informal, insouciant, *inf* laid-back, *derog* lax, leisurely, light-hearted, nonchalant, peaceful, reassuring, restful, serene, *derog* slack, tranquil, unconcerned, unhurried, untroubled. *Opp* TENSE.

relay *n* **1** shift, turn. **2** *live relay.* broadcast, programme, transmission. • *vb* broadcast, communicate, pass on, send out, spread, televise, transmit.

release *vb* **1** acquit, allow out, deliver, discharge, dismiss, emancipate, excuse, exonerate, free, let go, let loose, let off, liberate, loose, pardon, rescue, save, set free, set loose, unchain, unfasten, unfetter, unleash, unshackle, untie. *Opp* DETAIN. **2** fire off, launch, let fly, let off, send off. **3** *release information.* circulate, disseminate, distribute, issue, make available, present, publish, put out, send out, unveil.

relegate *vb* **1** consign to a lower position, demote, downgrade, put down. **2** banish, dispatch, exile.

relent *vb* acquiesce, become more lenient, be merciful, capitulate, give in, give way, relax, show pity, soften, weaken, yield.

relentless *adj* **1** dogged, fierce, hard-hearted, implacable, incessant, inexorable, intransigent, merciless, obdurate, obstinate, pitiless, remorseless, ruthless, uncompromising, unfeeling, unforgiving, unmerciful, unyielding. ▷ CRUEL. **2** unceasing, unrelieved, unstoppable, unyielding. ▷ CONTINUOUS.

relevant *adj* appertaining, applicable, apposite, appropriate, apropos, apt, connected, essential, fitting, germane, linked, material, pertinent, proper, related, relative, significant, suitable, suited, to the point. *Opp* IRRELEVANT.

reliable *adj* certain, conscientious, consistent, constant, dependable, devoted, efficient, faithful, honest, infallible, loyal, predictable, proven, punctilious, regular, reputable, responsible, safe, solid, sound, stable, staunch, steady, sure, trusted, trustworthy, trusty, unchanging, unfailing. *Opp* UNRELIABLE.

relic *n* heirloom, heritage, inheritance, keepsake, memento, remains, reminder, remnant, souvenir, survival, token, vestige.

relief *n* abatement, aid, alleviation, assistance, assuagement, comfort, cure, deliverance, diversion, ease, help, *inf* let-up, mitigation, palliation, relaxation, release, remedy, remission, respite, rest.

relieve *vb* abate, alleviate, anaesthetize, assuage, bring relief to, calm, comfort, console, cure, diminish, disburden, disencumber, dull, ease, lessen, lift, lighten, make less, mitigate, moderate, palliate, reduce, relax, release, rescue, soften, soothe, unburden. ▷ HELP. *Opp* INTENSIFY.

religion *n* **1** belief, creed, divinity, doctrine, dogma, *derog* pietism, theology. **2** creed, cult, denomination, faith, persuasion, sect. □ *Buddhism, Christianity, Hinduism, Islam, Judaism, Sikhism, Taoism, Zen.*

religious *adj* **1** devotional, divine, holy, sacramental, sacred, scriptural, theological. *Opp* SECULAR. **2** churchgoing, committed, dedicated, devout, God-fearing, godly, *derog* pietistic, pious, *derog* religiose, reverent, righteous, saintly, *derog* sanctimonious, spiritual. *Opp* IRRELIGIOUS. **3** *religious wars.* bigoted, doctrinal, fanatical, sectarian, schismatic.

relinquish *vb* concede, give in, hand over, part with, submit, surrender, yield.

relish *n* **1** appetite, delight, enjoyment, enthusiasm, gusto, pleasure, zest. **2** flavour, piquancy, savour, tang, taste. • *vb* appreciate, delight in, enjoy, like, love, revel in, savour, take pleasure in.

reluctant *adj* averse, disinclined, grudging, hesitant, loath, unenthusiastic, unwilling. *Opp* EAGER.

rely *vb* **rely on** *inf* bank on, count on, depend on, have confidence in, lean on, put your faith in, *inf* swear by, trust.

remain *vb* *old use* abide, be left, carry on, continue, endure, keep on, linger, live on, persevere, persist, stay, *inf* stay put, survive, tarry, wait. **remaining** ▷ RESIDUAL.

remainder *n* balance, excess, extra, remnant, residue, residuum, rest, surplus. ▷ REMAINS.

remains *plur n* **1** crumbs, debris, detritus, dregs, fragments, *inf* leftovers, oddments, *inf* odds and ends, offcuts, remainder, remnants, residue, rubble, ruins, scraps, traces, vestiges, wreckage. **2** *historic remains.* heirloom, heritage, inheritance, keepsake, memento, monument, relic, reminder, souvenir, survival. **3** *human remains.* ashes, body, bones, carcass, corpse.

remake *vb* piece together, rebuild, reconstitute, reconstruct, redo. ▷ RENEW.

remark *n* comment, mention, observation, opinion, reflection, statement, thought, utterance, word. • *vb* **1** assert, comment, declare, mention, note, observe, pass comment, reflect, say, state. **2** heed, mark, notice, observe, perceive, see, take note of.

remarkable *adj* amazing, astonishing, astounding, conspicuous, curious, different, distinguished, exceptional, extraordinary, important, impressive, marvellous, memorable, notable, noteworthy, odd, out-of-the-ordinary, outstanding, peculiar, phenomenal, prominent, signal, significant, singular, special, strange, striking, surprising, *inf* terrific, *inf* tremendous, uncommon, unforgettable, unusual, wonderful. *Opp* ORDINARY.

remedy *n inf* answer, antidote, corrective, countermeasure, cure, cure-all, drug, elixir, medicament, medication, medicine, nostrum, palliative, panacea, prescription, redress, relief, restorative, solution, therapy, treatment. • *vb* alleviate, *inf* ameliorate, answer, control, correct, counteract, *inf* fix, heal, help, mend, mitigate, palliate, put right, rectify, redress, relieve, repair, solve, treat. ▷ CURE.

remember *vb* **1** be mindful of, have a memory of, have in mind, keep in mind, recognize. **2** learn, memorize, retain. **3** *remember old times.* be nostalgic about, hark back to, recall, recollect, reminisce about, review, summon up, tell stories about, think back to. **4** *remember Christmas.* celebrate, commemorate, observe. *Opp* FORGET.

remind *vb* give a reminder to, jog the memory of, nudge, prompt.

reminder *n* **1** aide-mémoire, cue, hint, *inf* memo, memorandum, mnemonic, note, *inf* nudge, prompt, *inf* shopping list. **2** heirloom, inheritance, keepsake, memento, relic, souvenir, survival.

reminisce *vb* be nostalgic, hark back, look back, recall, remember, review, tell stories, think back.

reminiscence *n* account, anecdote, memoir, memory, recollection, remembrance.

reminiscent *adj* evocative, nostalgic, recalling, redolent, suggestive.

remiss *adj* careless, dilatory, forgetful, irresponsible, lax, negligent, slack, thoughtless. *Opp* CAREFUL.

remit *vb* **1** *remit a debt.* cancel, let off, settle. **2** abate, decrease, ease off, lessen, relax, slacken. **3** dispatch, forward, send, transmit. ▷ PAY.

remittance *n* allowance, fee, payment.

remnants *plur n* bits, fragments, *inf* leftovers, oddments, offcuts, residue, scraps, traces, vestiges. ▷ REMAINS.

remodel *vb* ▷ RENEW.

remorse *n* bad conscience, compunction, contrition, grief, guilt, mortification, pangs of conscience, penitence, pricking of conscience, regret, repentance, sadness, self-accusation, self-reproach, shame, sorrow.

remorseful *adj* ashamed, conscience-stricken, contrite, grief-stricken, guilt-ridden, guilty, penitent, regretful, repentant, rueful, sorry. *Opp* UNREPENTANT.

remorseless *adj* dogged, implacable, inexorable, intransigent, merciless, obdurate, pitiless, relentless, ruthless, uncompromising, unforgiving, unkind, unmerciful, unremitting. ▷ CRUEL.

remote *adj* 1 alien, cut off, desolate, distant, far-away, foreign, God-forsaken, hard to find, inaccessible, isolated, lonely, outlying, out of reach, out of the way, secluded, solitary, unfamiliar, unfrequented, *inf* unget-at-able, unreachable. *Opp* CLOSE. 2 *a remote chance*. doubtful, implausible, improbable, negligible, outside, poor, slender, slight, small, unlikely. *Opp* SURE. 3 *a remote manner*. abstracted, aloof, cold, cool, detached, haughty, preoccupied, reserved, standoffish, uninvolved, withdrawn. *Opp* FRIENDLY.

removal *n* 1 relocation, removing, taking away, transfer, transportation. 2 elimination, eradication, extermination, liquidation, purge, purging. ▷ KILLING. 3 *removal from a job*. deposition, dethronement, dislodgement, dismissal, displacement, ejection, expulsion, *inf* firing, making redundant, ousting, redundancy, *inf* sacking, transference, unseating. 4 *removal of teeth*. drawing, extraction, pulling, taking out, withdrawal.

remove *vb* 1 abolish, abstract, amputate (*limb*), banish, clear away, cut off, cut out, delete, depose, detach, disconnect, dismiss, dispense with, displace, dispose of, do away with, eject, eliminate, eradicate, erase, evict, excise, exile, expel, expunge, *inf* fire, *inf* get rid of, *inf* kick out, kill, oust, purge, root out, rub out, *inf* sack, send away, separate, strike out, sweep away, take out, throw out, turn out, undo, unfasten, uproot, wash off, wipe (*tape-recording*), wipe out. 2 *remove furniture*. carry away, convey, move, take away, transfer, transport. 3 *remove a tooth*. draw out, extract, pull out, take out. 4 *remove clothes*. doff (*a hat*), peel off, strip off, take off.

rend *vb* cleave, lacerate, pull apart, rip, rupture, shred, split, tear.

render *vb* 1 cede, deliver, furnish, give, hand over, offer, present, proffer, provide, surrender, tender, yield. 2 *render a song*. execute, interpret, perform, play, produce, sing. 3 *rendered me speechless*. cause to be, make.

rendezvous *n* appointment, assignation, date, engagement, meeting, meeting-place, *old use* tryst.

renegade *n* apostate, backslider, defector, deserter, fugitive, heretic, mutineer, outlaw, rebel, runaway, traitor, turncoat.

renege *vb* **renege on** abjure, abrogate, *inf* back out of, break, default on, fail to keep, go back on, *sl* rat on, repudiate, *sl* welsh on.

renew *vb* 1 bring up to date, *inf* do up, *inf* give a face-lift to, improve, mend, modernize, overhaul, recondition, reconstitute, recreate, redecorate, redesign, redevelop, redo, refit, refresh, refurbish, regenerate, reintroduce, rejuvenate, remake, remodel, renovate, repaint, repair, replace, replenish, restore, resume, resurrect, revamp, revitalize, revive, touch up, transform, update. 2 *renew an activity*. come back to, pick up again, recommence, restart, resume, return to. 3 *renew vows*. confirm, reaffirm, reiterate, repeat, restate.

renounce *vb* 1 abandon, abjure, abstain from, declare your opposition to, deny, desert, discard, disown, eschew, forgo, forsake, forswear, give up, reject, repudiate, spurn. 2 *renounce the throne*. abdicate, *inf* quit, relinquish, resign, surrender.

renovate *vb* ▷ RENEW.

renovation *n* improvement, modernization, overhaul, reconditioning, redevelopment, refit, refurbishment, renewal, repair, restoration, transformation, updating.

renowned *adj* celebrated, distinguished, eminent, illustrious, noted, prominent, well-known. ▷ FAMOUS.

rent *n* 1 fee, hire, instalment, payment, rental. 2 *a rent in a garment*. ▷ SPLIT. ● *vb* charter, farm out, hire, lease, let.

reorganize *vb* rationalize, re-arrange, re-deploy, reshuffle, restructure.

repair *vb* **1** *inf* fix, mend, overhaul, patch up, put right, rectify, refit, restore, service. ▷ RENEW. **2** darn, patch, sew up.

repay *vb* **1** compensate, give back, pay back, recompense, refund, reimburse, remunerate, settle. **2** avenge, get even, *inf* get your own back, reciprocate, requite, retaliate, return, revenge.

repeal *vb* abolish, abrogate, annul, cancel, invalidate, nullify, rescind, reverse, revoke.

repeat *vb* **1** do again, duplicate, redo, rehearse, replay, replicate, reproduce, re-run, show again. **2** echo, quote, recapitulate, re-echo, regurgitate, reiterate, restate, retell, say again.

repel *vb* **1** check, drive away, fend off, fight off, hold off, *inf* keep at bay, parry, push away, rebuff, repulse, resist, ward off, withstand. **2** *repel water.* be impermeable to, exclude, keep out, reject. **3** *cruelty repels us.* alienate, be repellent to, disgust, nauseate, offend, *inf* put off, revolt, sicken, *inf* turn off. *Opp* ATTRACT.

repellent *adj* **1** impermeable, impervious, resistant, unsusceptible. **2** ▷ REPULSIVE.

repent *vb* bemoan, be repentant about, bewail, feel repentance for, lament, regret, reproach yourself for, rue.

repentance *n* contrition, guilt, penitence, regret, remorse, self-accusation, self-reproach, shame, sorrow.

repentant *adj* apologetic, ashamed, conscience-stricken, contrite, grief-stricken, guilt-ridden, guilty, penitent, regretful, remorseful, rueful, sorry. *Opp* UNREPENTANT.

repertory *n* collection, repertoire, repository, reserve, stock, store, supply.

repetitive *adj* boring, incessant, iterative, monotonous, recurrent, repeated, repeating, repetitious, tautologous, tedious, unchanging, unvaried. ▷ CONTINUAL.

replace *vb* **1** make good, put back, reinstate, restore, return. **2** be a replacement for, come after, follow, oust, succeed, supersede, supplant, take over from, take the place of. ▷ DEPUTIZE. **3** *replace worn parts.* change, renew, substitute.

replacement *n inf* fill-in, proxy, stand-in, substitute, successor, understudy.

replenish *vb* fill up, refill, renew, restock, top up.

replete *adj inf* bursting, crammed, gorged, *inf* jam-packed, overloaded, sated, stuffed. ▷ FULL.

replica *n inf* carbon copy, clone, copy, duplicate, facsimile, imitation, likeness, model, reconstruction, reproduction.

reply *n* acknowledgement, answer, *inf* come-back, reaction, rejoinder, response, retort, riposte. ● *vb* answer, give a reply, react, rejoin, respond. **reply to** ▷ ACKNOWLEDGE, COUNTER.

report *n* **1** account, announcement, article, communication, communiqué, description, dispatch, narrative, news, record, statement, story, *inf* write-up. **2** backfire, bang, blast, boom, crack, detonation, discharge, explosion, noise. ● *vb* **1** announce, broadcast, circulate, communicate, declare, describe, disclose, divulge, document, give an account of, notify, present a report on, proclaim, publish, put out, record, recount, reveal, state, tell. **2** *report for duty.* announce yourself, check in, clock in, introduce yourself, make yourself known, present yourself, sign in. **3** *report someone to the police.* complain about, denounce, inform against, *inf* tell on.

reporter *n* columnist, commentator, correspondent, journalist, newscaster, newsman, newspaperman, newspaperwoman, news presenter, newswoman, photojournalist.

repose *n* calm, calmness, comfort, ease, inactivity, peace, peacefulness, poise, quiescence, quiet, quietness, relaxation, respite, rest, serenity, stasis, stillness, tranquillity. ▷ SLEEP. *Opp* ACTIVITY.

reprehensible *adj* blameworthy, culpable, deplorable, disgraceful, immoral, objectionable, regrettable, remiss, shameful, unworthy, wicked. ▷ GUILTY. *Opp* INNOCENT.

represent *vb* **1** act out, assume the guise of, be an example of, embody, enact, epitomize, exemplify, exhibit, express, illustrate, impersonate, incarnate, masquerade as, personify, pose as, present, pretend to be, stand for, symbolize, typify. **2** characterize, define, delineate, depict, describe, draw, paint, picture, portray, reflect, show, sketch. **3** act for, speak for, stand up for.

representation *n* depiction, figure, icon, image, imitation, likeness, model, picture, portrait, portrayal, resemblance, semblance, statue.

representative *adj* **1** archetypal, average, characteristic, illustrative, normal, typical. *Opp* ABNORMAL. **2** *representative government.* chosen, democratic, elected, elective, popular. *Opp* TOTALITARIAN. • *n* **1** delegate, deputy, proxy, spokesman, spokeswoman, stand-in, substitute. **2** agent, *inf* rep, salesman, salesperson, saleswoman, *inf* traveller. **3** ambassador, consul, diplomat, emissary, envoy, legate. **4** *Amer* congressman, councillor, Member of Parliament, MP, ombudsman.

repress *vb* **1** control, crush, curb, keep down, limit, oppress, overcome, put down, quell, restrain, subdue, subjugate. **2** *repress emotion. inf* bottle up, frustrate, inhibit, stifle, suppress.

repressed *adj* **1** cold, frigid, frustrated, inhibited, neurotic, *inf* prim and proper, tense, unbalanced, undemonstrative, *inf* uptight. *Opp* UNINHIBITED. **2** *repressed emotion. inf* bottled up, hidden, latent, subconscious, suppressed, unconscious, unfulfilled.

repression *n* **1** authoritarianism, censorship, coercion, control, despotism, dictatorship, oppression, restraint, subjugation, totalitarianism, tyranny. **2** *repression of emotion. inf* bottling up, frustration, inhibition, suffocation, suppression.

repressive *adj* authoritarian, autocratic, brutal, coercive, cruel, despotic, dictatorial, fascist, harsh, illiberal, oppressive, restricting, severe, totalitarian, tyrannical, undemocratic, unenlightened. *Opp* LIBERAL.

reprieve *n* amnesty, pardon, postponement, respite, stay of execution. • *vb* commute a sentence, forgive, let off, pardon, postpone execution, set free, spare.

reprimand *n* admonition, castigation, censure, condemnation, criticism, *inf* dressing-down, *inf* going-over, *inf* lecture, lesson, *inf* rap on the knuckles, rebuke, remonstration, reproach, reproof, scolding, *inf* slap on the wrist, *inf* slating, *inf* talking-to, *inf* telling-off, *inf* ticking-off, upbraiding, *inf* wigging. • *vb* admonish, berate, blame, *inf* carpet, castigate, censure, chide, condemn, correct, criticize, disapprove of, *inf* dress down, find fault with, *inf* haul over the coals, *inf* lecture, *inf* rap, rate, *inf* read the riot act to, rebuke, reprehend, reproach, reprove, scold, *inf* slate, *inf* take to task, *inf* teach a lesson, *inf* tell off, *inf* tick off, upbraid. *Opp* PRAISE.

reprisal *n* counter-attack, getting even, redress, repayment, retaliation, retribution, revenge, vengeance.

reproach *n* blame, disapproval, disgrace, scorn. • *vb* censure, criticize, scold, show disapproval of, upbraid. ▷ REPRIMAND. *Opp* PRAISE.

reproachful *adj* admonitory, censorious, condemnatory, critical, disapproving, disparaging, reproving, scornful, withering.

reproduce *vb* **1** copy, counterfeit, duplicate, forge, imitate, mimic, photocopy, print, redo, reissue, reprint, simulate. ▷ REPEAT. **2** beget young, breed, increase, multiply, procreate, produce offspring, propagate, regenerate, spawn.

reproduction *n* **1** breeding, cloning, increase, multiplying, procreation, proliferation, propagation, spawning. **2** *inf* carbon copy, clone, copy, duplicate, facsimile, fake, forgery, imitation, likeness, print, replica.

repudiate *vb* **1** deny, disagree with, dispute, rebuff, refute, reject, scorn, turn down. *Opp* ACKNOWLEDGE. **2** *repudiate an agreement.* abrogate, discard, disown, go back on, recant, renounce, rescind, retract, reverse, revoke.

repugnant *adj* ▷ REPULSIVE.

repulsive *adj* abhorrent, abominable, beastly, disagreeable, disgusting, distasteful, distressing, foul, gross, hateful, hideous, loathsome, nasty, nauseating, nauseous, objectionable, obnoxious, odious, offensive, *inf* off-putting, repellent, repugnant, revolting, *inf* sick, sickening, unattractive, unpalatable, unpleasant, unsavoury, unsightly, vile. ▷ UGLY. *Opp* ATTRACTIVE.

reputable *adj* creditable, dependable, esteemed, famous, good, highly regarded, honourable, honoured, prestigious, reliable, respectable, respected, trustworthy, unimpeachable, *inf* up-market, well-thought-of, worthy. *Opp* DISREPUTABLE.

reputation *n* character, fame, name, prestige, recognition, renown, repute, standing, stature, status.

reputed *adj* alleged, assumed, believed, considered, deemed, famed, judged, purported, reckoned, regarded, rumoured, said, supposed, thought.

request *n* appeal, application, call, demand, entreaty, petition, plea, prayer, question, requisition, solicitation, suit, supplication. • *vb* adjure, appeal, apply (for), ask, beg, beseech, call for, claim, demand, desire, entreat, implore, importune, invite, petition, pray for, require, requisition, seek, solicit, supplicate.

require *vb* **1** be missing, be short of, depend on, lack, need, want. **2** *require a response.* call for, coerce, command, compel, direct, force, insist, instruct, make, oblige, order, put pressure on. ▷ REQUEST. **required** ▷ REQUISITE.

requirement *n* condition, demand, essential, necessity, need, precondition, prerequisite, provision, proviso, qualification, *Lat* sine qua non, stipulation.

requisite *adj* compulsory, essential, imperative, indispensable, mandatory, necessary, needed, obligatory, prescribed, required, set, stipulated. *Opp* OPTIONAL.

requisition *n* application, authorization, demand, mandate, order, request, voucher. • *vb* **1** demand, order, *inf* put in for, request. **2** appropriate, commandeer, confiscate, expropriate, occupy, seize, take over, take possession of.

rescue *n* deliverance, emancipation, freeing, liberation, recovery, release, relief, salvage. • *vb* **1** deliver, emancipate, extricate, free, let go, liberate, loose, ransom, release, save, set free. **2** get back, recover, retrieve, salvage.

research *n* analysis, enquiry, examination, experimentation, exploration, fact-finding, inquiry, investigation, *inf* probe, scrutiny, searching, study. • *vb inf* check out, *inf* delve into, experiment, investigate, *inf* probe, search, study.

resemblance *n* affinity, closeness, coincidence, comparability, comparison, conformity, congruity, correspondence, equivalence, likeness, similarity, similitude.

resemble *vb* approximate to, bear resemblance to, be similar to, compare with, look like, mirror, sound like, *inf* take after.

resent *vb* begrudge, be resentful about, dislike, envy, feel bitter about, grudge, grumble at, object to, *inf* take exception to, *inf* take umbrage at.

resentful *adj* aggrieved, annoyed, begrudging, bitter, disgruntled, displeased, embittered, envious, grudging, hurt, indignant, irked, jaundiced, jealous, malicious, offended, *inf* peeved, *inf* put out, spiteful, unfriendly, ungenerous, upset, vexed, vindictive. ▷ ANGRY.

resentment *n* animosity, bitterness, discontent, envy, grudge, hatred, hurt, ill-will, indignation, irritation, jealousy, malevolence, malice, pique, rancour, spite, unfriendliness, vexation, vindictiveness. ▷ ANGER.

reservation *n* **1** condition, doubt, hedging, hesitation, misgiving, proviso, qualification, qualm, reluctance, reticence, scepticism, scruple. **2** *hotel reservation.* appointment, booking. **3** *a wildlife reservation.* ▷ RESERVE.

reserve *n* **1** cache, fund, hoard, *inf* nest-egg, reservoir, savings, stock, stockpile, store, supply. **2** *inf* backup, deputy, *plur* reinforcements, replacement, stand-by, *inf* stand-in, substitute, understudy. **3** *a wildlife reserve.* enclave, game park, preserve, protected area, reservation, safari-park, sanctuary. **4** aloofness, caution, modesty, quietness, reluctance, reticence, self-consciousness, self-effacement, shyness, *derog* stand-offishness, taciturnity, timidity. • *vb* **1** earmark, hoard, hold back, keep, keep back, preserve, put aside, retain, save, set aside, stockpile, store up. **2** *reserve seats. inf* bag, book, order, pay for. **reserved** ▷ RETICENT.

reside *vb* **reside in** dwell in, inhabit, live in, lodge in, occupy, settle in.

residence *n old use* abode, address, domicile, dwelling, dwelling-place, habitation, home, quarters, seat. ▷ HOUSE.

resident *adj* in residence, livingin, permanent, remaining, staying. • *n* citizen, denizen, dweller, householder, houseowner, inhabitant, *inf* local, native.

residual *adj* abiding, continuing, left over, outstanding, persisting, remaining, surviving, unconsumed, unused.

resign *vb* abandon, abdicate, *sl* chuck in, forsake, give up, leave, quit, relinquish, renounce, retire, stand down, step down, surrender, vacate. **resigned** ▷ PATIENT. **resign yourself to** ▷ ACCEPT.

resilient *adj* **1** bouncy, elastic, firm, plastic, pliable, rubbery, springy, supple. *Opp* BRITTLE. **2** *a resilient person.* adaptable, buoyant, irrepressible, strong, tough, unstoppable. *Opp* VULNERABLE.

resist *vb* avoid, be resistant to, check, confront, counteract, defy, face up to, hinder, *inf* hold out against, *inf* hold your ground against, impede, inhibit, keep at bay, oppose, prevent, rebuff, refuse, stand up to, withstand. ▷ FIGHT. *Opp* ASSIST, YIELD.

resistant *adj* defiant, hostile, intransigent, invulnerable, obstinate, opposed, refractory, stubborn, uncooperative, unresponsive, unyielding. **resistant to** against, impervious to, invulnerable to, opposed to, proof against, repellent of, unaffected by, unsusceptible to, unyielding to. *Opp* SUSCEPTIBLE.

resolute *adj* adamant, bold, committed, constant, courageous, decided, decisive, determined, dogged, firm, immovable, immutable, indefatigable, *derog* inflexible, *derog* obstinate, persevering, persistent, pertinacious, relentless, resolved, single-minded, staunch, steadfast, strong-minded, strong-willed, *derog* stubborn, tireless, unbending, undaunted, unflinching, unshakable, unswerving, untiring, unwavering. *Opp* IRRESOLUTE.

resolution *n* **1** boldness, commitment, constancy, determination, devotion, doggedness, firmness, *derog* obstinacy, perseverance, persistence, pertinacity, purposefulness, resolve, single-mindedness, staunchness, steadfastness, *derog* stubbornness, tenacity, will-power. ▷ COURAGE. **2** commitment, oath, pledge, promise, undertaking, vow. **3** *resolu-*

tion at a meeting. decision, motion, proposal, proposition, statement. **4** *resolution of a problem.* answer, denouement, disentangling, resolving, settlement, solution, sorting out.

resolve *n* ▷ RESOLUTION. ● *vb* **1** agree, conclude, decide formally, determine, elect, fix, make a decision, make up your mind, opt, pass a resolution, settle, undertake, vote. **2** *resolve a problem.* answer, clear up, disentangle, figure out, settle, solve, sort out, work out.

resonant *adj* booming, echoing, full, pulsating, resounding, reverberant, reverberating, rich, ringing, sonorous, thunderous, vibrant, vibrating.

resort *n* **1** alternative, course of action, expedient, option, recourse, refuge, remedy, reserve. **2** *a seaside resort.* holiday town, retreat, spa, *old use* wateringplace. ● *vb* **resort to 1** adopt, *inf* fall back on, have recourse to, make use of, turn to, use. **2** frequent, go to, *inf* hang out in, haunt, invade, patronize, visit.

resound *vb* boom, echo, pulsate, resonate, reverberate, ring, rumble, thunder, vibrate. **resounding** ▷ RESONANT.

resourceful *adj* clever, creative, enterprising, imaginative, ingenious, innovative, inspired, inventive, original, skilful, *inf* smart, talented. *Opp* SHIFTLESS.

resources *plur n* **1** assets, capital, funds, possessions, property, reserves, riches, wealth. ▷ MONEY. **2** *natural resources.* materials, raw materials.

respect *n* **1** admiration, appreciation, awe, consideration, courtesy, deference, esteem, homage, honour, liking, love, politeness, regard, reverence, tribute, veneration. **2** *perfect in every respect.* aspect, attribute, characteristic, detail, element, facet, feature, particular, point, property, quality, trait, way. ● *vb* admire, appreciate, be polite to, defer to, esteem, have high regard for, honour, look up to, pay homage to, revere, reverence, show respect to, think well of, value, venerate. *Opp* DESPISE.

respectable *adj* **1** decent, genteel, honest, honourable, law-abiding, refined, respected, unimpeachable, upright, worthy. **2** *respectable clothes.* chaste, clean, decorous, dignified, modest, presentable, proper, seemly. *Opp* DISREPUTABLE. **3** *a respectable sum.* ▷ CONSIDERABLE.

respectful *adj* admiring, civil, considerate, cordial, courteous, deferential, dutiful, gentlemanly, gracious, humble, ladylike, obliging, polite, proper, reverent, reverential, *derog* servile, subservient, thoughtful, well-mannered. *Opp* DISRESPECTFUL.

respective *adj* individual, own, particular, personal, relevant, separate, several, special, specific.

respite *n* break, *inf* breather, delay, hiatus, holiday, intermission, interruption, interval, *inf* let-up, lull, pause, recess, relaxation, relief, remission, rest, time off, time out, vacation.

resplendent *adj* brilliant, dazzling, glittering, shining, splendid. ▷ BRIGHT.

respond *vb* **respond to 1** acknowledge, answer, counter, give a response to, react to, reciprocate, reply to. **2** *respond to need.* ▷ SYMPATHIZE.

response *n* acknowledgement, answer, *inf* comeback, counter, counterblast, feedback, reaction, rejoinder, reply, retort, riposte.

responsible *adj* **1** at fault, culpable, guilty, liable, to blame. **2** *a responsible person.* accountable, answerable, concerned, conscientious, creditable, dependable, diligent, dutiful, ethical, honest, in charge, law-abiding, loyal, mature, moral, reliable, sensible, sober, steady, thinking, thoughtful, trustworthy, unselfish. *Opp* IRRESPONSIBLE. **3** *a responsible job.* burdensome, decision-making, executive, *inf* frontline, important, managerial, *inf* top. *Opp* MENIAL.

responsive *adj* alert, alive, aware, impressionable, interested, open, perceptive, receptive, sensitive, sharp, sympathetic, warm-hearted, wideawake, willing. *Opp* UNINTERESTED.

rest *n* **1** break, *inf* breather, breathing-space, comfort, ease, hiatus, idleness, inactivity, indolence, interlude, intermission, interval, leisure, *inf* let-up, *inf* lie-down, *inf* loafing, lull, nap, pause, quiet, recess, relaxation, relief, remission, repose, respite, siesta, tea-break, time off, vacation. ▷ SLEEP. **2** base, brace, bracket, holder, prop, stand, support, trestle, tripod. **3** ▷ REMAINDER. • *vb* **1** be still, doze, have a rest, idle, laze, lie back, lie down, lounge, nod off, *inf* put your feet up, recline, relax, snooze, *inf* take a nap, *inf* take it easy, unwind. ▷ SLEEP. **2** lean, place, position, prop, set, stand, support. **3** *It all rests on the weather.* depend, hang, hinge, rely, turn. **come to rest** ▷ HALT.

restaurant *n* eating-place. □ *bistro, brasserie, buffet, café, cafeteria, canteen, carvery, diner, dining-room, grill, refectory, snack-bar, steak-house.*

restful *adj* calm, calming, comfortable, leisurely, peaceful, quiet, relaxed, relaxing, reposeful, soothing, still, tranquil, undisturbed, unhurried, untroubled. *Opp* EXHAUSTING.

restless *adj* **1** agitated, anxious, edgy, excitable, fidgety, highly-strung, impatient, *inf* jittery, jumpy, nervous, *inf* on tenterhooks, restive, skittish, uneasy, worked up, worried. ▷ ACTIVE. **2** *a restless night.* disturbed, interrupted, sleepless, *inf* tossing and turning, troubled, uncomfortable, unsettled. *Opp* RESTFUL.

restore *vb* **1** bring back, give back, make restitution, put back, reinstate, replace, return. **2** *restore antiques.* clean, *inf* do up, fix, *inf* make good, mend, rebuild, recondition, reconstruct, refurbish, renew, renovate, repair, touch up. **3** *restore good relations.* re-establish, rehabilitate, reinstate, reintroduce, rekindle, revive. **4** *restore to health.* cure, nurse, rejuvenate, resuscitate, revitalize.

restrain *vb* **1** check, control, curb, govern, hold back, inhibit, keep back, keep under control, limit, regulate, rein in, repress, restrict, stifle, stop, strait-jacket, subdue, suppress. **2** arrest, bridle, confine, detain, fetter, handcuff, harness, imprison, incarcerate, jail, *inf* keep under lock and key, lock up, manacle, muzzle, pinion, tie up. **restrained** ▷ CALM, DISCREET.

restrict *vb* circumscribe, confine, control, cramp, delimit, enclose, impede, imprison, inhibit, keep within bounds, limit, regulate, shut. ▷ RESTRAIN. *Opp* FREE.

restriction *n* ban, check, constraint, control, curb, curfew, inhibition, limit, limitation, proviso, qualification, regulation, restraint, rule, stipulation.

result *n* **1** conclusion, consequence, effect, end-product, fruit, issue, outcome, repercussion, sequel, upshot. **2** *result of a trial.* decision, judgement, verdict. **3** *result of a sum.* answer, product, score, total. • *vb* arise, be produced, come about, develop, emanate, emerge, ensue, eventuate, follow, happen, issue, occur, proceed, spring, stem, take place, turn out. **result in** ▷ CAUSE.

resume *vb* begin again, carry on, continue, *inf* pick up the threads, proceed, recommence, reconvene, re-open, restart.

resumption *n* continuation, recommencement, re-opening, *inf* restart.

resurrect *vb* breathe new life into, bring back, raise (from the dead), reawaken, restore, resuscitate, revitalize, revive. ▷ RENEW.

retain *vb* **1** *inf* hang on to, hold, hold back, keep, keep control of, maintain, preserve, reserve, save. *Opp* LOSE. **2** *retain moisture.* absorb, soak up. **3** *retain facts.* keep in mind, learn, memorize, remember. *Opp* FORGET.

retaliate *vb* avenge yourself, be revenged, counter-attack, exact retribution, *inf* get even, *inf* get your own back, *inf* give tit for tat, hit back, pay back, repay, revenge yourself, seek retribution, *inf* settle a score, strike back, *inf* take an eye for an eye, take revenge, wreak vengeance.

retaliation *n* counter-attack, reprisal, retribution, revenge, vengeance.

retard *vb* check, handicap, hinder, hold back, hold up, impede, obstruct, postpone, put back, set back, slow down. ▷ DELAY. **retarded** ▷ BACK-WARD.

reticent *adj* aloof, *derog* antisocial, bashful, cautious, *derog* cold, cool, demure, diffident, discreet, distant, modest, quiet, remote, reserved, restrained, retiring, secretive, self-conscious, self-effacing, shy, silent, *derog* standoffish, taciturn, timid, uncommunicative, undemonstrative, unemotional, unforthcoming, unresponsive, unsociable, withdrawn. *Opp* DEMONSTRATIVE.

retinue *n* attendants, company, entourage, followers, *inf* hangerson, servants, suite, train.

retire *vb* **1** give up, leave, quit, resign. **2** *retire from society*. become reclusive, cloister yourself, go away, go into retreat, retreat from the world, sequester yourself, withdraw. **3** aestivate, go to bed, hibernate, *sl* hit the hay. ▷ SLEEP.

retort *n* answer, *inf* comeback, rebuttal, rejoinder, reply, response, retaliation, riposte. • *vb* answer, counter, react, rejoin, reply, respond, retaliate, return.

retract *vb* **1** draw in, pull back, pull in. **2** abandon, cancel, disclaim, disown, forswear, *inf* have second thoughts about, recant, renounce, repeal, repudiate, rescind, reverse, revoke, withdraw.

retreat *n* **1** departure, escape, evacuation, exit, flight, retirement, withdrawal. **2** *a secluded retreat*. asylum, den, haven, *inf* hideaway, hideout, hiding-place, refuge, resort, sanctuary, shelter. • *vb* **1** back away, back down, climb down, decamp, depart, evacuate, fall back, flee, give ground, go away, leave, move back, pull back, retire, *inf* run away, take flight, *inf* take to your heels, *inf* turn tail, withdraw. **2** *the floods retreated*. ebb, flow back, recede, shrink back. *Opp* ADVANCE.

retribution *n* compensation, *Lat* quid pro quo, recompense, redress, reprisal, retaliation, revenge, *old use* satisfaction, vengeance. *Opp* FORGIVENESS.

retrieve *vb* bring back, come back with, fetch back, find, get back, make up for, recapture, reclaim, recoup, recover, regain, repossess, rescue, restore, return, salvage, save, take back, trace, track down.

retrograde *adj* backward, negative, regressive, retreating, retrogressive, reverse.

retrospective *adj* backwardlooking, looking back, looking behind, nostalgic, with hindsight.

return *n* **1** advent, arrival, homecoming, reappearance, re-entry. **2** *return to normality*. re-establishment (of), regression, reversion. **3** *return of a problem* recrudescence, recurrence, re-emergence, repetition. **4** *return of stolen goods*. replacing, restitution, restoration, retrieval. **5** *return on an investment*. benefit, earnings, gain, income, interest, proceeds, profit, yield. • *vb* **1** backtrack, come back, do a U-turn, double back, go back, reassemble, reconvene, re-enter, regress, retrace your steps, revert, turn back. **2** put back, readdress, repatriate, replace, restore, send back. **3** *return money*. exchange, give back, refund, reimburse, repay. **4** *return a verdict*. *inf* come up with, deliver, give, proffer, report. **5** *The problem returned*. *inf* crop up again, happen again, reappear, recur, resurface.

reveal *vb* announce, bare, betray, bring to light, communicate, confess, declare, denude, dig up, disclose, display, divulge, exhibit, expose, *inf* give the game away, lay bare, leak, *inf* let on, *inf* let out, *inf* let slip, make known, open, proclaim, produce, publish, show, show up, *inf* spill the beans about, *inf* take the wraps off, tell, uncover, undress, unearth, unfold, unmask, unveil. *Opp* HIDE.

revel *n* carnival, festival, fête, *inf* jamboree, *inf* rave-up, *inf* spree. ▷ REVELRY. ● *vb* carouse, celebrate, *inf* have a spree, have fun, indulge in revelry, *inf* live it up, make merry, *inf* paint the town red. **revel in** ▷ ENJOY.

revelation *n* admission, announcement, communiqué, confession, declaration, disclosure, discovery, exposé, exposure, information, *inf* leak, news, proclamation, publication, revealing, unmasking, unveiling.

revelry *n* carousing, celebration, conviviality, debauchery, festivity, fun, gaiety, *inf* high jinks, jollification, jollity, *inf* junketing, *inf* living it up, merry-making, revelling, revels, roistering, *inf* spree. ▷ PARTY.

revenge *n* reprisal, retaliation, retribution, spitefulness, vengeance, vindictiveness. ● *vb* avenge, repay. **be revenged** ▷ RETALIATE.

revenue *n* gain, income, interest, money, proceeds, profits, receipts, returns, takings, yield.

reverberate *vb* boom, echo, pulsate, resonate, resound, ring, rumble, throb, thunder, vibrate.

revere *vb* admire, adore, adulate, beatify, esteem, feel reverence for, glorify, honour, idolize, pay homage to, praise, respect, reverence, value, venerate, worship. *Opp* DESPISE.

reverence *n* admiration, adoration, adulation, awe, deference, devotion, esteem, glorification, homage, honour, idolization, praise, respect, veneration, worship.

reverent *adj* adoring, awed, awestruck, deferential, devoted, devout, pious, prayerful, religious, respectful, reverential, solemn, worshipful. *Opp* IRREVERENT.

reverie *n inf* brown study, daydream, dream, fantasy, meditation.

reverse *adj* back, back-to-front, backward, contrary, converse, inverse, inverted, opposite, rear. ● *n* **1** antithesis, contrary, converse, opposite. **2** back, rear, underside, verso, wrong side. **3** defeat, difficulty, disaster, failure, misfortune, mishap, problem, reversal, setback, *inf* upset, vicissitude. ● *vb* **1** change, invert, overturn, transpose, turn round, turn upsidedown. **2** *reverse a car.* back, drive backwards, go into reverse. **3** *reverse a decision.* abandon, annul, cancel, countermand, invalidate, negate, nullify, overturn, quash, recant, repeal, rescind, retract, revoke, undo.

review *n* **1** examination, *inf* look back, *inf* post-mortem, reappraisal, reassessment, recapitulation, reconsideration, re-examination, report, retrospective, study, survey. **2** *book review.* appreciation, assessment, commentary, criticism, critique, evaluation, judgement, notice, *inf* write-up. ● *vb* **1** appraise, assess, consider, evaluate, examine, *inf* go over, inspect, reassess, recapitulate, reconsider, re-examine, scrutinize, study, survey, take stock of, *inf* weigh up. **2** *review a book.* criticize, write a review of.

revise *vb* **1** adapt, alter, change, correct, edit, emend, improve, modify, overhaul, *inf* polish up, reconsider, rectify, *inf* redo, *inf* rehash, rephrase, revamp, reword, rework, rewrite, update. **2** *revise for exams.* brush up, *inf* cram, learn, study, *inf* swot.

revival *n* advance, progress, quickening, reanimation, reawakening, rebirth, recovery, renaissance, renewal, restoration, resurgence, resurrection, resuscitation, return, revitalization, upsurge.

revive *vb* **1** awaken, come back to life, *inf* come round, *inf* come to, quicken, rally, reawaken, recover, resurrect, rouse, waken. *Opp* RELAPSE. **2** bring back to life, *inf* cheer up, freshen, invigorate, refresh, renew, restore, resuscitate, revitalize, strengthen. *Opp* WEARY.

revolt *n* civil war, coup, coup d'état, insurrection, mutiny, putsch, rebellion, reformation, revolution, rising, *inf* take-over, uprising. • *vb* **1** disobey, dissent, mutiny, rebel, riot, rise up. **2** appal, disgust, nauseate, offend, outrage, repel, sicken, upset. **revolting** ▷ OFFENSIVE.

revolution *n* **1** ▷ REVOLT. **2** circuit, cycle, gyration, orbit, rotation, spin, turn. **3** change, reorganization, reorientation, shift, transformation, *inf* turn-about, upheaval, *inf* upset, *inf* U-turn.

revolutionary *adj* **1** insurgent, mutinous, rebel, rebellious, seditious, subversive. **2** *revolutionary ideas.* avant-garde, challenging, creative, different, experimental, extremist, innovative, new, novel, progressive, radical, *inf* unheard-of, upsetting. *Opp* CONSERVATIVE. • *n* anarchist, extremist, freedom fighter, insurgent, mutineer, rebel, terrorist.

revolve *vb* circle, go round, gyrate, orbit, pirouette, pivot, reel, rotate, spin, swivel, turn, twirl, wheel, whirl.

revulsion *n* abhorrence, aversion, disgust, hatred, loathing, nausea, outrage, repugnance.

reward *n* award, bonus, bounty, compensation, decoration, favour, honour, medal, payment, prize, recompense, remuneration, requital, return, tribute. *Opp* PUNISHMENT. • *vb* compensate, decorate, give a reward to, honour, recompense, remunerate, repay. *Opp* PENALIZE, PUNISH. **rewarding** ▷ PROFITABLE, WORTHWHILE.

rhapsodize *vb* be expansive, effuse, enthuse, *inf* go into raptures.

rhetoric *n derog* bombast, eloquence, expressiveness, *inf* gift of the gab, grandiloquence, magniloquence, oratory, rhetorical language, *derog* speechifying.

rhetorical *adj* [*most synonyms derog*] artifical, bombastic, florid, *inf* flowery, fustian, grandiloquent, grandiose, highflown, insincere, oratorical, ornate, pretentious, verbose, wordy.

rhyme *n* doggerel, jingle, poem. ▷ VERSE.

rhythm *n* accent, beat, measure, metre, movement, pattern, pulse, stress, tempo, throb, time.

rhythmic *adj* beating, measured, metrical, predictable, pulsing, regular, repeated, steady, throbbing. *Opp* IRREGULAR.

ribald *adj* bawdy, coarse, disrespectful, earthy, naughty, racy, rude, scurrilous, *inf* smutty, vulgar. ▷ OBSCENE.

ribbon *n* band, braid, line, strip, stripe, tape, trimming. **in ribbons** ▷ RAGGED.

rich *adj* **1** affluent, *inf* flush, *inf* loaded, moneyed, opulent, plutocratic, prosperous, wealthy, *inf* well-heeled, well-off, well-to-do. *Opp* POOR. **2** *rich furnishings.* costly, elaborate, expensive, lavish, luxurious, precious, priceless, splendid, sumptuous, valuable. **3** *rich land.* fecund, fertile, fruitful, lush, productive. **4** *a rich harvest.* abundant, ample, bountiful, copious, plenteous, plentiful, profuse, prolific, teeming. **5** *rich colours.* deep, full, intense, strong, vibrant, vivid, warm. **6** *rich food.* cloying, creamy, fat, fattening, fatty, full-flavoured, heavy, highly-flavoured, luscious, sumptuous, sweet. **rich person** billionaire, capitalist, millionaire, plutocrat, tycoon.

riches *plur n* affluence, fortune, means, money, opulence, plenty, possessions, prosperity, resources, wealth.

rickety *adj* dilapidated, flimsy, frail, insecure, ramshackle, shaky, tottering, tumbledown, unsteady, wobbly. ▷ WEAK.

rid *vb* clear, deliver (from), free, purge, rescue, save. **get rid of** ▷ DESTROY, REMOVE.

riddle *n* **1** *inf* brain-teaser, conundrum, enigma, mystery, *inf* poser, problem, puzzle, question. **2** filter, screen, sieve. • *vb* **1** filter, screen, sieve, sift, strain. **2** *riddle with holes.*

honeycomb, *inf* pepper, perforate, pierce, puncture.

ride *n* ▷ JOURNEY. • *vb* **1** *ride a bike*. control, handle, manage, sit on, steer. **2** *ride on a bike*. be carried, freewheel, pedal. **3** *ride on a horse*. amble, canter, gallop, trot. ▷ TRAVEL.

ridge *n* arête, bank, crest, edge, embankment, escarpment. ▷ HILL.

ridicule *n* badinage, banter, burlesque, caricature, contumely, derision, invective, jeering, jibing, lampoon, laughter, mockery, parody, raillery, *inf* ribbing, sarcasm, satire, scorn, sneers, taunts, teasing. • *vb* be sarcastic, be satirical about, burlesque, caricature, chaff, deride, gibe at, guy, hold up to ridicule, jeer at, jibe at, joke about, lampoon, laugh at, make fun of, make jokes about, mimic, mock, parody, pillory, *inf* poke fun at, *inf* rib, satirize, scoff at, *inf* send up, sneer at, subject to ridicule, *inf* take the mickey, taunt, tease, travesty.

ridiculous *adj* absurd, amusing, comic, comical, *inf* crazy, *inf* daft, eccentric, farcical, foolish, grotesque, hilarious, illogical, irrational, laughable, ludicrous, mad, nonsensical, preposterous, senseless, silly, unbelievable, unreasonable, weird, *inf* zany. ▷ FUNNY, STUPID. *Opp* SENSIBLE.

rife *adj* abundant, common, endemic, prevalent, widespread.

rift *n* **1** breach, break, chink, cleft, crack, fracture, gap, gulf, opening, split. **2** *a rift between friends*. alienation, conflict, difference, disagreement, disruption, division, opposition, schism, separation.

rig *n* **1** ▷ RIGGING. **2** *oil rig*. platform. **3** [*inf*] *sporting rig*. apparatus, clothes, equipment, gear, kit, outfit, stuff, tackle. • *vb* **rig out** equip, fit out, kit out, outfit, provision, set up, supply.

rigging *n* rig, tackle. □ *halyards, ropes and pulleys, sails*.

right *adj* **1** decent, ethical, fair, good, honest, honourable, just, law-abiding, lawful, moral, principled, responsible, righteous, right-minded, upright, virtuous. **2** *right answers*. accurate, apposite, appropriate, apt, correct, exact, factual, faultless, fitting, genuine, perfect, precise, proper, sound, suitable, true, truthful, valid, veracious. **3** *the right way*. advantageous, beneficial, best, convenient, good, normal, preferable, preferred, recommended, sensible, usual. **4** *your right side*. right-hand, starboard [= *right facing bow of ship*]. **5** *right wing in politics*. conservative, fascist, reactionary, Tory. *Opp* LEFT, WRONG. • *n* **1** decency, equity, ethics, fairness, goodness, honesty, integrity, justice, morality, propriety, reason, truth, virtue. **2** *right to free speech*. entitlement, facility, freedom, liberty, prerogative, privilege. **3** *right to give orders*. authority, commission, franchise, licence, position, power, title. • *vb* **1** amend, correct, make amends for, put right, rectify, redress, remedy, repair, set right. **2** pick up, set upright, stand upright, straighten up.

righteous *adj* blameless, ethical, God-fearing, good, guiltless, *derog* holier-than-thou, honest, just, law-abiding, moral, pure, *derog* sanctimonious, upright, upstanding, virtuous. *Opp* SINFUL.

rightful *adj* authorized, *Lat* bona fide, correct, just, lawful, legal, legitimate, licensed, licit, proper, real, true, valid. *Opp* ILLEGAL.

rigid *adj* **1** adamantine, firm, hard, inelastic, inflexible, set, solid, steely, stiff, strong, unbending, wooden. **2** *rigid discipline*. harsh, intransigent, punctilious, stern, strict, uncompromising, unkind, unrelenting, unyielding. ▷ OBSTINATE, RIGOROUS. *Opp* FLEXIBLE.

rigorous *adj* **1** conscientious, demanding, exact, exacting, meticulous, painstaking, precise, punctilious, rigid, scrupulous, strict, stringent, structured, thorough, tough, uncompromising, undeviating, unsparing, unswerving. *Opp* LAX. **2** *rigorous climate*. extreme, hard, harsh, inclement, inhospitable, severe, unfriendly, unpleasant. ▷ COLD. *Opp* MILD.

rim *n* brim, brink, circumference, edge, lip, perimeter, periphery.

rind *n* crust, husk, outer layer, peel, skin.

ring *n* **1** annulus, band, bracelet, circle, circlet, collar, corona, eyelet, girdle, halo, hoop, loop, O, ringlet. **2** *boxing ring.* arena, enclosure, rink. **3** *drugs ring.* association, band, gang, mob, organization, syndicate. ▷ GROUP. **4** *the ring of a bell.* boom, buzz, chime, clang, clink, *inf* ding-a-ling, jangle, jingle, knell, peal, ping, resonance, reverberation, tinkle, tintinnabulation, tolling. **5** *give me a ring sometime. inf* bell, *inf* buzz, call, *inf* tinkle. • *vb* **1** bind, circle, embrace, encircle, enclose, encompass, gird, surround. **2** boom, buzz, chime, clang, clink, jangle, jingle, peal, ping, resonate, resound, reverberate, sound (the knell), tinkle, toll. **3** call, *inf* give a buzz, phone, ring up, telephone.

rinse *vb* bathe, clean, cleanse, drench, flush, sluice, swill, wash.

riot *n* affray, anarchy, brawl, chaos, commotion, demonstration, disorder, disturbance, fracas, fray, hubbub, imbroglio, insurrection, lawlessness, mass protest, mêlée, mutiny, pandemonium, *inf* punch-up, revolt, rioting, riotous behaviour, rising, row, *inf* rumpus, *inf* shindy, strife, tumult, turmoil, unrest, uproar, violence. • *vb* brawl, create a riot, *inf* go on the rampage, *inf* go wild, mutiny, rampage, rebel, revolt, rise up, run riot, *inf* take to the streets. ▷ FIGHT.

riotous *adj* anarchic, boisterous, chaotic, disorderly, lawless, mutinous, noisy, obstreperous, rampageous, rebellious, rowdy, tumultuous, uncivilized, uncontrollable, undisciplined, ungovernable, unrestrained, unruly, uproarious, violent, wild. *Opp* ORDERLY.

rip *vb* gash, lacerate, pull apart, rend, rupture, shred, slit, split, tear.

ripe *adj* mature, mellow, ready to use.

ripen *vb* age, become riper, come to maturity, develop, mature, mellow.

ripple *n* ▷ WAVE. • *vb* agitate, disturb, make waves, purl, ruffle, stir.

rise *n* **1** acclivity, ascent, bank, camber, climb, elevation, hill, hump, incline, ramp, ridge, slope. **2** *a rise in prices.* escalation, gain, increase, increment, jump, leap, upsurge, upswing, upturn, upward movement. • *vb* **1** arise, ascend, climb, fly up, go up, jump, leap, levitate, lift, lift off, mount, soar, spring, take off. **2** get to your feet, get up, stand up. **3** *prices rise each year.* escalate, grow, increase, spiral. **4** *cliffs rise above us.* loom, stand out, stick up, tower. **rise up** ▷ REBEL.

risk *n* **1** chance, likelihood, possibility. **2** danger, gamble, hazard, peril, speculation, uncertainty, venture. • *vb* **1** chance, dare, endanger, hazard, imperil, jeopardize. **2** *risk money.* gamble, speculate, venture.

risky *adj inf* chancy, *inf* dicey, hazardous, *inf* iffy, perilous, precarious, unsafe. ▷ DANGEROUS. *Opp* SAFE.

ritual *n* ceremonial, ceremony, custom, formality, liturgy, observance, practice, rite, routine, sacrament, service, set procedure, solemnity, tradition.

rival *n* adversary, antagonist, challenger, competitor, contender, contestant, enemy, opponent, opposition. • *vb* **1** challenge, compete with, contend with, contest, emulate, oppose, struggle with, undercut, vie with. *Opp* COOPERATE. **2** be as good as, compare with, equal, match, measure up to.

rivalry *n* antagonism, competition, competitiveness, conflict, contention, feuding, opposition, strife. *Opp* COOPERATION.

river *n* brook, rivulet, stream, watercourse, waterway. □ *channel, confluence, delta, estuary, lower reaches, mouth, source, tributary, upper reaches.*

road *n* roadway, route, way. □ *alley, arterial road, avenue, boulevard, bridle-path, bridle-way, bypass, byroad, byway, cart-track, causeway, clearway, crescent, cul-de-sac, drive, driveway, dual carriageway,* Amer *freeway, highway, lane, motorway, one-way street, path, pathway, ring road, service road, side-road, side-street, slip-road, street, thoroughfare, tow-path, track, trail, trunk road,* old use *turnpike.*

roam *vb* amble, drift, meander, prowl, ramble, range, rove, saunter, stray, stroll, *inf* traipse, travel, walk, wander.

roar *vb* bellow, cry out, growl, howl, shout, snarl, thunder, yell, yowl. ▷ SOUND.

rob *vb* burgle, *inf* con, defraud, hold up, loot, *inf* mug, *old use* mulct, pick pockets, pilfer from, pillage, plunder, ransack, rifle, steal from. ▷ STEAL.

robber *n* bandit, brigand, burglar, cat burglar, *inf* con-man, defrauder, embezzler, *old use* highwayman, housebreaker, looter, *inf* mugger, pickpocket, pirate, shoplifter, swindler, thief.

robbery *n* breaking and entering, burglary, *inf* con, confidence trick, embezzlement, fraud, hijacking, *inf* hold-up, larceny, looting, *inf* mugging, pilfering, pillage, plunder, sacking, *inf* scrumping, shoplifting, stealing, *inf* stick-up, theft, thieving.

robe *n* cloak, dress, frock, gown. □ *bathrobe, caftan, cassock, dressing-gown, habit, housecoat, kimono, peignoir, surplice, vestment.* ● *vb* ▷ DRESS.

robot *n* android, automated machine, automaton, bionic man, bionic woman, computerized machine, mechanical man.

robust *adj* **1** athletic, brawny, fit, *inf* hale and hearty, hardy, healthy, hearty, muscular, powerful, rugged, sound, strong, sturdy, tough, vigorous. **2** durable, serviceable, strongly-made, well-made. *Opp* WEAK.

rock *n* boulder, crag, ore, outcrop, scree, stone. □ *igneous, metamorphic, sedimentary.* □ *basalt, chalk, clay, flint, gneiss, granite, gravel, lava, limestone, marble, obsidian, pumice, quartz, sandstone, schist, shale, slate, tufa, tuff.* ● *vb* **1** lurch, move to and fro, pitch, reel, roll, shake, sway, swing, toss, totter, wobble. **2** ▷ SHOCK.

rocky *adj* **1** barren, inhospitable, pebbly, rough, rugged, stony. **2** ▷ UNSTEADY.

rod *n* bar, baton, cane, dowel, pole, rail, shaft, spoke, staff, stick, strut, wand.

rogue *n* blackguard, charlatan, cheat, *inf* con-man, fraud, *old use* knave, mischief-maker, *inf* quack, rapscallion, rascal, ruffian, scoundrel, swindler, trickster, villain, wastrel, wretch. ▷ CRIMINAL.

role *n* **1** character, impersonation, lines, part, portrayal. **2** *role in a business.* contribution, duty, function, job, position, post, task.

roll *n* **1** cylinder, drum, reel, scroll, spool, tube. **2** catalogue, directory, index, inventory, list, listing, record, register. ● *vb* **1** go round, gyrate, move round, revolve, rotate, run, somersault, spin, tumble, turn, twirl, whirl. **2** coil, curl, furl, make into a roll, twist, wind, wrap. **3** *roll the lawn.* flatten, level off, level out, smooth. **4** *ship rolled in the storm.* lumber, lurch, pitch, reel, rock, stagger, sway, toss, totter, wallow, welter. **rolling** ▷ WAVY. **roll in, roll up** ▷ ARRIVE.

romance *n* **1** idyll, love story, novel. ▷ WRITING. **2** adventure, colour, excitement, fascination, glamour, mystery. **3** affair, amour, attachment, intrigue, liaison, love affair, relationship.

romantic *adj* **1** colourful, dream-like, exotic, fabulous, fairy-tale, glamorous, idyllic, nostalgic, picturesque. **2** *romantic feelings.* affectionate, amorous, emotional, erotic, loving, passionate, *inf* sexy, *inf* soppy, tender. **3** *romantic fiction.* emotional, escapist, heart-warming, nostalgic, reassuring, sentimental, *derog* sloppy, tender, unrealistic. **4** *romantic ideals.*

chimerical, *inf* head in the clouds, idealistic, illusory, impractical, improbable, quixotic, starry-eyed, unworkable, Utopian, visionary. *Opp* REALISTIC.

room *n* **1** *inf* elbow-room, freedom, latitude, leeway, margin, scope, space, territory. **2** *a room in a house.* apartment, cell, *old use* chamber. □ *ante-room, attic, audience chamber, bathroom, bedroom, boudoir, cell, cellar, chapel, classroom, cloakroom, conservatory, corridor, dining-room, dormitory, drawing-room, dressing-room, gallery, guest-room, hall, kitchen, kitchenette, laboratory, landing, larder, laundry, lavatory, library, living-room, loft, lounge, music-room, nursery, office, pantry, parlour, passage, play-room, porch, salon, saloon, scullery, sick-room, sitting-room, spare room, stateroom, store-room, studio, study, toilet, utility room, waiting-room, ward, washroom, WC, workroom, workshop.*

roomy *adj* capacious, commodious, large, sizeable, spacious, voluminous. ▷ BIG. *Opp* SMALL.

root *n* **1** radicle, rhizome, rootlet, tap root, tuber. **2** *the root of a problem.* base, basis, bottom, cause, foundation, fount, origin, seat, source, starting-point. ● *vb* **root out** ▷ REMOVE.

rope *n* cable, cord, line, strand, string. □ *halyard, hawser, lanyard, lariat, lasso, tether.* ● *vb* bind, hitch, lash, moor, tether, tie. ▷ FASTEN.

rot *n* **1** corrosion, corruption, decay, decomposition, deterioration, disintegration, dry rot, mould, mouldiness, putrefaction, wet rot. **2** *What rot!* ▷ NONSENSE. ● *vb* become rotten, corrode, crumble, decay, decompose, degenerate, deteriorate, disintegrate, fester, go bad, *inf* go off, perish, putrefy, rust, spoil.

rota *n* list, roster, schedule, timetable.

rotary *adj* gyrating, revolving, rotating, rotatory, spinning, turning, twirling, twisting, whirling.

rotate *vb* **1** go round, gyrate, have a rotary movement, move round, pirouette, pivot, reel, revolve, roll, spin, swivel, turn, turn anticlockwise, turn clockwise, twiddle, twirl, twist, wheel, whirl. **2** *rotate duties.* alternate, pass round, share out, take in turn, take turns.

rotten *adj* **1** bad, corroded, crumbling, decayed, decaying, decomposed, disintegrating, foul, mouldering, mouldy, *inf* off, overripe, perished, putrid, rusty, smelly, tainted, unfit for consumption, unsound. *Opp* SOUND. **2** ▷ IMMORAL.

rough *adj* **1** broken, bumpy, coarse, craggy, irregular, jagged, knobbly, lumpy, pitted, rocky, rugged, rutted, stony, uneven. **2** *rough skin.* bristly, callused, chapped, coarse, hairy, harsh, leathery, ragged, scratchy, shaggy, unshaven, wrinkled. **3** *a rough sea.* agitated, choppy, stormy, tempestuous, turbulent, violent, wild. **4** *a rough voice.* cacophonous, discordant, grating, gruff, harsh, hoarse, husky, rasping, raucous, strident, unmusical, unpleasant. *Opp* SMOOTH. **5** *rough manners, a rough fellow.* badly-behaved, bluff, blunt, brusque, churlish, ill-bred, impolite, loutish, rowdy, rude, surly, *inf* ugly, uncivil, uncivilized, undisciplined, unfriendly. **6** *rough treatment.* brutal, cruel, painful, ruffianly, thuggish, violent. **7** *rough work.* amateurish, careless, clumsy, crude, hasty, imperfect, inept, *inf* rough and ready, unfinished, unpolished, unskilful. **8** *a rough estimate.* approximate, general, hasty, imprecise, inexact, sketchy, vague. *Opp* EXACT, GENTLE, SMOOTH.

roughly *adv* about, approximately, around, close to, nearly.

round *adj* **1** [*two-dimensional*] annular, circular, curved, discshaped, hoop-shaped, orbicular, ring-shaped. **2** [*three-dimensional*] ball-shaped, bulbous, cylindrical, globelike, globoid, globular, orb-shaped, spherical, spheroid. **3** *a round figure.* ample, full, plump, rotund, rounded, well-padded. ▷ FAT. ● *n* bout, contest, game, heat, stage. ● *vb* skirt, travel round, turn. **round off** ▷ COMPLETE. **round on** ▷ ATTACK. **round the bend** ▷ MAD. **round the clock** ▷ CONTINUOUS. **round up** ▷ ASSEMBLE.

roundabout *adj* circuitous, circular, devious, indirect, long, meandering, oblique, rambling, tortuous, twisting, winding. *Opp* DIRECT. • *n* **1** carousel, merry-go-round, *old use* whirligig. **2** traffic island.

round-shouldered *adj* hunchbacked, humpbacked, stooping.

rouse *vb* **1** arise, arouse, awaken, call, get up, wake up. **2** *rouse to a frenzy*. agitate, animate, electrify, excite, galvanize, goad, incite, inflame, provoke, spur on, stimulate, stir up, *inf* wind up, work up.

rout *vb* conquer, crush, overpower, overwhelm, put to flight, *inf* send packing. ▷ DEFEAT.

route *n* course, direction, itinerary, journey, path, road, way.

routine *adj* accustomed, commonplace, customary, everyday, familiar, habitual, normal, ordinary, perfunctory, planned, run-of-the-mill, scheduled, uneventful, wellrehearsed. • *n* **1** course of action, custom, *inf* drill, habit, method, pattern, plan, practice, procedure, schedule, system, way. **2** *comedy routine*. act, number, performance, programme, set piece.

row *n* **1** [rhyme with *crow*] chain, column, cordon, file, line, queue, rank, sequence, series, string, tier. **2** [rhyme with *cow*] ado, commotion, fuss, hubbub, hullabaloo, *inf* racket, rumpus, tumult, uproar. ▷ NOISE. **3** altercation, argument, controversy, disagreement, dispute, fight, fracas, *inf* ructions, *inf* slanging match, squabble. ▷ QUARREL. • *vb* **1** [rhyme with *crow*] *row a boat*. move, propel, scull. **2** [rhyme with *cow*] ▷ QUARREL.

rowdy *adj* badly-behaved, boisterous, disorderly, ill-disciplined, irrepressible, lawless, obstreperous, riotous, rough, turbulent, undisciplined, unruly, violent, wild. ▷ NOISY. *Opp* QUIET.

royal *adj* imperial, kingly, majestic, princely, queenly, regal, stately. • *n* [*inf*] member of royal family. □ *consort, Her/His Majesty, Her/His Royal Highness, king, monarch, prince, princess, queen, queen mother, regent, sovereign*. ▷ NOBLE.

rub *vb* **1** caress, knead, massage, smooth, stroke. **2** abrade, chafe, graze, scrape, wear away. **3** *rub clean*. buff, burnish, polish, scour, scrub, shine, wipe. **rub it in** ▷ EMPHASIZE. **rub out** ▷ ERASE. **rub up the wrong way** ▷ ANNOY.

rubbish *n* **1** debris, detritus, dregs, dross, filth, flotsam and jetsam, garbage, junk, leavings, *inf* left-overs, litter, lumber, muck, *inf* odds and ends, offal, offcuts, refuse, rejects, rubble, scrap, slops, sweepings, trash, waste. **2** ▷ NONSENSE.

rubble *n* broken bricks, debris, fragments, remains, ruins, wreckage.

ruddy *adj* flushed, fresh, glowing, healthy, red, sunburnt.

rude *adj* **1** abrupt, abusive, badmannered, bad-tempered, blasphemous, blunt, boorish, brusque, cheeky, churlish, coarse, common, condescending, contemptuous, discourteous, disparaging, disrespectful, foul, graceless, gross, ignorant, ill-bred, ill-mannered, impertinent, impolite, improper, impudent, in bad taste, inconsiderate, indecent, insolent, insulting, loutish, mocking, naughty, oafish, offensive, offhand, patronizing, peremptory, personal (*remarks*), saucy, scurrilous, shameless, tactless, unchivalrous, uncivil, uncomplimentary, uncouth, ungracious, *old use* unmannerly, unprintable, vulgar. ▷ OBSCENE. *Opp* POLITE. **2** *rude workmanship*. awkward, basic, bumbling, clumsy, crude, inartistic, primitive, rough, rough-hewn, simple, unpolished, unskilful, unsophisticated, unsubtle. *Opp* SOPHISTICATED. **be rude to** ▷ INSULT.

rudeness *n* abuse, *inf* backchat, bad manners, boorishness, *inf* cheek, churlishness, condescension, contempt, discourtesy, disrespect, ill-breeding, impertinence, impudence, incivility, insolence, insults, oafishness, tactlessness, uncouthness, vulgarity.

rudiments *plur n* basic principles, basics, elements, essentials, first principles, foundations, fundamentals.

rudimentary *adj* basic, crude, elementary, embryonic, immature, initial, introductory, preliminary, primitive, provisional, undeveloped. *Opp* ADVANCED.

ruffian *n inf* brute, bully, desperado, gangster, hoodlum, hooligan, lout, mugger, rogue, scoundrel, thug, *inf* tough, villain, *inf* yob.

ruffle *vb* **1** agitate, disturb, ripple, stir. **2** *ruffle your hair.* derange, disarrange, dishevel, disorder, *inf* mess up, rumple, tangle, tousle. **3** *ruffle your composure.* annoy, confuse, disconcert, disquiet, fluster, irritate, *inf* nettle, *inf* rattle, *inf* throw, unnerve, unsettle, upset, vex, worry. *Opp* SMOOTH.

rug *n* blanket, coverlet, mat, matting.

rugged *adj* **1** bumpy, craggy, irregular, jagged, pitted, rocky, rough, stony, uneven. **2** *rugged conditions.* arduous, difficult, hard, harsh, onerous, rough, severe, tough. **3** *rugged good looks.* burly, hardy, husky, muscular, robust, rough, strong, sturdy, ungraceful, unpolished, weather-beaten.

ruin *n* bankruptcy, breakdown, collapse, *inf* crash, destruction, downfall, end, failure, fall, ruination, undoing, wreck. • *vb* damage, demolish, destroy, devastate, flatten, overthrow, shatter, spoil, wreck. **ruins** debris, havoc, remains, rubble, wreckage.

ruined *adj* crumbling, derelict, dilapidated, fallen down, in ruins, ramshackle, ruinous, tumbledown, uninhabitable, unsafe, wrecked.

ruinous *adj* **1** apocalyptic, calamitous, cataclysmic, catastrophic, crushing, destructive, devastating, dire, disastrous, fatal, harmful, injurious, pernicious, shattering. **2** ▷ RUINED.

rule *n* **1** axiom, code, decree, *plur* guidelines, law, ordinance, practice, precept, principle, regulation, ruling, statute. **2** administration, ascendancy, authority, command, control, domination, dominion, empire, government, influence, jurisdiction, management, mastery, oversight, power, regime, reign, sovereignty, supervision, supremacy, sway. **3** *as a general rule.* convention, custom, norm, routine, standard. • *vb* **1** administer, be the ruler of, command, control, direct, dominate, govern, guide, hold sway, lead, manage, predominate, reign, run, superintend. **2** adjudicate, decide, decree, deem, determine, find, judge, pronounce, resolve. **rule out** ▷ EXCLUDE.

ruler *n* administrator, *inf* Big Brother, law-maker, leader, manager. □ *autocrat, Caesar, demagogue, despot, dictator, doge, emir, emperor, empress, governor, kaiser, king, lord, monarch, potentate, president, prince, princess, queen, rajah, regent, satrap, sovereign, sultan, suzerain, triumvirate* [= three ruling jointly], *tyrant, tsar, viceroy.* ▷ CHIEF.

rumour *n* chat, *inf* chit-chat, gossip, hearsay, *inf* low-down, news, prattle, report, scandal, *inf* tittletattle, whisper.

run *n* **1** canter, dash, gallop, jog, marathon, race, sprint, trot. **2** *a run in the car.* drive, excursion, jaunt, journey, joyride, ride, *inf* spin, trip. **3** *run of bad luck.* chain, sequence, series, stretch. **4** *chicken run.* compound, coop, enclosure, pen. • *vb* **1** bolt, canter, career, dash, gallop, hare, hurry, jog, race, rush, scamper, scoot, scurry, scuttle, speed, sprint, tear, trot. **2** *buses run hourly.* go, operate, ply, provide a service, travel. **3** *car runs well.* behave, function, perform, work. **4** *water runs downhill.* cascade, dribble, flow, gush, leak, pour, spill, stream, trickle. **5** *Who runs the country?* administer, conduct, control, direct, govern, look after, maintain, manage, rule, supervise. **run across** ▷ MEET. **run after** ▷ PURSUE. **run away** ▷ ESCAPE. **run into** ▷ MEET.

runner *n* **1** athlete, competitor, entrant, hurdler, jogger, participant, sprinter. **2** courier, dispatch-rider, errand-boy, errand-girl, messenger. **3** *plant sends out runners*. offshoot, shoot, sprout, sucker, tendril.

runny *adj* fluid, free-flowing, liquid, running, thin, watery. *Opp* SOLID, VISCOUS.

rupture *n* **1** breach, break, burst, cleavage, fracture, puncture, rift, split. **2** *rupture between friends*. break-up, disunity, schism, separation. **3** [*medical*] hernia. • *vb* break, burst, fracture, part, separate, split.

rural *adj* agrarian, agricultural, Arcadian, bucolic, countrified, pastoral, rustic, sylvan. *Opp* URBAN.

rush *n* **1** bustle, dash, haste, hurry, panic, pressure, race, scramble, speed, turmoil, urgency. **2** *rush of water*. cataract, flood, gush, spate, surge. **3** *rush of people*. charge, onslaught, stampede. • *vb* bolt, burst, bustle, canter, career, charge, dash, fly, gallop, *inf* get a move on, hare, hasten, hurry, jog, make haste, move fast, race, run, scamper, *inf* scoot, scramble, scurry, scuttle, shoot, speed, sprint, stampede, *inf* step on it, *inf* tear, trot, *inf* zoom.

rust *vb* become rusty, corrode, crumble away, oxidize, rot.

rustic *adj* **1** ▷ RURAL. **2** *rustic simplicity*. artless, clumsy, crude, naïve, *derog* oafish, plain, rough, simple, uncomplicated, uncultured, unpolished, unsophisticated.

rusty *adj* **1** corroded, oxidized, rotten, tarnished. **2** [*inf*] *My French is rusty*. dated, forgotten, out of practice, unused.

rut *n* **1** channel, furrow, groove, indentation, pothole, track, trough, wheel-mark. **2** *in a rut*. dead end, habit, pattern, routine, treadmill.

ruthless *adj* bloodthirsty, brutal, callous, cruel, dangerous, ferocious, fierce, hard, heartless, inexorable, inhuman, merciless, pitiless, relentless, sadistic, unfeeling, unrelenting, unsympathetic, vicious, violent. *Opp* MERCIFUL.

S

sabotage *n* disruption, vandalism, wilful damage, wrecking. • *vb* cripple, damage, destroy, disable, disrupt, incapacitate, put out of action, *inf* throw a spanner in the works (of), vandalize, wreck.

sack *n* **1** bag, pouch. **2** *inf* the boot, *inf* the chop, dismissal, firing, redundancy, *inf* your cards. • *vb* **1** *inf* axe, discharge, dismiss, *inf* fire, give someone notice, *inf* give someone the boot, *inf* give someone the chop, *inf* give someone the sack, lay off, make redundant. **2** ▷ DESTROY, PLUNDER. **get the sack** be dismissed, be sacked, *inf* get your cards, get your marching orders, lose your job.

sacred *adj* blessed, blest, consecrated, dedicated, divine, godly, hallowed, holy, religious, revered, sacrosanct, sanctified, venerable, venerated. *Opp* SECULAR.

sacrifice *n* immolation, oblation, offering, propitiation, votive offering. • *vb* **1** immolate, kill, offer up, slaughter, yield up. **2** abandon, forfeit, forgo, give up, let go, lose, relinquish, renounce, surrender.

sacrilege *n* blasphemy, desecration, disrespect, heresy, impiety, irreverence, profanation.

sacrilegious *adj* atheistic, blasphemous, disrespectful, heretical, impious, irreligious, irreverent, profane, ungodly. ▷ WICKED. *Opp* REVERENT.

sacrosanct *adj* inviolable, inviolate, protected, respected, secure, untouchable. ▷ SACRED.

sad *adj* **1** abject, *inf* blue, broken-hearted, careworn, cheerless, crestfallen, dejected, depressed, desolate, despairing, desperate, despondent, disappointed, disconsolate, discontented, discouraged, disgruntled, disheartened, disillusioned, dismal, dispirited, dissatisfied, distressed, doleful, dolorous, *inf* down, downcast, downhearted, dreary, forlorn, friendless, funereal, gloomy, glum, grave, grief-stricken, grieving, grim, guilty, heartbroken, *inf* heavy, heavy-hearted, homesick, hopeless, in low spirits, *inf* in the doldrums, joyless, lachrymose, lonely, *inf* long-faced, *inf* low, lugubrious, melancholy, miserable, moody, moping, morose, mournful, pathetic, penitent, pessimistic, piteous, pitiable, pitiful, plaintive, poignant, regretful, rueful, saddened, serious, sober, sombre, sorrowful, sorry, tearful, troubled, unhappy, unsatisfied, upset, wistful, woebegone, woeful, wretched. **2** *sad news.* calamitous, deplorable, depressing, disastrous, discouraging, dispiriting, distressing, grievous, heartbreaking, heart-rending, lamentable, morbid, moving, painful, regrettable, *inf* tear-jerking, touching, tragic, unfortunate, unsatisfactory, unwelcome, upsetting. **3** *a sad state of disrepair.* ▷ UNSATISFACTORY. *Opp* HAPPY.

sadden *vb* aggrieve, *inf* break someone's heart, deject, depress, disappoint, discourage, dishearten, dismay, dispirit, distress, grieve, make sad, upset. *Opp* CHEER.

sadistic *adj* barbarous, beastly, brutal, inhuman, monstrous, perverted, pitiless, ruthless, vicious. ▷ CRUEL.

sadness *n* bleakness, care, dejection, depression, desolation, despair, despondency, disappointment, disillusionment, dissatisfaction, distress, dolour, gloom, glumness, grief, heartbreak, heaviness, homesickness, hopelessness, joylessness, loneliness, melancholy, misery, moping, moroseness, mournfulness, pessimism, poignancy, regret, ruefulness, seriousness, soberness, sombreness, sorrow, tearfulness, trouble, unhappiness, wistfulness, woe. *Opp* HAPPINESS.

safe *adj* **1** defended, foolproof, guarded, immune, impregnable, invulnerable, protected, secured, shielded. ▷ SECURE. *Opp* VULNERABLE. **2** *inf* alive and well, *inf* all right, *inf* in one piece, intact, sound, undamaged, unharmed, unhurt, uninjured, unscathed, well, whole. **3** *safe drivers.* cautious, circumspect, dependable, reliable, trustworthy. **4** *safe pets.* docile, friendly, harmless, innocuous, tame. **5** *safe to drink.* decontaminated, drinkable, eatable, fit for human consumption, fresh, good, non-poisonous, non-toxic, pasteurized, potable, pure, purified, uncontaminated, unpolluted, wholesome. **6** *safe vehicle.* airworthy, roadworthy, seaworthy, tried and tested. *Opp* DANGEROUS. **make safe** ▷ SECURE. **safe keeping** care, charge, custody, guardianship, keeping, protection.

safeguard *vb* care for, defend, keep safe, look after, protect, shelter, shield.

safety *n* **1** cover, immunity, invulnerability, protection, refuge, sanctuary, security, shelter. **2** *safety of air travel.* dependability, harmlessness, reliability.

sag *vb* be limp, bend, dip, droop, fall, flop, hang down, sink, slump. ▷ DROP.

sail *n* **1** canvas. □ *foresail, gaffsail, jib, lateen sail, lugsail, mainsail, mizzen, spinnaker, spritsail, topsail.* **2** cruise, sea-passage, voyage. ▷ JOURNEY. • *vb* **1** captain, navigate, paddle, pilot, punt, row, skipper, steer. **2** cruise, go sailing, put to sea, set sail, steam. ▷ TRAVEL.

sailor *n* mariner, *old use* sea dog, seafarer, seaman. □ *able seaman, bargee, boatman, boatswain, bosun, captain, cox, coxswain,* plur *crew, deck-hand, helmsman, mate, midshipman, navigator, pilot, rating, rower, skipper, yachtsman, yachtswoman.*

saintly *adj* angelic, blessed, blest, chaste, godly, holy, innocent, moral, pious, pure, religious, righteous, seraphic, sinless, virginal, virtuous. ▷ GOOD. *Opp* SATANIC.

sake *n* account, advantage, behalf, benefit, gain, good, interest, welfare.

salary *n* compensation, earnings, emolument, income, pay, payment, remuneration, stipend, wages.

sale *n* marketing, selling, trade, traffic, transaction, vending. □ *auction, bazaar, closing-down sale, fair, jumble sale, market, rummage sale, spring sale.*

salesperson *n* assistant, auctioneer, representative, salesman, saleswoman, shop-boy, shop-girl, shopkeeper.

saliva *n inf* dribble, *inf* spit, spittle, sputum.

sallow *adj* anaemic, bloodless, colourless, etiolated, pale, pallid, pasty, unhealthy, wan, yellowish.

salt *adj* brackish, briny, saline, salted, salty, savoury. *Opp* FRESH.

salubrious *adj* health-giving, healthy, hygienic, invigorating, nice, pleasant, refreshing, sanitary, wholesome. *Opp* UNHEALTHY.

salute *n* acknowledgement, gesture, greeting, salutation, wave. • *vb* accost, acknowledge, address, greet, hail, honour, pay respects to, recognize. ▷ GESTURE.

salvage *n* **1** reclamation, recovery, rescue, retrieval, salvation, saving. **2** recyclable material, waste. • *vb* conserve, preserve, reclaim, recover, recycle, redeem, rescue, retrieve, reuse, save, use again.

salvation *n* deliverance, escape, help, preservation, redemption, rescue, saving, way out. *Opp* DAMNATION.

salve *n* balm, cream, demulcent, embrocation, emolient, liniment, lotion, ointment, unguent. • *vb* alleviate, appease, assuage, comfort, ease, mitigate, mollify, soothe.

same *adj* **1** actual, identical, selfsame. **2** *two women wearing the same jacket.* analogous, comparable, consistent, corresponding, duplicate, equal, equivalent, indistinguishable, interchangeable, matching, parallel, similar, synonymous [= *having same meaning*], twin, unaltered, unchanged, uniform, unvaried. *Opp* DIFFERENT.

sample *n* bit, demonstration, example, foretaste, free sample, illustration, indication, instance, model, pattern, representative piece, selection, snippet, specimen, taste, trailer (*of film*), trial offer. • *vb* experience, inspect, take a sample of, taste, test, try.

sanatorium *n* clinic, convalescent home, hospital, nursing home, rest-home.

sanctify *vb* beatify, bless, canonize, consecrate, hallow, justify, purify.

sanctimonious *adj* canting, holier-than-thou, hypocritical, insincere, moralizing, pharisaical, *sl* pi, pietistic, pious, self-righteous, sententious, *inf* smarmy, smug, superior, unctuous.

sanction *n* agreement, approval, authorization, *inf* blessing, confirmation, consent, encouragement, endorsement, legalization, licence, permission, ratification, support, validation. • *vb* agree to, allow, approve, authorize, confirm, consent to, endorse, *inf* give your blessing to, give permission for, legalize, legitimize, licence, permit, ratify, support, validate.

sanctity *n* divinity, godliness, grace, holiness, piety, sacredness, saintliness.

sanctuary *n* **1** asylum, haven, protection, refuge, retreat, safety, shelter. **2** *wildlife sanctuary*. conservation area, park, preserve, reservation, reserve. **3** *a holy sanctuary*. chapel, church, holy of holies, holy place, sanctum, shrine, temple.

sands *plur n* beach, seaside, shore, *poet* strand.

sane *adj inf* all there, balanced, *Lat* compos mentis, *inf* in your right mind, level-headed, lucid, normal, of sound mind, rational, reasonable, sensible, sound, stable, well-balanced. *Opp* MAD.

sanguine *adj* buoyant, cheerful, confident, expectant, hopeful, *inf* looking on the bright side, optimistic, positive. *Opp* PESSIMISTIC.

sanitary *adj* aseptic, bacteria-free, clean, disinfected, germfree, healthy, hygienic, pure, salubrious, sterile, sterilized, uncontaminated, unpolluted, wholesome. *Opp* UNHEALTHY.

sanitation *n* drainage, drains, lavatories, sanitary arrangements, sewage disposal, sewers.

sap *n* fluid, life-blood, moisture, vigour, vitality, vital juices. • *vb* bleed, drain. ▷ EXHAUST.

sarcasm *n* acerbity, asperity, contumely, derision, irony, malice, mockery, ridicule, satire, scorn.

sarcastic *adj* acerbic, acidulous, biting, caustic, contemptuous, cutting, demeaning, derisive, disparaging, hurtful, ironic, ironical, mocking, satirical, scathing, sharp, sneering, spiteful, taunting, trenchant, venomous, vitriolic, withering, wounding. ▷ HUMOROUS.

sardonic *adj* bitter, black, cruel, cynical, grim, heartless, malicious, mordant, wry. ▷ HUMOROUS.

sash *n* band, belt, cummerbund, girdle, waistband.

satanic *adj* demonic, devilish, diabolical, fiendish, hellish, infernal, Mephistophelian. ▷ WICKED. *Opp* SAINTLY.

satchel *n* bag, pouch, school-bag, shoulder-bag.

satellite *n* **1** moon, planet. **2** *man-made satellite*. spacecraft, sputnik.

satire *n* burlesque, caricature, derision, invective, irony, lampoon, mockery, parody, ridicule, satirical comedy, scorn, *inf* send-up, *inf* spoof, *inf* take-off, travesty. ▷ WRITING.

satirical *adj* critical, derisive, disparaging, disrespectful, ironic, irreverent, mocking, scornful. ▷ HUMOROUS, SARCASTIC.

satirize *vb* be satirical about, burlesque, caricature, criticize, deride, hold up to ridicule, lampoon, laugh at, make fun of, mimic, mock, parody, pillory, *inf* send up, *inf* take off, travesty. ▷ RIDICULE.

satisfaction *n* comfort, content, contentment, delight, enjoyment, fulfilment, gratification, happiness, joy, pleasure, pride, self-satisfaction. *Opp* DISSATISFACTION.

satisfactory *adj* acceptable, adequate, *inf* all right, competent, fair, *inf* good enough, *inf* not bad, passable, pleasing, satisfying, sufficient, suitable, tolerable, *inf* up to scratch. *Opp* UNSATISFACTORY.

satisfy *vb* appease, assuage, comfort, comply with, content, fill, fulfil, gratify, make happy, meet, pacify, placate, please, put an end to, quench, sate, satiate, serve (*a need*), settle, slake (*thirst*), solve, supply. *Opp* FRUSTRATE. **satisfied** ▷ CONTENT.

saturate *vb* drench, fill, impregnate, permeate, soak, souse, steep, suffuse, waterlog, wet.

sauce *n* **1** condiment, gravy, ketchup, relish. **2** ▷ INSOLENCE.

saucepan *n* cauldron, pan, pot, skillet, stockpot.

savage *adj* **1** barbarian, barbaric, cannibal, heathen, pagan, primitive, uncivilized, uncultivated, uneducated. *Opp* CIVILIZED. **2** *savage beasts.* feral, fierce, undomesticated, untamed, wild. **3** *savage attack.* angry, atrocious, barbarous, beastly, bestial, blistering, bloodthirsty, bloody, brutal, callous, cold-blooded, cruel, demonic, diabolical, ferocious, fierce, heartless, inhuman, merciless, murderous, pitiless, ruthless, sadistic, unfeeling, vicious, violent. *Opp* TAME. ● *n* barbarian, beast, brute, cannibal, fiend, savage person. ● *vb* attack, bite, claw, lacerate, maul, mutilate.

save *vb* **1** be sparing with, collect, conserve, economize, hoard, hold back, hold on to, invest, keep, *inf* lay aside, *inf* put by, put in a safe place, reserve, retain, scrape together, set aside, *inf* stash away, store up, take care of, use wisely. *Opp* WASTE. **2** *save from captivity.* bail out, deliver, free, liberate, ransom, redeem, release, rescue, set free. **3** *save from destruction.* recover, retrieve, salvage. **4** *save from danger.* defend, deliver, guard, keep safe, preserve, protect, safeguard, screen, shelter, shield. **5** *saved me from looking a fool.* check, deter, preclude, prevent, spare, stop. *Opp* ABANDON.

saving *n* **1** economizing, frugality, parsimony, prudence, *inf* scrimping and scraping, thrift. **2** cut, discount, economy, reduction.

savings *n* capital, funds, investments, *inf* nest-egg, reserves, resources, riches, wealth.

saviour *n* **1** champion, defender, deliverer, *inf* friend in need, guardian, liberator, rescuer. **2** [*theological*] Christ, Our Lord, The Messiah, The Redeemer.

savour *n* flavour, piquancy, relish, smell, tang, taste, zest. ● *vb* appreciate, delight in, enjoy, relish, smell, taste.

savoury *adj* appetizing, delicious, flavoursome, piquant, salty. ▷ TASTY. *Opp* SWEET.

saw *n* **1** □ *chain-saw, hack-saw, jigsaw, ripsaw.* **2** [*old use*] *just an old saw.* ▷ SAYING. ● *vb* ▷ CUT.

say *vb* affirm, allege, announce, answer, articulate, assert, asseverate, aver, *old use* bruit abroad, *inf* come out with, comment, communicate, convey, declare, disclose, divulge, ejaculate, enunciate, exclaim, express, intimate, maintain, mention, mouth, phrase, pronounce, *inf* put it about, read out, recite, rejoin, remark, repeat, reply, report, respond, retort, reveal, signify, state, suggest, tell, utter. ▷ SPEAK, TALK, TELL.

saying *n* adage, aphorism, apophthegm, axiom, catch-phrase, catchword, cliché, dictum, epigram, expression, formula, maxim, motto, phrase, precept, proverb, quotation, remark, *old use* saw, slogan, statement, tag, truism, watchword.

scab *n* clot of blood, crust, sore.

scale *n* **1** dandruff, flake, plate, scurf. **2** *remove scale from teeth.* caking, coating, crust, deposit, encrustation, *inf* fur, plaque, tartar. **3** *the scale on a thermometer.* calibration, gradation, graduation. **4** *the social scale.* hierarchy, ladder, order, ranking, spectrum. **5** *small/large scale.* proportion, ratio. ▷ SIZE. **6** *musical scale.* sequence, series. □ *chromatic scale, diatonic scale, major scale, minor scale.* • *vb* ascend, clamber up, climb, go up, mount. **scales** balance, weighing-machine.

scamper *vb* dash, frisk, frolic, gambol, hasten, hurry, play, romp, run, rush, scuttle.

scan *vb* **1** check, examine, explore, eye, gaze at, investigate, look at, pore over, scrutinize, search, stare at, study, survey, view, watch. **2** *scan the papers.* flip through, glance at, read quickly, skim, thumb through.

scandal *n* **1** discredit, disgrace, dishonour, disrepute, embarrassment, ignominy, infamy, notoriety, obloquy, outrage, reproach, sensation, shame. **2** calumny, defamation, gossip, innuendo, libel, rumour, slander, slur, *inf* smear, *inf* tittle-tattle.

scandalize *vb* affront, appal, disgust, horrify, offend, outrage, shock, upset.

scandalous *adj* **1** disgraceful, disgusting, dishonourable, disreputable, ignominious, immodest, immoral, improper, indecent, indecorous, infamous, licentious, notorious, outrageous, shameful, shocking, sinful, sordid, unmentionable, unspeakable, wicked. **2** *a scandalous lie.* calumnious, defamatory, libellous, scurrilous, slanderous, untrue.

scansion *n* metre, prosody, rhythm. ▷ VERSE.

scanty *adj* **1** inadequate, insufficient, meagre, mean, *sl* measly, *inf* mingy, minimal, scant, scarce, *inf* skimpy, sparing, sparse, stingy. ▷ SMALL. *Opp* PLENTIFUL. **2** *scanty clothes.* indecent, revealing, *inf* see-through, thin.

scapegoat *n* dupe, *sl* fall guy, *inf* front, victim, whipping-boy.

scar *n* blemish, brand, burn, cicatrice, cicatrix, cut, disfigurement, injury, mark, scab, scratch. ▷ WOUND. • *vb* blemish, brand, burn, damage, deface, disfigure, injure, leave a scar on, mark, scratch, spoil.

scarce *adj inf* few and far between, *inf* hard to come by, *inf* hard to find, inadequate, infrequent, in short supply, insufficient, lacking, meagre, rare, scant, scanty, sparse, *inf* thin on the ground, uncommon, unusual. *Opp* PLENTIFUL.

scarcely *adv* barely, hardly, only just.

scarcity *n* dearth, famine, inadequacy, insufficiency, lack, need, paucity, poverty, rarity, shortage, want. *Opp* PLENTY.

scare *n* alarm, jolt, shock, start. ▷ FRIGHT. • *vb* **1** alarm, dismay, intimidate, make someone afraid, *inf* make someone jump, menace, panic, shake, shock, startle, terrorize, threaten, unnerve. ▷ FRIGHTEN. *Opp* REASSURE.

scarf *n* headscarf, muffler, shawl, stole.

scary *adj* [*inf*] creepy, eerie, hair-raising, horrible, scaring, unnerving. ▷ FRIGHTENING.

scathing *adj* biting, caustic, critical, humiliating, mordant, satirical, savage, scornful, tart, withering. *Opp* COMPLIMENTARY.

scatter *vb* **1** break up, disband, disintegrate, dispel, disperse, divide, send in all directions, separate. **2** *scatter seeds.* broadcast, disseminate, intersperse, shed, shower, sow, spread, sprinkle, strew, throw about. *Opp* GATHER.

scatterbrained *adj* absent-minded, careless, crazy, disorganized, forgetful, frivolous, hare-brained, inattentive, muddled, *inf* not with it, *inf* scatty, thoughtless, unreliable, unsystematic, vague. ▷ SILLY.

scavenge *vb* forage, rummage, scrounge, search.

scenario *n* design, framework, layout, outline, plan, scheme, storyline, structure, summary.

scene *n* **1** area, background, context, locale, locality, location, place, position, setting, site, situation, spot, whereabouts. **2** *a beautiful scene.* picture, sight, spectacle. ▷ SCENERY. **3** *scene from a film.* act, chapter, *inf* clip, episode, part, section, sequence. **4** *a nasty scene.* altercation, argument, *inf* carry-on, commotion, disturbance, furore, fuss, quarrel, row, tantrum, *inf* to-do, *inf* upset.

scenery *n* **1** landscape, outlook, panorama, prospect, scene, terrain, view, vista. **2** *stage scenery.* backdrop, flats, set, setting.

scenic *adj* attractive, beautiful, breathtaking, grand, impressive, lovely, panoramic, picturesque, pretty, spectacular.

scent *n* **1** aroma, bouquet, fragrance, nose, odour, perfume, redolence, smell. **2** after-shave, eau de cologne, lavender water, perfume. **3** *an animal's scent.* spoor, track, trail. ● *vb* ▷ SMELL. **scented** ▷ SMELLING.

sceptic *n* agnostic, cynic, doubter, *inf* doubting Thomas, disbeliever, scoffer, unbeliever. *Opp* BELIEVER.

sceptical *adj* agnostic, cynical, disbelieving, distrustful, doubting, dubious, incredulous, mistrustful, questioning, scoffing, suspicious, uncertain, unconvinced, unsure. *Opp* CONFIDENT.

scepticism *n* agnosticism, cynicism, disbelief, distrust, doubt, dubiety, incredulity, lack of confidence, mistrust, suspicion. *Opp* FAITH.

schedule *n* agenda, calendar, diary, itinerary, list, plan, programme, register, scheme, timetable. ● *vb* appoint, arrange, assign, book, earmark, fix a time, organize, outline, plan, programme, time, timetable.

scheme *n* **1** approach, blueprint, design, draft, idea, method, plan, procedure, programme, project, proposal, scenario, strategy, system. **2** *a dishonest scheme.* conspiracy, *inf* dodge, intrigue, machinations, manoeuvre, plot, *inf* ploy, *inf* racket, ruse, stratagem, subterfuge, tactic. **3** *colour scheme.* arrangement, design. ● *vb* collude, connive, conspire, *inf* cook something up, *inf* hatch a plot, intrigue, machinate, manoeuvre, plan, plot.

scholar *n* academic, *inf* egghead, expert, highbrow, intellectual, professor, pundit, savant. ▷ PUPIL.

scholarly *adj* **1** academic, bookish, *inf* brainy, *inf* deep, erudite, highbrow, intellectual, knowledgeable, learned, lettered, widely-read. **2** *scholarly treatise.* documented, researched, rigorous, scientific, well-argued, well-informed.

scholarship *n* **1** academic achievement, education, erudition, intellectual attainment, knowledge, learning, research, schooling, scientific rigour, wisdom. **2** *a scholarship to Oxford.* award, bursary, endowment, exhibition, fellowship, grant.

school *n* **1** educational institution. □ *academy, boarding-school, coeducational school, college, comprehensive (school), first school, grammar school, high school, infant school, junior school, kindergarten, nursery school, playgroup, preparatory school, primary school, public school, secondary school, seminary.* **2** *a school of whales.* shoal. ▷ GROUP. ● *vb* ▷ EDUCATE.

science *n* organized knowledge, systematic study. □ *acoustics, aeronautics, agricultural science, anatomy, anthropology, artifical intelligence, astronomy, astrophysics, behavioural science, biochemistry, biology, biophysics, botany, chemistry, climatology, computer science, cybernetics, dietetics, domestic science, dynamics, earth science, ecology, economics, electronics, engineering, entomology, environmental science, food science, genetics, geographical science, geology, geophysics, hydraulics, informa-*

tion technology, life science, linguistics, materials science, mathematics, mechanics, medical science, metallurgy, meteorology, microbiology, mineralogy, ornithology, pathology, pharmacology, physics, physiology, political science, psychology, robotics, sociology, space technology, telecommunications, thermodynamics, toxicology, veterinary science, zoology.

scientific *adj* analytical, methodical, meticulous, orderly, organized, precise, rational, regulated, rigorous, systematic.

scientist *n inf* boffin, researcher, scientific expert, technologist.

scintillating *adj* brilliant, clever, coruscating, dazzling, effervescent, flashing, glittering, lively, sparkling, vivacious, witty. *Opp* DULL.

scoff *vb* **1** belittle, be sarcastic, be scornful, deride, disparage, gibe, jeer, jibe, laugh, mock, *inf* poke fun, ridicule, sneer, taunt, tease. **2** ▷ EAT.

scold *vb* admonish, berate, blame, *inf* carpet, castigate, censure, chide, criticize, disapprove of, find fault with, *inf* jump down someone's throat, *inf* lecture, *inf* nag, rate, rebuke, reprehend, reprimand, reproach, reprove, *inf* slate, *inf* tell off, *inf* tick off, upbraid.

scoop *n* **1** bailer, ladle, shovel, spoon. **2** *news scoop*. exclusive, inside story, *inf* latest, revelation. • *vb* dig, excavate, gouge, hollow, scrape, shovel, spoon.

scope *n* **1** ambit, area, breadth, compass, competence, extent, field, limit, range, reach, span, sphere, terms of reference. **2** *scope for expansion*. capacity, chance, *inf* elbow-room, freedom, latitude, leeway, liberty, opportunity, outlet, room, space, spread.

scorch *vb* blacken, brand, burn, char, heat, roast, sear, singe.

score *n* **1** account, amount, count, marks, points, reckoning, result, sum, tally, total. **2** *score on furniture*. cut, groove, incision, line, mark, nick, scrape, scratch, slash. • *vb* **1** account for, achieve, add up, *inf* chalk up, earn, gain, *inf* knock up, make, tally, win. **2** *score a groove*. cut, engrave, gouge, incise, mark, scrape, scratch, slash. **3** *score music*. orchestrate, write out. **settle a score** ▷ RETALIATE.

scorn *n* contempt, contumely, derision, detestation, disdain, disgust, dislike, dismissal, disparagement, disrespect, jeering, mockery, rejection, ridicule, scoffing, sneering, taunt-ing. *Opp* ADMIRATION. • *vb* be scornful about, contemn, deride, despise, disapprove of, disdain, dislike, dismiss, disparage, hate, insult, jeer at, laugh at, look down on, make fun of, mock, reject, ridicule, *inf* scoff at, sneer at, spurn, taunt, *inf* turn up your nose at. *Opp* ADMIRE.

scornful *adj* condescending, contemptuous, contumelious, deprecative, derisive, disdainful, dismissive, disparaging, disrespectful, haughty, insulting, jeering, mocking, patronizing, sarcastic, satirical, scathing, scoffing, sneering, *inf* snide, *inf* snooty, supercilious, superior, taunting, withering. *Opp* RESPECTFUL.

scoundrel *n* blackguard, blighter, bounder, cad, good-for-nothing, heel, knave, miscreant, rascal, rogue, ruffian, scallywag, scamp, villain, wretch.

scour *vb* **1** abrade, buff up, burnish, clean, cleanse, polish, rub, scrape, scrub, shine, wash. **2** *scour the house*. comb, forage through, hunt through, rake through, ransack, rummage through, search, *inf* turn upside down.

scourge *n* **1** affliction, bane, curse, evil, misery, misfortune, plague, torment, woe. **2** ▷ WHIP. • *vb* beat, belt, flagellate, flog, horsewhip, lash, whip.

scout *n* lookout, spy. • *vb* explore, get information, hunt around, investigate, look about, reconnoitre, search, *inf* snoop, spy.

scowl *vb* frown, glower, grimace, *inf* look daggers, lower.

scraggy *adj* bony, emaciated, gaunt, lanky, lean, scrawny, skinny, starved, thin, underfed. *Opp* PLUMP.

scramble *n* commotion, confusion, *inf* free-for-all, haste, hurry, mêlée, race, rush, scrimmage, struggle. • *vb* **1** clamber, climb, crawl, grope, move awkwardly, scrabble. **2** *scramble for gold.* compete, contend, dash, fight, hasten, hurry, jostle, push, run, rush, scuffle, strive, struggle, tussle, vie. **3** *scramble a message.* confuse, jumble, mix up.

scrap *n* **1** atom, bit, crumb, fraction, fragment, grain, hint, iota, jot, mite, molecule, morsel, particle, piece, rag, scintilla, shard, shred, sliver, snippet, speck, trace. **2** *inf* junk, leavings, litter, odds and ends, offcuts, refuse, rejects, remains, remnants, residue, rubbish, salvage, waste. **3** *a friendly scrap.* argument, quarrel, scuffle, *inf* set-to, squabble, tiff, tussle, wrangle. ▷ FIGHT. • *vb* **1** abandon, cancel, discard, *inf* ditch, drop, give up, jettison, throw away, write off. **2** *scrap over trifles.* argue, bicker, flare up, quarrel, spar, squabble, tussle, wrangle. ▷ FIGHT.

scrape *n* **1** abrasion, graze, injury, laceration, scratch, scuff, wound. **2** *an awkward scrape.* difficulty, escapade, *inf* kettle of fish, piece of mischief, plight, prank, predicament, trouble. • *vb* **1** abrade, bark, bruise, damage, graze, injure, lacerate, scratch, scuff, skin, wound. **2** *scrape clean.* clean, file, rasp, rub, scour, scrub. **scrape together** ▷ COLLECT.

scrappy *adj* bitty, careless, disjointed, fragmentary, hurriedly done, imperfect, incomplete, inconclusive, sketchy, slipshod, unfinished, unpolished, unsatisfactory. *Opp* PERFECT.

scratch *n* abrasion, damage, dent, gash, gouge, graze, groove, indentation, injury, laceration, line, mark, score, scoring, scrape, scuff, wound. • *vb* abrade, claw at, cut, damage the surface of, dent, gash, gouge, graze, groove, incise, injure, lacerate, mark, rub, scarify, score, scrape, scuff, wound. **up to scratch** ▷ SATISFACTORY.

scrawl *vb* doodle, scribble, write hurriedly. ▷ WRITE.

scream *n & vb* bawl, caterwaul, cry, howl, roar, screech, shout, shriek, squeal, wail, yell, yowl.

screen *n* **1** blind, curtain, divider, partition. **2** camouflage, concealment, cover, disguise, protection, shelter, shield, smokescreen. **3** *sift through a screen.* filter, mesh, riddle, sieve, strainer. • *vb* **1** divide, partition off, subdivide, wall off. **2** camouflage, cloak, conceal, cover, disguise, guard, hide, mask, protect, safeguard, shade, shelter, shield, shroud, veil. **3** *screen employees for security. inf* check out, examine, investigate, process, sift out, vet.

screw *n* **1** bolt, screw-bolt. **2** rotation, spiral, turn, twist. • *vb* rotate, turn, twist. **screw down** ▷ FASTEN. **screw up** ▷ BUNGLE, TWIST.

scribble *vb* ▷ SCRAWL.

scribe *n* amanuensis, clerk, copyist, secretary, transcriber, writer.

script *n* **1** calligraphy, handwriting, penmanship. **2** *script of a play.* libretto, screenplay, text, words.

scripture *n* bible, holy writ, sacred writings, Word of God. □ *Bhagavad-Gita, inf the Good Book, the Gospel, Holy Bible, Koran, Upanishad.*

scrounge *vb* beg, cadge, importune.

scrub *vb* **1** brush, clean, rub, scour, wash. **2** ▷ CANCEL.

scruffy *adj* bedraggled, dirty, dishevelled, disordered, dowdy, frowsy, messy, ragged, scrappy, shabby, slatternly, slovenly, tatty, ungroomed, unkempt, untidy, worn out. *Opp* SMART.

scruple *n* compunction, conscience, doubt, hesitation, misgiving, qualm, reluctance, *inf* second thought. • *vb* [*usu neg*] be reluctant, have a conscience (about), have scruples (about), hesitate, hold back (from), *inf* think twice (about).

scrupulous *adj* **1** careful, cautious, conscientious, diligent, exacting, fastidious, *inf* finicky, meticulous, minute, neat, painstaking, precise, punctilious, rigid, rigorous, strict, systematic, thorough. **2** *scrupulous honesty*. ethical, fair-minded, honest, honourable, just, moral, principled, proper, upright, upstanding. *Opp* UNSCRUPULOUS.

scrutinize *vb* analyse, check, examine, *inf* go over with a toothcomb, inspect, investigate, look closely at, *inf* probe, sift, study.

scrutiny *n* analysis, examination, inspection, investigation, probing, search, study.

sculpture *n* three-dimensional art. □ *bas-relief, bronze, bust, carving, caryatid, cast, effigy, figure, figurine, maquette, marble, moulding, plaster cast, relief, statue, statuette*. • *vb* carve, cast, chisel, fashion, form, hew, model, mould, *inf* sculpt, shape.

scum *n* dirt, film, foam, froth, impurities, suds.

scurrilous *adj* abusive, calumnious, coarse, defamatory, derogatory, disparaging, foul, indecent, insulting, libellous, low, obscene, offensive, opprobrious, scabrous, shameful, slanderous, vile, vulgar.

sea *adj* aquatic, marine, maritime, nautical, naval, ocean-going, oceanic, salt-water, seafaring, seagoing. • *n* *inf* briny, *poet* deep, lake, *old use* main, ocean.

seal *n* **1** sea-lion, walrus. **2** *royal seal*. badge, coat of arms, crest, emblem, escutcheon, impression, imprint, mark, monogram, sign, stamp, symbol, token. • *vb* **1** close, fasten, lock, make airtight, make watertight, plug, secure, shut, stick down, stop up. **2** *seal an agreement*. affirm, authenticate, *inf* clinch, conclude, confirm, corroborate, decide, endorse, finalize, guarantee, ratify, settle, sign, validate, verify.

seam *n* **1** join, stitching. **2** *seam of coal*. bed, layer, lode, stratum, thickness, vein.

seamy *adj* disreputable, distasteful, nasty, repulsive, shameful, sordid, squalid, unattractive, unpleasant, unsavoury, unwholesome.

search *n* check, enquiry, examination, hunt, inspection, investigation, look, *inf* probe, pursuit, quest, scrutiny. • *vb* **1** cast about, explore, ferret about, hunt, investigate, *inf* leave no stone unturned, look, nose about, poke about, prospect, pry, seek. **2** *search suspects*. check, examine, *inf* frisk, inspect, scrutinize. **3** *search a house*. comb, go through, ransack, rifle, rummage through, scour. **searching** ▷ INQUISITIVE, THOROUGH.

seaside *n* beach, coast, coastal resort, sands, sea-coast, sea-shore, shore.

season *n* period, phase, time. • *vb* **1** add seasoning to, flavour, *inf* pep up, salt, spice. **2** *season wood*. age, harden, mature, ripen.

seasonable *adj* appropriate, apt, convenient, favourable, fitting, normal, opportune, propitious, suitable, timely, well-timed.

seasoning *n* additives, condiments, flavouring, relish, zest. □ *dressing, herbs, mustard, pepper, salt, sauce, spice, vinegar*.

seat *n* **1** place, sitting-place. □ *armchair, bench, carver, chair, chaise longue, couch, deck-chair, dining-chair, easy chair*, Fr *fauteuil, form, pew, pillion, pouffe, reclining chair, rocking-chair, saddle, settee, settle, sofa, squab, stall, stool, throne, window seat*. **2** *a country seat*. ▷ RESIDENCE. **3** ▷ BUTTOCKS. **seat yourself** ▷ SIT.

secateurs *plur n* clippers, cutters, pruning shears.

secluded *adj* cloistered, concealed, cut off, hidden, inaccessible, isolated, lonely, monastic, *inf* off the beaten track, private, remote, retired, screened, sequestered, sheltered, shut away, solitary, unfrequented, unvisited. *Opp* PUBLIC.

seclusion *n* concealment, hiding, isolation, loneliness, privacy, remoteness, retirement, separation, shelter, solitariness.

second *adj* added, additional, alternative, another, complementary, duplicate, extra, following, further, later, matching, next, other, repeated, subsequent, twin. • *n* **1** flash, instant, *inf* jiffy, moment, *inf* tick, *inf* twinkling, *inf* wink. **2** *second in a fight.* assistant, deputy, helper, *inf* number two, *inf* right-hand man, right-hand woman, second-in-command, *inf* stand-in, subordinate, supporter, understudy, vice-. • *vb* **1** aid, assist, back, encourage, give approval to, help, promote, side with, sponsor, support. **2** *second to another job.* move, reassign, relocate, shift, transfer.

secondary *adj* **1** alternative, ancillary, auxiliary, *inf* backup, extra, inessential, inferior, lesser, lower, minor, nonessential, reinforcing, reserve, second, second-rate, spare, subordinate, subsidiary, supplementary, supporting, supportive, unimportant. **2** *secondary sources.* copied, derivative, second-hand, unoriginal.

second-hand *adj* **1** *inf* hand-me-down, old, used, worn. *Opp* NEW. **2** *second-hand experience.* indirect, secondary, vicarious. *Opp* DIRECT.

second-rate *adj* commonplace, indifferent, inferior, low-grade, mediocre, middling, ordinary, poor, second-best, second-class, undistinguished, unexciting, uninspiring.

secret *adj* **1** clandestine, concealed, covert, disguised, hidden, *inf* hushed up, *inf* hush-hush, invisible, private, secluded, shrouded, stealthy, undercover, underground, unknown. ▷ SECRETIVE. **2** *secret papers.* classified, confidential, inaccessible, intimate, personal, restricted, sensitive, top-secret, undisclosed, unpublished. **3** *secret meanings.* arcane, cryptic, encoded, esoteric, incomprehensible, mysterious, occult, recondite. **4** *secret about his private life.* ▷ SECRETIVE. *Opp* OPEN, PUBLIC.

secretary *n* amanuensis, clerk, filing-clerk, personal assistant, scribe, shorthand-typist, stenographer, typist, word-processor operator.

secrete *vb* **1** cloak, conceal, cover up, disguise, enshroud, hide, mask, put away, put into hiding. **2** *secrete fluid.* discharge, emit, excrete, exude, give off, leak, ooze, produce, release.

secretion *n* discharge, emission, escape, excretion, leakage, release.

secretive *adj* close-lipped, enigmatic, furtive, mysterious, quiet, reserved, reticent, secret, shifty, silent, taciturn, tight-lipped, uncommunicative, unforthcoming, withdrawn. *Opp* COMMUNICATIVE.

sect *n* cult, denomination, faction, order, party, persuasion. ▷ GROUP.

sectarian *adj* bigoted, clannish, cliquish, cultic, denominational, dogmatic, exclusive, factional, fanatical, inflexible, narrow, narrow-minded, partial, partisan, prejudiced, rigid, schismatic.

section *n* bit, branch, chapter, compartment, component, department, division, element, fraction, fragment, group, instalment, leg (*of journey*), part, passage, piece, portion, quarter, sample, sector, segment, slice, stage, subdivision, subsection.

sector *n* area, district, division, part, quarter, region, zone. ▷ SECTION.

secular *adj* civil, earthly, lay, material, mundane, non-religious, temporal, terrestrial, worldly. *Opp* RELIGIOUS.

secure *adj* **1** cosy, defended, guarded, immune, impregnable, invulnerable, protected, safe, sheltered, shielded, snug, unharmed, unhurt, unscathed. **2** *secure doors.* bolted, burglarproof, closed, fast, fastened, fixed, foolproof, immovable, locked, shut, solid, tight, unyielding. **3** *secure faith.* certain, confident, firm, stable, steady, strong, sure, unquestioning. • *vb* **1** defend, guard, make safe, preserve, protect, shelter, shield. **2** anchor, attach, bolt, close, fix, lock, make fast, screw down, tie down. ▷ FASTEN. **3** *secure a loan.* acquire, be promised, come by, gain, get, obtain, procure, win.

sedate *adj* calm, collected, composed, controlled, conventional, cool, decorous, deliberate, dignified, equable, even-tempered, formal, grave, imperturbable, level-headed, peaceful, *derog* prim, proper, quiet, sensible, serene, serious, slow, sober, solemn, staid, strait-laced, tranquil, unruffled. *Opp* LIVELY. ● *vb* calm, put to sleep, tranquillize, treat with sedatives.

sedative *adj* anodyne, calming, lenitive, narcotic, relaxing, soothing, soporific, tranquillizing. ● *n* anodyne, barbiturate, calmative, depressant, narcotic, opiate, sleeping-pill, soporific, tranquillizer.

sedentary *adj* desk-bound, immobile, inactive, seated, sitting down. *Opp* ACTIVE.

sediment *n* deposit, dregs, grounds, lees, precipitate, remains, residue, *inf* sludge.

sedition *n* agitation, incitement, insurrection, mutiny, rabblerousing, revolt, treachery, treason. ▷ REBELLION.

seduce *vb* **1** allure, beguile, charm, corrupt, deceive, decoy, deprave, ensnare, entice, inveigle, lead astray, lure, mislead, tempt. **2** debauch, deflower, dishonour, rape, ravish, *old use* ruin, violate.

seduction *n* **1** allurement, attraction, charm, temptation. **2** rape, ravishing. ▷ SEX.

seductive *adj* alluring, appealing, attractive, bewitching, captivating, charming, coquettish, enchanting, enticing, flirtatious, inviting, irresistible, persuasive, provocative, *inf* sexy, tantalizing, tempting. *Opp* REPULSIVE.

see *vb* **1** behold, catch sight of, descry, discern, discover, distinguish, espy, glimpse, identify, look at, make out, mark, note, notice, observe, perceive, recognize, regard, sight, spot, spy, view, watch, witness. **2** *see what someone means.* appreciate, apprehend, comprehend, fathom, follow, *inf* get the hang of, grasp, know, perceive, realize, take in, understand. **3** *see problems ahead.* anticipate, conceive, envisage, foresee, foretell, imagine, picture, visualize. **4** *see what can be done.* consider, decide, discover, investigate, mull over, reflect on, think about, weigh up. **5** *see a play.* attend, be a spectator at, watch. **6** *seeing him tonight.* court, go out with, *inf* have a date with, meet, socialize with, visit, woo. **7** *see you home.* accompany, conduct, escort. **8** *saw fighting in the war.* endure, experience, go through, suffer, survive, undergo. **9** *Guess who I saw today!* encounter, face, meet, run into, talk to, visit. **see to** ▷ ORGANIZE.

seed *n* **1** egg, embryo, germ, ovule, ovum, semen, spawn, sperm, spore. **2** *seed in fruit.* pip, pit, stone. ● *vb* ▷ SOW.

seek *vb* aim at, apply for, ask for, aspire to, beg for, demand, desire, go after, hope for, hunt for, inquire after, look for, pursue, quest after, request, search for, solicit, strive after, try for, want, wish for.

seem *vb* appear, feel, give an impression of being, have an appearance of being, look, pretend to be, sound.

seep *vb* dribble, drip, exude, flow, leak, ooze, percolate, run, soak, trickle.

seer *n* clairvoyant, fortune-teller, oracle, prophet, prophetess, psychic, sibyl, soothsayer, vaticinator.

seethe *vb* be agitated, be angry, boil, bubble, erupt, foam, froth up, rise, simmer, stew, surge.

segment *n* bit, compartment, department, division, element, fraction, fragment, part, piece, portion, quarter, section, sector, slice, subdivision, subsection, wedge.

segregate *vb* compartmentalize, cut off, exclude, isolate, keep apart, put apart, separate, sequester, set apart, shut out.

segregation *n* **1** apartheid, discrimination. **2** isolation, quarantine, seclusion, separation.

seize *vb* **1** abduct, apprehend, arrest, capture, catch, clutch, *inf* collar, detain, grab, grasp, grip, hold, *inf* nab, pluck, possess, snatch, take, take into custody, take prisoner. **2** *seize a country*. annex, invade. **3** *seize property*. appropriate, commandeer, confiscate, hijack, impound, steal, take away. *Opp* RELEASE. **seize up** ▷ STICK.

seizure *n* **1** abduction, annexation, appropriation, arrest, capture, confiscation, hijacking, invasion, sequestration, theft, usurpation. **2** [*medical*] apoplexy, attack, convulsion, epileptic fit, fit, paroxysm, spasm, stroke.

seldom *adv* infrequently, occasionally, rarely.

select *adj* best, choice, chosen, élite, excellent, exceptional, exclusive, favoured, finest, first-class, first-rate, *inf* hand-picked, preferred, prime, privileged, rare, selected, special, top-quality. *Opp* ORDINARY. • *vb* appoint, cast (*actor for role*), choose, decide on, elect, nominate, opt for, pick, prefer, settle on, single out, vote for.

selection *n* **1** choice, option, pick, preference. **2** *a selection of goods*. assortment, range, variety. **3** *selection from the classics*. excerpts, extracts, passages, quotations.

selective *adj* careful, *inf* choosy, discerning, discriminating, particular, specialized. *Opp* COMPREHENSIVE, IMPERCEPTIVE.

self-confident *adj* assertive, assured, collected, cool, fearless, independent, outgoing, poised, positive, self-assured, self-possessed, self-reliant, sure of yourself. ▷ BOLD. *Opp* SELF-CONSCIOUS.

self-conscious *adj* awkward, bashful, blushing, coy, diffident, embarrassed, ill at ease, insecure, nervous, reserved, self-effacing, sheepish, shy, uncomfortable, unnatural. ▷ TIMID. *Opp* SELF-CONFIDENT.

self-contained *adj* **1** complete, independent, separate. **2** aloof, cold, reserved, self-reliant, uncommunicative, undemonstrative, unemotional.

self-control *n* calmness, composure, coolness, patience, resolve, restraint, self-command, self-denial, self-discipline, self-possession, self-restraint, will-power.

self-denial *n* abstemiousness, fasting, moderation, self-abnegation, self-sacrifice, temperance, unselfishness. *Opp* SELFINDULGENCE.

self-employed *adj* freelance, independent.

self-esteem *n* **1** ▷ SELF-RESPECT. **2** arrogance, *inf* big-headedness, conceit, egotism, overconfidence, self-admiration, self-importance, self-love, smugness, vanity.

self-explanatory *adj* apparent, axiomatic, blatant, clear, conspicuous, eye-catching, flagrant, glaring, inescapable, manifest, obvious, patent, plain, recognizable, self-evident, understandable, unmistakable, visible.

self-governing *adj* autonomous, free, independent, sovereign.

self-important *adj* arrogant, bombastic, conceited, grandiloquent, haughty, magisterial, ostentatious, pompous, pontifical, pretentious, self-centred, sententious, smug, *inf* snooty, *inf* stuckup, supercilious, vainglorious.

self-indulgence *n* extravagance, gluttony, greed, hedonism, pleasure, profligacy, self-gratification. ▷ SELFISHNESS. *Opp* SELF-DENIAL.

self-indulgent *adj* dissipated, epicurean, extravagant, gluttonous, gourmandizing, greedy, hedonistic, immoderate, intemperate, pleasure-loving, profligate, sybaritic. ▷ SELFISH. *Opp* ABSTEMIOUS.

selfish *adj* acquisitive, avaricious, covetous, demanding, egocentric, egotistic, grasping, greedy, inconsiderate, mean, mercenary, miserly, self-absorbed, self-centred, self-indulgent, self-interested, self-seeking, self-serving, *inf* stingy, thoughtless, uncaring, ungenerous, unhelpful, unsympathetic, worldly. *Opp* UNSELFISH.

selfishness *n* acquisitiveness, avarice, covetousness, egotism, greed, meanness, miserliness, niggardliness, possessiveness, self-indulgence, self-interest, selflove, self-regard, *inf* stinginess, thoughtlessness.

self-reliant *adj* autonomous, independent, self-contained, self-sufficient, self-supporting.

self-respect *n Fr* amour propre, dignity, honour, integrity, morale, pride, self-confidence, self-esteem.

self-righteous *adj* complacent, *inf* goody-goody, *inf* holier-than-thou, mealy-mouthed, pharisaical, pietistic, pious, pompous, priggish, proud, sanctimonious, self-important, self-satisfied, sleek, smug, superior, vain.

self-sufficient *adj* autonomous, independent, self-reliant, self-supporting.

self-willed *adj* determined, dogged, forceful, headstrong, inflexible, intractable, intransigent, *inf* mulish, obstinate, *inf* pigheaded, single-minded, *inf* stiffnecked, stubborn, uncontrollable, uncooperative, wilful.

sell *vb* **1** auction, barter, deal in, exchange, give in part-exchange, handle, hawk, *inf* keep, *inf* knock down, offer for sale, peddle, *inf* put under the hammer, retail, sell off, stock, tout, trade, *inf* trade in (*traded in my car*), traffic in, vend. **2** *sell hard.* advertise, market, merchandise, package, promote, *inf* push.

seller *n* dealer, merchant, stockist, supplier, trader, vendor. □ *agent, barrow-boy, broker,* old use *colporteur, costermonger,* old use *hawker, market-trader, pedlar,* inf *rep, representative, retailer, salesman, salesperson, saleswoman, shop assistant, shopkeeper, storekeeper, street trader, tradesman, traveller, wholesaler.* ▷ SHOP.

seminal *adj* basic, constructive, creative, fertile, formative, imaginative, important, influential, innovative, new, original, primary, productive.

send *vb* **1** address, consign, convey, deliver, direct, dispatch, fax, forward, mail, post, remit, ship, transmit. **2** *send a rocket to the moon.* fire, launch, project, propel, release, shoot. **send away** ▷ DISMISS. **send down** ▷ IMPRISON. **send for** ▷ SUMMON. **send-off** *n* ▷ GOODBYE. **send out** ▷ EMIT. **send round** ▷ CIRCULATE. **send up** ▷ PARODY.

senile *adj* declining, doddery, *inf* in your dotage, old, *derog* past it.

senior *adj* chief, elder, higher, high-ranking, major, older, principal, revered, superior, well-established. *Opp* JUNIOR.

sensation *n* **1** awareness, feeling, perception, sense. **2** *affair caused a sensation.* commotion, excitement, furore, outrage, scandal, stir, thrill.

sensational *adj* **1** blood-curdling, hair-raising, lurid, melodramatic, overwritten, scandal-mongering, shocking, startling, stimulating, violent. **2** [*inf*] *a sensational result.* amazing, astonishing, astounding, breathtaking, electrifying, exciting, extraordinary, *inf* fabulous, *inf* fantastic, *inf* great, incredible, marvellous, remarkable, spectacular, spine-tingling, stirring, superb, surprising, thrilling, unbelievable, unexpected, wonderful.

sense *n* **1** awareness, consciousness, faculty, feeling, sensation. □ *hearing, sight, smell, taste, touch.* **2** brains, cleverness, gumption, intellect, intelligence, intuition, judgement, logic, *inf* nous, perception, reason, reasoning, understanding, wisdom, wit. **3** *the sense of a message.* coherence, connotations, denotation, *inf* drift, gist, import, intelligibility, interpretation, meaning, message, point, purport, significance, signification, substance. ● *vb* be aware (of), detect, discern, divine, feel, guess, *inf* have a hunch, intuit, notice, perceive, *inf* pick up vibes, realize, respond to, suspect, understand. ▷ FEEL, HEAR, SEE, SMELL, TASTE. **make sense of** ▷ UNDERSTAND.

senseless *adj* **1** anaesthetized, asleep, comatose, insensate, insensible, knocked out, numb, *inf* out like a light, stunned, unconscious. **2** absurd, crazy, fatuous, meaningless, pointless, purposeless, silly. ▷ STUPID.

sensible *adj* **1** calm, common-sense, commonsensical, cool, discreet, discriminating, intelligent, judicious, level-headed, logical, prudent, rational, realistic, reasonable, reasoned, sage, sane, serious-minded, sound, straightforward, thoughtful, wise. *Opp* STUPID. **2** *sensible phenomena.* corporeal, existent, material, palpable, perceptible, physical, real, tangible, visible. **3** *sensible clothes.* comfortable, functional, *inf* no-nonsense, practical, useful. *Opp* FASHIONABLE, IMPRACTICAL. **sensible of** acquainted with, alert to, alive to, appreciative of, aware of, cognizant of, in touch with, mindful of, responsive to, *inf* wise to.

sensitive *adj* **1** considerate, perceptive, reactive, receptive, responsive, susceptible, sympathetic, tactful, thoughtful, understanding. **2** *a sensitive temperament.* emotional, hypersensitive, impressionable, temperamental, thin-skinned, touchy, volatile, vulnerable. **3** *sensitive skin.* delicate, fine, fragile, painful, soft, sore, tender. **4** *a sensitive topic.* confidential, controversial, delicate, *inf* tricky. *Opp* INSENSITIVE. **sensitive to** affected by, attuned to, aware of, considerate of, perceptive about, receptive to, responsive to, understanding about.

sensual *adj* animal, bodily, carnal, fleshly, physical, pleasure-loving, self-indulgent, voluptuous, worldly. ▷ SEXY. *Opp* ASCETIC.

sensuous *adj* beautiful, emotional, gratifying, lush, luxurious, rich, richly embellished.

sentence *n* **1** exclamation, question, statement, thought, utterance. **2** decision, judgement, pronouncement, punishment, ruling. ● *vb* condemn, pass judgement on, pronounce sentence on.

sentiment *n* **1** attitude, belief, idea, judgement, opinion, outlook, thought, view. **2** *sentiment of a poem.* emotion, feeling, sensibility.

sentimental *adj* **1** compassionate, emotional, nostalgic, romantic, soft-hearted, sympathetic, tearful, tender, warm-hearted, *inf* weepy. **2** [*derog*] gushing, *inf* gushy, indulgent, insincere, maudlin, mawkish, *inf* mushy, overdone, over-emotional, *inf* sloppy, *inf* soppy, *inf* sugary, tear-jerking, *inf* treacly, unrealistic, *sl* yucky. *Opp* CYNICAL.

sentimentality *n* bathos, emotionalism, insincerity, *inf* kitsch, mawkishness, nostalgia, *inf* slush.

sentry *n* guard, lookout, patrol, picket, sentinel, watch, watchman.

separable *adj* detachable, distinguishable, fissile, removable.

separate *adj* apart, autonomous, cloistered, cut off, detached, different, discrete, disjoined, distinct, divided, divorced, fenced off, free-standing, independent, individual, isolated, particular, peculiar, secluded, segregated, separated, shut off, solitary, unattached, unconnected, unique, unrelated, unshared, withdrawn. ● *vb* **1** break up, cut off, detach, disconnect, disengage, disentangle, disjoin, dismember, dissociate, divide, fence off, fragment, hive off, isolate, keep apart, part, pull apart, segregate, sever, split, sunder, take apart, uncouple, unfasten, unhook, unravel, unyoke. **2** *The paths separate here.* bifurcate, branch, diverge, fork. **3** *separated the grain from the chaff.* abstract, distinguish, filter out, remove, set apart, sift out, winnow. **4** *He separated from his partner.* become estranged, disband, divorce, part company, *inf* split up. *Opp* COMBINE, UNITE.

separation *n* **1** amputation, cutting off, detachment, disconnection, dismemberment, dissociation, division, fission, fragmentation, parting, rift, severance, splitting. *Opp* CONNECTION. **2** *separation of partners.* break, *inf* break-up, divorce, estrangement, rift, split. *Opp* UNION.

septic *adj* diseased, festering, infected, inflamed, poisoned, purulent, putrefying, putrid, suppurating.

sequel *n* consequence, continuation, development, *inf* follow-up, issue, outcome, result, upshot.

sequence *n* **1** arrangement, chain, concatenation, course, cycle, line, order, procession, programme, progression, range, row, run, series, set, string, succession, train. **2** *a sequence from a film. inf* clip, episode, excerpt, extract, scene, section.

serene *adj* **1** calm, idyllic, peaceful, placid, pleasing, quiet, restful, still, tranquil, unclouded, undisturbed, unperturbed, unruffled, untroubled. **2** *serene temperament.* collected, composed, contented, cool, easy-going, equable, even-tempered, imperturbable, pacific, peaceable, poised, self-possessed, *inf* unflappable. *Opp* BOISTEROUS, EXCITABLE.

series *n* **1** arrangement, chain, concatenation, course, cycle, line, order, procession, programme, progression, range, row, run, sequence, set, string, succession, train. **2** *TV series.* mini-series, serial, *inf* soap, soap-opera.

serious *adj* **1** dignified, grave, grim, humourless, long-faced, pensive, poker-faced, sedate, sober, solemn, sombre, staid, stern, straight-faced, thoughtful, unsmiling. *Opp* CHEERFUL. **2** *serious discussion.* deep, earnest, heavy, honest, important, intellectual, momentous, profound, significant, sincere, weighty. **3** *serious illness.* acute, appalling, awful, calamitous, critical, dangerous, dreadful, frightful, ghastly, grievous, hideous, horrible, *inf* life-and-death, nasty, severe, shocking, terrible, unfortunate, unpleasant, urgent, violent. *Opp* TRIVIAL. **4** *serious worker.* careful, committed, conscientious, diligent, hard-working.

sermon *n* address, discourse, homily, lecture, lesson, talk.

serpentine *adj* labyrinthine, meandering, roundabout, sinuous, snaking, tortuous, twisting, vermicular, winding. *Opp* STRAIGHT.

serrated *adj* cogged, crenellated, denticulate, indented, jagged, notched, saw-like, toothed, zigzag. *Opp* STRAIGHT.

servant *n* assistant, attendant, *derog* dogsbody, *inf* domestic, *derog* drudge, helper, *derog* hireling, *derog* menial, *old use* servitor, *inf* skivvy, slave, *old use* vassal. □ *au pair, barmaid, barman, batman,* inf *boots, butler, chamber-maid,* inf *char, charwoman, chauffeur, chef, cleaner,* old use *coachman, commissionaire, cook,* inf *daily, errand boy, factotum,* derog *flunkey, footman, governess, groom, home help, houseboy, housemaid, housekeeper, kitchenmaid,* derog *lackey, lady-in-waiting, maid, maidservant, major-domo, manservant, nanny, page, parlour-maid,* old use *postilion,* old use *retainer,* plur *retinue, scout, scullery maid,* old use *scullion,* old use *seneschal, slave, steward, stewardess, valet, waiter, waitress.*

serve *vb* **1** accommodate, aid, assist, attend, *inf* be at someone's beck and call, further, help, look after, minister to, wait upon, work for. **2** *serve in the forces.* be employed, do your duty, enlist, fight, sign on. **3** *serve goods.* deal out, distribute, dole out, give out, make available, provide, sell, supply. **4** *serve at table.* carve, *inf* dish up, officiate, wait. **5** *serve a sentence.* complete, endure, go through, pass, spend, survive.

service *n* **1** aid, assistance, benefit, favour, help, kindness, office. **2** *service of the community.* attendance (on), employment (by), ministering (to), work (for). **3** *a bus service.* business, organization, provision, system, timetable. **4** *give the car a service.* check-over, maintenance, overhaul, repair, servicing. **5** *church service.* ceremony, liturgy, meeting, rite, ritual, worship. □ *baptism, christening, communion, compline, evensong, fu-*

neral, marriage, Mass, matins, Requiem Mass, vespers. • *vb service a vehicle*. check, maintain, mend, overhaul, repair, tune.

serviceable *adj* dependable, durable, functional, hard-wearing, lasting, practical, strong, tough, usable.

servile *adj* abject, acquiescent, base, *inf* boot-licking, craven, cringing, deferential, fawning, flattering, grovelling, humble, ingratiating, low, menial, obsequious, slavish, submissive, subservient, sycophantic, *inf* time-serving, toadying, unctuous. *Opp* BOSSY. **be servile** ▷ GROVEL.

serving *n* helping, plateful, portion, ration.

session *n* **1** assembly, conference, discussion, hearing, meeting, sitting. **2** *a session at the baths*. period, term, time.

set *adj* **1** *set price*. advertised, agreed, arranged, defined, definite, fixed, prearranged, predetermined, prepared, scheduled, standard. **2** *set in your ways*. established, invariable, predictable, regular, stable, unchanging, unvarying. • *n* **1** batch, bunch, category, class, clique, collection, combination, kind, series, sort. ▷ GROUP. **2** *a TV set*. apparatus, receiver. **3** *set for a play*. scene, scenery, setting, stage. • *vb* **1** arrange, assign, deploy, deposit, dispose, lay, leave, locate, lodge, park, place, plant, *inf* plonk, put, position, rest, set down, set out, settle, situate, stand, station. **2** *set a clock*. adjust, correct, put right, rectify, regulate. **3** *set a post in concrete*. embed, fasten, fix. **4** *set like concrete*. become firm, congeal, *inf* gel, harden, *inf* jell, stiffen, take shape. **5** *set a problem*. ask, express, formulate, frame, phrase, pose, present, put forward, suggest, write. **6** *set a target*. allocate, allot, appoint, decide, designate, determine, establish, identify, name, ordain, prescribe, settle. **set about** ▷ ATTACK, BEGIN. **set free** ▷ LIBERATE. **set off** ▷ DEPART, EXPLODE. **set on** ▷ ATTACK. **set on fire** ▷ IGNITE. **set out** ▷ DEPART. **set up** ▷ ESTABLISH.

set-back *n inf* blow, check, complication, defeat, delay, difficulty, disappointment, hindrance, *inf* hitch, hold-up, impediment, misfortune, obstacle, problem, relapse, reverse, snag, upset.

settee *n* chaise longue, couch, sofa.

setting *n* **1** background, context, environment, environs, frame, habitat, locale, location, place, position, site, surroundings. **2** *setting for a play*. backcloth, backdrop, scene, scenery, set.

settle *vb* **1** arrange, conclude, deal with, decide, organize, put in order, straighten out. **2** alight, come to rest, land, light, *inf* make yourself comfortable, *inf* park yourself, pause, rest, roost, sit down. **3** *settle things in place*. assign, deploy, deposit, dispose, lay, locate, lodge, park, place, plant, position, put, rest, set, set down, situate, stand, station. **4** *the dust settled*. calm down, clear, compact, go down, sink, subside. **5** *settle what to do*. agree, choose, decide, establish, fix. **6** *settle differences*. end, negotiate, put an end to, reconcile, resolve, sort out, square. **7** *settle debts*. clear, discharge, pay, pay off. **8** *settle new territory*. become established in, colonize, immigrate, make your home in, occupy, people, set up home in, stay in.

settlement *n* **1** camp, colony, community, encampment, kibbutz, outpost, post, town, village. **2** agreement, arbitration, arrangement, contract, payment.

settler *n* colonist, frontiersman, immigrant, newcomer, pioneer, squatter.

sever *vb* **1** amputate, break, cut off, detach, disconnect, disjoin, part, remove, separate, split, terminate. ▷ CUT. **2** *sever a relationship*. abandon, break off, discontinue, end, put an end to, suspend, terminate.

several *adj* assorted, certain, different, divers, a few, a handful of, many, miscellaneous, a number of, some, sundry, a variety of, various.

severe *adj* **1** aloof, brutal, cold, cold-hearted, cruel, disapproving, dour, exacting, forbidding, glowering, grave, grim, hard, harsh, inexorable, merciless, obdurate, pitiless, relentless, rigorous, stern, stony, strict, unbending, uncompromising, unkind, unsmiling, unsympathetic, unyielding. **2** *severe illness.* acute, critical, dangerous, drastic, fatal, great, intense, keen, life-threatening, mortal, nasty, serious, sharp, terminal, troublesome. **3** *severe penalties.* draconian, extreme, maximum, oppressive, punitive, stringent. **4** *severe weather.* adverse, bad, inclement, violent, *inf* wicked. ▷ COLD, STORMY. **5** *a severe challenge.* arduous, demanding, difficult, onerous, punishing, taxing, tough. **6** *severe style.* austere, bare, chaste, plain, simple, spartan, stark, unadorned. *Opp* FRIENDLY, MILD, ORNATE.

sew *vb* baste, darn, hem, mend, repair, stitch, tack.

sewage *n* effluent, waste.

sewer *n* drain, drainage, sanitation, septic tank, soak-away.

sewing *n* dressmaking, embroidery, mending, needlepoint, needlework, tapestry.

sex *n* **1** gender, sexuality, **2** carnal knowledge, coition, coitus, congress, consummation of marriage, copulation, coupling, fornication, *inf* going to bed, incest, intercourse, intimacy, love-making, masturbation, mating, orgasm, perversion, rape, seduction, sexual intercourse, sexual relations, union. **have sex (with)** be intimate (with), consummate marriage, copulate (with), couple (with), fornicate (with), have sexual intercourse (with), make love (to), mate (with), rape, ravish, *sl* screw, seduce, unite (with).

sexism *n inf* chauvinism, discrimination, prejudice.

sexual *adj* **1** genital, procreative, progenitive, reproductive. **2** ▷ SEXY.

sexuality *n* gender. □ *bisexuality, hermaphroditism, heterosexuality, homosexuality.*

sexy *adj* **1** amorous, carnal, concupiscent, erotic, lascivious, lecherous, *derog* lewd, libidinous, *derog* lubricious, lustful, passionate, provocative, *derog* prurient, *inf* randy, seductive, sensual, sexual, *inf* sultry, venereal, voluptuous. **2** attractive, *inf* beddable, desirable, *sl* dishy, flirtatious. **3** *sexy books.* aphrodisiac, arousing, pornographic, *sl* raunchy, salacious, *inf* steamy, suggestive, titillating, *inf* torrid. ▷ OBSCENE.

shabby *adj* **1** bedraggled, dilapidated, dingy, dirty, dowdy, drab, faded, frayed, *inf* grubby, mangy, *inf* moth-eaten, ragged, run-down, *inf* scruffy, seedy, tattered, *inf* tatty, threadbare, unattractive, worn, worn-out. *Opp* SMART. **2** *shabby behaviour.* base, contemptible, despicable, disagreeable, discreditable, dishonest, dishonourable, disreputable, ignoble, *inf* low-down, mean, nasty, shameful, shoddy, unfair, unfriendly, ungenerous, unkind, unworthy. *Opp* HONOURABLE.

shack *n* cabin, hovel, hut, lean-to, shanty, shed.

shade *n* **1** ▷ SHADOW. **2** awning, blind, canopy, covering, curtain, parasol, screen, shelter, shield, umbrella, Venetian blind. **3** *a shade of blue.* colour, hue, intensity, tinge, tint, tone. **4** *shades of meaning.* degree, difference, nicety, nuance, variation. • *vb* **1** camouflage, conceal, cover, hide, mask, obscure, protect, screen, shield, shroud, veil. **2** *shade with pencil.* black out, block in, cross-hatch, darken, fill in, make dark.

shadow *n* **1** darkness, dimness, dusk, gloom, obscurity, penumbra, semi-darkness, shade, umbra. **2** *The sun casts shadows.* outline, shape, silhouette. **3** *a shadow of doubt.* ▷ HINT. • *vb* dog, follow, hunt, *inf* keep tabs on, keep watch on, pursue, stalk, *inf* tag onto, tail, track, trail, watch.

shadowy *adj* **1** dark, dim, faint, hazy, ill-defined, indefinite, indistinct, nebulous, obscure, unclear, unrecognizable, vague. ▷ GHOSTLY. **2** ▷ SHADY.

shady *adj* **1** *poet* bosky, cool, dark, dim, dusky, gloomy, leafy, shaded, shadowy, sheltered, sunless. *Opp* SUNNY. **2** *a shady character.* devious, dishonest, disreputable, dubious, *inf* fishy, questionable, shifty, suspicious, unreliable, untrustworthy. *Opp* HONEST.

shaft *n* **1** arrow, column, handle, helve, pillar, pole, post, rod, shank, stanchion, stem, stick, upright. **2** duct, mine, pit, tunnel, well, working. **3** *shaft of light.* beam, gleam, laser, pencil, ray, streak.

shaggy *adj* bushy, dishevelled, fibrous, fleecy, hairy, hirsute, matted, rough, tousled, unkempt, unshorn, untidy, woolly. *Opp* SMOOTH.

shake *vb* **1** convulse, heave, jump, quake, quiver, rattle, rock, shiver, shudder, sway, throb, totter, tremble, vibrate, waver, wobble. **2** *shake your umbrella.* agitate, brandish, flourish, gyrate, jar, jerk, *inf* jiggle, *inf* joggle, jolt, oscillate, sway, swing, twirl, twitch, vibrate, wag, *inf* waggle, wave, *inf* wiggle. **3** *The bad news shook us.* alarm, distress, disturb, frighten, perturb, *inf* rattle, shock, startle, *inf* throw, unnerve, unsettle, upset. ▷ SURPRISE.

shaky *adj* **1** decrepit, dilapidated, feeble, flimsy, frail, insecure, precarious, ramshackle, rickety, rocky, shaking, unreliable, unsound, unsteady, weak, wobbly. **2** *a shaky voice.* faltering, quavering, quivering, trembling, tremulous. **3** *a shaky start.* nervous, tentative, uncertain, underconfident, unimpressive, unpromising. *Opp* STEADY, STRONG.

shallow *adj* **1** *shallow water.* [There are no apt synonyms for this sense.] **2** *shallow argument.* empty, facile, foolish, frivolous, glib, insincere, puerile, silly, simple, *inf* skin-deep, slight, superficial, trivial, unconvincing, unscholarly, unthinking. *Opp* DEEP.

sham *adj* artificial, bogus, counterfeit, ersatz, fake, false, fictitious, fraudulent, imitation, make-believe, mock, *inf* pretend, pretended, simulated, synthetic. • *n* counterfeit, fake, fiction, fraud, hoax, imitation, make-believe, pretence, *inf* put-up job, simulation. • *vb* counterfeit, fake, feign, imitate, make believe, pretend, simulate.

shambles *plur n* **1** battlefield, scene of carnage, slaughterhouse. **2** [*inf*] chaos, confusion, devastation, disorder, mess, muddle, *inf* pigsty, *inf* tip.

shame *n* **1** chagrin, degradation, discredit, disgrace, dishonour, distress, embarrassment, guilt, humiliation, ignominy, infamy, loss of face, mortification, obloquy, opprobrium, remorse, stain, stigma, vilification. **2** *a shame to mistreat him so.* outrage, pity, scandal, wickedness. • *vb* abash, chagrin, chasten, discomfit, disconcert, discountenance, disgrace, embarrass, humble, humiliate, make someone ashamed, mortify, *inf* put someone in his/her place, *inf* show someone up.

shamefaced *adj* **1** abashed, ashamed, chagrined, *inf* hang-dog, humiliated, mortified, penitent, *inf* red-faced, remorseful, repentant, sorry. **2** bashful, coy, embarrassed, modest, self-conscious, sheepish, shy, timid. *Opp* SHAMELESS.

shameful *adj* **1** *a shameful crime.* base, contemptible, deplorable, disgraceful, ignoble, infamous, low, mean, outrageous, reprehensible, scandalous, unworthy. ▷ WICKED. **2** *shameful to be found out.* compromising, degrading, demeaning, discreditable, dishonourable, embarrassing, humiliating, ignominious, *sl* infra dig, inglorious, lowering, mortifying, undignified. *Opp* HONOURABLE.

shameless *adj* **1** barefaced, bold, brazen, cheeky, cool, defiant, flagrant, hardened, impenitent, impudent, incorrigible, insolent, unabashed, unashamed, unrepentant. **2** *shameless nudity.* frank, honest, immodest, improper, indecorous, open, rude, shocking, unblushing, unconcealed, undisguised, unselfconscious. *Opp* SHAMEFACED.

shape *n* **1** body, build, figure, physique, profile, silhouette. **2** *geometrical shape.* configuration, figure, form, format, model, mould, outline, pattern. □ [two-dimensional] *circle, diamond, ellipse, heptagon, hexagon, lozenge, oblong, octagon, oval, parallelogram, pentagon, polygon, quadrant, quadrilateral, rectangle, rhomboid, rhombus, ring, semicircle, square, trapezium, trapezoid, triangle.* [three-dimensional] *cone, cube, cylinder, decahedron, hemisphere, hexahedron, octahedron, polyhedron, prism, pyramid, sphere.* • *vb* adapt, adjust, carve, cast, cut, fashion, form, frame, give shape to, model, mould, *inf* sculpt, sculpture, whittle.

shapeless *adj* **1** amorphous, formless, indeterminate, irregular, nebulous, undefined, unformed, unstructured, vague. **2** *a shapeless figure.* deformed, distorted, *inf* dumpy, flat, misshapen, twisted, unattractive, unshapely. *Opp* SHAPELY.

shapely *adj* attractive, comely, *inf* curvaceous, elegant, good-looking, graceful, neat, trim, *inf* voluptuous, well-proportioned. *Opp* SHAPELESS.

share *n* allocation, allotment, allowance, bit, cut, division, due, fraction, helping, part, percentage, piece, portion, proportion, quota, ration, serving, *sl* whack. • *vb* **1** allocate, allot, apportion, deal out, distribute, divide, dole out, *inf* go halves or shares (with), halve, partake of, portion out, ration out, share out, split. **2** *share work.* be involved, cooperate, join, participate, take part. **shared** ▷ JOINT.

sharp *adj* **1** acute, arrow-shaped, cutting, fine, jagged, keen, knife-edged, needle-sharp, pointed, razor-sharp, sharpened, spiky, tapering. **2** *sharp bend, drop.* abrupt, acute, angular, hairpin, marked, precipitous, sheer, steep, sudden, surprising, unexpected, vertical. **3** *sharp focus.* clear, defined, distinct, focused, well-defined. **4** *a sharp storm.* extreme, heavy, intense, serious, severe, sudden, violent. **5** *sharp frost.* biting, bitter, keen, nippy. ▷ COLD. **6** *sharp pain.* acute, excruciating, painful, stabbing, stinging. **7** *sharp rejoinder.* acerbic, acid, acidulous, barbed, biting, caustic, critical, cutting, hurtful, incisive, malicious, mocking, mordant, sarcastic, sardonic, scathing, spiteful, tart, trenchant, unkind, venomous, vitriolic. **8** *sharp mind.* acute, agile, alert, artful, astute, bright, clever, crafty, *inf* cute, discerning, incisive, intelligent, observant, penetrating, perceptive, probing, quick-witted, searching, shrewd, *inf* smart. **9** *sharp eyes.* attentive, eagle-eyed, observant, *inf* peeled (*keep your eyes peeled*), quick, watchful, wide-open. **10** *sharp taste, smell.* acid, acrid, bitter, caustic, hot, piquant, pungent, sour, spicy, tangy, tart. **11** *sharp sound.* clear, detached, ear-splitting, high, high-pitched, penetrating, piercing, shrieking, shrill, staccato, strident. *Opp* BLUNT, DULL, SLIGHT.

sharpen *vb* file, grind, hone, make sharp, strop, whet. *Opp* BLUNT.

sharpener *n* file, grindstone, hone, pencil-sharpener, strop, whetstone.

shatter *vb* blast, break, break up, burst, crack, crush, dash to pieces, demolish, destroy, disintegrate, explode, pulverize, shiver, smash, *inf* smash to smithereens, splinter, split, wreck. **shattered** ▷ SURPRISED, WEARY.

sheaf *n* bunch, bundle, file, ream.

shear *vb* clip, strip, trim. ▷ CUT.

sheath *n* casing, covering, scabbard, sleeve.

sheathe *vb* cocoon, cover, encase, enclose, put away, put in a sheath, wrap.

shed *n* hut, hutch, lean-to, outhouse, penthouse, potting-shed, shack, shelter, storehouse. • *vb* abandon, cast off, discard, drop, let fall, moult, pour off, scatter, shower, spill, spread, throw off. **shed light** ▷ SHINE.

sheen *n* brightness, burnish, glaze, gleam, glint, gloss, lustre, patina, polish, radiance, reflection, shimmer, shine.

sheep *n* ewe, lamb, mutton, ram, wether.

sheepish *adj* abashed, ashamed, bashful, coy, docile, embarrassed, guilty, meek, mortified, reticent, self-conscious, self-effacing, shamefaced, shy, timid. *Opp* SHAMELESS.

sheer *adj* **1** absolute, arrant, complete, downright, out-and-out, plain, pure, simple, thoroughgoing, total, unadulterated, unalloyed, unmitigated, unmixed, unqualified, utter. **2** *a sheer cliff*. abrupt, perpendicular, precipitous, steep, vertical. **3** *sheer silk*. diaphanous, filmy, fine, flimsy, gauzy, gossamer, *inf* see-through, thin, translucent, transparent.

sheet *n* **1** bedsheet, duvet cover. **2** [*paper*] folio, leaf, page. **3** [*glass, etc*] pane, panel, plate. **4** [*ice, etc*] blanket, coating, covering, film, lamina, layer, membrane, skin, veneer. **5** [*water*] area, expanse, surface.

shelf *n* ledge, shelving.

shell *n* **1** carapace (*of tortoise*), case, casing, covering, crust, exterior, façade, hull, husk, outside, pod. **2** *fired shells at them*. cartridge, projectile. ● *vb* attack with gunfire, barrage, bomb, bombard, fire at, shoot at, strafe.

shellfish *n* bivalve, crustacean, mollusc. □ *barnacle, clam, cockle, conch, crab, crayfish, cuttlefish, limpet, lobster, mussel, oyster, prawn, scallop, shrimp, whelk, winkle.*

shelter *n* **1** asylum, cover, haven, lee, protection, refuge, safety, sanctuary, security. **2** barrier, concealment, cover, fence, hut, roof, screen, shield. **3** *seek shelter for the night*. accommodation, home, housing, lodging, resting-place. ▷ HOUSE. **4** *air-raid shelter*. bunker. ● *vb* **1** defend, enclose, guard, keep safe, protect, safeguard, screen, secure, shade, shield. **2** *shelter a runaway*. accommodate, give shelter to, harbour, hide, *inf* put up. **sheltered** ▷ QUIET.

shelve *vb* **1** defer, hold in abeyance, lay aside, postpone, put off, put on ice. **2** ▷ SLOPE.

shield *n* **1** barrier, bulwark, defence, guard, protection, safeguard, screen, shelter. **2** *a warrior's shield*. buckler, *heraldry* escutcheon. ● *vb* cover, defend, guard, keep safe, protect, safeguard, screen, shade, shelter.

shift *n* **1** adjustment, alteration, change, move, switch, transfer, transposition. **2** *night shift*. crew, gang, group, period, *inf* stint, team, workforce. ● *vb* adjust, alter, budge, change, displace, reposition, switch, transfer, transpose. ▷ MOVE. **shift for yourself** ▷ MANAGE.

shiftless *adj* idle, indolent, ineffective, inefficient, inept, irresponsible, lazy, unambitious, unenterprising. *Opp* RESOURCEFUL.

shifty *adj* artful, canny, crafty, cunning, deceitful, designing, devious, dishonest, evasive, *inf* foxy, furtive, scheming, secretive, *inf* shady, *inf* slippery, sly, treacherous, tricky, untrustworthy, wily. *Opp* STRAIGHTFORWARD.

shimmer *vb* flicker, glimmer, glisten, ripple. ▷ SHINE.

shine *n* brightness, burnish, coruscation, glaze, gleam, glint, gloss, glow, luminosity, lustre, patina, phosphorescence, polish, radiance, reflection, sheen, shimmer, sparkle, varnish. ● *vb* **1** beam, be luminous, blaze, coruscate, dazzle, emit light, flare, flash, glare, gleam, glint, glisten, glitter, glow, phosphoresce, radiate, reflect, scintillate, shed light, shimmer, sparkle, twinkle. **2** *used to shine at maths*. be brilliant, be clever, do well, excel, *inf* make your mark, stand out. **3** *shine your shoes*. brush, buff up, burnish, clean, polish, rub up. **shining** ▷ BRIGHT, CONSPICUOUS.

shingle *n* **1** gravel, pebbles, stones. **2** *roofing shingle*. tile.

shiny *adj* bright, brilliant, burnished, gleaming, glistening, glossy, glowing, luminous, lustrous, phosphorescent, polished, reflective, rubbed, shimmering, shining, sleek, smooth. *Opp* DULL.

ship *n* boat. ▷ VESSEL. ● *vb* carry, *inf* cart, convey, deliver, ferry, freight, move, send, transport.

shirk *vb* avoid, dodge, duck, evade, get out of, neglect, shun. **shirk work** be lazy, malinger, *inf* skive, slack.

shiver *n* flutter, frisson, quiver, rattle, shake, shudder, thrill, tremor, vibration. ● *vb* chatter, flap, flutter, quake, quaver, quiver, rattle, shake, shudder, tremble, twitch, vibrate.

shock *n* **1** blow, collision, concussion, impact, jolt, thud. **2** *came as a shock. inf* bombshell, surprise, *inf* thunderbolt. **3** *state of shock.* dismay, distress, fright, trauma, upset. ● *vb* **1** alarm, amaze, astonish, astound, confound, daze, dismay, distress, dumbfound, frighten, *inf* give someone a turn, jar, jolt, numb, paralyse, petrify, rock, scare, shake, stagger, startle, stun, stupefy, surprise, *inf* throw, traumatize, unnerve. **2** *Sadism shocks us.* appal, disgust, horrify, nauseate, offend, outrage, repel, revolt, scandalize, sicken.

shoddy *adj* **1** cheap, flimsy, *inf* gimcrack, inferior, jerry-built, meretricious, nasty, poor quality, *inf* rubbishy, second-rate, shabby, *sl* tacky, *inf* tatty, tawdry, *inf* trashy. **2** *shoddy work.* careless, messy, negligent, slipshod, *inf* sloppy, slovenly, untidy. *Opp* SUPERIOR.

shoe *n plur* footwear. □ *boot, bootee, brogue, clog, espadrille,* inf *flip-flop, galosh, gum-boot,* inf *lace-up, moccasin, plimsoll, pump, sabot, sandal,* inf *slip-on, slipper, trainer, wader, wellington.*

shoemaker *n* bootmaker, cobbler.

shoot *n* branch, bud, new growth, offshoot, sprout, sucker, twig. ● *vb* **1** *shoot a gun.* aim, discharge, fire. **2** *shoot the enemy.* aim at, bombard, fire at, gun down, hit, hunt, kill, *inf* let fly at, open fire on, *inf* pick off, shell, snipe at, strafe, *inf* take potshots at. **3** *shoot from your chair.* bolt, dart, dash, fly, hurtle, leap, move quickly, race, run, rush, speed, spring, streak. **4** *plants shoot in the spring.* bud, burgeon, develop, flourish, grow, put out shoots, spring up, sprout.

shop *n* boutique, cash-and-carry, department store, *old use* emporium, establishment, market, outlet, retailer, seller, store, wholesaler. □ *baker, betting shop, bookshop, butcher, chandler, chemist, confectioner, couturier, creamery, dairy, delicatessen, draper, fishmonger, florist, garden-centre, greengrocer, grocer, haberdasher, herbalist, hypermarket, ironmonger, jeweller, launderette, minimarket, newsagent, off-licence, outfitter, pawnbroker, pharmacy, post office, poulterer, stationer, supermarket, tailor, take-away, tobacconist, toyshop, video shop, vintner, watchmaker.*

shopkeeper *n* dealer, merchant, retailer, salesgirl, salesman, saleswoman, stockist, storekeeper, supplier, trader, tradesman.

shopper *n* buyer, customer, patron.

shopping *n* **1** buying, *inf* spending-spree. **2** goods, purchases.

shopping-centre *n* arcade, complex, hypermarket, mall, precinct.

shore *n* bank, beach, coast, edge, foreshore, sands, seashore, seaside, shingle, strand. ● *vb* **shore up** ▷ SUPPORT.

short *adj* **1** diminutive, *inf* dumpy, dwarfish, little, midget, *fem* petite, *derog* pint-sized, slight, small, squat, *inf* stubby, *inf* stumpy, stunted, tiny, *inf* wee, undergrown. **2** *a short visit.* brief, cursory, curtailed, ephemeral, fleeting, momentary, passing, quick, short-lived, temporary, transient, transitory. **3** *a short book.* abbreviated, abridged, compact, concise, cut, pocket, shortened, succinct. **4** *in short supply.* deficient, inadequate, insufficient, lacking, limited, low, meagre, scanty, scarce, sparse, wanting. **5** *a short manner.* abrupt, bad-tempered, blunt, brusque, cross, curt, gruff, grumpy, impolite, irritable, laconic, sharp, snappy, taciturn, terse, testy, uncivil, unfriendly, unkind, unsympathetic. *Opp* EXPANSIVE, LONG, PLENTIFUL, TALL. **cut short** ▷ SHORTEN.

shortage *n* absence, dearth, deficiency, deficit, insufficiency, lack, paucity, poverty, scarcity, shortfall, want. *Opp* PLENTY.

shortcoming *n* bad habit, defect, deficiency, drawback, failing, failure, fault, flaw, foible, imperfection, limitation, vice, weakness, weak point.

shorten *vb* abbreviate, abridge, compress, condense, curtail, cut, cut down, cut short, diminish, dock, lop, précis, prune, reduce, shrink, summarize, take up (*clothes*), telescope, trim, truncate. *Opp* LENGTHEN.

shortly *adv old use* anon, before long, by and by, directly, presently, soon.

short-sighted *adj* **1** myopic, near-sighted. **2** unadventurous, unimaginative, without vision.

short-tempered *adj* abrupt, acerbic, brusque, crabby, cross, crusty, curt, gruff, irascible, irritable, peevish, peremptory, shrewish, snappy, testy, touchy, waspish. *Opp* GOOD-TEMPERED.

shot *n* **1** ball, bullet, discharge, missile, pellet, projectile, round, *inf* slug. **2** *heard a shot.* bang, blast, crack, explosion, report. **3** *a first-class shot.* marksman, markswoman, sharpshooter. **4** *give it a shot.* attempt, chance, *inf* crack, effort, endeavour, *inf* go, hit, kick, *inf* stab, stroke, try. **5** *photographic shot.* angle, photograph, picture, scene, sequence, snap, snapshot.

shout *vb* bawl, bellow, *inf* belt, call, cheer, clamour, cry out, exclaim, howl, rant, roar, scream, screech, shriek, talk loudly, vociferate, whoop, yell, yelp, yowl. *Opp* WHISPER.

shove *vb inf* barge, crowd, drive, elbow, hustle, impel, jostle, nudge, press, prod, push, shoulder, thrust.

shovel *vb* clear, dig, scoop, shift.

show *n* **1** drama, performance, play, presentation, production. ▷ ENTERTAINMENT. **2** *flower show.* competition, demonstration, display, exhibition, *inf* expo, exposition, fair, presentation. **3** *show of strength.* appearance, demonstration, façade, illusion, impression, pose, pretence, threat. **4** *just for show.* affectation, exhibitionism, flamboyance, ostentation, pretentiousness, showing off. • *vb* **1** bare, betray, demonstrate, display, divulge, exhibit, expose, make public, make visible, manifest, open up, present, produce, reveal, uncover. **2** *Let your feelings show.* appear, be seen, be visible, catch the eye, come out, emerge, make an appearance, materialize, *inf* peep through, stand out, stick out. **3** *show the way.* conduct, direct, escort, guide, indicate, lead, point out, steer, usher. **4** *show kindness.* accord, bestow, confer, grant, treat with. **5** *This photo shows us at work.* depict, give a picture of, illustrate, picture, portray, represent, symbolize. **6** *Show me how.* clarify, describe, elucidate, explain, instruct, make clear, teach, tell. **7** *Tests show I was right.* attest, bear out, confirm, corroborate, demonstrate, evince, exemplify, manifest, prove, substantiate, verify, witness. **show off** ▷ BOAST. **show up** ▷ ARRIVE, HUMILIATE.

showdown *n* confrontation, crisis, *inf* decider, decisive encounter, *inf* moment of truth.

shower *n* **1** drizzle, sprinkling. ▷ RAIN. **2** douche, shower-bath. • *vb* **1** deluge, drop, rain, spatter, splash, spray, sprinkle. **2** *shower with gifts.* heap, inundate, load, overwhelm.

show-off *n inf* big-head, boaster, braggart, conceited person, egotist, exhibitionist, *inf* poser, poseur, *inf* showman, swaggerer.

showy *adj* bright, conspicuous, elaborate, fancy, flamboyant, flashy, florid, fussy, garish, gaudy, lavish, *inf* loud, lurid, ornate, ostentatious, *inf* over the top, pretentious, striking, trumpery, vulgar. *Opp* DISCREET.

shred *n* atom, bit, fragment, grain, hint, iota, jot, piece, scintilla, scrap, sliver, snippet, speck, trace. • *vb* cut to shreds, destroy, grate, rip up, scrap, tear. **shreds** rags, ribbons, strips, tatters.

shrewd *adj* acute, artful, astute, calculating, *inf* canny, clever, crafty, cunning, discerning, discriminating, *inf* foxy, ingenious, intelligent, knowing, observant, perceptive, percipient, perspicacious, quick-witted, sage, sharp, sly, smart, wily, wise. *Opp* STUPID.

shriek *vb* cry, scream, screech, squawk, squeal.

shrill *adj* ear-splitting, high, high-pitched, jarring, penetrating, piercing, piping, screaming, screeching, screechy, sharp, shrieking, strident, treble, whistling. *Opp* GENTLE, SONOROUS.

shrine *n* altar, chapel, holy of holies, holy place, place of worship, reliquary, sanctum, tomb. ▷ CHURCH.

shrink *vb* **1** become smaller, contract, decrease, diminish, dwindle, lessen, make smaller, narrow, reduce, shorten. ▷ SHRIVEL. *Opp* EXPAND. **2** *shrink with fear*. back off, cower, cringe, flinch, hang back, quail, recoil, retire, shy away, wince, withdraw. *Opp* ADVANCE.

shrivel *vb* become parched, become wizened, curl, dehydrate, desiccate, droop, dry out, dry up, pucker up, wilt, wither, wrinkle. ▷ SHRINK.

shroud *n* blanket, cloak, cloud, cover, mantle, mask, pall, veil, winding-sheet. • *vb* camouflage, cloak, conceal, cover, disguise, enshroud, envelop, hide, mask, screen, swathe, veil, wrap up.

shrub *n* bush, tree. □ *berberis, blackthorn, broom, bryony, buckthorn, buddleia, camellia, daphne, forsythia, gorse, heather, hydrangea, japonica, jasmine, lavender, lilac, myrtle, privet, rhododendron, rosemary, rue, viburnum.*

shudder *vb* be horrified, convulse, jerk, quake, quiver, rattle, shake, shiver, squirm, tremble, vibrate.

shuffle *vb* **1** confuse, disorganize, intermix, intersperse, jumble, mix, mix up, rearrange, reorganize. **2** *shuffle along*. drag your feet, scrape, shamble, slide. ▷ WALK.

shun *vb* avoid, disdain, eschew, flee, *inf* give the cold shoulder to, keep clear of, rebuff, reject, shy away from, spurn, steer clear of, turn away from. *Opp* SEEK.

shut *vb* bolt, close, fasten, latch, lock, push to, replace, seal, secure, slam. **shut in** ▷ CONFINE, IMPRISON. **shut off** ▷ ISOLATE. **shut out** ▷ EXCLUDE. **shut up** ▷ CONFINE, IMPRISON, SILENCE.

shutter *n* blind, louvre, screen.

shy *adj* apprehensive, backward, bashful, cautious, chary, coy, diffident, hesitant, inhibited, introverted, modest, *inf* mousy, nervous, reserved, reticent, retiring, self-conscious, self-effacing, sheepish, timid, timorous, underconfident, wary, withdrawn. *Opp* ASSERTIVE, UNINHIBITED. • *vb* ▷ THROW.

sibling *n* brother, sister, twin. ▷ FAMILY.

sick *adj* **1** afflicted, ailing, bedridden, diseased, ill, indisposed, infirm, *inf* laid up, *inf* poorly, *inf* queer, sickly, *inf* under the weather, unhealthy, unwell. ▷ ILL. **2** airsick, bilious, carsick, likely to vomit, nauseated, nauseous, queasy, seasick, squeamish. **3** *sick of rudeness*. annoyed (by), bored (with), disgusted (by), distressed (by), *inf* fed up (with), glutted (with), nauseated (by), sated (with), sickened (by), tired, troubled (by), upset (by), weary. **4** [*inf*] *a sick joke*. ▷ MORBID. **be sick** ▷ VOMIT.

sicken *vb* **1** *inf* catch a bug, fail, fall ill, take sick, weaken. **2** appal, be sickening to, disgust, make someone sick, nauseate, offend, repel, revolt, *inf* turn someone off, *inf* turn someone's stomach. **sickening** ▷ REPULSIVE.

sickly *adj* **1** ailing, anaemic, delicate, drawn, feeble, frail, ill, pale, pallid, *inf* peaky, unhealthy, wan, weak. ▷ ILL. *Opp* HEALTHY. **2** *sickly sentiment*. cloying, maudlin, mawkish, *inf* mushy, nasty, nauseating, obnoxious, *inf* off-putting, syrupy, treacly, unpleasant. *Opp* REFRESHING.

sickness *n* biliousness, nausea, queasiness, vomiting. ▷ ILLNESS.

side *n* **1** *sides of a cube.* elevation, face, facet, flank, surface. **2** *side of the road.* border, boundary, brim, brink, edge, fringe, limit, margin, perimeter, rim, verge. **3** *sides in a debate.* angle, aspect, attitude, perspective, point of view, position, school of thought, slant, standpoint, view, viewpoint. **4** *sides in a quarrel.* army, camp, faction, interest, party, sect, team. ● *vb* **side with** ally with, favour, form an alliance with, *inf* go along with, join up with, partner, prefer, support, team up with. ▷ HELP.

sidestep *vb* avoid, circumvent, dodge, *inf* duck, evade, skirt round.

sidetrack *vb* deflect, distract, divert.

sideways *adj* **1** crabwise, indirect, lateral, oblique. **2** *a sideways glance.* covert, sidelong, sly, *inf* sneaky, unobtrusive.

siege *n* blockade. ● *vb* ▷ BESIEGE.

sieve *n* colander, riddle, screen, strainer. ● *vb* ▷ SIFT.

sift *vb* **1** filter, riddle, screen, separate, sieve, strain. **2** *sift evidence.* analyse, examine, investigate, pick out, review, scrutinize, select, sort out, weed out, winnow.

sigh *n* breath, exhalation, murmur, suspiration. ▷ SOUND.

sight *n* **1** eyesight, seeing, vision, visual perception. **2** *within sight.* field of vision, gaze, range, view, visibility. **3** *a brief sight of it.* glimpse, look. **4** *an impressive sight.* display, exhibition, scene, show, show-piece, spectacle. ● *vb* behold, descry, discern, distinguish, espy, glimpse, make out, notice, observe, perceive, recognize, see, spot. **catch sight of** ▷ SEE.

sightseer *n* globe-trotter, holiday-maker, tourist, tripper, visitor.

sign *n* **1** augury, forewarning, hint, indication, indicator, intimation, omen, pointer, portent, presage, warning. ▷ SIGNAL. **2** *sign that someone was here.* clue, *inf* giveaway, indication, manifestation, marker, proof, reminder, spoor (*of animal*), suggestion, symptom, token, trace, vestige. **3** *put up a sign.* advertisement, notice, placard, poster, publicity, signboard. **4** *identifying sign.* badge, brand, cipher, device, emblem, flag, hieroglyph, ideogram, ideograph, insignia, logo, mark, monogram, rebus, symbol, trademark. ● *vb* **1** autograph, countersign, endorse, inscribe, write. **2** ▷ SIGNAL. **sign off** ▷ FINISH. **sign on** ▷ ENLIST. **sign over** ▷ TRANSFER.

signal *n* **1** communication, cue, gesticulation, gesture, *inf* goahead, indication, motion, sign, signal, *inf* tip-off, token, warning. □ *alarm-bell, beacon, bell, burglar-alarm, buzzer, flag, flare, gong, green light, indicator, password, red light, reveille, rocket, semaphore signal, siren, smoke-signal, tocsin,* old use *trafficator, traffic-lights, warning-light, whistle, winker.* **2** *radio signal.* broadcast, emission, output, transmission, waves. ● *vb* beckon, communicate, flag, gesticulate, give or send a signal, indicate, motion, notify, sign, wave. ▷ GESTURE.

signature *n* autograph, endorsement, mark, name.

signet *n* seal, stamp.

significance *n* denotation, force, idea, implication, import, importance, message, point, purport, relevance, sense, signification, usefulness, value, weight. ▷ MEANING.

significant *adj* **1** eloquent, expressive, indicative, informative, knowing, meaningful, pregnant, revealing, suggestive, symbolic, *inf* tell-tale. **2** *significant event.* big, consequential, considerable, historic, important, influential, memorable, newsworthy, noteworthy, relevant, salient, serious, sizeable, valuable, vital, worthwhile. *Opp* INSIGNIFICANT.

signify *vb* **1** announce, be a sign of, betoken, communicate, connote, convey, denote, express, foretell, impart, imply, indicate, intimate, make known, reflect, reveal, signal, suggest, symbolize, tell, transmit. **2** *It doesn't signify.* be significant, count, matter, merit consideration.

signpost *n* finger-post, pointer, road-sign, sign.

silence *n* **1** calm, calmness, hush, noiselessness, peace, quiet, quietness, quietude, soundlessness, stillness, tranquillity. *Opp* NOISE. **2** *Her silence puzzled us.* dumbness, muteness, reticence, speechlessness, taciturnity, uncommunicativeness. • *vb* **1** gag, hush, keep quiet, make silent, muzzle, repress, shut up, suppress. **2** *silence engine noise.* damp, deaden, muffle, mute, quieten, smother, stifle. **Silence!** Be quiet! Be silent! *inf* Hold your tongue! Hush! Keep quiet! *inf* Pipe down! Shut up! Stop talking!

silent *adj* **1** hushed, inaudible, muffled, muted, noiseless, quiet, soundless. **2** dumb, laconic, *inf* mum, reserved, reticent, speechless, taciturn, tight-lipped, tongue-tied, uncommunicative, unforthcoming, voiceless. **3** *silent listeners.* attentive, rapt, restrained, still. **4** *silent agreement.* implicit, implied, mute, tacit, understood, unexpressed, unspoken, unuttered. *Opp* EXPLICIT, NOISY, TALKATIVE. **be silent** keep quiet, *inf* pipe down, say nothing, *inf* shut up.

silhouette *n* contour, form, outline, profile, shadow, shape.

silky *adj* delicate, fine, glossy, lustrous, satiny, sleek, smooth, soft, velvety.

silly *adj* **1** absurd, asinine, brainless, childish, crazy, daft, *inf* dopey, *inf* dotty, fatuous, feather-brained, feeble-minded, flighty, *old use* fond, foolish, frivolous, grotesque, *inf* half-baked, hare-brained, idiotic, ill-advised, illogical, immature, impractical, imprudent, inadvisable, inane, infantile, irrational, *inf* jokey, laughable, light-hearted, ludicrous, mad, meaningless, mindless, misguided, naïve, nonsensical, playful, pointless, preposterous, ridiculous, scatter-brained, *inf* scatty, senseless, shallow, simple, simple-minded, simplistic, *inf* soppy, stupid, thoughtless, unintelligent, unreasonable, unsound, unwise, wild, witless. *Opp* SERIOUS, WISE. **2** [*inf*] *knocked silly.* ▷ UNCONSCIOUS.

silt *n* alluvium, deposit, mud, ooze, sediment, slime, sludge.

silvan *adj* arboreal, leafy, tree-covered, wooded.

similar *adj* akin, alike, analogous, comparable, compatible, congruous, co-ordinating, corresponding, equal, equivalent, harmonious, homogeneous, identical, indistinguishable, like, matching, parallel, related, resembling, the same, toning, twin, uniform, well-matched. *Opp* DIFFERENT.

similarity *n* affinity, closeness, congruity, correspondence, equivalence, homogeneity, kinship, likeness, match, parallelism, relationship, resemblance, sameness, similitude, uniformity. *Opp* DIFFERENCE.

simmer *vb* boil, bubble, cook, seethe, stew.

simple *adj* **1** artless, basic, candid, childlike, elementary, frank, fundamental, guileless, homely, honest, humble, ingenuous, innocent, lowly, modest, *derog* naïve, natural, *derog* silly, simple-minded, sincere, unaffected, unassuming, unpretentious, unsophisticated. *Opp* SOPHISTICATED. **2** *simple instructions.* clear, comprehensible, direct, easy, fool-proof, intelligible, lucid, straightforward, uncomplicated, understandable. *Opp* COMPLEX. **3** *a simple dress.* austere, classical, plain, severe, stark, unadorned, unembellished. *Opp* ORNATE.

simplify *vb* clarify, explain, make simple, paraphrase, prune, *inf* put in words of one syllable, streamline, unravel, untangle. *Opp* COMPLICATE.

simplistic *adj* [*always derog*] facile, inadequate, naïve, oversimple, oversimplified, shallow, silly, superficial.

simulate *vb* act, counterfeit, dissimulate, enact, fake, feign, imitate, *inf* mock up, play-act, pretend, reproduce, sham.

simultaneous *adj* coinciding, concurrent, contemporaneous, parallel, synchronized, synchronous.

sin *n* blasphemy, corruption, depravity, desecration, devilry, error, evil, fault, guilt, immorality, impiety, iniquity, irreverence, misdeed, offence, peccadillo, profanation, sacrilege, sinfulness, transgression, *old use* trespass, ungodliness, unrighteousness, vice, wickedness, wrong, wrongdoing. • *vb* be guilty of sin, blaspheme, do wrong, err, fall from grace, go astray, lapse, misbehave, offend, stray, transgress.

sincere *adj* candid, direct, earnest, frank, genuine, guileless, heartfelt, honest, open, real, serious, simple, *inf* straight, straightforward, true, truthful, unaffected, unfeigned, upright, wholehearted. *Opp* INSINCERE.

sincerity *n* candour, directness, earnestness, frankness, genuineness, honesty, honour, integrity, openness, straightforwardness, trustworthiness, truthfulness, uprightness.

sinewy *adj* brawny, muscular, strapping, tough, wiry. ▷ STRONG.

sinful *adj* bad, blasphemous, corrupt, damnable, depraved, erring, evil, fallen, guilty, immoral, impious, iniquitous, irreligious, irreverent, profane, sacrilegious, ungodly, unholy, unrighteous, vile, wicked, wrong, wrongful. *Opp* RIGHTEOUS.

sing *vb* carol, chant, chirp, chorus, croon, descant, hum, intone, serenade, trill, vocalize, warble, whistle, yodel.

singe *vb* blacken, burn, char, scorch, sear.

singer *n* songster, vocalist. □ *alto, balladeer, baritone, bass, carol-singer, castrato,* plur *choir, choirboy, choirgirl, chorister,* plur *chorus, coloratura, contralto, counter-tenor, crooner,* It *diva, folk singer, minstrel, opera singer, pop star, precentor,* It *prima donna, soloist, soprano, tenor, treble, troubadour.*

single *adj* **1** exclusive, individual, isolated, lone, odd, one, only, personal, separate, singular, sole, solitary, unique, unparalleled. **2** *a single person.* celibate, *inf* free, unattached, unmarried. • *vb* **single out** ▷ CHOOSE.

single-handed *adj* alone, independent, solitary, unaided, unassisted, without help.

single-minded *adj* dedicated, determined, devoted, dogged, *derog* fanatical, *derog* obsessive, persevering, resolute, steadfast, tireless, unswerving, unwavering.

singular *adj* **1** ▷ SINGLE. **2** abnormal, curious, different, distinct, eccentric, exceptional, extraordinary, odd, outstanding, peculiar, rare, remarkable, strange, unusual. ▷ DISTINCTIVE. *Opp* COMMON.

sinister *adj* **1** dark, disquieting, disturbing, evil, forbidding, foreboding, frightening, gloomy, inauspicious, malevolent, malignant, menacing, minatory, ominous, threatening, upsetting. **2** *sinister motives.* bad, corrupt, criminal, dishonest, furtive, illegal, nefarious, questionable, *inf* shady, suspect, treacherous, unworthy, villainous.

sink *n* basin, stoup, washbowl. • *vb* **1** collapse, decline, descend, diminish, disappear, droop, drop, dwindle, ebb, fade, fail, fall, go down, go lower, plunge, set (*sun sets*), slip down, subside, vanish, weaken. **2** be engulfed, be submerged, founder, go down, go under. **3** *sink a ship.* scupper, scuttle. **4** *sink a borehole.* bore, dig, drill, excavate.

sinner *n* evil-doer, malefactor, miscreant, offender, reprobate, transgressor, wrongdoer.

sip *vb* drink, lap, sample, taste.

sit *vb* **1** be seated, perch, rest, seat (yourself), settle, squat, take a seat, *inf* take the weight off your feet. **2** *sit for a portrait.* pose. **3** *sit an exam.* be a candidate in, *inf* go in for, take, write. **4** *Parliament sat for 12 hours.* assemble, be in session, convene, gather, get together, meet.

site *n* area, campus, ground, location, place, plot, position, setting, situation, spot. ● *vb* ▷ SITUATE.

sitting-room *n* drawing-room, living-room, lounge.

situate *vb* build, establish, found, install, locate, place, position, put, set up, site, station.

situation *n* **1** area, locale, locality, location, place, position, setting, site, spot. **2** *an awkward situation.* case, circumstances, condition, *inf* kettle of fish, plight, position, predicament, state of affairs. **3** *situations vacant.* employment, job, place, position, post.

size *n* amount, area, bigness, breadth, bulk, capacity, depth, dimensions, extent, gauge, height, immensity, largeness, length, magnitude, mass, measurement, proportions, scale, scope, volume, weight, width. ▷ MEASURE. ● *vb* **size up** ▷ ASSESS.

sizeable *adj* considerable, decent, generous, largish, significant, worthwhile. ▷ BIG.

skate *vb* glide, skim, slide.

skeleton *n* bones, frame, framework, structure.

sketch *n* **1** description, design, diagram, draft, drawing, outline, picture, plan, *inf* rough, skeleton, vignette. **2** *comic sketch.* performance, playlet, scene, skit, turn. ● *vb* depict, draw, indicate, outline, portray, represent. **sketch out** ▷ OUTLINE.

sketchy *adj* bitty, crude, cursory, hasty, hurried, imperfect, incomplete, inexact, perfunctory, rough, scrappy, undeveloped, unfinished, unpolished. *Opp* DETAILED, PERFECT.

skid *vb* aquaplane, glide, go out of control, slide, slip.

skilful *adj* able, accomplished, adept, adroit, apt, artful, capable, competent, consummate, crafty, cunning, deft, dexterous, experienced, expert, gifted, handy, ingenious, masterful, masterly, practised, professional, proficient, qualified, shrewd, smart, talented, trained, versatile, versed, workmanlike. ▷ CLEVER. *Opp* UNSKILFUL.

skill *n* ability, accomplishment, adroitness, aptitude, art, artistry, capability, cleverness, competence, craft, cunning, deftness, dexterity, experience, expertise, facility, flair, gift, handicraft, ingenuity, knack, mastery, professionalism, proficiency, prowess, shrewdness, talent, technique, training, versatility, workmanship.

skilled *adj* experienced, expert, qualified, trained, versed. ▷ SKILFUL.

skim *vb* **1** aquaplane, coast, fly, glide, move lightly, plane, sail, skate, ski, skid, slide, slip. **2** *skim a book.* dip into, leaf through, look through, read quickly, scan, skip, thumb through.

skin *n* casing, coat, coating, complexion, covering, epidermis, exterior, film, fur, hide, husk, integument, membrane, outside, peel, pelt, rind, shell, surface. ● *vb* excoriate, flay, pare, peel, shell, strip.

skin-deep *adj* insubstantial, shallow, superficial, trivial, unimportant.

skinny *adj* bony, emaciated, gaunt, half-starved, lanky, scraggy, wasted. ▷ THIN.

skip *vb* **1** bound, caper, cavort, dance, frisk, gambol, hop, jump, leap, prance, romp, spring. **2** *skip the boring bits.* avoid, forget, ignore, leave out, miss out, neglect, omit, overlook, pass over, skim through. **3** *skip lessons.* be absent from, cut, miss, play truant from.

skirmish *n* brush, fight, fray, scrimmage, *inf* set-to, tussle. ● *vb* ▷ FIGHT.

skirt *vb* avoid, border, bypass, circle, encircle, go round, pass round, *inf* steer clear of, surround.

skit *n* burlesque, parody, satire, sketch, spoof, *inf* take-off.

sky *n* air, atmosphere, *poet* blue, *poet* empyrean, *poet* firmament, *poet* heavens, space, stratosphere, *poet* welkin.

slab *n* block, chunk, hunk, lump, piece, slice, wedge, *inf* wodge.

slack *adj* **1** drooping, limp, loose, sagging, soft. *Opp* TIGHT. **2** *slack attitude*. careless, dilatory, disorganized, easy-going, flaccid, idle, inattentive, indolent, lax, lazy, listless, neglectful, negligent, permissive, relaxed, remiss, slothful, unbusinesslike, uncaring, undisciplined. *Opp* RIGOROUS. **3** *slack trade*. inactive, quiet, slow, slow-moving, sluggish. *Opp* BUSY. ● *vb* be lazy, idle, malinger, neglect your duty, shirk, *inf* skive.

slacken *vb* **1** ease off, loosen, relax, release. **2** *slacken speed*. abate, decrease, ease, lessen, lower, moderate, reduce, slow down.

slacker *n inf* good-for-nothing, idler, lazy person, malingerer, *sl* skiver, sluggard.

slake *vb* allay, assuage, cool, ease, quench, relieve, satisfy.

slam *vb* **1** bang, shut. **2** [*inf*] ▷ CRITICIZE.

slander *n* backbiting, calumny, defamation, denigration, insult, libel, lie, misrepresentation, obloquy, scandal, slur, smear, vilification. ● *vb* blacken the name of, calumniate, defame, denigrate, disparage, libel, malign, misrepresent, slur, smear, spread tales about, tell lies about, traduce, vilify.

slanderous *adj* abusive, calumnious, cruel, damaging, defamatory, disparaging, false, hurtful, insulting, libellous, lying, malicious, mendacious, scurrilous, untrue, vicious.

slang *n* argot, cant, jargon. ● *vb* ▷ INSULT. **slanging match** ▷ QUARREL.

slant *n* **1** angle, bevel, camber, cant, diagonal, gradient, incline, list, pitch, rake, ramp, slope, tilt. **2** *slant on a problem*. approach, attitude, perspective, point of view, standpoint, view, viewpoint. **3** *slant to the news*. bias, distortion, emphasis, imbalance, one-sidedness, prejudice. ● *vb* **1** be at an angle, be skewed, incline, lean, shelve, slope, tilt. **2** *slant the news*. bias, colour, distort, prejudice, twist, weight. **slanting** ▷ OBLIQUE.

slap *vb* smack, spank. ▷ HIT.

slash *vb* gash, slit. ▷ CUT.

slaughter *n* bloodshed, butchery, carnage, killing, massacre, murder. ● *vb* annihilate, butcher, massacre, murder, slay. ▷ KILL.

slaughterhouse *n* abattoir, shambles.

slave *n old use* bondslave, drudge, serf, thrall, vassal. ▷ SERVANT. ● *vb* drudge, exert yourself, grind away, labour, *inf* sweat, toil, *inf* work your fingers to the bone. ▷ WORK.

slave-driver *n* despot, hard taskmaster, tyrant.

slaver *vb* dribble, drool, foam at the mouth, salivate, slobber, spit.

slavery *n* bondage, captivity, enslavement, serfdom, servitude, subjugation, thraldom, vassalage. *Opp* FREEDOM.

slavish *adj* **1** abject, cringing, fawning, grovelling, humiliating, menial, obsequious, servile, submissive. **2** *slavish imitation*. close, flattering, strict, sycophantic, unimaginative, unoriginal. *Opp* INDEPENDENT.

slay *vb* assassinate, bump off, butcher, destroy, dispatch, execute, exterminate, *inf* finish off, martyr, massacre, murder, put down, put to death, slaughter. ▷ KILL.

sleazy *adj* cheap, contemptible, dirty, disreputable, low-class, mean, mucky, run-down, seedy, slovenly, sordid, squalid, unprepossessing.

sledge *n* bob-sleigh, sled, sleigh, toboggan.

sleek *adj* **1** brushed, glossy, graceful, lustrous, shining, shiny, silken, silky, smooth, soft, trim, velvety, well-groomed. *Opp* UNTIDY. **2** *a sleek look*. complacent, contented, fawning, self-satisfied, *inf* slimy, *inf* smarmy, smug, suave, thriving, unctuous, well-fed.

sleep *n inf* beauty sleep, catnap, coma, dormancy, doze, *inf* forty winks, hibernation, *sl* kip, *inf* nap, repose, rest, *inf* shut-eye, siesta, slumber, snooze, torpor, unconsciousness. ● *vb* aestivate, be sleeping, be unconscious, catnap, *inf* doss down, doze, *inf* drop off, drowse, fall asleep, go to bed, *inf* have forty winks, hibernate, *sl* kip, *inf* nod off, rest, slumber, snooze, *inf* take a nap. **sleeping** ▷ ASLEEP.

sleepiness *n* drowsiness, lassitude, lethargy, somnolence, tiredness, torpor.

sleepless *adj* awake, conscious, disturbed, insomniac, restless, *inf* tossing and turning, wakeful, watchful, wide awake. *Opp* ASLEEP.

sleepwalker *n* noctambulist, somnambulist.

sleepy *adj* **1** comatose, *inf* dopey, drowsy, heavy, lethargic, ready to sleep, sluggish, somnolent, soporific, tired, torpid, weary. **2** *a sleepy village*. boring, dull, inactive, quiet, restful, slowmoving, unexciting. *Opp* LIVELY.

slender *adj* **1** fine, graceful, lean, narrow, slight, svelte, sylphlike, trim. ▷ THIN. **2** *slender thread*. feeble, fragile, tenuous. **3** *slender means*. inadequate, meagre, scanty, small. *Opp* FAT, LARGE.

slice *n* carving, layer, piece, rasher, shaving, sliver, wedge. ● *vb* carve, shave off. ▷ CUT.

slick *adj* **1** adroit, artful, clever, cunning, deft, dextrous, efficient, quick, skilful, smart. **2** *a slick talker*. glib, meretricious, plausible, *inf* smarmy, smooth, smug, specious, suave, superficial, *inf* tricky, unctuous, untrustworthy, urbane, wily. **3** *slick hair*. glossy, oiled, plastered down, shiny, sleek, smooth.

slide *n* **1** avalanche, landslide, landslip. **2** *photographic slide*. transparency. ● *vb* aquaplane, coast, glide, glissade, plane, skate, ski, skid, skim, slip, slither, toboggan.

slight *adj* **1** imperceptible, inadequate, inconsequential, inconsiderable, insignificant, insufficient, little, minor, negligible, scanty, slim (*chance*), small, superficial, trifling, trivial, unimportant. **2** *slight build*. delicate, diminutive, flimsy, fragile, frail, petite, sickly, slender, slim, svelte, sylphlike, thin, tiny, weak. *Opp* BIG. ● *n*, *vb* ▷ INSULT.

slightly *adv* hardly, moderately, only just, scarcely. *Opp* VERY.

slim *adj* **1** fine, graceful, lean, narrow, slender, svelte, sylphlike, trim. ▷ THIN. **2** *a slim chance*. little, negligible, remote, slight, unlikely. ● *vb* become slimmer, diet, lose weight, reduce.

slime *n* muck, mucus, mud, ooze, sludge.

slimy *adj* clammy, greasy, mucous, muddy, oily, oozy, slippery, *inf* slippy, slithery, *inf* squidgy, *inf* squishy, wet.

sling *vb* cast, *inf* chuck, fling, heave, hurl, launch, *inf* let fly, lob, pelt, pitch, propel, shoot, shy, throw, toss.

slink *vb* creep, edge, move guiltily, prowl, skulk, slither, sneak, steal.

slinky *adj* [*inf*] *a slinky dress*. clinging, close-fitting, graceful, *inf* sexy, sinuous, sleek.

slip *n* **1** accident, *inf* bloomer, blunder, error, fault, *Fr* faux pas, impropriety, inaccuracy, indiscretion, lapse, miscalculation, mistake, oversight, *inf* slip of the pen, slip of the tongue, *inf* slip-up. **2** *slip of paper*. note, piece, sheet, strip. ● *vb* **1** aquaplane, coast, glide, glissade, move out of control, skate, ski, skid, skim, slide, slither, stumble, trip. **2** *slipped into the room*. creep, edge, move quietly, slink, sneak, steal. **give someone the slip** ▷ ESCAPE. **let slip** ▷ REVEAL. **slip away, slip the net** ▷ ESCAPE. **slip up** ▷ BLUNDER.

slippery *adj* **1** glassy, greasy, icy, lubricated, oily, slimy, *inf* slippy, slithery, smooth, wet. **2** *a slippery customer*. crafty, cunning, devious, evasive, *inf* hard to pin down, shifty, sly, *inf* smarmy, smooth, sneaky, specious, *inf* tricky, unreliable, untrustworthy, wily.

slipshod *adj* careless, disorganized, lax, messy, slapdash, *inf* sloppy, slovenly, untidy.

slit *n* aperture, breach, break, chink, cleft, crack, cut, fissure, gap, gash, hole, incision, opening, rift, slot, split, tear, vent. ● *vb* cut, gash, slice, split, tear.

slither *vb* creep, glide, *inf* skitter, slide, slink, slip, snake, worm.

sliver *n* chip, flake, shard, shaving, snippet, splinter, strip. ▷ PIECE.

slobber *vb* dribble, drool, salivate, slaver.

slogan *n* battle-cry, catch-phrase, catchword, jingle, motto, war-cry, watchword. ▷ SAYING.

slope *n* angle, bank, bevel, camber, cant, gradient, hill, incline, pitch, rake, ramp, scarp, slant, tilt. □ [upwards] *acclivity, ascent, rise.* □ [downwards] *decline, declivity, descent, dip, drop, fall.* ● *vb* ascend, bank, decline, descend, dip, fall, incline, lean, pitch, rise, shelve, slant, tilt, tip. **sloping** ▷ OBLIQUE.

sloppy *adj* **1** liquid, messy, runny, *inf* sloshy, slushy, *inf* splashing about, squelchy, watery, wet. **2** *sloppy work.* careless, dirty, disorganized, lax, messy, slapdash, slipshod, slovenly, unsystematic, untidy. **3** ▷ SENTIMENTAL.

slot *n* **1** aperture, breach, break, channel, chink, cleft, crack, cut, fissure, gap, gash, groove, hole, incision, opening, rift, slit, split, vent. **2** *slot on a schedule.* place, position, space, spot, time.

sloth *n* apathy, idleness, indolence, inertia, laziness, lethargy, sluggishness, torpor.

slouch *vb* droop, hunch, loaf, loll, lounge, sag, shamble, slump, stoop.

slovenly *adj* careless, *inf* couldn't-care-less, disorganized, lax, messy, shoddy, slapdash, slatternly, *inf* sloppy, thoughtless, unmethodical, untidy. *Opp* CAREFUL.

slow *adj* **1** careful, cautious, crawling, dawdling, delayed, deliberate, dilatory, gradual, lagging, late, lazy, leisurely, lingering, loitering, measured, moderate, painstaking, plodding, protracted, slow-moving, sluggardly, sluggish, steady, tardy, torpid, unhurried, unpunctual. **2** *slow learner.* backward, dense, dim, dull, obtuse, *inf* thick. ▷ STUPID. **3** *slow worker.* phlegmatic, reluctant, unenthusiastic, unwilling. ▷ SLUGGISH. *Opp* FAST. ● *vb* **slow down** brake, decelerate, *inf* ease up, go slower, hold back, reduce speed. **be slow** ▷ DAWDLE, DELAY.

sludge *n* mire, muck, mud, ooze, precipitate, sediment, silt, slime, slurry, slush.

sluggish *adj* apathetic, dull, idle, inactive, indolent, inert, lazy, lethargic, lifeless, listless, phlegmatic, slothful, torpid, unresponsive. ▷ SLOW. *Opp* LIVELY.

sluice *vb* flush, rinse, swill, wash.

slumber *n*, *vb* ▷ SLEEP.

slump *n* collapse, crash, decline, depression, dip, downturn, drop, fall, falling-off, plunge, recession, trough. *Opp* BOOM. ● *vb* **1** collapse, crash, decline, dive, drop, fall off, plummet, plunge, recede, sink, slip, *inf* take a nosedive, worsen. *Opp* PROSPER. **2** *slump in a chair.* be limp, collapse, droop, flop, hunch, loll, lounge, sag, slouch, subside.

slur *n* affront, aspersion, calumny, imputation, innuendo, insinuation, insult, libel, slander, smear, stigma. ● *vb* garble, lisp, mumble.

slurry *n* mud, ooze, slime.

sly *adj* artful, *inf* canny, *inf* catty, conniving, crafty, cunning, deceitful, designing, devious, disingenuous, *inf* foxy, furtive, guileful, insidious, knowing, scheming, secretive, *inf* shifty, shrewd, *inf* sneaky, *inf* snide, stealthy, surreptitious, treacherous, tricky, underhand, wily. *Opp* CANDID, OPEN.

smack *vb* pat, slap, spank. ▷ HIT.

small *adj* **1** *inf* baby, bantam, compact, concise, cramped, diminutive, *inf* dinky, dwarf, exiguous, fine, fractional, infinitesimal, lean, lilliputian, little, microscopic, midget, *inf* mini, miniature, minuscule, minute, narrow, petite, *inf* pint-sized, *inf* pocket-sized, *inf* poky, portable, pygmy, short, slender, slight, *inf* teeny, thin, tiny, toy, undergrown, undersized, *inf* wee, *inf* weeny. **2** *small helpings.* inadequate, insufficient, meagre, mean, *inf* measly, miserly, modest, niggardly, parsimonious, *inf* piddling, scanty, skimpy, stingy, ungenerous, unsatisfactory. **3** *a small problem.* inconsequential, insignificant, minor, negligible, nugatory, slim (*chance*), slight, trifling, trivial, unimportant. *Opp* BIG. **small arms** ▷ WEAPON.

small-minded *adj* bigoted, grudging, hidebound, illiberal, intolerant, narrow, narrowminded, old-fashioned, parochial, petty, prejudiced, rigid, selfish, trivial, unimaginative. ▷ MEAN. *Opp* BROAD-MINDED.

smart *adj* **1** acute, adept, artful, astute, bright, clever, crafty, *inf* cute, discerning, ingenious, intelligent, perceptive, perspicacious, quick, quickwitted, shrewd, *sl* streetwise. *Opp* DULL. **2** *smart appearance.* bright, chic, clean, dapper, *inf* dashing, elegant, fashionable, fresh, modish, *inf* natty, neat, *inf* posh, *inf* snazzy, *Fr* soigné, spruce, stylish, tidy, trim, well-dressed, well-groomed, well-looked-after. *Opp* SCRUFFY. **3** *a smart pace.* brisk, *inf* cracking, fast, forceful, quick, rapid, *inf* rattling, speedy, swift. **4** *a smart blow.* painful, sharp, stinging, vigorous. ● *vb* ▷ HURT.

smash *vb* **1** *smash to pieces.* crumple, crush, demolish, destroy, shatter, squash, wreck. ▷ BREAK. **2** *smash into a wall.* bang, bash, batter, bump, collide, crash, hammer, knock, pound, ram, slam, strike, thump, wallop. ▷ HIT.

smear *n* **1** blot, daub, mark, smudge, stain, streak. **2** *a smear on your name.* aspersion, calumny, defamation, imputation, innuendo, insinuation, libel, slander, slur, stigma, vilification. ● *vb* **1** dab, daub, plaster, rub, smudge, spread, wipe. **2** *smear a reputation.* attack, besmirch, blacken, calumniate, defame, discredit, libel, malign, slander, stigmatize, tarnish, vilify.

smell *n* odour, redolence. □ [pleasant] *aroma, bouquet, fragrance, incense, nose, perfume, scent.* □ [unpleasant] *fetor, mephitis, miasma,* inf *pong, pungency, reek, stench, stink, whiff.* ● *vb* **1** *inf* get a whiff of, scent, sniff. **2** *onions smell. inf* hum, *inf* pong, reek, stink, whiff.

smelling *adj* [*Smelling* is usually used in combination: sweet-smelling, etc.] **1** *pleasant-smelling.* aromatic, fragrant, musky, odoriferous, odorous, perfumed, redolent, scented, spicy. **2** *unpleasantsmelling.* fetid, foul, gamy, *inf* high, malodorous, mephitic, miasmic, musty, noisome, *inf* off, *sl* pongy, pungent, putrid, rank, reeking, rotten, smelly, stinking, *inf* whiffy. *Opp* ODOURLESS.

smelly *adj* ▷ SMELLING.

smile *n, vb* beam, grin, leer, simper, smirk, sneer.

smoke *n* **1** air pollution, exhaust, fog, fumes, gas, smog, steam, vapour. **2** cigar, cigarette, cheroot, *inf* fag, pipe, tobacco. ● *vb* **1** emit smoke, fume, reek, smoulder. **2** *smoke cigars.* inhale, puff at.

smoky *adj* clouded, dirty, foggy, grimy, hazy, sooty. *Opp* CLEAR.

smooth *adj* **1** even, flat, horizontal, level, plane, regular, unbroken, unruffled. **2** *smooth sea.* calm, peaceful, placid, quiet, restful. **3** *a smooth finish.* burnished, glassy, glossy, polished, satiny, shiny, silken, silky, sleek, soft, velvety. **4** *smooth progress.* comfortable, easy, effortless, fluent, steady, uncluttered, uneventful, uninterrupted, unobstructed. **5** *a smooth taste.* agreeable, bland, mellow, mild, pleasant, soft, soothing. **6** *a smooth mixture.* creamy, flowing, runny. **7** *a smooth talker.* convincing, facile, glib, insincere, plausible, polite, self-assured, self-satisfied, slick, smug, sophisticated, suave, untrustworthy, urbane. *Opp* ROUGH. ● *vb* buff up, burnish, even out, file, flatten, iron, level, level off, plane, polish, press, roll out, sand down, sandpaper.

smother *vb* **1** asphyxiate, choke, cover, kill, snuff out, stifle, strangle, suffocate, throttle. **2** ▷ SUPPRESS.

smoulder *vb* burn, smoke. **smouldering** ▷ ANGRY.

smudge *vb* blot, blur, dirty, mark, smear, stain, streak.

smug *adj* complacent, conceited, *inf* holier-than-thou, pleased, priggish, self-important, selfrighteous, self-satisfied, sleek, superior. *Opp* HUMBLE.

snack *n* bite, *inf* elevenses, *inf* nibble, refreshments. ▷ MEAL.

snack-bar *n* buffet, café, cafeteria, fast-food restaurant, transport café.

snag *n* catch, complication, difficulty, drawback, hindrance, hitch, impediment, obstacle, obstruction, problem, set-back, *inf* stumbling-block. • *vb* catch, jag, rip, tear.

snake *n* ophidian, serpent. □ *adder, anaconda, boa constrictor, cobra, copperhead, flying-snake, grass snake, mamba, python, rattlesnake, sand snake, sea snake, sidewinder, tree snake, viper.* • *vb* crawl, creep, meander, twist and turn, wander, worm, zigzag. **snaking** ▷ TWISTY.

snap *adj* ▷ SUDDEN. • *vb* **1** break, crack, fracture, give way, part, split. **2** *snap your fingers.* click, crack, pop. **3** *dog snapped at me.* bite, gnash, nip, snatch. **4** *snap orders.* bark, growl, *inf* jump down someone's throat, snarl, speak angrily.

snare *n* ambush, booby-trap, *old use* gin, noose, springe, trap. • *vb* capture, catch, decoy, ensnare, entrap, net, trap.

snarl *vb* **1** bare the teeth, growl. **2** *snarl up rope.* confuse, entangle, jam, knot, tangle, twist.

snatch *vb* **1** catch, clutch, grab, grasp, lay hold of, pluck, seize, take, wrench away, wrest away. **2** abduct, kidnap, remove, steal.

sneak *vb* **1** creep, move stealthily, prowl, skulk, slink, stalk, steal. **2** [*inf*] *sneak on someone.* *sl* grass, inform (against), report, *sl* snitch, *inf* tell tales (about).

sneaking *adj* furtive, half-formed, intuitive, lurking, nagging, *inf* niggling, persistent, private, secret, uncomfortable, unconfessed, undisclosed, unproved, worrying.

sneaky *adj* cheating, contemptible, crafty, deceitful, despicable, devious, dishonest, furtive, *inf* low-down, mean, nasty, shady, *inf* shifty, sly, treacherous, underhand, unorthodox, unscrupulous, untrustworthy. *Opp* STRAIGHTFORWARD.

sneer *vb* be contemptuous, be scornful, boo, curl your lip, hiss, hoot, jeer, laugh, mock, scoff, sniff. **sneer at** ▷ DENIGRATE, RIDICULE.

sniff *vb* **1** *inf* get a whiff of, scent, smell. **2** ▷ SNIVEL. **3** ▷ SNEER.

snigger *vb* chuckle, giggle, laugh, snicker, titter.

snip *vb* clip, dock, nick, nip. ▷ CUT.

snipe *vb* fire, shoot, *inf* take potshots. **snipe at** ▷ CRITICIZE.

snippet *n* fragment, morsel, particle, scrap, shred, snatch. ▷ PIECE.

snivel *vb* blubber, cry, grizzle, mewl, sob, sniff, sniffle, snuffle, whimper, whine, *inf* whinge. ▷ WEEP.

snobbish *adj* affected, condescending, disdainful, élitist, haughty, highfalutin, *inf* hoitytoity, lofty, lordly, patronizing, pompous, *inf* posh, presumptuous, pretentious, *inf* putting on airs, self-important, smug, *inf* snooty, *inf* stuck-up, supercilious, superior, *inf* toffee-nosed. ▷ CONCEITED. *Opp* UNPRETENTIOUS.

snoop *vb* be inquisitive, butt in, do detective work, interfere, intrude, investigate, meddle, *inf* nose about, pry, sneak, spy, *inf* stick your nose in.

snooper *n* busybody, detective, investigator, meddler, sneak, spy.

snout *n* face, muzzle, nose, nozzle, proboscis, trunk.

snub *vb* be rude to, brush off, cold-shoulder, disdain, humiliate, insult, offend, *inf* put someone down, rebuff, reject, scorn, *inf* squash.

snuff *vb* extinguish, put out. **snuff it** ▷ DIE. **snuff out** ▷ KILL.

snug *adj* **1** comfortable, *inf* comfy, cosy, enclosed, friendly, intimate, protected, reassuring, relaxed, relaxing, restful, safe, secure, sheltered, soft, warm. **2** *a snug fit.* close-fitting, exact, well-tailored.

soak *vb* bathe, drench, *inf* dunk, immerse, marinate, penetrate, permeate, pickle, saturate, souse, steep, submerge, wet thoroughly. **soaked, soaking** ▷ WET. **soak up** ▷ ABSORB.

soar *vb* **1** ascend, climb, float, fly, glide, hang, hover, rise, tower. **2** *prices soared.* escalate, increase, rise, rocket, shoot up, spiral.

sob *vb* blubber, cry, gasp, snivel, *inf* sob your heart out, whimper. ▷ WEEP.

sober *adj* **1** calm, clear-headed, composed, dignified, grave, in control, level-headed, lucid, peaceful, quiet, rational, sedate, sensible, serene, serious, solemn, steady, subdued, tranquil, unexciting. *Opp* SILLY. **2** *sober habits.* abstemious, moderate, *inf* on the wagon, restrained, self-controlled, staid, teetotal, temperate. *Opp* DRUNK. **3** *sober dress.* colourless, drab, dull, plain, sombre.

sociable *adj* affable, approachable, *old use* clubbable, companionable, convivial, extroverted, friendly, gregarious, hospitable, neighbourly, outgoing, warm, welcoming. ▷ SOCIAL. *Opp* UNFRIENDLY, WITHDRAWN.

social *adj* **1** civilized, collaborative, gregarious, organized. **2** *social events.* collective, communal, community, general, group, popular, public. ▷ SOCIABLE. *Opp* SOLITARY. • *n* dance, disco, *inf* do, gathering, *inf* get-together, party, reception, reunion, soirée. ▷ PARTY.

socialize *vb* associate, be sociable, entertain, fraternize, get together, *inf* go out together, join in, keep company, mix, relate.

society *n* **1** civilization, the community, culture, the human family, mankind, nation, people, the public. **2** *the society of our friends.* camaraderie, companionship, company, fellowship, friendship, togetherness. **3** *a secret society, etc.* academy, alliance, association, brotherhood, circle, club, confraternity, fraternity, group, guild, league, organization, sisterhood, sodality, sorority, union.

sofa *n* chaise longue, couch, settee, sofa bed. ▷ SEAT.

soft *adj* **1** compressible, crumbly, cushiony, elastic, flabby, flexible, floppy, limp, malleable, mushy, plastic, pliable, pliant, pulpy, spongy, springy, squashable, squashy, squeezable, supple, tender, yielding. **2** *soft ground.* boggy, marshy, muddy, sodden, waterlogged. **3** *a soft bed.* comfortable, cosy. **4** *soft texture.* downy, feathery, fleecy, fluffy, furry, satiny, silky, sleek, smooth, velvety. **5** *soft music.* dim, faint, low, mellifluous, muted, peaceful, quiet, relaxing, restful, soothing, subdued. **6** *soft breeze.* balmy, delicate, gentle, light, mild, pleasant, warm. **7** [*inf*] *a soft option.* easy, undemanding. **8** *soft feelings.* ▷ SOFT-HEARTED. *Opp* HARD, HARSH, VIOLENT.

soften *vb* **1** abate, alleviate, buffer, cushion, deaden, decrease, deflect, diminish, lower, make softer, mellow, mitigate, moderate, muffle, pacify, palliate, quell, quieten, reduce the impact of, subdue, temper, tone down, turn down. **2** dissolve, fluff up, lighten, liquefy, make softer, melt. **3** *soften in attitude.* become softer, concur, ease up, give in, give way, *inf* let up, relax, succumb, weaken, yield. *Opp* HARDEN, INTENSIFY.

soft-hearted *adj* benign, compassionate, conciliatory, easygoing, generous, indulgent, kind-hearted, *derog* lax, lenient, merciful, permissive, sentimental, *inf* soft, sympathetic, tender, tender-hearted, tolerant, understanding. ▷ KIND. *Opp* CRUEL.

soggy *adj* drenched, dripping, heavy (*soil*), saturated, soaked, sodden, *inf* sopping, wet through. ▷ WET. *Opp* DRY.

soil *n* clay, dirt, earth, ground, humus, land, loam, marl, topsoil. • *vb* befoul, besmirch, blacken, contaminate, defile, dirty, make dirty, muddy, pollute, smear, stain, sully, tarnish.

solace *n* comfort, consolation, reassurance, relief. ● *vb* ▷ CONSOLE.

soldier *n* fighter, fighting man, fighting woman, *old use* man at arms, serviceman, servicewoman, warrior. □ *cadet, cavalryman, centurion, commando, conscript, guardsman, gunner, infantryman, lancer, marine, mercenary, NCO, officer, paratrooper, private, recruit, regular, rifleman, sapper, sentry, trooper,* plur *troops, warrior.* ▷ FIGHTER, RANK. ● *vb* **soldier on** ▷ PERSIST.

sole *adj* exclusive, individual, lone, one, only, single, singular, solitary, unique.

solemn *adj* **1** earnest, gloomy, glum, grave, grim, long-faced, reserved, sedate, serious, sober, sombre, staid, straight-faced, thoughtful, unsmiling. *Opp* CHEERFUL. **2** *a solemn occasion.* august, awe-inspiring, awesome, ceremonial, ceremonious, dignified, ecclesiastical, formal, grand, holy, important, imposing, impressive, liturgical, momentous, pompous, religious, ritualistic, stately. *Opp* FRIVOLOUS.

solicit *vb* appeal for, ask for, beg, entreat, importune, petition, seek.

solicitous *adj* **1** attentive, caring, concerned, considerate, sympathetic. **2** ▷ ANXIOUS.

solid *adj* **1** concrete, hard, impenetrable, impermeable, rigid, unmoving. **2** *a solid crowd.* compact, crowded, dense, jammed, packed. **3** *solid gold.* authentic, genuine, pure, real, unadulterated, unalloyed, unmixed. **4** *a solid hour.* continual, continuous, entire, unbroken, uninterrupted, unrelieved, whole. **5** *solid foundations.* firm, fixed, immovable, robust, sound, stable, steady, stout, strong, sturdy, substantial, unbending, unyielding, well-made. **6** *a solid shape.* cubic, rounded, spherical, thick, three-dimensional. **7** *solid evidence.* authoritative, cogent, coherent, convincing, genuine, incontrovertible, indisputable, irrefutable, provable, proven, real, sound, tangible, weighty. **8** *solid support.* complete, dependable, effective, like-minded, reliable, stalwart, strong, trustworthy, unanimous, undivided, united, unwavering, vigorous. *Opp* FLUID, FRAGMENTARY, WEAK.

solidarity *n* accord, agreement, coherence, cohesion, concord, harmony, like-mindedness, unanimity, unity. *Opp* DISUNITY.

solidify *vb* cake, clot, coagulate, congeal, crystallize, freeze, harden, jell, set, thicken. *Opp* LIQUEFY.

soliloquy *n* monologue, speech.

solitary *adj* **1** alone, antisocial, cloistered, companionless, friendless, isolated, lonely, lonesome, reclusive, unsociable, withdrawn. **2** *a solitary survivor.* individual, one, only, single, sole. **3** *a solitary place.* desolate, distant, hidden, inaccessible, isolated, out-of-the-way, private, remote, secluded, sequestered, unfrequented, unknown. *Opp* NUMEROUS, PUBLIC, SOCIAL. ● *n* anchorite, hermit, *inf* loner, recluse.

solitude *n* aloneness, friendlessness, isolation, loneliness, privacy, remoteness, retirement, seclusion.

solo *adv* alone, individually, on your own, unaccompanied.

soloist *n* performer, player, singer. ▷ MUSICIAN.

soluble *adj* **1** explicable, manageable, solvable, tractable, understandable. **2** *soluble in water.* dispersing, dissolving, melting. *Opp* INSOLUBLE.

solution *n* **1** answer, clarification, conclusion, denouement, elucidation, explanation, explication, key, outcome, resolution, solving, unravelling, working out. **2** *a chemical solution.* blend, compound, emulsion, infusion, mixture, suspension.

solve *vb* answer, clear up, *inf* crack, decipher, elucidate, explain, explicate, figure out, find the solution to, interpret, puzzle out, resolve, unravel, work out.

solvent *adj* creditworthy, in credit, profitable, reliable, self-supporting, solid, sound, viable. *Opp* BANKRUPT.

sombre *adj* black, bleak, cheerless, dark, dim, dismal, doleful, drab, dreary, dull, funereal, gloomy, grave, grey, joyless, lowering, lugubrious, melancholy, morose, mournful, serious, sober. ▷ SAD. *Opp* CHEERFUL.

somewhat *adv* fairly, moderately, *inf* pretty, quite, rather, *inf* sort of.

song *n* air, *inf* ditty, *inf* hit, lyric, number, tune. □ *anthem, aria, ballad, blues, calypso, cantata, canticle, carol, chant, chorus, descant, folk-song, hymn, jingle,* Ger *lied* [plur *lieder*], *lullaby, madrigal, nursery rhyme, plainsong, pop song, psalm, reggae, rock, serenade, shanty, soul, spiritual, wassail.*

sonorous *adj* deep, full, loud, powerful, resonant, resounding, reverberant, rich, ringing. *Opp* SHRILL.

soon *adv old use* anon, *inf* any minute now, before long, *inf* in a minute, presently, quickly, shortly, straight away.

sooner *adv* **1** before, earlier. **2** *sooner have tea than coffee.* preferably, rather.

soot *n* dirt, grime.

soothe *vb* allay, appease, assuage, calm, comfort, compose, ease, mollify, pacify, quiet, relieve, salve, settle, still, tranquillize.

soothing *adj* **1** balmy, balsamic, comforting, demulcent, emollient, healing, lenitive, mild, palliative. **2** *soothing music.* calming, gentle, peaceful, pleasant, reassuring, relaxing, restful, serene.

sophisticated *adj* **1** adult, *sl* cool, cosmopolitan, cultivated, cultured, elegant, fashionable, *inf* grown-up, mature, polished, *inf* posh, *derog* pretentious, refined, stylish, urbane, worldly. *Opp* UNSOPHISTICATED. **2** *sophisticated ideas.* advanced, clever, complex, complicated, elaborate, hard to understand, ingenious, intricate, involved, subtle. *Opp* PRIMITIVE, SIMPLE.

soporific *adj* boring, deadening, hypnotic, sedative, sleep-inducing, sleepy, somnolent. *Opp* LIVELY.

sorcerer *n* conjuror, enchanter, enchantress, magician, magus, medicine man, necromancer, sorceress, *old use* warlock, witch, witch-doctor, wizard.

sorcery *n* black magic, charms, conjuring, diabolism, incantations, magic, *inf* mumbo jumbo, necromancy, the occult, spells, voodoo, witchcraft, wizardry.

sordid *adj* **1** dingy, dirty, disreputable, filthy, foul, miserable, *inf* mucky, nasty, offensive, polluted, putrid, ramshackle, seamy, seedy, *inf* sleazy, *inf* slummy, squalid, ugly, unclean, undignified, unpleasant, unsanitary, wretched. *Opp* CLEAN. **2** *sordid dealings.* avaricious, base, corrupt, covetous, degenerate, despicable, dishonourable, ignoble, ignominious, immoral, mean, mercenary, rapacious, selfish, *inf* shabby, shameful, unethical, unscrupulous. *Opp* HONOURABLE.

sore *adj* **1** aching, burning, chafing, delicate, hurting, inflamed, painful, raw, red, sensitive, smarting, stinging, tender. **2** aggrieved, hurt, irked, *inf* peeved, *inf* put out, resentful, upset, vexed. ▷ ANNOYED. ● *n* abrasion, abscess, boil, bruise, burn, carbuncle, gall, gathering, graze, infection, inflammation, injury, laceration, pimple, rawness, redness, scrape, spot, swelling, ulcer. ▷ WOUND. **make sore** abrade, bruise, burn, chafe, chap, gall, graze, hurt, inflame, lacerate, redden, rub.

sorrow *n* **1** affliction, anguish, dejection, depression, desolation, despair, desperation, despondency, disappointment, discontent, disgruntlement, dissatisfaction, distress, dolour, gloom, glumness, grief, heartache, heartbreak, heaviness, homesickness, hopelessness, loneliness, melancholy, misery, misfortune, mourning, sad feelings, sadness, suffering, tearfulness, tribulation, trouble, unhappiness, wistfulness, woe, wretchedness. *Opp* HAPPINESS. **2** *sorrow for wrongdoing.* apologies, guilt, penitence, regret, remorse, repentance. • *vb* agonize, be sorrowful, be sympathetic, bewail, grieve, lament, mourn, weep. *Opp* REJOICE.

sorrowful *adj* broken-hearted, dejected, disconsolate, distressed, doleful, grief stricken, heartbroken, long faced, lugubrious, melancholy, miserable, mournful, regretful, rueful, saddened, sombre, tearful, unhappy, upset, woebegone, woeful, wretched. ▷ SAD, SORRY. *Opp* HAPPY.

sorry *adj* **1** apologetic, ashamed, conscience-stricken, contrite, guilt-ridden, penitent, regretful, remorseful, repentant, shamefaced. **2** *sorry for the homeless.* compassionate, concerned, merciful, pitying, sympathetic, understanding.

sort *n* **1** brand, category, class, classification, description, form, genre, group, kind, make, mark, nature, quality, set, type, variety. **2** breed, class, family, genus, race, species, strain, stock, variety. • *vb* arrange, assort, catalogue, categorize, classify, divide, file, grade, group, order, organize, put in order, rank, systematize, tidy. *Opp* MIX. **sort out 1** choose, *inf* put on one side, segregate, select, separate, set aside. **2** *sort out a problem.* attend to, clear up, cope with, deal with, find an answer to, grapple with, handle, manage, organize, put right, resolve, solve, straighten out, tackle.

soul *n* **1** psyche, spirit. **2** [*inf*] *poor soul!* ▷ PERSON.

soulful *adj* deeply felt, eloquent, emotional, expressive, fervent, heartfelt, inspiring, moving, passionate, profound, sincere, spiritual, stirring, uplifting, warm. *Opp* SOULLESS.

soulless *adj* cold, inhuman, insincere, mechanical, perfunctory, routine, spiritless, superficial, trite, unemotional, unfeeling, uninspiring, unsympathetic. *Opp* SOULFUL.

sound *adj* **1** durable, fit, healthy, hearty, *inf* in good shape, robust, secure, solid, strong, sturdy, tough, undamaged, uninjured, unscathed, vigorous, well, whole. **2** *sound food.* eatable, edible, fit for human consumption, good, wholesome. **3** *sound ideas.* balanced, coherent, common-sense, convincing, correct, judicious, logical, orthodox, prudent, rational, reasonable, reasoned, sane, sensible, well-founded, wise. **4** *a sound business.* dependable, established, profitable, recognized, reliable, reputable, safe, secure, trustworthy, viable. *Opp* BAD, WEAK. • *n* din, noise, resonance, timbre, tone. □ [Most of these words can be used as either *nouns* or *verbs*.] *bang, bark, bawl, bay, bellow, blare, blast, bleat, bleep, boo, boom, bray, buzz, cackle, caw, chime, chink, chirp, chirrup, chug, clack, clamour, clang, clank, clap, clash, clatter, click, clink, cluck, coo, crack, crackle, crash, creak, croak, croon, crow, crunch, cry, drone, echo, explosion, fizz, grate, grizzle, groan, growl, grunt, gurgle, hiccup, hiss, honk, hoot, howl, hum, jabber, jangle, jeer, jingle, lisp, low, miaow, moan, moo, murmur, neigh, patter, peal, ping, pip, plop, pop, purr, quack, rattle, report, reverberation, ring, roar, rumble, rustle, scream, screech, shout, shriek, sigh, sizzle, skirl, slam, slurp, smack, snap, snarl, sniff, snore, snort, sob, splutter, squawk, squeak, squeal, squelch, swish, throb, thud, thump, thunder, tick, ting, tinkle, toot, trumpet, twang, tweet, twitter, wail, warble, whimper, whine, whinny, whir, whistle, whiz, whoop, woof, yap, yell, yelp, yodel, yowl.* ▷ NOISE. • *vb* **1** become audible, be heard, echo, make a noise, resonate, resound, reverberate. **2** *sound a signal.* activate, cause, create, make, make audible, produce, pronounce, set off, utter. **sound out** check, examine, inquire into, investigate, measure, plumb, probe, research, survey, test, try.

soup *n* broth, consommé, stock.

sour *adj* **1** acid, acidic, acidulous, bitter, citrus, lemony, pungent, sharp, tangy, tart, unripe, vinegary. **2** *sour milk.* bad, curdled, *inf* off, rancid, stale, turned. **3** *sour remarks*. acerbic, bad-tempered, bitter, caustic, cross, crusty, curmudgeonly, cynical, disaffected, disagreeable, grudging, grumpy, ill-natured, irritable, jaundiced, peevish, petulant, snappy, testy, unpleasant.

source *n* **1** author, begetter, cause, creator, derivation, informant, initiator, originator, root, starting-point. **2** *source of river*. head, origin, spring, start, well-head, well-spring. ▷ BEGINNING.

souvenir *n* heirloom, keepsake, memento, relic, reminder.

sovereign *adj* **1** absolute, all-powerful, dominant, highest, royal, supreme, unlimited. **2** *sovereign state*. autonomous, independent, self-governing. ● *n* emperor, empress, king, monarch, prince, princess, queen. ▷ RULER.

sow *vb* broadcast, disseminate, plant, scatter, seed, spread.

space *adj* extraterrestrial, interplanetary, interstellar, orbiting. ● *n* **1** emptiness, endlessness, infinity, ionosphere, stratosphere, the universe. **2** *space to move about*. *inf* elbow-room, expanse, freedom, latitude, leeway, margin, room, scope, spaciousness. **3** *an empty space*. area, blank, break, chasm, concourse, distance, duration, gap, hiatus, hole, intermission, interval, lacuna, lapse, opening, place, spell, stretch, time, vacuum, wait. ● *vb space things out*. ▷ ARRANGE.

spacious *adj* ample, broad, capacious, commodious, extensive, large, open, roomy, sizeable, vast, wide. ▷ BIG. *Opp* SMALL.

span *n* breadth, compass, distance, duration, extent, interval, length, period, reach, scope, stretch, term, width. ● *vb* arch over, bridge, cross, extend across, go over, pass over, reach over, straddle, stretch over, traverse.

spank *vb* slap, slipper, smack. ▷ HIT, PUNISH.

spar *vb* box, exchange blows, scrap, shadow-box. ▷ FIGHT.

spare *adj* **1** additional, auxiliary, extra, free, inessential, in reserve, leftover, odd, remaining, superfluous, supernumerary, supplementary, surplus, unnecessary, unneeded, unused, unwanted. *Opp* NECESSARY. **2** *a spare figure*. ▷ THIN. ● *vb* **1** be merciful to, deliver, forgive, free, have mercy on, let go, let off, liberate, pardon, redeem, release, reprieve, save. **2** *spare money, time, etc*. afford, allow, donate, give, give up, manage, part with, provide, sacrifice. **sparing** ▷ ECONOMICAL, MISERLY.

spark *n* flash, flicker, gleam, glint, scintilla, sparkle. ● *vb* **spark off** ignite, kindle. ▷ PROVOKE.

sparkle *vb* burn, coruscate, flash, flicker, gleam, glint, glitter, reflect, scintillate, shine, spark, twinkle, wink. ▷ LIGHTEN.

sparkling *adj* **1** brilliant, flashing, glinting, glittering, scintillating, shining, shiny, twinkling. ▷ BRIGHT. *Opp* DULL. **2** *sparkling drinks*. aerated, bubbling, bubbly, carbonated, effervescent, fizzy, foaming.

sparse *adj inf* few and far between, inadequate, light, little, meagre, scanty, scarce, scattered, sparing, spread out, thin, *inf* thin on the ground. *Opp* PLENTIFUL.

spartan *adj* abstemious, ascetic, austere, bare, bleak, disciplined, frugal, hard, harsh, plain, rigid, rigorous, severe, simple, stern, strict. *Opp* LUXURIOUS.

spasm *n* attack, contraction, convulsion, eruption, fit, jerk, outburst, paroxysm, seizure, *plur* throes, twitch.

spasmodic *adj inf* by fits and starts, erratic, fitful, intermittent, interrupted, irregular, jerky, occasional, *inf* on and off, periodic, sporadic. *Opp* CONTINUOUS, REGULAR.

spate *n* cataract, flood, flow, gush, inundation, onrush, outpouring, rush, torrent.

spatter *vb* bespatter, besprinkle, daub, pepper, scatter, shower, slop, speckle, splash, splatter, spray, sprinkle.

speak *vb* answer, argue, articulate, ask, communicate, complain, converse, declaim, declare, deliver a speech, discourse, ejaculate, enunciate, exclaim, express yourself, fulminate, harangue, hold a conversation, hold forth, object, *inf* pipe up, plead, pronounce words, read aloud, recite, say something, soliloquize, *inf* speechify, talk, tell, use your voice, utter, verbalize, vocalize, voice. ▷ SAY, TALK. **speak about** ▷ MENTION. **speak to** ▷ ADDRESS. **speak your mind** be honest, say what you think, speak honestly, speak out, state your opinion, voice your thoughts.

speaker *n* lecturer, mouthpiece, orator, public speaker, spokesperson.

spear *n* assegai, harpoon, javelin, lance, pike.

special *adj* **1** different, distinguished, exceptional, extraordinary, important, infrequent, momentous, notable, noteworthy, odd, *inf* out-of-the-ordinary, rare, red-letter (*day*), remarkable, significant, strange, uncommon, unconventional, unorthodox, unusual. *Opp* ORDINARY. **2** *Petrol has a special smell.* characteristic, distinctive, idiosyncratic, memorable, peculiar, singular, unique, unmistakable. **3** *my special chair.* especial, individual, particular, personal. **4** *a special tool for the job.* bespoke, proper, specialized, specific.

specialist *n* **1** authority, connoisseur, expert, fancier (*pigeon fancier*), master, professional, *inf* pundit, researcher. **2** [*medical*] consultant. ▷ MEDICINE.

speciality *n inf* claim to fame, expertise, field, forte, genius, *inf* line, specialization, special knowledge, special skill, strength, strong point, talent.

specialize *vb* **specialize in** be a specialist in, be best at, concentrate on, devote yourself to, have a reputation for.

specialized *adj* esoteric, expert, specialist, unfamiliar.

species *n* breed, class, genus, kind, race, sort, type, variety.

specific *adj* clear-cut, defined, definite, detailed, exact, explicit, express, fixed, identi-fied, individual, itemized, known, named, particular, peculiar, precise, predetermined, special, specified, unequivocal. *Opp* GENERAL.

specify *vb* be specific about, define, denominate, detail, enumerate, establish, identify, itemize, list, name, particularize, *inf* set out, spell out, stipulate.

specimen *n* example, exemplar, illustration, instance, model, pattern, representative, sample.

specious *adj* casuistic, deceptive, misleading, plausible, seductive.

speck *n* bit, crumb, dot, fleck, grain, mark, mite, *old use* mote, particle, speckle, spot, trace.

speckled *adj* blotchy, brindled, dappled, dotted, flecked, freckled, mottled, patchy, spattered (with), spotted, spotty, sprinkled (with), stippled.

spectacle *n* ceremonial, ceremony, colourfulness, display, exhibition, extravaganza, grandeur, magnificence, ostentation, pageantry, parade, pomp, show, sight, spectacular effects, splendour. **spectacles** ▷ GLASS.

spectacular *adj* beautiful, breathtaking, colourful, dramatic, elaborate, eye-catching, impressive, magnificent, *derog* ostentatious, sensational, showy, splendid, stunning.

spectator *n plur* audience, beholder, bystander, *plur* crowd, eyewitness, looker-on, observer, onlooker, passer-by, viewer, watcher, witness.

spectre *n* apparition, ghost, phantom, presentiment, vision, wraith. ▷ SPIRIT.

spectrum *n* compass, extent, gamut, orbit, range, scope, series, span, spread, sweep, variety.

speculate *vb* **1** conjecture, consider, hypothesize, make guesses, meditate, ponder, reflect, ruminate, surmise, theorize, weigh up, wonder. ▷ THINK. **2** *speculate in shares.* gamble, invest speculatively, *inf* play the market, take a chance, wager.

speculative *adj* **1** abstract, based on guesswork, conjectural, doubtful, *inf* gossipy, hypothetical, notional, suppositional, suppositious, theoretical, unfounded, uninformed, unproven, untested. *Opp* PROVEN. **2** *speculative investments. inf* chancy, *inf* dicey, *inf* dodgy, hazardous, *inf* iffy, risky, uncertain, unpredictable, unreliable, unsafe. *Opp* SAFE.

speech *n* **1** articulation, communication, declamation, delivery, diction, elocution, enunciation, expression, pronunciation, speaking, talking, using words, utterance. **2** dialect, idiolect, idiom, jargon, language, parlance, register, tongue. **3** *a public speech.* address, discourse, disquisition, harangue, homily, lecture, oration, paper, presentation, sermon, *inf* spiel, talk, tirade. **4** *speech in a play.* dialogue, lines, monologue, soliloquy.

speechless *adj* dumb, dumbfounded, dumbstruck, inarticulate, *inf* mum, mute, nonplussed, silent, thunderstruck, tongue-tied, voiceless. *Opp* TALKATIVE.

speed *n* **1** pace, rate, tempo, velocity. **2** alacrity, briskness, celerity, dispatch, expeditiousness, fleetness, haste, hurry, quickness, rapidity, speediness, swiftness. • *vb* **1** *inf* belt, *inf* bolt, *inf* bowl along, canter, career, dart, dash, flash, flit, fly, gallop, *inf* go like the wind, hasten, hurry, hurtle, make haste, move quickly, *inf* nip, *inf* put your foot down, race, run, rush, shoot, sprint, stampede, streak, tear, *inf* zoom. **2** *speed on the road.* break the speed limit, go too fast. **speed up** ▷ ACCELERATE.

speedy *adj* **1** expeditious, fast, *old use* fleet, nimble, quick, rapid, swift. **2** *a speedy exit.* hasty, hurried, immediate, precipitate, prompt, unhesitating. *Opp* SLOW.

spell *n* **1** bewitchment, charm, conjuration, conjuring, enchantment, incantation, magic formula, sorcery, witchcraft, witchery. **2** *the spell of the theatre.* allure, captivation, charm, enthralment, fascination, glamour, magic. **3** *a spell of rain.* interval, period, phase, season. **4** *a spell at the wheel.* session, stint, stretch, term, time, tour of duty, turn, watch. • *vb* augur, bode, foretell, indicate, mean, portend, presage, signal, signify, suggest. **spell out** ▷ CLARIFY.

spellbound *adj* bewitched, captivated, charmed, enchanted, enthralled, entranced, fascinated, hypnotized, mesmerized, overcome, overpowered, transported.

spend *vb* **1** *inf* blue, consume, *inf* cough up, disburse, exhaust, expend, *inf* fork out, fritter, *inf* get through, invest, *inf* lash out, pay out, *inf* shell out, *inf* splash out, *inf* splurge, squander. **2** *spend time.* devote, fill, occupy, pass, use up, waste.

spendthrift *n inf* big spender, prodigal, profligate, wasteful person, wastrel. *Opp* MISER.

sphere *n* **1** ball, globe, globule, orb, spheroid. **2** *sphere of influence.* area, department, discipline, domain, field, province, range, scope, speciality, subject, territory. **3** *social sphere.* caste, class, domain, milieu, position, rank, society, station, stratum, walk of life.

spherical *adj* ball-shaped, globe-shaped, globular, rotund, round, spheric, spheroidal.

spice *n* **1** flavouring, piquancy, relish, seasoning. □ *allspice, bayleaf, capsicum, cardamom, cassia, cayenne, chilli, cinnamon, cloves, coriander, curry powder, ginger, grains of paradise, juniper, mace, nutmeg, paprika, pepper, pimento, poppy seed, saffron, sesame, turmeric.* **2** *add spice to life.* colour, excitement, gusto, interest, *inf* lift, *inf* pep, sharpness, stimulation, vigour, zest.

spicy *adj* aromatic, fragrant, gingery, highly flavoured, hot, peppery, piquant, pungent, seasoned, spiced, tangy, zestful. *Opp* BLAND.

spike *n* barb, nail, pin, point, projection, prong, skewer, spine, stake, tine. ● *vb* impale, perforate, pierce, skewer, spear, spit, stab, stick.

spill *vb* **1** overturn, slop, splash about, tip over, upset. **2** brim, flow, overflow, pour, run. **3** *lorry spilled its load*. discharge, drop, scatter, shed, tip.

spin *vb* **1** gyrate, pirouette, revolve, rotate, swirl, turn, twirl, twist, wheel, whirl. **2** *head was spinning*. be giddy, reel, suffer vertigo, swim. **spin out** ▷ PROLONG.

spindle *n* axis, axle, pin, rod, shaft.

spine *n* **1** backbone, spinal column, vertebrae. **2** *hedgehog's spines*. barb, bristle, needle, point, prickle, prong, quill, spike, spur, thorn.

spineless *adj* cowardly, craven, faint-hearted, feeble, helpless, irresolute, *inf* lily-livered, pusillanimous, *inf* soft, timid, unheroic, weedy, *inf* wimpish. ▷ WEAK. *Opp* BRAVE.

spiral *adj* cochlear, coiled, corkscrew, turning, whorled. ● *n* coil, curl, helix, screw, whorl. ● *vb* **1** turn, twist. **2** *spiralling prices*. ▷ FALL, RISE.

spire *n* flèche, pinnacle, steeple.

spirit *n* **1** *Lat* anima, breath, mind, psyche, soul. **2** *supernatural spirits*. apparition, *inf* bogy, demon, devil, genie, ghost, ghoul, gremlin, hobgoblin, imp, incubus, nymph, phantasm, phantom, poltergeist, *poet* shade, shadow, spectre, *inf* spook, sprite, sylph, vision, visitant, wraith, zombie. **3** *spirit of a poem*. aim, atmosphere, essence, feeling, heart, intention, meaning, mood, purpose, sense. **4** *fighting spirit*. animation, bravery, cheerfulness, confidence, courage, daring, determination, dynamism, energy, enthusiasm, fire, fortitude, *inf* get-up-and-go, *inf* go, *inf* guts, heroism, liveliness, mettle, morale, motivation, optimism, pluck, resolve, valour, verve, vivacity, will-power, zest. **5** ▷ ALCOHOL.

spirited *adj* active, animated, assertive, brave, brisk, buoyant, courageous, daring, determined, dynamic, energetic, enterprising, enthusiastic, frisky, gallant, *inf* gutsy, intrepid, lively, mettlesome, plucky, positive, resolute, sparkling, sprightly, vigorous, vivacious. *Opp* SPIRITLESS.

spiritless *adj* apathetic, cowardly, defeatist, despondent, dispirited, dull, irresolute, lacklustre, languid, lethargic, lifeless, listless, melancholy, negative, passive, slow, unenterprising, unenthusiastic. *Opp* SPIRITED.

spiritual *adj* devotional, divine, eternal, heavenly, holy, incorporeal, inspired, other-worldly, religious, sacred, unworldly, visionary. *Opp* TEMPORAL.

spit *n* **1** dribble, saliva, spittle, sputum. ● *vb* dribble, expectorate, salivate, splutter. **spit out** ▷ DISCHARGE. **spitting image** ▷ TWIN.

spite *n* animosity, animus, antagonism, *inf* bitchiness, bitterness, *inf* cattiness, gall, grudge, hate, hatred, hostility, ill-feeling, ill will, malevolence, malice, maliciousness, malignity, rancour, resentment, spleen, venom, vindictiveness. ● *vb* ▷ ANNOY.

spiteful *adj* acid, acrimonious, *inf* bitchy, bitter, *inf* catty, cruel, cutting, hateful, hostile, hurtful, ill-natured, invidious, malevolent, malicious, nasty, poisonous, punitive, rancorous, resentful, revengeful, sharp, *inf* snide, sour, unforgiving, venomous, vicious, vindictive. *Opp* KIND.

splash *vb* **1** bespatter, besprinkle, shower, slop, *inf* slosh, spatter, spill, splatter, spray, sprinkle, squirt, wash. **2** *splash about in water*. bathe, dabble, paddle, wade. **3** *splash news across the front page*. blazon, display, exhibit, flaunt, *inf* plaster, publicize, show, spread. **splash out** ▷ SPEND.

splay *vb* make a V-shape, slant, spread.

splendid *adj* admirable, aweinspiring, beautiful, brilliant, costly, dazzling, dignified, elegant, fine, first-class, glittering, glorious, gorgeous, grand, great, handsome, imposing, impressive, lavish, luxurious, magnificent, majestic, marvellous, noble, ornate, *derog* ostentatious, palatial, *inf* posh, refulgent, regal, resplendent, rich, royal, *derog* showy, spectacular, *inf* splendiferous, stately, sublime, sumptuous, *inf* super, superb, supreme, wonderful. ▷ EXCELLENT.

splendour *n* beauty, brilliance, ceremony, costliness, display, elegance, *inf* glitter, glory, grandeur, luxury, magnificence, majesty, nobility, ostentation, pomp, pomp and circumstance, refulgence, richness, show, spectacle, stateliness, sumptuousness.

splice *vb* bind, conjoin, entwine, join, knit, marry, tie together, unite.

splinter *n* chip, flake, fragment, shard, shaving, shiver, sliver. • *vb* chip, crack, fracture, shatter, shiver, smash, split. ▷ BREAK.

split *n* **1** break, chink, cleavage, cleft, crack, cranny, crevice, fissure, furrow, gash, groove, leak, opening, rent, rift, rip, rupture, slash, slit, tear. **2** breach, dichotomy, difference, dissension, divergence of opinion, division, divorce, estrangement, schism, separation. ▷ QUARREL. • *vb* **1** break up, disintegrate, divide, divorce, go separate ways, move apart, separate. **2** *split logs*. burst, chop, cleave, crack, rend, rip apart, rip open, slash, slice, slit, splinter, tear. ▷ CUT. **3** *split profits*. allocate, allot, apportion, distribute, divide, halve, share. **4** *road splits*. bifurcate, branch, diverge, fork. **split on** ▷ INFORM.

spoil *vb* **1** blight, blot, blotch, bungle, damage, deface, destroy, disfigure, *inf* dish, harm, injure, *inf* make a mess of, mar, *inf* mess up, ruin, stain, undermine, undo, upset, vitiate, worsen, wreck. *Opp* IMPROVE. **2** *food spoiled in the heat*. become useless, curdle, decay, decompose, go bad, *inf* go off, moulder, perish, putrefy, rot, *inf* turn. **3** *spoil children*. coddle, cosset, dote on, indulge, make a fuss of, mollycoddle, over-indulge, pamper.

spoken *adj* oral, unwritten, verbal, *Lat* viva voce. *Opp* WRITTEN.

spokesperson *n* mouthpiece, representative, spokesman, spokeswoman.

sponge *vb* **1** clean, cleanse, mop, rinse, sluice, swill, wash, wipe. **2** [*inf*] *sponge on friends*. be dependent (on), cadge (from), scrounge (from).

spongy *adj* absorbent, compressible, elastic, giving, porous, soft, springy, yielding. *Opp* SOLID.

sponsor *n inf* angel, backer, benefactor, donor, patron, promoter, supporter. • *vb* back, be a sponsor of, finance, fund, help, patronize, promote, subsidize, support, underwrite.

sponsorship *n* aegis, auspices, backing, benefaction, funding, guarantee, patronage, promotion, support.

spontaneous *adj* **1** *inf* ad lib, extempore, impromptu, impulsive, *inf* off-the-cuff, unplanned, unpremeditated, unprepared, unrehearsed, voluntary. **2** *a spontaneous reaction*. automatic, instinctive, instinctual, involuntary, mechanical, natural, reflex, unconscious, unconstrained, unforced, unthinking. *Opp* PREMEDITATED.

spooky *adj* creepy, eerie, frightening, ghostly, haunted, mysterious, scary, uncanny, unearthly, weird.

spool *n* bobbin, reel.

spoon *n* dessert-spoon, ladle, tablespoon, teaspoon.

spoon-feed *vb* cosset, help, indulge, mollycoddle, pamper, spoil.

spoor *n* footprints, scent, traces, track.

sporadic *adj* erratic, fitful, intermittent, irregular, occasional, periodic, scattered, separate, unpredictable.

sport *n* **1** activity, amusement, diversion, enjoyment, entertainment, exercise, fun, games, pastime, play, pleasure, recreation. □ *aerobics, angling, archery, athletics, badminton, base-ball, basketball, billiards, blood sports, bobsleigh, bowls, boxing, canoeing, climbing, cricket, croquet, cross-country, curling, darts, decathlon, discus, fishing, football, gliding, golf, gymnastics, hockey, hunting, hurdling, ice-hockey, javelin, jogging, keep-fit, lacrosse, marathon, martial arts, mountaineering, netball, orienteering, pentathlon,* inf *ping-pong, polo, pool, pot-holing, quoits, racing, rock-climbing, roller-skating, rounders, rowing, Rugby, running, sailing, shooting, shot, show-jumping, skating, skiing, skin-diving, sky-diving, snooker, soccer, squash, street-hockey, surfing, surf-riding, swimming, table-tennis, tennis, tobogganing, trampolining, volley-ball, water-polo, water-skiing, wind-surfing, winter sports, wrestling, yachting.* ▷ ATHLETICS, RACE. **2** badinage, banter, humour, jesting, joking, merriment, raillery, teasing. ● *vb* **1** caper, cavort, divert yourself, frisk about, frolic, gambol, lark about, rollick, romp, skip about. **2** *sport new clothes.* display, exhibit, flaunt, show off, wear.

sporting *adj* considerate, fair, generous, good-humoured, honourable, sportsmanlike.

sportive *adj* coltish, frisky, kittenish, light-hearted, playful, waggish. ▷ SPRIGHTLY.

sportsperson *n* contestant, participant, player, sportsman, sportswoman.

sporty *adj* **1** active, athletic, energetic, fit, vigorous. **2** *sporty clothes.* casual, informal, *inf* loud, rakish, showy, *inf* snazzy.

spot *n* **1** blemish, blot, blotch, discoloration, dot, fleck, mark, patch, smudge, speck, speckle, stain, stigma. **2** *spot on the skin.* birthmark, boil, freckle, *plur* impetigo, mole, naevus, pimple, pock, pock-mark, *plur* rash, sty, whitlow, *sl* zit. **3** *spots of rain.* bead, blob, drop. **4** *spot for a picnic.* locale, locality, location, neighbourhood, place, point, position, scene, setting, site, situation. **5** *an awkward spot.* difficulty, dilemma, embarrassment, mess, predicament, quandary, situation. **6** *spot of bother.* bit, small amount, *inf* smidgen. ● *vb* **1** blot, discolour, fleck, mark, mottle, smudge, spatter, speckle, splash, spray, stain. **2** ▷ SEE.

spotless *adj* **1** clean, fresh, immaculate, laundered, unmarked, unspotted, white. **2** *spotless reputation.* blameless, faultless, flawless, immaculate, innocent, irreproachable, pure, unblemished, unsullied, untarnished, *inf* whiter than white.

spotty *adj* blotchy, dappled, flecked, freckled, mottled, pimply, pockmarked, pocky, spattered, speckled, speckly, *inf* splodgy, spotted.

spouse *n* better half, *old use* helpmate, husband, partner, wife.

spout *n* duct, fountain, gargoyle, geyser, jet, lip, nozzle, outlet, rose (*of watering-can*), spray, waterspout. ● *vb* **1** discharge, emit, erupt, flow, gush, jet, pour, shoot, spew, spit, spurt, squirt, stream. **2** ▷ TALK.

sprawl *vb* **1** flop, lean back, lie, loll, lounge, recline, relax, slouch, slump, spread out, stretch out. **2** be scattered, branch out, spread, straggle.

spray *n* **1** drizzle, droplets, fountain, mist, shower, splash, sprinkling. **2** *spray of flowers.* arrangement, bouquet, branch, bunch, corsage, posy, sprig. **3** *spray for paint.* aerosol, atomizer, spray-gun, sprinkler, vaporizer. ● *vb* diffuse, disperse, scatter, shower, spatter, splash, spread in droplets, sprinkle.

spread *n* **1** broadcasting, broadening, development, diffusion, dispensing, dispersal, dissemination, distribution, expansion, extension, growth, increase, passing on, proliferation, promotion, promulgation. **2** *spread of a bird's wings.* breadth, compass, extent, size, span, stretch, sweep. **3** ▷ MEAL. ● *vb* **1** arrange, display, lay out, open out, unfold, unfurl, unroll. **2** broaden, enlarge, expand, extend, fan out, get bigger, get longer, get wider, lengthen, *inf* mushroom, proliferate, straggle, widen. **3** *spread news.* advertise, broadcast, circulate, diffuse, dispense, disperse, disseminate, distribute, divulge, give out, make known, pass on, pass round, proclaim, promote, promulgate, publicize, publish, scatter, sow, transmit. **4** *spread butter.* apply, cover a surface with, smear.

spree *n inf* binge, debauch, escapade, *inf* fling, frolic, *inf* orgy, outing, revel. ▷ REVELRY.

sprightly *adj* active, agile, animated, brisk, *inf* chipper, energetic, jaunty, lively, nimble, *inf* perky, playful, quickmoving, spirited, sportive, spry, vivacious. *Opp* LETHARGIC.

spring *n* **1** bounce, buoyancy, elasticity, give, liveliness, resilience. **2** *clock spring.* coil, mainspring. **3** *spring of water.* fount, fountain, geyser, source (*of river*), spa, well, well-spring. ● *vb* bounce, bound, hop, jump, leap, pounce, vault. **spring from** come from, derive from, proceed from, stem from. **spring up** appear, arise, burst forth, come up, develop, emerge, germinate, grow, shoot up, sprout.

springy *adj* bendy, elastic, flexible, pliable, resilient, spongy, stretchy, supple. *Opp* RIGID.

sprinkle *vb* drip, dust, pepper, scatter, shower, spatter, splash, spray, strew.

sprint *vb* dash, *inf* hare, race, speed, *inf* tear. ▷ RUN.

sprout *n* bud, shoot. ● *vb* bud, come up, develop, emerge, germinate, grow, shoot up, spring up.

spruce *adj* clean, dapper, elegant, groomed, *inf* natty, neat, *inf* posh, smart, tidy, trim, well-dressed, well-groomed, *inf* well-turned-out. *Opp* SCRUFFY. ● *vb* **spruce up** ▷ TIDY.

spur *n* **1** encouragement, goad, impetus, incentive, incitement, inducement, motivation, motive, prod, prompting, stimulus, urging. **2** *motorway spur.* branch, projection. ● *vb* animate, egg on, encourage, impel, incite, motivate, pressure, pressurize, prick, prod, prompt, provide an incentive, stimulate, urge.

spurn *vb* disown, give (someone) the cold shoulder, jilt, rebuff, reject, renounce, repel, repudiate, repulse, shun, snub, turn your back on.

spy *n* contact, double agent, fifth columnist, *sl* grass, infiltrator, informant, informer, *inf* mole, private detective, secret agent, snooper, stool-pigeon, undercover agent. ● *vb* **1** be a spy, be engaged in spying, eavesdrop, gather intelligence, inform, *inf* snoop. **2** ▷ SEE. **spy on** keep under surveillance, *inf* tail, trail, watch.

spying *n* counter-espionage, detective work, eavesdropping, espionage, intelligence, snooping, surveillance.

squabble *vb* argue, bicker, clash, *inf* row, wrangle. ▷ QUARREL.

squalid *adj* **1** dingy, dirty, disgusting, filthy, foul, insalubrious, mean, mucky, nasty, poverty-stricken, repulsive, run-down, *inf* sleazy, slummy, sordid, ugly, uncared-for, unpleasant, wretched. *Opp* CLEAN. **2** *squalid behaviour.* corrupt, degrading, dishonest, dishonourable, disreputable, immoral, scandalous, *inf* shabby, shameful, unethical, unworthy. *Opp* HONOURABLE.

squander *vb inf* blow, *inf* blue, dissipate, *inf* fritter, misuse, spend unwisely, *inf* splurge, use up, waste. *Opp* SAVE.

square *adj* **1** perpendicular, rectangular, right-angled. **2** *a square deal. inf* above-board, decent, equitable, ethical, fair, honest, honourable, proper, *inf* right and proper, *inf* straight. ● *n* **1** piazza, plaza. **2** [*inf*] *an old-fashioned square.* bourgeois, conformist, conservative, conventional person, die-hard, *inf* fuddy-duddy, *inf* old fogy, *inf* stick-in-the-mud, traditionalist. ● *vb square an account.* ▷

SETTLE. **squared** chequered, criss-crossed, marked in squares.

squash *vb* **1** compress, crumple, crush, flatten, mangle, mash, pound, press, pulp, smash, stamp on, tamp down, tread on. **2** *squash into a room.* cram, crowd, pack, push, ram, shove, squeeze, stuff, thrust, wedge. **3** *squash an uprising.* control, put down, quash, quell, repress, suppress. **4** *squash with a look.* humiliate, *inf* put down, silence, snub.

squashy *adj* mashed up, mushy, pulpy, shapeless, soft, spongy, squelchy, yielding. *Opp* FIRM.

squat *adj* burly, dumpy, plump, podgy, short, stocky, thick, thickset. *Opp* TALL. ● *vb* crouch, sit.

squeamish *adj inf* choosy, dainty, fastidious, finicky, over-scrupulous, particular, *inf* pernickety, prim, *inf* prissy, prudish, scrupulous.

squeeze *vb* **1** clasp, compress, crush, embrace, enfold, exert pressure on, flatten, grip, hug, mangle, pinch, press, squash, stamp on, tread on, wring. **2** cram, crowd, pack, push, ram, shove, squash, stuff, tamp, thrust, wedge. **squeeze out** expel, extrude, force out.

squirm *vb* twist, wriggle, writhe.

squirt *vb* ejaculate, eject, gush, jet, send out, shoot, spit, splash, spout, spray, spurt.

stab *n* **1** blow, cut, jab, prick, puncture, thrust, wound, wounding. **2** *stab of pain.* ▷ PAIN. ● *vb* bayonet, cut, injure, jab, lance, perforate, pierce, puncture, skewer, spike, stick, thrust, transfix, wound. **have a stab at** ▷ TRY.

stability *n* balance, constancy, durability, equilibrium, firmness, immutability, permanence, reliability, solidity, soundness, steadiness, strength. *Opp* INSTABILITY.

stabilize *vb* balance, become stable, give stability to, keep upright, make stable, settle. *Opp* UPSET.

stable *adj* **1** balanced, firm, fixed, solid, sound, steady, strong, sturdy. **2** constant, continuing, durable, established, immutable, lasting, long-lasting, permanent, predictable, resolute, steadfast, unchanging, unwavering. **3** *a stable personality.* balanced, even-tempered, reasonable, sane, sensible. *Opp* UNSTABLE.

stack *n* **1** accumulation, heap, hill, hoard, mound, mountain, pile, quantity, stock, stockpile, store. **2** chimney, pillar, smokestack. **3** *stack of hay. old use* cock, haycock, haystack, rick, stook. ● *vb* accumulate, amass, assemble, build up, collect, gather, heap, load, mass, pile, *inf* stash away, stockpile.

stadium *n* amphitheatre, arena, ground, sports-ground.

staff *n* **1** baton, cane, crook, crosier, flagstaff, pike, pole, rod, sceptre, shaft, stake, standard, stave, stick, token, wand. **2** *staff of a business.* assistants, crew, employees, *old use* hands, personnel, officers, team, workers, workforce. ● *vb* man, provide with staff, run.

stage *n* **1** apron, dais, performing area, platform, podium, proscenium, rostrum. **2** *stage of a journey.* juncture, leg, phase, period, point, time. ● *vb* arrange, *inf* get up, mount, organize, perform, present, produce, *inf* put on, set up, stage-manage.

stagger *vb* **1** falter, lurch, pitch, reel, rock, stumble, sway, teeter, totter, walk unsteadily, waver, wobble. **2** *price staggered us.* alarm, amaze, astonish, astound, confuse, dismay, dumbfound, flabbergast, shake, shock, startle, stun, stupefy, surprise, worry.

stagnant *adj* motionless, sluggish, stale, standing, static, still, without movement. *Opp* MOVING.

stagnate *vb* achieve nothing, become stale, be stagnant, degenerate, deteriorate, idle, languish, stand still, stay still, vegetate. *Opp* PROGRESS.

stain *n* **1** blemish, blot, blotch, discoloration, mark, smear, smudge, speck, spot. **2** *a wood stain.* colouring, dye, paint, pigment, tinge, tint, varnish. • *vb* **1** blacken, blemish, blot, contaminate, dirty, discolour, make dirty, mark, smudge, soil, tarnish. **2** *stain your reputation.* besmirch, damage, defile, disgrace, shame, spoil, sully, taint. **3** *stain wood.* colour, dye, paint, tinge, tint, varnish.

stair *n* riser, step, tread. **stairs** escalator, flight of stairs, staircase, stairway, steps.

stake *n* **1** paling, palisade, pike, pile, pillar, pole, post, rod, sceptre, shaft, standard, stave, stick, upright. **2** *a gambler's stake.* bet, pledge, wager. • *vb* **1** fasten, hitch, secure, tether, tie up. **2** *stake a claim.* establish, put on record, state. **3** *stake my life on it.* bet, chance, gamble, hazard, risk, venture, wager. **stake out** define, delimit, demarcate, enclose, fence in, mark off, outline.

stale *adj* **1** dry, hard, limp, mouldy, musty, *inf* off, old, *inf* past its best, tasteless. **2** *stale ideas.* banal, clichéd, familiar, hackneyed, old-fashioned, out-of-date, overused, stock, threadbare, *inf* tired, trite, uninteresting, unoriginal, worn out. *Opp* FRESH.

stalemate *n* deadlock, impasse, standstill.

stalk *n* branch, shaft, shoot, stem, trunk, twig. • *vb* **1** chase, dog, follow, haunt, hound, hunt, pursue, shadow, tail, track, trail. **2** *stalk about.* prowl, rove, stride, strut. ▷ WALK.

stall *n* booth, compartment, kiosk, stand, table. • *vb* be obstructive, delay, hang back, haver, hesitate, pause, *inf* play for time, postpone, prevaricate, procrastinate, put off, stonewall, stop, temporize, waste time.

stalwart *adj* courageous, dependable, determined, faithful, indomitable, intrepid, redoubtable, reliable, resolute, robust, staunch, steadfast, sturdy, tough, trustworthy, valiant. ▷ BRAVE, STRONG. *Opp* WEAK.

stamina *n* endurance, energy, *inf* grit, indomitability, resilience, staunchness, staying power, *inf* stickability.

stammer *vb* falter, hesitate, hem and haw, splutter, stumble, stutter. ▷ TALK.

stamp *n* **1** brand, die, hallmark, impression, imprint, print, punch, seal. **2** *stamp of genius.* characteristic, mark, sign. **3** *stamp on a letter.* franking, postage stamp. • *vb* **1** bring down, strike, thump. **2** *stamp a mark.* brand, emboss, engrave, impress, imprint, label, mark, print, punch. **stamp on** ▷ SUPPRESS. **stamp out** ▷ ELIMINATE.

stampede *n* charge, dash, flight, panic, rout, rush, sprint. • *vb* **1** bolt, career, charge, dash, gallop, panic, run, rush, sprint, *inf* take to your heels, tear. **2** *stampede cattle.* frighten, panic, rout, scatter.

stand *n* **1** base, pedestal, rack, support, tripod, trivet. **2** booth, kiosk, stall. **3** grandstand, terraces. • *vb* **1** arise, get to your feet, get up, rise. **2** *Stand it on the floor.* arrange, deposit, erect, locate, place, position, put up, set up, situate, station, upend. **3** *Trees stand along the avenue.* be, be situated, exist. **4** *My offer stands.* be unchanged, continue, remain valid, stay. **5** *Can't stand onions.* abide, bear, endure, put up with, suffer, tolerate, *inf* wear. **stand by** ▷ SUPPORT. **stand for** ▷ SYMBOLIZE. **stand in for** ▷ DEPUTIZE. **stand out** ▷ SHOW. **stand up for** ▷ PROTECT, SUPPORT. **stand up to** ▷ RESIST.

standard *adj* accepted, accustomed, approved, average, basic, classic, common, conventional, customary, definitive, established, everyday, familiar, habitual, normal, official, ordinary, orthodox, popular, prevailing, prevalent, recognized, regular, routine, set, staple (*diet*), stock, traditional, typical, universal, usual. *Opp* UNUSUAL. • *n* **1** archetype, benchmark, criterion, example, exemplar, gauge, grade, guide, guideline, ideal, level of achievement, measure, measurement, model, paradigm, pattern, requirement, rule, sample, specification, touchstone, yardstick. **2** average, level, mean, norm. **3** *standard of* *a regiment*. banner, colours, ensign, flag, pennant. **4** *lamp standard*. column, pillar, pole, post, support, upright. **standards** ▷ MORALITY.

standardize *vb* average out, conform to a standard, equalize, homogenize, normalize, regiment, stereotype, systematize.

standoffish *adj* aloof, antisocial, cold, cool, distant, frosty, haughty, remote, reserved, reticent, retiring, secretive, self-conscious, *inf* snooty, taciturn, unapproachable, uncommunicative, unforthcoming, unfriendly, unsociable, withdrawn. *Opp* FRIENDLY.

standpoint *n* angle, attitude, belief, opinion, perspective, point of view, position, stance, vantage point, view, viewpoint.

standstill *n inf* dead end, deadlock, halt, *inf* hold-up, impasse, jam, stalemate, stop, stoppage.

staple *adj* basic, chief, important, main, principal. ▷ STANDARD.

star *n* **1** celestial body, sun. □ *asteroid, comet, evening star, falling star, lodestar, morning star, nova, shooting star, supernova*. **2** asterisk, pentagram. **3** *TV star*. attraction, big name, celebrity, *It* diva, *inf* draw, idol, leading lady, leading man, personage, *It* prima donna, starlet, superstar. ▷ PERFORMER.

starchy *adj* aloof, conventional, formal, prim, stiff. ▷ UNFRIENDLY.

stare *vb* gape, *inf* gawp, gaze, glare, goggle, look fixedly, peer. **stare at** contemplate, examine, eye, scrutinize, study, watch.

stark *adj* **1** austere, bare, bleak, depressing, desolate, dreary, gloomy, grim. **2** *stark contrast*. absolute, clear, complete, obvious, perfect, plain, sharp, sheer, thoroughgoing, total, unqualified, utter.

start *n* **1** beginning, birth, commencement, creation, dawn, establishment, founding, fount, inauguration, inception, initiation, institution, introduction, launch, onset, opening, origin, outset, point of departure, setting out, spring, springboard. *Opp* FINISH. **2** *an unfair start*. advantage, edge, head-start, opportunity. **3** *bankloan gave me a start*. assistance, backing, financing, help, *inf* leg-up, *inf* send-off, sponsorship. **4** *a nasty start*. jump, shock, surprise. ● *vb* **1** depart, embark, *inf* get going, *inf* get under way, *sl* hit the road, *inf* kick off, leave, move off, proceed, set off, set out. **2** *start something*. activate, beget, begin, commence, create, embark on, engender, establish, found, *inf* get cracking on, *inf* get off the ground, *inf* get the ball rolling, give birth to, inaugurate, initiate, instigate, institute, introduce, launch, open, originate, pioneer, set in motion, set up. *Opp* FINISH. **3** *start at sudden noise*. blench, draw back, flinch, jerk, jump, quail, recoil, shy, spring up, twitch, wince. **make someone start** ▷ STARTLE.

startle *vb* agitate, alarm, catch unawares, disturb, frighten, give you a start, jolt, make you jump, make you start, scare, shake, shock, surprise, take aback, take by surprise, upset. **startling** ▷ SURPRISING.

starvation *n* deprivation, famine, hunger, malnutrition, undernourishment, want.

starve *vb* die of starvation, go hungry, go without, perish. **starve yourself** diet, fast, go on hunger strike, refuse food. **starving** ▷ HUNGRY.

state *n* **1** *plur* circumstances, condition, fitness, health, mood, *inf* shape, situation. **2** agitation, excitement, *inf* flap, panic, plight, predicament, *inf* tizzy. **3** *a sovereign state*. land, nation. ▷ COUNTRY. ● *vb* affirm, announce, assert, asseverate, aver, communicate, declare, express, formulate, proclaim, put into words, report, specify, submit, testify, voice. ▷ SAY, SPEAK, TALK.

stately *adj* august, dignified, distinguished, elegant, formal, grand, imperial, imposing, impressive, lofty, majestic, noble, pompous, regal, royal, solemn, splendid, striking. *Opp* INFORMAL. **stately home** ▷ MANSION.

statement *n* account, affirmation, announcement, annunciation, assertion, bulletin, comment, communication, communiqué, declaration, disclosure, explanation, message, notice, proclamation, proposition, report, testament, testimony, utterance.

statesman *n* diplomat, politician.

static *adj* constant, fixed, immobile, immovable, inert, invariable, motionless, passive, stable, stagnant, stationary, steady, still, unchanging, unmoving. *Opp* MOBILE, VARIABLE.

station *n* **1** calling, caste, class, degree, employment, level, location, occupation, place, position, post, rank, situation, standing, status. **2** *fire station.* base, depot, headquarters, office. **3** *radio station.* channel, company, transmitter, wavelength. **4** *railway station.* halt, platform, stopping-place, terminus, train station. • *vb* assign, garrison, locate, place, position, put, site, situate, spot, stand.

stationary *adj* at a standstill, at rest, halted, immobile, immovable, motionless, parked, pausing, standing, static, still, stock-still, unmoving. *Opp* MOVING.

stationery *n* paper, office supplies, writing materials.

statistics *n* data, figures, information, numbers.

statue *n* carving, figure, statuette. ▷ SCULPTURE.

statuesque *adj* dignified, elegant, imposing, impressive, poised, stately, upright.

stature *n* **1** build, height, size, tallness. **2** *artist of international stature.* esteem, greatness, recognition. ▷ STATUS.

status *n* class, degree, eminence, grade, importance, level, position, prestige, prominence, rank, reputation, significance, standing, station, stature, title.

staunch *adj* ▷ STEADFAST.

stay *n* **1** holiday, *old use* sojourn, stop, stop-over, visit. **2** *stay of execution.* ▷ DELAY. **3** ▷ SUPPORT. • *vb* **1** *old use* bide, carry on, continue, endure, *inf* hang about, hold out, keep on, last, linger, live on, loiter, persist, remain, survive, *old use* tarry, wait. **2** *stay in a hotel. old use* abide, be accommodated, be a guest, be housed, board, dwell, live, lodge, reside, settle, *old use* sojourn, stop, visit. **3** *stay judgement.* ▷ DELAY.

steadfast *adj* committed, constant, dedicated, dependable, determined, devoted, faithful, firm, loyal, patient, persevering, reliable, resolute, resolved, single-minded, sound, stalwart, staunch, steady, true, trustworthy, trusty, unchanging, unfaltering, unflinching, unswerving, unwavering. ▷ STRONG. *Opp* UNRELIABLE.

steady *adj* **1** balanced, confident, fast, firm, immovable, poised, safe, secure, settled, solid, stable, substantial. **2** *a steady flow.* ceaseless, changeless, consistent, constant, continuous, dependable, endless, even, incessant, invariable, never-ending, nonstop, perpetual, persistent, regular, reliable, repeated, rhythmic, *inf* round-the-clock, unbroken, unchanging, undeviating, unfaltering, unhurried, uniform, uninterrupted, unrelieved, unremitting, unvarying. *Opp* UNSTEADY. **3** ▷ STEADFAST. • *vb* **1** balance, brace, hold steady, keep still, make steady, secure, stabilize, support. **2** *steady your nerves.* calm, control, soothe, tranquillize.

steal *vb* **1** annex, appropriate, arrogate, burgle, commandeer, confiscate, embezzle, expropriate, *inf* filch, hijack, *inf* knock off, *inf* lift, loot, *inf* make off with, misappropriate, *inf* nick, peculate, pick pockets, pilfer, pillage, *inf* pinch, pirate, plagiarize, plunder, poach, purloin, *inf* rip you off, rob, seize, shop-lift, *inf* sneak, *inf* snitch, *inf* swipe, take, thieve, usurp, walk off with. **2** *steal quietly upstairs.*

creep, move stealthily, slink, slip, sneak, tiptoe.

stealing *n* robbery, theft, thieving. □ *break-in, burglary, embezzlement, fraud, hijacking, housebreaking, larceny, looting, misappropriation, mugging, peculation, pilfering, pillage, piracy, plagiarism, plundering, poaching, purloining, scrumping, shop-lifting.*

stealthy *adj* clandestine, concealed, covert, disguised, furtive, imperceptible, inconspicuous, quiet, secret, secretive, *inf* shifty, sly, *inf* sneaky, surreptitious, underhand, unobtrusive. *Opp* BLATANT.

steam *n* condensation, haze, mist, smoke, vapour.

steamy *adj* **1** blurred, clouded, cloudy, fogged over, foggy, hazy, misted over, misty. **2** *a steamy atmosphere.* close, damp, humid, moist, muggy, *inf* sticky, sultry, sweaty, sweltering. **3** [*inf*] *steamy sex scenes.* ▷ SEXY.

steep *adj* **1** abrupt, bluff, headlong, perpendicular, precipitous, sharp, sheer, sudden, vertical. *Opp* GRADUAL. **2** *steep prices.* ▷ EXPENSIVE. ● *vb* ▷ SOAK.

steeple *n* pinnacle, point, spire.

steer *vb* be at the wheel, control, direct, drive, guide, navigate, pilot. **steer clear of** ▷ AVOID.

stem *n* peduncle, shoot, stalk, stock, trunk, twig. ● *vb* arise, come, derive, develop, emanate, flow, issue, originate, proceed, result, spring, sprout. **2** *to stem the flow.* ▷ CHECK.

stench *n* mephitis, *inf* pong, reek, stink. ▷ SMELL.

step *n* **1** footfall, footstep, pace, stride, tread. **2** doorstep, rung, stair, tread. **3** *a step forward.* advance, move, movement, progress, progression. **4** *step in a process.* action, initiative, manoeuvre, measure, phase, procedure, stage. ● *vb* put your foot, stamp, stride, trample, tread. ▷ WALK. **steps** ladder, stairs, staircase, stairway, stepladder. **step down** ▷ RESIGN. **step in** ▷ ENTER, INTERVENE. **step on it** ▷ HURRY. **step up** ▷ INCREASE. **take steps** ▷ BEGIN.

stereoscopic *adj* solid-looking, three-dimensional, *inf* 3-D.

stereotype *n* formula, model, pattern, stereotyped idea.

stereotyped *adj* clichéd, conventional, formalized, hackneyed, predictable, standard, standardized, stock, typecast, unoriginal.

sterile *adj* **1** arid, barren, childless, dry, fruitless, infertile, lifeless, unfruitful, unproductive. **2** *sterile bandage.* antiseptic, aseptic, clean, disinfected, germ-free, hygienic, pure, sanitary, sterilized, uncontaminated, uninfected, unpolluted. **3** *a sterile attempt.* abortive, fruitless, hopeless, pointless, unprofitable, useless. *Opp* FERTILE, FRUITFUL, SEPTIC.

sterilize *vb* **1** clean, cleanse, decontaminate, depurate, disinfect, fumigate, make sterile, pasteurize, purify. **2** *sterilize animals.* caponize, castrate, emasculate, geld, neuter, perform a vasectomy on, spay, vasectomize.

stern *adj* adamant, austere, authoritarian, critical, dour, forbidding, frowning, grim, hard, harsh, inflexible, obdurate, resolute, rigid, rigorous, severe, strict, stringent, tough, unbending, uncompromising, unrelenting, unremitting. ▷ SERIOUS. *Opp* SOFT-HEARTED. ● *n stern of ship.* aft, back, rear end.

stew *n* casserole, goulash, hash, hotpot, ragout. ● *vb* boil, braise, casserole, simmer. ▷ COOK.

steward, stewardess *ns* **1** attendant, waiter. ▷ SERVANT. **2** marshal, officer, official.

stick *n* branch, stalk, twig. □ *bar, baton, cane, club, hockey-stick, pike, pole, rod, staff, stake, walking-stick, wand.* ● *vb* **1** bore, dig, impale, jab, penetrate, pierce, pin, poke, prick, prod, punch, puncture, run through, spear, spike, spit, stab, thrust, transfix. **2** *stick with glue.* adhere, affix, agglutinate, bind, bond, cement, cling, coagulate, fuse together, glue, gum, paste, solder, weld. ▷ FASTEN. **3** *stick in your mind.* be fixed, continue, endure, keep on, last, linger, persist, remain, stay. **4** *stick in mud.* become trapped, get bogged down, seize up, jam, wedge. **5** ▷ TOLERATE. **stick at** ▷ PERSIST. **stick in** ▷ PENETRATE. **stick out** ▷ PROTRUDE. **stick together** ▷ UNITE. **stick up** ▷ PROTRUDE. **stick up for** ▷ DEFEND. **stick with** ▷ SUPPORT.

sticky *adj* **1** adhesive, glued, gummed, self-adhesive. **2** *sticky paint.* gluey, glutinous, *inf* gooey, gummy, tacky, viscous. **3** *sticky weather.* clammy, close, damp, dank, humid, moist, muggy, steamy, sultry, sweaty. *Opp* DRY.

stiff *adj* **1** compact, dense, firm, hard, heavy, inelastic, inflexible, rigid, semi-solid, solid, solidified, thick, tough, unbending, unyielding, viscous. **2** *stiff joints.* arthritic, immovable, painful, paralysed, rheumatic, taut, tight. **3** *a stiff task.* arduous, challenging, difficult, exacting, exhausting, hard, laborious, tiring, tough, uphill. **4** *stiff opposition.* determined, dogged, obstinate, powerful, resolute, stubborn, unyielding, vigorous. **5** *a stiff manner.* artificial, awkward, clumsy, cold, forced, formal, graceless, haughty, inelegant, laboured, mannered, pedantic, self-conscious, standoffish, starchy, stilted, *inf* stuffy, tense, turgid, ungainly, unnatural, wooden. **6** *stiff penalties.* cruel, drastic, excessive, harsh, hurtful, merciless, pitiless, punishing, punitive, relentless, rigorous, severe, strict. **7** *stiff wind.* brisk, fresh, strong. **8** *stiff drink.* alcoholic, potent, strong. *Opp* EASY, RELAXED, SOFT.

stiffen *vb* become stiff, clot, coagulate, congeal, dry out, harden, jell, set, solidify, thicken, tighten, toughen.

stifle *vb* **1** asphyxiate, choke, smother, strangle, suffocate, throttle. **2** *stifle laughter.* check, control, curb, dampen, deaden, keep back, muffle, restrain, suppress, withhold. **3** *stifle free speech.* crush, destroy, extinguish, kill off, quash, repress, silence, stamp out, stop.

stigma *n* blot, brand, disgrace, dishonour, mark, reproach, shame, slur, stain, taint.

stigmatize *vb* brand, condemn, defame, denounce, disparage, label, mark, pillory, slander, vilify.

still *adj* at rest, calm, even, flat, hushed, immobile, inert, lifeless, motionless, noiseless, pacific, peaceful, placid, quiet, restful, serene, silent, smooth, soundless, stagnant, static, stationary, tranquil, unmoving, unruffled, untroubled, windless. *Opp* ACTIVE, NOISY. ● *vb* allay, appease, assuage, calm, lull, make still, pacify, quieten, settle, silence, soothe, subdue, suppress, tranquillize. *Opp* AGITATE.

stimulant *n* antidepressant, drug, *inf* pick-me-up, restorative, *inf* reviver, *inf* shot in the arm, tonic. ▷ STIMULUS.

stimulate *vb* activate, arouse, awaken, cause, encourage, excite, fan, fire, foment, galvanize, goad, incite, inflame, inspire, instigate, invigorate, kindle, motivate, prick, prompt, provoke, quicken, rouse, set off, spur, stir up, titillate, urge, whet. *Opp* DISCOURAGE.

stimulating *adj* arousing, challenging, exciting, exhilarating, inspirational, inspiring, interesting, intoxicating, invigorating, provocative, provoking, rousing, stirring, thought-provoking, titillating. *Opp* UNINTERESTING.

stimulus *n* challenge, encouragement, fillip, goad, incentive, inducement, inspiration, prompting, provocation, spur, stimulant. *Opp* DISCOURAGEMENT.

sting *n* bite, prick, stab. ▷ PAIN. ● *vb* **1** bite, nip, prick, wound. **2** smart, tingle. ▷ HURT.

stingy *adj* **1** avaricious, cheeseparing, close, close-fisted, covetous, mean, mingy, miserly, niggardly, parsimonious, penny-pinching, tight-fisted, ungenerous. **2** *stingy helpings.* inadequate, insufficient, meagre, *inf* measly, scanty. ▷ SMALL. *Opp* GENEROUS.

stink *n*, *vb* ▷ SMELL.

stipulate *vb* demand, insist on, make a stipulation, require, specify.

stipulation *n* condition, demand, prerequisite, proviso, requirement, specification.

stir *n* ▷ COMMOTION. • *vb* **1** agitate, beat, blend, churn, mingle, mix, move about, scramble, whisk. **2** *stir from sleep*. arise, bestir yourself, *inf* get a move on, *inf* get going, get up, move, rise, *inf* show signs of life, *inf* stir your stumps. **3** *stir emotions*. activate, affect, arouse, awaken, challenge, disturb, electrify, excite, exhilarate, fire, impress, inspire, kindle, move, resuscitate, revive, rouse, stimulate, touch, upset.

stirring *adj* affecting, arousing, challenging, dramatic, electrifying, emotional, emotion-charged, emotive, exciting, exhilarating, heady, impassioned, inspirational, inspiring, interesting, intoxicating, invigorating, moving, provocative, provoking, rousing, spirited, stimulating, thought-provoking, thrilling, titillating, touching. *Opp* UNEXCITING.

stitch *vb* darn, mend, repair, sew, tack.

stock *adj* accustomed, banal, clichéd, common, commonplace, conventional, customary, expected, hackneyed, ordinary, predictable, regular, routine, run-of-the-mill, set, standard, staple, stereotyped, *inf* tired, traditional, trite, unoriginal, usual. *Opp* UNEXPECTED. • *n* **1** cache, hoard, reserve, reservoir, stockpile, store, supply. **2** *stock of a shop*. commodities, goods, merchandise, range, wares. **3** *farm stock*. animals, beasts, cattle, flocks, herds, livestock. **4** *ancient stock*. ancestry, blood, breed, descent, dynasty, extraction, family, forebears, genealogy, line, lineage, parentage, pedigree. **5** *meat stock*. broth, soup. • *vb* carry, deal in, handle, have available, *inf* keep, keep in stock, market, offer, provide, sell, supply, trade in. **out of stock** sold out, unavailable. **take stock** ▷ REVIEW.

stockade *n* fence, paling, palisade, wall.

stockings *n* nylons, panti-hose, socks, tights.

stockist *n* merchant, retailer, seller, shopkeeper, supplier.

stocky *adj* burly, compact, dumpy, heavy-set, short, solid, squat, stubby, sturdy, thickset. *Opp* THIN.

stodgy *adj* **1** filling, heavy, indigestible, lumpy, soggy, solid, starchy. *Opp* SUCCULENT. **2** *a stodgy lecture*. boring, dull, ponderous, *inf* stuffy, tedious, tiresome, turgid, unexciting, unimaginative, uninteresting. *Opp* LIVELY.

stoical *adj* calm, cool, disciplined, impassive, imperturbable, long-suffering, patient, philosophical, phlegmatic, resigned, stolid, uncomplaining, unemotional, unexcitable, *inf* unflappable. *Opp* EXCITABLE.

stoke *vb* fuel, keep burning, mend, put fuel on, tend.

stole *n* cape, shawl, wrap.

stolid *adj* bovine, dull, heavy, immovable, impassive, lumpish, phlegmatic, unemotional, unexciting, unimaginative, wooden. ▷ STOICAL. *Opp* LIVELY.

stomach *n* abdomen, belly, *inf* guts, *inf* insides, *derog* paunch, *derog* pot, *inf* tummy. • *vb* ▷ TOLERATE.

stomach-ache *n* colic, *inf* collywobbles, *inf* gripes, *inf* tummy-ache.

stone *n* **1** boulder, cobble, *plur* gravel, pebble, rock, *plur* scree. ▷ ROCK. **2** block, flagstone, sett, slab. **3** *a memorial stone*. gravestone, headstone, memorial, monolith, obelisk, tablet. **4** *precious stone*. ▷ JEWEL. **5** *stone in fruit*. pip, pit, seed.

stony *adj* **1** pebbly, rocky, rough, shingly. **2** *stony silence*. adamant, chilly, cold, coldhearted, expressionless, frigid, hard, *inf* hardboiled, heartless, hostile, icy, indifferent, insensitive, merciless, pitiless, steely, stony-hearted, uncaring, unemotional, unfeeling, unforgiving, unfriendly, unresponsive, unsympathetic.

stooge *n* butt, dupe, *inf* fall-guy, lackey, puppet.

stoop *vb* **1** bend, bow, crouch, duck, hunch your shoulders, kneel, lean, squat. **2** condescend, degrade yourself, deign, humble yourself, lower yourself, sink.

stop *n* **1** ban, cessation, close, conclusion, end, finish, halt, shut-down, standstill, stoppage, termination. **2** *a stop for refreshments.* break, destination, pause, resting-place, stage, station, stopover, terminus. **3** *a stop at a hotel.* holiday, *old use* sojourn, stay, vacation, visit. • *vb* **1** break off, call a halt to, cease, conclude, cut off, desist from, discontinue, end, finish, halt, *inf* knock off, leave off, *inf* pack in, pause, quit, refrain from, rest from, suspend, terminate. **2** *stop the flow.* bar, block, check, curb, cut off, delay, frustrate, halt, hamper, hinder, immobilize, impede, intercept, interrupt, *inf* nip in the bud, obstruct, put a stop to, stanch, staunch, stem, suppress, thwart. **3** *stop in a hotel.* be a guest, have a holiday, *old use* sojourn, spend time, stay, visit. **4** *stop a gap. inf* bung up, close, fill in, plug, seal. **5** *stop a thief.* arrest, capture, catch, detain, hold, seize. **6** *the rain stopped.* be over, cease, come to an end, finish, peter out. **7** *the bus stopped.* come to rest, draw up, halt, pull up.

stopper *n* bung, cork, plug.

store *n* **1** accumulation, cache, fund, hoard, quantity, reserve, reservoir, stock, stockpile, supply. ▷ STOREHOUSE. **2** *a grocery store.* outlet, retail business, retailers, supermarket. ▷ SHOP. • *vb* accumulate, aggregate, deposit, hoard, keep, lay by, lay in, lay up, preserve, put away, reserve, save, set aside, *inf* stash away, stockpile, stock up, stow away.

storehouse *n* depository, repository, storage, store, store-room. □ *armoury, arsenal, barn, cellar, cold-storage, depot, granary, larder, pantry, safe, silo, stock-room, strong-room, treasury, vault, warehouse.*

storey *n* deck, floor, level, stage, tier.

storm *n* **1** disturbance, onslaught, outbreak, outburst, stormy weather, tempest, tumult, turbulence. □ *blizzard, cloudburst, cyclone, deluge, dust-storm, electrical storm, gale, hailstorm, hurricane, mistral, monsoon, rainstorm, sandstorm, simoom, sirocco, snowstorm, squall, thunderstorm, tornado, typhoon, whirlwind.* **2** *storm of protest.* ▷ CLAMOUR. • *vb* ▷ ATTACK.

stormy *adj* angry, blustery, choppy, fierce, furious, gusty, raging, rough, squally, tempestuous, thundery, tumultuous, turbulent, vehement, violent, wild, windy. *Opp* CALM.

story *n* **1** account, anecdote, chronicle, fiction, history, narration, narrative, plot, recital, record, scenario, tale, yarn. □ *allegory, children's story, crime story, detective story, epic, fable, fairy-tale, fantasy, folk-tale, legend, mystery, myth, novel, parable, romance, saga, science fiction, SF, thriller,* inf *whodunit.* **2** *story in newspaper.* article, dispatch, exclusive, feature, news item, piece, report, scoop. **3** falsehood, *inf* fib, lie, tall story, untruth.

storyteller *n* author, biographer, narrator, raconteur, teller.

stout *adj* **1** *inf* beefy, big, bulky, burly, *inf* chubby, corpulent, fleshy, heavy, *inf* hulking, overweight, plump, portly, solid, stocky, *inf* strapping, thick-set, *inf* tubby, well-built. ▷ FAT. *Opp* THIN. **2** *stout rope.* durable, reliable, robust, sound, strong, sturdy, substantial, thick, tough. **3** *stout fighter.* bold, brave, courageous, fearless, gallant, heroic, intrepid, plucky, resolute, spirited, valiant. *Opp* WEAK.

stove *n* boiler, cooker, fire, furnace, heater, oven, range.

stow *vb* load, pack, put away, *inf* stash away, store.

straggle *vb* be dispersed, be scattered, dangle, dawdle, drift, fall behind, lag, loiter, meander, ramble, scatter, spread out, stray, string out, trail, wander. **straggling** ▷ DISORGANIZED, LOOSE.

straight *adj* **1** aligned, direct, flat, linear, regular, smooth, true, unbending, undeviating, unswerving. **2** neat, orderly, organized, right, *inf* shipshape, sorted out, spruce, tidy. **3** *a straight sequence.* consecutive, continuous, non-stop, perfect, sustained, unbroken, uninterrupted, unrelieved. **4** ▷ STRAIGHTFORWARD. *Opp* CROOKED, INDIRECT, UNTIDY. **straight away** at once, directly, immediately, instantly, now, without delay.

straighten *vb* disentangle, make straight, put straight, rearrange, sort out, tidy, unbend, uncurl, unravel, untangle, untwist.

straightforward *adj* blunt, candid, direct, easy, forthright, frank, genuine, honest, intelligible, lucid, open, plain, simple, sincere, straight, truthful, uncomplicated. *Opp* DEVIOUS.

strain *n* **1** anxiety, difficulty, effort, exertion, hardship, pressure, stress, tension, worry. **2** *genetic strain.* ▷ ANCESTRY. • *vb* **1** haul, heave, make taut, pull, stretch, tighten, tug. **2** *strain to succeed.* attempt, endeavour, exert yourself, labour, make an effort, strive, struggle, toil, try. **3** *strain yourself.* exercise, exhaust, overtax, *inf* push to the limit, stretch, tax, tire out, weaken, wear out, weary. **4** *strain a muscle.* damage, hurt, injure, overwork, pull, rick, sprain, tear, twist, wrench. **5** *strain liquid.* clear, drain, draw off, filter, percolate, purify, riddle, screen, separate, sieve, sift.

strained *adj* **1** artificial, constrained, distrustful, embarrassed, false, forced, insincere, self-conscious, stiff, tense, uncomfortable, uneasy, unnatural. **2** *strained look.* drawn, tired, weary. **3** *strained interpretation.* far-fetched, incredible, laboured, unlikely, unreasonable. *Opp* NATURAL, RELAXED.

strainer *n* colander, filter, riddle, sieve.

strand *n* fibre, filament, string, thread, wire. • *vb* **1** abandon, desert, forsake, leave stranded, lose, maroon. **2** *strand a ship.* beach, ground, run aground, wreck. **stranded** ▷ AGROUND, HELPLESS.

strange *adj* **1** abnormal, astonishing, atypical, bizarre, curious, eerie, exceptional, extraordinary, fantastic, *inf* funny, grotesque, irregular, odd, out-of-the-ordinary, outré, peculiar, quaint, queer, rare, remarkable, singular, surprising, surreal, uncommon, unexpected, unheard-of, unique, unnatural, untypical, unusual. **2** *strange neighbours. inf* cranky, eccentric, sinister, unconventional, weird, *inf* zany. **3** *a strange problem.* baffling, bewildering, inexplicable, insoluble, mysterious, mystifying, perplexing, puzzling, unaccountable. **4** *strange places.* alien, exotic, foreign, little-known, off the beaten track, outlandish, out-of-the-way, remote, unexplored, unmapped. **5** *strange experience.* different, fresh, new, novel, unaccustomed, unfamiliar. *Opp* FAMILIAR, ORDINARY.

strangeness *n* abnormality, bizarreness, eccentricity, eeriness, extraordinariness, irregularity, mysteriousness, novelty, oddity, oddness, outlandishness, peculiarity, quaintness, queerness, rarity, singularity, unconventionality, unfamiliarity.

stranger *n* alien, foreigner, guest, newcomer, outsider, visitor.

strangle *vb* **1** asphyxiate, choke, garrotte, smother, stifle, suffocate, throttle. **2** *strangle a cry.* ▷ SUPPRESS.

strangulate *vb* bind, compress, constrict, squeeze.

strangulation *n* asphyxiation, garrotting, suffocation.

strap *n* band, belt, strop, tawse, thong, webbing. • *vb* ▷ FASTEN.

stratagem *n* artifice, device, *inf* dodge, manoeuvre, plan, ploy, ruse, scheme, subterfuge, tactic, trick.

strategic *adj* advantageous, critical, crucial, deliberate, key, planned, politic, tactical, vital.

strategy *n* approach, design, manoeuvre, method, plan, plot, policy, procedure, programme, *inf* scenario, scheme, tactics.

stratum *n* layer, seam, table, thickness, vein.

straw *n* corn, stalks, stubble.

stray *adj* **1** abandoned, homeless, lost, roaming, roving, wandering. **2** *stray bullets*. accidental, casual, chance, haphazard, isolated, lone, occasional, odd, random, single. • *vb* **1** get lost, get separated, go astray, meander, move about aimlessly, ramble, range, roam, rove, straggle, wander. **2** *stray from the point*. deviate, digress, diverge, drift, get off the subject, *inf* go off at a tangent, veer.

streak *n* **1** band, bar, dash, line, mark, score, smear, stain, stria, striation, strip, stripe, stroke, vein. **2** *a selfish streak*. component, element, strain, touch, trace. **3** *streak of good luck*. period, run, series, spate, spell, stretch, time. • *vb* **1** mark with streaks, smear, smudge, stain, striate. **2** *streak past*. dart, dash, flash, fly, gallop, hurtle, move at speed, rush, *inf* scoot, speed, sprint, tear, *inf* whip, zoom.

streaky *adj* barred, lined, smeary, smudged, streaked, striated, stripy, veined.

stream *n* **1** beck, brook, brooklet, burn, channel, freshet, *poet* rill, river, rivulet, streamlet, watercourse. **2** cascade, cataract, current, deluge, effluence, flood, flow, fountain, gush, jet, outpouring, rush, spate, spurt, surge, tide, torrent. • *vb* cascade, course, deluge, flood, flow, gush, issue, pour, run, spill, spout, spurt, squirt, surge, well.

streamer *n* banner, flag, pennant, pennon, ribbon.

streamlined *adj* **1** aerodynamic, elegant, graceful, hydrodynamic, sleek, smooth. **2** ▷ EFFICIENT.

street *n* avenue, roadway, terrace. ▷ ROAD.

strength *n* **1** brawn, capacity, condition, energy, fitness, force, health, might, muscle, power, resilience, robustness, sinew, stamina, stoutness, sturdiness, toughness, vigour. **2** *strength of purpose*. *inf* backbone, commitment, courage, determination, firmness, *inf* grit, perseverance, persistence, resolution, resolve, spirit, tenacity. *Opp* WEAKNESS.

strengthen *vb* **1** bolster, boost, brace, build up, buttress, encourage, fortify, harden, hearten, increase, make stronger, prop up, reinforce, stiffen, support, tone up, toughen. **2** *strengthen an argument*. back up, consolidate, corroborate, enhance, justify, substantiate. *Opp* WEAKEN.

strenuous *adj* **1** arduous, backbreaking, burdensome, demanding, difficult, exhausting, gruelling, hard, laborious, punishing, stiff, taxing, tough, uphill. *Opp* EASY. **2** *strenuous efforts*. active, committed, determined, dogged, dynamic, eager, energetic, herculean, indefatigable, laborious, pertinacious, resolute, spirited, strong, tenacious, tireless, unremitting, vigorous, zealous. *Opp* CASUAL.

stress *n* **1** anxiety, difficulty, distress, hardship, pressure, strain, tenseness, tension, trauma, worry. **2** accent, accentuation, beat, emphasis, importance, significance, underlining, urgency, weight. • *vb* **1** accent, accentuate, assert, draw attention to, emphasize, feature, highlight, insist on, lay stress on, mark, put stress on, repeat, spotlight, underline, underscore. **2** *stressed by work*. burden, distress, overstretch, pressure, pressurize, push to the limit, tax, weigh down.

stressful *adj* anxious, difficult, taxing, tense, tiring, traumatic, worrying. *Opp* RELAXED.

stretch *n* **1** period, spell, stint, term, time, tour of duty. **2** *stretch of country*. area, distance, expanse, length, span, spread, sweep, tract. • *vb* **1** broaden, crane (*your neck*), dilate, distend, draw out, elongate, enlarge, expand, extend, flatten out, inflate, lengthen, open out, pull out, spread out, swell, tauten, tighten, widen. **2** *stretch into the distance.* be unbroken, continue, disappear, extend, go, reach out, spread. **3** *stretch resources.* overextend, overtax, *inf* push to the limit, strain, tax.

strew *vb* disperse, distribute, scatter, spread, sprinkle.

strict *adj* **1** austere, authoritarian, autocratic, firm, harsh, merciless, *inf* no-nonsense, rigorous, severe, stern, stringent, tyrannical, uncompromising. *Opp* EASYGOING. **2** *strict rules.* absolute, binding, defined, *inf* hard and fast, inflexible, invariable, precise, rigid, stringent, tight, unchangeable. *Opp* FLEXIBLE. **3** *strict truthfulness.* accurate, complete, correct, exact, meticulous, perfect, precise, right, scrupulous.

stride *n* pace, step. • *vb* ▷ WALK.

strident *adj* clamorous, discordant, grating, harsh, jarring, loud, noisy, raucous, screeching, shrill, unmusical. *Opp* SOFT.

strife *n* animosity, arguing, bickering, competition, conflict, discord, disharmony, dissension, enmity, friction, hostility, quarrelling, rivalry, unfriendliness. ▷ FIGHT. *Opp* COOPERATION.

strike *n* **1** go-slow, industrial action, stoppage, walk-out, withdrawal of labour. **2** assault, attack, bombardment. • *vb* **1** bang against, bang into, beat, collide with, hammer, impel, knock, rap, run into, smack, smash into, *inf* thump, *inf* whack. ▷ ATTACK, HIT. **2** *strike a match.* ignite, light. **3** *tragedy struck us forcibly.* affect, afflict, *inf* come home to, impress, influence. **4** *clock struck one.* chime, ring, sound. **5** *strike for more pay. inf* come out, *inf* down tools, stop work, take industrial action, withdraw labour, work to rule. **6** *strike a flag, tent.* dismantle, lower, pull down, remove, take down.

striking *adj* affecting, amazing, arresting, conspicuous, distinctive, extraordinary, glaring, imposing, impressive, memorable, noticeable, obvious, out-of-the-ordinary, outstanding, prominent, showy, stunning, telling, unmistakable, unusual. *Opp* INCONSPICUOUS.

string *n* **1** cable, cord, fibre, line, rope, twine. **2** chain, file, line, procession, progression, queue, row, sequence, series, stream, succession, train. • *vb string together* connect, join, line up, link, thread. **stringed instruments** strings. □ *banjo, cello, clavichord, double-bass,* inf *fiddle, guitar, harp, harpsichord, lute, lyre, piano, sitar, spinet, ukulele, viola, violin, zither.*

stringy *adj* chewy, fibrous, gristly, sinewy, tough. *Opp* TENDER.

strip *n* band, belt, fillet, lath, line, narrow piece, ribbon, shred, slat, sliver, stripe, swathe. • *vb* **1** bare, clear, decorticate, defoliate, denude, divest, *old use* doff, excoriate, flay, lay bare, peel, remove the covering, remove the paint, remove the skin, skin, uncover. *Opp* COVER. **2** *strip to the waist.* bare yourself, disrobe, expose yourself, get undressed, uncover yourself. *Opp* DRESS. **strip down** ▷ DISMANTLE. **strip off** ▷ UNDRESS.

stripe *n* band, bar, chevron, line, ribbon, streak, striation, strip, stroke, swathe.

striped *adj* banded, barred, lined, streaky, striated, stripy.

strive *vb* attempt, *inf* do your best, endeavour, make an effort, strain, struggle, try. ▷ FIGHT.

stroke *n* **1** action, blow, effort, knock, move, swipe. ▷ HIT. **2** *a stroke of the pen.* flourish, gesture, line, mark, movement, sweep. **3** [*medical*] apoplexy, attack, embolism, fit, seizure, spasm, thrombosis. • *vb* caress, fondle, massage, pass your hand over, pat, pet, rub, soothe, touch.

stroll *n, vb* amble, meander, saunter, wander. ▷ WALK.

strong *adj* **1** durable, hard, hard-wearing, heavy-duty, impregnable, indestructible, permanent, reinforced, resilient, robust, sound, stout, substantial, thick, unbreakable, well-made. **2** *strong physique.* athletic, *inf* beefy, *inf* brawny, burly, fit, *inf* hale and hearty, hardy, *inf* hefty, *inf* husky, mighty, muscular, powerful, robust, sinewy, stalwart, *inf* strapping, sturdy, tough, well-built, wiry. **3** *strong personality.* assertive, committed, determined, domineering, dynamic, energetic, forceful, independent, reliable, resolute, stalwart, steadfast, *inf* stout, strong-minded, strong-willed, tenacious, vigorous. ▷ STUBBORN. **4** *strong commitment.* active, assiduous, deep-rooted, deep-seated, *derog* doctrinaire, *derog* dogmatic, eager, earnest, enthusiastic, fervent, fierce, firm, genuine, intense, keen, loyal, passionate, positive, rabid, sedulous, staunch, true, vehement, zealous. **5** *strong government.* decisive, dependable, *derog* dictatorial, fearless, *derog* tyrannical, unswerving, unwavering. **6** *strong measures.* aggressive, draconian, drastic, extreme, harsh, high-handed, ruthless, severe, tough, unflinching, violent. **7** *a strong army.* formidable, invincible, large, numerous, powerful, unconquerable, well-armed, well-equipped, well-trained. **8** *strong colour, light.* bright, brilliant, clear, dazzling, garish, glaring, vivid. **9** *strong taste, smell.* concentrated, highly-flavoured, hot, intense, noticeable, obvious, overpowering, prominent, pronounced, pungent, sharp, spicy, unmistakable. **10** *strong evidence.* clear-cut, cogent, compelling, convincing, evident, influential, persuasive, plain, solid, telling, undisputed. **11** *strong drink.* alcoholic, concentrated, intoxicating, potent, undiluted. *Opp* WEAK.

stronghold *n* bastion, bulwark, castle, citadel, *old use* fastness, fort, fortification, fortress, garrison.

structure *n* **1** arrangement, composition, configuration, constitution, design, form, formation, *inf* make-up, order, organization, plan, shape, system. **2** complex, construction, edifice, erection, fabric, framework, pile, superstructure. ▷ BUILDING. • *vb* arrange, build, construct, design, form, frame, give structure to, organize, shape, systematize.

struggle *n* **1** challenge, difficulty, effort, endeavour, exertion, labour, problem. **2** ▷ FIGHT. • *vb* **1** endeavour, exert yourself, labour, make an effort, move violently, strain, strive, toil, try, work hard, wrestle, wriggle about, writhe about. **2** *struggle through mud.* flail, flounder, stumble, wallow. **3** ▷ FIGHT.

stub *n* butt, end, remains, remnant, stump. • *vb* ▷ HIT.

stubble *n* **1** stalks, straw. **2** beard, bristles, *inf* five-o'clock shadow, hair, roughness.

stubbly *adj* bristly, prickly, rough, unshaven.

stubborn *adj* defiant, determined, difficult, disobedient, dogged, dogmatic, headstrong, inflexible, intractable, intransigent, mulish, obdurate, obstinate, opinionated, persistent, pertinacious, *inf* pig-headed, recalcitrant, refractory, rigid, self-willed, tenacious, uncompromising, uncontrollable, uncooperative, unmanageable, unreasonable, unyielding, wayward, wilful. *Opp* AMENABLE.

stuck *adj* **1** bogged down, cemented, fast, fastened, firm, fixed, glued, immovable. **2** *stuck on a problem.* baffled, beaten, held up, *inf* stumped, *inf* stymied.

stuck-up *adj* arrogant, *inf* big-headed, bumptious, *inf* cocky, conceited, condescending, *inf* high-and-mighty, patronizing, proud, self-important, snobbish, *inf* snooty, supercilious, *inf* toffee-nosed. *Opp* MODEST.

student *n* apprentice, disciple, learner, postgraduate, pupil, scholar, schoolchild, trainee, undergraduate.

studied *adj* calculated, conscious, contrived, deliberate, intentional, planned, premeditated.

studious *adj* academic, assiduous, attentive, bookish, brainy, earnest, hard-working, intellectual, scholarly, serious-minded, thoughtful.

study *vb* **1** analyse, consider, contemplate, enquire into, examine, give attention to, investigate, learn about, look closely at, peruse, ponder, pore over, read carefully, research, scrutinize, survey, think about, weigh. **2** *study for exams. inf* cram, learn, *inf* mug up, read, *inf* swot, work.

stuff *n* **1** ingredients, matter, substance. **2** fabric, material, textile. ▷ CLOTH. **3** *all sorts of stuff.* accoutrements, articles, belongings, *inf* bits and pieces, *inf* clobber, effects, *inf* gear, impedimenta, junk, objects, *inf* paraphernalia, possessions, *inf* tackle, things. • *vb* **1** compress, cram, crowd, force, jam, pack, press, push, ram, shove, squeeze, stow, thrust, tuck. **2** *stuff a cushion.* fill, line, pad. **stuff yourself** ▷ EAT.

stuffing *n* **1** filling, lining, padding, quilting, wadding. **2** *stuffing in poultry.* forcemeat, seasoning.

stuffy *adj* **1** airless, close, fetid, fuggy, fusty, heavy, humid, muggy, musty, oppressive, stale, steamy, stifling, suffocating, sultry, unventilated, warm. *Opp* AIRY. **2** [*inf*] *a stuffy old bore.* boring, conventional, dreary, dull, formal, humourless, narrow-minded, old-fashioned, pompous, prim, staid, *inf* stodgy, strait-laced. *Opp* LIVELY.

stumble *vb* **1** blunder, flounder, lurch, miss your footing, reel, slip, stagger, totter, trip, tumble. ▷ WALK. **2** *stumble in speech.* become tongue-tied, falter, hesitate, pause, stammer, stutter.

stumbling-block *n* bar, difficulty, hindrance, hurdle, impediment, obstacle, snag.

stump *vb* baffle, bewilder, *inf* catch out, confound, confuse, defeat, *inf* flummox, mystify, outwit, perplex, puzzle, *inf* stymie. **stump up** ▷ PAY.

stun *vb* **1** daze, knock out, knock senseless, make unconscious. **2** amaze, astonish, astound, bewilder, confound, confuse, dumbfound, flabbergast, numb, shock, stagger, stupefy. **stunning** ▷ BEAUTIFUL, STUPENDOUS.

stunt *n inf* dare, exploit, feat, trick. • *vb stunt growth.* ▷ CHECK.

stupendous *adj* amazing, colossal, enormous, exceptional, extraordinary, huge, incredible, marvellous, miraculous, notable, phenomenal, prodigious, remarkable, *inf* sensational, singular, special, staggering, stunning, tremendous, unbelievable, wonderful. *Opp* ORDINARY.

stupid *adj* [*Most synonyms derog*] **1** addled, bird-brained, bone-headed, bovine, brainless, clueless, cretinous, dense, dim, doltish, dopey, drippy, dull, dumb, empty-headed, feather-brained, feeble-minded, foolish, gormless, half-witted, idiotic, ignorant, imbecilic, imperceptive, ineducable, lacking, lumpish, mindless, moronic, naïve, obtuse, puerile, senseless, silly, simple, simple-minded, slow, slow in the uptake, slowwitted, subnormal, thick, thick-headed, thick-skulled, thickwitted, unintelligent, unthinking, unwise, vacuous, weak in the head, witless. **2** *a stupid thing to do.* absurd, asinine, barmy, crack-brained, crass, crazy, fatuous, feeble, futile, half-baked, hare-brained, ill-advised, inane, irrational, irrelevant, irresponsible, laughable, ludicrous, lunatic, mad, nonsensical, pointless, rash, reckless, ridiculous, risible, scatterbrained, thoughtless, unjustifiable. **3** *stupid after a knock on the head.* dazed, in a stupor, semi-conscious, sluggish, stunned, stupefied. *Opp* INTELLIGENT. **stupid person** ▷ FOOL.

stupidity *n* absurdity, crassness, denseness, dullness, *inf* dumbness, fatuity, fatuousness, folly, foolishness, futility, idiocy, ignorance, imbecility, inanity, lack of intelligence, lunacy, madness, mindlessness, naïvety, pointlessness, recklessness, silliness, slowness, thoughtlessness. *Opp* INTELLIGENCE.

stupor *n* coma, daze, inertia, lassitude, lethargy, numbness, shock, state of insensibility, torpor, trance, unconsciousness.

sturdy *adj* **1** athletic, brawny, burly, hardy, healthy, hefty, husky, muscular, powerful, robust, stalwart, stocky, *inf* strapping, vigorous, well-built. **2** *sturdy shoes, etc.* durable, solid, sound, substantial, tough, well-made. **3** *sturdy opposition.* determined, firm, indomitable, resolute, staunch, steadfast, uncompromising, vigorous. ▷ STRONG. *Opp* WEAK.

stutter *vb* stammer, stumble. ▷ TALK.

style *n* **1** dash, elegance, flair, flamboyance, panache, polish, refinement, smartness, sophistication, stylishness, taste. **2** *not my style.* approach, character, custom, habit, idiosyncrasy, manner, method, way. **3** *style in writing.* diction, mode, phraseology, phrasing, register, sentence structure, tenor, tone, wording. **4** *style in clothes.* chic, cut, design, dress-sense, fashion, look, mode, pattern, shape, tailoring, type, vogue.

stylish *adj Fr* à la mode, chic, *inf* classy, contemporary, *inf* dapper, elegant, fashionable, modern, modish, *inf* natty, *inf* posh, smart, *inf* snazzy, sophisticated, *inf* trendy, up-to-date. *Opp* OLD-FASHIONED.

subconscious *adj* deep-rooted, hidden, inner, intuitive, latent, repressed, subliminal, suppressed, unacknowledged, unconscious. *Opp* CONSCIOUS.

subdue *vb* check, curb, hold back, keep under, moderate, quieten, repress, restrain, suppress, temper. ▷ SUBJUGATE.

subdued *adj* **1** chastened, crestfallen, depressed, downcast, grave, reflective, repressed, restrained, serious, silent, sober, solemn, thoughtful. ▷ SAD. *Opp* EXCITED. **2** *subdued music.* calm, hushed, low, mellow, muted, peaceful, placid, quiet, soft, soothing, toned down, tranquil, unobtrusive.

subject *adj* **1** captive, dependent, enslaved, oppressed, ruled, subjugated. **2** *subject to interference.* exposed, liable, prone, susceptible, vulnerable. *Opp* FREE. • *n* **1** citizen, dependant, national, passport-holder, taxpayer, voter. **2** *subject for discussion.* affair, business, issue, matter, point, proposition, question, theme, thesis, topic. **3** *subject of study.* area, branch of knowledge, course, discipline, field. □ *anatomy, archaeology, architecture, art, astronomy, biology, business, chemistry, computing, craft, design, divinity, domestic science, drama, economics, education, electronics, engineering, English, environmental science, ethnology, etymology, geography, geology, heraldry, history, languages, Latin, law, linguistics, literature, mathematics, mechanics, medicine, metallurgy, metaphysics, meteorology, music, natural history, oceanography, ornithology, penology, pharmacology, pharmacy, philology, philosophy, photography, physics, physiology, politics, psychology, religious studies, science, scripture, social work, sociology, sport, surveying, technology, theology, topology, zoology.* • *vb* **1** *subject a thing to scrutiny.* expose, lay open, submit. **2** ▷ SUBJUGATE.

subjective *adj* biased, emotional, *inf* gut (*reaction*), idiosyncratic, individual, instinctive, intuitive, personal, prejudiced, self-centred. *Opp* OBJECTIVE.

subjugate *vb* beat, conquer, control, crush, defeat, dominate, enslave, enthral, *inf* get the better of, master, oppress, overcome, overpower, overrun, put down, quash, quell, subdue, subject, tame, triumph over, vanquish.

sublimate *vb* channel, convert, divert, idealize, purify, redirect, refine.

sublime *adj* ecstatic, elated, elevated, exalted, great, heavenly, high, high-minded, lofty, noble, spiritual, transcendent. *Opp* BASE.

submerge *vb* **1** cover with water, dip, drench, drown, *inf* dunk, engulf, flood, immerse, inundate, overwhelm, soak, swamp. **2** dive, go down, go under, plummet, sink, subside.

submission *n* **1** acquiescence, capitulation, compliance, giving in, surrender, yielding. ▷ SUBMISSIVENESS. **2** contribution, entry, offering, presentation, tender. **3** *a legal submission.* argument, claim, contention, idea, proposal, suggestion, theory.

submissive *adj* accommodating, acquiescent, amenable, biddable, *derog* boot-licking, compliant, deferential, docile, humble, meek, obedient, obsequious, passive, pliant, resigned, servile, slavish, supine, sycophantic, tame, tractable, unassertive, uncomplaining, unresisting, weak, yielding. *Opp* ASSERTIVE.

submissiveness *n* acquiescence, assent, compliance, deference, docility, humility, meekness, obedience, obsequiousness, passivity, resignation, servility, submission, subservience, tameness.

submit *vb* **1** accede, bow, capitulate, concede, give in, *inf* knuckle under, succumb, surrender, yield. **2** *submit a proposal.* advance, enter, give in, hand in, offer, present, proffer, propose, propound, put forward, state, suggest. **submit to** ▷ ACCEPT, OBEY.

subordinate *adj* inferior, junior, lesser, lower, menial, minor, secondary, subservient, subsidiary. • *n* aide, assistant, dependant, employee, inferior, junior, menial, *inf* underling. ▷ SERVANT.

subscribe *vb* **subscribe to 1** contribute to, covenant to, donate to, give to, patronize, sponsor, support. **2** *subscribe to a magazine.* be a subscriber to, buy regularly, pay a subscription to. **3** *subscribe to a theory.* advocate, agree with, approve of, *inf* back, believe in, condone, consent to, endorse, *inf* give your blessing to.

subscriber *n* patron, regular customer, sponsor, supporter.

subscription *n* due, fee, payment, regular contribution, remittance.

subsequent *adj* coming, consequent, ensuing, following, future, later, next, resultant, resulting, succeeding, successive. *Opp* PREVIOUS.

subside *vb* **1** abate, calm down, decline, decrease, die down, diminish, dwindle, ebb, fall, go down, lessen, melt away, moderate, quieten, recede, shrink, slacken, wear off. **2** *subside into a chair.* collapse, descend, lower yourself, settle, sink. *Opp* RISE.

subsidiary *adj* additional, ancillary, auxiliary, complementary, contributory, inferior, lesser, minor, secondary, subordinate, supporting.

subsidize *vb* aid, back, finance, fund, give subsidy to, maintain, promote, sponsor, support, underwrite.

subsidy *n* aid, backing, financial help, funding, grant, maintenance, sponsorship, subvention, support.

substance *n* **1** actuality, body, concreteness, corporeality, reality, solidity. **2** chemical, fabric, make-up, material, matter, stuff. **3** *substance of an argument.* core, essence, gist, import, meaning, significance, subject-matter, theme. **4** [*old use*] *a person of substance.* ▷ WEALTH.

substandard *adj inf* below par, disappointing, inadequate, inferior, poor, shoddy, unworthy.

substantial *adj* **1** durable, hefty, massive, solid, sound, stout, strong, sturdy, well-built, well-made. **2** big, consequential, considerable, generous, great, large, significant, sizeable, worthwhile. *Opp* FLIMSY, SMALL.

substitute *adj* **1** acting, deputy, relief, reserve, stand-by, surrogate, temporary. **2** alternative, ersatz, imitation. • *n* alternative, deputy, locum, proxy, relief, replacement, reserve, stand-in, stopgap, substitution, supply, surrogate, understudy. • *vb* **1** change, exchange, interchange, replace, *inf* swop, *inf* switch. **2** *substitute for an absentee.* act as a substitute, cover, deputize, double, stand in, supplant, take the place of, take over the role of, understudy.

subtle *adj* **1** delicate, elusive, faint, fine, gentle, mild, slight, unobtrusive. **2** *subtle argument.* arcane, clever, indirect, ingenious, mysterious, recondite, refined, shrewd, sophisticated, tactful, understated. ▷ CUNNING. *Opp* OBVIOUS.

subtract *vb* debit, deduct, remove, take away, take off. *Opp* ADD.

suburban *adj* outer, outlying, residential.

suburbs *n* fringes, outer areas, outskirts, residential areas, suburbia.

subversive *adj* challenging, disruptive, insurrectionary, questioning, radical, seditious, traitorous, treacherous, treasonous, undermining, unsettling. ▷ REVOLUTIONARY. *Opp* CONSERVATIVE, ORTHODOX.

subvert *vb* challenge, corrupt, destroy, disrupt, overthrow, overturn, pervert, ruin, undermine, upset, wreck.

subway *n* tunnel, underpass.

succeed *vb* **1** accomplish your objective, *inf* arrive, be a success, do well, flourish, *inf* get on, *inf* get to the top, *inf* make it, prosper, thrive. **2** be effective, *inf* catch on, produce results, work. **3** be successor to, come after, follow, inherit from, replace, take over from. *Opp* FAIL. **succeeding** ▷ SUBSEQUENT.

success *n* **1** fame, good fortune, prosperity, wealth. **2** *success of a plan.* accomplishment, achievement, attainment, completion, effectiveness, successful outcome. **3** *a great success.* *inf* hit, *inf* sensation, triumph, victory, *inf* winner. *Opp* FAILURE.

successful *adj* **1** booming, effective, effectual, flourishing, fruitful, lucrative, money-making, productive, profitable, profit-making, prosperous, rewarding, thriving, useful, well-off. **2** best-selling, celebrated, famed, famous, high-earning, leading, popular, top, unbeaten, victorious, well-known, winning. *Opp* UNSUCCESSFUL.

succession *n* chain, flow, line, procession, progression, run, sequence, series, string.

successive *adj* consecutive, continuous, in succession, succeeding, unbroken, uninterrupted.

successor *n* heir, inheritor, replacement.

succinct *adj* brief, compact, concise, condensed, epigrammatic, pithy, short, terse, to the point. *Opp* WORDY.

succulent *adj* fleshy, juicy, luscious, moist, mouthwatering, palatable, rich.

succumb *vb* accede, be overcome, capitulate, give in, give up, give way, submit, surrender, yield. *Opp* SURVIVE.

suck *vb* **suck up** absorb, draw up, pull up, soak up. **suck up to** ▷ FLATTER.

sudden *adj* **1** abrupt, brisk, hasty, hurried, impetuous, impulsive, precipitate, quick, rash, *inf* snap, swift, unconsidered, unplanned, unpremeditated. *Opp* SLOW. **2** *a sudden shock.* acute, sharp, startling, surprising, unannounced, unexpected, unforeseeable, unforeseen, unlooked-for. *Opp* PREDICTABLE.

suds *n* bubbles, foam, froth, lather, soapsuds.

sue *vb* **1** indict, institute legal proceedings against, proceed against, prosecute, summons, take legal action against. **2** *sue for peace.* ▷ ENTREAT.

suffer *vb* **1** bear, cope with, endure, experience, feel, go through, live through, *inf* put up with, stand, tolerate, undergo, withstand. **2** *suffer from a wound.* ache, agonize, feel pain, hurt, smart. **3** *suffer for a crime.* atone, be punished, make amends, pay.

suffice *vb* answer, be sufficient, *inf* do, satisfy, serve.

sufficient *adj* adequate, enough, satisfactory. *Opp* INSUFFICIENT.

suffocate *vb* asphyxiate, choke, smother, stifle, stop breathing, strangle, throttle.

sugar *n* □ *brown sugar, cane sugar, caster sugar, demerara, glucose, granulated sugar, icing sugar, lump sugar, molasses, sucrose, sweets, syrup, treacle.* • *vb* sweeten.

sugary *adj* **1** glazed, iced, sugared, sweetened. ▷ SWEET. **2** *sugary sentiments*. cloying, honeyed, sickly. ▷ SENTIMENTAL.

suggest *vb* **1** advise, advocate, counsel, moot, move, propose, propound, put forward, raise, recommend, urge. **2** call to mind, communicate, hint, imply, indicate, insinuate, intimate, make you think (of), mean, signal.

suggestion *n* **1** advice, counsel, offer, plan, prompting, proposal, recommendation, urging. **2** breath, hint, idea, indication, intimation, notion, suspicion, touch, trace.

suggestive *adj* **1** evocative, expressive, indicative, reminiscent, thought-provoking. **2** ▷ INDECENT.

suicidal *adj* **1** hopeless, *inf* kamikaze, self-destructive. **2** ▷ DESOLATE.

suit *n* outfit. ▷ CLOTHES. ● *vb* **1** accommodate, be suitable for, conform to, fill your needs, fit in with, gratify, harmonize with, match, please, satisfy, tally with. *Opp* DISPLEASE. **2** *That colour suits you*. become, fit, look good on.

suitable *adj* acceptable, applicable, apposite, appropriate, apt, becoming, befitting, congenial, convenient, correct, decent, decorous, fit, fitting, handy, *old use* meet, opportune, pertinent, proper, relevant, right, satisfactory, seemly, tasteful, timely, well-chosen, well-judged, well-timed. *Opp* UNSUITABLE.

sulk *vb* be sullen, brood, mope, pout.

sullen *adj* **1** antisocial, bad-tempered, brooding, churlish, crabby, cross, disgruntled, dour, glum, grim, grudging, ill-humoured, lugubrious, moody, morose, *inf* out of sorts, petulant, pouting, resentful, silent, sour, stubborn, sulking, sulky, surly, uncommunicative, unforgiving, unfriendly, unhappy, unsociable. ▷ SAD. **2** *a sullen sky*. cheerless, dark, dismal, dull, gloomy, grey, leaden, sombre. *Opp* CHEERFUL.

sultry *adj* **1** close, hot, humid, *inf* muggy, oppressive, steamy, stifling, stuffy, warm. *Opp* COLD. **2** *sultry beauty*. erotic, mysterious, passionate, provocative, seductive, sensual, sexy, voluptuous.

sum *n* aggregate, amount, number, quantity, reckoning, result, score, tally, total, whole. ● *vb* **sum up** ▷ SUMMARIZE.

summarize *vb* abridge, condense, digest, encapsulate, give the gist, make a summary, outline, précis, *inf* recap, recapitulate, reduce, review, shorten, simplify, sum up. *Opp* ELABORATE.

summary *n* abridgement, abstract, condensation, digest, epitome, gist, outline, précis, recapitulation, reduction, résumé, review, summation, summing-up, synopsis.

summery *adj* bright, sunny, tropical, warm. ▷ HOT. *Opp* WINTRY.

summit *n* **1** apex, crown, head, height, peak, pinnacle, point, top. *Opp* BASE. **2** *summit of success*. acme, apogee, climax, culmination, high point, zenith. *Opp* NADIR.

summon *vb* **1** command, demand, invite, order, send for, subpoena. **2** assemble, call, convene, convoke, gather together, muster, rally.

sunbathe *vb* bake, bask, *inf* get a tan, sun yourself, tan.

sunburnt *adj* blistered, bronzed, brown, peeling, tanned, weather-beaten.

sundry *adj* assorted, different, *old use* divers, miscellaneous, mixed, various.

sunken *adj* **1** submerged, underwater, wrecked. **2** *sunken cheeks*. concave, depressed, drawn, hollow, hollowed.

sunless *adj* cheerless, cloudy, dark, dismal, dreary, dull, gloomy, grey, overcast, sombre. *Opp* SUNNY.

sunlight *n* daylight, sun, sunbeams, sunshine.

sunny *adj* **1** bright, clear, cloudless, fair, fine, summery, sunlit, sunshiny, unclouded. *Opp* SUNLESS. **2** ▷ CHEERFUL.

sunrise *n* dawn, daybreak.

sunset *n* dusk, evening, gloaming, nightfall, sundown, twilight.

sunshade *n* awning, canopy, parasol.

superannuated *adj* **1** discharged, *inf* pensioned off, *inf* put out to grass, old, retired. **2** discarded, disused, obsolete, thrown out, worn out. ▷ OLD.

superannuation *n* annuity, pension.

superb *adj* admirable, excellent, fine, first-class, first-rate, grand, impressive, marvellous, superior. ▷ SPLENDID. *Opp* INFERIOR.

superficial *adj* **1** cosmetic, external, exterior, on the surface, outward, shallow, skin-deep, slight, surface, unimportant. **2** careless, casual, cursory, desultory, facile, frivolous, hasty, hurried, inattentive, lightweight, *inf* nodding (*acquaintance*), oversimplified, passing, perfunctory, simple-minded, simplistic, sweeping (*generalization*), trivial, unconvincing, uncritical, undiscriminating, unquestioning, unscholarly, unsophisticated. *Opp* ANALYTICAL, DEEP.

superfluous *adj* excess, excessive, extra, needless, redundant, spare, superabundant, surplus, unnecessary, unneeded, unwanted. *Opp* NECESSARY.

superhuman *adj* **1** god-like, herculean, heroic, phenomenal, prodigious. **2** *superhuman powers.* divine, higher, metaphysical, supernatural.

superimpose *vb* overlay, place on top of.

superintend *vb* administer, be in charge of, be the supervisor of, conduct, control, direct, look after, manage, organize, oversee, preside over, run, supervise, watch over.

superior *adj* **1** better, *inf* classier, greater, higher, higher-born, loftier, more important, more impressive, nobler, senior, *inf* up-market. **2** *superior quality.* choice, exclusive, fine, first-class, first-rate, select, top, unrivalled. **3** *superior attitude.* arrogant, condescending, contemptuous, disdainful, élitist, haughty, *inf* high-and-mighty, lofty, paternalistic, patronizing, self-important, smug, snobbish, *inf* snooty, stuck-up, supercilious. *Opp* INFERIOR.

superlative *adj* best, choicest, consummate, excellent, finest, first-rate, incomparable, matchless, peerless, *inf* tip-top, *inf* top-notch, unrivalled, unsurpassed. ▷ SUPREME.

supernatural *adj* abnormal, ghostly, inexplicable, magical, metaphysical, miraculous, mysterious, mystic, occult, other-worldly, paranormal, preternatural, psychic, spiritual, uncanny, unearthly, unnatural, weird.

superstition *n* delusion, illusion, myth, *inf* old wives' tale, superstitious belief.

superstitious *adj* credulous, groundless, illusory, irrational, mythical, traditional, unfounded, unprovable.

supervise *vb* administer, be in charge of, be the supervisor of, conduct, control, direct, govern, invigilate (*an exam*), *inf* keep an eye on, lead, look after, manage, organize, oversee, preside over, run, superintend, watch over.

supervision *n* administration, conduct, control, direction, government, invigilation, management, organization, oversight, running, surveillance.

supervisor *n* administrator, chief, controller, director, executive, foreman, *inf* gaffer, head, inspector, invigilator, leader, manager, organizer, overseer, superintendent, timekeeper.

supine *adj* **1** face upwards, flat on your back, prostrate, recumbent. *Opp* PRONE. **2** ▷ PASSIVE.

supplant *vb* displace, dispossess, eject, expel, oust, replace, *inf* step into the shoes of, supersede, *inf* topple, unseat.

supple *adj* bending, *inf* bendy, elastic, flexible, flexile, graceful, limber, lithe, plastic, pliable, pliant, resilient, soft. *Opp* RIGID.

supplement *n* **1** additional payment, excess, surcharge. **2** *a newspaper supplement, etc.* addendum, addition, annexe, appendix, codicil, continuation, endpiece, extra, insert, postscript, sequel. • *vb* add to, augment, boost, complement, extend, reinforce, *inf* top up.

supplementary *adj* accompanying, added, additional, ancillary, auxiliary, complementary, excess, extra, new, supportive.

supplication *n* appeal, entreaty, petition, plea, prayer, request, solicitation.

supplier *n* dealer, provider, purveyor, retailer, seller, shopkeeper, vendor, wholesaler.

supply *n* **1** cache, hoard, quantity, reserve, reservoir, stock, stockpile, store. **2** equipment, food, necessities, provisions, rations, shopping. **3** *a regular supply.* delivery, distribution, provision, provisioning. • *vb* cater to, contribute, deliver, distribute, donate, endow, equip, feed, furnish, give, hand over, pass on, produce, provide, purvey, sell, stock.

support *n* **1** aid, approval, assistance, backing, back-up, bolstering, contribution, cooperation, donation, encouragement, fortifying, friendship, help, interest, loyalty, patronage, protection, reassurance, reinforcement, sponsorship, succour. **2** brace, bracket, buttress, crutch, foundation, frame, pillar, post, prop, sling, stanchion, stay, strut, substructure, trestle, truss, underpinning. **3** *financial support.* expenses, funding, keep, maintenance, subsistence, upkeep. • *vb* **1** bear, bolster, buoy up, buttress, carry, give strength to, hold up, keep up, prop up, provide a support for, reinforce, shore up, strengthen, underlie, underpin. **2** *support someone in trouble.* aid, assist, back, be faithful to, champion, comfort, defend, encourage, favour, fight for, give support to, help, rally round, reassure, side with, speak up for, stand by, stand up for, stay with, *inf* stick up for, *inf* stick with, take someone's part. **3** *support a family.* bring up, feed, finance, fund, keep, look after, maintain, nourish, provide for, sustain. **4** *support a charity.* be a supporter of, be interested in, contribute to, espouse (*a cause*), follow, give to, patronize, pay money to, sponsor, subsidize, work for. **5** *support a point of view.* accept, adhere to, advocate, agree with, allow, approve, argue for, confirm, corroborate, defend, endorse, explain, justify, promote, ratify, substantiate, uphold, validate, verify. *Opp* SUBVERT, WEAKEN. **support yourself** lean, rest.

supporter *n* **1** adherent, admirer, advocate, aficionado, apologist, champion, defender, devotee, enthusiast, *inf* fan, fanatic, follower, seconder, upholder, voter. **2** ally, assistant, collaborator, helper, henchman, second.

supportive *adj* caring, concerned, encouraging, favourable, heartening, helpful, interested, kind, loyal, positive, reassuring, sustaining, sympathetic, understanding. *Opp* SUBVERSIVE.

suppose *vb* **1** accept, assume, believe, conclude, conjecture, expect, guess, infer, judge, postulate, presume, presuppose, speculate, surmise, suspect, take for granted, think. **2** daydream, fancy, fantasize, hypothesize, imagine, maintain, postulate, pretend, theorize. **supposed** ▷ HYPOTHETICAL, PUTATIVE. **supposed to** due to, expected to, having a duty to, meant to, required to.

supposition *n* assumption, belief, conjecture, fancy, guess, *inf* guesstimate, hypothesis, inference, notion, opinion, presumption, speculation, surmise, theory, thought.

suppress *vb* **1** conquer, *inf* crack down on, crush, end, finish off, halt, overcome, overthrow, put an end to, put down, quash, quell, stamp out, stop, subdue. **2** *suppress emotion.* bottle up, censor, choke back, conceal, cover up, hide, hush up, keep quiet about, keep secret, muffle, mute, obstruct, prohibit, repress, restrain, silence, smother, stamp on, stifle, strangle.

supremacy *n* ascendancy, dominance, domination, dominion, lead, mastery, predominance, pre-eminence, sovereignty, superiority.

supreme *adj* best, choicest, consummate, crowning, culminating, excellent, finest, first-rate, greatest, highest, incomparable, matchless, outstanding, paramount, peerless, predominant, pre-eminent, prime, principal, superlative, surpassing, *inf* tip-top, top, *inf* top-notch, ultimate, unbeatable, unbeaten, unparalleled, unrivalled, unsurpassable, unsurpassed.

sure *adj* **1** assured, certain, confident, convinced, decided, definite, persuaded, positive. **2** *sure to come.* bound, certain, compelled, obliged, required. **3** *a sure fact.* accurate, clear, convincing, guaranteed, indisputable, inescapable, inevitable, infallible, proven, reliable, true, unchallenged, undeniable, undisputed, undoubted, verifiable. **4** *a sure ally.* dependable, effective, established, faithful, firm, infallible, loyal, reliable, resolute, safe, secure, solid, steadfast, steady, trustworthy, trusty, undeviating, unerring, unfailing, unfaltering, unflinching, unswerving, unwavering. *Opp* UNCERTAIN.

surface *n* **1** coat, coating, covering, crust, exterior, façade, integument, interface, outside, shell, skin, veneer. **2** *cube has six surfaces.* face, facet, plane, side. **3** *a working surface.* bench, table, top, worktop. • *vb* **1** appear, arise, *inf* come to light, come up, *inf* crop up, emerge, materialize, *inf* pop up, rise. **2** coat, cover, laminate, veneer.

surfeit *n* excess, flood, glut, overabundance, overindulgence, oversupply, plethora, superfluity, surplus.

surge *n* burst, gush, increase, onrush, onset, outpouring, rush, upsurge. ▷ WAVE. • *vb* billow, eddy, flow, gush, heave, make waves, move irresistibly, push, roll, rush, stampede, stream, sweep, swirl, well up.

surgery *n* **1** biopsy, operation. **2** *a doctor's surgery.* clinic, consulting room, health centre, infirmary, medical centre, sick-bay.

surly *adj* bad-tempered, boorish, cantankerous, churlish, crabby, cross, crotchety, *inf* crusty, curmudgeonly, dyspeptic, gruff, *inf* grumpy, ill-natured, illtempered, irascible, miserable, morose, peevish, rough, rude, sulky, sullen, testy, touchy, uncivil, unfriendly, ungracious, unpleasant. *Opp* FRIENDLY.

surmise *vb* assume, believe, conjecture, expect, fancy, gather, guess, hypothesize, imagine, infer, judge, postulate, presume, presuppose, sense, speculate, suppose, suspect, take for granted, think.

surpass *vb* beat, better, do better than, eclipse, exceed, excel, go beyond, leave behind, *inf* leave standing, outclass, outdistance, outdo, outperform, outshine, outstrip, overshadow, top, transcend, worst.

surplus *n* balance, excess, extra, glut, oversupply, remainder, residue, superfluity, surfeit.

surprise *n* **1** alarm, amazement, astonishment, consternation, dismay, incredulity, stupefaction, wonder. **2** *a complete surprise.* blow, *inf* bolt from the blue, *inf* bombshell, *inf* eye-opener, jolt, shock. • *vb* **1** alarm, amaze, astonish, astound, disconcert, dismay, dumbfound, flabbergast, nonplus, rock, shock, stagger, startle, stun, stupefy, *inf* take aback, take by surprise, *inf* throw. **2** *surprise someone doing wrong.* capture, catch out, *inf* catch red-handed, come upon, detect, discover, take unawares.

surprised *adj* alarmed, amazed, astonished, astounded, disconcerted, dismayed, dumbfounded, flabbergasted, incredulous, *inf* knocked for six, nonplussed, *inf* shattered, shocked, speechless, staggered, startled, struck dumb, stunned, taken aback, taken by surprise, *inf* thrown, thunderstruck.

surprising *adj* alarming, amazing, astonishing, astounding, disconcerting, extraordinary, frightening, incredible, *inf* off-putting, shocking, staggering, startling, stunning, sudden, unexpected, unforeseen, unlooked-for, unplanned, unpredictable, upsetting. *Opp* PREDICTABLE.

surrender *n* capitulation, giving in, resignation, submission. • *vb* **1** acquiesce, capitulate, *inf* cave in, collapse, concede, fall, *inf* give in, give up, give way, give yourself up, resign, submit, succumb, *inf* throw in the towel, *inf* throw up the sponge, yield. **2** *surrender your ticket.* deliver up, give up, hand over, part with, relinquish. **3** *surrender your rights.* abandon, cede, renounce, waive.

surreptitious *adj* clandestine, concealed, covert, crafty, disguised, furtive, hidden, private, secret, secretive, shifty, sly, *inf* sneaky, stealthy, underhand. *Opp* BLATANT.

surround *vb* beset, besiege, cocoon, cordon off, encircle, enclose, encompass, engulf, environ, girdle, hedge in, hem in, ring, skirt, trap, wrap.

surrounding *adj* adjacent, adjoining, bordering, local, nearby, neighbouring.

surroundings *plur n* ambience, area, background, context, environment, location, milieu, neighbourhood, setting, vicinity.

surveillance *n* check, observation, reconnaissance, scrutiny, supervision, vigilance, watch.

survey *n* appraisal, assessment, census, count, evaluation, examination, inquiry, inspection, investigation, review, scrutiny, study, triangulation. • *vb* **1** appraise, assess, estimate, evaluate, examine, inspect, investigate, look over, review, scrutinize, study, view, weigh up. **2** do a survey of, map out, measure, plan out, plot, reconnoitre, triangulate.

survival *n* continuance, continued existence, persistence.

survive *vb* **1** *inf* bear up, carry on, continue, endure, keep going, last, live, persist, remain. **2** *survive disaster.* come through, live through, outlast, outlive, pull through, weather, withstand. *Opp* SUCCUMB.

susceptible *adj* affected (by), disposed, given, inclined, liable, open, predisposed, prone, responsive, sensitive, vulnerable. *Opp* RESISTANT.

suspect *adj* doubtful, dubious, inadequate, questionable, *inf* shady, suspected, suspicious, unconvincing, unreliable, unsatisfactory, untrustworthy. • *vb* **1** call into question, disbelieve, distrust, doubt, have suspicions about, mistrust. **2** *suspect that she's lying.* believe, conjecture, consider, guess, imagine, infer, presume, speculate, suppose, surmise, think.

suspend *vb* **1** dangle, hang, swing. **2** *suspend work.* adjourn, break off, defer, delay, discontinue, freeze, hold in abeyance, hold up, interrupt, postpone, put off, *inf* put on ice, shelve. **3** *suspend from duty.* debar, dismiss, exclude, expel, lay off, lock out, send down.

suspense *n* anticipation, anxiety, apprehension, doubt, drama, excitement, expectancy, expectation, insecurity, irresolution, nervousness, not knowing, tension, uncertainty, waiting.

suspicion *n* **1** apprehension, apprehensiveness, caution, distrust, doubt, dubiety, dubiousness, *inf* funny feeling, guess, hesitation, *inf* hunch, impression, misgiving, mistrust, presentiment, qualm, scepticism, uncertainty, wariness. **2** *suspicion of a smile.* glimmer, hint, inkling, shadow, suggestion, tinge, touch, trace.

suspicious *adj* **1** apprehensive, *inf* chary, disbelieving, distrustful, doubtful, dubious, incredulous, in doubt, mistrustful, sceptical, uncertain, unconvinced, uneasy, wary. *Opp* TRUSTFUL. **2** *suspicious character.* disreputable, dubious, *inf* fishy, peculiar, questionable, *inf* shady, suspect, suspected, unreliable, untrustworthy. *Opp* TRUSTWORTHY.

sustain *vb* **1** continue, develop, elongate, extend, keep alive, keep going, keep up, maintain, prolong. **2** ▷ SUPPORT.

sustenance *n* eatables, edibles, food, foodstuffs, nourishment, nutriment, provender, provisions, rations, *old use* victuals.

swag *n* booty, loot, plunder, takings.

swagger *vb* parade, strut. ▷ WALK.

swallow *vb* consume, *inf* down, gulp down, guzzle, ingest, take down. ▷ DRINK, EAT. **swallow up** absorb, assimilate, enclose, enfold, make disappear. ▷ SWAMP.

swamp *n* bog, fen, marsh, marshland, morass, mud, mud-flats, quagmire, quicksand, salt-marsh, *old use* slough, wetlands. ● *vb* deluge, drench, engulf, envelop, flood, immerse, inundate, overcome, overwhelm, sink, submerge, swallow up.

swampy *adj* boggy, marshy, muddy, soft, soggy, unstable, waterlogged, wet. *Opp* DRY, FIRM.

swarm *n* cloud, crowd, hive, horde, host, multitude. ▷ GROUP. ● *vb* cluster, congregate, crowd, flock, gather, mass, move in a swarm, throng. **swarm up** ▷ CLIMB. **swarm with** ▷ TEEM.

swarthy *adj* brown, dark, dark-complexioned, dark-skinned, dusky, tanned.

swashbuckling *adj* adventurous, aggressive, bold, daredevil, daring, dashing, *inf* macho, manly, swaggering. *Opp* TIMID.

sway *vb* **1** bend, fluctuate, lean from side to side, oscillate, rock, roll, swing, undulate, wave. **2** *sway opinions.* affect, bias, bring round, change (someone's mind), convert, convince, govern, influence, persuade, win over. **3** *sway from a chosen path.* divert, go off course, swerve, veer, waver.

swear *vb* **1** affirm, asseverate, attest, aver, avow, declare, give your word, insist, pledge, promise, state on oath, take an oath, testify, vouchsafe, vow. **2** blaspheme, curse, execrate, imprecate, use swearwords, utter profanities.

swear-word *n inf* bad language, blasphemy, curse, execration, expletive, *inf* four-letter word, imprecation, oath, obscenity, profanity, swearing.

sweat *vb* **1** *inf* glow, perspire, swelter. **2** ▷ WORK.

sweaty *adj* clammy, damp, moist, perspiring, sticky, sweating.

sweep *vb* brush, clean, clear, dust, tidy up. **sweep along** ▷ MOVE. **sweep away** ▷ REMOVE. **sweeping** ▷ GENERAL, SUPERFICIAL.

sweet *adj* **1** aromatic, fragrant, honeyed, luscious, mellow, perfumed, sweetened, sweetscented, sweet-smelling. **2** [*derog*] *sickly sweet.* cloying, saccharine, sentimental, sickening, sickly, sugary, syrupy, treacly. **3** *sweet sounds.* dulcet, euphonious, harmonious, heavenly, mellifluous, melodious, musical, pleasant, silvery, soothing, tuneful. **4** *a sweet nature.* affectionate, amiable, attractive, charming, dear, endearing, engaging, friendly, genial, gentle, gracious, lovable, lovely, nice, pretty, unselfish, winning. *Opp* ACID, BITTER, NASTY, SAVOURY. ● *n* **1** *inf* afters, dessert, pudding. **2** [*usu plur*] *old use* bon-bons, *Amer* candy, confectionery, *inf* sweeties, *old use* sweetmeats. □ *acid drop, barley sugar, boiled sweet, bull's-eye, butterscotch, candy, candyfloss, caramel, chewing-gum, chocolate, fondant, fruit pastille, fudge, humbug, liquorice, lollipop, marshmallow, marzipan, mint, nougat, peppermint, rock, toffee, Turkish delight.*

sweeten *vb* **1** make sweeter, sugar. **2** *sweeten your temper.* appease, assuage, calm, mellow, mollify, pacify, soothe.

sweetener *n* □ *artificial sweetener, honey, saccharine, sugar, sweetening, syrup.*

swell *vb* **1** balloon, become bigger, belly, billow, blow up, bulge, dilate, distend, enlarge, expand, fatten, fill out, grow, increase, inflate, mushroom, puff up, rise. **2** *swell numbers.* augment, boost, build up, extend, increase, make bigger, raise, step up. *Opp* SHRINK.

swelling *n* blister, boil, bulge, bump, distension, enlargement, excrescence, hump, inflammation, knob, lump, node, nodule, prominence, protrusion, protuberance, tumescence, tumour.

sweltering *adj* humid, muggy, oppressive, steamy, sticky, stifling, sultry, torrid, tropical. ▷ HOT.

swerve *vb* career, change direction, deviate, diverge, dodge about, sheer off, swing, take avoiding action, turn aside, veer, wheel.

swift *adj* agile, brisk, expeditious, fast, *old use* fleet, fleet-footed, hasty, hurried, nimble, *inf* nippy, prompt, quick, rapid, speedy, sudden. *Opp* SLOW.

swill *vb* **1** bathe, clean, rinse, sponge down, wash. **2** ▷ DRINK.

swim *vb* bathe, dive in, float, go swimming, *inf* take a dip.

swimming-bath *n* baths, leisure-pool, lido, swimming-pool.

swim-suit *n* bathing-costume, bathing-dress, bathing-suit, bikini, swimwear, trunks.

swindle *n* cheat, chicanery, *inf* con, confidence trick, deception, double-dealing, fraud, knavery, *inf* racket, *inf* rip-off, *inf* sharp practice, *inf* swizz, trickery. ● *vb inf* bamboozle, cheat, *inf* con, cozen, deceive, defraud, *inf* diddle, *inf* do, double-cross, dupe, exploit, *inf* fiddle, *inf* fleece, fool, gull, hoax, hoodwink, mulct, *inf* pull a fast one on you, *inf* rook, *inf* take you for a ride, trick, *inf* welsh (*on a bet*).

swindler *n* charlatan, cheat, cheater, *inf* con man, counterfeiter, double-crosser, extortioner, forger, fraud, hoaxer, impostor, knave, mountebank, quack, racketeer, scoundrel, *inf* shark, trickster, *inf* twister.

swing *n* change, fluctuation, movement, oscillation, shift, variation. ● *vb* **1** be suspended, dangle, flap, fluctuate, hang loose, move from side to side, move to and fro, oscillate, revolve, rock, roll, sway, swivel, turn, twirl, wave about. **2** *swing opinion.* affect, bias, bring round, change (someone's mind), convert, convince, govern, influence, persuade, win over. **3** *support swung to the opposition.* change, move across, shift, transfer, vary. **4** *swing from a path.* deviate, divert, go off course, swerve, veer, waver, zigzag.

swipe *vb* **1** lash out at, strike, swing at. ▷ HIT. **2** ▷ STEAL.

swirl *vb* boil, churn, circulate, curl, eddy, move in circles, seethe, spin, surge, twirl, twist, whirl.

switch *n* circuit-breaker, lightswitch, power-point. ● *vb* change, divert, exchange, redirect, replace, reverse, shift, substitute, *inf* swap, transfer, turn.

swivel *vb* gyrate, pirouette, pivot, revolve, rotate, spin, swing, turn, twirl, wheel.

swoop *vb* descend, dive, drop, fall, fly down, lunge, plunge, pounce. **swoop on** ▷ RAID.

sword *n* blade, broadsword, cutlass, dagger, foil, kris, rapier, sabre, scimitar.

sycophantic *adj* flattering, servile, *inf* smarmy, toadyish, unctuous.

syllabus *n* course, curriculum, outline, programme of study.

symbol *n* mark, sign, token. □ *badge, brand, character, cipher, coat of arms, crest, emblem, figure, hieroglyph, ideogram, ideograph, image, insignia, letter, logo, logotype, monogram, motif, number, numeral, pictogram, pictograph, trademark.*

symbolic *adj* allegorical, emblematic, figurative, meaningful, metaphorical, representative, significant, suggestive, symptomatic, token (*gesture*).

symbolize *vb* be a sign of, betoken, communicate, connote, denote, epitomize, imply, indicate, mean, represent, signify, stand for, suggest.

symmetrical *adj* balanced, even, proportional, regular. *Opp* ASYMMETRICAL.

sympathetic *adj* benevolent, caring, charitable, comforting, commiserating, compassionate, concerned, consoling, empathetic, friendly, humane, interested, kind-hearted, kindly, merciful, pitying, soft-hearted, solicitous, sorry, supportive, tender, tolerant, understanding, warm. *Opp* UNSYMPATHETIC.

sympathize *vb inf* be on the same wavelength, be sorry, be sympathetic, comfort, commiserate, condole, console, empathize, feel, grieve, have sympathy, identify (with), mourn, pity, respond, show sympathy, understand.

sympathy *n* affinity, commiseration, compassion, concern, condolence, consideration, empathy, feeling, fellow-feeling, kindness, mercy, pity, rapport, solicitousness, tenderness, understanding.

symptom *n* characteristic, evidence, feature, indication, manifestation, mark, marker, sign, warning, warning-sign.

symptomatic *adj* characteristic, indicative, representative, suggestive, typical.

synthesis *n* amalgamation, blend, coalescence, combination, composite, compound, fusion, integration, union. *Opp* ANALYSIS.

synthetic *adj* artificial, bogus, concocted, counterfeit, ersatz, fabricated, fake, *inf* made-up, man-made, manufactured, mock, *inf* phoney, simulated, spurious, unnatural. *Opp* GENUINE, NATURAL.

syringe *n* hypodermic, needle.

system *n* **1** network, organization, *inf* set-up, structure. **2** approach, arrangement, logic, method, methodology, *Lat* modus operandi, order, plan, practice, procedure, process, routine, rules, scheme, technique. **3** *system of government.* constitution, regime. **4** *system of knowledge.* categorization, classification, code, discipline, philosophy, science, set of principles, theory.

systematic *adj* according to plan, businesslike, categorized, classified, codified, constitutional, coordinated, logical, methodical, neat, ordered, orderly, organized, planned, rational, regimented, routine, scientific, structured, tidy, well-arranged, well-organized, well-rehearsed, well-run. *Opp* UNSYSTEMATIC.

systematize *vb* arrange, catalogue, categorize, classify, codify, make systematic, organize, rationalize, regiment, standardize, tabulate.

T

table *n* **1** bench, board, counter, desk, gate-leg table, kitchen table, worktop. **2** *table of information.* agenda, catalogue, chart, diagram, graph, index, inventory, list, register, schedule, tabulation, timetable. • *vb* bring forward, lay on the table, offer, proffer, propose, submit.

tablet *n* **1** capsule, drop, lozenge, medicine, pastille, pellet, pill. **2** *tablet of soap.* bar, block, chunk, piece, slab. **3** *tablet of stone.* gravestone, headstone, memorial, plaque, plate, tombstone.

taboo *adj* banned, censored, disapproved of, forbidden, interdicted, prohibited, proscribed, unacceptable, unlawful, unmentionable, unnamable. ▷ RUDE. • *n* anathema, ban, curse, interdiction, prohibition, proscription, taboo subject.

tabulate *vb* arrange as a table, catalogue, index, list, pigeon-hole, set out in columns, systematize.

tacit *adj* implicit, implied, silent, undeclared, understood, unexpressed, unsaid, unspoken, unvoiced.

taciturn *adj* mute, quiet, reserved, reticent, silent, tight-lipped, uncommunicative, unforthcoming. *Opp* TALKATIVE.

tack *n* **1** drawing-pin, nail, pin, tintack. **2** *the wrong tack.* approach, bearing, course, direction, heading, line, policy, procedure, technique. • *vb* **1** nail, pin. ▷ FASTEN. **2** sew, stitch. **3** *tack in a yacht.* beat against the wind, change course, go about, zigzag. **tack on** ▷ ADD.

tackle *n* **1** accoutrements, apparatus, *inf* clobber, equipment, fittings, gear, implements, kit, outfit, paraphernalia, rig, rigging, tools. **2** *a football tackle.* attack, block, challenge, interception, intervention. • *vb* **1** address (yourself to), apply yourself to, attempt, attend to, combat, *inf* come to grips with, concentrate on, confront, cope with, deal with, engage in, face up to, focus on, get involved in, grapple with, handle, *inf* have a go at, manage, set about, settle down to, sort out, take on, undertake. **2** *tackle an opponent.* attack, challenge, intercept, stop, take on.

tacky *adj* adhesive, gluey, *inf* gooey, gummy, sticky, viscous, wet. *Opp* DRY.

tact *n* adroitness, consideration, delicacy, diplomacy, discernment, discretion, finesse, judgement, perceptiveness, politeness, savoir-faire, sensitivity, tactfulness, thoughtfulness, understanding. *Opp* TACTLESSNESS.

tactful *adj* adroit, appropriate, considerate, courteous, delicate, diplomatic, discreet, judicious, perceptive, polite, politic, sensitive, thoughtful, understanding. *Opp* TACTLESS.

tactical *adj* artful, calculated, clever, deliberate, planned, politic, prudent, shrewd, skilful, strategic.

tactics *plur n* approach, campaign, course of action, design, device, manoeuvre, manoeuvring, plan, ploy, policy, procedure, ruse, scheme, stratagem, strategy.

tactless *adj* blundering, blunt, boorish, bungling, clumsy, discourteous, gauche, heavyhanded, hurtful, impolite, impolitic, inappropriate, inconsiderate, indelicate, indiscreet, inept, insensitive, maladroit, misjudged, thoughtless, uncivil, uncouth, undiplomatic, unkind. ▷ RUDE. *Opp* TACTFUL.

tactlessness *n* boorishness, clumsiness, gaucherie, indelicacy, indiscretion, ineptitude, insensitivity, lack of diplomacy, misjudgement, thoughtlessness, uncouthness. ▷ RUDENESS. *Opp* TACT.

tag *n* **1** docket, label, marker, name tag, price tag, slip, sticker, tab, ticket. **2** *a Latin tag.* ▷ SAYING. ● *vb* identify, label, mark, ticket. **tag along with** ▷ FOLLOW.

tail *n* appendage, back, brush (*of fox*), buttocks, end, extremity, rear, rump, scut (*of rabbit*), tail-end. ● *vb* dog, follow, hunt, pursue, shadow, stalk, track, trail. **tail off** ▷ DECLINE.

taint *vb* **1** adulterate, contaminate, defile, dirty, infect, poison, pollute, soil. **2** *taint a reputation.* besmirch, blacken, blemish, damage, dishonour, harm, ruin, slander, smear, spoil, stain, sully, tarnish.

take *vb* **1** acquire, bring, carry away, *inf* cart off, catch, clasp, clutch, fetch, gain, get, grab, grasp, grip, hold, pick up, pluck, remove, secure, seize, snatch, transfer. **2** *take prisoners.* abduct, arrest, capture, catch, corner, detain, ensnare, entrap, secure. **3** *take property.* appropriate, get away with, pocket. ▷ STEAL. **4** *take 2 from 4.* deduct, eliminate, subtract, take away. **5** *take passengers.* accommodate, carry, contain, have room for, hold. **6** *take a partner.* accompany, conduct, convey, escort, ferry, guide, lead, transport. **7** *take a taxi.* engage, hire, make use of, travel by, use. **8** *take a subject.* have lessons in, learn about, read, study. **9** *can't take pain.* abide, accept, bear, brook, endure, receive, *inf* stand, *inf* stomach, suffer, tolerate, undergo, withstand. **10** *take food, drink.* consume, drink, eat, have, swallow. **11** *It takes courage to own up.* necessitate, need, require, use up. **12** *take a new name.* adopt, assume, choose, select. **take aback** ▷ SURPRISE. **take after** ▷ RESEMBLE. **take against** ▷ DISLIKE. **take back** ▷ WITHDRAW. **take in** ▷ ACCOMMODATE, DECEIVE, UNDERSTAND. **take life** ▷ KILL. **take off** ▷ IMITATE. **take off, take out** ▷ REMOVE. **take on, take up** ▷ UNDERTAKE. **take over** ▷ USURP. **take part** ▷ PARTICIPATE. **take place** ▷ HAPPEN. **take to task** ▷ REPRIMAND. **take up** ▷ BEGIN, OCCUPY.

take-over *n* amalgamation, combination, incorporation, merger.

takings *plur n* earnings, gains, gate, income, proceeds, profits, receipts, revenue.

tale *n* account, anecdote, chronicle, narration, narrative, relation, report, *sl* spiel, story, yarn. ▷ WRITING.

talent *n* ability, accomplishment, aptitude, brilliance, capacity, expertise, facility, faculty, flair, genius, gift, ingenuity, knack, *inf* know-how, prowess, skill, strength, versatility.

talented *adj* able, accomplished, artistic, brilliant, distinguished, expert, gifted, inspired, proficient, skilful, skilled, versatile. ▷ CLEVER. *Opp* UNSKILFUL.

talisman *n* amulet, charm, fetish, mascot.

talk *n* **1** baby-talk, *inf* blarney, chat, *inf* chin-wag, *inf* chit-chat, confabulation, conference, conversation, dialogue, discourse, discussion, gossip, intercourse, language, palaver, *inf* powwow, *inf* tattle, *inf* tittle-tattle, words. **2** *a public talk.* address, diatribe, exhortation, harangue, lecture, oration, *inf* peptalk, presentation, sermon, speech, tirade. ● *vb* **1** address one another, articulate ideas, commune, communicate, confer, converse, deliver a speech, discourse, discuss, enunciate, exchange views, have a conversation, *inf* hold forth, lecture, negotiate, *inf* pipe up, pontificate, prate, pronounce words, say something, sermonize, speak, tell, use language, use your voice, utter, verbalize, vocalize. □ *babble, bawl, bellow, blab, blether, blurt out, breathe, burble, call out, chat, chatter, clamour, croak, cry, drawl, drone, gabble, gas, gibber, gossip, grunt, harp, howl, intone, jabber, jaw, jeer, lisp, maunder, moan, mumble, murmur, mutter, natter, patter, prattle, pray, preach, rabbit on, rant, rasp, rattle on, rave, roar,* *scream, screech, shout, shriek, slur, snap, snarl, speak in an undertone, splutter, spout, squeal, stammer, stutter, tattle, vociferate, wail, whimper, whine, whinge, whisper, witter, yell.* **2** *talk French.* communicate in, express yourself in, pronounce, speak. **3** *get someone to talk.* confess, give information, *inf* grass, inform, *inf* let on, *inf* spill the beans, *inf* squeal, *inf* tell tales. ▷ SAY, SPEAK. **talk about** ▷ DISCUSS. **talk to** ▷ ADDRESS.

talkative *adj* articulate, *inf* chatty, communicative, effusive, eloquent, expansive, garrulous, glib, gossipy, long-winded, loquacious, open, prolix, unstoppable, verbose, vocal, voluble, wordy. *Opp* TACITURN. **talkative person** chatter-box, *sl* gas-bag, gossip, *sl* wind-bag.

tall *adj* colossal, giant, gigantic, high, lofty, soaring, towering. ▷ BIG. *Opp* SHORT.

tally *n* addition, count, reckoning, record, sum, total. • *vb* **1** accord, agree, coincide, concur, correspond, match up, square. **2** *tally up the bill.* add, calculate, compute, count, reckon, total, work out.

tame *adj* **1** amenable, biddable, broken in, compliant, disciplined, docile, domesticated, gentle, manageable, meek, mild, obedient, safe, subdued, submissive, tamed, tractable, trained. **2** *tame animals.* approachable, bold, fearless, friendly, sociable, unafraid. **3** *a tame story.* bland, boring, dull, feeble, flat, insipid, lifeless, tedious, unadventurous, unexciting, uninspiring, uninteresting, vapid, *inf* wishy-washy. *Opp* EXCITING, WILD. • *vb* break in, conquer, curb, discipline, domesticate, house-train, humble, keep under, make tame, master, mollify, mute, quell, repress, subdue, subjugate, suppress, temper, tone down, train.

tamper *vb* **tamper with** alter, *inf* fiddle about with, interfere with, make adjustments to, meddle with, tinker with.

tan *n* sunburn, suntan. • *vb* bronze, brown, burn, colour, darken, get tanned.

tang *n* acidity, *inf* bite, *inf* edge, *inf* nip, piquancy, pungency, savour, sharpness, spiciness, zest.

tangible *adj* actual, concrete, corporeal, definite, material, palpable, perceptible, physical, positive, provable, real, solid, substantial, tactile, touchable. *Opp* INTANGIBLE.

tangle *n* coil, complication, confusion, jumble, jungle, knot, labyrinth, mass, maze, mesh, mess, muddle, scramble, twist, web. • *vb* **1** complicate, confuse, entangle, entwine, *inf* foul up, intertwine, interweave, muddle, ravel, scramble, *inf* snarl up, twist. **2** *tangle fish in a net.* catch, enmesh, ensnare, entrap, trap. *Opp* DISENTANGLE, FREE. **3** *tangle with criminals.* become involved with, confront, cross. **tangled** ▷ DISHEVELLED, INTRICATE.

tangy *adj* acid, appetizing, bitter, fresh, piquant, pungent, refreshing, sharp, spicy, strong, tart. *Opp* BLAND.

tank *n* **1** aquarium, basin, cistern, reservoir. **2** *army tank.* armoured vehicle.

tanned *adj* brown, sunburnt, suntanned, weather-beaten.

tantalize *vb* bait, entice, frustrate, *inf* keep on tenterhooks, lead on, plague, provoke, taunt, tease, tempt, titillate, torment.

tap *n* **1** *Amer* faucet, spigot, stopcock, valve. **2** knock, rap. • *vb* knock, rap, strike. ▷ HIT.

tape *n* **1** band, belt, binding, braid, fillet, ribbon, strip, stripe. **2** audiotape, cassette, magnetic tape, tape-recording, videotape.

taper *n* candle, lighter, spill. • *vb* attenuate, become narrower, narrow, thin. **taper off** ▷ DECLINE.

target *n* **1** aim, ambition, end, goal, hope, intention, objective, purpose. **2** *target of attack.* butt, object, quarry, victim.

tariff *n* **1** charges, menu, pricelist, schedule. **2** *tariff on imports.* customs, duty, excise, impost, levy, tax, toll.

tarnish *vb* **1** blacken, corrode, dirty, discolour, soil, spoil, stain, taint. **2** *tarnish a reputation.* blemish, blot, calumniate, defame, denigrate, disgrace, dishonour, mar, ruin, spoil, stain, sully.

tarry *vb* dawdle, delay, *inf* hang about, hang back, linger, loiter, pause, procrastinate, temporize, wait.

tart *adj* **1** acid, acidic, acidulous, astringent, biting, citrus, harsh, lemony, piquant, pungent, sharp, sour, tangy. **2** *a tart rejoinder.* ▷ SHARP. *Opp* BLAND, SWEET. ● *n* **1** flan, pastry, pasty, patty, pie, quiche, tartlet, turnover. **2** ▷ PROSTITUTE.

task *n* activity, assignment, burden, business, charge, chore, duty, employment, enterprise, errand, imposition, job, mission, requirement, test, undertaking, work. **take to task** ▷ REPRIMAND.

taste *n* **1** character, flavour, relish, savour. **2** bit, bite, morsel, mouthful, nibble, piece, sample, titbit. **3** *an acquired taste.* appetite, appreciation, choice, fancy, fondness, inclination, judgement, leaning, liking, partiality, preference. **4** *a person of taste.* breeding, cultivation, culture, discernment, discretion, discrimination, education, elegance, fashion sense, finesse, good judgement, perception, perceptiveness, polish, refinement, sensitivity, style, tastefulness. ● *vb* nibble, relish, sample, savour, sip, test, try. **in bad taste** ▷ TASTELESS. **in good taste** ▷ TASTEFUL.

tasteful *adj* aesthetic, artistic, attractive, charming, *Fr* comme il faut, correct, cultivated, decorous, dignified, discerning, discreet, discriminating, elegant, fashionable, in good taste, judicious, *inf* nice, polite, proper, refined, restrained, sensitive, smart, stylish, tactful, well-judged. *Opp* TASTELESS.

tasteless *adj* **1** cheap, coarse, crude, *inf* flashy, garish, gaudy, graceless, improper, inartistic, in bad taste, indecorous, indelicate, inelegant, injudicious, in poor taste, *inf* kitsch, *inf* loud, meretricious, ugly, unattractive, uncouth, uncultivated, undiscriminating, unfashionable, unimaginative, unpleasant, unrefined, unseemly, unstylish, vulgar. *Opp* TASTEFUL. **2** *tasteless food.* bland, characterless, flavourless, insipid, mild, uninteresting, watered-down, watery, weak, *inf* wishy-washy. *Opp* TASTY.

tasty *adj* appetizing, delectable, delicious, flavoursome, luscious, *inf* mouth-watering, *inf* nice, palatable, *inf* scrumptious, toothsome, *sl* yummy. □ *acid, bitter, creamy, fruity, hot, meaty, peppery, piquant, salty, savoury, sharp, sour, spicy, sugary, sweet, tangy, tart.* *Opp* TASTELESS.

tattered *adj* frayed, ragged, rent, ripped, shredded, tatty, threadbare, torn, worn out. *Opp* SMART.

tatters *plur n* bits, pieces, rags, ribbons, shreds, torn pieces.

tatty *adj* **1** frayed, old, patched, ragged, ripped, scruffy, shabby, tattered, torn, threadbare, untidy, worn out. **2** ▷ TAWDRY. *Opp* SMART.

taunt *vb* annoy, goad, insult, jeer at, reproach, tease, torment. ▷ RIDICULE.

taut *adj* firm, rigid, stiff, strained, stretched, tense, tight. *Opp* SLACK.

tautological *adj* long-winded, otiose, pleonastic, prolix, redundant, repetitious, repetitive, superfluous, tautologous, verbose, wordy. *Opp* CONCISE.

tautology *n* duplication, long-windedness, pleonasm, prolixity, repetition, verbiage, verbosity, wordiness.

tavern *n old use* alehouse, bar, hostelry, inn, *inf* local, pub, public house.

tawdry *adj inf* Brummagem, cheap, common, eye-catching, fancy, *inf* flashy, garish, gaudy, inferior, meretricious, poor quality, showy, tasteless, tatty, tinny, vulgar, worthless. *Opp* TASTEFUL.

tax *n* charge, due, duty, imposition, impost, levy, tariff, *old use* tribute. □ *airport tax, community charge, corporation tax, customs, death duty, estate duty, excise, income tax, poll tax, property tax, rates,* old use *tithe, toll, value added tax*. *vb* **1** assess, exact, impose a tax on, levy a tax on. **2** *tax someone's patience*. burden, exhaust, make heavy demands on, overwork, pressure, pressurize, strain, try. ▷ TIRE. **tax with** accuse of, blame for, censure for, charge with, reproach for, reprove for.

taxi *n* cab, *old use* hackney carriage, minicab.

teach *vb* advise, brainwash, coach, counsel, demonstrate to, discipline, drill, edify, educate, enlighten, familiarize with, give lessons in, ground in, impart knowledge to, implant knowledge in, inculcate habits in, indoctrinate, inform, instruct, lecture, school, train, tutor.

teacher *n* adviser, educator, guide. □ *coach, counsellor, demonstrator, don, governess, guru, headteacher, housemaster, housemistress, instructor, lecturer, maharishi, master, mentor, mistress, pedagogue, preacher, preceptor, professor, pundit, schoolmaster, schoolmistress, schoolteacher, trainer, tutor.*

teaching *n* **1** education, guidance, instruction, training. □ *brainwashing, briefing, coaching, computer-aided learning, counselling, demonstration, familiarization, grounding, indoctrination, lecture, lesson, practical, preaching, rote learning, schooling, seminar, tuition, tutorial, work experience, workshop.* **2** *religious teachings*. doctrine, dogma, gospel, precept, principle, tenet.

team *n* club, crew, gang, *inf* line up, side. ▷ GROUP.

tear *n* **1** [rhymes with *fear*] droplet, tear-drop. [*plur*] *inf* blubbering, crying, sobs, weeping. **2** [rhymes with *bear*] cut, fissure, gap, gash, hole, laceration, opening, rent, rip, slit, split. • *vb* claw, gash, lacerate, mangle, pierce, pull apart, rend, rip, rive, rupture, scratch, sever, shred, slit, snag, split. **shed tears** ▷ WEEP.

tearful *adj inf* blubbering, crying, emotional, in tears, lachrymose, snivelling, sobbing, weeping, *inf* weepy, wet-cheeked, whimpering. ▷ SAD.

tease *vb inf* aggravate, annoy, badger, bait, chaff, goad, harass, irritate, laugh at, make fun of, mock, *inf* needle, *inf* nettle, pester, plague, provoke, *inf* pull someone's leg, *inf* rib, tantalize, taunt, torment, vex, worry. ▷ RIDICULE.

teasing *n* badinage, banter, chaffing, joking, mockery, provocation, raillery, *inf* ribbing, ridicule, taunts.

technical *adj* **1** complicated, detailed, esoteric, expert, professional, specialized. **2** *technical skill*. engineering, industrial, mechanical, technological, scientific.

technician *n* engineer, mechanic, skilled worker, *plur* technical staff.

technique *n* **1** approach, dodge, knack, manner, means, method, mode, procedure, routine, system, trick, way. **2** *an artist's technique*. art, artistry, cleverness, craft, craftsmanship, expertise, facility, *inf* know-how, proficiency, skill, talent, workmanship.

technological *adj* advanced, automated, computerized, electronic, scientific.

tedious *adj* banal, boring, dreary, *inf* dry-as-dust, dull, endless, *inf* humdrum, irksome, laborious, long-drawn-out, long-winded, monotonous, prolonged, repetitious, slow, soporific, tiresome, tiring, unexciting, uninteresting, vapid, wearing, wearisome, wearying. *Opp* INTERESTING.

tedium *n* boredom, dreariness, dullness, ennui, long-windedness, monotony, repetitiousness, slowness, tediousness.

teem *vb* **1** abound (in), be alive (with), be full (of), be infested, be overrun (by), *inf* bristle, *inf* crawl, proliferate, seethe, swarm with. **2** ▷ RAIN.

teenager *n* adolescent, boy, girl, juvenile, minor, youngster, youth.

teetotal *adj* abstemious, abstinent, *sl* on the wagon, restrained, self-denying, self-disciplined, temperate.

teetotaller *n* abstainer, non-drinker.

telegram *n* cable, cablegram, fax, telex, wire.

telepathic *adj* clairvoyant, psychic.

telephone *n inf* blower, carphone, handset, phone. • *vb inf* buzz, call, dial, *inf* give someone a buzz, *inf* give someone a call, *inf* give someone a tinkle, phone, ring, ring up.

telescope *vb* abbreviate, collapse, compress, elide, shorten.

telescopic *adj* adjustable, collapsible, expanding, extending, retractable.

televise *vb* broadcast, relay, send out, transmit.

television *n inf* the box, monitor, receiver, *inf* small screen, *inf* telly, video.

tell *vb* **1** acquaint with, advise, announce, assure, communicate, describe, disclose, divulge, explain, impart, inform, make known, narrate, notify, portray, promise, recite, recount, rehearse, relate, reveal, utter. ▷ SPEAK, TALK. **2** *tell the difference.* calculate, comprehend, decide, discover, discriminate, distinguish, identify, notice, recognize, see. **3** *told me what to do.* command, direct, instruct, order. **tell off** ▷ REPRIMAND.

teller *n* **1** author, narrator, raconteur, storyteller. **2** *teller in a bank.* bank clerk, cashier.

telling *adj* considerable, effective, influential, potent, powerful, significant, striking, weighty.

temper *n* **1** attitude, character, disposition, frame of mind, humour, *inf* make-up, mood, personality, state of mind, temperament. **2** *watch your temper.* anger, churlishness, fit of anger, fury, hot-headedness, ill-humour, irascibility, irritability, *inf* paddy, passion, peevishness, petulance, rage, surliness, tantrum, unpredictability, volatility, *inf* wax, wrath. **3** *keep your temper.* calmness, composure, *sl* cool, coolness, equanimity, sang-froid, self-control, self-possession. • *vb* **1** assuage, lessen, mitigate, moderate, modify, modulate, reduce, soften, soothe, tone down. **2** *temper steel.* harden, strengthen, toughen.

temperament *n* attitude, character, *old use* complexion, disposition, frame of mind, *old use* humour, *inf* make-up, mood, nature, personality, spirit, state of mind, temper.

temperamental *adj* **1** characteristic, congenital, constitutional, inherent, innate, natural. **2** *temperamental moods.* capricious, changeable, emotional, erratic, excitable, explosive, fickle, highly-strung, impatient, inconsistent, inconstant, irascible, irritable, mercurial, moody, neurotic, passionate, sensitive, touchy, undependable, unpredictable, unreliable, *inf* up and down, variable, volatile.

temperance *n* abstemiousness, continence, moderation, self-discipline, self-restraint, sobriety, teetotalism.

temperate *adj* calm, controlled, disciplined, moderate, reasonable, restrained, self-possessed, sensible, sober, stable, steady. *Opp* EXTREME.

tempest *n* cyclone, gale, hurricane, tornado, tumult, typhoon, whirlwind. ▷ STORM.

tempestuous *adj* fierce, furious, tumultuous, turbulent, vehement, violent, wild. ▷ STORMY. *Opp* CALM.

temple *n* church, house of god, mosque, pagoda, place of worship, shrine, synagogue.

tempo *n* beat, pace, pulse, rate, rhythm, speed.

temporal *adj* earthly, fleshly, impermanent, material, materialistic, mortal, mundane, non-religious, passing, secular, sublunary, terrestrial, transient, transitory, worldly. *Opp* SPIRITUAL.

temporary *adj* **1** brief, ephemeral, evanescent, fleeting, fugitive, impermanent, interim, makeshift, momentary, passing, provisional, short, short-lived, short-term, stopgap, transient, transitory. **2** *temporary captain*. acting. *Opp* PERMANENT.

tempt *vb* allure, attract, bait, bribe, cajole, captivate, coax, decoy, entice, fascinate, inveigle, lure, offer incentives, persuade, seduce, tantalize, woo. **tempting** ▷ APPETIZING, ATTRACTIVE.

temptation *n* allure, allurement, appeal, attraction, cajolery, coaxing, draw, enticement, fascination, inducement, lure, persuasion, pull, seduction, snare, wooing.

tenable *adj* arguable, believable, conceivable, credible, creditable, defendable, defensible, feasible, justifiable, legitimate, logical, plausible, rational, reasonable, sensible, sound, supportable, understandable, viable. *Opp* INDEFENSIBLE.

tenacious *adj* determined, dogged, firm, intransigent, obdurate, obstinate, persistent, pertinacious, resolute, single-minded, steadfast, strong, stubborn, tight, uncompromising, unfaltering, unshakeable, unswerving, unwavering, unyielding. *Opp* WEAK.

tenant *n* inhabitant, leaseholder, lessee, lodger, occupant, occupier, resident.

tend *vb* **1** attend to, care for, cherish, cultivate, guard, keep, *inf* keep an eye on, look after, manage, mind, minister to, mother, protect, supervise, take care of, watch. **2** *tend the sick*. nurse, treat. **3** *tend to fall asleep*. be biased, be disposed, be inclined, be liable, be prone, have a tendency, incline.

tendency *n* bias, disposition, drift, inclination, instinct, leaning, liability, partiality, penchant, predilection, predisposition, proclivity, proneness, propensity, readiness, susceptibility, trend.

tender *adj* **1** dainty, delicate, fleshy, fragile, frail, green, immature, soft, succulent, vulnerable, weak, young. **2** *tender meat*. chewable, eatable, edible. **3** *a tender wound*. aching, inflamed, painful, sensitive, smarting, sore. **4** *a tender love-song*. emotional, heartfelt, moving, poignant, romantic, sentimental, stirring, touching. **5** *tender care*. affectionate, amorous, caring, compassionate, concerned, considerate, fond, gentle, humane, kind, loving, merciful, pitying, soft-hearted, sympathetic, tender-hearted, warm-hearted. *Opp* TOUGH, UNSYMPATHETIC.

tense *adj* **1** rigid, strained, stretched, taut, tight. **2** *a tense person*. anxious, apprehensive, edgy, excited, fidgety, highly-strung, intense, jittery, jumpy, *inf* keyed-up, nervous, on edge, *inf* on tenterhooks, overwrought, restless, strained, stressed, *inf* strung up, touchy, uneasy, *sl* uptight, worried. **3** *a tense situation*. exciting, fraught, *inf* nail-biting, nerve-racking, stressful, worrying. *Opp* RELAXED.

tension *n* **1** pull, strain, stretching, tautness, tightness. **2** *the tension of waiting*. anxiety, apprehension, edginess, excitement, nervousness, stress, suspense, unease, worry. *Opp* RELAXATION.

tent *n* □ *bell tent, big-top, frame tent, marquee, ridge tent, tepee, trailer tent, wigwam.*

tentative *adj* cautious, diffident, doubtful, experimental, exploratory, half-hearted, hesitant, inconclusive, indecisive, indefinite, nervous, preliminary, provisional, shy, speculative, timid, uncertain, uncommitted, unsure, *inf* wishywashy. *Opp* DECISIVE.

tenuous *adj* attenuated, fine, flimsy, fragile, insubstantial, slender, slight, weak. ▷ THIN. *Opp* STRONG.

tepid *adj* **1** lukewarm, warm. **2** *a tepid response*. ▷ APATHETIC.

term *n* **1** duration, period, season, span, spell, stretch, time. **2** *a school term*. *Amer* semester, session. **3** *technical terms*. appellation, designation, epithet, expression, name, phrase, saying, title, word. **terms 1** conditions, particulars, provisions, provisos, specifications, stipulations. **2** *a hotel's terms*. charges, fees, prices, rates, schedule, tariff.

terminal *adj* deadly, fatal, final, incurable, killing, lethal, mortal. • *n* **1** keyboard, VDU, work-station. **2** *passenger terminal*. airport, terminus. **3** *electric terminal*. connection, connector, coupling.

terminate *vb* bring to an end, cease, come to an end, discontinue, end, finish, *inf* pack in, phase out, stop, *inf* wind up. ▷ END. *Opp* BEGIN.

terminology *n* argot, cant, choice of words, jargon, language, nomenclature, phraseology, special terms, technical language, vocabulary.

terminus *n* destination, last stop, station, terminal, termination.

terrain *n* country, ground, land, landscape, territory, topography.

terrestrial *adj* earthly, mundane, ordinary, sublunary.

terrible *adj* **1** acute, appalling, awful, *inf* beastly, distressing, dreadful, fearful, fearsome, formidable, frightening, frightful, ghastly, grave, gruesome, harrowing, hideous, horrendous, horrible, horrific, horrifying, insupportable, intolerable, loathsome, nasty, nauseating, outrageous, revolting, shocking, terrific, terrifying, unbearable, vile. **2** ▷ BAD.

terrific *adj Terrific* may mean *causing terror* (▷ TERRIBLE). It is more often used *informally* of anything which is *extreme* in its own way: *a terrific problem* ▷ EXTREME; *terrific size* ▷ BIG; *a terrific party* ▷ EXCELLENT; *a terrific storm* ▷ VIOLENT.

terrify *vb* appal, dismay, horrify, *inf* make your blood run cold, petrify, shock, terrorize. ▷ FRIGHTEN. **terrified** ▷ FRIGHTENED. **terrifying** ▷ FRIGHTENING.

territory *n* area, colony, *old use* demesne, district, domain, dominion, enclave, jurisdiction, land, neighbourhood, precinct, preserve, province, purlieu, region, sector, sphere, state, terrain, tract, zone. ▷ COUNTRY.

terror *n* alarm, awe, consternation, dismay, dread, fright, *inf* funk, horror, panic, shock, trepidation. ▷ FEAR.

terrorist *n* assassin, bomber, desperado, gunman, hijacker.

terrorize *vb* browbeat, bully, coerce, cow, intimidate, menace, persecute, terrify, threaten, torment, tyrannize. ▷ FRIGHTEN.

terse *adj* abrupt, brief, brusque, compact, concentrated, concise, crisp, curt, epigrammatic, incisive, laconic, pithy, short, *inf* short and sweet, *inf* snappy, succinct, to the point. *Opp* VERBOSE.

test *n* analysis, appraisal, assay, assessment, audition, *inf* check-over, *inf* check-up, evaluation, examination, inspection, interrogation, investigation, probation, quiz, screen-test, trial, *inf* try-out. • *vb* analyse, appraise, assay, assess, audition, check, evaluate, examine, experiment with, inspect, interrogate, investigate, probe, *inf* put someone through their paces, put to the test, question, quiz, screen, try out.

testify *vb* affirm, attest, aver, bear witness, declare, give evidence, proclaim, state on oath, swear, vouch, witness.

testimonial *n* character reference, commendation, recommendation, reference.

testimony *n* affidavit, assertion, declaration, deposition, evidence, statement, submission.

tether *n* chain, cord, fetter, halter, lead, leash, painter, restraint, rope. • *vb* chain up, fetter, keep on a tether, leash, restrain, rope, secure, tie up. ▷ FASTEN.

text *n* **1** argument, content, contents, matter, subject matter, wording. **2** *a literary text*. book, textbook, work. ▷ WRITING. **3** *a text from scripture*. line, motif, passage, quotation, sentence, theme, topic, verse.

textile *n* fabric, material, stuff. ▷ CLOTH.

texture *n* appearance, composition, consistency, feel, grain, quality, surface, tactile quality, touch, weave.

thank *vb* acknowledge, express thanks, say thank you, show gratitude.

thankful *adj* appreciative, contented, glad, grateful, happy, indebted, pleased, relieved. *Opp* UNGRATEFUL.

thankless *adj* bootless, futile, profitless, unappreciated, unrecognized, unrewarded, unrewarding. *Opp* PROFITABLE.

thanks *plur n* acknowledgement, appreciation, gratefulness, gratitude, recognition, thanksgiving. **thanks to** as a result of, because of, owing to, through.

thaw *vb* become liquid, defrost, de-ice, heat up, melt, soften, uncongeal, unfreeze, unthaw, warm up. *Opp* FREEZE.

theatre *n* **1** auditorium, hall, opera-house, playhouse. **2** acting, dramaturgy, histrionic arts, show business, thespian arts. □ *ballet, masque, melodrama, mime, musical, music-hall, opera, pantomime, play*. ▷ DRAMA, ENTERTAINMENT, PERFORMANCE.

theatrical *adj* **1** dramatic, histrionic, thespian. **2** [*derog*] *a theatrical exit.* affected, artificial, calculated, demonstrative, exaggerated, forced, *inf* hammy, melodramatic, ostentatious, overacted, overdone, *inf* over the top, pompous, selfimportant, showy, stagy, stilted, unconvincing, unnatural. *Opp* NATURAL.

theft *n* burglary, larceny, pilfering, robbery, thievery. ▷ STEALING.

theme *n* **1** argument, core, essence, gist, idea, issue, keynote, matter, point, subject, text, thesis, thread, topic. **2** *a musical theme*. air, melody, motif, subject, tune.

theology *n* divinity, religion, religious studies.

theoretical *adj* abstract, academic, conjectural, doctrinaire, hypothetical, ideal, notional, pure (*science*), putative, speculative, suppositious, unproven, untested. *Opp* PRACTICAL, PROVEN.

theorize *vb* conjecture, form a theory, guess, hypothesize, speculate.

theory *n* **1** argument, assumption, belief, conjecture, explanation, guess, hypothesis, idea, notion, speculation, supposition, surmise, thesis, view. **2** *theory of a subject.* laws, principles, rules, science. *Opp* PRACTICE.

therapeutic *adj* beneficial, corrective, curative, healing, healthy, helpful, medicinal, remedial, restorative, salubrious. *Opp* HARMFUL.

therapist *n* counsellor, healer, physiotherapist, psychoanalyst, psychotherapist.

therapy *n* cure, healing, remedy, tonic, treatment. □ *chemotherapy, group therapy, hydrotherapy, hypnotherapy, occupational therapy, physiotherapy, psychotherapy, radiotherapy.* ▷ MEDICINE.

therefore *adv* accordingly, consequently, hence, so, thus.

thesis *n* **1** argument, assertion, contention, hypothesis, idea, opinion, postulate, premise, premiss, proposition, theory, view. **2** *a research thesis.* disquisition, dissertation, essay, monograph, paper, tract, treatise.

thick *adj* **1** broad, *inf* bulky, chunky, stout, sturdy, wide. ▷ FAT. **2** *a thick layer.* deep, heavy, substantial, woolly. **3** *a thick crowd.* compact, dense, impassable, impenetrable, numerous, packed, solid. **4** *thick liquid.* clotted, coagulated, concentrated, condensed, firm, glutinous, heavy, jellied, sticky, stiff, viscid, viscous. **5** *thick growth.* abundant, bushy, luxuriant, plentiful. **6** *thick with visitors.* alive, bristling, *inf* chock-full, choked, covered, crammed, crawling, crowded, filled, full, jammed, swarming, teeming. *Opp* THIN.

thicken *vb* coagulate, clot, concentrate, condense, congeal, firm up, gel, jell, reduce, solidify, stiffen.

thickness *n* **1** breadth, density, depth, fatness, viscosity, width. **2** *a thickness of paint, rock.* coating, layer, seam, stratum.

thief *n* bandit, brigand, burglar, cat-burglar, cutpurse, embezzler, footpad, highwayman, housebreaker, kleptomaniac, looter, mugger, peculator, pickpocket, pilferer, pirate, plagiarist, poacher, purloiner, robber, safe-cracker, shoplifter, stealer, swindler. ▷ CRIMINAL.

thieving *adj* dishonest, light-fingered, rapacious. • *n* ▷ STEALING.

thin *adj* **1** anorexic, attenuated, bony, cadaverous, emaciated, fine, flat-chested, gangling, gaunt, lanky, lean, narrow, pinched, rangy, scraggy, scrawny, skeletal, skinny, slender, slight, slim, small, spare, spindly, underfed, undernourished, underweight, wiry. *Opp* FAT. **2** *a thin layer.* delicate, diaphanous, filmy, fine, flimsy, gauzy, insubstantial, light, *inf* see-through, shallow, sheer (*silk*), superficial, translucent, wispy. **3** *a thin crowd.* meagre, scanty, scarce, scattered, sparse. **4** *thin liquid.* dilute, flowing, fluid, runny, sloppy, watery, weak. **5** *thin atmosphere.* rarefied. **6** *a thin excuse.* feeble, implausible, tenuous, transparent, unconvincing. *Opp* DENSE, STRONG, THICK. • *vb* dilute, water down, weaken. **thin out 1** become less dense, decrease, diminish, disperse. **2** make less dense, prune, reduce, trim, weed out.

thing *n* **1** apparatus, artefact, article, body, contrivance, device, entity, gadget, implement, invention, item, object, utensil. **2** affair, circumstance, deed, event, eventuality, happening, incident, occurrence, phenomenon. **3** *a thing on your mind.* concept, detail, fact, factor, feeling, idea, point, statement, thought. **4** *a thing to be done.* act, action, chore, deed, job, responsibility, task. **5** [*inf*] *a thing about snakes.* aversion, fixation, *inf* hang-up, mania, neurosis, obsession, passion, phobia, preoccupation. **things 1** baggage, belongings, clothing, equipment, *inf* gear, luggage, possessions, *inf* stuff. **2** *How are things?* circumstances, conditions, life.

think *vb* **1** attend, brood, chew things over, cogitate, concentrate, consider, contemplate, day-dream, deliberate, dream, dwell (on), fantasize, give thought (to), meditate, *inf* mull over, muse, ponder, *inf* rack your brains, reason, reflect, remind yourself of, reminisce, ruminate, use your intelligence, work things out, worry. **2** *Do you think it's true?* accept, admit, assume, be convinced, believe, be under the impression, conclude, deem, estimate, feel, guess, have faith, imagine, judge, presume, reckon, suppose, surmise. **think better of** ▷ RECONSIDER. **thinking** ▷ INTELLIGENT, THOUGHTFUL. **think up** ▷ DEVISE.

thinker *n inf* brain, innovator, intellect, inventor, *inf* mastermind, philosopher, sage, savant, scholar.

thirst *n* **1** drought, dryness, thirstiness. **2** *thirst for knowledge.* appetite, craving, desire, eagerness, hunger, itch, longing, love (of), lust, passion, urge, wish, yearning, *inf* yen. • *vb* be thirsty, crave, have a thirst, hunger, long, strive (after), wish, yearn. **thirst for** ▷ WANT.

thirsty *adj* **1** arid, dehydrated, dry, *inf* gasping, panting, parched. **2** *thirsty for news.* avid, craving, desirous, eager, greedy, hankering, itching, longing, voracious, yearning.

thorn *n* barb, bristle, needle, prickle, spike, spine.

thorny *adj* **1** barbed, bristly, prickly, scratchy, sharp, spiky, spiny. **2** ▷ DIFFICULT.

thorough *adj* **1** assiduous, attentive, careful, comprehensive, conscientious, deep, detailed, diligent, efficient, exhaustive, extensive, full, *inf* in-depth, methodical, meticulous, minute, observant, orderly, organized, painstaking, particular, penetrating, probing, scrupulous, searching, systematic, thoughtful, watchful. *Opp* SUPERFICIAL. **2** *a thorough rascal.* absolute, arrant, complete, downright, out-and-out, perfect, proper, sheer, thoroughgoing, total, unmitigated, unmixed, unqualified, utter.

thought *n* **1** *inf* brainwork, brooding, *inf* brown study, cerebration, cogitation, concentration, consideration, contemplation, day-dreaming, deliberation, intelligence, introspection, meditation, mental activity, musing, pensiveness, ratiocination, rationality, reason, reasoning, reflection, reverie, rumination, study, thinking, worrying. **2** *a clever thought.* belief, concept, conception, conclusion, conjecture, conviction, idea, notion, observation, opinion. **3** *no thought of gain.* aim, design, dream, expectation, hope, intention, objective, plan, prospect, purpose, vision. **4** *a kind thought.* attention, concern, consideration, kindness, solicitude, thoughtfulness.

thoughtful *adj* **1** absorbed, abstracted, anxious, attentive, brooding, contemplative, dreamy, grave, introspective, meditative, pensive, philosophical, rapt, reflective, serious, solemn, studious, thinking, wary, watchful, worried. **2** *thoughtful work.* careful, conscientious, diligent, exhaustive, intelligent, methodical, meticulous, observant, orderly, organized, painstaking, rational, scrupulous, sensible, systematic, thorough. **3** *a thoughtful kindness.* attentive, caring, compassionate, concerned, considerate, friendly, good-natured, helpful, obliging, public-spirited, solicitous, unselfish. ▷ KIND. *Opp* THOUGHTLESS.

thoughtless *adj* **1** absentminded, careless, forgetful, hasty, heedless, ill-considered, impetuous, inadvertent, inattentive, injudicious, irresponsible, mindless, negligent, rash, reckless, *inf* scatter-brained, unobservant, unthinking. ▷ STUPID. **2** *a thoughtless insult.* cruel, heartless, impolite, inconsiderate, insensitive, rude, selfish, tactless, uncaring, undiplomatic, unfeeling. ▷ UNKIND. *Opp* THOUGHTFUL.

thrash *vb* beat, birch, cane, flay, flog, lash, scourge, whip. ▷ DEFEAT, HIT.

thread *n* **1** fibre, filament, hair, strand. □ *cotton, line, silk, string, thong, twine, wool, yarn.* **2** *thread of a story.* argument, continuity, course, direction, drift, line of thought, plot, story line, tenor, theme. ● *vb* put on a thread, string together. **thread your way** file, pass, pick your way, wind.

threadbare *adj* frayed, old, ragged, scruffy, shabby, tattered, tatty, worn, worn-out.

threat *n* **1** commination, intimidation, menace, warning. **2** *threat of rain.* danger, forewarning, intimation, omen, portent, presage, risk, warning.

threaten *vb* **1** browbeat, bully, cow, intimidate, make threats against, menace, pressurize, terrorize. ▷ FRIGHTEN. *Opp* REASSURE. **2** *clouds threaten rain.* forebode, foreshadow, forewarn of, give warning of, portend, presage, warn of. **3** *the recession threatens jobs.* endanger, imperil, jeopardize, put at risk.

threatening *adj* forbidding, grim, impending, looming, menacing, minatory, ominous, portentous, sinister, stern, *inf* ugly, unfriendly, worrying. *Opp* SUPPORTIVE.

three *n* triad, trio, triplet, triumvirate.

three-dimensional *adj* in the round, rounded, sculptural, solid, stereoscopic.

threshold *n* **1** doorstep, doorway, entrance, sill. **2** *threshold of a new era.* ▷ BEGINNING.

thrifty *adj* careful, *derog* closefisted, economical, frugal, *derog* mean, *derog* niggardly, parsimonious, provident, prudent, skimping, sparing. *Opp* EXTRAVAGANT.

thrill *n* adventure, *inf* buzz, excitement, frisson, *inf* kick, pleasure, sensation, shiver, suspense, tingle, titillation, tremor. ● *vb* arouse, delight, electrify, excite, galvanize, rouse, stimulate, stir, titillate. **thrilling** ▷ EXCITING.

thriller *n* crime story, detective story, mystery, *inf* whodunit. ▷ WRITING.

thrive *vb* be vigorous, bloom, boom, burgeon, *inf* come on, develop strongly, do well, expand, flourish, grow, increase, *inf* make strides, prosper, succeed. *Opp* DIE. **thriving** ▷ PROSPEROUS, VIGOROUS.

throat *n* gullet, neck, oesophagus, uvula, windpipe.

throaty *adj* deep, gravelly, gruff, guttural, hoarse, husky, rasping, rough, thick.

throb *vb* beat, palpitate, pound, pulsate, pulse, vibrate.

throe *n* convulsion, effort, fit, labour, *plur* labour-pains, pang, paroxysm, spasm. ▷ PAIN.

thrombosis *n* blood-clot, embolism.

throng *n* assembly, crowd, crush, gathering, horde, jam, mass, mob, multitude, swarm. ▷ GROUP.

throttle *vb* asphyxiate, choke, smother, stifle, strangle, suffocate. ▷ KILL.

throw *vb* **1** bowl, *inf* bung, cast, *inf* chuck, fling, heave, hurl, launch, lob, pelt, pitch, propel, put (*the shot*), send, *inf* shy, *inf* sling, toss. **2** *throw light.* cast, project, shed. **3** *throw a rider.* dislodge, floor, shake off, throw down, throw off, unseat, upset. **4** ▷ DISCONCERT. **throw away** ▷ DISCARD. **throw out** ▷ EXPEL. **throw up** ▷ PRODUCE, VOMIT.

throw-away *adj* **1** cheap, disposable. **2** *throw-away remark.* casual, offhand, passing, unimportant.

thrust *vb* butt, drive, elbow, force, impel, jab, lunge, plunge, poke, press, prod, propel, push, ram, send, shoulder, shove, stab, stick, urge.

thug *n* assassin, *inf* bully-boy, delinquent, desperado, gangster, *inf* hoodlum, hooligan, killer, mugger, *inf* rough, ruffian, *inf* tough, troublemaker, vandal, *inf* yob. ▷ CRIMINAL.

thunder *n* clap, crack, peal, roll, rumble. ▷ SOUND.

thunderous *adj* booming, deafening, reverberant, reverberating, roaring, rumbling. ▷ LOUD.

thus *adv* accordingly, consequently, for this reason, hence, so, therefore.

thwart *vb* baffle, baulk, block, check, foil, frustrate, hinder, impede, obstruct, prevent, stand in the way of, stop, stump.

ticket *n* **1** coupon, pass, permit, token, voucher. **2** *price ticket.* docket, label, marker, tab, tag.

ticklish *adj* **1** *inf* giggly, responsive to tickling, sensitive. **2** *a ticklish problem.* awkward, delicate, difficult, risky, *inf* thorny, touchy, tricky.

tide *n* current, drift, ebb and flow, movement, rise and fall.

tidiness *n* meticulousness, neatness, order, orderliness, organization, smartness, system. *Opp* DISORDER.

tidy *adj* **1** neat, orderly, presentable, shipshape, smart, *inf* spick and span, spruce, straight, trim, uncluttered, well-groomed, well-kept. **2** *tidy habits.* businesslike, careful, house-proud, methodical, meticulous, organized, systematic, well-organized. *Opp* UNTIDY. • *vb* arrange, clean up, groom, make tidy, neaten, put in order, rearrange, reorganize, set straight, smarten, spruce up, straighten, titivate. *Opp* MUDDLE.

tie *vb* **1** bind, chain, do up, hitch, interlace, join, knot, lash, moor, rope, secure, splice, tether, truss up. ▷ FASTEN. *Opp* UNTIE. **2** *tie in a race.* be equal, be level, be neck and neck, draw.

tier *n* course (*of bricks*), layer, level, line, order, range, rank, row, stage, storey, stratum, terrace.

tight *adj* **1** close, fast, firm, fixed, immovable, secure, snug. **2** *a tight lid.* airtight, close-fitting, hermetic, impermeable, impervious, leakproof, sealed, waterproof, watertight. **3** *tight supervision.* harsh, inflexible, precise, rigorous, severe, strict, stringent. **4** *tight ropes.* rigid, stiff, stretched, taut, tense. **5** *a tight space.* compact, constricted, crammed, cramped, crowded, dense, inadequate, limited, packed, small. **6** ▷ DRUNK. **7** ▷ MISERLY. *Opp* FREE, LOOSE.

tighten *vb* **1** become tighter, clamp down, close, close up, constrict, harden, make tighter, squeeze, stiffen, tense. ▷ FASTEN. **2** *tighten ropes.* pull tighter, stretch, tauten. **3** *tighten screws.* give another turn to, screw up. *Opp* LOOSEN.

till *vb* cultivate, dig, farm, plough, work.

tilt *vb* **1** angle, bank, cant, careen, heel over, incline, keel over, lean, list, slant, slope, tip. **2** *tilt with lances.* joust, thrust. ▷ FIGHT.

timber *n* beam, board, boarding, deal, lath, log, lumber, plank, planking, post, softwood, tree, tree trunk. ▷ WOOD.

time *n* **1** date, hour, instant, juncture, moment, occasion, opportunity, point. **2** duration, interval, period, phase, season, semester, session, spell, stretch, term, while. □ *aeon, century, day, decade, eternity, fortnight, hour, lifetime, minute, month, second, week, weekend, year.* **3** *time of Nero.* age, days, epoch, era, period. **4** *time in music.* beat, measure, rhythm, tempo. • *vb* **1** choose a time for, estimate, fix a time for, judge, organize, plan, schedule, timetable. **2** *time a race.* clock, measure the time of.

timeless *adj* ageless, deathless, eternal, everlasting, immortal, immutable, indestructible, permanent, unchanging, undying, unending.

timely *adj* appropriate, apt, fitting, suitable.

timepiece *n* □ *chronometer, clock, digital clock, digital watch, hourglass, stop-watch, sundial, timer, watch, wristwatch.*

timetable *n* agenda, calendar, curriculum, diary, list, programme, roster, rota, schedule.

timid *adj* afraid, apprehensive, bashful, chicken-hearted, cowardly, coy, diffident, fainthearted, fearful, modest, *inf* mousy, nervous, pusillanimous, reserved, retiring, scared, sheepish, shrinking, shy, spineless, tentative, timorous, unadventurous, unheroic, wimpish. ▷ FRIGHTENED. *Opp* BOLD.

tingle *n* **1** itch, itching, pins and needles, prickling, stinging, throb, throbbing, tickle, tickling. **2** *a tingle of excitement.* quiver, sensation, shiver, thrill. • *vb* itch, prickle, sting, tickle.

tinker *vb* dabble, fiddle, fool about, interfere, meddle, *inf* mess about, *inf* play about, tamper, try to mend, work amateurishly.

tinny *adj* cheap, flimsy, inferior, insubstantial, poor-quality, shoddy, tawdry.

tinsel *n* decoration, glitter, gloss, show, sparkle, tinfoil.

tint *n* colour, colouring, dye, hue, shade, stain, tincture, tinge, tone, wash.

tiny *adj* diminutive, dwarf, imperceptible, infinitesimal, insignificant, lilliputian, microscopic, midget, *inf* mini, miniature, minuscule, minute, negligible, pygmy, *inf* teeny, unimportant, *inf* wee, *inf* weeny. ▷ SMALL. *Opp* BIG.

tip *n* **1** apex, cap, crown, end, extremity, ferrule, finial, head, nib, peak, pinnacle, point, sharp end, summit, top, vertex. **2** *tip for a waiter. inf* baksheesh, gift, gratuity, inducement, money, *inf* perk, present, reward, service-charge, *inf* sweetener. **3** *useful tips.* advice, clue, forecast, hint, information, pointer, prediction, suggestion, tip-off, warning. **4** *rubbish tip.* dump, rubbish-heap. • *vb* **1** careen, incline, keel, lean, list, slant, slope, tilt. **2** drop off, dump, empty, pour out, spill, unload, upset. **3** *tip a waiter.* give a tip to, remunerate, reward. **tip over** ▷ OVERTURN.

tire *vb* **1** become bored, become tired, flag, grow weary, weaken. **2** debilitate, drain, enervate, exhaust, fatigue, *inf* finish, *sl* knacker, make tired, overtire, sap, *inf* shatter, *inf* take it out of, tax, wear out, weary. *Opp* REFRESH. **tired** ▷ WEARY. **tired of**

bored with, *inf* fed up with, impatient with, sick of. **tiring** ▷ EXHAUSTING.

tiredness *n* drowsiness, exhaustion, fatigue, inertia, jet-lag, lassitude, lethargy, listlessness, sleepiness, weariness.

tireless *adj* determined, diligent, dogged, dynamic, energetic, hardworking, indefatigable, persistent, pertinacious, resolute, sedulous, unceasing, unfaltering, unflagging, untiring, unwavering, vigorous. *Opp* LAZY.

tiresome *adj* **1** boring, dull, monotonous, tedious, tiring, unexciting, uninteresting, wearisome, wearying. *Opp* EXCITING. **2** *tiresome delays*. annoying, bothersome, distracting, exasperating, inconvenient, infuriating, irksome, irritating, maddening, petty, troublesome, trying, unwelcome, upsetting, vexatious, vexing.

tiring *adj* debilitating, demanding, difficult, exhausting, fatiguing, hard, laborious, strenuous, taxing, wearying. *Opp* REFRESHING.

tissue *n* **1** fabric, material, structure, stuff, substance. **2** *tissuepaper*. □ *lavatory paper, napkin, paper handkerchief, serviette, toilet paper, tracing-paper*.

title *n* **1** caption, heading, headline, inscription, name, rubric. **2** appellation, designation, form of address, office, position, rank, status. □ *Baron, Baroness, Count, Countess, Dame, Doctor, Dr, Duchess, Duke, Earl, Lady, Lord, Marchioness, Marquis, Master, Miss, Mr, Mrs, Ms, Professor, Rev, Reverend, Sir, Viscount, Viscountess*. ▷ RANK, ROYAL. **3** *title to an inheritance*. claim, deed, entitlement, interest, ownership, possession, prerogative, right. ● *vb* call, designate, entitle, give a title to, label, name, tag.

titled *adj* aristocratic, noble, upper class.

titter *vb* chortle, chuckle, giggle, snicker, snigger. ▷ LAUGH.

titular *adj* formal, nominal, official, putative, *inf* so-called, theoretical, token. *Opp* ACTUAL.

toast *vb* **1** brown, grill. ▷ COOK. **2** *toast a guest*. drink a toast to, drink the health of, drink to, honour, pay tribute to, raise your glass to.

tobacco *n* □ *cigar, cigarette, pipe tobacco, plug, snuff*.

together *adv* all at once, at the same time, collectively, concurrently, consecutively, continuously, cooperatively, hand in hand, in chorus, in unison, jointly, shoulder to shoulder, side by side, simultaneously.

toil *n inf* donkey work, drudgery, effort, exertion, industry, labour, work. ● *vb* drudge, exert yourself, grind away, *inf* keep at it, labour, *inf* plug away, *inf* slave away, struggle, *inf* sweat. ▷ WORK.

toilet *n* **1** convenience, latrine, lavatory, *sl* loo, *old use* privy, urinal, water closet, WC. **2** [*old use*] *make your toilet*. dressing, grooming, making up, washing.

token *adj* cosmetic, dutiful, emblematic, insincere, nominal, notional, perfunctory, representative, superficial, symbolic. *Opp* GENUINE. ● *n* **1** badge, emblem, evidence, expression, indication, mark, marker, proof, reminder, sign, symbol, testimony. **2** *a token of esteem*. keepsake, memento, reminder, souvenir. **3** *a bus token*. coin, counter, coupon, disc, voucher.

tolerable *adj* **1** acceptable, allowable, bearable, endurable, sufferable, supportable. **2** *tolerable food*. adequate, all right, average, fair, mediocre, middling, *inf* OK, ordinary, passable, satisfactory. *Opp* INTOLERABLE.

tolerance *n* **1** broad-mindedness, charity, fairness, forbearance, forgiveness, lenience, open-mindedness, openness, patience, permissiveness. **2** *tolerance of others*. acceptance, sufferance, sympathy (towards), toleration, understanding. **3** *tolerance in moving parts*. allowance, clearance, deviation, fluctuation, play, variation.

tolerant *adj* big-hearted, broad-minded, charitable, easygoing, fair, forbearing, forgiving, generous, indulgent, *derog* lax, lenient, liberal, magnanimous, open-minded, patient, permissive, *derog* soft, sympathetic, understanding, unprejudiced. *Opp* INTOLERANT.

tolerate *vb* abide, accept, admit, bear, brook, concede, condone, countenance, endure, *inf* lump (*I'll have to lump it!*), make allowances for, permit, *inf* put up with, sanction, *inf* stand, *inf* stick, *inf* stomach, suffer, *inf* take, undergo, *inf* wear, weather.

toll *n* charge, dues, duty, fee, levy, payment, tariff, tax. • *vb* chime, peal, ring, sound, strike.

tomb *n* burial chamber, burial place, catacomb, crypt, grave, gravestone, last resting-place, mausoleum, memorial, monument, sepulchre, tombstone, vault.

tonality *n* key, tonal centre.

tone *n* **1** accent, colouring, expression, feel, inflection, intonation, manner, modulation, note, phrasing, pitch, quality, sonority, sound, timbre. **2** *tone of a poem, place.* air, atmosphere, character, effect, feeling, mood, spirit, style, temper, vein. **3** *colour tone.* colour, hue, shade, tinge, tint, tonality. **tone down** ▷ SOFTEN. **tone in** ▷ HARMONIZE. **tone up** ▷ STRENGTHEN.

tongue *n* dialect, idiom, language, parlance, patois, speech, talk, vernacular.

tongue-tied *adj* dumb, dumbfounded, inarticulate, *inf* lost for words, mute, silent, speechless.

tonic *n* boost, cordial, dietary supplement, fillip, *inf* pick-me-up, refresher, restorative, stimulant.

tool *n* apparatus, appliance, contraption, contrivance, device, gadget, hardware, implement, instrument, invention, machine, mechanism, utensil, weapon. □ [carpentry] *auger, awl, brace and bit, bradawl, chisel, clamp, cramp, drill, file, fretsaw, gimlet, glass-paper, hacksaw, hammer, jigsaw, mallet, pincers, plane, pliers, power-drill, rasp, sander, sandpaper, saw, screwdriver, spokeshave, T-square, vice, wrench.* □ [gardening] *billhook, dibber, fork, grass-rake, hoe, lawnmower, mattock, pruning knife, pruning shears, rake, roller, scythe, secateurs, shears, sickle, spade, Strimmer, trowel.* □ [various] *axe, bellows, chainsaw, chopper, clippers, crowbar, cutter, hatchet, jack, ladder, lever, penknife, pick, pickaxe, pitchfork, pocket-knife, scissors, shovel, sledgehammer, spanner, tape-measure, tongs, tweezers.*

tooth *n* □ *canine, eye-tooth, fang, incisor, molar, tusk, wisdom tooth.* **false teeth** bridge, denture, dentures, plate.

toothed *adj* cogged, crenellated, denticulate, indented, jagged, serrated. *Opp* SMOOTH.

top *adj inf* ace, best, choicest, finest, first, foremost, greatest, highest, incomparable, leading, maximum, most, peerless, pre-eminent, prime, principal, supreme, topmost, unequalled, winning. *n* **1** acme, apex, apogee, crest, crown, culmination, head, height, high point, peak, pinnacle, summit, tip, vertex, zenith. **2** *top of a table.* surface. **3** *top of a jar.* cap, cover, covering, lid, stopper. *Opp* BOTTOM. • *vb* **1** complete, cover, decorate, finish off, garnish, surmount. **2** beat, be higher than, better, cap, exceed, excel, outdo, outstrip, surpass, transcend.

topic *n* issue, matter, point, question, subject, talking-point, text, theme, thesis.

topical *adj* contemporary, current, recent, timely, up-to-date.

topography *n* features, geography, *inf* lie of the land.

topple *vb* **1** bring down, fell, knock down, overturn, throw down, tip over, upset. **2** collapse, fall, overbalance, totter, tumble. **3** *topple a rival.* oust, overthrow, unseat. ▷ DEFEAT.

torch *n* bicycle lamp, brand, electric lamp, flashlight, lamp, *old use* link.

torment *n* affliction, agony, anguish, distress, harassment, misery, ordeal, persecution, plague, scourge, suffering, torture, vexation, woe, worry, wretchedness. ▷ PAIN. • *vb* afflict, annoy, bait, be a torment to, bedevil, bother, bully, distress, harass, inflict pain on, intimidate, *inf* nag, persecute, pester, plague, tease, torture, vex, victimize, worry. ▷ HURT.

torpid *adj* apathetic, dormant, dull, inactive, indolent, inert, lackadaisical, languid, lethargic, lifeless, listless, passive, phlegmatic, slothful, slow, slow-moving, sluggish, somnolent, spiritless. *Opp* LIVELY.

torrent *n* cascade, cataract, deluge, downpour, effusion, flood, flow, gush, inundation, outpouring, overflow, rush, spate, stream, tide.

torrential *adj* copious, heavy, relentless, soaking, teeming, violent.

tortuous *adj* bent, circuitous, complicated, contorted, convoluted, corkscrew, crooked, curling, curvy, devious, indirect, involved, labyrinthine, mazy, meandering, roundabout, serpentine, sinuous, turning, twisted, twisting, twisty, wandering, winding, zigzag. *Opp* DIRECT, STRAIGHT.

torture *n* **1** cruelty, degradation, humiliation, inquisition, persecution, punishment, torment. **2** affliction, agony, anguish, distress, misery, pain, plague, scourge, suffering. • *vb* **1** be cruel to, brainwash, bully, cause pain to, degrade, dehumanize, humiliate, hurt, inflict pain on, intimidate, persecute, rack, torment, victimize. **2** *tortured by doubts.* afflict, agonize, annoy, bedevil, bother, distress, harass, *inf* nag, pester, plague, tease, vex, worry.

toss *vb* **1** bowl, cast, *inf* chuck, fling, flip, heave, hurl, lob, pitch, shy, sling, throw. **2** *toss about in a storm.* bob, dip, flounder, lurch, move restlessly, pitch, plunge, reel, rock, roll, shake, twist and turn, wallow, welter, writhe, yaw.

total *adj* **1** complete, comprehensive, entire, full, gross, overall, whole. **2** *total disaster.* absolute, downright, out-and-out, outright, perfect, sheer, thorough, thoroughgoing, unalloyed, unmitigated, unqualified, utter. • *n* aggregate, amount, answer, lot, sum, totality, whole. • *vb* **1** add up to, amount to, come to, make. **2** add up, calculate, compute, count, find the sum of, find the total of, reckon up, totalize, *inf* tot up, work out.

totalitarian *adj* absolute, arbitrary, authoritarian, autocratic, despotic, dictatorial, fascist, illiberal, one-party, oppressive, tyrannous, undemocratic, unrepresentative. *Opp* DEMOCRATIC.

totter *vb* dodder, falter, reel, rock, stagger, stumble, teeter, topple, tremble, waver, wobble. ▷ WALK.

touch *n* **1** feeling, texture, touching. **2** brush, caress, contact, dab, pat, stroke, tap. **3** *an expert's touch.* ability, capability, experience, expertise, facility, feel, flair, gift, knack, manner, sensitivity, skill, style, technique, understanding, way. **4** *a touch of salt.* bit, dash, drop, hint, intimation, small amount, suggestion, suspicion, taste, tinge, trace. • *vb* **1** be in contact with, brush, caress, contact, cuddle, dab, embrace, feel, finger, fondle, graze, handle, hit, kiss, lean against, manipulate, massage, nuzzle, pat, paw, pet, push, rub, stroke, tap, tickle. **2** *touch the emotions.* affect, arouse, awaken, concern, disturb, impress, influence, inspire, move, stimulate, stir, upset. **3** *touch 100 m.p.h.* attain, reach, rise to. **4** *I can't touch her skill.* be in the same league as, *inf* come up to, compare with, equal, match, parallel, rival. **touched** ▷ EMOTIONAL, MAD. **touching** ▷ EMOTIONAL. **touch off** ▷ BEGIN, IGNITE. **touch on** ▷ MENTION. **touch up** ▷ IMPROVE.

touchy *adj* edgy, highly strung, hypersensitive, irascible, irritable, jittery, jumpy, nervous, over-sensitive, peevish, querulous, quick-tempered, sensitive, short-tempered, snappy, temperamental, tense, testy, tetchy, thin-skinned, unpredictable, waspish.

tough *adj* **1** durable, hard-wearing, indestructible, lasting, rugged, sound, stout, strong, substantial, unbreakable, well-built, well-made. **2** *tough physique. inf* beefy, brawny, burly, hardy, muscular, robust, stalwart, strong, sturdy. **3** *tough opposition.* invulnerable, merciless, obdurate, obstinate, resilient, resistant, resolute, ruthless, stiff, stubborn, tenacious, unyielding. **4** *a tough taskmaster.* cold, cool, *inf* hardboiled, hardened, *inf* hard-nosed, inhuman, severe, stern, stony, uncaring, unsentimental, unsympathetic. **5** *tough meat.* chewy, hard, gristly, leathery, rubbery, uneatable. **6** *tough work.* arduous, demanding, difficult, exacting, exhausting, gruelling, hard, laborious, stiff, strenuous, taxing, troublesome. **7** *a tough problem.* baffling, intractable, *inf* knotty, mystifying, perplexing, puzzling, *inf* thorny. *Opp* EASY, TENDER, WEAK.

toughen *vb* harden, make tougher, reinforce, strengthen.

tour *n* circular tour, drive, excursion, expedition, jaunt, journey, outing, peregrination, ride, trip. • *vb* do the rounds of, explore, go round, make a tour of, visit. ▷ TRAVEL.

tourist *n* day-tripper, holidaymaker, sightseer, traveller, tripper, visitor.

tournament *n* championship, competition, contest, event, match, meeting, series.

tow *vb* drag, draw, haul, lug, pull, trail, tug.

tower *n* □ *belfry, campanile, castle, fort, fortress, keep, minaret, pagoda, skyscraper, spire, steeple, turret.* • *vb* ascend, dominate, loom, rear, rise, soar, stand out, stick up.

towering *adj* **1** colossal, gigantic, high, huge, imposing, lofty, mighty, soaring. ▷ TALL. **2** *a towering rage.* extreme, fiery, immoderate, intemperate, intense, mighty, overpowering, passionate, unrestrained, vehement, violent.

town *n* borough, city, community, conurbation, municipality, settlement, township, urban district, village.

toxic *adj* dangerous, deadly, harmful, lethal, noxious, poisonous. *Opp* HARMLESS.

trace *n* **1** clue, evidence, footprint, *inf* give-away, hint, indication, intimation, mark, remains, sign, spoor, token, track, trail, vestige. **2** ▷ BIT. • *vb* **1** detect, discover, find, get back, recover, retrieve, seek out, track down. ▷ TRACK. **2** *trace an outline.* copy, draw, go over, make a copy of, mark out, sketch. **kick over the traces** ▷ REBEL.

track *n* **1** footmark, footprint, mark, scent, spoor, trace, trail, wake (*of ship*). **2** *a farm track.* bridle-path, bridle-way, cart-track, footpath, path, route, trail, way. ▷ ROAD. **3** *a racing track.* circuit, course, dirt-track, race-track. **4** *railway track.* branch, branch line, line, mineral line, permanent way, rails, railway, route, tramway. • *vb* chase, dog, follow, hound, hunt, pursue, shadow, stalk, tail, trace, trail. **make tracks** ▷ DEPART. **track down** ▷ TRACE.

trade *n* **1** barter, business, buying and selling, commerce, dealing, exchange, industry, market, marketing, merchandising, trading, traffic, transactions. **2** *a skilled trade.* calling, career, craft, employment, job, *inf* line, occupation, profession, pursuit, work. • *vb* buy and sell, do business, have dealings, market goods, merchandise, retail, sell, traffic (in). **trade in** ▷ EXCHANGE. **trade on** ▷ EXPLOIT.

trader *n* broker, buyer, dealer, merchant, retailer, roundsman, salesman, seller, shopkeeper, stockist, supplier, tradesman, trafficker (*in illegal goods*), vendor.

tradition *n* **1** convention, custom, habit, institution, practice, rite, ritual, routine, usage. **2** *popular tradition.* belief, folklore.

traditional *adj* **1** accustomed, conventional, customary, established, familiar, habitual, historic, normal, orthodox, regular, time-honoured, typical, usual. *Opp* UNCONVENTIONAL. **2** *traditional stories*. folk, handed down, old, oral, popular, unwritten. *Opp* MODERN.

traffic *n* conveyance, movements, shipping, transport, transportation. ▷ VEHICLE. ● *vb* ▷ TRADE.

tragedy *n* adversity, affliction, *inf* blow, calamity, catastrophe, disaster, misfortune. *Opp* COMEDY.

tragic *adj* **1** appalling, awful, calamitous, catastrophic, depressing, dire, disastrous, dreadful, fatal, fearful, hapless, ill-fated, ill-omened, ill-starred, inauspicious, lamentable, terrible, tragical, unfortunate, unlucky. **2** *a tragic expression*. bereft, distressed, funereal, grief-stricken, hurt, pathetic, piteous, pitiful, sorrowful, woeful, wretched. ▷ SAD. *Opp* COMIC.

trail *n* **1** evidence, footmarks, footprints, marks, scent, signs, spoor, traces, wake (*of ship*). **2** path, pathway, route, track. ▷ ROAD. ● *vb* **1** dangle, drag, draw, haul, pull, tow. **2** chase, follow, hunt, pursue, shadow, stalk, tail, trace, track down. **3** ▷ DAWDLE.

train *n* **1** carriage, coach, diesel, *inf* DMU, electric train, express, inter-city, local train, railcar, steam train, stopping train. **2** *train of servants*. cortège, entourage, escort, followers, guard, line, retainers, retinue, staff, suite. **3** *train of events*. ▷ SEQUENCE. ● *vb* **1** coach, discipline, drill, educate, instruct, prepare, school, teach, tutor. **2** do exercises, exercise, *inf* get fit, practise, prepare yourself, rehearse, *inf* work out. **3** ▷ AIM.

trainee *n* apprentice, beginner, cadet, learner, *inf* L-driver, novice, pupil, starter, student, tiro, unqualified person.

trainer *n* coach, instructor, teacher, tutor.

trait *n* attribute, characteristic, feature, idiosyncrasy, peculiarity, property, quality, quirk.

traitor *n* apostate, betrayer, blackleg, collaborator, defector, deserter, double-crosser, fifth columnist, informer, *inf* Judas, quisling, renegade, turncoat.

tramp *n* **1** hike, march, trek, trudge, walk. **2** *a homeless tramp*. beggar, *inf* destitute person, *inf* dosser, *inf* down and out, drifter, homeless person, rover, traveller, vagabond, vagrant, wanderer. ● *vb inf* footslog, hike, march, plod, stride, toil, traipse, trek, trudge, *sl* yomp. ▷ WALK.

trample *vb* crush, flatten, squash, *inf* squish, stamp on, step on, tread on, walk over.

trance *n inf* brown study, daydream, daze, dream, ecstasy, hypnotic state, rapture, reverie, semi-consciousness, spell, stupor, unconsciousness.

tranquil *adj* **1** calm, halcyon (*days*), peaceful, placid, quiet, restful, serene, still, undisturbed, unruffled. *Opp* STORMY. **2** *a tranquil mood*. collected, composed, dispassionate, *inf* laid-back, sedate, sober, unemotional, unexcited, untroubled. *Opp* EXCITED.

tranquillizer *n* barbiturate, bromide, narcotic, opiate, sedative.

transaction *n* agreement, bargain, business, contract, deal, negotiation, proceeding.

transcend *vb* beat, exceed, excel, outdo, outstrip, rise above, surpass, top.

transcribe *vb* copy out, render, reproduce, take down, translate, transliterate, write out.

transfer *vb* bring, carry, change, convey, deliver, displace, ferry, hand over, make over, move, pass on, pass over, relocate, remove, second, shift, sign over, take, transplant, transport, transpose.

transform *vb* adapt, alter, change, convert, improve, metamorphose, modify, mutate, permute, rebuild, reconstruct, remodel, revolutionize, transfigure, translate, transmogrify, transmute, turn.

transformation *n* adaptation, alteration, change, conversion, improvement, metamorphosis, modification, mutation, reconstruction, revolution, transfiguration, transition, translation, transmogrification, transmutation, *inf* turn-about.

transgression *n* crime, error, fault, lapse, misdeed, misdemeanour, offence, sin, wickedness, wrongdoing.

transient *adj* brief, ephemeral, evanescent, fleeting, fugitive, impermanent, momentary, passing, *inf* quick, short, short-lived, temporary, transitory. *Opp* PERMANENT.

transit *n* conveyance, journey, movement, moving, passage, progress, shipment, transfer, transportation, travel.

transition *n* alteration, change, change-over, conversion, development, evolution, modification, movement, progress, progression, shift, transformation, transit.

translate *vb* change, convert, decode, elucidate, explain, express, gloss, interpret, make a translation, paraphrase, render, reword, spell out, transcribe. ▷ TRANSFORM.

translation *n* decoding, gloss, interpretation, paraphrase, rendering, transcription, transliteration, version.

translator *n* interpreter, linguist.

transmission *n* **1** broadcasting, communication, diffusion, dissemination, relaying, sending out. **2** *transmission of goods.* carriage, carrying, conveyance, dispatch, sending, shipment, shipping, transfer, transference, transport, transportation.

transmit *vb* **1** convey, dispatch, disseminate, forward, pass on, post, send, transfer, transport. **2** *transmit a message.* broadcast, cable, communicate, emit, fax, phone, radio, relay, telephone, telex, wire. *Opp* RECEIVE.

transparent *adj* **1** clear, crystalline, diaphanous, filmy, gauzy, limpid, pellucid, *inf* see-through, sheer, translucent. **2** *transparent honesty.* ▷ CANDID.

transplant *vb* displace, move, relocate, reposition, resettle, shift, transfer, uproot.

transport *n* carrier, conveyance, haulage, removal, shipment, shipping, transportation. □ *aircraft, barge, boat, bus, cable-car, car, chair-lift, coach, cycle, ferry, horse, lorry, Metro, minibus,* old use *omnibus, ship, space-shuttle, taxi, train, tram, van.* □ *air, canal, railway, road, sea, waterways.* ▷ VEHICLE, VESSEL. • *vb* **1** bear, carry, convey, fetch, haul, move, remove, send, shift, ship, take, transfer. **2** ▷ DEPORT.

transpose *vb* change, exchange, interchange, metathesize, move round, rearrange, reverse, substitute, swap, switch, transfer.

transverse *adj* crosswise, diagonal, oblique.

trap *n* ambush, booby-trap, deception, gin, mantrap, net, noose, pitfall, ploy, snare, trick. • *vb* ambush, arrest, capture, catch, catch out, corner, deceive, dupe, ensnare, entrap, inveigle, net, snare, trick.

trappings *plur n* accessories, accompaniments, accoutrements, adornments, appointments, decorations, equipment, finery, fittings, furnishings, *inf* gear, ornaments, paraphernalia, *inf* things, trimmings.

trash *n* **1** debris, garbage, junk, litter, refuse, rubbish, sweepings, waste. **2** ▷ NONSENSE.

travel *n* globe-trotting, moving around, peregrination, touring, tourism, travelling, wandering. □ *cruise, drive, excursion, expedition, exploration, flight, hike, holiday, journey, march, migration, mission, outing, pilgrimage, ramble, ride, safari, sail, sea-passage, tour, trek, trip, visit, voyage, walk.* • *vb inf* gad about, *inf* gallivant, journey, make a trip, move, proceed, progress, roam, *poet* rove, voyage, wander. ▷ GO. □ *aviate, circumnavigate (the world), commute, cruise, cycle, drive, emigrate, fly, free-wheel, hike, hitch-hike, march, migrate, motor, navigate,* *paddle, pedal, pilot, punt, ramble, ride, row, sail, shuttle, steam, tour, trek, walk.*

traveller *n* **1** astronaut, aviator, commuter, cosmonaut, cyclist, driver, flyer, migrant, motorcyclist, motorist, passenger, pedestrian, sailor, voyager, walker. **2** *a company traveller. inf* rep, representative, salesman, saleswoman. **3** *overseas travellers.* explorer, globe-trotter, hiker, hitchhiker, holidaymaker, pilgrim, rambler, stowaway, tourist, tripper, wanderer, wayfarer. **4** *live as travellers.* gypsy, itinerant, nomad, tinker, tramp, vagabond.

travelling *adj* homeless, itinerant, migrant, migratory, mobile, nomadic, peripatetic, restless, roaming, roving, touring, vagrant, wandering.

treacherous *adj* **1** deceitful, disloyal, double-crossing, double-dealing, duplicitous, faithless, false, perfidious, sneaky, unfaithful, untrustworthy. **2** *treacherous conditions.* dangerous, deceptive, hazardous, misleading, perilous, risky, shifting, unpredictable, unreliable, unsafe, unstable. *Opp* LOYAL, RELIABLE.

treachery *n* betrayal, dishonesty, disloyalty, double-dealing, duplicity, faithlessness, infidelity, perfidy, untrustworthiness. ▷ TREASON. *Opp* LOYALTY.

tread *vb* **tread on** crush, squash underfoot, stamp on, step on, trample, walk on. ▷ WALK.

treason *n* betrayal, high treason, mutiny, rebellion, sedition. ▷ TREACHERY.

treasure *n* cache, cash, fortune, gold, hoard, jewels, riches, treasure trove, valuables, wealth. • *vb* adore, appreciate, cherish, esteem, guard, keep safe, love, prize, rate highly, value, venerate, worship.

treasury *n* bank, exchequer, hoard, repository, storeroom, treasure-house, vault.

treat *n* entertainment, gift, outing, pleasure, surprise. • *vb* **1** attend to, behave towards, care for, look after, use. **2** *treat a topic.* consider, deal with, discuss, tackle. **3** *treat a patient, wound.* cure, dress, give treatment to, heal, medicate, nurse, prescribe medicine for, tend. **4** *treat food.* process. **5** *treat a friend to dinner.* entertain, give a treat, pay for, provide for, regale.

treatise *n* disquisition, dissertation, essay, monograph, pamphlet, paper, thesis, tract. ▷ WRITING.

treatment *n* **1** care, conduct, dealing (with), handling, management, manipulation, organization, reception, usage, use. **2** *treatment of illness.* cure, first aid, healing, nursing, remedy, therapy. ▷ MEDICINE, THERAPY.

treaty *n* agreement, alliance, armistice, compact, concordat, contract, covenant, convention, *inf* deal, entente, pact, peace, protocol, settlement, truce, understanding.

tree *n* bush, sapling, standard. □ *bonsai, conifer, cordon, deciduous tree, espalier, evergreen, pollard, standard.* □ *ash, banyan, baobab, bay, beech, birch, cacao, cedar, chestnut, cypress, elder, elm, eucalyptus, fir, fruit-tree, gum-tree, hawthorn, hazel, holly, horse-chestnut, larch, lime, maple, oak, olive, palm, pine, plane, poplar, redwood, rowan, sequoia, spruce, sycamore, tamarisk, tulip tree, willow, yew.*

tremble *vb* quail, quake, quaver, quiver, rock, shake, shiver, shudder, vibrate, waver.

tremendous *adj* alarming, appalling, awful, fearful, fearsome, frightening, frightful, horrifying, shocking, startling, terrible, terrific. ▷ BIG, EXCELLENT, REMARKABLE.

tremor *n* **1** agitation, hesitation, quavering, quiver, shaking, trembling, vibration. **2** earthquake, seismic disturbance.

tremulous *adj* **1** agitated, anxious, excited, frightened, jittery, jumpy, nervous, timid, uncertain. *Opp* CALM. **2** quivering, shaking, shivering, trembling, *inf* trembly, vibrating. *Opp* STEADY.

trend *n* **1** bent, bias, direction, drift, inclination, leaning, movement, shift, tendency. **2** *latest trend.* craze, *inf* fad, fashion, mode, *inf* rage, style, *inf* thing, vogue, way.

trendy *adj inf* all the rage, contemporary, fashionable, *inf* in, latest, modern, stylish, up-to-date, voguish. *Opp* OLD-FASHIONED.

trespass *vb* encroach, enter illegally, intrude, invade.

trial *n* **1** case, court martial, enquiry, examination, hearing, inquisition, judicial proceeding, lawsuit, tribunal. **2** attempt, check, *inf* dry run, experiment, rehearsal, test, testing, trial run, *inf* try-out. **3** *a sore trial.* affliction, burden, difficulty, hardship, nuisance, ordeal, *sl* pain in the neck, *inf* pest, problem, tribulation, trouble, worry.

triangular *adj* three-cornered, three-sided.

tribe *n* clan, dynasty, family, group, horde, house, nation, pedigree, people, race, stock, strain.

tribute *n* accolade, appreciation, commendation, compliment, eulogy, glorification, homage, honour, panegyric, praise, recognition, respect, testimony. **pay tribute to** ▷ HONOUR.

trick *n* **1** illusion, legerdemain, magic, sleight of hand. **2** *deceitful trick.* cheat, *inf* con, deceit, deception, fraud, hoax, imposture, joke, *inf* leg-pull, manoeuvre, ploy, practical joke, prank, pretence, ruse, scheme, stratagem, stunt, subterfuge, swindle, trap, trickery, wile. **3** *clever trick.* art, craft, device, dodge, expertise, gimmick, knack, *inf* know-how, secret, skill, technique. **4** *a trick of speech.* characteristic, habit, idiosyncrasy, mannerism, peculiarity, way. • *vb inf* bamboozle, bluff, catch out, cheat, *inf* con, cozen, deceive, defraud, *inf* diddle, dupe, fool, hoax, hoodwink, *inf* kid, mislead, outwit, *inf* pull your leg, swindle, *inf* take in.

trickery *n* bluffing, cheating, chicanery, deceit, deception, dishonesty, double-dealing, duplicity, fraud, *inf* funny business, guile, *inf* hocus-pocus, *inf* jiggerypokery, knavery, *inf* skulduggery, slyness, swindling, trick.

trickle *vb* dribble, drip, drizzle, drop, exude, flow slowly, leak, ooze, percolate, run, seep. *Opp* GUSH.

trifle *vb* behave frivolously, dabble, fiddle, fool about, play about. **trifling** ▷ TRIVIAL.

trill *vb* sing, twitter, warble, whistle.

trim *adj* compact, neat, orderly, *inf* shipshape, smart, spruce, tidy, well-groomed, well-kept, well-ordered. *Opp* UNTIDY. • *vb* **1** clip, crop, cut, dock, pare down, prune, shape, shear, shorten, snip, tidy. **2** ▷ DECORATE.

trip *n* day out, drive, excursion, expedition, holiday, jaunt, journey, outing, ride, tour, visit, voyage. • *vb* **1** blunder, catch your foot, fall, stagger, stumble, totter, tumble. **2** *trip along.* caper, dance, frisk, gambol, run, skip. **make a trip** ▷ TRAVEL.

trite *adj* banal, commonplace, ordinary, pedestrian, predictable, uninspired, uninteresting.

triumph *n* **1** accomplishment, achievement, conquest, coup, *inf* hit, knockout, master-stroke, *inf* smash hit, success, victory, *inf* walk-over, win. **2** *return in triumph.* celebration, elation, exultation, joy, jubilation, rapture. • *vb* be victorious, carry the day, prevail, succeed, take the honours, win. **triumph over** ▷ DEFEAT.

triumphant *adj* **1** conquering, dominant, successful, victorious, winning. *Opp* UNSUCCESSFUL. **2** boastful, *inf* cocky, elated, exultant, gleeful, gloating, immodest, joyful, jubilant, proud, triumphal.

trivial *adj inf* fiddling, *inf* footling, frivolous, inconsequential, inconsiderable, inessential, insignificant, little, meaningless, minor, negligible, paltry, pettifogging, petty, *inf* piddling, *inf* piffling, silly, slight, small, superficial, trifling, trite, unimportant, worthless. *Opp* IMPORTANT.

trophy *n* **1** booty, loot, mementoes, rewards, souvenirs, spoils. **2** *a sport-*

ing trophy. award, cup, laurels, medal, palm, prize.

trouble *n* **1** adversity, affliction, anxiety, burden, difficulty, distress, grief, hardship, illness, inconvenience, misery, misfortune, pain, problem, sadness, sorrow, suffering, trial, tribulation, unhappiness, vexation, worry. **2** *crowd trouble*. bother, commotion, conflict, discontent, discord, disorder, dissatisfaction, disturbance, fighting, fuss, misbehaviour, misconduct, naughtiness, row, strife, turmoil, unpleasantness, unrest, violence. **3** *engine trouble*. breakdown, defect, failure, fault, malfunction. **4** *took the trouble to get it right*. care, concern, effort, exertion, labour, pains, struggle, thought. • *vb* afflict, agitate, alarm, anguish, annoy, bother, cause trouble to, concern, discommode, distress, disturb, exasperate, grieve, harass, *inf* hassle, hurt, impose on, inconvenience, interfere with, irk, irritate, molest, nag, pain, perturb, pester, plague, *inf* put out, ruffle, threaten, torment, upset, vex, worry. *Opp* REASSURE. **troubled** ▷ WORRIED.

troublemaker *n Fr* agent provocateur, agitator, criminal, culprit, delinquent, hooligan, malcontent, mischief-maker, offender, rabble-rouser, rascal, ringleader, ruffian, scandalmonger, *inf* stirrer, vandal, wrongdoer.

troublesome *adj* annoying, badly-behaved, bothersome, disobedient, disorderly, distressing, inconvenient, irksome, irritating, naughty, *inf* pestiferous, pestilential, rowdy, tiresome, trying, uncooperative, unruly, upsetting, vexatious, vexing, wearisome, worrisome, worrying. *Opp* HELPFUL.

trousers *n inf* bags, breeches, corduroys, culottes, denims, dungarees, jeans, jodhpurs, *old use* knickerbockers, *inf* Levis, overalls, *Amer* pants, plus-fours, shorts, ski-pants, slacks, *Scot* trews, trunks.

truancy *n* absenteeism, desertion, malingering, shirking, *inf* skiving.

truant *n* absentee, deserter, dodger, idler, malingerer, runaway, shirker, *inf* skiver. **play truant** be absent, desert, malinger, *inf* skive, stay away.

truce *n* agreement, armistice, ceasefire, moratorium, pact, peace, suspension of hostilities, treaty.

true *adj* **1** accurate, actual, authentic, confirmed, correct, exact, factual, faithful, faultless, flawless, genuine, literal, proper, real, realistic, right, veracious, verified, veritable. *Opp* FALSE. **2** *a true friend*. constant, dedicated, dependable, devoted, faithful, firm, honest, honourable, loyal, reliable, responsible, sincere, staunch, steadfast, steady, trustworthy, trusty, upright. **3** *the true owner*. authorized, legal, legitimate, rightful, valid. **4** *true aim*. accurate, exact, perfect, precise, *inf* spot-on, unerring, unswerving. *Opp* INACCURATE.

truncheon *n* baton, club, cudgel, staff, stick.

trunk *n* **1** bole, shaft, stalk, stem, stock. **2** *a person's trunk*. body, frame, torso. **3** *an elephant's trunk*. nose, proboscis. **4** *a clothes' trunk*. box, case, casket, chest, coffer, crate, locker, suitcase.

trust *n* **1** assurance, belief, certainty, certitude, confidence, conviction, credence, faith, reliance. **2** *a position of trust*. responsibility, trusteeship. • *vb* **1** *inf* bank on, believe in, be sure of, confide in, count on, depend on, have confidence in, have faith in, *inf* pin your hopes on, rely on. **2** assume, expect, hope, imagine, presume, suppose, surmise. *Opp* DOUBT.

trustful *adj* confiding, credulous, gullible, innocent, trusting, unquestioning, unsuspecting, unsuspicious, unwary. *Opp* DISTRUSTFUL.

trustworthy *adj* constant, dependable, ethical, faithful, honest, honourable, loyal, moral, on the level, principled, reliable, responsible, *inf* safe, sensible, sincere, steadfast, steady, straightforward, true, *old use* trusty, truthful, upright. *Opp* DECEITFUL.

truth *n* **1** facts, reality. *Opp* LIE. **2** accuracy, authenticity, correctness, exactness, factuality, genuineness, integrity, reliability, truthfulness, validity, veracity, verity. **3** *an accepted truth.* axiom, fact, maxim, truism.

truthful *adj* accurate, candid, correct, credible, earnest, factual, faithful, forthright, frank, honest, proper, realistic, reliable, right, sincere, *inf* straight, straightforward, true, trustworthy, valid, veracious, unvarnished. *Opp* DISHONEST.

try *n* attempt, *inf* bash, *inf* crack, effort, endeavour, experiment, *inf* go, *inf* shot, *inf* stab, test, trial. • *vb* **1** aim, attempt, endeavour, essay, exert yourself, make an effort, strain, strive, struggle, venture. **2** *try something new.* appraise, *inf* check out, evaluate, examine, experiment with, *inf* have a go at, *inf* have a stab at, investigate, test, try out, undertake. **trying** ▷ ANNOYING, TIRESOME. **try someone's patience** ▷ ANNOY.

tub *n* barrel, bath, butt, cask, drum, keg, pot, vat.

tube *n* capillary, conduit, cylinder, duct, hose, main, pipe, spout, tubing.

tuck *vb* cram, gather, insert, push, put away, shove, stuff. **tuck in** ▷ EAT.

tuft *n* bunch, clump, cluster, tuffet, tussock.

tug *vb* drag, draw, haul, heave, jerk, lug, pluck, pull, tow, twitch, wrench, *inf* yank.

tumble *vb* **1** collapse, drop, fall, flop, pitch, roll, stumble, topple, trip up. **2** *tumble things into a heap.* disarrange, dump, jumble, mix up, rumple, shove, spill, throw carelessly, toss.

tumbledown *adj* badly maintained, broken down, crumbling, decrepit, derelict, dilapidated, ramshackle, rickety, ruined, shaky, tottering.

tumult *n* ado, agitation, chaos, commotion, confusion, disturbance, excitement, ferment, fracas, frenzy, hubbub, hullabaloo, rumpus, storm, tempest, upheaval, uproar, welter.

tumultuous *adj* agitated, boisterous, confused, excited, frenzied, hectic, passionate, stormy, tempestuous, turbulent, unrestrained, unruly, violent, wild. *Opp* CALM.

tune *n* air, melody, motif, song, strain, theme. • *vb* adjust, calibrate, regulate, set, temper.

tuneful *adj inf* catchy, euphonious, mellifluous, melodic, melodious, musical, pleasant, singable, sweet-sounding. *Opp* TUNELESS.

tuneless *adj* atonal, boring, cacophonous, discordant, dissonant, harsh, monotonous, unmusical. *Opp* TUNEFUL.

tunnel *n* burrow, gallery, hole, mine, passage, passageway, shaft, subway, underpass. • *vb* burrow, dig, excavate, mine, penetrate.

turbulent *adj* **1** agitated, boisterous, confused, disordered, excited, hectic, passionate, restless, seething, turbid, unrestrained, violent, volatile, wild. **2** *a turbulent crowd.* badly-behaved, disorderly, lawless, obstreperous, riotous, rowdy, undisciplined, unruly. **3** *turbulent weather.* blustery, bumpy, choppy (*sea*), rough, stormy, tempestuous, violent, wild, windy. *Opp* CALM.

turf *n* grass, grassland, green, lawn, *poet* sward.

turgid *adj* affected, bombastic, flowery, fulsome, grandiose, high-flown, overblown, pompous, pretentious, stilted, wordy. *Opp* ARTICULATE.

turmoil *n inf* bedlam, chaos, commotion, confusion, disorder, disturbance, ferment, *inf* hubbub, *inf* hullabaloo, pandemonium, riot, row, rumpus, tumult, turbulence, unrest, upheaval, uproar, welter. *Opp* CALM.

turn *n* **1** circle, coil, curve, cycle, loop, pirouette, revolution, roll, rotation, spin, twirl, twist, whirl. **2** angle, bend, change of direction, corner, deviation, *inf* dogleg, hairpin bend, junction, loop, meander, reversal, shift, turning-point, *inf* U-turn, zigzag. **3** *your turn in a game.* chance, *inf* go, innings, opportunity, shot, stint. **4** *a comic turn*. ▷ PERFORMANCE. **5** *a nasty turn*. ▷ ILLNESS. ● *vb* **1** circle, coil, curl, gyrate, hinge, loop, move in a circle, orbit, pivot, revolve, roll, rotate, spin, spiral, swivel, twirl, twist, whirl, wind, yaw. **2** bend, change direction, corner, deviate, divert, go round a corner, negotiate a corner, steer, swerve, veer, wheel. **3** *turn a pumpkin into a coach*. adapt, alter, change, convert, make, modify, remake, remodel, transfigure, transform. **4** *turn to and fro*. squirm, twist, wriggle, writhe. **turn aside** ▷ DEVIATE. **turn down** ▷ REJECT. **turn into** ▷ BECOME. **turn off** ▷ DEVIATE, DISCONNECT, REPEL. **turn on** ▷ ATTRACT, CONNECT. **turn out** ▷ EXPEL, HAPPEN, PRODUCE. **turn over** ▷ CONSIDER, OVERTURN. **turn tail** ▷ ESCAPE. **turn up** ▷ ARRIVE, DISCOVER.

turning-point *n* crisis, crossroads, new direction, revolution, watershed.

turnover *n* business, cash-flow, efficiency, output, production, productivity, profits, revenue, throughput, yield.

twiddle *vb* fiddle with, fidget with, fool with, mess with, twirl, twist.

twig *n* branch, offshoot, shoot, spray, sprig, sprout, stalk, stem, stick, sucker, tendril.

twilight *n* dusk, evening, eventide, gloaming, gloom, halflight, nightfall, sundown, sunset.

twin *adj* balancing, corresponding, double, duplicate, identical, indistinguishable, *inf* look-alike, matching, paired, similar, symmetrical. ● *n* clone, counterpart, double, duplicate, *inf* look-alike, match, pair, *inf* spitting image.

twirl *vb* **1** gyrate, pirouette, revolve, rotate, spin, turn, twist, wheel, whirl, wind. **2** *twirl an umbrella*. brandish, twiddle, wave.

twist *n* **1** bend, coil, curl, kink, knot, loop, tangle, turn, zigzag. **2** *a twist to a story*. revelation, surprise ending. ● *vb* **1** bend, coil, corkscrew, curl, curve, loop, revolve, rotate, screw, spin, spiral, turn, weave, wind, wreathe, wriggle, writhe, zigzag. **2** *twist ropes*. entangle, entwine, intertwine, interweave, tangle. **3** *twist a lid off*. jerk, wrench, wrest. **4** *twist out of shape*. buckle, contort, crinkle, crumple, distort, screw up, warp, wrinkle. **5** *twist meaning*. alter, change, falsify, misquote, misrepresent. **twisted** ▷ CONFUSED, PERVERTED, TWISTY.

twisty *adj* bending, bendy, circuitous, coiled, contorted, crooked, curving, curvy, *inf* in and out, indirect, looped, meandering, misshapen, rambling, roundabout, serpentine, sinuous, snaking, tortuous, twisted, twisting, *inf* twisting and turning, winding, zigzag. *Opp* STRAIGHT.

twitch *n* blink, convulsion, flutter, jerk, jump, spasm, tic, tremor. ● *vb* fidget, flutter, jerk, jump, start, tremble.

two *n* couple, duet, duo, match, pair, twosome.

type *n* **1** category, class, classification, description, designation, form, genre, group, kind, mark, set, sort, species, variety. **2** *He was the very type of evil*. embodiment, epitome, example, model, pattern, personification, standard. **3** *printed in large type*. characters, font, fount, lettering, letters, print, printing, typeface.

typical *adj* **1** characteristic, distinctive, particular, representative, special. **2** *a typical day*. average, conventional, normal, ordinary, orthodox, predictable, standard, stock, unsurprising, usual. *Opp* UNUSUAL.

tyrannical *adj* absolute, authoritarian, autocratic, *inf* bossy, cruel, despotic, dictatorial, domineering, harsh, high-handed, illiberal, imperious, oppressive, overbearing, ruthless, severe, totalitarian, tyrannous, undemocratic, unjust. *Opp* DEMOCRATIC, LIBERAL.

tyrant *n* autocrat, despot, dictator, *inf* hard taskmaster, oppressor, slave-driver. ▷ RULER.

U

ugly *adj* **1** deformed, disfigured, disgusting, dreadful, frightful, ghastly, grim, grisly, grotesque, gruesome, hideous, horrible, *inf* horrid, ill-favoured, loathsome, misshapen, monstrous, nasty, objectionable, odious, offensive, repellent, repulsive, revolting, shocking, sickening, terrible. **2** *ugly furniture.* displeasing, inartistic, inelegant, plain, tasteless, unattractive, unpleasant, unprepossessing, unsightly. **3** *an ugly mood.* angry, cross, dangerous, forbidding, hostile, menacing, ominous, sinister, surly, threatening, unfriendly. *Opp* BEAUTIFUL.

ulterior *adj* concealed, covert, hidden, personal, private, secondary, secret, undeclared, underlying, undisclosed, unexpressed. *Opp* OVERT.

ultimate *adj* **1** closing, concluding, eventual, extreme, final, furthest, last, terminal, terminating. **2** *ultimate truth.* basic, fundamental, primary, root, underlying.

umpire *n* adjudicator, arbiter, arbitrator, judge, linesman, moderator, official, *inf* ref, referee.

unable *adj* impotent, incompetent, powerless, unfit, unprepared, unqualified. *Opp* ABLE.

unacceptable *adj* bad, forbidden, illegal, improper, inadequate, inadmissible, inappropriate, inexcusable, insupportable, intolerable, invalid, taboo, unsatisfactory, unsuitable, wrong. *Opp* ACCEPTABLE.

unaccompanied *adj* alone, lone, single-handed, sole, solo, unaided, unescorted.

unaccountable *adj* ▷ INEXPLICABLE.

unaccustomed *adj* ▷ STRANGE.

unadventurous *adj* **1** cautious, cowardly, spiritless, timid, unimaginative. **2** *an unadventurous life.* cloistered, limited, protected, sheltered, unexciting. *Opp* ADVENTUROUS.

unalterable *adj* ▷ IMMUTABLE.

unambiguous *adj* ▷ DEFINITE.

unanimous *adj* ▷ UNITED.

unasked *adj* ▷ UNINVITED.

unassuming *adj* ▷ MODEST.

unattached *adj* autonomous, *inf* available, free, independent, separate, single, uncommitted, unmarried, *inf* unspoken for.

unattractive *adj* characterless, colourless, displeasing, dull, inartistic, inelegant, nasty, objectionable, *inf* off-putting, plain, repellent, repulsive, tasteless, uninviting, unpleasant, unprepossessing, unsightly. ▷ UGLY. *Opp* ATTRACTIVE.

unauthorized *adj* illegal, illegitimate, illicit, irregular, unapproved, unlawful, unofficial. *Opp* OFFICIAL.

unavoidable *adj* certain, compulsory, destined, fated, fixed, ineluctable, inescapable, inevitable, inexorable, mandatory, necessary, obligatory, predetermined, required, sure, unalterable.

unaware *adj* ▷ IGNORANT.

unbalanced *adj* **1** asymmetrical, irregular, lopsided, off-centre, shaky, uneven, unstable, wobbly. **2** biased, bigoted, one-sided, partial, partisan, prejudiced, unfair, unjust. **3** *unbalanced mind.* ▷ MAD.

unbearable *adj* insufferable, insupportable, intolerable, overpowering, overwhelming, unacceptable, unendurable. *Opp* TOLERABLE.

unbeatable *adj* ▷ INVINCIBLE.

unbecoming *adj* dishonourable, improper, inappropriate, indecorous, indelicate, offensive, tasteless, unattractive, unbefitting, undignified, ungentlemanly, unladylike, unseemly, unsuitable. *Opp* DECOROUS.

unbelievable *adj* ▷ INCREDIBLE.

unbelieving *adj* ▷ INCREDULOUS.

unbend *vb* **1** straighten, uncurl, untwist. **2** loosen up, relax, rest, unwind.

unbending *adj* ▷ INFLEXIBLE.

unbiased *adj* balanced, disinterested, enlightened, even-handed, fair, impartial, independent, just, neutral, non-partisan, objective, open-minded, reasonable, *inf* straight, unbigoted, undogmatic, unprejudiced. *Opp* BIASED.

unbreakable *adj* ▷ INDESTRUCTIBLE.

unbroken *adj* ▷ CONTINUOUS, WHOLE.

uncalled-for *adj* ▷ UNNECESSARY.

uncared-for *adj* ▷ DERELICT.

uncaring *adj* ▷ CALLOUS.

unceasing *adj* ▷ CONTINUOUS.

uncertain *adj* **1** ambiguous, arguable, *inf* chancy, confusing, conjectural, cryptic, enigmatic, equivocal, hazardous, hazy, *inf* iffy, imprecise, incalculable, inconclusive, indefinite, indeterminate, problematical, puzzling, questionable, risky, speculative, *inf* touch and go, unclear, unconvincing, undecided, undetermined, unforeseeable, unknown, unresolved, woolly. **2** *uncertain what to believe.* agnostic, ambivalent, doubtful, dubious, *inf* hazy, insecure, *inf* in two minds, self-questioning, unconvinced, undecided, unsure, vague, wavering. **3** *an uncertain climate.* changeable, erratic, fitful, inconstant, irregular, precarious, unpredictable, unreliable, unsettled, variable. *Opp* CERTAIN.

unchanging *adj* ▷ CONSTANT.

uncharitable *adj* ▷ UNKIND.

uncivilized *adj* anarchic, antisocial, backward, barbarian, barbaric, barbarous, brutish, crude, disorganized, illiterate, Philistine, primitive, savage, uncultured, uneducated, unenlightened, unsophisticated, wild. *Opp* CIVILIZED.

unclean *adj* ▷ DIRTY.

unclear *adj* ▷ UNCERTAIN.

unclothed *adj* ▷ NAKED.

uncomfortable *adj* **1** bleak, cold, comfortless, cramped, hard, inconvenient, lumpy, painful. **2** *uncomfortable clothes.* formal, restrictive, stiff, tight, tight-fitting. **3** *an uncomfortable silence.* awkward, distressing, embarrassing, nervous, restless, troubled, uneasy, worried. *Opp* COMFORTABLE.

uncommon *adj* ▷ UNUSUAL.

uncommunicative *adj* ▷ TACITURN.

uncomplimentary *adj* censorious, critical, deprecatory, depreciatory, derogatory, disapproving, disparaging, pejorative, scathing, slighting, unfavourable, unflattering. ▷ RUDE. *Opp* COMPLIMENTARY.

uncompromising *adj* ▷ INFLEXIBLE.

unconcealed *adj* ▷ OBVIOUS.

unconditional *adj* absolute, categorical, complete, full, outright, total, unequivocal, unlimited, unqualified, unreserved, unrestricted, wholehearted, *inf* with no strings attached. *Opp* CONDITIONAL.

uncongenial *adj* alien, antipathetic, disagreeable, incompatible, unattractive, unfriendly, unpleasant, unsympathetic. *Opp* CONGENIAL.

unconquerable *adj* ▷ INVINCIBLE.

unconscious *adj* **1** anaesthetized, *inf* blacked-out, comatose, concussed, *inf* dead to the world, insensible, *inf* knocked out, *inf* knocked silly, oblivious, *inf* out for the count, senseless, sleeping. **2** blind, deaf, ignorant, oblivious, unaware. **3** *unconscious humour.* accidental, inadvertent, unintended, unintentional, unwitting. **4** *an unconscious reaction.* automatic, *sl* gut, impulsive, instinctive, involuntary, reflex, spontaneous, unthinking. **5** *an unconscious desire.* repressed, subconscious, subliminal, suppressed. *Opp* CONSCIOUS.

unconsciousness *n inf* blackout, coma, faint, oblivion, sleep.

uncontrollable *adj* ▷ UNDISCIPLINED.

unconventional *adj* abnormal, atypical, *inf* cranky, eccentric, exotic, futuristic, idiosyncratic, independent, inventive, non-conforming, non-standard, odd, off-beat, original, peculiar, progressive, revolutionary, strange, surprising, unaccustomed, unorthodox, *inf* way-out, wayward, weird, zany. *Opp* CONVENTIONAL.

unconvincing *adj* implausible, improbable, incredible, invalid, spurious, unbelievable, unlikely. *Opp* PERSUASIVE.

uncooperative *adj* lazy, obstructive, recalcitrant, selfish, unhelpful, unwilling. *Opp* COOPERATIVE.

uncover *vb* bare, come across, detect, dig up, disclose, discover, disrobe, exhume, expose, locate, reveal, show, strip, take the wraps off, undress, unearth, unmask, unveil, unwrap. *Opp* COVER.

undamaged *adj* ▷ PERFECT.

undefended *adj* defenceless, exposed, helpless, insecure, unarmed, unfortified, unguarded, unprotected, vulnerable, weaponless. *Opp* SECURE.

undemanding *adj* ▷ EASY.

undemonstrative *adj* ▷ ALOOF.

underclothes *plur n* lingerie, *inf* smalls, underclothing, undergarments, underthings, underwear, *inf* undies. □ *bra, braces, brassière, briefs, camiknickers, corset, drawers, garter, girdle, knickers, panties, pantihose, pants, petticoat, slip, suspenders, tights, trunks, underpants, underskirt, vest.*

undercurrent *n* atmosphere, feeling, hint, sense, suggestion, trace, undertone.

underestimate *vb* belittle, depreciate, dismiss, disparage, minimize, miscalculate, misjudge, underrate, undervalue. *Opp* EXAGGERATE.

undergo *vb* bear, be subjected to, endure, experience, go through, live through, put up with, *inf* stand, submit yourself to, suffer, withstand.

underground *adj* **1** buried, hidden, subterranean, sunken. **2** clandestine, revolutionary, secret, subversive, unofficial, unrecognized.

undergrowth *n* brush, bushes, ground cover, plants, vegetation.

undermine *vb* burrow under, destroy, dig under, erode, excavate, mine under, ruin, sabotage, sap, subvert, tunnel under, undercut, weaken, wear away.

underprivileged *adj* deprived, destitute, disadvantaged, downtrodden, impoverished, needy, oppressed. ▷ POOR. *Opp* PRIVILEGED.

undersea *adj* subaquatic, submarine, underwater.

understand *vb* **1** appreciate, apprehend, be conversant with, *inf* catch on, comprehend, *inf* cotton on to, decipher, decode, fathom, figure out, follow, gather, *inf* get, *inf* get to the bottom of, grasp, interpret, know, learn, make out, make sense of, master, perceive, realize, recognize, see, take in, *inf* twig. **2** *understand animals.* be in sympathy with, empathize with, sympathize with.

understanding *n* **1** ability, acumen, brains, cleverness, discernment, insight, intellect, intelligence, judgement, penetration, perceptiveness, percipience, sense, wisdom. **2** *understanding of a problem.* appreciation, apprehension, awareness, cognition, comprehension, grasp, knowledge. **3** *understanding between people.* accord, agreement, compassion, consensus, consent, consideration, empathy, fellow feeling, harmony, kindness, mutuality, sympathy, tolerance. **4** *a formal understanding.* arrangement, bargain, compact, contract, deal, entente, pact, settlement, treaty.

understate *vb* belittle, *inf* make light of, minimize, *inf* play down, *inf* soft-pedal. *Opp* EXAGGERATE.

undertake *vb* **1** agree, attempt, consent, covenant, guarantee, pledge, promise, try. **2** *undertake a task.* accept responsibility for, address, approach, attend to, begin, commence, commit yourself to, cope with, deal with, embark on, grapple with, handle, manage, tackle, take on, take up.

undertaking *n* **1** affair, business, enterprise, project, task, venture. **2** agreement, assurance, contract, guarantee, pledge, promise, vow.

undervalue *vb* belittle, depreciate, dismiss, disparage, minimize, miscalculate, misjudge, underestimate, underrate.

underwater *adj* subaquatic, submarine, undersea.

undeserved *adj* unearned, unfair, unjustified, unmerited, unwarranted.

undesirable *adj* ▷ OBJECTIONABLE.

undisciplined *adj* anarchic, chaotic, disobedient, disorderly, disorganized, intractable, rebellious, uncontrollable, uncontrolled, ungovernable, unmanageable, unruly, unsystematic, untrained, wild, wilful. *Opp* OBEDIENT.

undiscriminating *adj* ▷ IMPERCEPTIVE.

undisguised *adj* ▷ OBVIOUS.

undistinguished *adj* ▷ ORDINARY.

undo *vb* **1** detach, disconnect, disengage, loose, loosen, open, part, separate, unbind, unbuckle, unbutton, unchain, unclasp, unclip, uncouple, unfasten, unfetter, unhook, unleash, unlock, unpick, unpin, unscrew, unseal, unshackle, unstick, untether, untie, unwrap, unzip. **2** *undo someone's good work.* annul, cancel out, destroy, mar, nullify, quash, reverse, ruin, spoil, undermine, vitiate, wipe out, wreck.

undoubted *adj* ▷ INDISPUTABLE.

undoubtedly *adv* certainly, definitely, doubtless, indubitably, of course, surely, undeniably, unquestionably.

undress *vb* disrobe, divest yourself, *inf* peel off, shed your clothes, strip off, take off your clothes, uncover yourself. **undressed** *adj* ▷ NAKED.

undue *adj* ▷ EXCESSIVE.

undying *adj* ▷ ETERNAL.

uneasy *adj* anxious, apprehensive, awkward, concerned, distressed, distressing, disturbed, edgy, fearful, insecure, jittery, nervous, restive, restless, tense, troubled, uncomfortable, unsettled, upsetting, worried.

uneducated *adj* ▷ IGNORANT.

unemotional *adj* apathetic, clinical, cold, cool, dispassionate, frigid, hard-hearted, heartless, impassive, indifferent, objective, unfeeling, unmoved, unresponsive. *Opp* EMOTIONAL.

unemployed *adj* jobless, laid off, on the dole, out of work, redundant, *inf* resting, unwaged. ▷ IDLE.

unendurable *adj* ▷ UNBEARABLE.

unenthusiastic *adj* ▷ APATHETIC, UNINTERESTED.

unequal *adj* **1** different, differing, disparate, dissimilar, uneven, varying. **2** *unequal treatment.* biased, prejudiced, unjust. **3** *an unequal contest.* ill-matched, one-sided, unbalanced, uneven, unfair. *Opp* EQUAL, FAIR.

unequalled *adj* incomparable, inimitable, matchless, peerless, supreme, surpassing, un-matched, unparalleled, unrivalled, unsurpassed.

unethical *adj* ▷ IMMORAL.

uneven *adj* **1** bent, broken, bumpy, crooked, irregular, jagged, jerky, pitted, rough, rutted, undulating, wavy. **2** *an uneven rhythm.* erratic, fitful, fluctuating, inconsistent, spasmodic, unpredictable, variable, varying. **3** *an uneven load.* asymmetrical, lopsided, unsteady. **4** *uneven contest.* illmatched, one-sided, unbalanced, unequal, unfair. *Opp* EVEN.

uneventful *adj* ▷ UNEXCITING.

unexciting *adj* boring, dreary, dry, dull, humdrum, monotonous, predictable, quiet, repetitive, routine, soporific, straightforward, tedious, trite, uneventful, uninspiring, uninteresting, vapid, wearisome. ▷ ORDINARY. *Opp* EXCITING.

unexpected *adj* accidental, chance, fortuitous, sudden, surprising, unforeseen, unhoped-for, unlooked-for, unplanned, unpredictable, unusual. *Opp* PREDICTABLE.

unfair *adj* ▷ UNJUST.

unfaithful *adj* deceitful, disloyal, double-dealing, duplicitous, faithless, false, fickle, inconstant, perfidious, traitorous, treacherous, treasonable, unreliable, untrue, untrustworthy. *Opp* FAITHFUL.

unfaithfulness *n* **1** duplicity, perfidy, treachery, treason. **2** adultery, infidelity.

unfamiliar *adj* ▷ STRANGE.

unfashionable *adj* dated, obsolete, old-fashioned, *inf* out, outmoded, passé, superseded, unstylish. *Opp* FASHIONABLE.

unfasten *vb* ▷ UNDO.

unfavourable *adj* **1** adverse, attacking, contrary, critical, disapproving, discouraging, hostile, ill-disposed, inauspicious, negative, opposing, uncomplimentary, unfriendly, unhelpful, unkind, unpromising, unpropitious, unsympathetic. **2** *an unfavourable reputation.* bad, undesirable, unenviable, unsatisfactory. *Opp* FAVOURABLE.

unfeeling *adj* ▷ CALLOUS.

unfinished *adj* imperfect, incomplete, rough, sketchy, uncompleted, unpolished. *Opp* PERFECT.

unfit *adj* **1** ill-equipped, inadequate, incapable, incompetent, unsatisfactory, useless. **2** *unfit for family viewing.* improper, inappropriate, unbecoming, unsuitable, unsuited. **3** *an unfit athlete.* feeble, flabby, out of condition, unhealthy. ▷ ILL. *Opp* FIT.

unflagging *adj* ▷ TIRELESS.

unflinching *adj* ▷ RESOLUTE.

unforeseen *adj* ▷ UNEXPECTED.

unforgettable *adj* ▷ MEMORABLE.

unforgivable *adj* inexcusable, mortal (*sin*), reprehensible, shameful, unjustifiable, unpardonable, unwarrantable. *Opp* FORGIVABLE.

unfortunate *adj* ▷ UNLUCKY.

unfriendly *adj* aggressive, aloof, antagonistic, antisocial, cold, cool, detached, disagreeable, distant, forbidding, frigid, haughty, hostile, ill-disposed, ill-natured, impersonal, indifferent, inhospitable, menacing, nasty, obnoxious, offensive, remote, reserved, rude, sour, standoffish, *inf* starchy, stern, supercilious, threatening, unapproachable, uncivil, uncongenial, unenthusiastic, unforthcoming, unkind, unneighbourly, unresponsive, unsociable, unsympathetic, unwelcoming. *Opp* FRIENDLY.

ungainly *adj* ▷ AWKWARD.

ungodly *adj* ▷ IRRELIGIOUS.

ungovernable *adj* ▷ UNDISCIPLINED.

ungrateful *adj* displeased, ill-mannered, rude, selfish, unappreciative, unthankful. *Opp* GRATEFUL.

unhappy *adj* **1** dejected, depressed, dispirited, down, downcast, gloomy, miserable, mournful, sorrowful. ▷ SAD. **2** *unhappy about losing.* bad-tempered, disaffected, discontented, disgruntled, disillusioned, displeased, dissatisfied, *inf* fed up, *inf* grumpy, morose, sulky, sullen, unsatisfied. **3** *an unhappy choice.* ▷ UNSATISFACTORY.

unhealthy *adj* **1** ailing, debilitated, delicate, diseased, feeble, frail, infected, infirm, *inf* poorly, sick, sickly, suffering, unwell, valetudinary, weak. ▷ ILL. **2** *unhealthy conditions.* deleterious, detrimental, dirty, harmful, insalubrious, insanitary, noxious, polluted, unhygienic, unwholesome. *Opp* HEALTHY.

unheard-of *adj* ▷ UNUSUAL.

unhelpful *adj* disobliging, inconsiderate, negative, slow, uncivil, uncooperative, unwilling. *Opp* HELPFUL.

unhygienic *adj* ▷ UNHEALTHY.

unidentifiable *adj* anonymous, camouflaged, disguised, hidden, undetectable, unidentified, unknown, unrecognizable. *Opp* IDENTIFIABLE.

unidentified *adj* anonymous, incognito, mysterious, nameless, unfamiliar, unknown, unmarked, unnamed, unrecognized, unspecified. *Opp* SPECIFIC.

uniform *adj* consistent, even, homogeneous, identical, indistinguishable, predictable, regular, same, similar, single, standard, unbroken, unvaried, unvarying. *Opp* DIFFERENT. • *n* costume, livery, outfit.

unify *vb* amalgamate, bring together, coalesce, combine, consolidate, fuse, harmonize, integrate, join, merge, unite, weld together. *Opp* SEPARATE.

unimaginative *adj* banal, boring, clichéd, derivative, dull, hackneyed, inartistic, insensitive, obvious, ordinary, prosaic, stale, trite, ugly, uninspired, uninteresting, unoriginal. *Opp* IMAGINATIVE.

unimportant *adj* ephemeral, forgettable, immaterial, inconsequential, inconsiderable, inessential, insignificant, irrelevant, lightweight, minor, negligible, peripheral, petty, secondary, slight, trifling, trivial, valueless, worthless. ▷ SMALL. *Opp* IMPORTANT.

uninhabitable *adj* condemned, in bad repair, unliveable, unusable. *Opp* HABITABLE.

uninhabited *adj* abandoned, deserted, desolate, empty, tenantless, uncolonized, unoccupied, unpeopled, unpopulated, untenanted, vacant.

uninhibited *adj* abandoned, candid, casual, easygoing, frank, informal, natural, open, outgoing, outspoken, relaxed, spontaneous, unbridled, unconstrained, unrepressed, unreserved, unrestrained, unselfconscious, wild. *Opp* REPRESSED.

unintelligent *adj* ▷ STUPID.

unintelligible *adj* ▷ INCOMPREHENSIBLE.

unintentional *adj* accidental, fortuitous, inadvertent, involuntary, unconscious, unintended, unplanned, unwitting. *Opp* INTENTIONAL.

uninterested *adj* apathetic, bored, incurious, indifferent, lethargic, passive, phlegmatic, unconcerned, unenthusiastic, uninvolved, unresponsive. *Opp* INTERESTED.

uninteresting *adj* boring, dreary, dry, dull, flat, monotonous, obvious, predictable, tedious, unexciting, uninspiring, vapid, wearisome. ▷ ORDINARY. *Opp* INTERESTING.

uninterrupted *adj* ▷ CONTINUOUS.

uninvited *adj* **1** unasked, unbidden, unwelcome. **2** *an uninvited comment.* gratuitous, unsolicited, voluntary.

uninviting *adj* ▷ UNATTRACTIVE.

union *n* **1** alliance, amalgamation, association, coalition, confederation, conjunction, federation, integration, joining together, merger, unanimity, unification, unity. **2** amalgam, blend, combination, combining, compound, fusion, grafting, marrying, mixture, synthesis, welding. **3** marriage, matrimony, partnership, wedlock.

unique *adj* distinctive, incomparable, lone, *inf* one-off, peculiar, peerless, *inf* second to none, single, singular, unequalled, unparalleled, unrepeatable, unrivalled.

unit *n* component, constituent, element, entity, item, module, part, piece, portion, section, segment, whole.

unite *vb* ally, amalgamate, associate, blend, bring together, coalesce, collaborate, combine, commingle, confederate, connect, consolidate, conspire, cooperate, couple, federate, fuse, go into partnership, harmonize, incorporate, integrate, interlock, join, join forces, link, link up, marry, merge, mingle, mix, stick together, tie up, unify, weld together. ▷ MARRY. *Opp* SEPARATE.

united *adj* agreed, allied, coherent, collective, common, concerted, coordinated, corporate, harmonious, integrated, joint, like-minded, mutual, *inf* of one mind, shared, *inf* solid, unanimous, undivided. *Opp* DISUNITED. **be united** ▷ AGREE.

unity *n* accord, agreement, coherence, concord, consensus, harmony, integrity, like-mindedness, oneness, rapport, solidarity, unanimity, wholeness. *Opp* DISUNITY.

universal *adj* all-embracing, all-round, boundless, common, comprehensive, cosmic, general, global, international, omnipresent, pandemic, prevailing, prevalent, total, ubiquitous, unbounded, unlimited, widespread, worldwide.

universe *n* cosmos, creation, the heavens, *old use* macrocosm.

unjust *adj* biased, bigoted, indefensible, inequitable, one-sided, partial, partisan, prejudiced, undeserved, unfair, unjustified, unlawful, unmerited, unreasonable, unwarranted, wrong, wrongful. *Opp* JUST.

unjustifiable *adj* excessive, immoderate, indefensible, inexcusable, unacceptable, unconscionable, unforgivable, unjust, unreasonable, unwarranted. *Opp* JUSTIFIABLE.

unkind *adj* abrasive, *inf* beastly, callous, caustic, cold-blooded, discourteous, disobliging, hard, hard-hearted, harsh, heartless, hurtful, ill-natured, impolite, inconsiderate, inhuman, inhumane, insensitive, malevolent, malicious, mean, merciless, nasty, pitiless, relentless, rigid, rough, ruthless, sadistic, savage, selfish, severe, sharp, spiteful, stern, tactless, thoughtless, uncaring, uncharitable, unchristian, unfeeling, unfriendly, unpleasant, unsympathetic, unthoughtful, vicious. ▷ ANGRY, CRITICAL, CRUEL. *Opp* KIND.

unknown *adj* **1** anonymous, disguised, incognito, mysterious, nameless, strange, unidentified, unnamed, unrecognized, unspecified. **2** *an unknown country*. alien, foreign, uncharted, undiscovered, unexplored, unfamiliar, unmapped. **3** *an unknown actor*. humble, insignificant, little-known, lowly, obscure, undistinguished, unheard-of, unimportant. *Opp* FAMOUS.

unlawful *adj* ▷ ILLEGAL.

unlikely *adj* **1** dubious, farfetched, implausible, improbable, incredible, suspect, suspicious, *inf* tall (*story*), unbelievable, unconvincing, unthinkable. **2** *an unlikely possibility*. distant, doubtful, faint, *inf* outside, remote, slight. *Opp* LIKELY.

unlimited *adj* ▷ BOUNDLESS.

unload *vb* disburden, discharge, drop off, *inf* dump, empty, offload, take off, unpack. *Opp* LOAD.

unloved *adj* abandoned, discarded, forsaken, hated, loveless, lovelorn, neglected, rejected, spurned, uncared-for, unvalued, unwanted. *Opp* LOVED.

unlucky *adj* **1** accidental, calamitous, chance, disastrous, dreadful, tragic, unfortunate, untimely, unwelcome. **2** *an unlucky person*. *inf* accident-prone, hapless, luckless, unhappy, unsuccessful, wretched. **3** *an unlucky number*. cursed, ill-fated, ill-omened, ill-starred, inauspicious, jinxed, ominous, unfavourable. *Opp* LUCKY.

unmanageable *adj* ▷ UNDISCIPLINED.

unmarried *adj inf* available, celibate, *inf* free, single, unwed. **unmarried person** bachelor, celibate, spinster.

unmentionable *adj* ▷ TABOO.

unmistakable *adj* ▷ DEFINITE, OBVIOUS.

unnamed *adj* ▷ UNIDENTIFIED.

unnatural *adj* **1** abnormal, bizarre, eccentric, eerie, extraordinary, fantastic, freak, freakish, inexplicable, magic, magical, odd, outlandish, preternatural, queer, strange, supernatural, unaccountable, uncanny, unusual, weird. **2** *unnatural feelings*. callous, cold-blooded, cruel, hard-hearted, heartless, inhuman, inhumane, monstrous, perverse, perverted, sadistic, savage, stony-hearted, unfeeling, unkind. **3** *unnatural behaviour*. actorish, affected, bogus, contrived, fake, feigned, forced, insincere, laboured, mannered, *inf* out of character, overdone, *inf* phoney, pretended, *inf* pseudo, *inf* put on, self-conscious, stagey, stiff, stilted, theatrical, uncharacteristic, unspontaneous. **4** *unnatural materials.* artificial, fabricated, imitation, man-made, manufactured, simulated, synthetic. *Opp* NATURAL.

unnecessary *adj* dispensable, excessive, expendable, extra, inessential, needless, nonessential, redundant, supererogatory, superfluous, surplus, uncalled-for, unjustified, unneeded, unwanted, useless. *Opp* NECESSARY.

unobtrusive *adj* ▷ INCONSPICUOUS.

unofficial *adj* friendly, informal, *inf* off the record, private, secret, unauthorized, unconfirmed, undocumented, unlicensed. *Opp* OFFICIAL.

unorthodox *adj* ▷ UNCONVENTIONAL.

unpaid *adj* **1** due, outstanding, owing, payable, unsettled. **2** *unpaid work.* honorary, unremunerative, unsalaried, voluntary.

unpalatable *adj* disgusting, distasteful, inedible, nasty, nauseating, *inf* off, rancid, sickening, sour, tasteless, unacceptable, unappetizing, uneatable, unpleasant. *Opp* PALATABLE.

unparalleled *adj* ▷ UNEQUALLED.

unpardonable *adj* ▷ UNFORGIVABLE.

unplanned *adj* ▷ SPONTANEOUS.

unpleasant *adj* abhorrent, abominable, antisocial, appalling, atrocious, awful, bad-tempered, beastly, bitter, coarse, crude, despicable, detestable, diabolical, dirty, disagreeable, disgusting, displeasing, distasteful, dreadful, evil, execrable, fearful, fearsome, filthy, foul, frightful, ghastly, grim, grisly, gruesome, harsh, hateful, *inf* hellish, hideous, horrible, horrid, horrifying, improper, indecent, inhuman, irksome, loathsome, *inf* lousy, malevolent, malicious, mucky, nasty, nauseating, objectionable, obnoxious, odious, offensive, *inf* off-putting, repellent, repugnant, repulsive, revolting, rude, shocking, sickening, sickly, sordid, sour, spiteful, squalid, terrible, ugly, unattractive, uncouth, undesirable, unfriendly, unkind, unpalatable, unsavoury, unwelcome, upsetting, vexing, vicious, vile, vulgar. ▷ BAD. *Opp* PLEASANT.

unpopular *adj* despised, disliked, friendless, hated, ignored, *inf* in bad odour, minority (*interests*), out of favour, rejected, shunned, unfashionable, unloved, unwanted. *Opp* POPULAR.

unpredictable *adj* changeable, surprising, uncertain, unexpected, unforeseeable, variable. *Opp* PREDICTABLE.

unprejudiced *adj* ▷ UNBIASED.

unpremeditated *adj* ▷ SPONTANEOUS.

unprepared *adj inf* caught napping, caught out, ill-equipped, surprised, taken off-guard, unready. *Opp* READY.

unpretentious *adj* humble, modest, plain, simple, straightforward, unaffected, unassuming, unostentatious, unsophisticated. *Opp* PRETENTIOUS.

unproductive *adj* **1** fruitless, futile, ineffective, pointless, unprofitable, unrewarding, useless, valueless, worthless. **2** *an unproductive garden.* arid, barren, infertile, sterile, unfruitful. *Opp* PRODUCTIVE.

unprofessional *adj* amateurish, casual, incompetent, inefficient, inexpert, lax, negligent, shoddy, *inf* sloppy, unethical, unfitting, unprincipled, unseemly, unskilful, unskilled, unworthy. *Opp* PROFESSIONAL.

unprofitable *adj* futile, lossmaking, pointless, uncommercial, uneconomic, ungainful, unproductive, unremunerative, unrewarding, worthless. *Opp* PROFITABLE.

unprovable *adj* doubtful, inconclusive, questionable, undemonstrable, unsubstantiated, unverifiable. *Opp* PROVABLE, PROVEN.

unpunctual *adj* behindhand, belated, delayed, detained, last-minute, late, overdue, tardy, unreliable. *Opp* PUNCTUAL.

unravel *vb* disentangle, free, solve, sort out, straighten out, undo, untangle.

unreal *adj* chimerical, false, fanciful, illusory, imaginary, imagined, make-believe, nonexistent, phantasmal, *inf* pretend, *inf* pseudo, sham. ▷ HYPOTHETICAL. *Opp* REAL.

unrealistic *adj* **1** inaccurate, non-representational, unconvincing, unlifelike, unnatural, unrecognizable. **2** *unrealistic ideas.* delusory, fanciful, idealistic, impossible, impracticable, impractical, over-ambitious, quixotic, romantic, silly, visionary, unreasonable, unworkable. **3** *unrealistic prices.* ▷ EXCESSIVE. *Opp* REALISTIC.

unreasonable *adj* ▷ IRRATIONAL.

unrecognizable *adj* ▷ UNIDENTIFIABLE.

unrelated *adj* **1** different, independent, unconnected, unlike. **2** ▷ IRRELEVANT. *Opp* RELATED.

unreliable *adj* **1** deceptive, false, flimsy, implausible, inaccurate, misleading, suspect, unconvincing. **2** *unreliable friends.* changeable, disreputable, fallible, fickle, inconsistent, irresponsible, treacherous, undependable, unpredictable, unsound, unstable, untrustworthy. *Opp* RELIABLE.

unrepentant *adj* brazen, confirmed, conscienceless, hardened, impenitent, incorrigible, incurable, inveterate, irredeemable, shameless, unapologetic, unashamed, unblushing, unreformable, unregenerate. *Opp* REPENTANT.

unripe *adj* green, immature, sour, unready. *Opp* RIPE.

unrivalled *adj* ▷ UNEQUALLED.

unruly *adj* ▷ UNDISCIPLINED.

unsafe *adj* ▷ DANGEROUS.

unsatisfactory *adj* defective, deficient, disappointing, displeasing, dissatisfying, faulty, frustrating, imperfect, inadequate, incompetent, inefficient, inferior, insufficient, lacking, not good enough, poor, *inf* sad (*state of affairs*), unacceptable, unhappy, unsatisfying, *inf* wretched. *Opp* SATISFACTORY.

unscrupulous *adj* amoral, conscienceless, corrupt, *inf* crooked, cunning, dishonest, dishonourable, immoral, improper, self-interested, shameless, *inf* slippery, sly, unconscionable, unethical, untrustworthy. *Opp* SCRUPULOUS.

unseemly *adj* ▷ UNBECOMING.

unseen *adj* ▷ INVISIBLE.

unselfish *adj* altruistic, caring, charitable, considerate, disinterested, generous, humanitarian, kind, liberal, magnanimous, open-handed, philanthropic, public-spirited, self-effacing, selfless, self-sacrificing, thoughtful, ungrudging, unstinting. *Opp* SELFISH.

unsightly *adj* ▷ UGLY.

unskilful *adj* amateurish, bungled, clumsy, crude, incompetent, inept, inexpert, maladroit, *inf* rough and ready, shoddy, unprofessional. *Opp* SKILFUL.

unskilled *adj* inexperienced, unqualified, untrained. *Opp* SKILLED.

unsociable *adj* ▷ UNFRIENDLY.

unsophisticated *adj* artless, childlike, guileless, ingenuous, innocent, lowbrow, naïve, plain, provincial, simple, simple-minded, straightforward, unaffected, uncomplicated, unostentatious, unpretentious, unrefined, unworldly. *Opp* SOPHISTICATED.

unsound *adj* ▷ WEAK.

unspeakable *adj* dreadful, indescribable, inexpressible, nameless, unutterable.

unspecified *adj* ▷ UNIDENTIFIED.

unstable *adj* capricious, changeable, fickle, inconsistent, inconstant, mercurial, shifting, unpredictable, unsteady, variable, volatile. *Opp* STABLE.

unsteady *adj* **1** flimsy, frail, insecure, precarious, rickety, *inf* rocky, shaky, tottering, unbalanced, unsafe, unstable, wobbly. **2** changeable, erratic, inconstant, intermittent, irregular, variable. **3** *an unsteady light.* flickering, fluctuating, quavering, quivering, trembling, tremulous, wavering. *Opp* STEADY.

unsuccessful *adj* **1** abortive, failed, fruitless, futile, ill-fated, ineffective, ineffectual, loss-making, sterile, unavailing, unlucky, unproductive, unprofitable, unsatisfactory, useless, vain, worthless. **2** *unsuccessful contestants.* beaten, defeated, foiled, hapless, losing, luckless, vanquished. *Opp* SUCCESSFUL.

unsuitable *adj* ill-chosen, ill-judged, ill-timed, inapposite, inappropriate, incongruous, inept, irrelevant, mistaken, unbefitting, unfitting, unhappy, unsatisfactory, unseasonable, unseemly, untimely. *Opp* SUITABLE.

unsure *adj* ▷ UNCERTAIN.

unsurpassed *adj* ▷ UNEQUALLED.

unsuspecting *adj* ▷ CREDULOUS.

unsympathetic *adj* apathetic, cool, cold, dispassionate, hardhearted, heartless, impassive, indifferent, insensitive, neutral, pitiless, reserved, ruthless, stony, stony-hearted, unaffected, uncaring, uncharitable, unconcerned, unfeeling, uninterested, unkind, unmoved, unpitying, unresponsive. *Opp* SYMPATHETIC.

unsystematic *adj* anarchic, chaotic, confused, disorderly, disorganized, haphazard, illogical, jumbled, muddled, *inf* shambolic, *inf* sloppy, unmethodical, unplanned, unstructured, untidy. *Opp* SYSTEMATIC.

unthinkable *adj* ▷ INCONCEIVABLE.

unthinking *adj* ▷ THOUGHTLESS.

untidy *adj* **1** careless, chaotic, cluttered, confused, disorderly, disorganized, haphazard, *inf* higgledy-piggledy, in disarray, jumbled, littered, *inf* messy, muddled, *inf* shambolic, slapdash, *inf* sloppy, slovenly, *inf* topsyturvy, unsystematic, upsidedown. **2** *untidy hair.* bedraggled, blowzy, dishevelled, disordered, rumpled, scruffy, shabby, tangled, tousled, uncared-for, uncombed, ungroomed, unkempt. *Opp* TIDY.

untie *vb* cast off (*boat*), disentangle, free, loosen, release, unbind, undo, unfasten, unknot, untether.

untried *adj* experimental, innovatory, new, novel, unproved, untested. *Opp* ESTABLISHED.

untroubled *adj* carefree, peaceful, straightforward, undisturbed, uninterrupted, unruffled.

untrue *adj* ▷ FALSE.

untrustworthy *adj* ▷ DISHONEST.

untruthful *adj* ▷ LYING.

unused *adj* blank, clean, fresh, intact, mint (*condition*), new, pristine, unopened, untouched, unworn. *Opp* USED.

unusual *adj* abnormal, atypical, curious, *inf* different, exceptional, extraordinary, *inf* freakish, *inf* funny, irregular, odd, out of the ordinary, peculiar, queer, rare, remarkable, singular, strange, surprising, uncommon, unconventional, unexpected, unfamiliar, *inf* unheard-of, *inf* unique, unnatural, unorthodox, untypical, unwonted. *Opp* USUAL.

unutterable *adj* ▷ INDESCRIBABLE.

unwanted *adj* ▷ UNNECESSARY.

unwarranted *adj* ▷ UNJUSTIFIABLE.

unwary *adj* ▷ CARELESS.

unwavering *adj* ▷ RESOLUTE.

unwelcome *adj* disagreeable, unacceptable, undesirable, uninvited, unpopular, unwanted. *Opp* WELCOME.

unwell *adj* ▷ ILL.

unwholesome *adj* ▷ UNHEALTHY.

unwieldy *adj* awkward, bulky, clumsy, cumbersome, inconvenient, ungainly, unmanageable. *Opp* HANDY, PORTABLE.

unwilling *adj* averse, backward, disinclined, grudging, half-hearted, hesitant, ill-disposed, indisposed, lazy, loath, opposed, reluctant, resistant, slow, uncooperative, unenthusiastic, unhelpful. *Opp* WILLING.

unwise *adj inf* daft, foolhardy, foolish, ill-advised, ill-judged, illogical, imperceptive, impolitic, imprudent, inadvisable, indiscreet, inexperienced, injudicious, irrational, irresponsible, mistaken, obtuse, perverse, rash, reckless, senseless, short-sighted, silly, stupid, thoughtless, unintelligent, unreasonable. *Opp* WISE.

unworldly *adj* ▷ SPIRITUAL.

unworthy *adj* contemptible, despicable, discreditable, dishonourable, disreputable, ignoble, inappropriate, mediocre, second-rate, shameful, substandard, undeserving, unsuitable. *Opp* WORTHY.

unwritten *adj* oral, spoken, verbal, *inf* word-of-mouth. *Opp* WRITTEN.

unyielding *adj* ▷ INFLEXIBLE.

upbringing *n* breeding, bringing-up, care, education, instruction, nurture, raising, rearing, teaching, training.

update *vb* amend, bring up to date, correct, modernize, review, revise.

upgrade *vb* enhance, expand, improve, make better.

upheaval *n* chaos, commotion, confusion, disorder, disruption, disturbance, revolution, *inf* to-do, turmoil.

uphill *adj* arduous, difficult, exhausting, gruelling, hard, laborious, stiff, strenuous, taxing, tough.

uphold *vb* back, champion, defend, endorse, maintain, preserve, protect, stand by, support, sustain.

upkeep *n* care, conservation, keep, maintenance, operation, preservation, running, support.

uplifting *adj* civilizing, edifying, educational, enlightening, ennobling, enriching, humanizing, improving, spiritual. *Opp* SHAMEFUL.

upper *adj* elevated, higher, raised, superior, upstairs.

uppermost *adj* dominant, highest, loftiest, supreme, top, topmost.

upright *adj* **1** erect, on end, perpendicular, vertical. **2** *an upright judge.* conscientious, fair, good, high-minded, honest, honourable, incorruptible, just, moral, principled, righteous, *inf* straight, true, trustworthy, upstanding, virtuous. • *n* column, pole, post, vertical.

uproar *n inf* bedlam, brawling, chaos, clamour, commotion, confusion, din, disorder, disturbance, furore, *inf* hubbub, *inf* hullabaloo, *inf* a madhouse, noise, outburst, outcry, pandemonium, *inf* racket, riot, row, *inf* ructions, *inf* rumpus, tumult, turbulence, turmoil.

uproot *vb* deracinate, destroy, eliminate, eradicate, extirpate, get rid of, *inf* grub up, pull up, remove, root out, tear up, weed out.

upset *vb* **1** capsize, destabilize, overturn, spill, tip over, topple. **2** *upset a plan.* affect, alter, change, confuse, defeat, disorganize, disrupt, hinder, interfere with, interrupt, jeopardize, overthrow, spoil. **3** *upset feelings.* agitate, alarm, annoy, disconcert, dismay, distress, disturb, excite, fluster, frighten, grieve, irritate, offend, perturb, *inf* rub up the wrong way, ruffle, scare, unnerve, worry.

upside-down *adj* inverted, *inf* topsy-turvy, upturned, wrong way up.

upstart *n Fr* nouveau riche, social climber, *inf* yuppie.

up-to-date *adj* **1** advanced, current, latest, modern, new, present-day, recent. **2** contemporary, fashionable, *inf* in, modish, stylish, *inf* trendy. *Opp* OLD-FASHIONED.

upward *adj* ascending, going up, rising, uphill. *Opp* DOWNWARD.

urban *adj* built-up, densely populated, metropolitan, suburban. *Opp* RURAL.

urge *n* compulsion, craving, desire, drive, eagerness, hunger, impetus, impulse, inclination, instinct, *inf* itch, longing, pressure, thirst, wish, yearning, *inf* yen. • *vb* accelerate, advise, advocate, appeal to, beg, beseech, *inf* chivvy, compel, counsel, drive, *inf* egg on, encourage, entreat, exhort, force, goad, impel, implore, importune, incite, induce, invite, move on, nag, persuade, plead with, press, prod, prompt, propel, push, recommend, solicit, spur, stimulate. *Opp* DISCOURAGE.

urgent *adj* **1** acute, compelling, compulsive, dire, essential, exigent, high-priority, immediate, imperative, important, inescapable, instant, necessary, pressing, top-priority, unavoidable. **2** *an urgent cry for help.* eager, earnest, forceful, importunate, insistent, persistent, persuasive, solicitous.

usable *adj* acceptable, current, fit to use, functional, functioning, operating, operational, serviceable, valid, working.

use *n* advantage, application, benefit, employment, function, necessity, need, *inf* point, profit, purpose, usefulness, utility, value, worth. • *vb* **1** administer, apply, deal with, employ, exercise, exploit, handle, make use of, manage, operate, put to use, utilize, wield, work. **2** consume, drink, eat, exhaust, expend, spend, use up, waste, wear out.

used *adj* cast-off, *inf* hand-medown, second-hand, soiled. *Opp* UNUSED.

useful *adj* **1** advantageous, beneficial, constructive, good, helpful, invaluable, positive, profitable, salutary, valuable, worthwhile. **2** *a useful tool.* convenient, effective, efficient, handy, powerful, practical, productive, utilitarian. **3** *a useful player.* capable, competent, effectual, proficient, skilful, successful, talented. *Opp* USELESS.

useless *adj* **1** fruitless, futile, hopeless, pointless, unavailing, unprofitable, unsuccessful, vain, worthless. **2** *inf* broken down, *inf* clapped out, dead, dud, impractical, ineffective, inefficient, unusable. **3** *a useless player.* incapable, incompetent, ineffectual, lazy, unhelpful, unskilful, unsuccessful, untalented. *Opp* USEFUL.

usual *adj* accepted, accustomed, average, common, conventional, customary, everyday, expected, familiar, general, habitual, natural, normal, official, ordinary, orthodox, predictable, prevalent, recognized, regular, routine, standard, stock, traditional, typical, unexceptional, unsurprising, well-known, widespread, wonted. *Opp* UNUSUAL.

usurp *vb* appropriate, assume, commandeer, seize, steal, take, take over.

utensil *n* appliance, device, gadget, implement, instrument, machine, tool.

utter *vb* articulate, *inf* come out with, express, pronounce, voice. ▷ SPEAK, TALK.

V

vacancy *n* job, opening, place, position, post, situation.

vacant *adj* **1** available, bare, blank, clear, empty, free, hollow, open, unfilled, unused, usable, void. **2** abandoned, deserted, uninhabited, unoccupied, untenanted. **3** *a vacant look.* absent-minded, abstracted, blank, deadpan, dreamy, expressionless, far-away, fatuous, inattentive, vacuous. *Opp* BUSY.

vacate *vb* abandon, depart from, desert, evacuate, get out of, give up, leave, quit, withdraw from.

vacuous *adj* apathetic, blank, empty-headed, expressionless, inane, mindless, uncomprehending, unintelligent, vacant. ▷ STUPID. *Opp* ALERT.

vacuum *n* emptiness, space, void.

vagary *n* caprice, fancy, fluctuation, quirk, uncertainty, unpredictability, *inf* ups and downs, whim.

vagrant *n* beggar, destitute person, *inf* down-and-out, homeless person, itinerant, tramp, traveller, vagabond, wanderer, wayfarer.

vague *adj* **1** ambiguous, ambivalent, broad, confused, diffuse, equivocal, evasive, general, generalized, imprecise, indefinable, indefinite, inexact, loose, nebulous, uncertain, unclear, undefined, unspecific, unsure, *inf* woolly. **2** amorphous, blurred, dim, hazy, ill-defined, indistinct, misty, shadowy, unrecognizable. **3** absent-minded, careless, disorganized, forgetful, inattentive, scatter-brained, thoughtless. *Opp* DEFINITE.

vain *adj* **1** arrogant, *inf* bigheaded, boastful, *inf* cocky, conceited, egotistical, haughty, narcissistic, proud, self-important, self-satisfied, *inf* stuck-up, vainglorious. *Opp* MODEST. **2** *a vain attempt.* abortive, fruitless, futile, ineffective, pointless, senseless, unavailing, unproductive, unrewarding, unsuccessful, useless, worthless. *Opp* SUCCESSFUL.

valiant *adj* bold, brave, courageous, doughty, gallant, heroic, plucky, stalwart, stout-hearted, valorous. *Opp* COWARDLY.

valid *adj* acceptable, allowed, approved, authentic, authorized, *Lat* bona fide, convincing, current, genuine, lawful, legal, legitimate, official, permissible, permitted, proper, ratified, rightful, sound, suitable, usable. *Opp* INVALID.

validate *vb* authenticate, authorize, certify, endorse, legalize, legitimize, make valid, ratify.

valley *n* canyon, chasm, coomb, dale, defile, dell, dingle, glen, gorge, gulch, gully, hollow, pass, ravine, vale.

valour *n* bravery, courage, pluck.

valuable *adj* **1** costly, dear, expensive, generous, irreplaceable, precious, priceless, prized, treasured, valued. **2** *valuable advice.* advantageous, beneficial, constructive, esteemed, helpful, invaluable, positive, profitable, useful, worthwhile. *Opp* WORTHLESS.

value *n* **1** cost, price, worth. **2** advantage, benefit, importance, merit, significance, use, usefulness. • *vb* **1** assess, estimate the value of, evaluate, price, *inf* put a figure on. **2** appreciate, care for, cherish, esteem, *inf* have a high regard for, *inf* hold dear, love, prize, respect, treasure.

vandal *n* barbarian, delinquent, hooligan, looter, marauder, Philistine, raider, ruffian, savage, thug, trouble-maker.

vanish *vb* clear, clear off, disappear, disperse, dissolve, dwindle, evaporate, fade, go away, melt away, pass. *Opp* APPEAR.

vanity *n* arrogance, *inf* bigheadedness, conceit, egotism, narcissism, pride, self-esteem.

vaporize *vb* dry up, evaporate, turn to vapour.

vapour *n* exhalation, fog, fumes, gas, haze, miasma, mist, smoke, steam.

variable *adj* capricious, changeable, erratic, fickle, fitful, fluctuating, fluid, inconsistent, inconstant, mercurial, mutable, protean, shifting, temperamental, uncertain, unpredictable, unreliable, unstable, unsteady, *inf* up-and-down, vacillating, varying, volatile, wavering. *Opp* INVARIABLE.

variation *n* alteration, change, conversion, deviation, difference, discrepancy, diversification, elaboration, modification, permutation, variant.

variety *n* **1** alteration, change, difference, diversity, unpredictability, variation. **2** array, assortment, blend, collection, combination, jumble, medley, miscellany, mixture, multiplicity. **3** brand, breed, category, class, form, kind, make, sort, species, strain, type.

various *adj* assorted, contrasting, different, differing, dissimilar, diverse, heterogeneous, miscellaneous, mixed, *inf* motley, multifarious, several, sundry, varied, varying. *Opp* SIMILAR.

vary *vb* **1** change, deviate, differ, fluctuate, go up and down, vacillate. **2** *vary your speed.* adapt, adjust, alter, convert, modify, reset, switch, transform, upset. *Opp* STABILIZE. **varied, varying** ▷ VARIOUS.

vast *adj* boundless, broad, colossal, enormous, extensive, gigantic, great, huge, immeasurable, immense, infinite, interminable, large, limitless, mammoth, massive, measureless, monumental, never-ending, titanic, tremendous, unbounded, unlimited, voluminous, wide. ▷ BIG. *Opp* SMALL.

vault *n* basement, cavern, cellar, crypt, repository, strongroom, undercroft. • *vb* bound over, clear, hurdle, jump, leap, leapfrog, spring over.

veer *vb* change direction, dodge, swerve, tack, turn, wheel.

vegetable *adj* growing, organic. • *n* □ *artichoke, asparagus, aubergine, bean, beet, beetroot, broad bean, broccoli, Brussels sprout, butter bean, cabbage, carrot, cauliflower, celeriac, celery, chicory, courgette, cress, cucumber, garlic, kale, kohlrabi, leek, lettuce, marrow, mushroom, onion, parsnip, pea, pepper, potato, pumpkin, radish, runner bean, salsify, shallot, spinach, sugar beet, swede, sweetcorn, tomato, turnip, watercress, zucchini.*

vegetate *vb* be inactive, do nothing, *inf* go to seed, idle, lose interest, stagnate.

vegetation *n* foliage, greenery, growing things, growth, plants, undergrowth, weeds.

vehement *adj* animated, ardent, eager, enthusiastic, excited, fervent, fierce, forceful, heated, impassioned, intense, passionate, powerful, strong, urgent, vigorous, violent. *Opp* APATHETIC.

vehicle *n* conveyance. □ *ambulance,* inf *buggy, bulldozer, bus, cab, camper, caravan, carriage, cart,* old use *charabanc, chariot, coach, dump truck, dustcart, estate car, fire-engine, float, gig, go-kart, hearse, horse-box, jeep, juggernaut, lorry, minibus, minicab,* inf *motor, motor car,* old use *omnibus, pantechnicon, patrol-car, pick-up, removal van, rickshaw, scooter, sedan-chair, side-car, sledge, snowplough, stage-coach, steamroller, tank, tanker, taxi, traction-engine, tractor, trailer, tram, transporter, trap, trolley-bus, truck, tumbrel, van, wagon,* sl *wheels.* ▷ CAR, CYCLE, TRAIN, VESSEL.

veil *vb* camouflage, cloak, conceal, cover, disguise, hide, mask, shroud.

vein *n* **1** artery, blood vessel, capillary. **2** *mineral vein.* bed, course, deposit, line, lode, seam, stratum. **3** ▷ MOOD.

veneer *n* coating, covering, finish, gloss, layer, surface. • *vb* ▷ COVER.

venerable *adj* aged, ancient, august, dignified, esteemed, estimable, honourable, honoured, old, respectable, respected, revered, reverenced, sedate, venerated, worshipped, worthy of respect.

venerate *vb* adore, esteem, hero-worship, honour, idolize, look up to, pay homage to, respect, revere, reverence, worship.

vengeance *n* reprisal, retaliation, retribution, revenge, *inf* tit for tat.

vengeful *adj* avenging, bitter, rancorous, revengeful, spiteful, unforgiving, vindictive. *Opp* FORGIVING.

venom *n* poison, toxin.

venomous *adj* deadly, lethal, poisonous, toxic.

vent *n* aperture, cut, duct, gap, hole, opening, orifice, outlet, passage, slit, slot, split. • *vb* articulate, express, give vent to, let go, make known, release, utter, ventilate, voice. ▷ SPEAK.

ventilate *vb* aerate, air, freshen, oxygenate.

venture *n* enterprise, experiment, gamble, risk, speculation, undertaking. • *vb* **1** bet, chance, dare, gamble, put forward, risk, speculate, stake, wager. **2** *venture out.* dare to go, risk going.

venturesome *adj* adventurous, bold, courageous, daring, doughty, fearless, intrepid.

venue *n* location, meeting-place, rendezvous.

verbal *adj* **1** lexical, linguistic. **2** *a verbal message.* oral, said, spoken, unwritten, vocal, wordof-mouth. *Opp* WRITTEN.

verbatim *adj* exact, faithful, literal, precise, word for word.

verbose *adj* diffuse, garrulous, long-winded, loquacious, prolix, rambling, repetitious, talkative, voluble. ▷ WORDY. *Opp* CONCISE.

verbosity *n inf* beating about the bush, circumlocution, diffuseness, garrulity, long-windedness, loquacity, periphrasis, prolixity, repetition, verbiage, wordiness.

verdict *n* adjudication, assessment, conclusion, decision, finding, judgement, opinion, sentence.

verge *n* bank, boundary, brim, brink, edge, hard shoulder, kerb, lip, margin, roadside, shoulder, side, threshold, wayside.

verifiable *adj* demonstrable, provable.

verify *vb* affirm, ascertain, attest to, authenticate, bear witness to, check out, confirm, corroborate, demonstrate the truth of, establish, prove, show the truth of, substantiate, support, uphold, validate, vouch for.

verisimilitude *n* authenticity, realism.

vermin *plur n* parasites, pests.

vernacular *adj* common, everyday, indigenous, local, native, ordinary, popular, vulgar.

versatile *adj* adaptable, allpurpose, all-round, flexible, gifted, multipurpose, resourceful, skilful, talented.

verse *n* lines, metre, rhyme, stanza. □ *blank verse, Chaucerian stanza, clerihew, couplet, free verse, haiku, hexameter, limerick, ottava rima, pentameter, quatrain, rhyme royal, sestina, sonnet, Spenserian stanza, terza rima, triolet, triplet, vers libre, villanelle.* ▷ POEM.

versed *adj* accomplished, competent, experienced, expert, knowledgeable, practised, proficient, skilled, taught, trained.

version *n* **1** account, description, portrayal, reading, rendition, report, story. **2** adaptation, interpretation, paraphrase, rendering, translation. **3** design, form, kind, mark, model, style, type, variant.

vertical *adj* erect, perpendicular, precipitous, sheer, upright. *Opp* HORIZONTAL.

vertigo *n* dizziness, giddiness, light-headedness.

very *adv* acutely, enormously, especially, exceedingly, extremely, greatly, highly, *inf* jolly, most, noticeably, outstandingly, particularly, really, remarkably, *inf* terribly, truly, uncommonly, unusually.

vessel *n* **1** ▷ CONTAINER. **2** bark, boat, craft, ship. □ *aircraftcarrier, barge, bathysphere, battleship, brigantine, cabin cruiser, canoe, catamaran, clipper, coaster, collier, coracle, corvette, cruise-liner, cruiser, cutter, destroyer, dhow, dinghy, dredger, dugout, ferry, freighter, frigate, galleon, galley, gondola, gunboat, houseboat, hovercraft, hydrofoil, hydroplane, ice-breaker, junk, kayak, ketch, landing-craft, launch, lifeboat, lighter, lightship, liner, longboat, lugger, man-of-war, merchant ship, minesweeper, motor boat, narrow-boat, oil-tanker, packet-ship, paddle-steamer, pontoon, power-boat, pram, privateer, punt, quinquereme, raft, rowing-boat, sailing-boat, sampan, schooner, skiff, sloop, smack, speed-boat, steamer, steamship, submarine, tanker, tender, torpedo boat, tramp steamer, trawler, trireme, troopship, tug, warship, whaler, wind-jammer, yacht, yawl.*

vet *vb inf* check out, examine, investigate, review, scrutinize.

veteran *adj* experienced, mature, old, practised. ● *n* experienced soldier, ex-serviceman, ex-servicewoman, old hand, old soldier, survivor.

veto *n* ban, block, embargo, prohibition, proscription, refusal, rejection, *inf* thumbs down. ● *vb* ban, bar, blackball, block, disallow, dismiss, forbid, prohibit, proscribe, quash, refuse, reject, rule out, say no to, turn down, vote against. *Opp* APPROVE.

vex *vb inf* aggravate, annoy, bother, displease, exasperate, harass, irritate, provoke, *inf* put out, trouble, upset, worry. ▷ ANGER.

viable *adj* achievable, feasible, operable, possible, practicable, practical, realistic, reasonable, supportable, sustainable, usable, workable. *Opp* IMPRACTICAL.

vibrant *adj* alert, alive, dynamic, electric, energetic, lively, living, pulsating, quivering, resonant, thrilling, throbbing, trembling, vibrating, vivacious. *Opp* LIFELESS.

vibrate *vb* fluctuate, judder, oscillate, pulsate, quake, quiver, rattle, resonate, reverberate, shake, shiver, shudder, throb, tremble, wobble.

vibration *n* juddering, oscillation, pulsation, quivering, rattling, resonance, reverberation, shaking, shivering, shuddering, throbbing, trembling, tremor.

vicarious *adj* delegated, deputed, indirect, second-hand, surrogate.

vice *n* **1** badness, corruption, degeneracy, degradation, depravity, evil, evil-doing, immorality, iniquity, lechery, profligacy, promiscuity, sin, venality, villainy, wickedness, wrongdoing. **2** bad habit, blemish, defect, failing, fault, flaw, foible, imperfection, shortcoming, weakness.

vicinity *n* area, district, environs, locale, locality, neighbourhood, outskirts, precincts, proximity, purlieus, region, sector, territory, zone.

vicious *adj* **1** atrocious, barbaric, barbarous, beastly, bloodthirsty, brutal, callous, cruel, diabolical, fiendish, heinous, hurtful, inhuman, merciless, monstrous, murderous, pitiless, ruthless, sadistic, savage, unfeeling, vile, violent. **2** *a vicious character.* bad, *inf* bitchy, *inf* catty, depraved, evil, heartless, immoral, malicious, mean, perverted, rancorous, sinful, spiteful, venomous, villainous, vindictive, vitriolic, wicked. **3** *vicious animals.* aggressive, bad-tempered, dangerous, ferocious, fierce, snappy, untamed, wild. **4** *a vicious wind.* cutting, nasty, severe, sharp, unpleasant. *Opp* GENTLE.

vicissitude *n* alteration, change, flux, instability, mutability, mutation, shift, uncertainty, unpredictability, variability.

victim *n* **1** casualty, fatality, injured person, patient, sufferer, wounded person. **2** *sacrificial victim.* martyr, offering, prey, sacrifice.

victimize *vb* bully, cheat, discriminate against, exploit, intimidate, oppress, persecute, *inf* pick on, prey on, take advantage of, terrorize, torment, treat unfairly, *inf* use. ▷ CHEAT.

victor *n* champion, conqueror, prizewinner, winner. *Opp* LOSER.

victorious *adj* champion, conquering, first, leading, prevailing, successful, top, top-scoring, triumphant, unbeaten, undefeated, winning. *Opp* UNSUCCESSFUL.

victory *n* achievement, conquest, knockout, mastery, success, superiority, supremacy, triumph, *inf* walkover, win. *Opp* DEFEAT.

vie *vb* compete, contend, strive, struggle.

view *n* **1** aspect, landscape, outlook, panorama, perspective, picture, prospect, scene, scenery, seascape, spectacle, townscape, vista. **2** angle, look, perspective, sight, vision. **3** *political views.* attitude, belief, conviction, idea, judgement, notion, opinion, perception, position, thought. • *vb* **1** behold, consider, contemplate, examine, eye, gaze at, inspect, observe, perceive, regard, scan, stare at, survey, witness. **2** *view TV.* look at, see, watch.

viewer *n plur* audience, observer, onlooker, spectator, watcher, witness.

viewpoint *n* angle, perspective, point of view, position, slant, standpoint.

vigilant *adj* alert, attentive, awake, careful, circumspect, eagle-eyed, observant, on the watch, on your guard, *inf* on your toes, sharp, wakeful, wary, watchful, wideawake. *Opp* NEGLIGENT.

vigorous *adj* active, alive, animated, brisk, dynamic, energetic, fit, flourishing, forceful, full-blooded, *inf* full of beans, growing, hale and hearty, healthy, lively, lusty, potent, prosperous, red-blooded, robust, spirited, strenuous, strong, thriving, virile, vital, vivacious, zestful. *Opp* FEEBLE.

vigour *n* animation, dynamism, energy, fitness, force, forcefulness, gusto, health, life, liveliness, might, potency, power, robustness, spirit, stamina, strength, verve, *inf* vim, virility, vitality, vivacity, zeal, zest.

vile *adj* bad, base, contemptible, degenerate, depraved, despicable, disgusting, evil, execrable, filthy, foul, hateful, horrible, immoral, loathsome, low, nasty, nauseating, obnoxious, odious, offensive, perverted, repellent, repugnant, repulsive, revolting, sickening, sinful, ugly, vicious, wicked.

vilify *vb* abuse, calumniate, defame, denigrate, deprecate, disparage, revile, *inf* run down, slander, *inf* smear, speak evil of, traduce, vituperate.

villain *n* blackguard, criminal, evildoer, malefactor, mischiefmaker, miscreant, reprobate, rogue, scoundrel, sinner, wretch. ▷ CRIMINAL.

villainous *adj* bad, corrupt, criminal, dishonest, evil, sinful, treacherous, vile. ▷ WICKED.

vindictive *adj* avenging, malicious, nasty, punitive, rancorous, revengeful, spiteful, unforgiving, vengeful, vicious. *Opp* FORGIVING.

vintage *adj* choice, classic, fine, good, high-quality, mature, mellowed, old, seasoned, venerable.

violate *vb* **1** breach, break, contravene, defy, disobey, disregard, flout, ignore, infringe, overstep, sin against, transgress. **2** *violate someone's privacy.* abuse, desecrate, disturb, invade, profane. **3** [*of men*] *violate a woman.* assault, attack, debauch, dishonour, force yourself on, rape, ravish.

violation *n* breach, contravention, defiance, flouting, infringement, invasion, offence (against), transgression.

violent *adj* **1** acute, damaging, dangerous, destructive, devastating, explosive, ferocious, fierce, forceful, furious, hard, harmful, intense, powerful, rough, ruinous, savage, severe, strong, swingeing, tempestuous, turbulent, uncontrollable, vehement, wild. **2** *violent behaviour.* barbaric, berserk, bloodthirsty, brutal, cruel, desperate, frenzied, headstrong, homicidal, murderous, riotous, rowdy, ruthless, uncontrolled, unruly, vehement, vicious, wild. *Opp* GENTLE.

VIP *n* celebrity, dignitary, important person.

virile *adj derog* macho, manly, masculine, potent, vigorous.

virtue *n* **1** decency, fairness, goodness, high-mindedness, honesty, honour, integrity, justice, morality, nobility, principle, rectitude, respectability, righteousness, right-mindedness, sincerity, uprightness, worthiness. **2** advantage, asset, good point, merit, quality, *inf* redeeming feature, strength. **3** *sexual virtue.* abstinence, chastity, honour, innocence, purity, virginity. *Opp* VICE.

virtuoso *n* expert, genius, maestro, prodigy, showman, *inf* wizard. ▷ MUSICIAN.

virtuous *adj* blameless, chaste, decent, ethical, exemplary, fair, God-fearing, good, *derog* goodygoody, high-minded, high-principled, honest, honourable, innocent, irreproachable, just, law-abiding, moral, noble, praiseworthy, principled, pure, respectable, right, righteous, right-minded, sincere, *derog* smug, spotless, trustworthy, uncorrupted, unimpeachable, unsullied, upright, virginal, worthy. *Opp* WICKED.

virulent *adj* **1** dangerous, deadly, lethal, life-threatening, noxious, pernicious, poisonous, toxic, venomous. **2** *virulent abuse.* acrimonious, bitter, hostile, malicious, malign, malignant, mordant, nasty, spiteful, splenetic, vicious, vitriolic.

viscous *adj* gluey, sticky, syrupy, thick, viscid. *Opp* RUNNY.

visible *adj* apparent, clear, conspicuous, detectable, discernible, distinct, evident, manifest, noticeable, observable, obvious, open, perceivable, perceptible, plain, recognizable, unconcealed, undisguised, unmistakable. *Opp* INVISIBLE.

vision *n* **1** eyesight, perception, sight. **2** apparition, chimera, day-dream, delusion, fantasy, ghost, hallucination, illusion, mirage, phantasm, phantom, spectre, spirit, wraith. **3** *a man of vision.* far-sightedness, foresight, imagination, insight, spirituality, understanding.

visionary *adj* dreamy, fanciful, far-sighted, futuristic, idealistic, imaginative, impractical, mystical, prophetic, quixotic, romantic, speculative, transcendental, unrealistic, Utopian. ● *n* dreamer, idealist, mystic, poet, prophet, romantic, seer.

visit *n* **1** call, *old use* sojourn, stay, stop, visitation. **2** day out, excursion, outing, trip. ● *vb* call on, come to see, *inf* descend on, *inf* drop in on, go to see, *inf* look up, make a visit to, pay a call on, *inf* pop in on, stay with. **visit regularly** ▷ HAUNT.

visitor *n* **1** caller, *plur* company, guest. **2** holiday-maker, sightseer, tourist, traveller, tripper. **3** *a visitor from abroad.* alien, foreigner, migrant, visitant.

visor *n* protector, shield, sun-shield.

vista *n* landscape, outlook, panorama, prospect, scene, scenery, seascape, view.

visualize *vb* conceive, dream up, envisage, imagine, picture.

vital *adj* **1** alive, animate, animated, dynamic, energetic, exuberant, life-giving, live, lively, living, sparkling, spirited, sprightly, vigorous, vivacious, zestful. *Opp* LIFELESS. **2** *vital information.* compulsory, current, crucial, essential, fundamental, imperative, important, indispensable, mandatory, necessary, needed, relevant, requisite. *Opp* INESSENTIAL.

vitality *n* animation, dynamism, energy, exuberance, *inf* go, life, liveliness, *inf* sparkle, spirit, sprightliness, stamina, strength, vigour, *inf* vim, vivacity, zest.

vitriolic *adj* abusive, acid, biting, bitter, caustic, cruel, destructive, hostile, hurtful, malicious, savage, scathing, vicious, vindictive, virulent.

vituperate *vb* abuse, berate, calumniate, censure, defame, denigrate, deprecate, disparage, reproach, revile, *inf* run down, slander, upbraid, vilify.

vivacious *adj* animated, bubbly, cheerful, ebullient, energetic, high-spirited, light-hearted, lively, merry, positive, spirited, sprightly. *Opp* LETHARGIC.

vivid *adj* **1** bright, brilliant, colourful, dazzling, fresh, *derog* gaudy, gay, gleaming, glowing, intense, rich, shining, showy, strong, vibrant. **2** *a vivid description.* clear, detailed, graphic, imaginative, lifelike, lively, memorable, powerful, realistic, striking. *Opp* LIFELESS.

vocabulary *n* **1** diction, lexis, words. **2** dictionary, glossary, lexicon, phrase book, word-list.

vocal *adj* **1** oral, said, spoken, sung, voiced. **2** *vocal in discussion.* communicative, forthcoming, loquacious, outspoken, talkative, vociferous. *Opp* TACITURN.

vocation *n* calling, career, employment, job, life's work, occupation, profession, trade.

vogue *n* craze, fad, fashion, *inf* latest thing, mode, rage, style, taste, trend. **in vogue** ▷ FASHIONABLE.

voice *n* accent, articulation, expression, idiolect, inflexion, intonation, singing, sound, speaking, speech, tone, utterance. • *vb* ▷ SPEAK.

void *adj* **1** blank, empty, unoccupied, vacant. **2** *a void contract.* annulled, cancelled, inoperative, invalid, not binding, unenforceable, useless. • *n* blank, emptiness, nothingness, space, vacancy, vacuum.

volatile *adj* **1** explosive, sensitive, unstable. **2** *volatile moods.* changeable, erratic, fickle, flighty, inconstant, lively, mercurial, temperamental, unpredictable, *inf* up and down, variable. *Opp* STABLE.

volley *n* barrage, bombardment, burst, cannonade, fusillade, salvo, shower.

voluble *adj* chatty, fluent, garrulous, glib, loquacious, talkative. ▷ WORDY.

volume *n* **1** *old use* tome. ▷ BOOK. **2** *volume of a container.* aggregate, amount, bulk, capacity, dimensions, mass, measure, quantity, size.

voluminous *adj* ample, billowing, bulky, capacious, cavernous, enormous, extensive, gigantic, great, huge, immense, large, mammoth, massive, roomy, spacious, vast. ▷ BIG. *Opp* SMALL.

voluntary *adj* **1** elective, free, gratuitous, optional, spontaneous, unpaid, willing. *Opp* COMPULSORY. **2** *a voluntary act.* conscious, deliberate, intended, intentional, planned, premeditated, wilful. *Opp* INVOLUNTARY.

volunteer *vb* **1** be willing, offer, propose, put yourself forward. **2** ▷ ENLIST.

voluptuous *adj* **1** hedonistic, luxurious, pleasure-loving, self-indulgent, sensual, sybaritic, **2** *voluptuous figure.* attractive, buxom, *inf* curvaceous, desirable, erotic, sensual, *inf* sexy, shapely, *inf* well-endowed.

vomit *vb* be sick, *inf* bring up, disgorge, *inf* heave up, *inf* puke, regurgitate, retch, *inf* spew up, *inf* throw up.

voracious *adj* avid, eager, fervid, gluttonous, greedy, hungry, insatiable, keen, ravenous, thirsty.

vortex *n* eddy, spiral, whirlpool, whirlwind.

vote *n* ballot, election, plebiscite, poll, referendum, show of hands. • *vb* ballot, cast your vote. **vote for** choose, elect, nominate, opt for, pick, return, select, settle on.

vouch *vb* **vouch for** answer for, back, certify, endorse, guarantee, speak for, sponsor, support.

voucher *n* coupon, ticket, token.

vow *n* assurance, guarantee, oath, pledge, promise, undertaking, word of honour. • *vb* declare, give an assurance, give your word, guarantee, pledge, promise, swear, take an oath.

voyage *n* cruise, journey, passage. • *vb* circumnavigate, cruise, sail. ▷ TRAVEL.

vulgar *adj* **1** churlish, coarse, common, crude, foul, gross, ill-bred, impolite, improper, indecent, indecorous, low, offensive, rude, uncouth, ungentlemanly, unladylike. ▷ OBSCENE. *Opp* POLITE. **2** *vulgar colour scheme*. crude, gaudy, inartistic, in bad taste, inelegant, insensitive, lowbrow, plebeian, tasteless, tawdry, unrefined, unsophisticated. *Opp* TASTEFUL.

vulnerable *adj* **1** at risk, defenceless, exposed, helpless, unguarded, unprotected, weak, wide open. **2** easily hurt, sensitive, thin-skinned, touchy. *Opp* RESILIENT.

W

wad *n* bundle, lump, mass, pack, pad, plug, roll.

wadding *n* filling, lining, packing, padding, stuffing.

wade *vb* ford, paddle, splash. ▷ WALK.

waffle *n* evasiveness, padding, prevarication, prolixity, verbiage, wordiness. • *vb inf* beat about the bush, *inf* blather on, hedge, prattle, prevaricate.

waft *vb* **1** be borne, drift, float, travel. **2** bear, carry, convey, puff, transmit, transport.

wag *vb* bob, flap, move to and fro, nod, oscillate, rock, shake, sway, undulate, *inf* waggle, wave, *inf* wiggle.

wage *n* compensation, earnings, emolument, honorarium, income, pay, pay packet, recompense, remuneration, reward, salary, stipend. • *vb* carry on, conduct, engage in, fight, prosecute, pursue, undertake.

wager *vb* bet, gamble.

wail *vb* caterwaul, complain, cry, howl, lament, moan, shriek, waul, weep, *inf* yowl.

waist *n* middle, waistline.

waistband *n* belt, cummerbund, girdle.

wait *n* delay, halt, hesitation, hiatus, *inf* hold-up, intermission, interval, pause, postponement, rest, stay, stop, stoppage. • *vb* **1** *old use* bide, delay, halt, *inf* hang about, *inf* hang on, hesitate, hold back, keep still, linger, mark time, pause, remain, rest, *inf* sit tight, stand by, stay, stop, *old use* tarry. **2** *wait at table.* serve.

waive *vb* abandon, cede, disclaim, dispense with, forgo, give up, relinquish, remit, renounce, resign, sign away, surrender.

wake *n* **1** funeral, vigil, watch. **2** *wake of a ship*. path, track, trail, turbulence, wash. • *vb* **1** arouse, awaken, bring to life, call, disturb, galvanize, rouse, stimulate, stir, waken. **2** become conscious, bestir yourself, *inf* come to life, get up, rise, *inf* stir, wake up. **wake up to** ▷ REALIZE. **waking** ▷ CONSCIOUS.

wakeful *adj* alert, awake, insomniac, *inf* on the qui vive, restless, sleepless.

walk *n* **1** bearing, carriage, gait, stride. **2** constitutional, hike, *old use* promenade, ramble, saunter, stroll, traipse, tramp, trek, trudge, *inf* turn. **3** *a paved walk*. aisle, alley, path, pathway, pavement. • *vb* **1** be a pedestrian, travel on foot. □ *amble, crawl, creep, dodder,* inf *foot-slog, hike, hobble, limp, lope, lurch, march, mince, sl mooch, pace, pad, paddle, parade, old use perambulate, plod, promenade, prowl, ramble, saunter, scuttle, shamble, shuffle, slink, stagger, stalk, steal, step, inf stomp, stride, stroll, strut, stumble, swagger, tiptoe, inf toddle, totter, traipse, tramp, trample, trek, troop, trot, trudge, waddle, wade.* **2** *don't walk on the flowers*. stamp, step, trample, tread. **walk away with** ▷ WIN. **walk off with** ▷ STEAL. **walk out** ▷ QUIT. **walk out on** ▷ DESERT.

walker *n* hiker, pedestrian, rambler.

wall *n* □ *barricade, barrier, bulkhead, bulwark, dam, dike, divider, embankment, fence, fortification, hedge, obstacle, paling, palisade, parapet, partition, rampart, screen, sea-wall, stockade.* **wall in** ▷ ENCLOSE.

wallet *n* notecase, pocketbook, pouch, purse.

wallow *vb* **1** flounder, lie, pitch about, roll about, stagger about, tumble, wade, welter. **2** *wallow in luxury.* glory, indulge yourself, luxuriate, revel, take delight.

wan *adj* anaemic, ashen, bloodless, colourless, exhausted, faint, feeble, livid, pale, pallid, pasty, sickly, tired, waxen, worn.

wand *n* baton, rod, staff, stick.

wander *vb* **1** drift, go aimlessly, meander, prowl, ramble, range, roam, rove, saunter, stray, stroll, travel about, walk, wind. **2** *wander off course.* curve, deviate, digress, drift, err, go off at a tangent, stray, swerve, turn, twist, veer, zigzag. **wandering** ▷ INATTENTIVE, NOMADIC.

wane *vb* decline, decrease, dim, diminish, dwindle, ebb, fade, fail, *inf* fall off, grow less, lessen, peter out, shrink, subside, taper off, weaken. *Opp* STRENGTHEN.

want *n* **1** demand, desire, need, requirement, wish. **2** *a want of ready cash.* absence, lack, need. **3** *war against want.* dearth, famine, hunger, insufficiency, penury, poverty, privation, scarcity, shortage. • *vb* **1** aspire to, covet, crave, demand, desire, fancy, hanker after, *inf* have a yen for, hunger for, *inf* itch for, like, long for, miss, pine for, please, prefer, *inf* set your heart on, thirst after, thirst for, wish for, yearn for. **2** *want manners.* be short of, lack, need, require.

war *n* campaign, conflict, crusade, fighting, hostilities, military action, strife, warfare. □ *ambush, assault, attack, battle, blitz, blockade, bombardment, counter-attack, engagement, guerrilla warfare, invasion, manoeuvres, operations, resistance, siege, skirmish.* **wage war** ▷ FIGHT.

ward *n* charge, dependant, minor. • *vb* **ward off** avert, beat off, block, chase away, check, deflect, fend off, forestall, parry, push away, repel, repulse, stave off, thwart, turn aside.

warder *n* gaoler, guard, jailer, keeper, prison officer.

warehouse *n* depository, depot, store, storehouse.

wares *plur n* commodities, goods, manufactures, merchandise, produce, stock, supplies.

warlike *adj* aggressive, bellicose, belligerent, hawkish, hostile, militant, militaristic, pugnacious, warmongering, warring.

warm *adj* **1** close, hot, lukewarm, subtropical, sultry, summery, temperate, tepid, warmish. **2** *warm clothes.* cosy, thermal, thick, winter, woolly. **3** *a warm welcome.* affable, affectionate, ardent, cordial, emotional, enthusiastic, excited, fervent, friendly, genial, impassioned, kind, loving, passionate, sympathetic, warm-hearted. *Opp* COLD, UNFRIENDLY. • *vb* heat, make warmer, melt, raise the temperature of, thaw, thaw out. *Opp* COOL.

warn *vb* admonish, advise, alert, caution, counsel, forewarn, give a warning, give notice, inform, notify, raise the alarm, remind, *inf* tip off.

warning *n* **1** advance notice, augury, forewarning, hint, indication, notice, notification, omen, portent, premonition, presage, prophecy, reminder, sign, signal, threat, *inf* tip-off, *inf* word to the wise. □ *alarm, alarm-bell, beacon, bell, fire-alarm, flashing light, fog-horn, gong, hooter, red light, siren, traffic-lights, whistle.* **2** *let off with a warning.* admonition, advice, caution, caveat, reprimand.

warp *vb* become deformed, bend, buckle, contort, curl, curve, deform, distort, kink, twist.

warrant *n* authority, authorization, certification, document, entitlement, guarantee, licence, permit, pledge, sanction, search-warrant, voucher, warranty. • *vb* ▷ JUSTIFY.

wary *adj* alert, apprehensive, attentive, *inf* cagey, careful, cautious, chary, circumspect, distrustful, heedful, observant, on the lookout, on your guard, suspicious, vigilant, watchful. *Opp* RECKLESS.

wash *n old use* ablutions, bath, rinse, shampoo, shower. ● *vb* **1** clean, cleanse, flush, launder, mop, rinse, scrub, shampoo, sluice, soap down, sponge down, swab down, swill, wipe. **2** bath, bathe, *old use* make your toilet, perform your ablutions, shower. **3** *The sea washes against the cliff.* break, dash, flow, lap, pound, roll, splash. **wash your hands of** ▷ ABANDON.

washing *n* cleaning, dirty clothes, laundry, *inf* the wash.

washout *n* débâcle, disappointment, disaster, failure, *inf* flop.

waste *adj* **1** discarded, extra, superfluous, unprofitable, unusable, unused, unwanted, worthless. **2** *waste land.* bare, barren, derelict, empty, overgrown, run-down, uncared-for, uncultivated, undeveloped, unproductive, wild. ● *n* **1** debris, dregs, effluent, excess, garbage, junk, leavings, *inf* left-overs, litter, offcuts, refuse, remnants, rubbish, scrap, scraps, trash, unusable material, unwanted material, wastage. **2** extravagance, indulgence, overprovision, prodigality, profligacy, self-indulgence. ● *vb* be wasteful with, dissipate, fritter, misspend, misuse, over provide, *sl* splurge, squander, use up, use wastefully. *Opp* CONSERVE. **waste away** become emaciated, become thin, become weaker, mope, pine, weaken.

wasteful *adj* excessive, expensive, extravagant, improvident, imprudent, lavish, needless, prodigal, profligate, reckless, spendthrift, thriftless, uneconomical, unthrifty. *Opp* ECONOMICAL. **wasteful person** ▷ SPENDTHRIFT.

watch *n* chronometer, clock, digital watch, stop-watch, timepiece, timer, wrist-watch. ● *vb* **1** attend, concentrate, contemplate, eye, gaze, heed, keep an eye open for, keep your eyes on, look at, mark, note, observe, pay attention, regard, see, spy on, stare, take notice, view. **2** *watch sheep.* care for, chaperon, defend, guard, keep an eye on, keep watch on, look after, mind, protect, safeguard, shield, superintend, supervise, take charge of, tend. **keep watch** ▷ GUARD. **on the watch** ▷ WATCHFUL. **watch your step** ▷ BEWARE.

watcher *n plur* audience, *inf* looker-on, observer, onlooker, spectator, viewer, witness.

watchful *adj* attentive, eagleeyed, heedful, observant, *inf* on the look-out, *inf* on the qui vive, on the watch, quick, sharp-eyed, vigilant. ▷ ALERT. *Opp* INATTENTIVE.

watchman *n* caretaker, custodian, guard, lookout, night-watchman, security guard, sentinel, sentry, watch.

water *n* **1** Adam's ale, bath water, brine, distilled water, drinking water, mineral water, rainwater, sea water, spa water, spring water, tap water. **2** lake, lido, ocean, pond, pool, river, sea. ▷ STREAM. ● *vb* damp, dampen, douse, drench, flood, hose, inundate, irrigate, moisten, saturate, soak, souse, spray, sprinkle, wet. **water down** ▷ DILUTE.

waterfall *n* cascade, cataract, chute, rapids, torrent, white water.

waterlogged *adj* full of water, saturated, soaked.

waterproof *adj* damp-proof, impermeable, impervious, water-repellent, water-resistant, watertight, weatherproof. *Opp* LEAKY. ● *n* cape, groundsheet, *inf* mac, mackintosh, sou'wester.

watertight *adj* hermetic, sealed, sound. ▷ WATERPROOF.

watery *adj* **1** aqueous, bland, characterless, dilute, diluted, fluid, liquid, *inf* runny, *inf* sloppy, tasteless, thin, watered-down, weak, *inf* wishy-washy. **2** *watery eyes.* damp, moist, tear-filled, tearful, *inf* weepy. ▷ WET.

wave *n* **1** billow, breaker, crest, heave, ridge, ripple, roller, surf, swell, tidal wave, undulation, wavelet, *inf* white horse. **2** flourish, gesticulation, gesture, shake, sign, signal. **3** *a wave of enthusiasm.* current, flood, ground swell, outbreak, surge, tide, upsurge. **4** *a new wave.* advance, fashion, tendency, trend. **5** *radio waves.* pulse, vibration. ● *vb* **1** billow, brandish, flail about, flap, flourish, fluctuate, flutter, move to and fro, ripple, shake, sway, swing, twirl, undulate, waft, wag, waggle, wiggle, zigzag. **2** gesticulate, gesture, indicate, sign, signal. **wave aside** ▷ DISMISS.

wavelength *n* channel, station, waveband.

waver *vb inf* be in two minds, be unsteady, change, falter, flicker, hesitate, quake, quaver, quiver, shake, shiver, shudder, sway, teeter, tergiversate, totter, tremble, vacillate, wobble.

wavy *adj* curling, curly, curving, heaving, rippling, rolling, sinuous, undulating, up and down, winding, zigzag. *Opp* FLAT, STRAIGHT.

way *n* **1** advance, direction, headway, journey, movement, progress, route. ▷ ROAD. **2** distance, length, measurement. **3** *a way to do something.* approach, avenue, course, fashion, knack, manner, means, method, mode, *Lat* modus operandi, path, procedure, process, system, technique. **4** *foreign ways.* custom, fashion, habit, *Lat* modus vivendi, practice, routine, style, tradition. **5** *funny ways.* characteristic, eccentricity, idiosyncrasy, oddity, peculiarity. **6** *in some ways.* aspect, circumstance, detail, feature, particular, respect.

waylay *vb* accost, ambush, await, buttonhole, detain, intercept, lie in wait for, pounce on, surprise. ▷ ATTACK.

wayward *adj* disobedient, headstrong, obstinate, self-willed, stubborn, uncontrollable, uncooperative, wilful. ▷ NAUGHTY. *Opp* COOPERATIVE.

weak *adj* **1** breakable, brittle, decrepit, delicate, feeble, flawed, flimsy, fragile, frail, frangible, inadequate, insubstantial, rickety, shaky, slight, substandard, tender, thin, unsafe, unsound, unsteady, unsubstantial. **2** *weak in health.* anaemic, debilitated, delicate, enervated, exhausted, feeble, flabby, frail, helpless, ill, infirm, listless, *inf* low, *inf* poorly, puny, sickly, slight, thin, tired out, wasted, weakly, *derog* weedy. **3** *a weak character.* cowardly, fearful, impotent, indecisive, ineffective, ineffectual, irresolute, poor, powerless, pusillanimous, spineless, timid, timorous, unassertive, weak-minded, wimpish. **4** *a weak position.* defenceless, exposed, unguarded, unprotected, vulnerable. **5** *weak excuses.* hollow, lame, *inf* pathetic, shallow, unbelievable, unconvincing, unsatisfactory. **6** *weak light.* dim, distant, fading, faint, indistinct, pale, poor, unclear, vague. **7** *weak tea.* dilute, diluted, tasteless, thin, watery. *Opp* STRONG.

weaken *vb* **1** debilitate, destroy, dilute, diminish, emasculate, enervate, enfeeble, erode, exhaust, impair, lessen, lower, make weaker, reduce, ruin, sap, soften, thin down, undermine, *inf* water down. **2** abate, become weaker, decline, decrease, dwindle, ebb, fade, flag, give in, give way, sag, wane, yield. *Opp* STRENGTHEN.

weakling *n* coward, *inf* milksop, *inf* pushover, *inf* runt, *inf* softie, weak person, *inf* weed, *inf* wimp.

weakness *n* **1** *inf* Achilles' heel, blemish, defect, error, failing, fault, flaw, flimsiness, foible, fragility, frailty, imperfection, inadequacy, mistake, shortcoming, softness, *inf* weak spot. **2** debility, decrepitude, delicacy, feebleness, impotence, incapacity, infirmity, lassitude, vulnerability. ▷ ILLNESS. **3** *a weakness for wine.* affection, fancy, fondness, inclination, liking, partiality, penchant, predilection, *inf* soft spot, taste. *Opp* STRENGTH.

wealth *n* **1** affluence, assets, capital, fortune, *old use* lucre, means, opulence, possessions, property, prosperity, riches, *old use* substance. ▷ MONEY. *Opp* POVERTY. **2** *a wealth of information.* abundance, bounty, copiousness, cornucopia, mine, plenty, profusion, store, treasury. *Opp* SCARCITY.

wealthy *adj* affluent, *inf* flush, *inf* loaded, moneyed, opulent, *joc* plutocratic, privileged, prosperous, rich, *inf* well-heeled, well-off, well-to-do. *Opp* POOR. **wealthy person** billionaire, capitalist, millionaire, plutocrat, tycoon.

weapon *n* bomb, gun, missile. □ *air-gun, arrow, atom bomb, ballistic missile, battering-ram, battleaxe, bayonet, bazooka, blowpipe, blunderbuss, boomerang, bow and arrow, bren-gun, cannon, carbine, catapult, claymore, cosh, crossbow, CS gas, cudgel, cutlass, dagger, depth-charge, dirk, flame-thrower, foils, grenade,* old use *halberd, harpoon, H-bomb, howitzer, incendiary bomb, javelin, knuckleduster, lance, land-mine, laser beam, longbow, machete, machine-gun, mine, mortar, musket, mustard gas, napalm bomb, pike, pistol, pole-axe, rapier, revolver, rifle, rocket, sabre, scimitar, shotgun, inf six-shooter, sling, spear, sten-gun, stiletto, sub-machine-gun, sword, tank, tear-gas, time-bomb, tomahawk, tommy-gun, torpedo, truncheon, warhead, water-cannon.* **weapons** armaments, armoury, arms, arsenal, magazine, munitions, ordnance, weaponry. □ *artillery, automatic weapons, biological weapons, chemical weapons, firearms, missiles, nuclear weapons, small arms, strategic weapons, tactical weapons.*

wear *vb* **1** be dressed in, clothe yourself in, don, dress in, have on, present yourself in, put on, wrap up in. **2** *wear a smile.* adopt, assume, display, exhibit, show. **3** *wears the carpet.* damage, fray, injure, mark, scuff, weaken, wear away. **4** *wear well.* endure, last, *inf* stand the test of time, survive. **wear away** ▷ ERODE. **wear off** ▷ SUBSIDE. **wear out** ▷ WEARY.

wearisome *adj* boring, dreary, exhausting, monotonous, repetitive, tedious, tiring, wearying. ▷ TROUBLESOME. *Opp* STIMULATING.

weary *adj* bone-weary, *inf* dead beat, *inf* dog-tired, *inf* done in, drained, drawn, drowsy, enervated, exhausted, *inf* fagged, fatigued, fed up, flagging, foot-sore, impatient, jaded, *inf* jetlagged, *sl* knackered, listless, prostrate, *inf* shattered, *inf* sick (of), sleepy, spent, tired out, travel-weary, wearied, *inf* whacked, worn out. *Opp* FRESH, LIVELY. ● *vb* **1** debilit-ate, drain, enervate, exhaust, fatigue, *inf* finish, make tired, *sl* knacker, overtire, sap, *inf* shatter, *inf* take it out of, tax, tire, wear out. *Opp* REFRESH. **2** become bored, become tired, flag, grow weary, weaken.

weather *n* climate, the elements, meteorological conditions. □ *blizzard, breeze, cloud, cyclone, deluge, dew, downpour, drizzle, drought, fog, frost, gale, hail, haze, heatwave, hoar-frost, hurricane, ice, lightning, mist, rain, rainbow, shower, sleet, slush, snow, snowstorm, squall, storm, sunshine, tempest, thaw, thunder, tornado, typhoon, whirlwind, wind.* ● *vb* ▷ SURVIVE. **under the weather** ▷ ILL.

weave *vb* **1** braid, criss-cross, entwine, interlace, intertwine, interweave, knit, plait, sew. **2** *weave a story.* compose, create, make, plot, put together. **3** *weave through a crowd.* dodge, make your way, tack, *inf* twist and turn, wind, zigzag.

web *n* criss-cross, lattice, mesh, net, network.

wedding *n* marriage, nuptials, union.

wedge *vb* cram, force, jam, pack, squeeze, stick.

weep *vb* bawl, *inf* blub, blubber, cry, *inf* grizzle, lament, mewl, moan, shed tears, snivel, sob, wail, whimper, whine.

weigh *vb* **1** measure the weight of. **2** *weigh evidence.* assess, consider, contemplate, evaluate, judge, ponder, reflect on, think about, weigh up. **3** *evidence weighed with the jury.* be important, carry weight, count, *inf* cut ice, have weight, matter. **weigh down** ▷ BURDEN. **weigh up** ▷ EVALUATE.

weighing-machine *n* balance, scales, spring-balance, weighbridge.

weight *n* **1** avoirdupois, burden, density, heaviness, load, mass, pressure, strain, tonnage. **2** *My voice has some weight.* authority, credibility, emphasis, force, gravity, importance, power, seriousness, significance, substance, value, worth. • *vb* ballast, bias, hold down, keep down, load, make heavy, weigh down.

weird *adj* **1** creepy, eerie, ghostly, mysterious, preternatural, scary, *inf* spooky, supernatural, unaccountable, uncanny, unearthly, unnatural. **2** *weird behaviour.* abnormal, bizarre, *inf* cranky, curious, eccentric, *inf* funny, grotesque, odd, outlandish, peculiar, queer, quirky, strange, unconventional, unusual, *inf* way-out, *inf* zany. *Opp* CONVENTIONAL, NATURAL.

welcome *adj* acceptable, accepted, agreeable, appreciated, desirable, gratifying, much-needed, *inf* nice, pleasant, pleasing, pleasurable. *Opp* UNWELCOME. • *n* greeting, hospitality, reception, salutation. • *vb* **1** give a welcome to, greet, hail, receive. **2** *They welcome criticism.* accept, appreciate, approve of, delight in, like, want.

weld *vb* bond, cement, fuse, join, solder, unite. ▷ FASTEN.

welfare *n* advantage, benefit, felicity, good, happiness, health, interest, prosperity, well-being.

well *adj* **1** fit, hale, healthy, hearty, *inf* in fine fettle, lively, robust, sound, strong, thriving, vigorous. **2** *All is well.* all right, fine, *inf* OK, satisfactory. • *n* fountain, shaft, source, spring, waterhole, well-spring. □ *artesian well, borehole, gusher, oasis, oil well, wishing-well.*

well-behaved *adj* cooperative, disciplined, docile, dutiful, good, hard-working, law-abiding, manageable, *inf* nice, polite, quiet, well-trained. ▷ OBEDIENT. *Opp* NAUGHTY.

well-bred *adj* courteous, courtly, cultivated, decorous, genteel, polite, proper, refined, sophisticated, urbane, well-brought-up, well-mannered. *Opp* RUDE.

well-built *adj* athletic, big, brawny, burly, hefty, muscular, powerful, stocky, *inf* strapping, strong, sturdy, upstanding. *Opp* SMALL.

well-known *adj* celebrated, eminent, familiar, famous, illustrious, noted, *derog* notorious, prominent, renowned. *Opp* UNKNOWN.

well-meaning *adj* good-natured, obliging, sincere, well-intentioned, well-meant. ▷ KIND. *Opp* UNKIND.

well-off *adj* affluent, comfortable, moneyed, prosperous, rich, *inf* well-heeled, well-to-do. *Opp* POOR.

well-spoken *adj* articulate, educated, polite, *inf* posh, refined, *inf* upper crust.

wet *adj* **1** awash, bedraggled, clammy, damp, dank, dewy, drenched, dripping, moist, muddy, saturated, sloppy, soaked, soaking, sodden, soggy, sopping, soused, spongy, submerged, waterlogged, watery, wringing. **2** *wet weather.* drizzly, humid, misty, pouring, rainy, showery, teeming. **3** *wet paint.* runny, sticky, tacky. • *n* dampness, dew, drizzle, humidity, liquid, moisture, rain. • *vb* dampen, douse, drench, irrigate, moisten, saturate, soak, spray, sprinkle, steep, water. *Opp* DRY.

wheel *n* circle, disc, hoop, ring. □ *bogie, castor, cog-wheel, spinning-wheel, steering-wheel.* • *vb* change direction, circle, gyrate, move in circles, pivot, spin, swerve, swing round, swivel, turn, veer, whirl.

wheeze *vb* breathe noisily, cough, gasp, pant, puff.

whereabouts *n* location, neighbourhood, place, position, site, situation, vicinity.

whiff *n* breath, hint, puff, smell.

whim *n* caprice, desire, fancy, impulse, quirk, urge.

whine *vb* complain, cry, *inf* grizzle, groan, moan, snivel, wail, weep, whimper, *inf* whinge.

whip *n* birch, cane, cat, cat-o'-nine-tails, crop, horsewhip, lash, riding-crop, scourge, switch. • *vb* **1** beat, birch, cane, flagellate, flog, horse-whip, lash, scourge, *inf* tan, thrash. ▷ HIT. **2** beat, stir vigorously, whisk.

whirl *vb* circle, gyrate, pirouette, reel, revolve, rotate, spin, swivel, turn, twirl, twist, wheel.

whirlpool *n* eddy, maelstrom, swirl, vortex, whirl.

whirlwind *n* cyclone, hurricane, tornado, typhoon, vortex, waterspout.

whisk *n* beater, mixer. • *vb* beat, mix, stir, whip.

whiskers *plur n* bristles, hairs, moustache.

whisper *n* **1** murmur, undertone. **2** *a whisper of scandal.* gossip, hearsay, rumour. • *vb* breathe, hiss, murmur, mutter. ▷ TALK.

whistle *n* hooter, pipe, pipes, siren. • *vb* blow, pipe.

white *adj* chalky, clean, cream, ivory, milky, off-white, silver, snow-white, snowy, spotless, whitish. ▷ PALE.

whiten *vb* blanch, bleach, etiolate, fade, lighten, pale.

whole *adj* coherent, complete, entire, full, healthy, in one piece, intact, integral, integrated, perfect, sound, total, unabbreviated, unabridged, unbroken, uncut, undamaged, undivided, unedited, unexpurgated, unharmed, unhurt, uninjured, unscathed. *Opp* FRAGMENTARY, INCOMPLETE.

wholesale *adj* comprehensive, extensive, general, global, indiscriminate, mass, total, universal, widespread. *Opp* LIMITED.

wholesome *adj* beneficial, good, healthful, health-giving, healthy, hygienic, nourishing, nutritious, salubrious, sanitary. *Opp* UNHEALTHY.

wicked *adj* abominable, *inf* awful, bad, base, beastly, corrupt, criminal, depraved, diabolical, dissolute, egregious, evil, foul, guilty, heinous, ill-tempered, immoral, impious, incorrigible, indefensible, iniquitous, insupportable, intolerable, irresponsible, lawless, lost (*soul*), machiavellian, malevolent, malicious, mischievous, murderous, naughty, nefarious, offensive, perverted, rascally, scandalous, shameful, sinful, sinister, spiteful, *inf* terrible, ungodly, unprincipled, unregenerate, unrighteous, unscrupulous, vicious, vile, villainous, violent, wrong. ▷ IRRELIGIOUS, OBSCENE. *Opp* MORAL. **wicked person** ▷ VILLAIN.

wickedness *n* baseness, depravity, enormity, guilt, heinousness, immorality, infamy, iniquity, irresponsibility, *old use* knavery, malice, misconduct, naughtiness, sin, sinfulness, spite, turpitude, ungodliness, unrighteousness, vileness, villainy, wrong, wrongdoing. ▷ EVIL.

wide *adj* **1** ample, broad, expansive, extensive, large, panoramic, roomy, spacious, vast, yawning. **2** *wide sympathies.* all-embracing, broad-minded, catholic, comprehensive, eclectic, encyclopedic, inclusive, wide-ranging. **3** *arms open wide.* extended, open, outspread, outstretched. **4** *a wide shot.* off-course, off-target. *Opp* NARROW.

widen *vb* augment, broaden, dilate, distend, enlarge, expand, extend, flare, increase, make wider, open out, spread, stretch.

widespread *adj* common, endemic, extensive, far-reaching, general, global, pervasive, prevalent, rife, universal, wholesale. *Opp* RARE.

width *n* beam (*of ship*), breadth, broadness, calibre (*of gun*), compass, diameter, distance across, extent, girth, range, scope, span, thickness.

wield *vb* **1** brandish, flourish, handle, hold, manage, ply, wave. **2** *wield power.* employ, exercise, exert, have, possess, use.

wild *adj* **1** *wild animals.* free, undomesticated, untamed. **2** *a wild moor.* deserted, desolate, *inf* God-forsaken, natural, overgrown, remote, rough, rugged, uncultivated, unenclosed, unfarmed, uninhabited, waste. **3** *wild behaviour.* aggressive, barbaric, barbarous, berserk, boisterous, disorderly, ferocious, fierce, frantic, hysterical, lawless, mad, noisy, obstreperous, on the rampage, out of control, rabid, rash, reckless, riotous, rowdy, savage, uncivilized, uncontrollable, uncontrolled, undisciplined, ungovernable, unmanageable, unrestrained, unruly, uproarious, violent. **4** *wild weather.* blustery, stormy, tempestuous, turbulent, violent, windy. **5** *wild enthusiasm.* eager, excited, extravagant, uninhibited, unrestrained. **6** *wild notions.* crazy, fantastic, impetuous, irrational, silly, unreasonable. **7** *a wild guess.* inaccurate, random, unthinking. *Opp* CALM, CULTIVATED, TAME.

wilderness *n* desert, jungle, waste, wasteland, wilds.

wile *n* artifice, gambit, *inf* game, machination, manoeuvre, plot, ploy, ruse, stratagem, subterfuge, trick.

wilful *adj* **1** calculated, conscious, deliberate, intended, intentional, premeditated, purposeful, voluntary. *Opp* ACCIDENTAL. **2** *a wilful character. inf* bloody-minded, determined, dogged, headstrong, immovable, intransigent, obdurate, obstinate, perverse, *inf* pigheaded, refractory, self-willed, stubborn, uncompromising, unyielding, wayward. *Opp* AMENABLE.

will *n* aim, commitment, desire, determination, disposition, inclination, intent, intention, longing, purpose, resolution, resolve, volition, will-power, wish. • *vb* **1** command, encourage, force, influence, inspire, persuade, require, wish. **2** *will a fortune.* bequeath, hand down, leave, pass on, settle on.

willing *adj* acquiescent, agreeable, amenable, assenting, complaisant, compliant, consenting, content, cooperative, disposed, docile, *inf* game, happy, helpful, inclined, pleased, prepared, obliging, ready, well-disposed. ▷ EAGER. *Opp* UNWILLING.

wilt *vb* become limp, droop, fade, fail, flag, flop, languish, sag, shrivel, weaken, wither. *Opp* THRIVE.

wily *adj* artful, astute, canny, clever, crafty, cunning, deceptive, designing, devious, disingenuous, furtive, guileful, ingenious, knowing, scheming, shifty, shrewd, skilful, sly, tricky, underhand. ▷ DISHONEST. *Opp* STRAIGHTFORWARD.

win *vb* **1** be the winner, be victorious, carry the day, come first, conquer, overcome, prevail, succeed, triumph. **2** *win a prize.* achieve, acquire, *inf* carry off, collect, *inf* come away with, deserve, earn, gain, get, obtain, *inf* pick up, receive, secure, *inf* walk away with. *Opp* LOSE.

wind *n* **1** air-current, blast, breath, breeze, current of air, cyclone, draught, gale, gust, hurricane, monsoon, puff, squall, storm, tempest, tornado, whirlwind, *poet* zephyr. **2** *wind in the stomach.* flatulence, gas, heartburn. • *vb* bend, coil, curl, curve, furl, loop, meander, ramble, reel, roll, slew, snake, spiral, turn, twine, twist, *inf* twist and turn, veer, wreathe, zigzag. **winding** ▷ TORTUOUS. **wind up** ▷ FINISH.

window *n* □ *casement, dormer, double-glazed window, embrasure, fanlight, French window, light, oriel, pane, sash window, skylight, shop window, stained-glass window, windscreen.*

windswept *adj* bare, bleak, desolate, exposed, unprotected. ▷ WINDY.

windy *adj* blowy, blustery, boisterous, breezy, draughty, fresh, gusty, squally, stormy, tempestuous. ▷ WINDSWEPT. *Opp* CALM.

wink *vb* **1** bat (*eyelid*), blink, flutter. **2** *lights winked.* flash, flicker, sparkle, twinkle.

winner *n inf* champ, champion, conquering hero, conqueror, first, medallist, prizewinner, title-holder, victor. *Opp* LOSER.

winning *adj* **1** champion, conquering, first, leading, prevailing, successful, top, top-scoring, triumphant, unbeaten, undefeated, victorious. *Opp* UNSUCCESSFUL. **2** *a winning smile.* ▷ ATTRACTIVE.

wintry *adj* arctic, icy, snowy. ▷ COLD. *Opp* SUMMERY.

wipe *vb* brush, clean, cleanse, dry, dust, mop, polish, rub, scour, sponge, swab, wash. **wipe out** ▷ DESTROY.

wire *n* **1** cable, coaxial cable, flex, lead, wiring. **2** cablegram, telegram. ▷ COMMUNICATION.

wiry *adj* lean, muscular, sinewy, strong, thin, tough.

wisdom *n* astuteness, common sense, discernment, discrimination, good sense, insight, judgement, judiciousness, penetration, perceptiveness, perspicacity, prudence, rationality, reason, sagacity, sapience, sense, understanding. ▷ INTELLIGENCE.

wise *adj* **1** astute, discerning, enlightened, erudite, fair, just, knowledgeable, penetrating, perceptive, perspicacious, philosophical, sagacious, sage, sensible, shrewd, sound, thoughtful, understanding, well-informed. ▷ INTELLIGENT. **2** *a wise decision*. advisable, appropriate, considered, diplomatic, expedient, informed, judicious, politic, proper, prudent, rational, reasonable, right. *Opp* UNWISE. **wise person** philosopher, pundit, sage.

wish *n* aim, ambition, appetite, aspiration, craving, desire, fancy, hankering, hope, inclination, *inf* itch, keenness, longing, objective, request, urge, want, yearning, *inf* yen. • *vb* ask, choose, crave, desire, hope, want, yearn. **wish for** ▷ WANT.

wisp *n* shred, strand, streak.

wispy *adj* flimsy, fragile, gossamer, insubstantial, light, streaky, thin. *Opp* SUBSTANTIAL.

wistful *adj* disconsolate, forlorn, melancholy, mournful, nostalgic, regretful, yearning. ▷ SAD.

wit *n* **1** banter, cleverness, comedy, facetiousness, humour, ingenuity, jokes, puns, quickness, quips, repartee, witticisms, wordplay. ▷ INTELLIGENCE. **2** comedian, comic, humorist, jester, joker, wag.

witch *n* enchantress, gorgon, hag, sibyl, sorceress, *plur* weird sisters.

witchcraft *n* black magic, charms, enchantment, *inf* hocus-pocus, incantation, magic, *inf* mumbo-jumbo, necromancy, the occult, occultism, sorcery, spells, voodoo, witchery, wizardry.

withdraw *vb* **1** abjure, call back, cancel, *inf* go back on, recall, rescind, retract, take away, take back. **2** *withdraw from the fight*. back away, back down, back out, *inf* chicken out, *inf* cry off, draw back, drop out, fall back, move back, pull back, pull out, *inf* quit, recoil, retire, retreat, run away, *inf* scratch, secede, shrink back. ▷ LEAVE. *Opp* ADVANCE, ENTER. **3** *withdraw teeth*. extract, pull out, remove, take out.

withdrawn *adj* bashful, diffident, distant, introverted, private, quiet, reclusive, remote, reserved, retiring, shy, silent, solitary, taciturn, timid, uncommunicative. *Opp* SOCIABLE.

wither *vb* become dry, become limp, dehydrate, desiccate, droop, dry out, dry up, fail, flag, flop, sag, shrink, shrivel, waste away, wilt. *Opp* THRIVE.

withhold *vb* check, conceal, control, hide, hold back, keep back, keep secret, repress, reserve, retain, suppress. *Opp* GIVE.

withstand *vb* bear, brave, confront, cope with, defy, endure, fight, grapple with, hold out against, last out against, oppose, *inf* put up with, resist, stand up to, *inf* stick, survive, take, tolerate, weather (*storm*). *Opp* SURRENDER.

witness *n* bystander, eyewitness, looker-on, observer, onlooker, spectator, viewer, watcher. • *vb* attend, behold, be present at, look on, note, notice, observe, see, view, watch. **bear witness** ▷ TESTIFY.

witty *adj* amusing, clever, comic, droll, facetious, funny, humorous, ingenious, intelligent, jocular, quick-witted, sarcastic, sharp-witted, waggish.

wizard *n* enchanter, magician, magus, sorcerer, *old use* warlock, witch-doctor.

wobble *vb* be unsteady, heave, move unsteadily, oscillate, quake, quiver, rock, shake, sway, teeter, totter, tremble, vacillate, vibrate, waver.

wobbly *adj* insecure, loose, rickety, rocky, shaky, teetering, tottering, unbalanced, unsafe, unstable, unsteady. *Opp* STEADY.

woe *n* affliction, anguish, dejection, despair, distress, grief, heartache, melancholy, misery, misfortune, sadness, suffering, trouble, unhappiness, wretchedness. ▷ SORROW. *Opp* HAPPINESS.

woebegone *adj* crestfallen, dejected, downhearted, forlorn, gloomy, melancholy, miserable, *inf* sorry for yourself, woeful, wretched. ▷ SAD. *Opp* CHEERFUL.

woman *n sl* bird, bride, *old use* dame, *old use* damsel, daughter, dowager, female, girl, girlfriend, *derog* hag, *derog* harridan, housewife, hoyden, *derog* hussy, lady, lass, madam, Madame, maid, *old use* maiden, matriarch, matron, mistress, mother, *derog* termagant, *derog* virago, virgin, widow, wife.

wonder *n* **1** admiration, amazement, astonishment, awe, bewilderment, curiosity, fascination, respect, reverence, stupefaction, surprise, wonderment. **2** *a wonder of science.* marvel, miracle, phenomenon, prodigy, *inf* sensation. ● *vb* ask yourself, be curious, be inquisitive, conjecture, marvel, ponder, question yourself, speculate. ▷ THINK. **wonder at** ▷ ADMIRE.

wonderful *adj* amazing, astonishing, astounding, extraordinary, impressive, incredible, marvellous, miraculous, phenomenal, remarkable, surprising, unexpected, *old use* wondrous. *Opp* ORDINARY.

woo *vb* **1** *sl* chat up, court, make love to. **2** *woo custom.* attract, bring in, coax, cultivate, persuade, pursue, seek, try to get.

wood *n* **1** afforestation, coppice, copse, forest, grove, jungle, orchard, plantation, spinney, thicket, trees, woodland, woods. **2** blockboard, chipboard, deal, planks, plywood, timber. □ *balsa, beech, cedar, chestnut, ebony, elm, mahogany, oak, pine, rosewood, sandalwood, sapele, teak, walnut.*

wooded *adj* afforested, *poet* bosky, forested, silvan, timbered, tree-covered, woody.

wooden *adj* **1** ligneous, timber, wood. **2** *wooden acting.* dead, emotionless, expressionless, hard, inflexible, lifeless, rigid, stiff, stilted, unbending, unemotional, unnatural. *Opp* LIVELY.

woodwind *n* □ *bassoon, clarinet, cor anglais, flute, oboe, piccolo, recorder.*

woodwork *n* carpentry, joinery.

woody *adj* fibrous, hard, ligneous, tough. ▷ WOODEN.

woolly *adj* **1** wool, woollen. **2** *woolly toy.* cuddly, downy, fleecy, furry, fuzzy, hairy, shaggy, soft. **3** *woolly ideas.* ambiguous, blurry, confused, hazy, ill-defined, indefinite, indistinct, uncertain, unclear, unfocused, vague.

word *n* **1** expression, name, term. **2** ▷ NEWS. **3** ▷ PROMISE. ● *vb* articulate, express, phrase. **word for word** ▷ VERBATIM.

wording *n* choice of words, diction, expression, language, phraseology, phrasing, style, terminology.

wordy *adj* chatty, diffuse, digressive, discursive, garrulous, long-winded, loquacious, pleonastic, prolix, rambling, repetitious, talkative, unstoppable, verbose, voluble, *inf* windy. *Opp* CONCISE.

work *n* **1** *inf* donkey-work, drudgery, effort, exertion, *inf* fag, *inf* graft, *inf* grind, industry, labour, *inf* plod, slavery, *inf* slog, *inf* spadework, strain, struggle, *inf* sweat, toil, *old use* travail. **2** *work to be done.* assignment, chore, commission, duty, errand, homework, housework, job, mission, project, responsibility, task, undertaking. **3** *regular work.* business, calling, career, employment, job, livelihood, living, métier, occupation, post, profession, situation, trade. ● *vb* **1** *inf* beaver away, be busy, drudge, exert yourself, *inf* fag, *inf* grind away, *inf* keep your nose to the grindstone, labour, make efforts, navvy, *inf* peg away, *inf* plug away, *inf* potter about, *inf* slave, *inf* slog away, strain, strive, struggle, sweat, toil, travail. **2** act, be effective, function, go, operate, perform, run, succeed, thrive. **3** *work slaves hard.* drive, exploit, utilize. **working** ▷ EMPLOYED, OPERATIONAL. **work out** ▷ CALCULATE. **work up** ▷ DEVELOP, EXCITE.

worker *n* artisan, breadwinner, coolie, craftsman, employee, *old use* hand, labourer, member of staff, navvy, operative, operator, peasant, practitioner, servant, slave, tradesman, wage-earner, working man, working woman, workman.

workforce *n* employees, staff, workers.

workmanship *n* art, artistry, competence, craft, craftsmanship, expertise, handicraft, handiwork, skill, technique.

workshop *n* factory, mill, smithy, studio, workroom.

world *n* **1** earth, globe, planet. **2** area, circle, domain, field, milieu, sphere.

worldly *adj* avaricious, covetous, earthly, fleshly, greedy, human, material, materialistic, mundane, physical, profane, secular, selfish, temporal. *Opp* SPIRITUAL.

worm *vb* crawl, creep, slither, squirm, wriggle, writhe.

worn *adj* **1** frayed, moth-eaten, old, ragged, *inf* scruffy, shabby, tattered, *inf* tatty, thin, threadbare, worn-out. **2** ▷ WEARY.

worried *adj* afraid, agitated, agonized, alarmed, anxious, apprehensive, bothered, concerned, distraught, distressed, disturbed, edgy, fearful, *inf* fraught, fretful, guilt-ridden, insecure, nervous, nervy, neurotic, obsessed (by), on edge, overwrought, perplexed, perturbed, solicitous, tense, troubled, uncertain, uneasy, unhappy, upset, vexed.

worry *n* **1** agitation, anxiety, apprehension, disquiet, distress, fear, neurosis, perplexity, perturbation, tension, unease, uneasiness. **2** affliction, annoyance, bother, burden, care, concern, misgiving, problem, *plur* trials and tribulations, trouble, vexation. ● *vb* **1** agitate, annoy, *inf* badger, bother, depress, disquiet, distress, disturb, exercise, *inf* hassle, irritate, molest, nag, perplex, perturb, pester, plague, tease, threaten, torment, trouble, upset, vex. *Opp* REASSURE. **2** *worry about money.* agonize, be anxious, be worried, brood, exercise yourself, feel uneasy, fret.

worsen *vb* **1** aggravate, exacerbate, heighten, increase, intensify, make worse. **2** *his health worsened.* decline, degenerate, deteriorate, fail, get worse, *inf* go downhill, weaken. *Opp* IMPROVE.

worship *n* adoration, adulation, deification, devotion, glorification, homage, idolatry, love, praise, reverence, veneration. ● *vb* admire, adore, adulate, be devoted to, deify, dote on, exalt, extol, glorify, hero-worship, idolize, kneel before, laud, lionize, look up to, love, magnify, pay homage to, praise, pray to, *inf* put on a pedestal, revere, reverence, venerate.

worth *n* benefit, cost, good, importance, merit, quality, significance, use, usefulness, utility, value. **be worth** be priced at, cost, have a value of.

worthless *adj* *old use* bootless, dispensable, disposable, frivolous, futile, *inf* good-for-nothing, hollow, insignificant, meaningless, meretricious, paltry, pointless, poor, *inf* rubbishy, *inf* trashy, trifling, trivial, trumpery, unimportant, unproductive, unprofitable, unusable, useless, vain, valueless. *Opp* WORTHWHILE.

worthwhile *adj* advantageous, beneficial, considerable, enriching, fruitful, fulfilling, gainful, gratifying, helpful, important, invaluable, meaningful, noticeable, productive, profitable, remunerative, rewarding, satisfying, significant, sizeable, substantial, useful, valuable. ▷ WORTHY. *Opp* WORTHLESS.

worthy *adj* admirable, commendable, creditable, decent, deserving, estimable, good, honest, honourable, laudable, meritorious, praiseworthy, reputable, respectable, worth supporting, worthwhile. *Opp* UNWORTHY.

wound *n* damage, hurt, injury, scar, trauma. □ *amputation, bite, bruise, burn, contusion, cut, fracture, gash, graze, laceration, lesion, mutilation, puncture, scab, scald, scar, scratch, sore, sprain, stab, sting, strain, weal, welt.* ● *vb* cause pain to, damage, harm, hurt, injure, traumatize. □ *amputate, bite, blow up, bruise, burn, claw, cut, fracture, gash, gore, graze, hit, impale, knife, lacerate, maim, make sore, mangle, maul, mutilate, scratch, shoot, sprain, strain, stab, sting, torture. Opp* HEAL, MEND.

wrap *n* cape, cloak, mantle, poncho, shawl, stole. ● *vb* bind, bundle up, cloak, cocoon, conceal, cover, do up, encase, enclose, enfold, enshroud, envelop, hide, insulate, lag, muffle, pack, package, shroud, surround, swaddle, swathe, wind.

wreathe *vb* adorn, decorate, encircle, festoon, intertwine, interweave, twist, weave.

wreck *n* **1** hulk, shipwreck. ▷ WRECKAGE. **2** *the wreck of all my hopes.* demolition, destruction, devastation, loss, obliteration, overthrow, ruin, termination, undoing. ● *vb* **1** annihilate, break up, crumple, crush, dash to pieces, demolish, destroy, devastate, ruin, shatter, smash, spoil, *inf* write off. **2** *wreck a ship.* capsize, founder, ground, scuttle, sink, shipwreck.

wreckage *n* bits, debris, *inf* flotsam and jetsam, fragments, pieces, remains, rubble, ruins.

wrench *vb* force, jerk, lever, prize, pull, rip, strain, tear, tug, twist, wrest, wring, *inf* yank.

wrestle *vb* grapple, strive, struggle, tussle. ▷ FIGHT.

wretch *n* **1** beggar, down-and-out, miserable person, pauper, unfortunate. **2** ▷ VILLAIN.

wretched *adj* **1** dejected, depressed, dispirited, downhearted, hapless, melancholy, miserable, pathetic, pitiable, pitiful, unfortunate. ▷ SAD. **2** ▷ UNSATISFACTORY.

wriggle *vb* crawl, snake, squirm, twist, waggle, wiggle, wobble, worm, writhe, zigzag.

wring *vb* **1** clasp, compress, crush, grip, press, shake, squeeze, twist, wrench, wrest. **2** coerce, exact, extort, extract, force.

wrinkle *n* corrugation, crease, crinkle, *inf* crow's foot, dimple, fold, furrow, gather, line, pleat, pucker, ridge, ripple. ● *vb* corrugate, crease, crinkle, crumple, fold, furrow, gather, make wrinkles, pleat, pucker up, ridge, ripple, ruck up, rumple, screw up.

wrinkled *adj* corrugated, creased, crinkly, crumpled, furrowed, lined, pleated, ridged, ripply, rumpled, screwed up, shrivelled, undulating, wavy, wizened, wrinkly. *Opp* SMOOTH.

write *vb* be a writer, compile, compose, copy, correspond, doodle, draft, draw up, engrave, indite, inscribe, jot, note, pen, print, put in writing, record, scrawl, scribble, set down, take down, transcribe, type. **write off** ▷ CANCEL, DESTROY.

writer *n* **1** amanuensis, clerk, copyist, *derog* pen-pusher, scribe, secretary, typist. **2** author, bard, composer, *derog* hack, littérateur, wordsmith. □ *biographer, columnist, contributor, copy-writer, correspondent, diarist, dramatist, essayist, freelancer, ghost-writer, journalist, leader-writer, librettist, novelist, playwright, poet, reporter, scriptwriter.*

writhe *vb* coil, contort, jerk, squirm, struggle, thrash about, thresh about, twist, wriggle.

writing *n* **1** calligraphy, characters, copperplate, cuneiform, handwriting, hieroglyphics, inscription, italics, letters, longhand, notation, penmanship, printing, runes, scrawl, screed, scribble, script, shorthand. **2** authorship, composition, journalism. **3** hard copy, literature, manuscript, opus, printout, text, typescript, work. □ *article, autobiography, belles-lettres, biography, comedy, copy-writing, correspondence, crime story, criticism, detective story, diary, dissertation, documentary, drama, editorial, epic, epistle, essay, fable, fairy-tale, fantasy, fiction, folk-tale, history, legal document, legend, letter, libretto, lyric, monograph, mystery, myth, newspaper column, non-fiction, novel, parable, parody, philosophy, play, poem, propaganda, prose, reportage, romance, saga, satire, science fiction, scientific writing, scriptwriting, SF, sketch, story, tale, thesis, thriller, tragedy, tragi-comedy, travel writing, treatise, trilogy, TV script, verse, inf whodunit, yarn.*

written *adj* documentary, *inf* in black and white, inscribed, in writing, set down, transcribed, typewritten. *Opp* SPOKEN.

wrong *adj* **1** base, blameworthy, corrupt, criminal, crooked, deceitful, dishonest, dishonourable, evil, felonious, illegal, illegitimate, illicit, immoral, iniquitous, irresponsible, mendacious, misleading, naughty, reprehensible, sinful, specious, unethical, unjustifiable, unlawful, unprincipled, unscrupulous, vicious, villainous, wicked, wrong-headed. **2** *wrong answers.* erroneous, fallacious, false, imprecise, improper, inaccurate, incorrect, inexact, misinformed, mistaken, unfounded, untrue. **3** *a wrong decision.* curious, illadvised, ill-considered, ill-judged, impolitic, imprudent, injudicious, misguided, misjudged, unacceptable, unfair, unjust, unsound, unwise, wrongful. **4** *go the wrong way.* abnormal, contrary, inappropriate, incongruous, inconvenient, misleading, opposite, unconventional, undesirable, unhelpful, unsuitable, worst. **5** *Something's wrong.* amiss, broken down, defective, faulty, out of order, unusable. ▷ BAD. *Opp* RIGHT. ● *vb* abuse, be unfair to, cheat, damage, do an injustice to, harm, hurt, injure, malign, maltreat, misrepresent, mistreat, traduce, treat unfairly. **do wrong** ▷ MISBEHAVE.

wrongdoer *n* convict, criminal, crook, culprit, delinquent, evil-doer, law-breaker, malefactor, mischief-maker, miscreant, offender, sinner, transgressor.

wrongdoing *n* crime, delinquency, disobedience, evil, immorality, indiscipline, iniquity, malpractice, misbehaviour, mischief, naughtiness, offence, sin, sinfulness, wickedness.

wry *adj* **1** askew, aslant, awry, bent, contorted, crooked, deformed, distorted, lopsided, twisted, uneven. **2** *a wry sense of humour.* droll, dry, ironic, mocking, sardonic.

Y

yard *n* court, courtyard, enclosure, garden, *inf* quad, quadrangle.

yarn *n* **1** fibre, strand, thread. **2** account, anecdote, fiction, narrative, story, tale.

yawning *adj* gaping, open, wide.

yearly *adj* annual, perennial, regular.

yearn *vb* ache, feel desire, hanker, have a craving, hunger, itch, long, pine. ▷ WANT.

yellow *adj* □ *chrome yellow, cream, gold, golden, orange, tawny.*

yield *n* **1** crop, harvest, output, produce, product. **2** earnings, gain, income, interest, proceeds, profit, return, revenue. • *vb* **1** acquiesce, agree, assent, bow, capitulate, *inf* cave in, cede, comply, concede, defer, give in, give up, give way, *inf* knuckle under, submit, succumb, surrender, *inf* throw in the towel, *inf* throw up the sponge. **2** *yield interest.* bear, earn, generate, pay out, produce, provide, return, supply. **yielding** ▷ FLEXIBLE, SPONGY, SUBMISSIVE.

young *adj* **1** baby, early, growing, immature, new-born, undeveloped, unfledged, youngish. **2** *young people.* adolescent, juvenile, pubescent, teenage, underage, youthful. **3** *young for your age.* babyish, boyish, callow, childish, girlish, *inf* green, immature, inexperienced, infantile, juvenile, naïve, puerile. • *n* brood, family, issue, litter, offspring, progeny. **young creatures** bullock, calf, chick, colt, cub, cygnet, duckling, fawn, fledgling, foal, gosling, heifer, kid, kitten, lamb, leveret, nestling, pullet, puppy, yearling. **young people** adolescent, baby, boy, *derog* brat, child, girl, infant, juvenile, *inf* kid, lad, lass, *inf* nipper, teenager, toddler, *derog* urchin, youngster, youth.

youth *n* **1** adolescence, babyhood, boyhood, childhood, girlhood, growing up, immaturity, infancy, minority, pubescence, *inf* salad days, *inf* teens. **2** adolescent, boy, juvenile, *inf* kid, *inf* lad, minor, stripling, teenager, youngster.

youthful *adj* fresh, lively, sprightly, vigorous, well-preserved, young-looking. ▷ YOUNG.

Z

zany *adj* absurd, clownish, crazy, eccentric, idiotic, *inf* loony, *inf* mad, madcap, playful, ridiculous, silly, *sl* wacky.

zeal *n derog* bigotry, earnestness, enthusiasm, fanaticism, fervour, partisanship.

zealot *n* bigot, extremist, fanatic, partisan, radical.

zealous *adj* conscientious, diligent, eager, earnest, enthusiastic, fanatical, fervent, keen, militant, obsessive, partisan, passionate. *Opp* APATHETIC.

zenith *n* acme, apex, apogee, climax, height, highest point, meridian, peak, pinnacle, summit, top. *Opp* NADIR.

zero *n cricket* duck, *tennis* love, naught, nil, nothing, nought, *sl* zilch. **zero in on** ▷ AIM.

zest *n* appetite, eagerness, energy, enjoyment, enthusiasm, exuberance, hunger, interest, liveliness, pleasure, thirst, zeal.

zigzag *adj* bendy, crooked, *inf* in and out, indirect, meandering, serpentine, twisting, winding. • *vb* bend, curve, meander, snake, tack, twist, wind.

zone *n* area, belt, district, domain, locality, neighbourhood, province, quarter, region, section, sector, sphere, territory, tract, vicinity.

zoo *n* menagerie, safari park, zoological gardens.

zoom *vb* career, dart, dash, hurry, hurtle, race, rush, shoot, speed, *inf* whiz, *inf* zip. ▷ MOVE.

A lexicon of hard words

A

aam a former liquid wine measure of 37 to 41 gallons; a cask.

abatis (also **abattis**) a defence made of felled trees with the boughs pointing outwards.

abecedarian **1** one occupied in learning the alphabet. **2** a teacher of the alphabet.

aberdevine a bird-fancier's name for the siskin, a small bird like a goldfinch.

aberrant diverging from the normal type or accepted standard.

abeyance a state of temporary disuse or suspension (*in abeyance*).

abiogenesis **1** the formation of living organisms from non-living substances. **2** the supposed spontaneous generation of living organisms.

ablation **1** the surgical removal of body tissue. **2** the evaporation or melting of part of the outer surface of a spacecraft, through heating by friction with the atmosphere.

abnegation **1** denial; the rejection or renunciation of a doctrine. **2** self-denial; self-sacrifice.

abomasum the fourth stomach of a ruminant.

abortifacient a drug or other agent that effects abortion.

abruption an interruption; a sudden break.

abseil to descend a steep rock face by using a doubled rope coiled round the body and fixed at a higher point.

abstemious (of a person, habit, etc.) moderate, not self-indulgent, especially in eating and drinking.

abstruse hard to understand; obscure; profound.

abysmal **1** extremely bad (*abysmal weather; the standard is abysmal*). **2** profound, utter (*abysmal ignorance*).

acaricide a preparation for destroying mites.

acceptation a particular sense, or the generally recognized meaning, of a word or phrase.

accidie laziness, sloth, apathy.

accolade **1** the awarding of praise; an acknowledgement of merit. **2** a touch made with a sword at the bestowing of a knighthood.

accoutrements (*US* also **accouterments**) **1** equipment, trappings. **2** a soldier's outfit other than weapons and garments.

accretion **1** growth by organic enlargement or by slow additions of extraneous matter. **2** the product of such growing.

accrue to come as a natural increase or advantage, especially financial.

acculturate to (cause to) adapt to or adopt a different culture.

acerbic **1** astringently sour. **2** bitter in speech, manner, or temper.

acme the highest point or period (of achievement, success, etc.); the peak of perfection (*displayed the acme of good taste*).

acolyte **1** a person assisting a priest in a service or procession. **2** an assistant; a beginner.

acuity (of a needle, senses, understanding) sharpness, acuteness.

acumen keen insight or discernment, penetration.

adduce to cite as an instance or as proof or evidence.

adiaphorism religious or theological indifference; latitudinarianism.

adipose of or characterized by fat; fatty.

adit a horizontal entrance or passage in a mine.

adminicle **1** a thing that helps. **2** (in Scottish law) collateral evidence of the contents of a missing document.

adobe an unburnt sun-dried brick, or the clay used for making these.

adscititious adopted from without; supplementary.

adulate to flatter obsequiously.

adumbrate **1** to indicate faintly. **2** to represent in outline. **3** to foreshadow, typify. **4** to overshadow.

adventitious **1** accidental, casual. **2** added from outside or unexpectedly. **3** *Biol.* formed accidentally or under unusual conditions.

advowson (in British ecclesiastical law) the right of recommending a member of the clergy for a vacant benefice, or of making the appointment.

adze a tool for cutting away the surface of wood, like an axe with an arched blade at right angles to the handle.

aegis protection, defence (*under the aegis of*=under the protection of).

aegrotat **1** a certificate that a British university student is too ill to attend an examination. **2** an examination pass awarded in such circumstances.

aeolipyle an instrument by which steam produces circular motion.

aerotrain a train that is supported on an air cushion and guided by a track.

aestival (*US* **estival**) belonging to or appearing in summer.

afflatus a divine creative impulse; inspiration.

aficionado a devotee of a sport or pastime.

agape **1** a Christian feast in token of fellowship, especially one held by early Christians in commemoration of the Last Supper. **2** Christian fellowship, especially as distinct from erotic love.

agitprop the dissemination of Communist political propaganda, especially in plays, films, books, etc.

aglet **1** a metal tag attached to each end of a shoelace etc. **2** an aiguillette.

agnate **1** descended especially by male line from the same male ancestor. **2** descended from the same forefather; of the same clan or nation.

agora a place of public assembly, especially the market place.

agraffe a kind of hook on a ring, used as a clasp.

ahimsa in the Hindu, Buddhist, and Jainist tradition, respect for all living things, and avoidance of violence towards others both in thought and deed.

aigrette **1** the white plume of an egret. **2** a tuft of feathers or hair. **3** a spray of gems or similar ornament.

aiguillette a tagged point hanging from the shoulder on the breast of some uniforms.

aikido a Japanese form of self-defence making use of the attacker's own movements without causing injury.

ait (also **eyot**) *Brit.* a small island, especially in a river.

akimbo (of the arms) with hands on the hips and elbows turned outwards.

alcalde a magistrate or mayor in a Spanish, Portuguese, or Latin American town.

aleatoric **1** depending on the throw of a die or on chance. **2** involving random choice by a performer or artist.

alembic **1** an apparatus formerly used in distilling, an early kind of retort. **2** a means of refining or extracting.

aliment food.

allele (also **allel**) one of the (usually two) alternative forms of a gene.

alluvium a deposit of usually fine fertile soil left during a time of flood, especially in a river valley or delta.

almagest the astronomical treatise of Ptolemy; in the Middle Ages also other books of astrology and astronomy.

alopecia baldness.

altruism regard for others; unselfishness, concern for other people.

amah (in the Far East and India) a nursemaid or maid.

amanuensis a person who writes from dictation or copies manuscripts; a literary assistant.

ambagious roundabout; circuitous.

ambient surrounding.

ambit **1** the scope, extent, or bounds of something. **2** precincts or environs.

ambivalent having opposing feelings, especially love and hate, in a single context.

amice **1** a white linen cloth worn on the neck and shoulders by a priest celebrating the Eucharist. **2** a cap, hood, or cape worn by members of certain religious orders.

amnesty a general pardon, especially for political offences.

ampersand the sign & (=*and*).

amphibology **1** a quibble. **2** an ambiguous wording.

amphigoric of or being nonsense verses.

amphora a Greek or Roman vessel with two handles and a narrow neck.

ampoule (*US* **ampul** or **ampule**) a small capsule in which measured quantities of liquids or solids, especially for injecting, are sealed ready for use.

amygdaloid shaped like an almond.

anabasis **1** the march of the younger Cyrus into Asia in 401 BC, as narrated by Xenophon in his work *Anabasis.* **2** a military up-country march.

anabiosis revival after apparent death.

anadromous (of a fish) swimming up a river to spawn.

anaglyph **1** a composite stereoscopic photograph printed in superimposed complementary colours. **2** an embossed object cut in low relief.

analects (also **analecta**) a collection of short literary extracts.

analeptic (of a drug etc.) restorative.

analgesia the absence or relief of pain, especially without loss of consciousness.

anamnesis **1** recollection, especially of a supposed previous existence. **2** a patient's account of his or her medical history. **3** the part of the Eucharist recalling Christ's Passion, Resurrection, and Ascension.

anathema **1** a detested person or thing (*is anathema to me*). **2** a curse of the Church, excommunicating someone or denouncing a doctrine, or a person or thing so cursed.

anchorite a hermit; a religious recluse.

ancillary **1** (of a person, activity, or service) providing essential support to a central service or industry, especially the medical service. **2** subordinate or subservient (*to*).

andiron a metal stand for supporting logs in a fireplace; a firedog.

androgynous having both male and female sexual organs; hermaphrodite.

anfractuosity **1** circuitousness. **2** intricacy.

ankh a device consisting of a looped bar with a shorter crossbar, used in ancient Egypt as a symbol of life.

annular ring-shaped.

anodyne **1** able to relieve pain. **2** mentally soothing (*anodyne remarks*).

anomalous having an irregular or deviant feature; abnormal.

anomy (also **anomie**) lack of the usual social or ethical standards in an individual or group.

anopheles a genus of mosquitoes, many of which carry the malarial parasite.

anthelmintic any drug or agent that destroys tapeworms, roundworms, flukes, etc.

anthropomorphic (of a god, animal, or thing) having a human form or personality.

anti-hero a central character in a story or drama who noticeably lacks conventional heroic attributes.

antihistamine a substance used especially in the treatment of allergies.

antinomy **1** a contradiction between two reasonable beliefs or conclusions; a paradox. **2** a conflict between two laws or authorities.

anuran any tailless amphibian of the order that includes frogs and toads.

apatetic (of markings or colourings) deceptively resembling those of another species or of the environment.

apiculture bee-keeping.

aplomb assurance; self-confidence.

apodictic **1** clearly established. **2** of clear demonstration.

apophthegm (*US* **apothegm**) a terse saying or maxim; an aphorism.

aposematic *Zool.* (of coloration, markings, etc.) serving to warn or repel.

appanage (also **apanage**) **1** provision for the maintenance of the younger children of kings. **2** a perquisite. **3** a natural accompaniment or attribute.

appetence longing, desire.

apteryx a kiwi.

arachnid any arthropod of the class including scorpions, spiders, mites, and ticks.

arbalest (also **arblast**) a crossbow with a mechanism for drawing the string.

arboretum a botanical garden devoted to trees.

arcane mysterious, secret; understood by few.

archaism **1** the retention or imitation of the old or obsolete, especially in language or art. **2** an antiquated word or expression.

archetypical being a typical specimen or recurrent symbol.

archimandrite 1 the superior of a large monastery or several monasteries in the Orthodox Church. **2** an honorary title given to a monastic priest.

arcuate shaped like a bow; curved.

areola 1 a circular pigmented area, especially that surrounding a nipple. **2** any of the spaces between lines on a surface, e.g. of a leaf or an insect's wing.

argil clay, especially that used in pottery.

argol crude potassium hydrogen tartrate; a crusty deposit that builds up in vats during winemaking.

argute 1 sharp, shrewd. **2** (of sounds) shrill.

arisings the secondary or waste products of industrial operations.

armiger a person entitled to heraldic arms.

arrack (also **arak**) an alcoholic spirit, especially distilled from coconut sap or rice.

arraign 1 to indict before a tribunal; accuse. **2** to call (an action or statement) into question.

arras a rich tapestry, formerly hung on the walls of a room or to conceal an alcove.

arrogate 1 (often followed by *to* oneself) to claim (power, responsibility, etc.) without justification. **2** to attribute unjustly *to* a person.

arroyo *US* 1 a brook or stream. **2** a gulley.

arthropod any invertebrate animal of the phylum that has a segmented body, jointed limbs, and an external skeleton, e.g. an insect, spider, or crustacean.

ascesis the practice of self-discipline.

ashram a place of religious retreat for Hindus.

askari an East African soldier or policeman.

aspergillum a brush for sprinkling holy water.

assay to test (a metal, ore, or other substance) to determine its ingredients, concentration, etc.

assegai (also **assagai**) a slender iron-tipped spear, especially as used by South African peoples.

asseverate to declare solemnly.

asthenic 1 of lean or long-limbed build. **2** weakened and debilitated.

astral of or consisting of stars.

ataraxy (also **ataraxia**) calmness or tranquillity; imperturbability.

atavistic reverting to an earlier type, or to remote ancestors.

atheling a prince or lord in Anglo-Saxon England.

atoll a ring-shaped coral reef enclosing a lagoon.

atrabilious melancholy; ill-tempered.

attenuate to make thinner; dilute or reduce in force, value, or virulence.

auctorial of or pertaining to an author.

audile of the sense of hearing.

aumbry **1** a small recess in a church wall. **2** an old word for a cupboard.

aureole **1** a halo, especially round the head or body of a portrayed religious figure. **2** a corona round the sun or moon.

auscultation the act of listening, especially to sounds from the heart, lungs, etc., as a part of medical diagnosis.

austral **1** southern. **2** of Australia or Australasia.

autarky **1** self-sufficiency, especially as an economic system. **2** a state etc. run according to such a system.

autochthons the original or earliest inhabitants of a country; aboriginals.

autocross motor-racing across country or on unmade roads.

autodidact a self-taught person.

autonomous **1** having self-government. **2** acting independently or free to do so.

autotomy the casting off of a body part when threatened, e.g. the tail of a lizard.

avatar **1** in Hindu mythology, the descent of a deity or released soul to earth in bodily form. **2** incarnation; manifestation. **3** a manifestation or phase.

avid eager, greedy.

avionics electronics as applied to aviation.

avocation **1** a minor occupation. **2** a vocation or calling.

avuncular like or of an uncle; kind and friendly, especially towards a younger person.

axolotl an aquatic Mexican salamander which retains its larval form for life but can breed.

ayatollah a Shi'ite Muslim religious leader in Iran.

ayurvedic of or being traditional Hindu medicine.

azoth the alchemists' name for mercury.

B

baasskaap domination, especially of South African non-Whites by Whites.

babushka a headscarf tied under the chin.

baccalaureate **1** the university degree of bachelor. **2** an examination intended to qualify successful candidates for higher education.

bacchanalia drunken revelry.

bacchant riotous, roistering.

badinage humorous or playful ridicule.

bagatelle **1** a game in which small balls are struck into numbered holes on a board, with pins as obstructions. **2** a mere trifle; a negligible amount (and see MUSIC).

bagel a hard ring-shaped bread roll.

bagnio **1** a brothel. **2** an oriental prison.

bailiwick **1** the district or jurisdiction of a bailiff or bailie. **2** a person's sphere of operations or particular area of interest.

baklava a rich sweetmeat of flaky pastry, honey, and nuts.

baksheesh (also **backsheesh**) (in some oriental countries) a small sum of money given as a tip or in alms.

baldachin (also **baldaquin**) **1** a ceremonial canopy over an altar, throne, etc., or carried in a procession. **2** a rich brocade.

balderdash senseless talk or writing; nonsense.

baldric a belt for a sword, bugle, etc. that hung from the shoulder across the body to the opposite hip.

baleen whalebone.

ballista a catapult used in ancient warfare for hurling large stones etc.

balneal relating to bathing and medicinal springs.

baltimore (also **baltimore-oriole**) a North American bird of the starling family.

banausic **1** uncultivated or materialistic. **2** suitable only for artisans.

banderole (also **banderol**) **1** a long narrow flag flown at a masthead, or a similar streamer on a knight's lance. **2** a ribbon-like scroll.

banket the gold-bearing rocks of the Transvaal.

banneret **1** a knight who commanded his own troops in battle under his own banner. **2** a knighthood given on the battlefield for courage.

banshee an Irish or Scottish female spirit whose wailing warns of death in a house.

banzai **1** a Japanese battle-cry. **2** a form of greeting used to the Japanese emperor.

barbel any of the fleshy filaments growing from the mouth of a fish.

barbule a minute filament projecting from the barb of a feather.

Barmecide illusory, imaginary; such as to disappoint.

barracoon a rough barrack in which negro slaves, convicts, etc. were temporarily housed.

barre a horizontal bar at waist level used in dance exercises.

barrette **1** the crossbar of a fencing foil or hilt of a rapier. **2** a woman's hair ornament or bar for supporting the back hair.

barton **1** a farmyard. **2** the demesne lands of a manor.

bascule a type of drawbridge raised and lowered by counterweights.

basinet a light metal headpiece of medieval times, with a visor.

bastinado punishment by beating with a stick on the soles of the feet.

bat-fowling the catching of roosting birds at night.

bathos an unintentional lapse from the sublime to the absurd or trivial; a commonplace or ridiculous feature offsetting an otherwise sublime situation; an anticlimax.

bathysphere a spherical vessel for deep-sea observation.

batik cloth decorated with coloured designs produced by applying wax to the parts to be left uncoloured.

bayou a marshy offshoot of a river etc. in the southern US.

beatific **1** blissful (*a beatific smile*). **2** of blessedness, or making blessed.

bedizened gaudily decked out.

beedi an Indian cigarette made of a leaf rolled and tied with thread.

beestings the first milk (especially of a cow) after giving birth.

behemoth an enormous creature or thing.

behest a command; an entreaty (*went at his behest*).

bellicose eager to fight; warlike.

bell-wether **1** the leading sheep of a flock, on whose neck a bell is hung. **2** an absurd chief or leader.

belvedere a summer house or open-sided gallery usually at rooftop level.

benignant **1** kindly, especially to inferiors. **2** salutary, beneficial. **3** *Med.* (of a disease, tumour, etc.) benign; not malignant.

benison a blessing.

bergschrund a crevasse or gap at the head of a glacier or névé.

berserk wild, frenzied; in a violent rage (*went berserk*).

bestiary a moralizing medieval treatise on real and imaginary beasts.

bethel a chapel or nonconformist meeting-house.

bey (in the former Ottoman Empire) the title of the governor of a province.

bezel **1** the sloped edge of a chisel. **2** the oblique faces of a cut gem. **3** a groove or rim holding a watch-glass or gem.

bib-cock a tap with a bent nozzle fixed at the end of a pipe.

bibelot a small curio or artistic trinket.

bibliopole a seller of (especially rare) books.

bicuspid having two cusps, horns, or points (*bicuspid tooth*).

bifurcate to fork into two branches.

bight **1** a curve or recess in a coastline, river, etc. **2** a loop of rope.

bigot an obstinate and intolerant believer in a religion, political theory, etc.

bilboes an iron bar with sliding shackles formerly used for securing a prisoner's ankles.

biltong *S.Afr.* boneless meat salted and dried in strips.

biodegradable capable of being decomposed by bacteria or other living organisms.

bionic having artificial body parts or the superhuman powers resulting from these.

biretta a square usually flat cap with three flat projections on top, worn by (especially Roman Catholic) clergymen.

bisque **1** a rich shellfish soup, especially from lobster. **2** an advantage of scoring one free point in tennis, croquet, and golf, or of taking an extra turn or stroke. **3** fired unglazed pottery; biscuit.

bissextile leap year.

bistoury a surgical scalpel.

bistre (*US* **bister**) (the colour of) a brownish pigment made from the soot of burnt wood.

bitumen a tarlike mixture of hydrocarbons derived from petroleum, used for road surfacing and roofing.

blasé **1** unimpressed or indifferent because of overfamiliarity. **2** tired of pleasure; surfeited.

blatherskite a foolish chatterer.

bleachers (especially *US*) the outdoor uncovered bench seats at a sports ground, arranged in tiers and very cheap.

bleb **1** a small blister on the skin. **2** a small bubble in glass or on water.

blet the form of near-decay seen in over-ripe pears etc.

blunger a machine to mix clay etc. with water.

blurb a (usually eulogistic) description of a book, especially printed on its jacket, as promotion by its publishers.

bodega a cellar or shop selling wine and food, especially in a Spanish-speaking country.

boletus a large edible fungus, spongy underneath.

bolide a large exploding meteor; a fireball.

bolus **1** a soft ball, especially of chewed food. **2** a large pill.

bombazine (also **bombasine**) a twilled worsted dress material with or without some silk or cotton, especially when black.

bonzai **1** the art of cultivating ornamental artificially dwarfed trees and shrubs. **2** a tree or shrub grown in this way.

boondocks *US slang* rough or isolated country.

boondoggle *US slang* a trifling, useless, or wasteful undertaking.

borak *Austral. & NZ slang* banter, ridicule.

borborygmus a rumbling of gas in the intestines.

boreal of the North, or the north wind.

bosky wooded, bushy.

boules a French form of bowls, played on rough ground with usually metal balls.

bouleversement a violent inversion.

bowdlerize to remove objectionable matter from (a book etc.); expurgate.

brachial of or like an arm.

brad a thin flat nail with a narrow head.

braggadocio empty boasting; a boastful manner of speech and behaviour.

brandreth **1** a tripod or trivet. **2** a wooden framework supporting a cask, hay-rick, etc.

branks a scold's bridle; an iron framework for the head with a sharp metal gag.

brassage a mint charge levied to cover the expense of coining money.

brassard a band worn on the sleeve, especially with a uniform.

brasserie a restaurant, originally one serving beer with food.

brattice a wooden partition or shaft lining in a coal mine.

bravura **1** a brilliant or ambitious action or display. **2** a style of (especially vocal) music requiring exceptional ability.

braxy (*Scot*) an apoplectic disease of sheep.

brevet a document conveying a privilege from a sovereign or government, especially a rank in the army, without the appropriate pay.

breviary *RC Ch.* a book containing the service for each day, to be recited by those in orders.

brevier the name of a rather small type size.

brewis bread soaked in broth.

bridewell an old word for a prison or reformatory.

brimstone an old word for the element sulphur.

brindled (especially of domestic animals) brownish or tawny with streaks of other colour.

Brobdingnagian huge, immense, gigantic.

Brummagem cheap and showy and perhaps counterfeit (*Brummagem goods*).

bruxism the involuntary grinding or clenching of the teeth.

buccinator a flat thin cheek muscle.

buckler a small round shield that was held by a handle.

bucolic of shepherds, the pastoral life, etc.; rural.

buhl furniture etc. decorated with inlays of brass, tortoiseshell, etc. cut in patterns.

bulla **1** a watery blister on the skin. **2** a genus of deep-water molluscs.

bunraku the traditional Japanese puppet theatre.

bunt **1** the baggy centre of a sail or fishing net. **2** a disease of wheat. **3** (*verb*) **a** to butt with the head or horns. **b** to stop (a ball in US baseball) with the bat without swinging.

burette (*US* **buret**) a graduated glass tube with an end-tap for measuring small volumes of liquid in chemical analysis.

burgoo a thick oatmeal gruel or porridge used by sailors.

burin **1** a steel tool for engraving on copper or wood. **2** a flint tool of the Stone Age with a chisel point.

burke **1** to murder by suffocation or strangulation, or for the purpose of selling the victim's body for dissection. **2** to suppress quietly; to evade or shirk.

burlap **1** a coarse canvas, especially of jute, used for sacking etc. **2** a similar lighter material for use in dressmaking or furnishing.

bursa *Anat.* a fluid-filled cavity to lessen friction.

bushwhacker *US, Austral., & NZ* someone who clears woods and bush country, or lives and travels there.

buskins **1** thick-soled laced boots worn by ancient Athenian tragic actors to gain height. **2** medieval calf- or knee-high cloth or leather boots.

bustee an Indian shanty town; a slum.

butter-bump a dialect name for the bittern.

butyraceous like butter; buttery.

bwana (*Afr.*) master; sir.

C

cabal **1** a secret intrigue. **2** a political clique or faction.

caballero a Spanish gentleman.

cabbala **1** the Jewish mystical tradition. **2** mystic interpretation; any esoteric doctrine or occult lore.

caboose **1** a kitchen on a ship's deck. **2** *US* a guard's van; a car on a freight train for workmen etc.

cabotage **1** coastal navigation and trade. **2** the reservation to a country of (especially air) traffic operation within its territory.

cabriole a kind of curved leg characteristic of Queen Anne and Chippendale furniture.

cabriolet **1** a light two-wheeled carriage with a hood, drawn by one horse. **2** a car with a folding top.

cache a hiding place for treasure, provisions, ammunition, etc., or its contents.

cachet **1** a distinguishing mark or seal. **2** prestige. **3** *Med.* a flat capsule enclosing a dose of unpleasant-tasting medicine.

cachinnate to laugh loudly.

cachou a lozenge to sweeten the breath.

cacique **1** a West Indian or American Indian native chief. **2** a Spanish or Latin American political boss.

cacoethes an urge to do something undesirable.

cacography bad handwriting or spelling.

cadastral of or showing the extent, value, and ownership of land for taxation.

cadaver a corpse.

cadre **1** a basic unit, especially of servicemen, forming a nucleus for expansion when necessary. **2** a group of activists in a revolutionary party, or a member of such a group.

caduceus an ancient Greek or Roman herald's wand, especially as carried by Hermes or Mercury.

caesura **1** (in Greek and Latin verse) a break between words within a metrical foot. **2** (in modern verse) a pause near the middle of the line.

caisson **1** a watertight chamber in which underwater construction work can be done. **2** a floating vessel used as a floodgate in docks. **3** an ammunition chest or wagon.

cajole to persuade by flattery, deceit, etc. *into* or *out of*.

calabash **1** an evergreen tree of tropical America, *Crescentia cujete*. **2** a gourd from this tree, whose shell is used to carry water, make a tobacco pipe, etc.

calash **1** a light low-wheeled carriage with a removable folding hood. **2** *Canadian* a two-wheeled horse-drawn vehicle. **3** a woman's hooped silk hood.

calcaneus the bone forming the heel.

calefacient a substance producing a sensation of warmth.

calender a machine in which cloth, paper, etc. is pressed by rollers to glaze or smooth it.

calibrate **1** to mark (a gauge) with a standard scale of readings. **2** to correlate the readings of (an instrument) with a standard. **3** to determine the calibre of (a gun). **4** to determine the correct capacity or value of.

callipers compasses with bowed legs for measuring the diameter of convex bodies or internal dimensions.

callipygian having beautiful buttocks.

calotte a skullcap as worn by Roman Catholic clergymen.

caltrop (also **caltrap**) **1** a four-spiked iron ball that used to be thrown on the ground to impede cavalry horses. **2** a creeping plant of the genus *Tribulus*, with hard spines.

calumet a North American Indian peace pipe.

calumny slander; malicious misrepresentation.

cambist **1** one who deals in bills of exchange. **2** a manual of foreign exchanges.

camelopard an old word for a giraffe.

cameralistics the management of German state property.

campestral pertaining to fields or open country.

canard **1** an unfounded rumour. **2** an extra surface attached to an aeroplane forward of the main lifting surface, for extra stability or control.

cancellate marked with crossing lines.

cancroid **1** crablike. **2** resembling cancer.

cangue a broad heavy wooden frame worn round the neck as a former punishment in China.

cannelure the groove round a bullet.

cannula a small tube for inserting into the body to allow fluid to enter or escape.

Canopic urn/jar an urn for holding the entrails of an embalmed body in an ancient Egyptian burial.

cantankerous bad-tempered, quarrelsome.

canterbury a piece of furniture with partitions for holding music etc.

cantharides a preparation of dried beetles, causing blistering of the skin and formerly used in medicine and as an aphrodisiac.

canthus either corner of the eye, where the eyelids meet.

cantle the part that sticks up at the back of a saddle.

canto a division of a long poem.

canton a subdivision of a country, especially of Switzerland.

cantor the leader of the singing in a church or synagogue.

cantoris (of music) to be sung by the north side of a church choir in antiphonal singing (compare DECANI).

caoutchouc raw rubber.

capitular **1** of a cathedral chapter. **2** of or being a lump on the end of a bone.

capote a long hooded cloak, formerly worn by soldiers and travellers.

capuche a monk's hood.

Capuchin **1** a Franciscan friar of the rule of 1529. **2** a cloak and hood formerly worn by women. **3** (**capuchin**) **a** a South American monkey with cowl-like head and hair. **b** a kind of pigeon with head and neck feathers like a cowl.

caracole a horse's half-turn to the right or left.

carapace the hard upper shell of a tortoise or crustacean.

caravanserai an Eastern inn with a central court where desert caravans may rest.

carboy a large globular glass bottle usually protected by a frame, for containing liquids.

carcanet an old word for a jewelled collar or headdress.

caret a mark (‸, ‸) indicating a proposed insertion in printing or writing.

caries decay and crumbling of a tooth or bone.

carillon **1** a set of bells sounded either from a keyboard or mechanically. **2** an organ stop imitating a peal of bells.

carminative relieving flatulence.

carnet **1** a customs permit to take a motor vehicle across a frontier for a limited period. **2** a permit allowing use of a campsite.

carob an evergreen Mediterranean tree whose edible pods are sometimes used as a substitute for chocolate.

carpet-bagger **1** (especially *US*) a political candidate in an area where the candidate has no local connections. **2** an unscrupulous opportunist.

carrel a small cubicle for a reader in a library, or formerly for study in a cloister.

carronade a short ship's gun of large calibre, with a chamber for the powder like a mortar.

cartography the drawing of maps.

cartouche an oval ring usually enclosing a king's name in Egyptian hieroglyphics.

caruncle a fleshy excrescence such as a turkeycock's wattles, or a similar outgrowth on a plant.

casern a building in a town to accommodate troops; a barrack.

casque a helmet.

caste **1** any of the Hindu hereditary classes. **2** a more or less exclusive social class, or the position this confers.

castigate to rebuke or punish severely.

casuistry the resolving of moral problems with clever but false reasoning.

cataclysm **1** a violent, especially social or political, upheaval or disaster. **2** a great flood.

catafalque a decorative wooden framework to support a coffin during a funeral or when lying in state.

catamite a boy kept for homosexual practices.

catchpole **1** a Roman publican; a tax-gatherer. **2** a sheriff's officer or sergeant.

catechumen a Christian convert under instruction before baptism.

cateran a Highland irregular fighting man; a marauder.

catharsis **1** an emotional release in drama or art. **2** purging of the bowels.

catholicon a universal remedy; a panacea.

catoptric of or being a mirror, a reflector, or reflection.

caucus **1** a meeting of US political party members to decide policy; or a bloc of such members. **2** a secret meeting of a group within any larger organization; or such a group.

caudal of a tail, or the hind parts of the body.

caudillo (in Spanish-speaking countries) a military or political leader.

caul the inner membrane enclosing a foetus, a part of which is sometimes found on a child's head at birth.

cay a low insular bank or reef of coral, sand, etc.

cedilla **1** a mark written under the letter ç, especially in French, to show that it is sibilant (as in *façade*). **2** a similar mark under ş in Turkish and other oriental languages.

ceilidh *Ir. & Sc.* an informal gathering for conversation, music, dancing, songs, and stories.

cenacle a supping room; an upper chamber, especially that in which the Last Supper was held.

cephalic of the head.

cerecloth waxed cloth formerly used as a waterproof covering or (especially) as a shroud.

certitude a feeling of absolute certainty; conviction.

cerulean deep blue like a clear sky.

cerumen earwax.

cervelat a kind of smoked pork sausage.

cetacean any marine mammal with a streamlined hairless body and a blowhole on the back for breathing, including whales, dolphins, and porpoises.

chador (also **chador, chuddar**) a large cloth worn in some countries by Muslim women, wrapped around the body to leave only the face exposed.

chalcedony a type of quartz occurring in several forms, e.g. onyx, agate, tiger's eye, etc.

Chaldean **1** of ancient Chaldea or its people or language. **2** of or relating to astrology.

chalybeate (of mineral water etc.) impregnated with iron salts.

chamfer a bevelled surface at a right-angled edge or corner.

chanterelle an edible fungus with a yellow funnel-shaped cap and smelling of apricots.

chaplet **1** a garland for the head. **2** a string of beads used for counting prayers or as a necklace.

charisma **1** the ability to inspire followers with devotion and enthusiasm; great charm. **2** a divinely conferred power or talent.

charpoy a light Indian bedstead.

chasuble a priest's usually ornate loose sleeveless outer vestment.

chauvinism **1** exaggerated or aggressive patriotism. **2** excessive or prejudiced support for one's own cause or group or sex (*male chauvinism*).

chela **1** a prehensile claw of crabs, scorpions, etc. **2** in Buddhism, a novice or disciple.

cheongsam a Chinese woman's dress with a high neck and slit skirt.

cheval glass a tall mirror swung on an upright frame.

cheverel **1** kid leather. **2** pliable and yielding.

chibouk a long Turkish tobacco pipe.

chiliad **1** a thousand. **2** a thousand years.

chiliasm the doctrine of or belief in Christ's prophesied reign of 1,000 years on earth.

chimera (also **chimaera**) **1** a female monster in Greek mythology, with a lion's head, a goat's body, and a serpent's tail. **2** a fantastic product of the imagination; a bogy. **3** an organism formed out of different parts by grafting.

chirography handwriting, calligraphy.

chiropody the treatment of the feet and their ailments.

chiropteran any creature such as the bats and flying foxes, whose membraned limbs serve as wings.

chitin the hornlike substance in the shells of crustaceans etc.

chondrify to turn into cartilage.

chopine (also **chopin**) a woman's high-heeled clog.

chop-logic pedantic argument.

choragus (also **choregus**) **1** the leader of an ancient Greek chorus. **2** a choir leader.

chrestomathy a selection of passages used to help in learning a language.

chrism consecrated oil used especially for anointing in Catholic and Greek Orthodox rites.

chrisom a baby's white baptismal robe that was used as its shroud if it died within the month.

chthonic (also **chthonian**) of the underworld.

chutzpah *slang* shameless audacity; cheek.

chyle milky fluid consisting of lymph and absorbed food from the intestine after digestion.

cicerone a guide who gives information to sightseers.

cicisbeo the recognized male escort of a married woman.

cilice haircloth, or a garment made of this.

Cimmerian dark; densely gloomy.

cineaste a cinema enthusiast.

cingulum *Anat.* a girdle or similar structure, especially the ridge round the base of the crown of a tooth.

circinate *Bot. & Zool.* rolled up with apex in the centre, e.g. of young fronds of ferns.

circumspect wary, cautious; taking everything into account.

circumvent **1** to evade (a difficulty); find a way round. **2** to baffle, outwit.

clade *Biol.* a group of organisms evolved from a common ancestor.

clairschach the old Celtic harp strung with wire.

clandestine surreptitious, secret.

clapperdudgeon a term of insult for a beggar.

claque a group of people hired to applaud in a theatre etc.

claymore **1a** an early Scottish broadsword. **b** a broadsword, often with a single edge, having a hilt with a basketwork design. **2** *US* a type of anti-personnel mine.

clemency mercy.

clepsydra an ancient time-measuring device worked by a flow of water.

clerihew a short comic or nonsensical verse in two rhyming couplets with lines of unequal length, about a famous person whose name usually provides one of the rhymes.

clerisy learned people as a body; scholars.

climacteric **1** *Med.* the period of life when fertility and sexual activity are in decline. **2** a supposed critical period in life (especially occurring every seven years).

cline a graded sequence of differences within a species etc.; a continuum.

clinquant glittering, as with tinsel or spangles.

cliometrics a method of historical research making much use of statistical information and methods.

cloaca the single genital and excretory passage in birds, reptiles, etc.

clone **1** a group of organisms produced asexually from one parent. **2** a person or thing regarded as identical with another.

cloture *US* the closure of a debate.

coalesce to come together and form one whole.

coaptation adaptation of parts to each other, e.g. the ends of a fractured bone.

cochleate shaped like a snail shell; spiral.

codex an ancient manuscript in book form.

coeliac of or affecting the belly.

coenobite a member of a monastic community.

coetaneous contemporary, simultaneous.

coeval **1** of the same age. **2** of the same duration. **3** existing at the same time.

cogent (of arguments, reasons, etc.) convincing, compelling.

cognomen **1** a nickname. **2** an ancient Roman's personal name or epithet, as in Marcus Tullius *Cicero*, Publius Cornelius Scipio *Africanus*.

cohere **1** (of parts or a whole) to stick together, remain united. **2** (of reasoning etc.) to be logical or consistent.

col a depression in a mountain ridge, generally affording a pass.

cold-short (of a metal) brittle in its cold state.

collogue to talk confidentially.

colloquium an academic conference or seminar.

collude to conspire, especially for a fraudulent purpose.

colophon **1** a publisher's device or imprint, especially on the title-page. **2** a tailpiece in a manuscript or book, often ornamental, giving the writer's or printer's name, the date, etc.

colophony rosin.

colostrum the first secretion from the mammary glands after giving birth.

colporteur an itinerant seller of (especially religious) books.

columbarium **1** a dovecote. **2** a vault with niches for funerary urns. **3** a hole left in a wall for the end of a beam.

comedo a blackhead.

commensurate having the same size, duration, etc.; coextensive or proportionate *with*.

commination the threatening of divine vengeance; the recital of divine threats against sinners.

commode **1** a chest of drawers. **2** a chamber-pot concealed in a chair with a hinged cover.

compliant disposed to comply; yielding, obedient.

complicity partnership in a crime or wrongdoing.

compunction the pricking of conscience; regret, scruples.

compurgation acquittal from a charge or accusation, formerly obtained by the oaths of witnesses.

concha *Anat.* any shell-like part, especially the outer ear.

concomitant going together; associated (*concomitant circumstances*).

concordance **1** agreement. **2** a book containing an alphabetical list of the important words used in a book or by an author, usually with citations of the passages concerned.

concordat an agreement, especially between the Roman Catholic church and a State.

concupiscence sexual desire.

condign (of a punishment etc.) severe and well-deserved.

condone **1** to forgive or overlook (an offence or wrongdoing). **2** to approve or sanction, usually reluctantly. **3** (of an action) to atone for (an offence); make up for.

conduit **1** a channel or pipe for conveying liquids. **2** a tube or trough for protecting insulated electric wires.

condyle (also **condyl**) a rounded projection at the end of a bone, forming a joint with another bone.

confluence **1** a place where two rivers meet. **2a** a coming together. **b** a crowd of people.

confrère a fellow member of a profession, scientific body, etc.

confute to prove (a person) to be in error or (an argument) to be false.

congeries a disorderly collection; a mass or heap.

connive **1** (followed by *at*) to disregard or tacitly consent to (a wrongdoing). **2** to conspire *with*.

connubial of marriage or the marital relationship.

conquistador a conqueror, especially one of the Spanish conquerors of Mexico and Peru in the 16th century.

consensus a general agreement of opinion, testimony, etc.; a majority view.

consign **1** to hand over; deliver to a person's possession or trust. **2** to commit decisively or permanently (*consigned it to the dustbin*).

consistory the council of Roman Catholic cardinals, or a court presided over by a bishop of the Church of England.

constrain **1** to compel, or bring about by compulsion. **2** to confine or restrict forcibly.

contentious **1** aggressive, quarrelsome. **2** likely to cause an argument; controversial.

contiguous touching, especially along a line; in contact *with*.

continuum anything seen as having a continuous, not discrete, structure (*space-time continuum*).

contrail a condensation trail, especially from an aircraft.

contumacious insubordinate; stubbornly disobedient, especially to a court order.

contumely insolent or reproachful language or treatment.

contusion a bruise.

conversant well experienced or acquainted *with*.

convoluted **1** coiled, twisted. **2** complex, intricate.

cony (also **coney**) a rabbit.

coprophagous *Zool.* dung-eating.

cordillera a system of parallel mountain ranges with intervening plateaux etc., especially of the Andes.

cordovan a kind of soft leather.

corniche a coastal road cut into the edge of a cliff.

corposant a luminous electric charge sometimes seen on a ship or aircraft during a storm.

corrida a bullfight.

corrigenda errors to be corrected in a printed book.

corsair a pirate, or pirate ship, especially formerly along the Barbary coast.

coruscate to sparkle; be brilliant.

corybantic wild, frenzied.

costive constipated.

coterminous having the same boundaries in space, time, or meaning *with*.

countervail to counterbalance; oppose forcefully and usually successfully.

couvade a custom by which a father appears to undergo labour and childbirth when his child is being born.

coven an assembly of witches.

cozen to cheat, defraud, beguile.

crambo a game in which a player gives a word or verse-line to which each of the others must find a rhyme.

cran a measure for fresh herrings ($37^1/_2$ gallons).

crapulent drunk, or resulting from drunkenness.

crepitate to make a crackling sound.

crepuscular **1** of twilight; dim. **2** appearing or active in twilight.

cromlech **1** a dolmen; a megalithic tomb. **2** a circle of upright prehistoric stones.

crosier a bishop's staff.

crural *Anat.* of the leg.

crux **1** the decisive point at issue. **2** a difficult matter; a puzzle.

cucking-stool a chair on which disorderly women were ducked as a punishment.

cudbear a purple dye derived from lichen.

culminate to reach the highest or final point (*the antagonism culminated in war*).

cuneiform the wedge-shaped writing impressed usually in clay in ancient Babylonian etc. inscriptions.

curmudgeon a bad-tempered person.

cursive (of writing) done with joined characters.

cursory hasty, hurried (*a cursory glance*).

cuspidor *US* a spitton.

cutaneous of the skin.

cwm a bowl-shaped hollow in the side of a hill.

D

dacha a Russian country house or cottage.

dacoit a member of a gang of armed robbers in India or Myanmar.

daedal **1** skilful; inventive. **2** (of the earth etc.) variously adorned.

dalmatic a wide-sleeved long loose ecclesiastical vestment.

daltonism colour-blindness, especially the inability to distinguish between red and green.

dariole a savoury or sweet dish cooked and served in a small cup-shaped mould.

dauphin the eldest son of the King of France.

deadlight **1** a shutter inside a ship's porthole. **2** *US* a skylight that cannot be opened.

deasil clockwise.

débâcle a sudden utter defeat or collapse.

debouch (of troops, a river, a road, etc.) to issue forth into an open area.

decanal of a dean or deanery.

decani (of music) to be sung by the south side of a church choir in antiphonal singing (compare CANTORIS).

deckle a device in a paper-making machine that limits the size of the sheet, leaving a rough edge.

decorticate to remove the bark, husk, or other outside layer from.

decretal a papal decree.

dedans the open gallery at the end of the service side of a real tennis court.

deemster a judge in the Isle of Man.

deeping each of the fathom-deep sections of a fishing net.

defalcation **1** misappropriation of money. **2** a shortcoming.

defeasance the act or process of rendering null and void.

defenestration the action of throwing (especially a person) out of a window.

defilade to secure (a fortification) against gunfire.

deft neatly skilful or dexterous; adroit.

deglutition the act of swallowing.

degust to taste attentively; savour.

deign to think fit; condescend.

deipnosophist a master of the art of dining.

delation reporting of an offence; impeachment.

delectation pleasure, enjoyment (*sang for his delectation*).

deleterious harmful to the mind or body.

demagogue **1** a political agitator appealing to the basest instincts of a mob. **2** a leader of the people in ancient times.

deme **1** a political or administrative division in both ancient and modern Greece. **2** a local population of closely related plants or animals.

demesne **1** a domain. **2** landed property attached to a mansion etc.

demiurge **1** according to Plato, the creator of the universe. **2** in Gnosticism etc., a heavenly being subordinate to the Supreme Being.

demivierge a woman of suspected unchastity who is still physiologically a virgin.

demography the study of the statistics of births, deaths, diseases, etc. in a community.

dendrite **1** a mineral with natural treelike markings. **2** a branching treelike crystal. **3** a branching outgrowth on a nerve cell.

denigrate to defame or disparage (someone's character); blacken.

denizen **1** a foreigner admitted to certain rights in the adopted country. **2** a naturalized word, animal, or plant.

deodand a personal chattel forfeited to the Crown for pious uses.

deontic of or relating to moral duty and obligation.

depilate to remove the hair from.

deploy **1** (of troops) to spread out from a column into a line. **2** to bring (arguments etc.) into effective action.

depredations despoiling, ravaging, or plundering.

deracinate to tear up by the roots.

dermabrasion the surgical removal of some layers of the skin with a revolving tool.

derogate (*from*) **1** to take away a part from; detract from (a merit, right, etc.). **2** to deviate from (correct behaviour etc.)

desalinate to remove salt from (especially sea water).

desiccate to dry out (especially food for preservation) (*desiccated coconut*).

desiderate to feel to be missing; regret the absence of; wish to have.

desist to abstain, cease (*please desist from interrupting*).

desuetude a state of disuse.

desultory going half-heartedly from one subject to another; unmethodical and superficial.

detent **1** a catch whose removal allows machinery to move. **2** a catch that regulates striking in a clock.

deuteragonist the second most important person in a drama.

Devanagari the alphabet used for Sanskrit, Hindi, and other Indian languages.

dewlap the loose fold of skin hanging from the throats of cattle, dogs, etc., or of old people.

dexter one of a small hardy breed of Irish cattle (and see HERALDRY).

dharma *Indian* **1** social custom; the right behaviour. **2** the Buddhist truth. **3** the Hindu social or moral law.

dhobi a washerman or washerwoman in India.

diacritical distinguishing; distinctive.

diaeresis (*US* **dieresis**) a mark (as in *naïve*) over a vowel to indicate that it is sounded separately.

dianetics the system of mental therapy associated with scientology.

diaphanous (of fabric etc.) light and delicate and almost transparent.

diaphoresis sweating, especially artificially induced.

diaphysis *Anat.* the shaft of a long bone.

Diaspora the dispersion of the Jews among the Gentiles, or any group of people similarly scattered.

diastema 1 an interval in ancient Greek music. **2** a space between two teeth.

diatribe a forceful verbal attack; a piece of bitter criticism.

dichotomy **1** a sharp division into two. **2** binary classification. **3** *Bot. & Zool.* repeated bifurcation.

dictum a formal utterance, saying, or maxim.

didicoy *slang* a gypsy; an itinerant tinker.

diktat a categorical decree, especially one imposed by a victor after a war.

dilatory given to or causing delay.

dilettante a person who studies a subject superficially.

dimity cotton fabric woven with stripes or checks.

dipnoan a fish with both gills and lungs.

dirigible a balloon or airship that can be guided.

discobolus a discus-thrower in ancient Greece.

discombobulate *US slang* to disturb, disconcert.

discrepancy difference; a failure to correspond; inconsistency.

discrete individually distinct; separate, discontinuous.

discursive **1** rambling or disgressive. **2** based on argument or reasoning rather than on immediate insight.

disembogue (of a river etc.) to pour forth (waters) at the mouth.

disparage **1** to speak slightingly of; depreciate. **2** to bring discredit on.

disparity inequality; difference; incongruity.

disquisition a long or elaborate treatise or discourse on a subject.

distich a pair of verse lines; a couplet.

dittography a copyist's mistaken repetition of a letter, word, or phrase.

diuretic causing increased output of urine.

divot a piece of turf cut out, as by a golf club in making a stroke.

doge the chief magistrate of the former States of Venice or Genoa.

dolmen a prehistoric tomb with a large flat stone laid on two upright ones.

dolorous **1** distressing, painful; doleful, dismal. **2** distressed, sad.

dominie a Scottish schoolmaster.

dorsal **1** of or on the back. **2** ridge-shaped.

dortour (also **dorter**) a dormitory in a monastery.

do-se-do (also **do-si-do**) a figure in which two dancers pass round each other back to back and return to their original positions.

dotal pertaining to a woman's dowry.

dottle a remnant of burnt tobacco in a pipe.

doxology a hymn or verse of praise to God.

Draconian (of laws, etc.) very harsh or severe.

dragoman an interpreter or guide, especially in countries speaking Arabic, Turkish, or Persian.

drail a fish-hook or line weighted with lead for dragging below the surface of the water.

dressage the training of a horse in obedience and deportment, especially for competition.

drogue **1** a buoy at the end of a harpoon line, or a sea anchor. **2** a funnel-shaped fabric device used as a wind-sock, a target for gunnery, etc.

dryad in Greek mythology, a nymph inhabiting a tree; a wood nymph.

ductile **1** (of a metal) capable of being drawn into wire. **2** (of a substance) easily moulded. **3** (of a person) docile, gullible.

duenna an older woman acting as a governess or companion in charge of girls, especially in a Spanish family; a chaperone.

dugong a marine mammal of Asian seas; the sea cow.

dulcet (especially of a sound) sweet and soothing.

dundrearies long side-whiskers worn without a beard.

dunnock the common hedge sparrow.

dysphemism the substitution of an unpleasant or derogatory expression for a pleasant or harmless one (opp. EUPHEMISM).

dysphoria unease; mental discomfort.

dystopia an imaginary place or condition in which everything is as bad as possible (opp. UTOPIA).

E

eagre a high tidal wave rushing up a narrow estuary; a bore.

ebullient exuberant, high-spirited.

ecdysiast a strip-teaser.

echinoderm a marine invertebrate usually with a spiny skin, e.g. starfish and sea urchins.

eclectic **1** deriving ideas, tastes, style, etc. from various sources. **2** selecting one's beliefs etc. from various sources; attached to no particular school of philosophy.

eclogue a short poem, especially a pastoral dialogue.

ectoplasm the supposed semi-fluid substance issuing from the body of a spiritualistic medium during a trance.

ecumene a nuclear centre of dense population and high culture.

ecumenical seeking or promoting worldwide Christian unity.

edacious voracious; greedy.

effendi a former title of respect for a man of standing in Turkey.

effete **1** feeble and incapable. **2** worn out; exhausted of its essential quality or vitality.

efficacious (of a thing) producing or sure to produce the desired effect.

effluvium an unpleasant smell or exhaled substance affecting the lungs.

effulgent radiant; shining brilliantly.

egregious outstandingly bad; shocking (*egregious folly; an egregious ass*).

eidetic (of a mental image) having unusual vividness and detail, as if actually visible.

eidolon **1** a spectre; phantom. **2** an idealized figure.

eirenicon a proposal made as a means of achieving peace.

eisteddfod a congress of Welsh bards; a national or local festival for musical competitions etc.

elation high spirits.

eld old age.

electuary medicinal powder etc. mixed with something sweet.

eleemosynary **1** of alms; charitable. **2** gratuitous.

elucidate to throw light on; explain.

elude **1** to escape adroitly from (a danger, difficulty, pursuer, etc.); dodge. **2** to avoid compliance with (a law). **3** (of a fact, solution, etc.) to baffle (a person's memory or understanding).

emanate to issue or originate (*from*).

emasculate **1** to deprive of force or vigour; make feeble or ineffective. **2** to castrate.

embroil **1** to involve (a person) in conflict or difficulties. **2** to bring (affairs) into confusion.

emmetropia the normal condition of the eye; perfect vision.

emollient something that soothes and softens the skin.

empennage an arrangement of stabilizing surfaces at the tail of an aircraft.

empirical based on observation, not on theory; deriving knowledge from experience alone.

empyrean **1** the highest heaven, as the sphere of fire in ancient cosmology or as the abode of God in early Christianity. **2** the visible heavens.

emulate to try to equal or excel; imitate zealously.

encaenia an annual celebration in memory of founders and benefactors, especially at Oxford University.

enchiridion a handbook.

enclave **1** a part of a foreign country surrounded by territory of another (compare EXCLAVE). **2** a group of people who are culturally etc. distinct from those surrounding them.

encomium a formal or high-flown expression of praise.

encryption the conversion of data into code.

endemic (of a disease, plant, etc.) regularly or only found among a particular people or in a certain region.

endorphin any of a group of pain-reducing substances occurring naturally in the brain.

energumen an enthusiast or fanatic.

enfilade gunfire directed along a line from end to end at troops, a road, etc.

ensconce to establish or settle (oneself) comfortably, safely, or secretly.

entourage **1** the people attending an important person. **2** surroundings.

enzootic regularly affecting animals in a particular district or at a particular season.

Eonism transvestism, especially by a man.

eparchy a province of the Orthodox Church.

ephemeris an astronomical almanac.

epicene **1** having characteristics of both sexes or of neither; neuter. **2** effete, effeminate.

epigone one of a later and less distinguished generation; an inferior follower.

epitome a person or thing embodying a quality, class, etc.; a typical example.

eponymous of or being the person after whom something is named (*Macbeth is the eponymous hero of the play*).

epyllion a miniature epic poem.

equilibrist an acrobat, especially on a tightrope.

equilibrium **1** the state of physical balance. **2** mental or emotional equanimity. **3** a state in which the energy in a system is evenly distributed and forces, influences, etc. balance each other.

equivocate to use double meaning or inexactness to conceal the truth.

eremite a hermit or recluse.

erethism **1** excessive sensitivity to sexual stimulation. **2** abnormal mental excitement or irritation.

ergonomics the study of human efficiency in the working environment.

ergot a fungus causing a disease of cereals, used as a medicine to aid childbirth.

erinaceous of or like a hedgehog.

eristic (of an argument or arguer) aiming at winning rather than at reaching the truth; disputatious.

erogenous (especially of a part of the body) sensitive to sexual stimulation.

erubescence blushing.

eructation belching.

eschar a brown or black layer of dead skin, caused by a burn etc.

escheat in former times, the reversion of property to the State, or to a feudal lord, on the owner's dying without legal heirs.

esculent fit to eat; edible.

esemplastic moulding into unity; unifying.

esoteric intelligible only to the initiated or those with special knowledge.

espalier a lattice work along which trees or shrubs are trained to grow flat against a wall; or a tree or shrub grown in this way.

espièglerie frolicsomeness.

estovers necessaries formerly allowed by law to a tenant (e.g. fuel, or wood for repairs).

esurient **1** hungry. **2** impecunious and greedy.

eth the name of an old English and Icelandic letter, /ð/ = th.

ethereal **1** light, airy. **2** highly delicate, especially in appearance. **3** heavenly, celestial. **4** of or relating to ether.

ethos the characteristic spirit or attitudes of a community, people, or system, or of a literary work etc.

etiolated pale and sickly.

eupeptic of or having a good digestion.

euphoria a feeling of well-being, especially one based on over-confidence or over-optimism.

evanescent (of an impression or appearance etc.) quickly fading.

evince to make (a quality) evident (*evinced indignation*).

exacerbate **1** to make (pain, anger, etc.) worse. **2** to irritate (a person).

excerpt a short extract from a book, film, piece of music, etc.

exclave a part of one's own country surrounded by territory of another (compare ENCLAVE).

excoriate **1** to rub, strip, or peel off (skin). **2** to censure severely.

exculpate to free (a person) from blame; clear of a charge.

execrable abominable, detestable.

exegesis critical explanation of a text, especially of Scripture.

exemplar **1** a model or pattern. **2** a typical instance of something.

exigent urgent, pressing, exacting.

exiguous scanty, small.

exonerate **1** to free or declare free from blame etc. **2** to release from a duty.

exorbitant (of a price, demand, etc.) grossly excessive.

exorcize to drive out (a supposed evil spirit) by holy words, or free (a person or place) from such a spirit.

expedite to hasten (an action etc.); accomplish (business) quickly.

expiate to pay the penalty for (wrongdoing); make amends for.

expletive a swear-word used in an exclamation.

exponent a person who favours, promotes, or interprets something.

expunge to erase, remove (especially a passage from a book or a name from a list).

extenuate to lessen the seeming seriousness of (guilt) by showing some mitigating factor (*extenuating circumstances*).

extirpate to root out; destroy completely.

exordium the introductory part of a discourse or treatise.

exude **1** to (cause to) ooze out; emit, give off. **2** to display (an emotion etc.) freely (*exuded displeasure*).

eyas a young hawk, especially one taken from the nest for training in falconry.

eyot an ait.

eyrie (also **aerie**) a nest of an eagle or other bird of prey, built high up.

F

fabulist **1** a composer of fables. **2** a liar.

facetious intending to be amusing; flippant.

facile (of speech, writing, theories, etc.) easily achieved but of little value; fluent, glib.

factitious not genuine or natural.

factotum an employee who does all kinds of work.

famulus an attendant on a magician or medieval scholar.

fard make-up; cosmetics.

fartlek a method of training for running, mixing fast with slow work.

fasces **1** the bundle of rods with an axe, carried by a lictor in ancient Rome as a symbol of a magistrate's power. **2** the emblems of authority in Fascist Italy.

fascicle **1** a separately published instalment of a book. **2** a bunch or bundle of fibres etc.

fatwa an authoritative Islamic ruling on a religious matter.

faucal of the throat, especially guttural.

favela a Brazilian shack or slum.

faveolate honeycombed, cellular.

febrile of fever; feverish.

feculent murky; containing sediments or dregs.

feisty *US slang* aggressive, exuberant.

fenestra a small hole in a bone etc., especially in the inner ear.

fenks the fibrous parts of a whale's blubber.

feral **1** (of an animal or plant) wild, untamed, uncultivated. **2** (of an animal) living in a wild state after escape from captivity or domesticity. **3** brutal.

ferial (of a day) ordinary; not a religious festival or fast day.

Festschrift a collection of writings published in honour of a scholar.

fetlock part of the back of a horse's leg above the hoof where a tuft of hair grows.

fibrillate **1** (of a fibre) to split up. **2** (of a muscle, especially in the heart) to quiver.

filibuster **1** to obstruct progress in a legislative assembly by making long speeches. **2** (formerly) to engage in unauthorized warfare against a foreign State.

finocchio a kind of dwarf fennel.

fipple a plug at the mouth end of a wind instrument.

firkin a small cask for liquids, butter, fish, etc.

firmament the sky regarded as a vault or arch.

firman an oriental sovereign's edict, grant, or permit.

fisc the Roman emperor's privy purse.

fissile **1** capable of undergoing nuclear fission. **2** tending to split.

flaccid limp, flabby, drooping.

flagitious deeply criminal; utterly villainous.

fleer to laugh impudently or mockingly; sneer, jeer.

flense to cut up (a whale or seal).

flews the hanging lips of a bloodhound etc.

flocculent like tufts of wool; downy.

flume **1** an artificial channel conveying water etc. for industrial use. **2** a ravine with a stream.

flustra sea matweed.

fontanelle a membraneous space at the top of an infant's skull.

forensic used in connection with courts of law (*forensic medicine*).

formic relating to ants.

fortuitous due to chance; accidental, casual.

foudroyant **1** thundering or dazzling. **2** (of a disease) beginning suddenly and severely.

fouetté a quick whipping movement of the raised leg in ballet.

fox-fire *US* the phosphorescent light emitted by decaying timber.

fraise **1** a ruff, as worn in the 16th century. **2** a horizontal or sloping palisade for defence. **3** a tool for enlarging a round hole, or for cutting teeth in a wheel.

frass the refuse or excrement left by insects.

frenetic frantic, frenzied.

freshet **1** a rush of fresh water flowing into the sea. **2** the flooding of a river.

friable easily crumbled.

frisket a thin iron frame keeping the sheet in position during printing on a hand-press.

froward perverse; difficult to deal with.

frugivorous feeding on fruit.

fugacious fleeting, evanescent; hard to capture or keep.

fulguration the destruction of tissue (e.g. warts) by means of high-voltage electric sparks.

fuliginous sooty, dusky.

fulvous reddish-yellow, tawny.

fumarole an opening in a volcano, through which hot vapours emerge.

fumatory a place for smoking or fumigating purposes.

funambulist a rope-walker.

furcula a forked bone, e.g. the wishbone.

furuncle a boil.

fustanella a man's stiff white kilt worn in Albania and Greece.

futhorc the Scandinavian runic alphabet.

futon a Japanese quilted mattress rolled out on the floor for use as a bed.

fylfot a swastika.

fyrd the English militia before 1066.

G

gadroon a decoration on silverware etc., consisting of convex curves forming an edge like inverted fluting.

gaff **1** a hooked stick for landing large fish. **2** a spar to which the head of a fore-and-aft sail is attached.

gaffe a social blunder.

galliard a lively dance usually in triple time for two people.

galligaskins breeches or trousers, originally as worn in the 16th–17th centuries.

gallimaufry a heterogeneous mixture; a jumble.

gambade **1** a leap or bound of a horse. **2** a prank, freak, frolic.

gamelan an orchestra of SE Asia (especially Indonesia) with strings, woodwind, and many percussion instruments.

gammadion a decorative pattern formed of combinations of the Greek letter gamma.

ganglion **1** a nerve-nucleus, or assemblage of nerve-cells. **2** a cyst, especially on a tendon sheath.

gangue valueless earth etc. in which ore is found.

ganja marijuana.

garbanzo the chickpea.

Garda the State police force of the Irish Republic.

garrotte to strangle, especially with an iron or wire collar.

garth **1** an open space between cloisters. **2** an old word for a yard or garden.

gavage force-feeding with a pump and a tube passing into the stomach.

gavel an auctioneer's or chairman's hammer.

gavelkind **1** a Kentish form of land-tenure. **2** any of various ways of dividing up the property of a deceased man.

gazump (of a seller) to raise the price of a property after having accepted an offer from (an intending buyer).

geek an American fairground entertainer whose act often includes biting the head off a live chicken, snake, etc.

gelation solidification by freezing.

geminate combined in pairs.

gemot a judicial or legislative assembly in Anglo-Saxon England.

genuflect to bend the knee, especially in worship or as a sign of respect.

Georgic relating to agriculture.

germane relevant (*to*) a subject under consideration.

gerrymander to manipulate the boundaries of (a constituency etc.) to the undue advantage of a party or class.

gestate **1** to carry (a foetus) in the womb. **2** to develop (an idea etc.).

ghat **1** the steps leading down to an Indian river. **2** an Indian mountain pass or chain.

ghee Indian clarified butter.

gherao in India and Pakistan, coercion of employers, by which their workers prevent them from leaving the premises until certain demands are met.

ghyll a narrow mountain torrent in a ravine.

gibbous **1** convex, protuberant. **2** (of a moon or planet) between half and full.

gibus a man's tall collapsible hat.

gigot a leg of mutton or lamb.

gimmal a ring made of two linked rings.

gingili sesame seed or its oil.

gingivae the gums.

ginglymus a hingelike joint, as in the elbow or knee, with motion in one plane only.

ginnel a long narrow passage between houses.

girandole **1** a revolving cluster of fireworks. **2** a branched candlestick. **3** an earring or pendant with a large stone surrounded by small ones.

gismo *slang* a gadget.

glabrous hairless; smooth-skinned.

glacis a bank sloping down from a fort.

glair (also **glaire**) **1** white of egg. **2** glue made from this, used in bookbinding etc.

glaive a broadsword.

glasnost (in the former Soviet Union) the policy or practice of more open consultative government and wider dissemination of information.

glaucous **1** of a dull greyish green or blue. **2** covered with a powdery bloom as of grapes.

glebe a piece of land granted to a clergyman as part of his benefice.

glendoveer one of a race of beautiful sprites in Southey's quasi-Hindu mythology.

glossal of the tongue.

gluteal of the buttocks.

gnathic of the jaws.

gnomic of or using aphorisms; sententious.

gnomon the rod etc. on a sundial that shows the time.

gnosis knowledge of spiritual mysteries.

gobemouche a gullible listener.

gobo a portable screen used to deflect light in filming.

goety sorcery; necromancy.

gofer *US slang* someone who runs errands; a dogsbody.

goffer to crimp, make wavy (a lace edge, a trimming, etc.) with a hot iron.

goliard an educated medieval jester and author of loose or satirical Latin verses.

gombeen *Irish* usury.

gombroon a kind of Persian pottery.

gonfalon a banner, often with streamers, hung from a crossbar.

googly an off-break ball in cricket, deceptively bowled with apparent leg-break action.

gorget **1a** a piece of armour for the throat. **b** a woman's wimple. **2** a patch of colour on the throat of a bird, insect, etc.

gorgonize to stare at so as to paralyse with fear.

grabble to sprawl on the floor and grope about to feel for something.

gradine **1** each of a series of low steps or a tier of seats. **2** a ledge at the back of an altar.

grallatorial of long-legged wading birds, e.g. flamingos.

gralloch to disembowel (a dead deer etc.).

graminivorous feeding on grass, cereals, etc.

grangerize to illustrate (a book) by sticking in pictures.

gravamen the most serious part of an argument or grievance.

greaves armour for the shins.

Greek Calends never.

gregarious fond of company.

grilse a young salmon that has returned to fresh water from the sea for the first time.

grommet a metal, plastic, or rubber eyelet fitted in a hole to protect a rope or cable etc.

groundling **1** a plant or animal that lives near the ground. **2** someone on the ground and not in an aircraft. **3** a spectator or reader of inferior taste.

grout a thin fluid mortar for filling gaps in tiling etc.

groyne a low wall built out from a shore to check erosion of a beach.

guacamole a salad or dip of mashed avocado mixed with onion, tomato, chilli, etc.

guano the excrement of sea-fowl, used as manure.

gubernatorial (especially *US*) of or relating to a governor.

guddle to catch fish with the hands.

gudgeon **1** a pivot working a wheel, bell, etc. **2** the tubular part of a hinge into which the pin fits to effect a joint. **3** a socket at the stern of a boat that holds the rudder.

guidon a pointed or forked pennant, especially one used as the standard of a regiment of dragoons.

guimpe a high-necked underblouse to be worn with a low-necked dress or pinafore dress.

gular of the throat or gullet.

gulosity gluttony.

gustatory of the sense of taste.

guttate having droplike markings; speckled.

guttler a glutton.

gymnotus an electric eel.

gynaecomastia enlargement of a man's breasts, usually due to hormone imbalance or hormone therapy.

H

haaf a deep-sea fishing ground.

habergeon a sleeveless coat of mail.

habile skilful, deft, dexterous.

hachures parallel lines used in hill-shading on maps, their closeness indicating the steepness of gradient.

hacienda (in Spanish-speaking countries) an estate or plantation with a dwelling-house, or a factory.

hagiography the writing of the lives of saints.

haik, haick an outer covering for head and body worn by Arabs.

haiku a Japanese three-part poem of usually 17 syllables.

hajji (also **haji**) a Muslim who has been to Mecca as a pilgrim.

haka a Maori ceremonial war dance accompanied by chanting.

halal to kill (an animal) as prescribed by Muslim law.

halitosis bad breath.

halitus vapour, exhalation.

hallux the big toe; or the corresponding digit in vertebrates.

hames the two curved iron or wooden pieces forming the collar of a draught-horse, to which the traces are attached.

haplography the accidental omission of letters when these are repeated in a word (e.g. *philogy* for *philology*).

haptic relating to the sense of touch.

hara-kiri ritual suicide by disembowelment with a sword, formerly practised by Samurai to avoid dishonour.

haras a breeding station for horses; a stud.

harbinger a forerunner that announces the approach of something (*crocuses are harbingers of spring*).

Harijan a member of the untouchable class in India.

harmala the plant wild rue.

harpy **1** (in Greek and Roman mythology) a monster with a woman's head and body and a bird's wings and claws. **2** a grasping unscrupulous person.

haruspex a Roman religious official who interpreted omens by inspecting animals' entrails.

haslet pieces of (especially pig's) offal cooked together and usually compressed into a meat loaf.

haulm (also **halm**) a stalk or stem of peas, beans, potatoes, etc.

havelock a covering for the cap, with a flap hanging over the neck as protection from the sun.

hebdomadal every week, weekly.

hebetude dullness.

hecatomb a great public sacrifice in ancient Greece or Rome, originally of 100 oxen.

heddle one of the sets of small cords or wires between which the warp is passed in a loom.

hedonism belief in pleasure as the highest good and mankind's proper aim.

hegemony leadership, especially by one State of a confederacy.

heinous (of a crime or criminal) utterly odious or wicked.

helot a serf, of a class in ancient Sparta.

helve the handle of a weapon or tool.

hemeralopia difficulty in seeing by daylight; day-blindness.

henge a prehistoric monument such as Stonehenge, consisting of a circle of massive uprights.

hepatic **1** of the liver. **2** dark brownish-red; liver-coloured.

heriot a tribute formerly paid to a lord on the death of a tenant, consisting of an animal, a chattel, etc.

herm a squared stone pillar with a head (especially of the god Hermes) on top, used by the ancient Greeks as a boundary marker etc.

hermeneutic concerning interpretation, especially of Scripture or literary texts.

hetman a Polish or Cossack military commander.

heuristic allowing or assisting to discover (and see COMPUTERS).

hiatus a break or gap in a series etc.

hibachi a portable Japanese pan or brazier in which charcoal is burnt for cooking or to heat a room.

hickwall the green woodpecker.

hidalgo a Spanish gentleman.

hidrosis perspiration.

hierophant an interpreter of sacred mysteries.

hilding **1** a worthless or vicious beast. **2** a contemptible or worthless person of either sex.

hinny (also **hinnie**) the offspring of a female donkey and a male horse.

hippocampus **1** a sea horse. **2** the elongated ridges on the floor of each lateral ventricle of the brain, thought to be the centre of emotion and the involuntary nervous system.

hippocras wine flavoured with spices.

hirsute hairy, shaggy.

hoggin a mixture of sand and gravel.

holistic **1** regarding the whole as greater than the sum of its parts. **2** giving medical treatment to the whole person rather than just to the symptoms of a disease.

holt **1** an animal's (especially an otter's) lair. **2** a wood or copse.

homily a sermon or tedious moralizing discourse.

hominid any member of the primate family Hominidae, including humans and their fossil ancestors.

homocentric having the same centre.

homunculus a little man, a manikin.

hone a whetstone, especially for razors.

hoplite a heavily armed foot soldier of ancient Greece.

horripilation goose-flesh.

hoveller an unlicensed boatman, especially on the Kentish coast.

howdah a seat for two or more, usually with a canopy, for riding on the back of an elephant or camel.

hoyden a boisterous girl.

hubble-bubble a rudimentary kind of hookah, the oriental tobacco pipe with a tube passing through water to cool the smoke.

hubris arrogant pride or presumption.

humectant a substance, especially a food additive, used to retain moisture.

humidor a room or container for keeping cigars or tobacco moist.

hurling an Irish game rather like hockey, played with broad sticks.

hustings **1** parliamentary election proceedings. **2** a platform from which, before 1872, parliamentary candidates were nominated and addressed electors.

hwyl an emotional quality inspiring impassioned eloquence, as in a Welsh poet.

hymeneal of or concerning marriage.

hyperborean of the extreme north of the earth.

hypnagogic inducing sleep, or accompanying the drowsy state leading to sleep.

hypocaust a hollow space under the floor of an ancient Roman house, into which hot air was sent for heating a room or bath.

hypocorism a pet name.

hypothecate to pledge, mortgage.

I

iatrogenic (of a disease etc.) caused by medical examination or treatment.

ichor in Greek mythology, fluid flowing like blood in the veins of the gods.

icon **1** a devotional painting or carving, usually on wood, of Christ or another holy figure, especially in the Eastern Church. **2** an image or statue.

iconoclastic destructive of holy images or of cherished beliefs.

ideogram a character symbolizing the idea of a thing without indicating the sequence of sounds in its name (e.g. a numeral, and many Chinese characters).

idiosyncrasy a mental constitution, view, feeling, or foible peculiar to a person.

idioticon a dictionary confined to a particular dialect, or containing words and phrases peculiar to one part of a country.

idolum a mental image; a phantom or fallacy.

ignominious **1** causing or deserving dishonour. **2** humiliating.

ikebana the art of Japanese flower arrangement.

illation a deduction or conclusion.

illicit unlawful, forbidden (*illicit dealings*).

illuminati people claiming to have special enlightenment.

imagism a movement in early 20th-century poetry which sought clarity of expression through the use of precise images.

imam **1** a leader of prayers in a mosque. **2** a title of various Muslim leaders, especially one succeeding Muhammad as leader of Islam.

imbricate to arrange (leaves, scales of a fish, etc.) so as to overlap like roof tiles.

imbroglio a confused or complicated situation.

imbrue to stain (one's hands, sword, etc.).

immanent **1** indwelling, inherent. **2** (of the supreme being) permanently pervading the universe (opp. TRANSCENDENT).

immarcescible unfading; incorruptible, imperishable.

immiscible that cannot be mixed.

immolate to kill or offer as a sacrifice.

immortelle a papery flower that keeps its shape and texture when dried.

impanate contained or embodied in bread.

impecunious having little or no money.

impedimenta **1** encumbrances. **2** travelling equipment, especially of an army.

impinge to make an impact, have an effect or encroach *on*.

implode to (cause to) burst inwards.

impost **1** a tax, duty, or tribute. **2** a weight carried by a horse in a handicap race.

imprest money advanced to someone for use in State business.

imprimatur an official licence by the Roman Catholic church to print a book.

impugn to challenge (a statement, action, etc.); call in question.

inane silly, senseless.

incarnate **1** embodied in flesh, especially in human form (*is the devil incarnate*). **2** represented in a recognizable or typical form (*folly incarnate*).

inchoate undeveloped, rudimentary.

incipient beginning; in an initial stage.

incivism lack of good citizenship.

incommunicado **1** without or deprived of the means of communication with others. **2** (of a prisoner) in solitary confinement.

incubus **1** an evil spirit supposed to lie on sleeping people, especially to have intercourse with sleeping women. **2** a nightmare, or something that oppresses like a nightmare.

inculpate **1** to involve in a charge. **2** to accuse, blame.

incunabula books printed very early, especially before 1501.

incursion an invasion or attack, especially when sudden or brief.

indite **1** to put (a speech etc.) into words. **2** to write (a letter etc.).

induct **1** to introduce formally into possession of a benefice. **2** to install (a person) into a room, position, etc.

indurate to harden.

ineffable **1** unutterable; too great for description in words. **2** too sacred to be uttered.

ineluctable unescapable.

infanta a daughter of the ruling monarch of Spain or Portugal, usually the eldest daughter who is not heir to the throne.

infarct a small localized area of dead tissue caused by an inadequate blood supply.

infibulation the fastening up of the sexual organs with a clasp etc., to prevent sexual intercourse.

inguinal of the groin.

insolation exposure to the sun's rays, especially for bleaching.

insouciant carefree, unconcerned.

inspissate to thicken, condense.

instauration restoration, renewal.

insurgent a rebel, a revolutionary.

integument a natural outer covering; a skin, rind, husk, etc.

intercalary (of a day or month) inserted in the calendar to harmonize it with the solar year, e.g. 29 February in leap years.

interim the time between two events (*in the interim he had died*).

internecine mutually destructive.

interregnum an interval between successive reigns or regimes, when the normal government is suspended.

intinction the dipping of the Eucharistic bread in the wine so that the communicant receives both together.

inveigh to speak or write with strong hostility *against*.

involute curled spirally, or rolled inwards at the edges.

irascible irritable; hot-tempered.

iridescent showing rainbow-like luminous or gleaming colours; shimmering.

irredentist a person, especially in 19th-century Italy, advocating the restoration to his or her country of any territory formerly belonging to it.

irrefragable **1** (of a statement, argument, or person) unanswerable, indisputable. **2** (of rules etc.) inviolable.

irrefutable impossible to refute or disprove.

irrision derision, mockery.

irrupt to enter forcibly or violently *into*.

isocheim a line on a map connecting places having the same average temperature in winter.

isomorphic having exactly the same form and relations.

istle fibre used for cord, nets, etc., obtained from the plant agave.

iterate to repeat; state repeatedly.

izard a chamois.

izzard an old name for the letter Z.

J

jabot an ornamental frill or lace ruffle on the front of a shirt or blouse.

jacobus an English gold coin struck in the reign of James I.

jacquerie the French peasants' revolt against the nobles in 1357–8.

jalousie a blind made of a row of angled slats.

janizary (also **janissary**) a member of the Turkish infantry forming the Sultan's guard in the 14th–19th centuries.

jarl a Norse or Danish chief.

jejune **1** (of ideas etc.) shallow, meagre, sparse. **2** (of the land) barren, poor.

jennet a small Spanish horse.

jeofail a mistake in a legal proceeding.

jeopardy danger, especially of severe harm or loss, or of conviction when on trial for a criminal offence.

jeremiad a doleful lamentation; a list of woes.

jeroboam a wine bottle of 4–12 times the ordinary size.

jerque to examine a ship's papers when checking the cargo for customs.

jeton a metal disc used, chiefly in France, instead of a coin for insertion in a public telephone box.

jihad (also **jehad**) a holy war undertaken by Muslims against unbelievers.

jingoism blustering patriotism in favour of war.

jocose **1** playful in style. **2** fond of joking; jocular.

jokul a permanently snow-covered mountain.

jugate having paired parts joined together.

juggernaut **1** a huge overwhelming force or object. **2** in Britain, a large heavy motor vehicle, especially an articulated lorry.

jugular of the neck or throat (*jugular vein*).

jugulate to kill by cutting the throat.

ju-ju a charm or fetish of some West African peoples.

jumbal a kind of sweet crisp cake.

junta a political or military group taking power after a revolution.

juxtapose to place side by side, especially for the sake of comparison.

jynx **1** a bird, the wryneck. **2** a charm or spell.

K

kabuki a form of popular traditional Japanese drama with highly stylized song, acted by males only.

kamikaze **1** a Japanese aircraft of World War II that was loaded with explosives and deliberately crashed on the target. **2** its suicide pilot.

kampong a Malayan enclosure or village.

kanaka a South Sea Islander, especially one of those formerly employed in forced labour in Australia.

kanga a patterned cotton cloth worn as a woman's garment in East Africa.

kaolin fine soft white clay used especially for making porcelain and in medicines; china clay.

kapok a firm fibrous cotton-like substance found surrounding the seeds of a tropical tree, *Ceiba pentandra*, used for stuffing things.

kaput *slang* broken, ruined, done for.

karma in Buddhism and Hinduism, the sum of a person's actions in previous lives, viewed as determining his or her future; one's fate or destiny.

kaross a sleeveless hairy mantle worn by Hottentots and other South African Negroid peoples.

kazoo a toy musical instrument that buzzes when the player sings or hums into it.

keelhaul **1** to drag (a person) under the keel of a ship as a punishment. **2** to scold severely.

keffiyeh an Arab headscarf.

keloid fibrous scar tissue.

kelp large broad-fronded brown seaweed suitable for use as manure.

kelpie a Scottish water-spirit, usually in the form of a horse, reputed to delight in the drowning of travellers.

kelt a salmon or sea trout after spawning.

kendo a Japanese form of fencing with two-handed bamboo swords.

kenning a compound expression in Old English and Old Norse poetry, e.g. *oar-steed* = ship.

kenosis the partial renunciation of the divine nature by Christ in the Incarnation.

kerf a slit made by sawing.

kibbutz a communal (especially farming) establishment in Israel.

kibitzer an onlooker at cards etc., especially a busybody who offers unwanted advice.

kiddle a barrier in a river fitted with nets to catch fish; or a similar arrangement of nets on stakes along the seashore.

kilderkin a 16- or 18-gallon cask for liquids.

kilim a pile-less woven Eastern rug or wall hanging.

kismet fate, destiny.

knag **1** a knot in wood. **2** a small dead branch. **3** a peg for hanging things on.

knobkerrie a short stick with a knobbed head used as a weapon, especially by South African tribes.

knout a scourge used in imperial Russia, often causing death.

koan a riddle used in Zen Buddhism to demonstrate the inadequacy of logical reasoning.

kohl a black powder used as eye make-up, especially in Eastern countries.

kris (also **crease, creese**) a Malay or Indonesian dagger with a wavy blade.

kukri a Gurka knife, curved and broadening towards the point.

kulak a peasant working for personal profit in Soviet Russia.

kymograph an instrument for recording variations in pressure, e.g. in sound waves or in blood within blood vessels.

L

laager **1** a camp or encampment in South Africa, especially one formed by a circle of wagons. **2** a park for armoured vehicles.

labial of, near, or using the lips.

labile unstable; liable to change.

labret a piece of shell, bone, etc. inserted in the lip as an ornament.

labrys the double-headed axe of ancient Crete.

lachrymal of or concerned with tears.

lachrymose given to weeping; tearful.

laconic (of speech or writing, or a speaker or writer) brief, concise, terse.

lactate (of mammals) to secrete milk.

lacuna a gap, blank, or cavity.

lacustrine of lakes; especially living or growing in lakes.

lagan goods or wreckage lying on the bed of the sea, sometimes with a marked buoy etc. for later retrieval.

lallation the pronunciation of *r* as *l*; or imperfect speech generally.

lama a Tibetan or Mongolian Buddhist monk.

lambaste **1** to thrash, beat. **2** to criticize severely.

lambent softly radiant.

lambrequin *US* a short piece of drapery hung over a door, window, or mantelpiece.

lamia a fabulous monster with a woman's body, supposed to prey on human beings.

lamina a thin plate of bone, stratified rock, vegetable tissue, etc.

lampion a usually coloured pot of oil with a wick, formerly used in illuminations.

lamprey an eel-like fish with a sucking mouth and horny teeth but no scales or jaws.

lanate woolly; covered with hairs like wool.

landau a four-wheeled enclosed carriage with a removable front cover and a back cover that can be raised and lowered.

langlauf cross-country skiing.

lansquenet **1** a German card game. **2** a German mercenary soldier in the 16th–17th centuries.

lanugo fine soft hair, especially that which covers a human foetus.

laparotomy a surgical incision into the abdominal cavity.

lapidary **1** concerned with, or engraved on, stone. **2** (of writing style) dignified and concise; suitable for inscriptions.

lapidate to pelt (someone) with stones.

lariat **1** a lasso. **2** a tethering-rope, especially used by cowboys.

lasque a flat piece of diamond.

lassitude **1** languor, weariness. **2** disinclination to exert or interest oneself.

latex the milky fluid found especially in the rubber tree and used for commercial purposes.

latifundia large estates or plantations.

latrant barking, snarling.

lauwine an avalanche.

lavabo **1** the ritual washing of the priest's hands at Mass. **2** a monastery washing trough.

lave **1** to wash, bathe. **2** (of water) to wash against; flow along.

laver bread a Welsh dish of boiled seaweed dipped in oatmeal and fried.

layette a set of clothing and equipment for a new baby.

lazaretto an isolation hospital or quarantine ship.

leach to remove (soluble matter) from bark, ore, ash, soil, etc. by the action of percolating liquid.

leat an open watercourse taking water to a mill.

lector **1** a reader, especially of lessons in church. **2** (*fem.* **lectrice**) a lecturer or reader, especially one employed in a foreign university to teach his or her native language.

lees the sediment of wine etc.

legerdemain sleight of hand; conjuring.

legume the seed pod of a pea, bean, etc. used as food.

lei **1** a Polynesian flower garland. **2** the plural of *leu*, the Romanian currency unit.

leister a pronged salmon-spear.

lemma **1** a proposition used in an argument or proof. **2** a heading indicating the subject of a literary composition, a dictionary entry, etc. **3** a motto appended to a picture etc.

lenitive soothing, palliative.

lenity mercy, gentleness.

lentigo a freckle or pimple.

lepidopterist an expert in or collector of butterflies and moths.

Lethe **1** in Greek mythology, a river in Hades producing forgetfulness of the past. **2** such forgetfulness.

leucoma a white opacity in the cornea of the eye.

levant *Brit. slang* to abscond or bolt, especially with betting or gaming losses unpaid.

levigate to reduce to smooth paste or powder.

levitate to (cause to) rise and float in the air (especially with reference to spiritualism).

lexigraphy a system of writing in which each character represents a word.

libation a drink-offering poured out to a god.

libidinous lustful.

lich-gate (also **lych-gate**) a roofed gateway to a churchyard where a coffin may be rested before a funeral.

Lilliputian tiny, diminutive.

limaceous of slugs or snails; snail-like.

limn to paint (especially a miniature portrait).

limpid (of water, eyes, etc.) clear, transparent.

linga a phallus, especially as the Hindu symbol of Shiva.

limpkin a water bird not unlike the cranes and rails.

lionize to treat as a celebrity.

lipography the omission of letters or words in writing.

lipper **1** a rippling of the sea. **2** a tool for forming the lip of a glass vessel.

lissom lithe, supple, agile.

littoral a region lying along the shore of the sea, a lake, etc.

llano a treeless grassy plain, especially in South America.

loblolly a thick gruel eaten especially by sailors.

lockage **1** the amount of rise and fall effected by canal locks. **2** a toll for the use of a lock. **3** the construction or use of locks.

logie *Scottish* the open space before a kiln fire.

logion a saying attributed to Christ, especially one not recorded in the recognized Gospels.

logistics the detailed planning and organization of an operation, especially of moving, lodging, and supplying troops and equipment.

logomachy a dispute about words; controversy turning on merely verbal points.

logorrhoea an excessive flow of words, especially in mental illness.

longanimity long-suffering; forbearance or patience under provocation.

loquacious talkative, chattering.

loricate having an armour of scales, plates, etc.

lorimer, loriner a maker of bits, spurs, and metal bridle mountings for horses.

loupe a small magnifying glass used by jewellers.

lovelock a curl or lock of hair worn on the temple or forehead.

lox *US* smoked salmon.

luau a feast with Hawaiian food and usually entertainment.

lubricious **1** slippery, smooth, oily. **2** lewd, prurient.

lucubration **1** nocturnal study. **2** pedantic or elaborate literary writings.

ludic of spontaneous play or games.

luge a light toboggan for one or two people, ridden in the sitting position.

lumbar of the lower back area.

lungi a length of cotton cloth, worn as a loincloth in India, or a skirt in Myanmar (where it is the national dress for both sexes).

lunula **1** the crescent-shaped area at the base of the fingernail. **2** a crescent-shaped Bronze Age ornament.

lustrate to purify by ceremonial sacrifice, washing, etc.

lustrum a period of five years.

lycanthrope a werewolf, or an insane person who thinks he or she is a wolf.

lycopod any of various clubmosses, especially of the genus *Lycopodium*.

lysis the disintegration of a cell.

M

macabre grim, gruesome.

macerate to make or become soft by soaking.

machete a broad heavy knife used in Central America and the West Indies as an implement and weapon.

machiavellian elaborately cunning; scheming, unscrupulous.

machismo exaggeratedly assertive manliness; a show of masculinity.

mackle a blurred impression in printing.

macramé the art of knotting string in patterns to make decorative articles.

macron a written or printed mark (¯) over a long or stressed vowel.

macroscopic **1** big enough to be visible to the naked eye. **2** regarded in terms of large units.

macula a dark spot, especially a permanent one, on the skin.

maelstrom **1** a great whirlpool. **2** a state of confusion.

maenad a female follower of the god Bacchus.

magnum a wine bottle of about twice the standard size.

magot **1** the tailless Barbary ape of Gibraltar. **2** a small grotesque Chinese or Japanese figure of porcelain, ivory, wood, etc.

maharishi a great Hindu sage or spiritual leader.

mahout in India etc. an elephant-driver or -keeper.

maieutic (of the Socratic mode of enquiry) serving to bring a person's latent ideas into clear consciousness.

maladroit clumsy; bungling.

malamute (also **malemute**) an Eskimo dog.

malediction a curse; cursing.

maleficent hurtful or criminal.

malign **1** (of a thing) injurious. **2** (of a disease) malignant. **3** malevolent.

malism the doctrine that the world is an evil one.

malversation corrupt behaviour in a position of trust, as by a public official.

mamilla (*US* **mammilla**) a nipple or teat.

mana **1** power, authority, prestige. **2** supernatural or magical power.

manacle a handcuff.

manciple an officer who buys provisions for a college, an Inn of Court, etc.

mandala a symbolic circular figure representing the universe in various religions.

mandor a foreman or overseer in Malaysia or Indonesia.

mandrel **1** a shaft in a lathe to hold work being turned. **2** a cylinder round which material is forged or shaped.

manes the deified souls of dead ancestors.

mangonel an ancient military engine for throwing stones, etc.

Manichee an adherent of a 3rd–5th century religious system representing Satan as in a state of everlasting conflict with God.

mansuetude meekness, docility, gentleness.

manumit to set (a slave) free.

marasmus a wasting away of the body.

marc brandy made from the refuse of pressed grapes.

marimba a xylophone played by natives of Africa and Central America, or a modern orchestral instrument derived from this.

marmoreal of or like marble.

marquois an apparatus for drawing equidistant parallel lines.

marram a kind of shore grass.

marshalsea a prison in Southwark abolished in 1842; also certain other London prisons.

martinet a strict (especially military or naval) disciplinarian.

martingale **1** a strap connecting a horses's noseband to the girth, to prevent rearing. **2** a gambling system of continually doubling the stakes.

martlet an old word for a swift or house-martin.

masochism **1** a form of (especially sexual) perversion characterized by pleasure derived from one's own pain or humiliation. **2** *colloq.* the enjoyment of what seems to be painful or tiresome.

mastaba **1** an ancient Egyptian tomb with sloping sides and a flat roof. **2** a bench outside a house in Islamic countries.

mastectomy the amputation of a breast.

matutinal of or in the morning.

maud a Scottish shepherd's grey striped plaid.

maudlin weakly or tearfully sentimental, especially in an effusive stage of drunkenness.

maulstick a light stick with a padded leather ball at one end, held by a painter in one hand to support the other.

maunder to talk or move dreamily or listlessly.

maverick **1** *US* an unbranded calf or yearling. **2** an unorthodox or independent-minded person.

mawkish sentimental in a feeble or sickly way.

maya *Hinduism* a marvel or illusion, especially perceptible to the senses.

meerschaum **1** a white clay-like mineral chiefly found in Turkey. **2** a tobacco pipe made of this.

megalopolis a great city.

megass the fibre left when sugar has been extracted from the cane.

megilp (also **magilp**) a mixture of mastic resin and linseed oil often added to oil paints in the 19th century.

melanin the dark pigment responsible for tanning the skin when exposed to sunlight.

melton cloth with a close-cut nap, used for overcoats etc.

menarche the onset of first menstruation.

menhir a tall upright usually prehistoric monumental stone.

mephitis a noxious emanation; a stench.

mercurial **1** sprightly, ready-witted, volatile. **2** of or containing mercury. **3** (**Mercurial**) of the planet Mercury.

meretricious **1** (of decorations, literary style, etc.) showily but falsely attractive. **2** of or befitting a prostitute.

merkin **1** false hair to cover the pudendum; a pubic wig. **2** a mop for cleaning out a cannon.

mesa *US* an isolated flat-topped hill with steep sides, found in landscapes with horizontal strata as in the south-west USA.

mestizo a Spaniard or Portuguese of mixed race, especially the offspring of a Spaniard and an American Indian.

metempsychosis the supposed transmigration of souls into a new body after death.

metheglin a kind of spiced mead, originally peculiar to Wales.

metopic of the forehead; frontal.

Mickey Finn a strong alcoholic drink adulterated with knockout drops.

micron one-millionth of a metre.

micturate to urinate.

mien a person's look or bearing, as showing character or mood.

mihrab a niche or slab in a mosque, used to show the direction of Mecca.

militate (of facts or evidence) to have force or effect *against* (*what you say militates against our opinion*).

milt **1** the spleen or spleen-like organ in vertebrates. **2** a sperm-filled reproductive gland of a male fish.

mimesis **1** deliberate imitation; mimicry. **2** *Biol.* a close external resemblance of an animal to another that is distasteful or harmful to predators of the first.

miniver (also **minever**) plain white fur used in ceremonial costume.

misandry the hatred of men.

miscegenation the interbreeding of races, especially of Whites and non-Whites.

miscreant a vile wretch; a villain.

misericord a shelving projection on the under side of a hinged seat in a choir stall serving (when the seat is turned up) to help support a person standing.

misogyny the hatred of women.

misprision **1** a misunderstanding. **2** failure to appreciate the value of something. **3** an old word for contempt.

mistigris a blank card used like a joker in a form of poker.

mithridatize to render proof against a poison by administering gradually increasing doses of it.

mitrailleuse a breech-loading 19th-century machine-gun.

mnemonic a phrase etc. designed to aid the memory, e.g. *face* for the musical notes F, A, C, E between the lines on the treble clef.

moiety each of two parts, especially halves, into which something is divided.

mollify to appease, pacify, soften.

moniker (also **monicker, monniker**) *slang* a person's name.

monition **1** a warning of danger. **2** a rebuke, admonishment.

monocoque an aircraft or vehicle structure in which the chassis is integral with the body.

monotreme any mammal of Australia and New Guinea, including the duckbill and spiny anteater, with a single opening for urine, faeces, and eggs.

monstrance in the Roman Catholic church, a vessel in which the Host is exposed for veneration.

mor humus formed under acid conditions.

mora **1a** a delay. **b** a unit of time equal to the duration of a short syllable. **2** a game in which one player guesses the number of fingers held up by another. **3** a division of the Spartan army. **4** a tree of Guiana and Trinidad. **5** a footstool.

moratorium **1** a temporary prohibition or suspension of an activity. **2** a legal authorization to debtors to postpone payment.

mordant **1** (of sarcasm etc.) caustic, biting. **2** corrosive or cleansing.

mores the customs and conventions of a community.

morganatic (of a marriage) between people of different social ranks, the spouse and children having no claim to the possessions or title of the person of higher rank.

morion a kind of military helmet of the 16th and 17th centuries.

moshav a cooperative association of Israeli smallholders.

motile capable of motion.

moxibustion a Chinese and Japanese method of treating various conditions by burning a herbal mixture on part of the body.

muckluck (also **mukluk**) a high Eskimo boot made of sealskin, canvas, etc.

muezzin a Muslim crier who proclaims the hours of prayer usually from a minaret.

mugient lowing, bellowing.

mugwump *US* **1** a great man; a boss. **2** a person who holds aloof, especially from party politics.

mulct **1** to extract money from by fine or taxation. **2** to swindle, or obtain by swindling.

muliebrity **1** womanhood; the common characteristics of a woman. **2** softness, effeminacy.

multipara a woman who has borne more than one child.

mumchance silent; dumbstruck.

mummiform shaped like a mummy.

mumpsimus an ignorant opponent of reform; an old fogey.

mundungus bad-smelling tobacco.

murex a shellfish that gives a purple dye.

muscular stomach any organ that grinds and squeezes to aid digestion, such as a bird's gizzard.

musth (of a male elephant or camel) in a state of frenzy.

mutch a woman's or child's linen cap.

muzhik a Russian peasant of tsarist times.

myrmidon **1** a hired ruffian. **2** a base servant.

N

nacre mother-of-pearl.

naevus (*US* **nevus**) a birthmark or mole.

naiad **1** in Greek mythology, a water-nymph. **2** the larva of a dragon-fly etc.

nainsook a fine soft cotton fabric, originally Indian.

naker an old word for a kettledrum.

napalm a jellied petrol used in incendiary bombs.

nappa (also **napa**) a soft leather made by a special process from the skins of sheep or goats.

narcosis insensibility induced by drugs.

nascent just beginning to be; not yet mature.

natality birth rate.

natation swimming.

nattier blue a soft shade of blue.

neap tide a tide just after the first and third quarters of the moon, when there is least difference between low and high water.

Nearctic of the Arctic and the temperate parts of North America as a zoogeographical region.

nefarious wicked, iniquitous.

Negritude **1** the state of being a Negro. **2** the affirmation of the value of Negro culture.

nemesis downfall caused by retributive justice.

nenuphar a water-lily.

neonate a newborn child.

neophyte **1** a new convert, especially to a religious faith. **2** *RC Ch.* a novice of a religious order or newly ordained priest. **3** a beginner; a novice.

nepenthe a drug causing forgetfulness of grief.

nepotism favouritism shown to relatives in conferring appointments or privileges.

nereid in Greek mythology, a sea nymph.

nescience lack of knowledge; ignorance.

nether lower.

netsuke a carved button-like Japanese ornament, especially of ivory or wood, formerly worn to suspend articles from a girdle.

névé an expanse of granular snow not yet compressed into ice, at the head of a glacier.

nexus **1** a connected group or series. **2** a bond; a connection.

nictitate to blink or wink.

nidicolous (of a bird) bearing helpless young that remain in the nest until they can live without parental care.

nidifugous (of a bird) bearing well-developed young that leave the nest almost immediately.

niello a black composition of sulphur with silver, lead, or copper, for filling engraved lines in silver or other metal ornamental work.

nimbus a bright cloud or halo investing a deity or person or thing.

nimiety excess, redundancy.

niveous like snow; snowy.

nobiliary (of a preposition) forming part of a title of nobility (e.g. French *de*, German *von*).

nock a notch in a bow to hold the bowstring, or on an arrow to receive it.

noctambulist a sleepwalker.

noetic **1** of the intellect. **2** intellectual, speculative.

Noh traditional Japanese drama with dance and song, evolved from Shinto rites.

noisette a small round piece of meat etc.

nonage an old word for legal minority; immaturity.

nonce the time being (*for the nonce*).

nonchalant calm and casual, unmoved, unexcited, indifferent.

nonentity a person or thing of no importance.

nonpareil unrivalled or unique.

noria a Spanish and Eastern device for raising water, consisting of a revolving chain of pots or buckets which are filled below and discharged as they reach the top.

nostrum **1** a quack remedy. **2** a pet scheme, especially for political or social reform.

Notogæa the zoological region comprising Australia, New Zealand, and tropical and South America.

novena *RC Ch.* a devotion consisting of special prayers or services on nine successive days.

noyade execution by drowning.

nuance a subtle difference in or shade of meaning, feeling, colour, etc.

nubile (of a woman) marriageable or sexually attractive.

nuchal of or relating to the nape of the neck.

nugatory trifling, worthless, not valid.

nullify to make null; neutralize, invalidate.

numdah an embroidered felt rug from India etc.

numinous **1** indicating the presence of a god. **2** spiritual and awe-inspiring.

numismatics the study of coins and medals.

nyctalopia night-blindness.

nympholepsy ecstasy or frenzy caused by desire of the unattainable.

nymphomania excessive sexual desire in women.

O

oakum a loose fibre obtained by picking old rope to pieces and used especially in waterproofing the seams of boats.

oast a kiln for drying hops.

obdurate stubborn; hardened against persuasion.

obeah a kind of sorcery practised especially in the West Indies.

obfuscate to confuse or bewilder (a mind, topic, etc.).

obi a broad sash worn with a Japanese kimono.

objurgation scolding, chiding.

oblate a person dedicated to a monastic or religious life.

oblation something offered to a divine being, e.g. the offering of bread and wine to God in the Eucharist.

obloquy **1** the state of being generally ill spoken of. **2** abuse, detraction.

obol an ancient Greek coin equal to one-sixth of a drachma.

obsecration earnest entreaty.

obsequies funeral rites.

obstetric of childbirth and associated processes.

obstreperous turbulent, vociferous; noisily resisting control.

obtrude to thrust forward (oneself, one's opinion, etc.) unduly.

obviate to get round or do away with (a need, inconvenience, etc.).

Occident Europe and America as distinct from the Orient.

occiput the back of the head.

occlude to block up, close (an orifice).

ocellus **1** a simple (not compound) eye of some insects etc. **2** an eye-like marking, as on a butterfly's wing or peacock's tail.

oche the line behind which darts players stand when throwing.

octroi a duty levied in some European countries on goods entering a town.

od a hypothetical power once thought to pervade nature and account for various scientific phenomena.

odalisque an Eastern female slave or concubine, especially in the former Turkish Sultan's harem.

odontoid toothlike.

oestrus a recurring period of sexual receptivity in many female mammals; heat.

officinal **1** (of a medicine) kept ready for immediate dispensing. **2** (of a plant etc.) used in medicine.

ogdoad a group of eight.

ogham (also **ogam**) an ancient British and Irish alphabet of twenty characters formed by parallel strokes on either side of or across a continuous line.

oleaginous oily, greasy.

olfactory of the sense of smell.

oliver a hammer with its arm attached to an axle, worked with the foot by a treadle and used in shaping nails, bolts, etc.

omphalos **1** a conical stone (especially that at Delphi) representing the navel of the earth. **2** a centre or hub, such as the boss on a shield.

onager **1** a wild ass of Central Asia. **2** an ancient military engine for throwing rocks.

onanism **1** masturbation. **2** coitus interruptus.

oneiric of dreams or dreaming.

ontogenesis the origin and development of an individual.

opine to express as one's opinion.

oppidan a town-dweller.

oppugn to call into question; contradict.

opsimath a person who learns only late in life.

optophone an instrument converting light into sound, and so enabling the blind to read print etc. by ear.

opuscule a minor (especially musical or literary) work.

oracy the ability to express oneself fluently in speech.

ordinand a candidate for admission to holy orders.

ordnance mounted guns and other military weapons, ammunition, and equipment.

ordonnance the systematic arrangement especially of literary or architectural work.

ordure **1** excrement, dung. **2** obscenity; filth; foul language.

oread in Greek and Roman mythology, a mountain nymph.

orectic concerning desire or appetite.

oreide a kind of shiny brass used for imitation jewellery etc.

orgeat a cooling drink made from barley or almonds and orange-flower water.

orgulous haughty, splendid.

oriflamme **1** the sacred scarlet banner of St Denis carried into war by early French kings. **2** a principle or ideal as a rallying point in a struggle.

origami the Japanese art of folding paper into decorative shapes and figures.

ormolu gilded metal alloy used to decorate furniture, clocks, etc.

orotund **1** (of the voice or phrasing) full, round, imposing. **2** (of language) pompous, pretentious.

Orphic of the mysteries associated with the legendary Greek poet Orpheus; oracular, occult.

orphrey an ornamental stripe or border or separate piece of ornamental needlework, especially on ecclesiastical vestments.

orris any plant of the genus *Iris*, whose fragrant rootstock is used in perfumery.

ortanique a cross between an orange and a tangerine.

orthodontics the treatment of irregularities in the teeth and jaws.

orthodromy the art of sailing or flying on a great circle route, the most direct course.

ortolan a small European bird, eaten as a delicacy.

orts fragments of food; leavings.

oscitant yawning, drowsy.

osculate to kiss.

osmic of the sense of smell.

ossuary a place for the bones of the dead; a charnel-house.

osteal of bone.

ostler a stableman at an inn.

otiose serving no practical purpose; functionless.

ottoman an upholstered seat without a back or sides.

oubliette a secret dungeon with access only through a trapdoor.

ovation **1** an enthusiastic reception, especially spontaneous and sustained applause. **2** in ancient Rome, a lesser form of triumph.

oviparous egg-laying.

oxbow **1** a horseshoe bend in a river. **2** a lake formed when the river cuts across the narrow end of this.

oxytocic accelerating childbirth.

P

pabulum food, especially for the mind.

pachinko a Japanese form of pinball.

pachyderm a thick-skinned mammal, especially an elephant or rhinoceros.

paduasoy a strong corded silk fabric.

paean a song of praise or triumph.

paedophilia (*US* **pedo-**) sexual desire directed towards children.

paladin a knight errant; a champion.

palanquin (also **palankeen**) a covered litter for one passenger, used in the East.

palfrey an old word for a horse for ordinary riding, especially for women.

palimony *US colloq.* an allowance made to one's unmarried partner after separation.

palimpsest a manuscript on which the original writing has been effaced to make room for other writing.

palingenesis the reproduction of ancestral characteristics in the development of an individual.

palinode a poem in which the writer retracts a view expressed in a former poem.

palliate **1** to alleviate (disease etc.) without curing it. **2** to excuse, extenuate.

palmer a medieval pilgrim who had returned from the Holy Land with a palm branch or leaf.

palpebral of the eyelids.

palps the segmented feelers at the mouths of some shellfish and insects.

palstave a type of ancient chisel made of bronze etc. and shaped to fit into a split handle.

palter **1** to haggle or equivocate. **2** to trifle.

paludal **1** of a marsh; marshy. **2** malarial.

panache **1** assertiveness or flamboyant confidence of style or manner. **2** a tuft of feathers on a medieval headdress.

panada **1** a thick flour paste. **2** bread boiled to a pulp and flavoured.

pandect a complete body of laws; especially a compendium in 50 books of the Roman civil law made by order of Justinian in the 6th century.

pandemic an epidemic ranging over a whole country or the whole world.

pandour a former kind of soldier or mounted constable in the Balkans.

Pangæa the original vast supercontinent that split up into the land-masses of today.

panhandle *US* **1** a narrow strip of land extending from one State into another. **2** *verb* to beg for money in the street.

pannage **1** the right of pasturing swine in a forest. **2** the acorns etc. on which the swine feed.

pantheism the belief that God is identifiable with nature and natural forces.

pantheon **1** a building in which the illustrious dead are buried or commemorated. **2** all the deities of a people; or a temple dedicated to them.

panurgic able or ready to do anything; crafty and subtle.

paparazzo a freelance photographer who pursues celebrities to photograph them.

papilloma a wart, corn, or other usually benign tumour.

Paraclete the Holy Spirit as advocate or counsellor.

paradigm an example or pattern, especially a set of the inflections of a noun, verb, etc.

paramount **1** supreme; requiring first consideration; pre-eminent (*of paramount importance*). **2** in supreme authority.

parang a large heavy Malayan knife used for clearing vegetation etc.

paraph a flourish after a signature, originally as a precaution against forgery.

paraquat a quick-acting herbicide.

paravane a torpedo-shaped device towed by a ship to cut the moorings of submerged mines.

parbuckle a rope sling for raising or lowering casks and cylindrical objects.

pard an old word for a leopard.

parergon **1** work secondary to one's main employment. **2** an ornamental accessory.

parget to plaster (a wall etc.) especially with an ornamental pattern.

parison a rounded mass of glass formed by rolling immediately after taking it from the furnace.

parlay *US* to use (money won on a bet) as a further stake.

parlous dangerous or difficult.

Parousia the supposed second coming of Christ.

parr a young salmon in the freshwater stage.

parturition childbirth.

parvis (also **parvise**) **1** an enclosed area in front of a cathedral, church, etc. **2** a room over a church porch.

paschal of Easter or the Jewish Passover.

pasquinade a lampoon or satire, originally one displayed in a public place.

pastern the part of a horse's foot just above the hoof.

pastiche a picture, musical composition, or literary work either composed in the style of a well-known earlier creator or made up as a medley of various borrowed fragments.

patagium the wing-membrane of a bat, flying squirrel, etc.

patella the kneecap.

paterfamilias the male head of a family or household.

patrial having the right to live in the UK through the British birth of a parent or grandparent.

patrimony **1** property inherited from one's father or ancestor. **2** a heritage. **3** the endowment of a church etc.

patristic of the early Christian writers or their work.

patronymic a name derived from the first name of a father or ancestor, e.g. *Johnson, O'Brien, Ivanovitch.*

paucity smallness of number or quantity.

pavane (also **pavan**) a stately dance, formerly danced in elaborate clothing.

pavonine of or like a peacock.

pawl a lever to lock a capstan, the teeth of a wheel, etc.

paxwax the tendon in the nape of the neck of a horse, ox, sheep, etc.

peccadillo a trifling offence; a small sin.

peccant **1** sinning. **2** inducing disease.

peccary a kind of American wild pig.

pectin a soluble jelly-forming substance found in ripe fruit and used as a setting agent in jam.

peculation the embezzling of money.

pedagogue a schoolmaster; a teacher.

pederasty (also **paederasty**) anal intercourse between a man and a boy.

pedicular infested with lice.

peen the wedge-shaped or curved end of a hammer head.

peggle a dialect word for the fruit of the hawthorn; a haw.

peignoir a woman's loose dressing gown.

pelf money; wealth.

pellucid **1** (of water, light, etc.) transparent, clear. **2** (of style, speech, etc.) not confused; clear.

pemmican dried pounded meat mixed with melted fat and currants etc. for use by Arctic travellers etc.

penchant an inclination or liking (*has a penchant for old films*).

penetralia innermost shrines or recesses; secret hidden parts.

pennate feathery, winged.

pennill an improvised stanza sung to a harp accompaniment at an eisteddfod etc.

pensile hanging down; pendulous.

pentad the number five; a group of five.

pentagram a five-pointed star, formerly used as a mystic symbol.

Pentateuch the first five books of the Old Testament.

pentathlon an athletic event comprising five different events for each competitor.

penumbra **1** the partially shaded region round the shadow of an opaque body, especially that around the total shadow of the moon or earth in an eclipse. **2** a partial shadow.

peptic concerning or promoting digestion.

perdurable permanent; eternal; durable.

peregrination a journey or wandering, especially extensive.

peremptory dogmatic, imperious; admitting no refusal.

perfidy breach of faith; treachery.

perfunctory done merely superficially for the sake of getting through a duty (*a perfunctory kiss*).

periapt a thing worn as a charm; an amulet.

peripatetic **1** (of a teacher) working in more than one school or college etc. **2** going from place to place; itinerant. **3** (**Peripatetic**) Aristotelian (from Aristotle's habit of walking in the Lyceum while teaching).

peripheral **1** of minor importance; marginal. **2** on the fringe. **3** *Anat.* near the surface of the body, with special reference to the circulation and nervous system.

Perique a strong dark Louisiana tobacco.

peristalith a ring or row of ancient standing stones.

permafrost subsoil which remains frozen all the year round, as in polar regions.

peroration the concluding part of a speech, forcefully summing up what has been said.

perquisite **1** an extra profit additional to a main income. **2** a customary extra right or privilege; a perk.

persiflage light raillery, banter.

persimmon a usually tropical evergreen tree bearing edible tomato-like fruits.

perspicacity mental penetration; discernment.

perspicuity clearness of expression.

pertinent relevant to the matter in hand; to the point.

pertussis whooping cough.

pestilence a fatal epidemic disease, especially bubonic plague.

petard a small bomb used in former times to blast down a door etc.

petasus an ancient Greek hat, as worn by Hermes.

peterman a safe-breaker.

petroglyph a rock-carving, especially a prehistoric one.

pettitoes pigs' trotters, regarded as food.

pharos a lighthouse or beacon to guide sailors.

pheromone a chemical secreted by an animal to attract or warn others of the same species.

philander (of a man) to flirt, womanize.

philately stamp-collecting.

philippic a bitter verbal attack.

phillumeny the collecting of matchbox labels.

phlogiston a substance formerly thought to exist in all combustible bodies and to be released in burning.

phratry a tribal or kinship division; a clan.

phrenetic **1** frantic. **2** fanatic.

phylactery **1** a small leather box containing Hebrew texts, worn by Jewish men at prayer. **2** an amulet or charm.

phylum a taxonomic rank below kingdom, comprising a class or classes and subordinate groups.

phytotron a laboratory where plants can grow and be studied under controlled conditions.

piacular **1** atoning, especially for sacrilege. **2** needing atonement; sacrilegious.

piaffe (of a horse) to move as in a trot, but slower.

pibroch a series of martial or funerary variations for the bagpipes.

picador a mounted man with a lance who goads the bull in a bullfight.

picaresque (of a style of fiction) dealing with the episodic adventures of rogues etc.

piceous of or like pitch; black and glossy.

pichiciago (also **pichiciego**) a small South American armadillo.

piggin a wooden bucket with one long stave serving as a handle.

pikelet a thin kind of Northern English crumpet.

pilose (also **pilous**) hairy.

pinchbeck an alloy of copper and zinc used in cheap jewellery as imitation gold.

pinguid fat, oily.

pintle a pin or bolt, especially one on which some other part turns.

Pinyin a system of romanized spelling for transcribing Chinese.

pique ill-feeling; enmity, resentment.

piscatory of fishermen or fishing.

pismire a dialect word for an ant.

piste a ski run of compacted snow.

pizzle an animal's penis, especially that of a bull, formerly used as a whip.

placate to pacify, conciliate.

placebo a pill, medicine, etc. having no physiological effect, prescribed for psychological reasons or as a control in testing new drugs.

placer a deposit of sand, gravel, etc. in the bed of a stream etc., containing valuable minerals in particles.

placket a slit in a garment, for fastenings or access to a pocket.

planchette a small usually heart-shaped board on castors with a pencil that supposedly writes spirit messages when someone's fingers rest lightly on it.

plangent (of a sound) **1** loud and reverberating. **2** plaintive.

plantar of the sole of the foot.

plasma (also **plasm**) the colourless fluid part of blood, lymph, or milk.

plaudit applause; emphatic approval.

pleach to entwine or interlace (especially branches to form a hedge).

plectrum a thin flat piece of plastic or horn etc. held in the hand to pluck the string of a guitar etc.

plenary **1** entire, unqualified (*plenary indulgence*). **2** (of an assembly) to be attended by all members.

plenitude fullness, completeness; abundance.

pleonastic using more words than are needed.

plethora an oversupply, e.g. an excess of any body fluid, or of red corpuscles in the blood.

plexor (also **plessor**) a small hammer used for testing reflexes and tapping the chest etc. for diagnosis.

pneuma the spirit or soul.

poco-curante careless, indifferent.

pogoniate bearded, unshaven.

pogrom an organized massacre (originally of Jews in Russia).

polder a piece of low-lying land reclaimed from the sea or a river, especially in the Netherlands.

polity **1** a form or process of civil government or constitution. **2** an organized society; a State as a political entity.

pollard **1** a hornless sheep, ox, or goat. **2** a tree, especially a riverside willow, whose branches have been cut off to encourage new growth.

pollex the thumb, or corresponding digit of a forelimb.

poltroon a spiritless coward.

polymath a person of much or varied learning; a great scholar.

polynya a stretch of open water surrounded by ice, especially in the Arctic seas.

pomace **1** the mass of crushed apples in cider-making, before or after the juice is pressed out. **2** the refuse of fish etc. after the oil has been extracted, generally used as a fertilizer.

pomander a spiced orange or ball of mixed aromatic substances to be placed in a cupboard etc.

pompadour a woman's hairstyle with the hair in a high turned-back roll round the face.

poniard a small slim dagger.

pontine of bridges.

porringer a small bowl, often with a handle, for soup, stew, etc.

posit to assume as a fact; postulate.

postprandial after dinner or lunch.

postulate to assume as a necessary condition; take for granted.

potable drinkable.

potamic of rivers.

poteen (also **potheen**) *Irish* alcohol distilled illicitly, usually from potatoes.

pother a noise; commotion; fuss.

potlatch among North American Indians, a ceremonial giving away or destruction of property to enhance status.

pragmatic dealing with matters with regard to their practical requirements or consequences.

praxis **1** accepted practice or custom. **2** the practising of an art or skill.

precedent a previous case or legal decision etc., taken as a guide for later cases or as a justification.

preclude to prevent, exclude, make impossible (*so as to preclude all doubt*).

predilection a preference or special liking.

pre-empt to forestall, acquire, or prevent by action in advance (*pre-empt an attack/my rival/the land*).

prehensile (of a tail, limb, elephant's trunk, etc.) capable of grasping.

premonition a forewarning; a presentiment.

prepuce the foreskin.

prequel a story, film, etc. whose events precede those of an existing work.

presbyopia long-sightedness, developing especially in middle and old age.

prescient having foreknowledge or foresight.

prestidigitation conjuring.

prevalent **1** generally occurring or existing. **2** predominant.

prevaricate to speak misleadingly; quibble.

priapic phallic; sexually licentious.

primogeniture the fact of being the first-born child, often with the consequent right of inheritance.

pristine in its original condition; unspoilt.

probang a flexible strip with a sponge or button at the end, for surgical introduction into the throat.

probity uprightness, honesty.

proclivity a tendency or inclination.

proem a preface, preamble, or prelude.

prognathous having a projecting jaw.

prognosis a forecast, as of the course of a disease etc.

prolegomena the introductory matter of a book etc., especially when critical or discursive.

prolepsis **1** the anticipation and answering of possible objections. **2** the representation of something as happening in advance, as in *he was a dead man when he entered.*

prolix (of speech, writing, etc.) lengthy; tedious.

promulgate **1** to make (a cause etc.) known to the public; disseminate, promote. **2** to proclaim (a decree, news, etc.)

prophylactic **1** a preventive medicine or course of action. **2** *US* a condom.

propitiate to appease (an offended person etc.)

proponent someone advocating a motion, theory, or proposal.

prorogue to discontinue the meetings of (a parliament etc.) without dissolving it.

proscribe **1** to banish, exile. **2** to reject or denounce (a practice etc.).

prosthesis an artificial leg, breast, tooth, etc. (and see LANGUAGE).

protean variable, versatile; taking many forms.

prothalamium a song or poem to celebrate a forthcoming wedding.

provenance the origin or history of especially a work of art.

pruritus severe itching of the skin.

psychokinesis the movement of objects supposedly by mental effort without the action of natural forces.

puce dark red or purple-brown.

pulchritude beauty.

pullulate **1** (of a seed, shoot, etc.) to bud, sprout, germinate. **2** (especially of animals) to swarm, throng, breed abundantly, abound.

pulmonary of the lungs.

pulverulent powdery, or likely to crumble.

punctate spotted, speckled.

punctilio petty overattention to ceremony and etiquette.

punty an iron rod used in glass-blowing.

purfle an ornamental border, especially on a violin etc.

purulent consisting of or discharging pus.

pusillanimous lacking courage; timid.

putative reputed, supposed.

putcher a conical basket or wicker trap for catching salmon.

puteal of a well or pit.

putsch an attempt at political revolution; a violent uprising.

pyknic (also **pycnic**) having a thick neck, large abdomen, and short limbs.

pyrexia fever.

pyx (also **pix**) **1** the vessel in which the bread of the Eucharist is kept. **2** a box at the Royal Mint in which specimen gold and silver coins are deposited for testing annually.

Q

quadrat a small area marked for ecological study.

quadrennium a period of four years.

quadroon a person with three White grandparents and one Negro one.

quagga an extinct zebra-like South African mammal with yellowish-brown stripes.

quandary a state of perplexity; a practical dilemma.

quant a punting-pole.

quantal composed of discrete units; varying in steps, not continuously.

quartan (of a fever etc.) recurring every fourth day.

quartile in statistics, one of three values of a variable dividing a population into four equal groups as regards the value of that variable.

quebracho any of several kinds of American trees, with very hard timber and medicinal bark.

quenelle a seasoned ball or roll of pounded fish or meat.

quern a hand-mill for grinding corn.

quiddity **1** the essence of a person or thing; what makes a thing what it is. **2** a quibble; a trivial objection.

quidnunc a newsmonger; a person given to gossip.

quietus **1** something which quiets or represses. **2** release from life; death, final riddance.

quincunx five objects (e.g. planted trees, or the five on a dice) set so that four are at the corners of a square or rectangle and the fifth is at its centre.

quintain a post set up as a mark for the medieval military exercise of tilting, often provided with a sandbag to swing round and strike an unsuccessful tilter.

quire **1** four sheets of paper folded to form eight leaves, as often in medieval manuscripts. **2** 25 (formerly 20) sheets of paper.

quittance **1** a release from something. **2** an acknowledgement of payment.

quodlibet **1** a topic for philosophical or theological discussion, as set for an exercise. **2** a light-hearted medley of well-known tunes.

R

rabid **1** furious, violent (*rabid hate; a rabid nationalist*). **2** (especially of a dog) affected with rabies.

rachitic suffering from rickets.

raddle the red ochre often used to mark sheep.

raddled worn out; untidy, unkempt.

rale an abnormal rattling sound as heard in unhealthy lungs.

ramose branched, branchy.

rancour (*US* **rancor**) inveterate bitterness, spitefulness.

raptor any bird of prey; an owl, falcon, etc.

raster a pattern of scanning lines for a cathode-ray tube picture.

rataplan a drumming sound.

ratiocination logical reasoning.

ratite a flightless bird, e.g. an ostrich, emu, or cassowary.

rattan (also **ratan**) the jointed pliable stem of an East Indian climbing plant, used for walking sticks, furniture, etc.

raucous harsh-sounding, loud and hoarse.

ravelin an outwork of early fortification, with two faces projecting outwards at an angle.

razzia a hostile incursion for conquest, plunder, capture of slaves, etc., as practised by the Muslim peoples in Africa.

realtor *US* an estate agent.

rebarbative repellent, unattractive.

rebato a kind of stiff collar worn by both sexes from about 1590 to 1630.

reboation a re-bellowing echo.

rebus a representation of a word or phrase (especially a name) by pictures etc. suggesting its parts, as in 'if the Gbmt put:' for 'if the grate be empty put coal on'.

recalesce to grow hot again (especially of iron allowed to cool from white heat, whose temperature rises at a certain point for a short time).

recension a particular form or version of a text resulting from revision.

recherché **1** carefully sought out; rare or exotic. **2** far-fetched, obscure.

recidivist a person who relapses into crime.

réclame popular fame, notoriety.

recondite abstruse; out of the way; obscure.

recoup **1** to recover or regain (a loss). **2** to compensate or reimburse (someone) for a loss.

recrudescence (of a disease or difficulty etc.) to break out again, especially after a dormant period.

recto **1** the right-hand page of a book. **2** the front of a page (opp. VERSO).

rectrix a bird's strong tail-feather directing flight.

recusant someone who refuses submission to an authority or compliance with a regulation; especially formerly, one who refused to attend services of the Church of England.

recuse to object, renounce; especially to object to (a judge) as prejudiced.

redact to put into literary form; edit for publication.

redound (of an action etc.) to make a great contribution (*it redounded to his credit*).

reflux **1** a backward flow. **2** a method of boiling a liquid so that any vapour is liquefied and returned to the boiler.

refulgent shining; gloriously bright.

regelate to freeze again (especially of pieces of ice etc. frozen together after temporary thawing of the surfaces).

regenerate **1** to bring or come into renewed existence. **2** to give or acquire new and better life; reform. **3** to regrow new tissue. **4** to restore to an initial state.

regimen **1** a prescribed course of exercise, way of life, and diet. **2** *archaic* a system of government.

regisseur the director of a theatrical production, especially a ballet.

regnant **1** reigning, not merely a consort (*Queen regnant*). **2** (of things, qualities, etc.) predominant, prevalent.

regulus **1** the purer or metallic part of a mineral that separates on reduction. **2** an impure metallic product formed during smelting.

reify to convert (a person, abstraction, etc.) into a thing; materialize.

reliquary a receptacle for a religious relic.

remontant blooming more than once a year.

remora any of various sea fish that attach themselves with sucker-like fins to other fish and to ships.

renal of the kidneys.

renege (also **renegue**) to go back on one's word; recant.

rennet curdled milk from the stomach of an unweaned calf (or a preparation made from its stomach-membrane) used in making cheese and junket.

repine to fret, be discontented.

rescind to abrogate (a law, contract, etc.); revoke, cancel.

respire **1** to breathe; inhale and exhale air. **2** to get rest or respite.

resurgent rising or arising again.

ret (also **rate**) **1** to soften (flax etc.) by soaking. **2** (of hay etc.) to be spoilt by wet or rot.

retiarius a Roman gladiator using a net and trident.

reticle a network of threads or lines in the focal plane of an optical instrument to help accurate observation.

retroussé (of a nose) turned up at the tip.

revanchism a political policy of seeking to retaliate, especially to recover lost territory.

revers the turned-up edge of a garment at a lapel or cuff, revealing the (often lined) under-surface.

revet to face (a rampart etc.) with masonry, especially in fortification.

rheum a watery discharge from the eyes or nose.

rhinal of a nostril or the nose.

rhonchus a snoring or whistling sound from the chest.

rhotacism excessive or peculiar pronunciation of the sound *r*.

rhumb **1** any of the 32 points of the compass. **2** the angle between two successive compass points.

rictus the gape of a mouth or beak.

rifampicin an antibiotic used to treat various diseases, especially pulmonary tuberculosis.

riffler a tool with a curved file-surface at each end, used by sculptors, metal-workers, and wood-carvers.

rile to anger, irritate.

rilletts a tinned preparation of minced ham, chicken, fat, etc.

rime frost, especially white frost deposited by cloud or fog.

rinderpest a virulent infectious disease of ruminants, especially cattle.

riparian of or on a river bank (*riparian rights*).

riprap *US* a collection of loose stones as a foundation for a structure.

risible laughable, ludicrous.

rivière a gem necklace, especially of more than one string.

roborant a strengthening drug.

roc a gigantic bird of Eastern legend.

rodomontade boastful bragging talk or behaviour.

roil to make (a liquid) muddy by stirring it.

Romany **1** a Gypsy. **2** the language of the Gypsies.

rondavel a South African round tribal hut usually with a thatched conical roof.

rondeau a poem of ten or thirteen lines with only two rhymes throughout and with the opening words used twice as a refrain.

roquelaure a man's knee-length cloak of the 18th and early 19th centuries.

rosarium a rose garden.

rotund **1** (of a person) large and plump, podgy. **2** (of language) sonorous, impressively highfalutin.

roué a debauchee, especially an elderly one; a rake.

rouleau **1** a cylindrical packet of coins. **2** a coil or roll of ribbon etc., especially as trimming.

rowen *US* a second growth of hay; an aftermath.

rubicund (of a face, or person in this respect) ruddy, rosy, high-coloured.

ruche a frill or gathering of lace, etc. as a trimming.

ruminate **1** to meditate; ponder. **2** (of ruminants) to chew the cud.

runagate a deserter, fugitive, runaway.

rundale a system by which land is divided into strips or patches of which several, not adjoining each other, are cultivated by each holder.

runt **1** a small pig, especially the smallest in a litter. **2** a weak undersized person. **3** a large domestic pigeon. **4** an ox or cow of various small breeds.

S

sabot a shoe hollowed out of a block of wood.

sabulous sandy, granular.

sacerdotal of priests; priestly.

sachem **1** the supreme chief of some American Indian tribes. **2** *US* a political leader.

saffian a leather made from goatskins or sheepskins dyed in bright colours.

saggar (also **sagger**) a protective fireclay box enclosing ceramic ware while it is being fired.

salangane a kind of swallow that makes edible nests.

salicylism aspirin poisoning.

salientian a frog or toad.

salmagundi **1** a salad of chopped meat, anchovies, eggs, onions, etc. **2** a general mixture; miscellaneous collection.

saltation **1** the act of leaping or dancing; a jump. **2** a sudden transition.

samite a rich medieval dress-fabric of silk sometimes interwoven with gold.

samizdat a system of underground publishing of banned literature in the former USSR.

samp *US* coarse maize porridge.

sandiver liquid scum formed in glass-making.

sanguinary delighting in bloodshed; bloodthirsty.

sans-culotte **1** a lower-class Parisian republican in the French Revolution. **2** an extreme republican or revolutionary.

sans serif (also **sanserif**) a form of printing type without serifs, the projections finishing off the strokes of the letters.

saponaceous of soap, soapy.

Sapphic **1** of the Greek poetess Sappho. **2** lesbian.

sardonic grimly jocular; bitterly mocking or cynical.

sartorial of tailoring, or men's clothes.

sastrugi wave-like irregularities, caused by winds, in the surface of hard polar snow.

satrap **1** a provincial governor in the ancient Persian empire. **2** a subordinate ruler, colonial governor, etc.

saturnine **1** sluggish, gloomy; dark and brooding. **2** an old word referring to the metal lead, or to lead poisoning.

satyagraha passive resistance; originally the policy of resistance to British rule advocated by Gandhi.

savannah (also **savanna**) a grassy plain in the tropics or subtropics.

sawder flattery, blarney.

scabrous **1** rough, scurfy. **2** indecent, salacious.

scapular **1** a monk's short cloak. **2** a bandage for the shoulders. **3** a bird's feather near the shoulder.

scaramouch an old word for a boastful coward.

scarify **1** to slit or scrape (the skin). **2** to hurt by severe criticism. **3** to loosen (soil) with a spiked tool.

scatophagous feeding on dung.

schlock *US colloq.* inferior goods; trash.

sciamachy (also **skiamachy**) fighting with shadows; imaginary or futile combat.

scintilla **1** a trace. **2** a spark.

sciolist a superficial pretender to knowledge.

scofflaw (especially *US*) one who treats the law with contempt, especially a person who avoids various kinds of not easily enforceable laws.

scorbutic of, or affected with, scurvy.

Scouse the dialect of Liverpool.

scrannel thin, meagre.

screeve **1** to write. **2** to draw coloured pictures on the pavement.

scrimshank *Brit. slang* to shirk duty.

scrimshaw shells, ivory, etc. adorned with carved or coloured designs as a sailors' pastime at sea.

scry to divine by crystal-gazing.

scut the short tail of especially a hare, rabbit, or deer.

scutage money formerly paid by a feudal landowner instead of personal service.

scuttlebutt **1** a water-butt on the deck of a ship, for drinking from. **2** *colloq.* rumour, gossip.

sebaceous fatty, oily.

sedulous persevering, painstaking, diligent.

seg a protective stud on the toe or heel of a boot.

seigniorage (also **seignorage**) a profit made by issuing currency, especially by issuing coins rated above the value of their metal.

seine a large fishing net with floats at the top and weights at the bottom edge.

seismic of earthquakes.

selvedge (also **selvage**) the edge of a cloth along the warp.

seminal **1** of seeds or semen. **2** (of ideas etc.) providing the basis for future development (*a seminal book*).

sempiternal eternal, everlasting.

seneschal the steward of a medieval great house.

sententious pompously moralizing; given to the use of maxims.

seppuku Japanese ritual disembowelment; hara-kiri.

sequacious **1** inconsequent, incoherent. **2** dependent, servile.

sequelae complications following a disease.

serac one of the tower-shaped masses into which a glacier is divided at steep points by crevasses crossing it.

serang the head of a crew of East Indian seamen.

sere (of leaves etc.) dried up, withered.

serendipity the faculty of making happy and unexpected discoveries by accident.

serialism the composing of music using a fixed arrangement of the twelve notes of the chromatic scale.

sericulture the breeding of silkworms.

sesquipedalian **1** (of a word or expression) of many syllables. **2** half a yard high or long.

setiferous (also **setigerous**) bristly.

sett **1** a badger's burrow. **2** a granite paving block.

shaddock the largest citrus fruit, with a thick yellow skin and bitter pulp.

shadoof a pole with a bucket and counterpoise, used especially in Egypt for raising water.

shagreen **1** a kind of rough untanned leather. **2** rough sharkskin used for rasping and polishing.

shaman a witch doctor or priest claiming to communicate with gods, etc.

shard **1** a broken piece of pottery or glass. **2** a beetle's wing-case.

sheading each of the six administrative divisions in the Isle of Man.

shibboleth a long-standing formula, doctrine, or phrase etc., held to be true by a party or sect (*must abandon outdated shibboleths*).

shikar hunting in India.

shillelagh a thick stick of blackthorn or oak, used in Ireland especially as a weapon.

shirr **1** to gather (fabric) with especially elastic parallel threads. **2** *US* to bake (eggs) without their shells.

shive a thin flat cork for a wide-mouthed bottle, or bung for a cask.

shofar a ram's-horn trumpet used in Jewish religious ceremonies and as an ancient battle-signal.

shoji a sliding paper-covered screen door in a Japanese house.

siccative a substance causing drying, especially mixed with oil-paint etc.

sigmoid crescent-shaped or S-shaped.

simony the buying or selling of ecclesiastical privileges.

simulacrum an image or likeness of something, often deceptive.

simulate **1** to pretend to have or feel or be. **2** to imitate, counterfeit (*simulated fur*).

simulcast simultaneous transmission of the same programme on radio and television.

singultus hiccups.

sjambok in South Africa, a rhinoceros-hide whip.

skald (also **scald**) in ancient Scandinavia, a composer and reciter of poems honouring the deeds of heroes.

skean-dhu a dagger worn in the stocking as part of Highland costume.

skerry *Scot.* a reef or rocky island.

skewbald (of an animal) with irregular patches of white and another colour, properly not black.

skilly a thin broth or gruel, usually of oatmeal flavoured with meat.

slalom **1** a ski race down a zigzag course between artificial obstacles. **2** an obstacle race for canoes, cars, skateboards, or water-skis.

slivovitz a plum brandy made especially in the Balkans.

slurry semi-liquid mud, cement, or manure.

smallage any of several kinds of celery or parsley.

smegma an oily secretion in the folds of the skin, especially of the foreskin.

snaffle a horse's simple bridle-bit, without a curb and usually with a single rein.

snood an ornamental net to hold a woman's back hair.

sobriquet (also **soubriquet**) **1** a nickname. **2** an assumed name.

sodality a confraternity or association, especially a Roman Catholic religious guild or brotherhood.

softa a Muslim student of sacred law and theology.

solarium a room with sun-lamps, or large glass areas, for sunbathing.

solidus an oblique stroke (/) used in writing fractions ($^3/_4$), or to denote alternatives (*and/or*) or ratios (*miles/day*).

solipsism the philosophical view that the self is all that exists or can be known.

somatic of the body, especially as distinct from the mind.

somite each body-division of an animal divided into similar segments.

somniferous inducing sleep; soporific.

somniloquent talking in one's sleep.

sophism a false argument, especially one intended to deceive.

sophomore *US* a second-year university or high-school student.

sorites a series of logical propositions in which the predicate of the first is the subject of the second, as in *all A=B, all B=C, therefore all A=C.*

sororal by or of a sister; sisterly.

sorority a female students' society in an American university or college.

sortilege divination by lots.

souk a market place in Muslim countries.

soutane a priest's cassock.

southpaw a left-handed person, especially in boxing.

spall a splinter or chip of rock.

spatchcock a chicken or especially game bird split open and grilled.

spatterdash a cloth or leather legging, formerly worn to protect the legs from mud etc.

spatulate broad with a rounded end (*a spatulate finger/leaf*).

speculum **1** a surgical instrument for stretching body cavities for inspection. **2** a mirror, especially of polished metal in a reflecting telescope. **3** a lustrous coloured area on the wing of especially ducks.

spermaceti a white waxy secretion from a sperm whale's head, used in making candles, ointments, etc.

speys thick woodland.

sphagnum a moss growing in bogs and peat, used in packing, as fertilizer, etc.

sphragistics the study of engraved seals.

spikenard a costly perfumed ointment, made in former times from an Indian plant.

spindrift spray blown along the surface of the sea.

spiracle an external vent for breathing, in insects, whales, and some fish.

spitchcock an eel split and broiled.

splanchnic of the viscera; intestinal.

splenetic ill-tempered; peevish.

spline a ridge fitting into a groove in the hub or shaft of a wheel to allow longitudinal play.

spoor the track or scent of an animal.

sporadic occurring only here and there or occasionally; separate, scattered.

sprocket each of several teeth on a wheel engaging with links of a chain, e.g. on a bicycle.

squamous scaly.

stacte a sweet spice used by the ancient Jews in making incense.

stanchion **1** a post or pillar; an upright support. **2** a bar or pair of bars for confining cattle in a stall.

stannary a tin-mine.

steatopygous having fat buttocks.

stein a large earthenware beer mug, typically with a lid.

stellate arranged like a star; radiating.

stentorian (of a voice or speech) very loud.

stercoraceous **1** consisting of dung or faeces. **2** living in dung.

sternum the breastbone.

sternutation sneezing.

stertorous (of breathing etc.) heavy; sounding like snoring.

stevedore a person employed in loading and unloading ships; a docker.

stichomythia in classical Greek drama, dialogue in alternate lines.

stigmata in Christian belief, marks corresponding to those left on Christ's body by the Crucifixion, said to have been impressed on the bodies of St Francis of Assisi and others.

stirk a yearling bullock or heifer.

stirps a classificatory group in biology.

stochastic **1** determined by a random distribution of probabilities. **2** governed by the laws of probability.

stoma **1** a small mouthlike opening in some lower animals, e.g. a hookworm. **2** a small orifice made surgically in the stomach.

stomatic good for diseases of the mouth.

stoush *Austral. & New Zealand* to fight with, attack.

stover winter food for cattle.

strabismus a squint.

strappado a form of torture in which the victim is secured to a rope and made to fall from a height almost to the ground and then stopped with a jerk.

strath a broad mountain valley in Scotland.

stricture a critical or censorious remark.

stridulate (of insects, especially the cicada and grasshopper) to make a shrill sound by rubbing the legs or wing-cases together.

strigil a skin-scraper used by ancient Greek and Roman bathers after exercise.

struma goitre.

struthious of or like an ostrich.

stultify to make useless or futile, especially as a result of tedious routine (*stultifying boredom*).

stupa a round usually domed building erected as a Buddhist shrine.

Stygian dark, gloomy, indistinct.

stylite an ancient or medieval ascetic living on top of a pillar.

suave 1 (of a person, especially a man) smooth; polite; sophisticated. **2** (of a wine etc.) bland, smooth.

subereous of cork; corky.

sublunary of this world; earthly.

suborn to induce by bribery etc. to commit perjury or any other unlawful act.

subreption the obtaining of something by surprise or misrepresentation.

subrogation the substitution of one party for another as creditor, with the transfer of rights and duties.

subsume to include (an instance, idea, category, etc.) within a larger class.

subvention a grant of money from a government etc.; a subsidy.

succedaneum a substitute, especially for a medicine or drug.

succotash a dish of green maize and beans boiled together.

succour (*US* **succor**) aid, assistance.

succubus a female demon believed to have intercourse with sleeping men.

succumb 1 to be forced to give way; be overcome (*succumbed to temptation*). **2** to be overcome by death (*succumbed to his injuries*).

succuss to shake (a patient) vigorously so as to hear any splashing sound in the lungs.

sudd floating vegetation impeding the navigation of the White Nile.

sudorific causing sweating.

sulcus a groove or furrow, especially on the surface of the brain.

sullage filth, refuse, sewage.

sumo a style of Japanese wrestling, in which a participant is defeated by touching the ground with any part of the body except the soles of the feet or by moving outside the marked area.

supererogation the performance of more than duty requires.

superfetation a second conception during pregnancy, giving rise to embryos of different ages.

supernal **1** heavenly, divine. **2** of or concerning the sky. **3** lofty.

supine **1** lying face upwards. **2** inert, indolent; morally inactive.

surcingle a band round a horse's body usually to keep a pack etc. in place.

surrogate a substitute, deputy.

suspire **1** to sigh, or utter with a sigh. **2** to breathe.

sussuration a sound of whispering or rustling.

sutler a person in the past who followed an army and sold provisions to the soldiers.

suture **1** the stitching of a wound or incision, or the thread or wire used for this. **2** the seamlike junction of two bones, especially in the skull.

suzerain **1** a feudal lord. **2** a sovereign or State having some control over another State that is internally autonomous.

swami a Hindu male religious teacher.

swarf fine chips or filings of stone, metal, plastic, etc. removed by cutting.

swatch a sample, especially of cloth.

swinge to strike hard, beat.

swingletree a pivoted crossbar to which the traces are attached in a cart, plough, etc.

sybarite a self-indulgent person; one devoted to sensuous luxury.

sycophant a servile flatterer; a toady.

syllabub a dessert made of cream or milk flavoured, sweetened, and whipped.

symbiosis an interaction between two different organisms living in close physical association, usually to the advantage of both.

synaesthesia (*US* **synesthesia**) **1** the production of a mental sense-impression relating to one sense by the stimulation of another sense, as when a sensation of colour is aroused by a smell. **2** a sensation produced in one part of the body by stimulation of another part.

syncretism the process of attempting to unify differing schools of thought.

synergism the combined effect of drugs, organs, etc. that exceeds the sum of their individual effects.

syphilophobia an abnormal fear of being infected with syphilis.

syrinx the song-organ of birds.

T

tabard **1** a herald's official coat bearing the arms of the sovereign. **2** a woman's sleeveless jerkin. **3** a medieval knight's short tunic bearing his arms and worn over armour.

tabouret (*US* **taboret**) **1** a low seat usually without arms or back. **2** an embroidery frame.

tacit understood or implied without being stated (*tacit consent*).

taciturn reserved in speech; saying little; incommunicative.

tactile of or perceived by the sense of touch.

tahina (also **tahini**) a paste of sesame seeds originally from the Middle East.

taiga coniferous forest lying between tundra and steppe, especially in Siberia.

taint a corrupt condition or trace of decay.

tampion (also **tompion**) a stopper or plug, e.g. for the muzzle of a gun or an organ-pipe.

tangential only slightly relevant; peripheral.

tangram a Chinese puzzle square cut into seven pieces to be combined into various figures.

tanist the heir apparent to a Celtic chief, usually his most vigorous adult relation, chosen by election.

tantalus a stand in which spirit-decanters may be locked up but visible.

tantamount (*to*) equivalent to (*was tantamount to a denial*).

tarantella a rapid whirling Southern Italian dance.

tare **1** an allowance made for the weight of the packing round goods. **2** the weight of an unladen goods vehicle without fuel.

tarot cards a pack of cards for fortune-telling, with symbolic pictures.

taw the game of marbles, a large marble, or the line from which players throw marbles.

taws (also **tawse**) a thong with a slit end formerly used for punishing children in Scottish schools.

taxidermy the art of stuffing and mounting the skins of animals.

taxonomy the science or practice of classifying living or extinct organisms.

tazza a saucer-shaped cup, especially one mounted on a foot.

tectonics **1** the production of practical and beautiful buildings. **2** the study of large-scale geological features.

telekinesis the movement of objects at a distance supposedly by mental powers.

telergy the supposed force operating in telepathy and directly affecting the brain or human organism.

tellurian of or inhabiting the earth.

telpher a system for transporting goods by cable-cars.

temporal **1** worldly rather than spiritual; secular. **2** of time. **3** of the temples of the head, between forehead and ear.

tenable that can be defended against attack (*a tenable position/theory*).

tendentious (of writing etc.) calculated to promote a particular cause or controversial viewpoint; having an underlying purpose.

tenebrous dark, gloomy.

tensile **1** of tension. **2** capable of being drawn out or stretched.

tenson (also **tenzon**) a contest in verse-making between troubadours.

teraph a small image as a domestic deity or oracle of the ancient Hebrews.

tercel a male hawk, especially a peregrine or goshawk to be used in falconry.

tergiversate **1** to change one's party or principles. **2** to equivocate; make conflicting or evasive statements.

tergum the back or upper surface of an articulated creature, e.g. a crayfish.

termitarium a termites' nest.

ternary composed of three parts.

Terpsichorean of dancing.

terret each of the rings on a harness-pad for the driving-reins to pass through.

tesseract a four-dimensional hypercube; extension of a cube into the fourth dimension.

testudo a overhead protection, either in the form of a portable screen or of their overlapping shields, for besieging troops in ancient Roman warfare.

Tetragrammaton the Hebrew name of God written in four letters, articulated as *Yahweh* etc.

thalassic of the sea or seas, especially small or inland seas.

thaumatrope a disc or card with two different pictures on its two sides, which merge into one when the disc is rapidly twirled.

thaumaturgy the working of miracles.

thegosis tooth-grinding in animals to sharpen the teeth.

theodicy the vindication of divine providence in view of the existence of evil.

theophany a visible manifestation of God or a god to man.

theriomorphic (especially of a deity) having an animal form.

thespian of tragedy or drama.

thimblerigger a trickster who uses sleight of hand in a game involving three inverted thimbles or cups, which are moved about, contestants having to spot which one has a pea or other object under it.

thrall **1** a slave. **2** a state of slavery; bondage (*in thrall*).

thrasonical bragging, boastful, vainglorious.

threnody a lamentation or song of lamentation, especially on a person's death.

thurible a container for burning incense in; a censer.

thurifer an acolyte carrying a vessel of incense in a service or procession.

thyrsus in Greek and Roman antiquity, a staff tipped with an ornament like a pine-cone, an attribute of Bacchus the god of wine.

tick-tack-toe *US* noughts and crosses.

tilde a mark (˜) put over a letter, e.g. over a Spanish *n* when pronounced *ny* (as in *señor*).

tine a prong of a fork.

tipcat a game with a short piece of wood tapering at the ends and struck with a stick.

tippet **1** a stole for the shoulders formerly worn by women. **2** a similar garment worn as part of some official uniforms, especially by the clergy.

tiro, tyro a beginner or novice.

tisane a tea-like infusion of dried herbs etc.

titillate **1** to excite pleasantly. **2** to tickle.

titivate (also **tittivate**) to adorn, smarten.

tomalley the fat of the North American lobster, which becomes green when cooked.

tong a Chinese guild, association, or secret society.

tonsorial of a hairdresser or hairdressing.

tontine an annuity shared by subscribers to a loan, the shares increasing as subscribers die till the last survivor gets all, or until a specified date when the remaining survivors share the proceeds.

toper an excessive (especially habitual) drinker.

topiary the art of clipping shrubs and trees into ornamental shapes.

tor a hill or rocky peak, especially in Devon or Cornwall.

torchère a tall stand with a small table for a candlestick etc.

torque a necklace of twisted metal, especially of the ancient Gauls and Britons.

torsade a twisted fringe or ribbon decorating a hat etc.

torus a solid in the shape of a ring doughnut or tyre.

toupee (also **toupet**) a wig to cover a bald spot.

tournedos a small round thick cut from a fillet of beef.

toxophilite an archer, or lover of archery.

traduce to speak ill of; misrepresent.

transient of short duration; momentary, passing, impermanent (*of transient interest; transient guests*).

transilient passing from one thing or condition to another.

translucent allowing light to pass through diffusely; semi-transparent, as with frosted glass.

transmogrify to transform, especially in a magical or surprising manner.

transvestite a person who likes to wear the clothes of the opposite sex, especially as a sexual stimulus; a cross-dresser.

trapunto a kind of quilting in which the design alone is padded.

trave a timber or wooden beam or enclosure of bars.

trebuchet (also **trebucket**) **1** a military machine formerly used for throwing stones etc. in siege warfare. **2** a tilting balance for accurately weighing light articles.

trematode a parasitic flatworm, especially a fluke.

trepan **1** a cylindrical saw formerly used by surgeons for removing part of the skull bone. **2** a borer for sinking shafts.

triage **1** the act of sorting out according to quality. **2** the assignment of degrees of urgency to decide the order of treatment of wounds, illnesses, etc.

tribade a woman who takes part in a simulation of sexual intercourse with another woman.

triskelion a symbolic figure of three legs or lines from a common centre, e.g. the Manx emblem.

triturate **1** to grind to a fine powder. **2** to masticate thoroughly.

triumvirate a ruling group of three men, especially in ancient Rome.

troche a small usually circular medicated tablet or lozenge.

troglodyte **1** a cave-dweller. **2** a wilfully obscurantist or old-fashioned person.

troika **1** a Russian vehicle with three horses harnessed abreast. **2** a group of three people, especially as an administrative council.

trommel a revolving cylindrical sieve for cleaning ore in mining.

trounce **1** to defeat heavily. **2** to beat, thrash.

truculent aggressively defiant; pugnacious.

trudgen a swimming stroke like the crawl, with a scissors movement of the legs.

trunnion a supporting pin on each side of a cannon or mortar, on which it can pivot.

tucket a flourish on a trumpet; a fanfare.

tumbril (also **tumbrel**) **1** an open cart that carried prisoners to the guillotine during the French Revolution. **2** a cart that tips to discharge its load, especially a dung cart.

tumescent becoming inflated; swelling.

tumid **1** (of parts of the body etc.) swollen, inflated. **2** (of a style etc.) inflated, bombastic.

tunicate clothed in concentric layers.

turbary the right of digging turf or peat.

turpitude baseness, depravity, wickedness.

twill a fabric so woven as to have a surface of diagonal parallel ridges.

U

ubiquitous present everywhere simultaneously; often encountered.

uhlan a cavalryman who was armed with a lance, especially in the former German army.

uhuru national independence of an African country.

ukase **1** an arbitrary command. **2** an edict of the Tsarist Russian government.

ulema a body of Muslim doctors of sacred law and theology.

ullage the amount by which a cask etc. falls short of being full, by evaporation or leakage.

ulotrichan having tightly curled hair, especially denoting a human type.

ultra-crepidarian going beyond one's proper province; giving opinions on matters beyond one's knowledge.

ululate to howl, wail; make a hooting cry.

umbles the edible offal of deer etc.

umbo **1** the boss of a shield. **2** a rounded knob.

umbrageous **1** shady; affording shade. **2** (of persons) suspicious, jealous.

umlaut a mark (¨) used over a vowel, especially in Germanic languages, to indicate a vowel change.

unau the South American two-toed sloth.

uncinate hooked, crooked.

unction **1** the act of anointing for religious or medical purposes. **2** the oil or ointment so used. **3** excessive or overfervent words.

ungulate hoofed; having hooves.

uniparous producing one offspring at a birth.

upcast a shaft through which air leaves a mine.

Uranian **1** celestial, heavenly. **2** of the planet Uranus. **3** homosexual.

urticate to sting like a nettle.

usquebaugh (*especially Irish & Scot.*) whisky.

uxorious greatly or excessively fond of one's wife.

V

vaccinia a virus used as vaccine against smallpox.

vacillate **1** to fluctuate in opinion or resolution. **2** to move from side to side; oscillate; waver.

vandyke each of a series of large points forming a border to a lace collar etc.

vaporetto a canal motor-boat in Venice, used for public transport.

vaquero a cowboy or herdsman in Spanish America.

variorum **1** (of an edition of a text) having notes by various editors or commentators. **2** (of an edition of an author's works) including variant readings.

variola smallpox.

vasectomy the surgical sterilization of a man by cutting the spermatic ducts.

vatic prophetic or inspired.

vavasour a vassal who owed allegiance to a great lord and had other vassals under him.

vedette **1** a mounted sentry positioned beyond an army's outposts to watch the enemy. **2** a motor launch. **3** a stage or film star.

vegan a vegetarian who also avoids milk and eggs.

vehmgericht a form of secret tribunal which exercised great power in Westphalia from the 12th–16th centuries.

velar **1** of a veil or membrane. **2** (of a sound) pronounced with the back of the tongue near the soft palate.

velleity a low degree of volition; a slight wish or inclination.

velodrome a track, often banked, for cycle-racing.

venatic of hunting.

venation **1** the arrangement of veins in a leaf or an insect's wing etc. **2** the system of venous blood vessels in an organism.

ventage a finger-hole on a wind instrument.

veracity **1** truthfulness, honesty. **2** accuracy (of a statement etc.).

verbatim in exactly the same words; word for word (*repeated it verbatim; a verbatim report*).

verglas a thin coating of ice or frozen rain.

veridical (of visions etc.) coinciding with reality.

verisimilitude the appearance of being true or real.

verjuice an acid liquor obtained from crab-apples, sour grapes, etc., and formerly used in cooking and medicine.

vernal of or in spring (*vernal equinox; vernal breezes*).

verso **1** the left-hand page of a book. **2** the back of a page, or of a coin (opp. RECTO).

vesicant a blistering agent.

vesicle a small bladder, bubble, or hollow structure.

vespertine (of flowers, insects, etc.) opening, or active, in the evening.

vespiary a wasps' nest.

vexillum **1** an ancient Roman military standard. **2** the vane of a feather.

viatical of a road or journey.

vibrissae **1** the stiff coarse hairs near the mouth of most mammals (e.g. a cat's whiskers) and in the human nostrils. **2** bristle-like feathers near the mouth of insect-eating birds.

vicarious **1** done or experienced through another person. **2** deputed, delegated.

vicegerent someone exercising delegated power; a deputy.

vicuña a South American mammal like a llama, or its fine silky wool.

videlicet viz.; namely, that is to say.

vignette **1** a short description or brief incident in a book, film, etc. **2** an illustration or decorative design, especially on the title-page of a book.

vinaceous wine-red.

viniculture the cultivation of grapevines.

virago a fierce or abusive woman.

virelay a short (especially old French) lyric poem with two rhymes to a stanza variously arranged.

virgule **1** a slanting line used to mark division of words or lines. **2** the stroke (/) used in writing fractions etc.; a solidus.

virid green, verdant.

viscid glutinous, sticky.

vitellus the yolk of an egg.

vivarium a place for keeping animals in (nearly) their natural state indoors.

viviparous bringing forth young alive, rather than laying eggs.

volar of the palm of the hand or sole of the foot.

volition **1** the exercise of the will. **2** the power of willing (*by one's own volition*).

vomer the small thin bone separating the nostrils in man and most vertebrates.

vomitory each of the passages to the seats in an ancient Roman theatre or amphitheatre.

voyeurism the obtaining of sexual satisfaction from observing others' sexual actions or organs.

W

wadi (also **wady**) a rocky watercourse in North Africa etc., dry except in the rainy season.

wainwright a wagon-builder.

wale **1** a ridge on a woven fabric, e.g. corduroy. **2** a stout horizontal timber along a ship's sides, supporting the piles of a dam, etc. **3** a strong band round a woven basket.

wampum shell beads used as money, decoration, or aids to memory by North American Indians.

wapentake a former division of a British shire in areas of England with a large Danish population; a hundred.

warlock a sorcerer; a male witch.

water-gall **1** a boggy tract in a field. **2** a secondary or imperfectly-formed rainbow. **3** a watery bubble in the liver of swine. **4** a flaw in an article caused by the settling of water.

wayzgoose an annual summer dinner or outing held by a printing-house for its employees.

welkin the sky; the upper air.

wether a castrated ram.

whitlow an inflammation near a fingernail or toenail.

widdershins (also **withershins**) anticlockwise.

windage **1** the friction of air against the moving part of a machine. **2** the effect of the wind in deflecting a missile. **3** the difference between the diameter of a gun's bore and that of its projectile.

windrow a row in which hay, peats, sheaves of corn, etc. are laid for drying.

winze a shaft connecting levels in a mine.

withe (also **withy**) a tough flexible shoot of willow or osier, used for tying a bundle of wood etc.

wittol a man aware of his wife's infidelity; a complaisant cuckold.

woggle a leather ring fastening a Scout's or Guide's neckerchief.

wok a bowl-shaped frying-pan used in especially Chinese cookery.

X

xanthochroid having light-coloured hair and a pale complexion.

xenoglossia the faculty of using intelligibly a language one has not learnt.

xeric having dry conditions, as of a desert.

xiphoid sword-shaped.

xystus **1** a covered portico where ancient Greek athletes exercised. **2** a garden walk or terrace in ancient Rome.

Y

yahoo a coarse bestial person.

yang in Chinese philosophy, the active male principle of the universe (compare YIN).

yapp a form of bookbinding with a limp leather cover projecting to fold over the edges of the leaves.

yare ready, prompt, brisk.

yarmulke (also **yarmulka**) a skullcap worn by Jewish men.

yean to bring forth (a lamb or kid).

yeti the Abominable Snowman; an unidentified manlike or bearlike animal said to exist in the Himalayas.

yin in Chinese philosophy, the passive female principle of the universe (compare YANG).

ylem the primordial matter of the universe, conceived as a gas of neutrons.

yogh a middle English letter used for certain values of *g* and *y*.

Z

ziggurat a rectangular stepped tower in ancient Mesopotamia, with a temple on top.

zillah an administrative district in India.

zoetrope an old-fashioned optical toy in the form of a picture-lined cylinder producing moving images when revolved and viewed through a slit.

zymosis fermentation.

zymurgy the branch of applied chemistry dealing with the use of fermentation in brewing etc.